THE MEṚTĪYO RĀṬHOṚS OF MEṚTO, RĀJASTHĀN: SELECT TRANSLATIONS BEARING ON THE HISTORY OF A RAJPŪT FAMILY, 1462-1660

Translated and Annotated by
Richard D. Saran and Norman P. Ziegler

Michigan Papers on South and Southeast Asian Studies
Number 51

THE UNIVERSITY OF MICHIGAN
CENTERS FOR SOUTH AND SOUTHEAST ASIAN STUDIES

Open access edition funded by the National Endowment for the Humanities/ Andrew W. Mellon Foundation Humanities Open Book Program.

Library of Congress Card Number: 2001091502

ISBN: 0-89148-085-4

Published by The Centers for South and Southeast Asian Studies
The University of Michigan
1080 South University, Suite 3640
Ann Arbor, MI 48109-1106

Printed and bound by CPI Group (UK) Ltd, Croydon, CR0 4YY

ISBN 978-0-89148-085-3 (hardcover)
ISBN 978-0-472-03821-3 (paper)
ISBN 978-0-472-12777-1 (ebook)
ISBN 978-0-472-90173-9 (open access)

VOLUME ONE

TRANSLATIONS AND NOTES

WITH

APPENDICES, GLOSSARY, INTRODUCTORY
MATERIAL,

AND INDEXES

Dedication

This work is dedicated to Nārāyaṇ Siṃh Bhāṭī, Sītāraṃ Lāḷas, Badrīprasād Sākariyā, and John D. Smith,

Who edited the texts,
Compiled the dictionaries,
And wrote the grammars

Without which our endeavors would have been impossible.

ACKNOWLEDGEMENTS

The translations and accompanying notes which make up this work were originally funded by the National Endowment for the Humanities (NEH grant no. RL-00052-80-0960, 4-1-1980-3-31-1981). We are deeply grateful to the Endowment and its staff, particularly Dr. Susan Mango, David J. Wallace, Joyce F. Wendell, and Carrie Wolf, for their constant support both during the period of the grant and afterward. We also wish to express our appreciation to the anonymous reviewers who examined our proposal and found it worthy of consideration.

A special word of thanks is due to Dr. John D. Smith, of Cambridge, who read an early version of the translations with their accompanying notes and presented us with an outstanding critical commentary of immense value. He has saved us from many errors. In no way can he be held responsible for those that remain.

Many other persons have helped us in a variety of ways over the twenty years we have worked on this project. Frances Taft provided us with rare books from Rajasthan and thoughtful queries that led us to expand several areas of our research. Kailash Dan Ujwal and the late Indranath Bohra of Jodhpur, Rajasthan have both been helpful answering our questions about local history and culture. Peter E. Hook never ceased to prod us toward getting these volumes published. John F. Richards, Thomas R. Trautmann, and Stewart Gordon were decent enough to read portions of our work and offer enthusiastic encouragement. Members of the Rajasthan Studies Group, by their periodic questions and unceasing curiosity, have provided us with a powerful incentive to do justice to our sources and publish our results.

The late Om P. Sharma, formerly South Asia Bibliographer at the University of Michigan, was instrumental in acquiring books and microfilms on Rajasthan which simplified much of our research. Maureen Patterson, during her tenure as South Asia Bibliographer at the University of Chicago, helped provide us with copies of texts otherwise impossible to acquire.

Finally, we owe much to our spouses, Patricia Saran and Judy Ziegler, our friends, and our families, who somehow managed to remain both supportive and sympathetic over so many years.

TABLE OF CONTENTS

LIST OF ILLUSTRATIONS

Illustration

Page

LIST OF MAPS

Map

Between Pages

LIST OF TABLES

Table

Page

INTRODUCTION

The edited translations that comprise Volume I of this publication, and the Marriage and Family Lists and Biographical Notes that make up Volume II have one primary purpose: to provide a basis for better understanding Rajpūts and the kingdoms of Rājasthān during the pre-modern period. Until recently, one major English language source has dominated this field: James Tod's ***Annals and Antiquities of Rajasthan***.[1] Tod was among the first British army officers of the early nineteenth century to gain an in-depth view of Rajpūts and Rājasthānī society. His comprehensive history of Rājasthān and its local kingdoms bespeaks his knowledge, gained through years of association with this area and painstaking work with local documents. Yet Tod himself was unaware of the sources used for the translations, the marriage lists, and the biographical notes which comprise these volumes. For his "Annals of Marwar," Tod relied primarily upon two poetic works from the period of Mahārājā Abhāysiṅghjī of Jodhpur (1724-49): ***Sūraj Prakās*** by Cāraṇ Kaviyā Karṇīdānjī,[2] and ***Rājrūpak*** by Ratnū Cāraṇ Kaviyā Vīrbhāṇ,[3] supplemented with material from Rāṭhoṛ genealogies (***vaṃśāvalīs***) and from local informants.[4] These works were greatly inadequate, even in Tod's own estimation, for the periods prior to the reign of Mahārājā Ajītsiṅghjī of Jodhpur (1707-24).[5]

The writings of a number of historians in the last century have, of course, added much information to Tod's ***Annals***. These include notably ***Vīr Vinod*** by Cāraṇ Kavirājā Śyāmaldās in Urdu (Devanāgarī script),[6] and the histories ***Rājpūtāne kā Itihās*** by Paṇḍit Gaurīśaṅkar Hīrācand Ojhā[7] and ***Mārvāṛ***

---

[1] James Tod, ***Annals and Antiquities of Rajasthan***, edited by William Crooke; 3 vols. (London: Oxford University Press, 1920).

[2] Karṇīdānjī, ***Sūraj Prakās***, edited by P. J. Muni; 3 vols. (Jodhpur: Rājasthān Prācyavidyā Pratiṣṭhān, 1961-1963).

[3] Vīrbhāṇ Ratnū, ***Rājrūpak***, edited by Paṇḍit Rāmkaraṇ Āsopā (Kāśī: Nāgarīpracāriṇī Sabhā, V.S. 1998 [A.D. 1941]).

[4] Tod, ***Annals*** , 2:929-933.

[5] ***Ibid***., 2:932.

[6] Śyāmaldās, Kavirāja, ***Vīr Vinod***, 2 vols. in 4 parts (Udaipur: Rājyantrālaya, V. S. 1943 [A. D. 1886]).

[7] G. H. Ojhā, ***Rājpūtāne kā Itihās***, 5 vols. in 9 parts (Ajmer: Vedic Yantrālaya, 1927-1941).

kā Itihās by Paṇḍit Biśveśvar Nāth Reu[8] in Hindi. These works now serve as basic reference tools for historians of Rājasthān. More recently, scholars have begun publishing research in English and Hindi based upon the use of local sources, thereby making information on Rājasthānī history and culture available to a wider and less specialized audience.[9] Only a very few original historical materials have been published in translation,[10] however, despite the importance of Rajpūts and their unique role in the history of pre-modern north India.

Richard Saran and I present here for the first time in English an integrated series of original documents dealing with the history of a Rajpūt kingdom during the "middle period."[11] The documents deal with the Rāṭhoṛ

---

[8] B. N. Reu, ***Mārvāṛ kā Itihās,*** 2 vols. (Jodhpur: Archaeological Department, 1938-1940).

[9] The bibliography following the two introductory sections includes a sampling of more recent works on Rajasthani history and culture. A full bibliography of English, Hindi, and Rājasthānī materials would require a separate volume.

[10] Recent publications include: ***Jagdev Parmār rī Vāt: Trividha-vīra Parmār Jagdev kī Mūl Rājasthānī Lok-kathā, Hindī Anuvād, Prakṛt, Saṃskṛt, va Gujarātī meṃ Prāpt Itivṛtta evaṃ Sarvāṅgīṇ Mūlyāṅkan = Tale of Jagdeva Parmar***, edited by Mahāvīr Siṃh Gahlot (Jodhpur: Rājasthān Sāhitya Mandīr, 1986); ***Selections from the Banera Archives: Civil War in Mewar (Baneṛā Saṅgrahālaya ke Abhilekh [1758-1770]),*** edited by K. S. Gupta & L. P. Mathur (Udaipur: Sahitya Sansthan Rajasthan Vidyapeeth,1967); John D. Smith, ***The Epic of Pābūjī: A Study, Transcription and Translation*** (Cambridge [England]: Cambridge University Press, 1991); Smith, ***The Vīsaḷadevarāsa: A Restoration of the Text*** (Cambridge: Cambridge University Press, 1976); ***Vīramde Sonīgarā rī Vāt: Pracīn Rājasthānī Lok Sāhitya kī Prasiddh Aitihāsik Kathā, Mūl Rājasthānī Pāṭh, evaṃ Hindī-Aṅgrejī Rūpāntar Sahit: Vāt (Kathā) kā Sarvāṅgīṇ Mūlyāṅkan = A Muslim Princess Becomes Sati: A Historical Romance of Hindu-Muslim Unity***, edited by Mahāvīr Siṃh Gahlot (Jālor: Śrī Mahāvīr Śodh-Saṃsthān, 1981).

[11] The term "middle period" designates a rather broad span of Rajpūt history extending roughly from the 12th century of the Christian Era into the late 17th and early 18th centuries. The period is defined according to Rajpūt traditions which mark its "beginning" in the 8th through 12th centuries. It was during this period that the Kṣatriya ancestors of the Rajpūts lost their kingdoms in northern and western India to the Muslims, and began their migrations into the area of Rājasthān. The period of migrations is seen as a time when authority was lost, when there was "mixing" among the castes, and when rank was cast in doubt. The middle period itself represents an era during which the Rajpūt successors to the Kṣatriyas re-established their former positions of rank through the conquest of new kingdoms and the reassertion of their authority. This period ends in the early 18th century with the decline of Mughal rule in north India and the Mahratta invasions of Rājasthān. It was during this time that the local sovereignties of Rājasthān once again came into jeopardy. The designation of middle period speaks to Rajpūt conceptions of history defined in terms of a cyclical alteration: rulership and order - loss of rank, distress and migration - re-conquest and reassertion of rank and authority.

For further comments, see: N. P. Ziegler, "Action, Power and Service in Rājasthānī Culture: A Social History of the Rajpūts of Middle Period Rājasthān"

Rajpūts of Mārvāṛ, western Rājasthān. They trace the history of a particular branch (*sākh*) of Rāṭhoṛs, the Meṛtīyos of Meṛto in eastern Mārvāṛ, over a period of some two hundred years from the mid-fifteenth to the mid-seventeenth century, and detail their relationship with the Jodho Rāṭhoṛ ruling house of Jodhpur and with other contemporary ruling houses of Rājasthān and north India.

We have chosen to focus on the Meṛtīyos for several reasons. Their story records the emergence of a Rajpūt brotherhood (*bhāībandh* - lit. "brother-bound") into local prominence and follows the establishment of their kingdom on the eastern edge of Mārvāṛ as a defined territorial unit. The evolution of the Meṛtīyos as a brotherhood passed through several clearly defined stages. With regard to Jodhpur, Meṛtīyo relations were characterized initially, in the mid-fifteenth century, by a mixture of mutual support among brothers and brothers' sons against outsiders, and by internal hostility over shares of ancestral lands, locally termed *grās-vedh* (lit. "share-battle"), among these same brothers. A second stage developed in the early sixteenth century and involved a clear separation of the Meṛtīyos from the house of Jodhpur, with Meṛtīyo attempts to consolidate their claims to ancestral lands within their own kingdom and to assert an equal precedence alongside Jodhpur. A study of the Meṛtīyos in this context allows a unique view of the formation of a strong and independent Rajpūt cadet line, of the establishment and defense of a local territory, and of the internal relations among Rajpūt brotherhoods regarding issues of precedence, honor, patronage and service. The hostilities with Jodhpur that the Meṛtīyo assertion of independence engendered occurred at a time of great political and social change in north India. This change included the collapse of the Delhi Sultānate before the Mughal advance under Bābur, the rise of the Afghan Sher Shāh Sūr (1540-45) to rule in Delhi, and the reconsolidation of Mughal authority under Akbar (1556-1605).

The long and bitter struggle between the Meṛtīyos and Jodhpur was not isolated from these events taking place in north India. Rāv Vīramde Dūdāvat, ruler of Meṛto (ca. 1497-1544) and son of one of the original founders of Meṛto, was among the first local rulers in Rājasthān to form an alliance with the Muslims. He sought out Sher Shāh in 1543 to petition for aid in the recovery of his lands in Mārvāṛ, which Rāv Mālde Gāṅgāvat of Jodhpur (1532-62) had usurped in ca. 1535. Sher Shāh agreed to help Rāv Vīramde to further his own ends in Rājasthān. Sher Shāh's victory against Rāv Mālde at the battle of Samel (near Ajmer) on January 5, 1544 was due in great part to Rāv Vīramde's support. Rāv Vīramde was then able to return to the rule of Meṛto.

With Akbar's succession to the Mughal throne in 1556, the nature of the conflict between these two Rāṭhoṛ brotherhoods shifted from a question of local force to that of the legitimizing sanction of the Mughal Emperor's grant of *jāgīr*. Rāv Jaimal Vīramdevot, Rāv Vīramde's son and successor to the rulership of Meṛto (ca. 1544-57, 1562), soon became involved with the Mughals in his own attempts to secure his rights to ancestral lands. When Rāv Mālde of Jodhpur

---

(unpublished Ph.D. dissertation, The University of Chicago, 1973), pp. 3-5; R. D. Saran, "Conquest and Colonization: Rajpūts and *Vasīs* in Middle Period Mārvāṛ" (unpublished Ph.D. dissertation, The University of Michigan, 1978), p. 3.

again usurped these lands, Jaimal joined Mughal service under Akbar and returned to Mārvāṛ with a force of Mughals under the command of Mīrzā Sharafu'd-Dīn Ḥusayn. They met Rāv Mālde's warriors before Meṛto in 1562 and defeated them with great loss. Rāv Jaimal afterwards received Meṛto in ***jāgīr*** from Akbar.

Six years later, in 1568, this same Rāv Jaimal stood against Akbar at the historic battle of Cītoṛ in Mevāṛ. Rāv Jaimal was related by marriage to the Sīsodīyo Gahlot ruling family. His father, Rāv Vīramde, had married a daughter of Sīsodīyo Rāṇo Rāymal Kūmbhāvat of Cītoṛ (ca. 1473-1509),[12] and a daughter of one of his paternal uncles, Ratansī Dūdāvat, had been married to the Sīsodīyo Bhojrāj Sāṅgāvat, a son of Rāṇo Sāṅgo Rāymalot (1509-28). This daughter was later to become the famous ***bhaktī*** poetess of Rājasthān known as Mīrāmbāī.[13] Rāv Jaimal was a leading commander of Rāṇo Sāṅgo's successor, Sīsodīyo Rāṇo Udaisiṅgh Sāṅgāvat (ca. 1537-72). There at Cītoṛ during the battle against Akbar, Rāv Jaimal was killed by Akbar himself while Jaimal supervised the filling of a breach in the walls of the fort. Because of Rāv Jaimal's display of great bravery at Cītoṛ, Akbar had his likeness carved in stone seated upon an elephant and placed at the entrance to the main gateway of the Red Fort in Agra, alongside that of Sīsodīyo Pato Jāgāvat, another distinguished Rajpūt warrior from this battle.

Rāv Jaimal's son, Kesodās Jaimalot, and a paternal nephew, Narhardās Īsardāsot, were among the first Rāṭhoṛs to enter Mughal service following the battle of Cītoṛ, and to give their daughters in marriage to the Mughals. Narhardās joined Akbar's service ca. 1570 and married his uterine sister, Purāṃ Bāī, to Akbar in return for Akbar's support of Kesodās' claims to rulership at Meṛto. Shortly thereafter, Kesodās himself married one of his daughters to Akbar's son, Prince Salīm (Jahāṅgīr).[14] A contemporary of theirs, Meṛtīyo Kesodās Bhīṃvot, known in Mughal circles as Kesodās Mārū, was also in Akbar's service. Under Akbar, he rose to considerable prominence.[15] Other

---

[12] Gopalsiṃh Rāṭhoṛ Meṛtiyā, ***Jaymalvaṃśprakāś, arthāt, Rājasthān Badnor kā Itihās = Jayamal Vansa Prakasha, or, The History of Badnore*** (Ajmer: Vaidik Yantrālay, 1932), p. 106.

[13] ***Khyāt***, 1:21; Reu, ***Mārvāṛ kā Itihās***, 1:103, n. 5.

[14] Regarding this marriage, see ***Vigat***, 2:70 of the translated text, ***infra***, and Biographical Note no. 119 for Meṛtīyo Kesodās Jaimalot. The details of this marriage are unfortunately shrouded in some uncertainty.

[15] Kesodās Mārū Bhīṃvot does not figure in the portions of text that we have translated. He is mentioned here because he was yet another among a number of Meṛtīyos and other Rāṭhoṛs whose careers were based upon service under the Mughals. Kesodās Mārū was a Meṛtīyo of the Varsiṅghot branch (***sākh***), descended from Varsiṅgh Jodhāvat, one of the founders of Meṛto. Under Mughal Emperor Akbar, he rose to a position of influence and held the ***jāgīr*** of Vadhnor in northern Mevāṛ over a period of years. He died sometime during the reign of Akbar's successor, Jahāṅgīr (1605-1628). See ***Rāṭhoṛoṃ kī Khyāt Purāṇī Kavirājjī Murārdānjī ke Yahāṃ se Likhī Gaī***, Ms. no. 15672, no. 2, Rājasthān Prācyavidyā Pratiṣṭhān, Jodhpur, p. 584.

members of this family in this and later generations were among the important Rajpūt warriors of the Mughals in campaigns in Gujarat, the Deccan and north India. These examples indicate not only the prominence to which Meṛtīyos rose in the middle period, but also their intimate involvement in both local affairs and in the affairs of north India. Their careers and those of other contemporary Rajpūts detailed in the translation material and in the biographical notes that accompany the translations, provide excellent data for the study of changing patterns and perspectives among individual Rajpūts of the period.

Although Akbar initially recognized Meṛtīyo claims to local lands, with time all of Meṛto became incorporated within the ***vatan jāgīr*** of the Jodho Rāṭhoṛ rulers of Jodhpur. Meṛtīyo responses to this subordination varied from cooperation and acceptance to outright protest and migration from Mārvāṛ itself. On the whole, however, most Meṛtīyos remained, for a time at least, outwardly accepting of Jodhpur authority. Then, after the death of Mahārājā Jasvantsiṅgh Gajsiṅghot of Jodhpur (1638-78), the Meṛtīyos again rebelled and sought to reassert rights as individuals and families to ancestral lands. This conflict occurred during a period of great local instability culminating in the Rajpūt wars against the Mughal Emperor Aurangzeb. This latter period of instability lies beyond the scope of the texts translated here, but its mention may serve to place in perspective the tenuous compromise of statecraft that evolved in Mārvāṛ over a century of Mughal suzerainty in the north. From the broader perspective of political and social change in north India in the middle period, the history of the Meṛtīyos offers, because of its integral connection with the fortunes of Jodhpur and Rājasthān as a whole, a deeper understanding of local rulership and authority, and of the impact of Muslim and particularly Mughal rule in north India on the organization and structure of a Rajpūt kingdom.

The companion Volume II that accompanies the translated material is organized in two parts. The first part provides detailed Marriage and Family Lists for the Jodho Rāṭhoṛ Rulers of Jodhpur. These lists extend over ten generations beginning with Rāv Jodho Riṇmalot (ca. 1453-89), the founder of Jodhpur, whose sons, Varsiṅgh and Dūdo Jodhāvat, settled Meṛto and laid the foundations for Meṛtīyo rule in eastern Mārvāṛ, and ending with Rājā Jasvantsiṅgh Gajsiṅghot (1638-78). The enumerations of wives, of sons, and of daughters and their places of marriage (where known), offer an important perspective on patterns of alliance within the ruling family of Rāṭhoṛs over a two-hundred-year period. They mark the manner in which these alliances evolved in relation to changing political fortunes in Mārvāṛ and neighboring Rajpūt kingdoms, and in the Muslim kingdoms of northern and western India, to the rulers of a number of which the Rāṭhoṛs of Jodhpur also gave daughters in marriage.

The Biographical Notes which follow the Marriage and Family Lists include entries for one hundred and sixty-three individuals mentioned in the translated texts. The majority of these notes (nos. 1-153) are about Rajpūts of different families (***kuḷ***) and branches (***sākhāṃ***) who played roles of varying importance in the history of Meṛto and Jodhpur during the period under review. There are also notes (nos. 154-163) about the Khānzādā Khān Muslims who controlled Nāgaur during the fifteenth and sixteenth centuries and interacted in varying degrees with the Rāṭhoṛs of Jodhpur and Meṛto, and about members of several administrative ***jātis*** of local importance including the Bhaṇḍārīs, Muṃhatos and Pañcolīs.

These notes draw on information from a variety of sources, among the most important of which are the genealogical materials in the ***khyāts*** of Naiṇsī[16] and Kavirājjī Murārdānjī.[17] Murārdān's ***khyāts*** were compiled contemporaneously with those of Naiṇsī, and one possesses an extensive genealogy of the Meṛtīyo Rāṭhoṛs[18] which has been particularly helpful in the identification of Meṛtīyos who otherwise would remain obscure figures in the historical texts. The genealogies also furnish biographical data about these Rajpūts and their families, and allow the placement of individuals firmly within a network of kinship. Supplemented with material from other sources, they greatly facilitate an understanding of individual actions within a generational perspective.

The biographical notes are organized according to the different Rajpūt families (***kuḷ***) and branches (***sākhāṃ***). They provide details about individuals who figure in the translated texts, and where appropriate, about the founders of particular branches. Three Jeso Bhāṭīs are mentioned in the translated material, for example (see Biographical Notes nos. 1-3). All were military servants of Rāv Mālde Gāṅgāvat of Jodhpur (1532-62). One was killed in 1544 while defending the fort of Jodhpur against attack from Sher Shāh Sūr and his forces following Rāv Mālde's defeat at the battle of Samel. The other two died fighting at the battle of Meṛto in 1562, when Rāv Mālde's forces at the Mālgaḍh came under attack from the combined forces of Meṛtīyo Rāv Jaimal Vīramdevot and the Mughal commander, Mīrzā Sharafu'd-Dīn Ḥusayn. Very little is known about these three men other than their places and dates of death. But the Jeso Bhāṭīs as a group played an important role as supporters of the Rāṭhoṛ house of Jodhpur beginning with Rāv Jodho Riṇmalot (ca. 1453-89), and one Jeso Bhāṭī, Goyanndās Mānāvat, later became ***pradhān*** of Jodhpur under Rājā Sūrajsiṅgh Udaisiṅghot (1595-1619). Information is provided, therefore, about the founding ancestor of the Jeso Bhāṭīs of Mārvāṛ, Jeso Kalikaraṇot, and his sons and

---

[16] Muṃhatā Naiṇsī, ***Muṃhatā Naiṇsi viracit Muṃhatā Naiṇsīrī Khyāt***, edited by Badrīprasād Sākariyā; 4 vols. (Jodhpur: Rājasthān Prācyavidyā Pratiṣṭhān, 1968-1974).

[17] ***Kavirāj Murārdānjī kī Khyāt kā Tarjumā***, Ms. no. 25658, no. 1, Rājasthān Prācyavidyā Pratiṣṭhān, Jodhpur; ***Rāṭhoṛoṃ kī Khyāt Purāṇī Kavirājjī Murārdānjī ke Yahāṃ se Likhī Gaī***, Ms. no. 15672, no. 2, Rājasthān Prācyavidyā Pratiṣṭhān, Jodhpur; ***Rajpūtoṃ kī Khyāt: Kavirājjī Murārdānjī kī Khyāt kā Tarjumā***, Ms. no. 15671, no. 3, Rājasthān Prācyavidyā Pratiṣṭhān, Jodhpur.

[18] ***Murārdān***, no. 2, pp. 444-643. Frances Taft has supplied us with another Meṛtīyo genealogy, copied from the ***Udaibhāṇ Cāmpāvat rī Khyāt***, but unfortunately too late to be used for these volumes. It appears that this text may have been the original Middle Mārvāṛī version of ***Murārdān***, no. 2, which is mostly written in Hindi.

grandsons in order to set forth a context from which to understand the lives and actions of those individuals named in the translated material.

Lastly, some Rajpūts mentioned in the translation were individuals of importance both locally and at the Mughal court. One such individual was Dhīrāvat Kachvāho Rāmdās Ūdāvat (see Biographical Note no. 19). Rāmdās rose from rather humble beginnings to a position of considerable power and influence at the Mughal court as a favorite of both Emperors Akbar and Jahāngīr. A broader range of information is, therefore, available about Rāmdās from both local documents and genealogies, and from Mughal Imperial writings including the works of Abū al-Fazl[19] and the ***Memoirs*** of Emperor Jahāngīr.[20] These materials provide a rich tapestry of information about the life of this important Rajpūt, which has been incorporated in his biographical note.

It is hoped that these two volumes together will offer the reader a unique opportunity to read and learn about Rajpūts and the history of Rājasthān from a local and individual perspective.

The remaining portions of this introductory section to Volume I provide information about the sources from which the translated materials were selected including a discussion of Muṃhato Naiṇsī, the methodology employed in the translations, and the conventions used. Lastly, there is a section of importance to the general reader on Rajpūt social organization during the middle period.

Norman Ziegler
Denver, Colorado

---

[19] Abū al-Fazl ibn Mubārak, ***The Akbar Nāma of Abu-l-Fazl***, translated by H. Beveridge; 3 vols. (reprint ed.; Delhi: Rare Books, 1972).

[20] Jahāngīr, ***The Tūzuk-i-Jahāngīrī; or, Memoirs of Jahāngīr***, translated by Alexander Rogers, edited by Henry Beveridge; 2 vols. (reprint ed.; Delhi: Munshiram Manoharlal,1968 [1909-1914]).

INTRODUCTION TO THE TRANSLATIONS

I. The Texts.

We have selected for translation six prose historical passages taken from three primary sources written in middle period Mārvāṛ. These texts, except for a few short poems in Ḍiṅgal,[1] are in the same language, Middle Mārvāṛī, and were composed during the reign of Rājā Jasvantsiṅgh (1638-1678) of Jodhpur. The passages translated all concern a ***pargano*** ("district") of Mārvāṛ, Meṛto, and its rulers, the Meṛtīyo Rāṭhoṛs. They describe the founding of Meṛtīyo rule at Meṛto town, the settling of the surrounding region, and events in the lives of leading Meṛtīyos in the subsequent history of the ***pargano***.

The longest of our selections is the ***Vāt Pargane Meṛte rī*** ("Account of Meṛto Pargano"). This ***vāt*** is contained in the ***Mārvāṛ rī Parganāṃ rī Vigat***,[2] an enormous gazetteer-like work compiled and at least in part written by Muṃhato Naiṇsī, an administrator who served both Rājā Gajsiṅgh (1619-38) and Rājā Jasvantsiṅgh of Jodhpur. The last year mentioned in this voluminous text is V.S. 1722/A.D. 1665-66; the data included within represent the efforts of several decades.

The ***Vigat*** ("List") gives historical and other information about seventeenth-century Jodhpur and its six adjoining ***parganos***: Meṛto, Sojhat, Phaḷodhī, Pokaraṇ, Jaitāraṇ, and Sīvāṇo. The text is divided into seven major sections, entitled ***vāt***, each of which concerns a particular ***pargano***. The sections are subdivided into numbered entries or paragraphs. The largest section, the ***Vāt Pargane Jodhpur rī*** ("Account of Jodhpur Pargano"), contains 313 such entries; the ***Vāt Pargane Meṛte rī*** has 111. Every section begins with a short narrative, usually legendary in nature, discussing the early history of the ***pargano***, and then continues in a chronological sequence of notes to record the coming to power of the Rāṭhoṛ Rajpūts within that ***pargano*** and subsequent events of local importance. The histories of Jodhpur and Meṛto ***parganos*** are much longer and more detailed than the others: the former comprises some 150 pages; the latter forty.

Following the chronicle entries, the sections each contain a mass of descriptive and statistical information. All the villages of the ***parganos*** are listed. Nearly every village is described in a brief note following its name, accompanied by statistics giving the yearly revenues produced by the village between V.S. 1715 and 1719 (A.D. 1658-59 to 1662-63). The ***kasbos***, or main towns, of the ***parganos*** are discussed in more detail, with a census of households according to ***jāti*** given for

---

[1] Ḍiṅgaḷ is an archaizing derivative of Middle Mārvāṛī. Cf. John D. Smith, "An Introduction to the Language of the Historical Documents from Rajasthan," ***Modern Asian Studies***, 9, 4 (1975), p. 375.

[2] Muṃhato Naiṇsī, ***Mārvāṛ rā Parganāṃ rī Vigat***, ed. Narayansiṃh Bhāṭī, 3 vols. (Jodhpur: Rājasthān Prācyavidyā Pratiṣṭhān, 1968-74).

every ***kasbo*** save Jodhpur city. Besides all this, the sections have a variety of miscellaneous data: lists of taxes, information about local fairs, administrative classifications of villages, etc. John Smith has called the ***Vigat*** a kind of Domesday Book,[3] and so it is. In its entirety, it provides more information about a region of India than does any other single source compiled prior to the advent of the British.

We have translated the first seventy entries of the ***Vāt Pargane Meṛte rī***.[4] These comprise the chronicle portion of this ***vāt***; the last forty-one entries are all statistical or descriptive in nature. The ***Vāt*** begins with a legend concerning the founding of Meṛto by the Purāṇic hero Rājā Māndhātā, then proceeds in the following sixty-nine entries to record the settlement of Meṛto town in 1462 by Dūdo and Varsiṅgh Jodhāvat, the rise of the Meṛtīyos as a regional Rāṭhoṛ brotherhood of some significance in Mārvāṛ, the struggles between the rulers of Meṛto and Rāv Mālde (1532-62) of Jodhpur, the intrusion of the Mughals in 1562, and the incorporation of Meṛto Pargano into the domain of the Jodhpur Rājās during the early seventeenth century. The chronicle ends with the accession of Rājā Jasvantsiṅgh in 1638.

The second and third selections translated come from the ***Rāv Mālde rī Bāt*** included in a collection of historical texts edited by N. S. Bhāṭī and entitled by him "Aitihāsik Bātāṃ" ("Historical Stories").[5] This collection

> ... contains short historical narratives about all of the Rathor rulers of Jodhpur from Rao Malde (1532-62) through Maharaja Surajsimgh (1595-1619), and also includes stories about Rao Jodho, the founder of Jodhpur city, and his father, Rao Rinmal. It is considered that all of these batam (tales) were written down in 1646, a date which is noted at the end of one of the stories. If this dating is correct for all of the stories, they were probably written under the direction or supervision of Nainsi, for the writer of the story which supplies the date has also noted that Mumhata Sumdardas, Nainsi's brother, had ordered him to prepare it. All of the stories also come from the same old bahi (register), and are written in the same hand. As a whole, the narratives complement the khyat of Nainsi by filling in material between the reigns of Rao Malde and Jasvamtsimgh, and they coincide with much of the later historical sections of the vigat of Nainsi. From the contents, these narratives are clearly official histories, written with the aid of state records.[6]

---

3 Smith, "An Introduction to the Language of the Historical Documents from Rajasthan," p. 437, n. 18.

4 ***Vigat***, 2:37-77.

5 "Aitihāsik Bātāṃ," in ***Paramparā***, part 11, pp. 17-109, ed. N. S. Bhāṭī (Caupāsnī: Rājasthānī Śodh Saṃsthān, 1961).

6 Norman P. Ziegler, "Marvari Historical Chronicles: Sources for the Social and Cultural History of Rajasthan," ***Indian Economic and Social History Review***, vol. 13,

Of the documents comprising the collection, the ***Rāv Mālde rī Bāt*** ("Story of Rāv Mālde")[7] is the longest and most valuable to the historian. The style of this ***bāt*** is very much like that of the ***Vāt Pargane Meṛte rī***; indeed, some passages are virtually identical, word for word. The account of Rāv Mālde's reign fills some forty pages of printed text and is probably the best source available concerning events in the life of this enigmatic and powerful Rāṭhoṛ.

The first passage selected for translation (pp. 42-44) discusses the invasion of Mārvāṛ by Sher Shāh in 1544, the flight of Rāv Mālde from the battlefield between Samel and Girrī on Mārvāṛ's eastern boundary, and the role played by the ruler of Meṛto, Vīramde Dūdāvat, in deceiving Mālde and causing him to flee. The second passage (pp. 48-56) gives an account of the battle of Meṛto in 1554, records Mālde's acquisition of the town in 1557 following the battle of Harmāṛo, and ends with the capture of Meṛto by Mughal troops aided by Jaimal Vīramdevot in 1562. Both passages from the ***Rāv Mālde rī Bāt*** nicely complement the material in the ***Vāt Pargane Meṛte rī***, adding valuable details and clarifying obscure events.

The last three selections translated are from Muṃhato Naiṇsī's ***Khyāt***,[8] an immense collection of tales, poems, historical stories, genealogies, descriptions of towns and regions, and other random facts pertaining to Rājasthān, Gujarat, and

---

no. 2 (April-June, 1976), p. 248. L. P. Tessitori mentions a chronicle entitled ***Vātāṃ Mārvāṛi rāṃ*** [*sic*] ***Rāṭhaurāṃ rī*** in his ***A Descriptive Catalogue of Bardic and Historical Manuscripts***, Section I: Prose Chronicles, Part I: Jodhpur State (Calcutta: The Asiatic Society of Bengal, 1917), p. 56, and he published and translated a portion of this ms. in ***idem***, "A Progress Report on the Work done during the year 1917 in connection with the Bardic and Historical Survey of Rajputana," ***Journal of the Asiatic Society of Bengal***, N.S. 15 (1919), pp. 47-48. This extract is identical to the beginning of the ***Rāv Jodhājī rā Beṭāṃ rī Bāt*** contained in "Aitihāsik Bātāṃ," pp. 35-38. Tessitori believed that the chronicle was compiled not long after the death of Rāv Mālde of Jodhpur in 1562. Thus at least one of the stories contained in "Aitihāsik Bātāṃ" may be considerably older than 1646.

[7] "Aitihāsik Bātāṃ," pp. 39-78.

[8] Muṃhato Naiṇsī, ***Muṃhatā Naiṇsī viracit Muṃhatā Naiṇsīrī Khyāt***, ed. Badrīprasād Sākariyā, 4 vols. (Jodhpur: Rājasthan Prācyavidyā Pratiṣṭhān, 1960-67). A partial edition of the ***Khyāt***, equivalent to most of vol. one of the Rājasthān Prācyavidyā Pratiṣṭhan edition, was edited by Rāmkaraṇ Āsopā under the title ***Naiṇsī kī Khyāt***, vol. 1 (n.p., n.d.). A good complete Hindi translation with notes and full index was done by Rāmnārāyaṇ Dūgaṛ and Gaurīśaṅkar Hīrācand Ojhā (***Muhaṇot Naiṇsī kī Khyāt, arthāt, Naiṇsī kī Mārvāṛi Bhāṣā kī Khyāt se Guhilot (Sīsodīyā), Cauhān, Solaṅkī (Caulukya), Paṛihār (Pratihār) aur Parmār (Paṃvār) Vaṃśoṃ kī Itihās kā Hindī Anuvād***, 2 vols., Allahabad: K. Mittra at the Indian Press, 1925-34). More recently, Manoharsiṃh Rāṇāvat has translated into Hindi vol. 1 only (***Muhaṇot Naiṇsī kī Khyāt***, vol. 1, Sītāmaū: Śrī Naṭnāgar Śodh-Saṃsthān, 1987). John D. Smith brilliantly translated into English with extensive annotations the ***Vāt Pābūjī rī*** (***Khyāt***, 3:58-79) in his remarkable book, ***The Epic of Pābūjī: A Study, Transcription and Translation*** (Cambridge [England]: Cambridge University Press, 1991), pp. 480-505.

central India compiled during the years Naiṇsī was in the service of the rulers of Jodhpur (1637-66).[9] The word ***khyāt*** probably is derived from the Sanskrit ***khyāti***, "fame," "renown." In middle period Rājasthān, a ***khyāt*** was a book of historical information, either taking the form of a chronicle or being a collection of miscellaneous data like Naiṇsī's or that of Bāṅkīdās, the court poet of Rājā Mānsiṅgh of Jodhpur (1803-43).[10]

The bulk of Naiṇsī's ***Khyāt*** consists of sections, also called ***khyāt***, which are devoted to particular Rajpūt ***kuḷ***s. The printed text begins with the ***Sīsodiyāṃ rī Khyāt***,[11] which concerns the Sīsodīyo Rajpūts of Mevāṛ and includes stories and poems about prominent Sīsodīyos, an annotated genealogy of the ruling line, brief genealogies of a few other major ***sākh***s, and a geographical account of Mevāṛ. Similar short ***khyāt***s follow, giving details about the Hāḍo Cahuvāṇs of Būndī and Koṭo, the Bhāṭīs of Jaisaḷmer and Pūgaḷ, the Kachvāhos of Āmber and Sekhāvaṭī, and other important Rajpūt ***kul*** and ***sākh***s of the middle period. The last quarter of the second volume of the printed text and about half of the third contain stories and other information about the Rāṭhoṛs.

Naiṇsī's ***Khyāt*** has a bias toward the ruling families of western Rājasthān: the Rāṭhoṛs, Bhāṭīs, Sācoro Cahuvāṇs, Sāṅkhlos, Soḍhos, etc. The information concerning certain Rajpūt families that had military obligations to the Rāṭhoṛs of Mārvāṛ is particularly full: we learn more about the Urjanot Bhāṭīs, a minor ***sākh*** serving the Jodhpur rulers, than we do about the Bundelos of Bundelkhaṇḍ. Clearly Naiṇsī had more information about such local ***sākh***s than he did about the major ruling families of eastern Rājasthān and central India. But there are curious omissions also. Presumably Naiṇsī had at hand a good deal of data pertaining to the Rāṭhoṛs of Bīkāner, yet his ***Khyāt*** contains only two short narratives about events there. Even more striking is the lack of information regarding the reigns of the Jodhpur rulers from Rāv Candrasen (1562-81) onward. One reason for these omissions may be that other documents (e.g., the ***Vigat***) existed to fill the gaps in the ***Khyāt***. Alternatively, perhaps the ***Khyāt*** was never finished (Naiṇsī was imprisoned in 1666 and committed suicide in disgrace in 1670).

We have selected and translated three stories from the ***Khyāt*** bearing upon events in the lives of leading Meṛtīyo Rāṭhoṛs. The first, ***Ath Vāt Dūdai Jodhāvat Megho Narsiṅghdāsot Sīndhaḷ Mārīyo tai Samai rī*** ("Now the Story of the Time that Dūdo Jodhāvat killed Sīndhaḷ [Rāṭhoṛ] Megho Narsiṅghdāsot"),[12] delineates an

---

[9] The ***Khyāt***, like the ***Vigat***, contains no date later than V.S. 1722 (1665-66), Naiṇsī's last full year of service. Hukamsiṃh Bhāṭī, "Muhaṇot Naiṇsī kī Khyāt meṃ āī huī Ghaṭnāoṃ kā Tithikram," in ***Muhaṇot Naiṇsī: Itihāsvid Muhaṇot Naiṇsī, Vyaktitva evaṃ Kṛtitva, Paramparā***, nos. 39-40, ed. Nārāyaṇsiṃh Bhāṭī (Caupāsnī: Rājasthānī Śodh Saṃsthān, 1974), p. 82.

[10] Bāṅkīdās, ***Bāṅkīdās rī Khyāt***, ed. Narottamdāsjī Svāmī (Jaypur: Rājasthān Purattvānvesaṇ Mandir, 1956).

[11] ***Khyāt***, 1:1-97.

[12] ***Khyāt***, 3:38-40.

episode in the life of Dūdo Jodhāvat just prior to the settling of Meṛto town in 1462. The second story, misleadingly titled ***Ath Vāt Hardās Ūhaṛ rī Likhyate*** ("Now the Story of Hardās Ūhaṛ is Written"),[13] mainly outlines the growing hostility between Rāv Mālde, the ruler of Jodhpur (1532-62) and the Rāv of Meṛto, Vīramde Dūdāvat (1497-1544) from the battle of Sevakī in 1529, when Mālde was ***kuṃvar*** ("prince"), to Sher Shāh's occupation of Mārvāṛ in 1544. The last selection, ***Ath Jaimal Vīramdevot nai Rāv Mālde rī Vāt Likhyate*** ("Now the Story of Jaimal Vīramdevot and Rāv Mālde is Written"),[14] continues the account of the hostility between Rāv Mālde and the Rāṭhoṛs of Meṛto, now under the leadership of Vīramde's son, Jaimal (Rāv of Meṛto, 1544-1557, 1562), during the years from Vīramde's death in 1544 to the battle of Meṛto in 1554.

The three stories are considerably different in style from the translated prose sections of the ***Vigat*** and "Aitihāsik Bātāṃ." They are more in the nature of oral traditions, with a corresponding undated, almost timeless quality. One has to be reminded that the events described are occuring over a period of years, not weeks or months. This is not to say that these stories are less useful to the historian than the other selections. On the contrary, they provide insights into matters of honor, shame, prestige, and duty among Rajpūts not as common in the more chronologically organized texts.

One problem of these texts for the historian, however, is that they mention events removed by one or two centuries from the lifetime of the man primarily responsible for them, Muṃhato Naiṇsī. As will be discussed below, Naiṇsī's family had a long connection with the Jodhpur rulers. He undoubtedly had access to a wide variety of documents and manuscripts from earlier periods. As a high-ranking official within the Jodhpur bureaucracy, he also knew many important contemporaries who supplied him with information, oral and written, over the many years of his service.[15] He often cites the source of his information.[16] Yet in many instances he does not,

---

[13] ***Khyāt***, 3:87-102.

[14] ***Khyāt***, 3:115-122.

[15] Ziegler ("Marvari Historical Chronicles ...," p. 247) has remarked that

> It seems clear from inspection of the text that Nainsi not only requested and collected oral traditions from a large number of contributors throughout Marvar and Rajasthan as a whole on the histories of the ruling houses of different Rajput clans, but also solicited genealogies from Bhats and others knowledgeable of them. In addition, he obtained materials such as the survey reports from Qanungos and other local administrative officials, as well as information from family and friends.

[16] Naiṇsī frequently begins a narration with the phrase "I heard a tale like this (***ek vāt yūṃ sūnī***)." At times the name of informant is given. For example, Naiṇsī records that the Cāraṇ Āḍho Mahes told him the ***bhed*** ("distinction," "secret") of the Sīsodīyo Rajpūts in 1649-50. In April-May of 1658 Cāraṇ Dhadhvāṛiyo Khīṃvrāj wrote down the story of the battle between Hājī Khān and Rāṇo Udaisiṅgh of Mevāṛ at Harmāṛo in 1557. And in March-April of 1663 Cāraṇ Jhūlo Rudradās, son of Bhāṇ and grandson of Sāīyo, recited some information

and so one is led to wonder if he merely selected, or actually wrote, those particular texts.

A partial answer to this question comes from the later ***Khyāt*** of Dayāldās Siṇḍhāyac. Dayāldās, who wrote in the mid-nineteenth century in Bīkāner, included without attribution and only slight modifications long passages also contained in Naiṇsī's ***Khyāt***, compiled nearly two hundred years earlier.[17] One may compare a portion of the ***Ath Vāt Hardās Ūhaṛ rī Likhyate*** with Dāyaldās's later version:

Naiṇsi:

> ***Tāhrāṃ Hardās chāḍiyo. Tāhrāṃ jāy Sojhat Rāymal Muṃhataisūṃ miḷiyo. Hardās Vīramderai vās vasiyo. Tāhrāṃ Hardās Rāymal nūṃ kahai: "Je the Rāv Gāṅgaisūṃ veḍh karo, to hūṃ thāṃrai rahīs, nahīṃ to nahīṃ rahūṃ." Tāhrāṃ Rāymal kahyo: "Jī, mhāṃrai to āṭh pohar laṛāīj chai."***[18]
>
> (Then Hardās left. He went to Sojhat and met with Muṃhato Rāymal. Hardās settled in the ***vās*** of Vīramde. Hardās told Rāymal: "If you would do battle with Rāv Gāṅgo, then I will stay with you; otherwise I shall not stay." Then Rāymal said: "***Jī***, for us there is only battle, twenty-four hours a day.")

Dayāldās:

> ***Pīche Hardās Koḍhṇo chāḍnai Sojhat gayo, nai Rāymalsūṃ miliyo. Aru Rāymalnūṃ kayo: "Jo the Rāv Gāṅgaisūṃ laṛāī karo, to hūṃ thāṃrai rahūṃ." Tad Rāymal kayo: "Jī mhārai to āṭh paur laṛāīj rahai." Tārāṃ Hardās Ūhaṛ Vīramderai vās vasiyo.***[19]
>
> (Afterward Hardās left Koḍhṇo and went to Sojhat, and he met with Rāymal. And he said to Rāymal: "If you would do battle with Rāv Gāṅgo, then I shall stay with you." Then Rāymal said: "***Jī***, for us there is only battle, twenty-four hours a day." Then Hardās Ūhaṛ settled in the ***vās*** of Vīramde.)

One might presume that Naiṇsī himself similarly included materials from much

---

concerning Sīrohī while "in front of Naiṇsī" in Jaitāraṇ village. ***Khyāt***, 1:8, 60, 88.

[17] Dayāldās Siṇḍhayac, ***Dayāldāsrī Khyāt: Bīkānerrai Rāṭhoṛāṃrī Khyāt***, ed. Daśrath Śarmā, vol. 1 (Bīkāner: Anūp Saṃskṛt Pustakālay, 1948). The accounts of the reigns of Rāv Jaitsī (1:37-63) and Rāv Kalyāṇsiṅgh (1:64-90) have the passages borrowed from Naiṇsī.

[18] ***Khyāt***, 3:87.

[19] Siṇḍhāyac, ***Dayāldāsrī Khyāt***, 1:46.

older, unattributed sources. He too may have rewritten them with slight modifications, such as more modern vocabulary or grammar in place of archaic terms or usages. Thus the three stories from his ***Khyāt*** that we have selected may indeed be contemporary with the events they mention.[20]

Alternatively, Naiṇsī may have composed entirely new stories, based on his knowledge and long experience. To explore this possibility, one may examine a text discussing events at the court of Rāvaḷ Mālo, ruler of Mahevo in western Mārvāṛ during the fourteenth century. The text concerns the arrival at court of Kumbho Kāmpaliyo, one of Rāvaḷ Mālo's Rajpūts, who happens to possess a fine mare that the Rāvaḷ wants:

> One branch (***sākh***) among the Cahuvāṇ [Rajpūt] branches is called Kāmpaliyo .... Formerly Kumbho Kāmpaliyo was a great Rajpūt .... Kumbho Kāmpaliyo possessed a very fine mare. In those days Rāvaḷ Mālo had acquired much land to the west [of Mahevo]. All the ***bhomiyo***s of the west accepted Rāvaḷ Mālo's authority. He decided to take Kumbho's mare. At that time Rāvaḷ Mālo's pradhan was Bhovo Nāī. The Rāvaḷ said to him: "This mare should be taken." Then Bhovo said: "Kumbho is not one who simply will hand over the mare." They summoned Kumbho and had [him] sit in court. 500 men, ***cīndhaṛ***s wearing armor, were seated in front. 500 men, gunners (***tobci***) remained standing, having touched off matches [for their guns] ....[21]

This story contains an anachronistic element which reveals that it cannot be contemporary with the events it describes. Fourteenth-century Mārvāṛ did not have gunners, who first appear in large numbers there only during the reign of Rāv Candrasen of Jodhpur (1562-81). Naiṇsī may have rewritten an old tale and added the gunners as a flourish that would make the events more plausible to his audience, but perhaps he simply told a new story containing some historical truths of which he was aware (Rāvaḷ Mālo ruled from Mahevo; he probably did conquer much land to the west, etc.).

Similar ambiguities surround other unattributed sections of his ***Khyāt*** and to a lesser extent, his ***Vigat***. And so, the historian using these sections cannot make easy judgements about their dates of composition.

---

[20] These stories lack any sort of statement of attribution, even the simple "I heard a story like this."

[21] ***Khyāt***, 1:247-248. The term ***cīndhaṛ*** mentioned in the text refers to a type of warrior serving for food, clothing, and (occasionally) money.

A. Muṃhato Naiṇsī.[22]

Naiṇsī was a member of the Muhaṇot family of Mārvāṛī Osvāḷs. The Osvāḷs are Mahājans who are named after Osian or Osīāṃ, as it is called in the ***Vigat***, a village thirty miles north-northwest of Jodhpur. According to a legend, half of the population of Osīāṃ converted to Jainism around V.S. 282 (225-26), and so the Osvāḷ ***jāti*** had its beginning. Over time others converted and joined, including many Rajpūts. The internal structure of the ***jāti*** at present is complex, with more than 1,800 subdivisions. Most of the Osvāḷs are Jains.[23]

The Muhaṇot family claims descent from Muhaṇ, brother of Kanhpāl, the son and successor of Rāv Rāypāl, a Rāṭhoṛ Rajpūt who ruled Kheṛ in Mārvāṛ in the early fourteenth century. Muhaṇ converted to Jainism, and his descendants following the Jain faith were called Muhaṇots and included in the Osvāḷ ***jāti***. This much is generally accepted by scholars; the circumstances of his conversion are not. According to one tradition, one day when Muhaṇ had gone hunting, he killed a pregnant doe. Stricken with remorse, he returned to Kheṛ. While standing at a well in this village, he encountered the Jain ascetic Śivsen. He pleaded with Śivsen to bring the deer back to life. When Śivsen did so, Muhaṇ converted to Jainism. This event supposedly took place in V.S. 1351 (1294-95).[24]

A second account of Muhaṇ's conversion relates that because of the hostility of his brothers, he had gone to Jaisaḷmer during his father's reign and had received the protection of the Rāvaḷ there. While in Jaisaḷmer he fell under the influence of the Jain scholar Śrī Jinmaṇikyasūri and converted to Jainism. Another version of Muhaṇ's conversion in Jaisaḷmer indicates that he became enamoured of the daughter of the Jaisaḷmer ***pradhān***, who was of the Śrīmal Vaiśya ***jāti***. When the ***pradhān*** complained to the Rāvaḷ, the Rāvaḷ decided to marry Muhaṇ to the daughter. Upon his marriage in V.S. 1351, Muhaṇ became a Jain. A son, Sampat, was born from this marriage; his descendants are the Muhaṇot Osvāls. A third version of the Jaisaḷmer episode indicates that the Rāvaḷ of Jaisaḷmer had forced Muhaṇ to marry a Jain girl in revenge for Rāv Rāypāl's previously forcing a Bhāṭī Rajpūt to become a Cāraṇ. The descendants of the Jain wife of Muhaṇ following the Jain faith are the Muhaṇots. This last is the account Manoharsiṃh Rāṇāvat himself prefers, but I see no real reason why it might be more credible than the others, all of which depend on the uncertain information about the fourteenth century provided by seventeenth-century

---

[22] The following account of Naiṇsī is based primarily upon Manorsiṃh Rāṇāvat's excellent study of his life entitled "Muhaṇot Naiṇsī: uskā Vyaktiva tathā uskā Kāl," in ***idem, Itihāskār Muhaṇot Naiṇsī tathā uske Itihās-Granth*** (Jodhpur: Rājasthān Sāhitya Mandir, 1981), pp. 16-46. Where possible I have examined the original sources that Rāṇāvat used.

[23] Munshi Hardyal Singh, ***The Castes of Marwar: Being Census Report of 1891***, 2nd edition, with an introduction by Komal Kothari (Jodhpur: Books Treasure, 1990), pp. 128-130.

[24] Rāṇāvat, p. 16.

sources.[25]

Very little can be said with authority about the Muhaṇots from Muhaṇ's death until the lifetime of Muhaṇot Acḷo Sūjāvat in the sixteenth century, but clearly they were in the service of the Rāṭhoṛ rulers of Maṇḍor and Jodhpur in those years.[26] Acḷo Sūjāvat himself was Naiṇsī's paternal great-grandfather and served under Rāv Candrasen (1562-81) of Jodhpur. He shared the Rāv's long, difficult life in exile while the Rāv wandered about Rājasthān, visiting Ḍūṅgarpur, Vāṃsvāḷo, and Mevāṛ. When Candrasen returned to Mārvāṛ and attacked Sojhat's Mughal garrison, Muhaṇot Acḷo died in the battle there on Sunday, June 30, 1578.[27] After Candrasen's death five years later, Acḷo's descendants and the other Muhaṇots transferred their allegiance to Candrasen's elder brother, Udaisiṅgh Māldevot (ruler of Jodhpur, 1583-95).

Inscriptions and ***khyāt***s mention the name of Muhaṇot Jeso, Acḷo's son, but tell us nothing else about him. Much more is known about Jeso's son, Muhaṇot Jaymal Jesāvat, who was Naiṇsī's father. Jaymal was born on Wednesday, January 31, 1582. He began his long period of service during the reign of Rājā Sūrajsiṅgh Udaisiṅghot, ruler of Jodhpur from 1595-1619. The Mughal Emperor Jahāṅgīr had ordered Sūrajsiṅgh to Gujarat in 1606 to repress some rebels there. He obtained some ***pargano***s in ***jāgīr***, including Baṛnagar, of which he made Jaymal the ***hākim***. Jaymal managed the affairs of Baṛnagar until 1615. In that year, Jahāṅgīr presented Sūrajsiṅgh with Phaḷodhī Pargano, and Muhaṇot Jaymal was appointed ***hākim*** of Phaḷodhī by Sūrajsiṅgh.

In February of 1621 Prince Khurram (later Shāh Jahān) gave Rājā Gajsiṇgh Sūrajsiṅghot (ruler of Jodhpur, 1619-38) Jāḷor Pargano. Gajsiṇgh appointed Jaymal ***hākim*** of Jāḷor. Subsquently Gajsiṅgh obtained Sācor Pargano (1622) and by 1624 or 1625 Muhaṇot Jaymal was the ***hākim*** there. Following a serious attack on Sācor by an army of Kachīs which he successfully repulsed, Jaymal had the walls of Sācor rebuilt.

After a series of military campaigns against rebellious Rajpūt chiefs in Surācand, Pokaraṇ, Rāṛdharā, and Mahevo, Gajsiṅgh appointed Jaymal to the post of ***des-dīvan*** in 1629, replacing Siṅghvī Sahasmal. The ***des-dīvān*** was the highest administrative office in the Jodhpur kingdom during the seventeenth century. Holders of the office had great control over the fiscal affairs of Jodhpur. They also had to function as military commanders in the absence of the rājās, who were often out of Mārvāṛ involved in Mughal wars. Jaymal performed as ***des-dīvān*** until 1633, when Gajsiṅgh replaced him with Siṅghvī Sukhmal. He had developed a reputation for severity. During the famine of 1630-31 in Jāḷor, Jaymal had refused to make any concessions in taxes and forced their full realization, a policy which drove the nearby chief of Rāṛdharā, Mahesdās, into rebellion. Perhaps Gajsiṅgh was displeased with Jaymal over this episode and so replaced him. Nothing more is heard of Jaymal after

---

[25] ***Ibid.***, pp. 17-18.

[26] ***Ibid.***, pp. 18-19.

[27] ***Vigat***, 1:73; Rāṇāvat, p. 19.

1633.[28]

Jaymal had made two marriages, the first to the daughter of Muṃhato Lālcand, Sarūpde, by whom he had four sons, Naiṇsī, Sundardās, Āskaraṇ, and Narsiṃhdās; the second to Suhāgde, daughter of Siṅghvī Biṛadsiṃh, who had one son, Jagmāl.[29]

Jaymal's eldest son, Naiṇsī, was born on Friday, November 9, 1610. Naiṇsī himself was married twice, the first time to the daughter of Bhaṇḍārī Nārāyaṇdās, the second to the daughter of Muṃhato Bhīmrāj.[30] An interesting story is told about Naiṇsī's attempt to make a third marriage with the daughter of Kamo, a ***kāmdār*** from Bāhaṛmer. At the time Naiṇsī was ***hākim*** of Jāḷor Pargano. His administrative duties kept him there, and so he sent only his sword to Bāhaṛmer along with some retainers to represent him at the marriage. The ***kāmdār***, Kamo, considered this an insult and married his daughter elsewhere. In revenge, an enraged Naiṇsi sent men to Bāhaṛmer, had the main gates of the fort there removed, brought to him, and installed at the main gate of Jāḷor.[31]

Not much is known of Naiṇsī's life before his first appointment in 1637. One may recall, however, that his ancestors had been in the service of the Rāṭhoṛs since the fourteenth century. The family undoubtedly possessed many private papers and manuscripts relating to the royal family. Naiṇsī probably received training in the use and composition of documents from his father, Jaymal, who had been involved in the Jodhpur administration for twenty-seven years. His early training must have involved military training as well, for he, like his father, took part in several campaigns within Mārvāṛ. His career may be studied by examining his activities in both administrative and military affairs.

On October 12, 1637, Muhaṇot Naiṇsī was appointed ***hākim*** of Phaḷodhī Pargano in western Mārvāṛ, a post previously held by Muṃhato Jagannāth. For several years previously, Baloc raiders had been stepping up their operations in this ***pargano***, and Jagannāth had been unable to suppress them. In March, 1634 Baloc Mughal Khān and Samāyal Khān looted two villages of Phaḷodhi. Then, in September of 1636 the Baloc penetrated again, looting animals and material goods. Jagannāth lost several men attempting to stop them. Finally, on October 5, 1637, Baloc Mudāphar Khān came upon Nenaū village of Phaḷodhī, killed two Rajpūts

---

[28] Jaymal was a munificent patron of the Jain Śvetambar sect. Several inscriptions from local temples in Jāḷor, Sācor, Nāḍol, Pālītāṇā, and Phaḷodhī attest to his generosity. His final inscription, found in the temple of Śāntināth in Phaḷodhī, is dated Tuesday, November 14, 1632 and refers to him as "Mantrīśvara," i.e., ***des-dīvān***. For Jaymal's career, see Rāṇāvat, pp. 20-23.

[29] Rāṇāvat, p. 23.

[30] ***Ibid.***

[31] Bāṅkīdās, ***Bāṅkīdās rī Khyāt***, ed. Narottamdāsjī Svāmī (Jaypur: Rājasthān Purātattvānveṣaṇ Mandir, 1956), p. 176, no. 2125. Rāṇāvat ("Muhaṇot Naiṇsī: uskā Vyaktiva tathā uskā Kāl," p. 24) states that Naiṇsī looted several areas of Bāhaṛmer as well, but Bāṅkīdās does not mention this.

there along with their men, and came away with many animals. One week later Naiṇsi replaced Jagannāth as ***hākim*** and made his way to Phaḷodhī, where he arrived on October 20, 1637. His mission was to end the Baloc raiding.[32]

The Baloc raider Mughal Khān Saroī returned to Phaḷodhī in December of 1637 and attacked Vāp village with over one hundred mounted companions. Rāv Mohandās of Vāp closed the gates and sent messengers to Naiṇsī in Phaḷodhī. Naiṇsī reached Vāp with a few soldiers, enough to drive away Mughal Khān. Naiṇsi tracked down the Khān and, in a coordinated attack involving not only Rāv Manohardās but also the Rāvaḷ of Jaisaḷmer , killed him at the Ahvācī River on December 14, 1637.[33] Many other Baloc were killed as well. For the moment, the raids were over. But then Rājā Gajsiṅgh died, and on Thursday, January 31, 1639, eight months into the reign of his young successor, Rājā Jasvantsiṅgh, the Baloc Mādo and Phatai Alī attacked Phaḷodhī with 750 men. Naiṇsi and his brother, Sundardās, confronted them; they fled without a battle. This was the last of the Baloc raids against Phaḷodhī during Naiṇsī's stay there.[34]

During the middle period, the rugged terrain of eastern Jaitāraṇ and Sojhat ***pargano***s was the homeland of the Mers, a ***jāti*** of diverse origin whose members were often not under the control of either the Jodhpur rājās or the local Rajpūt ***ṭhākur***s. In 1642-43 Rājā Jasvantsiṅgh sent Naiṇsī to Sojhat to suppress a Mer rebellion. He attacked and defeated them. Many of their villages were burned down. Then again, in 1645-46, Naiṇsī, along with his brother Sundardās, received Jasvantsiṅgh's order to proceed against the Mer leader Rāvat Nārāyaṇ, who had begun looting villages of Sojhat from his mountain retreat. Naiṇsī and Sundardās destroyed several Mer villages and put an end to the forays of Rāvat Nārāyaṇ.[35]

A more complex problem arose over Pokaraṇ in 1649 following the death of Rāvaḷ Manohardās of Jaisaḷmer on November 11. Pokaraṇ Pargano was situated on the boundary of the Jodhpur and Jaisaḷmer domains. The Rāvaḷs of Jaisaḷmer had held Pokaraṇ since the reign of Rāv Candrasen of Jodhpur (1562-81). In the seventeenth century, the Mughal Emperors began to include Pokaraṇ as part of the lands granted to the Jodhpur rājās, but the Jaisaḷmer Rāvaḷs retained their ***de facto*** control. Rājā Jasvantsiṅgh had acquired Pokaraṇ in 1638 when he succeeded Rājā Gajsiṅgh, but he made no attempt to exert authority over it. Then in 1650, Manbhāvatī Bāī, Rājā Gajsiṅgh's sister and the wife of the deceased Mughal prince Parvīz, petitioned Shāh Jahān to write a ***farmān*** ordering Pokaraṇ to be turned over to Jasvantsiṅgh. Jasvantsiṅgh's officers brought the ***farmān*** to the new Rāvaḷ of

---

[32] Rāṇāvat, pp.24-25.

[33] ***Vigat***, 1:118-123. See also Norman P. Ziegler, "Evolution of the Rathor State of Marvar: Horses, Structural Change and Warfare," in ***The Idea of Rajasthan: Explorations in Regional Identity***, edited by Karine Schomer et al., 2 vols. (Columbia, Mo.: South Asia Publications by arrangement with Manohar Publishers & Distributors; New Delhi: American Institute of Indian Studies, 1994), 2:208-209.

[34] Rāṇāvat, pp. 25-27.

[35] ***Ibid.***, p.27.

Jaisaḷmer, Rāmcandra, Manohardās's cousin, who rejected it with these words: "One does not obtain a fort upon demand. Pokaraṇ will come [into your hands] after ten Bhāṭī men have died."[36] Jasvantsiṅgh's response was to mobilize an army. Once assembled, this army consisted of several thousand men under three commanders. Naiṇsī himself was in the ***harāval***, or vanguard, led by Nāhar Khān Rājsiṅghot, a Kūmpāvat Rāṭhoṛ. They left Jodhpur on September 7, 1650, and arrived at Khāro village of Pokaraṇ Pargano on September 22, 1650.[37]

During this same period Shāh Jahān had inquired about the succession to the throne of Jaisaḷmer. The Rāṭhoṛ Rājā of Kisangaṛh, Rūpsiṅgh, had in his service Sabaḷsiṅgh Dayāḷdāsot, Rāvaḷ Manohardās's other cousin. He had him touch the feet of the Emperor in a gesture of obeisance. Shāh Jahān gave Sabaḷsiṅgh the throne and dispatched him to Jaisaḷmer. As Sabaḷsiṅgh had no military equipment or retinue, he went first to Jodhpur and met with Rājā Jasvantsiṅgh. Jasvantsiṅgh supplied him with a horse, a ***sirpāv***, expense money, and instructions: "You go to Phaḷodhī; my army is coming; they will help you."[38] Sabaḷsiṅgh remained in Phaḷodhī for some time, then joined Jasvantsiṅgh's army in Khāro with five or six hundred men. On September 29, 1650, the combined army, now numbering 6,000 men, encircled Pokaraṇ. An initial attack failed. Most of the army returned to camp. Naiṇsī, however, remained behind with some Bhāṭī and Rāṭhoṛ soldiers from Nāhar Khān's division. They attacked and penetrated the town of Pokaraṇ, took up a position in a temple, and began a gun-battle with the soldiers inside the fort.[39] After several more days of similar action, the enthusiam of the Bhāṭī soldiers inside the fort waned, and they came to an agreement to evacuate Pokaraṇ. A few loyal Bhāṭīs refused to surrender and died confronting Jasvantsiṅgh's army. After the capture of Pokaraṇ on October 4, 1650, Jasvantsiṅgh's army set out for Jaisaḷmer. Rāvaḷ Rāmcandra fled, and Sabaḷsiṅgh became the new Rāvaḷ of Jaisaḷmer.[40]

In 1659, Naiṇsī, now ***des-dīvan*** of Jodhpur, again became involved in a military conflict over Pokaraṇ with the Bhāṭīs of Jaisaḷmer. The second military campaign against Pokaraṇ has been described in minute detail by either Naiṇsī or one of his subordinates. The account has been published in the collection of documents entitled ***Jodhpur Hukūmat rī Bahī***.[41]

In the fall of 1657, the Mughal emperor Shāh Jahān fell ill. A war of

---

[36] ***Vigat***, 2:298.

[37] Rāṇāvat, pp. 27-28.

[38] ***Vigat***, 2:300.

[39] ***Ibid***., 2:302; Ziegler, , "Evolution of the Rathor State of Marvar: Horses, Structural Change and Warfare," 2:209.

[40] Rāṇāvat, pp. 28-30.

[41] "Jodhpur Hukūmat rī Bahī," in ***Marwar under Jaswant Singh (1658-1678): Jodhpur Hukumat ri Bahi***, ed. by Satish Chandra, Raghubir Sinh and G. D. Sharma (Meerut: Meenakshi Prakashan, 1976), pp. 39-74.

succession soon began between his sons. Jasvantsiṅgh was sent to confront Prince Aurangzeb, coming from the Deccan, and Prince Murād, coming from Gujarat. On April 16, 1658, Jasvantsiṅgh lost the battle of Dharmāṭ to Aurangzeb. Most of Jasvantsiṅgh's personal contingent was annihilated. Jasvantsiṅgh accepted Aurangzeb's authority temporarily, but then abandoned him. The Rāvaḷ of Jaisaḷmer, Sabaḷsiṅgh, took advantage of Aurangzeb's renewed hostility toward Jasvantsiṅgh and obtained a ***farmān*** for Pokaraṇ on February 24, 1659. On March 26, 1659, an army from Jaisaḷmer under the leadership of Kuṃvar Amarsiṅgh, Sabaḷsiṅgh's son, seized Pokaraṇ. But then Aurangzeb was forced to conclude an agreement with Jasvantsiṅgh in order to prevent him from joining forces with Dārā Shikoh, another of Shāh Jahān's sons. As part of this agreement, Jasvantsiṅgh received Pokaraṇ again.[42]

On March 31, 1659, Jasvantsiṅgh received the news that the Bhāṭīs had taken Pokaraṇ. He dispatched an army under the leadership of Naiṇsī to re-establish his authority there. Naiṇsī gathered together an impressive force of 2,071 horsemen, 811 camel riders, and 2,622 footsoldiers, collected the military equipment necessary, and took 20,000 rupees from the Jodhpur treasury for other expenses. He and his army departed from Jodhpur at dawn on April 9, 1659. Along the way they learned that the Bhāṭī army had evacuated Pokaraṇ but were continuing to loot villages in the area.[43]

Naiṇsī and his men reached Pokaraṇ on April 19. One may pause a moment to contemplate the difficulty of marching thousands of men nearly 100 miles in eleven days through desert terrain in the heat of a Rājasthān April.[44] Once in Pokaraṇ, Naiṇsī sent messengers to the Bhāṭīs to inform them about Aurangzeb's having given Pokaraṇ to Jasvantsiṅgh. After resupplying the army, Naiṇsī departed after the Bhāṭīs with approximately 4,000 soldiers. On April 26 they reached the Jaisaḷmer border. Naiṇsi gave the soldiers permission to begin looting the villages of Jaisaḷmer. They advanced slowly, looting and burning as they went. Finally they returned to Pokaraṇ on May 11, 1659. It had been an inconclusive but devastating campaign.[45]

After returning to Jodhpur, Naiṇsī received word that the Bhāṭīs had returned to the Pokaraṇ/Phaḷodhī area and were themselves looting villages. Once again Naiṇsī left Jodhpur. He had to re-unite his soldiers, who had disbanded and returned to their homes. He arrived at Phaḷodhī on June 10. A long period of raiding and counter-raiding began, with the Bhāṭīs gradually losing ground. Finally a peace agreement was signed with the aid of Rājā Karaṇ

---

[42] Rāṇāvat, pp. 30-31.

[43] ***Ibid.***, p. 31.

[44] The average maximum daily temperature in Jodhpur during April is over 100 degree Fahrenheit. Cf. K. D. Erskine, ed., ***Rajputana Gazetteers:*** Volume III-A, ***The Western Rajputana States Residency and the Bikaner Agency*** (Allahabad: The Pioneer Press, 1909), p. 20.

[45] Rāṇāvat, pp. 32-34.

of Bīkāner. Naiṇsī returned to Jodhpur on August 4, 1659. For four months he had carried out a successful military operation in the worst heat of the Indian summer.[46]

At the time Naiṇsī was appointed ***des-dīvān***, he had been in the service of Jodhpur for twenty-one years, almost entirely as a ***hākim*** of various ***parganos***. As noted, he had received his first appointment in October of 1637, when he was made ***hākim*** of Phaḷodhī. He remained in Phaḷodhī for at least two years, until 1639. From then until October, 1650, his status is unknown, although he did lead military operations against the Mers of Sojhat in May, 1642 and in 1645-46.[47] Then, on October 16, 1650, he was appointed ***hākim*** of Pokaraṇ. He held this position for about two months and then was transferred by Jasvantsiṅgh to Agra Province to become the new ***hākim*** of Udehī Pañcvār Pargano in the district of Hiṇḍaun. Possibly he stayed there until August, 1652. At that time he was appointed ***hākim*** of Malārṇo Pargano, where he remained until June, 1656. Evidently he then became ***hākim*** of Vadhnor Pargano, his last appointment before becoming ***des-dīvan***.[48]

During the years prior to his appointment, Naiṇsī gathered much of the information that fills his ***Vigat*** and ***Khyāt***. His accounts of the military campaigns in the Pokaraṇ and Phaḷodhī areas come from this period. Wherever he went, he collected anecdotes and documents.[49] His experience, coupled with his family's long association with the Jodhpur rulers and their undoubted access to administrative records dating back to the previous century if not further, made him uniquely placed to assume the duties of the office to which Jasvantsiṅgh appointed him on May 18, 1658. Jasvantsiṅgh established his salary at 9,000 rs. yearly and gave him in addition a ***paṭo*** or land grant. Naiṇsī was to remain ***des-dīvan*** until 1666.[50]

Probably one of his first tasks as ***des-dīvān*** was ordering the compilation of the ***paṭo bahī***, or register of land grants, of V.S. 1714/1657-58.[51] This document, which lists all holders of ***paṭo***s in V.S. 1714 and recipients of grants in succeeding years until V.S. 1729/1672-73, would give Naiṇsī a clear picture of who held what lands in Mārvāṛ, what those lands' current assessed values were, and the relative strengths of the Rajpūt landholding groups. One would

---

[46] ***Ibid.***, p. 34.

[47] Possibly Naiṇsī was ***hākim*** of Jāḷor between 1639 and 1650 and this was the period during which he had attempted to marry in Bāhaṛmer. Cf. p. 10, ***supra***.

[48] Rāṇāvat, p. 35.

[49] The collection of documents began as early as 1643-44, when Muṃhato Lakho had the ***hakīkat*** of Jaisalmer written for Naiṇsī while in the military camp at Meṛto. ***Khyāt***, 2:6.

[50] Rāṇāvat, p. 36.

[51] The ***paṭo bahī*** is contained in "Jodhpur Hukūmat rī Bahī," pp. 125-237.

assume a new ***des-dīvān*** would have great interest in such information. Conceivably it is not a mere coincidence that the first year of the ***bahī*** and Naiṇsī's first year of appointment are the same.

Certainly Naiṇsī began the compilation of his ***Vigat*** soon after he took office. The first year of village revenue statistics in the ***Vigat*** is V.S. 1715/1658-59. Evidently the village survey had been completed by the end of this year as V.S. 1715 revenue returns are given for every village (around 2,000 in all). Similar statistics are given for most of the villages for each of the following four years, V.S. 1716-19/1659-63. The ***Vigat*** also includes aggregate revenue statistics for seven ***parganos*** of Mārvāṛ from V.S. 1711/1654-55 to V.S. 1720/1663-64. An analysis of these statistics, presented in Tables One and Two,[52] reveals the success of Naiṇsī in increasing the revenues produced by the lands under his administration. The overall increase averaged 35.4% during the first six full years of Naiṇsī's tenure. Only in Sojhat Pargano was there a decline. If one assumes that V.S. 1715 may have been a transitional year during which the ***Vigat***'s village survey was completed, and that Naiṇsī may not have implemented any changes until the following year, the statistics become even more dramatic, as shown by Tables Three and Four, which demonstrate an average revenue increase of 74.2% during the four years V.S. 1716-19 as compared with the four years prior to V.S. 1715. Such a large difference in land revenue very likely was due to new, more efficient administrative methods and not to increased agricultural production or a change in weather conditions.[53] But efficiency in extracting land revenue from peasants on the margin of existence is not always welcomed, as Naiṇsī was to find out.

Before 1666 there was no indication that Muhaṇot Naiṇsī had been anything other than a valued soldier-administrator of the Jodhpur kingdom. But while in Lahore in December of that year Rājā Jasvantsiṅgh abruptly made some major changes. On December 9, he appointed Rāṭhoṛ Āskaraṇ his new ***pradhān***. Then, on December 24, he removed his ***des-dīvān***, Naiṇsī, and ***tan-dīvān***,[54] Muhaṇot Sundardās (Naiṇsī's brother), from office. After an investigation, Sundardās's wealth was found in the possession of Rāṭhoṛ Syāmsiṅgh Gopāḷdāsot. Syāmsiṅgh lost his land grant and had to leave service.[55]

Why did Jasvantsiṅgh dismiss the Muhaṇot brothers? Some have suggested that Naiṇsī appointed too many of his relations to important offices. It is true that Naiṇsī's two brothers, Āskaraṇ and Sundardās, and later his son,

---

[52] Tables One through Four are based on statistics given by the ***Vigat***, 1:168-169, 402, 500, 2:10, 80, 281, 322.

[53] Cf. Rāṇāvat, p. 42.

[54] ***Tan-dīvān***: an official of the Jodhpur kingdom whose main concerns were salaries and the reckoning of land grants. Sundardās was ***tan-dīvān*** from 1654 to 1666, and so he probably compiled the ***paṭṭā-bahī*** found in the "Jodhpur Hukūmat rī Bahī," pp. 125-237, on the orders of his brother, Naiṇsī.

[55] Rāṇāvat, pp. 40-41.

Muhaṇot Karamsī, held high positions within the Jodhpur administration, but this fact alone does not explain why Jasvantsiṅgh, who appointed them all, would suddenly become concerned enough to remove Naiṇsī and Sundardās. Others have suggested that Naiṇsī had his rivals within the administration, which is possible but undocumented. One story suggests that Rājsiṅgh Khiṃvāvat, Jasvantsiṅgh's famous ***pradhān***, had something to do with Naiṇsī's fall from favor in 1666. As Dr. Rāṇāvat has pointed out, Rājsiṅgh's death in 1640 removes him from this event by twenty-six years.[56]

One possible reason why Naiṇsī was dismissed comes from the ***Vigat*** itself. Amidst an account of ***pargano*** taxes in Meṛto is the following note:

> In January-February of 1662 the ***rait*** [of Meṛto Pargano] went to the Mughal court and complained [about taxes]. Then ***[va]kīl*** Manohardās made a reduction ... and Māhārājājī [Jasvantsiṅgh] agreed [to it].[57]

The previous autumn Naiṇsī had become aware that the Jāṭs of several villages were dissatisfied with local administration. He had attempted to placate them, but they refused to come and meet with him. Then, about a year later, in late 1662, the Jāṭs of Cāndārūṇ, Lavero, and Rāhīṇ villages assembled and appealed to the Mughal Emperor, Aurangzeb, about the heavy tax burden they bore.[58]

The appeals to Aurangzeb from the peasants of Meṛto in 1661 and 1662 probably did not disturb Aurangzeb as much as complaints from Haṃsār.[59] Jasvantsiṅgh had received this area after he was transferred from Gujarat in 1661. Naiṇsī had sent his son, Muhaṇot Karamsī, along with Pañcolī Bachraj to Haṃsār to assume control of the administration there. Haṃsar was not in Rājāsthan. It had been more a part of the Mughal Empire than Jasvantsiṅgh's Māṛvāṛ ***parganos***, and what happened in it was of considerable concern to Aurangzeb. Thus when the local people complained to him in 1666 about the administration of Jasvantsiṅgh's officials, Aurangzeb ordered the remission of 100,000 rupees (one ***lākh***) to mitigate their difficulties. Jasvantsiṅgh responded as well. He appointed Vyās Padmanābh the new ***hākim*** of Haṃsār and on December 24, 1666 removed Naiṇsi and Sundardās from office.[60]

On March 11, 1667 Aurangzeb ordered Jasvantsiṅgh to go to the Deccan. At this time Jasvantsiṅgh summoned Naiṇsī to him. He departed for the Deccan with both Naiṇsī and Sundardās, who had been with him since autumn, 1666. In the camp at Aurangābād on November 29, 1667, Jasvantsiṅgh

---

[56] ***Ibid.***, pp. 43-45.

[57] ***Vigat***, 2:93.

[58] ***Ibid***, 2:94.

[59] Haṃsar is in Haryana state, on the border of the old Bīkāner Princely State.

[60] Rāṇāvat, p. 42.

ordered that they be imprisoned. They were held for one year, then Jasvantsiṅgh released them and ordered that Naiṇsī deposit 100,000 rupees in the Jodhpur treasury, exactly the same amount Aurangzeb had returned to the petitioners in Haṃsār. Naiṇsī refused to pay, and so, on December 28, 1669, he was imprisoned along with his brother once again. On August 3, 1670, Naiṇsī and Sundardās, disgraced, killed themselves in Phūlmārī, a village not far from Aurangābād.[61]

The very methods by which Naiṇsī extracted an unprecedented amount of revenue from the Mārvāṛ ***pargano***s evidently had alienated those who paid the revenue. And so Jasvantsiṅgh, faced with repeated complaints to his Emperor, removed and imprisoned Naiṇsī and Sundardās. Historians may admire the documents left behind by Naiṇsī, but his efficiency in office had its punishments as well as its rewards.

II. Conventions.

A. Translation methodology.

Marshall G. S. Hodson has divided translations into three types: recreative, explanatory, and precise study translations. Our translations fall into the latter category. Hodgson has defined the precise study translation as one whose aim is

> ... to reproduce the information carried by the original work, for the purposes of special study by those who cannot read the original language. Such a translation attempts to provide an equivalent communication of the original which readers can then interpret for themselves. For study purposes, the translation has to be maximally precise.... The translator must find an equivalent for every personal turn of phrase of the original, however superfluous it may seem, and must leave ambiguities, so far as possible, ambiguous. Such a translation almost necessarily requires a certain number of explicitly technical terms and a few footnotes or square brackets to pinpoint untranslatable implications.[62]

In general, we have followed Hodgson's guidelines. As he suggested, the methodology demands the inclusion of technical terms, which for various reasons are better left untranslated. Instead, we have defined these terms at length in footnotes when they are first encountered in the texts. In addition, we have provided a glossary comprising definitions for all such terms followed by lists of passages in which they appear.

We have translated kinship terms, but have placed the corresponding Middle

---

[61] ***Ibid.***, pp. 45-46.

[62] Marshal G. S. Hodgson, ***The Venture of Islam: Conscience and History in a World Civilization***. 3 vols. (Chicago: The University of Chicago Press, 1974), 1:68.

Mārvāṛī words after them in parentheses to save footnotes, as; "mother's brother" (*māmo*). Occasionally we have followed other translated terms with Middle Mārvāṛī equivalents in parentheses, as, for example, "soul" (*jīv*), but this practice has been kept to a minimum, as has the reverse: following indigenous words with parenthetical translations.

We have tried to represent the original texts faithfully without being overly literal. Thus we have not translated every ***pachai*** ("afterwards," "subsequently") or ***tarai*** ("then"), recognizing that to have done so would have made the English too repetitive. Similarly, we have deleted obvious redundancies and noted their omission in footnotes. We have made considerable use of brackets to add material not given but implied by the original. Ambiguities, difficulties of interpretation, comments on editorial mistakes or on misprints, points of grammar, etc., are all duly noted. Finally, we have attempted to the greatest extent possible to standardize the translations so that the same terms or phrases are rendered identically each time they occur.

B. Transliteration.

We have used the following system for the transliteration of Middle Mārvāṛī words:

Vowels:	**a**	**ā**	**i**	**ī**	**u**	**ū**	
	e	**ai**	**o**	**au**			
Consonants:	**k**	**kh**	**g**	**gh**	**ṅ**		
	c	**ch**	**j**	**jh**	**ñ**		
	ṭ	**ṭh**	**ḍ**	**ḍh**	**ṇ**	**ḷ**	**ṛ**
	t	**th**	**d**	**dh**	**n**		
	p	**ph**	**b**	**bh**	**m**		
	y	**r**	**l**	**v**			
	s	**h**					
Anusvār:	**ṃ**						

1. The scribes of middle period Rājasthān used only the ***anusvār*** to indicate both a nasalized vowel and the nasal before a consonant. We have distinguished between the two instances in our transliteration system and have transliterated anusvar before consonants as follows:

ṅ before gutterals,
ñ before palatals,
ṇ before cerebrals,
n before dentals, and
m before labials.

Before semivowels and sibilants ***anusvār*** is transliterated as **ṃ**.

2. Nasalized vowels before nasal consonants are not indicated in transliteration (hence ***thāṇo*** instead of ***thāṃṇo***).

3. Final **au**, which is a scribal variant of final **o**, has in all instances been transliterated as **o**.

4. We have adopted a method for dealing with the unwritten vowel **a** similar to that used for modern Hindi: final **a** is considered unpronounced and hence not indicated; **a** deleted by rule[63] is similarly omitted.

5. The symbol ष is considered an orthographic equivalent of ख and is accordingly transliterated as **kh** except when in a Sanskrit word (hence ***khān*** and not ***ṣān***, but Viṣṇu, not Vikhṇu).

6. Finally, Sanskrit and Hindi words have been transliterated according to current scholarly conventions.

C. Spelling.

The beginning student of Middle Mārvāṛī cannot fail to be struck by the variant spellings so ubiquitous in the texts. For example, Lāḷas lists no less than fourteen additional forms of the proper name "Rāṭhoṛ."[64] Naiṇsī himself often spelled the same word differently in the same story. Faced with such variety, we have been forced to standardize terms and proper names, aware on the one hand of the need to do justice to the original texts and on the other of the necessity of eliminating confusion in the mind of the reader.

1. Terms not translated, such as ***sāth***, ***bhāībandh***, etc., are transliterated according to the spellings under which they are defined in Lāḷas's ***Rājasthānī Sabad Kos***, unless they are contrary to the usual (or only) spellings found in our texts (hence ***ṭhākur*** instead of ***ṭhākar***, the variant preferred by Lāḷas). Certain terms well-known to those with a knowledge of Indian society are given as they are commonly written and not as they are spelled in Middle Mārvāṛī. Thus, Brāhmaṇ is preferred to Bāmbhaṇ, ***jāti*** to ***jāt***, ***dharma*** to ***dharam***, and so forth. We have indicated the original Arabic and Persian forms of Middle Mārvāṛī words when known and where relevant.

2. Names of places are transliterated as they are ordinarily spelled in the texts. If there are but two dissimilar spellings to be found, we have given each as it occurs and footnoted the variant each time. Well-known names of places outside

---

[63] For a statement of this rule, see Bruce R. Pray, ***Topics in Hindi-Urdu Grammar***, Research Monograph Series no. 1 (Berkeley: Center for South and Southeast Asia Studies, University of California, 1976), pp. 41-43.

[64] Lāḷas, ***RSK***, 4:1:4135.

Rājasthān are given in their standard forms, as for example, Malwa, Delhi, Gujarat, etc. (not Māḷvā, Dilī, or Gujrāt).

3. Hindu personal names have been standardized according to the way they are most commonly spelled in the texts. Muslim personal names have been similarly treated; where possible we have identified Muslim individuals in footnotes and given therein the standard Persian/Arabic versions of their names. Extreme variant spellings of personal names are mentioned in footnotes also.

D. Abbreviations.

Jāti*, *kuḷ*,** and ***sākh names frequently are abbreviated in the chronicles: Rā. for Rāṭhoṛ, Bhā. for Bhāṭī, Kā. for Kachvāho, etc. In such cases we have simply included the full name without abbreviation or bracketing, e.g., Rāṭhoṛ Devīdās instead of Rā. Devīdās or Rā[ṭhoṛ] Devīdās.

E. Paragraphing.

In general we have followed in our translations the paragraphing chosen by the respective editors of the texts, Badrīprasād Sākariyā and Nārāyaṇsiṃh Bhāṭī. The ***Vigat*** has numbered entries or paragraphs as well as the paragraphing done by Bhāṭī. We have retained the numbers for quick reference and also to preserve more exactly the sense of the original.

F. Manuscript variants.

Both the ***Khyāt*** and the ***Rāv Mālde rī Bāt*** contained in "Aitihāsik Bātāṃ" were edited from single manuscripts, but N. S. Bhāṭī edited the ***Vigat*** from two, which he labelled **ka** and **kha**. His policy throughout was to consider the **ka** ms. the "ideal" (***adarś***) and list **kha** ms. variants in footnotes.[65] Our policy has been to indicate in footnotes wherever we have preferred **kha** ms. readings. We also have indicated variant spelling of proper names given in the **kha** ms. if the names appear in no other places in the texts.

G. Dates.

That chronicles indigenous to Rājasthān contain dates at all will perhaps surprise those whose only knowledge of the area's history comes from the hyperbolic prose of James Tod's ***Annals and Antiquities of Rajasthan***. That these dates are usually remarkably accurate, as is shown by the consistent corroboration by contemporary inscriptions and Persian chronicles, may surprise even the more knowledgeable students of the middle period. Still, the dating system used in our

---

[65] N. S. Bhāṭī, "Sampādakīya," in Muṃhatā Naiṇsī, ***Mārvāṛ Parganāṃ rī Vigat***, 3 vols., edited by Nārāyaṇsiṃh Bhāṭī (Jodhpur: Rājasthān Prācyavidyā Pratiṣṭhān, 1968-74), 1:37.

texts is not without its regional quirks, which require elucidation for the reader's benefit.

It is evident that all the dates in these texts are in the luni-solar Vikrama Era, which began in 57 B.C. The Vikrama Era was one of two major eras (there are several minor ones) used in pre-modern India; the other is the Śaka Era, beginning in A.D. 78. In north India, the Vikrama luni-solar year generally began with the month ***Caitra***, hence it was called ***Caitrādi*** Vikrama ("***Caitra***-first Vikrama"). But several regions in Rājasthān, including Mārvāṛ, used a different system according to which the year began with the month ***Śrāvaṇa*** (the ***Śrāvaṇādi*** or "***Śrāvaṇa***-first" Vikrama luni-solar year). The last four months of the ***Śrāvaṇādi*** year are the first four of the following ***Caitrādi*** year; thus, if we see the date Vikrama ***Saṃvat*** ("Year") 1600, ***Vaisākh***, in a text, and we know that the reckoning is ***Śrāvaṇādi***, we must recognize that this corresponds to Vikrama ***Saṃvat*** 1601, ***Vaisākh*** by the Caitrādi reckoning, for ***Vaisākh*** is the second month of the new ***Caitrādi*** year and the tenth month of the old ***Śrāvaṇādi*** year. As standard conversion tables all use the ***Caitrādi*** reckoning, all ***Śrāvaṇādi*** dates falling in the last four months of the year must be changed similarly to ***Caitrādi*** dates before converting them into dates in the Christian Era.

An example found in the compilation entitled "Jodhpur Hukūmat rī Bahī" provides proof of the usage of the ***Śrāvaṇādi*** Vikrama luni-solar year in seventeenth-century Mārvāṛ. The text describes the day by day encampments of one Muṃhato Kalo, who had been given a contingent of soldiers and sent to pillage the ***vasī*** of a certain Bhāṭī Dvārkādās, beginning at the end of Vikrama ***Saṃvat*** 1715 and continuing into 1716:

> ***Āsāḍh, sudi*** 13 Wednesday. In Phaḷodhī.
> ***Āsāḍh, sudi*** 14 Thursday. In Phaḷodhī.
> ***Āsāḍh, sudi*** 15 [Friday]. In Phaḷodhī.
> ***Śrāvaṇa, badi*** 1, 1716, Saturday. In Phaḷodhī.[66]

This sequence clearly indicates that the first day of the new year was the first day of the dark half (***badi***) of ***Śrāvaṇa***. The sequence also reveals that the lunar month in Mārvāṛ was reckoned as ***pūrṇimānta***, "ending in the full moon" (i.e., ***sudi*** 15), an important fact for the correct conversion of ***Śrāvaṇādi*** Vikrama luni-solar dates to dates in the Christian Era.

Unfortunately for the modern reader, the writers of the Middle Mārvāṛī chronicles do not always provide such a clear indication of which reckoning they used, but to our knowledge all the dates in our texts are in the ***Śrāvaṇādi*** or "***Śrāvaṇa***-first" Vikrama Era and the lunar month is always ***pūrṇimānta.***[67] Whenever we have been able to corroborate a date, the reckoning has proved to be ***Śrāvaṇādi/pūrṇimānta***. Yet there are many dates that cannot be corroborated, and so one can never be completely certain if they are in the ***Śrāvaṇādi*** or ***Caitrādi***

---

[66] "Jodhpur Hukūmat rī Bahī," p. 50.

[67] The lunar month was generally counted as ***pūrṇimānta*** in north India. See D. C. Sircar, ***Indian Epigraphy*** (Delhi: Motilal Banarsidass, 1965), p. 224.

Vikrama Year or if the lunar month is ***pūrṇimānta*** or ***amānta*** ("ending with the new moon"). With the knowledge that the present weight of the evidence favors the ***Śrāvanādi/pūrṇimānta*** reckoning, we have converted all dates into the Christian Era accordingly.

Another problem of dating is that the dates in the text are often incomplete: perhaps just the year is given, or just the year and the month. We have used the following system to convert such incomplete dates:

(1) If just the year is given, we give both years of the Christian Era in which the months of the ***Śrāvaṇādi*** Vikrama year fall. V.S. 1625 in the text therefore is converted to 1568-69. If we know from other sources in which year a specific event took place, we have converted the incomplete date accordingly. For example, the text usually states simply that the great battle between Sher Shāh Sūr and Rāv Mālde took place in V.S. 1600 (1543-44). As we know that this battle occurred in 1544 rather than in 1543, we have used only the former year in our conversion.

(2) When the year and months are given, we give both months of the Christian Era year in which the days of the month of the Vikrama year fall: V.S. 1600, ***Caitra***, is thus converted to March-April, 1544. If we know in which month an event occurred, we have given just that month and the year in our conversion.

We have used Cunningham's ***Book of Indian Eras***[68] and Swamikannu Pillai's ***Indian Ephemeris***[69] to convert all dates. Occasionally the corresponding Christian Era dates given by these authors are at variance with those given by G. H. Ojhā, the recognized expert on dates in Rājasthān's inscriptions and chronicles, in his ***Rājputāne kā Itihās*** (History of Rajputana).[70] In such cases we have placed Cunningham's or Pillai's dates in the text of the translation and Ojhā's conversions in footnotes. Also, some dates in the text are obviously incorrect; we have converted these as they are and suggested the more likely dates in footnotes.

Richard D. Saran

---

[68] Alexander Cunningham, ***Book of Indian Eras, with Tables for Calculating Indian Dates*** (1883; reprint ed., Varanasi: Indological Book House, 1970).

[69] Swamikannu Pillai, L. D., ***An Indian Ephemeris, A.D. 700 to A.D. 1799***, 7 vols. in 8 (Madras: Govt. Press, 1922-23).

[70] G. H. Ojhā, ***Rājputāne kā Itihās***, 5 vols. in 9 parts (Ajmer: Vedic Yantralaya, 1927-41).

TABLE 1. Yearly ***Pargano*** revenue totals (numbers represent rupees).

Pargano	1711	1712	1713	1714	**1715**	**1716**	**1717**	**1718**	**1719**	**1720**
Meṛto	348325	183415	257169	246411	**169520**	**512000**	**552309**	**571301**	**328576**	**160550**
Jodhpur	304582	263059	289221	287875	**155697**	**642202**	**432059**	**680464**	**424719**	**131829**
Sojhat	138600	168402	124573	120111	**94168**	**146410**	**169424**	**185550**	**157810**	**72187**
Jaitāraṇ	119565	109076	109794	107616	**94168**	**167517**	**226306**	**193978**	**133476**	**47732**
Phalodhī	17924	23465	23613	19815	**3920**	**37882**	**52299**	**71203**	**34400**	**12119**
Sīvāṇo	32275	34241	28515	20080	**13888**	**44540**	**54634**	**57708**	**33295**	**25491**
Pokaraṇ	9870	9320	9013	10910	**4028**	**8205**	**12036**	**16727**	**8320**	**0**
TOTALS	971141	792690	843611	814532	**537104**	**1560472**	**1500784**	**1778649**	**1122315**	**451628**

The totals in **bold** are those for the full Vikrama Saṃvat years that Naiṇsī was ***des-dīvān*** for which information is available (V.S. 1715-20/1658-59-1663-64). No revenue information was returned for Pokaraṇ Pargano in V.S. 1720.

TABLE 2. Increase in revenue totals during Naiṇsī's tenure as ***Des-Dīvān***.

Pargano	**Average 1711-14**	**Average 1715-20**	**Increase/Decrease**
Meṛto	258830	382376	+47.7%
Jodhpur	286184	411162	+43.7%
Sojhat	137922	137592	-2.4%
Jaitāraṇ	111513	143863	+29.0%
Phaḷodhī	21204	35304	+66.5%
Sīvāṇo	28778	38259	+32.9%
Pokaraṇ	9778	9863	+8.7%
TOTALS	855494	1158492	+35.4%

TABLE 3. V.S. 1715 is considered a transitional year when the ***Vigat*** village survey was undertaken and its revenue totals are omitted. The four years preceeding V.S. 1715 may then be compared with the four years following the survey (in ***bold***).

Pargano	1711	1712	1713	1714	**1716**	**1717**	**1718**	**1719**
Meṛto	348325	183415	257169	246411	**512000**	**552309**	**571301**	**328576**
Jodhpur	304582	263059	289221	287875	**642202**	**432059**	**680464**	**424719**
Sojhat	138600	168402	124573	120111	**146410**	**169424**	**185550**	**157810**
Jaitāraṇ	119565	109076	109794	107616	**167517**	**226306**	**193978**	**133476**
Phalodhī	17924	23465	23613	19815	**37882**	**52299**	**71203**	**34400**
Sīvāṇo	32275	34241	28515	20080	**44540**	**54634**	**57708**	**33295**
Pokaraṇ	9870	9320	9013	10910	**8205**	**12036**	**16727**	**8320**
TOTALS	971141	792690	843611	814532	**1560472**	**1500784**	**1778649**	**1122315**

TABLE 4. Percentage increase in revenue collected V.S. 1711-14 compared with four years (V.S. 1716-19) following the village survey year of V.S. 1715.

Pargano	**Average 1711-14**	**Average 1716-19**	**Increase/Decrease**
Merṭo	258830	491015	+89.7%
Jodhpur	286184	544861	+90.4%
Sojhat	137922	164799	+19.5%
Jaitāraṇ	111513	180319	+61.7%
Phaḷodhī	21204	48946	+130.8%
Sīvāṇo	28778	47544	+65.2%
Pokaraṇ	9778	11322	+15.8%
TOTALS	855494	1490555	+74.2%

Abbreviations

The following abbreviations are used for works frequently cited:

Ā'īn-i-Akbarī	Abū al-Fazl ibn Mubārak, ***Ā'īn-i-Akbarī***
"Aitihāsik Bātāṃ"	"Aitihāsik Bātāṃ." In ***Paramparā***, part 11, pp. 17-109
Akbar Nāma	Abū al-Fazl ibn Mubārak. ***The Akbar Nāma of Abu-l-Fazl***
Āsop kā Itihās	Āsopā, Rāmkaraṇ. ***Āsop kā Itihās***
Athar Ali, ***Apparatus***	Athar Ali, M. ***The Apparatus of Empire: Awards of Ranks, Offices, and Titles to the Mughal Nobility, 1574-1658***
Bāṅkīdās	Bāṅkīdās, ***Bāṅkīdās rī Khyāt***
Bhāṭī, ***Sarvekṣaṇ***	Bhāṭī, Nārāyaṇsiṃh. ***Rājasthān ke Aitihāsik Granthoṃ kā Sarvekṣaṇ***
Cāmpāvat Rāṭhauṛ	Bhagavatsiṃh, Ṭhākur. ***Cāmpāvat Rāṭhauṛ***
Census Report, 1891	"***Mārvāṛ kī Qaumoṃ kā Itihās***." ***Riporṭ Mardumśumārī Rāj Mārvāṛ bābat san 1891 Īsvī***, part 3
Gehlot, ***Mārvāṛ***	Gehlot, G. S. ***Mārvāṛ kā Saṅkṣipt Itihās***
Jahāngīr	Jahāngīr. ***The Tūzuk-i-Jahāngīrī; or, Memoirs of Jahāngīr***
Jaisalmer rī Khyāt	***Jaisalmer rī Khyāt***. ***Paramparā***, parts 57-58. Edited by Nārāyaṇsiṃh Bhāṭī

"Jodhpur Hukūmat rī Bahī"	"Jodhpur Hukūmat rī Bahī." In ***Marwar under Jaswant Singh (1658-1678): Jodhpur Hukumat ri Bahi***, pp. 1-237
Jodhpur Rājya kī Khyāt	***Jodhpur Rājya kī Khyāt***. Edited by Raghuvīr Siṃh and Manoharsiṃh Rāṇāvat
Khyāt	Naiṇsī, Muṃhato, ***Muṃhatā Naiṇsī viracit Muṃhatā Naiṇsīrī Khyāt***
Lāḷas, ***RSK***	Lāḷas, Sītārām, ***Rājasthānī Sabad Kos***
Maā͟thir-ul-Umarā	Shāhnavāz K͟hān Awrangābādī. ***The Maā͟thir-ul-Umarā***
Mūṇḍiyār rī Rāṭhoṛāṃ rī Khyāt	***Mūṇḍiyār rī Rāṭhoṛāṃ rī Khyāt***, MS no. 15635, no. 2
Murārdān, no. 1	***Kavirāj Murardānjī kī Khyāt kā Tarjumā***
Murārdān, no. 2	***Rāṭhoṛoṃ rī Khyāt Purāṇī Kavirājjī Murardānjī ke Yahāṃ se Likhī Gaī***
Murārdān, no. 3	***Rajpūtom kī Khyāt: Kavirājjī Murardānjī kī Khyāt kā Tarjumā***
Ojhā	Ojhā, G. H., ***Rājpūtāne kā Itihās***
Paṃvār Vaṃś Darpaṇ	Siṇḍhāyac, Dayāldās. ***Paṃvār Vaṃś Darpaṇ***. Edited by Daśrath Śarmā
Platts, ***Dictionary***	Platts, John A., ***A Dictionary of Urdū, Classical Hindī, and English***
Rāṭhoṛāṃ rī Vaṃśāvalī, ms. no. 20130	***Rāṭhoṛāṃ rī Vaṃśāvalī***. MS no. 20130, Rājasthān Prācyavidyā Pratiṣṭhān, Jodhpur.
Reu	Reu, B. N., ***Mārvāṛ kā Itihās***
Sākariyā, ***RHSK***	Sākariyā, Badrīprasād, and Sākariyā, Bhūpati Rām, eds. ***Rājasthānī Hindī Śabd Koś***

Tavārīkh Jaisalmer	Lakhmīcand. ***Tavārīkh Jaisalmer = The History of Jeysalmere***
Tod, ***Annals***	Tod, James, ***Annals and Antiquities of Rajasthan***
Vigat	Naiṇsī, Muṃhato. ***Mārvāṛ rā Parganāṃ rī Vigat***
Vīr Vinod	Śyāmaldās, Kavirājā. ***Vīr Vinod***

Full references will be found in the bibliography immediately following.

Other abbreviations:

B.N.	Biographical Notes
V.S.	Vikrama Saṃvat

BIBLIOGRAPHY

Dictionaries, Glossaries, etc.

Citrāv, Siddheśvarśāstrī. ***Bhāratavarṣīya Prācīn Caritrakoś***. Pūnā: Bhāratīya Caritrakoś Maṇḍal, 1964.

Lāḷas, Sītārām. ***Rājasthānī Sabad Kos***. Vol. 1, Jodhpur: Rājasthānī Śodh Saṃsthān, 1962. Vols. 2 and 3, vol. 4, part 1, Jodhpur: Upasamiti Rājasthānī Sabad Kos, 1967-73. Vol. 4, parts 2 and 3, Jodhpur: Caupāsnī Śikṣa Samiti, 1976-78.

McGregor, R. S. ed. ***The Oxford Hindi-English Dictionary***. Oxford: Oxford University Press, 1993.

Mani, Vettam. ***Purāṇic Encyclopaedia: A Comprehensive Dictionary with Special Reference to the Epic and Purāṇic Literature***. 4th ed., reprinted. Delhi: Motilal Banaridass, 1979 [1974].

Molesworth, J. T. compiler. ***A Dictionary, Marathi and English***. Corrected reprint ed. Poona: Shubhada-Saraswat, 1975 [1857].

Monier-Williams, Sir Monier. ***A Sanskrit-English Dictionary***. Reprint ed. London: Oxford University Press, 1970 [1899].

Platts, John A. ***A Dictionary of Urdū, Classical Hindī, and English***. 5th edition. Reprint ed. London: Oxford University Press, 1968 [1930].

Prasād, Kālikā. ***Bṛhat Hindī Koś***. 4th ed. Vārāṇasī: Jñānmaṇḍal, V.S. 2030 [1973].

Rose, H. A. ***A Glossary of the Tribes and Castes of the Punjab and North-west Frontier Province***. 3 vols. Reprint ed. Delhi: Punjab National Press, 1970 [1883].

Sākariyā, Badrīprasād. "Khyāt meṃ Prayukt Pad, Upadhi aur Virudādi Viśiṣṭ Saṅgyāoṃ ya Śabdoṃ kī Arth sahit Nāmāvalī." In Muṃhato Naiṇsī, ***Muṃhatā Naiṇsī viracit Muṃhatā Naiṇsīrī Khyāt***, vol. 4, pp. 194-208. Edited by Badrīprasād Sākariyā. Jodhpur: Rājasthān Prācyavidyā Pratiṣṭhān, 1967.

Sākariyā, Badrīprasād, and Sākariyā, Bhūpati Rām, eds. ***Rājasthānī Hindī Śabd Kos***. 3 vols. Jaypur: Pañcaśīl Prakāśan, 1977-82.

Steingass, F. ***A Comprehensive Persian-English Dictionary***. Reprint ed. New Delhi: Oriental Books Reprint Corporation, 1973.

Stutley, Margaret and James. ***Harper's Dictionary of Hinduism***. New York: Harper & Row, 1977.

Suthār, Bhaṃvarlāl and Gahlot, Sukhvīrsiṃh. ***Rājasthānī-Hindī-Aṅgreji Koś = Rājasthānī-Hindī-English Dictionary***. Jodhpur: Jagdiśsiṃh Gahlot Śodh Saṃsthān, 1995.

Wilson, H. H. ***A Glossary of Judicial and Revenue Terms***. Reprint ed. Delhi: Munshiram Manoharlal, 1968 [1855].

English

Ambastha, B. P. "Patal-Pota: Biographical Account of Ram Das Kachhawaha." In his ***Non-Persian Sources on Indian Medieval History*** (Delhi: Idarah-i Adabiyat-i Delli, 1984), pp 75-128.

Athar Ali, M. ***The Apparatus of Empire: Awards of Ranks, Offices, and Titles to the Mughal Nobility, 1574-1658***. [Aligarh?]: Centre of Advanced Study in History, Aligarh Muslim University, 1985.

Bhandari, M. M. ***Flora of the Indian Desert***. Jodhpur: Scientific Publishers, 1978.

Bhargava, V. S. ***Marwar and the Mughal Emperors***. Delhi: Munshiram Manoharlal, 1966.

---. ***The Rise of the Kachhawas in Dhundhār (Jaipur)***. Ajmer: Shabd Sanchar, 1979.

Bosworth, C. E. ***The Islamic Dynasties: A Chronological and Genealogical Handbook***. Islamic Surveys, 5. Edinburgh: At the University Press, 1967.

Brandreth. ***Brandreth's Treatise on the Law of Adoption in Rajpootana***. With notes by Col. J. C. Brooke. Calcutta: Foreign Dept. Press, 1871.

Carstairs, Morris. ***The Twice Born: A Study of a Community of High-Caste Hindus***. Bloomington: Indiana University Press, 1967.

Chaghta'i, M. A. "Nagaur--A Forgotten Kingdom." ***Bulletin of the Deccan College Research Institute***, vol. 2, nos. 1-2 (Nov., 1940), pp 166-183.

Commissariat, M. S. *A History of Gujarat*. Vol. 1, Bombay: Longmans, Green & Co., Ltd., 1938; vol. 2, Bombay: Orient Longmans, 1957.

Cunningham, Alexander. ***Book of Indian Eras, with Tables for Calculating Indian Dates***. Reprint ed. Varanasi: Indological Book House, 1970.

Day, Upendra Nath. ***Medieval Malwa: A Political and Cultural History, 1401-1562***. Delhi: Munshiram Manoharlal, 1965.

Dundlod, Harnath Singh. ***The Sheikhawats & their Lands***. Jaipur: Raj Educational Printers, 1970.

Erskine, Major K. D. ed. ***Rajputana Gazetteers:*** Volume III-A, ***The Western Rajputana States Residency and the Bikaner Agency***. Allahabad: The Pioneer Press, 1909.

Forbes, A. K. ***Rās-Mālā: Hindu Annals of Western India***. Reprint ed. New Delhi: Heritage Publishers, 1973 [1878].

Fox, Robin. ***Kinship and Marriage***. Baltimore: Penguin Books, 1967.

Fruzetti, L. M. ***The Gift of a Virgin***. Delhi: Oxford University Press, 1982.

Fruzetti, L., and Ostor, A., "Seed and Earth: A Cultural Analysis of Kinship in a Bengali Town," ***Contributions to Indian Sociology*** (NS), Vol. 10, No. 1 (1976), pp. 97-132.

Gazetteer of the Bombay Presidency: Volume V, ***Cutch, Palanpur, and Mahi Kantha***. Bombay: Government Central Press, 1908.

Habib, Irfan. ***The Agrarian System of the Mughal Empire, 1556-1707***. New York: Asia Publishing House, 1963.

---. "The Family of Nur Jahan during Jahangir's Reign: A Political Study." In ***Medieval India: A Miscellany***, vol. 1, pp. 74-95. London: Asia Publishing House, 1969.

Henige, D. P. ***The Chronology of Oral Tradition: Quest for a Chimera***. Oxford: Clarendon Press, 1974.

Hodgson, Marshall G. S. ***The Venture of Islam: Conscience and History in a World Civilization***. 3 vols. Chicago: The University of Chicago Press, 1974.

The Idea of Rajasthan: Explorations in Regional Identity. Edited by Karine Schomer et al. 2 vols. Columbia, Mo.: South Asia Publications by arrangement with Manohar Publishers & Distributors; New Delhi: American Institute of Indian Studies, 1994.

Inden, Ronald. *Marriage and Rank in Bengali Culture*. Berkeley: University of California Press, 1976.

Jain, K. C. *Ancient Cities and Towns of Rajasthan*. Delhi: Motilal Banarsidass, 1972.

---. *Jainism in Rajasthan*. Sholapur: Gulabchand Hirachand Doshi, 1963.

Khan, Refaqat Ali. *The Kachhwahas under Akbar and Jahangir*. New Delhi: Kitab Pub. House, 1976.

Khan, Yar Muhammad. *The Deccan Policy of the Mughals*. Lahore: United Book Corp., 1971.

Lane-Poole, Stanley. *The Mohammadan Dynasties: Chronological and Genealogical Tables with Historical Introductions* (New York: Frederick Ungar Publishing Co., republished 1965.

Letter from Major W. H. Richards, Political Agent, Jaipur, to Lt. Co. Sir H. M. Lawrence, Agent Governor General, Rajputana, April 29, 1853, in "Law and Practice in Castes of Adoption and Succession to Sovereignties in Rajputana," *Rajputana Agency Office Historical Record 27, 75/General*, 1846, 1853, 1859, 1:11-16.

Marriott, M., and Inden, R. "Caste Systems." *Encyclopaedia Britannica*, 15th ed., 1974.

Powlett, Captain P. W. *Gazetteer of the Bikaner State*. Calcutta: Office of the Superintendent of Government Printing, 1874.

Prasad, B. *History of Jahangir*. Allahabad: The Indian Press Ltd., 1940.

Pray, Bruce R. *Topics in Hindī-Urdu Grammar*. Research Monograph Series no. 1. Berkeley: Center for South and Southeast Asia Studies, University of California, 1976.

Qanungo, K. R. *Sher Shah and His Times*. Bombay: Orient Longmans Ltd., 1965.

---. *Studies in Rajput History*. Delhi: S. Chand & Co., 1960.

Qureshi, I. H. *The Administration of the Mughal Empire*. Patna: N. V. Publications, 1966.

The Rāmāyaṇa of Vālmīki: An Epic of Ancient India. Vol. 3. *Araṇyakāṇḍa*. Introduction, translation, and annotation by Sheldon I. Pollack; edited by Robert P. Goldman. Princeton: Princeton University Press, 1991.

Ray, H. C. *The Dynastic History of Northern India*. 2 vols. 1931-36; reprint edition, Delhi: Munshiram Manoharlal Publisher Pvt. Ltd., 1973.

Reu, B. N. *Glories of Marwar and the Glorious Rathors*. Jodhpur: Archaeological Department, 1943.

Saran, P. *The Provincial Government of the Mughals, 1526-1658*. Allahabad: Kitabistan, 1941.

Saran, Richard Davis. "Conquest and Colonization: Rajputs and *Vasīs* in Middle Period Mārvāṛ." Unpublished Ph.D. dissertation, The University of Michigan, 1978.

Sarda, H. B. *Ajmer: Historical and Descriptive*. Ajmer: Fine Art Printing Press, 1941.

Schneider, D. *American Kinship: A Cultural Account*. Englewood Cliffs: Prentice Hall, Inc., 1968.

Selections from Banera Archives: Civil War in Mewar (Baneṛā Saṅgrahālay ke Abhilekh [1758-1770]. Edited by K. S. Gupta & L. P. Mathur. Udaipur: Sahitya Sansthan, Rajasthan Vidyapeeth, 1967.

Sharma, Dasharatha. *Lectures on Rajput History and Culture*. Delhi: Motilal Banarsidass, 1970.

---, ed. *Rajasthan through the Ages*. Vol. 1. Bikaner: Rajasthan State Archives, 1966.

Sharma, G. D. *Rajput Polity: A Study of Politics and Administration of the State of Marwar, 1638-1749*. New Delhi: Manohar Book Service, 1977.

Sharma, G. N. *Rajasthan Studies*. Agra: Lakshmi Narain Agarwal Educational Publishers, 1970.

Sharma, S. R. *Mughal Government and Administration*. Bombay: Hind Kitab Ltd., 1951.

Shokoohy, Mehrdad and Shokoohy Natalie H. ***Nagaur: Sultanate and Early Mughal History and Architecture of the District of Nagaur, India***. London: Royal Asiatic Society, 1993.

Singh, Hardayal. ***Brief Account of Mallani***. Jodhpur: n.p., 1892.

Singh, Karni. ***The Relations of the House of Bikaner with the Central Powers, 1465-1949***. New Delhi: Munshiram Manoharlal Publishers Pvt. Ltd., 1974.

Singh, Munshi Hardyal. ***The Castes of Marwar: Being Census Report of 1891***. 2nd edition, with an introduction by Komal Kothari. Jodhpur: Books Treasure, 1990.

Smith, John D. ***The Epic of Pābūjī: A Study, Transcription and Translation***. Cambridge [England]: Cambridge University Press, 1991.

---. "An Introduction to the Language of the Historical Documents from Rajasthan." ***Modern Asian Studies***, 9, 4 (1975), pp. 433-464.

---. ***The Vīsaḷadevarāsa: A Restoration of the Text***. Cambridge: Cambridge University Press, 1976.

Srivastava, A. L. ***Akbar the Great***. Vol. 1, ***Political History: 1542-1605 A.D.*** 2nd ed. Agra: Shiva Lala Agarwala & Co., 1972.

Studies in Marwar History. Edited by N.S. Bhati. Chopasni, Jodhpur: Rajasthani Shodh Sansthan, 1979.

Swamikannu Pillai, L. D. ***An Indian Ephemeris, A.D. 700 to A.D. 1799***. 7 vols. in 8. Madras: Govt. Press, 1922-23.

Tessitori, L. P. ***A Descriptive Catalogue of Bardic and Historical Manuscripts***. Section I: Prose Chronicles. Part 1: Jodhpur State. Section II: Bardic Poetry. Part 1: Bikaner State. Calcutta: The Asiatic Society of Bengal, 1917-18.

---. "A Progress Report on the Preliminary Work done during the year 1915 in connection with the Proposed Bardic and Historical Survey of Rajputana." ***Journal of the Asiatic Society of Bengal***, N.S. 12 (1916), pp. 57-116.

---. "A Progress Report on the Work done during the year 1916 in connection with the Bardic and Historical Survey of Rajputana." ***Journal of the Asiatic Society of Bengal***, N.S. 13 (1917), pp. 195-252.

---. "A Progress Report on the Work done during the year 1917 in connection with the Bardic and Historical Survey of Rajputana." ***Journal of the Asiatic Society of Bengal***, N.S. 15 (1919), pp. 5-79.

---. "A Progress Report on the Work done during the year 1918 in connection with the Bardic and Historical Survey of Rajputana." ***Journal of the Asiatic Society of Bengal***, N.S., 16 (1920), pp. 251-279.

---. "A Scheme for the the Bardic and Historical Survey of Rajputana." ***Journal of the Asiatic Society of Bengal***, N.S. 10 (1914), pp. 373-410.

Tirmizi, S. ***Ajmer Through Inscriptions (1532-1852 A.D.)***. New Delhi: Indian Institute of Islamic Studies, 1968.

Tod, James. ***Annals and Antiquities of Rajasthan***. Edited with an introduction and notes by William Crooke. 3 vols. London: Oxford University Press, 1920.

Tripathi, R. P. ***The Rise and Fall of the Mughal Empire***. Reprint ed. Allahabad: Central Book Depot, 1966.

Ujwal, Kr. Kailash Dan S. ***Bhagwati Shri Karniji Maharaj: A Biography***. Ujlan (Marwar): N.p., n.d.

Zaidi, S. Inayat Ali. "The Pattern of Matrimonial Ties between the Kachawaha Clan and the Mughal Ruling Family." ***Indian History Congress: Proceedings of the 35th Session, Jadavpur (Calcutta), 1974***, pp. 131-149.

---. "The Rise of Rathor Family of Marwar under Shah Jahan." ***Islamic Culture*** (Hyderabad), 55, no. 1 (January, 1981), pp. 21-33.

Ziegler, Norman P. "Action, Power and Service in Rajasthani Culture: A Social History of the Rajpūts of Middle Period Rajasthan." Unpublished Ph.D. dissertation, The University of Chicago, 1973.

---. "Evolution of the Rathor State of Marvar: Horses, Structural Change and Warfare." In ***The Idea of Rajasthan: Explorations in Regional Identity***, edited by Karine Schomer et al., vol. 2, pp. 192-216. Columbia, Mo.: South Asia Publications by arrangement with Manohar Publishers & Distributors; New Delhi: American Institute of Indian Studies, 1994.

---. "Marvari Historical Chronicles: Sources for the Social and Cultural History of Rajasthan." ***Indian Economic and Social History Review***, 13, 2 (April-June, 1976), pp. 219-250.

---. "The Seventeenth Century Chronicles of Mārvāṛa: A Study in the Evolution and Use of Oral Traditions in Western India." ***History in Africa***, 3 (1976), pp. 127-153.

---. "Some Notes on Rajput Loyalties During the Mughal Period." In ***Kingship and Authority in South Asia***, edited by J. F. Richards, pp. 215-251. Publication #3, South Asian Studies: University of Wisconsin-Madison Publication Series, 1978.

Hindi

Āsopā, Rāmkaraṇ. ***Āsop kā Itihās***. Jodhpur: n.p., n.d.

---. ***Itihās Nībāj, arthāt, Marūdeśāntargat Svasthān Nībājādhipati Ūdāvat Rāṭhauṛ Rājvaṃś kā Itihās***. Mārvāṛ: Ṭhikānā Śrī Nībāj, [1931].

Bhagavatsiṃh, Ṭhākur. ***Cāmpāvat Rāṭhauṛ***. Jodhpur: Rajasthan Law Weekly Press, 1972.

Bhāṭī, Hukamsiṃh. ***Rājasthān ke Meṛtiyā Rāṭhauṛ, 1458-1707 Ī.: Mārvāṛ ke Itihās meṃ Meṛtiyā Rāṭhauṛoṃ kī Bhūmikā***. Jodhpur: Rājasthānī Granthāgār, 1986.

Bhāṭī, Nārāyaṇsiṃh. ***Rājasthān ke Aitihāsik Granthoṃ kā Sarvekṣaṇ***. 3 vols. Jodhpur: Rājasthānī Granthāgār, 1989.

Gehlot, G. S. ***Mārvāṛ kā Saṅkṣipt Itihās***. Jodhpur: Gehlot Bindery Works, n.d.

Jānā. ***Kyām Khāṃ Rāsā***. Edited with extensive notes by Daśarath Śarma, Agarcand Nāhṭā, and Bhaṃvarlāl Nāhṭā. Jaypur: Rājasthān Puratattva Mandir, 1953.

Kānotā, Mohansiṃh. ***Cāmpāvatoṃ kā Itihās***. 3 vols. Jaypur: Raṇbāṅkur Prakāśan, 1990-91.

Lakhmīcand. ***Tavārīkh Jaisalmer = The History of Jeysalmere***. Ajmer: Ciragh Rājisthān va Rājpūtānāgazaṭ Yantrālay, 1891.

"***Mārvāṛ kī Qaumoṃ kā Itihās***." ***Riporṭ Mardumśumārī Rāj Mārvāṛ bābat san 1891 Īsvī***, volume 3. Jodhpur: Census Press, 1895.

Meṛtiyā, Gopalsiṃh Rāṭhoṛ. ***Jaymalvaṃśprakāś, arthāt, Rājasthān Badnor kā Itihās = Jayamal Vansa Prakasha, or, The History of Badnore***. Ajmer: Vaidik Yantrālay, 1932.

Muhaṇot Naiṇsī: Itihāsvid Muhaṇot Naiṇsī, Vyaktitva evaṃ Kṛtitva. Paramparā, parts 39-40, edited by Nārāyaṇsiṃh Bhāṭī. Caupāsnī: Rājasthānī Śodh Saṃsthān, 1974.

Naiṇsī, Muṃhato. *Muhaṇot Naiṇsī kī Khyāt.* Edited and translated by Manoharsiṃh Rāṇāvat. Vol. 1. Sītāmaū: Śrī Naṭnāgar Śodh-Saṃsthān, 1987.

---. *Muhaṇot Naiṇsī kī Khyāt, arthāt, Naiṇsī kī Mārvāṛi Bhāṣā kī Khyāt se Guhilot (Sīsodīyā), Cauhān, Solaṅkī (Caulukya), Paṛihār (Pratihār) aur Parmār (Paṃvār) Vaṃśoṃ kī Itihās kā Hindī Anuvād.* 2 vols. Vol. 1 edited by Rāmnārāyaṇ Dūgaṛ and Vol. 2 edited by Gaurīśaṅkar Hīrācand Ojhā. Allahabad: K. Mittra at the Indian Press, 1925-34.

Ojhā, G. H. *Ḍūṅgarpur Rājya kā Itihās*. Ajmer: Vedic Yantralaya, V.S. 1992 (A.D. 1935).

---. *Rājpūtāne kā Itihās*. 5 vols. in 9 parts. Ajmer: Vedic Yantralaya, 1927-41.

---. *Sirohī Rājya kā Itihās*. Rev. 2nd. ed. Jodhpur: Rājasthānī Granthāgār, 1999.

Raghubīrsiṃh. *Ratlām kā Pratham Rājya: Uskī Sthāpnā evaṃ Ant [Īsā kī 17vīṃ Śatābdī].* Naī Dillī: Rājkamal Prakāśan, 1950.

Rāṇāvat, Manoharsiṃh. *Itihāskār Muhaṇot Naiṇsī tathā uske Itihās-Granth.* Jodhpur: Rājasthān Sāhitya Mandir, 1981.

Rāybahādur Mahtā Vijaysiṅghji, Dīvān, Riyāsat Jodhpur (Mārvāṛ), kā Jīvan Caritra. Ajmer: Vedic Yantralaya, n.d.

Reu, B. N. *Mārvāṛ kā Itihās*. 2 vols. Jodhpur: Archaeological Department, 1938-40.

Śarmā, Daśarath. "Phadiyā, Dukṛā aur Dugānī." *Maru-Bhāratī*, 8:2 (July, 1960), pp. 49-51.

Śarmā, Paṇḍit Badrī. *Dāsapoṃ kā Itihās*. Jodhpur: Seṇāsadana, V.S. 2011 (A.D. 1954).

Śekhāvat, Ṭhākur Surjan Siṃh. *Kharvā kā Vṛhad Itihas*. Kharvā: Rāv Candrasen Jī, 1998.

---. *Rāv Śekhā: Śekhāvāṭī-Saṅgh tathā Śekhāvat Vaṃś ke Pravarttak Rāv Śekhā kā Jīvan-Vṛtt*. Sīkar. Mahārāv Śekhā Smārak Samiti, V.S. 2030 [A.D. 1973].

Siṃh, Rājendra. *Bīdāvat Rāṭhauṛoṃ kā Itihās: 1475-1857 Ī*. Jaypur: Yūnik Ṭreḍars, 1988.

Śivnāthsiṃh. *Kūmpāvat Rāṭhauṛom kā Itihās*. Gārāsaṇī, Mārbāṛ: Rāṭhoṛ Bhimsiṃh Kumpāvat, 1946.

Somānī, Rāmvallabh. "Mālde aur Bīramde Meṛtiyā kā Saṅgarṣ." *Maru-Bhāratī*, 15:4 (January, 1968), pp. 17-19.

Śyāmaldās, Kavirājā. *Vīr Vinod*. 2 vols. in 4 parts. Udaipur: Rājyantrālaya, V.S. 1943 (A.D. 1886).

"Ṭippaṇiyeṃ: Pratham Bhāg (Mahatvapūrṇ Vyaktiyoṃ tathā Sthānoṃ ādi para Tippaṇiyeṃ)." In Muṃhato Naiṇsī, *Mārvāṛ ra Parganam rī Vigat*, vol. 3, pp. 64-128. Edited by N. S. Bhāṭī. Jodhpur: Rājasthan Prācyavidyā Pratiṣṭhān, 1974.

Ūdāvat, Kiśansiṃh. *Ūdāvat Rāṭhāuṛ Itihās*. Jaitāraṇ: Vīr Rāv Śrī Ratansiṃh Rāṭhauṛ Smṛti Bhavan Niyās, 1982-83.

Vyās, Maṅgilal. *Jodhpur Rājya kā Itihās*. Jaypur: Pañcśīl Prakāśan, 1975.

---. *Mārvāṛ ke Abhilekh*. Jodhpur: Hindī Sāhitya Mandir, 1973.

Manuscripts

Aitihāsik Tavarīkhvār Vārtā. MS no. 1234. Rājasthānī Śodh Saṃsthān, Caupāsnī .

Kavirāj Murardānjī kī Khyāt kā Tarjumā. MS no. 25658, no. 1. Rājasthān Prācyavidyā Pratiṣṭhān, Jodhpur.

Mahārāj Śrī Gajsiṅghjī kī Khyāt. MS no. 15666. Rājasthān Prācyavidyā Pratiṣṭhān, Jodhpur.

Mūndiyāṛ rī Rāṭhoṛāṃ rī Khyāt, MS no. 15635, no. 2. Rājasthān Prācyavidyā Pratiṣṭhān, Jodhpur.

Rajpūtoṃ kī Khyāt: Kavirājjī Murardānjī kī Khyāt kā Tarjumā, MS no. 15671, no. 3. Rājasthān Prācyavidyā Pratiṣṭhān, Jodhpur.

Rāṭhoṛāṃ rī Khyāt evaṃ Bhādrājaṇ rī Khyāt. Personal family papers of Ṭhākur Devīsiṅgh of Ṭhikāṇo Bhādrājaṇ, Mārvāṛ.

Rāṭhoṛāṃ rī Vaṃśāvalī. MS no. 20130, Rājasthān Prācyavidyā Pratiṣṭhān, Jodhpur.

Rāṭhoṛoṃ kī Khyāt Purāṇī Kavirājjī Murardānjī ke Yahāṃ se Likhī Gaī. MS no. 15672, no. 2. Rājasthān Prācyavidyā Pratiṣṭhān, Jodhpur.

Śrī Mahārāj Śrī Jasvantsiṅghjī kī Khyāt. MS no. 15661. Rājasthān Prācyavidyā Pratiṣṭhān, Jodhpur.

Persian Sources

'Abbās Khān Sarwānī. *Tarīkh-i-Śer Śāhī.* Translated by Brahmadeva Prasad Ambashthya. Patna: K.P. Jayaswal Research Institute, 1974.

Abū al-Fazl ibn Mubārak. *Ā'īn-i-Akbarī*. 3 vols. in 2. Vol. one translated into English by H. Blochmann, edited by D.C. Phillott; vols. 2-3 translated into English by H.S. Jarrett, corrected and further annotated by Sir Jadu-Nath Sarkar. Reprint ed. Delhi: Low Price Publications, 1997 [1871-1949].

---. *The Akbar Nāmā of Abu-l-Fazl*. Translated by H. Beveridge. 3 vols. Reprint ed. Delhi: Rare Books, 1972 [1907-1939].

Badā'ūnī, Abd al-Qādir ibn Mulūk Shāh. *Muntakhabut-Tawārikh*. Translated from the Original Persian and Edited by George S. A. Ranking. 3 vols. Reprint ed. Karachi: Karimsons, 1976 [1898-1925].

Husaini, Khwaja Kamgar. *Ma'asir-i-Jahangiri: A Contemporary Account of Jahangir*. Edited by Azra Alavi. Bombay: Asia Publishing House, 1978.

Jahāngīr. *The Jahangirnama: Memoirs of Jahangir, Emperor of India*. Translated, edited, and annotated by Wheeler M. Thackston. Washington, D.C.: Freer Gallery of Art, Arthur M Sackler Gallery; New York: Oxford University Press, 1999.

---. *The Tūzuk-i-Jahāngīrī; or, Memoirs of Jahāngīr*. Translated by Alexander Rogers. Edited by Henry Beveridge. 2 vols. Reprint ed. Delhi: Munshiram Manoharlal, 1968 [1909-1914].

Khwājah Nizāmuddīn Ahmad. T*he Tabaqāt-i-Akbarī of Khwājah Nizāmuddīn Ahmad: a history of India from the early Musalman invasions to the thirty-sixth year of the reign of Akbar*. Translated by B. De. 3 vols. Calcutta: Asiatic Society, 1927-40.

Shāhnavāz Khān Awrangābādī. ***The Maāthir-ul-Umarā: being Biographies of the Muhammadan and Hindu Officers of the Timurid Sovereigns of India from 1500 to about 1780 A.D.*** Translated by H. Beveridge. Revised, annotated and completed by Baini Prashad. 3 vols. Calcutta: The Asiatic Society, 1941-64.

Published Middle Mārvāṛī and Ḍiṅgaḷ Texts

"Aitihāsik Bātāṃ." In ***Paramparā***, part 11, pp. 17-109. Edited by N. S. Bhāṭī. Caupāsnī: Rājasthānī Śodh Saṃsthān, 1961.

Ajīt Vilās. ***Paramparā***, part 27. Edited by N. S. Bhāṭī. Caupāsnī: Rājasthānī Śodh Saṃsthān, 1969.

Bāṅkīdās. ***Bāṅkīdas rī Khyāt***. Edited by Narottamdāsjī Svāmī. Jaypur: Rājasthān Purattvānvesaṇ Mandir, 1956.

Bātāṃ ro Jhūmakho. 3 vols. Edited by Manohar Śarmā. Bisāū: Rājasthān Sāhitya Samiti, Saṃ 2021 [1964].

Daḷpat Vilās. Edited by Rāvat Sarasvat. Bīkāner: Sādūl Rājasthānī Risarc Insṭīṭyūṭ, 1960.

"Ḍāvī ne Jīvṇī Mislāṃ rī Vigat." In Muṃhato Naiṇsī, ***Mārvāṛ ra Parganam rī Vigat***, vol. 2, pp. 465-477. Edited by N. S. Bhāṭī. Jodhpur: Rājasthan Prācyavidyā Pratiṣṭhān, 1969.

Jagdev Parmār rī Vāt: Trividha-vīra Parmār Jagdev kī Mūl Rājasthānī Lok-kathā, Hindī Anuvād, Prakṛt, Saṃskṛt, va Gujarātī meṃ Prāpt Itivṛtta evaṃ Sarvāṅgīṇ Mūlyāṅkan = Tale of Jagdeva Parmar. Edited by Mahāvīr Siṃh Gahlot. Jodhpur: Rājasthān Sāhitya Mandīr, 1986.

Jaisalmer rī Khyāt. ***Paramparā***, parts 57-58. Edited by Nārāyaṇsiṃh Bhāṭī. Caupāsnī: Rājasthānī Śodh Saṃsthān, 1981.

"Jaitsī Ūdāvat." In ***Rājasthānī Vātāṃ: Rājasthānī Bhāṣā meṃ likhit Prācīn Kahāniyoṃ kā Saṅgrah***, pp. 155-175. Edited by Sūryakaraṇ Pārīk. Dillī: Navayug-Sāhitya-Mandir, 1934.

Jasvantsiṅgh rī Khyāt. Edited by Rāvat Sarasvat. Jaypur: Rājasthān Adhyayan Kendra, Rājasthān Viśvavidyālay, 1987.

"Jodhpur Hukūmat rī Bahī." In ***Marwar under Jaswant Singh (1658-1678): Jodhpur Hukumat ri Bahi***, pp. 1-237. Edited by Satish Chandra, Raghubir Sinh and G. D. Sharma. Meerut: Meenakshi Prakashan, 1976.

"Jodhpur rā Cākrāṃ rī Vigat." In Muṃhato Naiṇsī, ***Mārvāṛ ra Parganam rī Vigat***, vol. 2, pp. 478-481. Edited by N. S. Bhāṭī. Jodhpur: Rājasthān Prācyavidyā Pratiṣṭhān, 1969.

Jodhpur Rājya kī Khyāt. Edited by Raghuvīr Siṃh and Manoharsiṃh Rāṇāvat. Nayī Dillī: Bhāratīy Itihās Anusandhān Pariṣad, evaṃ Pañcśīl Prakāśan, Jaypur, 1988.

Karṇīdānjī. ***Sūrajprakās***. Edited by Sītārām Lāḷas. 3 vols. Jodhpur: Rājasthān Prācyavidyā Pratiṣṭhān, 1961-63.

Khiṛiyā Jagā. ***Bardic and Historical Survey of Rajputana: Vacanikā Rāṭhoṛa Ratana Siṅghaji rī Maheśadāsota rī Khiṛiyā Jagā rī Kahī***. Edited by L. P. Tessitori. Calcutta: The Asiatic Society of Bengal, 1917.

---. ***Vacnikā Rāṭhoṛ Ratansiṅghjī Mahesdāsot rī Khiṛiyā Jagā rī Kahī***. Edited by Kāśīrām Śarmā and Raghubīrsiṃh. Dillī: Rājkamal Prakāśan, 1960.

"Mahārāv Śrī Amarsiṅghjī Rāṭhoṛ rī Vāt." In ***Rājasthānī Vāt-Saṅgrah***, pp. 109-117. Edited by Manohar Śarmā, Śrīlāl Nathmaljī Jośī. Naī Dillī: Sāhitya Akādemī, 1984.

Naiṇsī, Muṃhato. ***Mārvāṛ rā Parganāṃ rī Vigat***. Edited by Narayansiṃh Bhāṭī. 3 vols. Jodhpur: Rājasthān Prācyavidyā Pratiṣṭhan, 1968-74.

---. ***Muṃhatā Naiṇsī viracit Muṃhatā Naiṇsīrī Khyāt***. Edited by Badrīprasād Sākariyā. 4 vols. Jodhpur: Rājasthan Prācyavidyā Pratiṣṭhān, 1960-67.

---. ***Naiṇsi kī Khyāt***. [Edited by Rāmakaraṇa Āsopa]. Vol. 1. N.p., n.d.

"Pargane Nāgor rau Hāl." In Muṃhato Naiṇsī, ***Mārvāṛ ra Parganam rī Vigat***, vol. 2, pp. 421-424. Edited by N. S. Bhāṭī. Jodhpur: Rājasthan Prācyavidyā Pratiṣṭhān, 1969.

Rājasthānī Vāt-Saṅgrah. Edited by Manohar Śarmā, Śrīlāl Nathmaljī Jośī. Naī Dillī: Sāhitya Akādemī, 1984.

Rājasthānī Vātāṃ: Rājasthānī Bhāṣā meṃ likhit Prācīn Kahāniyoṃ kā Saṅgrah. Edited by Sūryakaraṇ Pārīk. Dillī: Navayug-Sāhitya-Mandir, 1934.

Rāṭhauḍ Vaṃś rī Vigat evaṃ Rāṭhauḍāṃ rī Vaṃśāvalī. Edited by Phatahsiṃh. Jodhpur: Rājasthān Prācyavidyā Pratiṣṭhān, 1968.

Siṇḍhāyac, Dayāldās. *Dayāldāsrī Khyāt: Bīkānerrai Rāṭhoṛāṃrī Khyāt*. Vol. 1. Edited by Daśrath Śarmā. Bīkāner: Anūp Saṃskṛt Pustakālay, 1948.

---. *Deśdarpaṇ: Bikāner Rājya kā Itihās*. Edited by Je. Ke. Jain et al. Bīkāner: Rājasthan Rājya Abhilekhāgār, 1989.

---. *Paṃvār Vaṃś Darpaṇ*. Edited by Daśrath Śarmā. Bīkāner: Sādūl Rājasthānī Risarc Instīṭūṭ, 1960.

Sivdās. *Acaldās Khīcī rī Vacnīkā: Śodhpūrṇ Bhūmikā sahit*. Edited by Śambhusiṃh Manohar. Jodhpur: Rājasthān Prācyavidyā Pratiṣṭhān, 1991.

"Vāt Tīḍai Chāḍāvat rī." In *Bātāṃ ro Jhūmakho*, vol. 3, pp. 38-44. Edited by M. Śarmā. Bīsau: Rājasthān Sāhitya Saṃsthān, Saṃ 2021 [1964].

Velī Krisana Rukamaṇī rī Rāṭhoṛ rāja Prithī Rāja rī kahī. Edited by L. P. Tessitori. Calcutta: The Asiatic Society of Bengal, 1919.

Vīramde Sonīgarā rī Vāt: Pracīn Rājasthānī Lok Sāhitya kī Prasiddh Aitihāsik Kathā, Mūl Rājasthānī Pāṭh, evaṃ Hindī-Aṅgrejī Rūpāntar Sahit: Vāt (Kathā) kā Sarvāṅgīṇ Mūlyāṅkan = A Muslim Princess Becomes Sati: A Historical Romance of Hindu-Muslim Unity. Edited by Mahāvīr Siṃh Gahlot. Jālor: Śrī Mahāvīr Śodh-Saṃsthāṇ, 1981.

Vīrbhāṇ Ratnū. *Rājrūpak*. Edited by Paṇḍit Rāmkaraṇ Āsopā. Kāśī: Nāgarīpracāriṇī Sabhā, 1941.

Rajpūt Social Organization:
A
Historical Perspective

For the general reader of these volumes, some discussion of Rajpūt social organization during the middle period is necessary both to facilitate proper identification of individual Rajpūts mentioned in the texts, and to provide a better understanding of the social reality in which Rajpūts of this period lived. This social reality was defined in terms of a complex network of kinship based upon patrilineal units of descent and relationships through marriage. The following discussion is divided into two parts. The first part offers an overview of Rajpūt kinship[1] and focuses upon the Meṛtīyo Rāṭhoṛ Rajpūt, Rāv Jaimal Vīramdevot, ruler of Meṛto in eastern Mārvāṛ (1544-57, 1562), as an example of an individual Rajpūt of this period. The second part analyzes the terminology associated with Rajpūt units of descent and traces several important changes in the use of this terminology over time.

I

Meṛtīyo Rāv Jaimal Vīramdevot lived during the mid-sixteenth century. He and his family were surrounded by a world shaped by the Purāṇic traditions of the great Hindu epics. These epics with their king lists and Kṣatriya heroes provided not only an illustrious ancestry for Rajpūts, but also offered a conceptual framework within which they viewed the order of their own society. Central to this framework was the concept of time manifested in four cyclical ages (***yugas***), with each age involving a progressive disintegration of society. The fourth age (***Kālī Yuga***) in which Rāv Jaimal lived, was felt to be one of significant decline from former ages, a period of lasciviousness and loss of virtue, of the imperfect remembering of the sacred texts of the Vedas, and of the weakness of kings.[2] Rajpūts as "sons of kings" saw themselves as being of less

[1] This discussion is informed by the cultural style of analysis employed by David M. Schneider in his study of American kinship, and by the works of Ronald Inden, Ralph Nicholas, Lina Fruzzetti. and Akos Ostor on Bengali culture. See: D. M. Schneider, ***American Kinship: A Cultural Account*** (Englewood Cliffs, New Jersey: Prentice Hall, Inc., 1968); R. Inden, ***Marriage and Rank in Bengali Culture*** (Berkeley: University of California Press, 1977); R. Inden & R. Nicholas, ***Kinship in Bengali Culture*** (Chicago: University of Chicago Press, 1977); L. M. Fruzzetti, ***The Gift of a Virgin*** (Delhi: Oxford University Press, 1982); L. Fruzzetti & A. Ostor, "Seed and Earth: A Cultural Analysis of Kinship in a Bengali Town," ***Contributions to Indian Sociology*** (NS), Vol. 10, No. 1 (1976), pp. 97-132.

[2] "Rāṭhoḍāṃ rī Vaṃśāvalī," in ***Rāṭhauḍ Vaṃś rī Vigat evaṃ Rāṭhauḍāṃ rī Vaṃśāvalī***, ed. by Phatahsiṃh (Jodhpur: Rājasthān Prācyavidyā Pratiṣṭhān, 1968), p. 33; Richard D. Saran, "Conquest and Colonization: Rajputs and ***Vasīs*** in Middle Period Mārvāṛ" (Unpublished Ph.D. dissertation, The University of Michigan, 1978), pp. 34-35.

stature and rank than the great warriors and kings of the epics. Their clan histories contain traditions of the loss of great kingdoms of the past, of migration and distress, of the mixing of castes and of the uncertainty of rank.[3]

Within this conceptual framework of time, genealogies were of utmost importance to Rajpūts in defining rightful position and place in society. Elaborate family and caste genealogies had emerged by the mid-sixteenth century and early seventeenth centuries. These took two distinct forms.[4] Most important were the ***vaṃśāvalī***s (lit. "line of the ***vaṃś***), which placed emphasis upon ruling lines of local kingdoms and traced descent from forefathers who had lived both in the ***Kālī Yuga*** and in other ages of the world. Richard Saran has written that the composition of a ***vaṃśāvalī*** was felt to be a task equal in merit to making a pilgrimage to a sacred shrine or performing libations to the manes. Like these acts, the composition of the ***vaṃśāvalī*** was seen to purify the ***vaṃś*** (***vaṃśaśodhana***) by properly linking Rajpūts of the present age with their Kṣatriya ancestors of former ages and with the deities from whom they ultimately descended.[5] Associated with the ***vaṃśāvalī***s were ***pīḍhiyāṃ*** (lit. "generations"). These genealogies provided lists of the various males members of each generation of a particular family, supplemented with important details about their lives including battles they had fought, lands they had held in grant (***paṭo***) from local rulers, and occasional information about marriages.[6]

Together, these two forms of the genealogy served important social and political functions. By listing family members and detailing positions held and acts performed, and by tracing descent from kings of this and other ages, the ***pīḍhiyāṃ*** and ***vaṃśāvalī***s served broad political functions in defining rank and status, and in establishing rights to land and rulership. In addition, they provided an ideological framework with reference to which these social and political relationships were explained and sustained.[7]

---

[3] ***Khyāt***, 1:1-12, 97-98, 2:211-212, 266-267, 304-308; Norman P. Ziegler, Marvari Historical Chronicles: Sources for the Social and Cultural History of Rajasthan," ***Indian Economic and Social History Review***, Vol. 13, no. 2 (April-June, 1976), p. 243.

[4] L. P. Tessitori, "A Progress Report on the Work done in the year 1917 in connection with the Bardic and Historical Survey of Rajputana," ***Journal of the Asiatic Society of Bengal***, N.S. 15 (1919), pp. 19-26. It should be noted here that in the chronicles of Muṃhato Naiṇsī, which date from the mid-seventeenth century, the distinction between ***vaṃśāvalī*** and ***pīḍhiyāṃ*** as discussed here is indistinct. One finds examples of the term ***pīḍhiyāṃ*** being used interchangeably with ***vaṃśāvalī***. In general, however, the former term applies to lists of members of particular families, or more rarely, to short lists of the generations of the family of a local ruler. See: ***Khyāt***, 1:77, 3:182.

[5] Saran, "Conquest and Colonization ... ," pp. 33, 39-40.

[6] For some excellent examples of ***pīḍhiyāṃ***, see: ***Khyāt***, 1:293-332, 2:152-195.

[7] Ziegler, "Marvari Historical Chronicles ... ," pp. 237-238.

For Rajpūts of the middle period such as Rāv Jaimal Vīramdevot, questions of genealogy and descent pertained first of all to the ordered hierarchy of patrilineal clans and lineages into which the Rajpūt caste (*jāti*) was divided. These clans and lineages were defined by ties of male blood to a common male ancestor and provided the basic units of reference and identification. Rajpūts recognized six to seven different named units of descent. The most inclusive of these were the great ***vaṃś***. These were originally seen to have been six in number[8] and were distinguished by the particular guardian deities who gave them birth.[9] As with all things in the cycle of time, these great ***vaṃś***, being most powerful and pure, were seen to have emerged during the first or golden age (***sat yuga***). The ***vaṃś*** to which Meṛtīyo Rāv Jaimal Vīramdevot belonged was the Sūryavaṃś ("family or dynasty of the Sun"). This ***vaṃś*** had emerged with the birth of the sun, Sūrya,[10] and from this deity all Sūryavaṃśī Rajpūts traced direct descent.

Through time, the Sūryavaṃś was seen to segment into distinct lines from which emerged more particularistic ***vaṃś*** or ***kuḷ***, such as the Gahlot, Kachvāho, Rāṭhoṛ and others (see Figure 1, ***infra***, for specific terminology associated with the different levels of descent among Rajpūts). The Rāṭhoṛ ***vaṃś*** to which Rāv Jaimal belonged was felt to have originated during the second or silver age (***tretā yuga***) some 1,728,000 years after the birth of the Sun.[11] The founding ancestor of the Rāṭhoṛs was Rājā Rāṣṭesvar, a son of Rājā Jhalmalesvar. He was conceived in the body of his own father and was called "Rāṭhoṛ" because he was given birth through his father's spine (***rāṭho***).

The story[12] of Rāṣṭesvar's conception and birth tells that Rājā Jhalmalesvar originally had no sons. Being greatly concerned about the future of his line, he went into the forest with his wives to see the great sage (***ṛṣī***), Gotam. Gotam listened intently to the Rājā, and when he learned of the Rājā's plight, he immediately agreed to help. Gotam first ordered the Rājā to perform the great sacrifice and to feed the host of deities in attendance. Gotam then spoke a sacred ***mantra***, the name of Śrī Parameśvarjī, over a container of water, impregnating it with the power to produce a son. Finally, Gotam ordered the Rājā to give the water to his wives to drink, after which a son would be conceived and born. The

---

8 "Rāṭhoḍāṃ rī Vaṃśāvalī," p. 10.

9 ***Khyāt,*** 1:1, 128, 134, 291, 2:3, 15.

10 ***Ibid.***, 3:177; "Rāṭhoḍāṃ rī Vaṃśāvalī," pp. 7, 9-10.

11 "Rāṭhoḍāṃ rī Vaṃśāvalī," pp. 5-6, 12-13.

12 I am here following Saran, "Conquest and Colonization ... ," pp. 35-37, in his rendering of "Rāṭhoḍāṃ rī Vaṃśāvalī," pp. 12-14. Saran notes that the ***Vaṃśāvalī*** contains a variant version of this same story (pp. 14-16). Both of these stories date from the late 16th century. Another version dating from the early 18th century is found in "Rāṭhauḍ Vaṃś rī Vigat," in ***Rāṭhauḍ Vaṃś rī Vigat evaṃ Rāṭhauḍāṃ rī Vaṃśāvalī***, ed. by Phatahsiṃh (Jodhpur: Rājasthān Prācyavidyā Pratiṣṭhān, 1968), pp. 1-2.

Rājā agreed to follow Gotam's instructions, but during the night following, the Rājā awoke with great thirst and mistakenly drank from the container of water himself. A foetus then began to grow within Jhalmalesvar's own body. And when it was time for the child's birth, a family goddess came to the Rājā's aid. She split open Jhalmalesvar's spine (*rāṭho*) and removed a son from his body. The son was called Rāṣṭesvar. Afterwards, Gotam Ṛṣī gave this new Rājā his blessing and the family goddess granted him a kingdom. There Rāṣṭesvar is said to have founded the city of Kanauj as his capital and to have built a fort of gold.

Because of their close relationship with Gotam Ṛṣī, the Rāṭhoṛs assumed the ***gotra*** designation of Gotam.[13] This ***gotra*** designation was seen to apply to all Rāṭhoṛs, for Gotam Ṛṣī was considered responsible for instilling among them the particular customs and behaviors (***gotrācār***) appropriate for their members, which distinguished them from Rajpūts of different ***gotra***.[14] For Rāv Jaimal Vīramdevot, the ***gotra*** designation was important primarily with regard to marriage, for it defined the boundaries of exogamy. All marriages with members of the same ***gotra***, that is, with one's own ***gotī***, were prohibited.[15] In addition, hostility (***vair***) and murder within the ***gotra*** (***gotrakadamb*** - lit. "***gotra***-destruction") were enjoined.[16]

The Rāṭhoṛs were considered to be one of the thirty-six ***rājkulīs*** ("ruling or sovereignty possessing families")[17] which had emerged during the second age. Tradition held that six ***rājkulīs*** had emerged from each of the six original ***vaṃś***, and each was in turn associated with its own particular fort or town which was its homeland (***utan***). As noted above, the Rāṭhoṛs were associated with Kanauj

---

[13] "Rāṭhoḍāṃ rī Vaṃśāvalī," pp. 16, 30, 36.

[14] ***Ibid.***, pp. 20-22.

[15] Phatahsiṃh, "Bhūmikā," in ***Rāṭhauḍ Vaṃś rī Vigat evaṃ Rāṭhauḍāṃ rī Vaṃśāvalī***, p. 13; Ojhā, 1:348, 352-354; Ziegler, "Action, Power and Service ... ," pp. 38, 40. It should be noted here that during the middle period, the same ***gotra*** designation did not necessarily apply to all members at this level of segmentation (Level 3: see Figure 1, ***infra***). In actuality, different branches of a ***vaṃś*** or ***kuḷ*** often had distinct ***gotra*** names of their own.

[16] "Aitihāsik Bātāṃ," p. 58; ***Khyāt***, 2:266-275; Ziegler, "Action, Power and Service ... ," pp. 38, 40.

[17] "Rāṭhoḍāṃ rī Vaṃśāvalī," pp. 9-11; Saran, "Conquest and Colonization ... ," pp. 25-27. Saran remarks of the 36 ***rājkulīs*** that:

> The idea of the existence of thirty-six clans is quite old, developing at least as early as the twelfth century of the Christian Era. During subsequent centuries many lists ... were compiled in Rājasthān. An important facet of these lists is that no two seem to be identical: they differ according to when and where they were written .... One may consider the number thirty-six a conventional one expressing totality (p. 27).

in north India, where they were first seen to have established their sovereignty.[18] Rāṭhoṛ affiliation with a particular family goddess (***kuḷdevī***) was also established in this period. The ***kuḷdevī*** that the Rāṭhoṛs worshipped was Paṅkhnī Mātā, a goddess in the form of a black hawk who had been instrumental in helping the Rāṭhoṛs consolidate their authority within their kingdom.[19]

During the third age (***dvāpara yuga***), several important Kṣatriya ancestors of the Rāṭhoṛs emerged. These were Śrī Rāmcandrajī (the Hindu God, Rām) and his two sons, Liv (Lava) and Kus (Kuśa).[20] The Rāṭhoṛs of Mārvāṛ (and the Sīsodīyo Gahlots of Mevāṛ) trace descent from Liv, while the Kachvāhos of Amber are said to have descended from Kus.[21] Then in the fourth age (***kālī yuga***), the Rāṭhoṛs themselves divided into a number of different branches (***sākhāṃ***) which spread over north India. Thirteen branches are said to have emerged. The branch to which Rāv Jaimal Vīramdevot belonged was called "Kamdhaj" after Rājā Kamdhaj, one of the great Rāṭhoṛ kings of Kanauj.[22] Rājā Kamdhaj was considered the direct ancestor of the last Rāṭhoṛ king of Kanauj, Rājā Jaicand, who according to tradition, was killed defending his capital against the Muslim invasion of north India in the thirteenth century.

With specific reference to the Rāṭhoṛs of Mārvāṛ, their "genealogical" history properly begins with Rāv Sīho Setrāmot (d. 1273). Again according to tradition, Rāv Sīho is considered a grandson of Rājā Jaicand. He is said to have migrated to Mārvāṛ in Rājasthān following the Muslim invasion and the fall of Kanauj, and to have founded a new kingdom of the Kamdhaj Rāṭhoṛs.[23]

---

[18] "Rāṭhoḍāṃ rī Vaṃśāvalī," p. 10.

[19] Saran, "Conquest and Colonization ... ," p. 38. Saran notes that the "Rāṭhoḍāṃ rī Vaṃśāvalī," pp. 20-21 and pp. 21-24, contains variant versions of the story regarding the ***kuḷdevī*** of the Rāṭhoṛs.

[20] "Rāṭhoḍāṃ rī Vaṃśāvalī," p. 26.

[21] ***Ibid.***

[22] ***Ibid.***, pp. 30, 35-36; ***Khyāt***, 3:218-219.

[23] ***Khyāt***, 2:266; "Rāṭhoḍāṃ rī Vaṃśāvalī," p. 40; ***Vigat***, 1:5. Rāv Sīho is known epigraphically from a memorial stone found at the village of Bīṭhu near Pālī in central Mārvāṛ. The inscription on the stone records only that Sīho was a son of Rāṭhoṛ Kuṃvar Setrām, and that he died on ***V. S.*** 1330, ***Kārtik, vadi*** 12 (October 9, 1273). See: Ojhā, 4:1:156-158; Reu, ***Mārvāṛ kā Itihās***, 1:40.

Very little is known about the genealogical history of the Rāṭhoṛs of Mārvāṛ from the time of Sīho Setrāmot until roughly the time of Rāv Cūṇḍo Vīramot of Maṇḍor (d. ca. 1423). D. P. Henige, ***The Chronology of Oral Tradition: Quest for a Chimera*** (Oxford: Clarendon Press, 1974), states:

> ... Anyone inclined to accept the testimony of the Jodhpur ***khyāts*** regarding the names and numbers of rulers before Chunda must at the same time recognize that the chronicles have converted a kinglist into an ascendant genealogy (p. 205).

It is from Sīho Setrāmot that Rāv Jaimal Vīramdevot of Meṛto traced direct descent through some thirteen male ancestors to his own great-grandfather, Rāv Jodho Riṇmalot, the founder of Jodhpur (ca. 1453-89).[24] Over the two centuries between the time of Rāv Sīho Setrāmot and Rāv Jaimal of Meṛto, and during the following period into the mid-seventeenth century, the Kamdhaj Rāṭhoṛs of Mārvāṛ themselves became divided into numerous branches (*sākhāṃ*). These branches are sometimes referred to as "thirteen" in number.[25] But in actual fact there were many more. From Rāv Sīho and his immediate sons and descendants emerged the Sīndhaḷ, Ūhaṛ, Pethaṛ, Mūlū and other branches.[26] These branches spread widely throughout the lands of Mārvāṛ. mingling with the branches of other Rajpūt clans and settling territories that became known as their homelands (*utan*). These lands were often referred to by the name of the group inhabiting and controlling the area, with the suffix "*vaṭī*" attached, meaning "share or portion" of the group.[27]

In the early fourteenth century, the Mahevco Rāṭhoṛs emerged in the area of Mahevo and Kheṛ in western Mārvāṛ. It is from this branch that the Rāṭhoṛs of Jodhpur and Meṛto descend in direct line:

Rāv Salkho Tīḍāvat (Mahevo)
|
Vīram Salkhāvat
|
Rāv Cūṇḍo Vīramot (d. ca. 1423) (Maṇḍor)
|
Rāv Riṇmal Cūṇḍāvat (ca. 1428-38) (Maṇḍor)
|
Rāv Jodho Riṇmalot (ca. 1453-89) (Maṇḍor and Jodhpur)

For additional comments in this regard, see: Ojhā, 4:1:229-234; Saran, "Conquest and Colonization ... ," pp. 39-41; Norman P. Ziegler, "The Seventeenth Century Chronicles of Mārvāṛa: A Study in the Evolution and Use of Oral Tradition in Western India," ***History in Africa***, Vol. 3 (1976), pp. 143-146.

24 ***Daḷpat Vilās***, edited by Rāvat Sarasvat (Bīkāner: Sādūl Rajasthani Research Institute, 1960), pp. 1-3; ***Vigat***, 1:5-38.

25 "Vāt Tīḍai Chāḍāvat rī," in ***Vātāṃ ro Jhūmakho***, part 3, edited by M. Śarmā (Bīsau: Rājasthān Sāhitya Saṃsthān, n.d.), p. 40.

26 ***Ibid.***; G. S. Gehlot, ***Mārvāṛ kā Saṅkṣipt Itihās*** (Jodhpur: Gehlot Bindery Works, n.d.), pp. 72-79.

27 Names of territories in Mārvāṛ, such as Sīndhaḷāvaṭī ("share or portion of the Sīndhaḷs"), do appear in the texts designating areas held by these early groups of Rāṭhoṛs or by other Rajpūts of the area. See: ***Khyāt***, 2:308, 3:41, 48, 125; ***Vigat***, 2:235, 241.

From Rāv Riṇmal Cūṇḍāvat and his son, Rāv Jodho, emerged the branches of the Rāṭhoṛs of Mārvāṛ that became most prominent during the middle period and possessed sovereignty within the kingdom of Mārvāṛ. These branches include the Cāmpāvats, Jaitāvats, Jodhos, Kūmpāvats, Meṛtīyos, Ūdāvats and others. Each branch established its own homeland within Mārvāṛ. Some, like the Meṛtīyo branch to which Rāv Jaimal Vīramdevot belonged, took their names from the particular territory in which they became established. Other branches took their names from their founders. For example, the Cāmpāvats trace descent from Cāmpo Riṇmalot, one of the sons of Rāv Riṇmal Cūṇḍāvat of Maṇḍor. In like manner, the Jaitāvats trace descent from Jaito Pañcāiṇot, a grandson of Rāv Riṇmal, and the Jodhos from Rāv Jodho Riṇmalot, the founder of Jodhpur.[28]

Depending on context, other levels of segmentation might be invoked. All the Rāṭhoṛs who were descendants of Rāv Riṇmal Cūṇḍāvat, for example, were collectively referred to as "Riṇmals" or "Riṇmalots"[29] in contrast to other groups of Rāṭhoṛs, such as the Sīndhaḷs, against whom they often stood regarding control of lands in Mārvāṛ. In addition, these branches themselves became divided into more discrete units as particular families assumed importance through time. By the late seventeenth century, the Meṛtīyos were divided among several segments including the Varsiṅghots, descended from Varsiṅgh Jodhāvat, one of the original founders of Meṛto; the Jaimalots, descended from Rāv Jaimal Vīramdevot; and the Jagnāthots, descended from Jagnāth Goinddāsot, a grandson of Rāv Jaimal Vīramdevot.[30]

Among Rajpūts of the middle period, all of the units of descent as collectivities of individuals related through ties of male blood to a common ancestor were known as brotherhoods (***bhāībandhāṃ*** - lit. "brothers-bound").[31] The higher units of descent, such as the great ***vaṃś***, however, did not designate corporate brotherhoods in the sense that the collectivity of members possessed joint control over land or acted in concert. Membership at these levels was too widely dispersed over different territories in Rājasthān and Mārvāṛ. The functionally corporate brotherhoods were the smaller, named internal segments of these large units of descent, such as the Meṛtīyos, Cāmpāvats and Jaitāvats.[32] Even these groups did not necessarily include all members. In general, brotherhoods were from three to five generations in depth and controlled specified territories within which most of the members lived. These territories are often referred to in the texts as the collective heritage of the brotherhood

---

[28] Gehlot, ***Mārvāṛ kā Saṅkṣipt Itihās***, pp. 160-161, 201-203.

[29] "Aitihāsik Bātāṃ," pp. 44, 48, 50, 54; ***Khyāt***, 3:84; ***Vigat***, 1:67, 83, 2:66.

[30] Several of these named units of descent did not fully emerge among the Meṛtīyos until the 18th century. See: ***Bāṅkīdās***, pp. 57-67.

[31] For further discussion of this term, see: Ziegler, "Action, Power and Service ... ," pp. 45-47.

[32] ***Ibid.***, p. 47; ***Khyāt***, 1:64, 119, 248, 2:50, 213, 3:155.

handed down from fathers and grandfathers (***bāp-dādā***)[33] and held by brothers (***bhāyāṃ***), their sons (***beṭāṃ***), their brothers' sons (***bhatījāṃ***) and their grandsons (***potrāṃ***).[34] While these brotherhoods acknowledged broader ties of descent and paid varying degrees of deference to senior or ruling lines, for the most part they looked upon themselves as separate and distinct units with equal rights to precedence and land with relation to other, more "distant" brothers.[35]

Individual Rajpūts as members of these brotherhoods were thus included within and acknowledged a series of units of descent extending out from themselves. Rāv Jaimal Vīramdevot of Meṛto was first and foremost a Meṛtīyo and secondly a Rāṭhoṛ. With relation to Rajpūts of other ***vaṃś*** or ***kuḷ***, he recognized himself as a Rāṭhoṛ as distinct from a Gahlot, Kachvāho or Cahuvāṇ. But he also acknowledged more distant ties of male blood that existed among the Sūryavaṃśī Rajpūts.

As an individual, he was himself known by a personal name given at birth and by the name of his father. To the name of his father a suffix was added to indicate "son of." Depending on the final letter of the father's name, this suffix would be "ot," "āvat," "īyot," or "ūvot."[36] In the case of Rāv Jaimal, his full name was then:

Sūryavaṃśī (***vaṃś***)	Rāṭhoṛ (***sākh***)	Rajpūt (***jāti***)	
Kamdhaj (***sākh***)	Rāṭhoṛ Meṛtīyo (***sākh***)	Jaimal (personal name)	Vīramdevot (son of Vīramde)

The terms "clan" and "lineage" are generally employed in English to designate these different units of descent among Rajpūts. Though acceptable, they should be used with the understanding that Rajpūts of the middle period would not have recognized what is generally meant by these terms. "Putative

---

[33] ***Khyāt***, 1:87; ***Vigat***, 2:48.

[34] ***Khyāt***, 2:50, 290; "Vāt Tīḍai Chādāvat rī," p. 40; ***Vigat***, 1:51.

[35] For a more complete discussion of the Rajpūt brotherhood in the middle period, see: Ziegler, "Action, Power and Service ... ," pp. 36-55, 84-90; Norman P. Ziegler, "Some Notes on Rajpūt Loyalties During the Mughal Period," in ***Kingship and Authority in South Asia***, edited by J. F. Richards (Publication 3, South Asian Studies: University of Wisconsin-Madison Publication Series, 1978), pp. 223-231.

[36] For example: Jaimal Vīramdev*ot*, Prithīrāj Jait*āvat*, Prithīrāj Bal*ūot*/Bal*ūvot*, Sīghaṇ Khets*īyot*. See: ***Vigat***, 2:57-59, 74.

Genealogical listings also present the personal names of Rajpūts followed by that of the father with the suffix "***ro***" meaning "of" (e.g., ***Kesodās Jaimal ro***). In other cases, sons are listed as being "of the belly of" the individual listed as their father (e.g., ***Kesodās Jaimal rai peṭ ro***). See: ***Khyāt***, 1:355, 2:11, 162.

descent" from a common ancestor implied in the meaning of the term "clan"[37] was not a defining criterion of the ***vaṃś*** or any other Rajpūt unit of descent. If lines of specific descent to particular ancestors were questioned, the ***vaṃśāvalī*** or ***pīḍhiyāṃ*** provided the names and set out the relationships to each other. This was their purpose. In addition, membership in a Rajpūt brotherhood was defined differently from that generally understood under the term "lineage."[38] In contrast to the lineage which included members by birth only, the brotherhood defined membership through birth and through marriage. It included by birth all male descendants of the founder and all unmarried females, who were the daughters and sisters of the brotherhood. It also included by marriage all the wives of the male members of the group.

Rajpūts of the middle period considered marriage to be an act which transformed a woman's affiliation from a person related to her father and her father's brotherhood into a person related to her husband and her husband's brotherhood.[39] Marriage was a ***saṃskāra*** (lit. "polishing, refining"), a rite whose power affected substantial configurations in the world. The union of a woman with her husband was symbolized through the ***hāth-leva*** (lit. "hand-taking") rite

---

[37] For example, see: Robin Fox, ***Kinship and Marriage*** (Baltimore: Penguin Books, 1967), pp. 49-50.

[38] ***Ibid.***

[39] In my dissertation work at the University of Chicago in 1973, I stated, following Ronald Inden's work on Bengali culture, that a woman "became related to her husband by male blood [through marriage] and was seen to possess the same substance and code for conduct that he possessed" (Ziegler, "Action, Power and Service ... ," p. 48). This statement needs modification. The woman is not changed bodily/substantially through marriage into someone related by male blood to her husband, but she does change her kinship status and her group affiliation, thereby becoming a member of her husband's family and brotherhood. This change is similar to that which Fruzzetti defines for Bengali culture: "In Bengali marriage women undergo a change of status through a change of ***gotra***. Through the ritual a woman leaves her father's line and is adopted into the ***baṇgśa*** [line] of her husband and husband's father. The incoming wife of a male line is not seen, however, as undergoing a bodily transubstantiation at marriage; she neither changes to nor adopts her husband's blood (***rakta***). Married women continue to share their father's and brother's blood. Only the ***gotra*** ties with their father's side change at marriage." (Fruzzetti, ***The Gift of a Virgin***, p. 120).

I have not had opportunity, for many reasons, to define in greater detail the specific dimensions of this change in Rājasthānī culture. Central aspects of kinship among Rajpūts include, however, the definition of brotherhood as those who share descent from and male blood with a common male ancestor, the notion of the exclusively male transmission of blood and heredity, the inclusion within the brotherhood of all males born into it, all unmarried females, and all women brought into it through marriage, and finally, the fact that a woman's kinship status and some of her kinships relationships are changed through marriage, while she retains others including the blood link to her father and brothers.

Having been out of direct contact with the field for several years, I am indebted to Richard Saran for helping keep me abreast of developments in the literature.

of the marriage ceremony, when the right hands of the bride and groom were bound together, palm to palm, with a red thread. Between the palms a small ball of mahendī, referred to as the ***hāth-piṇḍ*** (lit. "hand-ball"), was placed. The red dye of the mahendī marked each palm as a mingling of the wife's blood with that of her husband. This joining of hands was accompanied by the transforming power of appropriate words from the sacred texts, and was seen to unite the woman with her husband, making them one. A woman left her father's home (***pīhar***) after marriage, and took up residence in her husband's father's home (***sāsro***), where she received a new personal name signifying her "birth" into her husband's brotherhood.[40]

Accompanying these ideas about marriage was the Rajpūt's belief in the exclusively male transmission of heredity within the marriage. Hereditary features were seen to be passed to children of the union through the seed (***bīj, karaṇ***) that a husband implanted in his wife's belly or womb (***peṭ***) during sexual intercourse.

Studies done during the British period provide support for the set of beliefs evident in local texts from the middle period. In his work on the laws of adoption and succession in Rājasthān done in 1853, Major W. H. Richards wrote, for example:

> . . . The Hindoo order of succession determines the nearness of kindred, with the exception that the adoption must be from among the lineal or collateral descendants of a common ancestor in the male line. Thus a brother's son, grandson, or great-grandson may be adopted, *but not a sister's son or wife's brother. Here the stirps or stock is considered changed by marriage.* On the same principle descendants of remote kindred are preferred to all descendants of the female line or maternal kindred. (*Italics added*) [41]

Some years later in 1871, Brandreth completed his ***Treatise on the Law of Adoption in Rajpootana***. He stated:

---

[40] Lists of the wives of the Rāṭhoṛ rulers of Jodhpur often indicate both the birth name of the wife (***pīhar ro nām***) and the new name she received upon marriage. For example, one wife of Rāv Sūjo Jodhāvat (ca. 1492-1515) had the birth-name, Likhmībāī, but was known at the Jodhpur court as Rāṇī Bhāṭiyāṇī Sāraṅgdejī. Similarly, a wife of Rāv Gāṅgo Vāghāvat (1515-32) had the birth-name, Padmāvatībāī, but was called Rāṇī Sīsodṇī Uttamdejī at the Jodhpur court. See: ***Murārdān***, no. 2. pp. 103, 112.

[41] Letter from Major W. H. Richards, Political Agent, Jaipur, to Lt. Col. Sir H. M. Lawrence, Agent Gevernor General, Rajputana, April 29, 1853, in "Law and Practice in Cases of Adoption and Succession to Sovereignties in Rajputana," ***Rajputana Agency Office Historical Record 27/General, 1846, 1853, 1859*** (National Archives of India, Delhi, India), 1 (1853), p. 11.

> ... A sister's son or daughter's son is not reckoned of the family at all.[42]

And:

> ... Blood relationship is calculated to be on the paternal side only. The female side is mere connexionship.[43]

While marriage changed a woman's kinship status and joined her with her husband's brotherhood, it was also seen to create a special relationship between her husband's family and her own paternal family, who became ***sago***s. The term ***sago*** is related to the abstract noun ***sagāī***, meaning both "betrothal" and "alliance."[44] ***Sago***s defined one's relations by marriage, that is, those to whom one gave and/or from whom one received daughters in marriage. In a more general sense, ***sago***s were allies and formed the other unit of primary reference and identification outside of the brotherhood for Rajpūts of the middle period.

Sagos included a range of individuals and groups: one's mother's and one's wife's families, the collective groups from which they came, and the relations by marriage of one's father and brothers. Genealogical entries for Rajpūts of this period often list the names of ***sago***s alongside the names of individual Rajpūts, an indication of the importance in which they were held. Rāv Jaimal Vīramdevot of Meṛto, for example, is listed as sister's son (***bhāṇej***) of the Tāṇko Rajpūts. His mother was a sister of the Tāṇkos.[45] Other Rajpūts are referred to as daughter's son (***dohitro***) of a particular Rajpūt clan, a segment thereof, or of a specific individual from that clan.[46]

A woman's ties with her father's home and with her brothers generally remained strong after marriage. She would continue to be called sister (***bāī***) or daughter (***beṭī***) of the brotherhood from which she had originally come,[47] and her offspring were entitled to special considerations from her relations. These bonds were particularly strong between a mother's brother (***māmo***) and his sister's son

---

[42] ***Brandreth's Treatise on the Law of Adoption in Rajpootana***, with notes by Col. J. C. Brooke (Calcutta: Foreign Dept. Press, 1871), p. 5.

[43] ***Ibid.***, p. 22.

[44] Kālikā Prasād, ***Bṛhat Hindī Koś*** (4th ed. Vārāṇasī: Jñānmaṇḍal, V.S. 2030 [1973]), p. 1419; Platts, ***Dictionary***, p. 667. The terms ***sago/sagā*** indicate "uterine or blood relationship" when used in compounds, such as ***sago bhāī*** ("uterine brother").

[45] ***Murārdān***, no. 2, p. 459.

[46] For examples, see: ***Khyāt***, 1:26, 28, 31, 2:141.

[47] ***Khyāt***, 2:41, 248, 292, 337, 3:64; ***Vigat***, 1:111. A wife also retained the name of the group from which she had come, and would be called "Rāṭhoṛ," "Bhāṭiyāṇī," Sāṅkhlī," or "Sīsodṇī," etc. For examples, see: ***Khyāt***, 3:144, 259.

(*bhāṇej*), the mother's brother holding strong obligations of support and assistance for his sister's offspring. In the Rajpūt literature of the period, this relationship figures most prominently alongside that between a son and his maternal grandparents (*nāno/nānī*).[48]

Bonds of alliance and support established between *sago*s through the act of marriage also provided an important means for the settlement of hostilities (*vair*) between rival Rajpūt brotherhoods in the middle period. The marriage of a sister or daughter to an opposing group was employed particularly when a murder had been committed. In such instances, the brotherhood that had lost a member received a woman from the brotherhood responsible for the killing. This woman was usually given to a son or a brother of the murdered man as a means of equalizing loss. In addition, the marriage itself established an alliance with on-going obligations of support.[49]

II

Figure 1, *infra*, sets out diagrammatically the different units of descent among Rajpūts and gives the Middle Mārvāṛī terms used to designate them. For purposes of analysis, I have included terms in the figure that occur both in texts from the middle period and in texts and usage from the eighteenth century and after. The latter have been marked with an asterisk (*) to distinguish them.

Below Level 1, the level of caste (*jāti*), only Level 2, that of the great clans (Sūryavaṃś, Somvaṃś, Agnīvaṃś, etc.), finds exclusive designation by the single term *vaṃś* (lit. "bamboo; bamboo pole"). The usage of *vaṃś* in this context appears to be a standard literary convention. For Levels 3-5, several terms find virtually synonymous usage. These terms include *jāti* (or the diminutive *jātiyo*), *vaṃś*, *kuḷ*, and *keḍ*. In addition, *gotī* ("a person of one's own *gotra*")[50] is also used in contexts that make reference to these same levels of descent.

In a general sense, all of these terms mean "offspring, progeny; family, dynasty; brotherhood," or more loosely "assemblage, group."[51] The lexicons define each of them in terms of the other, giving the following equation:

jāti = *vaṃś* = *kuḷ* = *keḍ* = *gotra*

---

[48] *Nānāṇo* is the Middle Mārvāṛī term for the maternal grandparent's home. A passage in *Vigat*, 1:51 specifically includes sisters' sons along with brothers and brothers' sons among the warriors of a local Rajpūt (x *rai bhāī bhatījāṃ bhāṇejāṃ* ...). See also: *Khyāt*, 1:26-27, 206-207, 2:141, 269-276, 288, 304-305, 3:63-64, 68-69, 151.

[49] *Khyāt*, 1:59, 2:336, 3:256-265; *Murārdān*, no. 2, p. 212.

[50] Lāḷas, *RSK*, 1:769.

[51] *Ibid.*, 1:525, 540, 605, 769; *Bṛhat Hindī Koś*, pp. 343, 399, 1207.

In a more specific sense, these terms define "those who share male blood (substance) and the particular inherent set of customs and behaviors (codes for conduct) within a moral order of caste."[52] The synonymous usage of these terms for the different levels indicates that the units which they designate are all of the same order, albeit of greater or lesser inclusiveness depending on the level of segmentation invoked.

Other lower levels are designated by the single term ***sākh*** (lit. "branch, as of a tree"),[53] although the term ***khāmp*** is occasionally found.[54] These lower levels are considered segments, branches or divisions of the higher and more inclusive units. During the middle period, the term ***sākh*** was employed almost exclusively to refer to Level 6-7, and in appropriate contexts, also to Level 5. The very occasional usage of the term ***khāmp*** for Level 6 presages a change in the application of terminology beginning in the latter half of the seventeenth century. In the "Jodhpur Hukūmat rī Bahī," a text compiled during the reign of Mahārājā Jasvantsiṅgh Gajsiṅghot of Jodhpur (1638-78), for example, the term ***khāmp*** appears only once to designate Level 6.[55] In contrast, the term ***sākh*** is an almost exclusive designation for this level in both this and other texts from the same period.[56] However, by the eighteenth century, ***khāmp*** has replaced ***sākh*** as the designation for both Level 6 and Level 7. ***Sākh*** remains in usage primarily as a referent for Level 5.[57]

The lexicons define ***khāmp*** like ***sākh*** in terms of ***jāti, vaṃś,*** and ***kuḷ***. But ***khāmp*** has the additional and more specific meaning of "a segment, a part, a piece, a slice."[58] During this change in terminology, the different branches of the Rāṭhoṛs, such as the Meṛtīyos, Cāmpāvats, and others, all became referred to as ***khāmp***s. Accompanying this change in terminology was a progressive modification in the presentation of Rajpūt names in the texts. This modification is evident in lists of Rajpūts found in material dealing with the sixteenth and seventeenth centuries. Such lists were compiled for varying reasons. But they sought primarily to preserve the names of Rajpūt warriors who fought in the

---

[52] Ziegler, "Action, Power and Service ... ," pp. 23-26, 36.

[53] Prasād, ***Bṛhat Hindī Koś***, pp. 1345, 1476; Lāḷas, ***RSK***, 4:3:5484-5485.

[54] "Jodhpur Hukūmat rī Bahī," p. 134.

[55] ***Ibid.***

[56] For examples, see: ***Ibid.***, p. 19; ***Khyāt***, 1:245, 248, 2:31, 112.

[57] For examples, compare the 18th century material from ***Ajīt Vilās*** (in ***Paramparā***, part 27, edited by N. S. Bhāṭī, Caupāsnī: Rājasthānī Śodh Saṃsthān, 1969), pp. 28, 31, 72, and "Rāṭhauḍ Vaṃś rī Vigat," pp. 6, 9, 17, with the 19th century material from ***Bāṅkīdās***, pp. 1-2, 87.

[58] Prasād, ***Bṛhat Hindī Koś***, p. 343; Lāḷas, ***RSK***, 1:605.

army of a local ruler and/or who died in important battles. Two examples illustrate the importance of this modification.

Lists dealing with the period of Rāv Mālde Gāṅgāvat of Jodhpur (1532-62) set forth names of Rajpūts in a haphazard manner.[59] The names of individual Rāṭhoṛs are mixed without seeming order or system among the names of Rajpūts of other clans, such as the Gahlots, Cahuvāṇs, or Bhāṭīs. In addition, named segments among the Rāṭhoṛs, such as the Meṛtīyo, Cāmpāvat, or Jodho, are rarely included as part of the identification of a Rajpūt. Only his personal name and the name of his father are given.

By contrast, lists of Rajpūts who served in the armies of Rājā Jasvantsiṅgh Gajsiṅghot of Jodhpur (1638-78) are presented in a very different manner. One such list in the "Jodhpur Hukūmat rī Bahī" sets forth the names of Rāṭhoṛ Rajpūts according to clearly defined segments: Cāmpāvat Rāṭhoṛs, Ūdāvat Jaitāraṇīyos (Ūdāvat Rāṭhoṛs of Jaitāraṇ Pargano), Jodho Rāṭhoṛs, etc.[60] Rajpūts of these segments are still mixed without seeming order among groups of Rajpūts from other clans, and all are classified as ***ṭhākur***s of different branches (***sākh-sākh rā ṭhākur***). But on the whole, these lists evidence a markedly increased formalization and systemization of material.

By the eighteenth century, Rajpūts were generally identified by ***khāmp*** designations in all such listings. In addition, even in textual passages where an individual Rajpūt is mentioned, the particular ***khāmp*** to which he belonged is noted.[61] This change shows a still greater attention to categorization than in earlier periods. It may be noted here that Rajpūts of the modern period have carried this classification system even further with the introduction of the term ***nakh*** to designate the lowest level of segmentation (Level 7). ***Nakh*** (lit. "nail of the finger") has the same meaning as ***khāmp*** in this context, that is, "a piece, a part, or a segment."[62]

This transition in the presentation of names and in the usage of terminology is significant. Several hypotheses present themselves as explanations. One relates to internal developments among Rāṭhoṛs and other Rajpūt clans over time. Most of the prominent branches of the Rāṭhoṛs of Mārvāṛ, for example, descend either from Rāv Riṇmal Cūṇḍāvat (ca. 1429-38) or his son and successor, Rāv Jodho Riṇmalot (ca. 1453-1489). By the mid-sixteenth century, these branches were well-defined groups with sizeable memberships and with varying territories under their control. Over the next century, most of these branches developed additional internal segments as new families and groups rose to prominence. Some of these segments retained their original names with the qualifying addition of a founder's name, as among the Jaimalot Meṛtīyos, mentioned above. Among others, the original names were

---

[59] For examples, see ***Vigat***, 2:59, 65-66, ***infra***, in the translated sections of this volume.

[60] "Jodhpur Hukūmat rī Bahī," pp. 19-24.

[61] ***Ajīt Vilās***, pp. 72, 80, 86-87.

[62] Prasād, ***Bṛhat Hindī Koś***, p. 682; Lāḷas, ***RSK***, 2:2:1985.

replaced with newer names of more recent "founders" or men of prominence. The relative stability in Mārvāṛ that followed Mughal domination of Rājasthān and north India under Akbar may itself have fostered this process of segmentation among groups that retained association with original lands and kingdoms. From one perspective then, increasing complexity of terminology and greater sophistication in the presentation of names can be seen as a response to the greater number and complexity of named groups themselves.

Complementing this segmentation process were other influences that affected the manner in which local groups and individuals perceived themselves. Some of these influences are seen in the emergence of a strong indigenous literature, particularly in the area of Mārvāṛ. Components of this literature are found in the lists of Rajpūts, such as those from the reign of Rāv Mālde Gāṅgāvat, which derive from a tradition of recording the names of important warriors and their deeds, usually in the form of stories or tales (***bātāṃ***) in the vernacular.[63] One passage in a text dealing with Rāv Mālde's reign specifically states that the Rāv ordered warriors chosen to fight in a battle "recorded name by name."[64] Passages in other material relating to even earlier periods also contain similar references.[65]

John D. Smith has recently discussed the origin and importance of this vernacular tradition in connection with his reconstruction of the ***Vīsaḷadevarāsa***, a poetic composition that Smith dates to ca. 1450.[66] Smith writes of this composition and its language of Middle Mārvāṛī:

> Until [the mid-fifteenth century] the culturally dominant region of Rājasthān had been the kingdom of Mewāṛ, but literature there was restricted to the 'classical' languages; vernacular Mewāṛī was not (and has never become) accepted as a literary medium. It would thus appear that the rise to unified power of the Rāṭhoṛs [with the founding of Jodhpur under Rāv Jodho Riṇmalot in 1459] was the impetus necessary to bring about the earliest vernacular composition in Rājasthān. It is hardly surprising if the first works to be composed were of a popular nature, and probably derive at no great distance from folk-song and ballad; nonetheless, from these humble beginnings was to come into being one of the greatest of the [New Indo-Aryan] literary languages.[67]

---

[63] Ziegler, "Marvari Historical Chronicles ... ," p. 233.

[64] "Aitihāsik Bātāṃ," p. 50.

[65] For an example, see: ***Khyāt***, 2:228.

[66] John D. Smith, ***The Vīsaḷadevarāsa: A Restoration of the Text*** (Cambridge: Cambridge Univeristy Press, 1976), p. 26.

[67] ***Ibid.***, pp. 45-46.

It is precisely this vernacular of Middle Mārvāṛī in which the prose chronicles compiled under Muṃhato Naiṇsī in the mid-seventeenth century were written.

During the sixteenth and seventeenth centuries, the loose collections of lists, the stories about the great deeds of warriors, and the compositions describing important events changed. L. P. Tessitori and following him, D. P. Henige, argue that the impetus for this change was political and was engendered specifically through Rajpūt contact with the Mughal court of Akbar (1556-1605). The compilation of much embellished genealogies and clan histories in this period is put forward as evidence.[68] With reference to Mārvāṛ and Bīkāner, Tessitori remarks:

> It is natural that there, before an Emperor [Akbar] who was ever ready to lend an interested and benevolent ear to stories, beliefs, and disputes of his subjects, the Princes of Rajputana brought all their mutual rivalries and their controversies about pre-eminence and seniority, and each tried to back his claim with pedigrees of his family. . . It was thus a spirit of emulation and ambition that awoke in the Rajput Princes who gathered at the Imperial Court, an interest in historical matters. . . now they began to inquire into the origins of their ancestors and the traditions concerning them, and to complete their pedigrees with long lists of *paurāṇika* names ....[69]

Tessitori argues further that even the format of the Rajpūt genealogies, especially the ***vaṃśāvalīs***, which trace descent of rulers back to Adi Narāyan, derived from the model provided in the ***Akbar Nāmā*** in which Akbar's ancestry is traced back to Adam.[70]

Mughal influence in Rājathān, Imperial concerns about ancestry and precedence, and Rajpūt attempts to emulate the traditions of the Imperial court for political advantage had an undoubted impact upon the forms and content of local compositions. I have also argued elsewhere that the emergence of local clan histories and genealogies during the sixteenth and seventeenth centuries may be seen as an adaptive response to the Muslim conquest and the threat it posed to local positions of precedence and power.[71] This process may have begun in the early part of the sixteenth century. The rather voluminous material

---

[68] Tessitori, "A Progress Report on the Work done during the year 1917... ," pp. 24-26; Henige, ***The Chronology of Oral Tradition***, pp. 201-202.

[69] Tessitori, "A Progress Report on the Work done during the year 1917 ... ," p. 25.

[70] L. P. Tessitori, "A Progress Report on the Work done in the year 1918 in connection with the Bardic and Historical Survey of Rajputana," ***Journal of the Asiatic Society of Bengal***, Vol. XVI, N.S. 1920, p. 263.

[71] Ziegler, "Marvari Historical Chronicles ... ," pp. 233-234; Ziegler, "The Seventeenth Century Chronicles of Mārvāṛa ... ," pp. 133-134.

in local chronicles about the reign of Rāv Mālde of Jodhpur, for example, may have been produced contemporaneously not only to commemorate Rāv Mālde's reign, in itself remarkable, but also to record position and deed in response to the continuing hostilities between Jodhpur and Meṛto.[72] Muslim rulers from north India entered into this conflict early on, for Sher Shāh Sūr (1540-45) became an outside arbiter at the behest of Meṛtīyo Rāv Vīramde Dūdāvat, ruler of Meṛto (ca. 1497-1544). Following his defeat of Rāv Mālde at the battle of Samel (near Ajmer) in January of 1544, Sher Shāh also occupied Jodhpur for a short period. Questions of precedence, rank and rights to land all figured prominently in these on-going hostilities.

Both emulation of Mughal customs and forms, and needs to re-define rank and precedence in response to outside threats speak to a process of objectification that occurred in Rājasthān during the sixteenth and seventeenth centuries. This process helps to explain much of the increased categorization and delineation of Rajpūt groups by name and level of segmentation which appears in the terminology applied to Rajpūt units of descent. One other type of influence that both Tessitori and Henige fail to note, however, also deserves mention. This influence I shall term simply "bureaucratic." It emerged secondarily from increasing Rajpūt contact with the Mughals. It is embodied in various Mughal regulations pertaining to the ordering of men. An example comes from the ***Ā'īn-ī-Akbarī***. Under the "Regulations Regarding the Branding of Animals" (Book II, ***Ā'īn*** 7), the following is written:

> When His Majesty had fixed the ranks of the army, and inquired into the quality of the horses, he ordered that upright *Bitikchīs* should make out descriptive rolls of the soldiers and write down their peculiar marks. Their ages, the names of their fathers, dwelling-places, and race, were to be registered.[73]

Coupled with general interest on the part of the Mughal Emperors in ancestry and genealogy, regulations such as this one must have had a considerable influence over time upon Rajpūt conceptions of themselves as individuals and as members of larger groups. These conceptions would have affected how they ordered information about themselves and the terms they used to describe themselves.

Norman P. Ziegler

[72] Librarians and other men of letters from the Delhi courts did occasionally seek attachments in the ***darbārs*** of Rājasthān, and they undoubtedly exerted their own influence on the form and content of local literature and composition. Mulla Surkh, a former librarian from Humāyūn's court, for example, is known to have served in Jodhpur during the time of Rāv Mālde Gāṅgāvat. However, no information is available about specific activities in which he may have been involved. See: Ziegler, "Marvari Historical Chronicles ... ," p. 233.

[73] ***A'īn-ī-Akbarī***, p. 265.

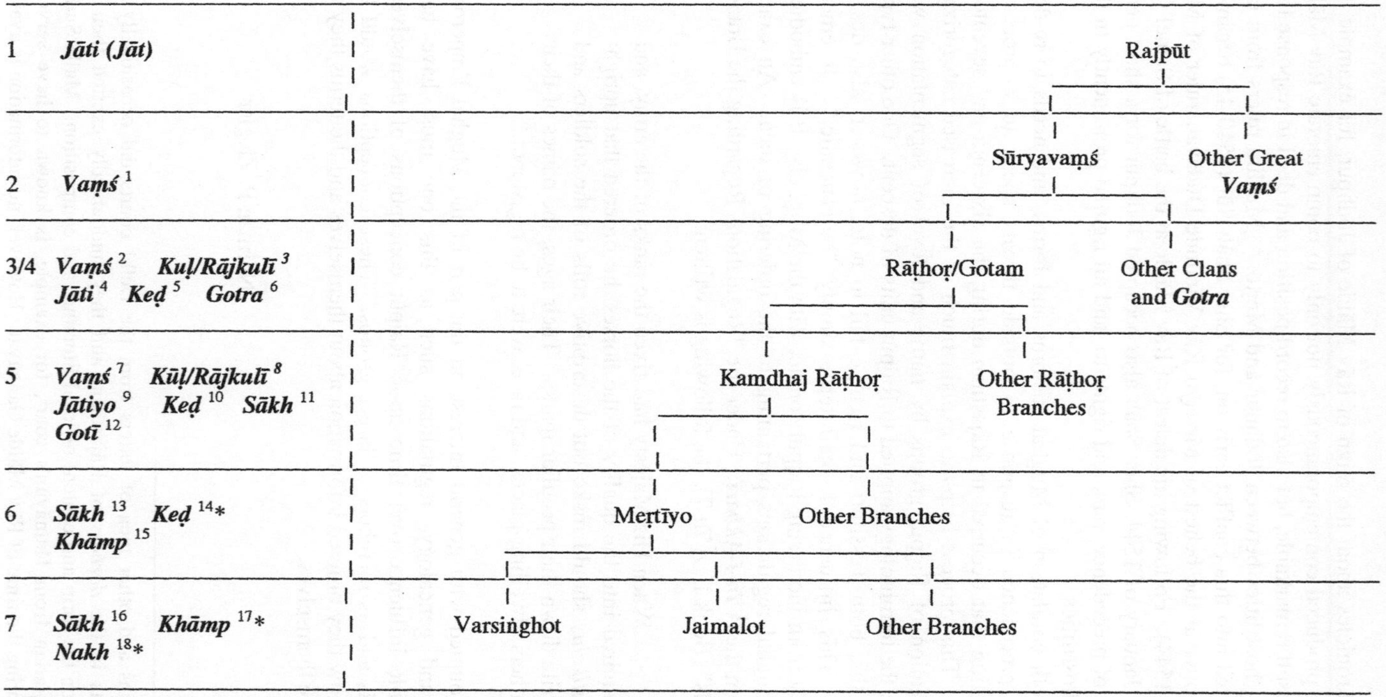

* Terms which occur in texts and usage from the eighteenth century and after.

Figure 1. Rajpūt Units of Descent

Endnotes for Figure 1

---

[1] ***Khyāt***, 1:1, 128, 134, 291, 2:3, 15, 3:177; "Rāṭhoḍāṃ rī Vaṃśāvalī," pp. 9-10; Khiṛiyā Jagā, ***Vacnikā Rāṭhoṛ Ratansiṅghjī Mahesdāsot rī Khiṛiyā Gagā rī Kahī***, edited by Kāśīrām Śarma and Raghubīrsiṃh (Dillī: Rājkamal Prakāśan, 1960), pp. 2, 8, 30, 36, 44.

[2] ***Khyāt***, 1:128, 2:3, 16, 209; "Rāṭhoḍāṃ rī Vaṃśāvalī," pp. 12, 18-19, 22, 24, 33-36.

[3] "Rāṭhoḍāṃ rī Vaṃśāvalī," pp. 7, 9-11; John D. Smith, ***The Vīsaḷadevarāsa: A Restoration of the Text*** (Cambridge: Cambridge University Press, 1976), pp. 68, 70, 95, 99.

[4] ***Khyāt***, 1:336, 2:287; Smith, ***The Vīsaḷadevarāsa*** ... , pp. 70, 96.

[5] "Rāṭhoḍāṃ rī Vaṃśāvalī," p. 14.

[6] ***Ibid***., pp. 16, 25, 30, 36; ***Khyāt***, 1:9, 23, 111, 128, 3:175.

[7] ***Khyāt***, 1:292, 2:1; "Rāṭhoḍāṃ rī Vaṃśāvalī," p. 30.

[8] ***Khyāt***, 1:2, 2:331, 3:104, 173; "Rāṭhoḍāṃ rī Vaṃśāvalī," pp. 9-11; ***Vacnikā Rāṭhoṛ Ratansiṅghjī*** ... , p. 2.

[9] ***Khyāt***, 2:287.

[10] "Rāṭhoḍāṃ rī Vaṃśāvalī," p. 14.

[11] ***Khyāt***, 1:88-90, 3:155, 218-219; "Rāṭhoḍāṃ rī Vaṃśāvalī," pp. 35-36.

[12] ***Khyāt***, 1:23, 111.

[13] ***Ibid.***, 1:245, 248, 2:31, 112; "Jodhpur Hukūmat rī Bahī," pp. 19-24; :Vāt Tīḍai Chāḍāvat rī," in ***Bātāṃ ro Jhūmakho***, part 3, edited by M. Śarmā (Bīsau: Rājasthān Sāhitya Saṃsthān, V. S. 2021 [1964]), p. 40.

[14] "Rāṭhauḍ Vaṃś rī Vigat," p. 9.

[15] ***Ibid.***, pp. 9, 18; ***Ajīt Vilās***, pp. 2, 31, 72; ***Bāṅkīdās***, pp. 1-2; "Jodhpur Hukūmat rī Bahī," p. 134.

[16] "Jodhpur Hukūmat rī Bahī," p. 22; ***Khyāt***, 2:11, 16, 33, 72, 112; ***Vigat***, 2:41, 68.

[17] ***Bāṅkīdās***, pp. 57, 62.

[18] Modern usage among Rajpūts in Mārvāṛ, based on information from a local informant, Ṭhākur Gopāḷsiṅghjī of Ṭhikāṇo Bhādrājuṇ, Mārvāṛ.

Succession Lists of the Major Rajpūt Ruling Families of Middle Period Rājasthān

Āhāṛo Gahlots of Ḍūṅgarpur
Āhāṛo Gahlots of Vāṃsvāḷo
Bhāṭīs of Jaisaḷmer
Bīkāvat Rāṭhoṛs of Bīkāner
Devṛo Cahuvāṇs of Sīrohī
Hāḍo Cahuvāṇs of Būndī
Jodho Rāṭhoṛs of Jodhpur
Meṛtīyo Rāṭhoṛs of Meṛto
Rājāvat Kachvāhos of Āmber
Sīsodīyo Gahlots of Mevāṛ

Āhāṛo Gahlots of Ḍūṅgarpur

Rāvaḷ Udaisiṅgh Gāṅgāvat	ca. 1497-1527
Rāvaḷ Prathīrāj Udaisiṅghot	ca. 1527-1549
Rāvaḷ Āskaraṇ Prathīrājot	ca. 1549-1580
Rāvaḷ Sahasmal Āskaraṇot	ca. 1580-1606
Rāvaḷ Puñjrāj Karamsiṅghot	ca. 1609-1657
Rāvaḷ Girdhardās Puñjrājot	ca. 1657-1661
Rāvaḷ Jasvantsiṅgh Girdhardāsot	ca. 1661-1691
Rāvaḷ Khumāṇsiṅgh Jasvantsiṅghot	ca. 1691-1702

Āhāṛo Gahlots of Vāṃsvāḷo

Rāvaḷ Jagmāl Udaisiṅghot	ca. 1518-1544
Rāvaḷ Jaisiṅgh Jagmālot	ca. 1544-1550
Rāvaḷ Pratāpsiṅgh Jaisiṅghot	ca. 1550-1579
Rāvaḷ Mānsiṅgh Pratāpsiṅghot	ca. 1579-1583
Rāvaḷ Ugrasen Mānsiṅghot	ca. 1586-1613
Rāvaḷ Udaibhāṇ Ugrasenot	ca. 1613-1614
Rāvaḷ Samarsī Udaibhāṇot	ca. 1614-1660
Rāvaḷ Kusalsiṅgh Samarsīyot	ca. 1660-1688
Rāvaḷ Ajabsiṅgh Kusalsiṅghot	ca. 1688-1706

Bhāṭīs of Jaisaḷmer

Rāvaḷ Kehar Devrājot	1361-1397
Rāvaḷ Lakhmaṇ Keharot	1397-1424 or 1437
Rāvaḷ Vairsī Lakhmaṇot	1424/37-1448
Rāvaḷ Cācag/Cācig Vairsīyot	1448-1464 or 1467
Rāvaḷ Devīdās Cācagot	1464/67-1491
Rāvaḷ Jaitsī Devīdāsot	1491-1528
Rāvaḷ Lūṇkaraṇ Jaitsīyot	1528-1551
Rāvaḷ Mālde Lūṇkaraṇot	1551-1561
Rāvaḷ Harrāj Māldevot	1561-1577
Rāvaḷ Bhīm Harrājot	1577-1613
Rāvaḷ Kalyāṇdās Harrājot	ca. 1613-1627
Rāvaḷ Manohardās Kalyāṇdāsot	1627-ca. 1650
Rāvaḷ Rāmcand Siṅghot	ca. 1650-(1651?)
Rāvaḷ Sabaḷsiṅgh Dayāḷdāsot	1651?-1660
Ravaḷ Amarsiṅgh Sabaḷsiṅghot	1660-1702

Bīkāvat Rāṭhoṛs of Bīkāner

Rāv Bīko Jodhāvat	ca. 1485-June 17, 1504
Rāv Naro Bīkāvat	ca. September, 1504-January 13, 1505
Rāv Lūṇkaraṇ Bīkāvat	January 23, 1505-June 28, 1526
Rāv Jaitsī Lūṇkaraṇot	ca. 1526-February 26, 1542
Rāv Kalyāṇmal Jaitsīyot	ca. 1542-January 24, 1574
Rājā Rāysiṅgh Kalyāṇmalot	ca. 1574-January 22, 1612
Rājā Dalpat Rāysiṅghot	March 28, 1612-January 25, 1614
Rājā Sūrsiṅghot Rāysiṅghot	ca. 1614-September 15, 1631
Rājā Karaṇsiṅgh Sūrsiṅghot	October 13, 1631-June 22, 1668
Rājā Anūpsiṅgh Karaṇsiṅghot	ca. 1668-1698
Rājā Svarūpsiṅgh Anūpsiṅghot	ca. 1698-December 15, 1700

<u>Devṛo Cahuvāṇs of Sīrohī</u>

Rāv Lākho Sahasmalot	Founded Sīrohī ca. 1395
Rāv Jagmal Lākhāvat	
Rāv Akhairāj Jagmālot	ca. 1532
Rāv Rāysiṅgh Akhairājot	
Rāv Dūdo Akhairājot	
Rāv Mānsiṅgh Dūdāvat	Died ca. 1575
Rāv Surtāṇ Bhāṇot	ca. 1575-1610
Rāv Kalo Mehājalot	ca. 1575-1575/ca. 1588
Rāv Rājsiṅgh Surtāṇot	ca. 1610-1618
Rāv Akhairāj Rājsiṅghot	ca. 1618-1665 (?)
Rāv Udaibhāṇ Akhairājot	ca. 1665-1676
Rāv Vairsal Udaibhāṇot	ca. 1676-1692

<u>Hāḍo Cahuvāns of Būndī</u>

Nāpo Ajītot	
Hāmo Nāpāvat	
Varsiṅgh Hāmāvat (Hamīrot)	
Rāv Nāraṇdās Bhāṇḍāvat	Died ca. 1527
Rāv Sūrajmal Nāraṇdāsot	ca. 1527-1531
Rāv Surtāṇ Sūrajmalot	ca. 1531-1554
Rāv Surjan Arjunot	ca. 1554-1578
Rāv Bhoj Surjanot	ca. 1578-1607
Rāv Ratansiṅgh Bhojāvat	ca. 1607-1631
Rāv Catrasāḷ Gopīnāthot	ca. 1631-1658
Rāv Bhāvsiṅgh Catrasāḷot	ca. 1658-1681
Rāv Aniruddsiṅgh Kisansiṅghot	ca. 1681-1695

Jodho Rāṭhoṛs of Jodhpur

Rāv Jodho Riṇmalot	May 12, 1459-April 6, 1489
Rāv Sātaḷ Jodhāvat	ca. 1489-March, 1492
Rāv Sūjo Jodhāvat	March, 1492-October 2, 1515
Rāv Gāṅgo Vāghāvat	November 8, 1515-May 9, 1532
Rāv Mālde Gāṅgāvat	May 21, 1532-November 7, 1562
Rāv Candrasen Māldevot	December 31, 1562-January 11, 1581[1]
Rājā Udaisiṅgh Māldevot	August 4, 1583-July 11, 1595
Rājā Sūrajsiṅgh Udaisiṅghot	July 23, 1595-September 7, 1619
Rājā Gajsiṅgh Sūrajsiṅghot	October 6, 1619-May 6, 1638.
Rājā Jasvantsiṅgh Gajsiṅghot	May 25, 1638-November 28, 1678

Meṛtīyo Rāṭhoṛs of Meṛto

Rāv Varsiṅgh Jodhāvat	March 7, 1462-ca.1492
Rāv Sīho Varsiṅghot	ca. 1492-ca. 1495
Rāv Dūdo Jodhāvat	ca. 1495-ca. 1497
Rāv Vīramde Dūdāvat	ca. 1497-1544
Rāv Jaimal Vīramdevot	1544-January 27, 1557; 1562
Kesodās Jaimalot	ca. 1570-ca. 1577 (half of Meṛto)
Surtāṇ Jaimalot	ca. 1572-ca. 1577 (half of Meṛto)
Kesodās Jaimalot	1586-1599 (half of Meṛto)
Kānhīdās Kesodāsot	ca. 1599-ca. 1601 (half of Meṛto)
Surtāṇ Jaimalot	February 12, 1586-ca. 1589 (half of Meṛto)
Balbhadar Surtāṇot	ca. 1589-ca.1596 (half of Meṛto)
Gopāḷdās Surtāṇot	ca. 1596-ca. 1599 (half of Meṛto)
Jagnāth Gopāḷdāsot	ca. 1599-ca. 1601 (half of Meṛto)

[1] Rāv Candrasen did not retain possession of Jodhpur after 1565; his son Āskaraṇ was designated his successor upon his death in 1581 by a group of Rāṭhoṛs in Sojhat but was killed on March 25, 1582. Another of Candrasen's sons, Rāysiṅgh, was in Mughal service but was killed on October 17, 1583. None of Candrasen's sons ever ruled Jodhpur.

Rājāvat Kachvāhos of Āmber

Rājā Prithvīrāj Candrasenot	January 17, 1503-November 4, 1527
Rājā Pūraṇmal Prithvīrājot	November 5, 1527-May 1536
Rājā Bhīm Prithvīrājot	Two and one-half months in 1536
Rājā Ratansiṅgh Bhīmot	1536-1547
Rājā Āskaraṇ Bhīmot	Ruled only a few days in 1547
Rājā Bhārmal Prithvīrājot	June 25, 1547-1574
Rājā Bhagvantdās Bhārmalot	1574?-November 14, 1589
Rājā Mānsiṅgh Bhagvantdāsot	November 26, 1589-July 6, 1614
Rājā Bhāvsiṅgh Mānsiṅghot	July, 1614-December 13, 1621
Rājā Jaisiṅgh (I) Mahāsiṅghot	December 18, 1621-August 28, 1667
Rājā Rāmsiṅgh Jaisiṅghot	September 10, 1667-April, 1688

Sīsodīyo Gahlots of Mevāṛ

Rāṇo Lākho Khetsot	ca. 1382-1420
Rāṇo Mokal Lākhāvat	ca. 1421-1433
Rāṇo Kūmbho Mokalot	ca. 1433-1468
Rāṇo Udaisiṅgh Kūmbhāvat	ca. 1468-1473
Rāṇo Rāymal Kūmbhāvat	ca. 1473-May 24, 1509
Rāṇo Sāṅgo Rāymalot	May 24, 1509-January 30, 1528
Rāṇo Ratansiṅgh Sāṅgāvat	February, 1528-1531
Rāṇo Vikramāditya Sāṅgāvat	ca. 1531-1536
Rāṇo Udaisiṅgh Sāṅgāvat	ca. 1537-February 28, 1572
Rāṇo Pratāp Udaisiṅghot	ca. 1572-January 19, 1597
Rāṇo Amarsiṅgh Pratāpot	January 19, 1597-January 26, 1620
Rāṇo Karansiṅgh Amarsiṅghot	January 26, 1620-March, 1628
Rāṇo Jagatsiṅgh Karaṇsiṅghot	March, 1628-April 10, 1652
Rāṇo Rājsiṅgh Jagatsiṅghot	October 10, 1652-October 22, 1680

Chronology of Important Events

Year	Month and Day	Event
1459	May 12	Founding of Jodhpur by Rāv Jodho Riṇmalot
1462	March 7	Settlement of Meṛto Town by Varsiṅgh and Dūdo Jodhāvat
1489	April 6	Death of Rāv Jodho
1489		Accession of Rāv Sātaḷ Jodhāvat in Jodhpur
1492	March 1	Battle of Kusāṇo; death of Rāv Sātaḷ
1492		Accession of Rāv Sūjo Jodhāvat in Jodhpur
ca. 1492		Death of Varsiṅgh Jodhāvat
ca. 1492		Accession of Sīho Varsiṅghot in Meṛto
ca. 1495		Sīho Varsinghot sent to Rāhīṇ by Dūdo Jodhāvat, who replaces him in Meṛto
ca. 1497		Death of Dūdo Jodhāvat; accession of Vīramde Dūdāvat in Meṛto
1515	October 2	Death of Rāv Sūjo
1515	November 8	Accession of Rāv Gāṅgo Vāghāvat in Jodhpur
1529	November 2	Battle of Sevakī; death of Sekho Sūjāvat
1531-32		Rāv Gāṅgo takes Sojhat
1532	May 9	Death of Rāv Gāṅgo
1532	May 21	Accession of Rāv Mālde Gāṅgāvat in Jodhpur

ca. 1535		Rāv Mālde captures Meṛto from Vīramde Dūdavat
ca. 1535		Battle of Reyāṃ
1536		Conquest of Nāgaur by Rāv Mālde
1544	January 5	Battle of Samel; defeat of Rāṭhoṛs by Sher Shāh Sūr
1544	End of January	Occupation of Jodhpur by Afghans
1544	February or March	Death of Vīramde Dūdāvat
1544		Accession of Jaimal Vīramdevot in Meṛto
1545		Death of Sher Shāh Sūr
1546-47		Reoccupation of Jodhpur by Rāv Mālde Gāṅgāvat
1554	March 21	Battle of Meṛto
1556		Accession of Mughal Emperor Akbar
1557	January 24	Battle of Harmāṛo
1557	January 27	Rāv Mālde Gāṇgāvat retakes Meṛto from Jaimal Vīramdevot
1558-59		Construction of the Mālgaḍh in Meṛto begun
1559	July 28	Jagmāl Vīramdevot receives half of Meṛto Pargano in ***paṭo*** from Rāv Mālde Gāṅgāvat
1560-61		Completion of the Mālgaḍh in Meṛto
1562		Emperor Akbar gives Jaimal Vīramdevot Meṛto
1562	January 27	Siege of Meṛto by Mughal troops begins
1562	March 20	Battle of Sātaḷvās; Mughals gain complete control over Meṛto and its surrounding region

1562	December 31	Accession of Rāv Candrasen Māldevot in Jodhpur
1562-63		Jaimal Vīramdevot abandons Meṛto and flees to Mevāṛ in the wake of Mīrzā Sharafu'd-Dīn Ḥusayn's rebellion
1565		Rāv Candrasen Māldevot abandons Jodhpur to Mughal troops
1568	February 23	Jaimal Vīramdevot is killed by Mughals at the siege of Cītoṛ
ca. 1570		Kesodās Jaimalot receives one-half of Meṛto Pargano in *jāgīr* from the Mughal Emperor Akbar
1572		Surtāṇ Jaimalot receives the other half of Meṛto Pargano from the Mughal Emperor Akbar
ca. 1577		Akbar removes Meṛto from the possession of Kesodās and Surtāṇ Jaimalot
1581	January 11	Death of Rāv Candrasen Māldevot
1581		Āskaraṇ Candrasenot designated successor to Rāv Candrasen by Rāṭhoṛ commanders at Sojhat
1582	March 25	Assassination of Āskaraṇ Candrasenot by his brother, Ugrasen Candrasenot
1582		Accession of Rāysiṅgh Candrasenot to throne of Jodhpur with Emperor Akbar's support
1583	October 17	Death of Rāysiṅgh Candrasenot
1583		Accession of Udaisiṅgh Māldevot (Moṭo Rājā) to throne of Jodhpur
1586	February 11	Surtāṇ Jaimalot again receives one-half Meṛto Pargano from Akbar
1586		Kesodās Jaimalot again receives the other half of Meṛto Pargano from Akbar

ca. 1589		Death of Surtāṇ Jaimalot; Balbhadar Surtāṇot receives his half of Meṛto in ***jāgīr*** from Akbar
1595	July 11	Death of Udaisiṅgh Māldevot
1595	July 23	Accession of Rājā Sūrajsiṅgh Udaisiṅghot to throne of Jodhpur
ca. 1596		Death of Balbhadar Surtāṇot; Gopāḷdās Surtāṇot receives his half of Meṛto Pargano from Akbar.
ca. 1599		Death of Kesodās Jaimalot, Gopāḷdās Surtāṇot, and several other leading Meṛtīyos at the battle of Bīḍ in the Deccan; Kānhīdās Kesodāsot receives Kesodās's half of Meṛto Pargano in ***jāgīr*** from Akbar, and Jagnāth Gopāḷdāsot receives Gopāḷdās's half
ca. 1601		Death of Kānhīdās Kesodāsot; Akbar transfers Jagnāth Gopāḷdāsot from Meṛto
ca. 1602		Rājā Sūrajsiṅgh Udaisiṅghot receives all of Meṛto Pargano in ***jāgīr*** from Akbar
1605		Death of Emperor Akbar; accession of Jahāngīr
1619	September 7	Death of Rājā Sūrajsiṅgh Udaisiṅghot
1619	October 6	Accession of Rājā Gajsiṅgh Sūrajsiṅghot to throne of Jodhpur
1619		Meṛto transferred from the house of Jodhpur and given to Prince Khurram in ***jāgīr*** by his father, Jahāngīr
1623	May-June	Prince Parvīz asserts control over Meṛto after Khurram's rebellion
1623	August 8	Rājā Gajsiṅgh receives all of Meṛto in ***jāgīr***, but from Mahābat Khān, not the Mughal Emperor

1625-26		Rājā Gajsiṅgh's possession of Meṛto is confirmed by the Mughal Emperor, Jahāngīr
1638	May 6	Death of Rājā Gajsiṅgh Sūrajsiṅghot
1638	May 25	Accession of Rājā Jasvantsiṅgh Gajsiṅghot to throne of Jodhpur
1678	November 28	Death of Rājā Jasvantsiṅgh Gajsiṅghot

MAP 1

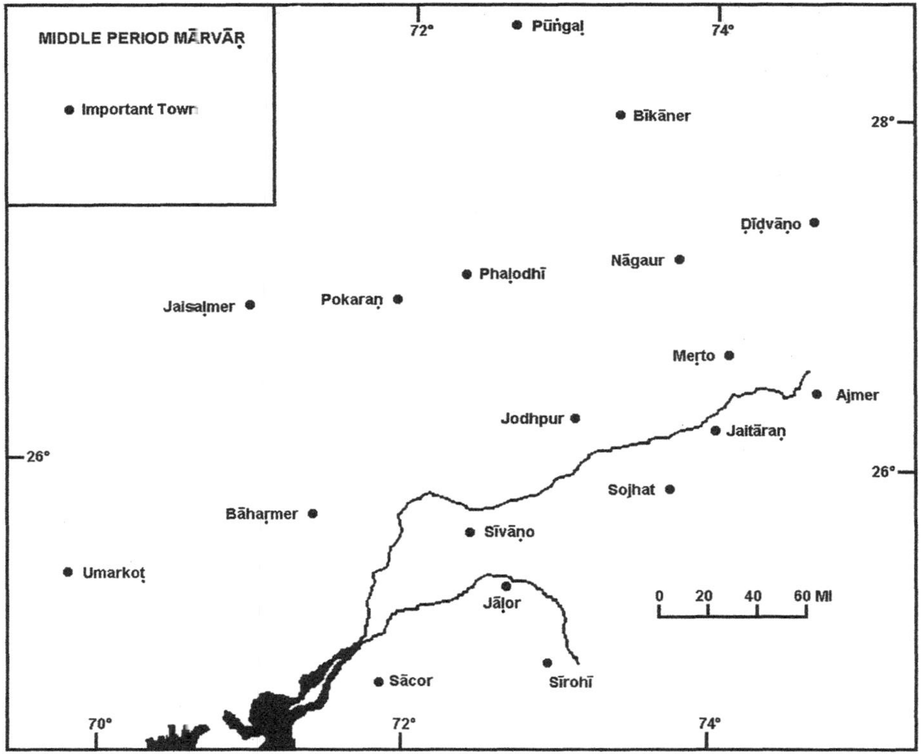

MAP 1. MIDDLE PERIOD MĀRVĀṚ.

Vigat, 2:37

An Account of Meṛto Pargano

1. Meṛto[1] was the first city[2] [in] the ***pargano***.[3] [It] was founded by Rājā Māndhātā.[4] So everyone says. I have heard also that for some time it was as follows: when Rāv[5] Kānhaṛde[6] had much land, people say that he once had authority [over Meṛto]. After that this place remained deserted [and] desolate for many days. Here it became [overgrown with] many trees [and] shrubs.

2. Subsequently Rāv Jodho[7] took Mārvāṛ [and] on May 13, 1459, founded Jodhpur.[8] Then he decided to give land to [his] brothers [and] sons. Rāv Jodho had two sons, Dūdo[9] [and] Varsiṅgh,[10] [who were] uterine brothers of

---

[1] For an account of the early history of Meṛto, see Appendix A.

[2] ***Ād sahar***. The ***ād sahar*** was the initial settlement in a region. Cf. ***Vigat***, 1.1, 493.

[3] ***Pargano***: an administrative and revenue unit or division of a district (***sarkār***). The term came into prominent use in Rājasthān only during the Mughal period.

[4] Rājā Māndhātā: the Purāṇic hero Māndhātṛ, ruler of Ayodhyā.

[5] ***Rāv***: a title held by many Rajpūt rulers in middle period Rājasthān, including the Rāṭhoṛs of Jodhpur (until 1583), Meṛto, and Bīkāner; the Bhāṭīs of Pūṅgaḷ and Vairsaḷpur; the Cahuvāṇs of Būndī, Koṭo, Sīrohī, and Jāḷor, and numerous others.

[6] Rāv Kānhaṛde: The Sonagaro Cahuvāṇ ruler of Jāḷor during the reign of 'Ala-ad-dīn Khiljī of Delhi (1296-1316). The Sonagaro branch (***sākh***) of the Cahuvāṇ Rajpūt family (***kuḷ***) takes its name from Suvarṇagiri, an ancient name for Jālor, a town situated sixty-five miles south-southeast of Jodhpur.

[7] Rāṭhoṛ Jodho Riṇmalot, born April 1, 1416, Rāv of Maṇḍor and Jodhpur, ca. 1453-April 6, 1489.

[8] V.S. 1515, ***Jeṭh***, ***Sudi*** 11. Ojhā, 4:1:241, converts the date to May 12, 1459, a Saturday. The ***Indian Ephemeris*** of L.D. Swamikannu Pillai (reprint edition; Delhi: Agam Prakashan, 1982 [1922]), 5:120, indicates this day was May 13, 1459, a Sunday. ***Vigat***, 1:38, gives the date V.S. 1515, ***Jeṭh***, ***Sudi*** 11, ***Sanīvār*** (Saturday), which suggests that the day Jodhpur was founded probably was Saturday, May 12, 1459, and that whoever recorded the date did not use the ***tithi*** current at daybreak, ***Sudi*** 10, but rather the one beginning after the first ***pohar*** (three-hour period) of the day had expired, ***Sudi*** 11.

[9] Meṛtīyo Rāṭhoṛ Dūdo Jodhāvat (no. 104).

[10] Varsiṅgh Jodhāvat (no. 146), ancestor of the Varsiṅghot Meṛtīyo Rāṭhoṛs

the womb of Sonagarī Cāmpā, daughter of Khīṃvo Satāvat.[11] The Rāv said to them: "I give you Meṛto; you go [there] and settle." They accepted. He gave them a horse [and a] ***sirpāv***[12] and dispatched them. They took their carts, brought them to Cokṛī,[13] and made camp. They went to inspect the hill of Cokṛī. At that time Rāṭhoṛ Ūdo Kānhaṛdevot, a Jaitmāl,[14] had left Nāgaur,[15] come to Gagrāṇo,[16] and left [his] carts [there]. Rāṭhoṛ Ūdo would go in all directions to hunt and also would wander about inspecting the whole land. While wandering, he had seen the site of Meṛto. Someone informed Ūdo: "Rāv Jodho's two sons have come to settle this[17] land; they are of a mind to have a fort constructed on the hill of Cokṛī. They intend to settle a city on the lowland."[18]

Vigat, 2:38

3. Then Rāṭhoṛ Ūdo Kānhaṛdevot himself mounted [his horse] and went to Rāṭhoṛs Varsiṅgh [and] Dūdo. For several days he paid [his] respects. He became acquainted [with them]. Then he said to Rāṭhoṛ Varsiṅgh Jodhāvat: "I hear, ***rāj***,[19] that you desire to settle this land. Have you thought of a place somewhere?" Then Varsiṅgh said: "We are resolved." Then Ūdo said: "***Rāj***! What place have you decided on?" Then Varsiṅgh [and] Dūdo came, mounted [their horses], and showed Rāṭhoṛ Ūdo the hill of Cokṛī. Then they asked Ūdo: "What sort of place is this?" Ūdo said: "The place is well and good. [But] I have seen a fine site [for a settlement]. ***Rāj***! Go there one time." Rāṭhoṛ Ūdo took Rāṭhoṛs Varsiṅgh [and] Dūdo Jodhāvat to where Meṛto city is situated.

---

[11] The text has "of the Sonagarī, Cāmpo Khīṃvāvat's daughter," which is either a textual or printing error. ***Vigat***, 1:39 gives the correct reading, which we have followed here.

[12] ***Sirpāv*** (Persian sar-o-pā): literally, "head-foot," a long dress or cloth such as a cloak reaching the length of the body, given by a ruler to a subordinate for particular actions of service, such as bravery in battle, etc. By the beginning of the nineteenth century ***sirpāv*** had also come to mean more generally an honorary gift, favor, or reward.

[13] Cokṛī: the village Cokṛī Baḍī, situated twenty-four miles southwest of Meṛto. There is a large hill directly east of the village.

[14] Jaitmālot Rāṭhoṛ Ūdo Kānhaṛdevot (no. 67).

[15] For a historical account of Nāgaur, see Appendix A.

[16] Gagrāṇo: a village located ten miles east of Meṛto.

[17] The text has ***āṇ***, apparently a mistake for ***ā***, "this."

[18] ***Taḷhaṭī***: The lowland around a hill or fort.

[19] ***Rāj***: ruler, sovereign, king, kingdom; a form of address conveying respect.

They saw the Kuṇḍaḷ [and] the Bejpo, two early tanks.[20] Afterward they saw the place where the *koṭṛī*[21] is in present-day Meṛto. Rāṭhoṛs Varsiṅgh [and] Dūdo were pleased. They brought [their] carts here and laid the foundations of a fort.

4. When they came to this place to live, two lions were standing at the site of the [future] ***koṭṛī***. One of them was a large lion; one a smaller lion. The large lion there roared. They drove [it] off; it went away from there. And the small lion sat in a cave there. Then an augur who was with them shook [his] head. At this moment Varsiṅgh saw [him]. He said: "Why did you shake [your] head?" [The augur] objected several times [to answering], but Varsiṅgh became obstinate and asked [again]. Then the augur said: "An omen of a singular nature has occurred." Then Varsingh said: "What do you think of this omen?" The augur said: "***Rāj***! As long as you live, you will enjoy this place. Afterward Dūdo's descendants will live here; this place will not remain [the possession of] your sons [and] grandsons."

Vigat, 2:39

At that time Dūdo [and] Varsiṅgh were one. Within [them] the souls (***jīv***) were not separate. Varsiṅgh said: "Dūdo [and] I are one." Afterward he had the foundations laid for the ***koṭṛī*** at the site [of] the [present] ***koṭṛī***. They say Varsiṅgh [and] Dūdo settled this place on Sunday, March 7, 1462, ***Hasat Nakhatr***.[22]

5. They made Rāṭhoṛ Ūdo Kānhaṛdevot ***pradhān***.[23] All responsibility [for governing] was on Ūdo's head. At that time the entire land of Meṛto was depopulated, so Rajpūts were coming [there]. They kept on settling. At that

---

[20] The text, ***kuṇḍaḷ bejpo taḷāv ād tho su dīṭhā***, is unclear, for ***tho*** is masc. sing. while ***dīṭhā*** is masc. pl. The Kuṇḍaḷ and the Bejpo were two separate tanks. Our translation is merely a considered suggestion.

[21] ***Koṭṛī***: the male section of a Rajpūt house; a courtyard surrounded by high walls; a small fort.

[22] ***Hasat Nakhatr*** (Sanskrit ***Hasta Nakṣatra***): the thirteenth of the twenty-seven ***nakṣatras***. A ***nakṣatra*** is a star or cluster of stars, or a constellation representing one of the twenty-seven divisions of the lunar zodiac. ***Nakṣatras*** also represent phases of the moon during its orbit of the earth, and are divided into auspicious (associated with the waxing moon) and inauspicious (associated with the waning moon). Margaret and James Stutley, ***Harper's Dictionary of Hinduism*** (New York: Harper and Row, 1977), pp. 200-201. The word ***riv*** (= ***ravi***, "Sunday") appears in the ***kha*** ms. only. March 7, 1462 was indeed a Sunday.

[23] ***Pradhān***: literally, "foremost," "chief," "principal," "most eminent." A chief minister, commander-in-chief, a general or leader of an army. Within the Rajpūt kingdoms, a Rajpūt generally held the post of ***pradhān***, and this individual could be either from the same family (***kuḷ***) as the ruler of the kingdom, or from a different family.

time the Ḍāṅgo [Jāṭs][24] were in Nāgaur, in the direction of Savāḷakh.[25] [Thīr] Rāj, son of Delo, lived in Kaṭhotī [village] of Jāyel;[26] a ***vair***[27] occurred there. Then Thīr[28] Rāj Ḍāṅgo approached Rāv Varsiṅgh [and] Dūdo. He said: "If you bring me, I shall cause all of the [empty] ***kheṛos***[29] to be settled." Then they favored Thīr Rāj as he had proposed. They settled Thīr Rāj right in Meṛto at the site of old Ḍāṅgāvās[30] and made him the ***desmukh caudhrī***[31] of the whole

---

[24] The text has ***Ḍīgā, Dāṅgo*** (sing.), and ***Ḍāgā***; the ***kha*** ms. has ***Ḍāgā***. ***Vigat***, 2:41, has ***Ḍāṅgā***. Apparently ***Ḍāṅgo*** (pl. ***Ḍāṅgā***) is the correct reading, as this form is used in the name of the ward of Meṛto town occupied by these Jāṭs, Dāṅgāvās.

[25] Savāḷakh: an area located to the northeast of Meṛto and to the southeast of Nāgaur. In ancient times this area was known as Sapādalakṣa, which became Savāḷakh in Apabhraṃśa. Formerly the Cahuvāṇ Rajpūts had a kingdom here, for which reason they were known as the "Sapādalakṣīya Kings." The area is still called Savāḷakh to this day. It is widely known for its black soil, rain-fed wheat, and excellent bullocks. ***Vigat***, 3:109.

[26] Kaṭhotī: a village thirty-five miles east of Nāgaur and forty-four miles north of Meṛto. Jāyel is seven miles west of Kaṭhotī. From the context of the sentence, Kaṭhotī village appears to have been part of an administrative subdivision of Nāgaur with its headquarters at Jāyel. In an earlier period, Jāyel was the homeland of the Khīcī branch (***sākh***) of the Cahuvāṇ family (***kuḷ***) of Rajpūts. ***Vigat***, 3:109.

[27] ***Vair***: the debt of vengeance owed upon the murder of a family member, kinsman, or dependent.

[28] The text has ***Ghar***; the ***kha*** ms. has ***Thir***. The correct reading apparently is ***Thīr***, which is the form given in the genealogy of the Ḍāṅgos (***Vigat***, 2:41). Also, in the ***kha*** ms., there is a textual addition that comes after ***tarai*** ("then"): "They left there, came to Ghāṭo village of Harsīr, and stayed. [But] they could not be contained there."

[29] ***Kheṛo***: outlying village land on which temporary huts are built during the growing season; a small site more or less permanently inhabited but attached to a larger village often at some distance; a deserted site, either of a former small village or of land previously cultivated.

[30] ***Purāṇo Ḍāṅgāvās*** (literally, "old ward of the Ḍāṅgos"). The town of Meṛto was originally comprised of three wards (***vās***): (1) Meṛto proper, inhabited in the mid-seventeenth century by many ***jātis***; (2) Ḍāṅgāvās, inhabited by Jāṭs; (3) Sodhāvās, inhabited by Jāṭs and Turks. The nineteenth-century text "Pargano Meṛto" notes that the Ḍāṅgo Jāṭs constructed a tank known as Ḍāṅgoḷāī in Ḍāṅgāvās during the time of Rāv Dūdo Jodhāvat and also remarks that for many years after its establishment Ḍāṅgāvās was a ***ḍhāṇī***, a settlement of huts near the fields of the inhabitants, situated some distance from the mother village. "Pargano Meṛto," in Naiṇsī, ***Mārvāṛ rā Parganāṃ rī Vigat***, vol. 2, edited by N. S. Bhāṭī (Jodhpur: Rājasthān Prācyavidyā Pratiṣṭhān, 1968), p. 437; ***Vigat***, 2:116-117.

[31] ***Desmukh caudhrī***: literally, "the country's chief ***caudhrī***." In middle period Mārvāṛ, ***caudhrī*** was a title taken by the headmen of Jāṭ lineages.

country. Thīr Rāj was a powerful man. Afterward the Jāṭs of Savāḷakh were favored and kept coming and settling in the villages of Meṛto.[32] All the villages of Meṛto were settled; the land became populous.

6. Jārauṛo Sāh Śrīmal had the temple of Śrī Phaḷodhī[33] Parasnāthjī[34] built in 1134-35. Afterward, in 1498-99, Surāṇo Hemrāj, son of Devrāj, restored [the temple]. In the Surāṇo *jāti* [are those of] the Paṃvār *jāti* [descended from Moḷaṇ, who was] converted to [Jainism] by Dharamghokh Sur.[35]

7. Rāṭhoṛs Varsiṅgh [and] Ūdo killed some Sāṅkhlo [Rajpūts] and settled in Cokṛī. They killed some Sāṅkhlos [at] Kusāṇo[36] [and] Mādḷīyo[37] also.

8. They brought Jāṭs from these villages [and] these places and settled them in these villages:[38]

---

[32] There is grammatical inconsistency in the text. ***Dilāsa kar-kar nai*** and ***āṇ-āṇ*** are transitive and have as their object the Jāṭs of Savāḷakh; ***bastā gayā*** is instransitive and has as its object these same Jāṭs. We have given one possible "compromise" translation; another would be "They kept favoring and bringing the Jāṭs of Savāḷakh and settling them in the villages of Meṛto."

[33] Śrī Phaḷodhī: The village Phaḷodhī, situated nine miles northwest of Meṛto.

[34] Parasnāthjī: the twenty-third Jain ***tīrthaṃkara***, Pārśvanātha.

[35] The text has a cryptic ***jāt Surāṇai dharam dhokh [sic] surpatbodhīyā jāt Puṃvār***. However, ***Vigat***, 2:115 gives the following information:

> In the city of Ujjain was Madhudev Paṃvār. His son, Surdev. His son, Sāṃvaḷ. His son was Moḷaṇ. Śrī Dharamghokh Sur converted him and established the Jain religion. He named the ***gotra*** [the descendants of Moḷaṇ] Surāṇā.

Thus the Surāṇo (sing.) ***jāti*** consisted of Paṃvārs descended from Moḷaṇ, who was converted to Jainsim by Śrī Dharamghokh Sur. The Paṃvār (Sanskrit Paramāra) Rajpūts ruled Ujjain and Malwa until the first decade of the fourteenth century, when they lost their main centers of power to invading Muslim armies. Dharamghokh Sur is a variant of Dharmaghoṣa Sūri, the name of the founder of a chapter of Jain monks, the Dharmaghoṣa Gaccha, which became prominent in Jaisaḷmer and Nāgaur in the fourteenth, fifteenth, and sixteenth centuries. See K. C. Jain, ***Jainism in Rajasthan*** (Sholapur: Gulabchand Hirachand Doshi, 1963), p. 62.

[36] Kusāṇo: a village twenty-eight miles southwest of Meṛto and thirty-eight miles east-northeast of Jodhpur.

[37] Mādḷīyo: probably Mādsīyo village, located two or three miles south of Kusāṇo.

[38] We have arranged the names given in the text into a table for the reader's convenience. When identifiable, the villages whence the Jāṭs came and those in which they settled are indicated on Map 2, "Jāṭ Migrations and Settlements."

Vigat, 2:40

[Jāṭ Lineage]	[From]	[Settled in]
Ḍāṅgo	Kaṭhotī	Ḍāṅgāvās, Lohṛoyāh,[39] Rāysalvās, Īḍvo.[40]
Thīrodo	Thīro [village] of Nāgaur	Sātaḷvās.
Vaḍīvaro	Ratāū	Phālo,[41] Baḍgāṃv.
Cāndelīyo	Cuvo	Mahevṛo.
Dugsato	Dustāū	Bhovālī.[42]
Ḍīḍel[43] Rāvṇo	Bugraṛo	Lāmbīyāṃ.
Kameḍīyo	Bhādu	Kairo.
Kasṇīyo	Kasṇo	Reyāṃ.

[39] Lyoṛīyāū in the ***kha*** ms.

[40] Iṭīvo is the name given in the text; Iḍbo is given in the ***kha*** ms. There are two possible identifications:

> (1) Probably Īḍvo, a village in Modṛo subdivision of Meṛto Pargano (***Vigat***, 2:167).
> (2) Possibly one of several villages of Deghāṇo subdivision of Meṛto Pargano, all in the same general area,which have Īṭāvo as the first part of their names (***Vigat***, 2:191-193).

[41] Phālo (Kālo in the ***kha*** ms.): Probably the village Phālko Baḍo, located in Āṇandpur subdivision of Meṛto Pargano (***Vigat***, 2:121).

[42] Bhovālī: there are two possible identifications:

> (1) Probably Bhavāḷ (Bhauvāl in the ***kha*** ms.), located in Āṇandpur subdivision of Meṛto Pargano (***Vigat***, 2:121).
> (2) Possibly Bhāṃvali (Bhavalī in the ***kha*** ms.), located in Deghāṇo subdivision of Meṛto Pargano (***Vigat***, 2:198).

[43] Ḍīḍelar in the ***kha*** ms.

Radu[44] Gvālro	Tago [village] of Nāgaur	Rāhaṇ.
Tetarvāl	Tetāro[45] [village] of Nāgaur	Jhaṛāū.
A Godāro [Jāṭ, son] of Pāṇḍo.[46]	Bīkāner	Jhīthīyā, Vaḍālī.
Somaḍvāl	Somṛā[47] [village] of Nāgaur	Rohīyo.[48]
Bohaṛīyo	Kaṭhotī; they came with the Ḍāṅgo [Jāṭs]	Mokālo, A[ṛ]ṇīyāḷo, Sahesṛo.

Vigat, 2:41

Goro	...	Pādubaṛī,[49] Tāmbṛaulī.
Laṭīyāl Thīrodo	Nāgaur	Lāmpoḷāī, Kākaṛkhī.
Cohīlo	***Sūbo***[50] of Nāgaur	Moḍrī.[51]

---

[44] Ratu in the ***kha*** ms.

[45] Tetāro in the ***kha*** ms. is preferable to Tītrī in the text.

[46] Pāṇḍo Godāro was a Jāṭ of Lādhaṛīyo village of Bīkāner. The Godāro Jāṭs of Lādhaṛīyo village became involved in a feud with the Sāharaṇ Jāṭs of Bhāraṅg village which resulted in the death of Pāṇḍo. The Godāros then appealed to their protector, Rāv Bīko Jodhāvat (no. 42), the founder and ruler of Bīkāner (ca. 1485-1504), who avenged Pāṇḍo. ***Khyāt***, 3:13-15.

[47] Somṛā in the ***kha*** ms. is preferable to to Somṛī in the text.

[48] Rohīyo: probably Rohīso village, located in Āṇandpur subdivision of Meṛto Pargano. There are two villages named Rohīso situated very near to each other in this area. The larger one is probably the village the Jāṭs originally settled. The two villages are one or two miles apart. ***Vigat***, 2:121-122.

[49] Pādubaṛī: probably the village Pad[u]māvatī Vaḍī, located in Reyāṃ subdivision of Meṛto Pargano (***Vigat***, 2:199).

Vāt Gohīlot	Ajmer	Nīlīyāṃ.

9. In those villages are all the Āñjaṇā Jāṭs.[52] In ancient times the Ḍāṅgo [Jāṭs] were Cahuvāṇ Rajpūts. Subsequently their ancestor, Jagsī, [grandson] of Chāju,[53] became a Jāṭ. [A genealogy]:

1. Māhārīkh.
2. Sam.[54]
3. Phokaṭ.
4. Vālāyo.
5. Chāju
6. Delū.[55]

---

[50] ***Sūbo*** (Persian ṣūba): a province; the largest administrative and revenue division of territory under the Mughal administrative system.

[51] Moḍrī: Probably Moḍro, the head village of Moḍro subdivision of Meṛto Pargano (***Vigat***, 2:166).

[52] Āñjaṇā Jāṭs: according to tradition, the Āñjaṇā Jāṭs emerged as a designated ***jāti*** at the time of Rājā Prithīrāj Cahuvāṇ (late twelfth century). The Rājā is said to have assembled all the Jāṭs during his reign for the purpose of performing a census. Many other people of different ***jātis*** came along with the Jāṭs, and, at meal time, the Rāja is said to have ordered those who were Jāṭs to sit and eat together while those of other ***jātis*** stood nearby and ate. All were counted with the Jāṭs in the census, but those who ate standing were called "Āñjaṇā." The saying "ūbho jiko āñjaṇā jīmā so Jāṭ" ("those who stand and eat cleanly/purely, they are Jāṭs") comes from this tradition.

Census reports and gazetteers from the late nineteenth and early twentieth centuries indicate that the Jāṭs of Mārvāṛ originally came from the north and were divided into three main divisions: (1) the Aslī or pure Jāṭs, claiming no Rajpūt ancestry, being descended from a strand of hair (*jaṭ*) of the God Śiva's head, and having two endogamous subdivisions, the Godāros and the Punīyos; (2) those Jāṭs of Rajpūt ancestry; and (3) the Āñjaṇā Jāṭs of inferior rank. The nineteenth century census report indicates that the Jāṭs of higher rank and the Āñjaṇā Jāṭs mingle and intermarry, but that their internal subdivisions (***khāmp***) are separate and distinct. The names of the Āñjaṇā ***khāmps*** derive from the names of forefathers or from the ***gotras*** of Rajpūts.

In the text, the Ḍāṅgo Jāṭs, who are referred to as descendants of Cahuvāṇ Rajpūts, are also equated with Āñjaṇā Jāṭs, perhaps indicating a less strict division of rank in the seventeenth century. ***Census Report***, 1891, 1:41-48; Major K. D. Erskine, ed., ***Raputana Gazetteers: Volume III-A, The Western Rajputana States Residency and the Bikaner Agency*** (Allahabad: The Pioneer Press, 1909), p. 83.

[53] The text indicates that Jagsī was Chāju's descendant; the genealogy following suggests that he was Chāju's grandson.

[54] Sām in the ***kha*** ms.

7. Jagsī.
8. Dulorāv.[56]
9. Thīr Rāj.
10. Ḍugar.
11. Vīko.
12. Chītar.
13. Hemo.
14. Jālap.
15. Khīṃvrāj.

10. In the ancient period Rājā Māndhātā had the temple of Mātājī[57] of Śrī Phaḷodhījī[58] constructed. After that there is a pillar dated 1026-27. There is one large pillar dated 1019-20. Afterward, in 1498-99, Surāṇo Hemrāj renovated [the temple] on the order of Rāṭhoṛs Varsiṅgh [and] Dūdo.

11. All the land was settled. Rajpūts of many different ***sākhs***[59] also settled. The responsibility [for governing] was the Jaitmāl's. Ūdo controlled all the affairs of state.[60] After awhile discord arose between Rāṭhoṛs Varsiṅgh and Dūdo. Rāṭhoṛ Dūdo left and went to Bīkāner. Back [in Meṛto] a famine occurred. Not very much was obtained to eat.

Vigat, 2:42

Then the military and domestic servants (***cākar-bābar***), ***hīṛāgars***,[61] and [other] subjects[62] who had come with Varsiṅgh from Jodhpur all began to go away.

---

55 Delo in the ***kha*** ms.

56 Dulerāv in the ***kha*** ms.

57 Mātājī: Mother Goddess.

58 Śrī Phaḷodhījī: the village Phaḷodhī, located nine miles northwest of Meṛto.

59 ***Sākh***: literally, "branch." Rajpūts perceived their ***jāti*** as divided into thirty-six great lineages, called either ***rājkuḷīs*** ("royal families") or ***rājvaṃś*** ("royal lineages"). The word ***vaṃś*** also means "bamboo shoot," and the Rajpūts extend the imagery equating their royal lineages with the bamboo even further: subdivisions of the ***vaṃś*** were known as ***sākhs*** ("branches"), and, by the late seventeenth century, the word ***khāmp*** ("twig"), used for subdivisions of the ***sākh***, had become common in Rājasthān. See the introductory section "Rajpūt Social Organization: A Historical Perspective" for a full discussion of these terms.

60 ***Udāvadu sārā rāj ro kām chai***. ***Udāvadu*** perhaps is a mistake for ***Udāa nūṃ***.

61 ***Hīṛāgar***: "one who performs ***hīṛo***." ***Hīṛo*** is service performed with respect and devotion. In middle period Mārvāṛ, the term ***hīṛāgar*** referred to a member of a class of military servants (Rajpūts and others) doing the more menial tasks, such as carrying rockets, attending to the accountrements of the Rajpūts of higher rank, etc.

Then Rāṭhor Varsiṅgh observed: "Why should we die this way?" Rāṭhoṛ Varsiṅgh assembled a ***sāth***[63] and sacked Navlakhī Sāmbhar.[64] He looted much booty. Gold coins were carried off.[65] In those days Ajmer[66] was under the authority of the Pātsāh of Māṇḍū.[67] Malū Khān[68] was here, in charge of the ***sūbo*** of Ajmer. He took [Varsiṅgh's raid] very badly, but he remained seated [in Ajmer].[69] A commemorative ***kavitt***[70] of the sacking of Sāmbhar:

> Implacably rending the lowland asunder, he made [as it were] a great mountain pass.[71]

---

[62] ***Paraj log***, ***Paraj*** refers to the non-Rajpūt subjects of a ruler. Coupled with ***log***, a word meaning both "people" and "people engaged in agriculture," "peasants," ***paraj*** may indicate the non-Rajpūt peasantry.

[63] ***Sāth***: one who accompanies or follows, a companion. In middle period Mārvāṛ, the term was used in a technical sense to designated a contingent of soldiers comprised of both cavalrymen and footmen. Among Rajpūts, a ***sāth*** was usually composed of kinsmen (brothers and sons) of the leaders as well as other men attached to them or their subordinates as servants or retainers.

[64] Navlakhī Sāmbhar: "Nine-***lākh*** Sāmbhar." ***Navlakhī*** ("nine ***lākhs***," "900,000") is an adjective of deliberate exaggeration used to indicate large numbers. Here the intent is to indicate that Sāmbhar was a populous, wealthy town. Sāmbhar is located fifty miles northeast of Ajmer and eighty miles east-northeast of Meṛto. For details concerning the early history of Sāmbhar and its local importance, see Appendix A.

[65] ***Sovan mor uḍīyā***: literally, "gold coins flew away." ***Mor*** is a variant of ***mohar***, a type of gold coin, but it also means "peacock." Perhaps a pun was intended.

[66] For details concerning the early history of Ajmer and its strategic importance, see Appendix A.

[67] ***Pātsāh*** (Persian pādshāh): a title assumed by Muslim rulers of the first rank in north India, such as the rulers of Malwa, Gujarat, and Hindustan. The Pātsāh referred to here is Ghiyāth Shāh Khiljī of Malwa (1469-1501). See U. N. Day, ***Medieval Malwa: A Political and Cultural History, 1401-1562*** (Delhi: Munshiram Manoharlal, 1965), pp. 220-248, for details of his reign. Māṇḍū was the capital of the Malwa rulers.

[68] Malū Khān (d. 1505) was governor of Ajmer at this time. His governorship is attested to by a tank called Malūsar, which he had constructed at the base of Tārāgaḍh, the hill fort at Ajmer (Ojhā, 4:1:261, n. 4).

[69] I.e., he took no action.

[70] ***Sākh ro kavitt***. ***Kavitt***: a type of Ḍiṅgaḷ poem, the first four line of which are in one meter, the last two in another.

[71] The text has ***dhaṇo kīyo ghāṭo***; evidently ***dhaṇo*** is a misprint for ***ghaṇo***, "much," "great."

Breaking the fort to pieces, [like] a clay pot, shredding
[it like] the bodice [and] petticoat [of a woman],
he set up a market place and served a liquor,[72]
the nectar of immortality (***amīras***), to the enemy soldiers.[73]
In perverse manner she played colors[74] [with him] there,
bearing the burden of [her heavy] breasts.[75]
A Gopī,[76] in the form of Sāmbhar;[77] Kānh [Kṛṣṇa]the
cowherd, [in the form of] Varsiṅgh.

12. Still the provincial governor of Ajmer remained seated. At that time discord arose between Rāv Sātal[78] and Kuṃvar[79] Varsiṅgh. Varsiṅgh said to Sātal: "I too should obtain something out of [our] father's estate,[80] Jodhpur." Then both their ***pradhān***s came to Ajmer. Malū Khān said: "You both come here. I will advise [you]."

I have heard one story like this: Rāv Sātal and Rāṭhoṛ Varsiṅgh went to Ajmer. Rāṭhoṛ Varsiṅgh made a proposal to Malū Khān: "You give me Jodhpur; I shall give [you] a tribute of 50,000 rupees." Afterward, [some]

---

[72] ***Madā gāḷiyā***. ***Madā*** perhaps is a poetic variant of the Sanskrit ***mada***: "any exhilarating or intoxicating drink, spirituous liquor, wine, Soma." M. Monier-Williams, ***A Sanskrit-English Dictionary*** (1899; reprint edition, London: Oxford University Press, 1970), p. 777.

[73] I.e., sent them to the next world.

[74] ***Raṅg ramī***. This is a reference to the Holī festival, when red dye and powder are throne upon people (often by women upon men). The ***kavitt*** suggests that Kṛṣṇa, in the form of Varsiṅgh, and a Gopī (see n. 16, ***infra***), in the form of Sāmbhar, celebrated Holī, as it were, with Kṛṣṇa (Varsiṅgh) breaking pots, ripping women's clothes, and pouring out liquor, while the Gopī (Sāmbhar) responds by throwing red dye (her soldiers' blood). We are indebted to John Smith for this inference.

[75] ***Bhār bharat joban bharī***: literally, "bearing a burden, filled with youth."

[76] Gopī: a herdswoman, one of the women with whom the youthful Kṛṣṇa lived. Margaret and James Stutley, ***Harper's Dictionary of Hinduism*** (New York: Harper and Row, 1977), p. 101.

[77] ***Sāmbhar jyarī***. ***Jyarī*** perhaps is a feminine variant of ***jehro*** ("like," "similar to"). Lāḷas, ***RSK***, 2:1:1162.

[78] Rāv Sātal Jodhāvat, ruler of Jodhpur, ca. 1489-92.

[79] ***Kuṃvar***: prince; title of the son of a ruler.

[80] ***Bāp kī*** in the text probably is a mistake for ***bāpī*** or ***bāpikā***, "father's estate."

Rāṭhoṛs mediated and reconciled Rāv Sātal and Rāv Varsiṅgh. They came from there without meeting Malū Khān.[81]

13. Some say they themselves did not come; the ***pradhāns*** came; the ***pradhāns*** had held this conversation [with Malū Khān].

Vigat, 2:43

But Malū Khān only was concerned with Varsiṅgh.[82] He said: "First, he sacked my [town], Sāmbhar; I demand my [looted] goods from him. Second, he had agreed to [pay] me a tribute; I helped him." At that time Rāv Sātal gave Varsiṅgh Kelāvo[83] along with several [other] villages of Jodhpur. [Malū Khān] heard about these. He said: "You achieved your intent; why did you withhold this tribute of mine? Give me what you agreed upon."[84] Malū Khān demanded; [Varsiṅgh] refused. Malū Khān gathered together an army. They came to the border of Meṛto [Pargano]. Then [Varsiṅgh] sent word to Rāv Sātal at Jodhpur. The Rāv said: "You must not do battle there. Bring [your] men quickly to Jodhpur." Then Varsiṅgh came to Jodhpur. Malū Khān came after [him]. He ravaged the land of Meṛto and also the land of Jodhpur. He made camp at Pīmpāṛ,[85] pillaged the whole countryside as far as Sathlāṇo,[86] and took prisoners.[87]

14. Rāv Sātal received this news. Then Rāv Sātal, Sūjo,[88] [and] Varsiṅgh, the three brothers, mounted [for battle]. All of the ***sāth*** of Mārvāṛ came and was assembled. The Rāv's camp was in Bīsalpur.[89] That day all the

---

[81] The text has ***uṭhai āyā***, "they came there," which makes little sense, as the sentence begins with ***uṭhī thī***, "from there." Perhaps ***uṭhai*** is a mistake for ***aṭhai***, "here," "this way." If so, the translation would read: "They came here/this way from there without meeting Malū Khān."

[82] ***Malū Khān [V]arsiṅgh suṃ lāgto tho hīj***: literally, "Malū Khān only was attached/adhering to Varsiṅgh."

[83] Kelāvo: the village Kelāvo Baḍo, situated sixty-five miles west of Meṛto and twenty-two miles north of Jodhpur.

[84] ***Sudo*** in the text is a misprint for ***su do***, "give it."

[85] Pīmpāṛ: a village located thirty-three miles east-northeast of Jodhpur and thirty-six miles southwest of Meṛto.

[86] Sathlāṇo: a village twenty-two miles due south of Jodhpur.

[87] ***Bandh kī***: literally, "made an imprisonment." The term ***bandh*** ("bondage," "imprisonment") is used with the verbs ***karṇo*** ("to make, do") and ***pakaṛṇo*** ("to take, capture") with the meaning "to take prisoners."

[88] Sūjo Jodhāvat, Rāv Sātal's successor and the ruler of Jodhpur, ca. 1492-1515.

[89] Bīsalpur: a village twenty miles due east of Jodhpur.

responsibility [for decision-making] was on the head [of] Rāv Varjāṅg Bhīṃvot.[90] The Rāvjī said to Varjāṅg: "You decide about the battle." That day Varjāṅg was discontent. Varjāṅg sent word with a ***pradhān***: "I am not considering doing battle [today]."[91] Then the Rāv[92] said to [his] ***pradhān***s: "What should be done?" The ***pradhān***s said: "He is a treacherous man, and self-interest is everything [for him]. Today the responsibility for the whole country is on his head. He should be appeased in every way [possible]." Then the Rāv asked: "How would he be appeased?" The ***pradhān***s said: "He demands Bhāvī [village].[93] Strike Bhāvī on his head."[94] Then [the Rāv] wrote a ***paṭo***[95] for Bhāvī and gave it [to Varjāṅg] Varjāṅg was pleased. He was considerably more enthusiastic.[96]

Vigat, 2:44

He said to the Rāv: "I am going to spy on the [Muslim] army. The Mughals[97] have encamped at Kusāṇo.[98] You come and wait at such-and-such a place, one

---

[90] Bhīṃvot Rāṭhoṛ Varjāṅg Bhīṃvot (no. 41).

[91] These two sentences appear in the ***kha*** ms. only.

[92] The text has ***Rāvāṃ***, the oblique plural of ***Rāv***, but the context suggests that only Rāv Sātal was speaking.

[93] Bhāvī: a village located twelve miles south of Pīmpāṛ village and thirty-six miles east of Jodhpur.

[94] ***Iṇ rai māthai māro***. Freely translated, the phrase would mean something to the effect of "give the bastard the village." As the editor of the ***Vigat***, N. S. Bhāṭī, notes (n. 11), the phrase is idiomatic: it indirectly refers to the Rajpūt custom of raising the ***paṭo***, or paper upon which the grant of land is written (see n. 95 ***infra***), to the forehead (***māthai paṭo caṛhāṇo***) when it is received from the ruler.

[95] ***Paṭo***: a written deed or title to land; lands granted by a ruler to a subordinate by such a deed in return for the obligation of military service.

[96] ***Su orhī begī chai***. ***Begī*** is not in Lāḷas's ***RSK***; it probably is a derivation from the Sanskrit ***vegin***: "having velocity, swift, rapid, impetuous." M. Monier-Williams, ***A Sanskrit-English Dictionary***, p. 1013. In the context, "enthusiastic" seems an appropriate translation of ***begī***.

[97] The term "Mughal" refers not to the Mughals who later achieved an empire in north India, but rather was a generic term used to describe Muslims of Central Asian origin.

[98] Kusāṇo: a village located twenty-eight miles southwest of Meṛto and thirty-eight miles east-northeast of Jodhpur.

kos[99] from Kusāṇo. When night is over, I shall look over [their army, then] come to the rendez-vous." Varsiṅgh, Sātal, [and] Sūjo stayed behind. Alone, Varjāṅg approached the army. Then he cut a large bundle of grass. He became a [grass]-bearer in the army and observed the entire army. The whole day he went back and forth [from] the exit to the entrance [of the camp], made estimates, and then, returning when night fell, came to the Rāv at the rendez-vous. He reported on the particulars of the [Muslim] army: "Malū Khān, along with such-and-such size *sāth*, has pitched tents behind the tank at Kusāṇo. All the prisoners[100] of our land are [being held] in [their] army."

15. Varjāṅg said: "Now there is no use delaying." Saying [this], he had two *aṇīs*[101] of the [Rāṭhoṛ] army formed. He provided a kettle-drum for both positions. They drew near, rushed [the camp], and fell upon [the Muslims]. The night was dark;[102] panic broke out in the [Muslim] army. The Rāṭhoṛs also fought well.[103] Rāv Varjāṅg Bhīṃvot was particularly outstanding.[104] Rāv Sūjo Jodhāvat fell badly wounded.[105] Malū Khān fled; they killed the Mughal Ghaduko.[106] The prisoners were freed. They killed many Mughals. Victory was Rāv Sātal's. Rāv Varsiṅgh came back to Meṛto and settled.

---

[99] ***Kos***: a unit of distance equal to approximately two miles.

[100] ***Band*** in the text is a variant of ***bandh*** (see n. 87 to ***Vigat***, 2:43 ***supra*** re: ***bandh***).

[101] ***Aṇī***: the point of a spear, arrow, etc., the end, the tip; piece, fragment; a division of an army.

[102] ***Andhīhārī*** (***āndhī rī*** in the ***kha*** ms.) is a variant of ***andhīyār*** ("dark," "darkness").

[103] ***Bhalo loh bāhyo***: literally, "struck a fine blow."

[104] Literally, "Rāv Varjāṅg Bhīṃvot possessed much ***viśeṣ***." ***Viśeṣ*** is "specialness," "outstanding quality." Those who are/have ***viśeṣ*** are distinct from others.

[105] Other sources indicate that Rāv Sātal was mortally wounded in this battle, but the ***Vigat***, both here and on p. 40 of vol. 1, omits any reference to Sātal's death and only refers to Rāv Sūjo being wounded. The ***Jodhpur Rājya kī Khyāt*** has the following information:

> Rāv Sātal died fighting in this battle [at Kusāṇo] on [Thursday], 1 March 1492. They cremated Sātal at the tank of Kusāṇo .... Rāv Jodho had given Sojhat to Sūjo, and while at Sojhat, Sūjo fought a battle with the Turks .... Sūjo was with [Sātal] in the battle of Kusāṇo [and] was wounded [there].

Bāṅkīdās, p. 8; ***Jodhpur Rājya kī Khyāt***, pp. 56-57; Ojhā, 4:1:262; Reū, 1:106-107. There is a cenotaph (***chatrī***) for Rāv Sātal at the tank in Kusāṇo village. ***Vīr Vinod***, 2:806-807.

[106] Ghaduko: this Muslim is referred to in other sources as "Ghaṛulā." He was an important officer in the army and a noble from Sindh. In Mārvāṛ, there is a large festival held each year to commemorate his death. During the festival, women of the

16. Malū Khān wrote a petition and sent it to the Pātsāh of Māṇḍū. Again an army came from Māṇḍū. Then they negotiated with Rāv Varsiṅgh. He too decided to make a pact. The Rajpūts forbade Rāv Varsiṅgh, but he did not accept [their] opinion. The Mughals also demanded concessions; he gave them. Varsiṅgh met Malū Khān in Ajmer.[107] [Malū Khān] cordially[108] honored the Rāṭhoṛ.

Vigat, 2:45

In noble fashion he continually gave [Varsiṅgh] presents.[109] He captured [Varsiṅgh's] trust. [Varsiṅgh] gave leave to [most of his] ***sāth***. Varsiṅgh stayed [in Ajmer] with just a small ***sāth***. Part of a month went by; then one day the Mughals summoned Varsiṅgh to the fort and seized him. Hul Jaito, [the son] of Pritham Rāv, [and] Sehlot Ajo Narbhāmot, a Cahuvāṇ, both died fighting.[110] A ***sākh***[111] of [this]:

> A scuffle[112] occurred between Varsiṅgh [and] the fierce warriors[113] [of Malū Khān]; there were "words" between the Hul and an elephant.

Kūmbhār ***jāti*** carry pitchers made with holes in them, in which candles have been placed. Mir Ghaṛulā's presence is conjured up from these pots, the openings signifying the arrow wounds in his body. Each day the women wander through the villages carrying the pots on their heads and singing the song of Ghaṛulā. On the last day of the festival, the pots are destroyed. Ojhā, 4:1:262, n. 1; ***Vīr Vinod***, 2:806-807.

[107] The text has ***[V]arsiṅgh Ajmer Malūkhān nuṃ melīyo***, "Varsiṅgh sent Malū Khān to Ajmer," clearly incorrect. Possibly ***nuṃ melīyo*** is a mistake for ***nuṃ milīyo***, "met with"; we have based our translation on this possibility.

[108] ***Dilī***: "Of the heart, cordial, sincere, true, intimate." Platts, ***Dictionary***, p. 525.

[109] ***Basat***: literally, "material," "stuff."

[110] The names of Hul Jaito, son of Pritham Rāv, and the Sehlot Cahuvāṇ, Ajo Narbhāmot, appear only here and in one other source available to us. We have not been able to trace them genealogically. We know only that they were Rajpūts serving under Varsiṅgh Jodhāvat. See also ***Bāṅkīdās***, p. 57.

[111] ***Sākh***: literally, "evidence," "testimony"; one or more lines of verse commemorating some event.

[112] ***Bāth***: embrace, scuffle, hand-to-hand combat, duel.

[113] ***Bāṅglāṃ***. Lāḷas, ***RSK***, 3:2:2956 (under ***bāṅghlo***), glosses this word as "warrior" (***yoddh***); actually it means "the one like a tiger."

A ***dūho***:[114]

Upon [him] were the "immovable ones" (***agam***); he saw the course (***gam***) of the army of elephants (***gai ghar***)
Ajīyo![115] From the top of [your] head[116] to the tips of [your] toes the son of Narbharāv.[117]

A ***kavitt***:

The maddened elephant was circling round.
White-tusked, monstrous,
like a high mountain, very intoxicated with liquor, black,
now that elephant trumpeted: "Hey boy!" (***Putā re***!)
With [his] ***sābaḷ***[118] lance [the Hul] strikes defiantly, [saying]: "Hey father!" (***Bābā re***!)
In Ajmer fort [were] the demon-host (i.e., the Muslim army) [and] the lion (i.e., Varsiṅgh) with [his] beloved companion, [the Hul].
The [Muslim] army, in a rage, strikes treacherously.
The elephant attacked Hul Jait[o].

17. News of Rāv Varsiṅgh's capture reached Rāṭhoṛ Dūdo Jodhāvat in Bīkāner. Then Dūdo told Rāv Bīko[119] the whole story, and he said: "Give me leave." In those days Rajpūts were fortresses of shame,[120] so Rāv Bīko said: "Varsiṅgh is just [as important] to me as he is to you." Rāv Bīko pitched tents outside [Bīkāner] He told Dūdo: "You go the the vicinity of Meṛto and gather

---

[114] ***Dūho***: a rhymed verse possessing two lines; a couplet.

[115] Ajīyo: a poetic form of Ajo.

[116] ***Ākāsāṃh***: literally, "from the skies." In Yoga, ***ākāśa*** refers to the space between the eyebrows and the top of the head. M. Eliade, ***Yoga: Immortality and Freedom*** (second edition; Princeton: Princeton University Press, 1969), p. 131.

[117] Ajo is referred to as Ajo Narbhāmot ("son of Narbhām") in the paragraph preceding the poems.

[118] ***Sābaḷ***: a type of lance (perhaps derived from ***sabaḷ***, "powerful).

[119] Rāv Bīko Jodhāvat (no. 42), founder and ruler of Bīkāner, ca. 1485-1504, and the ancestor of the Bīkāvat Rāṭhoṛs.

[120] ***Lāj rā koṭ***. ***Lāj*** ("shame") was used in Middle Mārvāṛī as one would use "honor" in English: the noble Rajpūts were those who possessed much shame (i.e., honor), as opposed to having little shame or being shameless.

your ***sāth***." Dūdo came to Meṛto and gathered [his] ***sāth***. Bīko reached Meṛto in four days.[121]

Vigat, 2:46

In addition, Rāv Sātal had [his] ***sāth*** readied[122] in Jodhpur and mounted [for battle]. Rāv Bīko [and] Dūdo took a large ***sāth*** and advanced on Ajmer from Meṛto. The news was received at Malū Khān's [residence].[123] Malū Khān assembled a ***sāth***. The fort was prepared [for siege]. A ***pradhān*** mediated. There was an agreement; [Malū Khān] quickly released Varsiṅgh and handed him over to Rāv Bīko [and] Dūdo. But he had given Varsiṅgh a poison from which one dies in the sixth month.[124] Rāv Bīko [and] Dūdo brought Varsiṅgh to Meṛto. Varsiṅgh kept Rāv Bīko [and] Dūdo in Meṛto seven days, showed them hospitality, then gave them leave.[125]

18. Rāv Dūdo went to Sarvāṛ[126] He subdued and took the best villages in all directions.[127] [His] ***bhāībandh***[128] settled in the various villages. Rāv Dūdo lived in Sarvāṛ. After six months, Varsiṅgh died. Varsiṅgh's son, Sīho,[129] was

---

[121] We have preferred "four," the variant found in the ***kha*** ms., to "fourteen," the number in the text. Bīkāner is roughly one hundred miles from Meṛto; twenty-five miles per day would not be unreasonable for a short march.

[122] ***Sāth nūṃ cheṛā***. ***Cheṛā*** evidently is a conjunctive participle formed from ***cheṛāṇo***, "to cause [someone] to stir up, incite, stimulate."

[123] The word ***piṇ*** ("too," "also") following ***Malūkhān rai*** in the text is redundant; we have left it untranslated.

[124] Literally, "... a six-month poison, from which one dies in the sixth month." We have eliminated the redundancy in the text.

[125] The last two sentences are rather garbled; we have combined them into what we consider the most probable reading and translated them accordingly.

[126] Sarvāṛ: a village located twenty-five miles east-northeast of Nāgaur and forty-nine miles due north of Meṛto.

[127] We have preferred the Hindī variant given in the ***kha*** ms., ***cyārūṃ taraph kā*** ("of all directions") to the reading ***capā catug karā*** (?) in the text.

[128] ***Bhāībandh***: literally, "bound as brothers"; a brotherhood; those related through ties of male blood to a common male ancestor. Among Rajpūts, membership in a ***bhāībandh*** included all males sharing common descent, their unmarried daughters, and their wives, who became members through the act of marriage. See the introductory section "Rajpūt Social Organization: A Historical Perspective" for a full discussion.

[129] Varsiṅghot Meṛtīyo Rāṭhoṛ Sīho Varsiṅghot (no. 147).

not so intelligent, but, thinking that the eldest son possessed experience,[130] the ***pañco***[131] [and] military servants of Varsiṅgh convened and gave the throne to him. Sīho was quite simple-minded. Four months passed, [then] Rāv Sātal heard about the weak characteristics of Sīho's sovereignty. Then Rāv Sātal [and] Sūjo established jurisdiction over [Sīho and] Meṛto.[132] They provided their ***hujdārs***[133] with some ***sāth*** and sent them to the grain market.[134] They came and established their authority. They made camp in the city. They began to set up a form of rulership[135] over the villages [and] hamlets[136] also.

19. Then Varsiṅgh's wife, Sīho's mother,[137] assembled her five men,[138] the Rajpūts, [and] the ***kāmdārs***.[139] When she inquired, everyone said: "There is no auspiciousness in your son, and Sātal [and] Sūjo, the rulers [of] Jodhpur, [are] powerful; who will respond to them?" Then Sīho's mother asked the ***pañco***: "What should be done?"

---

[130] ***Baḍai ro bairo jāṇ nai***. There is a remote possibility that the reading should be ***baḍairo bairo jāṇ nai***, "knowing the elder (***baḍairo***) [to be] a deaf person." ***Bairo*** means both "experience" and "deaf person."

[131] ***Pañco***: the committee of five important Rajpūts that convened upon the death of a ruler to aid in the succession; more generally, a council of elders.

[132] The text has ***iṇ Meṛtā suṃ***; presumably ***iṇ*** refers to Sīho.

[133] ***Hujdār***: an administrative official primarily concerned with the collection of revenue.

[134] The text has ***māḍhī dhānāṃ rī***; the ***kha*** ms. has ***maḍhī dāṇ rī***. The correct reading probably is ***maṇḍhī dāṇā rī***, "grain market."

[135] ***Dhāṇ[ī]yāp-sī***: literally, "[something] like rulership."

[136] ***Gāṃv-goṭhāṃ***. ***Goṭh***: a small village, a hamlet.

[137] ***Bāṅkīdās***, p. 57, indicates that Sīho's mother was a Sāṅkhlī Paṃvār (a woman of the Sāṅkhlo branch (***sākh***) of the Paṃvār Rajpūt family (***kuḷ***).

[138] I.e., the five men of the ***pañco***.

[139] ***Kāmdār***: literally, "one who has work." ***Kāmdārs*** (or ***kāmetī***) were generally drawn from among a number of non-Rajpūt ***jātis*** such as the Brāhmaṇ, Pañcolī (Kāyastha), and Osvāḷ Jain and Vaiṣṇava (Muṃhatos, Bhaṇḍārīs, Siṅghavīs, Lodhos, etc.). These officials performed not only record-keeping functions relating to the fiscal administration of local areas, but also police and military functions in the settlement and control of lands.

Vigat, 2:47

Then the *pañco* said: "You see the whole situation: today they took the market; tomorrow they will take the whole *pargano*. A recovery party must be formed; you must do this." Then this proposal pleased everyone: [that] they should agree upon a half-portion [of Meṛto's revenue] for Rāv Dūdo and bring him from Bīkāner. Sīho's mother also decided on this arrangement. Then they secretly sent men to Dūdo in Bīkāner and summoned him. Afterward, within six or seven days, Rāv Dūdo came to Meṛto at midnight. Some say he slaughtered Rāv Sātal's men while they were sleeping. Some say he put them to flight.

20. For two years Rāv Dūdo took exactly half of the revenue of Meṛto for Sīho. All responsibility was in Dūdo's hands. And I have heard a story like this, too: There was no auspicious quality in Sīho. While Sīho was drunk[140] [and] sleeping, Dūdo[141] had [his] *ḍholīyo*[142] removed from Meṛto and sent to Rāhaṇ[143] during the night. In the morning Sīho awoke in a *māḷīyo*[144] in Rāhaṇ. There were several servants [with him], whom he asked; "How [is] this?" They said: "Dūdo took Meṛto and gave you Rāhaṇ." Then [Sīho] said: "Dūdo will eat ghee and *bāṭī*,[145] [but] we too will eat." Dūdo sat on the throne [in Meṛto], and Bārhaṭh[146] Mahes Caturāvat, the Bārhath of the Meṛtīyos, said: "Dūdo preserved the dignity on Sīho's head."[147]

---

[140] The variant reading *matvāle* ("while drunk") in the *kha* ms. is preferable to the meaningless *tavāvai* in the text.

[141] *Sude* in the text is a misprint or a mistake for *Dūdai*.

[142] *Ḍholīyo*: a type of bed larger and more luxurious than the ordinary bed.

[143] Rāhaṇ: a village located ten miles north-northeast of Meṛto.

[144] *Māḷīyo*: a large bedroom built on the second floor of a large house or mansion (*havelī*), generally decorated with plaster, painting, and other embellishments.

[145] *Bāṭī*: small balls of heavy wheat flour cooked to form bread balls, which are served on feast occasions. The implication of this sentence is that Meṛto was a valuable and and lucrative acquisition for Dūdo, allowing him to live in style.

[146] Bārhaṭh ("obstinacy at the gate"): a synonym for Pauḷpāt ("recipient of the gate"), a title given to trusted Cāraṇs who, during times of siege, stood at the main gates (*pauḷ*) of forts and were the first to fight and give their lives in its defense. These same Cāraṇs were also those who stood first in line (even before the Brāhmaṇ) during a wedding to receive gifts and offerings (*neg, tyāg*) from the members of the bride's party.

[147] Ziegler has noted that "the position of one's head with relation to others was ... of great importance to the Rajpūt .... The head ... symbolized authority, leadership and more generalized notions of power, virility and manhood, and by extension that ability to assert oneself over others and rule." N. P. Ziegler, "Action, Power and Service in Rajasthani Culture: A Social History of the Rajpūts of Middle Period Rajasthan" (Unpublished Ph.D. dissertation, The University of Chicago, 1973), p. 78.

21. Dūdo Jodhāvat, born September 28, 1440.[148] Dūdo died in 1497-98. Rāv Vīramde[149] sat on the throne [in Meṛto]. Then he sent Sīho to Rāhaṇ.[150] Sīho was simple-minded; Sīho's three sons grew up [to be] great, fearsome warriors:[151] Rāv Jeso, Rāv Gāṅgo, [and] Rāv Bhojo.[152] Within the breasts of men like [these] three there was no room for Meṛto [in the possession of another].[153] They went and met with Rāv Mālde.[154] Rāv Mālde also greatly disfavored Rāv Vīramde.

Vigat, 2:48

The Rāv goaded them. He said: "Meṛto belongs to your father." Then they proposed to Vīramde: "We should obtain the share of our father [and] grandfather." Vīramde said: "The share is now based upon [the abilities of] swordsmen."[155] Then they too decided to fight. They removed [their] carts from

---

[148] The ***kha*** ms. gives the variant date V.S. 1497, ***Asoj***, ***Sudi*** 9 (October 5, 1440). There is general agreement among sources regarding the year of Dūdo Jodhāvat's birth, but there are differences about the month and day. Reū, 1:103, n. 5., gives the date V.S. 1497, ***Aśvin***, ***Sudi*** 15 (October 10, 1440), and notes that ***Āsāḍh*** (the fourth month of the Hindu calender) has also been given as the month of birth, which would make the V.S. date correspond to July 4, 1441.

[149] Meṛtīyo Rāṭhoṛ Vīramde Dūdāvat (no. 105), Rāv of Meṛto ca. 1497-1544. Dūdo Jodhāvat had five sons: Vīramde, Pañcāiṇ, Rāymal, Rāysal, and Ratansī.

[150] The statement that Rāv Vīramde sent Sīho to Rāhaṇ contradicts the preceding assertion that it was Dūdo Jodhāvat who sent Sīho to Rāhaṇ (***Vigat***, 2:47 ***supra***).

[151] ***Baḍī balāye uṭhīyā***. ***Balāy***, although feminine, was commonly used in Middle Mārvāṛī texts for male Rajpūts, in the sense of "one who inspires fear or awe by his presence," "a warrior," "a hero."

[152] Varsiṅghot Meṛtīyo Rāṭhoṛs Jeso Sīhavat (no. 150), Gāṅgo Sīhāvat (no. 149), and Bhojo Sīhāvat (no. 148), respectively.

[153] I.e., they could not tolerate Vīramde's possession of Meṛto.

[154] Rāv Mālde Gāṅgāvat, son of Rāv Gāṅgo Vāghāvat and ruler of Jodhpur, 1532-62. The events referred to in the text actually took place before Mālde became Rāv of Jodhpur, during the reign of his father, Rāv Gāṅgo of Jodhpur (1515-32).

[155] ***Tarvārīyāṃ***. This probably is the oblique plural of ***tarvārīyo***, "swordsman," "man who carries a sword." However, ***tarvāryāṃ*** is given as the oblique plural of ***tarvār*** ("sword") in ***Khyāt***, 3:117, line eight from the top of the page. Possibly, then, ***tarvārīyāṃ*** should be translated as "swords" instead of "swordsmen" in the sentence in ***Vigat***, 2:48. Then the translation of the line would be: "The share is now based upon [the power of] swords." The editor of the ***Vigat***, N. S. Bhāṭī, has followed this hypothesis in his n. 3 to ***Vigat***, 2:48.

Rāhaṇ. They engaged in much written correspondence with Rāv Mālde. Written assurance came from Rāv Mālde. They drove [their] carts toward Pīmpāṛ.[156] When two ***ghaṛīs***[157] of the day were spent, fifty or sixty superior horsemen mounted up, came to the market square of Meṛto, and raided it. A pursuit party was sent after [them].[158] Subsequently it caught up to [them] as they were going to Kusāṇo.[159] Their ***sāth*** also rejoined them. Here a great battle occurred. A large ***sāth*** from both sides died fighting. The three sons of Sīho were wounded. All [battle-field] responsibility was [placed] upon Rāṭhoṛ Khaṅgār Jogāvat[160] [by] Rāv Vīramde.[161] This Khaṅgār Jogāvat [and] Rāṭhoṛ Bhādo Mokaḷot[162] fell [under] heavy blows.[163] Sāndho Mokaḷot,[164] others too--the entire ***rāhavṇo***[165] of Vīramde--everyone was in this battle.[166] There was no ***sirdār***[167] like Vīramde in

---

[156] Pīmpāṛ village lies forty-five miles southwest of Rāhaṇ village.

[157] ***Ghaṛī***: a period of time equal to twenty-four minutes.

[158] ***Bāṃse bāhar choḍ huī***. We have found no other instance of a verb stem plus ***hoṇo***; ***choḍ huī*** probably is a mistake for ***choḍī huī***, a past participle. (Literally, the sentence might then be translated: "Behind, a released/dispatched pursuit party.")

[159] Kusāṇo village is situated seven miles northeast of Pīmpāṛ and thirty-six miles southwest of Rāhaṇ.

[160] Jodho Rāṭhoṛ Khaṅgār Jogāvat (no. 82) was the son of Jogo Jodhāvat and the grandson of Rāv Jodho Riṇmalot.

[161] The text has ***Rāv Vīramde sārī mudār Rā. Khaṅgār Jogāvat par thī***, literally, "Rāv Vīramde--all responsibility was upon Rā[ṭhoṛ] Khaṅgār Jogāvat." Our translation suggests the probable intent of this sentence.

[162] Jaitmāl Rāṭhoṛ Bhādo Mokalot (no. 68).

[163] ***Pūre lohāṃ paṛīyā***: literally, "fell [under] full/complete blows." ***Loh*** means both "blow" and "weapon" in Middle Mārvāṛī. Lāḷas, ***RSK***, 4:1:4446.

[164] Jaitmāl Rāṭhoṛ Sāndho Mokalot (no. 71). Sāndho Mokalot was Bhādo Mokalot's brother.

[165] ***Rāhavṇo***: the members of the household of an important Rajpūt, including his wives and concubines, their offspring, the descendants of offspring produced by Rajpūt liaisons with women of different ***jāt***is in the past who formed part of the body of household servants, and other personal servants of various ranks.

[166] ***Ar hīsā ro*** in the text is a mistake for ***ar hī, sāro***; ***siko*** is a mistake for ***sako***.

[167] ***Sirdār*** (P. sardār): headman, chief, leader; representative of a community or group.

[it].[168] He struck down the three brothers on the battlefield.[169] Vīramde's ***sāth*** won the battle.

22. Afterward, on April 20, 1532, Rāv Gāṅgo died.[170] Rāv Mālde sat on the throne.[171] In four or five years Mālde roared [like a lion]. He increased in strength.[172] Within Rāv Mālde's breast there was no room for Meṛto in the house of another. Rāv Mālde plotted[173] a great deal [against Vīramde], but Rāṭhoṛs Jaito,[174] Kūmpo,[175] Rāv Jeso,[176] [and] Rāṭhoṛ Khīṃvo[177] would not get involved

---

[168] The text has ***Vīramde Īsar sirdār māhe ko na chai***, which makes little sense. Perhaps ***Īsar*** ("God," a personal name) is a mistake for ***isṛo*** ("such as," "like"); we have based our translation on this possibility.

[169] ***Iṇ tīnāṃ hī bhāyāṃ nai khet pāṛīyā*** in the ***kha*** ms. is preferable to ***iṇ tīṇāṃ hī bhāṇṭ paṛīyā*** in the text.

[170] April 20, 1532 = V.S. 1588, ***Jeṭh***, ***Vadi*** 1 (see also ***Vigat***, 1:42). There is some disagreement regarding the date of Rāv Gāṅgo Vāghāvat's death. Ojhā, following ***Bāṅkīdās***, gives the date V.S. 1588, ***Jeṭh***, ***Sudi*** 5 = May 9, 1532, which we have preferred and which is the ***Śrāvaṇādi*** reckoning, but Reu and ***Vīr Vinod*** convert this to May 21, 1531, which is the ***Caitrādi*** reckoning. "Aitihāsik Bātāṃ," p. 38, gives the date V.S. 1589, ***Jeṭh***, ***Sudi*** 5 = May 9, 1532, if the reckoning is ***Caitrādi***, but May 28, 1533, if the reckoning is ***Śrāvaṇādi***. The circumstances of Rāv Gāṅgo's death also are open to question. Some sources say he was killed from a fall out of a window of the palace. Others indicate that his son, Mālde, pushed him from the window when he was drunk. ***Bāṅkīdās***, p. 11; V. S. Bhargava, ***Marwar and the Mughal Emperors*** (Delhi: Munshiram Manoharlal, 1966), p. 18 and n. 6; ***Murārdān***, no. 2, p. 106; Ojhā, 4:1:281; Reū, 1:115 and n. 1; ***Vīr Vinod***, 2:808

[171] The ceremony enthroning Rāv Mālde took place at Sojhat. Varying dates are given for the accession, including V.S. 1588, ***Āsāḍh***, ***Vadi 2*** = May 21, 1532 (***Śrāvaṇādi*** reckoning; Ojhā, 4:1:284), V.S. 1588, ***Āsāḍh***, ***Vadi*** 5 = June 5, 1531 (***Caitrādi*** reckoning) or May 24, 1532 (***Śrāvaṇādi*** reckoning; cf. Reu, 1:116), and V.S. 1588, ***Śrāvaṇ***, ***Sudi*** 15 = July 29, 1531 (***Bāṅkīdās***, p. 12; ***Jodhpur Rājya kī Khyāt***, p. 76). We have preferred Ojhā's conversion, May 21, 1532. See also ***Murārdān***, no. 2, p. 114.

[172] ***Jorai*** in the ***kha*** ms. is preferable to ***jarai*** in the text.

[173] ***Dāv-ghāv*** in the ***kha*** ms. is preferable to ***ghāv*** in the text.

[174] Rāṭhoṛ Jaito Pañcāiṇot (no. 61), founder of the Jaitāvat branch of Rāṭhoṛs.

[175] Rāṭhoṛ Kūmpo Mahirājot (no. 95), founder of the Kūmpāvat branch of Rāṭhoṛs.

[176] Cāmpāvat Rāṭhoṛ Rāv Jeso Bhairavdāsot (no. 48).

[177] Ūdāvat Rāṭhoṛ Khīṃvo Ūdāvat (no. 140).

in this matter. Rāv [Mālde] had formed an army [to fight] against the Sīndhaḷs.[178] Rāv Vīramde Dūdāvat also brought his ***rāhavṇo***.

Vigat, 2:49

He was with this army. Rāv Mālde was a wily ***ṭhākur***.[179] He sent word to Daulatīyo[180] in Nāgaur: "Rāv Vīramde is with me. All the great Rajpūts [of Meṛto] are with Vīramde. Vīramde lives having captured your elephant.[181] You must come behind [the back of Vīramde], pillage Meṛto, imprison all of Vīramde's men [and] close kinsmen,[182] and take them away. They will give back your elephant, too. And they will give other retribution as well." And he had Paṃvār Pañcāiṇ[183] informed: "You have Akho's ***vair*** [to settle].[184] And now the land of Meṛto is empty. Vīramde is with me with all of his ***sāth***. What are you doing sitting down?" He summoned Rāṭhoṛ Gāṅgo Sīhāvat and secretly told him: "Now there is an opportunity; you go and confiscate the fort of Meṛto." He employed these three stratagems. The Rāv did so in secret from Jaito [and] Kūmpo.

23. Four days went by; he held [these] conferences in secret. Then [Vīramde] asked some ***khavās***[185] [and] ***pāsvān***s:[186] "These days the Rāv does

---

[178] The Sīndhaḷs are a branch (***sākh***) of Mārvāṛ Rāṭhoṛs. They were powerful in eastern Mārvāṛ during the fifteenth and sixteenth centuries, particularly in the Jaitāraṇ and Bhādrājaṇ areas.

[179] ***Ṭhākur***: God; master, ruler, sovereign; one who rules a kingdom (among Rajpūts, the term is applied equally to the clan deity of a local kingdom, to the Rajpūt ruler himself, who is felt to rule as a subordinate and servant of this deity, and to other Rajpūts, who rule their lands directly under the ruler and who receive their authority from him.

[180] Daulatīyo: a diminutive nickname for Khānzāda Muḥammad Daulat Khān (no. 154), the ruler of Nāgaur, ca. 1516-36.

[181] A reference to a great war elephant, belonging to Muḥammad Daulat Khān and named "Dariyājoīs," which was captured by Vīramde after the battle of Sevakī in 1529. See ***Khyāt***, 3:93-94.

[182] ***Caco-baco***. This compound is derived from ***caco***, "father's younger brother," and ***baco***, "son," "young male," and was used as a generic term to indicate all the junior agnates who lived with and served an important Rajpūt.

[183] Paṃvār Pañcāiṇ Karamcandot (no. 24) of Cāṭsū, a town located thirty-five miles south of Jaipur.

[184] Meṛtīyo Rāṭhoṛ Ratansī Dūdāvat, Vīramde's brother, had murdered a Paṃvār of Pīsāṅgaṇ village named Akho Soḍhāvat (no. 23).

[185] ***Khavās*** (Arabic k͟hawāṣṣ): a male or female attendant or personal servant of a Rajpūt ruler or important land-holder.

not speak to me; what is he conferring about in secret?" Someone told [him] what news there was. Then [Vīramde] wrote letters and sent them to Meṛto. A Raibārī[187] brought the letters to Meṛto a watch before Daulatīyo [arrived]. Rāṭhoṛ Akhairāj Bhādāvat[188] had come to Meṛto without requesting leave from Rāṭhoṛ Vīramde. [The Raibārī] put the letters in Akhairāj's hands. Akhairāj prepared the fort for defense. He closed the gates. He sent scouts before [the enemy]; they brought back the information [that] the army had advanced to about four ***kos*** [from Meṛto]. He closed the main gates of the fort, climbed up on top of a tower, and stayed ready. Not very many retainers were inside the fort. Daulatīyo came[189] and sacked and looted the city. And he came and began to reduce the fort. [His] ***sāth*** penetrated the fort.[190] Then Akhairāj Bhādāvat observed: "There is no ***sāth*** [to aid us] nearby, and today Vīramde's men are being captured. I see with my own eyes [that] there is no dignity in this situation.[191] Today I must die." Then Akhairāj leaped from the wall of the fort [along with] fifteen to twenty men.[192] Akhairāj wielded a nine-digit long lance[193] in a dash [through the ranks of the enemy; some men] were struck, [others] warded it off.[194]

---

[186] ***Pāsvān*** (Persian pās-bān): literally, "one who stands beside or in attendance"; a male body servant or a female concubine of a Rajpūt ruler or important landholder.

[187] Raibārī: a member of a ***jāti*** having as its traditional occupation the transhumant herding of camels, sheep, and goats. Raibārīs were often used as messengers also.

[188] Jaitmāl Rāṭhoṛ Akhairāj Bhādāvat (no. 69). Akhairāj was Vīramde's ***pradhān***.

[189] ***Āj*** in the text apparently is a misprint for the conjunctive participle ***āy***.

[190] ***Koṭ num̩ sāth vaḷīyo***. The verb ***vaḷno*** has many meanings, including "to penetrate," "to pierce." See Lāḷas, ***RSK***, 4:2:4549, entry no. 15 under ***vaḷno***.

[191] I.e., there was no dignity in Akhairāj's standing idly by while Vīramde's men were being captured.

[192] We have preferred the variant reading ***koṭ rī bhīṇt thā kūdīyo*** in the ***kha*** ms. to the reading ***kūdīyā*** in the text.

[193] ***Barchī***: a short lance, usually made of iron, much favored by Rajpūts, which could be used as a stabbing weapon or hurled in battle.

[194] ***Ke lāgī ke ṭaḷī***: literally, "either it stuck or was warded off."

Vigat, 2:50

They joined weapons [in battle]. Daulatīyo fled. Victory was Akhairāj's. Rāṭhoṛ Bhairavdās Bhādāvat[195] died fighting. Paṃvār Pañcāiṇ, [son] of Karamcand, came. They[196] attacked Ālṇīyāvās,[197] [but] they fled before Rāysal.[198]

24. Rāṭhoṛ Gāṅgo Sīhāvat was coming to Meṛto with 500 horsemen. He was coming in [the bed of] the river of Bāñjhāṅkuṛī.[199] The ***ṭhākurs*** were sleeping; he suddenly became separated from them all.[200] When they came to a quarter ***kos*** [from Meṛto], Gāṅgo heard the palanquins of the ***ṭhākurs***, then--no palanquins. They turned back. For two ***ghaṛīs*** [Gāṅgo] searched for the ***ṭhākurs*** [and] palanquins, [but] he did not find them. Then Gāṅgo turned back from there. Vīramde's men brought this news to where Vīramde's tents were in the army of the Rāvjī and secretly gave [Vīramde] written reports. Upon looking at the reports, Vīramde took a small ***sāth*** and, using the pretext of having to relieve himself, mounted up and departed. He said to the small ***sāth***: "You must assemble at the third watch in such-and-such a place."[201] He had kept several

---

[195] Jaitmāl Rāṭhoṛ Bhairavdās Bhādāvat (no. 70), brother of Akhairāj Bhādāvat (no. 69).

[196] "They" refers to Paṃvār Pañcāiṇ Karamcandot (no. 24) of Cāṭsū, and his brother, Rāvat Jagmāl Karamcandot (no. 25) of Cāṭsū, who is mentioned in section 24, ***infra***, as taking part in the attack on Ālṇīyāvās.

[197] Ālṇīyāvās in the ***kha*** ms. is preferable to Lohīyāvās (?) in the text. Ālṇīyāvās is a village twenty miles southeast of Meṛto.

[198] Meṛtīyo Rāṭhoṛ Rāysal Dūdāvat (no. 106), brother of Rāv Vīramde Dūdāvat (no. 105) and son of Dūdo Jodhāvat (no. 104).

[199] Bāñjāṅkuṛī: a village located five miles north of Jaitāraṇ and situated one-half mile north of the Lilṛī River, an offshoot of the Lūṇī River of Mārvāṛ. This river would be dry except during the rainy season. Meṛto is twenty-eight miles north of the village.

[200] The text has ***chīṇṭ kapaṛīyo***, "caught a drop," clearly irrelevant to the rest of the passage. The correct reading probably is ***chīṇṭak paṛīyo***, a compound verb: ***chīṇṭakṇo*** ("to become separated") plus ***paṛṇo***, which adds a degree of suddenness or violence to the main verb. See J. D. Smith, "An Introduction to the Language of the Historical Documents from Rajasthan, ***Modern Asian Studies***, 9, 4 (1975), p. 457, for a brief discussion of compound verbs in Middle Mārvāṛī.

[201] The text has ***amakṛī ṭhauṛ***, "***amakṛī*** place." We have been unable to locate any place called ***amakṛī***. Although it is not listed in either Lāḷas's or Sākariyā's dictionary, perhaps ***amakṛo/-ī*** is a synonym for the adjective ***phaḷāṇo/-ī*** ("such-and-such"), which appears in identical contexts twice in this same passage.

umrāvs[202] [and] shrewd *kāmdārs* right in the camp.[203] He had told them: "In the morning[204] at this time demand leave from the Rāvjī and come [to me]. When the Rāvjī has you asked, 'Where is Vīramde?', then you must say: 'He informed us as follows: "I am going to relieve myself; afterward, if a hunt is to be found, I will go hunting too."'" And so, the Rāv's men came. They said: "Where is Vīramdejī?" [Vīramde's] servants said: "He has gone to relieve himself; he will come soon." At the second watch a man came again. Then they said: "He has not come; we think he must be hunting." At dusk they had the news reported [to Mālde]. Then the shrewd *ṭhākurs* who were in the camp sent word [to Mālde's men]: "As long as we were together, there was no news [of Vīramde]. But [afterward] a man came, who said: '[Vīramde] was hunting at such-and-such a place. Twenty-two horsemen came there from Meṛto; they said: "Paṃvārs Pañcāiṇ [and] Jagmāl[205] attacked such-and-such a place; much of Vīramde's *sāth* died fighting."' We hear that is where Vīramde went."

Vigat, 2:51

During the night Vīramde's *sāth* remained in [Mālde's] army. In the morning the tent was loaded, and they went to the main entrance [of Mālde's tent] and informed the Rāvjī: "Vīramde, in this [manner],[206] suddenly mounted up and departed. If we receive [your] order, we shall take leave." Then the Rāv summoned them into his presence and hastily[207] gave them leave. Vīramde came to Meṛto. None of the strategems Rāv Mālde had employed was successful. The Rāv also was disgraced in Jaito [and] Kūmpo's presence.[208]

---

[202] ***Umrāv*** (from umarā', pl. of Arabic amīr): a man of high rank; a noble. Under the Mughals, only those officers with a ***mansab*** rank of 1,000 ***jāt*** or more were considered to belong among the ***umrāvs*** or nobility of the Empire.

[203] The text has ***umrāv 2 pukhtā kāmdār deṛai hī rākh gayā thā***. Possibly the translation should be: He kept two ***umrāvs***, shrewd ***kamdārs***, right in the camp." However, to our knowledge, ***umrāv*** and ***kāmdār*** were two separate categories.

[204] ***Savārai*** in the ***kha*** ms. is preferable to ***su khārai*** in the text.

[205] Paṃvār Rāvat Jagmāl Karamcandot of Cāṭsū (no. 25).

[206] The text has ***Vīramde to iṇ acuk caḍh khaḍīyā***. Apparently the word ***bhānt*** or ***tarai*** ("way," "manner") should have followed ***iṇ***.

[207] ***Haḷbhaḷ kar***. ***Haḷbhaḷ karṇo***: "to make haste, to hurry; to make a commotion; to flatter, to pay compliments to, to treat with respect and deference; to welcome cordially."

[208] ***Rāv hī Kumpā Jaitā bīc besāṇ paṛīyā***. ***Besāṇ***: The Persian prefix ***be-*** ("without," "devoid of") plus ***sāṇ***, the Middle Mārvāṛī version of the Arabic ***shān***, "rank, dignity, state, pomp, grandeur, glory; radiance, lustre." Platts, ***Dictionary***, p. 719.

25. In the middle of that day the Pātsāh of Māṇḍū[209] died. There was a certain ***kiledār***[210] at Ajmer; because of [the Pātsāh's death] he abandoned the fort during the night and went away. The news reached Vīramde: "The ***thānedār***[211] of Ajmer, [who] was inside [the fort], went away; the fort has fallen vacant." Then Rāv Vīramde took his ***sāth*** and mounted up. Ajmer came into his hands. The fort came into his hands.[212] Mālde heard of this matter. Within the Rāv's

---

[209] The text has Maṇḍovar; Māṇḍū, the capital of the Malwa Sultāns, is meant. See n. 212, ***infra***.

[210] ***Kiledār*** (Persian qil'a-dār): a person in charge of a fort. The ***kiledār*** was Sham Sheru'l-Mulk, a noble serving the Sultān of Gujarat, Bahādur Shāh (1526-37). See n. 212, ***infra***.

[211] ***Thāṇedar***: a person in charge of a garrison (***thāṇo***).

[212] Meṛtīyo Rāv Vīramde Dūdāvat's fortuitous and apparently bloodless takeover of Ajmer occurred as a result of changes in political fortunes in north India, Malwa, and Gujarat in 1534-35, of which he took full advantage. The local chronicles supply no details about these changes. From their viewpoint, Ajmer was suddenly left unguarded due to the death of the ruler of Māṇḍū, a not uncommon occurrence on the death of a king. Later historians such as Ojhā and Reu do not explain this event either, appearing rather to take the chronicles at face value. Ojhā, for example, states only that "for some reason" the ***hākīm*** of Ajmer left the city unprotected.

The specific reasons are to be found in the relations between the Mughal Emperor Humāyūn of north India and Sultān Bahādur Shāh of Gujarat in this period. Shortly after his accession to the throne of Gujarat, Sultān Bahādur (1526-37) began to expand his territory into areas of Malwa and Rājasthān. In 1531, he attacked and captured Māṇḍū. Shortly thereafter, the ruler of Māṇḍū, Maḥmūd Shāh Khiljī (1511-31), was killed, bringing to an end the Khiljī dynasty of Malwa, which had ruled since 1436. Within the year, Sultān Bahādur had extended his authority over areas adjacent to Māṇḍū and had additional plans to lay siege to Cītoṛ. However, the siege was postponed until 1533, when Sultān Bahādur marched a large army into southern Rājasthān, sending forces at the same time against Riṇthambhor under Mālik Burhān'l-Mulk and Mujāhid Khān and against Ajmer under Sham Sheru'l-Mulk. Ajmer was taken from the Paṃvār Rajpūts under Rāv Jagmāl Karamcandot (no. 25) by the 12,000 troops of Sham Sheru'l-Mulk in 1533. In March of 1535, Sultān Bahādur also besieged and captured Cītoṛ from Sīsodīyo Rāṇo Vikramāditya Sāṅgāvat (ca. 1531-36; see biographical note for Sīsodīyo Gahlot Rāṇo Udaisiṅgh Sāṅgāvat, no. 17).

Aware of the developments in Malwa, Emperor Humāyūn had travelled to Gwālior in 1533 or 1534, but he had not ventured further against Sultān Bahādur. Then in late 1534, he marched toward Cītoṛ. When his army drew near in 1535, Sultān Bahādur's commander at Cītoṛ, Mālik Burhān'l-Mulk, withdrew from the fort (which was soon reoccupied by the Sīsodīyos) and fled to Māṇḍū, where he joined Sultān Bahādur. Humāyūn then attacked Māṇḍū, which he captured by the middle of 1535, forcing Sultān Bahādur to flee to Cāmpāner and then to Div on the coast of Gujarat.

With the fall of Māṇḍū in 1535 (the event that the local chronicles interpret as the death of the king of Māṇḍū), Sham Sheru'l-Mulk, the ***kiledār*** of Ajmer, withdrew from the city and travelled to Gujarat with his forces. The political vacuum created by his flight opened the city of Ajmer to Rāv Vīramde Dūdāvat and allowed him to take

breast there was no room for Merṭo [under the authority of Vīramde]. When he heard that Ajmer had come into Vīramde's hands, a fire flared up within the Rāv's body. Rāv Mālde sent [his] ***pradhāns*** to Rāv Vīramde and had them say: "Merṭo is yours, but in the house [of the Rāṭhoṛs] I am the ***ṭīkāyat***;[213] you are my ***bhāībandh*** servant.[214] You yourself give Ajmer to me; the city [and] the fort[215] are not for you to take." The ***pradhāns*** came to Merṭo. They told Vīramde [Mālde's] words. Vīramde did not comply with [Mālde's] statement. The ***pradhāns*** came back. The Rāv assembled [his] ***sāth***. Rāv Vīramde's ***sāth*** came too. Rāv [Vīramde] assembled [his] ***sāth***. At one time Vīramde, ready to die [in battle], was preparing the ***koṭṛī***[216] [and] the city [of Merṭo] for siege. Subsequently Vīramde's Rajpūts [and] ***kāmdārs*** remonstrated with Vīramde:

Vigat, 2:52

"We have no walls [or] fort [in Merṭo].[217] If there is a siege of ten days or so, then Merṭo is [as defenseless as] a village of the plains. If you die, you will be salt in flour.[218] Do not give an enemy a bundle of straw."[219] Afterward Rāv Mālde attacked Merṭo. Rāv Vīramde had gone away four days previously,

---

control virtually uncontested. M. S. Commissariat, *A History of Gujarat*, vol. 1 (Bombay: Longmans, Green & Co., Ltd., 1938), pp. 328-333, 350-356; Day, *Medieval Malwa*, pp. 319-327; Ojhā, 2:706-712, 4:1:285, ns. 2 and 3; Reu, 1:118-119; S. Tirmizi, *Ajmer through inscriptions [1532-1852 A.D.]* (New Delhi: Indian Institute of Islamic Studies, 1968), p. 12.

213 ***Ṭīkāyat***: a chosen successor; one designated to receive the throne and to have the ***ṭīko*** or red mark placed upon his forehead upon succession; one who has received the ***ṭīko***.

214 ***Bhāībandh cākar***: a military servant (***cākar***) who is also a member of one's brotherhood (***bhāībandh***).

215 ***Gaḍh koṭ***. In most contexts, there is no substantial difference in meaning between ***gaḍh*** and ***koṭ***; both usually mean "fort." Here, however, ***koṭ*** evidently means "walls" and, by extension, Ajmer city.

216 ***Koṭṛī*** in the ***kha*** ms. is preferable to ***lī*** in the text.

217 ***Gaḍh koṭ***. See n. 215 to ***Vigat***, 2:51, ***supra***. At this time Merṭo had only a small fort, the ***koṭṛī***, constructed during the time of Rāv Varsiṅgh Jodhāvat.

218 I.e., of no consequence.

219 I.e., do not give an enemy even the slightest advantage. The text has ***puro***; the ***kha*** ms. ***puḷo***. ***Pūḷo*** is the correct reading: "a tied bundle of straw or grass."

leaving Meṛto as it was.[220] He went to Ajmer with [his] men [and] ***vasī***.[221] The Rāvjī proceeded to Meṛto and established [his] authority [there]. This event occurred around 1538-39.[222] [Rāv Mālde] divided up the villages facing Ajmer among various important ***umrāvs***. He kept a garrison in Meṛto. He gave a large ***paṭo*** to Rāṭhoṛ Sahaiso Tejsīyot[223] (Tejsī [was] the son of Varsiṅgh),[224] a Meṛtīyo, and settled him in Reyāṃ rī Vaḍī.[225] Vīramde was very angry with Sahaiso. He said: "I shall kill Sahaiso today, in the morning." Rāṭhoṛs Sīdho Mokaḷot,[226] Akhairāj Bhādāvat, Rāysal[227]--all the Meṛtīyos[228]--persistently restrained Vīramde and kept him [in Ajmer, saying]: "Sahaiso is your son.[229]

---

[220] ***Meṛto ūbho mel nīsarīyo. Ūbho melṇo***: to leave (a town, fort, etc.) as it is without making defensive preparations; to abandon (a town, fort, etc.) without a fight.

[221] ***Vasī***: the people or subjects bound to an important Rajpūt who lived either in his village or town of residence (***vās***, q.v.) or in nearby villages under his control and who performed various services for him according to their status, receiving in exchange his protection. Typically the ***vasī*** of an important man contained persons of many ***jātis***, including a contingent of Rajpūt warriors, peasants such as Jāṭs, Sīrvīs, Paṭels, etc., Vāṇīyos, Brāhmaṇs, Cāraṇs, and members of the lower ***jātis***: Kumbhārs, Māḷīs, Sutrārs, and others. ***Vasīs*** were divided among sons either before or upon the death of a Rajpūt ***ṭhākur***, each inheriting son taking his part of the ***vasī*** and going to live on his share (***vaṇṭ***, ***grās***) of the paternal lands, a process referred to in the sources as ***judāī*** ("separation").

When Rajpūts were forced to flee, as was Rāv Vīramde, they frequently took their ***vasīs*** with them. For a discussion of the ***vasī***, see R. D. Saran, "Conquest and Colonization: Rajpūts and ***Vasīs*** in Middle Period Mārvāṛ" (unpublished Ph.D. dissertation, The University of Michigan, 1978), chapters 2, 3, and 4.

[222] The date given here is incorrect. Authorities place Rāv Mālde's conquest of Meṛto in 1534-35. ***Vigat***, 1:43, has 1542-43, also incorrect. See Tirmizi, ***Ajmer through Inscriptions***, pp. 12, 16.

[223] Varsiṅghot Meṛtīyo Rāṭhoṛ Sahaiso Tejsīyot (no. 151).

[224] A parenthetical remark by the author of the ***Vigat***, Naiṇsī.

[225] Reyāṃ rī Vaḍī: another name for Reyāṃ village, located fifteen miles southeast of Meṛto.

[226] Jaitmāl Rāṭhoṛ Sīdho Mokaḷot (no. 72).

[227] Meṛtīyo Rāṭhoṛ Rāysal Dūdāvat (no. 106), Vīramde's brother.

[228] In a strict sense, "all the Meṛtīyos" does not include Sīdho or Akhairāj, who were Jaitmāl Rāṭhoṛs. But in a general sense, the phrase would include both Meṛtīyo Rāṭhoṛs and those in their service, such as the Jaitmāls.

[229] I.e., Vīramde's relationship to Sahaiso, a junior member of Vīramde's ***bhāībandh***, is that of a father to a son.

Rāv Mālde has divided Meṛto among so many [other] Rāṭhoṛs; kill them first, then kill Sahaiso." But within Vīramde's breast there was no room for Sahaiso.

26. The scouts who had been sent by Vīramde came [back]. They gave [their] news; they said: "Sahaiso is sitting in Reyāṃ with his ***sāth***." When the night was a watch spent, Rāṭhoṛ Vīramde himself mounted up and departed, not giving very much information to anyone. Sahaiso's scouts also were in action; they came and gave [him] the news [of Vīramde's departure]. Rāv Sahaiso Tejsīyot and Rāṭhoṛ Vairsī Rāṇāvat[230] were friendly; Vairsī had come to Reyāṃ. Rāv [Mālde's] ***sāth***, [including] Rāṭhoṛs Kūmpo Mahirājot, Rāṇo Akhairājot,[231] Jeso Bhairavdāsot, [and] Bhado Pañcāiṇot,[232] was at the garrison in Raṛod[233] Vairsī had a she-camel, one that stayed fast for hours.[234] He had his ***khavās*** mount it and sent him to Rāṭhoṛs Kūmpojī [and] Rāṇo. He said: "[If you do not hurry], you might come when we have [already] died [or] killed [them], so come quickly!"[235]

Vigat, 2:53

The camel-rider arrived at midnight. Those ***ṭhākurs***, upon looking over the written message,[236] mounted up and took the reins. Just before daybreak[237] Rāṭhoṛ Sahaiso Tejsīyot donned the saffron robe[238] and [with] five hundred men went outside Reyāṃ, spread cloths [on the ground], and sat down. At that time the Rāvjī's ***sāth*** also had come near Reyāṃ. Rāṭhoṛs Kūmpo, Rāṇo, [and] Jeso, while still advancing [on the road to Reyāṃ], had sent ahead scouts, four riders [who were] owners of fine horses, off the road in the direction of Ajmer [and the

---

[230] Akhairājot Rāṭhoṛ Vairsī Rāṇāvat (no. 31).

[231] Akhairājot Rāṭhoṛ Rāṇo Akhairājot (no. 28).

[232] Akhairājot Rāṭhoṛ Bhado Pañcāiṇot (no. 32).

[233] Raṛod in the ***kha*** ms. is preferable to ***der*** (?) in the text. Raṛod is a village located thirty-five miles west of Meṛto and six miles west of Āsop village.

[234] ***Ghaṛīyāṃ jovaṇ***. ***Jovaṇ*** is a variant of ***javaṇ/javan***, "speed," "quickness"; "quick"; "fast." Lāḷas, ***RSK***, 2:1:1084.

[235] I.e., hurry or miss the battle.

[236] ***Kagaḷ dīṭhāṃ sāmā***. ***Sāmā*** probably is a mistake for ***samāṃ***, "at the time of."

[237] ***Rāt ghaṛī 1 rai jhāñjharkhai***. ***Jhāñjharkho***: "dawn," "early morning." The editor of the ***Vigat***, N. S. Bhāṭī, translates this phrase as "one ***ghaṛī*** of the night remaining" (n. 1); we have followed his suggestion.

[238] ***Kesarīyā kar nai***. Rajpūts put on saffron robes (***kesarīyo***) to indicate their commitment to die in battle.

approaching] Vīramde. These *ṭhākur*s came to the open field[239] of Reyāṃ, and the scouts on horseback came and gave the news: "*Rāj*![240] Vīramde is coming." Then that *ṭhākur* [to whom the news was told] did not go to the village [or] to Sahaiso; he made [all the men] go straight to where Vīramde was coming. A battle took place near the village. There was a great clash of weapons. Here a large *sāth* from both sides died fighting. That day [was] a great day for Rāv Mālde, a great glory. The Rāv's *sāth* won the battle; fifty of Rāṭhoṛ Vīramde's men died fighting. Rāvat[241] Bhojo, [who was the son] of Gāṅgo [and] a Jaitmāl [Rāṭhoṛ],[242] died fighting. Rāṭhor Sīdho Mokaḷot again fell wounded. Vīramde also showed outstanding prowess that day. He killed on five separate occasions with a knife[243] and all alone urged [his] horse into the Rāv's *sāth*. The knife having splintered, Vīramde snatched up eleven lances thrust by the Rāv's *sāth*. He held them together with the reins in [his] left hand. With difficulty a Bīhārī *sirdār* from Jāḷor[244] brought Vīramde twenty paces from the battlefield. That day Rāṭhoṛ Bhado Pañcāiṇot showed much prowess. Bhado jostled Vīramde and

---

[239] *Gorvo*: the open field outside a village; the open field where the village cattle are gathered before being taken out to graze in the scrub-brush.

[240] The text has *rājā*, the vocative plural of *rāj*, indicating that several *ṭhākur*s were being addressed, but the next sentence begins with *o ṭhākur*, "that *ṭhākur*." Perhaps *rājā* is simply a mistake for *rāj*.

[241] *Rāvat*: a title held by many petty rulers in middle period Rājasthān, including the Rāṭhoṛs of Ketū, Setrāvo, and Dechū, the Sīsodīyos of Devaḷīyo, and the Mers of Cāṅg.

[242] Jaitmāl Rāṭhoṛ Rāvat Bhojo Gāṅgāvat (no. 76).

[243] *Churī kār* in the text is a variant of *churīkā*, "knife." *Churīkā pherṇo*: to turn the knife, to kill with a knife.

[244] The text has *Jāḷorī ro ek Bīhārī sirdār*; evidently *Jāḷorī* is a mistake for Jāḷor. Possibly, however, the translation could be: "a Bīhārī *sirdār*, [son/military servant] of the Jāḷorī." The Bīhārīs were Paṭhāṇs (Afghans) of the Lohanī tribe. They claimed to have held the governorship of Bihar under the Tughluq Sultāns of Delhi, hence their name. In the late fourteenth century, the head of the family, Mālik Yūsuf, together with kinsmen and retainers, migrated during the course of a pilgrimage from Bihar to Jāḷor, where he seized power from the local Cahuvāṇ ruler. Mālik Yūsuf died in ca. 1395 and was succeeded by his son, Mālik Ḥasan, who was recognized by the Tughluqs as the governor of Jāḷor. The Bīhārī Paṭhāṇs subsequently became supporters of the rulers of Gujarat, serving them with 7,000 horsemen. They continued to hold Jāḷor until 1538-39, when they were driven out by a Baloc adventurer, who in turn was forced to flee by an army sent by Rāv Mālde. After Mālde was defeated by Sher Shāh Sūr in 1544, the Bīhārīs regained control of Jāḷor, which they held with brief interruptions until the second decade of the seventeenth century. ***Gazetteer of the Bombay Presidency:*** Volume V, ***Cutch, Pālanpur, and Mahi Kāntha*** (Bombay: Government Central Press, 1908), pp. 318-320; M. Vyās, ***Jodhpur Rājya kā Itihās*** (Jaypur: Pañcasīl Prakāśan, 1975), pp. 95-96.

knocked him away from the lances. He did [him] the honor of striking [his] body.[245] Rāṭhoṛs Bhado [and] Kūmpo spared [Vīramde]. Rāṭhoṛs Jeso Bhairavdāsot [and] Rāṇo Akhairājot fell badly wounded. Vīramde put his wounded in stretchers[246] and, having summoned [his] strength, departed. Rāṭhoṛs Kūmpo [and] Bhado had *saidānos*[247] played and remained standing right where they won the battle.[248]

Vigat, 2:54

They bandaged the wounded, came to Reyāṃ, and helped them dismount.[249] When Rāv Mālde heard of this affair, he touched heaven.[250] From this battle [onward], Meṛto became succulent for the Rāvjī.[251]

---

[245] ***Dīl māraṇ ro kāydo kīyo***. ***Kāydo*** (Persian qā'ida): a dignity, an honor. Striking the body of another Rajpūt warrior (particularly a highly esteemed warrior) in battle without killing him, was part of the Rajpūt etiquette of battle, from which one gained great honor. For a more detailed discussion of Rajpūt battle etiquette, see Norman P. Ziegler, "Evoluton of the Rathor State of Marvar: Horses, Structural Change and Warfare," in ***The Idea of Rajasthan: Explorations in Regional Identity***, ed. by Karine Schomer ***et al.***, 2 vols. (Columbia, MO: South Asia Publications by arrangement with Manohar Publishers & Distributors; New Delhi, India: American Institute of Indian Studies, 1994), 2:192-216.

[246] ***Jhālīyāṃ māṃhe***. ***Jhālīyā***: wooden sticks or boards used to load goods into oxcarts. Here they apparently were used as stretchers to carry the wounded men.

[247] ***Saidāno*** (Persian shādiyāna): a musical instrument played on an auspicious occasion as a form of celebration.

[248] Literally, "in that place [where] the field [of battle] had come into their hands." It is evident that Kūmpo and Bhado chose not to follow up their victory; they allowed Vīramde to regain his strength and leave the battlefield. ***Bāṅkīdās***, p. 12, no. 126 notes that on another, subsequent occasion in Bāṃvaḷī village Jaito Pañcāiṇot restrained Kūmpo Mahirājot from killing Vīramde, saying

> Do not kill Vīramde! Vīramde is a great Rajpūt. If he remains alive, he will bring someone [to aid him against Rāv Mālde] and fashion his own death.

The ***Jodhpur Rājya kī Khyāt*** (p. 80) has a similar version of events but substitutes Cāṭsū village for Bāṃvaḷī.

[249] The text has ***ghāv līyāṃ thā vāṃh nai Reyāṃ āī utārīyā***. Our translation is conjectural, based on ***ghāv līyāṃ*** being a mistake for ***ghāyalīyā*** and ***vāṃh*** being a variant of ***bāndh***. Literally, the translation would then be: "There were wounded men; they bandaged [them], came to Reyāṃ, and set them down/helped them dismount."

[250] ***Ābh lāgo***. The editor of the ***Vigat***, N. S. Bhāṭī, translates this phrase as "became very pleased" (***ati prasann huā***) in n. 1, but it is possible Mālde may have been less than pleased with his commanders' failure to follow up their victory and capture Vīramde.

27. Rāv Mālde, having passed the time for a year afterward,[252] formed an army [to attack] Ajmer. He drove Rāṭhoṛ Vīramde from Ajmer also. Ajmer came into his hands.[253] Afterward Vīramde went to Nahāṛṇo[254] one time. The Sekhāvat Kachvāhos[255] protected [him] for some time. Day by day Rāv Mālde increased in strength. He gave Ajmer to Rāṭhoṛ Mahes Ghaṛsīyot[256] in ***paṭo***. He took Ḍīḍvāṇo.[257] He gave Ḍīḍvāṇo to Rāṭhoṛ Kūmpo Mahirājot in ***paṭo***. He took Sāmbhar. The Rāv's ***kāmdārs*** continuously came and stayed in Sāmbhar. Then Rāṭhoṛ Vīramde went to Cāṭsū[258] There too the armies of the Rāv came

---

[251] Rajpūts often expressed their relationships toward land in terms of food; land was "eaten" or "consumed" (***dhartī khāṇo, dhartī bhogṇo***) by the ruler in the symbolic language of the Rajpūts, and thus the remark concerning the land's becoming succulent or tasty (***ras paṛiyo***) for Mālde is an indication that he had acquired full authority over it. For a discussion of Rajpūt tenets concerning land, see R. D. Saran, "Conquest and Colonization," pp. 88-90, 102.

[252] Rāv Mālde's conquest of Ajmer may have come much sooner than one year after his defeat of Vīramde at Reyāṃ, as Vīramde was in no position to defend the city.

[253] Rāv Mālde captured Ajmer in 1535. He held the city until it was taken by Sher Shāh Sūr in 1543. There are still remains at Ajmer of a massive unfinished water-lift said to have been begun by Rāv Mālde to carry water to the top of the fort Tārāgaḍh, which overlooks the city. V. S. Bhargava, ***Marwar and the Mughal Emperors***, p. 22, n. 1; ***Murārdān***, no. 2, p. 135; Ojhā, 4:1:286, n. 4; Reu, 1:119; Tirmizi, ***Ajmer through Inscriptions***, pp. 12, 16. ***Vigat***, 1:43-44, gives 1533-34 as the date for Mālde's conquest of Ajmer, which is incorrect.

[254] Nahāṛṇo/Narāiṇo: a town located forty-five miles northeast of Ajmer. During this period, the town was ruled by Kachvāho Khaṅgār Jagmālot, from whom the Khaṅgārot Kachvāho branch (***sākh***) emerged. The Khaṅgārots are a cadet line of the Kachvāho rulers of Āmber. The Mughal Emperor Akbar gave this town to Khaṅgār's son, Narāiṇdās, in ***jāgīr***, hence its name, Narāiṇo. ***Khyāt***, 1:297, 304.

[255] The Sekhāvat Kachvāhos stem from Sekho Mokalot, son of Mokal Bālāvat and great-grandson of Rājā Udaikaraṇ Juṇsīyot, ruler of Āmber. Sekho Mokalot founded Amarsar and Sikargaḍh, towns sixty miles northwest of Āmber in the area known as Sekhāvaṭī. For an interesting account of the origin of the Sekhāvat branch of the Kachvāho family, see Refaqat Ali Khan, ***The Kachhwahas under Akbar and Jahangir*** (New Delhi: Kitab Pub. House, 1976), p. 155.

Elswewhere it is noted that Vīramde Dūdāvat was taken in by Kachvāho Rāysal Sekhāvat, son of Sekho Mokalot. ***Khyāt***, 1:296, 318-319, 3:98.

[256] Cūṇḍāvat Rāṭhoṛ Mahes Ghaṛsīyot (no. 58).

[257] Ḍīḍvāṇo: a town 125 miles northeast of Jodhpur and sixty miles north of Ajmer. See Appendix A for a discussion of the local importance of Ḍīḍvāṇo and its early history.

after [him].[259] Rāṭhoṛ Vīramde went to Lālsoṭ.[260] [Rāv Mālde] would not allow [him] to stay there either. Afterward Vīramde went to Bāṃvaḷī[261] and left [his] carts [there].

28. He sent his ***pradhāns***, Rāṭhoṛ Akhairāj and Muṃhato Khīṃvo,[262] to the ***sūbedār***[263] of Riṇthambhor,[264] who was a certain ***umrāv***. Here no one went inside just to pay respects to this [***umrāv***]. They grew weary striving [to see him]. The Navāb[265] never came outside the vault[266] [of the fort]. They had nothing [with them] to give; [nothing] that they might give to the ***dīvāṇ***[267] [and]

---

[258] Cāṭsū: a town located thirty-five miles south of Jaipur city and Āmber. This reference to Rāv Vīramde's staying in Cāṭsū is peculiar, as it was previously stated that a ***vair*** existed between the Meṛtīyos and the Paṃvār rulers of Cāṭsū. See ***Vigat***, 2:49, and Biographical Notes under "Paṃvārs of Cāṭsū."

[259] Rāv Mālde's armies conquered Cāṭsū in 1541-42.

[260] Lālsoṭ: a town located thirty-five miles east of Cāṭsū.

[261] Bāṃvaḷī: a town located twenty miles east of Lālsoṭ.

[262] Muṃhato Khīṃvo Lālāvat (no. 157).

[263] ***Sūbedār*** (Persian ṣūbedār): an officer in charge of a province (***sūbo***).

[264] Riṇthambhor: a large fort and town situated forty miles south of Bāṃvaḷī village and sixty-five miles southeast of Jaipur, near Savāī Mādhopur. Because of its strategic location near the Bānas River, Riṇthambhor controlled the passageway into the valley of the Chambal River (southern Rājasthān). Historically, its fortress was one of the most formidable in all India.

In 1541 Riṇthambhor was captured by Sher Shāh Sūr from ʻUṣmān Khān, its governor under Qādir Shāh, ruler of Malwa. Sher Shāh then gave the fortress to his son, Salīm Shāh, in ***jāgīr***. During this period, it was administered by Khizr Khān. Governorship of the ***sūbo*** was at the same time given to Shujāʻat Khān, to whom Sher Shāh had assigned the whole territory following his conquest of Gwalior and Malwa. Jain, ***Ancient Cities***, pp. 330-334; P. Saran, ***The Provincial Government of the Mughals, 1526-1658*** (Allahabad: Kitabistan, 1941), p. 58; R. P. Tripathi, ***The Rise and Fall of the Mughal Empire*** (reprint edition, Allahabad: Central Book Depot, 1966), pp. 121-122.

[265] ***Navāb*** (Arabic nawwāb): a governor of a town, district, or province; a lord; a prince, a deputy, one who rules in place of another.

[266] ***Tekhāṇo*** (Persian tah-k͟hāna): a vault, a cellar, a room underground.

[267] ***Dīvāṇ*** (Persian dīwān): a minister or head of a department at either the state level or the provincial level. In seventeenth-century Mārvāṛ, the ***dīvāṇ*** was the chief minister over fiscal affairs and also performed military tasks on occasion.

the ***bagsīs***[268] and [thereby] have [them] make entreaties [and] requests [on Vīramde's behalf].

29. The Navāb had a son of fifteen [or] sixteen years. He would come outside to play for a short time.[269] Rāṭhoṛ Akhairāj Bhādāvat [and] the other Rajpūts as well all said: "Let us leave; we shall go away." Then Muṃhato Khīṃvo, [the son] of Lālo, said:

Vigat, 2:55

"There is no place to go back to. Driven from Mārvāṛ , we have come to Bāṃvaḷī, a hundred ***kos*** from Meṛto. In this region,[270] this Navāb has the full authority of the Pātsāh. There is no place for us to put our feet." Then the Rajpūts said: "What should be done?" Muṃhato Khīṃvo said: "I shall make one [more] attempt." [They said]: "Do as you think best." Then, in the morning, Muṃhato Khīṃvo kept the Rajpūts in the camp, placed a betrothal coconut[271] in a ***doykāṇṭhro***,[272] put in some satin cloth [and] four expensive silk cloths,[273] and himself took it to where the Navāb's son was playing. His men asked: "Who are you?" Muṃhato Khīṃvo said: "I am the servant of Rājā Vīramde, and Vīramde is the brother[274] of Rāv Mālde. He has become angry with Jodhpur and has come to the Navābjī. Rājā Vīramde has sent me to offer his daughter [in marriage] to the Mirjojī.[275] I have come with the betrothal coconut to make the ***sagāī***."[276] [The Navāb's son] heard the name of Rāv Mālde.

---

268 ***Bagsī*** (Persian bakhshī): "a paymaster, an officer whose special duty it was to keep an account of all disbursements connected with military tenures." H. H. Wilson, ***A Glossary of Judicial and Revenue Terms*** (1855; reprint edition, Delhi: Munshiram Manoharlal, 1968), p. 49.

269 ***Sāyto***: probably this word is derived from the Persian sā'at, "time; an hour; a short time, a little while; a minute; a moment." Platts, ***Dictionary***, p. 625.

270 ***Maṇḍaḷ***: a district, region, area, realm.

271 It was customary among Rajpūts to send a coconut (***nāḷer***) to the family of a prospective groom to express their willingness to betroth a daughter in marriage.

272 ***Doykāṇṭhro***: probably this word is a variant of ***dokāṭhro***, "possessing two sticks," evidently a name for a type of box or platform used to carry the betrothal coconut.

273 ***Mīsrū***: "a type of expensive silk cloth." Lāḷas, ***RSK***, 3:3:3757 (glossed under ***misru***). ***A'īn-ī-Akbari***, p. 100, notes that ***miṣrī*** is a type of silk cloth.

274 I.e., a kinsman of Mālde's; a fellow Rāṭhoṛ.

275 ***Mirjo*** (Persian mīrzā): a Muslim prince; a Muslim of high birth.

276 ***Sagāī***: betrothal; alliance of marriage between two families or clans (***kuḷ***, ***vaṃśa***).

Then he realized: "The betrothal coconut of the daughter of Rājā Vīramde, brother of Rāv Mālde, has come." The various important men near the Mirjo[277] offered [their] blessings: "They are very powerful men,[278] a Rājā [and] a Rāv. Today among the Hindus no one else has such a dynasty. The betrothal coconut has come to the Mirjojī from a very excellent place." The Mirjo was very pleased. He took [Muṃhato Khīṃvo] with him into the fort. The Mirjo had him sit by the main entrance and went into [the Navāb's quarters]. The servants of the Mirjo informed the Navāb: "Vīramde's *pradhān* has come, bringing the betrothal coconut of Rājā Vīramde, brother of Rāv Mālde." The Navāb was very pleased. He quickly summoned Muṃhato Khīṃvo into [his] presence. He honored the betrothal coconut. He gave him a *sirpāv*. Khīṃvo said: "Vīramde's brothers, who are *umrāv*s, are in [his] camp." [The Navāb] ordered: "Bring them; I will have them pay respects [to me]."[279] He sent a welcome to their camp. The Rajpūts said to Khīṃvo: "What are you doing? We do not understand this matter." Then Muṃhato Khīṃvo said: "I will answer to Vīramdejī about this matter." Then at dusk the *dīvān*, Rāṭhoṛ Akhairāj, and the other Rajpūts went to the *darbār*[280] [of the Navāb].

Vigat, 2:56

The Navāb summoned [them] into [his] presence and asked all about Rāṭhoṛ Vīramde. He allowed [Vīramde] to leave [his] carts in Bāṃvaḷī. He made out a *parvāno*[281] giving rulership rights to [some] *pargano*s. He gave all of them *sirpāv*s and dispatched them. He said: "May Vīramde come to me quickly. After Vīramde and I are [together] in one place, I shall write a petition to the Pātsāhjī just as [Vīramde] tells [me] to." After coming here,[282] they described everything in detail to Vīramdejī. Vīramdejī listened to [their] story and was pleased.

Within five or six days Rāṭhoṛ Vīramdejī, along with 400 horsemen, went to an audience with the Navāb. Vīramde told his whole story in detail to

---

[277] The text has *Navāb*, but presumably *Mirjo* is meant, as the Navāb was at this time inside the fort of Riṇthambhor. Possibly the implication is that the important men close to the Navāb, who at that time were looking after the Mirjo, offered their blessings.

[278] *Bunīyādī* (Persian bunyādī): literally, "men possessing a firm foundation (*bunyād*)," i.e., "strong men," "powerful men."

[279] *Nīmasyāṃ* in the text is an apparent misprint for *namāsyāṃ* (first person plural of *namāsṇo*, "to cause to bow down," "to have [someone] pay respects."

[280] *Darbār* (Persian): the hall of audience of a ruler.

[281] *Parvāno* (Persian parwāna): a written order addressed to a subordinate.

[282] I.e., back from the Navāb's *darbār* to where Vīramde was.

the Navāb. The Navāb had this story [and] all current news[283] delivered to the Pātsāhjī, then petitioned [him on Vīramde's behalf]. The Pātsāhjī's order came back: "You did a noble deed giving Vīramde Bāṃvaḷī; now give Rāṭhor Vīramde some expense money and quickly send [him] into my presence."

30. Afterward the Navāb sent Vīramde to the Pātsāh. Rāṭhoṛ Vīramde went to the ***dargāh***.[284] He paid respects to the Pātsāhjī.[285] He met with the ***dīvāṇ*** [and] the ***bagsīs***. He made known to the Pātsāhjī, together with the ***dīvāṇ*** [and] the ***bagsīs***, all the details about himself [and] Rāv Mālde. The Pātsāhjī was pleased with Rāṭhoṛ Vīramde. Even before this the Pātsāh had become irritated with Rāv Mālde, [for] at that time the ruler of Bīkāner[286] as well as Kuṃvar Bhīmrāj Jaitsīyot[287] [and] Muṃhato Nago[288] had also gone [to the Pātsāh] with complaints.[289] But Rāṭhoṛ Vīramde, a wily man, told the Pātsāh a thousand tales. He made the next battle appear easy.[290] The Pātsāh came to Agra from Sahasrām.[291] He made complete military preparations[292] and established a war-camp outside Agra.

---

[283] ***Sārī vākā***. ***Vākā*** probably is from the Arabic wāqi'a, "news," "intelligence."

[284] ***Dargāh*** (Persian): the court of a ruler, including the various departments of his administration and their heads.

[285] The Pātsāh whom Vīramde met was Sher Shāh Sūr, Afghan ruler of Delhi and north India, 1540-45.

[286] Bīkāvat Rāṭhoṛ Rāv Kalyāṇmal Jaitsīyot (no. 46), ruler of Bīkāner, ca. 1542-74.

[287] Bīkāvat Rāṭhoṛ Bhīmrāj Jaitsīyot (no. 47).

[288] Muṃhato Nago (no. 158).

[289] A local Rajpūt source mentions that Sher Shāh had once gone to Bīkāner during a period of difficulty (before he assumed the rulership of Delhi) and had come to know the family of Rāv Jaitsī Lūṇkaraṇot (no. 45; ruler of Bīkāner, ca. 1526-42), which gave him some personal assistance. Sher Shāh's extension of help now to Rāv Kalyāṇmal and Kuṃvar Bhīmrāj, who had come to Delhi with Muṃhato Nago, would indicate a personal reason for Sher Shāh's enmity for Rāv Mālde relating to Rāv Jaitsī's death and Mālde's conquest of Bīkāner in 1542. ***Daḷpat Vilās***, edited by Rāvat Sārasvat (Bīkāner: Sādūl Rājāsthānī Research Institute, 1960), pp. 4-5.

[290] ***Āglo māmlo sahal kar dikhāyo***: literally, "having made the next battle easy, caused [him] to see [it]."

[291] Sahasrām: a town in what is now Bihar State, located ninety miles southwest of Patna.

[292] ***Sulmān*** in the text evidently is an abbreviation of ***sūḷ-sāmān***, "[military] supplies."

31. The news reached Rāv Mālde also. The Rāv's messengers[293] went back and forth [summoning his *sāth*]. There were preparations for battle. The Pātsāh set out from Agra. The Pātsāh encamped at Hīḍvāṇ.[294] The Rāv also mounted up and came to Meṛto from Jodhpur.

Vigat, 2:57

At that time 80,000 horse[295] belonging to Rāv Mālde were assembled. The Pātsāh came to the vicinity of Mojābād.[296] Rāv Mālde came to Ajmer. The [opposing] camps drew nearer and nearer. ***Pradhān*s** mediated; no pact was made. ***Pradhān*s** mediated separately between Vīramde [and] Rāv Mālde. Men negotiated between Rāṭhoṛs Kūmpo [and] Jaito and created suspicion between master [and] servant.[297] Rāv Mālde moved the camp back twice. The Pātsāh's camp was on the near side of Samel.[298] The Rāv's camp was at Girrī.[299] Rāv

---

[293] ***Charo***: a single man, single rider. ***Charo*s** were sent to the ***ṭhākur*s** in the service of a ruler to summon them to battle.

[294] Hīḍvāṇ: a town seventy-five miles east-southeast of Jaipur (Hindaun on modern maps).

[295] According to Brahmadeva Prasad Ambashthya and V.S. Bhargava, who have explored both Middle Mārvāṛī and Persian chronicles, Rāv Mālde only had a force of 50,000 men at Samel. The local chronicles of Mārvāṛ disagree. Some record that Mālde had a force of 80,000, while others indicate that it was Sher Shāh who had an army of this size. The ***Tabaqāt-i-Akbarī*** states that Sher Shāh's army numbered 50,000; other Muslim sources do not specify its size, noting only that it was very large. The actual size of both armies at Samel remains in some doubt. 'Abbās Khān Sarwānī, ***Tārīkhi-i-Śer Śāhī***, translated by Brahmadeva Prasad Ambashthya (Patna: K. P. Jayaswal Research Institute, 1974), p. 662, "Aitihāsik Bātāṃ," p. 42; ***Bāṅkīdās***, p. 12; Bhargava, ***Marwar and the Mughal Emperors***, p. 29; Khwājah Nizāmuddīn Ahmad, ***The Tabaqāt-i-Akbarī of Khwājah Nizāmudīin Ahmad: A History of India from the early Musalman Invasions to the Thirty-sixth Year of the Reign of Akbar***, 3 vols., translated by B. De (Calcutta: Asiatic Society, 1927-40), 2:171; Mur***ārdān***, no. 2, p. 119; Ojhā, 4:1:302, n. 2.; Reu, 1:218; ***Vīr Vinod***, 2:810.

[296] Mojābād: the town Mozābād or Mozāmābād, situated forty-five miles northeast of Ajmer.

[297] I.e., between Rāv Mālde and Rāṭhoṛs Jaito and Kūmpo.

[298] Samel: a village located in the Arāvalī hills twenty-four miles southwest of Ajmer and twenty-three miles east of Jaitāraṇ. The site of the battle is indicated by Map 3, "Mārvāṛ Terrain of the Battle of Samel, 1544."

[299] Girrī: a village located ten miles west-southwest of Samel village and fifty miles from Ajmer. The village lies on the edge of the plains near the western side of the Arāvalī hills.

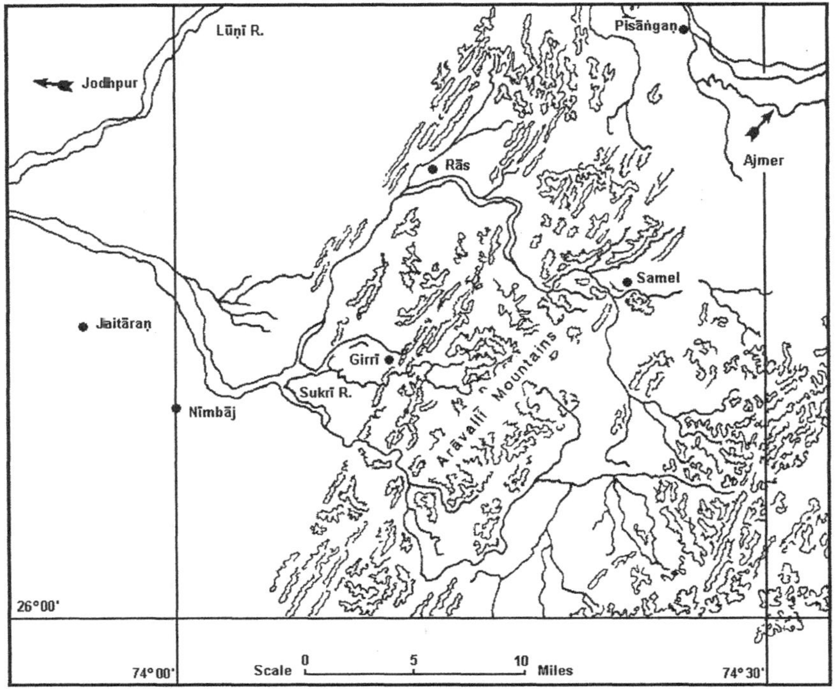

MAP 3. MĀRVĀṚ TERRAIN OF THE BATTLE OF SAMEL, 1544.

Mālde said to Kūmpo [and] Jaito: "Move the camp back once more." Then they said: "In the direction of the land beyond here [to the east] that the Rāvjī, a good son, had conquered, we did what the Rāvjī commanded. [But] we are not about to abandon and flee from the land beyond here [to the west] that your ancestors[300] and our ancestors together had conquered." There was much arguing[301] between the Rāv and the Rajpūts. Rāṭhoṛ Vīramde sent his Bārhaṭh, Pāto,[302] to the Rāv and had him tell [the Rāv] something. The Rāv, without having asked Jaito [and] Kūmpo [their advice], mounted a horse belonging to the guard-post and, when the night was a watch and a half spent, went away. Rāṭhoṛ Jaito Pañcāiṇot, Rāṭhoṛ Kūmpo Mahirājot, Rāṭhoṛ Khīṃvo,[303] Rāṭhoṛ Jaitsī Ūdāvat,[304] Sonagaro Akhairāj Riṇdhīrot,[305] Rāṭhoṛ Pañcāiṇ Karamsīyot,[306] Rāṭhoṛ Vīdo Bhārmalot,[307] and a large additional ***sāth*** as well, 20,000 men,[308] remained behind, ready to die. Another ***sāth*** left with the Rāvjī. In the morning the battle took place on the bank of the Samel River.[309] The ***ṭhākur***s mentioned above died fighting, along with 5,000 of Rāv Mālde's men.[310]

---

300 ***Māīt***: literally, "mother-father," used in Middle Mārvāṛī in the sense of "ancestors" or "respected elders," i.e., those persons whom one treats with the respect accorded one's mother and father.

301 ***Gāḍh***: stubbornness, firmness, argument.

302 Rohaṛīyo Cāraṇ Pāto Devāit. Meṛtīyo Rāv Dūdo Jodhāvat had granted Pāto the village Bījolī in Altavo Subdivision (***tapho***) of Meṛto Pargano (***Vigat***, 2:108).

303 Ūdāvat Rāṭhoṛ Khīṃvo Ūdāvat (no. 140).

304 Ūdāvat Rāṭhoṛ Jaitsī Ūdāvat (no. 139).

305 Sonagaro Cahuvāṇ Akhairāj Riṇdhīrot (no. 9).

306 Karamsot Rāṭhoṛ Pañcāiṇ Karamsīyot (no. 92).

307 Bālāvat Rāṭhoṛ Vīdo Bharmalot (no. 37).

308 Various numbers are given in the texts, ranging from 12,000 to 20,000 men. "Aitihāsik Bātāṃ," p. 44; Bhargava, ***Marwar and the Mughal Emperors***, p. 32; Reu, 1:130.

309 The battle of Samel between the forces of Rāv Mālde Gāṅgāvat, ruler of Jodhpur and western Rājasthān, and Sher Shāh Sūr, Afghan ruler of Delhi and north India, took place on January 5, 1544.

310 Various counts of the dead appear in the texts, ranging from 1,000 to 11,000 of Rāv Mālde's Rajpūts, plus a large number of Sher Shāh's troops. Most of the local chronicles contain a fairly detailed listing of the more important warriors of Rav Malde's who were killed. Appendix B contains a composite list compiled from the various sources.

32. Rāṭhoṛ Vīramde brought the Pātsāh to Jodhpur.[311] A small ***sāth***--Rāṭhoṛ Acḷo Sivrājot,[312] Rāṭhoṛ Tiloksī Varjāṅgot,[313] Bhāṭī Sāṅkar Sūrāvat,[314] Rāṭhoṛ Sīṅghaṇ Khetsīyot[315]--died fighting at the Jodhpur fort.[316]

33. The Pātsāh stayed in Jodhpur for some time. Then the Pātsāh, having stationed Saids[317] Hāsam [and] Kāsam[318] in Mārvāṛ and kept Khavās Khān[319] [there] as the only ***umrāv***,[320] set out from Jodhpur. He encamped in Meṛto.

---

[311] Sher Shāh had occupied Jodhpur by the end of January, 1544. Bhargava, ***Marwar and the Mughal Emperors***, p. 34.

[312] Jodho Rāṭhoṛ Acḷo Sivrājot (no. 80).

[313] The text has Tilok Sivrājot, which is incorrect. This Rajpūt was Ūdāvat (Baiṭhvāsīyo) Rāṭhoṛ Tiloksī Varjāṅgot (no. 143), whose name appears in other lists referring to the battle at the fort of Jodhpur.

[314] Jeso Bhāṭī Sāṅkar Sūrāvat (no. 2).

[315] Riṇmalot Rāṭhoṛ Sīṅghaṇ Khetsīyot (no. 129).

[316] The chronicles contain lists of varying length and completeness regarding those Rajpūts who died at the fort of Jodhpur fighting against the army of Sher Shāh. For a composite list, see Appendix B.

[317] Said (Arabic Saiyid): one who claims descent from the prophet Muḥammad.

[318] Hāsam and Kāsam: probably a reference to Saiyids Hāshim and Qāsim, sons of Saiyid Maḥmūd Khān of Barhā. Māḥmūd Khān was an important noble in the service of the Sūrs who subsequently switched his allegiance to the Mughals. He was the first of the famous Saiyids of Barhā to enter the service of the Mughal Emperors, and he became a personal favorite of Akbar's. Hāshim, Qāsim, and Aḥmad, Maḥmūd's brother, also were in Mughal service, and Maḥmūd, Hāshim, and Qāsim all took part in several Mughal military campaigns in Rājasthān, perhaps because they knew the region well from prior experience under Sher Shāh. ***Ā'īn-i-Akbari***, 1:424-425, 447, 461.

[319] Khavās Khān: the Afghan Khawāṣ Khān Masnād-ī-Ālī, one of Sher Shāh's most important knobles. Khawāṣ Khān first distinguished himself in the siege of Gaur in 1537. Subsequently he took part in the decisive battles fought by Sher Shāh against Humāyūn in 1539-40. He was placed in command of the ***sarkār*** of Sirhind after Sher Shāh's conquest of the Panjab and by the time of Sher Shāh's invasion of Mārvāṛ in 1543-44 had become the premier military commander in the service of the Sūr Emperor. 'Abbās Khān Sarwānī, ***Tārīkhi-i-Śer Śāhī***, pp. 261-262, 373-374, 377, 380, 445, 449-450, 455-456, 459, 465-467, 539, 600, 656-657.

[320] The ***Tārīkhi-i-Śer Śāhī*** notes that Sher Shāh left Khawāṣ Khān, Īsā Khān Niyāzī, and "certain other chiefs" in the region around Nāgaur. Khawāṣ Khān is said to have brought the regions of Nāgaur, Ajmer, and Mārvāṛ under his control. ***Ibid***., pp. 656-657.

Vigat, 2:58

34. Vīramde obtained Meṛto. Rāv Kalyāṇmal[321] obtained Bīkāner. The Pātsāh departed for Agra. While going to Agra,[322] he gave leave to Vīramde. Shortly thereafter Vīramde died.

35. Rāṭhoṛ Vīramde, born on November 19, 1477. The great battle occurred in January of 1544. In February or March of 1544 Vīramde passed away.[323]

The Cāraṇ[324] who mediated between Rāv Mālde [and Vīramde] was Vīramde's Bārhaṭh, Pāto. [A genealogy]:

1. Pāto.
2. Gāṅgo.
3. Jaimal.
4. Catro.
5. Mahes.

Once while Vīramde was [still] living Jaimal[325] had settled in the Pātsāh's ***vās***.[326] He obtained Muthrājī[327] in ***jāgīr***.[328-329]

---

[321] Bīkāvat Rāṭhoṛ Rāv Kalyāṇmal Jaitsīyot (no. 46), son of Rāv Jaitsī Lūṇkaraṇot (no. 45) and ruler of Bīkāner, ca. 1542-74.

[322] ***Āgre se jātāṃ***. The oblique form ***se*** (properly, ***sai***), from the adjective particle ***so*** ("like," "similar to"), is used in locative expressions of this type to add a slight degree of vagueness, as in the sentence ***mhai aṭhai sai dorāṃ chāṃ***: "we are raiding (literally, "running") hereabouts" (***Khyāt***, 3:125, line 1 at the top).

[323] ***Bāṅkīdās***, p. 60, gives the following dates for Vīramde:

Birth: V.S. 1534, ***Migsar***, ***Sudi*** 14 (November 19, 1477).
Death: V.S. 1600, ***Kātī*** (October-November, 1543).

[324] Cāraṇ (f. Cāraṇī): A person belonging to a ***jāti*** whose traditional occupation is the composition of poems and songs of praise in honor of heroes and rulers; a bard.

[325] Meṛtīyo Rāṭhoṛ Rāv Jaimal Vīramdevot (no. 107).

[326] ***Vās***: the town or village of residence of an important man; the residential area or ward of a ***jāti*** or group within a town or village. To settle in someone's ***vās*** meant to enter his service and place oneself under his protection.

[327] Muthrājī: probably the large town Mathurā, located thirty miles northwest of Āgrā

[328] ***Jāgīr*** (Persian): a technical term from the Mughal period designating an assignment of revenue on land based on moveable or prebendal tenure.

36. After Vīramde died, the Meṛtīyos met and gave the throne to Rāṭhoṛ Jaimal Vīramdevot. The Pātsāhjī also gave [Jaimal] Meṛto in ***jāgīr***. For ten years Rāṭhoṛ Jaimal enjoyed Meṛto in peace.

37. For three years Rāv Mālde lived on the mountain of Pīplāṇ[330] during a period of distress.[331] In 1546-47[332] the Sūr Pātsāh died. The Pātsāh's people who were the garrison in the fort of Jodhpur left the fort empty and went to Khavās Khān Masādalī.[333] They went to Khavāspur.[334] Back [in Jodhpur] the fort lay vacant. The Māḷīs[335] of Maṇḍor[336] received the news [that] the fort was vacant. Then the Māḷīs entered [the fort]. They sent the news to the Rāvjī at Pīplāṇ.

---

[329] The two sentences beginning with "once" and ending with ***jāgīr*** are found only in the ***kha*** ms.

[330] Sher Shāh's death occurred on May 22, 1545, some one and one-half years after the conquest of Jodhpur. During this period, Rāv Mālde apparently went first to Sīvāṇo, where he stayed in the fort and hills nearby, then travelled in southern Mārvāṛ near Jāḷor and Parbatsar collecting men and materials. ***Vigat***, 2:252, states that Mālde lived for awhile on the large hill or mountain (***vaḍo bhākar***) of Pīplāṇ, a village four or five miles southwest of Sīvāṇo, during the Muslim occupation of Jodhpur. While there, he had a fort and a tank, the Rāytaḷāv, constructed on the mountain. Ojhā, 4:1:308; Reu, 1:132, ***Vigat***, 1:180; ***Vīr Vinod***, 2:811.

[331] ***Vikho***: a period of distress during which a Rajpūt must leave his homeland. A ***vikho*** may occur during a military occupation, as in Rāv Mālde's case, or because of local adversities such as famine. Implied in the term are confusion of order and rank, as Rajpūts without land may be forced to take up new occupations. For an extended discussion of the ***vikho***, see Ziegler, "Action, Power and Service ...," pp. 112-126, and ***idem***, "Some notes on Rajpūt Loyalties during the Mughal Period," in ***Kingship and Authority in South Asia***, edited by John Richards (Publication no. 3, [Madison]: [Dept. of] South Asian Studies, University of Wisconsin-Madison, 1978), pp. 236-237.

[332] The date given in the text, V.S. 1603 (1546-47) is incorrect. Sher Shāh died in 1545.

[333] Masādalī: a corruption of Masnad-ī-'Alī, "Throne of 'Alī," a title held by a number of Sher Shāh's nobles, including Khawāṣ Khān.

[334] Khavāspur: the village Khuvāspuro of Meṛto Pargano, located forty-five miles northeast of Jodhpur. The ***Tārīkhi-i-Śer Śāhī***, p. 657, states that Khawāṣ Khān built a "city" called Khawāṣpuro near the fort of Jodhpur.

[335] Māḷī (f. Māḷaṇ/Māḷṇī): a person of the gardener ***jāti***.

[336] Maṇḍor: a town situated five miles north of Jodhpur. Maṇḍor was the original seat of Rāṭhoṛ rule in Mārvāṛ.

38. The Rāv came to the fort. Five or six years passed, then, on March 21, 1554,[337] Rāv Mālde once again attacked Merto. A battle occurred between Jaimal and Rāv Mālde at the Kuṇḍal [Tank].[338] There was a twist of fate. The Rāvjī lost the battle; Jaimal won.

Vigat, 2:59

The following ***sāth*** of the Rāvjī's died fighting:

1. Rāṭhoṛ Prithīrāj Jaitāvat.[339]
1. Rāṭhoṛ Dhano Bhārmalot.[340]
1. Sīndhal Ḍūṅgarsī.[341]
1. Pañcolī Abho.[342]
1. Sohaṛ Pītho Jesāvat.[343]

---

[337] V.S. 1610, ***Vaisākh***, ***Vadi*** 2, the date also given by "Aitihāsik Bāṭāṃ," p. 48, ***Bāṅkīdās***, p. 13, and ***Vigat***, 1:59. The ***kha*** ms. gives the date V.S. 1610, ***Vaisākh***, ***Vadi*** 12 (March 30, 1554). Other dates given for this battle are:

> (a) ***Śrāvaṇādi*** V.S. 1610 (***Caitrādi*** V.S. 1611), ***Vaisākh***, ***Sudi*** 2 (April 4, 1554). ***Jodhpur Rājya kī Khyāt***, p. 87; ***Murārdān***, no. 2, p. 131; Ojhā, 4:1:316, n. 2.
> (b) V.S. 1610. Reu, 1:134.

The Meṛtīyos had formed an alliance with Rāṭhoṛ Rāv Kalyāṇmal Jaitsīyot (no. 46) of Bīkāner (ca. 1542-74) at this time, and he came to their aid during the battle. Ojhā, 4:1:315; ***Vīr Vinod***, 2:811.

[338] Kuṇḍal: an ancient tank in Meṛto. See ***Vigat***, 2:38.

[339] Jaitāvat Rāṭhoṛ Prithīrāj Jaitāvat (no. 63).

[340] Bālāvat Rāṭhoṛ Dhano Bhārmalot (no. 39).

[341] Sīndhal Rāṭhoṛ Ḍūṅgarsī (no. 133).

[342] Pañcolī Abho Jhājhāvat (no. 161), one of Rāv Mālde's ***kāmdārs***.

[343] Sohaṛ Rāṭhoṛ Pītho Jesāvat. Variant lists present this individual as "Pītho Jagāvat" and Pītho Jasvantot (see ***Bāṅkīdās***, p. 13, and ***Vigat***, 1:59, respectively). We have found no other information concerning Pītho. According to G. D. Sharma, the Sohaṛ Rāṭhoṛs stem from Sohaṛ, great-grandson of Dhāndhal, son of Rāv Āsthān Sīhāvat. Rāv Āsthān was the Rāṭhoṛ ruler of Kheṛ, a village sixty-two miles southwest of Jodhpur, and the son of Sīho Setrāmot (d. ca. 1273), the founding ancestor of the Mārvāṛ Rāṭhoṛs. J. S. Gahlot states that Sobhat Salkhāvat, son of Salkho Tīḍāvat, a fourteenth-century Rāṭhoṛ ruler, was the progenitor of the Sohaṛ Rāṭhoṛs. "Jodhpur Hukūmat rī Bahī," p. 145, n. 1; J. S. Gahlot, ***Mārvāṛ kā Saṅkṣipt Itihās*** (Jodhpur: Gahlot Bindery Works, n.d.), pp 81-82.

1. Rāṭhoṛ Nago Bhārmalot.[344]
1. Rāṭhoṛ Jagmāl Udaikaraṇot.[345]
1. Cahuvāṇ Megho.[346]
1. Pañcolīs Rato [and] Neto.[347]
1. Rāṭhoṛ Sūjo Tejsīyot.[348]

39. Six persons, Rāṭhoṛ Jaimal's Rajpūts, died fighting:

1. Rāṭhoṛ Akhairāj Bhādāvat.[349]
1. Rāṭhoṛ Moṭo Jogāvat.[350]
1. Rāṭhoṛ Narāiṇdās, [son] of Candrāv.[351]
1. Rāṭhoṛ Candrāv, [son] of Jodho.[352]
1. Rāvat Sagto, [son] of Sāṅgo.[353]
1. Rāṭhoṛ Sāṅgo, [son] of Bhojo.[354]

40. In the year 1557, on January 24,[355] discord arose between Hājī Khān[356] and Rāṇo[357] Udaisiṅgh.[358] Rāv Mālde helped Hājī Khān. He provided

---

[344] Bālāvat Rāṭhoṛ Nago Bhārmalot (no. 38).

[345] Karamsot Rāṭhoṛ Jagmāl Udaikaraṇot (no. 91).

[346] Sācoro Cahuvāṇ Megho Bhairavdāsot (no. 8).

[347] The text has Rato and Neto; the ***kha*** ms. omits Neto. A variant list presents only Rato's name. Rato (no. 163) and Neto (no. 162) were sons of Pañcolī Abho Jhājhāvat (no. 161; see n. 342 for ***Vigat***, 2:59, ***supra***).

[348] The ***kha*** ms. presents this name as "Rāṭhoṛ Sūjo Netsiṃhot"; another list gives "Rāṭhoṛ Sūjo Jaitsiṅghot" (***Bāṅkīdās***, p. 13). The name is obscure, and we have not been able to trace it to a particular Rāṭhoṛ branch (***sākh***).

[349] Jaitmālot Rāṭhoṛ Akhairāj Bhādāvat (no. 69).

[350] Jaitmālot Rāṭhoṛ Moṭo Jogāvat (no. 79).

[351] Jaitmālot Rāṭhoṛ Narāiṇdās Candrāvat (no. 75).

[352] Jaitmālot Rāṭhoṛ Candrāv Jodhāvat (no. 74).

[353] We have been unable to identify this Jaitmālot Rāṭhoṛ with certainty. Possibly he was the son of Jaitmālot Rāṭhoṛ Sāṅgo Bhojvat, ***infra***.

[354] Jaitmālot Rāṭhoṛ Sāṅgo Bhojāvat (no. 77).

[355] The date given is the date of the subsequent battle of Harmāṛo between Hājī Khān and Rāṇo Udaisiṅgh.

[356] Hājī Khān was a noble of Sher Shāh Sūr's (see note 375 for ***Vigat***, 2:60, ***infra***).

1,500 horsemen: Rāṭhoṛ Devīdās Jaitāvat,[359] Rāvaḷ[360] Meghrāj Hāpāvat,[361] Rāṭhoṛ Jagmāl Vīramdevot,[362] Rāṭhoṛ Jaitmāl Jesāvat,[363] Rāṭhoṛ Lakhmaṇ Bhadāvat[364]--a large ***sāth***--and sent [them to Hājī Khān]. On Rāṇo Udaisiṅgh's side also so many Hindūs--with some military servants [and] some ***sagos***[365]--came and assembled:

Vigat, 2:60

1. Rāṇo Udaisiṅgh.
1. Jaimal Vīramdevot, Meṛtīyo Rāṭhoṛ.
1. Rāvaḷ Pratāp, master of Vāṃsvāḷo.[366]
1. Rāvaḷ Rāmcand Solaṅkī, master [of] Toḍaṛī.[367]

---

[357] Rāṇo: A title held by several Rajpūt rulers in middle period Rājasthān, including the Sīsodīyos of Mevāṛ, the Rāṭhoṛs of Sīvāṇo, the Sāṅkhlo Paṃvārs of Rūṇ, the Paṛihāṛs of Maṇḍor, and the Soḍho Paṃvārs of Umarkoṭ (in modern Sindh). Rāṇo is also a personal name (e.g., Rāṇo Akhairājot).

[358] Sīsodīyo Gahlot Rāṇo Udaisiṅgh Sāṅgāvat (no. 17), ruler of Mevāṛ, ca. 1537-72.

[359] Jaitāvat Rāṭhoṛ Devīdās Jaitāvat (no. 65).

[360] Rāvaḷ: a title held by several Rajpūt rulers of middle period Rājasthān, including the Rāṭhoṛs of Mahevo, the Bhāṭīs of Jaisaḷmer, the Āhāṛo Gahlots of Ḍūṅgarpur, and the Āhāṛo Gahlots of Vāṃsvāḷo.

[361] Maheco Rāṭhoṛ Rāvaḷ Meghrāj Hāpāvat (no. 103), ruler of Mahevo (western Mārvāṛ).

[362] Meṛtīyo Rāṭhoṛ Jagmāl Vīramdevot (no. 124).

[363] Cāmpāvat Rāṭhoṛ Jaitmāl Jesāvat (no. 49).

[364] Akhairājot Rāṭhoṛ Lakhmaṇ Bhadāvat (no. 33).

[365] ***Sago***: a relation by marriage; one to whom one gives or from whom receives a daughter or daughters in marriage.

[366] Āhāṛo Gahlot Rāval Pratāpsiṅgh Jaisiṅghot (no. 12), ruler of Vāṃsvāḷo ca. 1550-79. The territory of Vāṃsvāḷo lies directly to the south of Mevāṛ.

[367] "Aitihāsik Bāṭāṃ," p. 51, calls this ruler "Rāv Rāmcand [of] Toḍo"; ***Bāṅkīdās***, p. 14, refers to him as "Rāv Ramcandra of Toḍarī." Naiṇsī (***Khyāt***, 1:280) notes that there were branches of the Solaṅkī Rajpūt family (***kuḷ***) at both Toḍo (the Bālhaṇot Solaṅkīs) and Toḍaṛī (the Mahilgot Solaṅkīs). The title of ***rāv*** was held by the ruling lines of both branches. Naiṇsī's genealogy of the Mahilgot branch does not include a Rāv Rāmcand, so perhaps he was a Bālhaṇot Solaṅkī from Toḍo, located sixty-five miles south-southwest of Ajmer, on the northeastern edge of Mevāṛ. Toḍaṛī lies sixty miles southeast of Ajmer, near Tonk city.

1. Rāv Kalyāṇmal, master of Bīkāner.
1. Rāvaḷ Āskaraṇ, master of Ḍūṅgarpur.[368]
1. Rāv Surjan, master of Būndī.[369]
1. Rāv Durgo, master of Rāmpuro.[370]
1. Rāv Narāyaṇdās Īḍarīyo.[371]
1. Rām Khairāṛo, master of Jājpur.[372]
1. Rāvat[373] Tejo, master of Devaḷīyo.[374]

This battle occurred in Harmāṛo.[375] It occurred twelve ***kos*** from Ajmer. Rāṇo Udaisiṅgh fled. Rāṭhoṛ Tejsī Ḍūṅgarsīyot[376] [and] Bālīso Sūjo Sāṃvatot,[377]

---

[368] Āhāṛo Gahlot Rāvaḷ Āskaraṇ Prithīrājot (no. 11), ruler of Ḍūṅgarpur ca. 1549-80. Ḍūṅgarpur is located to the south of Mevāṛ and directly west of Vāṃsvāḷo.

[369] Hāḍo Cahuvāṇ Rāv Surjan Urjaṇot (no. 6), ruler of Būndī ca. 1554-85. Būndī town lies ninety-five miles southeast of Ajmer.

[370] Candrāvat Sīsodīyo Rāv Durgo Acḷāvat (no. 18), ruler of Rāmpuro. The territory of Rāmpuro lies east of Mevāṛ; Rāmpuro town is 145 miles south-southeast of Ajmer.

[371] Īḍareco Rāṭhoṛ Rāv Narāyaṇdās Pūñjāvat (no. 60), ruler of Īḍar. The territory of Īḍar lies to the southwest of Mevāṛ and is directly west of Ḍūṅgarpur.

[372] Solaṅkī Rām Khairāṛo, ruler of Jājpur (modern Jahāzpur). Very little information is available concerning Rām. He and (his brother?) Kūmbho founded the city of Jājpur in southern Rājasthān, located seventy miles south-east of Ajmer. "Aitihāsik Bāṭāṃ," p. 51; ***Bāṅkīdās***, pp. 13-14; ***Khyāt***, 1:279-280; ***Vigat***, 2:60.

[373] Rāvat: A title held by a large number of petty rulers, both Rajpūt and non-Rajpūt, in middle period Rājasthān.

[374] Sīsodīyo Gahlot Rāvat Tejo Bīkāvat (no. 16), ruler of Devaḷīyo ca. 1564-93. Devaḷīyo town is situated seventy-two miles southeast of Ajmer.

[375] The battle of Harmāṛo took place on January 24, 1557. Harmāṛo is located fifty-five miles south-southwest of Ajmer and six miles south of Vadhnor. It is said that the battle was precipitated by a quarrel that broke out between Rāṇo Udaisiṅgh Sāṅgāvat, Sīsodīyo ruler of Mevāṛ, ca. 1537-72, and Hājī Khān, a noble of Sher Shāh Sūr's, over the Rāṇo's demand for one of Hājī Khān's dancing girls.

With the conquest of Jodhpur, Sher Shāh had stationed Hājī Khān at the garrison of Bhāṅgesar (ten miles northwest of Sojhat) during the occupation of Mārvāṛ. Hājī Khān proceeded to launch his own conquest of the area upon Sher Shāh's death in 1545, and moved against Ajmer and Nāgaur in 1556 with the aid of both Sīsodīyo Rāṇo Udaisiṅgh Sāṅgāvat of Mevāṛ and Rāṭhoṛ Rāv Kalyāṇmal Jaitsīyot of Bīkāner. The alliance was short-lived, however, and broke up soon after Ajmer, Nāgaur, and surrounding territories were occupied. When Hājī Khān left Mārvāṛ for Gujarat with 5,000 horse and 150 war elephants in train, Rāṇo Udaisiṅgh stopped him with a large force of his own Rajpūts, demanding spoils from his recent conquests, including among

famous ***umrāv***s of the Rāṇo's, died fighting. Bālīso Sūjo remained [on the battlefield, killed] by the hand of Rāṭhoṛ Devīdās Jaitāvat. The Rāvjī's ***sāth*** was very noble. Hājī Khān won the battle. Rāv Māldejī had come and stayed in Jaitāraṇ[378] in order to send forth this army. The news reached the Rāvjī: "The Rāṇo fled; Hājī Khān won."

41. The Rāvjī was preparing to go against Meṛto. Just then the Rāvjī's spies, who had gone to Meṛto, brought news: "Rāṭhoṛ Jaimal's men, who were ***vasī*** Rajpūts, all fled during the night and went to the Rāṇo's territories or to Bīkāner [and] Ḍhūṇḍhāṛ."[379] The Rāvjī proceeded to Meṛto from Jaitāraṇ on January 27, 1557.[380] [His] authority was established there. Afterward the Rāvjī thoroughly despised the Meṛtīyos.[381] He knocked down the homes of the Meṛtīyos, made a level field [of them], had [them] plowed under, and had radishes sown [there].[382]

Vigat, 2:61

Afterward, in 1558-59, he had [the construction of] the Mālgaḍh[383] begun. In 1560-61 it was completed.[384] He kept a garrison--Rāṭhoṛ Devīdās Jaitāvat with a great ***sāth***--in the Mālgaḍh.

---

other things one of his dancing girls. Hājī Khān then appealed to Rāv Mālde for aid, promising Ajmer in return.

Rāv Mālde had captured the garrison of Bhāṅgesar from Hājī Khān's men left in Mārvāṛ on the death of Sher Shāh in 1545. "Aitihāsik Bāṭāṃ, p. 50; ***Akbar Nāma***, 2:72; ***Bāṅkīdās***, p. 14; Ojhā, 4:1:319-320; Reu, 1:136-137; Tirmizi, ***Ajmer through Inscriptions***, p. 12; ***Vigat***, 1:63.

[376] Ūdāvat Rāṭhoṛ Tejsī Ḍūṅgarsīyot (no. 138).

[377] Bālīso Cahuvāṇ Sūjo Sāṃvatot (no. 4).

[378] Jaitāraṇ: a town located fifty-six miles east of Jodhpur.

[379] Ḍhūṇḍhāṛ: the name for the territory around Āmber and Jaipur.

[380] January 27, 1557 = V.S. 1613, ***Phāguṇ***, ***Vadi*** 12, the date preferred by Ojhā, 4:1:320, for Rāv Mālde's conquest of Meṛto, also given by ***Vigat***, 1:60, and by ***Jodhpur Rājya kī Khyāt***, p. 89. ***Vigat***, 1:65 and 2:60 have V.S. 1613, ***Phāguṇ***, ***Sudi*** 12 = February 10, 1557.

[381] ***Rāvjī rai Meṛtīyāṃ suṃ kas ghaṇo huto***. ***Kas*** (Arabic qaṣ'): "despising, treating with contempt." F. Steingass, ***A Comprehensive Persian-English Dictionary*** (reprint edition, New Delhi: Oriental Books Reprint Corporation, 1973), p. 973.

[382] ***Mūḷā bavāṛīyā***. The radish is a symbol for anything worthless or good for nothing. Platts, ***Dictionary***, p. 1094.

[383] The name of this fort appears as both Mālgaḍh and Mālkoṭ in the ***Vigat*** and other texts from this period. We have standardized the name in our translation, using

42. On July 28, 1559, he gave half of Meṛto [Pargano] to Rāṭhoṛ Jagmāl Vīramdevot in *paṭo*. A copy of this [*paṭo*]:[385]

List:

Thirteen [villages including] Nīlīyāṃ:

1. Nīlīyāṃ.
1. Īṭāvo.
1. Mherasṇī.
1. Goṭhṛo.
2. Vās Makāmpā.
1. Barno.
1. Vāvaḷalo.
1. Nībṛī.

....

(The above document tore. I have had the [names of the] villages following below copied from another document.)[386]

1. Rāhaṇ.
1. Hīrādṛo.
1. Ākelī.
1. Cāndāruṇ.
1. Pālṛī.
1. Dhanāpo.
1. Khīndāvṛo.
1. Gonarṛo.
1. Pālṛī Sīndhaḷe.
1. Lāmbo.
1. Altavo.
1. Durgāvās.
1. Gothṛī.
1. Vagaṛ.
1. Ghagharṇo.
1. Phālko.
1. Bhīmḷīyo.
1. Īṭāvo Khīyāṃ ro.
1. Nathāvro.
1. Bollo.
1. Kurlāī.

Mālgaḍh to avoid confusion. Tod, ***Annals and Antiquities of Rajasthan***, 2:856-857, notes that the Mālgaḍh lies "about a gun-shot to the south-west of the town and encloses an area of a mile and a half."

[384] There is general agreement on dates for the start and the completion of the Mālgaḍh fort in Meṛto. One source ("Aitihāsik Bāṭāṃ, p. 52) gives a more detailed date for the start, March 1, 1558. ***Bāṅkīdās***, p. 15; Ojhā, 4:1:320; ***Vigat***, 1:60.

[385] The villages listed are shown on Maps 4A-B, "***Paṭo*** of Meṛtīyo Jagmāl Vīramdevot, 1559." Problems of identification are discussed in Appendix C.

[386] This sentence is a parenthetical remark by the copyist of the ***kha*** ms.

MAP 4A

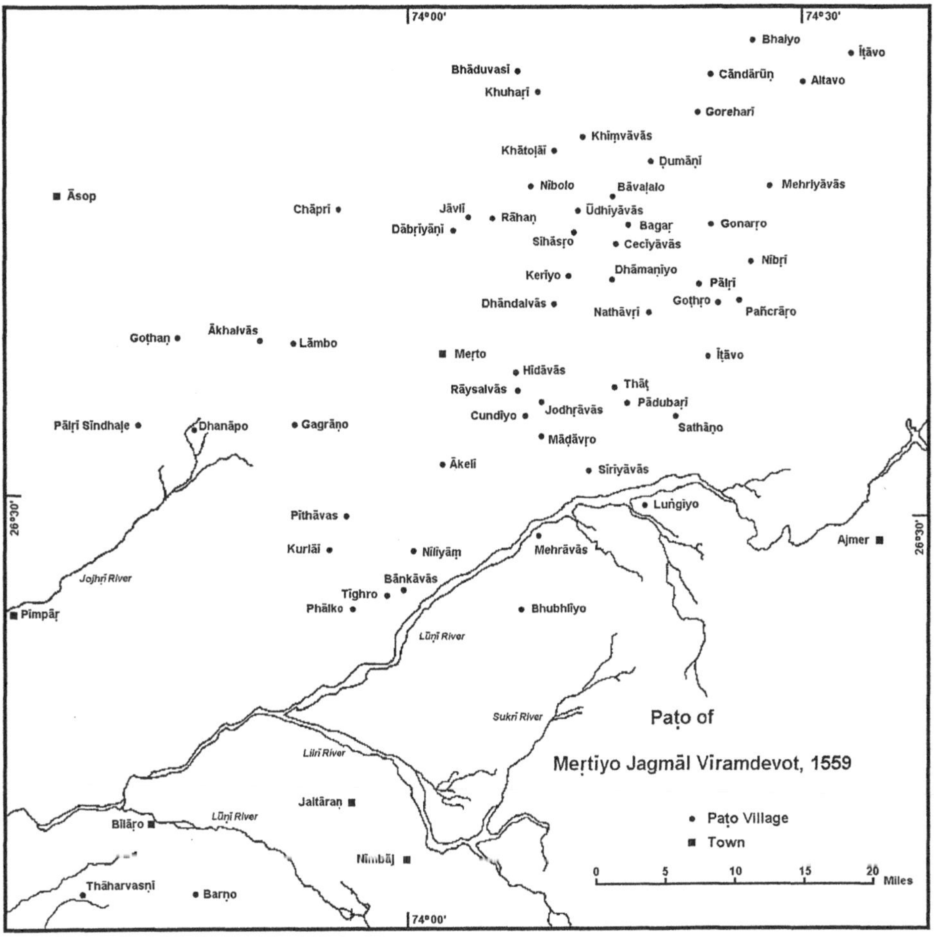

MAP 4A. PAṬO Of MEṚTĪYO JAGMĀL VĪRAMDEVOT, 1559

MAP 4B

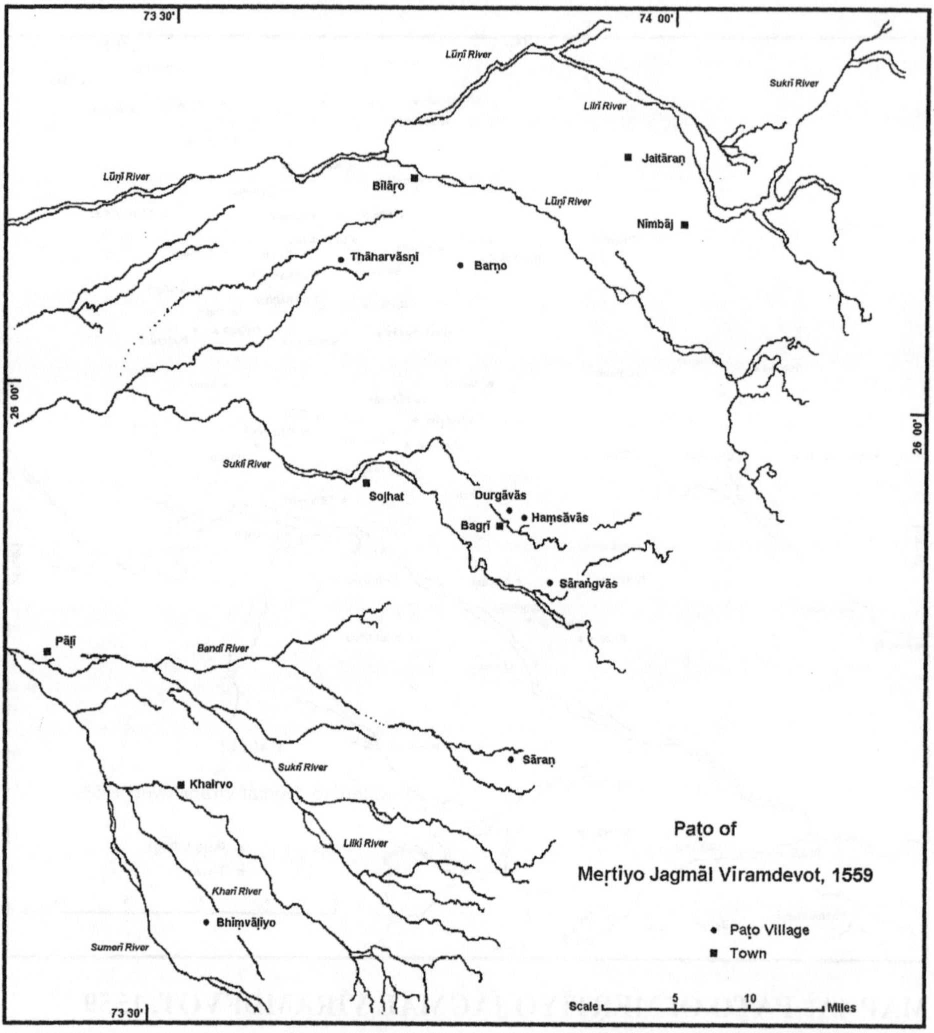

MAP 4B. PAṬO Of MEṚTĪYO JAGMĀL VĪRAMDEVOT, 1559

Vigat, 2:62

1. Ānolī.
1. Pīthāvas.
1. Julāṇo.
1. Goṭhaṇ.
1. Sarṇu.
1. Dābṛīyāṇī.
1. Ūdhīyāvas.
1. Pāñcīyāvas.
1. Chāprī.
1. Cocīyāvas.
1. Dhāmaṇīyo.
1. Ḍumāṇī.
1. Pādubaṛī.
1. Gorharī.
1. Luṅgīyo.
1. Hīdāvas.
1. Kālṇī.
1. Bhāduvasṇī.
1. Khīdāvas.
1. Dhāndalvās.
1. ....
1. Pacīplo.
1. Cundhīyāṃ.
1. Tīghrīyo.
1. Māṅkīyāvas.
1. Sāyarvas.
1. Rāysalvās.
1. Khuhaṛī.
1. Jāvlī.
1. Bhaiyo.
1. Jodhṛāvas.
1. Khāteḷāī.
1. Hāsāvas.
1. Vākhalvas.
1. Sathāṇo.
1. Kerīyo.
1. Thāṭi.
1. Maḍāvro.
1. Thāharvasṇī.
1. Sāraṅgvāsṇī.
1. Sirīyārī[387] of Sojhat.
1. ....

[Subtotal]: 58.
[Total]: 71.[388]

[Mālde] set up a second arrangement, given below, to which he had [Jagmāl][389] swear a ***devaco***[390] in the temple of Mahāmāyā[391] at Phaḷodhī.[392] He

---

[387] Sīyārī in the ***kha*** ms.

[388] The numbers 58 and 71 are given in the text. Apparently the intent was to divide the villages into two groups: those connected with Nīlīyāṃ (13) and those not (58). However, only nine villages are in the Nīlīyāṃ group and sixty-one, not fifty-eight, are in the second group. Possibly some of these sixty-one should be included in the Nīlīyāṃ group. The grand total is seventy instead of seventy-one.

[389] Mālde had made Meṛtīyo Jagmāl Vīramdevot ***kiledār*** of the Meṛto fort (the Mālgaḍh) at the time he granted him the villages in ***paṭo*** (see B.N. no. 124 for Jagmāl). Devīdās Jaitāvat served alongside Jagmāl as commander of the troups of the garrison.

[390] ***Devaco***: an oath sworn in the name of a god or goddess. Such an oath need not be sworn in a temple, although that is the case in this passage.

[391] Mahāmāyā: the transcendant power of illusion personified as the goddess Mahāmāyā, who is also identified with Durgā. Margaret and James Stutley, ***Harper's Dictionary of Hinduism***, p. 171.

swore [the ***devaco***] in front of Kuṃvar Candrasen,[393] Māṅglīyo Vīram,[394] Cahuvāṇ Jhāñjhaṇ,[395] and Pañcolī Neto.[396]

Vigat, 2:63

He swore [the ***devaco***] standing at the side of Rāṭhoṛ Jaitmāl Pañcāiṇot[397] [and] Purohit Bhānīdās.[398] Jagmāl swore the ***devaco*** to the following arrangement:[399]

[1]. He would never turn [his] back on the Rāvjī or Kuṃvar Candrasen.

[2]. [He][400] would not retain Rāṭhoṛ[401] Cāndo Vīramdevot[402] [or] Rāṭhoṛ Vāgh Jagmālot[403] in [his] ***vās***.

---

[392] Phaḷodhī: the village Phaḷodhī of Meṛto Pargano, situated nine miles northwest of Meṛto.

[393] Candrasen Māldevot, son of Rāv Mālde Gāṅgāvat and ruler of Jodhpur, 1562-81.

[394] Māṅglīyo Gahlot Vīram Devāvat (no. 14). Vīram held the position of ***hujdār*** in Rāv Mālde's service.

[395] Sācoro Cahuvāṇ Jhāñjhaṇ Bhairavdāsot (no. 7).

[396] Pañcolī Neto Abhāvat (no. 162), the son of Pañcolī Abho Jhajhāvat (no. 161), a ***kāmdār*** of Rāv Mālde's. ***Vigat***, 2:59, lists Pañcolī Neto as having been killed at the battle of Meṛto in 1554 against Meṛtīyo Rāṭhoṛ Jaimal Vīramdevot, along with his father Abho and his brother Rato.

[397] Meṛtīyo Rāṭhoṛ Jaitmāl Pañcāiṇot (no. 127) was the son of Pañcāiṇ Dūdāvat and the grandson of Dūdo Jodhāvat.

[398] The Brāhmaṇ Purohit Bhānīdās Tejsīyot Sīvaṛ, to whom Meṛtīyo Rāṭhoṛ Jagmāl Vīramdevot gave one-half of the village Cāṃvaḍīyo of Meṛto Pargano.

[399] The text includes items 5-8 of our enumeration under Section no. **43**. We have not included this section number in order to retain the unity of the passage.

[400] The text has ***na rākho*** ("you won't retain"), an apparent misprint for ***na rākhai*** ("he would not retain").

[401] The text has ***Rāv***, but there is no other indication that Cāndo ever held this title. Probably ***Rāv*** is a mistake for ***Ra.***, the standard abbreviation for Rāṭhoṛ.

[402] Meṛtīyo Rāṭhoṛ Cāndo Vīramdevot (no. 123).

[403] Meṛtīyo Rāṭhoṛ Vāgh Jagmālot (no. 125).

[3]. He would not retain any military servant of the Rāvjī's without orders.

[4]. The grain of [each] Mahājan[404] who comes back [to Meṛto] has been buried; of this, three portions belong to [Mālde], one portion of the grain belongs to the owners [of the grain].

[5]. [Each] Rajpūt of Jagmāl's now will reside in Meṛto; after one year, [conditions] being peaceful, he will go to the village of [his] ***paṭo*** and reside.

[6]. Māṅglīyo Vīram, a ***hujdār*** of [Rāv Mālde's], will stay in Meṛto.

[7]. Then the fort will come down. They[405] will retain the moat. They will tear apart two tanks, the Kuṇḍal [and] the Kukso.

[8]. [Mālde's] ***kāmdar***s will make a camp in the city and live [there].

(The name of the Kalyāṇsar Tank was Kukso).[406]

44. [Mālde's men] levelled the entire village of Meṛto; they made fields of the [former] rulers' homes. They had established a [new] settlement,[407] a city near the Dorāṇī Nāḍī.[408] [People] say [the old settlement] had become various ruins.[409] They had given the city the name "Navo Nagar" ("New Town").

45. On February 10, 1557,[410] Meṛto had come into the Rāvjī's hands. It stayed [his] for five years, one month, [and] three days.[411] Subsequently, during

---

[404] Mahājan: literally, "great man." The name of a division of the Vāṇīyo ***jāti***; a grain merchant.

[405] The subject of this and the following sentence is unspecified; presumably the Rāv's officials in the city are the agents.

[406] A parenthetical remark inserted by the author or by the copyist.

[407] ***Vāsvāṇo***. Lāḷas, ***RSK***, 4:2:4640, merely glosses this word as "a place to live." ***Vāṇo/vāhṇo*** is a fairly common noun in Middle Mārvāṛī, defined by Lāḷas, ***RSK***, 4:2:4583, as: (1) "a collection of water-vessels kept on a vehicle for bringing water"; (2) "the method or act of bringing water by the above means." Possibly one could translate the sentence in the ***Vigat*** as "They had established a [new] settlement [and] water supply, a city near the Dorāṇī Nāḍī."

[408] ***Nāḍī***: a small tank.

[409] The text has ***vaīk***, evidently a misprint for ***kaīk*** ("several," "various").

[410] February 10, 1557 = V.S. 1613, ***Phāguṇ***, ***Sudi*** 12, the date also given by ***Vigat***, 1:65. Concerning the date of Rāv Mālde's conquest of Meṛto, see n. 380, ***supra***.

the year 1562, Rāṭhoṛ Jaimal Vāramdevot went to the *dargāh* again. The Pātsāhjī[412] gave [him] Meṛto. He sent in aid the Mughal Saraphdīn[413] with 7,000 horse. The Rāvjī received the news [that] the Pātsāh's army was approaching. Rāṭhoṛ Devīdās Jaitāvat always stayed at the garrison in the Mālgaḍh of Meṛto. Upon [receiving] the news [of the advancing army], the Rāvjī sent Kuṃvar Candrasen, Rāṭhoṛ Prithīrāj Kūmpāvat,[414] Sonagaro Mānsiṅgh,[415] Rāṭhoṛ Sāṃvaḷdās,[416] and an additional *sāth*, along with 2,000 horsemen.

Vigat, 2:64

[Mālde] said [to them]: "If you see some opportunity[417] for a [successful] battle, then you should do battle. If not, then take Rāṭhoṛ Devīdās [with you] and come [back] here." These *ṭhākurs* came to Meṛto. The Pātsāhjī's army was powerful; they moved the camp back. Rāṭhoṛ Devīdās Jaitāvat, along with a large *sāth*,[418] turned around[419] and entered the Mālgaḍh. The Mughals and Jaimal came and camped, besieging the Mālgaḍh. Kuṃvar Candrasen's camp was [at Sātaḷvās and Indāvaṛ].[420] Sāṃvaḷdās came back [to Meṛto from there] and fell upon the

---

[411] According to Ojhā, 4:1:320, Rāv Mālde captured Meṛto from Jaimal Vīramdevot on V.S. 1613, *Phāguṇ*, *Vadi* 12 = January 27, 1557, and held it until shortly after the beginning of Akbar's seventh regnal year, which began on March 11, 1562. See also *Akbar Nāma*, 2:247.

[412] The Mughal Emperor Akbar (1556-1603).

[413] Mīrzā Sharafu'd-Dīn Ḥusayn, a descendant of Timur through his mother and hence a very distant relation of the Mughal Emperor Akbar. He was an important noble of Akbar's, acquiring a rank of 5,000 in Mughal service. In 1560, Akbar gave Sharafu'd - Dīn his sister Bakhshī Bānū Begum in marriage and made him governor of Ajmer and Nāgaur, a position he held at the time of the Mughal attack on Meṛto. *Ā'īn-ī-Akbarī*, 1:339-340, *Akbar Nāma*, 2:196-197.

[414] Kūmpāvat Rāṭhoṛ Prithīrāj Kūmpāvat (no. 97).

[415] Sonagaro Cahuvāṇ Mānsiṅgh Akhairājot (no. 10).

[416] Varsiṅghot Meṛtīyo Rāṭhoṛ Sāṃvaḷdās Udaisiṅghot (no. 152).

[417] *Gam*: probably from the Sanskrit word *gama*, "a going," "a course," "a road," and by extension, "a way," "a chance," "an opportunity."

[418] *Akbar Nāma*, 2:248, notes that the Rajpūt force was about 500 warriors.

[419] I.e., Devīdās refused to take part in the retreat; he turned around and entered the Mālgaḍh in order to confront the Mughals.

[420] This sentence, literally "Candrasen's camp became/was," is incomplete. "Aitihāsik Bātāṃ," p. 53, states that Candrasen moved the camp back to Sātaḷvās and Indāvaṛ,

[Mughal] camp.[421] [He and his men] killed a hundred Mughals. Sāṃvaḷdās's leg was struck by a weapon. Then Rāṭhoṛ Sāṃvaḷdās's Rajpūts took [him] and left [the battlefield]. Rāṭhoṛ Jaimal [and] Saraphdīn rode after [them]. They caught up to [them] after coming fourteen *kos*.[422] There Sāṃvaḷdās turned around[423] [to face them] and died fighting in noble fashion.

46. [The Mughals] besieged the Mālgaḍh. There were assaults[424] [on the fort]. Rāv Mālde's letters were continually coming to Devīdās, [saying]: "You certainly are making a name for yourself, [but] you are causing the loss of my *ṭhākurāī*."[425] [The Mughals] besieged the fort on January 27, 1562.[426] A tower exploded from a mine.[427] So Rāṭhoṛ Devīdās made a pact with the

---

villages lying within four miles of each other and four and eight miles respectively to the southwest of Meṛto.

[421] Once again the account in "Aitihāsik Bātāṃ," pp. 53-54, is more detailed. This source states that Sāṃvaḷdās remained behind after Candrasen had gone back to Jodhpur and carried out a night attack on the Mughal army surrounding Meṛto.

[422] According to "Aitihāsik Bātāṃ," p. 54, Sāṃvaḷdās proceeded in the direction of Reyāṃ village, located fifteen or sixteen miles southeast of Meṛto. It was near this village that the battle took place.

[423] ***Vaḷ nai*** in the ***kha*** ms. is preferable to ***nai*** in the text.

[424] ***Ḍhovo***: an assault upon a fortified position. Cf. ***Khyāt***, 2:26, 50, 56, 83, 108.

[425] ***Ṭhākurāī***: the quality or essence of a ***ṭhākur***; rulership, sovereignty, authority, kingdom, domain.

[426] January 27, 1562 = V.S. 1618, ***Phāguṇ***, ***Vadi*** 7 (see also ***Jodhpur Rājya kī Khyāt***, p. 92). Apparently the siege began on this date ("Aitihāsik Bātāṃ," p. 55, give the alternate date V.S 1619, ***Phāguṇ***, ***Vadi Amāvas*** = February 22, 1563, which is incorrect). Mughal operations against Meṛto ended with the annihilation of Rāv Mālde's ***sāth*** under the command of Devīdās Jaitāvat near Sātaḷvās on V.S. 1618, ***Cait***, ***Sudi*** 15 = March 20, 1562, a date given by several sources, including ***Bāṅkīdās***, p. 17 (twice), and ***Vigat***, 1:61, 2:65-66. Variant dates include: V.S. 1618, ***Cait***, ***Sudi*** 2 = March 7, 1562 (***Jodhpur Rājya kī Khyāt***, p. 92); V.S. 1618, ***Cait***, ***Sudi*** 5 = March 10, 1562 (***Bāṅkīdās***, p. 16); V.S. 1619 ***Cait***, ***Sudi*** 2 = March 7, 1562, ***Caitrādi*** reckoning, or March 26, 1563, ***Śrāvaṇādi*** reckoning ("Aitihāsik Bātāṃ," p. 55); V.S. 1619, ***Cait***, ***Sudi*** 5 = March 29, 1563, ***Śrāvaṇādi*** reckoning (***Vigat***, 1:61, n. 3); V.S. 1619, ***Cait***, ***Sudi*** 15 = March 20, 1562, ***Caitrādi*** reckoning, or April 8, 1563, ***Śrāvaṇādi*** reckoning ("Aitihāsik Bātāṃ," p. 55).

[427] ***Sābāt*** (Arabic sābāṭ): a covered approachway protecting the besiegers attempting to mine the towers or walls of a fortress; a mine. ***Akbar Nāma***, 2:248-249, gives the following description of the Mughal advance and their attack on the fort at Meṛto:

> When the army of victory arrived at the town the soldiers travel-stained as they were and with their swift coursers all in a sweat donned the armour of endeavor and upreared the flag of daring and without hesitation advanced to

Mughals and withdrew from [the fort].[428] The Mughal Saraphdīn [and] Rāṭhoṛ Jaimal were seated on the ***khāndho***[429] of the main gate [of the fort]. A footsoldier was in front of[430] Rāṭhoṛ Devīdās. In his hands was a gun,[431] a personal possession of the Rāvjī's. A Mughal laid [his] hands on it. Devīdās had a ***kaṛīyāḷī*** stick[432] in [his] hands; he struck [the Mughal] a blow on the head with the stick near Rāṭhoṛ Jaimal [and] Saraphdīn. [The Mughal's] brains gushed out and ran down toward [his] nose. Rāṭhoṛ Jaimal said to Saraphdīn: "Devīdās is leaving [the fort] through the door of ***dharma***,[433] [as] you saw well."[434]

---

the foot of the fortress. The garrison [of Rajputs] crept into the fort of fear and did not venture to come out. Meanwhile four champion horsemen of the army advanced the foot of boldness and discharged some arrows against the gate of the fortress. Suddenly the Rajputs became restless under the discharge of arrows and come out on the walls. They made the battlements their shields and discharged confusedly bricks, stones, arrows and bullets, and also boiling pitch. Two of the horsemen obtained martyrdom and the other two came back wounded. Muḥammad Sharafu-d-Dīn Ḥusain and the other officer saw wisdom in proceeding slowly and so they established themselves in the city of Mīrthā and stations here and there. They applied thought and deliberation to the business of taking the fort and cautiously invested it. They erected batteries according to the proper rules and drove mines on various sides of the fort. The garrison opposed them and everyday there were hot engagements. Occasionally, they watched their opportunity and made sallies, and after showing their valour again withdrew themselves. At length, a mine, which had been carried up to under the tower was filled with gunpowder and set fire to. The tower fell to pieces like cotton when it is carded and a great breach was made. The heroes of fortune's army got an open road for battle and rushed on.

428 Both Jagmāl Vīramdevot and Devīdās Jaitāvat made an agreement with the Mughals after much deliberation to relinquish the fort and leave all property behind. Jagmāl did leave with a small contingent, while Devīdās set fire to the property and emerged from the fort with several hundred Rajpūts to confront the Mughal army.

429 ***Khāndho***: a wall standing out from the main wall and blocking or covering the main gate of a fort in order to shelter the entrance from direct attack.

430 ***Devīdās rai moṇḍai āgai***: literally, "before the face of Devīdās." One could also translate this fragment as "under Devīdas's supervision."

431 The text has ***bardukh***; the ***kha*** ms. ***bandakī***. The correct reading probably should be ***bandukh***, a Middle Mārvāṛī form of the Arabic word bandūq, "gun."

432 ***Kaṛīyāḷī gedi*** in the ***kha*** ms. is preferable to ***kaṛīyā lāgai*** in the text. A ***kaṛīyāḷī*** stick was a type of wooden stick banded with metal rings (***kaṛī***).

433 ***Devīdās dharam duār nīsrai chai***. ***Dharma dvār nīsarṇo***: to leave/go out through the door of ***dharma***, i.e., to leave a besieged fort with one's life intact after making a pact with the enemy. Cf. "Aitihāsik Bātāṃ," p. 55; James Tod, ***Annals and Antiquities of Rajasthan***, edited by William Crooke, 3 vols. (London: Oxford University Press,

Saraphdīn said: "I saw!" Jaimal began to speak: "He is not the sort of Rajpūt who abandons a fort and goes away, but Rāv Mālde was telling him: 'You are causing the loss of my domain.' [Devīdās] is going unwillingly. If he reached Jodhpur, he would get Rāv Mālde and attack [us] during the night."[435]

Vigat, 2:65

47. Saying these things took time. In the interim Rāṭhoṛ Devīdās went 200 paces. Then Saraphdīn said to Jaimal: "What should be done?" Jaimal said: "If you wish [to preserve] our safety, then catch up to Devīdās from behind and kill him."[436] Then the kettledrum was struck.[437] Rāṭhoṛ Jaimal [and] Mughal Saraphdīn rode after [Devīdās]. Devīdās and the Rāv's ***sāth***, hearing the striking of the kettledrum, turned around and stood waiting [for Jaimal and Saraphdīn]. A battle occurred on this side of Sātaḷvas[438] on March 20, 1562. A list of the Rāv's ***sāth*** that died fighting, as follows:[439]

1. Rāṭhoṛ Devīdās Jaitāvat, in [his] thirty-fifth year.[440]

1920), 2:1006; ***Vigat***, 2:219. The connotation is not quite honorable, as the remark by Jaimal following in the text indicates.

[434] The reading ***ruṛā dīṭhā*** in the ***kha*** ms. is preferable to ***uḍdoge*** (?) in the text.

[435] ***Rāv Mālde nuṃ rāt āpāṛ ūpar āvsī***: literally, "he would catch up to Rāv Mālde and attack during the night."

[436] The ***Akbar Nāma***, 2:249, notes that Rāṭhoṛ Jaimal Vīramdevot and other Rajpūts present with the Mughals had an old quarrel with Devīdās Jaitāvat and the Rajpūts of the garrison (perhaps a reference to Devīdās's participation in the battle of Harmāṛo and the subsequent occupation of Meṛto). After Devīdās burned the property of the fort (see n. 428 to ***Vigat***, 2:64, ***supra***), they considered the agreement with the Mughals broken and urged the Mughals to attack.

[437] ***Tarai nagāro huo***. ***Nagāro hoṇo*** is a synonym for ***nagāro vajṇo***, "kettledrum to be struck." The kettledrum was struck to announce the commencement of battle or attack.

[438] Sātaḷvas: a village located four miles southwest of Meṛto. Reu, 1:140, mentions that the battle took place between Meṛto and the village of Sogāvas [Sodhāvas], located one mile due west of Meṛto.

[439] The chronicles contain lists of varying length and completeness regarding those Rajpūts who died at the battle of Sātaḷvas. For a composite list, see Appendix B.

[440] The ***Akbar Nāma*** contains a story about Devīdās that also appears in the ***khyāt*** literature about this Rajpūt. This story relates that Devīdās was indeed not killed at Meṛto, but only wounded, and that he survived and appeared locally some ten to twelve years later in the dress of a wandering holy man. See B.N., no. 65. "Aitihāsik Bātāṃ," pp. 83-84; ***Akbar Nāma***, 2:250; "Bāt Rāṭhoṛ Deīdās Jaitāvat rī," in ***Aitihāsik***

1. Rāṭhoṛ Bhākharsī Jaitāvat.[441]
1. Rāṭhoṛ Pūraṇmal, [son] of Prithīrāj Jaitāvat.[442]
1. Rāṭhoṛ Tejsī, [son] of Urjan Pañcāiṇot.[443]
1. Rāṭhoṛ Īsardās, [son] of Rāṇo Akhairājot.[444]
1. Rāṭhoṛ Goind, [son] of Rāṇo Akhairājot.[445]
1. Rāṭhoṛ Pato, [son] of Kūmpo Mahirājot.[446]
1. Rāṭhoṛ Bhāṇ, [son] of Bhojrāj, [who was the son] of Sādo Rūpāvat.[447]
1. Rāṭhoṛ Amro Rāmāvat.[448]
1. Rāṭhoṛ Netsī Sīhāvat.[449]
1. Rāṭhoṛ Jaimal Tejsīyot.[450]
1. Rāṭhoṛ Rāmo Bhairavdāsot.[451]
1. Rāṭhoṛ Bhākharsī Ḍūṅgarsīyot.[452]
1. Rāṭhoṛ Acḷo Bhāṇot.[453]
1. Rāṭhoṛ Mahes Pañcāiṇot.[454]

Tavārīkhvār Vārtā (MS no. 1234, Rājasthānī Śodh Saṃsthān, Caupāsnī), ff. 71-74; Reu, 1:139, n. 2.

[441] Jaitāvat Rāṭhoṛ Bhākharsī Jaitāvat (no. 66).

[442] Jaitāvat Rāṭhoṛ Pūraṇmal Prithīrājot (no. 64).

[443] Akhairājot Rāṭhoṛ Tejsī Urjanot (no. 34).

[444] Akhairājot Rāṭhoṛ Īsardās Rāṇāvat (no. 30).

[445] Akhairājot Rāṭhoṛ Goind Rāṇāvat (no. 29).

[446] Kūmpāvat Rāṭhoṛ Pato Kūmpāvat (no. 96).

[447] Riṇmalot Rāṭhoṛ Bhāṇ Bhojrājot (no. 130). ***Rūpāvat*** in the ***kha*** ms. is preferable to ***Kūmpāvat*** in the text.

[448] Cāmpāvat Rāṭhoṛ Amro Rāmāvat (no. 51).

[449] Akhairājot Rāṭhoṛ Netsī Sīhāvat (no. 36). ***Bāṅkīdās***, p. 16, lists him as Tejsī Sīhāvat, and on p. 17, has Netsī Sodāvat.

[450] We have been unable to identify this Rāṭhoṛ with any certainty. He is listed as Jaimal Jaitsīyot in the ***kha*** ms.

[451] Cāmpāvat Rāṭhoṛ Rāmo Bhairavdāsot (no. 50).

[452] Jodho Rāṭhoṛ Bhākharsī Ḍūṅgarsīyot (no. 81).

[453] We have been unable to identify this Rāṭhoṛ with certainty. He probably was the son of Bhāṇ Bhojrājot (see n. 447, ***supra***).

[454] Karamsot Rāṭhoṛ Mahes Pañcāiṇot (no. 93).

Vigat, 2:66

1. Meṛtīyo Rāṭhoṛ Jaitmāl, [son] of Pañcāiṇ Dūdāvat.[455]
1. Rāṭhoṛ Riṇdhīr Rāysiṅghot.[456]
1. Rāṭhoṛ Sāṅgo Riṇdhīrot.[457]
1. Rāṭhoṛ Īsar Gharsīyot.[458]
1. Rāṭhoṛ Rāṇo Jagnāthot.[459]
1. Bhāṭī Pirāg Bhārmalot.[460]
1. Māṅglīyo Dedo.[461]
1. Rāṭhoṛ Mahes Gharsīyot.[462]
1. Rāṭhoṛ Rājsiṅgh Gharsīyot.[463]
1. Māṅglīyo Vīram.[464]
1. Sāṅkhlo Tejsī.[465]
1. Bhāṭī Tiloksī.[466]

---

[455] Meṛtīyo Rāṭhoṛ Jaitmāl Pañcāiṇot (no. 127).

[456] This Rāṭhoṛ is listed as Riṇdhīr Rāysalot in the ***kha*** ms. ***Vigat***, 1:62, says that he was a military servant of Meṛtīyo Jagmāl Vīramdevot. We have been unable to identify him with certainty.

[457] This Rāṭhoṛ probably was the son of Riṇdhīr Rāysiṅghot (see no. 456, ***supra***).

[458] Cūṇḍāvat Rāṭhoṛ Īsar Gharsīyot (no. 57). The identity of this Rajpūt is uncertain, but he appears to be the brother of Rāṭhoṛ Mahes Gharsīyot, ***infra***.

[459] We have been unable to identify this Rāṭhoṛ.

[460] Bhāṭī Pirāg Bhārmalot was the son of Bhārmal Jesāvat, a descendant of Rāvaḷ Dūdo of Jaisaḷmer (early fourteenth century). ***Khyāt***, 2:66, states that Pūno, Rāvaḷ Dūdo's grandson, died fighting in a battle at Cāṅg village during the time of Rāv Riṇmal of Maṇḍor (ca. 1427-38). Subsequently the family of Puno's son, Jaito, became military servants in the service of Jodhpur. Pirāg Bhārmalot was fifth in descent from Jaito. ***Vigat***, 1:62, also lists Pirāg among those killed at Sātaḷvas.

[461] Māṅglīyo Gahlot Dedo (no. 13).

[462] Cūṇḍāvat Rāṭhoṛ Mahes Gharsīyot (no. 58).

[463] Cūṇḍāvat Rāṛhoṛ Rājsiṅgh Gharsīyot (no. 59).

[464] Māṅglīyo Gahlot Vīram Devāvat (no. 14).

[465] Sāṅkhlo Paṃvār Tejsī Bhojāvat (no. 27).

[466] Jeso Bhāṭī Tiloksī Parbatot (no. 3).

1. Bhāṭī Pītho.[467]
3. Bārhaṭhs: 1. Jālap. 1. Jīvo. 1. Colo.[468]
1. A Turk, Hamjo.[469]
1. A Sutrār, Bhānīdās.[470]

48. Afterward, Rāv Mālde formed no army [to attack] Meṛto. Eight months thereafter, on November 7, 1562, Rāv Mālde passed away.[471] Rāv Candrasen sat on the throne.[472] Candrasen's brothers, ***grāsīyos***,[473] attacked [him].[474] There was enmity between the Rajpūts, the Riṇmals,[475] and Rāv [Candrasen]. Rāv Candrasen did not take the name of Meṛto.

---

[467] Jeso Bhāṭī Pītho Āṇandot (no. 1).

[468] We have no additional information concerning these three Cāraṇs.

[469] The term Turk (***Turak***) was used in seventeenth century texts from Mārvāṛ to indicate a Muslim soldier, not necessarily one of Turkish extraction (for example, even Rajpūts who converted to Islam were called "Turks"). Cf. ***Khyāt***, 1:89. We have no information concerning Hamjo.

[470] Sutrār (f. Sutrārī/Sutārī): a carpenter. We have no additional information concerning Bhānīdās.

[471] Rāv Mālde's date of death, V.S. 1619, ***Kātī, Sudi 12*** = November 7, 1562 is generally agreed upon as given in the text. ***Vigat***, 1:42, says that he ruled thirty-one years. ***Jodhpur Rājya kī Khyāt***, p. 76; Ojhā, 4:1:325; Reu, 1:141; ***Vigat***, 1:42. . ***Bāṅkīdās***, p. 18, has V.S. 1619, ***Kātī, Sudi 15*** = November 10, 1562.

[472] Rāv Candrasen Māldevot (1562-81) was Rāv Mālde's chosen successor. According to most sources, he ascended the throne of Jodhpur on December 31, 1562 (V.S. 1619, ***Pos, Sudi*** 6). "Aitihāsik Bātāṃ," p. 78; ***Jodhpur Rājya kī Khyāt***, p. 104; Ojhā, 4:1:332-333. ***Bāṅkīdās***, p. 20, has V.S. 1618, ***Pos, Sudi*** 6 = December 12, 1561 (incorrect); Reu, 1:148, gives the date November 11, 1562 (V.S. 1619, ***Mṛgsar, Vadi*** 1).

[473] ***Grāsīyo***: a holder of a share of land (***grās***); a bandit, a robber. Though chosen successor of Rāv Mālde, Rāv Candrasen was not unanimously accepted as ruler of Jodhpur. Factions quickly developed around Candrasen's elder uterine brother, Udaisiṅgh (later the Moṭo Rājā of Jodhpur, 1583-95), who held Phaḷodhī in northern Mārvāṛ in ***paṭo*** from Rāv Mālde (confirmed at Candrasen's accession), and Rām Māldevot, an elder half-brother whom Rāv Mālde had banished from Mārvāṛ, and who coveted rulership over Sojhat. Upon accession, Candrasen held just the three areas of Sojhat, Jodhpur proper, and Jaitāraṇ. Jaitāraṇ was then under the Ūdāvat Rāṭhoṛs, who were military servants of the Jodhpur rulers. The presence of the Mughals and their intervention locally added much to the confusion and turmoil. Rām Māldevot shortly thereafter received Sojhat from the Mughals and consolidated his control there with their assistance. "Aitihasik Bātāṃ," pp. 78-79; ***Bāṅkīdās***, pp. 20-21; ***Murārdān***, no. 2, pp. 154-158, 176; ***Vigat***, 1:67-68.

[474] ***Jor lāgā***: literally, "were forcefully fastened/attached [to him]."

[49]. On March 20, 1562, Rāṭhoṛ Devīdās Jaitāvat died fighting. Very soon thereafter Rāv Mālde passed away. Jaimal enjoyed [the rule of] Meṛto, which he had obtained from the Pātsāh.[476]

Vigat, 2:67

Rāṭhoṛ Vīṭhaḷdās Jaimalot[477] was doing military service at the ***dargāh***. With Rāṭhoṛ Jaimal [ruling] in Meṛto, the Mughal Saraphdīn, having finished up the business involving Rāṭhoṛ Devīdās, quickly went to the ***dargāh***. There was much affection between Jaimal and Saraphdīn. While [Saraphdīn] was there,[478] he did much to tend to the personal affairs of Jaimal.[479] As he was doing so, an offense of Saraphdīn's came to the attention of the Pātsāh.[480] Saraphdīn fled

---

[475] Riṇmal: in the broadest sense, any Rāṭhoṛ descended from Rāv Riṇmal, ruler of Maṇḍor, ca. 1427-38. By the end of the sixteenth century, however, the term Riṇmal had come to indicate those Rāṭhoṛs who did not fall within a more restrictive classification, such as Jodho, Meṛtīyo, etc. See Vol. 2 under "Riṇmalot Rāṭhoṛs" for an extended discussion.

[476] Literally, "from the Pātsāh's side" (***Pātsāhī taraph***).

[477] Meṛtīyo Rāṭhoṛ Vīṭhaḷdās Jaimalot (no. 117). Vīṭhaḷdās was Jaimal Vīramdevot's son.

[478] "There" (***uṭhai***) refers to the Mughal court.

[479] "He did much to tend to the personal affairs of Jaimal" is a conjectural translation of ***Jaimal ro khasmāno ... ghaṇo karai chai***. ***Khasmāno*** is not to be found in either Lālas's or Sākariyā's dictionary; it is perhaps derived from the Arabic word k͟haṣmāna: "inimically; --like a good husband; economically; attending to domestic affairs; husbanding; --s.m. housewifery." Platts, ***Dictionary***, p. 490.

[480] Literally, "a defect/fault (***khāmī***) in Saraphdīn came to the Pātsāh's side." ***Khāmī*** is from the Persian word k͟hāmī, ""rawness, unripeness, immaturity; inexperience; imperfection, defect, fault." ***Ibid***., p. 485.

With the victory over Devīdās Jaitāvat, Meṛto and portions adjacent came under Mīrzā Sharafu'd-Dīn's control. Rāv Jaimal Vīramdevot held Meṛto in ***jāgīr*** at this time with his approval. According to the ***Ā'īn-ī-Akbarī***, the Mīrzā rebelled shortly after his return to Agra with Akbar, after the conquest of Meṛto and shortly after his own father had come to Agra and been received with great honor by Akbar. The Mīrzā's father, Khwāja Mu'īn, had been on a pilgrimage to Mecca. There was strain in the relationship between father and son, and the Mīrzā is said to have been suspicious of danger to himself, particularly after the fine welcome Akbar had given the Khwāja. Mīrzā Sharafu'd-Dīn fled Agra in October of 1562, going first to Ajmer and Nāgaur, his ***jāgīrs***, and then on to southern Mārvāṛ (Jāḷor) and Gujarat. In Gujarat, he remained for some time with a Gujarati noble, Changiz Khān, and then joined the rebellion of the Mīrzās against Akbar in 1572-73.

When Mīrzā Sharafu'd-Dīn rebelled, Akbar appointed Ḥusayn Qulī Khān ***jāgīrdār*** in his place and sent him to Nāgaur. The Mīrzā left Ajmer under the control of

from there; he brought Rāṭhoṛ Vīṭhaḷdās with him. Saraphdīn camped at the Ḍāṅgoḷāī.[481] Rāṭhoṛ Vīṭhaḷdās abruptly came to where Jaimal was seated in the ***darbār*** and remained standing. He [then] touched the feet [of Jaimal].[482] Jaimal, observing [Vīṭhaḷdās], grew worried. Quickly he rose from the ***darbār***, went into the ***mahal***s,[483] and asked [Vīṭhaḷdās]: "Why have you come?" Then Vīṭhaḷdās told Jaimal in detail the news of Saraphdīn.[484] Jaimal said: "You did wrong." [Vīṭhaḷdās] said: "It [was] unavoidable. There was no remedy [for what happened]." Then [Jaimal] asked: "Where is Saraphdīn?" [Vīṭhaḷdās] said: "He is camped[485] at the Ḍāṅgoḷāī." Jaimal went and met with Saraphdīn. They conversed. [Saraphdīn] said: "My men are in Nāgaur; send for them quickly."

50. Then Jaimal provided Rāṭhoṛ Sādūḷ Jaimalot[486] with a small ***sāth*** and also a few military servants of Saraphdīn's and sent them to Nāgaur. They went [there], took [Saraphdīn's] men from the fort, and sent [them] off. Sādūḷ was coming behind [them]; meanwhile, the Pātsāh's ***ahadhīs***[487] ran up from the post-station. They brought a ***pharmān***[488] to a certain ***jāgīrdār***[489] in Nāgaur:

---

a servant, Tarkhān Dīvāna, and fled to Jāḷor, which he held for a short time before proceeding to Gujarat. ***Ā'īn-ī-Akbarī***, 1:339-340; ***Akbar Nāma***, 2:302-305; R. P. Tripathi, ***The Rise and Fall of the Mughal Empire*** (reprint edition, Allahabad: Central Book Depot, 1966), pp. 186, 189.

[481] Ḍāṅgoḷāī: a tank near Ḍāṅgāvās, one of the three original wards (***vās***) of Meṛto town. See n. 30 to ***Vigat***, 2:39, ***supra***.

[482] ***Page lāgṇo***: to touch the feet [of someone], to show subordination [to someone].

[483] ***Mahal*** (Arabic maḥall): residence, palace; room or chamber of the residence of an important man; the wife or consort of a noble.

[484] ***Saraphdīn ro uvāko. Uvāko*** probably is derived from the Arabic wāqi'a, "news," "intelligence."

[485] Literally, "seated" (***baiṭho***).

[486] Meṛtīyo Rāṭhoṛ Sādūḷ Jaimalot (no. 108). Sādūḷ was Jaimal's son.

[487] ***Ahadhī*** (Arabic aḥadī): literally, "single man." A soldier under the Mughal Emperor Akbar's immediate orders who was paid in cash and held no ***jāgīr***. ***Ā'īn-ī-Akbarī***, 1:20, 255.

[488] ***Pharmān*** (Persian farmān): a royal decree, directive, or writ, issued to a subordinate from the hands of the Emperor only and requiring (under the Mughals) his seal for validity.

[489] ***Jāgīrdār*** (Persian): the holder of an assignment of revenue on land (***jāgīr***) during the Mughal period. This particular ***jāgīrdār*** perhaps was Ḥusayn Qulī Khān, assigned Nāgaur after the flight of Sharafu'd-Dīn (see n. 480 to ***Vigat***, 2:67, ***supra***).

"Saraphdīn has fled; Saraphdīn's men [in Nāgaur] cannot go." [The ***jāgīrdār***], a ***mansabdār***,[490] rode after [them] with two to four hundred horsemen. He caught up to [them] going into Meṛto. Saraphdīn's men reached Meṛto safely. Rāv[491] Sādūḷ Jaimalot was going along a fraction of a ***kos*** behind [them]. [The ***jāgīrdār*** and his horsemen] killed Sādūḷ along with forty [of his] men and turned back. Rāv Jaimal quickly gave leave to Saraphdīn. [Saraphdīn] perceived Rāṭhoṛ Jaimal's thoughts:

Vigat, 2:68

"My breach with the Pātsāh[492] is complete. First, Vīṭhaḷdās left and came from the ***dargāh*** with Saraphdīn; next, Sādūḷ was killed[493] in this way. There is no [safe] place left to talk [in Meṛto]."

51. In 1562-63 Jaimal went to Mevāṛ, abandoning Meṛto without a fight. The Rāṇo[494] gave [him] Vadhnor.[495] Afterward, on February 23, 1568, Akbar Pātsāh attacked Cītoṛ.[496] Rāṭhoṛ Jaimal died fighting then. Cāraṇs,

---

490 ***Mansabdār*** (Arabic manṣab plus the Persian suffix -dār): the holder of a ***mansab*** in the Mughal service. The term ***mansab*** (literally, "post," "office") designated a military rank and an office in the administrative service of the Mughal Empire. The rank consisted of both a personal or ***jāt*** (Arabic zāt) rank, which marked the status of a person among the nobles of the Empire, and a trooper or ***asvār*** (Persian suwār) rank, indicating the number of cavalrymen and horses an official or ***mansabdār*** was to maintain. All persons within the administrative system of the Empire were graded according to this rank order and given either military or civilian responsibilities. Payment on the basis of rank for duties performed was either in cash (***naqda***) or by an assignment of revenue on land (***jāgīr***).

491 The text has ***Rāv***, but this may be a mistake for ***Rā***., the abbreviation used for Rāṭhoṛ. No other source indicates Sādūḷ held the title of Rāv.

492 Literally, "with the Pātsāh's side" (***Pātsāhī taraph thā***).

493 ***Marāṇo*** in the text evidently is a mistake for ***mārāṇo*** ("was killed"), a perfect passive participle.

494 Sīsodīyo Gahlot Rāṇo Udaisiṅgh Sāṅgāvat (no. 17), ruler of Mevāṛ ca. 1537-72.

495 Vadhnor: a northern district of Mevāṛ with its headquarters at the town of the same name, located forty-seven miles south-southwest of Ajmer.

496 Ojhā notes that Akbar reached the plain before Cītoṛ and encamped on October 23, 1567, and soon thereafter ordered the investment of the fort. Smith states that Akbar formed his camp on October 20 and completed his investment of the fort in the course of a month. The date given in the text, February 23, 1568, is in fact the date of Jaimal Vīramdevot's death. While directing operations to mine the walls of Cīṭor, Akbar noticed a man dressed in a chief's cuirass standing at the breach in the wall and shot him. This man was Jaimal, who died from the wound. Ojhā and ***Vīr Vinod*** assert that he was shot in the leg and died shortly thereafter; A. L. Srivastava maintains that Jaimal

servants of the Meṛtīyos, say [that] Jaimal had gone to Cītoṛ from Vadhnor with 500 men. The five hundred men, of various ***sākhs***, had gone up into the fort. Their [Cāraṇs] speak as follows: "Jaimal died fighting with the five hundred men, but [just] 200 men of Jaimal's, Jaimal's ***sāth***, died fighting; [some of the other 300][497] men who also died fighting were Jaitmāl Rāṭhoṛs, great Rajpūts of [the Meṛtīyos]."

52. An account of Saraphdīn's becoming estranged from the ***dargāh***:[498] the Pātsāh's mother had gone on a pilgrimage to Mecca. He had sent Saraphdīn with the ***begam***.[499] There [in Mecca] a woman would have a viewing[500] of the ***pīrs***[501] [only] if she "tied the edges"[502] with a man, otherwise the ***mujāvar***[503]

---

was killed instantly and that Ojhā and ***Vīr Vinod*** are categorically wrong, but he does not indicate specifically where he learned otherwise. Jaimal's death much weakened the resistance of the Rajpūts against the Mughals.

Jaimal Vīramdevot died at Cītoṛ along with his brother, Īsardās Vīramdevot, and two close paternal relations, Meṛtīyo Rūpsī Surjaṇot and Meṛtīyo Karamcand Rāysalot. By all standards, Cītoṛ was an extremely bloody victory for the Mughals. In addition to some 8,000 Rajpūts and 1,000 musketeers, over 40,000 peasants and servants attached to the fort and the soldiers were killed in the battle. ***Murārdān***, no. 2, pp. 461-462, 507, 568, 572; Ojhā, 2:727-728; V. A. Smith, ***Akbar the Great Mogul, 1542-1605*** (second edition, 1927; reprint edition, Delhi: S. Chand & Co., 1966), p. 63; A. L. Srivastava, ***Akbar the Great***, vol. 1, ***Political History: 1542-1605 A.D.*** (second edition, Agra: Shiva Lala Agarwalla & Co., 1972), pp. 108-109; Tripathi, ***The Rise and Fall of the Mughal Empire***, p. 205; ***Vīr Vinod***, 2:80, 82.

[497] There is a gap in the text; we have supplied what seems to be a reasonable replacement for the missing words.

[498] For the rebellion of Sharafu'd-Dīn, see n. 480 to ***Vigat***, 2:67, ***supra***. The story given here is probably a good example of the inevitably garbled chain of communication, for it was the Mīrzā's father who had gone to Mecca and returned and who was close to Akbar. He has apparently become confused somehow with Akbar's mother in this story.

[499] ***Begam*** (Persian): "a title of Mughal ladies." Platts, ***Dictionary***, p. 210. Here, ***begam*** refers to the Pātsāh's mother.

[500] ***Darsaṇ***: a respectful glimpse or viewing of someone or something.

[501] ***Pīr*** (Persian): an old man; a saint; a spiritual guide.

[502] ***Cheṛo***: the upper edge of a woman's sari. The editor of the ***Vigat***, N. S. Bhāṭī, remarks (n. 5) that the edge of the wife's sari was tied to the husband's shoulder in order that the two might make a request of a ***devatā*** together, and he suggests that this custom is still current in Rājasthān. It is not known whether or not this was a custom among Muslims in the Mughal period, however.

[503] ***Mujāvar*** (Arabic mujāwir): the attendant at a Muslim shrine or mosque.

would not have [her] perform the viewing. The ***begam*** said to Saraphdīn: "You tie the edges with me." He objected very much, but the ***begam***, the Pātsāh's mother, tied the edges [of her garment] to [his] headdress and they made the pilgrimage.[504] They came [back]. The Pātsāh, who for some time disfavored [Saraphdīn], conspired against [him]. The Pātsāhjī was highly displeased [with Saraphdīn]. He began to speak: "First he was my slave; now he has become my father.[505] Summon [him] from wherever he is and tell [him] I will behead [him]." Saraphdīn's agent at court wrote and sent Saraphdīn this information. For this reason Saraphdīn fled.

Vigat, 2:69

53. Rāṭhoṛ Jaimal himself went with Saraphdīn as far as Sīrohī[506] in order to have him reach [there safely]. He told [his] ***bhāībandh*** back [in Meṛto]: "All of you must take the ***vasī***, go[507] to the lowland of Vadhnor, and stay [there]." Jaimal, returning [from Sīrohī], came to Vadhnor via Bāṛal.[508] Rāṇo Udaisiṅgh also had come [near Vadhnor] in the direction of the mountains of Rūpjī[509] [village] to hunt. He approached Jaimal, showed [him] favor, gave [him] Vadhnor, Karheṛo,[510] [and] Koṭhārīyo[511] [in grant], and retained [him] in his ***vās***, [Cītoṛ]. Rāṭhoṛ Jaimal died fighting in Cītoṛ. There occurred a period of distress in the land for the Rāṇo. The Rāṇo had given Rāṭhoṛs Surtāṇ[512] [and] Kesodās[513] the fort Bor[514] on a mountain three ***kos*** from the village Rūpjī.

---

504 Lāḷas, ***RSK***, 3:3:3655, interprets ***māṇḍ*** in this sentence as a variant of ***mauṛ***, "headdress." But it might be a variant of ***māṇḍāṃ***, "with force," "forcefully." If so, the translation would be as follows: "He objected very much, but the ***begam***, the Pātsāh's mother, forced [him] to tie the edges and they made the pilgrimage."

505 I.e., by tying edges with Akbar's mother, he usurped the father's role.

506 Sīrohī: a town ninety-five miles south of Jodhpur.

507 Literally, "come."

508 Bāṛal: we have been unable to locate this village on modern maps of Mevāṛ.

509 Rūpjī: the village Rūpnagar, located fifty miles north-northwest of Udaipur.

510 Karheṛo: a town forty-five miles north-northeast of Udaipur.

511 Koṭhārīyo: a town twenty-six miles north-northeast of Udaipur.

512 Meṛtīyo Rāṭhoṛ Surtāṇ Jaimalot (no. 113), son of Jaimal Vīramdevot. The text has Surtāṇ Kesodāsot, but this is a mistake. Kesodās was Surtāṇ's half-brother.

513 Meṛtīyo Rāṭhoṛ Kesodās Jaimalot (no. 119), son of Jaimal Vīramdevot.

514 The fort Bor is located five miles east of Rūpjī and forty-seven miles north of Udaipur.

Their[515] ***vasī*** remained there for some time. The Śrī Catarbhujjī[516] Temple, [which] the Meṛtīyos had constructed, is there.

54. Four or five years thereafter, Rāṭhoṛ Jaimal's sons, Rāṭhoṛs Surtāṇ [and] Kesodās, went to the ***dargāh***.[517] [The Pātsāh] did not give them Meṛto right away. For a while the Pātsāhjī gave Rāṭhoṛ Surtāṇ Jaimalot the ***pargano*** of Malārṇo[518] near Riṇthambhor in ***jāgīrī*** [tenure].[519] While [the Meṛtīyos] were staying in Malārṇo [Pargano], a fight broke out with ***bhomīyos***[520] living there [who were] ***kiledārs*** living in the main town (***kasbo***). Rāṭhoṛ Surtāṇ's servants, [about] one hundred men [who were] ***beldārs***,[521] killed a Turk who was a ***bhomīyo*** there.

55. I have heard a story like this: in 1580-81[522] or 1582-83, Rāṭhoṛ Surtāṇ Jaimalot obtained Sojhat [Pargano], given in ***jāgīr*** by the Pātsāh,[523] for a

---

515 The text has ***iṇ rī*** ("his"), but perhaps it should have ***iṇāṃ rī*** ("their"), since both Surtāṇ and Kesodās were in Bor.

516 Śrī Catarbhujjī: the four-armed manifestation of Viṣṇu and the patron deity of the Meṛtīyo Rāṭhoṛs. Tod, ***Annals and Antiquities of Rajasthan***, 1:331, n. 1.

517 The genealogy of the Meṛtīyos included in the ***Khyāt*** of Murārdān indicates that after Jaimal was killed at Cītoṛ, Akbar sent word via Kachvāho Rājā Bhagvantdās Bhārmalot to Meṛtīyo Surtāṇ Jaimalot in Mevāṛ, informing him that he would receive Meṛto upon his coming to the Mughal court and showing his obeisance to the Mughal throne. Surtāṇ is said to have sent word back that he would not leave the service of the Sīsodīyo Rāṇo for one year because this was against his ***dharma***.

In the meantime, Meṛtīyo Rāṭhoṛ Narhardās Īsardāsot (no. 120), Surtāṇ's paternal cousin, met with Akbar on behalf of Surtāṇ's half-brother, Kesodās. Akbar then granted one-half of Meṛto to Kesodās. Narhardās is said to have married his own sister, Purāṃ Bāī, to Akbar at this time (1568-69). Sometime later, Surtāṇ met with Akbar and received the other half of Meṛto in ***jāgīr***. After a few years, it was revoked and he was given Sojhat in ***jāgīr*** in 1578-79; he also held Malārṇo near Riṇthambhor. He obtained Meṛto originally in 1572-73. ***Murārdān***, no. 2, pp. 462-464; 471-472, 512-513; ***Vigat***, 1:389-390.

518 Malārṇo: a town twenty miles north of Riṇthambhor.

519 ***Jāgīrī*** (Persian): the technical term used to indicate the tenure of land held by a ***jāgīrdār***; relating to or pertaining to a ***jāgīr*** (see Glossary).

520 ***Bhomīyo***: literally, "one of the soil (***bhom***)"; a local; one who controls or asserts a dominant right over a small area of land.

521 ***Beldār***: a person belonging to a ***jāti*** whose traditional occupation is excavating.

522 The ***kha*** ms. gives the variant date 1581-82.

523 The text has ***Pātsāhī rī dīvī jāgīr***; evidently ***Pātsāhī*** is an abbreviation of ***Pātsāhī taraph***, the standard phrase in such contexts.

time.[524] During 1580-81, Rāṭhoṛ Surtāṇ went to the ***dargāh***. The Pātsāh[525] gave [Surtāṇ] Meṛto [Pargano]. When [Surtāṇ] was dividing villages among [the Meṛtīyos], discord arose with Rāṭhoṛ Narhardās Īsardāsot.[526] Narhardās was in the faction of Rāṭhoṛ Kesodās Jaimalot.[527] Narhardās took Rāṭhoṛ Kesodās and left.[528] No petition [put forth] there[529] was successful.

Vigat, 2:70

Then Rāṭhoṛ Kesodās married his daughter to the Pātsāh and took away half of Meṛto Pargano [in *jāgīr*].[530]

56. Subsequently a certain wet-nurse of the Pātsāh's, who had gone to Gujarat, came to Meṛto. Rāv Surtāṇ,[531] master of Sīrohī, had come with the wet-nurse as far as Meṛto. And the Pātsāh's wet-nurse said to Rāṭhoṛs Surtāṇ [and] Kesodās: "Escort me as far as Āmber."[532] Then they said: "Many

---

[524] Surtāṇ received Sojhat in *jāgīr* in 1578-79, as is noted in the account of Sojhat Pargano given in the ***Vigat*** (1:389-390). He held it for about one year, then it was overrun by Rāv Candrasen Māldevot and his band of followers just shortly before Candrasen's death in 1581.

[525] The text has ***Pātsāhī*** once again. See n. 523 ***supra***.

[526] Meṛtīyo Rāṭhoṛ Narhardās Īsardāsot (no. 120).

[527] See n. 517 ***supra***. Narhardās held the villages Reyāṃ and Pādu of Meṛto Pargano in grant from Kesodās Jaimalot.

[528] The respective accounts given by the ***Khyāt*** of Murārdān and the ***Vigat*** conflict. ***Murārdān*** has no mention of Kesodās or Narhardās quitting Meṛto at any time. From this source, Kesodās's holding of one-half of Meṛto in *jāgīr* appears to have been continuous from his reception of it just after Jaimal Vīramdevot's death at Cītoṛ in 1568 until his own death in the Deccan in 1599-1600. Narhardās held the *jāgīr* of Vadhnor in Mevāṛ from Akbar, and it may have been here that they went for some time. ***Murārdān***, no. 2, pp. 471, 512-513.

[529] It is not clear where "there" was. It could have been either Meṛto or the Mughal ***dargāh***.

[530] Literally, "Then, marrying Rāṭhoṛ Kesodās's daughter to the Pātsāh, Kesodās took away half of Meṛto [Pargano in grant]." This section is in disagreement with ***Murārdān***, no. 2, p. 512, which states that it was Narhardās Īsardāsot who married his sister to Akbar (see n. 517 to ***Vigat***, 2:69, ***supra***). For a discussion of the marriage, see B.N. under "Meṛtīyo Rāṭhoṛs," s.v. "Kesodās Jaimalot" (no. 119), n. 1.

[531] Devṛo Cahuvāṇ Rāv Surtāṇ Bhāṇot (no. 5), ruler of Sīrohī, ca. 1575-1610.

[532] Literally, "Have me reach/send me as far as Āmber."

whores[533] like this one come and go." They would not escort her. Afterward she went to Agra. She went and told the Pātsāh: "No one treats me the way the Meṛtīyos treated me. Tell [me your preference]: either you take Meṛto away from them,[534] or I shall cut off the nipples of my breasts." Afterward [the Pātsāh] removed Meṛto [from their authority].[535] He gave Rāṭhoṛ Surtāṇ Sarvāṛ again.[536] [Surtāṇ's] *vasī* went there. And Rāṭhoṛ Kesodās's *vasī* stayed in Nāgeḷāv.[537] Surtan's *vasī* stayed in Sarvāṛ ten or twelve years afterward. After that, in 1586, the Pātsāh gave [Surtāṇ and Kesodās] Meṛto again. Again Surtāṇ [and] Kesodās returned to Meṛto.

57. In 1584 the Navāb Khānkhāno[538] received the ***sūbo*** of Gujarat.[539] Rāṭhoṛ Surtāṇ Jaimalot was in the contingent of the Navāb. In those days Jago

---

533 ***Rāṇḍ***: a widow; a woman whose husband is dead but who has not become a ***satī*** ("virtuous woman"); a whore.

534 ***Iṇāṃ thā Meṛto tāgīr karo***. ***Tāgīr*** (Arabic taghīr) is a technical term used to refer to the transfer of ***jāgīr***s in the Mughal period; here we have translated ***tagīr karo*** as "take away" rather than "transfer" in order to emphasize the brothers' loss of Meṛto.

535 This curious episode involving the Pātsāh's wet-nurse is paralleled by an event that occurred in the mid-seventeenth century in Meṛto, described by the traveller Jean-Baptiste Tavernier:

> Mirda [Meṛto] is a large town, but badly built. When I arrived there, during one of my journeys in India, all the caravansarāīs were full of people, because the aunt of Shāhjahān, wife of Shāista Khān, was then on her way, taking her daughter to marry her to Sultān Shujā, second son of Shāhjahān. I was obliged to order my tent to be pitched upon a bank where there were large trees on both sides, and two hours afterwards I was much surprised to see fifteen or twenty elephants which came to break off as much as they could of these great trees. It was a strange thing to seem them break large branches with their trunks, as we break a piece of faggot. This injury was done by order of the Begam to avenge herself of an affront by the inhabitants of Mirda, who had not received her, and had not made a present as they ought to have done.

Jean-Baptiste Tavernier, ***Travels in India***, trans. V. Hall (1889; second edition, ed. W. Crooke, Oxford: Oxford University Press, 1925, p. 72.

536 Sarvāṛ: (1) a town thirty-five miles southeast of Ajmer; (2) a village located twenty-five miles east-northeast of Nāgaur and forty-nine miles due north of Meṛto. There is no indication that Surtāṇ had held either place previously, but Meṛtiyo Rāṭhoṛ Dūdo Jodhāvat (no. 104) had held Sarvāṛ village, located to the north of Meṛto, in the fifteenth century.

537 Nāgeḷāv: a town eighteen miles southwest of Ajmer.

538 Khān Khānān Mīrzā 'Abdu'r-Rahīm, the son of Akbar's famous regent, Bairam Khān. Mīrzā 'Abdu'r-Rahīm was one of Akbar's most important nobles, a commander of five thousand in the Mughal service. For a detailed account of his career, see ***Ā'īn-ī-Akbarī***, 1:354-361.

Jāṛeco[540] was a great ***bhomīyo*** in Gujarat. He caused nothing but harm to Ahmadabad city, skipping one day only to resume the next. ***Phaujdārs***,[541] ***sikdārs***,[542] ***koṭvāḷs***,[543]--they all died striving [to capture him];[544] Jago came into no one's hands. He repeatedly would take forty to fifty horsemen and by means of trickery[545] raid[546] the bazaar [and] the market place at the main gate. Deer lost [their] tails [just] from mentioning Jago's name.[547]

---

539 Mīrzā 'Abdu'r-Rahīm twice held the ***sūbo*** of Gujarat: from 1575 to 1578 and from 1584 to 1589. M. S. Commissariat, ***A History of Gujarat***, vol. 2 (Bombay: Orient Longmans, 1957), p. 16.

540 The Jāṛecos were very powerful Rajpūts in Kutch (around Bhuj city) and Saurashtra (around Navnagar city) at the time of the events described in the ***Vigat***. Akbar had conquered Gujarat in 1573, but many areas of the province remained outside Mughal authority for over twenty years afterward. We have found no additional information concerning Jago Jāṛeco himself; evidently he was head of a local Jāṛeco branch in the vicinity of Ahmadabad.

541 ***Phaujdār*** (Persian faujdār): literally, "one who has an army (***phauj***)." A subordinate military official under the Mughals, responsible for the maintenance of law and order within a district (***sarkār***) of a province (***sūbo***); more generally, a military official responsible for a local area. During the reign of Shāh Jahān the ***phaujdār***s of the Empire became involved with revenue collection as well. See Appendix D.

542 ***Sikdār*** (Arabic shiqq plus the Persian suffix -dār): under Sher Shāh, the revenue officer of a single ***pargano***, whether appointed by the state or by the holder of a land grant; in the Mughal period, a synonym for ***kiroṛī*** (see Appendix D); within the territory under the administrative control of the Rājās of Jodhpur during the Mughal period, an official placed in charge of maintaining order within a town.

543 ***Koṭvāḷ***: during the Mughal period, the chief officer of police within a city or large town; the superintendent of the market.

544 ***Sārā pañc muā***. ***Pañc*** probably is a mistake for ***pac***, from the verb ***pacṇo***, "to strive," "to labor."

545 ***Bhāgale***. Lāḷas, ***RSK***, 3:3:3338, glosses ***bhāgaḷ/bhāgal*** as "coward," "one who flees from the battlefield." Possibly the translation of the sentence could be: "The coward, taking along forty to fifty horsemen, repeatedly would raid the bazaar [and] the market place at the main gate." The problem with this translation is that ***bhāgale*** is oblique; one would have to assume that ***bhāgal*** was meant. Our translation is conjectural, based on ***bhāgale*** being a mistake for or a variant of ***bhagale***. ***Bhagal***: "trick," "deceit," "fraud." Platts, ***Dictionary***, p. 190; Lāḷas, ***RSK***, 3:3:3268 (under ***bhagaḷ***).

546 ***Karai*** in the ***kha*** ms. is preferable to ***pherai*** in the text.

547 ***Hiraṇ bāṇḍā huvai chai***. The editor of the ***Vigat***, N. S. Bhāṭī, suggests (n. 8) that this phrase is an idiom (***muhāvrā***) signifying that people were terrified by the very name of Jago.

One day Rāṭhoṛ Vīṭhaḷdās Jaimalot[548] [and] Sīndhaḷ Campo,[549] [son] of Karamsī, had gone on a hunting trip along the bank of the Samarmatī River.[550]

Vigat, 2:71

On the opposite side came people who had fled from [Ahmadabad] city. [Vīṭhaḷdās], having finished [his] hunting trip, was coming back. Meanwhile, the multitude of people who had fled were approaching. He asked: "You come fleeing in this manner--what sort of army comes behind you?" Among them was an intelligent fellow; he remained standing [before Vīṭhaḷdās] and said: "Jago Jāṛeco, who is always doing great damage to Ahmadabad, is coming." Then Vīṭhaḷdās [and] Cāmpo said: "Which one is Jago?" Then [the people] said: "Jago is not hidden." [Vīṭhaḷdās and Cāmpo] said: "He is not hidden from you, but we do not recognize [him]." Meanwhile the Jāṛeco, Jago, came near. He became visible. Those whom they were asking said: "He is mounted on a bay-colored horse, wearing a red turban [and] chain-mail.[551] He sparkles [in the sun]. He is the ***sirdār*** among the horsemen.[552] Another one [is Ratno]. So-and-so [is] Ratno, so-and-so [is] Jago, riding the horses--Ratno [and] Jago [who] are destruction [to] all Gujarat."[553] Talking took time; [Jago and Ratno] bore down on them. A skirmish[554] occurred there. Rāṭhoṛ Vīṭhaḷdās [and] Sīndhal Cāmpo killed Jago [and] Ratno along with ten to fifteen [other] men.

58. Rāṭhoṛ Surtāṇ did not receive the news. First[555] the Navāb received word [that] some Hindu had killed Jago. The Navāb himself mounted up and

---

548 Meṛtīyo Rāṭhoṛ Vīṭhaḷdās Jaimalot (no. 117).

549 Sīndhaḷ Rāṭhoṛ Campo Karamsīyot (no. 136).

550 The Samarmatī River flows south from the Arāvalī hills, from which it finds its source, travelling through Ahmadabad and on into the Gulf of Cambay.

551 ***Hajār meṅkhī***: literally, "having a thousand metal nails"; a type of chain mail. ***Akbar Nāma***, 2:472, notes that wearing hazār mīkhī armor was a mark of chieftainship among Rajpūts.

552 Literally, "he is the ***sirdār*** among so many horsemen (***itrai asvār***)."

553 The beginning of this sentence, ***dūjo Ratno Jago***, is confusing; we have given what seems to be the most logical translation of the entire sentence.

554 ***Māmlo***, from the Arabic mu'āmala, "trading, negotiating, bargaining with," etc. (Steingass, ***Persian-English Dictionary***, p. 1266), is used in Middle Mārvāṛī with the meaning "battle" or "skirmish" as well.

555 The text has ***Rā. Surtāṇ nuṃ khabar huī nahīṃ tā paihlī Navāb nuṃ khabar huī***, literally, "Rāṭhoṛ Surtāṇ did not receive the news; before that the Navāb received the news." We have translated ***tā paihlī*** simply as "first" to avoid confusion.

came there. The entire ***sāth*** of the ***sūbo*** mounted up and came. [Then] Rāṭhoṛ Surtāṇ mounted up and came. The Navāb asked [Vīṭhaḷdās and Cāmpo]: "Who are you?" Rāṭhoṛ Vīṭhaḷdās [and] Sīndhaḷ Cāmpo said: "We are Surtāṇ Jaimalot's military servants." The Navāb was very pleased. The Navāb cut off the heads of Jago [and] Ratno and brought [them] into the city. He asked responsible men in the city [to tell] the story of [Jago and Ratno]. The people of the city said: "Great glory for the Pātsāh! Good fortune for the Navāb! Today, [through] the killing of Jago [and] Ratno, Gujarat fell completely under the Pātsāhjī's control."[556]

Vigat, 2:72

The Navāb commanded Rāṭhoṛ Vīṭhaḷdās: "Make whatever request you have; I will petition the Pātsāh and have it given to you." Then Rāṭhoṛ Vīṭhaḷdās [and] Cāmpo made [this] request: "We are Rāṭhoṛ Surtāṇ Jaimalot's military servants. Navābjī, if you have been pleased, have Meṛto given[557] to Rāṭhoṛ Surtāṇ." Thereafter the Navābjī had [Meṛto] given [to him].

59. On February 11, 1586, their ***vasī*** came to Meṛto. They say Rāṭhoṛ Surtāṇ passed away in 1589-90.[558] Half of Meṛto [Pargano] was Surtāṇ's. Half of Meṛto [Pargano] was Rāṭhoṛ Kesodās Jaimalot's. Rāṭhoṛ Surtāṇ's men stayed where the ***koṭṛī*** [is] in Meṛto City. And Rāṭhoṛ Kesodās's men stayed in the Mālgaḍh. In 1589-90 Surtāṇ passed away. Balbhadar[559] received [half of] Meṛto [Pargano], transferred from Surtāṇ.[560]

60. In 1596-97 Balbhadar Surtāṇot passed away.[561] Rāṭhoṛ Gopāḷdās Surtāṇot[562] received Meṛto [City] with Surtāṇ's share [of the villages]. And

---

[556] ***Pātsāhjī rai Gujrāt kharī ras paṛī***. For ***ras paṛno***, see n. 251 to ***Vigat***, 2:54 ***supra***.

[557] ***Dirāvo*** in the ***kha*** ms. is preferable to ***diyo*** in the text.

[558] ***Murārdān***, no. 2, p. 464, says that the Emperor sent Surtāṇ with Rājā Mānsiṅgh Kachvāho to the east and that he died near Gokal in 1589-90.

[559] Meṛtīyo Rāṭhoṛ Balbhadar Surtāṇot (no. 114), one of the sons of Surtāṇ Jaimalot.

[560] ***Surtāṇ rī tāgīrī***. ***Tāgīrī***: that which has been transferred. Cf. n. 534 to ***Vigat***, 2:70, ***supra***.

[561] ***Murārdān***, no. 2, p. 465, notes that Balbhadar died in the Deccan from a wound received from a Turk during a fight at his camp. No date of death is given, but the date in the ***Vigat***, 1596-97, would be a period of active Mughal campaigning in the Deccan against Ahmadnagar, Bijapur, and Berar, in the final years before the death of Akbar (1605).

[562] Meṛtīyo Rāṭhoṛ Gopāḷdās Surtāṇot (no. 115). Balbhadar Surtāṇot had no sons, and therefore the land of Meṛto passed to his brother, Gopāḷdās.

Kesodās [continued] enjoying [his] share.[563] In 1599-1600, in the Deccan outside Bīḍ city,[564] a battle occurred between Cānd Bībī's[565] people and Ser Khojo,[566] who was a ***sirdār*** in the Pātsāh's army. The Pātsāh's army lost.[567] Rāṭhoṛ Gopāḷdās Surtāṇot, Rāṭhoṛ Kesodās Jaimalot, [and] Rāṭhoṛ Dvārkādās Jaimalot,[568] three Meṛtīyos, died fighting there.[569] Kachvāho Rājā Jagnāth's son Jagrūp[570] also died fighting there. This battle occurred at the river that is outside Bīḍ City. Kachvāho Jagrūp's ***chatrī***[571] is [there]. [When] he lost the battle, Ser

---

563 Literally, "And Kesodās [continued] enjoying Kesodās's share." Cf. n. 530 to ***Vigat***, 2:70, ***supra***.

564 Bīḍ city lies in the western Deccan sixty-five miles east of Ahmadnagar.

565 Sultāna Cānd Bībī, wife of the Nizām Shāh of Bijapur and sister to the deceased ruler of Ahmadnagar, Burhānu'd-Dīn. Burhānu'd-Dīn had succeeded to the throne of Ahmadnagar in 1590 with Akbar's assistance and then had repudiated the Mughals. Within a short time, Burhānu'd-Dīn died, and the state became split into four rival factions for the throne, with civil war emerging. Then, in 1595, the Mughals attacked, having been invited in by the Deccani faction, and a treaty was signed in 1596, with Ahmadnagar as a Mughal vassal state. The treaty lasted only a short time, and the Mughals returned to take Ahmadnagar in 1599-1600. In the interim period, Cānd Bībī had ruled a portion of the territory of Ahmadnagar including the fort at Ahmadnagar city. She was eventually killed by her own troops before the fall of Ahmadnagar in 1600. Y. M. Khan, ***The Deccan Policy of the Mughals*** (Lahore: United Book Corp., 1971), p. 62-65, 85-87; Srivastava, ***Akbar the Great***, 1:391-422; Tripathi, ***The Rise and Fall of the Mughal Empire***, p. 329.

566 ***Ser Khojo tho*** in the ***kha*** ms. is preferable to ***Ser Khāṃ Jodhā*** in the text. This man was Sher Khwāja, a Saiyid of Itāwa. For some details concerning his career, see ***Ā'īn-ī-Akbarī***, 1:510-511.

567 In the months of mid-1599, Bīḍ was occupied by Mughal troops under Sher Khwāja after their defeat outside the city and was under heavy attack from the forces of Ahmadnagar. Bīḍ was hard pressed at this time, but was eventually relieved by reinforcements sent by Abu'l Fazl, whom Akbar had deputed to military duty in the Deccan. Khan, ***The Deccan Policy of the Mughals***, p. 83; Srivastava, ***Akbar the Great***, 1:438-439; Tripathi, ***The Rise and Fall of the Mughal Empire***, p. 329.

568 Meṛtīyo Rāṭhoṛ Dvārkādās Jaimalot (no. 118). ***Murārdān***, no. 2, pp. 504-505, indicates that Dvārkādās died fighting along with Kachvāho Ramcandro.

569 In addition to these three Meṛtīyo Rāṭhoṛs, six other Meṛtīyos, Narbad Rāymalot, Prayāgdās Arjunot, Cakrasen Rāysiṅghot, Narsiṅghdās Rūpsīyot, Tātar Khān Acḷāvat, and Devīdās Vairsīyot, were also killed at Bīḍ. ***Ibid.***, pp. 556, 557, 559, 569.

570 The text has Mantup; the ***kha*** ms. Manrūp. This Rajpūt was in fact Rājāvat Kachvāho Jagrūp Jagnāthot (no. 21), son of Rājā Jagnāth Bhārmalot of Toḍo and grandson of Rājā Bhārmal Prithīrājot of Āmber.

571 ***Chatrī***: a cenotaph; a memorial erected for a fallen Rajpūt warrior.

Khojo fled and re-entered the fort [of Bīḍ]. Afterward Rāṭhoṛ Jagnāth Gopāḷdāsot[572] received Rāṭhoṛ Gopāḷdās's half share and Kānhīdās Kesodāsot[573] received Rāṭhoṛ Kesodās['s] half.

Vigat, 2:73

61. Thereafter discord arose between Rāṭhoṛ Jagnāth Gopāḷdāsot and the Kachvāho Rājā, Rāmdās Ūdāvat.[574] Then Akbar Pātsāh gave Jagnāth's half share [of] Meṛto [Pargano] to Rājā Sūrajsiṅgh, [starting] from the spring crop of 1602.[575] Rāṭhoṛ Kānhīdās Kesodāsot had [the other] half. In those days Kānhīdās's men stayed in the city's ***koṭṛī***. The Rājājī's ***kāmdār*** stayed in the Mālgaḍh.

62. Afterward, in 1604-05, Rāṭhoṛ Kānhīdās passed away.[576] Then the various important Meṛtīyo ***ṭhākurs*** took a ***sāth*** of 2,000 horsemen and went to the ***dargāh***. The Pātsāhjī would not accept Indrabhāṇ[577] [as Kānhīdās's heir].

---

[572] Meṛtīyo Rāṭhoṛ Jagnāth Gopāḷdāsot (no. 116).

[573] Meṛtīyo Rāṭhoṛ Kānhīdās Kesodāsot (no. 121).

[574] Dhīrāvat Kachvāho Rājā Rāmdās Ūdāvat (no. 19), who was a favored servant of Emperor Akbar's.

[575] Jodho Rāṭhoṛ Rājā Sūrajsiṅgh Udaisiṅghot, ruler of Jodhpur, 1595-1619, had succeeded to the throne of Jodhpur in 1595 while at Lahore, to which he had travelled with his father, Moṭo Rājā Udaisiṅgh Māldevot (1583-95), to meet with the Emperor, Akbar. There is some slight confusion about the exact date of succession. ***Vigat***, 1:92, has V.S. 1651, ***Āsāḍh, Vadi*** 13, corresponding to June 25, 1595. ***Jodhpur Rājya kī Khyāt***, p. 131, and Reu, 1:181, have V.S. 1652, ***Sāvaṇ, Vadi*** 12 (July 23, 1595), with which Ojhā (4:1:364) agrees. ***Bāṅkīdās***, p. 25, has both V.S. 1651, ***Āsāḍh, Sudi*** 15 = July 11, 1595, and V.S. 1657, ***Āsāḍh, Vadi*** 11 = June 16, 1601. "Aitihāsik Bātāṃ," p. 74, has V.S. 1642, ***Āsāḍh, Vadi*** 12, corresponding to June 3, 1586. The last two dates are clearly wrong; the choice appears to be between the date given by the ***Jodhpur Rājya kī Khyāt*** and accepted by Ojhā and Reu, the date given in the ***Vigat***, and ***Bāṅkidās***'s earlier date.

Sūrajsiṅgh received the first half of Meṛto in 1602, and then in 1605 received the other half. Ojhā, 4:1:370, gives the date May 30, 1605, for his receipt of all of Meṛto (see also "Aitihāsik Bātāṃ," p. 95).

With regard to the receipt of the first half of Meṛto, Sūrajsiṅgh had been on maneuvers with the Mughal army in the Deccan and had participated in the battle with Amarcampu on May 3, 1602. Here he played a prominent part in the winning of the battle. In return, he received the raiment of red and white, which became his colors, and one-half of Meṛto. In the same year he also obtained the title of Savāī Rājā. See Reu, 1:185, and ***Vigat***, 1:96.

[576] ***Murārdān***, no. 2, p. 472, states that Kānhīdās died in 1601-02.

[577] Meṛtīyo Rāṭhoṛ Indrabhāṇ Kānhīdāsot (no. 122), son of Kānhīdās Kesodāsot.

Later, in 1605, Akbar Pātsāh gave Rājā Sūrajsiṅgh Rāṭhoṛ Kānhīdās's half, too.[578] Meṛto remained [a possession of] Rājā Sūrajsiṅghjī's as long as he lived.[579]

63. On September 7, 1619, [Sūrajsiṅgh] passed away in Mahaikar.[580] Rājā Gajsiṅgh received the throne of Jodhpur.[581] Then Meṛto was transferred. Sāhjādo[582] Khuram[583] received [Meṛto, starting] from the ***māl***[584] [and] ***ghāsmārī***[585] [of 1619].[586] Abu, an ***amīn***, came [to Meṛto]. He entrusted the [two] halves of the ***pargano*** to the custody of ***kiroṛīs***: one, Hājī Itbārī; the other, Mīr Sako.[587] Abu's ***hākmī***[588] lasted two years. Afterward, [beginning] with the

---

[578] See n. 575 ***supra***. Akbar died on October 16, 1605, shortly after making this grant to Rājā Sūrajsiṅgh. Jahāṅgīr ascended the throne several days after Akbar's death, on October 24, 1605.

[579] Literally, "It--as long as Rājā Sūrajsiṅgh lived--Meṛto remained."

[580] Mahaikar is located in the Deccan eighty miles east-northeast of Aurangabad.

[581] On the death of Rājā Sūrajsiṅgh at Mahaikar, Gajsiṅgh (Jodho Rāṭhoṛ Gajsiṅgh Sūrajsiṅghot, Rājā of Jodhpur, 1619-38) was in the Deccan with his father in the service of Jahāṅgīr. When the Emperor heard of Sūrajsiṅgh's death, he sent a ***sirpāv*** from Agra to Gajsiṅgh consisting of an elephant, horses with gold trappings, and other things. On October 6, 1619, he received the ***ṭīko*** of succession at Burhanpur from the son of Navāb Khānkhānān, Darāb Khān.

At the time of succession, Gajsiṅgh received a ***mansab*** rank of 3,000 ***zāt***, 2,000 ***suwār***. Along with the rank came the following ***parganos*** in ***jāgīr***: Jodhpur, Sojhat, Sīvāṇo, Jaitāraṇ, Sātalmer, and Pokaraṇ (included but not under direct administration due to the occupation of the area by the Bhāṭīs of Jaisaḷmer), all in Mārvāṛ, and Tervāṛo-Mervāṛo in Gujarat. ***Bāṅkīdās***, p. 27 (he gives the date of V.S. 1676, ***Āsoj, Sudi*** 10 = October 8, 1619, for the succession); ***Mahārāj Śrī Gajsiṅgh kī Khyāt*** (MS no. 15666, Rājasthān Prācyavidyā Pratiṣṭhān, Jodhpur), pp. 1-2; Ojhā, 4:1:388; ***Vigat***1, 1:95, 105.

[582] ***Sāhjādo*** (Persian shāhzāda): the son of a shāh, a prince.

[583] Sāhjādo Khuram: Prince Khurram (later Shāh Jahān), son of Jahāṅgīr. Khurram was ***subedār*** of Ajmer at this time.

[584] ***Māl*** (Arabic): literally, "money"; the land revenue.

[585] ***Ghāsmārī***: literally, "grass-struck." A local tax levied on domestic animals at so much cash per type of animal. See ***Vigat***, 2:95, for an example from Meṛto Pargano.

[586] ***Vigat***, 1:106, says that only the ***ghāsmārī*** tax was granted at this time.

[587] ***Amīn*** (Arabic) and ***kiroṛī*** are names of Mughal revenue officials entrusted with the assessment and collection of land revenue. These two functionaries stand in an interesting relationship to each other in this passage. The period referred to in the text is 1619, during the middle of the reign of Emperor Jahāṅgīr (1605-27). The

year 1621-22, Sāhjādo Khuram divided up the entire ***pargano*** and gave [it] to his military servants [and] Rajpūts in ***jāgīrī*** [tenure].[589] So it remained for two years. Details[590] [and] a list of the villages in April-May, 1623 ....[591]

64. [Khuram] gave Rājā Bhīm Amrāvat, a Sīsodīyo [Rajpūt],[592] the town [of Meṛto] along with 204 villages. Rājā Bhīm himself came to Meṛto.

On November 11, 1619, Abu came to Meṛto and established [his] authority [there]. With Abu Kābo, the ***amīn***, were the two ***kiroṛīs***. Entrusted to him [were] five ***paṭīs***[593] [in the charge of] Hājī Itbārī:

1. Havelī.
1. Āṇandpur.
1. Kalro.[594]
1. Moḍro.[595]

---

terminology used and the relationships defined, however, stem from the reign of Emperor Shāh Jahān (1628-58) and after, near the time this account was set to writing. Properly designated, Abu Kābo should be the ***'amīl*** or ***kiroṛī***, and Hājī Itbārī and Mīr Sako the ***amīns*** serving under his authority.

For an overview of the Mughal land revenue administration and its development and functioning over time, see Appendix D.

We have no further information about the review officials mentioned in this passage.

588 ***Hākmī***: an abstract noun formed from ***hākīm*** (Arabic ḥākim). A ***hākīm*** was an administrative official encharged with the authority over a district on behalf of an outsider. In this instance, Abu was an agent acting on behalf of Prince Khurram.

589 Khurram appears to have kept Meṛto in ***khālso*** tenure (see glossary) long enough to allow for surveying and assessment and then to have changed it into ***jāgīr*** land based upon what one supposes was a reasonably realistic assessment of actual revenue and value of land.

590 ***Tahal*** in the text has no relevant meaning. The word might be a mistake for the term ***taphsīl*** (Arabic tafṣīl), "details," "particulars," which appears in similar contexts. Cf. ***Vigat***, 1:113, 171.

591 There appears to be a gap in the text, as only the grant to Rājā Bhīm Amrāvat is mentioned.

592 Sīsodīyo Gahlot Rājā Bhīm Amrāvat (no. 15).

593 ***Paṭī***: a term used for the administrative subdivisions of Meṛto, Nāgaur, and Jāḷor ***parganos***. The word ***tapho*** was also used for the Meṛto Pargano subdivisions, which are located on Map 5, "Administrative Divisions of Meṛto Pargano, ca. 1660."

594 The text has Phaldu, evidently a mistake for Kalro/Kalru, one of the subdivisions of Meṛto Pargano.

MAP 5

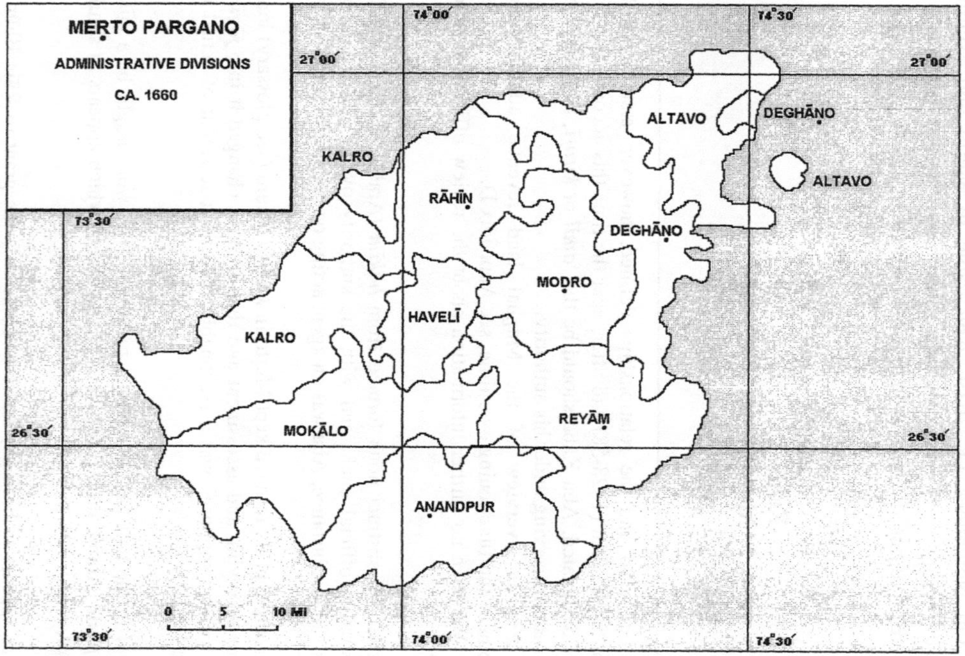

MAP 5. MEṚTO PARGANO: ADMINISTRATIVE DIVISIONS, CA. 1660.

1. Rāhaṇ.

[And] four ***paṭīs*** [that] were in the charge of Mīr Sako:

1. Reyāṃ.
1. Mokālo.
1. Deghāṇo.
1. Altavo.

Vigat, 2:74

Abu's custodianship lasted two years.
[Estimated revenue] produced[596] in 1619-20 [and] 1620-21:

Rs. 325,000 in 1619-20.
Rs. 475,000 in 1620-21.

In May-June of 1623, Pātsāh Jahāngīr came to Ajmer. Khuram rebelled.[597] Then [Jahāngīr] placed all of [Khuram's] responsibilities on

---

[595] The text has Māṇḍro, a mistake for Moḍro, one of the subdivisions of Meṛto Pargano.

[596] The text has only ***ūpnā*** ("produced"); the round numbers suggest an estimate.

[597] The revolt of Khurram/Shāh Jahān (Khurram had been given the title "Shāh Jahān" in 1617 by Jahāngīr at the time he was made ***sūbedār*** of the Deccan) began in 1621. Jahāngīr's health had begun failing as early as 1618, while he was in Gujarat. He had suffered attacks of fever with signs of asthma, and in 1619, his eye problems reappeared. Then in 1620, he again suffered a relapse from asthma and became very ill while returning to Āgrā from Kashmīr. This condition worsened from much drinking. From this time forward, his health remained very delicate and he relied more and more upon his wife, Nūr Jahān, to run the government. In addition, in late January of 1621, the Prime Minister (***vākīl***) of the Empire, I'timadu'd-Daulah, Nūr Jahān's father, died, leaving Nūr Jahān with virtually complete control over the Empire.

Nūr Jahān feared Shāh Jahān's power from his base in the Deccan, and she quickly moved to entrench her candidate for succession, Shāhriyār, the youngest son of Jahāngīr, in a position of power. The court itself became divided into three factions around Nūr Jahān and Shāhriyār, Khurram/Shāh Jahān, and Khusrau. Shāh Jahān, upon learning of his father's illness in 1621 and of Nūr Jahān's rise to supreme power in the Empire, quickly took measures to protect his own position. He first had his half-brother, Khusrau, strangled to death at Burhanpur in February of 1621. He later told Jahāngīr that Khusrau had died of colic (which the Emperor appears to have accepted), but the infamy of this deed clung to Shāh Jahān throughout the rest of his life.

In the meantime, Qandahar was attacked by Shāh 'Abbās of Persia, and Shāh Jahān, militarily the ablest of the Mughal princes and the most powerful, was ordered to the north by Jahāngīr, who was in Kashmir at the time because of his health. Shāh Jahān refused to move beyond Māṇḍū unless he was put in full command of the army of the Panjab and given Riṇthambhor in ***jāgīr***, for the protection of his family. While

Parvej.[598] He gave Meṛto to Parvej. The ***phaujdār***, Sādat Beg, attacked the ***kiroṛī***, Sekh, in May-June [of 1623].[599] He took the ***ghāsmārī*** [tax] in 1623-24.

[1]. Rāṭhoṛ Bhīṃv Kilāṇdāsot [received] Āṇandpur village.[600]
[1]. Rāṭhoṛ Prithīrāj Baluvot [received] Reyāṃ [village].[601]
[1]. Rāṭhoṛ Mahesdās Dalpatot [received] Baḍālī [village].[602]
[1]. Rāṭhoṛ Īsardās Kalyāṇdāsot [received] Rohīso [village].[603]

65. Rājājī [Gajsiṅgh's] ***jāgīrdārs*** had seized the ***māl*** [and] ***ghāsmārī*** [tax] in 1619-20. Rāṭhoṛ Rājsiṅgh Khīṃvāvat[604] approached Abu, [the ***amīn***], and stayed in Meṛto twenty days in negotiations[605] over this [seizure]. He paid

---

these negotiations were taking place, Qandahar fell to the Persians, raising Jahāngīr's ire at Shāh Jahān (to Nūr Jahān's pleasure).

Then in 1623, Shāh Jahān rose in revolt, supported by most of the great ***amīrs*** in the Deccan, Malwa, and Gujarat. He advanced from Māṇḍū with the large army and reached Fatehpur Sikr and Agra, which he partially looted. He also seized Dholpur (near Agra), which had been assigned in ***jāgīr*** to Shāhriyār, and other tracts belonging to the ***jāgīr*** of Nūr Jahān. Afterwards, he marched toward Delhi, where he was defeated in battle and forced to retreat to Māṇḍū, pursued by the army under his half-brother, Parvīz, and Mahābat Khān. Jahāngīr himself came to Ajmer at this time for some months to oversee operations against Shāh Jahān, eventually retreating to Kashmir, the only place he could now live in his worsening physical condition, before the end of the year. B. Prasad, ***History of Jahangir*** (Allahabad: The Indian Press Ltd., 1940), pp. 292-342; Tripathi, ***The Rise and Fall of the Mughal Empire***, pp. 393-397.

[598] Parvej: Prince Parvīz, son of Jahāngīr and half-brother of Khurram.

[599] We have been unable to identify either one of these officials. Presumably the ***kiroṛī***, Sekh, was Khurram's representative, whose local functions were taken away by the ***phaujdār***, Sādat Beg, upon the outbreak of the rebellion and Parvīz's reception of Meṛto.

[600] Ūdāvat Rāṭhoṛ Bhīṃv Kilāṇdāsot (no. 142). Āṇandpur village was the head village of the Āṇandpur subdivision (***paṭī/tapho***) of Meṛto and is located twenty miles south of Meṛto.

[601] Bhārmalot Rāṭhoṛ Prithīrāj Baluvot (no. 40). Reyāṃ village was the headquarters of the Reyāṃ subdivision of Meṛto Pargano is located fifteen miles southeast of Meṛto.

[602] Jodho Rāṭhoṛ Mahesdās Dalpatot (no. 89). Baḍālī village is located thirteen miles south-southeast of Meṛto.

[603] Jodho Rāṭhoṛ Īsardās Kalyāṇdāsot (no. 88). Rohīso village is located two miles southeast of Baḍālī village and fifteen miles south-southeast of Meṛto.

[604] Kūmpāvat Rāṭhoṛ Rājsiṅgh Khīṃvāvat (no. 101).

[605] In this sentence, ***māmlo*** is used in the sense of "negotiations" or "bargaining." See n. 554 to ***Vigat***, 2:71, ***supra***, for another sense of this word in Middle Mārvāṛī texts.

rs. 50,000 cash and stationed Muṃhato Velo[606] with Abu [in Meṛto]. A fight occurred between some of Velo's and Abu's servants. [Velo said]: "Draw up a deed of discharge[607] and give [it] to me." [Abu] had the deed of discharge made and brought [it to Velo].

66. Thereafter, in February-March of 1623, Sāhjādo Khuram rebelled against the Pātsāh, Jahāngīr. Śrījī[608] was in the ***des***.[609] A battle occurred between the Pātsāh's [forces and] Khuram's [forces] near Delhi. Mahābat Khān[610] fought [the battle] there. Rājā Vikmādīt, a Brāhmaṇ,[611] was killed. Khuram fled. Jahāngīr, the Pātsāh, was coming to Ajmer. Mahārājā Śrī Gajsiṅghjī went and met with Pātsāh Jahāngīr near Cāṭsū.[612]

Vigat, 2:75

He paid [his] respects. The Pātsāh came to Ajmer. He designated Sāhjādo Parvej [his] heir-apparent,[613] made Mahābat Khān the commander [of a military

---

[606] Muṃhato Velo (no. 160).

[607] ***Phārkatī*** (Arabic fār-khaṭī): "A deed of release or discharge." Platts, ***Dictionary***, p. 775.

[608] Śrījī: Naiṇsī's term of address for the rulers of Jodhpur under whom he served (Gajsiṅgh and Jasvantsiṅgh).

[609] ***Des***: land, geographic region; a term used by Naiṇsī in his ***Khyāt*** and ***Vigat*** to refer to the lands in Mārvāṛ under the authority of the Jodhpur Rājā.

[610] Mahābat Khān was one of the most powerful nobles in the service of Jahāngīr. He was widely known for his patronage of Rajpūts (he had four or five thousand in his service) and his opposition to the Iranian (Khurāsānī) faction at the Mughal court. For a detailed discussion of Mahābat Khān's career, see Shāh Nawāz Khan, ***Maāthir-ul-Umarā***, translated by H. Beveridge, revised, annotated, and completed by Baini Prashad, 3 vols. (Calcutta: The Asiatic Society, 1941-52-64), 2:9-28.

[611] Rājā Vikmādīt (Bikramājīt in Persian sources) was the title of the Brāhmāṇ Sundar Dās, who rose from the position of writer for Prince Khurram to that of Mīr Sāman under Jahāngīr. He was a native of Bandhū in the Allahabad District. He attained the rank of 5,000 ***zāt***, 5,000 ***suwār*** in the Mughal service, took part in several military expeditions (most notably the siege of Kangra in 1620), and was killed by a bullet received in battle here, which the ***Vigat*** records. For some details of the Rājā's career, see ***ibid.***, 1:412-419.

[612] Bhargava, ***Marwar and the Mughal Emperors***, p. 72, gives the date May 1, 1623, for this meeting.

[613] ***Sāhjādo Parvej nuṃ vaḷe āhad kar nai***. ***Vaḷe āhad*** (Arabic walī-'ahd): "heir-apparent, destined or acknowledged successor." Platts, ***Dictionary***, p. 1201.

expedition] under [Parvej's] supervision,[614] and dispatched them from [Ajmer] after Khuram. Then the Navāb, [Mahābat Khān], highly recommended the Rājājī and had [his rank] increased one thousand ***jāt*** [and] one thousand ***asvār***.[615] [His] ***mansab***[616] was increased.[617] The Navāb [and] Parvej took [him] with them. But [Gajsiṅgh] did not obtain his full claim.[618] At that time he obtained Phaḷodhī[619] [Pargano] assessed at rs. 67,000 and Sāhjādo Parvej received all of

---

614 ***Navāb Mohobatkhān muṃhaḍai āgai mudāit kar nai***. This sentence fragment may be interpreted in two ways:

> (a) "He made [Parvej] the commander [of a military expedition] under Mahābat Khān['s] supervision and ...."
> (b) "He made Mahābat Khān the commander [of a military expedition] under [Parvej's] supervision and ...."

Either translation is problematic: the first is grammatically preferable (one would assume that the postposition ***nuṃ*** would follow Mahābat Khān's name if he were being made commander [***mudait***]); the second is preferable on historical grounds (Mahābat Khān was the commander of this expedition; he was under Parvīz's nominal supervision) and for lexical reasons (***mudāit*** is used in Middle Mārvāṛī texts to refer to one who has real, as opposed to nominal, responsibilities for decision-making). We have chosen the second alternative based on a parallel passage occurring in ***Vigat***, 1:108, where it is stated clearly that Jahāṅgīr, at the time he made Parvīz heir-apparent, "gave Mahābat Khān full responsibility (***sārī madār***) under Parvej's supervision (***Parvej rai muṃhaḍai āgai***)" and dispatched them after Khurram.

615 ***Jāt*** (Arabic ẕat) and ***asvār*** (Persian Suwar) were the two indices of rank (***mansab***) in the Mughal administration. See n. 490 to ***Vigat***, 2:67, ***supra***.

616 ***Mansab*** (Arabic manṣab): literally, "post," "office." See n. 490 to ***Vigat***, 2:67, ***supra***.

617 Rājā Gajsiṅgh was in the Deccan at the time of Shāh Jahān's revolt and had shown initial sympathies toward his cause. He had then returned to Jodhpur, having been granted leave from Mahaikar where he had been posted in action against the Deccanis since early 1622. At the time of which the text speaks, he had just returned to the Deccan from Jodhpur. His rank was raised to 5,000 ***ẕat***, 4,000 ***suwār***.

Gajsiṅgh's initial sympathy for Shāh Jahān's cause may have been due to the fact that Shāh Jahān was the son of Jodh Bāī, daughter of Gajsiṅgh's grandfather, Moṭo Rājā Udaisiṅgh Māldevot of Jodhpur (ruled 1583-95). ***Bāṅkīdās***, p. 27; ***Mahārāj Śrī Gajsiṅghjī kī Khyāt***, pp. 21-22; Khan, ***The Deccan Policy of the Mughals***, p. 155; Ojhā, 4:1:390-392; ***Vigat***, 1:107-108.

618 ***Talab*** (Arabic ṭalab): the pay claim on a ***mansab***.

619 Phaḷodhī: a town situated seventy-two miles northwest of Jodhpur.

the *parganos* comprising the *khālso*[620] of the *sūbo* of Ajmer. Parvej received Meṛto among these [*parganos*] as well.

67. Afterward Sāhjādo Parvej gave Meṛto to a Said in *jāgīrī* [tenure].[621] Then the Rājājī had [his] negotiator,[622] Rāṭhoṛ Rājsiṅgh Khīṃvāvat, adamantly[623] tell the Navāb four or five times: "For many days I have enjoyed [the lands] obtained by Rājā Sūrajsiṅgh. I have enjoyed [them] and have retained the entire *jamīyat*[624] so that the Navāb would have Meṛto given [to me] in the near future. My[625] Rajpūts have stayed with me so many days in the hope of [my receiving] Meṛto. Now my Rajpūts heard in the *darbār* that the Sāhjādo is giving Meṛto to someone else, so all my Rajpūts are going away. And the Navābjī had my *mansab* increased, [but] I have not even obtained the [full] claim of this [*mansab*]." Afterward the Navāb petitioned Sāhjādo Parvej and had Meṛto given by the Sāhjādojī. He wrote out a *tālīko*[626] and gave [it to Gajsiṅgh]. The Rājājī sent the *tālīko* to the *des*. Subsequently Rāṭhoṛ Kānh Khīṃvāvat[627] [and] Bhaṇḍārī Lūṇo[628] brought the *tālīko* to Meṛto. At first Parvej's men in Meṛto raised an objection. Then Rāṭhoṛ Kānh [and] Bhaṇḍārī Lūṇo sent men to negotiate with them, and, after a little give-and-take, gave them leave. [Gajsiṅgh] established [his] authority [over Meṛto] on August 8,

---

[620] ***Khālso*** (Persian khāliṣa): literally, "pure." Land directly administered and taxed by a ruler and his personal officials.

[621] The text, ***Pachai Meṛto Sāhājādo Parvej Said nuṃ jāgīrī māṃhai tho***, is unclear. Literally, the translation would be: "Afterward, Meṛto--Sāhjādo Parvej--was to a Said in *jāgīrī* [tenure]." The ***kha*** ms. differs, but it also confusing: ***Sāhjādāṃ nuṃ jāgīr meṃ deto tho***, "He was giving [Meṛto] in *jāgīr* to the Sāhjādos (?)." Our translation suggests what might have been the intention of the author.

[622] ***Bīc***: middleman, negotiator.

[623] The editor of the ***Vigat***, N. S. Bhāṭī, takes ***gāḍhpur*** in the text to be a place-name (***Vigat***, 3:210); we believe ***-pur*** to be a variant of the suffix ***-pūr***, "filled with," joined with ***gāḍh*** ("stubborn," "obstinate," etc.) to form an adverb, ***gāḍhpur***, "stubbornly," "adamantly," "obstinately," etc.

[624] ***Jamīyat*** (Persian jam'īyat): the assemblage of men and horses in the service of a chief.

[625] ***Yāṃhrā*** in the text evidently is a misprint for ***māṃhrā***, "my."

[626] ***Tālīko*** (Persian ta'līqa): the certificate of appointment to all posts that required the approval of the Mughal Emperor. In this instance, however, Parvīz wrote the ***tālīko*** upon the petition of the Navāb, Mahābat Khān, hence the ensuing difficulties with the Mughal administration.

[627] Kūmpāvat Rāṭhoṛ Kānh Khīṃvāvat (no. 100).

[628] Bhaṇḍārī Lūṇo (no. 156).

1623. He did not obtain it in ***dargāhī mansab***.[629] It was given by the Sāhjādo personally,[630] assessed at rs. 200,000, ***dāms***[631] 8,000,000.

Vigat, 2:76

68. Two years later Mahābat Khān was in the Deccan under the supervision of Parvej. The Khurāsāṇīs[632] misled the Pātsāh, Jahāṅgīr, and had [Mahābat Khān] called back from there. Phidāī Khān[633] came to Burhānpur[634] in 1625-26, bringing a ***pharmān*** from the person of the Pātsāh to all the ***umrāv***s. The Sāhjādo [and] all the ***umrāv***s prepared to leave with the Navāb. They came outside the city and made camp. The Rājījī stayed where he was in [his] camp. Then the Sāhjādo [and] the ***umrāv***s all came back.[635] The Sāhjādo [and] all the ***umrāv***s persuaded [Rājā Gajsiṅgh to take the recall] very well. He went to the ***dargāh***.[636] Then Phidāī Khān, after speaking to Śrījī, took Rāṭhoṛ Rājsiṅghjī with him to Lahore. Phidāī Khān went to Lahore and paid [his] respects [to the Pātsāh]. He had Rāṭhoṛ Rājsiṅgh Khīṃvāvat touch the feet of the Śrī Pātsāhjī.

---

629 ***Dargāhī mansab***: a ***mansab*** given by the Mughal Emperor.

630 ***Sāhājādī rī āprī taraph sūṃ***: literally, "from the Sāhjādo's own side."

631 ***Dām***: a copper coin equal to one-fortieth of a rupee.

632 Khurāsāṇī: a person from the Iranian province of Khurasan; an Iranian. The reference is to the Iranian faction at the Mughal court, centering around Nūr Jahān, Jahāngīr's wife, and her brother, Asaf Khān. For an account of this faction and its importance in contemporary politics, see Irfan Habib, "The Family of Nur Jahan during Jahangir's reign: A Political Study," in ***Medieval India: A Miscellany***, vol. 1 (London: Asia Publishing House, 1969), pp. 74-95.

633 Phidāī Khān: Fidāī Khan (Hedāyat Ullah), a protégé of Mahābat Khān's (at one time his ***vakīl***), who later became a servant of the Mughal Emperors Jahāngīr and Shāh Jahān. For an account of his career, see ***Maāthir-ul-Umarā***, 1:559-563. Ojhā, 4:1:395, indicates that this Muslim possibly was an advisor regarding ***mansabdār***s at the ***darbār*** of Jahāngīr.

634 Burhanpur: an important town 110 miles north-northeast of Aurangabad. Burhanpur was the central base of operations for the Mughals in their campaigns against the Deccan Sultānates.

635 This sentence is found only in the ***kha*** ms.

636 Ojhā, 4:1:395, notes that Gajsiṅgh had refused to leave camp out of fear for the anger of Navāb Mahābat Khān, who, he felt, would berate him at court and place him in a difficult position with the Emperor. Although Ojhā is not explicit about the reasons for this feeling, it may have been due to Gajsiṅgh's initial sympathy for the cause of Shāh Jahān when he was in the Deccan (see n. 617 to ***Vigat***, 2:75, ***supra***).

Phidāī Khān highly praised Rājsiṅghjī. At that time Khojo Abdal Hasan[637] was the Patsah's ***dīvān*** of the ***kaceṛī***.[638] Khojo Abdal Hasan prepared an accounting of the ***mansab*** [of Gajsiṅgh] and made [it] known to the Pātsāh: "Meṛto was not given to the Rājājī in ***dargāhī mansab***. Mahābat Khān showed favor [to Gajsiṅgh] and had [Meṛto] given by Sāhjādo [Parvej]." [The Pātsāh] wrote out [a notice of] transfer for Meṛto.[639] Afterward Phidāī Khān informed the Pātsāhjī: "The Rājājī had paid [his] respects [to you]; he was a candidate for an increase [in ***mansab***]. Why in this instance[640] are you deciding to the contrary[641] and transferring Meṛto?" Then the Pātsāh reversed Abdal Hasan and made a command. He had Meṛto kept as it was.[642] [However], the assessment [of Mer to] was increased 2,000,000 ***dams*** (rs. 50,000). By this means Meṛto was assessed at rs. 250,000.

---

[637] Khojo Abdal Hasan (Abal Husen in the ***kha*** ms.; Abal Hasan farther down on ***Vigat***, 2:76): Khāja Abū-l-Hasan of Turbat, a district of Khurasan. He was an important member of the Iranian faction at the Mughal court (see n. 632 to ***Vigat***, 2:75, ***supra***). Beginning his career in the service of Prince Dānyāl, one of Akbar's sons, he later attained the position of ***dīwān*** of the Deccan under Akbar. Subsequently he became ***mīr bakhshī*** under Jahāngīr (1613) and then was appointed chief ***dīwān*** with a rank of 5,000 ***ẕāt***, 5,000 ***suwār***. He died in 1632-33, after attaining a rank of 6,000/6,000 under Shāh Jahān.

Vigat, 1:109 remarks that the Khwāja bore ill-will toward Gajsiṅgh. He was an opponent of Mahābat Khān, and as such he may have objected to the Khān's petitioning Parvīz and having Meṛto given to Gajsiṅgh.

For additional details concerning the career of Khwāja Abū-l-Hasan, see ***Maāthir-ul-Umarā***, 1:128-130.

[638] ***Kaceṛī***: the department of the Mughal administration encharged with reviewing documents.

[639] ***Meṛto tāgīr meṃ likhīyo***: literally, "He wrote Meṛto in transfer." ***Mahārāj Śrī Gajsiṅgh kī Khyāt***, pp. 33-39, notes that Parvīz was angry with Gajsiṅgh because of Mahābat Khān's favoring him and his words of praise for him. The ***Khyāt*** intimates that Khwāja Abū-l-Hasan was a person of the Prince and in his accounting made special note of the fact that Meṛto had not been an imperial grant, but had been given by Mahābat Khān. This tradition is in conflict with the details in the ***Vigat***, which do not indicate that Parvīz was angry with Gajsiṅgh.

[640] Literally, "there" (***taṭhai***). The literal translation of the entire sentence thus would be "Why are you deciding to the contrary there and transferring Meṛto?"

[641] ***Sāmo*** in this clause apparently is used in the sense of "contrary" or "opposite," meanings given by Lāḷas, ***RSK***, 4:3:5472.

[642] ***Barkarār*** (Persian barqa-rār): "continuing as heretofore." Platts, ***Dictionary***, p. 147.

69. Thereafter, in 1632-33, Pātsāh Shāh Jahān sent Asap Khān[643] along with many Hindus [and] Muslims against Bījāpur. At that time he had sent Rājā Gajsiṅghjī[644] with Asap Khān too.[645] There was no accord between Asap Khān and the Rājājī.

Vigat, 2:77

Asap Khān came back. He complained a great deal about the Śrī Mahārājājī. Then [the Pātsāh] increased [the assessment] on all the lands [held by Gajsiṅgh].[646] Once again he increased [the assessment] on Meṛto 2,000,000 ***dāms***. The total ***rekh***[647] became 12,000,000 ***dāms***, the rupee [value] of which [was] 300,000.

70. On May 6, 1638, Rājā Gajsiṅghjī passed away in Agra.[648] On May 25, 1638, Pātsāh Shāh Jahān gave Rājā Śrī Jasvantsiṅghjī the throne of Jodhpur.[649] On that day [the assessment] on Meṛto was again increased

---

643 Asap Khān: the noble Āṣaf Khān, Nūr Jahān's brother and the most powerful noble in the Iranian faction at the Mughal court. His daughter was the famous Mamtāz Maḥal, the favorite wife of Shāh Jahān, for whom he built the Tāj Maḥal. Āṣaf Khān continued in favor after the death of Jahāngīr and acquired a rank of 9,000 ***zāt***, 9,000 ***suwār*** under Shāh Jahān. He died in 1641. For some details of his career, see ***Maāthir-ul-Umarā***, 1:287-295.

644 The text has ***Rājsiṅghjī***, clearly incorrect. Gajsiṅgh is meant.

645 Bhargava, ***Marwar and the Mughal Emperors***, p. 76, notes that Gajsiṅgh was deputed along with Āṣaf Khān against Muḥammad Adīl Khān, Sultān of Bījāpur, in December of 1631.

646 The assessments of the ***parganos*** Sojhat, Jaitāraṇ, and Meṛto were increased at this time.

647 ***Rekh***: assessment, evaluation.

648 At the time of Gajsiṅgh's death, he had spent one ***lākh*** twelve ***kroṛs*** of rupees, taken out of the treasury built up by his father, Rājā Sūrajsiṅgh, and had in addition taken out a loan of Rs. 1,300,000, for which he had mortgaged Jāḷor Pargano to the imperial treasury. These debts were left to his son and successor, Jasvantsiṅgh, to pay back. ***Bāṅkīdās***, p. 27; ***Mahārāj Śrī Gajsiṅgh kī Khyāt***, p. 139; Ojhā, 4:1:407; ***Vigat***, 1:105.

649 Jasvantsiṅgh had been to Būndī to marry at the time he received the news of his father's death in Āgrā. Immediately after the marriage, he proceeded to Delhi, where he was given the throne of Jodhpur by Shāh Jahān himself. At the time of his succession, his ***mansab*** rank was raised to 4,000 ***zāt***, 4,000 ***suwar***, and he received the ***parganos*** Jodhpur, Sīvāṇo, Meṛto, Sojhat, Phaḷodhī, and Sātalmer (Pokaraṇ) in ***jāgīr***. ***Bāṅkīdās***, p. 29; ***Jasvantsiṅghjī kī Khyāt*** (MS no. 15661, Rājasthān Prācyavidyā Pratiṣṭhān, Jodhpur), pp. 1-2; Ojhā, 4:1:413-414; ***Vigat***, 1:123-124.

2,000,000 ***dāms***.[650] [The total assessment] there became 14,000,000 ***dāms***, the rupee [value] of which was 350,000.

[650] The text has ***dām lākh 2,000,000***; apparently the word ***bīs*** ("twenty") should have followed ***lākh*** (100,000).

"Aitihāsik Bātāṃ," p. 42

A great battle came up in the month of January, 1544,[1] between [the villages of] Samel [and] Khāp.[2] There is a river [flowing] before Samel. Its [flow is] toward Girrī [and] Bābro.[3] On its near side[4] are two small hills. The ***sāth*** of Rāv [Mālde]jī came [to the battle] between them. There was brush there. The entire battlefield there consisted of terraces.[5] Now they have fallen. On the far side of the river of Samel are the ***chatrīs*** of the Meṛtīyos. Once during the battle[6] both Jaito[7] [and] Kūmpo[8] dismounted while in the safety of the river bank and ate opium with the water of the river.[9] They rinsed their mouths. Tightening the reins [of their horses], they urged [them] up again and spurred [them] on into [the opposing army].

---

[1] The battle of Samel between the forces of Rāv Mālde of Jodhpur and those of Sher Shāh Sūr took place on January 5, 1544.

[2] The text has ***Amel Khāpas***, evidently a printer's mistake for Samel and Khāp, two villages located twenty-four miles southwest of Ajmer and twenty-three miles east of Jaitāraṇ town. Khāp is listed as "Khāp of Samel" in ***Vigat***, 1:555.

[3] Literally, "its direction [is] to Girrī [and] Bābro." Bābro is situated seven miles to the west of Samel; Girrī lies eight miles southwest of Bābro. The site of the battle is indicated by Map 3, "Mārvāṛ Terrain of the Battle of Samel, 1544."

[4] ***Ulai kānai***: the near side; the side nearest Jodhpur.

[5] ***Cautro***: a raised platform; a terrace. Lands near the hills, particularly where there are potential waterways or streams, are often terraced with mud walls around them to contain water from runoff and rains. James Tod, ***Annals and Antiquities of Rajasthan***, edited by William Crooke, 3 vols. (London: Oxford University Press, 1920), 2:774, has an excellent description of terrace cultivation in the Arāvalīs:

> From the margin of the stream on each side to the mountain's base they have constructed a series of terraces rising over each other, whence by simple and ingenious methods they raise the waters to irrigate the rich crops of sugarcane, cotton, and rice, which they cultivate upon them .... Wherever soil could be found, or time decomposed these primitive rocks, a barrier was raised.

[6] Literally, "having done battle" (***veḍh kar nai***).

[7] Rāṭhoṛ Jaito Pañcāiṇot (no. 61), one of Rāv Mālde's ***pradhāns*** and the founder of the Jaitāvat branch of Mārvāṛ Rāṭhoṛs.

[8] Rāṭhoṛ Kūmpo Mahirājot (no. 95), Rāv Mālde's ***senāpati***, or army commander, and the founder of the Kūmpāvat branch of Mārvāṛ Rāṭhoṛs.

[9] It was a common custom among Rajpūts to take opium before or during a battle, both to steady nerves and to alleviate or deaden pain.

The Sūr Pātsāh, a Paṭhāṇ,[10] and the Rāṭhoṛ, Vīramde Dūdāvat,[11] advanced against Rāv Mālde. Vīramde Dūdāvat brought [the Pātsāh's] armies [to Mārvāṛ]. Then Rāv Mālde, [having gone] as far as Harmāṛo,[12] [a village] of Ajmer, confronted [them] with 80,000 horse.[13] The encampments of the Pātsāh drew near. Then [Rāv Mālde] moved [his camp] back two or three ***kos***. Samel became the Pātsāh's camp. Girrī became the Rāv's camp. Here the Rāv decided to move the camp back once more. He told Rāṭhoṛ Jaito Pañcāiṇot [and] Rāṭhoṛ Kūmpo Mahirājot [this]. They said: "The land beyond [here] you obtained. And the land to the rear of here your ancestors and our ancestors obtained together. We shall not move back from here." Then Vīramde Dūdāvat played a trick and confused the Rāv.

It was dusk. [The first] four ***gharīs*** of the night were gone. The Rāvjī had lain down on a ***ḍholiyo*** in [his] tent. He was wearing a ***sūthaṇ***.[14] He was covered with a fine ***dupaṭo***.[15] Rāṭhoṛ Pato Kūmpāvat[16] [and] Rāṭhoṛ Udaisiṅgh Jaitāvat[17] both were sleeping on the ground near the Rāvjī's ***ḍholiyo***. Meanwhile, a Cāraṇ of Rāṭhoṛ Vīramde Dūdāvat's came and had [his] respects paid [to the Rāvjī while standing] at the entrance [to the tent]. Then the Rāvjī said: "Come inside." The Cāraṇ sent word: "Vīramde has had [me] make a request. He has had [me] make [it] in secret. ***Rāj***! Stand outside at the entrance." Then the Rāvjī went outside wearing the ***sūthaṇ***, covered with the ***dupaṭo***.

"Aitihāsik Bātāṃ," p. 43

He conversed with that Cāraṇ while standing near the tent-rope. Rāṭhoṛ Vīramde had fabricated a lie and sent word with the Cāraṇ: "The Rāvs [of Jodhpur] drove us away, but even so we wish the throne [of Jodhpur to be] yours. Your Rajpūts have all met with the Pātsāh." Then the Rāvjī said: "Why should one think [so]?" The Cāraṇ said: "The Pātsāh has given ***mohars***[18] to the ***umrāvs***." Then the Rāvjī said: "The

---

[10] Sher Shāh Sūr, the Afghan (Paṭhāṇ) ruler of Delhi and north India, 1540-45.

[11] Meṛtīyo Rāṭhoṛ Rāv Vīramde Dūdāvat (no. 105).

[12] Harmāṛo: a village situated fifty-five miles south-southwest of Ajmer.

[13] For the size of the armies present at Samel, see n. 295 to ***Vigat***, 2:57.

[14] ***Sūthaṇ***: a type of pajama covering the lower portion of the body; a type of chain mail fulfilling the same function.

[15] The text has ***dupaṭī*** here and ***dupaṭo*** farther down the page. We have standardized the usage to avoid confusion. A ***dupaṭo*** was a type of shawl or cover-cloth commonly worn by Rajpūts.

[16] Kūmpāvat Rāṭhoṛ Pato (Pratāpsiṅgh) Kūmpāvat (no. 96).

[17] Jaitāvat Rāṭhoṛ Udaisiṅgh Jaitāvat (no. 62).

[18] ***Mohar*** (Persian muhr): a gold coin. In Akbar's time, the ***mohar*** had an accounting

umrāv*s are not the sort of men [who can be bribed]." The Cāraṇ said: "[Their] tents cannot be searched, but send a Sāhūkār;[19] have the Modīs[20] of the ***umrāv*s estimate the ***mohar*s." So the Rāvjī sent the Sāhūkār. Previously Vīramde had withheld ***mohar*s from the hands of his own Modīs, having promised[21] [them to] the Modīs [of the ***umrāv*s]. And so [the Sāhūkār] came and told the Rāvjī: "They have ready as many ***mohar*s as they need." Then [concern] entered the mind of the Rāvjī. He came back [into his tent], quickly put on a ***vāgo,[22] tied on a dagger, tied on a sword, and did not even ask anyone [about the ***mohar*s]. There was a horse of the guardpost standing [nearby]; he mounted [it] and set out himself. He told the ***kāmdār*s: "Come quickly with the camp equipment."

Then they began to take down the camp equipment. Rāṭhoṛ Pato Kānhāvat,[23] Rāṭhoṛ Udaisiṅgh Jaitāvat, [and] Rāṭhoṛ Kūmpojī received this news. These ***ṭhākur*s did not believe [what they had heard]. They sent for [additional] information; yet another man came and said: "The Rāvjī departed." Then both brothers,[24] Kūmpojī [and] Jaitojī, came and sat down in one place. [Someone] had set free an elephant of the Rāv's; [men] had to search for it. It [was] the elephant [carrying] the Rāv's throne[25] [and] had been injured.[26] It [could] not be saved, [no matter] what they did.

---

value of nine silver rupees. Its exact value at the time of the battle of Samel in 1544 is unknown. For a discussion of the relationship between the ***mohar*** and the rupee in Mughal times, see Irfan Habib, ***The Agrarian System of Mughal India, 1556-1707*** (Bombay: Asia Publishing House, 1963), pp. 384-387.

[19] Sāhūkār: a person who deals with money, a banker.

[20] Modī: a grain merchant. H. H. Wilson, ***A Glossary of Judicial and Revenue Terms*** (1855: reprint edition, Delhi: Munshiram Manoharlal, 1968), p. 344, has the following: "[Modī] most usually denotes the village shopkeeper, a sort of grocer or chandler and grain dealer, who sells a variety of of articles of necessity to the villagers, ... who are generally in his debt at an usurious rate of interest." Apparently Modīs also handled funds for important Rajpūts in middle period Mārvāṛ.

[21] ***Sadvāy***: perhaps this conjunctive participle is from the verb ***sandāvṇo***, a variant form of ***sandhāṇo***, "to join," "to connect," "to promise," "to vow." Our translation is based upon this possibility.

[22] ***Vāgo***: a garment bound at the waist and extending down to the knees.

[23] Akhairājot Rāṭhoṛ Pato Kānhāvat (no. 35). There may be some confusion of names in the text between Pato Kānhāvat and Pato Kūmpāvat, who is mentioned on p. 42, ***supra***, as sleeping outside the Rāv's tent along with Udaisiṅgh Jaitāvat.

[24] Kūmpo and Jaito were not actual brothers, but rather paternal cousins. The term "brothers" is used in a broader sense here, indicating those Rajpūts of close male blood belonging to the same brotherhood (***bhāībandh***).

[25] ***Pāṭ ro hāthī***. Literally, "the elephant of the throne," i.e., the elephant the Rāv would have ridden into battle.

Then Kūmpojī [and] Jaitojī had [it] shot by the men who searched [for it]. Afterward, they sent a man to the [Rāv's] tent and had [him] report how large a ***sāth*** had left [and] how large a ***sāth*** had stayed. The man came [back] and informed [them]: "A large ***sāth*** went with the Rāvjī. There are various important ***ṭhākur***s [still here], and, up until now, quite a large ***sāth*** has remained. Twenty thousand horse have stayed." Then both ***ṭhākur***s, Jaitojī [and] Kūmpojī, spread floor-cloths and sat down. They pondered: "What should be done?" Then they summoned all the great ***ṭhākurs***. They asked [their opinion]; all thought this: "If we let Mārvāṛ be lost now, where would we go?" And [so] thinking, they perceived: "Rāv Mālde left; the ***sāth*** [left] behind [is] small; we cannot match [the enemy] in a daytime battle." Then they mounted to carry out a night attack. There was some twist of fate. They wandered around all night [but still] did not find the innumerable[27] horse of the Pātsāh.

Meanwhile, it became morning. The Pātsāh's kettledrum was struck. [As] the Pātsāh's kettledrum was being struck, [the Rāṭhoṛs], as they wandered around, came to the bank of the river of Samel.

"Aitihāsik Bātāṃ," p. 44

They did not find [the Pātsāh's army] during the night[28] [because] Vīramde told the Pātsāh: "The Rajpūts will attack [our] tents [during the night]; take down the tents." So the Pātsāh took down the tents, retreated, and set up [the tents again].

Then [the Rāṭhoṛs] came to the bank of the river of Samel. Even before [they came there] the ***sāth*** of the [Pātsāh's] guardpost saw [them]. The Pātsāhjī prepared for battle also.[29] Here both armies rushed forward[30] and joined [in battle]. The

---

[26] ***Vīraṛiyo*** in the text is a misprint for ***vīgaṛiyo*** ("injured," "spoiled"), as the editor, N. S. Bhāṭī, suggests in n. 5.

[27] ***Navlākh***: literally, "nine ***lākh***s," "900,000," an adjective of deliberate exaggeration used to indicate very large numbers.

[28] The text has ***rāte lābh nahīṃ***; apparently the reading should be ***rate lābho/lābhai nahīṃ***.

[29] The Rāṭhoṛs were already prepared to fight, as they had been trying to carry out a night attack.

[30] ***Kaṭhaṭh nai***. Lāḷas, ***RSK***, 1:399, defines ***kāṭhaṭhṇo*** thus:

> (1) To leave; (2) to come outside; (3) to move making the "***kaṭhaṭh***" sound; (4) to move being in a frenzy/boil.

Sākarīya, ***RHSK***, p. 192, defines ***kaṭhaṭhṇo*** in this way:

> (1) To be ready/prepared; (2) to be ready/prepared for attack; (3) to attack; (4) to be in a frenzy/boil; (5) to surge/overflow.

The verb may be onomatopoeic, suggesting the bubbling of a liquid or (perhaps) the

kettledrums sounded. These ***ṭhākur***s, Jaitojī [and] Kūmpojī, destroyed an ***aṇī***, a large ***harol***[31] of the Pātsāh's army, and remained standing unharmed [on the battlefield]. Afterward there was a skirmish[32] with Jalāl Jalūko.[33] Jaitojī struck Jalāl's chest [a blow] with [his] lance. Jalāl had full armor, so the lance did not break through, but Jalāl's foot left the stirrups from the magic[34] of the lance. Jalāl, [knocked back] on the hairs of [his] horse's tail, fell down, and both front feet of Jaitojī's horse broke [from Jaitoji's] hurling the lance. Such strength Jaitojī showed! These ***ṭhākur***s died fighting. Another ***sāth*** died fighting. Rāṭhoṛ Jaitojī died fighting in [his] sixtieth year. Kūmpojī died fighting in [his] thirty-fifth year. Rāṭhoṛ Pato Kānhāvat fought so [fiercely] that the blood of Pato's body got on the Pātsāh's body. The Pātsāh himself was in the battle, mounted on a very fine horse. He won the battle. Afterward, the Pātsāhjī came upon [the bodies of] Jaitojī [and] Kūmpojī. He looked at [them]. He stood Jaitojī up and looked at [him]. He told Rāṭhoṛ Vīramde Dūdāvat: "This Rajpūt did so much—I might have lost the Empire of Delhi. Perhaps if Rāv Mālde had stayed, I would have lost the battle."[35]

---

sound of armored men marching forward in step.

[31] ***Harol*** (Persian harāwal): an advance guard of an army, a vanguard.

[32] ***Kām***: literally, "an action."

[33] Jalāl Jalūko: Jalāl Khān Jalvāṇī, an Afghan chief in the service of Sher Shāh.

[34] ***Jāḷ***: magic, magical power.

[35] One may contrast the description of the battle of Samel given here with that given by the Muslim historian, ʻAbd al-Qadīr ibn Mulūk Shāh Badā'ūnī:

> In short Shīr Shāh, who would not give the head of one of his soldiers for a kingdom, and to whom the Afghāns were far dearer than can be expressed, was by no means willing to involve his army in calimity with the ignorant, boar-natured, currish Hindūs. Accordingly he devised an artifice, and wrote fictitious letters purporting to emanate from the generals of Māldeo's army, to himself, couched in enigmatic language, the substance of them being that there would be no need for the king in person to superintend the fighting, when the armies were drawn up for battle, because they themselves would take Māldeo alive and deliver him up, upon the condition that such and such place should be given them as a reward. Having done this he so arranged that those letters fell into Māldeo's hands, with the result that Māldeo became utterly suspicious of all his generals, and, in the dead of night, fled alone without looking behind him; and, notwithstanding that his generals denied their complicity with oath upon oath, saying that they never could have been guilty of such dastardly conduct, and that this was all the handiwork of Shīr Shāh in his desire to raise dissension between them, it was of no use, and had no effect upon Māldeo's mind. Kanhaiyā [Kūmpo], who was his minister and agent, abused Māldeo in violent terms, and taking four thousand resolute men devoted to death, or even more than this number, came down upon the army of Shīr Shāh, with the intention of surprising them by night, but missed his way, and after marching

Five thousand Rāṭhoṛs out of twenty thousand died fighting. Fifteen thousand left [only] after having fought [with the enemy]. Rāṭhoṛ Jaitsī Vāghot,[36] Rāṭhoṛ Jeso Bhairavdāsot,[37] Rāṭhoṛ Mahes Gharsīyot[38]--these great *ṭhākurs* left. Many others left. The Rāv left and came toward Sīvāṇo to the mountains of Pīplāṇ. [Thereafter] the *guṛos*[39] of the Riṇmals were in the hills. Kūmpojī's [wife] became a *satī*[40] [near the statue of] Mahākāḷ[41] in Sāraṇ.[42]

---

the whole night, when morning broke became aware that he had left the camp far in rear. After striving to the utmost of their powers, when they had abandoned all hope of life, at the very moment when the army of Shīr Shāh came in sight, as a result of their own stupidity, by the good luck of Shīr Shāh or by the superior good fortune of Islām, the infidels in a body dismounted from their horses, and renewing their vows of singleness of purpose and mutual assistance, binding their sashes together and joining hand to hand, attacked the army of the Afghāns with their short spears, which they call *Barchcha*, and with their swords. Shīr Shāh had given orders saying that if any man ventured to fight with the sword with this swinish horde, his blood would be on his own head. He accordingly ordered the elephant troops to advance and trample them down. In the rear of the elephants, the artillery and archers gave them a taste of the bowstring, and admitting them to the banquet of death, gave them the hospitality of the land of extinction. The bright surface of the world's page was polished, and freed from the dark lines of the land of infidels, and not one of the infidels got off with his life, nor was a single Muslim lost in that encounter.

'Abd al-Qadīr ibn Mulūk Shāh Badā'ūnī, ***Muntakhabu't-Tawārīkh***, vol. 1, translated and edited by George S. A. Ranking (1898; reprint edition, Delhi: Idarah-i Adabiyat-i Delli, 1973), pp. 477-479.

[36] Jodho Rāṭhoṛ Jaitsī Vāghāvat (no. 85).

[37] Cāmpāvat Rāṭhoṛ Jeso Bhairavdāsot (no. 48).

[38] Cūṇḍāvat Rāṭhoṛ Mahes Gharsīyot (no. 58).

[39] ***Guṛo***: a hideout; a temporary village which may grow into a permanent settlement; a type of long-term camp, different from the ***ḍero*** or short-term camp in that it included all of the dependents of its Rajpūt master—peasants, Cāraṇs, Brāhmaṇs, potters, etc.—and not just those persons concerned with military service. Livestock was also kept in the ***guṛo***. See R. Saran, "Conquest and Colonization: Rajpūts and ***Vasīs*** in Midde Period Mārvāṛ (unpublished Ph.D. dissertation, The University of Michigan, 1978), pp. 88-89.

[40] ***Satī***: a "virtuous woman"; a woman who has immolated herself on her husband's funeral pyre.

[41] Mahākāḷ: (1) Śiva as Lord of Time and hence of Death; (2) an image or statue of Śiva in this destructive aspect. The text has a cryptic ***Kūmpājī ri satī Sāraṇ Māhkāḷ huī***, but "Aitihāsik Bātāṃ," p. 85, has the following:

> Rāv Candrasen was cremated near the banyan tree (*vaṛ*) of Mahākāḷ of Sāraṇ [village]. There were three ***satīs***. Their ***chatrīs*** are near [the statue of] Mahākāḷ.

From this passage, one might hypothesize that it was a tradition (during the sixteenth century, at least) for important Rāṭhoṛs to be cremated and their wives to become ***satīs*** near the statue of Mahākāḷ in Sāraṇ village. See also "Aitihāsik Bātāṃ," pp. 87-89; ***Vigat***, 1:465.

[42] Sāraṇ: a village located eighteen miles southeast of Sojhat.

"Aitihāsik Bātāṃ," p. 48

Thereafter Rāv Mālde recalled again the enmity with the Meṛtīyos. The Rāvjī went against Meṛto in 1554. At that time these great *ṭhākurs* were with [him]: Prithīrāj Jaitāvat,[1] Cāndo Vīramdevot,[2] Ratansī Khīṃvāvat,[3] Nago Bhārmalot,[4] Prithīrāj Kūmpāvat,[5] and Mānsiṅgh.[6] There was another large *sāth* too. They came to Indāvaṛ[7] and made camp. Jaimal[8] sent a man to Prithīrāj and had [him] say: "We are the Rāvjī's Rajpūts. Have us perform services; why kill us?" He as well as the five *ṭhākurs*[9] entreated with the Rāvjī, but the Rāv, in a hostile mood, would not consider [their request]. On March 20, 1554,[10] he carried out an attack [against Meṛto]. These [men]—Rāv Mālde himself, Prithārāj, and Nago Bhārmalot—[were] at the Jodhpur Gate.[11] The large *aṇī*[12] was on this side. Cāndo Vīramdevot had not joined [them] at the time of the battle. He had camped at Vaḍāgāṃv.[13] He procrastinated a bit; [then] he came and joined [them] at Sātaḷvās[14] [after the battle].

---

[1] Jaitāvat Rāṭhoṛ Prithīrāj Jaitāvat (no. 63).

[2] Meṛtīyo Rāṭhoṛ Cāndo Vīramdevot (no. 123).

[3] Ūdāvat Rāṭhoṛ Ratansī Khīṃvāvat (no. 141).

[4] Bālāvat Rāṭhoṛ Nago Bhārmalot (no. 38)

[5] Kūmpāvat Rāṭhoṛ Prithīrāj Kūmpāvat (no. 97).

[6] Sonagaro Cahuvāṇ Mānsiṅgh Akhairājot (no. 10).

[7] Indāvaṛ: a village situated eight miles southwest of Meṛto.

[8] Meṛtīyo Rāṭhoṛ Jaimal Vīramdevot (no. 107), Rāv of Meṛto, 1544-57 and also briefly in 1562.

[9] The "five *ṭhākurs*" referred to apparently were the Rāṭhoṛ *ṭhākurs* with Rāv Mālde at this time.

[10] See n. 337 to *Vigat*, 2:58, for the date of the second attack on Meṛto.

[11] I.e., the gate of Meṛto town facing Jodhpur.

[12] Apparently the Rāv's army was divided into two *aṇīs*: one, referred to as the "Rāv's *sāth*" or the "large *aṇī*," situated near the Jodhpur Gate; the second, called the *"anī* of the Riṇmals" or simply the "other *aṇī*," situated near the Bejpo Tank and the *koṭṛī*.

[13] Vaḍāgāṃv: a village situated eleven miles south-southwest of Meṛto and five miles due south of Indāvaṛ, mentioned above.

[14] Sātaḷvās: a village situated four miles southwest of Meṛto.

Ratansī Khīṃvāvat, Jagmāl,[15] [and] another large ***sāth*** as well, forming a [smaller] ***aṇī*** in the direction of the Bejpo [Tank],[16] had told [him]: "Come to the ***koṭṛī***."

[Meanwhile] Jaimal was performing many religious devotions[17] for Śrī Catarbhujjī.[18] The Ṭhākur[19] was pleased. There was a command: "Do battle; victory will be yours." So Jaimal himself came in front of the large ***aṇī*** and remained [concealed] among some shrubs.[20] The Rāv's ***sāth*** did not even take very much notice [of him], and Jaimal's men went back and forth in between. They came and told Jaimal: "Prithīrāj [is] by himself, [sub]dividing the [large] ***aṇī***. The [smaller] ***aṇī*** of the Rinmals is separate [near the Bejpo Tank]. The ***sāth*** is inattentive. If you rush upon [them] now, there is a chance. Also, Prithīrāj will come before you now to divide the [large] ***aṇī***." Then all of a sudden they made a quick attack. When Prithīrāj saw them, he dismounted. His ***aṇī*** remained separate. A skirmish occurred here. Śrī Caturbhujjī was Jaimal's ally. The fight began with Prithārāj Jaitāvat. Prithārāj showed great prowess. Fourteen men were struck down by his hand. The sword of his military servant, Hīṅgoḷo Pīpāṛo,[21] broke. Then he snatched Surtāṇ Jaimalot's[22] sword, one embellished with silk,[23] from [Surtāṇ's] waist,[24] took [it] away with him, summoned Hīṅgoḷo, and gave [it to him].

Nago Bhārmalot died fighting.

---

[15] Meṛtīyo Rāṭhoṛ Jagmāl Vīramdevot (no. 124).

[16] The Bejpo was an ancient tank in Meṛto town (see ***Vigat***, 2:38).

[17] ***Sevā***: service of a religious or devotional nature performed for a god, goddess, or religious teacher.

[18] Śrī Catarbhujjī: the patron deity of the Meṛtīyo Rāṭhoṛs (see n. 516 to ***Vigat***, 2:69).

[19] I.e., Śrī Catarbhujjī.

[20] ***Āk*** (Calotropis Procera): a much-branched shrub, usually two or three meters high, common throughout Rājasthān. M. M. Bhandari, ***Flora of the Indian Desert*** (Jodhpur: Scientific Publishers, 1978), p. 219.

[21] Pīpāṛo is the designation of a branch (***sākh***) of the Gahlot Rajpūt family (***kuḷ***). We have no additional information concerning Hīṅgoḷo.

[22] Meṛtīyo Rāṭhoṛ Surtāṇ Jaimalot (no. 113).

[23] ***Sājh resmī tho***: literally, "the embellishment/decoration was silken."

[24] ***Kaṛīyāṃ suṃ***. ***Kaṛīyāṃ*** is "waist," but also is the plural of ***kaṛī***, "metal ring/band." Possibly ***kaṛīyāṃ*** in this sentence refers to the embellishment (***sājh***) of Surtāṇ's sword. If so, the translation would read; "Then he snatched Surtāṇ's sword, one embellished with silk [and] with metal bands, took [it] away with him, summoned Hīṅgoḷo, and gave [it to him]."

"Aitihāsik Bātāṃ," p. 49

Caturbhujjī himself mounted a horse and joined Jaimal's faction.[25] The Rāvjī's ***sāth***, the [large] ***aṇī***, fled. The Rāvjī withdrew from there and remained standing to the rear. Jaimal, having won the battle, immediately turned back. He came before the gate near the ***koṭṛī***.[26] Just then [the men of] the other ***aṇī***, which was coming to this entrance of the Bejpo [Tank] after having taken the [nearby] villages under control and looted the city, perceived Jaimal returning. They thought: "He has come from there having lost [the battle]." This ***aṇī*** and Jaimal joined [in battle]. There Devīdās Jaitāvat[27] was about to strike Jaimal a blow with a lance when out of the mouth of Ratansī Khīṃvāvat [came the words]: "Rāv [Jaimal] should be spared." That ***ṭhākur***, [Devīdās], did not thrust the lance. Jaimal was a perceptive man. He realized: "I have acquired the backing of a powerful man."[28] Then he went inside the gate. A ***dūho*** concerning this [occurrence], the ***sākh*** of Ratansī Khīṃvāvat:

> Jaimal, man of battle, one who troubled the land of Maṇḍovar,[29]
> the son of Khīṃvo[30] defeated the weapon before you.

Jaimal closed the gate and remained seated [inside]. [The men of the ***aṇī***] looted the market square and the city again, then came outside [the walls]. Previously [they] received the news [that] the Rāv had fled. Many men wrung [their] hands in regret over this occurrence. The ***sāth*** came to Sātaḷvās and joined the Rāv. Then Rāṭhoṛ Cāndo Vīramdevot said a great deal to Rāv Mālde: "Make camp right here. Tomorrow we will attack. We will kill Jaimal." But the Rāvjī did not consider [Cāndo's] proposal. He made camp back at Gāṅgāṛo.[31]

In this battle [at Meṛto] the following ***sāth*** of Rāv Mālde's died fighting:[32]

---

[25] ***Bhīr***: crowd, faction.

[26] ***Koṭṛī kanai najīk pauḷ rai muṃhaḍai āyo***. The word ***najīk*** is redundant in this sentence.

[27] Jaitāvat Rāṭhoṛ Devīdās Jaitāvat (no. 65).

[28] ***Mhai sabaḷo bol bāṃsai nāṅkhīyo chai***. We are uncertain of the precise meaning of the fragment ***bol bāṃsai nāṅkhīyo chai***; the sense of the entire phrase seems to be that Jaimal had put or placed strong words or a firm promise on his side (literally, "behind [him]"), i.e., that he had acquired the support of a powerful man (Ratansī Khīṃvāvat).

[29] Maṇḍovar: another name for Maṇḍor, a town situated five miles north of Jodhpur.

[30] Khemāl: apparently this is a poetic form of Khīmāvāḷo/Khīṃvāvat, "son of Khīmo/Khīṃvo," a reference to Ratansī Khīṃvāvat.

[31] Gāṅgāṛo: a village situated seven miles west of Meṛto.

[32] This list contains several redundancies, which we have eliminated for the reader's convenience.

Prithārāj Jaitāvat died fighting. He fought well. His ***sākh:***

Destruction[33] [itself] in hand-to-hand combats,[34] a warrior with a collection [of] twelve lances [belonging to fallen enemies],

Pīthal (Prithīrāj), destroying the renown[35] [of others], killed so many in battle.

There, in the Rāṭhoṛ family, several became men a second time,[36]

but none [your] equal in profound virtues, Pīthal!

Rāṭhoṛ Prithīrāj Jaitāvat [was] thirty years [old].
Rāṭhoṛs Nago Bhārmalot [and] Dhano Bhārmalot, two brothers.
Rāṭhoṛ Jagmāl Udaikaraṇot.[37]
Rāṭhoṛ Dhanrāj.[38]
Ḍūṅgarsī.[39]
Megho.[40]
Abho.[41]
Rato.[42]
Sohaṛ Pītho Jesāvat.[43]
Sūjo Tejsīyot.[44]

---

[33] ***Bibhaṛ***: probably this is a variant of ***vibhāṛ***, "destruction."

[34] ***Vāthāṃ***: the oblique plural of ***vāth/bāth***, "scuffle," "embrace," "duel," etc.

[35] ***Virad***: a laudatory title held by men of renown (e.g., ***kāḷ-bhujāḷ***, "warrior capable of fighting Death/Time itself").

[36] I.e., "died fighting." ***Bhaḷaih*** in the text is glossed by Lāḷas (***RSK***, 3:3:3317) as a variant of ***vaḷe***, "again," "a second time."

[37] Karamsot Rāṭhoṛ Jagmāl Udaikaraṇot (no. 91).

[38] Probably Bālāvat Rāṭhoṛ Dhanrāj (Dhano) Bhārmalot (no. 39). If so, this would be yet another redundancy in this somewhat garbled list.

[39] Sīndhaḷ Rāṭhoṛ Ḍūṅgarsī (no. 133).

[40] Sācoro Cahuvāṇ Megho Bhairavdāsot (no. 8).

[41] Pañcolī Abho Jhājhāvat (no. 161).

[42] Pañcolī Rato Abhāvat (no. 163), son of Abho Jhājhāvat.

[43] Sohaṛ Rāṭhoṛ Pītho Jesāvat. See n. 343 to ***Vigat***, 2:59.

[These men] fell [on the battlefield].

"Aitihāsik Bātāṃ," p. 50

Then the Rāv left [Gāṅgārṛo]. A military servant of Jaimal's, Sīsodīyo Megho,[45] came near to thrust a weapon at the Rāvjī. Rāṭhoṛ Kisandās Gāṅgāvat[46] [and] Rāṭhoṛ Ḍūṅgarsī Ūdāvat[47] realized: "He will strike the Rāv with [his] lance." Then they killed [Megho].

Afterward Jaimal [and] several [others] heard of this affair. Then Rāṭhoṛ Kisandās came to the Rāv's ***vās*** [for protection]. Jaimal was infuriated. After that the Rāvjī proceeded to Jodhpur.

At that time there was no Rajpūt like [Prithārāj Jaitāvat in the Rāv's service], for which [reason] the Rāvjī [was] very worried. The Rāvjī gave Bagṛī[48] to Prithārāj's son, Pūraṇmal.[49] At that time Rāṭhoṛ Devīdās Jaitāvat was in the ***sāth*** of Ratansī Khīṃvāvat. He had Bāñjhāṅkūṛī[50] in ***pato***. Devīdās left there and came to the Rāvjī. The Rāvjī highly honored Devīdās. Devīdās greatly strengthened the Rāvjī. The Rāvjī thought: "He will achieve the aim of Prithīrāj for me." Devīdās requested orders from the Rāvjī: "If [you] command [me], I shall depart one time and end the ***vair*** of Prithīrāj."[51] Then he went[52] to [his] home, dispatched one thousand horsemen of the Riṇmals, came [with them] to Reyāṃ,[53] and invested [it]. [After] they had stayed [there] an entire day, Jaimal received word. Then the entire Meṛtīyo ***colāvaṭ***[54]

---

[44] Rāṭhoṛ Sūjo Tejsīyot. See n. 348 to ***Vigat***, 2:59.

[45] No additional information is available concerning this Sīsodīyo Rajpūt.

[46] Jodho Rāṭhoṛ Kisandās Gāṅgāvat (no. 87).

[47] Ūdāvat Rāṭhoṛ Ḍūṅgarsī Ūdāvat (no. 137). Both Ḍūṅgarsī and Kisandās were Jaimal's military servants at this time.

[48] Bagṛī: a village situated fifty-two miles southeast of Jodhpur, near Sojhat.

[49] Jaitāvat Rāṭhoṛ Pūraṇmal Prithīrājot (no. 64).

[50] Bāñjhāṅkuṛī: a village situated five miles north of Jaitāraṇ and fifty-two miles due east of Jodhpur.

[51] ***Vair ekarsuṃ khaṛ bhāñjhāṃ***. ***Vair bhāñjṇo***: "to break a ***vair***"; i.e., to end the state of tension or hostility that exists for a lineage or an individual upon the murder of a kinsman or retainer.

[52] Literally, "came."

[53] Reyāṃ: a village situated twenty-eight miles northeast of Bāñjhāṅkuṛī and eighty miles east-northeast of Jodhpur.

[54] ***Colāvaṭ***: perhaps this word is a compound formed from ***colā*** ("bodies") plus ***vaṭ***

prepared for [battle] and came [to Meṛto] for an attack [on Devīdās]. Jaimal stopped [them]. He said: "This [situation] is very favorable to them [now]. In the morning have the kettledrum struck." Devīdās passed near Meṛto with [his] supplies loaded into one hundred plowman's carts. Even then no one came to oppose [him].

Subsequently Hājī Khān,[55] [who had been] an ***umrāv*** of the Pātsāh's,[56] was going to Gujarāt. Discord arose between him [and] Rāṇo Udaisiṅgh.[57] Then Hājī Khān sent word to the Rāvjī: "If you send a ***sāth*** to help me, then I will give you Ajmer." The Rāvjī became very thoughtful: "Who shall I send? Who will go?" Rāṭhoṛ Devīdās Jaitāvat said to the Rāvjī: "I shall go. ***Rāj***! Why do you worry?" The Rāvjī was very pleased. He praised [Devīdās] much. He said: "Indeed you are my [man]! First, last, and always the shame[58] of Mārvāṛ is on your shoulders." Then the Rāvjī said to Rāṭhoṛ Devīdās: "Take with you the ***sāth*** you decide upon; you are dismissed." Devīdās decided upon 1,500 horsemen. He had the ones selected recorded name by name.[59] The Rāvjī gave Devīdās a horse [and] a ***sirpāv*** and dispatched [him]. The following great ***ṭhākur***s were in the ***sāth***:

"Aitihāsik Bātāṃ," p. 51

Rāṭhoṛ Devīdās Jaitāvat.
Rāṭhoṛ Jagmāl Vīramdevot.[60]
Rāvaḷ Meghrāj Hāpāvat.[61]
Rāṭhoṛ Prithīrāj Kūmpāvat.[62]
Rāṭhoṛ Mahes Gharsīyot.[63]

("share," "portion"), signifying the living members of the Meṛtīyo ***sākh***.

[55] See n. 356 to ***Vigat***, 2:60.

[56] Sher Shāh Sūr, Afghan ruler of north India, 1540-45.

[57] Sīsodīyo Gahlot Rāṇo Udaisiṅgh Sāṅgāvat (no. 17), ruler of Mevāṛ, ca. 1537-72.

[58] Re: "shame" (***lāj***), see n. 120 to ***Vigat***, 2:45.

[59] The Rāṭhoṛ rulers of Mārvāṛ were in the habit of recording the names of those men taking part in military endeavors. A passage in Naiṇsī's ***Khyāt*** (2:288) suggests that this may have been a practice since the reign of Rāvaḷ Mālojī (fourteenth century):

> Then they decided on a night attack. Mālojī ordered: "Write down the names of the ***sirdārs***." He had the names of one hundred and forty ***sirdārs*** written down.

[60] Meṛtīyo Rāṭhoṛ Jagmāl Vīramdevot (no. 124).

[61] Maheco Rāṭhoṛ Meghrāj Hāpāvat (no. 103).

[62] Kūmpāvat Rāṭhoṛ Prithīrāj Kūmpāvat (no. 97).

Rāṭhoṛ Lakhmaṇ Bhādāvat.[64]
Rāṭhoṛ Jaitmāl Jesāvat.[65]

Rāṭhoṛ Mahes Kūmpāvat,[66] a military servant of the Rāṇo's, was in the opposing ***sāth***. At that time Mahes had little material wealth. [He] had one village of Mevāṛ, Nīpraṛ,[67] in ***paṭo***. In the battle Mahesjī protected the Rāṇo's elephants, which were being seized. He brought [them back], for which [reason] Mahes gained esteem. Afterward the Rāṇo gave Mahesjī Bālī[68] with seventeen [other] villages.

The Rāvjī's ***sāth*** came from [one direction]; Hājī Khān came from [another].[69] The Rāṇo also came to Harmāṛo.[70] Here preparations for battle began. At that time Rāṭhoṛ Tejsī Ḍūṅgarsīyot[71] was in the opposing army of the Rāṇo. He had come to meet [his] brothers.[72] Afterward the Rāṇojī asked Tejsī for information concerning [Rāv Mālde's] army: "Tell [me] the information [you have]." Then [Tejsī] said: "***Rāj***! I shall tell you what you ask." The Rāṇojī said: "If the opposing army were to be defeated,[73] how large a ***sāth*** [of theirs] would die fighting?" Tejsī said: "Five hundred Rāṭhoṛs would die fighting." And the Rāṇojī said: "If our army were to be defeated, how large a ***sāth*** [of ours] would die fighting?" Then Tejsī said: "Five [to] seven men would die fighting."[74] The Rāṇojī said: "You are speaking very well[75] of your brothers!" Then he said: "Tejsī! This [battle] will end quickly!"

---

[63] Cūṇḍāvat Rāṭhoṛ Mahes Gharsīyot (no. 58).

[64] Akhairājot Rāṭhoṛ Lakhmaṇ Bhādāvat (no. 33).

[65] Cāmpāvat Rāṭhoṛ Jaitmāl Jesāvat (no. 49).

[66] Kūmpāvat Rāṭhoṛ Mahes Kūmpāvat (no. 98).

[67] Nīpraṛ: we have been unable to find this village of Mevāṛ on modern maps.

[68] Bālī: a large village forty-eight miles northwest of Udaipur and seventy-six miles south-southeast of Jodhpur.

[69] Literally, "The Rāvjī's ***sāth*** came from here; Hājī Khān came from there."

[70] Harmāṛo: a village situated fifty-five miles south-southwest of Ajmer.

[71] Ūdāvat Rāṭhoṛ Tejsī Ḍūṅgarsīyot (no. 138).

[72] I.e., his fellow Rāṭhoṛs who were in Rāv Mālde's army.

[73] Literally, "flee" or "be destroyed" (***bhājai***).

[74] Tejsī is saying that if the Rāṭhoṛs were to lose, five hundred Rāṭhoṛs would die because, being great warriors, they would all stay on the battlefield and fight to the death. But if the Rāṇo's army were to lose, only five or six Sīsodīyos would die because most would run away and not fight.

[75] Literally, "very fully" (***nipaṭ pūro***).

Very soon afterward the battle occurred. Rāṭhoṛ Tejsī Ḍūṅgarsīyot, of firm resolve[76] [and] world-famous, [said]: "I shall kill the ***sirdār***, Hājī Khān."

After [that], Hājī Khān sat in an iron compartment on an elephant. He took many precautions.[77] Even so Tejsī came and struck Hājī Khān a blow. Rāṭhoṛ Devīdās Jaitāvat killed Bālīso Sūjo.[78] Hājī Khān [and] the Rāvjī's ***sāth*** won the battle. The Rāṇo lost. He fled. At that time the following other ***desots***[79] were in the Rāṇo's army:

Rāv Kalyāṇmal, the Bīkā[ner]īyo.[80]
Rāv Rāmcand Soḷaṅkī [of] Toḍaṛī.[81]
Rāv Durgo of Rāmpuro.[82]
Rāv Tejo of Devaḷīyo.[83]
Rāv Rām Khairāṛo of Jājpur.[84]
Rāv Narāyāṇ[dās] of Īḍar.[85]

---

[76] ***Vadievād***: this word is problematic; it seems to be a compound adjective formed from ***vadie***, which perhaps is the oblique past participle of ***vadṇo***, "to say," "to speak," "to decide," "to be stubborn," "to insist," etc. (Lāḷas, ***RSK***, 4:2:4501), plus the noun ***vād***, "obstinacy," "promise," "word," etc. (Lāḷas, ***RSK***, 4:2:4611), used to qualify Tejsī. Cf. "Aitihāsik Bātāṃ," p. 67, where the variant form ***vādiyevād*** appears in another passage concerning the same events. Our translation suggests one possible meaning of ***vadievād***; others might be "of firm promise," "of spoken word," of determined stubbornness," etc.

[77] ***Ghaṇā jatan kiyā***: literally, "made many efforts [to defend himself]."

[78] Bālīso Cahuvāṇ Sūjo Sāṃvatot (no. 4).

[79] ***Desot***: the ruler of a ***des*** ("country").

[80] Bīkāvat Rāṭhoṛ Rāv Kalyāṇmal Jaitsīyot (no. 46), son of Rāv Jaitsī Lūṇkaraāot (no. 45) and ruler of Bīkāner, ca. 1542-74.

[81] The text has Toḍā, evidently a mistake for Toḍaṛī. Cf. n. 367 for ***Vigat***, 2:60. Toḍaṛī lies sixty miles southeast of Ajmer, near Tonk.

[82] Candrāvat Sīsodīyo Gahlot Rāv Durgo Acḷāvat (no. 18), ruler of Rāmpuro. The territory of Rāmpuro lies east of Mevāṛ; Rāmpuro town is 155 miles south-southeast of Ajmer.

[83] Sīsodīyo Gahlot Rāv (or Rāvat; see ***Vigat***, 2:60) Tejo Bīkāvat (no. 16), ruler of Devaḷīyo ca. 1564-93. Devaḷīyo town is situated seventy-two miles southeast of Ajmer.

[84] Solāṅkī Rāv Rām Khairāṛo, ruler of Jājpur (modern Jahāzpur). See n. 372 to ***Vigat***, 2:60. Jājpur lies seventy miles southeast of Ajmer.

[85] Īḍareco Rāṭhoṛ Rav Narāyaṇdās Pūñjāvat of Īḍar (no. 60). The territory of Īḍar lies to

Rāv Surjan, master of Būndī.[86]
Rāv Jaimal Vīramdevot [of Meṛto].
Rāvaḷ Āskaraṇ of Ḍūṅgarpur.[87]
Rāval Pratāpsiṅgh of Vāṃsvāḷo.[88]

[The Sīndhaḷs] Riṇdhīr [and] Dedo Kojhāvat died fighting.[89]

"Aitihāsik Bātāṃ," p. 52

This battle occurred on January 24, 1557, a Sunday.[90] It was perceived [that] the Rāvjī's ***sāth*** possessed much excellence. On the Rāvjī's side the Sīndhaḷs Dedo [and] Riṇdhīr died fighting. Afterward Hājī Khān gave leave to the [Rāṭhoṛ] ***ṭhākur***s. The Rāvjī thought very well of Rāṭhoṛ Devīdās. He had decided to give [him] Khairvo[91] along with eighty-four [other] villages. The ***hujdār***s said to the Rāvjī: "Their house is one of a kind.[92] One should ask [Devīdās] one time [what he wants]." Then the ***hujdār***s said[93] to Devīdās: "The Rāvjī is saying that you performed a great deed. We shall give you what[ever] lands you want." Devīdās said: "If you would favor me, then have Bagṛī given to me." Then Devīdās was given Bagṛī with eighty villages. Pūraṇmal Prithīrājot[94] was given Paclāk[95] with

---

the southwest of Mevāṛ and is directly west of Ḍūṅgarpur.

[86] Hāḍo Cahuvāṇ Rāv Surjan Urjaṇot, ruler of Būndī ca. 1554-85 (no. 6). Būndī is situated to the east of Mevāṛ. Būndī town lies ninety-five miles southeast of Ajmer.

[87] Āhāṛo Gahlot Rāvaḷ Āskaraṇ Prithīrājot, ruler of Ḍūṅgarpur ca. 1549-80 (no. 11). Ḍūṅgarpur is located to the south of Mevāṛ and directly west of Vāṃsvāḷo.

[88] Āhāṛo Gahlot Rāvaḷ Pratāpsiṅgh Jaisiṅghot, ruler of Vāṃsvāḷo ca. 1550-79 (no. 12). The territory of Vāṃsvāḷo lies directly to the south of Mevāṛ. The text mistakenly lists Rāvaḷ Pratāpsiṅgh as ruler of Ḍūṅgarpur and Rāvaḷ Āskaraṇ (n. 87, ***supra***) as ruler of Vāṃsvāḷo.

[89] Sīndhaḷ Rāṭhoṛs Riṇdhīr and Dedo Kojhāvat (nos. 135 and 134, respectively).

[90] See n. 375 to ***Vigat***, 2:60.

[91] Khairvo: a village situated fifty miles south-southeast of Jodhpur.

[92] ***Ek bhānt ro***: "one of a kind," "unique," "singular," "strange." The "house" referred to is the Jaitāvat Rāṭhoṛ house.

[93] Literally, "asked" (***pūchīyo***).

[94] Jaitāvat Rāṭhoṛ Pūraṇmal Prithīrājot (no. 64). Rāv Mālde had given Pūraṇmal, Devīdās's paternal nephew, Bagṛī village upon the death of Prithīraj Jaitāvat. See "Aitihāsik Bātāṃ," p. 50.

[95] Paclāk: a village located twenty-three miles north of Bagṛī and three miles north of

twelve villages.

A few days thereafter Rāv Mālde quickly formed an army [to attack] Meṛto. Jaimal left Meṛto without a fight and went away. Rāv Mālde took Meṛto. The Rāvjī had attacked from a camp in Jaitāraṇ.[96] [Before] a battle occurred,[97] Jaimal went away. The Rāv took Meṛto. He had the ***koṭṛī*** [and] the place [where] Jaimal's houses [were] knocked down. He knocked down the houses. He had radishes sown in the place [where] the houses [were].[98] He took Meṛto in 1557.[99]

On March 1, 1558, Rāv Mālde began to have the Mālgaḍh constructed.[100] And when he asked Rāṭhoṛ Devīdās [his advice], Devīdāsjī restrained [him]. He said: "[Meṛto] is a village of the open field. The Meṛtīyos are attached to it. They will constantly be bringing armies against Meṛto. If there is to be a fort, a few men[101] will [have to] stay here. They will have to die. Otherwise, they will come [to you] when you summon [them]."[102] But Rāv Mālde did not accept [what] Devīdās said. He had the Mālgaḍh begun in 1558. In 1560 it was completed.

After having the fort made, he said to Rāṭhoṛ Devīdās Jaitāvat: "You stay at the garrison in the Mālgaḍh." Devīdās said: "Soon the Meṛtīyos will bring armies [to Meṛto]. Then you will tell me: 'Come near [me] now.' Then I will not come.[103] For that reason you must keep another [there]." The Rāvjī began to talk: "Meṛto [is] in the face of attacks by the Pātsāh's armies. The Meṛtīyos are strongly attached [to it]. Who else is the sort of man who would stay [there]?" The Rāvjī was very obstinate and kept Devīdās at the garrison in Meṛto.

"Aitihāsik Bātāṃ," p. 53

In 1562 the Meṛtīyo, Jaimal, went to the [Mughal] ***darbār*** and was

---

Bīlāṛo.

[96] Jaitāraṇ: a town located thirty-two miles south of Meṛto.

[97] The text has ***veḍh huī***, "a battle occurred," but there was no battle at this time.

[98] The text has ***mūḷā vāḍīyā***, "cut the radishes/roots." All the other sources suggest that Mālde sowed radishes on the site of the Meṛtīyos' house. ***Vāḍīyā*** therefore probably is a mistake for ***vāvīyā/bāvīya***, "sowed."

[99] Rāv Mālde took Meṛto on January 27, 1557. See ***Vigat***, 2:60, n. 380.

[100] Re: the dates for the contruction of the Mālgaḍh, see n. 384 to ***Vigat***, 2:61.

[101] Literally, "four men."

[102] In other words, of what use is a fort in Meṛto if the men stationed there either must leave when attacked or die fighting in a losing cause?

[103] Devīdās is implying that he prefers dying in battle to abandoning Meṛto to the enemy.

dispatched from the ***darbār*** [with] the ***sirdār*** Saraphdīn[104] [and] an army of the Pātsāh's.[105] Rāv Mālde received the news. Then he sent an army in aid to Meṛto, [dispatching] Kuṃvar Candrasen[106] along with Rāṭhoṛ Prithārāj Kūmpāvat, Mānsiṅgh Akhairājot, [and] Sāṃvaḷdās, a Varsiṅghot Meṛtīyo,[107] [and] providing [him] with an additional large ***sāth***. He told Devīdās along with Candrasen: "If an opportunity arises, then you should do battle, otherwise you [Candrasen] come back with Devīdās." Candrasen came to Meṛto. The opposing armies drew near also. Then Candrasen decided: "There is no opportunity for battle. The Pātsāh's armies [are] strong." Then Kuṃvar Candrasen said to Devīdās: "Come, we shall go to the Rāvjī's presence." Devīdās said: "I pleaded with the Rāvjī at the very time [he built the Mālgaḍh]: 'Do not have the fort built and do not keep me at the garrison [in Meṛto].' Yesterday[108] Prithīrāj[109] died fighting in this way at Meṛto. I would not appear noble coming [back to Jodhpur] having left Meṛto without a fight." Candrasen remonstrated with Devīdās a great deal, but Devīdās turned around and went into the Mālgaḍh. Rāṭhor Sāṃvaḷdās Varsiṅghot conversed with Devīdāsjī during the night. Then he went to his ***vasī***, which was somewhere nearby. Candrasen made camp back at Sātaḷvās [and] Indāvaṛ.[110] Rāṭhoṛ Sāṃvaḷdās Varsiṅghot came there.

Rāṭhoṛ Jaimal came to Meṛto too, bring the Pātsāh's army. Then once again Candrasen assembled the entire ***sāth*** and deliberated. Rāṭhoṛ Sāṃvaḷdās Varsiṅghot was an overly talkative ***ṭhākur***. He said: "Now how should one decide? Devīdās was a Rajpūt equal to [many] Rajpūts."[111] He deliberated: "Who are the Rajpūts near you? One [is] a little one-eyed man! One is a Vāṇīyo!"[112] The one-eyed man was Mānsiṅgh Akhairājot, and Rāṭhoṛ Prithīrāj Kūmpāvat, who was lazy, Sāṃvaḷdās called a Vāṇīyo. Afterward the talk became disagreeable. Rāṭhoṛ Prithīrāj Kūmpāvat [and] Sonagaro Mānsiṅgh rose up behind [the back of Sāṃvaḷdās], filled with anger.

---

104 Mīrzā Sharafu'd-Dīn Ḥusayn (see n. 413 to ***Vigat***, 2:63).

105 The Mughal Emperor Akbar (1556-1605).

106 Candrasen Māldevot, Rāv Mālde's successor and Rāv of Jodhpur, 1562-81.

107 Varsiṅghot Meṛtīyo Rāṭhoṛ Sāṃvaḷdās Udaisiṅghot (no. 152).

108 ***Kāle***. Prithīrāj actually had died eight years earlier.

109 Jaitāvat Rāṭhoṛ Prithīrāj Jaitāvat (no. 63).

110 Sātaḷvas and Indāvaṛ lie within four miles of each other, and four and eight miles respectively southwest of Meṛto.

111 Devīdās was not dead at this point but he no longer was with Candrasen's ***sāth*** to offer his advice.

112 ***Ek kāṇīyo, ek vāṇīyo chai***: a sneering rhyme in the original. ***Kāṇīyo***: diminutive of ***kāṇo***, "one-eyed man." Vāṇīyo: a merchant or moneylender, a Baniya.

They complained about Sāṃvaḷdāsjī's dishonorable action in the affair involving Māṇḍaṇ Kūmpāvat.[113]

[113] ***Rāṭhoṛ Māṇḍaṇ Kūmpāvat vāḷī kām rī Sāṃvaḷdāsjī māṃhai khāmī thī, tiṇ bāt ro gilo kīyo***: literally, "There was a fault (***khāmī***) of action of Sāṃvaḷdāsjī's [in the affair/matter] involving Rāṭhoṛ Māṇḍaṇ Kūmpāvat; they complained about that affair/matter." This sentence and the following paragraph contain several obscure references, elucidated only by Norman Ziegler's discovery of a story about Kūmpāvat Rāṭhoṛ Māṇḍaṇ Kūmpāvat (no. 99) and Sāṃvaḷdās Udaisiṅghot. The story is of interest because it speaks directly to issues of honor and dishonor that stem from slights of behavior and actions that result from such slights. Māṇḍaṇ is portrayed in the story as a great warrior, while Sāṃvaḷdās is presented as a rather obtuse, boorish Rajpūt, constantly getting himself into trouble through thoughtless acts. The dishonorable action to which the text refers is Sāṃvaḷdās's flight before Māṇḍaṇ, leaving his wife to confront him in his stead and allowing Māṇḍaṇ to kill his mother and wound one of his elephants. The substance of the story is as follows:

Māṇḍaṇ Kūmpāvat and Sāṃvaḷdās Udaisiṅghot were both Rajpūts of prominence who moved about offering military service to local rulers in return for land. As the story opens, Māṇḍaṇ Kūmpāvat had gone to Mevāṛ with a large ***sāth*** to attend a wedding at which the Sīsodiyo Rāṇo, Udaisiṅgh Sāṅgāvat (ca. 1537-72) was also present. While he was there, the Mevār people insulted him, suggesting that the ***sāth*** was not his own, but rather belonged to his brotherhood. The Rāṇo himself added further insult by suggesting that the ***sāth*** belonged to Abho Sāṅkhlo. These remarks angered Māṇḍaṇ greatly. He promptly left Mevāṛ for Vāṃsvāḷo, where he took service under the ruler there in return for a sizeable ***paṭo***. Māṇḍaṇ remained in Vāṃsvāḷo for one year.

During this time Sāṃvaḷdās Udaisiṅghot left Mārvāṛ for Mevāṛ, where he sought military service under Rāṇo Udaisiṅgh. The Rāṇo was pleased to receive Sāṃvaḷdās. He honored him and later sent him some of his personal servants. Sāṃvaḷdās insulted these servants by ordering one old man to warm water for his bath and putting his hands on another. News of these actions quickly reached the Rāṇo, who was infuriated and refused to retain Sāṃvaḷdās in his service.

Sāṃvaḷdās in turn went to Vāṃsvāḷo, arriving there shortly after Māṇḍaṇ Kūmpāvat had departed following his term of service. The Rāvaḷ of Vāṃsvāḷo took Sāṃvāḷdās into his service and gave him Māṇḍaṇ's old ***paṭo*** along with additional lands. The Rāvaḷ remarked when he granted these lands that Sāṃvaḷdās had a great honor to uphold, for he had received the ***paṭo*** of Māṇḍaṇ Kūmpāvat, a great Rajpūt of Mārvāṛ, along with another ***paṭo*** formerly belonging to a great Rajpūt of Vāṃsvāḷo. Sāṃvaḷdās replied that he had received many such ***paṭo***s and that he did not know a Rajpūt named Māṇḍaṇ, son of Kūmpo.

A servant of Māṇḍaṇ's happened to overhear the slur and informed Māṇḍaṇ, who resolved to confront Sāṃvaḷdās. Some of Māṇḍaṇ's Rajpūts cautioned him against involving the two Rāṭhoṛ ***bhāībandh***s (his own and Sāṃvaḷdās's) in a fight, but he was not dissuaded, despite the sanctions for such actions (see n. 118 ***infra***).

Māṇḍaṇ proceeded to ride to Sāṃvaḷdās's village with his ***sāth***. He and his men killed thirty of Sāṃvaḷdās's Rajpūts during an initial confrontation. Māṇḍaṇ then entered Sāṃvaḷdas's house and climbed up to the ***māḷiyo*** where Sāṃvaḷdās and his wife, a Vaḍgūjar Rajpūt woman, had been sleeping. Sāṃvaḷdās had heard the approach of Māṇḍaṇ and his men as they rode in on horseback, and had awakened. He was able to escape at the last moment by leaping down from the ***māḷiyo*** into the house of a

A certain servant of Sāṃvaḷdās's, Kevāṅgīn, who was standing [nearby], heard [their complaint]. He went to where Sāṃvaḷdās had pitched [his] tent and quarreled with [him, saying]: "Why did you say such a petty thing to that ***ṭhākur***?"

"Aitihāsik Bātāṃ," p. 54

Then he told Sāṃvaḷdās the slanderous remark [they had made]:[114] "They are talking too, [saying]: 'Up to this point there is no fault of ours equivalent to Sāṃvaḷdās['s].'" When he heard these words, a fire flared up in Sāṃvaḷdās's body. He rose up from his tent and went[115] to the ***darbār***. Sāṃvaḷdās said to Prithīrāj [and] Mānsiṅgh: "You complained about me; you did well. The world knows [that] I was offended [and] you were offended.[116] Even at the time [of the incident involving Māṇḍaṇ Kūmpāvat] I was not the sort of Rajpūt [who] would flee, but Kūmpo's ***dharma*** drove me away.[117] Otherwise, Māṇḍaṇ would have received the penance [imposed by] the ***bhāībandh***, and up until now why hasn't he gone?"[118]

The Rāv's ***darbār*** was convened. Within were the various important

---

neighboring Brāhmaṇ. Sāṃvaḷdas left his wife to confront Māṇḍaṇ wearing one of his garments (***vāgo***). She said: "Your brother indeed has fled; I stand [before you]." Māṇḍaṇ then went away, but before leaving he killed Sāṃvaḷdās's mother and wounded an elephant.

The Rāṇo of Mevāṛ heard of Māṇḍaṇ Kūmpāvat's deeds soon afterward. He then summoned Māṇḍaṇ into his presence and rewarded him with a large grant of lands.

For the story concerning Māṇḍaṇ and Sāṃvaḷdās, see "Vāt Māṇḍaṇjī Kūmpāvat rī," in ***Aitihāsik Tavārīkhvār Vārtā*** (MS no. 1234, Rājasthānī Śodh Saṃsthān, Caupāsnī), ff. 67-68.

[114] ***Tarai Sāṃvaḷdās kahaṇ nai kahyo***. ***Kahaṇ***: "a word, saying"; "a proverb"; "a slanderous remark, public slander."

[115] Literally, "came."

[116] ***Ek [vāt] uvāṃ tathā monuṃ lāgī***. ***Uvāṃ*** ("they") apparently refers to Prithīrāj and Mānsiṅgh. Since Sāṃvaḷdās is speaking to them, we have substituted "you" for "they" in the translation.

[117] ***Piṇ Kūmpā rai dharam monuṃ ṭhel kāḍhīyo***. Sāṃvaḷdās is suggesting that that his respect for Kūmpo Mahirājot, Māṇḍaṇ's father (no. 95 under "Kūmpāvat Rāṭhoṛs") led him to avoid a conflict with Māṇḍaṇ. See also n. 118, ***infra***.

[118] Sāṃvaḷdās is saying that had he stood his ground and allowed Māṇḍaṇ to kill him, Māṇḍaṇ would have incurred the penance imposed by the ***bhāībandh*** (***bhāībandh ro prācit***) for intra-lineage murder (***gotrakadamb***), which was a pilgrimage to Dvārkā, a town in Saurāṣṭra. Because Sāṃvaḷdās fled, Māṇḍaṇ did not have to go to Dvārkā to atone for killing him.

Re: pilgrimage to Dvārkā as a penance for ***gotrakadamb*** among Rajpūts, see A. K. Forbes, ***Rās-Mālā: Hindu Annals of Western India*** (1878; reprint edition, New Delhi: Heritage Publishers, 1973), p. 312; ***Khyāt***, 1:111, 2:266-268.

Rajpūts. [Sāṃvaḷdās said]: "Devīdās is in the fort with many Rinmals. The Mughal army is on all sides. We might proceed with deliberate speed[119] to the fort. Or we might join up with Devīdās after killing the Mughals. Let him who would do as I do come forth. I shall proceed with deliberate speed[120] [to the fort]." Candrasen departed and went to Jodhpur. Sāṃvaḷdās assembled his ***sāth*** in two [or] three days and [then] decided to attack the Pātsāh's army. Sāṃvaḷdās sent word to Rāṭhoṛ Devīdās too: "I shall come to [you], ***rāj***, if I am able. Have the door to the main gate [of the fort] kept open." Sāṃvaḷdās carried out a night attack on the Pātsāh's army. He killed a large ***sāth*** there, people of the Pātsāh's. He killed fourteen ***sirdārs***. He destroyed the campsite of the fourteen ***sirdārs***. He killed fourteen ***sirdārs*** [and] many [other] people. Rāṭhoṛ Sāṃvaḷdās received a severe blow on the foot there as well. Many other [men of] the ***sāth*** were wounded also. Then Rajpūt Sāṃvaḷdās's military servants remonstrated with him and brought him away [from the battle].

In the morning Jaimal came and appealed to Saraphdīn: "If the Rāṭhoṛs are stubborn about this matter,[121] they will strike constantly, time after time. We will not be able to stay in place here. Alternatively, come [with me now]; we shall ride after Sāṃvaḷdās and kill [him]." Then Jaimal took Saraphdīn [with him] and reached Sāṃvaḷdās at Reyāṃ [village]. A skirmish occurred there. Sāṃvaḷdās fought very nobly. Sāṃvaḷdās died fighting at Reyāṃ.

Rāṭhoṛ Devīdās took refuge in the fort at Meṛto.[122] Rāv Mālde's men constantly were coming to Devīdās [with the message]: "Today you are making a name for yourself, but you are destroying all I have achieved.[123] [If you] die today, my ***rāj*** will become weak." And Rāṭhoṛ Devīdās Jaitāvat took refuge in the Mālgaḍh in Meṛto.

"Aitihāsik Bātāṃ," p. 55

Then the Turks attached a mine[124] to a tower and exploded [it]. After that there was a pact [between Devīdās and the Mughals]. Rāṭhoṛ Gopāḷdāsjī[125] told this story: the

---

[119] ***Cāl suṃ cāl bāndh***: literally, "binding/joining motion with motion."

[120] ***Hūṃ sāthaḷ suṃ sāthaḷ bāndhūṃ***: literally, "I shall bind/join thigh with thigh."

[121] ***Je iṇ bāt māthai Rāṭhoṛ āyā***. The perfective (***āyā***) is used here as a tense of possible condition. See J. D. Smith, "An Introduction to the Language of the Historical Documents from Rājasthān," ***Modern Asian Studies***, 9, 4 (1975), pp. 456, 458. ***Bāt māthai āṇo***: "to do what one has said; to be stubborn." Lāḷas, ***RSK***, 3:2:2997.

[122] ***Meṛto ro koṭ jhālīyo***. ***Koṭ/gaḍh jhālṇo***: "to take refuge in a fort" (literally, "to catch hold of a fort").

[123] Literally, "you are destroying my entire creation (***bandh***)."

[124] ***Sīdhṛo***: a variant of ***sīndhṛo***, "a vessel made of camel skin for storing ***ghī*** or oil." Lāḷas, ***RSK***, 4:3:5623. In this instance, the vessel evidently was filled with gunpowder.

[125] Rāṭhoṛ Gopāḷdāsjī: probably Meṛtīyo Rāṭhoṛ Gopāḷdās Sundardāsot (no. 128), the

Mughals made a pact with Devīdāsjī. The Mughals said: "You take what is yours and leave. And do not burn the stores behind [you]." They made a pact in this way. [However], Devīdās burned the stores [left] behind.

Saraphdīn and Jaimal came and sat on the main gate. Devīdās mounted up along with the entire ***sāth*** and left. A servant was going along in front of Devīdāsjī carrying a gun [that was] a personal possession of the Rāvjī's. Saraphdīn [and] Jaimal were sitting on the main gate. When Devīdās left, a servant of one of the Mughals put [his] hands on the Rāvjī's gun. Just then some ***ṭhākur***'s horse kicked out; [the blow] struck the shin-bone of Devīdās's leg. [His] leg broke. Then someone said: "The ***ṭhākur***'s leg broke." Then Devīdāsjī said: "Indeed this one [leg] is broken. [But], if I abandon Meṛto like this and go away, then, if there is justice in the house of Parameśvar,[126] both my legs should break." Just then the Turk put [his] hands on the gun. And it fired. Devīdās perceived: "You seize[d] the gun." He gave the Turk a blow on the head with a stick he had taken up[127] in one hand. The [Turk's] brains began to come out inside [his] nose. Devīdās went outside the fort. Then Jaimal said to Saraphdīn: "You see, Devīdās is leaving through the door of ***dharma***.[128] He is not the sort of Rajpūt who abandons a fort and goes away, but Rāv Mālde wrote Devīdās again and again, [saying]: 'Why are you weakening my ***ṭhākurāī***?' So he has left. But you should see now how quickly Rāv Mālde comes. Devīdās is bringing [him] upon us." Then Saraphdīn said: "We will kill [Devīdās] right now."

Saraphdīn and Jaimal mounted up. The kettledrum was struck. Devīdās heard. He turned around and remained ready [for battle] once more. The battle occurred between[129] Sātaḷvas [and] Meṛto. The Mughals took the fort in February, 1563,[130] on the last day of the dark fortnight [the twenty-second]. Some [people] say the battle [of Sātaḷvas] occurred on March 26; [others say it occurred] on the last day of the bright fortnight [April 8].[131]

---

pradhān of Jodhpur under Rājā Jasvantsiṅgh during the years V.S. 1699-1705 (1642/43-1648/49). Gopāḷdās was a contemporary of Muṃhato Sundardās, Naiṇsī's brother, who is said to have had the last ***bāt*** (and possibly all the others) in the "Aitihāsik Bātāṃ" collection written down in V.S. 1703 (1646-47). See "Aitihāsik Bātāṃ," p. 109. It is Gopāḷdās who related the story concerning Devīdās in the text to the writer.

[126] Parameśvar: the highest or supreme lord; God; a powerful or illustrious man.

[127] ***Sāmbī thī. Sāmbṇo***: a variant of sambhāṇo, "to take up," "to raise up."

[128] See n. 433 to ***Vigat***, 2:64.

[129] The text has ***bichai***, evidently a misprint for ***bicai***, "between."

[130] The siege of Meṛto had begun on January, 1562. See ***Vigat***, 2:64.

[131] See n. 426 to ***Vigat***, 2:64, for a discussion of these dates. All are incorrect if the reckoning is ***Śrāvaṇādi***; if the reckoning is Caitrādī the last date, V.S. 1619, ***Cait***, ***Sudi*** 15, would convert to March 20, 1562, which is the date we have preferred for the battle of Sātaḷvās. See also ***Vigat***, 1:61, n. 3.

There Devīdāsjī died fighting along with the following *sāth*; a list of this [*sāth*] is written [below]:[132]

Rāṭhoṛ Devīdās Jaitāvat, [age] thirty-five years.
Rāṭhoṛ Bhākharsī Jaitāvat.[133]
Rāṭhoṛ Pūraṇmal, [son] of Prithīrāj Jaitāvat.
Rāṭhoṛ Tejsī, [son] of Urjan Pañcāiṇot.[134]
Rāṭhoṛ Goind, [son] of Rāṇo Akhairājot.[135]
Rāṭhoṛ Pato, [son] of Kūmpo Mahirājot.[136]
Rāṭhoṛ Bhāṇ, son of Bhojrāj, [who was the son of] Sado Rūpāvat.[137]

"Aitihāsik Bātāṃ" p. 56

Rāṭhoṛ Amro Rāmāvat.[138]
Rāṭhoṛ Sahso Rāmāvat.[139]
Rāṭhoṛ Netsī Sīhāvat.[140]
Rāṭhoṛ Jaimal Tejsīyot.[141]
Rāṭhoṛ Rāmo Bhairavdāsot.[142]
Rāṭhoṛ Bhākharsī Ḍūṅgarsīyot.[143]
Rāṭhoṛ Aclo Bhāṇot.[144]

---

[132] The chronicles contain lists of varying length and completeness regarding those Rajpūts who died at the battle of Sātaḷvas. For a composite list, see Appendix B.

[133] Jaitāvat Rāṭhoṛ Bhākharsī Jaitāvat (no. 66).

[134] Akhairājot Rāṭhoṛ Tejsī Urjanot (no. 34).

[135] Akhairājot Rāṭhoṛ Goind Rāṇāvat (no. 29).

[136] Kūmpāvat Rāṭhoṛ Pato Kūmpāvat (no. 96).

[137] Riṇmalot Rāṭhoṛ Bhāṇ Bhojrājot (no. 130).

[138] Cāmpāvat Rāṭhoṛ Amro Rāmāvat (no. 51).

[139] Cāmpāvat Rāṭhoṛ Sahso Rāmāvat (no. 52).

[140] Akhairājot Rāṭhoṛ Netsī Sīhāvat (no. 36). See also n. 449 to ***Vigat***, 2:65.

[141] We have been unable to identify this Rāṭhoṛ.

[142] Cāmpāvat Rāṭhoṛ Rāmo Bhairavdāsot (no. 50).

[143] Jodho Rāṭhoṛ Bhākarsī Ḍūṅgarsīyot (no. 81).

[144] We have been unable to identify this Rāṭhoṛ with certainty. He probably was the son of Bhāṇ Bhojrājot (see n. 137 to "Aitihāsik Bātāṃ," p. 55, ***supra***.

Rāṭhoṛ Mahes Pañcāiṇot.[145]
Rāṭhoṛ Jaitmāl Pañcāiṇot, [son of] Pañcāiṇ Dūdāvat, a Meṛtīyo.[146]
Rāṭhoṛ Riṇdhīr Rāysiṅghot.[147]
Rāṭhoṛ Mahes Gharsīyot.[148]
Rāṭhoṛ Sāṅgo Riṇdhīrot.[149]
Rāṭhoṛ Rājsiṅgh Gharsīyot.[150]
Rāṭhoṛ Īsar Gharsīyot.[151]
Māṅglīyo Vīram.[152]
Rāṭhoṛ Rāṇo Jagnāthot.[153]
Pirāg Bhārmalot.[154]
Tejsī.[155]
Tiloksī.[156]
Dedo.[157]
Pītho.[158]
A Turk, Hamjo.[159]

---

145 Karamsot Rāṭhoṛ Mahes Pañcāiṇot (no. 93).

146 Meṛtīyo Rāṭhoṛ Jaitmāl Pañcāiṇot (no. 127). The text has "Rāṭhoṛ Jaimal Pañcāiṇot, Pañcāiṇ Dūdāvat, a Meṛtīyo," which is incorrect.

147 We have been unable to identify this Rāṭhoṛ with certainty. See n. 456 to ***Vigat***, 2:66.

148 Cūṇḍāvat Rāṭhoṛ Mahes Gharsīyot (no. 58).

149 We have been unable to identify this Rāṭhoṛ with certainty. See n. 457 to ***Vigat***, 2:66.

150 Cūṇḍāvat Rāṭhoṛ Rājsiṅgh Gharsīyot (no. 59).

151 Cūṇḍāvat Rāṭhoṛ Īsar Gharsīyot (no. 57).

152 Māṅglīyo Gahlot Vīram Devāvat (no. 14).

153 We have been unable to identify this Rāṭhoṛ.

154 Bhāṭī Pirāg Bhārmalot. See n. 460 to ***Vigat***, 2:66.

155 Sāṅkhlo Paṃvār Tejsī Bhojrājot (no. 27).

156 Jeso Bhāṭī Tiloksī Parbatot (no. 3).

157 Māṅglīyo Gahlot Dedo (no. 13).

158 Jeso Bhāṭī Pītho Āṇandot (no. 1).

159 Re: the Turk, Hamjo, see n. 469 to ***Vigat***, 2:66.

A Sutrār, Bhavānīdās.[160]
Jīvo, a Bārhaṭh.[161]
Jalap [and] Colo.[162]

So many men died fighting.[163] Afterward Rāv Mālde did not form any army [to attack] Meṛto.

---

[160] This man is called Bhānīdās on ***Vigat***, 2:66. We have no additional information concerning him.

[161] No other information is available concerning Jīvo.

[162] Jālap and Colo are listed as Bārhaṭhs on ***Vigat***, 2:66. We have no additional information concerning them.

[163] The text has ***āsāṃsī--itrā kām āyā***, a mistake for ***āsāmī itrā kām āyā***. ***Āsāmī***: man, person.

Khyāt, 3:38

Now the Story of the Time that Dūdo Jodhāvat Killed Megho Narsiṅghdāsot Sīndhaḷ

Rāv Jodho[1] had lain down. The storytellers were conversing. They were telling stories about those who rule.[2] One said: "The Bhāṭīs do not have a single ***vair*** remaining [unsettled]." [Another] one spoke up: "The Rāṭhoṛs have a ***vair***." [A third] one stated: "One Rāṭhoṛ ***vair*** remains [unsettled]." [Someone] said: "Which one?" They said: "The ***vair*** of Āskaraṇ Satāvat[3] remains [unsettled]. The ***vair*** of the time that Narbadjī[4] captured Supiyārde."[5] Then Rāv Jodhojī heard the conversation. He asked them: "What are you saying?" They said: "***Jī***, nothing at all." Then he spoke up: "No, no! Tell [me]!" Then they said: "***Jī***, Āskaraṇ himself had no son, and Narbadjī also had no son. Thus this ***vair*** remains [unsettled]." Hearing this statement, Rāv Jodhojī kept [it] in mind.

In the morning, when [Rāv Jodhojī] was seated in the ***darbār***, Kuṃvar Dūdo[6] came and paid [his] respects. The Rāvjī was displeased with Dūdo. The Rāvjī said: "Dūdo! Megho Sīndhaḷ[7] should be killed." Dūdo performed ***salām***.[8] The Rāvjī spoke: "Dūdo! Narbadjī captured Supiyārde; in exchange, Narsiṅghdās Sīndhaḷ[9] killed Āskaraṇ Satāvat. Narsiṅghdās has a son, Megho; go and kill him."

---

[1] Rāv Jodho Riṇmalot, ruler of Maṇḍor and founder of Jodhpur, ca. 1453-89.

[2] ***Rājviyāṃ***. There were two major ranks within the Rajpūt ***jāti***: a higher rank consisting of those from ruling families, termed either ***rājviyāṃ*** ("those who rule") or ***vaḍā gharāṃ rā chorū*** ("sons of great houses"); and a lower rank consisting of the Rajpūt peasantry (***gaṃvār or padhrā*** Rajpūts) and other minor or petty Rajpūts (***chuṭā*** Rajpūts). For a discussion of internal ranking among Rajpūts, see N. P. Ziegler, "Action, Power and Service in Rajasthani Culture: A Social History of the Rajpūts of Middle Period Rajasthan" (unpublished Ph.D. dissertation, The University of Chicago, 1973), pp. 84-106.

[3] Cūṇḍāvat Rāṭhoṛ Āskaraṇ Satāvat (no. 55).

[4] Cūṇḍāvat Rāṭhoṛ Narbad Satāvat (no. 56), Āskaraṇ Satāvat's elder brother.

[5] Sāṅkhlī Paṃvār Supiyārde, daughter of the Rūṇeco Sāṅkhlo Rāṇo Sīhaṛ Cācāgot, master of Rūṇ village of Jāṅgaḷū, an area of southern Bīkāner. Rūṇ lies twenty-eight miles south-southeast of Nāgaur and twenty miles northwest of Meṛto.

[6] Meṛtīyo Rāṭhoṛ Dūdo Jodhāvat (no. 104).

[7] Sīndhaḷ Rāṭhoṛ Megho Narsiṅghdāsot (no. 132).

[8] ***Salām***: literally, "peace." A salutation, either of parting or of greeting; an act of bowing to or acknowledging in some manner the superiority of someone.

[9] Sīndhaḷ Rāṭhoṛ Narsiṅghdās Khīndāvat (no. 131).

Dūdo performed ***salām*** and started off.

Khyāt, 3:39

Then the Rāvjī said: "Dūdo! Don't go like this! You make preparations! Megho Sīndhaḷ is before [you]. You haven't heard Megho with your own ears." Then Dūdo said: "Either Megho [will kill] Dūdo, or Dūdo Megho."

Then Dūdo came to [his] camp, took his ***sāth***, and mounted [his horse]. He went and camped three ***kos*** from Jaitāraṇ.[10] He sent a man. [The man] went and told Megho: "Dūdo Jodhāvat has come. He demands [revenge for the death of] Āskaraṇ Satāvat."[11] The man went and told Megho [this]. Then Megho said: "Why did he come [so] late?" [The man] said: "After he found out, Dūdo did not drink water until he came before [you]."[12]

Then Megho climbed up into a ***mālīyo***. He called out: "Hey! Don't graze mares in this direction.[13] Dūdo Jodhāvat has come; he will steal the mares." Then Dūdo spoke. He said: "Who is that speaking?" They said: "***Jī***, Megho is speaking." Then he said: "Oh? He can be heard at such a distance?" Then they said: "***Jī***, have you heard Megho Sīndhaḷ with your own ears, or not?" Then [Dūdo] sent word to Megho: "I have no concern with mares. [I have] no concern with wealth. My concern is with your head. We will fight one another."[14]

On the next[15] day Megho formed a ***sāth*** and came forth. Dūdo approached from the other direction.[16] Megho said: "Dūdojī! You found an opportunity; all of my Rajpūts departed in my son's marriage procession. I am [on my own] here." Then Dūdo said: "Meghojī! We two will fight one another. Why should we kill [other] Rajpūts?

[10] Jaitāraṇ: a town situated fifty-six miles east of Jodhpur. Megho Sīndhaḷ was master of Jaitāraṇ at the time of the events described in the text.

[11] "To demand [x]" (x ***māṅgṇo***, x ***nūṃ māṅgṇo***) is a stock phrase in tales of vengeance; cf. ***Jodhpur Rājya kī Khyāt***, p. 90, ***Khyāt***, 1:350.

[12] ***Dūdai pāṇī āgai āy pīyo chai***: literally, Dūdo, having come before [you], has drunk water." Constructions of this sort are common in Middle Mārvāṛī texts and serve to emphasize the commencement of one activity or state of being only upon the completion or cessation of another, as in the sentence ***tūṃ gaḍh mar nai dai***, literally, "die, then give up the fort," but much better translated as "don't give up the fort until you die." For this example, see ***Vigat***, 2:219, line five counting from the top of the page.

[13] I.e., toward Jaitāraṇ. Megho obviously is a man endowed with a very loud voice; he is shouting this insult to the entire countryside around Jaitāraṇ.

[14] ***Parat rī veḍh karasyāṃ***. ***Parat***: reciprocal, mutal. Lāḷas, ***RSK***, 3:1:2365.

[15] Literally, "second" (***bījai***).

[16] Literally, "from this direction" (***iyai taraph sūṃ***).

Khyāt, 3:40

Either Megho [will kill] Dūdo, or Dūdo Megho. We two alone will acquire the fruits of our actions."[17] Then the ***sāth*** of both ***sirdār***s remained standing apart [from the two]. Megho came from one side; Dūdo came from the other side. Then Dūdo said: "Megho! Strike a blow." Megho said: "Dūdo! You strike a blow." Then Dūdo said again: "Megho! You strike the blow."[18] Megho struck a blow; Dūdo warded it off with [his] shield. Dūdo remembered Pābūjī[19] and struck Megho a blow. [Megho's] head was severed from [his] body and fell. Megho died fighting. Then Dūdo took Megho's head and started off.

Then his Rajpūts said: "Put Megho's head on [his] body. He is a great Rajpūt." Dūdo put the head on the body. Afterward Dūdo said: "Do not pillage a single village. Our business was with Megho." Having killed Megho, Dūdo turned back. He came and performed ***taslīm***[20] to Rāvjī Śrī Jodhojī. The Rāvjī was very pleased. The Rāvjī gave Dūdo a horse [and] a ***sirpāv***.

The Story of Dūdo Jodhāvat is concluded.

---

[17] ***Āmpāṃhīj sāmphaḷ husī. Sāmphaḷ***: a fight, battle, combat; less specifically, any action (***kām***) that has its karmic reward, or "fruit" (***phaḷ***).

[18] The following account of a similar encounter suggests that striking the first blow may have been a sign of inferior or lower rank based on age, position, or reputation:

> Then Hemo said: "Kūmbho! You strike a blow." Kūmbho said: "Hemoji! You strike a blow." Hemo said: "Kūmbho! You are a child. I have bandaged many [wounds with] ***nīm*** [leaves]." Then Kūmbho said: "Hemojī1 you strike the blow." Hemo said: "Kūmbho! Up until now a weapon hasn't touched your body; you are a child. You strike the blow. I am an elder; why should I strike the blow?" Kūmbho said: "Hemojī! You are senior in years, but I am senior in rank.... You strike the blow." ***Khyāt***, 2:296.

[19] Dhāndhalot Rāṭhoṛ Pābūjī Dhāndhalot, a Rajpūt warrior of the early fourteenth century. He is believed to have been the son of Dhāndhal Āsthānot, grandson of Rāv Sīho Setrāmot (d. 1273), who is considered the ancestor of the Mārvāṛ Rāṭhoṛs. Pābūjī is associated with Koḷū village (located eighteen miles south of Phaḷodhī), where there are two small temples dedicated to him. He is credited with many heroic deeds. For an account of Pābūjī, see John D. Smith, ***The Epic of Pābūjī: A Study, Transcription and Translation*** (Cambridge: Cambridge University Press, 1990) pp. 71-102; L. P. Tessitori, "A Progress Report on the Preliminary Work done during the year 1915 in connection with the Proposed Bardic and Historical Survey of Rajputana," ***Journal of the Asiatic Society of Bengal***, N.S. 12 (1916), pp. 106-114.

[20] ***Taslīm***: a salutation consisting of placing the back of the right hand on the ground and raising gently until the person stands erect, when he puts the palm of his hand upon the crown of his head. The salute indicates that one is ready to give himself as an offering. ***Āʿīn-ī-Akbarī***, 1:167.

Khyāt, 3:87

Now the Story of Hardās Ūhaṛ is Written

Hardās Mokaḷot[1] had Koḍhṇo[2] with one hundred forty [other] villages. This Hardās would not do the simplest military service;[3] he would [merely] come during Dasrāho[4] and perform ***salām***. Mālde,[5] the Kuṃvar, would not tolerate [this] sham. He gave Koḍhṇo to Bhāṇ.[6]

Hardās [was] such a fearsome man [that] no one whosoever would tell him.[7] Bhāṇ would perform the military service; Hardās enjoyed [the rule of] Koḍhṇo. Three years passed in this manner. Then Bhāṇ's and Hardās's ***hujdārs*** fought. Bhāṇ's ***hujdārs*** said: "***Jī***, you may rule. But do not speak to us. Bravo! For we allow you to live in the village with a revoked ***paṭo***." Hardās heard. He said: "Hey! What is [this]?" Then they said: "Your ***paṭo*** is revoked." Having heard this statement, Hardās said: "Ah! I ate filth;[8] I live in the village with a revoked ***paṭo***." Then

---

[1] Ūhaṛ Rāṭhoṛ Hardās Mokaḷot (no. 144).

[2] Koḍhṇo: a village located twenty-eight miles west-southwest of Jodhpur.

[3] ***Tiko Hardās lākaṛ cākrī na karai***. There are two ways to interpret this clause. One may consider ***lakaṛ*** ("stick") a reference to Hardās, as the editor of the ***Khyāt***, B. P. Sākariyā, has done (n. 2). By this reasoning, Hardās was a "stick": a rigid, unyielding person. It is also possible to consider (as we have done) ***lākaṛ cākrī*** a unit meaning "stick military service," i.e., the simplest form of military service, which could have been performed even by the untrained village Rajpūt peasantry.

[4] Dasrāho: a festival held in the month of ***Āsoj*** (September-October) to commemorate the victory of Rāma, King of Ayodhyā, over Rāvaṇa, the demon-king of Sri Lanka. It was often customary at the time of this festival for Rajpūts in the service of a local ruler to pay court at an official ***darbār***, during which vows of loyalty and service were reaffirmed.

[5] Mālde Gāṅgāvat, son and successor of Rāv Gāṅgo Vāghāvat, ruler of Jodhpur 1515-32.

[6] Ūhaṛ Rāṭhoṛ Bhāṇ Kājāvat (no. 145).

[7] ***Tāhrāṃ Hardās isṛī balāy nahīṃ jo koī iyainūṃ kahai***. The structure of this sentence is peculiar: either ***nahīṃ*** is in the wrong clause or the conjunction ***ju*** ("that"), which should precede ***nahīṃ***, has been omitted.

[8] Among Rajpūts, relationships between a ruler and subordinate warriors in his service were seen in forms of bonds between a master (***dhaṇī***) and a servant (***cākar***). These bonds were often symbolized by and expressed through the idiom of food, the master being obliged to feed and sustain his servant in return for the servant's loyalty and support. Land itself within this idiom became equated with grain, or more generally, with food, sustenance, and protection. A Rajpūt who had eaten another's grain was automatically indebted for the gift of life and support to serve in order to equalize the

Hardās left.

He went to Sojhat[9] and met with Muṃhato Rāymal.[10] Hardās settled in the *vās* of Vīramde.[11] Hardās told Rāymal: "If you would do battle with Rāv Gāṅgo,[12] then I will stay with you; otherwise I shall not stay." Then Rāymal said: "*Jī*, for us there is only battle, twenty-four hours a day."

Khyāt, 3:88

Then one day a battle occurred. A horse from Vīram[de]jī's stable had been given to Hardās to ride; here both Hardās and the horse were badly wounded. Bhāṇ picked up Hardās and sent him to Sojhat. Hardās came to Sojhat. He had the wounds bandaged. Then Vīramde said: "Be off, Hardās! You caused my five-thousand [rupee] horse injury." Hardās said: "Worthless Rajpūt! I caused injury to my own body as well." Hardās, offended, set off without [his] wounds having healed. He left the *vās* [of Vīramde]. He set off in the direction of Sarkhel Khān[13] [in Nāgaur].

At that time Sekho Sūjāvat[14] lived in Pīmpāṛ.[15] Sekho stopped Hardās. He

---

exchange.

In this passage, the dissolution of this bond is also couched in the idiom of food, as if to say that the Rajpūt, Hardās, had swallowed a bitter pill, or that the symbolic food, the land, had turned sour in his stomach. For further discussion of this idiom and its importance for Rajpūt culture of the middle period, see N. P. Ziegler, "Action, Power and Service in Rajasthani Culture: A Social History of the Rajpūts of Middle Period Rajasthan" (unpublished Ph.D. dissertation, The University of Chicago, 1973), pp. 84-97.

[9] Sojhat: a large town situated forty-six miles southeast of Jodhpur.

[10] Muṃhato Rāymal Khetāvat (no. 159).

[11] Jodho Rāṭhoṛ Rāv Vīramde Vāghāvat (no. 84). Vīramde was the half-brother of Rāv Gāṅgo Vāghāvat of Jodhpur (1515-32). Their father Vāgho Sūjāvat, who was designated successor to Rāv Sūjo Jodhāvat (ca. 1492-1515), died during the lifetime of Rāv Sūjo. Gāṅgo then emerged as heir and upon Rāv Sūjo's death, succeeded to the throne of Jodhpur. The texts indicate conflict between Gāṅgo and Vīramde at the time of succession, with final selection by the powerful Rāṭhoṛ ***ṭhākur***s of Mārvāṛ resting upon Gāṅgo. Vīramde was given the rule of Sojhat and surrounding territory in compensation along with the title of ***rāv***. He remained in opposition to the ruling house for some years afterwards. ***Khyāt***, 3:80-88; ***Murārdān***, no. 2, pp. 104-106; ***Vigat***, 1:41.

[12] Rāv Gāṅgo Vāghāvat, son of Vāgho Sūjāvat and ruler of Jodhpur, 1515-32.

[13] Khānzādā Khān Sarkhel Khān (no. 155).

[14] Jodho Rāṭhoṛ Sekho Sūjāvat (no. 86).

[15] Pīmpāṛ: a village located thirty-three miles east-northeast of Jodhpur.

said: "They will say there are no Rajpūts in Mārvāṛ at all, for they did not have Hardās's wounds bandaged."[16] Then Hardās said: "Sekho! Would you consider and retain me? If you would fight with Rāv Gāṇgo, then retain me, otherwise do not retain me." Sekho said: "Parameśvar will set things right. You may stay [with me]." Then Hardās stayed in Pīmpāṛ, the ***vās*** of Sekho.

Now Hardās and Sekho would confer in the ***mahal***s all night.[17] Sekho's wives would stay sitting up wearing saris all night. Because of [their] fine clothes, they would suffer in the cold.[18] Then one day Sekho's wives said: "Husband's mother (***sāsūjī***)![19] We [nearly] died in the cold!" [Sekho's mother] said: "Wives! Why [so]?" They said: "Husband's mother! Your son confers with Hardāsjī [while] we sit all night suffering in the cold."[20]

Khyāt, 3:89

Then [Sekho's] mother said: "Wives! Today when Hardās returns, inform me."[21]

The wife whose turn it was stood blocking the path [of Hardās]. As soon as Hardās returned the succeeding night, she said: "Husband's mother! Hardās returns." Sekho's mother also was standing [nearby]. Hardās came down from above. The path [was] in the ***rāy-āṅgaṇ***.[22] Hardās came into the ***rāy-āṅgaṇ***. Sekho's mother had him called inside; then she went and performed ***salām*** [to him]. She said: "Hardās [my] son! Take care; are you not bringing ruin upon the hut[23] of Sekho's mother?" Then he said: "Mājī![24] First the hut of Hardās's mother will be ruined, [only] after

---

[16] Rank as a Rajpūt and among Rajpūts as a group was closely associated with a complex ideology relating to the body (***deh***, ***piṇḍ***) and its preservation and sustenance. Threats to the body (either individual or collective) through loss of substance (blood/***lohī*** or land/***dhartī***) were seen in terms of a threat to rank and power. For further discussion of this ideology, see N. P. Ziegler, "Action, Power and Service ..., pp. 67-83.

[17] ***Cār pohar***: literally, "four watches' or "half the day." Here the meaning is "all night."

[18] Literally, "die in the cold" (***sīyāṃ marai***).

[19] A reference to the mother of Sekho Sūjāvat, daughter of Rāv Tejsī Varjāṅgot, the Sācoro Cahuvāṇ ruler of Sāñcor in southern Mārvāṛ. ***Jodhpur Rājya kī Khyāt***, p. 67.

[20] It was customary among Rajpūts for young wives to await the retirement of their husband dressed in finery and ready to receive him in bed. This is an amusing reference to this custom, the fine clothes of the wives being either silks or muslins.

[21] ***Monūṃ khabar diyā***. ***Diyā*** is a plural imperative in this sentence.

[22] ***Rāy-āṅgaṇ***: the courtyard of a ruler's residence.

[23] ***Ṭāpro***. The connotation of this word, a diminutive for home (***ghar***), might be likened to that of the phrase "humble home" in English.

[24] ***Mājī***: a polite address for a female elder (***mā***, "mother" + respectful particle ***jī***).

that will the hut of Sekho's mother be ruined. Jodhpur will not be obtained without the ruin of [someone's] hut, Mājī! Either [our] hut will be destroyed, or Jodhpur will be obtained."[25]

Then Rāv Gāṅgo's ***pradhāns*** came to Sekho, and they told Sekho: "Sekho! All the land containing ***karaṛ*** [grass] shall be yours; all the land containing ***bhuraṭ*** [grass] shall be ours."[26] Then Sekho said: "Excellent!"

Then Hardās came. Sekho said: "Hardās! They are proposing an excellent division of the land." Hardās would not accept the proposition.

Then [a Cāraṇ], Jhūṭo Āsiyo,[27] recited a ***dūho***:

> The Ūhaṛ, Hardās, would not consider a single pledge [of Rāv Gāṅgo's].
>
> Either all the ***sāmaṭho*** for Sekho, or all the ***grās*** for Gāṅgo.[28]

---

[25] The point of this passage is that Hardās is subjecting Sekho to no more danger than he faces himself, and that one has to take chances to get what one wants.

[26] ***Karaṛ*** grass (***Iseilema laxum***) is a tall, thin-leaved grass much used as fodder in Mārvāṛ; ***bhuraṭ*** grass (***Cenchrus catharthicus***) is a burr grass, particularly abundant in years of scarcity, when it is used as food. The seeds are about the size of a pin's head and are enclosed in a prickly husk which readily clings to clothing or to animal hair or fur. The seeds are ground to use as flour. ***Bhuraṭ*** is more common in the sandy, dry tracts of Mārvāṛ than is ***karaṛ***. The division of land proposed would have given Sekho the agriculturally more productive eastern region of Mārvāṛ but would have left Jodhpur in Rāv Gāṅgo's possession. Major K. D. Erskine, ed., ***Rajputana Gazetteers***: Vol. III-A, ***The Western Rajputana States Residency and the Bikaner Agency*** (Allahabad: The Pioneer Press, 1909), p. 49.

[27] Cāraṇ Jhūṭo Bīkāvat of the Āsiyo branch (***sākh***) of Cāraṇs, who was attached to the court of Jodhpur. Rāv Mālde Gāṅgāvat (ruler of Jodhpur, 1532-62) gave Jhūṭo the small village called "Jhūṭā rī Vāsṇī," located seventeen miles south-southwest of Jodhpur, in perpetuity (***sāṃsaṇ*** tenure). ***Vigat***, 1:242.

Cāraṇ Jhūṭo appears in this passage as a go-between. Cāraṇs in Rājasthān, because of their sacred status, often assumed this role in negotiations between hostile or warring groups.

[28] ***Sekhai siglo sāmaṭho, (kā) Gāṅgai siglo grās. Sāmaṭho*** is defined by Lāḷas (***RSK***, 4:3:5473) as: (1) high place, platform; (2), more, much, many; (3) strong, powerful. ***Grās*** literally means "mouthful" or "sustenance." By extension, the term came to mean a share of land given to a Rajpūt for his maintenance (such shares were also called ***vaṇṭ***, which simply means "share" or "porton"). In Mārvāṛ during the pre-Mughal period it was customary for one son of a Rajpūt ruler to inherit his father's title, residence, and the majority of his lands, while the other sons received smaller territorial shares termed ***grās*** for their livelihood. The word ***grāsiyo*** was used to designate a holder of one of these shares.

The sense of the ***dūho*** is that either Sekho will get "the high place" (i.e., Jodhpur), in addition to his share, or Gāṅgo will get the "mouthful" (i.e., Sekho's share)

Khyāt, 3:90

Then Hardās said: "What two divisions shall we make of the single [city of] Jodhpur? Jodhpur is but a small hill;[29] shall I fix it on a lance and carry it behind you?"

Then the ***pradhān*** went back. He said: "***Jī***! They would not consider an agreement. They will fight."

Rāv Gāṅgo assembled a ***sāth***. He summoned Rāv Jaitsījī[30] from Bīkāner. [Jaitsī] assembled another large ***sāth***. Sekho and Hardās approached Sarkhel Khān in Nāgaur. [Hardās] told Sarkhel Khān: "We shall marry [our daughters] to you and Daulat Khān.[31] Come to our aid." Then Sekho spoke: "Hey, Hardās! Whose daughters will you give? I have no daughter; you have no daughter." Then Hardās spoke: "Whose daughters? It will be raining swords on [us].[32] If we win, there are many Riṇmals; we will marry two of their girls [to the two Khāns]. And if we [all] die fighting, who will be married [anyway]? Whose concern [will it be]?" Having [spoken] thus,[33] Sekho, [Hardās, and] Daulat Khān came to the ***drah***s[34] of Bairāī[35] and camped.

An informant came [to Rāv Gāṅgo]. Then Rāv Gāṅgo asked: "Where did Daulatiyo come?" [The informant] said: "***Rāj***! He came to Bairāī and camped. Victory is in your hands."

Rāv Gāṅgojī came to Ghāṅghāṇī[36] and camped. [Ghāṅghāṇī] is within two ***kos*** [of Bairāī]. After that, Rāv Gāṅgojī sent word [to Sekho]: "***Rāj***! Come yourself

---

in adition to Jodhpur: Hardās will accept no compromise. There is alliteration involved as well: ***grās*** for Gāṅgo, ***sāmaṭho*** for Sekho.

[29] The original settlement of Jodhpur was essentially a fort and houses built on and immediately around a hill.

[30] Bīkāvat Rāṭhoṛ Jaitsī Lūṇkaraṇot (no. 45), Rāv of Bīkāner ca. 1526-42.

[31] Khānzāda Khān Muhammad Daulat Khān (no. 154).

[32] ***Tarvārāṃrā māthai bhoṭh paṛsī***: literally, "showers (***bhoṭh***) of swords will be falling on [us]."

[33] ***Yuṃ kar nai***: literally, "having done thus." ***Yuṃ kar nai*** and ***yuṃ kartāṃ*** ("while doing thus") were stock phrases in Middle Mārvāṛī, translatable in a variety of ways according to the context.

[34] ***Drah***: a deep pool, a ditch.

[35] Bairāī: a village located twenty-five miles northeast of Jodhpur.

[36] Ghāṅghāṇī: a village located seventeen miles northeast of Jodhpur and eight miles southwest of Bairāī village. The text indicates two ***kos*** (about four miles), which is inaccurate.

and camp [here]. This [shall be] the border [between] us. ***Rāj***! That much [is] yours. You are the elder, ***rāj***, you are [my] father's brother (***kāko***)." [Gāṅgo] had his ***pradhāns*** speak in such a way.[37] The ***pradhāns*** negotiated, but [Sekho] would not consider [the proposal].

Khyāt, 3:91

[Sekho] said: "***Jī***, a brother's son (***bhātrījo***) enjoying [the rule of] the land while [his] father's brother sits [quietly by]? In such a situation I would not sleep." He sent word to Rāv Gāṅgojī: "I have prepared a field of [the village] Sevakī[38] [for combat].[39] You and I will fight a battle there." Rāv Gāṅgo said: "All right. I am ready just as I am, ***rāj***!"[40] [Sekho] said: "The battle is tomorrow."

Then the Josīs[41] said to Gāṅgo: "***Rāj***! Tomorrow a Jogṇī[42] is facing us, [her] back to them." Rāv Gāṅgojī said[43] to Rāv Jaitsījī: "Rāvjī! Tomorrow a Jogṇī is facing us, [her] back to them." Rāv Jaitsī said: "***Rāj***! [Tomorrow] the battle is not under our control, it is under theirs. [That is why] they [wish to] fight tomorrow only." Then a Cāraṇ, Khemo Kiniyo,[44] spoke: "***Rāj***! There may be a Jogṇī, but

---

[37] ***Iso pardhāngo kiyo***. This sentence is problematic; ***go*** may be Persian, meaning "word," "speech," "saying," etc. If so, the literal translation of the passage would be: "He caused/made a ***pradhān***-statement of this sort," i.e., Gāṅgo had his ***pradhān*** make such a statement.

[38] Sevakī village is located approximately midway between Bairāī and Ghāṅghāṇī.

[39] ***Sevakīro khetr mhe buhāriyo chai***. ***Khet buhārṇo***: to remove the underbrush and other impediments from a field in order to prepare the area for the movements of men and horses in battle.

[40] We have based our translation on the theory that ***rāji*** in the text is a variant form of the term of address ***rāj*** and not of the adjective ***rājī*** ("pleased"). The editor's punctuation is therefore incorrect. For an example of ***rāji*** used in place of the term of address ***rāj***, see Lāḷas, ***RSK***, 4:1:4131, example no. 4 under ***rāji***. Gāṅgo's use of the term ***rāj*** for Sekho also is consistent with the form of address Gāṅgo used for his father's brother (***kāko***) on ***Khyāt***, 3:90.

[41] Josī: an astrologer.

[42] Jogṇī: any woman thought to possess magical powers; a witch or demoness; a female spirit ruling over periods of good and bad fortune. It was commonly believed that there were sixty-four Jogṇīs, located in different places on different dates. It was considered unlucky to travel in the direction of the Jogṇīs. H. A. Rose, ***A Glossary of the Tribes and Castes of the Punjab and North-West Frontier Province***, 3 vols. (1883; reprint edition, Delhi: Punjab National Press, 1970), 1:243-248; Margaret and James Stutley, ***Harper's Dictionary of Hinduism*** (New York: Harper and Row, 1977), p. 350.

[43] Literally, "asked" (***puchīyo***).

[44] Khemo Kiniyo was a Cāraṇ of the Kiniyo branch (***sākh***). We have found no

what does the Jogṇī ride?" Then [the Josīs] said: "*Jī*, the Jogṇī is riding a lion." [The Cāraṇ] said: "*Jī*, summon a Brāhmaṇ, ask if the Jogṇī is riding some other mount." Then the Brāhmaṇ said: "Tomorrow the Jogṇī rides a crow." Then he said: "The crow flees from arrows. There are arrows in battle, so it will flee from the arrows of both Gāṅgo [and] Sekho."

While [they were speaking] in this way, day broke. Sarkhel Khān had an elephant, whose name was "Dariyājoīs". He had forty elephants on one flank [and] forty elephants on the other flank. He had weighted down the elephants, armoring them with iron and fastening weapons to them. The elephants were in the front of [his] army.

Rāv Gāṅgo approached from [Ghāṅghāṇī]. Rāv Gāṅgojī, having formed [his] army, came before [the opposing army].

Khyāt, 3:92

Sekho had told Daulat Khān: "The Dīvāṇ[45] will flee." On the day of battle,[46] as the entire ***sāth*** [of Rāv Gāṅgo] used [its] weapons and [thus] showed its strength, Daulat Khān said: "Sekhojī! You were saying they would flee." Sekhojī said: "Khān Sāhib! Jodhpur is [in the balance], so why would they flee?" [Daulat Khān] thought: "Might there not be a trick?" Daulat Khān grew inwardly afraid.

Meanwhile the Rāv spoke: "If you [so] advise, I shall strike the [lead] elephant with an arrow, [or], if you [so] advise, I shall strike the mahout with an arrow." The [lead] elephant was approaching. The mahout was shouting. Then [Gāṅgo] hit the mahout with an arrow; the mahout fell. And he hit the elephant's temple with a second arrow. The elephant fled; Daulat Khān also fled. And Sekho stood his ground. Sekho did not consider fleeing. Sekho dismounted along with seven hundred men; there was a battle. Sekho died fighting along with [his] son. Hardās died fighting along with [his] son. The Turks fled. Many died. Many turned back.

[Before he died] Sekhojī was gasping convulsively on the battlefield. Then Rāv Gāṅgo asked: "Sekhojī! Whose land [is it now]?" Then Rāv Jaitsī had shade provided for Sekhojī. He had [Sekho] take opium. He served water [to Sekho]. Then Sekhojī asked: "Who are you?" He said: "I am Rāv Jaitsī." Sekho said:

---

additional information concerning Khemo; perhaps he was a descendant of the Kiniyo Cāraṇ Vīko, who was given the village Buṭeḷāv by Rāv Jodho Riṇmalot (ca. 1453-89). Buṭeḷāv is approximately eight miles north of Sojhat. *Vigat*, 1.488.

[45] Dīvāṇ: a reference to Rāv Gāṅgo, ruler of Jodhpur. The rulers of Jodhpur were referred to as ***dīvāṇs***, or "deputies," of the god Śiva, from whom their ancestors received their respective sovereignties. The rulers of Mevāṛ also were known as ***dīvāṇs*** for a similar reason.

[46] Literally, "tomorrow" (***savarai***). The battle of Sevakī took place on November 2, 1529 (V.S. 1586, ***Migsar***, ***Sudi*** 1). "Aitihāsik Bātāṃ," p. 37; ***Bāṅkīdās***, p. 11; ***Vigat***, 1:41. ***Jodhpur Rājya kī Khyāt***, p. 72, and ***Vigat***, 1:41, both have V.S. 1596, ***Migsar***, ***Sudi*** 1 = November 11, 1539, which is incorrect.

"Rāvjī! What have I harmed of yours? We—father's brother [and] brother's son—were quarreling over land." Then Sekho said: "Jaitsījī! Your fate shall be what mine has been."[47] As [he spoke] in such a way, Sekho's soul (*jīv*) departed.

Khyāt, 3:93

Kuṃvar Mālde took the best of what elephants there were. And the great elephant of the Khān's stable that had run away went to Meṛto. The Meṛtīyos took it. Rāv Mālde became hostile to the Meṛtīyos over [the issue of] this elephant.

Now a *Ghūmar*[48]

The wife asks: "Hey Daulatīyo! What did you do with [your] elephants?

[Daulat Khān replies]: "The Rāv took all the best ones; he gave back the 'buffalo calves'."

The wife asks: "Hey Daulatīyo! What did you do with [your] Muslim nobles?"

[Daulat Khān replies]: "I had a grave dug on a high hill; I embraced each one."[49]

---

[47] Rāv Jaitsī was killed February 26, 1542, when Rāv Mālde Gāṅgāvat of Jodhpur sent his Rajpūts under Rāṭhoṛ Kūmpo Mahirājot (no. 95; founder of the Kūmpāvat branch of Mārvāṛ Rāṭhoṛs) to attack Bīkāner. Rāv Mālde's forces conquered and occupied Bīkāner city, which they held for two years. Ojhā, 5:1:135-136.

[48] ***Ghūmar***: (1) a variant of ***ghūmaro***, "flock," "herd," "heap," "siege," "encirclement"; (2) a type of folk dance performed by women in a circle; (3) a folk song used to accompany this dance.

[49] The rhyme of the ***ghūmar*** is based upon a repeating pattern of ***kiyā/diyā***, the wife's questions ending in ***kiyā***, the Khān's answers in ***diyā***. Other points:

(a) The wife addresses the Khān disrespectfully using the term ***re*** ("hey!") and also refers to him as Daulatīyo ("Little Daulat").

(b) The editor suggests that ***kethā*** in the text is to be translated as "how many" (***kitne***). However, ***kethā/kitho*** used with ***karṇo*** forms a unit meaning "what to do with?" For an example, see ***Khyāt***, 1:2, where a Brāhmaṇ asks: "What shall I do with this son of a Rajpūt?" (***O Rajpūt ro beṭo kitho karūṃ***?). In the ***ghūmar***, the wife is asking what happened to all the elephants and Muslim nobles (***mīyā***) the Khān went into battle with, and not, as the editor suggests in his translation (bottom of ***Khyāt***, 3:93), how many Muslims the Khān "made" and how many elephants he took.

(c) ***Bāthai bāthai diyā*** in the last line of the ***ghūmar*** is problematic. Lāḷas, ***RSK***, 3:2:3002, suggests that ***bāthai*** is a variant of ***bāthāṃ***, "wrestling," "arm-embrace," "duel," etc. (***RSK***, 3:2:3001). Probably "arm-embrace" is the correct sense of ***bāthai*** in the ***ghūmar***, its repetition therein indicating distribution of the embraces among the dead Muslims.

Now the elephant went to the Meṛtīyos' [residence]. Then the Meṛtīyos bound the wounds of the elephant. They were bringing the elephant inside; it would not fit through the entrance gate. Then they had the gate dug up and took the elephant inside. The augurs said: "You have done wrong in digging up the gate." They said: "It's done. What now?"

While they were so engaged, Rāv Gāṅgojī and Mālde heard that the elephant went to Meṛto, [the residence] of Vīramde.[50] Mālde demanded the elephant. He said: "*Jī*, the elephant is ours; we fought [for it] and took it." The Meṛtīyos would not give [them] the elephant. Then Vīramdejī said: "Give the elephant to Rāv Gāṅgo." Then the [other] Meṛtīyos said: "We shall not just hand over the elephant. [But], if he would be our guest, we would feed him and give him the elephant." Then Mālde mounted up and came [to Meṛto]. They had food for Mālde.

Khyāt, 3:94

At that time the elephant was in Reyāṃ.[51] Then the food was ready. They said: "Kuṃvarjī! Come, partake of the meal.[52] In the meantime, the elephant, which was in Reyāṃ, is now coming [here]." Then [Mālde] said: "*Jī*, first we will take the elephant, then we will eat." Then Rāysal Dūdāvat[53] spoke up. "*Jī*, we too have [among us] obstinate boys like [you]. We will not give [you] the elephant. You must depart."[54]

Then the Kuṃvar became infuriated and said: "Indeed you are not giving [me] the elephant, but my name is Mālde. I, Mālde, will have radishes sown on the site of Meṛto." Mālde came back to Jodhpur.

Then Rāv Gāṅgojī sent word to Vīramdejī: "What [is] this you have done? As long as I live, you are my *parameśvar*.[55] But I was not a match for [you]. Mālde has been insulted by you; he will cause you distress. Give the elephant its freedom." Then Vīramde sent word: "Fine, if it pleases you, we will send back the elephant." He sent horses for Rāv Gāṅgojī [and] the elephant for Māldejī. When the elephant came to Pīmpāṛ, [its] wounds split open and the elephant died. The men brought the

---

[50] Meṛtīyo Rāṭhoṛ Rāv Vīramde Dūdāvat (no. 105), ruler of Meṛto.

[51] Reyāṃ: a village located fifteen miles southeast of Meṛto.

[52] ***The padhāṇo, bhagat ārogo***. The two verbs in this sentence, ***padhārṇo*** and ***ārogṇo***, are special forms used to indicate respect for the individual addressed or the actor involved. They replace respectively the verbs ***āṇo*** ("to come") and ***khāṇo*** ("to eat") in this sentence.

[53] Meṛtīyo Rāṭhoṛ Rāysal Dūdāvat (no. 106), Vīramde Dūdāvat's brother.

[54] Despite the stubborn words, Rāysal addresses Mālde politely, using the verb ***padhārṇo*** in his command.

[55] I.e., his superior.

horses and presented them. And they said: "*Jī*, the elephant died coming into Pīmpāṛ." Then Rāv Gāṅgojī said: "An elephant came into my land and died. It [was] my [elephant] that came."

Then Kuṃvar Mālde spoke: "*Jī*, your elephant came, but my elephant did not come. When I can take [my] elephant, then I will take it." Rāv Gāṅgojī lived only one year after that.[56]

Khyāt, 3:95

When Rāv Gāṅgojī attained the ***devlok***,[57] Māldejī sat on the throne.[58]

Mālde was intent upon Vīramde now; so intent he would not allow him to draw a breath. He said: "Abandon Meṛto and go to Ajmer and settle." Then Vīramdejī abandoned Meṛto. The Paṃvār [Rajpūts] used to live in Ajmer; Vīramdejī killed them and took Ajmer.[59] Then Sahaiso[60] fled and approached Mālde. Mālde gave [him] Reyāṃ with five [other] villages.

When Rāysal had prepared a feast at the Ānāsāgar,[61] he summoned the entire ***sāth***. Then he told Muṃhato Khīṃvo:[62] "We are going to eat the feast. You must not allow Rāv [Vīramde] to ascend the Vīṇṭḷī [Hill].[63] Whenever he will ascend the

---

[56] Rāv Gāṅgo Vāghāvat died in 1532.

[57] ***Devlok***: the realm of the ***devs***, or gods; Paradise.

[58] Re: Rāv Mālde's succession to the Jodhpur throne, see n. 171 to ***Vigat***, 2:48.

[59] Naiṇsī's chronology here is incorrect, with confusion both about time and events. The Paṃvār Rajpūts did control of Ajmer in this period, but their rule ended when Sultān Bahādur Shāh of Gujarat extended his authority into central Rajasthan and occupied Ajmer. Meṛtīyo Vīramde did not assert his authority over Ajmer until ca. 1535, and then only upon the fall of Māṇḍū to the Mughal Emperor Humāyun and the subsequent departure of Bahādur Shāh's forces under Sham Sheru'l-Mulk from Ajmer. For further details, see n. 212 to ***Vigat***, 2:51.

[60] Varsiṅghot Meṛtīyo Rāṭhoṛ Sahaiso Tejsīyot (no. 151).

[61] Ānāsāgar: a large man-made lake situated on the northern side of Ajmer city. It was built in the mid-twelfth century by Arṇorājā Cāhamāna to purify the land, which had become polluted from the blood of Muslims killed there during a battle. Jain, ***Ancient Cities***, p. 302.

[62] Muṃhato Khīṃvo Lālāvat (no. 157), Vīramde Dūdāvat's ***pradhān***.

[63] Vīṇṭḷī: a sizable hill of sandstone and granite situated on the western side of Ajmer city. It is an outlier of the Arāvalī hill system, in a low saddle of which Ajmer is built. The hill provides a view of the city to the east and of the plains of Mārvāṛ extending westward across the far side of the Arāvalīs. The great fortress Tārāgaḍh (also called Gaḍh Vīṇṭḷī) is atop this hill. H. B. Sarda, ***Ajmer: Historical and Descriptive*** (Ajmer: Fine Art Printing Press, 1941), pp. 49-59.

Vīṃṭḷī [Hill], he will see the hill of Reyāṃ. Then Sahaiso will come to mind. Then he will say: 'I shall not drink water without [first] having killed Sahaiso.'" After telling the Muṃhato [this], Rāysal went to eat the feast.

And [Rāv Vīramde] said to Muṃhato Khīṃvo: "You and I will go to the Vīṃṭḷī [Hill] and send for sweets." Muṃhato Khīṃvo forbade [him] one or two times, but he would not stay; he went and ascended the Vīṃṭḷī [Hill]. Having ascended [it], he saw Mārvāṛ before [him]. Looking, he said: "Isn't that the hill of Reyāṃ?" He said: "Indeed this hill is near. If I don't kill this Sahaiso, then he is my father."[64] Afterward Rāysal came with [him] too. The ***pradhāns*** told [Rāysal] a great deal.

And Rāv Mālde was in Nāgaur.[65] Rāv Māldejī said: "Vīramde is on my chest." At that time ten thousand horse were at the Raṛod[66] garrison, and within [were] these ***ṭhākurs***: Jaito,[67] Kūmpo,[68] Akhairāj Sonagaro,[69] [and] Vīdo Bhārmalot.[70]

Khyāt, 3:96

They came to Reyāṃ and camped. Their orders were: "Drive Vīramde from Ajmer."

Vīramde departed [from Ajmer] during the night. He came to Reyāṃ.[71] And ahead, unknown [to him, Mālde's] ***sāth*** was already prepared [for him].

---

[64] Two interpretations of this sentence are possible:

(a) It may mean something to the effect of "I'll be damned if I don't kill this Sahaiso."
(b) Or it may mean that Sahaiso would be considered Vīramde's superior if Vīramde didn't kill him.

[65] This reference to Nāgaur appears incorrect. Rāv Mālde did not capture Nāgaur until January of 1536. The events being referred to in the text took place ca. 1535. Ojhā, 4:1:286-287.

[66] Raṛod: a village located thirty-five miles west of Meṛto and six miles west of Āsop.

[67] Jaito Pañcāiṇot (no. 61), founder of the Jaitāvat branch of Mārvāṛ Rāṭhoṛs.

[68] Kūmpo Mahirājot (no. 95), founder of the Kūmpāvat branch of Mārvāṛ Rāṭhoṛs.

[69] Sonagaro Cahuvāṇ Akhairāj Riṇdhīrot (no. 9).

[70] Bālāvat Rāṭhoṛ Vīdo Bhārmalot (no. 37).

[71] ***Tiko rātiro khaṛiyo Vīramde Reyāṃ āyo***: literally, "he departed during the night, Vīramde came to Reyāṃ." This phrasing doesn't make very good sense; perhaps the reading should have been ***tikā rātiro khaṛiyo Vīramde Reyāṃ āyo*** and the translation then "Vīramde, departing that night, came to Reyāṃ" (literally, "that-night-departed, Vīramde came to Reyāṃ").

Thereafter a battle occurred. Adversity befell Vīramde.[72]

Many of Vīramde's *sāth* died fighting. Three horses were cut down under Vīramde. He mounted a horse [wielding] a knife. He snatched up ten of the opponents' lances and held them together with the reins. He suffered four wounds on the head. Streams of blood went down into [his] beard.

Both armies, becoming satiated with battle, were standing [apart] on the far side [of the battlefield].

Vīramde was tending to his wounded men.

Then Pañcāyaṇ[73] came. He came and said: "Wherever will you find Vīramde in such a state [again] that you are not killing him today?" Then the *sirdār*s said: "Brother! Once [already] we have with difficulty averted misfortune on [our] chests.[74] Brother! Vīramde will not die by our doing. And, if you would kill [him], that one [over there] is Vīramde."

Then Pañcāyaṇ came upon Vīramde with thirty horsemen. And he called out to Vīramdejī. Then Vīramdejī said: "Hey, Pañcāyaṇ! Is it you? Very well, come forth! Pañcāyaṇ! There are many boys like you in Mārvāṛ; if any one [of them] could press the back of Vīr[amde],[75] then [why hasn't he]?" Pañcāyaṇ drew the reins [of his horse] and remained standing right there.

***Khyāt*, 3:97**

Then Vīramdejī said: "One such as [you] I might kill even while he stands [over] there. But, be off!" Then Pañcāyaṇ turned the reins [of his horse] right back [around].[76]

Then Kūmpojī said: "*Rāj*! Vīramde won't die easily like this!" Afterward Vīramde, having picked up his wounded men, came to Ajmer. [Mālde's] army also advanced to Nāgaur. Much adversity befell Vīramde. [His] entire *sāth* died fighting.

Rāv [Mālde] greatly feared Rāysal; he always held [Rāysal in] awe. Someone said Rāysal died fighting; someone said he did not die fighting. Then [Mālde] sent Mūḷo the Purohit[77] [to find out]. He came; he met Vīramde. He began

---

[72] ***Vīramdenūṃ aḷvī paṛi***. ***Aḷvī***: distress, difficulty, adversity. Sākariyā, ***RHSK***, p. 65, indicates that ***aḷvī*** is an adjective meaning "difficult," "unbearable", "adverse"; here it is used as a noun.

[73] The identity of this Rajpūt is uncertain, but he is probably Karamsot Rāṭhoṛ Pañcāiṇ Karamsīyot (no. 92), son of Karamsī Jodhāvat.

[74] I.e., they had avoided being killed by Vīramde.

[75] I.e., subdue or defeat Vīramde.

[76] I.e., he turned the horse right around and galloped away.

[77] Purohit Mūḷo Kūmpāvat, a Sīvaṛ Brāhmaṇ. Mūḷo held five villages in grant from Rāv Mālde: Ḍhaṇḍharīyo and Kheṛāpo of Jodhpur Pargano (Lavero Subdivision), Dhuhaṛīyo Vāsṇī and Cāhaṛvas of Sojhat Pargano, and Vīkarlāī of Jaitāraṇ Pargano. ***Vigat***, 1:349, 479-480, 546.

to speak: "Burn, [Vīramde]![78] This very land [has become] harmful to you.[79] It caused Rāysal to die."

Then [Vīramde] said: "Wait [a moment], for Rāysal has quite minor wounds. A wound of this sort is not serious." And he sent word to Rāysal: "You must provide [yourself with] a cushion and sit [where you are]. I am sending Mūḷo to you." Then he said to Purohit Mūḷo: "Go to Rāysal yourself." Then Rāysal had a Kachī[80] horse saddled, tied on [his] weapon himself, mounted,[81] and approached them, all the while making [his] horse gallop at full speed. Then they[82] mounted up and came to Rāv Mālde. They came and said: "*Jī*, Rāysal is going about galloping [his] horse at full speed."

Khyāt, 3:98

Then Rāysal came back. [His] wounds burst open. Rāysal died. When the news of Rāysal's dying arrived, the armies [of Mālde] came again [to Ajmer]. They came and drove off Vīramdejī.

Then [the Meṛtīyos] approached Rāymal, a Sekhāvat Kachvāho [Rajpūt].[83] Rāymal performed many services for them. They stayed at Rāymal's for one year. He made many arrangements for [their] safety.[84] [The Sekhāvats' servants] performed various services [for the Meṛtīyos] according to the types of servants they were. Then Vīramdejī said: "Rāymaljī! You [are] our great *sago*;[85] you have

---

[78] ***Baḷo***! This imperative apparently has the same connotation as ***jaḷo***! in Marāṭhī: "Burn thee! Burn it! used in expressions of anger or scorn." J. T. Molesworth, compiler, ***A Dictionary, Marāṭhī and English*** (1857; corrected reprint edition, Poona: Shubhada-Saraswat, 1975), p. 311.

[79] ***Ā dhartīj thāṃhīnūṃ jyān āyo***. Literally, "this very land, harm come to you." ***Jyān*** is from the Persian ***ziyān***, "harm," "loss."

[80] Kachī: from the region of Kutch. This area is situated to the southwest of Rajasthan and comprises the westernmost part of Gujarat fronting the Arabian Sea directly south of the Rann of Kutch.

[81] ***Asvār huy***: literally, "became a rider."

[82] "They" (***ai***) apparently refers to Mūḷo and his unspecified companions.

[83] Sekhāvat Kachvāho Rāmal Sekhāvat (no. 22).

[84] ***Ghaṇī jābtā kīvī***. ***Jābtā***: arrangement for protection. Sakariya, ***RHSK***, p. 441.

[85] Meṛtīyo Rāṭhoṛ Rāymal Dūdāvat of Rāhīṇ village had married a daughter to Sūjo, Rāymal Sekhāvat's son. Other marriage connections between the Meṛtīyo Rāṭhoṛs and the Sekhāvat Kachvāhos are uncertain. It is possible that Meṛtīyo Vīramde Dūdāvat's son, Jaimal, had married among the Sekhāvats. Five of Jaimal's sons were born of Kachvāho wives; three of the five were uterine brothers and daughter's sons of Kachvāho Rājā Āskaraṇ of Gwālior. The other two sons may have been of different

performed important services for us." Afterward Vīramdejī took leave of that place.

Afterward Vīramdejī took Baumḷī [village].[86] He took Vaṇhaṭo [village].[87] He took Varvāṛo [village].[88] After taking [Varvāṛo], he stayed there.

Then Māldejī received [this] information. He said: "Vīramdejī has acquired a greater domain." Again he dispatched armies against Vīramdejī. The armies came to Mojābād.[89] Vīramdejī got word [that] the armies had come to Mojābād. Then Vīramdejī said: "This time I will die fighting. This time I shall not leave [the battlefield]. Many times [previously] I left [it]. But this time I shall not abandon [the field of battle]. I shall not abandon [the battlefield] many times [again]. This time I will die fighting."

Then Muṃhato Khīṃvo said: "Inspect the battlefield site. Look at the place where we will do battle." Then Vīramdejī [and] Muṃhato Khīṃvo mounted [their horses] and went[90] to inspect the site. Then Muṃhato Khīṃvo went forward a bit.

Khyāt, 3:99

Khīṃvo said: "If you were [meant] to die [in battle], then you would have died in a battle for Meṛto. Why die in an alien land [now]?" Then he dragged [Vīramde] ahead and departed.

At Malārṇo[91] there was a ***thāṇedār***, some Muslim, whom they went and met. This Muslim said: "I will have you meet the ***kiledār*** of Riṇthambhor;[92] he will have you meet the Pātsāh."[93] Next they met the ***kiledār*** of Riṇthambhor. Then he took Vīramde into the presence of the Pātsāh. He had [him] meet the Pātsāh. The

---

mothers, but details are lacking. The specific connection with the Kachvāhos is also unspecified. Jaimal's father, Rāv Vīramde Dūdāvat, does not appear to have had any Kachvāho wives himself. See Harnath Singh Dundlod, ***The Sheikawats & their Lands*** (Jaipur: Raj. Educational Printers, 1970), p. 12; ***Murārdān***, no. 2, pp. 473, 502, 504-507.

[86] Baumḷī (spelled Bāṃvaḷī on ***Vigat***, 2:54): a village fifty miles southeast of Jaipur.

[87] Vaṇhaṭo: a village ten miles south-southeast of Baumḷī.

[88] Varvāṛo: a village fourteen miles south-southwest of Baumḷī.

[89] Mojābād: the town Mozābād or Mozāmābād, situated forty-five miles northeast of Ajmer.

[90] Literally, "came" (***āyā***).

[91] Malārṇo: a town ten miles east of Baumḷī and twenty miles north of Riṇthambhor.

[92] Riṇthambhor: a large fort and town situated forty miles south of Baumḷī and sixty-five miles southeast of Jaipur. Re: the ***kiledār*** of Riṇthambhor, see n. 264 to ***Vigat***, 2:54.

[93] Sher Shāh Sūr, Afghan ruler of Delhi and north India, 1540-45.

Pātsāhjī was kind to Vīramdejī. Subsequently Vīramdejī brought the Sūr Pātsāh against Māldejī. With eighty thousand horses Mālde confronted [them] at Ajmer.[94]

Then Vīramdejī devised a stratagem. He sent twenty thousand rupees to Kūmpo's camp. He said: "Please send us blankets." And he sent twenty thousand rupees to Jaito's camp. He said: "Please send us swords from Sīrohī." He played tricks like these.[95] And he sent word to Mālde: "Jaito [and] Kūmpo have met with the Pātsāh. They will capture you and give you to the Pātsāh. An illustration of this: If you see a surplus of rupees in their camp, then [you will] know [that] he provided expense money for them."

In the meantime Jalāl Jalūko[96] began to speak: "Pātsāh ***salāmat***![97] Have one summoned from their side; I will be [the one] from the Pātsāh's side, and we will summon a soldier from their side [for a single combat]. Decide victory [or] defeat on this [basis]."

Khyāt, 3:100

Then the Pātsāh said to Vīramde: "Does this arrangement one of my Paṭhāṇs is talking about meet with your approval or not?" Vīramdejī said: "Pātsāh ***salamāt***! I have seen the Paṭhāṇ [but] once; summon the Paṭhāṇ once again so that I might look at [him]." [The Pātsāh] summoned the Paṭhāṇ. The Paṭhāṇ came. Then Vīramdejī, after looking [him over], said: "Pātsāh ***salāmat***! Summon two more Paṭhāṇs like [this one]. Send these three from our side. And the other side will send Vīdo Bhārmalot. He will kill all these three, take their weapons, and go off safe and sound. Pātsāh ***salāmat***! Indeed you must not decide [victory or defeat] on this [basis]!"

Vīramdejī had sent information to Māldejī. The information [Vīramde] had sent, that there was a surplus of rupees in the camp of the ***umrāvs***, was in Māldejī's mind. Considerable fear arose in Mālde's mind. The fear was from the various things Vīramdejī had suggested.[98]

Afterward, when it was the evening watch, Jaito, Kūmpo, [and] Akhairāj Sonagaro were seated in Kūmpojī's tent. Jait[sī] Ūdāvat[99] [and] Khīṃvo Ūdāvat[100]

---

[94] Re: the number of warrior in the army of Rāv Mālde, see n. 295 to ***Vigat***, 2:57.

[95] ***Isṛā sā cinh kiyā***. ***Cinh*** usually means "mark" or "sign." Molesworth, ***Dictionary***, p. 287, notes that one meaning for ***cinh/cihn*** is "pranks." This meaning seems more appropriate here in the context of Vīramde's actions.

[96] Jalāl Khān Jalvāṇī, an Afghan chief in the service of Sher Shāh. Ojhā, 4:1:306.

[97] ***Salāmat***: a salutation literally meaning "safety," "salvation," "health," etc. ***Salāmat*** was used to address both Hindus and Muslims of high rank.

[98] Literally, "had implanted (***ṭhahrāī***) [in Mālde's mind]."

[99] Ūdāvat Rāṭhoṛ Jaitsī Ūdāvat (no. 139).

[100] Ūdāvat Rāṭhoṛ Khīṃvo Ūdāvat (no. 140).

were negotiating for the Rāvjī. Whatever the Rāvjī said they would come and tell [Jaito, Kūmpo, and Akhairāj]. They went and told the Rāvjī what [Jaito, Kūmpo, and Akhairāj] said: "We will see that you reach Jodhpur." Hearing their answer, the Rāvjī set out seated in a ***sukhpāḷ***.[101] The Rāvjī's hand was on Khīṃvo's hand, and they were going along. Then Jaitsī Ūdāvat spoke: "Take leave, [Khīṃvo], people are expecting us." Khīṃvojī did not speak. Then Jaitsī spoke again.

Khyāt, 3:101

He said: "Khīṃvojī! You cannot manage[102] such a distance. It is very far from Samel to Jodhpur."[103] Then Khīṃvojī withdrew [his] hand and came back. The Rāv said: "Very well, it will be seen what happens." In the morning the battle occurred. People died fighting.[104]

Then the Rāv went into the mountains of Ghūghroṭ[105] and stayed. The Sūr Pātsāh came to Jodhpur.[106] Tiloksī Varjāṅgot[107] was the ***kiledār*** in Jodhpur. He died fighting with three hundred Rajpūts. The Sūr Pātsāh stayed in Jodhpur four months.[108] Māldejī cut down the acacia trees (***bāvaḷ***)[109] of Meṛto; he told Vīramde

---

[101] ***Sukhpāḷ***: a type of palanquin.

[102] ***Lābho***. ***Lābhṇo***: to gain, acquire, obtain, find, attain.

[103] Samel village lies eighty miles east of Jodhpur. The implication of Jaitsī's statement is that Khīṃvo cannot escort the Rāv to Jodhpur and come back in time to take part in the battle with Sher Shāh.

[104] For comments regarding numbers killed in the battle of Samel, see n. 308 to ***Vigat***, 2:57.

[105] Ghughroṭ: a village four miles south-southwest of Sīvāṇo on the northern edge of a large chain of rugged hills. ***Vigat***, 2:255, notes that Ghughroṭ was a place to stay during a ***vikho***, or period of distress during which a ruler must leave his realm and take refuge. ***Vigat***, 2:58, states that Rāv Mālde went ot the village of Pīplāṇ (located two or three miles west of Ghughroṭ) during this time of troubles.

[106] Sher Shāh occupied Jodhpur in late January, 1544.

[107] Ūdāvat Rāṭhoṛ (Baiṭhvāsiyo) Tiloksī Varjāṅgot (no. 143).

[108] The actual length of Sher Shāh's residence in Jodhpur is unknown. Some sources give a time of up to one year. While at the fort of Jodhpur, he had a small mosque built in the place of a temple which was levelled. ***Bāṅkīdās***, p. 13; ***Murārdān***, no. 2, pp. 126-127; ***Vigat***, 1:58.

[109] ***Bāvaḷ*** trees (***Acacia arabica***): an important indigenous source of timber. The leaves and pods are used for fodder in the hot weather; the bark is valuable in tanning and dyeing and the gum from the tree is an exportable item. Erskine, ***Rajputana Gazetteers, III-A***, p. 48.

[this]. Then Vīramde said: "I will cut down the mango trees of Jodhpur." Then the people said: "It is not proper[110] for you [to do] this." Then he took [his] knife and cut off a small mango-tree branch for a walking-stick. Afterward everyone went to his own residence (*ṭhikāṇo*).[111] And the Sūr Pātsāh went to Delhi.[112]

He kept a garrison in Harvāṛo,[113] a garrison in which he had stationed Paṭhāṇs and [also] Vīramde Dūdāvat [and] Kalyāṇmal, master of Droṇpur.[114] One day they rode out and imprisoned the ***vasī*** of Rāv Māldejī, which was in the mountains of Ghūghroṭ. After imprisoning [it], they came [back] to Harvāṛo. There

---

[110] ***Haisāb***: Lāḷas, ***RSK***, vol. 4:3:221, gives the meanings "proper" (***ucit***) and "correct" (***ṭhīk***) for ***haisāb*** in this sentence, but he quotes no other context. Apparently this word is a variant of the Persian *ḥisābī*, "proper", "accurate," "just." Platts, ***Dictionary***, p. 477.

[111] I.e., the ***sāth*** disbanded and the ***sirdār***s went back to their own lands.

[112] Sher Shāh seems to have remained in Jodhpur only long enough to organize his administration of the area and to establish an outpost of some 5,000 strong at Bhāṅgesar village near Sojhat. He then marched against Ajmer, which he conquered, only to return to Mārvāṛ to pillage Pāḷī. He finally quit Mārvāṛ in the latter part of 1544. V. S. Bhargava, ***Marwar and the Mughal Emperors*** (Delhi: Munshiram Manoharlal, 1966), pp. 34-35; ***Murārdān***, no. 2, pp. 126-127; Ojhā, 4:1:308; R. P. Tripathi, ***The Rise and Fall of the Mughal Empire*** (reprint edition, Allahabad: Central Book Depot, 1966), p. 126.

[113] Harvāṛo: a variant of Harmāṛo, a village located fifty-five miles south-southwest of Ajmer city. The last three paragraphs of this sections (***Khyāt***, 3:101-102) are suspect as historical material for several reasons:

> (a) There is no other reference to an outpost of Sher Shāh's at the village of Harvāṛo/Harmāṛo in Mevāṛ. There seems to be some confusion with the battle of Harmāṛo, which took place in 1557.
> (b) These paragraphs contain the only reference to Vīramde's being stationed at an outpost of Sher Shāh's, an unlikely development given that most indications are he went directly to Meṛto to consolidate his foothold there.
> (c) Time sequences are incorrect. If one assumes that the reference to Mālde's attack on a village is correct but that the village was Bhāṅgesar, the only large outpost of Sher Shāh's in Mārvāṛ, and not Harvāṛo, then the attack would have occurred after the death of Sher Shāh in 1545. Vīramde was already dead at this time, having died shortly after his return to Meṛto in 1544.

[114] Vīdāvat Rāṭhoṛ Kalyāṇmal Udaikaraṇot (no. 153). Kalyāṇmal was connected through ties of marriage with the Sekhāvat Kachvāhos of Amarsar and Sīkargaḍh. Kachvāho Rāymal Sekhāvat was his maternal grandfather, and it is to Rāymal that Vīramde Dūdāvat went after his flight from Ajmer. Both Rāymal and Kalyāṇmal served under Rāv Lūṇkaraṇ of Bīkāner (1505-26) and were reputed to have been good friends and companions. Vīramde was a ***sago*** of Rāymal's (see ***Khyāt***, 3:98, ***supra***, and n. 85 to same), and also a distant paternal cousin of Kalyāṇmal's. ***Khyāt***, 3:151, 166; Ojhā, 5:1:117-118.

was some old woman, who began to speak: "Who is he?" Then they told [her]: "Kalyāṇmal, master of Droṇpur." Then the old woman said: "Bravo! The noble one departed after causing the imprisonment of our fathers' mothers (***dādiyāṃ***) [and] fathers' sisters (***kākiyāṃ***) and putting female clothing on [his] head." Kalyāṇmal heard this retort. Then he made a vow [not to eat] grain.

Khyāt, 3:102

He said: "I will not eat[115] [grain] until I cause the release of the prisoners." Then Vīramde began to talk: "They were our enemies and still you say [this]! A fine thing!" On the seventh day [of Kalyāṇmal's fast, Vīramde] had [him] drink milk; they got up. Whereupon Vīramde began to speak: "I will go there, to the Paṭhāṇ's [residence], and petition on behalf of the prisoners." Kalyāṇmal was cognizant of omens. He said: "***Rāj***! Do not petition for the prisoners. In the morning Rāv Mālde's army will attack; all of the prisoners will be freed. Whoever has to die will die. And the Paṭhāṇs will flee." Then Vīramde said: "Then, ***rāj***, why do you not eat?" Kalyāṇmal[116] said: "Vīramdejī! I will die fighting."

While they [talked] like this, day broke. Rāv Māldejī's army attacked the garrison. The Paṭhāṇs did flee. Kalyāṇ[mal] confronted [Mālde]. Then Rāv Māldejī said: "Kalyāṇmaljī! Why should you die? We have come just because of you." Then [Kalyāṇmal] said: "No, Sāhib! When [the men of] the Pātsāh's garrison flee, then a few good men die." Kalyāṇmal died fighting there. Udaikaraṇ Rāymalot[117] died fighting. The Paṭhāṇs who fled went to Delhi.

Rāv Māldejī took the prisoners and went to the mountains of Ghūghroṭ. Vīramdejī came [back] to Meṛto and stayed. Afterward Rāv Māldejī came [back] to Jodhpur. A few Turks were [there]; they ran away.

Concluded.

---

115 The text has ***jamīs***, a misprint for ***jīmīs***, "I will eat."

116 The text has Kalyāṇdās, a mistake for Kalyāṇmal.

117 Udaikaraṇ Rāymalot: we cannot identify this Rajpūt with any certainty. He could be a son of Kachvāho Rāymal Sekhāvat, but he is not listed in Sekhāvat genealogies available to us. He might also be a son of Vīramde Dūdāvat's brother, Rāymal, but he is not listed in the available Meṛtīyo genealogies either. Perhaps the name is simply wrong.

Khyāt 3:115

Now the Story of Jaimal Vīramdevot and Rāv Mālde is Written

When Vīramde[1] attained the ***devlok***, Jaimal[2] obtained the throne of Meṛto. Then Rāv Mālde had word sent from Jodhpur. He said to Jaimal: "Men like me are your enemies. You must not give the entire ***pargano*** [of Meṛto] to [your] military servants. Keep something in the ***khālso*** as well."[3]

Then Arjaṇ Rāymalot[4] obtained Īḍvo[5] from Jaimal. Jaimaljī sent a man to Arjaṇ. He told [the man]: "Summon the brother[6] and bring [him to me]." And Arjaṇ had promised [that] when a summons came [from Jaimal], he would not go to [his] home, he would go to Jaimaljī. When the man came, Arjaṇ was in [Īḍvo] village.

The man came and said: "Arjaṇjī! Jaimal has summoned you. A letter of the Rāvjī's has come from Jodhpur; you must depart." Then Arjaṇ spoke; he said: "***Rāj***! What has the Rāvjī written in the letter?" [The man] said: "The Rāvjī has written: 'You are giving the entire realm to [your] military servants. Are you keeping anything in the ***khālso*** as well?' And finally: 'Is there any such man [among Jaimal's military servants], anyone at all who would stand firm in the middle [of battle]?'"[7] Arjaṇjī said: "***Rāj***! My ***paṭo*** is secure;[8] I will stand firm." [The man] said again: "Is there any such man who would stand firm in the middle [of battle]?" Arjaṇjī felt insulted. He, [Arjaṇ], not stand [firm], even a single time? He would speak in this way [to Mālde]: "Rāvjī! When you and we fight, would any [man of yours] stand

---

[1] Meṛtīyo Rāṭhoṛ Rāv Vīramde Dūdāvat (no. 105).

[2] Meṛtīyo Rāṭhoṛ Rāv Jaimal Vīramdevot (no. 107).

[3] The implication of this statement is that Jaimal's military servants may be disloyal when faced with an enemy like Mālde; Jaimal would do better to keep his lands directly under his own authority.

[4] Meṛtīyo Rāṭhoṛ Arjaṇ Rāymalot (no. 111).

[5] Īḍvo: a village located eighteen miles northeast of Meṛto.

[6] ***Bhāī***: brother; a member of one's brotherhood (***bhāībandh***); in this instance, a fellow Meṛtīyo.

[7] ***Vicai hī ūbho rahai***. ***Ūbho rahṇo***: literally, "to remain standing." In the context of battle, this phrase often is used in the sense of "standing firm" in the face of the enemy. It also implies taking an active role in battle, as opposed to fleeing or remaining inactive (in the idiom of the period, "seated." ***Baiṭho rahṇo***: to remain seated or inactive [on the day of battle]).

[8] ***Sabaḷo***: strong; large, extensive; powerful; firm, secure.

firm in the middle [of battle]?"[9] Then Arjaṇjī said: "Yes, *rāj*! I will stand firm. My *paṭo*, at least, is secure."[10]

Khyāt **3:116**

Then Arjaṇjī came to [his] camp and said: "I have made a grand vow.[11] They say one forgets in a single moment of battle[12] [the saying]: 'Noble is he who performs nobly; ignoble is he who performs ignobly.'"[13] At that time a Sāṅkhlo [Rajpūt][14] of Jāḷsū[15] was in [Arjaṇ's] *vās*. He said: "*Jī*, I will remind [you]." [Arjaṇ] said: "Bravo, great Rajpūt!" Then [the Sāṅkhlo Rajpūt] said: "Be cautious. They must have been offended by this [statement of yours]."[16]

[Rāv Mālde] performed the Dasrāho *pūjā*[17] during [the month] *Āsoj*,[18] then

---

[9] The language of this passage is rather cryptic, to say the least, and a summary may be of use to the reader:

> Jaimal's man comes to Arjaṇ Rāymalot, a loyal Meṛtīyo who has promised to go directly to Jaimal when summoned, and tells him about Mālde's remarks disparaging Jaimal's military servants. At first, Arjaṇ is puzzled. His *paṭo* is secure; he will stand firm in battle. The man repeats Mālde's final insult: is there anyone at all among Jaimal's men who will stand firm? Arjaṇ realizes this demeans him; he decides to throw Mālde's words back at him: is there any among Mālde's retainers who will stand firm when the Meṛtīyos and Mālde fight?

[10] ***Mhāro īj paṭo sabaḷo chai.*** The particle ***īj*** has restrictive force in this sentence: Arjaṇ is saying his own ***paṭo*** is secure; others may not be.

[11] ***Mhai mhoṭo bol boliyo. Bol***: word, statement, promise, vow.

[12] ***Riṇaktāḷ palakekmeṃ. Riṇaktāḷ*** apparently is a compound formed from ***riṇak***, "the soud of a weapon or musical instrument") and ***tāḷ*** ("time," "occasion") used metaphorically to mean "battle." It may simply be a variant of ***riṇtāḷ/raṇtāḷ***, "battle," "battlefield." ***Palakekmeṃ*** appears to be ***palak ek meṃ*** ("in one instant/moment") run together.

[13] ***Bhalo chai jakaṇ ro bhalo; bhūṇḍo chai jairo bhūṇḍo***: literally, "noble is he who possesses nobility/of whom there is nobility; ignoble is he who possesses ignobility/of whom there is ignobility." The editor of the ***Khyāt***, B. P. Sākariyā, translates this saying (n. 2) as: "good is the outcome of goodness; bad the outcome of badness."

[14] I.e., a man of the Sāṅkhlo branch (***sākh***) of the Pāṃvar family (***kuḷ***)

[15] Jāḷsū: a village situated twenty-two miles northeast of Meṛto.

[16] ***Īyāṃrai ā [bāt] lāgī hutīj. Bāt lāgṇo***: words to be felt or to hurt; words to offend.

[17] ***Pūjā***: worship, homage. For an account of the Dasrāho ***pūjā*** as performed in early ninteenth-century Mevāṛ, see James Tod, ***Annals and Antiquities of Rajasthan***, edited by William Crooke, 3 vols. (London: Oxford University Press, 1920), pp. 680-685.

prepared an expeditionary force[19] [to attack Meṛto]. Mālde came [to Meṛto Pargano] directly after forming the large army. He came to the village Gāṅgāṛro[20] and made camp. [His] army raided in all directions. The ***rait log***[21] of Meṛto were being driven away. The land was being ruined. The land was being destroyed. And Acḷo Rāymalot[22] was saying: "Jaimaljī is summoning me, but here I shall sit during the day tomorrow." And Jaimaljī was being very firm, [saying]: "Acḷo! You must come and come quickly!" Then Acḷo sent word [to Mālde's camp]: "Prithīrājjī![23] Summon Akhairājjī,[24] so that I will stand firm during the day tomorrow.[25] If you would favor me, do [so] well, otherwise I will join Jaimaljī in the morning."

Then [Prithīrāj] said: "First we will kill Jaimal and afterward we will kill Acḷo. And, if they join together, we will kill them together."

At that time Jaimal was saying: "If our [conflict] with the Rāv were settled, [it would be] good." The responsibility [for negotiating] was held by [Jaimal's] ***pradhān***s, the Jaitmāl [Rāṭhoṛs] Akhairāj Bhādāvat [and] Cāndrāj Jodhāvat,[26] [the sons] of brothers.[27] (Both Bhādo [and] Jodho were [sons] of Mokaḷ.)[28] On them was [placed] the responsibility for Meṛto.

---

[18] ***Āsoj***: the seventh month of the Hindu luni-solar year (days 163-192), which may begin either in August or in September, depending on the initial day of the luni-solar year. The Dasrāho festival begins on the first day of ***Āsoj***.

[19] ***Muhim*** (Arabic muhimm): expeditionary force; an army prepared to take part in a distant campaign. Cf. ***Khyāt***, 1:39-40.

[20] Gāṅgāṛro: a village situated seven mileswest-northwest of Meṛto.

[21] ***Rait*** (Persian ra'īyat) in middle period Mārvāṛ referred to the non-Rajpūt population that was not part of the ***vasī*** of any particular Rajpūt ***ṭhākur***. ***Rait*** in itself does not always imply the peasantry; coupled with ***log*** ("people"; "people engaged in agriculture"), it does.

[22] Meṛtīyo Rāṭhoṛ Acḷo Rāymalot (no. 110).

[23] Jaitāvat Rāṭhoṛ Prithīrāj Jaitāvat (no. 63), a military servant of Rāv Mālde's.

[24] Jaitmālot Rāṭhoṛ Akhairāj Bhādāvat (no. 69), one of the Meṛtīyos' ***pradhān***s.

[25] Apparently Acḷo is suggesting that he would join Rāv Mālde's forces only if Prithīrāj Jaitāvat could persuade Akhairāj Bhādāvat to do the same.

[26] Jaitmālot Rāṭhoṛ Cāndrāj Jodhāvat (no. 74).

[27] ***Kākā-bāba rā***: literally, "[sons] of father's brother [and] father." Akhairāj and Cāndrāj were related as paternal cousins.

[28] We have changed the word order slightly and treated this sentence as a parenthetical remark.

Khyāt 3:117

Jaimaljī said: "Akhairājjī! You go [to Mālde]." Then Akhairājjī said: "***Rāj***! For what reason do you send me? And, if you are sending me, make provisions for battle." Then Akhairājjī [and] Cāndrājjī set out.

Prithīrāj had some familial tie[29] with Akhairāj. These ***ṭhākurs***, [Cāndrāj and Akhairāj], came to Prithīrājjī's camp. They came and sent [the greeting] "Rām Rām"[30] to Prithīrājjī. Prithīrajjī send word [back]: "I am bathing; afterward I also will come to the ***darbār*** [of Rāv Mālde]." In Prithīrājjī's camp swords were being sharpened.[31] Several Rajpūts were [practicing] firing guns. A great uproar was going on. These ***sirdārs***, [Cāndrāj and Akhairāj], observed [all this] and grew worried. Meanwhile Prithīrājjī put on a ***vāgo***, got ready, and went outside. He took these ***ṭhākurs*** to the ***darbār***.

Previously Rāv Māldejī's ***darbār*** had been convened. These ***ṭhākurs*** went and paid respects to Rāv Māldejī. Nago Bhārmalot[32] was seated on one side [of the Rāv]; Prithīrājjī was seated on the other side. They seated these ***sirdārs***, [Cāndrāj and Akhairāj], facing [the Rāv]. Then Prithīrāj spoke: "Rāvjī ***salāmat***! The ***pradhāns*** of Meṛto have come." Then the Rāvjī was talking. He said: "What are the ***pradhāns*** saying?" Prithīrāj spoke: "They are speaking in this manner, ***mahārāj***:[33] 'Give Meṛto to us. We will perform military service for you.'" Then the Rāv said: "We shall not give [them] Meṛto; we will give [them] another ***paṭo***." Just then Akhairāj spoke: "***Rāj***! Are you speaking [for yourself], or are you saying what someone [else] said? Who gives Meṛto and who takes [it]?

Khyāt 3:118

He who has given you Jodhpur has given us Meṛto."[34] Then Nago Bhārmalot spoke: "Take care, [or] even the Rāv's Pāṇḍavs[35] will kill you." Then Cāndrāj spoke; he

---

[29] ***Nātro***: relationship, connection, familial tie. Perhaps Prithīrāj and Akhairāj had married into the same family.

[30] Rām Rām: a form of salutation used among Hindus only.

[31] ***Tarvāryāṃ nūṃ vāḍh lāgai chai***: literally, "[sharp] edges were being applied to swords."

[32] Bālāvat Rāṭhoṛ Nago Bhārmalot (no. 38).

[33] ***Mahārāj***: a respectful term of address slightly more honorific than ***rāj***.

[34] The implication of these two sentences is that the giving of Meṛto was not in the hands of Rāv Mālde, and its acceptance was not in the hands of Jaimal: both Meṛto and Jodhpur were given as shares (*vaṇṭ*) by Rāv Jodho Riṇmalot to his sons. Cf. ***Vigat***, 1:38-40, for a list of the lands Jodho divided among these sons.

[35] Pāṇḍav: a stable hand, a groom.

said: "*Jī*, either the Rāvjī's Pāṇḍavs will kill Jaimaljī's Pāṇḍavs, or Jaimal's Pāṇḍavs will kill the Rāvjī's Pāṇḍavs. You will kill us, or we will kill you."[36] Meanwhile Māldejī spoke: "O Prithīrāj! Are these [men] really the ***pradhāns*** of Meṛto, or are there others?" Prithīrāj said: "[Long] live the ***mahārāj***! These [men] are indeed [the ***pradhāns***]." Then the Rāvjī said: "The feet of the Meṛto ***pradhāns*** are weak, brother!"

At that moment they became irritated and stood up. Akhairāj violently jerked [his] ***dupaṭo***. The ***dupaṭo*** came apart in threads. And Cāndrāj tightened the leather cinch[37] of a horse. All four feet of the horse came up [in the air]. Then these ***ṭhākurs*** mounted [their own horses] and came [back] to Meṛto.

Back [in the Rāv's ***darbār***], the Rāvjī had his people jerk [their] ***dupaṭos***, but only Jaimal's Rajpūt jerked [his] in such a way [that it came apart in threads].

Then these ***ṭhākurs*** came to Jaimaljī. They came and told [their] story before Jaimaljī. Jaimaljī said: "Why would you have me fear dying? This is not to be." Then Īsardās[38] [stole and] brought the Rāvjī's horses, which had come to the tank in Gāṅgārṛo to drink the water. Then Jaimaljī said: "You openly humbled a great man.

Khyāt 3:119

Don't you know the Rāv will not give way to you?"

On the next day the besieging army[39] advanced. Then the ***aṇīs*** of both armies joined [in combat]. Shot [and] powder were being discharged. Then that [Sāṅkhlo] Rajpūt reminded Arjaṇ Rāymalot [of his] vow. And he said: "***Rāj***! You were saying, 'I have made a grand vow.' The time [to remember it] is today."

Then Arjaṇjī came in front of Nago Bhārmalot. And meanwhile Akhairāj, going forward, came in front of the Rāvjī's elephants. Akhairāj drew near the elephants. Then two ribs of an elephant broke from a blow of Akhairāj's. Then Akhairāj said: "My concern is with Prithīrāj." At this moment Prithīrāj spoke. He said: "Dwarf![40] Why did you delay coming?" Akhairāj said: "I performed a service for the Rāvjī's elephants." In the meantime Prayāgdās[41] came [to battle] mounted on

---

[36] Nago Bhārmalot has suggested that a mere stable hand could kill the ***pradhāns*** of Meṛto; Cāndrāj corrects him by saying that stable hands kill only other stable hands, not Rajpūt warriors: Rajpūts alone kill other Rajpūts.

[37] ***Ūkaṭo***. Lāḷas, ***RSK***, p. 326, notes that the ***ukaṭo*** is a leather cinch fastened to a camel's saddle. Here it is used with a horse's saddle.

[38] Meṛtīyo Rāṭhoṛ Īsardās Vīramdevot (no. 109), Jaimal Vīramdevot's younger brother.

[39] ***Lāgtī hī phoj***: literally, "the touching/contiguous army."

[40] ***Khāṭro***: dwarf, pigmy.

[41] Meṛtīyo Rāṭhoṛ Prayāgdās Arjuṇot (no. 112).

an Iraqi horse. Even as the horse was galloping, he came and performed ***salām*** to Jaimaljī. Then Jaimal spoke: "Prayāgīyo[42] comes! I [always] would forgive his offences for this reason."[43] Meanwhile the men of Rāv Māldejī's army approached. And four blows fell on Prayāgdās's head. And he went after [the men of] the army. At the moment he reached them, he raised [his] lance [to strike]. He said: "I shall thrust [the lance] into the Rāv's head." At that very moment he braced the lance.[44] Then—God knows why[45]—he took out [his] bow and strove to force [it] onto the Rāv's neck.

Khyāt 3:120

The first time [he tried] the bow lay lightly[46] on the [Rāv's] neck. On the second occasion, he whipped [his] horse and forced the bow onto the [Rāv's] neck. Then someone came from behind and struck Prayāgdās a blow. Prayāgdās fell in two pieces.[47] And the bow remained right on Rāv Māldejī's neck. [The Rāv's men] went ahead a bit. And he fell down.

Prithīrāj was fighting. Nago Bhārmalot was fighting. The rest of Rāv Māldejī's army fled. The two ***sirdārs*** were fighting. At that time Prithīrājjī had a military servant, Hīṅgoḷo Pīpāṛo,[48] whom Prithīrājjī had promised[49] a sword.[50]

---

[42] Prayāgīyo: a diminutive or affectionate nickname for Prayāgdās.

[43] I.e., Jaimal forgives Prayāgdās his offenses because Prayāgdās shows up when there is a battle.

[44] ***Itrai māṃhai to barchī kasīsī***. The editor of the ***Khyāt***, B. P. Sākariyā, suggests (n. 19) that ***kasīsī*** is to be translated as "slipped" ***(phisal gaī)***, which is certainly plausible. However, in his own dictionary (Sākariyā, ***RHSK***, p. 216, he gives ***kasnā*** ("to draw tight," "to tighten," "to brace," "to tie, strap, or fasten"), ***khīṃcnā*** ("to draw," "to pull," "to fasten"), and ***kasā jānā*** ("to be drawn tight, "to be tightened," etc.) as meanings for the verb ***kasīsṇo***. Lāḷas, ***RSK***, p. 449, gives the meanings ***kasā jānā*** and ***pratyañcā caṛhānā*** ("to string the bow," "to get ready to fight") under ***kasīsṇo***. The context suggests that Prayāgdās is something of a comic figure. Evidently he was about to kill Rāv Mālde with his lance, but then inexplicably took out his bow and attempted to strangle the Rāv with it.

[45] ***Koī Paramesvar ro khyāl huvo***: literally, "it was some notion of Paramesvar's."

[46] ***Ūpar sai***: externally, superficially, lightly.

[47] This sentence suggests that Prayāgdās was killed, but ***Murārdān***, no. 2, pp. 465, 557, indicates that Prayāgdās died in 1598-99 in the Deccan during the battle of Bīḍ city. It may be that the characterization given here in this story has gained in the telling: i.e., Prayāgdās was only wounded.

[48] Pīpāṛo is the designation of a branch (***sākh***) of the Gahlot family (***kuḷ***). We have no additional information concerning Hīṅgoḷo.

[49] Literally, "awarded" (***bagsī***). ***Bagasṇo***: to give, grant, bestow, award.

Hīṅgoḷo said: "Prithīrājjī! You promised me a sword. Give it [to me now]." Prithīrājjī said: "O Hīṅgoḷo! You demanded [it] at a fine time!" But a man mounted on a dark-colored horse was coming; in fact it was Surtāṇ Jaimalot[51] [who] came. He came; just as he was coming [near] he thrust a lance at Prithīrāj. Prithīrāj warded off the lance. He said: "Little boy! Don't you come [to fight me]; tell your father that he should strike Prithīrāj a blow." After [saying that], Prithīrāj plucked [Surtāṇ's] sword from [his] waist and awarded [it] to Hīṅgoḷo Pīpāṛo. [Hīṅgoḷo] said: "Noble [is] Prithīrāj! A ***sāmant***[52] of Mārvāṛ." Then Prithīrājjī said: "No, brother! Just the Kuṃvar of Meṛto[53] [is] noble."

Prithīrāj, a great Rajpūt. A weapon could not strike Prithīrāj in the front; [he] had received a boon from a Jogī.[54] Then Akhairāj Bhādāvat came and thrust a weapon at Prithīrājjī from behind.

Khyāt 3:121

Prithīrāj said: "A curse on you, son of Bhādo! You licked a fine pot."[55] Then [Akhairāj] said: "The pot I licked belonged to a great house. Inside [that house] the ***khīc***[56] is plentiful."[57] Prithīrāj died fighting there. Nago Bhārmalot also died fighting. Rāv Māldejī's army fled.

Then they gave Jaimaljī the good news. They said: "***Jī***! Rāv Mālde fled." Jaimaljī said: "He backed off before [our superior] courage.[58] Announce the good news in Meṛto of his having gone."

The kettledrums left behind by Rāv Māldejī came into [their] hands. [Jaimal] gave the kettledrums to Juglo, who was a Bāmbhī[59] of Meṛto, and sent him

---

[50] Cf. "Aitihāsik Bātāṃ," p. 48.

[51] Meṛtīyo Rāṭhoṛ Surtāṇ Jaimalot (no. 113), son of Jaimal Vīramdevot.

[52] ***Sāmant***: subordinate ruler (Sanskrit ***sāmanta***).

[53] I.e., Jaimal's son, Surtāṇ Jaimalot.

[54] Jogī: a yogī; a practitioner of yoga.

[55] I.e., Akhairāj had finished off a fine man.

[56] ***Khīc***: a food prepared by cooking wheat or millet with various sorts of pulse.

[57] I.e., Prithīrāj was a member of a great Rajpūt house (the Jaitāvat Rāṭhoṛ house) and there were many other Rajpūts in that house.

[58] ***Chātī āgā sūṃ khisiyo chai***. ***Chātī***, literally "chest" or "breast," was sometimes used metaphorically to mean "courage" or "spirit." Cf. ***Vigat***, 1:50, line ten from the top of the page.

[59] Bāmbhī: a leather-worker (hence untouchable); one fit to handle or touch leather drums.

[to Mālde]. When that Bāmbhī came near the village Lāmbiyo,[60] he observed: "I'll strike the kettledrums. These are Rāv Mālde's kettledrums, so they will go away [to him]."[61] Then the Bāmbhī struck a kettledrum. Then he observed: "Be off to his [place], if you must go!"[62]

Then Cāndo[63] said [to Mālde]: "[Jaimal] is my brother. Why are you so alarmed? I will reason with him." Rāv Mālde then said: "Cāndo! See that I reach Jodhpur somehow." Cāndo said: "You must not give in to fear. He is no god. You must not fear Jaimal. I will see that you enter the fort of Jodhpur." Then Cāndo took everything that was with Rāv Māldejī—horses, elephants, wounded men—with him and sent Rāv Māldejī to Jodhpur.

Khyāt 3:122

Rāv Māldejī went to Jodhpur and stayed there. Jaimaljī ruled Meṛto contentedly.

The Story of Māldejī [and] Jaimal is concluded.

---

[60] Lāmbiyo: a village situated eighteen miles due south of Meṛto.

[61] Apparently this passage is meant as a joke: the Bāmbhī perhaps is tired from carrying the drums (Lāmbiyo being eighteen miles from Meṛto) and so he facetiously remarks that since they are Rāv Mālde's drums, they will go back on their own if he strikes them. However, there may be a cultural idiom involved here that we do not understand.

[62] *Jā* ("be off") *iyairai* ("to his [place]") *je jāijai* ("if you must go").

[63] Meṛtīyo Rāṭhoṛ Cāndo Vīramdevot (no. 123).

APPENDIX A

Some Important Towns of Middle Period Rājasthān

I. Ajmer Town (26° 27' N., 74° 37' E.)

Ajmer is situated at the base of a low saddle in the Arāvallī hills which strike northeast and southwest across the center of Rājasthān. This strategic location eighty-five miles due east of Jodhpur made Ajmer one of the more contested towns of the region. Ajmer controlled the trade routes moving from north India west to Gujarat and the Arabian Sea, and into Sindh.

Originally known as Ajayameru or Ajayapura, the town was founded in the twelfth century by the Cāhamāna ruler, Ajayarājā, as his new capitol, which he moved from Sāmbhar in the north. Ajmer became a premium town in north India under Cāhamāna rule, and withstood several attacks from Muslim invaders. Then in 1192 Mu'izz al-Dīn Muḥammad of Ghūr defeated Pṛthvīrāja III and took possession of the city. It returned to Cāhamāna rule soon after, but was then seized by Quṭb al-Dīn Aybeg in 1195. From this time forward, control over the city changed hands many times among the various Muslim rulers of the Delhi Sultānate and prominent Rajpūt rulers such as the Sīsodīyo Rāṇos of Cītoṛ. Maḥmūd Shāh Khaljī I, ruler of Māṇḍū (in Malwa), 1436-1469, took control of the town in 1452 and rule remained with him and members of his family until 1531, when Bahādur Shāh of Gujarat asserted possession following his conquest of Malwa. Then in 1535 control again changed hands when Rāṭhoṛ Rāv Vīramde Dūdāvat of Meṛto occupied the town following the withdrawal of the ***kiledār***, Sham Sheru'l-Mulk, who was a subordinate of Sultān Bahādur Shāh of Gujarat.

> K. C. Jain, ***Ancient Cities and Towns of Rajasthan*** (Delhi: Motilal Banarsidass, 1972, pp. 301-303; Upendra Nath Day, ***Medieval Malwa: A Political and Cultural History, 1401-1562*** (Delhi: Munshiram Manoharlal, 1965), p. 135; Ojhā, 4:1:607-608.

II. Ḍīḍvāṇo Town (27° 24' N., 74° 35' E.)

Ḍīḍvāṇo town lies alongside a salt lake one hundred and twenty-five miles northeast of Jodhpur city and sixty miles north of Ajmer. An ancient town, it was under the rule of the Pratihāras and then the Cāhamānas from the eighth into the twelfth century. The Sultāns of Delhi subsequently occupied the town, and then, with the fall of the Sultānate, it became like Sāmbhar to its east, a contested prize fought over by the Sīsodīyo Rāṇos of Cītoṛ, the Khānzāda Khāns of Nāgaur, and the Sultāns of Malwa and Gujarat because of its salt industry. By the mid-fifteenth century, control over the town passed to the Khānzāda Khāns of Nāgaur, who held nominal control over the area until the time of Rāṭhoṛ Rāv Mālde Gāṅgāvat of Jodhpur (1532-62).

Jain, ***Ancient Cities and Towns of Rajasthan***, pp. 192-193; Major K. D. Erskine, ed., ***Rajputana Gazetteers:*** Volume III-A, ***The Western Rajputana States Residency and the Bikaner Agency*** (Allahabad: The Pioneer Press, 1909), pp. 184-185.

III. Meṛto Town (26° 39' N., 74° 2' E.)

Meṛto was referred to both as Meḍantaka and Meḍatapura in the pre-Muslim period, but in the early Muslim period (12th century), its name changed to Medanipura. Its significance in this early period appears to stem from the fact that it was an important religious center and occupied a place on the trade routs moving from north India toward Sindh and Gujarat. Epigraphically, the earliest reference to Meṛto is found in the Jodhpur inscription of Pratihāra Bauka, ca. 837. The inscription notes that one of Bauka's predecessors, Nāgabhaṭa, had established his capital at Meḍantaka. Pratihāra Nāgabhaṭa was the son of Narabhaṭa and the grandson of Rajilla, who originally established Pratihāra rule at Māṇḍor in central Mārvāṛ in the sixth century.

Pratihāra rule in this area eventually fell to the Cāhamānas. A certain Rāṇā Māladeva Cāhamāna had his capital at Meḍantaka around 1319. This same Māladeva is associated with Javālipura (Jāḷor) in southern Mārvāṛ and Citrakūṭa (Cītoṛ) in Mevāṛ.

Temporary Muslim rule extended over Meṛto at the turn of the fourteenth century. The Pāṇḍukhā inscription of the V.S. year 1358 (A.D. 1301-02) mentions the rule of Alāvadī of Joginīpura ('Alā' al-Dīn of Delhi) and his viceroy, Tājadī (Tāj al-Dīn) at Meḍantaka (Meṛto).

No other references to Meṛto in inscriptions or local texts have been found until the time of Rāv Jodho Riṇmalot and his sons, Varsiṅgh and Dūdo Jodhāvat.

Archaeologically, there are few extant remains in Meṛto proper dating from the pre-Muslim period. Those present include two eleventh century pillars and other structures in the temple of Lakṣmī, and the remains of a temple of Mahāvīra, built in 1113 by Abhayadevasuri in tribute to Jainism which flourished in this area from the twelfth century onwards. The town was of undoubted importance as a religious center from this time.

For reasons which are unclear, the town fell into obscurity during the second half of the fourteenth century and the first half of the fifteenth, for it was uninhabited at the time the Rāṭhoṛ brothers Varsiṅgh and Dūdo came to this area around 1462.

Jain, ***Ancient Cities and Towns of Rajasthan***, pp. 177-179, ***Khyāt***, 1:204-205; H. C. Ray, ***The Dynastic History of Northern India***. 2 vols. (1931-36; reprint edition, Delhi: Munshiram Manoharlal Publisher Pvt. Ltd., 1973), 2:1205; Dasharatha Sharma, ed., ***Rajasthan through the Ages***, vol. 1 (Bikaner: Rajasthan State Archives, 1966), pp. 701, 723.

IV. Nāgaur Town (27° 4' N., 73° 49' E.)

Nāgaur is an important town on the trade route from north India west into Sindh. It is situated sixty miles north-northeast of Jodhpur city. Prior to 1198 when control over it passed into Muslim hands, the town was held by a series of Hindu dynasties extending back into the eighth century. Nāgaur had several Turkish governors between 1198-1270 and was a minto town for the Sultāns of Delhi. Rule passed to Rāṭhoṛ Rāv Cūṇḍo Vīramot, the ruler of Maṇḍor in central Mārvāṛ, ca. 1399, after the fall of the Tughluq empire. Rāv Cūṇḍo was subsequently killed at Nāgaur[1] fighting against a coalition of Bhāṭī Rajpūts from Pūgaḷ and Muslim Paṭhāṇs from the north including Khyām Khān from Hisāṛ and Khiḍr Khān of Multān, who sought to assert control over the area. Nāgaur then became an independent seat of rule under a local Khānzāda Khān dynasty founded by Shams Khān Dandānī, a noble of Fīrūz Shāh of Gujarat. Shams Khān was a younger brother of Ẓafar Khān, the founder of the independent Sultānate of Gujarat, and he had established himself at Nāgaur by ousting its governor, Jalāl Khān Khokhar.

Later, following Shams Khān's death, Nāgaur became subject to inroads from the Rāṇos of Cītoṛ, and to conflict among various branches of the Khānzāda Khān family. Rāv Mālde Gāṅgāvat of Jodhpur conquered Nāgaur in 1536 and again brought it under Rāṭhoṛ rule. Rāv Mālde's rule lasted for eight years, then passed into Muslim hands following Rāv Mālde's defeat at the battle of Samel in 1544 at the hands of Sher Shāh Sūr.

Jain, ***Ancient Cities and Towns of Rajasthan***, p. 242-246.

V. Sāmbhar Town (26° 55' N., 75° 11' E.)

Sāmbhar is an ancient town which remained of considerable importance throughout the pre-modern period because of its position on trade routes and its value as a source of revenue from salt. The town is located at the southern extremity of a large salt lake lying some fifty miles northeast of Ajmer and eighty miles east-northeast of Meṛto. The salt lake extends northwest from the town for about twenty miles and varies in breadth from two to seven miles. It covers an area of nearly ninety square miles. Although dry much of the year, the lake fills with water during the rainy season, and may have water all year if the rains are exceptionally heavy.

Sāmbhar first came into prominence during the eighth and ninth centuries when the early Cāhamāna rulers controlled the area as subordinates of the Pratihāras. The Cāhamānas gained independence in the early tenth century during the rule of Sinharājā, and this independence lasted into the twelfth century when Ajayarājā Cāhamāna transferred his seat of rule to his newly founded city of Ajayameru (Ajmer).

Control over Sāmbhar passed to the Sultāns of Delhi in 1198, but again

---

[1] For a discussion of the dating of this event, see "Cūṇḍāvat Rāṭhoṛs" in the B.N.

changed hands in the following centuries in response to the political fortunes of the Sultānate. Bālhaṇadeva, ruler of Riṇthambhor, held the rule of Sāmbhar for some time during the early thirteenth century, then in 1226 it again came under Sultānate rule when Iltutmish led an army successfully against Riṇthambhor and Sāmbhar. Inscriptions indicate that Fīrūz Shāh Tughluq of Delhi governed Sāmbhar in 1363. Sīsodīyo Rāṇo Mokaḷ Lākhāvat (ca. 1421-33) of Cītoṛ then took control, only to be pushed out by the Muslim ruler of Nāgaur, Mujāhid Khān. Rāṇo Mokaḷ's son, Rāṇo Kūmbho Mokaḷot (ca. 1433-1468), reconquered the area not long after his succession to rulership. Some time during the latter part of Rāṇo Kūmbho's rule, control passed under the authority of the Muslim ruler of Māṇḍū.

Jain, ***Ancient Cities and Towns of Rajasthan***, pp. 250-254;
Erskine, ***Rajputana Gazetters***, III-A, pp. 214-216.

APPENDIX B

Lists of Men Killed in Various Battles

According to Available Sources

I. Battle of Samel, January 5, 1544.

A. From *Vigat*, 1:56-57:

Bhāṭī Pañcāiṇ Jodhāvat
Bhīṃvot Kalo Surjanot
Nīmbo Āṇandot, Jeso [Bhāṭī]
Rāṭhoṛ Bhavānīdās Sūrāvat, Akhairājot
Rāṭhoṛ Bhojo Pañcāiṇot, Akhairājot
Rāṭhoṛ Hamīr Sīhāvat, Akhairājot
Rāṭhoṛ Jaimal, [son] of Vīdo Parbatot, Ḍūṅgarot
Rāṭhoṛ Jaito Pañcāiṇot, Akhairājot
[Rāṭhoṛ] Jogo Rāvaḷot, Akhairājot
Rāṭhoṛ Khīmvo, [son] of Ūdo Sūjāvat
Rāṭhoṛ Kūmpo Mahirājot, Akhairājot
Rāṭhoṛ Pañcāiṇ Karamsīyot
Rāṭhoṛ Pato Kānhāvat, Akhairājot
Rāṭhoṛ Rāymal Akhairājot, Rīṇmal
Rāṭhoṛ Surtāṇ Gāṅgāvat, Ḍūṅgarot
Rāṭhoṛ Udaisiṅgh Jaitāvat, Akhairājot
Rāṭhoṛ Vīdo Bhārmalot, Bālāvat
Rāṭhoṛ Vairsī Rāṇāvat, Akhairājot
Sonagaro Akhairāj Riṇdhīrot

B. From *Vigat*, 2:57:

Rāṭhoṛ Jaito Pañcāiṇot
Rāṭhoṛ Jaitsī
Rāṭhoṛ Khīṃvo Ūdāvat
Rāṭhoṛ Kūmpo Mahirājot
Rāṭhoṛ Pañcāiṇ Karamsīyot
Rāṭhoṛ Vīdo Bhārmalot
Sonagaro Akhairāj Riṇdhīrot

C. From ***Jodhpur Rājya kī Khyāt***, pp. 83-84:

Bhāṭī Bhairī [i.e., Mero] Acḷāvat
Bhāṭī Gāṅgo Varjāṅgot
Bhāṭī Hamīr Lākhāvat
Bhāṭī Kelhaṇ Āpmal Hamīrot

Bhāṭī Mādhodās Rāghodāsot
Bhāṭī Nīmbo Patāvat
Bhāṭī Pañcāiṇ Jodhāvat
Bhāṭī Sūro Parbatot
Bhāṭī Sūro Patāvat
Cāraṇ Bhāno Khetāvat Dhadhvāṛiyo
Devṛo Akhairāj Banāvat
Īndo Kisno
Jaitmal Vīdāvat Ḍūṅgarot
Māṅglīyo Hemo Nīmbāvat
Paṭhāṇ Oledādkhān
Rāṭhoṛ Bhārmal Bājāvat
Rāṭhoṛ Bhado Pañcāiṇot
Rāṭhoṛ Bhavānīdās, [son] of Sūro Akhairājot
Rāṭhoṛ Bhojo Pañcāiṇot
Rāṭhoṛ Bhojrāj Pañcāiṇot, Akhairājot
Rāṭhoṛ Hāmo Sīhāvat
Rāṭhoṛ Hardās Khaṅgārot
Rāṭhoṛ Harpāl Jodhāvat
Rāṭhoṛ Jaimal, [son] of Vīdo Parbatot
Rāṭhoṛ Jaito Pañcāiṇot
Rāṭhoṛ Jaitsī Rāghāvat
Rāṭhoṛ Jaitsī Ūdāvat
Rāṭhoṛ Jogo, [son] of Rāvaḷ Akhairājot
Rāṭhoṛ Kalo Urjanot, Bhīṃvot
Rāṭhoṛ Khīṃvo Ūdāvat of Jaitāraṇ
Rāṭhoṛ Khīṃvo Ūdāvat's military servant
Rāṭhoṛ Kūmpo Mahirājot
Rāṭhoṛ Mahes Dedāvat
Rāṭhoṛ Nīmbo Aṇandot
Rāṭhoṛ Pañcāiṇ Karamsīyot
Rāṭhoṛ Pato Kānhāvat
Rāṭhoṛ Rāymal Akhairājot, Riṇmal
Rāṭhoṛ Surtāṇ Gāṅgāvat
Rāṭhoṛ Udaisiṅgh Jaitāvat
Rāṭhoṛ Vīdo Bhārmalot, Bāl[āvat]
Rāṭhoṛ Vairsī Rāṇāvat
Sāṅkhlo Ḍūṅgarsī Dhāmāvat
Sāṅkhlo Dhanrāj Dhāmāvat
Soḍho Nātho Dedāvat
Sonagaro Akhairāj Riṇdhīrot
Sonagaro Bhojrāj Akhairājot
Ūhaṛ Surjan Narhardāsot
Ūhaṛ Vīro Lākhāvat

II. Siege of Jodhpur Fort, 1544.

A. From *Vigat*, 2:59:

Bhāṭī Sāṅkar Sūrāvat
Rāṭhoṛ Acḷo Sivrājot
Rāṭhoṛ Sīṅghaṇ Khetsīyot
Rāṭhoṛ Tiloksī Varjāṅgot

B. From *Vigat*, 1:58:

Bhāṭī Mālo Jodhāvat, a Jesāvat
Rāṭhoṛ Acḷo Sivrājot
Rāṭhoṛ Pato Durjaṇsāḷot
Rāṭhoṛ Tiloksī Varjāṅgot, an Ūdāvat

C. From ***Jodhpur Rājya kī Khyāt***, pp. 85-86:

Bhāṭī Bhojo Jodhāvat
Bh[āṭī] Mālo Jodhāvat, brother of Rāmo
Bhāṭī Nāthū Mālāvat
Bhāṭī Sāṅkar Sūrāvat
Īndo Sekho Dhaṇrājot
Jaimal
Nāyak Bhīkhū
Nāyak Jhājhaṇ
Rāṭhoṛ Acḷo Sivrājot
Rāṭhoṛ Rāmo Vīramot
Rāṭhoṛ Sīṅghaṇ Khetsīyot
Rāṭhoṛ Tiloksī Varjāṅgot
Sohaṛ Bhairav, son of Bhīṃv Sīhāvat
Ūdavat Sāṅkar Jaitsīyot

III. Battle of Meṛto, March 21, 1554.

A. Rāv Mālde Gāṅgāvat's men.

1. From *Vigat*, 2:59:

Cahuvāṇ Megho
Pañcolī Abho
Pañcolī Neto
Pañcolī Rato
Rāṭhoṛ Dhano Bhārmalot
Rāṭhoṛ Jagmāl Udaikaraṇot
Rāṭhoṛ Nago Bhārmalot
Rāṭhoṛ Prithīrāj Jaitāvat

Rāṭhoṛ Sūjo Tejsīyot
Sīndhaḷ Ḍūṅgarsī
Sohaṛ Pītho Jesāvat

2. From "Aitihāsik Bātāṃ", p. 49:

Abho
Ḍūṅgarsī
Megho
Rāṭhoṛ Dhano Bhārmalot
Rāṭhoṛ Dhanrāj
Rāṭhoṛ Jagmāl Udaikaraṇot
Rāṭhoṛ Nago Bhārmalot
Rāṭhoṛ Prithīrāj Jaitāvat
Rato
Sohaṛ Pītho Jesāvat
Sūjo Tejsīyot

3. From *Vigat*, 1:59:

Cahuvāṇ Megho Bhairavdāsot
Pañcolī Abho Jhājhāvat
Pañcolī Rato, [son] of Abho
Rāṭhoṛ Bhārmal Devīdāsot
Rāṭhoṛ Dhano Bhārmalot, a Bālāvat
Rāṭhoṛ Dhanrāj Bhārmalot
Rāṭhoṛ Ḍūṅgarsī
Rāṭhoṛ Jagmāl Udaikaraṇot [of] Khīṃvasar
Rāṭhoṛ Nago Bhārmalot, a Bālāvat
Rāṭhoṛ Prithīrāj Jaitāvat
Rāṭhoṛ Rāghavde Barsalot, an Ūdāvat
Rāmo Pīpāṛo
[Rāmo] Bhairavdāsot, a Cāmpāvat
Sohāṛ Pītho Jagāvat

4. From ***Jodhpur Rājya kī Khyāt***, 87-88:

Cahuvāṇ Śārdūl
Cahuvāṇ Megho
Pīpāṛo Hoglo
Pīpāṛo Rāmo
Pañcolī Abho Jhājhāvat
Pañcolī Rato, Abho's son
Rāṭhoṛ Dhanrāj Bhārmalot, a Bāl[āvat]
Rāṭhoṛ Jagmāl Udaikaraṇot of Khīṃvasar
Rāṭhoṛ Nago Bhārmalot, a Bālāvat
Rāṭhoṛ Prithīrāj Jaitāvat

Rāṭhoṛ Rāghavde Versal[ot], an Ūdāvat
Rāṭhoṛ Rāmo Bhairavdāsot, a Cāmpāvat
Rāṭhoṛ Sūjo Jaitsīyot
Sīndhaḷ Dūṅgarsī
Ūhaṛ Prithīrāj

B. Rāv Jaimal's Rajpūts.

1. From *Vigat*, 2:59:

Rāṭhoṛ Akhairāj Bhādāvat
Rāṭhoṛ Candrāv, [son] of Jodho
Rāṭhoṛ Moṭo Jogāvat
Rāṭhoṛ Narāiṇdās, [son] of Candrāv
Rāṭhoṛ Sāṅgo, [son] of Bhojo
Rāvat Sagto, [son] of Sāṅgo

2. From *Vigat*, 1:60:

Akhairāj Bhādāvat
Rāṭhoṛ Cāndrāv Jodhāvat
Rāṭhoṛ Moṭo, [son] of Jogo
Rāṭhoṛ Nāraṇdās Cāndrāvat
Rāṭhoṛ Sāṅgo Bhojāvat
Rāvat Sagto Sāṅgāvat

3. From ***Jodhpur Rājya kī Khyāt***, p. 88:

Jaitmālot Akhairāj Bhadāvat
Jaitmāl[ot] Candrāj Jodhāvat
Jaitmāl[ot] Sāṅgo Bhadāvat

IV. Battle of Sātaḷvās, March 20, 1562.

A. From *Vigat*, 2:65-66:

Bārhaṭh Colo
Bārhaṭh Jālap
Bārhaṭh Jīvo
Bhāṭī Pirāg Bhārmalot
Bhāṭī Pītho
Bhāṭī Tiloksī
Hamjo, a Turk
Māṅglīyo Dedo
Māṅglīyo Vīram
Rāṭhoṛ Acḷo Bhāṇot
Rāṭhoṛ Amro Rāmāvat

Rāṭhoṛ Bhāṇ, [son] of Bhojrāj, [who was the son] of Sādo Rūpāvat
Rāṭhoṛ Bhākharsī Ḍūṅgarsīyot
Rāṭhoṛ Bhākharsī Jaitāvat
Rāṭhoṛ Devīdās Jaitāvat
Rāṭhoṛ Goind, [son] of Rāṇo Akhairājot
Rāṭhoṛ Īsar Gharsīyot
Rāṭhoṛ Īsardās, [son] of Rāṇo Akhairājot
Rāṭhoṛ Jaimal Tejsīyot
Rāṭhoṛ Jaitmāl, [son] of Pañcāiṇ Dūdāvat, a Meṛtīyo
Rāṭhoṛ Mahes Gharsīyot
Rāṭhoṛ Mahes Pañcāiṇot
Rāṭhoṛ Netsī Sīhāvat
Rāṭhoṛ Pato, [son] of Kūmpo Mahirājot
Rāṭhoṛ Pūraṇmal, [son] of Prithīrāj Jaitāvat
Rāṭhoṛ Rājsiṅgh Gharsīyot
Rāṭhoṛ Rāmo Bhairavdāsot
Rāṭhoṛ Rāṇo Jagnāthot
Rāṭhoṛ Riṇdhīr Rāysiṅghot
Rāṭhoṛ Sāṅgo Riṇdhīrot
Rāṭhoṛ Tejsī, [son] of Urjan Pañcāiṇot
Sāṅkhlo Tejsī
Sutrār Bhānīdās

B. From *Vigat*, 1:61-63:

Bārhaṭh Coḷo
Bārhaṭh Jālap
Bārhaṭh Jīvo
Bhāṭī Pirāg Bhārmalot
Bhāṭī Pītho Āṇandot
Bhāṭī Tiloksī, [son of] Parbat Āṇandot
Cahuvāṇ Vīram Ūdāvat
Hamīr Ūdāvat, Bālāvat
Hamjo, Turk
Māṅglīyo Dedo
Māṅglīyo Vīram Devāvat
Rāṭhoṛ Acḷo Bhāṇot
Rāṭhoṛ Akho Jagmālot, [descendant] of Kānho Cūṇḍāvat
Rāṭhoṛ Amro Rāmāvat
Rāṭhoṛ Bhākharsī Ḍūṅgarsīyot
Rāṭhoṛ Bhākharsī Jaitāvat
Rāṭhoṛ Bhāṇ, [son of] Bhojrāj, [who was the son] of Sādo Rūpāvat
Rāṭhoṛ Bhīṃv Ūdāvat, Bāl[āvat?]
Rāṭhoṛ Devīdās Jaitāvat
Rāṭhoṛ Goind, [son] of Rāṇo Akhairājot

[Rāṭhoṛ] Īsar Gharṣīyot
Rāṭhoṛ Īsardās, [son of] Rāṇo Akhairājot
Rāṭhoṛ Jaimal Tejsīyot
Rāṭhoṛ Jaitmāl Pañcāiṇot, [son of] Pañcāiṇ [D]ūdāvat
Rāṭhoṛ Mahes Gharṣīyot
Rāṭhoṛ Mahes Pañcāiṇot
Rāṭhoṛ Netsī Sīhāvat, Akhairāj[ot]
Rāṭhoṛ Pato, [son] of Kūmpo Mahirājot
Rāṭhoṛ Prithīrāj, [son of] Sīṅghaṇ Akhairājot
Rāṭhoṛ Pūraṇmal, [son] of Prithīrāj Jaitāvat
Rāṭhoṛ Rāmo Bhairavdāsot
[Rāṭhoṛ] Rāṇo Jagnāthot
Rāṭhoṛ Riṇ[?] Rāysalot, military servant of Meṛtīyo Jagmāl
Rāṭhoṛ Sāṅgo Riṇdhīrot
Rāṭhoṛ Sehso Rāmāvat
Rāṭhoṛ Sehso, [son of] Urjan Pañcāiṇot
Rāṭhoṛ Tejsī, [son of] Urjan Pañcāiṇot
Sāṅkhlo Tejsī Bhojuvot
Suthār Bhānīdās

C. From "Aitihāsik Bātāṃ", pp. 55-56:

Bārhaṭh Colo
Bārhaṭh Jālap
Bārhaṭh Jīvo
Dedo
Hamjo, a Turk
Māṅglīyo Vīram
Pītho
Pirāg Bhārmalot
Rāṭhoṛ Īsar Gharṣīyot
Rāṭhoṛ Acḷo Bhaṇot
Rāṭhoṛ Amro Rāmāvat
Rāṭhoṛ Bhāṇ, son of Bhojrāj, [who was the son of] Sado Rūpāvat
Rāṭhoṛ Bhākharsī Ḍūṅgarsīyot
Rāṭhoṛ Bhākharsī Jaitāvat
Rāṭhoṛ Devīdās Jaitāvat
Rāṭhoṛ Goind, [son] of Rāṇo Akhairājot
Rāṭhoṛ Jaimal Tejsīyot
Rāṭhoṛ Jaitmāl Pañcāiṇot, [son of] Pañcāiṇ Dūdāvat, a Meṛtīyo.
Rāṭhoṛ Mahes Gharṣīyot
Rāṭhoṛ Mahes Pañcāiṇot
Rāṭhoṛ Netsī Sīhāvat
Rāṭhoṛ Pato, [son] of Kūmpo Mahirājot
Rāṭhoṛ Pūraṇmal, [son] of Prithīrāj Jaitāvat

Rāṭhoṛ Rājsiṅgh Gharsīyot
Rāṭhoṛ Rāṇo Jagnāthot
Rāṭhoṛ Riṇdhīr Rāysiṅghot
Rāṭhoṛ Sahso Rāmāvat
Rāṭhoṛ Sāṅgo Riṇdhīrot
Rāṭhoṛ Tejsī, [son] of Urjan Pañcāiṇot
Sutrār Bhavānīdās
Tejsī
Tiloksī

D. From *Jodhpur Rājya kī Khyāt*, pp. 93-94:

Bārhaṭh Colo
Bārhaṭh Jālap
Bārhaṭh Jīvo
Bhāṭī Pīrāg Bhārmalot
Bhāṭī Pītho
Bhāṭī Tiloksī
Hamjo
Māṅglīyo Dedo
Māṅglīyo Vīram
Rāṭhoṛ Īsar Gharsīyot
Rāṭhoṛ Īsardās Rāṇāvat
Rāṭhoṛ Acḷo Bhāṇot
Rāṭhoṛ Amro Rāṇāvat
Rāṭhoṛ Bhāṇ Bhojrājot
Rāṭhoṛ Bhākharsī Ḍūṅgarsīyot
Rāṭhoṛ Devīdās Jaitāvat
Rāṭhoṛ Goind Rāṇāvat
Rāṭhoṛ Jagmāl Vīramdevot
Rāṭhoṛ Mahes Gharsīyot
Rāṭhoṛ Mahes Pañcāiṇot
Rāṭhoṛ Netsī Sīhāvat
Rāṭhoṛ Pato Kūmpāvat
Rāṭhoṛ Pūraṇmal Prithīrājot
Rāṭhoṛ Rājsiṅgh Gharsīyot
Rāṭhoṛ Rāṇo Jagannāthot
Rāṭhoṛ Rāmo Bhairavdāsot
Rāṭhoṛ Sahso Rāmāvat
Rāṭhoṛ Sahso Urjanot
Rāṭhoṛ Sāṅgo Rīṇdhīrot
Rāṭhoṛ Vīram
Sāṅkhlo Tejsī
Suthhār Bhānīdās
V[ī]ṭhū Meho

E. From ***Bāṅkīdās***, p. 16:

Bhāṭī Pītho Āṇandot
Bhāṭī Tiloksī Parbatot
Cahuvāṇ Jaitsī
Jagmāljī's military servant
Kāk Cāndāvat's [son]
Māṅglīyo Dedo
Māṅglīyo Vīramdev
Rāṭhoṛ Acḷo Bhāṇot
Rāṭhoṛ Akho Jagmālot
Rāṭhoṛ Amro Āsāvat
Rāṭhoṛ Amro Rāmāvat
Rāṭhoṛ Amro Rāyāvat
Rāṭhoṛ Bhākharsī Ḍūṅgarsīyot
Rāṭhoṛ Bhākharsī Jaitāvat
Rāṭhoṛ Bhāṇ Bhojrājot, a Rūp[āvat]
Rāṭhoṛ Bhīm Dūdāvat, a Bāl[āvat]
Rāṭhoṛ Devīdās Jaitāvat
Rāṭhoṛ Goind Rāṇāvat
Rāṭhoṛ Hamīr Ūdāvat, Bāl[āvat]
Rāṭhoṛ Īsardās Gharsīyot
Rāṭhoṛ Īsardās, [son] of Rāṇo Akhairājot
Rāṭhoṛ Jaimal Tejsīyot
Rāṭhoṛ Jaitmāl Pañcāiṇot, a Meṛtīyo
Rāṭhoṛ Mahes Gharsīyot
Rāṭhoṛ Mahes Pañcāiṇot, a Karamsīyot
Rāṭhoṛ Pūraṇmal Prithīrājot
Rāṭhoṛ Pato, [son] of Kūmpo Mahirājot
Rāṭhoṛ Prithīrāj
Rāṭhoṛ Pūraṇmal Prithīrājot
Rāṭhoṛ Rāṇo Jagnāthot
Rāṭhoṛ Rāysiṅgh Gharsīyot
Rāṭhoṛ Riṇdhīr Rāymalot
Rāṭhoṛ Sahso Rāmāvat
Rāṭhoṛ Sāṅgo Riṇdhīrot
Rāṭhoṛ Sīṅghaṇ, [son] of Akhairāj
Rāṭhoṛ Tejsī Sīhāvat
Sāṅkhlo Tejsī Bhojāvat
Vīram Dūdāvat's [son]

F. From ***Bāṅkīdās***, p. 17:

Bārhaṭh Jālap
Bārhaṭh Jīvo
Bhāṭī Pīrāgdās Bhārmalot
Bhāṭī Pītho

Bhāṭī Tiloksī
Hamlo, a Turk
Jaimal Tejsīyot
Khātī Bhānīdās
Māṅgḷīyo Vīram
Rāṭhoṛ Acḷo Bhāṇot
Rāṭhoṛ Amro Rāmāvat
Rāṭhoṛ Bhākharsī Ḍūṅgarot
Rāṭhoṛ Bhākharsī Jaitāvat
Rāṭhoṛ Bhāṇ Bhojrājot
Rāṭhoṛ Devīdās Jaitāvat
Rāṭhoṛ Goinddās Rāṇāvat
Rāṭhoṛ Īsardās Gharsīyot
Rāṭhoṛ Īsardās Rāṇāvat
Rāṭhoṛ Jaitsī, [son of] Urjaṇ Pañcāiṇot
Rāṭhoṛ Mahes Gharsīyot
Rāṭhoṛ Mahes Pañcāiṇot
Rāṭhoṛ Netsī Sodāvat
Rāṭhoṛ Pato Kūmpo Mahirājot's [son]
Rāṭhoṛ Pūraṇmal Prithīrājot
Rāṭhoṛ Rājsī Gharsīyot
Rāṭhoṛ Rāmo Bhairavdāsot
Rāṭhoṛ Rāṇo Jagnāthot
Rāṭhoṛ Riṇdhīr Rāysiṅghot
Rāṭhoṛ Sahso Rāmāvat
Rāṭhoṛ Sahso Urjaṇot
Rāṭhoṛ Sāṅgo Riṇdhīrot
Sāṅkhlo Tejsī

V. Composite Lists.

A. Battle of Samel, January 5, 1544.

Bhāṭīs

Bhāṭī Hamīr Lākhāvat
Bhāṭī Mādhodās Rāghodāsot
Bhāṭī Nīmbo Patāvat
Bhāṭī Sūro Parbatot
Bhāṭī Sūro Patāvat
Jeso Bhāṭī Gāṅgo Varjāṅgot
Jeso Bhāṭī Mero Acḷāvat
Jeso Bhāṭī Nīmbo Āṇandot
Jeso Bhāṭī Pañcāiṇ Jodhāvat
Kelhaṇ Bhāṭī Āpmal Hamīrot

Cāraṇs

Dhadhvāṛīyo Cāraṇ Bhāno Khetāvat

Cahuvāṇs

Devṛo Cahuvāṇ Akhairāj Banāvat
Sonagaro Cahuvāṇ Akhairāj Riṇdhīrot
Sonagaro Cahuvāṇ Bhojrāj Akhairājot

Gahlots

Māṅglīyo Gahlot Hemo Nīmbāvat

Paṃvārs

Sāṅkhlo Paṃvār Dhanrāj Dhāmāvat
Sāṅkhlo Paṃvār Ḍūṅgarsī Dhāmāvat
Soḍho Paṃvār Nātho Dedāvat

Paṛihārs

Īndo Paṛihār Kisno

Paṭhāṇs

Oledād Khān

Rāṭhoṛs

Akhairājot Rāṭhoṛ Bhado Pañcāiṇot
Akhairājot Rāṭhoṛ Bhavānīdās Sūrāvat
Akhairājot Bhojo Pañcāiṇot
Akhairājot Rāṭhoṛ Hamīr Sīhāvat
[Akhairājot] Rāṭhoṛ Jaito Pañcāiṇot[1]
Akhairājot Rāṭhoṛ Jogo Rāvaḷot
[Akhairājot] Rāṭhoṛ Kūmpo Mahirājot[2]
Akhairājot Rāṭhoṛ Pato Kānhāvat
Akhairājot Rāṭhoṛ Rāymal Akhairājot
Akhairājot Rāṭhoṛ Udaisiṅgh Jaitāvat
Akhairājot Rāṭhoṛ Vairsī Rāṇāvat
Bālāvat Rāṭhoṛ Vīdo Bhārmalot
Bhīṃvot Rāṭhoṛ Kalo Urjanot

---

[1] Founder of the Jaitāvat branch of Mārvāṛ Rāṭhoṛs.

[2] Founder of the Kūmpāvat branch of Mārvāṛ Rāṭhoṛs.

Ḍūṅgarot Rāṭhoṛ Jaitmāl Vīdāvat
Ḍūṅgarot Rāṭhoṛ Surtāṇ Gāṅgāvat
Karamsot Rāṭhoṛ Pañcāiṇ Karamsīyot
Rāṭhoṛ Bhārmal Bājāvat
Rāṭhoṛ Hardās Khaṅgarot
Rāṭhoṛ Harpāl Jodhāvat
Rāṭhoṛ Jaitsī Rāghāvat
Rāṭhoṛ Mahes Dedāvat
Ūdāvat Rāṭhoṛ Jaitsī Ūdāvat
Ūdāvat Rāṭhoṛ Khīṃvo Ūdāvat
Ūhaṛ Rāṭhoṛ Surjan Narhardāsot
Ūhaṛ Rāṭhoṛ Vīro Lākhāvat

Others

Ūdāvat Rāṭhoṛ Khīṃvo Ūdāvat's military servant

B. Siege of Jodhpur Fort, 1544.

Bhāṭīs

Jeso Bhāṭī Bhojo Jodhāvat
Jeso Bhāṭī Mālo Jodhāvat
Jeso Bhāṭī Nāthū Mālāvat
Jeso Bhāṭī Sāṅkar Sūrāvat

Nāyaks

Nāyak Bhīkhū
Nāyak Jhājhaṇ

Paṛihārs

Īndo Paṛihār Sekho Dhanrājot

Rāṭhoṛs

Jodho Rāṭhoṛ Acḷo Sivṛājot
Rāṭhoṛ Pato Durjaṇsāḷot
Rāṭhoṛ Rāmo Vīramot
Riṇmalot Rāṭhoṛ Sīṅghaṇ Khetsīyot
Sohaṛ Rāṭhoṛ Bhairav Bhīṃvot
Ūdāvat Rāṭhoṛ Sāṅkar Jaitsīyot
Ūdāvat (Baiṭhvāsīyo) Rāṭhoṛ Tiloksī Varjāṅgot

Others

Jaimal

C. Battle of Merto, March 21, 1554.

1. Rāv Mālde Gāṅgāvat's men:

Cahuvāṇs

Cahuvāṇ Śārdūl
Sācoro Cahuvāṇ Megho Bhairavdāsot

Gahlots

Pīpāṛo Gahlot Hoglo
Pīpāṛo Gahlot Rāmo

Pañcolīs

Pañcolī Abho Jhājhāvat
Pañcolī Neto
Pañcolī Rato Abhāvat

Rāṭhoṛs

Bālāvat Rāṭhoṛ Dhano Bharmalot
Bālāvat Rāṭhoṛ Nago Bharmalot
Cāmpāvat Rāṭhoṛ Rāmo Bhairavdāsot
Jaitāvat Rāṭhoṛ Prithīrāj Jaitāvat
Karamsot Rāṭhoṛ Jagmal Udaikaraṇot
Rāṭhoṛ Bhārmal Devīdāsot
Rāṭhoṛ Sūjo Jaitsīyot/Tejsīyot
Sīndhaḷ Rāṭhoṛ Ḍūṅgarsī
Sohaṛ Rāṭhoṛ Pītho Jesāvat
Ūdāvat Rāṭhoṛ Rāghavde Vairsalot
Ūhaṛ Rāṭhoṛ Prithīrāj

2. Rāv Jaimal Vīramdevot's men:

Jaitmāl Rāṭhoṛ Akhairāj Bhādāvat
Jaitmāl Rāṭhoṛ Candrāv Jodhāvat
Jaitmāl Rāṭhoṛ Moṭo Jogāvat
Jaitmāl Rāṭhoṛ Nārāiṇdās Candrāvat
Jaitmāl Rāṭhoṛ Sāṅgo Bhojāvat
Rāṭhoṛ Sagto Sāṅgāvat, Rāvat

D. Battle of Sātaḷvās, March 20, 1562.

Bārhaṭhs

Colo
Jālap
Jīvo

Bhāṭīs

Bhāṭī Pirāg Bhārmalot
Jeso Bhāṭī Pītho Āṇandot
Jeso Bhāṭī Tiloksī Parbatot

Cahuvāṇs

Cahuvāṇ Jaitsī
Cahuvāṇ Vīram Ūdāvat

Cāraṇs

Vīṭhū Cāraṇ Meho

Gahlots

Māṅglīyo Gahlot Dedo
Māṅglīyo Gahlot Vīram Devāvat

Paṃvārs

Sāṅkhlo Tejsī Bhojāvat

Rāṭhoṛs

Akhairājot Rāṭhoṛ Goind Rāṇāvat
Akhairājot Rāṭhoṛ Īsardās Rāṇāvat
Akhairājot Rāṭhoṛ Netsī Sīhāvat
Akhairājot Rāṭhoṛ Prithīrāj Sīṅghāṇot
Akhairājot Rāṭhoṛ Sahso Urjanot
Akhairājot Rāṭhoṛ Tejsī Urjanot
Bālāvat Rāṭhoṛ Bhīṃv Ūdāvat
Bālāvat Rāṭhoṛ Hamīr Ūdāvat
Cūṇḍāvat Rāṭhoṛ Akho Jagmālot
Cūṇḍāvat Rāṭhoṛ Īsar Gharsīyot
Cūṇḍāvat Rāṭhoṛ Mahes Gharsīyot
Cūṇḍāvat Rāṭhoṛ Rājsiṅgh Gharsīyot

Cāmpāvat Rāṭhoṛ Amro Rāmāvat
Cāmpāvat Rāṭhoṛ Rāmo Bhairavdāsot
Cāmpāvat Rāṭhoṛ Sahso Rāmāvat
Jaitāvat Rāṭhoṛ Bhākharsī Jaitāvat
Jaitāvat Rāṭhoṛ Devīdās Jaitāvat
Jaitāvat Rāṭhoṛ Pūraṇmal Prithīrājot
Jodho Rāṭhoṛ Bhākharsī Ḍūṅgarsīyot
Karamsot Rāṭhoṛ Mahes Pañcāiṇot
Kūmpāvat Rāṭhoṛ Pato Kūmpāvat
Meṛtīyo Rāṭhoṛ Jaitmāl Pañcāiṇot
Rāṭhoṛ Acḷo Bhāṇot
Rāṭhoṛ Jaimal Tejsīyot
Rāṭhoṛ Rāṇo Jagnāthot
Rāṭhoṛ Riṇdhīr Rāysiṅghot
Rāṭhoṛ Sāṅgo Riṇdhīrot
Rūpāvat Rāṭhoṛ Bhāṇ Bhojrājot

Sutrārs

Sutrār Bhānīdās

Turks

Hamjo, Turk

APPENDIX C

Paṭo of Meṛtīyo Jagmāl Vīramdevot, 1559

Identification of Villages

Village as Listed	Village Identified	Administrative Area	***Rekh***[1]	***Vigat*** Page
1. Ākelī	Ākelī	Mokālo Tapho	6000	2:133
2. Altavo	Altavo	Altavo Tapho	5000	2:176
3. Ānolī	(Akolī Baṛī)	Moḍro Tapho	3000	2:169
4. Barṇo	Barṇo	Sojhat Pargano	3000	1:433
5. Bhāduvāsṇī	Bhāduvāsī	Rāhīṇ Tapho	700	2:158
6. Bhaiyo	Bhaiyo	Altavo Tapho	3000	2:177
7. Bhīmlīyo	(Bhūbhliyo)	Āṇandpur Tapho	2500	2:127
8. Bollo	(Nībolo Baṛo)	Rāhīṇ Tapho	1300	2:153

[1] The ***rekh*** statistics date from the mid-seventeenth century; the ***paṭo*** was given in 1559.

Village as Listed	Village Identified	Administrative Area	***Rekh***	***Vigat*** Page
9. Cāndārūṇ	Cāndārūṇ	Altavo Tapho	2000	2:177
10. Chāprī	Chāprī Baṛī	Rāhīṇ Tapho	1000	2:159
11. Cocīyāvās	Cecīyāvās	Moḍro Tapho	1500	2:173
12. Cundhīyāṃ	Cundhīyo	Mokālo Tapho	2000	2:133
13. Dābṛīyāṇī	Dābṛīyāṇī	Rāhīṇ Tapho	2500	2:156
14. Dhāndhalvās	(Dhāndhalvās Jālap)	Moḍro Tapho	800	2:174
	(Dhāndhalvās Ūdo)	Moḍro Tapho	900	2:174
15. Dhāmaṇīyo	(Dhāmaṇīyo)	Moḍro Tapho	1500	2:170
	(Dhāmaṇīyo)	Reyāṃ Tapho	1000	2:206
16. Dhanāpo	Dhanāpo	Kalro Tapho	1200	2:147
17. Dumāṇī	Dumāṇī	Moḍro Tapho	3000	2:170
18. Durgāvas	Durgāvas	Sojhat Pargano	...	1:475
19. Ghagharṇo	(Gagrāṇo)	Mokālo Tapho	3000	2:133
20. Gonarṛo	Gonarṛo	Deghāṇo Tapho	4000	2:187

Village as Listed	Village Identified	Administrative Area	***Rekh***	***Vigat* Page**
21. Gorharī	(Goreharī Karaṇāṃ)	Deghāṇo Tapho	800	2:195
	(Goreharī Cāñcā)	Deghāṇo Tapho	500	2:195
22. Goṭhaṇ	Goṭhaṇ	Kalro Tapho	2200	2:145
23. Goṭhṛī	Goṭhṛo	Deghāṇo Tapho	500	2:186
24. Goṭhṛo	Goṭhṛo	Deghāṇo Tapho	500	2:186
25. Hāsāvas	(Hāṃsavās)	Kalro Tapho	600	2:150
	(Haṃsāvas)	Sojhat Pargano	...	1:475
26. Hīdāvās	(Hīdāvās Gurṛī ro)	Reyāṃ Tapho	500	2:210
	(Hīdāvās Codhrīyāṃ ro)	Reyāṃ Tapho	1000	2:206
27. Hīrādṛo	(Sīhāsṛo)	Reyāṃ Tapho	3000	2:200
28. Īṭāvo	Īṭāvo	Deghāṇo Tapho	2000	2:193
29. Īṭāvo Khīyām rī	Īṭāvo Khīcīyāṃ rī	Deghāṇo Tapho	500	2:195
30. Jāvlī	Jāvlī	Rāhīṇ Tapho	1400	2:156
31. Jodhṛāvas	Jodhṛāvas Baṛo	Reyāṃ Tapho	500	2:205

Village as Listed	Village Identified	Administrative Area	***Rekh***	***Vigat*** Page
32. Julāṇo	Julāṇo	Moḍro Tapho	2500	2:168
33. Kālṇī	Kāḷṇī	Reyāṃ Tapho	500	2:207
34. Kerīyo	Kerīyo	Moḍro Tapho	2000	2:171
35. Khāteḷāī	Khātoḷāī	Rāhīṇ Tapho	500	2:166
36. Khīdāvas	(Khīdāvās) (Khīdāvās)	Moḍro Tapho Reyāṃ Tapho	300 100	2:175 2:211
37. Khīndāvṛo	(Khīṃvāvās)	Rāhīṇ Tapho	300	2:158
38. Khuhaṛī	Khuhaṛī Baṛī	Rāhīn Tapho	2000	2:154
39. Kurlāī	Kurlāī	Mokālo Tapho	4000	2:130
40. Lāmbo	Lāmbo Jāṭāṃ ro	Kalro Tapho	5000	2:146
41. Luṅgīyo	Luṅgīyo	Reyāṃ Tapho	1250	2:212
42. Maḍāvro	Māḍāvṛo	Reyāṃ Tapho	400	2:205
43. Māṇkīyāvas	Māṇkīyāvās Baṛo	Reyāṃ Tapho	600	2:209

Village as Listed	Village Identified	Administrative Area	***Rekh***	***Vigat*** Page
44. Mherāsṇī	(Mehrāvās)	Āṇandpur Tapho	3000	2:124
	(Mehrīyāvās)	Deghāṇo Tapho	2500	2:189
45. Nathāvṛo	Nathāvṛī	Moḍro Tapho	1500	2:173
46. Nībṛī	(Nībṛī Kothārīyā rī)	Deghāṇo Tapho	2500	2:190
	(Nībṛī Kalāṃ)	Deghāṇo Tapho	2500	2:188
47. Nīlīyāṃ	Nīlīyāṃ	Āṇandpur Tapho	7000	2:121
48. Pacīplo	Pacīplo	Altavo Tapho	2000	2:177
49. Pāḍubaḍī	Paḍukhāṃ rī Vāsṇī	Havelī Tapho	400	2:117
50. Pālṛī	Pālṛī Baṛī	Moḍro Tapho	5000	2:168
51. Pālṛī Sindhale	Pālṛī Sidh	Kalro Tapho	2300	2:143
52. Pāñcīyāvas	(Pāñcrāṛo)	Deghāṇo Tapho	1000	2:194
53. Phālko	Phālko Baṛo	Āṇandpur Tapho	2500	2:124
54. Pīthāvas	Pīthāvās	Mokālo Tapho	500	2:114
55. Rāṃhaṇ	Rāhaṇ Khās	Rāhīṇ Tapho	11000	2:153
56. Rāysalvās	Rāysalvās	Reyāṃ Tapho	1700	2:203

Village as Listed	Village Identified	Administrative Area	***Rekh***	***Vigat*** Page
57. Sāraṅgvāsṇī	(Sāraṅgvāsṇī)	Havelī Tapho	400	2:117
	(Sāraṅgvās)	Sojhat Pargano	600	1:459
58. Sarṇu	(Saraṇ)	Sojhat Pargano	2000	1:464
59. Sathāṇo	(Sathāṇo Saraṅgvās)	Reyāṃ Tapho	300	2:211
	(Sathāṇo Khurad)	Reyāṃ Tapho	2000	2:204
60. Sāyarvas	(Sīrīyāvās)	Reyāṃ Tapho	1000	2:204
61. Sīrīyārī Sojhat rī	(Sīrīyārī Mahelī)	Sojhat Pargano	2200	1:470
	(Sīrīyārī Vāsṇī)	Sojhat Pargano	...	1:472
62. Thāharvasṇī	Thāharvāsṇī	Sojhat Pargano	800	1:450
63. Thāṭi	Thāṭ	Reyāṃ Tapho	3500	2:204
64. Tīghrīyo	(Tīghro)	Āṇandpur Tapho	1200	2:126
	(Tīghro)	Moḍro Tapho	800	2:170
65. Ūdhīyāvas	Ūdhīyāvās	Moro Tapho	400	2:174
66. Vagaṛ	Bagaṛ	Moḍro Tapho	5000	2:167
67. Vākhalvas	(Ākhalvās)	Kalro Tapho	500	2:148

Village as Listed	Village Identified	Administrative Area	***Rekh***	***Vigat*** Page
68. Vās Makāmpā	Bāṅkāvās	Āṇandpur Tapho	3000	2:124
69. Vāvaḷalo	Bāvaḷalo	Moḍro Tapho	2000	2:172

69 villages of the total 71 were listed. In all cases where the identification is uncertain the village names are placed in parentheses. The corresponding numbers on Map 5, "***Paṭo*** of Meṛtīyo Jagmāl Vīramdevot, 1559", are also in parentheses if uncertain.

APPENDIX D

Mughal Land Revenue Administration: An Overview

Land revenue administration in Mughal India was concerned with two primary activities: the assessment of revenue on lands and the collection of this revenue. The revenue system was based on a variety of methods inherited from previous rulers of north India during the early years of Emperor Akbar's reign (1556-1605). These included varying methods of assessing production for both the autumn (*kharīf*) and the spring (*rabī'*) crops, and fixing revenue demands. One method called ***hast-o-būd*** involved a rough estimate of the area of all cultivated land in a village without any kind of measurement of the area under crops, an estimate of production, and finally a fixing of the revenue demand in cash and kind. Alongside this very crude method was another called ***kankūt***. ***Kankūt*** involved a stricter assessment based upon actual field measurement using a rope (*jarīb*) or walking off distances, then estimating crop yields by unit through first-hand observation. Demands under this method were fixed primarily in kind through various methods of share-cropping, referred to locally as ***baṭāī*** or ***bhāoli*** (or by the Persian term *ghalla-bakhshī*). Several methods of share-cropping were in evidence, including division of a field of standing crop, division of the crop after it had been cut and stacked in readiness for threshing, and finally ***baṭāī*** proper or division of the crop on the threshing floor. Revenue farming with grants of land to locals at fixed prices was also current in some areas.

These methods of fixing demand and collecting revenue, while workable, posed inherent difficulties. Share-cropping divided the risks between the peasants and the state, and provided a relatively simple and easy method of fixing demand. However, it was expensive and cumbersome to operate because it required an army of officials to administer. These officials had to watch local village lands and crops and do the actual collection, in itself a major task. Additional problems were present because of the necessity of transport and storage of goods over large areas of the Empire.

The methods of assessment were also crude, there being no standardized measures, and were equally hard to administer. The assessments generally did not distinguish adequately between lands of differing quality, nor did they have a means of adjusting demand in relation to yearly fluctuations in crops, yields and prices at local levels. The fixing of demand was, in addition, open to serious abuses. Reliance was placed entirely on the fairness of the assessor who estimated land area and production. Corruption and inefficiency compounded difficulties present in the systems of assessment and collection.

By the thirteenth year of Akbar's reign (1569-70), a situation had emerged in the Empire which rendered the functioning of the land revenue system, particularly as this affected assignments of revenue on land (*jāgīr*s), virtually impossible. Land revenue assignments (*jama'*) no longer bore any relation to the amounts of revenue actually collected (*ḥāṣil*). Emperor Akbar had, in essence, an inflated paper valuation of his empire which bore little relation to land areas under production and the revenues derived from these lands.

Akbar had attempted to correct some of the shortcoming in his land revenue administration in his eleventh regnal year. He had placed his Imperial ***dīvān***, Muẕaffar Khān, and then Muẕaffar Khān's successor, Rājā Todār Mal, in charge of all revenue affairs for the Empire. They began a more consistent gathering of information about lands and crop production from the local hereditary officials concerned with village revenue accounts (***qānūngo***s) and other knowledgeable men. The new assessment (***jama'***) which emerged was an improvement, but it still remained far from actual collection figures (***ḥāṣil***).

Akbar finally initiated a series of reforms beginning in his nineteenth regnal year (1575-76) which fundamentally altered the Imperial revenue system. He first resumed all ***jāgīr***s throughout the Empire with the exception of those assigned in Bengal, Bihar, and Orissa. He then ordered the establishment of a system for fixing permanent local cash rates for different crops and assessing values on land. The latter was finally accomplished in his twenty-fourth regnal year, based on a ten-year schedule (***jama'-i dah-sāla***) determined through actual field measurement using bamboo rods linked with iron loops (an innovation of Akbar's to ensure uniform measurement), yields by year and crop prices. Actual field measurement did not extend to all parts of the Empire, but included only the Punjab, Uttar Pradesh, Malwa, and portions of Ajmer and Gujarat.

The new ***jama'*** based upon the ten-year schedule allowed the development of a system called ***ẕabṭ***, a payment of land revenue in cash based upon actual measurement of land and assessment of production. The ***ẕabṭ*** system involved the preparation and use of cash rates (***dastūr-al 'amal***s or ***dastūr***s) derived from information the local ***qānūngo***s had provided about lands, crops and revenues. New valuations were determined yearly, and cash rates eventually became fixed for particular areas. Revenue assessment and the fixing of the revenue demand became a matter of establishing a proportion of average production multiplied by averaged cash rates for an area.

Akbar reorganized the machinery of revenue administration in order to facilitate the compilation of a new and more accurate ***jama'***. He first had all crown lands (***khālisa***) divided into administrative districts (***parganā***s, ***mahal***s). These small administrative unites were grouped, in turn, into larger divisions (***sarkār***s) and finally unified into provinces (***ṣubā***s). There were one hundred and eighty-five ***parganā***s designated, each of which was expected to yield one ***kroṛ*** of ***ṭanka***s, or 250,000 rupees.

An ***'amīl*** (also called ***'amalguzār***) was appointed over each administrative district (***parganā***). This ***'amīl*** was initially responsible for both revenue assessment and revenue collection. It is this official, the ***'amīl***, who became known as the ***kiroṛī*** (the official associated with/responsible for a ***kroṛ*** of ***ṭanka***s). ***Kiroṛī***s were placed over one or more ***parganā***s and had wide powers to settle the boundaries of lands under their jurisdiction, assess production on the land, set revenue demands based on local prices, and administer the collection of the revenue itself. Subordinate to the ***kiroṛi/'amīl*** were officials known as ***amīn***s who were in charge of the revenue parties sent to local villages to carry out the actual measurement and assessment of lands. The ***amīns*** reported back to the ***kiroṛīs***, who in turn conveyed local information to the Imperial ***dīvāns*** posted at each of the provincial headquarters, where all revenue accounts were audited.

This system of land revenue administration functioned in all crown lands (***khālisa***) during the latter years of Akbar's reign and during the reign of his successor, Jahāngīr (1605-27). Then, when Shāh Jahān (1628-58) succeeded to the Mughal throne, there was a reversal of roles among local revenue officials. Shāh Jahān had his ***dīvān***, Islām Khān, make several changes in the land revenue system in order to curb abuses which had grown up (indeed the system as a whole had been fraught with abuse since its inception, due in large measure to the heavy-handedness of the ***kiroṛīs***/***'amīls***). Islām Khān transferred the work of the ***kiroṛīs***/***'amīls*** to the ***amīns***, whose duty it became to assess the revenue. Actual collection became a separate function under the ***kiroṛīs***.

Islām Khān's successor, Sa'adullah Khān, later reduced the powers of the ***kiroṛīs*** even further. This change was made in order to counter the local practice which had emerged of combining the functions of the ***kiroṛī*** and the ***faujdār***, the local official charged with the maintenance of law and order. The practice of combining these two functions in one person had led to a great increase in local abuse of the land revenue system.

***

It seems evident from the material about Meṛto that not only were ***qānūngos*** involved in the development and administration of the local land revenue system, but that a ***ẕabṭ*** system based on ***dastūrs*** evolved which extended both to Meṛto Pargano and to other nearby areas of Mārvāṛ (see ***Vigat***, 2:83-84, 2:88, 2:96 for mention of ***qānūngos***, ***ẕabṭī***, and the ***'amal dastūr*** for Meṛto).

Irfan Habib has written of the extension of the Mughal revenue system into Rājasthān that

> Some of the Rajput states seem to have been influenced considerably by the general pattern of Mughal administration. In the kingdom of Jodhpur, for example, a kind of ***jagirdari*** system existed. The Raja held a few villages in each ***pargana*** for his own treasury, while he assigned the rest in ***paṭṭas***, equivalent to ***jagirs***, to his officers in lieu of their pay.... It even appears from the ***Ain*** that in some Rajput states, especially Ambir and Jodhpur, an attempt was made to copy the ***Zabt*** method of revenue assessment established in the imperial territories. But if these states copied the Mughal system, they did so of their own volition. Nor was the copying ever one hundred per cent. Jodhpur, for example, did not have ***qānūngos***, officials whose functions were vital for the working of the ***jagirdari*** system. Nor did it enforce the ***Zabt***, for though it had established cash revenue rates it did not apparently come round to measuring the land, and the ***Ain*** fails to provide areas statistics for its territory. Finally, these states were, after all, exceptions, and there

is no reasons to believe that the chiefs in general ever followed their example.[1]

Based on material in the *Vigat*, a reassessment of Habib's observations appears to be in order.

[1] Irfan Habib, ***The Agrarian System of the Mughal Empire, 1556-1707*** (New York: Asia Publishing House, 1963), p. 186. For a complete discussion of the Mughal land revenue system and its operation over time, see also the following sources: I. H. Qureshi, ***The Administration of the Mughal Empire*** (Patna: N. V. Publications, 1966), pp. 227-238; P. Saran, ***The Provincial Government of the Mughals, 1526-1658*** (Allahabad: Kitabistan, 1941), pp. 63-82, 125-138, 165-212; S. R. Sharma, ***Mughal Government and Administration*** (Bombay: Hind Kitab Ltd., 1951), pp. 69-94; A. L. Srivastava, ***Akbar the Great***, vol. 1, ***Political History*** (2nd ed., Agra: Shiva Lala Agarwala & Co., 1972), pp. 95-96, 142, 162-165, 228-229.

GLOSSARY

A

ahadhī [A. aḥadī] — Literally, "single man." A soldier under the Mughal Emperor Akbar's immediate orders who was paid in cash and held no ***jāgīr***. ***Vigat***, 2:67.

āk (calotropis procera) — A much-branched shrub, usually two or three meters high, common throughout Rajasthan. "Aitihāsik Bātāṃ," p. 48.

amīn [A.] — See Appendix D. ***Vigat***, 2:73.

aṇī — The point of a spear, arrow, etc., the end, the tip; piece, fragment; a division of an army. ***Vigat***, 2:44; "Aitihāsik Bātāṃ," pp. 44, 48-49; ***Khyāt***, 3:119.

Āsoj — The seventh month of the ***Caitrādi*** Vikrama and the third month of the ***Śrāvaṇādi*** Vikrama luni-solar year. ***Āsoj*** may begin either in August or in September, depending upon the initial day of the luni-solar year. ***Khyāt***, 3:116.

asvār [P. suwār] — One of the two indices of rank in the Mughal administration. See also ***jāt*** and ***mansab***. ***Vigat***, 2:75.

B

bagsī [P. ba<u>khsh</u>ī] — A paymaster, an officer whose special duty it was also to keep an account of all disbursements connected with military tenures. ***Vigat***, 2:54, 2:56.

Bāmbhī (f. Bāmbhaṇ) — A leatherworker. ***Khyāt***, 3:121.

Bārhaṭh — Literally, "Obstinacy at the gate." A synonym for ***Pauḷpāt*** ("Recipient of the gate"), a title given to trusted Cāraṇs who, during times of siege, stood at the main gates (***pauḷ***) of forts and were the first to fight and give their lives in the fort's defense. These same Cāraṇs were also those who stood first in line (even before the Brāhmaṇ) during a wedding to receive gifts and offerings (***neg***, ***tyāg***) from the members of the bride's party. ***Vigat***, 2:47, 2:57-58, 2:66; "Aitihāsik Bātāṃ," p. 56.

bāṭī — Small balls of heavy wheat flour cooked to form bread balls, which are served on feast occasions among the well-to-do. ***Vigat***, 2:47.

begam [P.] — A title of Mughal women. ***Vigat***, 2:68.

Beldār (f. ***Beldārī***) — An excavator. ***Vigat***, 2:69.

bhāībandh — Literally, "bound as brothers"; a brotherhood; those related through ties of male blood to a common male ancestor. Among Rajpūts, membership in a ***bhāībandh*** included all males sharing common descent, their unmarried daughters, and their wives, who became members through the act of marriage. ***Vigat***, 2:46, 2:51, 2:69; "Aitihāsik Bātāṃ," p. 54.

bhomīyo — Literally, "one of the soil (***bhom***)"; one with intimate knowledge of a local area, a local; one who controls or asserts a dominant right over a small area of land. ***Vigat***, 2:69-70.

bhuraṭ (cenchrus biflorus) — A burr grass, particularly abundant in years of scarcity, when it is used as food. The seeds are about the size of a pin's head and are enclosed in a prickly husk which readily clings to clothing or animal hair or fur. The seeds are ground to use as flour. ***Khyāt***, 3:89.

C

Cāraṇ (f. ***Cāraṇī***) — A person belonging to a ***jāti*** whose traditional occupation is the composition of poems and songs of praise in honor of heroes and rulers; a bard. ***Vigat***, 2:58, 2:68; "Aitihāsik Bātāṃ," pp. 42-43; ***Khyāt***, 3:91.

(Śrī) Catarbhujjī The four-armed manifestation of Viṣṇu and the patron deity of the Meṛtīyo Rāṭhoṛs. ***Vigat***, 2:69; "Aitihāsik Bātāṃ," pp. 48-49.

caudhrī A title taken by the headmen of Jāṭ lineages. ***Vigat***, 2:39.

chatrī A cenotaph; a memorial erected for a fallen Rajpūt warrior. ***Vigat***, 2:72; "Aitihāsik Bātāṃ," p. 42.

colāvaṭ The living members of a lineage. "Aitihāsik Bātāṃ," p. 50.

D

dām A copper coin equal to one-fortieth of a rupee. ***Vigat***, 2:75-77.

darbār [P.] The hall of audience of a ruler. ***Vigat***, 2:55, 2:67, 2:75; "Aitihāsik Bātāṃ," pp. 53-54; ***Khyāt***, 3:38, 3:117.

dargāh [P.] The court of a ruler, including the various departments of his administration and their heads. ***Vigat***, 2:56, 2:63, 2:67-69, 2:73, 2:76.

dargahī mansab A ***mansab*** (q.v.) given by the Mughal Emperor. ***Vigat***, 2:75-76.

Dasrāho A festival held in the month of ***Āsoj*** (August-September) to commemorate the victory of Rāma, king of Ayodhyā, over Rāvaṇa, the demon king of Śrī Laṅka. It was often customary at the time of this festival for Rajpūts in the service of a local ruler to pay court at an official ***darbār*** (q.v.), during which vows of loyalty and service were reaffirmed. ***Khyāt***, 3:87, 3:116.

des	Land, geographic region; a term used by Naiṇsī in his ***Vigat*** and ***Khyāt*** to refer to the lands in Mārvāṛ under the authority of the Jodhpur rājā. ***Vigat***, 2:74-75.
desot	The ruler of a ***des***, q.v. "Aitihāsik Bātāṃ," p. 51.
devaco	An oath sworn in the name of a god or goddess. ***Vigat***, 2:62-63.
devlok	The realm of the ***dev***s, or gods; Paradise. ***Khyāt***, 3:95, 3:115.
dharma	Obligation, duty, code of conduct. In middle period Mārvāṛ, ***dharma*** was considered to be inherent in one's ***jāti*** and to be maintained by acts (***kām***) appropriate for that ***jāti***. ***Vigat***, 2:64; "Aitihāsik Bātāṃ," pp. 54-55.
dīvāṇ [P. dīwān]	(1) A minister or head of a department at either the state or provincial level. ***Vigat***, 2:54-56, 2:76. (2) A title held by the Rāṭhoṛ rulers of Jodhpur and the Sīsodīyo rulers of Cītoṛ and Udaipur, who were considered ***dīvāṇ***s or "deputies" of the god Śiva, from whom their ancestors were believed to have received their respective sovereignties. ***Khyāt***, 3:92.
doykāṇṭro	A type of box or platform. ***Vigat***, 2:55 (see also n. 2 for ***Vigat***, 2:55).
drah	A deep pool, a ditch. ***Khyāt***, 3:90.
dūho	A rhymed verse generally possessing two lines; a couplet. ***Vigat***, 2:45; "Aitihāsik Bātāṃ," p. 49; ***Khyāt***, 3:89.
dupaṭo	A type of shawl or cover-cloth commonly worn by Rajpūts. "Aitihāsik Bātāṃ," p. 42; ***Khyāt***, 3:89.

G

ghaṛī A period of time equal to twenty-four minutes. *Vigat*, 2:48, 2:50; "Aitihāsik Bātāṃ," p. 42.

ghāsmārī Literally, "grass-struck." A local tax levied on domestic animals at so much cash per type of animal. *Vigat*, 2:73-74.

ghūmar Flock, herd, heap, siege; a type of folk dance performed by women in a circle; a folk song concerning this dance. *Khyāt*, 3:93.

grās Literally, "mouthful" or "sustenance." By extension, the term came to mean a share of land given to a Rajpūt for his maintenance (such shares were also called ***vaṇṭ***, which simply means "share" or "portion"). In Mārvāṛ during the pre-Mughal period it was customary for one son of a Rajpūt ruler to inherit his father's title, residence, and the largest share of his lands and retainers, while the other sons received smaller territorial shares termed ***grās*** for their livelihood. *Khyāt*, 3:89.

grāsīyo A holder of a share of land (***grās***, q.v.); a bandit, a robber. *Vigat*, 2:66.

guṛo A hideout; a temporary village which might grow into a permanent settlement; a type of long-term camp, different from the ***ḍeṛo*** or short-term camp in that it included all of the dependents of its Rajpūt master—peasants, Cāraṇs, Brāhmaṇs, potters, etc.—and not just those persons concerned with military affairs. Livestock was also kept in the ***guṛo***. "Aitihāsik Bātāṃ," p. 44.

H

hākmī An abstract noun formed from ***hākīm*** [A. ḥākim]. A ***hākīm*** was an administrative official encharged with the authority over a district on behalf of an outsider. ***Vigat***, 2:73.

harol [P. harāwal]
An advance guard of an army, a vanguard. "Aitihāsik Bātāṃ," p. 44.

Hasat Nakhtar (S. Hasta nakṣatra)
The thirteenth of the twenty-seven ***nakṣatra***s. A ***nakṣatra*** is a star or cluster of stars, or a constellation representing one of the twenty-seven divisions of the lunar zodiac. ***Nakṣatra***s also represent phases of the moon during its orbit of the earth, and are divided into auspicious (associated with the waxing moon) and inauspicious (associated with the waning moon). ***Vigat***, 2:39.

hīṛāgar
"One who performs ***hīṛo***." ***Hīṛo*** is service performed with respect and devotion. In middle period Mārvāṛ, the term ***hīṛāgar*** referred to a member of a class of military servants (Rajpūts and others) doing the more menial tasks, such as carrying rockets, attending to the accoutrements of the Rajpūts of higher rank, etc. ***Vigat***, 2:42.

hujdār
An administrative official concerned primarily with the collection of revenues. ***Vigat***, 2:46, 2:63; "Aitihāsik Bātāṃ," p. 52; ***Khyāt***, 3:87.

J

jāgīr [P.]
A technical term from the Mughal period designating an assignment of revenue on land, based on moveable or prebendal tenure. ***Vigat***, 2:58, 2:69.

jāgīrdār [P.]
The holder of an assignment of revenue on land (***jāgīr***, q.v.) during the Mughal period. ***Vigat***, 2:67, 2:74.

jāgīrī [P.] — The technical term used to indicate the tenure of land held by a ***jāgīrdār***; relating to or pertaining to a ***jāgīr***. ***Vigat***, 2:69, 2:73, 2:75.

jamīyat [P. jam'īyat] — The assemblage of men and horses in the services of a chief. ***Vigat***, 2:75.

jāt [A. ẕāt] — One of the two indices of rank in the Mughal administration. See also ***asvār*** and ***mansab***. ***Vigat***, 2:75.

jāti — Genus, type, community, caste. ***Vigat***, 2:39.

Jogī — A yogi; a practitioner of yoga. ***Khyāt***, 3:120.

Jogṇī — Any women believed to possess magical powers; a witch or demoness; a female spirit ruling over period of good and bad fortune. It was commonly believed that there were sixty-four Jogṇīs, located in different places on different dates. To travel in the direction of the Jogṇīs was considered unlucky. ***Khyāt***, 3:91.

Josī (f. ***Josaṇ***) — An astrologer. ***Khyāt***, 3:91.

K

kaceṛī — The department of the Mughal administration encharged with reviewing documents. ***Vigat***, 2:76.

kāmdār — Literally, "one who has work." ***Kāmdār***s (or ***kāmetī***) were generally drawn from among a number of non-Rajpūt ***jāti***s such as the Brāhmaṇ, Pañcolī (Kāyastha), and Osvāḷ Jain and Vaiṣṇava (Muṃhatos, Bhaṇḍārīs, Siṅghavīs, Lodhos, etc.). These officials performed not only record-keeping functions relating to the fiscal administration of local areas, but also police and military functions in the settlement and control of lands. ***Vigat***,

2:46, 2:50-51, 2:54, 2:63, 2:73; "Aitihāsik Bātāṃ," p. 43.

karaṛ (Dicanthium annulatum) — A tall, thin-leafed grass much used as fodder in Mārvāṛ. ***Khyāt***, 3:89.

kaṛiyāḷī — A type of wooden stick banded with metal rings (***kaṛī***). ***Vigat***, 2:64.

kavitt — A type of Ḍiṅgaḷ poem, the first four lines of which are in one meter, the last two in another. ***Vigat***, 2:42.

khālso [P k͟hāliṣa] — Literally, "pure." Land directly administered and taxed by a ruler and his personal officials. ***Vigat***, 2:75; ***Khyāt***, 3:115.

khāṇḍo — A wall outside the gate of a fort made to shelter the entrance from direct attack. ***Vigat***, 2:64.

khavās [A. k͟hawāṣṣ] — A male or female attendant or personal servant of a Rajpūt ruler or important landholder. ***Vigat***, 2:49, 2:52.

kheṛo — Outlying village land on which temporary huts are built during the growing season; a small site more or less permanently inhabited but attached to a larger village often at some distance; a deserted site, either of a former small village or of land previously cultivated. ***Vigat***, 2:39.

khīc — A food prepared by cooking wheat or millet with various sorts of pulse. ***Khyāt***, 3:115.

kiledār [P. qil'adār] — A person in charge of a fort. ***Vigat***, 2:51, 2:69; ***Khyāt***, 3:99.

kiroṛī — See Appendix D. ***Vigat***, 2:73-74.

kos — A unit of distance measurement equal to approximately two miles. ***Vigat***, 2:44,

2:49, 2:54, 2:60, 2:64, 2:69; "Aitihāsik Bātāṃ," p. 42; ***Khyāt***, 3:90.

koṭṛī — The male section of a Rajpūt house; a courtyard surrounded by high walls; a small fort. ***Vigat***, 2:38-39, 2:51, 2:73; "Aitihāsik Bātāṃ," pp. 48-49.

koṭvāḷ — During the Mughal period, the chief officer of police within a city or large town; the superintendent of the market. ***Vigat***, 2:70.

kuṃvar — Prince; title of the son of a ruler. ***Vigat***, 2:42, 2:56, 2:62-64; ***Khyāt***, 3:87, 3:93-94, 3:120.

M

Mahājan — Literally, "great man." The name of a division of the Vāṇīyo ***jāti***; a grain merchant. ***Vigat***, 2:63.

Mahākāḷ — Śiva as Lord of Time and hence of Death; an image or statue of Śiva in this destructive aspect. "Aitihāsik Bātāṃ," p. 44.

mahal [A. maḥall] — Residence, palace; room or chamber of the residence of an important man; the wife or consort of a noble. ***Vigat***, 2:67; ***Khyāt***, 3:88.

mahārāj — A respectful term of address slightly more honorific than ***rāj*** (q.v.). ***Khyāt***, 3:117-118.

mājī — A respectful term of address for a female elder. ***Khyāt***, 3:89.

māl [A.] — Literally, "money"; the land revenue. ***Vigat***, 2:73-74.

Māḷī (f. ***Māḷaṇ/Māḷṇī***) — A person belonging to a ***jati*** whose traditional occupation is gardening. ***Vigat***, 2:58.

māḷīyo — A large bedroom built on the second floor of a large house or mansion (***havelī***), generally decorated with plaster, painting, and other embellishments. *Vigat*, 2:47; *Khyāt*, 3:39.

mansab [A. manṣab] — Literally, "post," "office." The term ***mansab*** designated a military rank and an office in the administrative service of the Mughal Empire. The rank consisted of both a personal or ***jāt*** [A. ẕāt] rank, which marked the status of a person among the nobles of the Empire, and a trooper or ***asvār*** [P. suwār] rank, indicated the number of cavalrymen and horses an official or ***mansabdār*** was to maintain. All persons within the administrative system of the Empire were graded according to this rank order and given either military or civilian responsibilities. Payment on the basis of rank for duties performed was either in cash (***naqda***) or by an assignment of revenue on land (***jāgīr***). *Vigat*, 2:75-76.

mansabdār [A. manṣab + the P. suffix -dār] — The holder of a rank (***mansab***) in the Mughal service. *Vigat*, 2:67.

mirjo [P. Mirzā] — A Muslim prince; a Muslim of high birth. *Vigat*, 2:55.

Modī — A village grain merchant or grocer. "Aitihāsik Bātāṃ," p. 43.

mohar [P. muhr] — A gold coin. *Vigat*, 2:42; "Aitihāsik Bātāṃ," p. 43.

mujāvar [A. mujāwir] — The attendant at a Muslim shrine or mosque. *Vigat*, 2:68.

N

nāḍī — A small tank. *Vigat*, 2:63.

navāb [A. nawwāb] — A governor of a town, district, or province; a lord, a prince; one who rules in place of another. ***Vigat***, 2:54-56, 2:70-72, 2:75-76.

P

pañco — The committee of five important Rajpūts that convened upon the death of a ruler to aid in the succession; more generally, a council of elders. ***Vigat***, 2:46-47.

Pāṇḍav — A stable hand, a groom. ***Khyāt***, 3:118.

parameśvar — The highest or supreme lord; God; a powerful or illustrious man. "Aitihāsik Bāṭāṃ," p. 55; ***Khyāt***, 3:88, 3:94.

pargano — An administrative and revenue unit or division of a district (***sarkār***). The term came into prominent use in Rajasthan only during the Mughal period. ***Vigat***, 2:37, 2:56, 2:69, 2:73, 2:75; ***Khyāt***, 3:115.

parvāno [P. parwāna] — A written order addressed to a subordinate. ***Vigat***, 2:56.

pāsvān [P. pās-bān] — Literally, "one who stands beside or in attendance"; a male body servant or female concubine of a Rajpūt ruler or important landholder. ***Vigat***, 2:49.

paṭī — A term used for the administrative subdivisions of Meṛto, Nāgaur, and Jāḷor ***pargano***s. ***Vigat***, 2:73.

paṭo — A written deed or title to land; lands granted by a ruler to a subordinate by such a deed in return for the obligation of military service. See also n. 13 for ***Vigat***, 2:43. ***Vigat***, 2:43, 2:52, 2:54, 2:61, 2:63; "Aitihāsik Bātāṃ," pp. 50-51; ***Khyāt***, 3:87, 3:115, 3:117.

pātsāh [P. pādshāh] — A title assumed by Muslim rulers of the first rank in northern India, such as the rulers of Mālwā, Gujarāt, and Hindustān. *Vigat*, 2:42-43, 2:51, 2:54, 2:56-58, 2:63-64, 2:66-67, 2:70-77; "Aitihāsik Bātāṃ," pp. 42-44, 50, 52-54; *Khyāt*, 3:99-102.

pharmān [P. farmān] — A royal decree, directive, or writ, issued to a subordinate from the hands of the emperor only and requiring (under the Mughals) his seal for validity. *Vigat*, 2:67, 2:76.

phaujdār [P. faujdār] — Literally, "one who has an army." A subordinate military official under the Mughals, responsible for the maintenance of law and order and for the collection of revenue within a district (***sarkār***) of a province (***sūbo***); more generally, a military offical responsible for a local area. *Vigat*, 2:70, 2:74.

pīr [P.] — An old man; a saint; a spiritual guide. *Vigat*, 2:68.

pradhān — Literally, "foremost," "chief," "principal," "most eminent." A chief minister, commander-in-chief, a general or leader of the army. Among Rajpūts, the post of ***pradhān*** was held predominately by Rajpūts themselves, either of the same clan or of a different clan than the ruler of a local state. *Vigat*, 2:42-43, 2:46, 2:51, 2:54-55, 2:57; *Khyāt*, 3:89-90, 3:95, 3:116-18.

pūjā — Worship, homage. *Khyāt*, 3:116.

Purohit — A Brāhmaṇ employed as a family priest. *Vigat*, 2:63; *Khyāt*, 3:97.

R

rāhavṇo — The members of the household of an important Rajpūt, including his wives and concubines, their offspring, the descendants of offspring produced by Rajpūt liaisons with women of different

	jātis in the past who formed part of the body of household servants, and other personal servants of various ranks. ***Vigat***, 2:48.
Raibārī (f. ***Raibāraṇ***)	A member of a *jāti* whose traditional occupation was that of transhumant herding of camels, sheep, and goats. Raibārīs were often used as messengers also. ***Vigat***, 2:49.
rait [A. ra'iyyat] *log*	The non-Rajpūt peasantry in middle period Mārvāṛ. ***Khyāt***, 3:116.
rāj	Ruler, sovereign, king, kingdom; a form of address conveying respect. ***Vigat***, 2:38, 2:53; "Aitihāsik Bātāṃ," pp. 42, 50-51, 54; ***Khyāt***, 3:90-91, 3:97, 3:102, 3:115, 3:117, 3:119.
Rām Rām	A form of salutation used among Hindus only. ***Khyāt***, 3:117.
rāṇo	A title held by several Rajpūt rulers in middle period Rājasthān, including the Sīsodīyos of Mevāṛ, the Rāṭhoṛs of Sīvāṇo, the Sāṅkhlo Paṃvārs of Rūṇ, the Paṛihāṛs of Maṇḍor, and the Soḍho Paṃvārs of Umarkoṭ (in modern Sindh). Rāṇo is also a personal name (e.g., Rāṇo Akhairājot). ***Vigat***, 2:59 60, 2:68-69; "Aitihāsik Bātāṃ," pp. 50-51.
rāv	A title held by many Rajpūt rulers in middle period Rājasthān, including the Rāṭhoṛs of Jodhpur (until 1583), Meṛto, and Bīkāner; the Bhāṭīs of Pūṅgaḷ and Vairsalpur; the Cahuvāṇs of Būndī, Koṭo, Sīrohī, and Jāḷor, and numerous others. ***Vigat***, 2:37, 2:39, etc.
rāvaḷ	A title held by several Rajpūt rulers in middle period Rājasthān, including the Bhāṭīs of Jaisaḷmer, the Rāṭhors of Mahevo, and the Āhāṛos of Ḍūṅgarpur and Vāṃsvāhḷo. ***Vigat***, 2:59-60; "Aitihāsik Bātāṃ," p. 51.

rāvat — A title held by a large number of petty rulers, both Rajpūt and non-Rajpūt, in middle period Rājasthān. *Vigat*, 2:60.

rāyāṅgaṇ — The courtyard of a ruler's residence. *Khyāt*, 3:89.

rekh — Assessment, evaluation. *Vigat*, 2:77.

S

sābaḷ — A type of lance (perhaps derived from *sabaḷ*, "powerful"). *Vigat*, 2:45.

sagāī — Betrothal; alliance of marriage between two families or clans (*kuḷ*, *vaṃś*). *Vigat*, 2:55.

sago — A relation through marriage; one to who one gives or from whom receives a daughter or daughters in marriage. *Vigat*, 2:59; *Khyāt*, 3:98.

sāhjādo [P. s̲h̲āhzāda] — The son of a shāh, a prince. *Vigat*, 2:73-76.

Sāhūkār — A person who deals with money, a banker. "Aitihāsik Bātāṃ," p. 43.

saidāno [P s̲h̲ādiyāna] — A musical instrument played on an auspicious occasion as a form of celebration. *Vigat*, 2:53.

sākh — (1) Literally, "branch." Rajpūts perceived their *jāti* as divided into thirty-six great lineages, called either *rājkuḷīs* ("royal families") or *rājvaṃś* ("royal lineages"). The word *vaṃś* also means "bamboo shoot," and the Rajpūts extend the imagery equating their royal lineages with the bamboo even further: subdivisions of the *vaṃś* were known as *sākh*s ("branches"), and, by the late seventeenth century, the word *khāmp* ("twig"), used for subdivisions of the *sākh*, had become common in Rajasthan. *Vigat*, 2:41, 2:68. (2) Literally, "evidence," "testimony." A term used to describe poetry containing historical information. *Vigat*, 2:45; "Aitihāsik Bātāṃ," p. 49.

salām [A.] — Literally, "peace." A salutation, either of parting or greeting; an act of bowing to or acknowledging in some manner the superiority of someone. ***Khyāt***, 3:38, 3:119.

salāmat [A.] — A salutation literally meaning "safety," "salvation," "health," etc., used to address both Hindus and Muslims of high rank. ***Khyāt***, 3:99-100, 3:117.

sāmant [S. sāmanta] — Subordinate ruler of high rank. ***Khyāt***, 3:120.

sāmaṭho — High place; platform. ***Khyāt***, 3:89.

sāth — One who accompanies or follows, a companion. In middle period Mārvāṛ, the term was used in a technical sense to designate a contingent of soldiers comprised of both cavalrymen and footmen. Among Rajpūts, a ***sāth*** usually was composed of kinsmen (brothers and sons) of the leaders as well as other men attached to them or their subordinates as servants or retainers. *Vigat*, 2:42-46, 2:48-53, 2:56-57, 2:59-61, 2:63-65, 2:67-68, 2:71, 2:73; "Aitihāsik Bātāṃ," pp. 42-44, 48-55; ***Khyāt***, 3:39-40, 3:90, 3:92, 3:95-97.

satī — A woman who has immolated herself on her husband's funeral pyre. "Aitihāsik Bātāṃ," p. 44.

sikdār [A. shiqq + the P. suffix -dār] — Under Sher Shāh, the revenue officer of a single ***pargano***, whether appointed by the state or by the holder of a land grant; in the Mughal period, a synonym for ***kiroṛī*** (q.v.); within the territory under the administrative control of the rājās of Jodhpur during the Mughal period, an official placed in charge of maintaining order within a town. *Vigat*, 2:70.

sirdār [P. sardār] — Headman, chief, leader, commander; representative of a community or group. *Vigat*, 2:48, 2:53, 2:71-72; "Aitihāsik Bātāṃ," pp. 51, 53-54; *Khyāt*, 3:40, 3:96, 3:117, 3:119.

sirpāv [P. sar-o-pā] — Literally, "head-foot," a long dress or cloth such as a cloak reaching the length of the body, given by a ruler to a subordinate for particular actions of service, such as bravery in battle, etc. By the beginning of the nineteenth century ***sirpāv*** had also come to mean more generally an honorary gift or reward. *Vigat*, 2:37, 2:55-56; "Aitihāsik Bātāṃ," p. 50; *Khyāt*, 3:40.

Śrījī — A phrase by which Muṃhato Naiṇsī referred to the rulers of Jodhpur under whom he served (Rājā Gajsiṅgh (1619-38) and Rājā Jasvantsiṅgh (1638-1678)). *Vigat*, 2:74.

sūbedār [P. ṣūbahdār] — An officer in charge of a ***sūbo*** (q.v.). *Vigat*, 2:54.

sūbo [P. ṣūbah] — A province; the largest administrative and revenue division of territory under the Mughal administrative system. *Vigat*, 2:41-42, 2:70-71, 2:75.

sukhpāḷ — A type of palanquin. *Khyāt*, 3:100.

sūthaṇ — A type of pajama covering the lower portion of the body; a type of chain mail fulfilling the same function. "Aitihāsik Bātāṃ," p. 42.

Sutrār (f. ***Sutrārī/Sutārī***) — A person belonging to a ***jāti*** whose traditional occupation is carpentry. *Vigat*, 2:66; "Aitihāsik Bātāṃ," p. 56.

T

tālīko [P. ta'līqa] — The certificate of appointment to all posts that required the approval of the Mughal emperor. ***Vigat***, 2:75.

taslīm [A.] — A salutation consisting of placing the back of the right hand on the ground and then raising it gently until the person stands erect, when he puts the palm of his hand upon the crown of his head. The salute indicates that one is ready to give himself as an offering. ***Khyāt***, 3:40.

ṭhākur — God; master, ruler, sovereign; one who rules a kingdom (among Rajpūts, the term is applied equally to the clan deity of a local kingdom, to the Rajpūt ruler himself, who is felt to rule as a subordinate and servant of this deity, and to other Rajpūts, who rule lands directly under the ruler and who receive their authority from him). ***Vigat***, 2:49-50, 2:53, 2:57, 2:64, 2:73; "Aitihāsik Bātāṃ," pp. 43-44, 48, 50, 52-53, 55; ***Khyāt***, 3:95, 3:117-118.

ṭhākurāī — The quality or essence of a ***ṭhākur***; rulership, sovereignty, authority; kingdom, domain. ***Vigat***, 2:64; "Aitihāsik Bātāṃ," p. 55.

thaṇedār — A person in charge of a garrison (***thāṇo***). ***Vigat***, 2:51; ***Khyāt***, 3:99.

ṭīkāyat — A chosen successor; one designated to receive the throne and to have the ***ṭīko*** or red mark placed upon his forehead upon succession; one who has received the ***ṭīko***. ***Vigat***, 2:51.

U

umrāv {A. umāra', pl. of amīr] — A man of high rank; a noble. Under the Mughals, only those officers with a ***mansab*** rank of 1,000 ***jāt*** or more were considered to belong among the ***umrāv***s or nobility of the Empire. *Vigat*, 2:50, 2:52, 2:54-55, 2:57, 2:60, 2:76; "Aitihāsik Bātāṃ," pp. 43, 50; ***Khyāt***, 3:100.

V

vāgo — A garment bound at the waist and extending down to the knees. "Aitihāsik Bātāṃ," p. 43; ***Khyāt***, 3:117.

vair — The debt of vengeance owed upon the murder of a family member, kinsman, or dependent. ***Vigat***, 2:39, 2:49; "Aitihāsik Bātāṃ," p. 50; ***Khyāt***, 3:38.

Vāṇīyo (f. ***Vaniyāṇ***) — A merchant or moneylender; a Baniya. "Aitihāsik Bātāṃ," p. 53.

vās — The town or village of residence of an important man; the residential area or ward of a ***jāti*** or group within a town or village. ***Vigat***, 2:58, 2:63, 2:69; "Aitihāsik Bātāṃ," p. 50; ***Khyāt***, 3:87-88, 3:116.

vasī — The people or subjects bound to an important Rajpūt who lived either in his village or town of residence (***vās***, q.v.) or in nearby villages under his control and who performed various services for him according to their status, receiving in exchange his protection. Typically the ***vasī*** of an important man contained persons of many ***jāti***s, including a contingent of Rajpūt warriors, peasants such as Jāṭs, Sīrvīs, Paṭels, etc., Vāṇīyos, Brāhmaṇs, Cāraṇs, and members of the lower ***jāti***s: Kumbhāṛs, Māḷīs, Sutrārs, and others. ***Vasī***s were divided among sons either before or upon the death of a Rajpūt ***ṭhākur***, each inheriting son taking his part of the ***vasī*** and going to live on his share (***vaṇṭ, grās***, q.v.) of the paternal lands, a process referred to in the sources as ***juḍāī*** ("separation"). ***Vigat***, 2:52, 2:60, 2:69-70, 2:72; "Aitihāsik Bātāṃ," p. 53;

265

Khyāt, 3:101.

INDEX OF PERSONAL NAMES

A

B

C

D

G

H

Hāḍo Cahuvāṇ Surjan Arjuṇot, Rāv *Vigat*, 2:60; "Aitihāsik Bātāṃ," p. 51
Hājī Itbārī, *kiroṛī* *Vigat*, 2:73
Hājī Khān *Vigat*, 2:59-60; "Aitihāsik Bātāṃ," pp. 50-52
Hamjo, Turk *Vigat*, 2:66; "Aitihāsik Bātāṃ," p. 56
Hardās Mokaḷot, Ūhaṛ Rāṭhoṛ *Khyāt*, 3:87-90, 3:92
Hīṅgoḷo Pīpāṛo *Vigat*, 3:120; "Aitihāsik Bātāṃ," p. 48
Huḷ, Jaito Prithamrāvat *Vigat*, 2:45

I

Īḍareco Rāṭhoṛs
Īḍareco Rāṭhoṛ Nārāyaṇdās Pūñjāvat, Rāv *Vigat*, 2:60; "Aitihāsik Bātāṃ," p. 51
Indrabhāṇ Kānhīdāsot, Meṛtīyo Rāṭhoṛ *Vigat*, 2:73
Īsar Ghaṛsīyot, Cūṇḍāvat Rāṭhoṛ *Vigat*, 2:66; "Aitihāsik Bātāṃ," p. 56
Īsardās Kalyāṇdāsot, Jodho Rāṭhoṛ *Vigat*, 2:74
Īsardās Rāṇāvat, Akhairājot Rāṭhoṛ *Vigat*, 2:65
Īsardās Vīramdevot, Meṛtīyo Rāṭhoṛ *Khyāt*, 3:118

J

Jagmāl, Paṃvār, Rāvat *Vigat*, 2:50
Jagmāl Udaikaraṇot, Karamsot Rāṭhoṛ *Vigat*, 2:59; "Aitihāsik Bātāṃ," p. 49
Jagmāl Vīramdevot, Meṛtīyo Rāṭhoṛ *Vigat*, 2:59, 2:61-63; "Aitihāsik Bātāṃ," pp. 48, 51
Jagnāth Bhārmalot, Rājāvat Kachvāho, Rājā *Vigat*, 2:72
Jagnāth Gopāḷdāsot, Meṛtīyo Rāṭhoṛ *Vigat*, 2:72-73
Jago, Jaṛeco *Vigat*, 2:70-71
Jagrūp Jagnāthot, Rājāvat Kachvāho, Kuṃvar *Vigat*, 2:72
Jahāṅgīr, Mughal Emperor *Vigat*, 2:73-76
Jaimal Gāṅgāvat, Rohaṛīyo Cāraṇ *Vigat*, 2:58
Jaimal Tejsīyot, Rāṭhoṛ [*sākh* unknown] *Vigat*, 2:65; "Aitihāsik Bātāṃ," p. 56
Jaimal Vīramdevot, Meṛtīyo Rāṭhoṛ, Rāv *Vigat*, 2:58-60, 2:63-69; "Aitihāsik Bātāṃ," pp. 48-55; *Khyāt*, 3:115-119, 3:121-122
Jaitāvat Rāṭhoṛs
Bhākharsī Jaitāvat *Vigat*, 2:65; "Aitihāsik Bātāṃ," p. 55
Devīdās Jaitāvat *Vigat*, 2:59-61, 2:63-67; "Aitihāsik Bātāṃ," pp. 49-55
Jaito Pañcāiṇot *Vigat*, 2:48-49, 2:51, 2:57; "Aitihāsik Bātāṃ," pp. 42-44; *Khyāt*, 3:95, 3:99-100
Prithīrāj Jaitāvat *Vigat*, 2:59; "Aitihāsik Bātāṃ," pp. 48-50, 53; *Khyāt*, 3:116-121
Pūraṇmal Prithīrājot *Vigat*, 2:65; "Aitihāsik Bātāṃ," pp. 50, 52, 55

K

N

P

Purohits
Bhānīdās Tejsīyot, Sīvaṛ, Brāhmaṇ *Vigat*, 2:63
Mūḷo, Brāhmaṇ *Khyāt*, 3:97

R

Raibārī *Vigat*, 2:49
Rājā Māndhātā *Vigat*, 2:37, 41
Rajpūt *Vigat*, 2:39, 2:41, 2:44-46, 2:49, 2:51, 2:54-55, 2:57, 2:63-64, 2:66, 2:68, 2:73, 2:75; "Aitihāsik Bātāṃ," pp. 43-44, 48, 50, 53-55;*Khyāt*, 3:39-40, 3:87-88, 3:101, 3:116, 3:119-120.
Rājsiṅgh Ghaṛsīyot, Cūṇḍāvat Rāṭhoṛ *Vigat*, 2:66; "Aitihāsik Bātāṃ," p. 56
Rājsiṅgh Khīṃvāvat, Kūmpāvat Rāṭhoṛ 2:74-76
Rām, Khairaṛo Soḷaṅkī, Rāv *Vigat*, 2:60; "Aitihāsik Bātāṃ," p. 51
Rāmcand, Bālhaṇot Soḷaṅkī, Rāvaḷ *Vigat*, 2:60; "Aitihāsik Bātāṃ," p. 51
Rāmdās Ūdāvat, Dhīrāvat Kachvāho, Rājā *Vigat*, 2:73
Rāmo Bhairavdāsot, Cāmpāvat Rāṭhoṛ *Vigat*, 2:65; "Aitihāsik Bātāṃ," p. 56
Rāṇo Akhairājot, Akhairājot Rāṭhoṛ 2:52-53
Rāṇo Jagnāthot, Rāṭhoṛ [*sākh* unknown] *Vigat*, 2:66; "Aitihāsik Bātāṃ," p. 56
Ratansī Khīṃvāvat, Ūdāvat Rāṭhoṛ "Aitihāsik Bātāṃ," pp. 48-50
Rāṭhoṛ Rajpūts *Vigat*, 2:42, 2:44, 2:52; "Aitihāsik Bātāṃ," pp. 51, 54; *Khyāt*, 3:38
Acḷo Bhāṇot [*sākh* unknown] *Vigat*, 2:65; "Aitihāsik Bātāṃ," p. 56
Jaimal Tejsīyot [*sākh* unknown] *Vigat*, 2:65; "Aitihāsik Bātāṃ," p. 56
Rāṇo Jagnāthot [*sākh* unknown] *Vigat*, 2:66; "Aitihāsik Bātāṃ," p. 56
Riṇdhīr Rāysiṅghot [*sākh* unknown] *Vigat*, 2:66; "Aitihāsik Bātāṃ," p. 56
Sāṅgo Riṇdhīrot [*sākh* unknown] *Vigat*, 2:66; "Aitihāsik Bātāṃ," p. 56
Sūjo Tejsīyot [*sākh* unknown] *Vigat*, 2:59; "Aitihāsik Bātāṃ," p. 49
See also individual listings under:
Akhairājot Rāṭhoṛs
Bālāvat Rāṭhoṛs
Bhārmalot Rāṭhoṛs
Bhīṃvot Rāṭhoṛs
Bīkāvat Rāṭhoṛs
Cāmpāvat Rāṭhoṛs
Cūṇḍāvat Rāṭhoṛs
Dhāndhalot Rāṭhoṛs
Īḍareco Rāṭhoṛs
Jaitāvat Rāṭhoṛs
Jaitmāl Rāṭhoṛs
Jodho Rāṭhoṛs
Karamsot Rāṭhoṛs
Kūmpāvat Rāṭhoṛs
Mahevo Rāṭhoṛs

S

T

U

V

Vāgh Jagmālot, Meṛtīyo Rāṭhoṛ *Vigat*, 2:63

Vairsī Rāṇāvat, Akhairājot Rāṭhoṛ *Vigat*, 2:52

Varjāṅg Bhīṃvot, Bhīṃvot Rāṭhoṛ *Vigat*, 2:43-44

Varsiṅgh Jodhāvat, Varsiṅghot Meṛtīyo Rāṭhoṛ, Rāv *Vigat*, 2:37-39, 2:41-46

Varsiṅghot Meṛtīyo Rāṭhoṛs

Bhojo Sīhāvat, Rāv *Vigat*, 2:47-48

Gāṅgo Sīhāvat, Rāv *Vigat*, 2:47-50

Jeso Sīhāvat, Rāv *Vigat*, 2:47-48

Sahaiso Tejsīyot *Vigat*, 2:52-53; ***Khyāt***, 3:95

Sāṃvaḷdās Udaisiṅghot *Vigat*, 2:63-64; "Aitihāsik Bātāṃ," pp. 53-54

Sīho Varsiṅghot, Rāv *Vigat*, 2:46-48

Varsiṅgh Jodhāvat, Rāv *Vigat*, 2:37-39, 2:41-46

Velo, Muṃhato *Vigat*, 2:74

Vīdāvat Rāṭhoṛs

Kalyāṇmal Udaikaraṇot ***Khyāt***, 3:101-102

Vīdo Bhārmalot, Bālāvat Rāṭhoṛ *Vigat*, 2:57; ***Khyāt***, 3:95, 3:100

Vikmādīt, Brāhmaṇ, Rājā *Vigat*, 2:74

Vīram Devāvat, Māṅgliyo Gahlot *Vigat*, 2:62-63, 2:66; "Aitihāsik Bātāṃ," p. 56

Vīramde Dūdāvat, Meṛtīyo Rāṭhoṛ, Rāv *Vigat*, 2:47-58; "Aitihāsik Bātāṃ," pp. 42-44; ***Khyāt***, 3:93-102, 3:115

Vīramde Vāghāvat, Jodho Rāṭhoṛ, Rāv ***Khyāt***, 3:87-88

Vīṭhaḷdās Jaimalot, Meṛtīyo Rāṭhoṛ *Vigat*, 2:67-68, 2:70-72

INDEX OF PLACE NAMES

A

B

C

D

G

H

I

J

K

L

M

N

P

R

V

END

THE MEṚTĪYO RĀṬHOṚS OF MEṚTO, RĀJASTHĀN:

SELECT TRANSLATIONS BEARING ON THE HISTORY OF

A RAJPŪT FAMILY, 1462-1660

Translated and Annotated by
Richard D. Saran and Norman P. Ziegler

Michigan Papers on South and Southeast Asian Studies
Number 51

THE UNIVERSITY OF MICHIGAN
CENTERS FOR SOUTH AND SOUTHEAST ASIAN STUDIES

Open access edition funded by the National Endowment for the Humanities/ Andrew W. Mellon Foundation Humanities Open Book Program.

Library of Congress Card Number: 2001091502

ISBN: 0-89148-085-4

Published by The Centers for South and Southeast Asian Studies
The University of Michigan
1080 South University, Suite 3640
Ann Arbor, MI 48109-1106

Printed in the United States of America

ISBN 978-0-89148-085-3 (hardcover)
ISBN 978-0-472-03821-3 (paper)
ISBN 978-0-472-12777-1 (ebook)
ISBN 978-0-472-90173-9 (open access)

VOLUME TWO

BIOGRAPHICAL NOTES

WITH

INTRODUCTION, GLOSSARY OF KINSHIP TERMS,

AND INDEXES

TABLE OF CONTENTS

INTRODUCTION

Volume II provides supplementary information to the translations about the history of Meṛto and the Meṛtīyo Rāṭhoṛs of Mārvāṛ, Rājasthān. The translations include mention of many individuals who played roles of varying importance in the history of Meṛto and Jodhpur. Some held prominent positions, while others were warriors whose names appear only once in a list of men killed in a particular battle. In all cases, it is important to know something about their lives and their families in order to understand better the context in which they lived and their motivations for action. These pages are offered in the hope that they will facilitate such an understanding.

The material is organized into two sections:

1. Marriage and Family Lists of the Rulers of Jodhpur
2. Biographical Notes

Marriage and Family Lists of the Rulers of Jodhpur

This section presents a detailed listing of the wives (***rāṇīs***), sons, and daughters of the Rāṭhoṛ rulers of Maṇḍor and Jodhpur over nine generations from Rāv Jodho Riṇmalot (ca. 1453-89) to Rājā Jasvantsiṅgh Gajsiṅghot (1638-78). While general information is available in English language publications about the reigns of these rulers, detailed information about their families is not so readily available. These listings attempt to rectify this situation, and include (where known):

1. The name of the branch (***sākh***) and clan (***vaṃś, kuḷ***) from which the wife came;
2. The wife's birth name, by which she was known at her paternal home (***pīhar***);
3. The new name given to the wife upon her marriage, by which she was known at her husband's father's home (***sāsro***);
4. The dates of marriage, birth of children, and of death;
5. The names of all sons born to the wife, with brief mention of significant events in the lives of the more important sons. If a son has been included in the Biographical Notes, the number of his Note, e. g., (no. 105), follows his name;
6. The names of all daughters born to the wife, with their dates and places of marriage.

This information provides important information about Rāṭhoṛ patterns of alliance through marriage, and details the manner in which these patterns developed over time in relation to the changing political fortunes of Rājasthān and north India.

Biographical Notes

The Biographical Notes provide information about the lives of all individuals mentioned in the translated texts, with the exception of the following:

1. Rāṭhoṛ rulers of Maṇḍor and Jodhpur, and important Muslim rulers of north India, such as Sher Shāh Sūr (1540-45) and Mughal Emperor Akbar (1556-1605). Information about these individuals is readily available in English language sources;
2. A small number of Rajpūts and other individuals, about whom only minimal information is known from sources available. Such individuals are treated in a footnote to the translated texts themselves.

The Biographical Notes include entries of varying length for one hundred and sixty-three different individuals referenced in the translations. The entries are numbered sequentially no. 1 - no. 163, and are divided into three groupings to facilitate location of specific notes: **Rajpūts**, **Muslims**, and **Administrative *Jātis***.

Rajpūts: The section on Rajpūts covers Notes no. 1 - no. 153. Individual Rajpūts are identified by a four-part name. The first two elements are the names of the branch (***sākh***) and the clan (***vaṃś, kuḷ***) to which the Rajpūt belonged, such as Hāḍo Cahuvāṇ, Sīsodīyo Gahlot, or Meṛtīyo Rāṭhoṛ. The third and fourth elements are the personal name of the individual followed by his father's name with the suffix meaning "son of." For example:

Jaitāvat Rāṭhoṛ Jaito Pañcāiṇot (Jaito, son of Pañcāiṇ)
Kūmpāvat Rāṭhoṛ Kūmpo Mahirājot (Kūmpo, son of Mahirāj)
Meṛtīyo Rāṭhoṛ Vīramde Dūdāvat (Vīramde, son of Dūdo)

These four elements provide the structure for the organization of the Notes themselves. The section is ordered first alphabetically by clan, and then within the clan, alphabetically by branch. The Notes for individual Rajpūts within subsections are placed in approximate chronological order according to family groupings.

To facilitate the location of specific Notes, two devices have been employed. First, all Notes are numbered sequentially, and the number of a Rajpūt's specific Biographical Note accompanies him wherever his name is mentioned either in a footnote to the translated texts or in different sections of the Biographical Notes where his name may appear in discussion. The reader can easily turn to the specific number in the Notes for that individual and locate the information about him.

Second, there is an alphabetical listing by personal name at the front of each subsection pertaining to the branch of a clan, of all individuals included in the subsection. Knowing a Rajpūt's personal name and the name of the branch and clan to which he belongs, the reader can turn to the appropriate subsection of the Notes and locate the number of the Note for the individual from the listing at the front of the subsection.

To site an example, in order to locate the Biographical Note for Meṛtīyo Rāṭhoṛ Jaimal Vīramdevot, the reader can turn either directly to the Note for Meṛtīyo Jaimal (no. 107), or turn to the Meṛtīyo subsection for the Rāṭhoṛs, then look at the listing at the front of the subsection for Jaimal Vīramdevot. The number of Jaimal's Note (no. 107) is listed in front of Jaimal's name, allowing easy location of the Note itself.

If the reader knows only the personal name of the Rajpūt along with his father's name, he or she may refer to the general index of names at the end of the volume. This index provides listing of all individuals in the Biographical Notes by personal name, and gives the number of the individual's specific Biographical Note.

Biographical subsections (Jeso Bhāṭī, Hāḍo Cahuvāṇ, Sīsodīyo Gahlot, etc.) also include genealogical charts, placed at the end of the subsections. These charts list all of the individuals with Notes along with some close family members, and trace their relationships to each other. Each individual is numbered on the genealogical chart by generation and by placement within the generation on the chart itself for easy reference and location. This number locator follows the names of the individuals in the alphabetical listing at the front of each subsection. A listing will appear as follows:

(no. 107) **Jaimal Vīramdevot** (8-1)

with the number of the individual's Biographical Note (i.e, no. 107), the personal name, (son of) father's name, and then the location on the genealogical chart (i.e., generation 8, position 1, beginning on the left).

Note: for Rāṭhoṛs, genealogical charts generally begin with Rāv Salkho (1-1) and his son, Vīram Salkhāvat (2-1), ancestors dating from the fourteenth century whose genealogical position in relation to later generations is known with certainty.

The subsections on branches of different Rajpūt clans include not only information about individuals belonging to this branch who are mentioned in the translated texts, but also material about the origin and early history of the branch. The subsection on the Jeso Bhāṭīs, for example, includes short Notes on three Jeso Bhāṭīs (no. 1 - no. 3) mentioned in the translated texts, and a somewhat longer lead section on Bhāṭī Jeso Kalikaraṇot. Bhāṭī Jeso was the founding ancestor of the Jeso Bhāṭīs of Mārvāṛ. It was he and his sons who established ties of service with the Rāṭhoṛ rulers of Jodhpur following the marriage of Jeso Kalikaraṇot's sister to Jodhpur ruler, Rāv Sūjo Jodhāvat (ca. 1492-1515).

The founders of different branches, as in the case of the Jeso Bhāṭīs, were often separated by several generations from the individuals who are included in the Notes. In other cases, the founders of branches are Rajpūts who lived during the period discussed in the translations. Rāṭhoṛs Jaito Pañcāiṇot and Kūmpo Mahirājot, for example, were founders of the Jaitāvat and Kūmpāvat ***sākh***s of Mārvāṛ Rāṭhoṛs. Both of these Rajpūts served under Rāṭhoṛ Rāv Mālde Gāṅgāvat of Jodhpur (1532-62) and were killed at the battle of Samel in January of 1544, fighting against the Afghan Sher Shāh Sūr. Properly speaking, these individuals belonged to branches of Rāṭhoṛs other than Jaitāvat and Kūmpāvat, for these groupings did not emerge until after their deaths. They are referred to in the texts under discussion as Akhairājot Rāṭhoṛs. However, material about them belongs with that for their descendants, who were Jaitāvat ("son of" Jaito) and Kūmpāvat ("son of" Kūmpo). This organization provides a better and more coherent ordering for the Notes.

Information about origins and founders offers an important and necessary context for understanding the lives of individual members of a brotherhood, who may have lived generations apart. Both immediate family relations and the larger network of kinship through time provided the context from which individual actions emerged.

Muslims and Administrative *Jātis*: This section consists of Notes no. 154 - no. 163. It includes a brief section on the family of Khānzāda Khān Muslims who ruled at Nāgaur for a period of years during the fifteenth and early sixteenth centuries, and sections on the members of three different administrative ***jāti***s who played roles of varying importance in the history of Meṛto and Jodhpur. Because less is known from local sources about these individuals, the sections themselves are devoted more to a general discussion of the ***jāti*** than to the lives of the individuals mentioned in the texts, about whom often only a personal name and a few other facts are in evidence.

Source References

Considerable attention has been given to the notation of sources from which material has been gathered for both the Marriage and Family Lists and the Biographical Notes.

Sources for the Marriage Lists have been arranged by individual wives of rulers and placed in footnotes. This ordering should facilitate the investigation of particular marriages and children of marriages which readers may wish to pursue.

Source references for the Biographical Notes have generally been placed at the end of individual sections, so the reader may go immediately to sources for that individual. The only exceptions are where there is limited information about a group of related individuals. In such cases, the sources have been placed together at the end of the section for these individuals.

List of Figures

(Genealogical Charts)

Abbreviations

The following abbreviations are used for works frequently cited:

Ā'īn-i-Akbarī	Abū al-Fazl ibn Mubārak, ***Ā'īn-i-Akbarī***
"Aitihāsik Bātāṃ"	"Aitihāsik Bātāṃ." In ***Paramparā***, part 11, pp. 17-109
Akbar Nāma	Abū al-Fazl ibn Mubārak. ***The Akbar Nāma of Abu-l-Fazl***
Āsop kā Itihās	Āsopā, Rāmkaraṇ. ***Āsop kā Itihās***
Athar Ali, ***Apparatus***	Athar Ali, M. ***The Apparatus of Empire: Awards of Ranks, Offices, and Titles to the Mughal Nobility, 1574-1658***
Bāṅkīdās	Bāṅkīdās, ***Bāṅkīdās rī Khyāt***
Bhāṭī, ***Sarvekṣaṇ***	Bhāṭī, Nārāyaṇsiṃh. ***Rājasthān ke Aitihāsik Granthoṃ kā Sarvekṣaṇ***
Cāmpāvat Rāṭhauṛ	Bhagavatsiṃh, Ṭhākur. ***Cāmpāvat Rāṭhauṛ***
Census Report, 1891	"***Mārvāṛ kī Qaumoṃ kā Itihās.***" ***Riporṭ Mardumśumārī Rāj Mārvāṛ bābat san 1891 Īsvī***, part 3
Gehlot, ***Mārvāṛ***	Gehlot, G. S. ***Mārvāṛ kā Saṅkṣipt Itihās***
Jahāngīr	Jahāngīr. ***The Tūzuk-i-Jahāngīrī; or, Memoirs of Jahāngīr***
Jaisalmer rī Khyāt	***Jaisalmer rī Khyāt. Paramparā***, parts 57-58. Edited by Nārāyaṇsiṃh Bhāṭī

"Jodhpur Hukūmat rī Bahī"	"Jodhpur Hukūmat rī Bahī." In ***Marwar under Jaswant Singh (1658-1678): Jodhpur Hukumat ri Bahi***, pp. 1-237
Jodhpur Rājya kī Khyāt	*Jodhpur Rājya kī Khyāt*. Edited by Raghuvīr Siṃh and Manoharsiṃh Rāṇāvat
Khyāt	Naiṇsī, Muṃhato, ***Muṃhatā Naiṇsī viracit Muṃhatā Naiṇsīrī Khyāt***
Lāḷas, ***RSK***	Lāḷas, Sītārām, ***Rājasthānī Sabad Kos***
Maāthir-ul-Umarā	Shāhnavāz Khān Awrangābādī. ***The Maāthir-ul-Umarā***
Mūndiyāṛ rī Rāṭhoṛāṃ rī Khyāt	*Mūndiyāṛ rī Rāṭhoṛāṃ rī Khyāt*, MS no. 15635, no. 2
Murārdān, no. 1	***Kavirāj Murardānjī kī Khyāt kā Tarjumā***
Murārdān, no. 2	***Rāṭhoṛoṃ rī Khyāt Purāṇī Kavirājjī Murardānjī ke Yahāṃ se Likhī Gaī***
Murārdān, no. 3	***Rajpūtom kī Khyāt: Kavirājjī Murardānjī kī Khyāt kā Tarjumā***
Ojhā	Ojhā, G. H., ***Rājpūtāne kā Itihās***
Paṃvār Vaṃś Darpaṇ	Siṇḍhāyac, Dayāldās. ***Paṃvār Vaṃś Darpaṇ***. Edited by Daśrath Śarmā
Platts, ***Dictionary***	Platts, John A., ***A Dictionary of Urdū, Classical Hindī, and English***
Rāṭhoṛāṃ rī Vaṃśāvalī, ms. no. 20130	*Rāṭhoṛāṃ rī Vaṃśāvalī*. MS no. 20130, Rājasthān Prācyavidyā Pratiṣṭhān, Jodhpur.
Reu	Reu, B. N., ***Mārvāṛ kā Itihās***
Sākariyā, ***RHSK***	Sākariyā, Badrīprasād, and Sākariyā, Bhūpati Rām, eds. ***Rājasthānī Hindī Śabd Koś***

Tavārīkh Jaisalmer	Lakhmīcand. *Tavārīkh Jaisalmer = The History of Jeysalmere*
Tod, *Annals*	Tod, James, *Annals and Antiquities of Rajasthan*
Vigat	Naiṇsī, Muṃhato. *Mārvāṛ rā Parganāṃ rī Vigat*
Vīr Vinod	Śyāmaldās, Kavirājā. *Vīr Vinod*

Full references will be found in the bibliography (vol. one, pp. 37-50)

Other abbreviations:

B.N.	Biographical Notes
V.S.	Vikrama Saṃvat

MARRIAGE AND FAMILY LISTS OF THE RULERS OF JODHPUR

Rāv Jodho Riṇmalot (ca. 1453-89)	(5-1)
Rāv Sātal Jodhāvat (ca. 1489-92)	(6-2)
Rāv Sūjo Jodhāvat (ca. 1492-1515)	(6-3)
Rāv Gāṅgo Vāghāvat (1515-32)	(8-1)
Rāv Mālde Gāṅgāvat (1532-62)	(9-1)
Rāv Candrasen Māldevot (1562-81)	(10-1)
Moṭo Rājā Udaisiṅgh Māldevot (1583-95)	(10-2)
Rājā Sūrajsiṅgh Udaisiṅghot (1595-1619)	(11-1)
Rājā Gajsiṅgh Sūrajsiṅghot (1619-38)	(12-1)
Rājā Jasvantsiṅgh Gajsiṅghot (1638-78)	(13-1)

Figure 1. Rāṭhoṛ Rulers of Jodhpur

(1-1) Rāv Salkho

(2-1) Vīram Salkhāvat

(3-1) Rāv Cūṇḍo Vīramot

(4-1) Rāv Riṇmal Cūṇḍāvat

(5-1) Rāv Jodho Riṇmalot

(6-1) Nīmbo Jodhāvat | (6-2) Rāv Sātal Jodhāvat | (6-3) Rāv Sūjo Jodhāvat

(7-1) Vāgho Sūjāvat

(8-1) Rāv Gāṅgo Vāghāvat

(9-1) Rāv Mālde Gāṅgāvat

(10-1) Rāv Candrasen Māldevot | (10-2) Moṭo Rājā Udaisiṅgh Māldevot

(11-1) Rājā Sūrajsiṅgh Udaisinghot

(12-1) Rājā Gajsiṅgh Sūrajsiṅghot

(13-1) Rājā Jasvantsiṅgh Gajsiṅghot

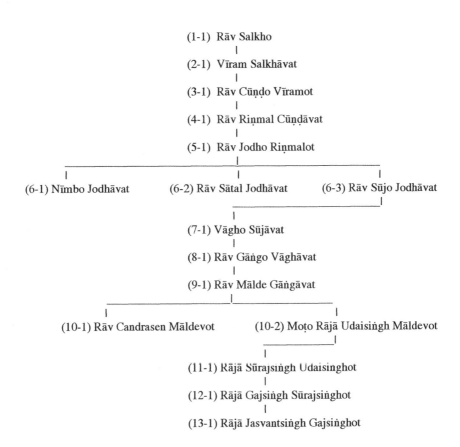

Rāv Jodho Riṇmalot (5-1)

Born: Tuesday, April 1, 1416[1]
Died: April 6, 1489 (unconfirmed by inscriptional evidence)
Ruled: ca. 1453 - April 6, 1489
Mother: Rāṇī Bhāṭiyāṇī Koṛamde, daughter of Bhāṭī Rāv Rāṇagde Lakhamsīyot of Pūṅgaḷ.

The following section on Rāv Jodho Riṇmalot is divided into two parts. The first provides a composite listing of Rāv Jodho's brothers. Many of these men played roles of importance in the history of Mārvāṛ and Bīkāner. Their exact number is unknown, but sources list twenty-five to twenty-seven brothers. Virtually no information is available about their mothers. The listing of these brothers is organized, therefore, into four alphabetical groupings based on what is known of their activities.

The second part of this section presents a detailed listing of all of Rāv Jodho's wives, sons and daughters.

Brothers[2]

A. Brothers who died in childhood:

1. Goyand
2. Karamcand: died of smallpox.
3. Sagto
4. Sāyar: drowned in a tank at the village of Dhaṇlo[3]; is said to have become a spirit (***pitar***).

B. Brothers included in Rāv Jodho's division of the lands of Mārvāṛ following the founding of Jodhpur in 1459:

1. Akhairāj: received Bagṛī village[4] (see "Akhairājot Rāṭhoṛs," ***infra***).

2. Bhākhar: died before the founding of Jodhpur; his son, Bālo, received the three villages of Khārlo, Khāṛī, and

[1] We are following Ojhā, 4:1:235, here. ***Jodhpur Rājya kī Khyāt***, p. 55, gives the date of Saturday, March 28, 1416 for Rāv Jodho's birth.

[2] General sources for this section include: Gehlot, ***Mārvāṛ***, pp. 160-162; ***Khyāt***, 3:40; ***Murārdān***, no. 1, pp. 205-208; Ojhā, 4:1:225-226; Reu, 1:80; ***Vigat***, 1:38-39; ***Vīr Vinod***, 2:805-806.

[3] Dhaṇlo village: located twenty-seven miles south of Sojhat in eastern Mārvāṛ.

[4] Bagṛī village: located nine miles east-southeast of Sojhat.

Sāhlī (located to the south of Jodhpur; see "Bālāvat Rāṭhoṛs," ***infra***).

3. Cāmpo: received Kāparṛo[5] and Baṇāṛ[6] villages (see "Cāmpāvat Rāṭhoṛs," ***infra***).

4. Ḍūṅgarsī: received Bhādrājuṇ village[7]; the Ḍūṅgarot ***sākh*** of Mārvāṛ Rāṭhoṛs emerged from his descendants (see "Riṇmalot Rāṭhoṛs," ***infra***).

5. Jagmāl: died before the founding of Jodhpur; his son, Khetsī, received the village of Netṛāṃ.[8] Two ***sākh***s of Mārvāṛ Rāṭhoṛs descend from Jagmāl: the Jagmālot and the Khetsīyot (see "Riṇmalot Rāṭhoṛs," ***infra***).

6. Karṇo: received Lūṇāvās village[9]; founder of the Karaṇot ***sākh*** of Mārvāṛ Rāṭhoṛs.

7. Maṇḍalo: received Sānduṛo village in the area that later became Bīkāner; founder of the Maṇḍalot ***sākh*** of Bīkāner and Mārvāṛ Rāṭhoṛs.

8. Pāto: received Karṇu village[10]; founder of the Pātāvat ***sākh*** of Mārvāṛ Rāṭhoṛs.

9. Rūpo: received Cāḍī village[11]; founder of the Rūpāvat ***sākh*** of Mārvāṛ Rāṭhoṛs (see "Riṇmalot Rāṭhoṛs," ***infra***).

10. Vairo: received Dudhvaṛ village[12] from Rāv Jodho; founder of the Vairāvat ***sākh*** of Mārvāṛ Rāṭhoṛs.

C. Brothers who left Jodhpur with Rāv Jodho's son, Bīko Jodhāvat, and participated in the founding of Bīkāner:

1. Kāndhaḷ: founder of the Kāndhaḷot ***sākh*** of Bīkāner Rāṭhoṛs.

2. Lākho: founder of the Lākhāvat ***sākh*** of Bīkāner Rāṭhoṛs.

---

[5] Kāparṛo village: located twenty-eight miles east of Jodhpur.

[6] Baṇāṛ village: located eight miles east-northeast of Jodhpur.

[7] Bhādrājuṇ village: located forty-eight miles south-southwest of Jodhpur.

[8] Netṛāṃ village: located twenty-one miles north-northeast of Jodhpur.

[9] Lūṇāvās village: located twenty miles southwest of Jodhpur.

[10] Karṇu village: located sixty miles north of Jodhpur.

[11] Cāḍī village: located fifty-eight miles north of Jodhpur.

[12] Dudhvaṛ village: located eleven miles south of Sojhat in eastern Mārvāṛ.

3. Nātho: founder of the Nāthāvat *sākh* of Bīkāner Rāṭhoṛs.

4. Ūdo: founder of the Ūdāvat *sākh* of Bīkāner Rāṭhoṛs.

D. Brothers whose activities are unknown:

1. Aḍvāḷ: founder of the Aḍvāḷot *sākh* of Mārvāṛ Rāṭhoṛs.

2. Hāpo: his descendants are known as both "Riṇmalots" and "Hāpāvats" in Mārvāṛ.

3. Jaitmāl: his son, Bhojrāj, was founder of the Bhojrājot *sākh* of Mārvāṛ Rāṭhoṛs.

4. Māṇḍaṇ: founder of the Māṇḍaṇot *sākh* of Mārvāṛ Rāṭhoṛs.

5. Sāṇḍo: founder of the Sāṇḍāvat *sākh* of Mārvāṛ Rāṭhoṛs.

6. Sīndho: his descendants are called "Riṇmalots."

7. Tejsī: founder of the Tejsīyot *sākh* of Mārvāṛ Rāṭhoṛs.

8. Vaṇvīr: founder of the Vaṇvīrot *sākh* of Mārvāṛ Rāṭhoṛs.

Rāṇīs, Sons, and Daughters

1. **Rāṇī Hāḍī Jasmādejī**[13]

The texts list this Rāṇī's name as both "Jasmāde" and "Koṛamde." Jasmāde appears to be the name she received upon marriage to Rāv Jodho. Koṛamde may have been her *pīhar* name, but this name was also the name of Rāv Jodho's mother, Rāṇī Bhāṭiyāṇī Koṛamdejī. Its ascription to one of Rāv Jodho's wives may indicate some confusion in the sources.

The name of Hāḍī Jasmādejī's father is uncertain. The texts list his name variously as Hāḍo Cahuvāṇ Jītmal Devot, Ajīt Māldevot, and Devīdās Jaitmālot of Būndī. Jītmal Devot's name appears in the genealogy for the Hāḍo Cahuvāṇs recorded in the *Khyāt* of Naiṇsī, 1:101. Jītmal was a son of Hāḍo Devo Bāṅgāvat, the founder of Hāḍo rule in Būndī, 1342-43. Given Rāv Jodho's birth in 1416, it would appear on genealogical grounds alone that Hāḍo Jītmal Devot could not have been Jasmāde's father. The name Ajīt Māldevot appears to be a corruption of Jītmal Devot. It does not appear in the Hāḍo genealogy in Naiṇsī's *Khyāt*, nor does the name Devīdās Jaitmālot. Without further information, it is not possible to know the identity of this Rāṇī's father with certainty.

S - Nīmbo: designated successor to the Jodhpur throne; died while a *kuṃvar* (see "Jodho Rāṭhoṛs," *infra*).

---

[13] "Aitihāsik Bātāṃ," pp. 36-37; ***Bāṅkīdās***, p. 8; ***Khyāt***, 1:101, 3:31, 216; ***Murārdān***, no. 2, pp. 401-402; Ojhā, 4:1:251-252; ***Vigat***, 1:39.

S - Sātal: Rāv Jodho's successor to the Jodhpur throne ca. 1489.

S - Sūjo: born August 2, 1439; succeeded Rāv Sātal Jodhāvat to the Jodhpur throne in March of 1492.

2. **Rāṇī Bhāṭiyāṇī Pūrāṃjī** [14]

Daughter of Kelhaṇ Bhāṭī Rāv Vairsal Cācāvat of Pūṅgaḷ and Vairsalpur (ca. 1448-64).

S - Karamsī: (see "Karamsot Rāṭhoṛs," ***infra***).
S - Rāypāḷ: founded the Rāypāḷot ***sākh*** of Mārvāṛ Rāṭhoṛs
S - Vaṇvīr: founded the Vaṇvīrot ***sākh*** of Mārvāṛ Rāṭhoṛs.
S - Jasvant
S - Kūmpo
S - Candrāv

D - Bhāgāṃ: married to Khānzāda Khān Salho Khān (Ṣalāh Khān, ca. 1467-69) of Nāgaur in 1464-65 by her two uterine brothers, Karamsī and Rāypāḷ. Her brothers received from Salho Khān, in turn, the important villages of Khīṃvsar and Āsop[15] in ***sāḷā kaṭārī*** (lit. "wife's brother-dagger").[16]

D - Rājāṃbāī: married to Mohil Cahuvāṇ Ajīt Sāṃvatsīyot of Chāpar-Droṇpur.

3. **Rāṇī Sāṅkhlī Nāraṅgdejī** [17]

There is uncertainty about the identity of this Rāṇī's father. This uncertainty extends both to the name of her father and to the branch of Sāṅkhlos (Rūṇeco or Jāṅgaḷvo) from which he came. ***Jodhpur Rājya kī Khyāt***, pp. 55, 57, states that Nāraṅgde Sāṅkhlī was a daughter of Sāṅkhlo Paṃvār Māṇḍo Jaitāvat, and refers to her as a Rūṇecī, of the Sāṅkhlos of Rūṇ village[18] in Mārvāṛ. ***Khyāt***, 3:8, confirms that Jodho Riṇmalot married among the Rūṇeco Sāṅkhlos, stating:

---

[14] ***Bāṅkīdās***, p. 8; ***Khyāt***, 2:117, 3:158-159; ***Murārdān***, no. 2, pp. 431, 600-601; Ojhā, 4:1:252; ***Vigat***, 1:40.

[15] Khīṃvsar and Āsop are located sixteen miles apart from each other some fifty-four miles north-northeast and fifty miles northeast of Jodhpur, respectively.

[16] ***Sāḷā kaṭārī***: the customary gifts which the brother(s) of the bride claim from the groom at the end of the marriage, following the couple's circumambulation of the fire. At this time, the wife's brother (***sāḷo***) takes up a sword or dagger and grabs hold of the groom's ear, demanding his presents or gifts (***neg***). These generally consist of weapons and/or money, but can also take the form of parcels of land or villages. See: ***Census Report, 1891***, 3:1:33-34.

[17] ***Bāṅkīdās***, pp. 8, 74; ***Khyāt***, 1:340-341, 346, 353, 3:8, 31; Ojhā, 4:1:252-253, 5:1:72-73. 90; Reu, 1:103, n. 3; ***Vigat***, 1:31, 39.

[18] Rūṇ village: located twenty miles northwest of Meṛto and fifty-nine miles northeast of Jodhpur.

> [Jodho] proceeded to [the home of] the Sāṅkhlos of Rūṇ. The Sāṅkhlos took a betrothal coconut and came before the Rāvjī. The designated successor (*ṭīkāyat*) of the Sāṅkhlos was called Rāvat; his daughter was married to the Rāvjī.

Rāṭhoṛāṃ rī Vaṃśāvalī, MS no. 20130, f. 35, gives Nāraṅgdejī's father's name as Māṇḍaṇ Jaitāvat, while ***Khyāt***, 3:31, in a section entitled "Ath Vāt Rāv Sīhojī (rai Vaṃś) rī" (Now the Story of Rāv Sīhojī's ***Vaṃś***), includes the following entry:

> Rāv Jodhojī's wife (***antevar***), Nāraṅgde Sāṅkhlī, [was] Rāṇo Māṇḍaṇ Ruṇāvat's daughter.

The Māṇḍaṇ referred to here was a Sāṅkhlo of Rūṇ, "Rāṇo" being a common title assumed by the Rūṇeco Sāṅkhlos. ***Vigat***, 1:39, lists two alternative names for the father, Rāṇo Maḍājetsot and Rāṇo Māḍāsiṅghot, both of which appear simply to be corruptions of Māṇḍo/Māṇḍaṇ Jaitāvat.

Khyāt, 1:341, lists an individual by the name of "Rāṇo Māṇḍo, [son] of Jaitsī," in its genealogy of the Rūṇeco Sāṅkhlos. This individual is presumably Māṇḍo Jaitāvat, but the ***Khyāt*** gives no information about him, listing only his name.

Elsewhere in ***Vigat***, 1:31, Naiṇsī provides a cryptic entry about Sāṅkhlī Nāraṅgde's father. As if writing a note to himself, he refers to two different Sāṅkhlos who might have been the father: Sāṅkhlo Māṇḍo [Jaitāvat] and Sāṅkhlo Nāpo Māṇakrāvat (no. 26) of the Sāṅkhlos of Jāṅgaḷu.[19] He states:

> Previously Sāṅkhlo Nāpo Māṇakrāvat - Māṇḍo [Jaitāvat] was the ***dhaṇī*** - [either] his daughter [or] Nāpo's, Nāraṅgde Sāṅkhlī, ... was married [to Rāv Jodho].

In support of Nāpo Sāṅkhlo as the father, ***Bāṅkīdās***, p. 74, records that Sāṅkhlī Nāraṅgdejī's eldest son, Bīko Jodhāvat, was a sister's son (***bhāṇej***) of the Sāṅkhlos of Jāṅgaḷu.

It is difficult to evaluate this information. Jāṅgaḷvo Sāṅkhlo Nāpo Māṇakrāvat was closely associated with Rāv Jodho and with Sāṅkhlī Nāraṅgde's two sons, Bīko and Vīdo. It may be that for this reason, he became, over time, Nāraṅgdejī's father.[20] The weight of the evidence rests, however, with Rūṇeco Sāṅkhlo Māṇḍo/Māṇḍaṇ Jaitāvat/Jaitsīyot as the father.

The date of this marriage is also uncertain. According to ***Khyāt***, 3:8, it took place sometime during Jodho Riṇmalot's period of distress (***vikhau***)

[19] Jāṅgaḷu village: located sixty-five miles northeast of Phaḷodhī and forty-five miles northwest of Nāgaur.

[20] See ***infra***, "Sāṅkhlo Paṃvārs," for more information about Nāpo Sāṅkhlo (no. 26).

following his father Rāv Riṇmal Cūṇḍāvat's murder at Cītoṛ ca. 1438. This dating is problematic, however, given at least one of the dates of birth for Nāraṅgde's eldest son, Bīko.

S - Bīko: different dates are given for Bīko's birth including August 5, 1438 and July 14, 1440 (***adhika vaiś***) or August 14, 1440 (***nija vaiś***). Bīko founded the kingdom of Bīkāner, and a Rāṭhoṛ ***sākh*** bearing his name emerged after him (see "Bīkāvat Rāṭhoṛs," no. 42, ***infra***).

S - Vīdo: (see "Vīdāvat Rāṭhoṛs," ***infra***).

4. **Rāṇī Sonagarī Cāmpābāī** (***pīhar*** name) [21]

Daughter of Sonagaro Cahuvāṇ Khīṃvo Satāvat of Pālī village[22] in eastern Mārvāṛ.

S - Varsiṅgh: born sometime prior to 1440 (see "Varsiṅghot Meṛtīyo Rāṭhoṛs," no. 146, ***infra***).

S - Dūdo: varying dates appear in the texts for Dūdo's birth, including June 15, September 28, October 6 and October 10, 1440, and July 4, 1441 (see "Meṛtīyo Rāṭhoṛs," no. 104, ***infra***, and ***Vigat***, 2:47, n. 148 of the **translated text**).

5. **Rāṇī Hulṇī Jamnādejī** (or **Jāṇāndejī**) [23]

Daughter of Hul Gahlot Vaṇvīr Bhojāvat (or Vīrbhāṇ Bhojāvat).

S - Jogo: (see "Jodho Rāṭhoṛs," ***infra***).

S - Bhārmal: (see "Bhārmalot Rāṭhoṛs," ***infra***).

6. **Rāṇī Vāghelī Vināṃjī** [24]

Daughter of Vāghelo Solaṅkī Urjaṇ Bhīmrājot.

S - Sāṃvatsī

S - Sivrāj (see "Jodho Rāṭhoṛs," no. 80, ***infra***).

7. **Rāṇī Soḷaṅkaṇī** [25]

---

[21] ***Khyāt***, 1:207; ***Murārdān***, no. 2, pp. 444, 583; Ojhā, 4:1:253-254; Reu, 1:103, n. 5; ***Vigat***, 1:39, 2:37.

[22] Pālī village: located forty miles south-southeast of Jodhpur.

[23] ***Khyāt***, 3:31; ***Murārdān***, no. 2, pp. 403, 422; Ojhā, 4:1:253; ***Vigat***, 1:39.

[24] ***Murārdān***, no. 2, p. 417; Ojhā, 4:1:254; ***Vigat***, 1:39.

[25] ***Murārdān***, no. 2, p. 98.

8. **Rāṇī Cahuvāṇ** [26]

9. **Rāṇī Sīsodṇī** [27]

Daughter of Sīsodīyo Gahlot Rāṇo Mokaḷ Lākhāvat, ruler of Cītoṛ (ca. 1421-33), and uterine sister of Rāṇo Kūmbho Mokaḷot, ruler of Cītoṛ (ca. 1433-68); given to Rāv Jodho in marriage, ca. 1453.

Miscellaneous

Several additional sons of Rāv Jodho, whose mothers are not known with certainty, are mentioned in the sources. [28] These sons include:

S - Abhāyrāj
S - Jagmāl
S - Lakhmaṇ
S - Nātho
S - Rūpsiṅgh

The texts also list several daughters of Rāv Jodho, whose mothers are not known. The names of these daughters and their places of marriage are:

D - Sundarbāī: married to Sonagaro Cahuvāṇ Lolo Rāṇāvat by Rāv Jodho's father, Rāv Riṇmal Cūṇḍāvat (ca. 1428-38). Sonagaro Lolo married a daughter to Rāv Riṇmal in exchange. [29]

D - Śriṅgārdevī: married to Sīsodīyo Gahlot Rāṇo Rāymal Kūmbhāvat, ruler of Cītoṛ (ca. 1473-1509). [30]

D - Rūpkuṃvarbāī: married to Bhāṭī Rāvaḷ Cāco Vairsīyot, ruler of Jaisaḷmer (1448-64 or 1467). Her son by Rāvaḷ Cāco was Rāvaḷ Devīdās Cācāvat, ruler of Jaisaḷmer (1464 or 1467-91). [31]

---

[26] *Ibid.*

[27] Paṇḍit Badrī Śarma, ***Dāsapoṃ kā Itihās*** (Jodhpur: Seṇāsadana, V.S. 2011 [A.D. 1954]), p. 13; ***Cāmpāvat Rāṭhaur***, p. 6. This marriage is not included in the lists of Rāv Jodho's marriages found in other primary sources. References to it appear only in the two above noted secondary sources that deal with the history of the Cāmpāvat Rāṭhoṛs of Mārvāṛ.

[28] ***Bāṅkīdās***, p. 7; Reu, 1:103; "Rāṭhauḍ Vaṃś rī Vigat," in ***Rāṭhauḍ Vaṃś rī Vigat evaṃ Rāṭhauḍāṃ rī Vaṃśāvalī***, edited by Phatahsiṃh (Jodhpur: Rājasthān Prācyavidyā Pratiṣṭān, 1968), pp. 10-11.

[29] ***Khyāt***, 1:206-207, 3:133.

[30] Dasharatha Sharma, ***Lectures on Rajput History and Culture*** (Delhi: Motilal Banarsidass, 1970), p. 81.

[31] ***Jaisalmer rī Khyāt***, pp. 64-65; ***Tavārīkh Jaisalmer***, p. 47.

D - (name unknown) married to Shams Khān Kyāṃ Khān, the master of Jhūñjhaṇūṃ.[32]

Marriage Lists

Lists of Rāv Jodho's marriages and of his sons and daughters are contained in the following primary sources. These sources reference all marriages except those for Rāṇīs no. 7, no. 8, and no. 9. The sources are:

Jodhpur Rājya kī Khyāt, pp. 55-58.
Murārdān, no. 2, pp. 98-99.
Rāṭhoṛāṃ rī Vaṃśāvalī, MS no. 20130, ff. 35-36.

Other references include:

L. P. Tessitori, "A Progress Report on the Work done during the year 1916 in connection with the Bardic and Historical Survey of Rajputana," ***Journal of the Asiatic Society of Bengal***, N.S. 12 (1917), p. 218; ***Murārdān***, no. 2, pp. 93-97, no. 3. p. 23; Ojhā, 4:1:235, 239, 267; "Rāṭhauḍ Vaṃś rī Vigat," pp. 10-11; Reu, 1:103; ***Vīr Vinod***, 2:806.

[32] ***Kyāṃ Khāṃ Rāsā***, pp. 36-37, as noted in S. Inayat Ali Zaidi, "The Pattern of Matrimonial Ties between the Kachawaha Clan and the Mughal Ruling Family," ***Indian Historical Congress: Proceedings of the 35th Session, Jadavpur (Calcutta), 1974***, pp. 133, 140.

Rāv Sātal Jodhāvat (6-2)

Born: (?)
Died: March of 1492
Ruled: ca. 1489 - March, 1492
Mother: Rāṇī Hāḍī Jasmādejī of Būndī [1]

Rāṇīs, Sons, and Daughters

1. **Rāṇī Bhāṭiyāṇī Harakhbāī** (***pīhar*** name)
   Daughter of the Kelhaṇ Bhāṭīs of Vikūmpur.

2. **Rāṇī Bhāṭiyāṇī Phūlāṃ**

Miscellaneous

Rāv Sātal is said to have had five other wives. There are no references to these wives by name among the sources available. All are said to have become ***satī***s following Rāv Sātal's death. There are no sons or daughters listed in any of the chronicles.

General References

Jodhpur Rājya kī Khyāt, p. 57; ***Murārdān***, no. 2, p. 100; Ojhā, 4:1:259-260, 262-263; ***Vigat***, 1:39.

[1] See ***supra***, Rāv Jodho Riṇmalot, Rāṇī no. 1, for a discussion of the confusion surrounding the identity of Rāṇī Jasmādejī's father.

Rāv Sūjo Jodhāvat (6-3)

Born: Sunday, August 2, 1439
Died: Tuesday, October 2, 1515
Ruled: March, 1492 - October 2, 1515
Mother: Rāṇī Hāḍī Jasmādejī of Būndī [1]

Rāṇīs, Sons, and Daughters

1. **Rāṇī Bhāṭiyāṇī Sāraṅgdejī** (***pīhar*** name Likhmībāī)[2]

The name of this Rāṇī's father is variously given in the sources as Bhāṭī Jīvo Urjanot, Kalikaraṇ Keharot and Jeso Kalikaraṇot, a son of Kalikaraṇ Keharot's.

No listing is found for a Jīvo Urjanot in the genealogy of the Bhāṭīs in the ***Khyāt*** of Naiṇsī. The name Jīvo is possibly a corruption of Jeso. Most references associate Bhāṭiyāṇī Likhmībāī with Jeso Kalikaraṇot and his father, Kalikaraṇ Keharot. From textual evidence, it appears that this Rāṇī's father was Kalikaraṇ Keharot of Jaisaḷmer, a son of Rāvaḷ Kehar Devrājot (1361-97). Likhmībāī's brother, Jeso Kalikaraṇot, was the founder of the Jeso ***sākh*** of Mārvāṛ Bhāṭīs (see "Jeso Bhāṭīs," ***infra***).

S - Vāgho: born December 16, 1457[3] (see "Jodho Rāṭhoṛs," no. 83, ***infra***).
S - Naro: founder of the Narāvat ***sākh*** of Mārvāṛ Rāṭhoṛs.

2. **Rāṇī Cahuvāṇjī** [4]

Daughter of Sācoro Cahuvāṇ Rāv Pithamrāv Tejsīyot of Sācor.

S - Sekho: (see "Jodho Rāṭhoṛs," no. 86, ***infra***).
S - Devīdās

---

[1] See ***supra***, Rāv Jodho Riṇmalot, Rāṇī no. 1, for a discussion of the confusion surrounding the identity of Hāḍī Jasmādejī's father.

[2] "Aitihāsik Bātāṃ," p. 37; ***Bāṅkīdās***, pp. 9, 119; ***Khyāt***, 2:152-153, 3:34, 104-105, 215; ***Murārdān***, no. 2, p. 431; Ojhā, 4:1:269; ***Vigat***, 1:40-41. The ***Vigat*** of Naiṇsī references Vāgho Sūjāvat as the son of Rāṇī Māṅgliyāṇī Sāraṅgde, the daughter of Māṅglīyo Gahlot Pāñcū Vīramdevot. This information is incorrect. It probably involves confusion with Rāṇī no. 3, ***infra***.

[3] This date is from Ojhā, 4:1:269. ***Jodhpur Rājya kī Khyāt***, p. 68, records a date of birth of Friday, April 15, 1468, which appears to be in error. See: Ojhā, 4:1:260-270, n. 5, for his discussion of issues surrounding the dating of Vāgho's birth.

[4] ***Bāṅkīdās***, pp. 9, 163; ***Khyāt***, 1:241-242; Ojhā, 4:1:270.

3. **Rāṇī Māṅgliyāṇī Sarvandejī** [5]

Daughter of Māṅglīyo Gahlot Rāṇo Pātū Hamīrot (Rāṇāvat)

S - Ūdo: (see "Ūdāvat Rāṭhoṛs," *infra*).
S - Pirāg (or Prāg)
S - Sāṅgo

4. **Rāṇī Sāṅkhlī Sahodrāṃjī** (or Soharadejī)[6]

Some uncertainty surrounds the name of this Rāṇī's father. ***Murārdān***, no. 2, p. 103, refers to him as Gopāḷ Mahirājot. However, no listing for an individual of this name is found in the genealogy of the Sāṅkhlo Paṃvārs in the ***Khyāt*** of Naiṇsī. This genealogy does list a Mahirāj Gopāḷdevot, a Sāṅkhlo of the Jāṅgaḷvo ***sākh***, closely associated with Rāṭhoṛ Rāv Cūṇḍo Vīramot of Maṇḍor (d. ca. 1423). Although this Mahirāj was too far removed genealogically from Rāv Sūjo to have married a daughter to him, it is possible that this "daughter" came from one of his sons or grandsons.

S - Prithīrāj
S - Nāpo

Miscellaneous

The sources list two more sons and a daughter for Rāv Sūjo:

S - Tiloksī: (mother unknown).[7]

S - Nātho: ***Bāṅkīdās***, p. 112, records that Nātho was the daughter's son (***dohitro***) of Bhāṭī Rāvaḷ Harrāj Māldevot of Jaisaḷmer (1561-77). This information is incorrect. From other sources, it is evident that Nātho was not Rāv Sūjo's son, but rather a daughter of Bhāṭī Rāvaḷ Harrāj named Nāthūkuṃvar. Nāthūkuṃvar lived in Jodhpur at the court of her maternal grandfather, Rāṭhoṛ Rāv Mālde Gāṅgāvat (see ***infra***, Rāv Mālde Gāṅgāvat, Rāṇī no. 3, D - Sajnāṃbāī).[8]

D - Khetūbāī (mother unknown): married to Hāḍo Cahuvāṇ Rāv Nāraṇdās Bhāṇḍāvat of Būndī (d. ca. 1527). Khetūbāī's son by Rāv Nāraṇdās was Sūrajmal Nāraṇdāsot, ruler of Būndī, ca. 1527-31.[9]

---

[5] ***Bāṅkīdās***, pp. 8-9; Ojhā, 4:1:270.

[6] ***Khyāt***, 1:347; Ojhā, 4:1:270.

[7] ***Bāṅkīdās***, p. 9; Reu, 1:110.

[8] ***Bāṅkīdās***, p. 112; ***Tavārīkh Jaisalmer***, p. 53.

[9] ***Khyāt***, 1:102.

The chronicles record an interesting story about Khetūbāī and Rāv Nārandās. The Rāv is said to have been addicted to opium and accustomed to taking exceedingly large amounts each day. Khetūbāī found her husband in an open field on one occasion, where he had fallen asleep in a stupor while urinating. She threw the end of her ***sāṛī*** over him to cover him and to hide his shame. The following morning when the Rāv awoke and found his wife standing over him, he was pleased and granted her one wish that was within his power to fulfill. Khetūbāī asked only that she be allowed to keep his opium pouch. Khetūbāī gradually reduced the amount of opium the Rāv consumed each day thereafter. Before long, she also gave birth to a son named Sūrajmal.[10]

Marriage Lists

Lists of Rāv Sūjo's marriages, and his sons and daughters are contained in the following primary sources:

Jodhpur Rājya kī Khyāt, pp. 67-68.
Murārdān, no. 2, pp. 102-104.
Rāṭhoṛāṃ rī Vaṃśāvalī, MS no. 20130, ff. 46-47.

Other general references include:

Ojhā, 4:1:262, 264, 269; "Rāṭhauḍ Vaṃś rī Vigat," pp. 10-11; Reu, 1:110; ***Vigat***, 1:39; ***Vīr Vinod***, 2:807.

[10] ***Bāṅkīdās***, p. 144; ***Jodhpur Rājya kī Khyāt***, p. 69; ***Khyāt***, 1:102, 107; ***Rāṭhoṛāṃ rī Vaṃśāvalī***, MS no. 20130, f. 48. ***Bāṅkīdās***, ***Jodhpur Rājya kī Khyāt*** and ***Rāṭhoṛāṃ rī Vaṃśāvalī*** refer to Khetubāī as the daughter of another of Rāv Jodho Riṇmalot's sons, Sāṃvatsī. This information appears incorrect.

Rāv Gāṅgo Vāghāvat (8-1)

Born: Thursday, May 6, 1484
Died: May 9, 1532
Ruled: November 8, 1515 - May 9, 1532
Mother: Kuṃvrāṇī Cahuvāṇ Udanbāī (Udaikuṃvar - *pīhar* name), daughter of Cahuvāṇ Rām Kaṃvrāvat (or Rāvat Rāmkaraṇ).

Rāṇīs, Sons, and Daughters

1. **Rāṇī Sāṅkhlī Gāṅgādejī** [1]

2. **Rāṇī Sīsodṇī Uttamdejī** ***(pīhar*** name Padmāvatībāī)[2]
Daughter of Sīsodīyo Gahlot Rāṇo Sāṅgo Rāymalot of Cītoṛ (1509-28).

Uttamdejī was at her paternal home (***pīhar***) at Cītoṛ when Rāv Gāṅgo died in 1532. Her uterine brother, Udaisiṅgh Sāṅgāvat (Rāṇo of Cītoṛ, ca. 1537-72), would not allow her to become a ***satī***. Uttamdejī then waited, and when Cītoṛ came under attack from the Mughals in 1568, she took part in the ***jauhar*** within the fort.

3. **Rāṇī Devṛī Māṇakdejī** ***(pīhar*** name Padmābāī)[3]
Daughter of Devṛo Cahuvāṇ Rāv Jagmāl Lākhāvat of Sīrohī.

S - Mālde: born Friday, December 5, 1511; succeeded Rāv Gāṅgo to the Jodhpur throne.
S - Vairsal
S - Mānsiṅgh
D - Sonbāī: married to Bhāṭī Rāvaḷ Lūṇkaraṇ Jaitsīyot of Jaisaḷmer (1528-51).

4. **Rāṇī Bhāṭiyāṇī Phulāṃbāī** (***pīhar*** name)[4]
She became a ***satī*** at the time of Rāv Gāṅgo's death.

D - Rājkuṃvar (or Rāykuṃvarbāī): married to Sīsodīyo Gahlot Rāṇo Vikramaditya Sāṅgāvat of Cītoṛ (ca. 1531-36).

---

[1] Ojhā, 4:1:282.

[2] ***Bāṅkīdās***, p. 11; Ojhā, 4:1:282.

[3] ***Bāṅkīdās***, pp. 12, 154-155; ***Khyāt***, 1:136, 160-161, 2:87-89, 3:215; ***Murārdān***, no. 1, pp. 628, 637; Ojhā, 4:1:282.

[4] ***Bāṅkīdās***, p. 12; Ojhā, 4:1:282.

5. **Rāṇī Bhāṭiyāṇī Lāḍbāī** (*pīhar* name)[5]

S - Kisandās: (see "Jodho Rāṭhoṛs," no. 87, *infra*).

6. **Rāṇī Kachvāhī Candrāvaḷbāī** (*pīhar* name)[6]
She became a *satī* at the time of Rāv Gāṅgo's death.

7. **Rāṇī Sonagarī Sabīrābāī** (*pīhar* name)[7]
She became a *satī* at the time of Rāv Gāṅgo's death.

D - Cāmpābāī: married to Devṛo Cahuvāṇ Rāv Rāysiṅgh Akhairājot of Sīrohī. Her son by Rāv Rāysiṅgh was Udaisiṅgh Rāysiṅghot, who succeeded to the throne of Sīrohī.

The ***Khyāt*** of Naiṇsī records that Cāmpābāī was a wise and respected wife of Rāv Rāysiṅgh's. She was murdered in Sīrohī, however, some years after Rāv Rāysiṅgh's death as a result of conflict over succession to rule in Sīrohī.

Cāmpābāī's son, Udaisiṅgh, was a minor when Rāv Rāysiṅgh died. The Rāv had ordered before his death that the throne pass to his brother, Dūdo Akhairājot, and that Dūdo should protect and raise his son, Udaisiṅgh, to assume rulership in Sīrohī when he came of age. Dūdo Akhairājot became ***rāv*** with the support of the ***pāñc Rajpūt*** (lit. "the five Rajpūts"; the council of elders), and he fulfilled Rāv Rāysiṅgh's order, raising Udaisiṅgh to rule and keeping his own son, Mānsiṅgh Dūdāvat, away from the throne.

When Rāv Dūdo died, the ***pradhān*** and ***pāñc Rajpūt*** gave the ***ṭīko*** of succession to Cāmpābāī's son, Ūdaisiṅgh Rāysiṅghot. Rāv Udaisiṅgh had his father's brother's son, Mānsiṅgh, given the village of Lohiyāṇo for his maintenance, but soon after, had him driven from the land. Mānsiṅgh went to Mevāṛ and took service under the Rāṇo of Cītoṛ, under whom he became a devoted military servant.

Rāv Udaisiṅgh died childless not long thereafter from smallpox, and the leading Rajpūts of Sīrohī called Mānsiṅgh back from Mevāṛ and seated him on the throne. Cāmpābāī learned shortly after Rāv Mānsiṅgh's accession, however, that her son Udaisiṅgh's wife was pregnant. She sent a message to the wife, saying: "Tomorrow our grandson will be born. Who is Mānsiṅgh to enjoy the rule of this land?" This message fell into Rāv Mānsiṅgh's hands and he had both Cāmpābāī and Udaisiṅgh's pregnant wife killed.

---

5 ***Murārdān***, no. 1, p. 632; Ojhā, 4:1:282.

6 Ojhā, 4:1:282.

7 "Aitihāsik Bātāṃ," p. 38; ***Bāṅkīdās***, p. 155; ***Khyāt***, 1:135-137, 141; Ojhā, 4:1:283.

8. **Rāṇī Devṛī Jevantābāī** (or Jaivantāṃ) (*pīhar* name)[8]

S - Sāḍūl
S - Kānho

9. **Rāṇī Jhālī Premaldejī** (or Premdejī)[9]
She became a *satī* at the time of Rāv Gāṅgo's death.

10. **Rāṇī Bhāṭiyāṇī Karametījī** [10]
She became a *satī* at the time of Rāv Gāṅgo's death.

Marriage Lists

Lists of Rāv Gāṅgo's marriages, and of his sons and daughters by these marriages, are contained in the following primary sources. These sources reference all marriages except that of Rāṇī no. 10:

Jodhpur Rājya kī Khyāt, pp. 71-76.
Murārdān, no. 2, pp. 112-113.
Rāṭhoṛāṃ rī Vaṃśāvalī, MS no. 20130, ff. 52-53.

Other general references include:

Bāṅkīdās, p. 11; *Khyāt*, 3:215; *Murārdān*, no. 1, pp. 238-239, 628, 632, 637-639, no. 2, pp. 106-112, 114; Ojhā, 4:1:270-271, 281-283; "Rāṭhauḍ Vaṃś rī Vigat," p. 11; Reu, 1:115; *Vīr Vinod*, 2:807-808; *Vigat*, 1:41-42.

---

8 *Murārdān*, no. 1, pp. 638-639; Ojhā, 4:1:283.

9 Ojhā, 4:1:283.

10 "Aitihāsik Bātāṃ," p. 38.

Rāv Mālde Gāṅgāvat (9-1)

Born: Friday, December 5, 1511
Died: November 7, 1562[1]
Ruled: May 21, 1532 - November 7, 1562
Mother: Rāṇī Devṛī Māṇakdejī (*pīhar* name Padmābāī), daughter of Devṛo Cahuvāṇ Rāv Jagmāl Lākhāvat of Sīrohī.

Rāṇīs, Sons, and Daughters

1. **Baṛī Rāṇī Cūṇḍāvat Sīsodṇī Pohpāvatījī** (*pīhar* name Parvatībāī)
She went to her *pīhar* to live, and died there.

2. **Rāṇī Bhāṭiyāṇī Ūmādejī** (*pīhar* name Rāmkuṃvar)[2]
Daughter of Bhāṭī Rāvaḷ Lūṇkaraṇ Jaitsīyot of Jaisaḷmer (1528-51). Rāvaḷ Lūṇkaraṇ was himself a daughter's son of the Bāhaṛmer Rāṭhoṛs. His mother was Bāhaṛmerī Rāṭhoṛ Lāchamdejī (*pīhar* name Sītābāī).

Ūmādejī was married to Rāv Mālde on Friday, March 30, 1537 at Jaisaḷmer. She became angry with the Rāv in 1538-39 while at Ajmer, and thereafter remained apart from him. When Rāv Mālde drove his son, Rām Māldevot (see Rāṇī no. 16, S - Rām, *infra*), from Mārvāṛ in 1547-48, Ūmādejī joined this son in exile in Mevāṛ. Ūmādejī was at the village of Kelvo in Mevāṛ, which was a village of Rām's *vasī*, on Tuesday, November 10, 1562 when news of Rāv Mālde's death arrived, and she became a *satī* there. Rām Māldevot made preparations to ride to Jodhpur even before the rite of Ūmādejī's *satī* had begun, and Ūmādejī is said to have cursed Rām at the time of her burning, saying that a woman should never entrust herself to a co-wife's (*sok*'s) son.

A cenotaph (*chatrī*) was built for Ūmādejī at Kelvo village.

Sources do not specify the reasons for Ūmādejī's anger at Rāv Mālde. Informants of the author's in Jodhpur indicate that this anger grew out of Rāv Mālde's favoritism for a court singer/dancing girl (*oḷgaṇī*).

3. **Rāṇī Jhālī Nāraṅgdejī** (or Navraṅgdejī; *pīhar* name Ardhanbāī)[3]
Some uncertainty surrounds the identity of this Rāṇī's father. ***Rāṭhoṛāṃ rī Vaṃśāvalī***, MS no. 20130, f. 63, lists him as Jhālo Mero Sūjāvat. No individual by this name appears in the genealogy of the Jhālos in the ***Khyāt*** of

---

[1] This date is from Ojhā, 4:1:325, and ***Jodhpur Rājya kī Khyāt***, p. 76. ***Bāṅkīdās***, p. 18, provides the alternate date of November 10, 1562.

[2] "Aitihāsik Bātāṃ," p. 56; ***Bāṅkīdās***, p. 18; ***Jaisalmer rī Khyāt***, p. 67; ***Khyāt***, 2:86, 88; Ojhā, 4:1:326, n. 1; ***Tavārīkh Jaisalmer***, pp. 49-50; ***Vigat***, 1:53-55.

[3] "Aitihāsik Bātāṃ," p. 56; ***Khyāt***, 2:264; ***Vigat***, 1:55.

Naiṇsī. The name Mālo Siṅghot does appear in this genealogy, and one of Mālo's sons was a military servant of Rāv Mālde, holding several villages in ***paṭo*** from him. Mālo himself was also a close relation of other Jhālos who married daughters to Rāv Mālde. It is possible that the name of Rāṇī Nāraṅgdejī's father was Mālo Siṅghot, not Mero Sūjāvat. Without further evidence, however, his identity remains in doubt.

Rāṇī Nāraṅgdejī became a ***satī*** at the time of Rāv Mālde's death.

D - Rājkuṃvarbāī[4]: married to Hāḍo Cahuvāṇ Rāv Surtāṇ Sūrajmalot of Būndī (ca. 1531-54). Rāv Mālde murdered a daughter of the Hāḍos who had been given to him in marriage (see ***infra***, Rāṇī no. 21) sometime after Rājkuṃvarbāī was married. The Hāḍos killed Rājkuṃvarbāī in retaliation. The exchange of brides between the Hāḍos of Būndī and the Rāṭhoṛs of Jodhpur ceased for some time thereafter.

D - Pohpāṃvatībāī[5]: married to Āhāṛo Gahlot Rāvaḷ Āskaraṇ Prithīrājot of Ḍūṅgarpur (ca. 1549-80). She became a ***satī*** at the time of the Rāvaḷ's death.

D - Kankāvatībāī[6]: married to the Pātsāh of Gujarat, Maḥmūd III (1537-54). Her married name was Nāraṅgdejī. Kankāvatībāī went to live with her sister, Sajnāṃbāī (see ***infra***) in Jaisaḷmer after the Pātsāh's death, bringing much wealth with her. She died in Jaisaḷmer.

D - Haṃsbāī[7]: married to Sekhāvat Kachvāho Rāv Lūṇkaraṇ Sūjāvat of Amarsar.[8] Her son by Rāv Lūṇkaraṇ was Māṇakrāv Lūṇkaraṇot.

D - Ratanāvatībāī[9]: married to Paṭhāṇ Hājī Khān. She came in mourning to her half-brother, Rāv Candrasen Māldevot, at Jodhpur after Hājī Khān's death. She followed Rāv Candrasen into exile from Jodhpur in southern Mārvāṛ and the Arāvallīs in the 1570s and remained with him thereafter. Rāv Candrasen's successor, Moṭo Rājā Udaisiṅgh Māldevot (1583-95), sent her to Nāgaur to live. She died there in 1592-93. A ***chatrī*** was built at Nāgaur in her memory.

---

[4] ***Bāṅkīdās***, p. 20; ***Khyāt***, 1:109; Ojhā, 4:1:327; ***Vigat***, 1:53.

[5] ***Bāṅkīdās***, pp. 20, 107; Ojhā, 4:1:327; ***Vigat***, 1:52.

[6] ***Bāṅkīdās***, p. 20; ***Vigat***, 1:52. Neither ***Jodhpur Rājya kī Khyāt*** nor ***Rāṭhoṛāṃ rī Vaṃśāvalī***, MS no. 20130, reference this daughter or her marriage.

[7] ***Bāṅkīdās***, p. 20; ***Khyāt***, 1:319; Ojhā, 4:1:328; ***Vigat***, 1:52.

[8] Amarsar: located forty miles due north of Jaipur in central Rājasthān.

[9] ***Bāṅkīdās***, p. 20; ***Vigat***, 1:52. Neither ***Jodhpur Rājya kī Khyāt*** nor ***Rāṭhoṛāṃ rī Vaṃśāvalī***, MS no. 20130, reference this daughter or her marriage.

D - Sajnāṃbāī[10]: married to Bhāṭī Rāvaḷ Harrāj Māldevot of Jaisaḷmer (1561-77). Rāvaḷ Harrāj was himself a daughter's son of the Bāhaṛmer Rāṭhoṛs. His mother was the daughter of Bāhaṛmer Rāṭhoṛ Rāv Punrāj. Sajnāṃbāī's married name was Harakhāndejī. Her son by Rāvaḷ Harrāj was Bhīṃv Harrājot, successor to the Jaisaḷmer throne (1577-1613). One of her daughters by Rāvaḷ Harrāj named Nāthūkaṃvar, lived at her maternal grandfather Rāv Mālde's court at Jodhpur.

D - Manāvatībāī[11]: married to Vāghelo Soḷaṅkī Vīrbhadro Rāmcandrāvat, Rāv of Bāndhavgaḍh.

Rāṇī Jhālī Nāraṅgdejī had three or four other daughters, all of whom died young.

4. **Rāṇī Jhālī Hīrādejī** [12]

Granddaughter of Jhālo Jaito Sajāvat, a military servant of Rāv Mālde holding the village of Khairvo[13] in eastern Mārvāṛ in *paṭo*, and daughter of Jaito's son, Māno Jaitāvat of Haḷvad. Jhālo Jaito Sajāvat also married a daughter to Rāv Mālde (see *infra*, Rāṇī no. 5).

The ***Vigat*** of Naiṇsī, 1:55, lists this Rāṇī's father incorrectly as Jhālo Rāysiṅgh Mānsiṅghot of Haḷvad. Jhālo Rāysiṅgh's son, Candrasen Rāysiṅghot, received a daughter in marriage from one of Rāv Mālde's sons, Udaisiṅgh Māldevot (see ***infra***, Moṭo Rājā Udaisiṅgh Māldevot, Rāṇī no. 9, D - Satyabhāmābāī). This marriage may account for the confusion in the ***Vigat***.

S - Rāymal: one of his daughters was married to Prince Dānyāl on October 2, 1595.

D - Indrāvatībāī: married to Rājāvat Kachvāho Rājā Āskaraṇ Bhīṃvrājot of Gwalior.

5. **Rāṇī Jhālī Sarūpdejī** [14]

Daughter of Jhalo Jaito Sajavat, a military servant of Rāv Mālde's holding the village of Khairvo in *paṭo*.

---

[10] ***Bāṅkīdās***, pp. 20, 112; ***Jaisalmer rī Khyāt***, p. 42; ***Khyāt***, 2:92, 98; Ojhā, 4:1:328; ***Tavārīkh Jaisalmer***, p. 53; ***Vigat***, 1:52.

[11] ***Khyāt***, 1:133; Ojhā, 4:1:329; ***Murārdān***, no. 2, does not reference this daughter or her place of marriage.

[12] ***Akbar Nāma***, 3:1041; ***Bāṅkīdās***, p. 20; ***Khyāt***, 1:303, 2:256, 264; ***Murārdān***, no. 1, p. 605; Ojhā, 4:1:326, n. 4, 329; ***Vigat***, 1:55.

[13] Khairvo village: located eleven miles southeast of Pālī in eastern Mārvāṛ.

[14] "Aitihāsik Bātāṃ," p. 56; ***Bāṅkīdās***, p. 18; ***Khyāt***, 2:262, 264; ***Murārdān***, no. 1, p. 598; Ojhā, 4:1:326, n. 1; ***Vigat***, 1:47-48, 55, 65, 76, 2:5.

Several sources list Rāṇī Sarūpdejī's father incorrectly as Jhālo Sūjo Rājāvat (or Rājo Sūjāvat). ***Rāṭhoṛāṃ rī Vaṃśāvalī***, MS no. 20130, f. 63, records that Sarūpde was sent in ***ḍoḷo*** to Rāv Mālde.

Sarūpdejī attempted to become a ***satī*** at the time of Rāv Mālde's death in November of 1562, but her son, Candrasen, who succeeded to the Jodhpur throne, prevented her and had her put in confinement in order to keep her alive. Candrasen eventually released Sarūpdejī, and she then became a ***satī***. She is said to have cursed Rāv Candrasen and his kingdom because he prevented her from burning with Rāv Mālde.[15]

S - Udaisiṅgh: born Sunday, January 13, 1538. He succeeded his younger brother to the Jodhpur throne in 1583 as the Moṭo Rājā.

S - Candrasen: born Saturday, July 30, 1541. He succeeded Rāv Mālde to the Jodhpur throne.

6. **Rāṇī Cahuvāṇ Indrādejī** (***pīhar*** name Indāṃbāī)[16]
Daughter of Cahuvāṇ Rāv Daḷpat (identity uncertain).
Indrādejī became a ***satī*** at the time of Rāv Mālde's death.

D - Durgāvatībāī: married to Kachvāho Rājā Bhagvantdās Bhārmalot of Āmber (ca. 1574-89).

7. **Rāṇī Jādam/Jādav Rājbāī** (***pīhar*** name)[17]
Sister of Rāv Maṇḍlik (identity uncertain). She became a ***satī*** at the time of Rav Malde's death.

S - Āskaraṇ: born on Thursday, October 15, 1551. He died at the age of five years.

8. **Rāṇī Vāghelī Pohpāṃvatībāī** (***pīhar*** name)
She died at her ***pīhar***.

9. **Rāṇī Bhāṭiyāṇī Ratanbāī** (***pīhar*** name)[18]
Daughter of Bhāṭī Mahirāvaṇ Jaitsīyot of Jaisaḷmer. Bhāṭī Mahirāvaṇ was a son of Rāvaḷ Jaitsī Devīdāsot (1491-1528) and a brother of Rāvaḷ Lūṇkaraṇ Jaitsīyot (1528-51).

Rāṇī Ratanbāī went to Mathurajī on a pilgrimage and died there.

---

[15] The ***Vigat*** of Naiṇsī, 1:76, records incorrectly that Udaisiṅgh's and Candrasen's mother was Devṛī Padmā, the daughter of Devṛo Cahuvāṇ Rāv Jagmāl Lākhāvat of Sīrohī. Devṛī Padmābāī (married name Māṇakdejī) was their grandmother (see ***supra***).

[16] "Aitihāsik Bātāṃ," p. 54; ***Khyāt***, 1:297; Ojhā, 4:1:329; ***Vigat***, 1:56.

[17] "Aitihāsik Bātāṃ," p. 56; ***Murārdān***, no. 1, p. 626; Ojhā, 4:1:327, n. 3; ***Vigat***, 1:56.

[18] ***Khyāt***, 2:28; ***Tavārīkh Jaisalmer***, p. 49.

10. **Rāṇī Kelhaṇ Bhāṭiyāṇī Kisnāvatījī**
She became a *satī* at the time of Rāv Mālde's death.

11. **Rāṇī Jāmvāḷī Kaṭhiyāṃjī** [19]
Daughter of Bālo Jagmāl Sūrāvat. She went to Puṣkarjī and died there in 1607-08.

12. **Rāṇī Bhāṭiyāṇī Jashar** [20]
She was married at Meṛto and became a *satī* at Reyāṃ village[21] at the time of Rāv Mālde's death.

13. **Rāṇī Sonagarī Dammājī** [22]
She died during Rāv Mālde's lifetime.

S - Gopāḷdās: he became angry with Rāv Mālde and went to Īḍar to live. While there, he became involved with Vāghelī Udhal, wife of Cāvṛo Rāvaḷ Āso. Vāghelī Udhal eventually came to live in Gopāḷdās's home, and in retaliation, the Cāvṛos killed Gopāḷdās. The *vair* which then arose between the Rāṭhoṛs of Jodhpur and the Cāvṛos of Īḍar was not settled until the time of Rāv Mālde's successor, Rāv Candrasen Māldevot (1562-81). The Cāvṛos married a daughter to Rāv Candrasen's son, Āskaraṇ, and then to Rāv Candrasen's elder uterine brother, Moṭo Rājā Udaisiṅgh Māldevot (see *infra*, Rāv Candrasen Māldevot, Rāṇī no. 4, S - Āskaraṇ, and Moṭo Rājā Udaisiṅgh Māldevot, Rāṇī no. 12).

14. **Rāṇī Sonagarī Lāḍbāī** (*pīhar* name)[23]
She died during Rāv Mālde's lifetime.

S - Prithīrāj: Rāv Mālde sent Prithīrāj and his paternal relation, Pratāpsī Vāghāvat,[24] with Prithīrāj's uterine sister, Lālbāī (see *infra*), when he gave Lālbāī to Sher Shāh Sūr in *ḍoḷo* following the battle of

---

[19] *Vigat*, 1:56.

[20] "Aitihāsik Bātāṃ," p. 56; *Vigat*, 1:56.

[21] Reyāṃ village: located fifteen miles southeast of Meṛto in eastern Mārvāṛ.

[22] *Murārdān*, no. 1, pp. 626-627; Ojhā, 4:1:327, n. 4.

[23] *Bāṅkīdās*, p. 20; *Murārdān*, no. 1, p. 626.

[24] Pratāpsī Vāghāvat was a son of Jodho Rāṭhoṛ Vāgho Sūjāvat. See *infra*, "Jodho Rāṭhoṛs," Vāgho Sūjāvat (no. 83).

Samel[25] in January of 1544. Prithīrāj apparently remained outside of Mārvāṛ for the remainder of his life, for he later died in north India.

S - Kānho

D - Lālbāī: given to Sher Shāh Sūr in *ḍoḷo* in January of 1544 following Rāv Mālde's defeat at the battle of Samel.

15. **Rāṇī Sonagari Pūrbāī** (or Purāṃbāī) (***pīhar*** name)[26]

Daughter of Sonagaro Cahuvāṇ Akhairāj Riṇdhīrot, a military servant of Rāv Mālde's holding the village of Pālī[27] in ***paṭo*** (see ***infra***, "Sonagaro Cahuvāṇs," no. 9).

Rāṇī Pūrbāī became a ***satī*** at the time of Rāv Mālde's death.

16. **Rāṇī Kachvāhī Lāchapdejī** (or Lāchaḷdejī)[28]

Daughter of Sekhāvat Kachvāho Ratansī Sekhāvat of Amarsar.

Rāṇī Lāchapdejī was living in the village of Kelvo of Mevāṛ at the time of Rāv Mālde's death. She had gone there to live with her son, Rām Māldevot (see ***infra***), who was in exile from Mārvāṛ. Rāṇī Bhāṭiyāṇī Ūmādejī (see ***supra***, Rāṇī no. 2) was with her in Kelvo, and both she and Rāṇī Ūmādejī became ***satīs*** at Kelvo upon receipt of the news of the Rāv's death.

S - Rām: two dates of birth are given for Rām, February 12, 1530 and 1531-32 (month and day unspecified).

Rāv Mālde drove Rām from Mārvāṛ following Rām's attempt to usurp power at Jodhpur in 1547-48. Rām went first to Mevāṛ, where he remained for some years with his mother and Rāṇī Bhāṭiyāṇī Ūmādejī, who had become disaffected with the Rāv very shortly after her marriage and had joined him in his exile. Rām eventually took service under the Mughals, from whom he received Sojhat in eastern Mārvāṛ in ***jāgīr***. He came into direct conflict with Rāv Mālde's successor to the Jodhpur throne, Rāv Candrasen Māldevot (1562-81), over control of lands in Mārvāṛ, and it was only with Mughal assistance that this dispute was resolved. Rām died at Sojhat on either May 9 or May 23, 1574.

D - Jasodābāī: married to Khānzāda Khān Muḥammad Daulat Khān of Nāgaur (see "Khānzāda Khāns," no. 154, ***infra***).

---

[25] Samel village: located twenty-four miles southwest of Ajmer.

[26] "Aitihāsik Bātāṃ," p. 56; ***Vigat***, 1:56.

[27] Pālī village: located forty miles southeast of Jodhpur.

[28] ***Bāṅkīdās***, pp. 18, 20; ***Jodhpur Rājya kī Khyāt***, p. 103; ***Khyāt***, 1:327; ***Murārdān***, no. 1, p. 591; Ojhā, 4:1:326, n. 3; Reu, 1:144, n. 1; ***Vigat***, 1:55.

17. **Rāṇī Kachvāhī Sahodrāṃjī** [29]

Daughter of Kachvāho Bhīṃvrāj Prithīrājot of Āmber. Bhīṃvrāj was a daughter's son (*dohitro*) of Bīkāner Rāṭhoṛ Rāv Lūṇkaraṇ Bīkāvat (1505-26) and son of Kachvāho Rājā Prithīrāj Candrasenot (1503-27).

Rāṇī Sahodrāṃjī made an oath to Rāv Mālde that she would not remain behind him after his death. She was at her *pīhar* when news of the Rāv's death came, and members of her paternal family would not allow her to become a *satī*. She then began to fast, refusing all foods except buttermilk (*chāch*) to drink. She died three months later.

18. **Rāṇī Soḍhī Kasūmbhābāī** (*pīhar* name)[30]

Daughter of Soḍho Paṃvār Rāṇo Pato (or Pātaḷ) Gāṅgāvat of Ūmarkoṭ. This Rāṇī was brought from Ūmarkoṭ to Maṇḍor in *ḍoḷo* and married there. She became a *satī* at the time of Rāv Mālde's death.

19. **Rāṇī Soḍhī Lohaṛījī**

She died at Sīvāṇo in Mārvāṛ during the time of Rāv Mālde's exile from Jodhpur following his defeat at the battle of Samel in January of 1544.

D - (name unknown): died very young in 1555-56.

20. **Rāṇī Āhāṛī Ratanādejī** (*pīhar* name Lachbāī)[31]

Daughter of Āhāṛo Gahlot Rāvaḷ Prithīrāj Udaisiṅghot (Gāṅgāvat) of Ḍūṅgarpur (ca. 1527-1549).

S - Ratansī: born on Sunday, October 6, 1532.
S - Bhojrāj: born January 24, 1534.

21. **Rāṇī Hāḍī Rambhāvatījī** (*pīhar* name Dropdābāī)[32]

Daughter of Hāḍo Cahuvāṇ Rāv Sūrajmal Nāraṇdāsot of Būndī (ca. 1527-31). Rāv Sūrajmal was a daughter's son (*dohitro*) of Rāṭhoṛ Rāv Sūjo Jodhāvat of Jodhpur (ca. 1492-1515) (see *supra*, Sūjo Jodhāvat, D - Khetūbāī [mother unknown]).

Rāv Mālde drove this Rāṇī from the palace at Jodhpur and had her killed when he saw her laughing at his younger uterine brother, Mānsiṅgh (see *supra*, Rāv Gāṅgo Vāghāvat, Rāṇī no. 3, S- Mānsiṅgh). In retaliation, the Hāḍos killed

---

[29] ***Khyāt***, 1:290, 302.

[30] "Aitihāsik Bātāṃ," p. 56; ***Khyāt***, 1:358; ***Vigat***, 1:56.

[31] ***Bāṅkīdās***, p. 19; G. H. Ojhā, ***Ḍūṅgarpur Rājya kā Itihās*** (Ajmer: Vedic Yantralaya, V. S. 1992 [A. D. 1935]), pp. 84-89; ***Khyāt***, 1:70; ***Murārdān***, no. 1, pp. 613, 617; Ojhā, 4:1:327, n. 1, n. 3; Reu, 1:144, n. 2, n. 3; ***Vigat***, 1:55.

[32] ***Bāṅkīdās***, p. 20; ***Khyāt***, 1:102; ***Murārdān***, no. 1, p. 622; Ojhā, 4:1:327; ***Vigat***, 1:59.

Rājkuṃvarbāī, a daughter of Rāv Mālde's who had been married to Hāḍo Rāv Sūrajmal's son, Surtāṇ Sūrajmalot (see ***supra***, Rāṇī no. 3, D - Rājkuṃvarbāī).

S - Vikramādit

22. **Rāṇī Bhāṭiyāṇī Dharbāī** (***pīhar*** name)[33]

There is some confusion in the texts regarding the identity of this Rāṇī's father. His name is variously given as both Bhāṭī Prithīrāj Dujaṇsalot of Vikūmpur and simply Bhāṭī Prithīrāj. There is no listing for a Bhāṭī Prithīrāj Dujaṇsalot in the genealogy of the Kelhaṇ Bhāṭīs recorded in the ***Khyāt*** of Naiṇsī. This name appears, therefore, to be incorrect. A Bhāṭī Prithīrāj Netsīyot does appear in this genealogy. He was a Khīṃvo Bhāṭī and Rāv of Vairsalpur, fourth in line of descent from Rāv Jaitsī Khīṃvāvat. This Bhāṭī Prithīrāj was probably Bhāṭiyāṇī Dharbāī's father.

The confusion about names and designation of the proper branch of Bhāṭīs may be related to the following: a Kelhaṇ Bhāṭī named Rāv Dujaṇsal Varsiṅghot did marry a daughter to Rāv Mālde's son, Udaisiṅgh Māldevot (see ***infra***, Moṭo Rājā Udaisiṅgh Māldevot, Rāṇī no. 4). The Khīṃvo Bhāṭīs of Vairsalpur are a branch of the Kelhaṇ Bhāṭīs of Vikūmpur.

Rāṇī Bhāṭiyāṇī Dharbāī was married at Maṇḍor and died in 1599-1600.

S - Bhāṇ
D - Mīrāṃbāī: married to the Bagṛīyo Cahuvāṇs of the Bāgaṛ region of Mevāṛ.

23. **Rāṇī Ṭāṅkaṇī Jamnādejī**[34]

This Rāṇī's father is variously listed in the texts as Kisno Kalhaṇot and Vīko Kisnāvat. It has not been possible to identify him further from sources available.

Rāṇī Jamnādejī became a ***satī*** at the time of Rāv Mālde's death.

D - Bālhabāī: married either to Soḍho Paṃvār Rāysal Gāṅgāvat, a son of Rāṇo Gāṅgo Cāmpāvat of Ūmarkoṭ, or to Soḍho Paṃvār Rāṇo Varsiṅgh (Vairsī) Nāraṇot of Ūmarkoṭ (sources are unclear). She came back to Jodhpur to live after her marriage and was given the village of Sāṃvatkuvo[35] in ***paṭo*** for her maintenance. She died in 1603-04.

---

[33] ***Khyāt***, 2:121, 128; ***Murārdān***, no. 1, p. 617; Ojhā, 4:1:327; ***Vigat***, 1:56.

[34] "Aitihāsik Bātāṃ," p. 56; ***Bāṅkīdās***, p. 20; ***Khyāt***, 1:358; Ojhā, 4:1:329; ***Vigat***, 1:52-53, 55.

[35] Sāṃvatkuvo village: located thirty-two miles north-northeast of Jodhpur.

24. **Rāṇī Candrāvatījī** [36]
Daughter of Candrāvat Sīsodīyo Gahlot Rāv Acḷo Rāymalot of Rāmpuro.

25. **Rāṇī Sīsodṇī Likhmī** (***pīhar*** name)[37]
Daughter of Sīsodīyo Gahlot Rāṇo Udaisiṅgh Sāṅgāvat of Cītoṛ (ca. 1537-72).

Miscellaneous

The texts list varying numbers of sons for Rāv Mālde, ranging between twelve and twenty-two. The total number appears to be twenty-one or twenty-two. Several of these sons were born of court concubines or prostitutes (***pātar***), and of court singers (***oḷgaṇī***). Sons born of the latter include[38]:

Of ***pātar***: Ḍūṅgarsī and Mahesdās, born of Ṭīpū (or Ṭīvū) Guḍī, a daughter of Māno Guḍo of Rohila.

Of ***oḷgaṇī***: Īsardās, Jaimal, Likhmīdās, Netsī, Rūpsiṅgh, Tejsiṅgh, Ṭhākursī, Tiloksī.

(Unknown): Rāypāḷ, Jasvantsiṅgh, Kalyāṇdās.

Rāv Mālde had one daughter who was born of a concubine, and several others whose mothers' names are unknown. These were:

D - Bāghrāva (mother unknown): sent in ***ḍoḷo*** to the Vāghelos.[39]

D - Sūjkuṃvarbāī (mother unknown): married to Bhāṭī Rāvaḷ Mālde Lūṇkaraṇot of Jaisaḷmer (1551-1561). Rāvaḷ Mālde's mother was Īḍarecī Rāṭhoṛ Haṃsābāī, the daughter of Rāv Jaimal of Īḍar.[40]

D - Kalāvatībāī (mother unknown): married to Bhāṭī Akhairāj.

D - Gāṅgābāī (mother unknown): married to Devṛo Cahuvāṇ Mero.

D - Rukhmāvatī: daughter of Ṭīpū (or Ṭīvū) Guḍī, a ***pātar*** of Rāv Mālde. Rukhmāvatī was sent in ***ḍoḷo*** to the Mughal Emperor Akbar.[41]

---

[36] ***Khyāt***, 3:246, 248.

[37] ***Rāṭhoṛāṃ rī Vaṃśāvalī***, MS no. 20130, f. 64.

[38] ***Bāṅkīdās***, p. 19; ***Murārdān***, no. 1, pp. 586, 591, 598-599, 605, 615-617, 622-623; Ojhā, 4:1:326-327; Reu, 1:144.

[39] ***Vigat***, 1:53.

[40] ***Khyāt***, 2:91; ***Tavārīkh Jaisalmer***, pp. 50, 52.

[41] ***Bāṅkīdās***, p. 20; Ojhā, 4:1:327, n. 6; ***Murārdān***, no. 2, pp. 148-149; ***Rāṭhoṛāṃ rī Vaṃśāvalī***, MS no. 20130, f. 64.

Marriage Lists

Lists of Rāv Mālde's marriages and of his sons and daughters are contained in the following primary texts, which reference all marriages except that of Rāṇī no. 25:

Jodhpur Rājya kī Khyāt, pp. 76, 96-101.
Murārdān, no. 2, pp. 139-147.
Rāṭhoṛāṃ rī Vaṃśāvalī, MS no. 20130, ff. 62-64.

Other general references include:

Dasharatha Sharma, *Lectures on Rajput History and Culture* (Delhi: Motilal Banarsidass, 1970), p. 144; *Murārdān*, no. 1, pp. 586, 591, 598-599, 605, 615-617, 622-623, 625-628, no. 2, pp. 137-138; Ojhā, 4:1:284, 325-329; "Rāṭhauḍ Vaṃś rī Vigat," pp. 11-13; Reu, 1:144; *Vīr Vinod*, 2:809-813.

Rāv Candrasen Māldevot (10-1)

Born: Saturday, July 30, 1541
Died: January 11, 1581
Ruled: December 31, 1562 - January 11, 1581
Mother: Rāṇī Jhālī Sarūpdejī, daughter of Jhālo Jaito Sajāvat, a military servant of Rāv Mālde's holding the village of Khairvo[1] in ***paṭo***.

Rāṇīs, Sons, and Daughters

1. **Baṛī Rāṇī Cahuvāṇ Kalyāṇdejī** [2]
Daughter of Sācoro Cahuvāṇ Hamīr Vīkāvat. Kalyāṇdejī died during Rāv Candrasen's lifetime.

S - Ugrasen: born on Wednesday, August 2, 1559. Ugrasen was killed in 1582-83 following his murder of his younger half-brother, Āskaraṇ (see ***infra***, Rāṇī no. 4, S - Āskaraṇ).

D - Jāmotībāī: married to Ḍūṅgarot Devṛo Cahuvāṇ Vījo Harrājot at Bhādrājuṇ[3] in Mārvāṛ while Rāv Candrasen lived there during his exile from Jodhpur.[4] Jāmotībāī became a ***satī*** at the time of Vījo Harrājot's death in 1588.

2. **Rāṇī Narūkī Kachvāhī Suhāgdejī** [5]
Daughter of Narūko Kachvāho Vīro.
Rāṇī Narūkī remained behind Rāv Candrasen after his death. She went to live at her ***pīhar*** in the village of Phāgī.

---

[1] Khairvo village: located eleven miles southeast of Pālī in eastern Mārvāṛ, and fifty miles south-southeast of Jodhpur.

[2] ***Bāṅkīdās***, p. 22; ***Khyāt***, 1:163; ***Murārdān***, no. 1, p. 600; Ojhā, 4:1:350-351, n. 3.

[3] Bhādrājuṇ village: located forty-eight miles south-southwest of Jodhpur.

[4] ***Bāṅkīdās***, p. 22, gives the date ***V. S.*** 1636 (1579-80) for this marriage at Bhādrājuṇ. This date appears incorrect. Rāv Candrasen began his exile from Jodhpur in December of 1565 when he vacated the fort and took up residence at Bhādrājuṇ. His exile continued until November of 1570, when he met with Emperor Akbar at Nāgaur and submitted to him. Rāv Candrasen gave up Bhādrājuṇ to the Mughals shortly thereafter in February of 1571 (Cf. Ojhā, 4:1:335-338). The correct date for this marriage is perhaps 1569. A half-sister of Jāmotībāī's named Karametībāī was married at Bhādrājuṇ in 1569 (see ***infra***, Rāṇī no. 3, D - Karametībāī).

[5] ***Bāṅkīdās***, pp. 22, 159; ***Khyāt***, 1:297; ***Murārdān***, no. 1, pp. 599-600, no. 2, p. 164; Ojhā, 4:1:351.

S - Rāysiṅgh: born in 1557-58.

D - Āskuṃvarbāī: married to Kachvāho Rājā Mānsiṅgh Bhagvantdāsot of Āmber (1589-1614).

D - Rukhmāvatībāī: sent in *ḍoḷo* to the Mughal Emperor Akbar.[6]

3. **Rāṇī Bhāṭiyāṇī Sobhāgdejī** (*pīhar* name Kankānde)[7]
Daughter of Bhāṭī Rāvaḷ Harrāj Māldevot of Jaisaḷmer (1561-77). Sobhāgdejī became a *satī* at the time of Rāv Candrasen's death.

D - Karametībāī: married to Sīsodīyo Gahlot Rāṇo Udaisiṅgh Sāṅgāvat of Cītoṛ (ca. 1537-72) on either December 9 or December 13, 1569 at Bhādrājuṇ in Mārvāṛ, during Rāv Candrasen's exile from Jodhpur.

4. **Rāṇī Sīsodṇī Sūrajdejī** (*pīhar* name Cāndābāī) [8]
Daughter of Sīsodīyo Gahlot Rāṇo Udaisiṅgh Sāṅgāvat of Cītoṛ.
Sūrajdejī was married to Rāv Candrasen on Tuesday, April 23, 1560 at Cītoṛ. She survived Rāv Candrasen and received the village of Sivrāṛ[9] in *paṭo* for her maintenance from Rāv Candrasen's successor to the Jodhpur throne, Moṭo Rājā Udaisiṅgh Māldevot (1583-95). Pañcolī Neto and Bhaṇḍārī Māno went with her from Jodhpur to Sivrāṛ and served under her there. She left Mārvāṛ in 1584-85 and settled in Mathurajī, where she died in 1613-14.

S - Āskaraṇ: born on Monday, June 19, 1570. Āskaraṇ's half-brother, Ugrasen Candrasenot (see *supra*, Rāṇī no. 1, S - Ugrasen), killed Āskaraṇ on March 25, 1582 when he was but twelve years old. *Murārdān*, no. 1, p. 600, records that the murder took place while Āskaraṇ lay asleep on a cot at the village of Sirīyārī,[10] and that Khetsīyot Rāṭhoṛ Sekho Sāṅkarot killed Ugrasen in turn in 1582-83. Āskaraṇ's wife, Cāvṛī Gopāḷdejī, became a *satī* at Jodhpur following Āskaraṇ's murder.

---

[6] Neither *Jodhpur Rājya kī Khyāt* nor *Rāṭhoṛāṃ rī Vaṃśāvalī*, MS no. 20130, list Rukhmāvatībāī as a daughter of Rāv Candrasen's.

[7] "Aitihāsik Bātāṃ," p. 80; *Bāṅkīdās*, p. 22; *Khyāt*, 2:92, 97; Ojhā, 4:1:351; *Vigat*, 1:69.

[8] "Aitihāsik Bātāṃ," pp. 78, 87-89; *Bāṅkīdās*, pp. 21-22; *Murārdān*, no. 1, p. 600; Ojhā, 4:1:350, n. 4, 351; *Vigat*, 1:70.

[9] Sivrāṛ village: located nine miles southeast of Sojhat.

[10] Sirīyārī village: located twenty miles southeast of Sojhat in eastern Mārvāṛ.

5. **Rāṇī Kachvāhī Kaṅkūndebāī** (or Kukamdebāī; ***pīhar*** name)
The identity of this Rāṇī's father is uncertain. The texts list him by the name of Kachvāho Jogī. It has not been possible to identify him further from materials available.

6. **Rāṇī Devṛī Ahaṅkārdejī** [11]
Daughter of Devṛo Cahuvāṇ Rāv Mānsiṅgh Dūdāvat of Sīrohī (d. ca. 1575).
Ahaṅkārdejī was married on Tuesday, June 22, 1568 at Sīrohī. She survived Rāv Candrasen. She went to Mathurajī in 1602-03 and she died there.

D - Kamlāvatībāī: married to Rājāvat Kachvāho Gordhan Āskaraṇot, a son of Rājā Āskaraṇ Bhīṃvrājot of Gwalior.
D - Rāykuṃvarbāī: married to Kachvāho Sabaḷsiṅgh Mānsiṅghot, a son of Rājā Mānsiṅgh Bhagvantdāsot of Āmber (1589-1614). She became a ***satī*** at the time of Sabaḷsiṅgh's death.
D - (name unknown): married to Sīsodīyo Gahlot Rāṇo Udaisiṅgh Sāṅgāvat of Cītoṛ (ca. 1537-72).

7. **Rāṇī Bhāṭiyāṇī Harakhāndejī** (***pīhar*** name Sahodarāṃbāī)[12]
Daughter of Kelhaṇ Bhāṭī Rām Pañcāiṇot of Vairsalpur.
Harakhāndejī survived Rāv Candrasen, and Rāv Candrasen's successor, Moṭo Rājā Udaisiṅgh Māldevot (1583-95), gave her the village of Gopāsar[13] in ***paṭo*** for her maintenance. She died at Gopāsar in November or December of 1640.

8. **Rāṇī Bhāṭiyāṇī Premaldejī** [14]
The identity of this Rāṇī's father is uncertain. The texts list both Kelhaṇ Bhāṭī Rāv Jaiso Varsiṅghot of Pūṅgaḷ and Rāv Jaiso's paternal nephew, Rāv Ḍūṅgarsī Dujaṇsalot, as her father. Rāv Jaiso Varsiṅghot appears to be correct. Textual confusion may result from the fact that Rāv Ḍūṅgarsī also married a daughter of Rāv Candrasen's (see ***infra***, Rāṇī no. 12).
Premaldejī died at Vikūmpur in 1626-27.

---

[11] ***Khyāt***, 1:140-142, 298, 303.

[12] ***Ibid.***, 2:119.

[13] ***Vigat***, 1:333, lists a village by the name of Gopāsarīyo, located twenty-seven miles north-northwest of Jodhpur. Gopāsar and Gopāsarīyo are probably the same village.

[14] ***Khyāt***, 2:127-128.

9. **Rāṇī Bhāṭiyāṇī Jagīsāṃbāī** (*pīhar* name)[15]
Daughter of Jeso Bhāṭī Meho Tejsīyot, a military servant of Rāv Candrasen's.

Jagīsāṃbāī became a *satī* at the time of Rāv Candrasen's death.

10. **Rāṇī Soḍhījī Meghāṃbāī** (*pīhar* name)
Daughter of the Soḍho Paṃvārs of Ūmarkoṭ. Meghāṃbāī became a *satī* at the time of Rāv Candrasen's death.

11. **Rāṇī Cahuvāṇ Pūrbāṇījī**[16]
Pūrbāṇījī became a *satī* at the time of Rāv Candrasen's death.

12. **Rāṇī Kelhaṇ Bhāṭiyāṇī**[17]
Daughter of Kelhaṇ Bhāṭī Rāv Ḍūṅgarsī Dujaṇsalot of Vikūmpur.

13. **Rāṇī Hāḍī**[18]
Daughter of Hāḍo Cahuvāṇ Rāv Surjan Urjaṇot (Narbadot) of Būndī (ca. 1554-68).

Rāṇī Hāḍī was married on February 21, 1569 at Riṇthambhor. Rāv Surjan gave Rāv Candrasen an elephant, fifteen horses and jewelry worth *rs*. 15,000 in dowry.

Marriage Lists

Lists of Rāv Candrasen's marriages and of his sons and daughters are contained in the following primary texts. These texts reference all marriages except those of Rāṇīs no. 12 and no. 13:

Jodhpur Rājya kī Khyāt, pp. 104, 113-114.
Murārdān, no. 2, pp. 164-166.
Rāṭhoṛāṃ rī Vaṃśāvalī, MS no. 20130, ff. 69-70.

Other general sources include:

"Aitihāsik Bātāṃ," pp. 78, 85; *Murārdān*, no. 1, pp. 589-600, no. 2, pp. 154-163; Ojhā, 4:1:332-333, 350; Reu, 1:160; *Vīr Vinod*, 2:813-814.

---

[15] *Ibid.*, 2:194.

[16] "Aitihāsik Bātāṃ," p. 85.

[17] *Khyāt*, 2:128, 132.

[18] *Ibid.*, 1:110-111; *Vigat*, 1:69.

Moṭo Rājā Udaisiṅgh Māldevot (10-2)

Born: Sunday, January 13, 1538
Died: Friday, July 11, 1595
Ruled: August 4, 1583[1] - July 11, 1595
Mother: Rāṇī Jhālī Sarūpdejī, daughter of Jhālo Jaito Sajāvat, a military servant of Rāv Mālde's holding the village of Khairvo[2] in eastern Mārvāṛ in *paṭo*.

Rāṇīs, Sons, and Daughters

1. **Baṛī Rāṇī Soḷaṅkaṇī Nachraṅgdejī** (***pīhar*** name Kaṅkāde)[3]
Daughter of Soḷaṅkī Sāṃvatsī Rāymalot of Desurī in Goḍhvāṛ.[4]
Nachraṅgdejī was married to Udaisiṅgh while he was a ***kuṃvar*** to settle a ***vair*** that had arisen between the Rāṭhoṛs of Jodhpur and the Soḷaṅkīs. She died at Jodhpur in 1589-90, while the Moṭo Rājā was in Sīrohī.

S - Narhardās: two different dates are given for his birth: Thursday, December 17, 1556 and October 10, 1557.
D - Rambhāvatībāī: married to Bhāṭī Khetsī Māldevot, a son of Bhāṭī Rāvaḷ Mālde Lūṇkaraṇot of Jaisaḷmer (1551-61). Khetsī Māldevot was himself a daughter's son (***dohitro***) of Bīkāner Rāṭhoṛ Rāv Jaitsī Lūṇkaraṇot (ca. 1526-42).
D - Dhanbāī: married to Chirmī Khān of Nāgaur.[5]
D - Rāykuṃvar: married to Rājāvat Kachvāho Rājā Rājsiṅgh Āskaraṇot of Gwalior.

---

[1] This date is from Ojhā, 4:1:354, and ***Jodhpur Rājya kī Khyāt***, p. 118. "Aitihāsik Bātāṃ," p. 91, gives the date of October 14, 1583.

[2] Khairvo village: located eleven miles southeast of Pālī in eastern Mārvāṛ, and fifty miles south-southeast of Jodhpur.

[3] ***Bāṅkīdās***, pp. 22-23, 25, 112, 134; Dasharatha Sharma, ***Lectures on Rajput History and Culture*** (Delhi: Motilal Banarsidass, 1970), p. 145; ***Khyāt***, 1:284-285, 303, 2:93, 96; ***Murārdān***, no. 2, p. 178; Ojhā, 4:1:362; Reu, 1:178, n. 3; ***Tavārīkh Jaisalmer***, p. 52; ***Vigat***, 1:89.

[4] Desūrī: located ten miles southeast of Nāḍūl in Goḍhvāṛ.

[5] Neither ***Jodhpur Rājya kī Khyāt*** nor ***Rāṭhoṛāṃ rī Vaṃśāvalī***, MS no. 20130, mention this daughter or her marriage to Chirmī Khān.

2. **Rāṇī Sīsodṇī Apuravdejī** [6]

Daughter of Sīsodīyo Gahlot Rām (or Pharasrām) Udaisiṅghot, a son of Rāṇo Udaisiṅgh Sāṅgvat of Cītoṛ (ca. 1537-72).

Apuravdejī died in 1596-97.

S - Bhagvāndās: born on Tuesday, September 21, 1557[7] and died on October 1, 1594.

S - Bhopatsiṅgh: two different dates of birth are given in the texts: Monday, October 17, 1558 and October 26, 1568. Bhopatsiṅgh was killed at Masudo village (near Ajmer) by either Paṃvār Sādūḷ Māldevot or his son on November 25, 1596 or December 4, 1606 (sources conflict). Paṃvār Sādūḷ was a Rajpūt from the Paṃvārs of Cāṭsū in central Rājasthān. He had held several villages of Jaitāraṇ Pargano in Mārvāṛ in *jāgīr* from the Mughal Emperor Akbar.

D - Candramatī: died young.

3. **Rāṇī Kachvāhī Aṅkārdejī** (*pīhar* name Pūrbāī)[8]

Daughter of Sekhāvat Kachvāho Mānsiṅgh Tejsīyot, a brother of Rāmsiṅgh Tejsīyot, who also married a daughter to Udaisiṅgh Māldevot (see *infra*, Rāṇī no. 5).

Aṅkārdejī died while she was in Phaḷodhī with Kuṃvar Udaisiṅgh, during the early years following Rāv Mālde's death in 1562.

S - Akhairāj: died in battle while his father was at Samāvalī in north India, prior to Udaisiṅgh's succession to the throne of Jodhpur in 1583.

4. **Rāṇī Bhāṭiyāṇī Jasvantdejī** (*pīhar* name Harakhāṃbāī)[9]

Daughter of Kelhaṇ Bhāṭī Rāv Dujaṇsal Varsiṅghot of Vikūmpur.

Some uncertainty exists in the texts regarding this Rāṇī's name. Jasvantde appears to be the name she received at the time of her marriage to Udaisiṅgh Māldevot. However, sources also refer to her both by her *pīhar* name, Harakhāṃbāī, and by the name Pohpāvatī. The latter name appears incorrect. This was the name of Rāv Dujaṇsal's son Rāymal Dujaṇsalot's daughter, who was also married to Udaisiṅgh Māldevot (see *infra*, Rāṇī no. 14).

---

6 "Aitihāsik Bātāṃ," p. 96; ***Bāṅkīdās***, p. 24; ***Khyāt***, 1:21; Ojhā, 4:1:362.

7 This date comes from ***Jodhpur Rājya kī Khyāt***, p. 124. This same text (p. 128) gives the alternate date of June 15, 1558, and ***Bāṅkīdās***, p. 24, records the date of September 12, 1557.

8 ***Bāṅkīdās***, p. 24; ***Khyāt***, 1:326; Ojhā, 4:1:362.

9 ***Akbar Nāma***, 3:594-596; ***Khyāt***, 1:312, 2:128; ***Vigat***, 1:83.

The texts also display some discrepancy regarding the date of this Rāṇī's death. One source indicates that she died following her marriage, before reaching Jodhpur, and another that she died in 1600-01 at Jodhpur. The latter date appears correct. It was again Rāv Dujaṇsal's son Rāymal's daughter who died before reaching Jodhpur.

D - Dāmetībāī: married to Kachvāho Jaimal Rūpsīyot, a grandson of Rājā Prithīrāj Candrasenot of Āmber (1503-27).

The Mughal Emperor Akbar sent Kachvāho Jaimal on an expedition to Bengal in 1583, during which he took ill near Causa and died from heat prostration and over-exertion. Dāmetībāī's son and his Kachvāho relations attempted to force Dāmetībāī to become a ***satī*** when they received word of Jaimal's death. News of this situation reached Akbar, who took it upon himself to stop the Kachvāhos and allow Dāmetībāī to live. She died some years later in 1626-27.

5. **Rāṇī Kachvāhī Uttamdejī** (***pīhar*** name Ratanāvatībāī)[10]

Daughter of Sekhāvat Kachvāho Rāmsiṅgh Tejsīyot of Amarsar,[11] who was a brother of Mānsiṅgh Tejsīyot (see ***supra***, Rāṇī no. 3).

S - Kīratsiṅgh: born on December 15, 1567.

S - Mohaṇdās: born in 1571-72. He stabbed himself with a dagger (***kaṭārī khāy***) in 1620-21 and died.

S - Mādhosiṅgh: born on September 24, 1575 or October 16, 1581.

S - Jaitsiṅgh: died in 1631-32.

D - Jasodābāī: married to Kachvāho Sūrsiṅgh Bhagvantdāsot, a son of Rājā Bhagvantdās Bhārmalot of Āmber (ca. 1574-89). She became a ***satī*** at the time of Sūrsiṅgh's death.

D - Kamlāvatībāī: married to Khīcī Cahuvāṇ Rāv Gopāḷdās of Mau (modern Mhow).

D - Pemāvatībāī: married to Rāv Bhāro of Bhuj.

6. **Rāṇī Rājāvat Kachvāhī** (***pīhar*** name Sītābāī)

Rāṇī Kachvāhī died at Jodhpur during the Moṭo Rājā's lifetime. Her father's name is unknown.

S - (name unknown): died young.

7. **Rāṇī Cahuvāṇ Ajāyabdejī** (***pīhar*** name Kaṅkābāī)[12]

---

[10] ***Bāṅkīdās***, pp. 24-25, 142; ***Khyāt***, 1:300, 326; ***Murārdān***, no. 1, p. 586; Ojhā, 4:1:362-363.

[11] Amarsar village: located forty miles due north of Jaipur in central Rājasthān.

[12] ***Bāṅkīdās***, pp. 24-25, 146, 162; ***Khyāt***, 1:233, 312; Ojhā, 4:1:363.

Daughter of Sācoro Cahuvāṇ Mahkaraṇ Rāṇāvat, a military servant of Rāv Mālde.

This Rāṇī died in 1617-18.

S - Daḷpat: born on Sunday, July 18, 1568. Daḷpat's daughter's son (*dohitro*) was Hāḍo Rāvrājā Bhāvsiṅgh Catrasāḷot of Būndī (ca. 1658-81).

S - (name unknown): died young.

D - Kisnāvatībāī: married to Kachvāho Tiloksī Rūpsīyot, a grandson of Rājā Prithīrāj Candrasenot of Āmber (1503-27). Tiloksī's father, Rūpsī Vairāgī, was a Mughal ***mansabdār*** holding Parbatsar in ***jāgīr*** from Emperor Akbar. Kisnāvatībāī became a ***satī*** at the time of Tiloksī's death.

8. **Rāṇī Bhāṭiyāṇī Kapūrdejī**[13]

Daughter of Gāḍāḷo Kelhaṇ Bhāṭī Kamo Goyandot.

S - Sakatsiṅgh: born on Saturday, November 29, 1567 or Monday, December 15, 1567 as Udaisiṅgh's third or fourth son, while Udaisiṅgh held Phaḷodhī[14] as his share of the lands of Mārvāṛ.

At a relatively early age, Udaisiṅgh granted Sakatsiṅgh the ***paṭo*** of Hūngāṃv village[15] for his maintenance, and Sakatsiṅgh went there to live with his family and retainers. Local chronicles speak of Sakatsiṅgh as a dutiful son (***sapūt***) and state that Udaisiṅgh presented him to Emperor Akbar, who took him into his service and granted him a ***mansab*** of 500 ***zāt***. Sakatsiṅgh rose steadily in the Emperor's esteem, and ***Jodhpur Rājya kī Khyāt***, p. 128, records that he attained a rank of 3,000 ***zāt*** by the time of his death. He also received the title of ***rāv***.

Suspicion of Sakatsiṅgh began to grow due to the favor in which he was held at the Mughal court, and Jeso Bhāṭī Goyanddās, ***pradhān*** of Jodhpur under Rājā Sūrajsiṅgh Udaisiṅghot (1595-1619), secretly administered poison to him outside the Red Fort at Agra one day because Sakatsiṅgh "desired to have Jodhpur written [into his ***jāgīr***]" (***ibid.***). The date of this murder is uncertain, but it would have occurred between March of 1605, when Sakatsiṅgh received an increase in

---

[13] ***Akbar Nāma***, 3:1252; Athar Ali, ***Apparatus***, p. 32; ***Bāṅkīdās***, p. 24; ***Jodhpur Rājya kī Khyāt***, pp. 128-129; ***Khyāt***, 2:140; ***Murārdān***, no. 2, pp. 655-658; Ojhā, 4:1:363, n. 4; Surjan Siṃh Śekhāvat, ***Kharvā kā Vṛhad Itihās*** (Kharvā: Rāv Candrasen Jī, V.S. 2055 [A.D. 1998]), pp. 18-24; ***Vigat***, 1:73-75, 111.

[14] Phaḷodhī: located seventy-two miles north-northwest of Jodhpur.

[15] Hūngāṃv village: located twenty-two miles northwest of Sojhat in eastern Mārvāṛ.

mansab rank to 1600/300, and May of 1615, when Bhāṭī Goyanddās was killed at Ajmer.[16]

A daughter of Sakatsiṅgh named Līlāvatībāī was married to Prince Khurram (Shāh Jahān). The date of this marriage is uncertain. A single reference to Līlāvatībāī in ***Vigat***, 1:111, places her with Shāh Jahān at Juner in the Deccan in 1627-28. This source notes that Shāh Jahān sent her to Jodhpur with a message of conciliation for Rājā Gajsiṅgh Sūrajsiṅghot (1619-38) following Emperor Jahāngīr's death in October of 1627.

Frances Taft (personal communication) believes that in all likelihood this marriage took place between the years 1623-27, during the time Shāh Jahān was in rebellion against his father and sought to strengthen ties with Jodhpur.

9. **Rāṇī Bhāṭiyāṇī Santokhdejī** (***pīhar*** name Sajnāṃbāī)[17]

Daughter of Bhāṭī Sūrajmal Lūṇkaraṇot, a son of Rāvaḷ Lūṇkaraṇ Jaitsīyot of Jaisaḷmer (1528-51).

Santokhdejī died in 1620-21.

D - Rājkuṃvar: married to Saktāvat Sīsodīyo Gahlot Bhāṇ Saktāvat of Mevāṛ.

D - Satyabhāmābāī: married to Jhālo Rāṇo Candrasen Rāysiṅghot of Haḷvad. Udaisiṅgh's brother, Rāv Candrasen Māldevot (1562-81), arranged this marriage.

10. **Rāṇī Rājāvat Kachvāhī Manraṅgdejī**[18]

Daughter of Rājāvat Kachvāho Rājā Āskaraṇ Bhīṃvrājot of Gwalior.

Manraṅgdejī died at Lahore on Monday, May 21, 1593.

S - Jasvantsiṅgh: died young.

S - Sūrajsiṅgh: born on Tuesday, April 24, 1571. Sūrajsiṅgh succeeded the Moṭo Rājā to the Jodhpur throne. He was adopted by an ***oḷgaṇī*** ("court singer") of the Moṭo Rājā's named Harbolāṃ while he was young. This ***oḷgaṇī*** became a ***satī*** at Lahore at the time of the Moṭo Rājā's death. When Sūrajsiṅgh ascended the throne in 1595, he had a stepwell built in Harbolāṃ's name near Bālsamand Lake at Jodhpur.

S - Pūraṇmal: died at the age of nine years.

---

[16] Surjan Siṃh Śekhāvat, ***Kharvā kā Vṛhad Itihās***, p. 23, gives May 30, 1606 (***V.S.*** 1662, ***Jeṭh***, ***Sudi*** 4) as the date of Saktasiṅgh's death, but offers no source for this date.

[17] ***Bāṅkīdās***, p. 93; ***Khyāt***, 1:26, 2:90, 256.

[18] "Aitihāsik Bātāṃ," p. 91; ***Akbar Nāma***, 3:677-678, 880, 921, 1094; ***Bāṅkīdās***, pp. 23, 25; G. H. Ojhā, ***Ḍūṅgarpur Rājya kā Itihās*** (Ajmer: Vedic Yantralaya, V. S. 1992 [A. D. 1935]), pp. 104-106; Jahāngīr, 1:19; ***Khyāt***, 1:79, 303; ***Murārdān***, no. 1, pp. 588-589, no. 2, pp. 187-188; Ojhā, 4:1:363-364; ***Vigat***, 1:92.

S - Kisansiṅgh: born April 28, 1583. He founded the kingdom of Kisangaḍh in central Rājasthān.

S - Kesodās: died young.

S - Rāmsiṅgh: died young.

D - Manāvatībāī (Mānībāī): born on Wednesday, May 13, 1573; married to Prince Salīm (Jahāngīr), who gave her the name Tāj Bībī.[19] Her son by Jahāngīr was Prince Khurram (Shāh Jahān), born September 5, 1592. She was called Jagat Gosā'in at the Mughal court, and was popularly known as Jodhbāī.

D - Rāmkuṃvarbāī: died young.

D - Tiloksībāī (or Lilāvatībāī): died young.

D - Prāṇmatībāī: married to Āhāṛo Gahlot Karamsī Sahasmalot, a son of Rāvaḷ Sahasmal Āskaraṇot of Ḍūṅgarpur (ca. 1580-1606). Prāṇmatībāī died at Jodhpur on Monday, August 10, 1640.

11. **Rāṇī Cahuvāṇ Suhāgdejī** (*pīhar* name Pūrbānībāī)[20]

The identity of this Rāṇī's father is uncertain. The texts list him by the names Vais Dhūṇḍhaṇjī and Surtāṇjī. They also note that Suhāgdejī was the brother's daughter (***bhatījī***) of a Devsen. From sources available, it had not been possible to identity these men further.

Suhāgdejī was married in Īḍar in 1584-85. She died some years later in 1599-1600 at Jodhpur.

D - Gāṅgābāī: married to Narūko Kachvāho Rāmcandro Rāymalot at Samāvalī in north India. She became a ***satī*** at the time of Rāmcandro's death.

---

[19] ***Bāṅkīdās***, p. 25, and ***Murārdān***, no. 2, pp. 187-188, 199, offer three different dates for Manāvatībāī's marriage to Prince Salīm: V.S. 1643 (1586-1587). V.S. 1644 (1587-1588), and V.S. 1645 (1588-1589). It is known that the marriage occurred sometime after February of 1585, the date Prince Salīm celebrated his first marriage to a daughter of Kachvāho Rājā Bhagvantdās Bhārmalot of Āmber. Frances Taft (personal communication) places this marriage in late 1586 based on her investigation of Mughal sources. The ***Akbar Nāma*** does not give a date for this marriage, but both the ***Jahāngīrnāma*** and the ***Ma'asir-i-Jahangiri*** give the date of A.H. 994 (December, 1585 -December, 1586). See Khwaja Kamgar Husaini, ***Ma'asir-i-Jahangiri: A Contemporary Account of Jahangir***, edited by Azra Alavi (Bombay: Asia Publishing House, 1978), p. 13 (text) and p. 26 (Introduction), and Jahāngīr, ***The Jahangirnama: Memoirs of Jahangir, Emperor of India***, translated, edited, and annotated by Wheeler M. Thackston (Washington, D.C.: Freer Gallery of Art, Arthur M. Sackler Gallery; New York: Oxford University Press, 1999), p. 6. The marriage was celebrated at Lahore, and because Akbar did not reach Lahore until May of 1586, it can therefore be dated to 1586. Taft also notes that Prince Salīm was married to a daughter of Rāṭhoṛ Rājā Rāysiṅgh Kalyānmalot of Bīkāner (ca. 1574-1612) at Lahore in 1586 (***Akbar Nāma***, 3:748-749).

[20] ***Khyāt***, 1:318.

12. **Rāṇī Cāvṛī Sīgārdejī** [21]

Daughter of Cāvṛo Āso of Īḍar. Sīgārdejī was married in 1584-85 to settle the ***vair*** between the Cāvṛos of Īḍar and the Rāṭhoṛs of Jodhpur that had arisen when the Cāvṛos killed Gopāḷdās Māldevot, a son of Rāv Māldev Gāṅgāvat of Jodhpur (see ***supra***, Rāv Mālde Gāṅgāvat, Rāṇī no. 13, S - Gopāḷdās). She died in 1618-19.

D - Rukhmāvatībāī: married to Kachvāho Rājā Mahāsiṅgh Jagatsiṅghot on Sunday, November 26, 1598 at Jodhpur. She became a ***satī*** at the time of Rājā Mahāsiṅgh's death in 1616-17 at Balapur in the Deccan.

13. **Rāṇī Cahuvāṇjī** [22]

Daughter of Sācoro Cahuvāṇ Vaṇvīr Siṅghāvat, a grandson of Vāgho Pithamrāvat's. Vaṇvīr was a military servant of Rāv Mālde's of Jodhpur, and he founded the village of Vāghāvās nead Koḍhṇo[23] in western Mārvāṛ. His daughter was married on Tuesday, December 29, 1589 at the village of Sathlāṇo.[24] She became a ***satī*** at Lahore at the time of the Moṭo Rājā's death.

14. **Rāṇī Bhāṭiyāṇī Pohpāvatījī**

Daughter of Kelhaṇ Bhāṭī Rāymal Dujaṇsalot, a son of Rāv Dujaṇsal Varsiṅghot of Vikūmpur.

Pohpāvatījī died following her marriage, while enroute from her paternal home (***pīhar***) to Jodhpur.

15. **Rāṇī Sonagarī Jasodājī** [25]

Daughter of Sonagaro Cahuvāṇ Bhāṇ Akhairājot, a son of Akhairāj Riṇdhīrot's (see ***infra***, "Sonagaro Cahuvāṇs," no. 9). Bhāṇ was a military servant of the Rāṇo of Mevāṛ.

Jasodājī became a ***satī*** at Maṇḍor upon the arrival of the Moṭo Rājā's turban from Lahore with news of his death.

---

[21] ***Bāṅkīdās***, p. 25; ***Khyāt***, 1:297; Ojhā, 4:1:363, n. 7.

[22] ***Bāṅkīdās***, p. 163; ***Khyāt***, 1:242.

[23] Koḍhṇo village: located twenty-eight miles west-southwest of Jodhpur. Vāghāvās is situated eight miles further southwest from Koḍhṇo.

[24] Sathlāṇo village: located twenty-two miles south of Jodhpur.

[25] ***Bāṅkīdās***, p. 152; ***Khyāt***, 1:207. 209-210.

16. Rāṇī Devṛī Lāḍījī (*pīhar* name Rāṇībāī)[26]

Daughter of Devṛo Cahuvāṇ Rāv Kalo Mehājalot. Rāv Kalo was a military servant of the Moṭo Rājā during the latter part of his life, and he held several villages in Mārvāṛ in ***paṭo*** from the Rājā.

Lāḍījī was married in 1589-90. She became a ***satī*** at Lahore at the time of the Moṭo Rājā's death.

17. Rāṇī Cahuvāṇ Tārāmatījī [27]

Daughter of Cahuvāṇ Jīvo. The ***Khyāt*** of Naiṇsī, 1:241, 243, lists two Cahuvāṇ Jīvos in its genealogy of the Sācoro Cahuvāṇs, a Jīvo Gāṅgāvat and a Jīvo Goyanddāsot. The ***Khyāt*** provides no information about Jīvo Goyanddāsot. Jīvo Gāṅgāvat was a military servant of Udaisiṅgh Māldevot's before he succeeded to the throne of Jodhpur in 1583. Following Udaisiṅgh's accession and return to Mārvāṛ from Samāvalī in north India, he granted Jīvo Gāṅgāvat the ***paṭo*** of Māṇaklāv village.[28] It is probable that this Jīvo was Tārāmatījī's father.

Tārāmatījī became a ***satī*** at Lahore at the time of the Moṭo Rājā's death.

18. Rāṇī Bhāṭiyāṇī [29]

Some doubt exists about the identity of this Rāṇī's father. The ***Khyāt*** of Naiṇsī, 2:132, lists a Bhāṭī Jaimal Kalāvat as father in its section detailing marriage ties between the Rāṭhoṛs of Jodhpur and the Kelhaṇ Bhāṭīs of Vikūmpur. However, ***Khyāt*** does not list a Bhāṭī by the name of Jaimal Kalāvat in its genealogy of the Kelhaṇs of Vikūmpur.

Elsewhere, ***Khyāt***, 2:199, lists a Bhāṭī Kalo Jaimalot in its genealogy of the Rūpsī Bhāṭīs. Kalo Jaimalot's father, Jaimal Devrājot, was a military servant of Rāv Mālde of Jodhpur, who died in the defense of the fort of Jodhpur following Rāv Mālde's defeat at the battle of Samel in January of 1544.

It is possible that Rūpsī Bhāṭī Kalo was the father of this Rāṇī Bhāṭiyāṇī, and not Kelhaṇ Bhāṭī Jaimal Kalāvat.

19. Rāṇī Bhāṭiyāṇījī [30]

Daughter of Khīṃvo Bhāṭī Jagmāl Sāṅgāvat (Khīṃvāvat) of Vairsalpur.

---

[26] ***Bāṅkīdās***, p. 155; ***Khyāt***, 1:160.

[27] ***Khyāt***, 1:241, 243.

[28] Māṇaklāv village: located eleven miles north of Jodhpur.

[29] ***Khyāt***, 2:132, 199.

[30] ***Ibid.***, 2:121, 132.

Miscellaneous

One additional son of the Moṭo Rājā's is listed:

S - Karaṇsiṅgh (mother unknown).[31]

Marriage Lists

Lists of the Moṭo Rājā's marriages and of his sons and daughters are contained in the following primary sources. These sources reference all marriages except those of Rāṇīs no. 18 and no. 19:

Jodhpur Rājya kī Khyāt, pp. 118, 124-131.
Murārdān, no. 2, pp. 193-201.
Rāṭhoṛāṃ rī Vaṃśāvalī, MS no. 20130, ff. 76-79.

Other general references include:

Murārdān, no. 1, pp. 586, 588, 590, no. 2, pp. 174-200; Ojhā, 4:1:327, 354; "Rāṭhauḍ Vaṃś rī Vigat," pp. 13-14; Reu, 1:178-180; ***Vīr Vinod***, 2:815-816.

[31] Reu, 1:180.

Rājā Sūrajsiṅgh Udaisiṅghot (11-2)

Born: Tuesday, April 24, 1571[1]
Died: Tuesday, September 7, 1619[2]
Ruled: July 23, 1595 - September 7, 1619
Mother: Rāṇī Kachvāhī Manraṅgdejī, daughter of Rājāvat Kachvāho Rājā Āskaraṇ Bhīṃvrājot of Gwalior.

Rāṇīs, Sons, and Daughters

1. **Baṛī Rāṇī Sīsodṇī Manorathdejī** [3]

Daughter of Sīsodīyo Gahlot Sakatsiṅgh Udaisiṅghot, a son of Rāṇo Udaisiṅgh Sāṅgāvat of Cītoṛ (ca. 1537-72).

Manorathdejī was married to Sūrajsiṅgh while he was living with his father, Kuṃvar Udaisiṅgh Māldevot, at Phaḷodhī in northern Mārvāṛ. She died young at her ***pīhar***.

2. **Rāṇī Bhāṭiyāṇī Sūjāṇdejī** (***pīhar*** name Gulābkuṃvarbāī or Bāḷbāī)[4]

Daughter of Kelhaṇ Bhāṭī Goyanddās Pañcāiṇot of Pūṅgaḷ and Vairsaḷpur.

Sūjāṇdejī was sent in ***ḍoḷo*** to Sūrajsiṅgh and married to him while he was a ***kuṃvar***. The marriage took place at Maṇḍor on Saturday, April 24, 1585. Sūjāṇdejī became a ***satī*** at the time of Rājā Sūrajsiṅgh's death. She was with him in the Deccan when he died.

S - (unnamed): aborted at eight months in 1586-87.

S - Pratāpsiṅgh: born in September or October, 1592 at Lahore. He died at the age of eight months. His wet-nurse (***dhāy***) was the wife of ***sikdār*** Sobho (tentatively identified as Jāṅgaḷvo Sāṅkhlo Paṃvār Sobho Harbhāmot).

---

[1] We are following Ojhā, 4:1:364, here. ***Jodhpur Rājya kī Khyāt***, p. 131, gives the date of Wednesday, April 25, 1571 for Sūrajsiṅgh's birth. Other dates given in the sources include April 5, 1570, and April 15 and April 16, 1571. See: "Aitihāsik Bātāṃ," p. 94; ***Bāṅkīdās***, p. 25; ***Vigat***, 1:92, n. 2.

[2] This is the date given in Ojhā, 4:1:364; ***Bāṅkīdās***, p. 25, gives the alternate date of September 6, 1619.

[3] ***Khyāt***, 1:26.

[4] ***Bāṅkīdās***, pp. 27, 115; ***Khyāt***, 1:351-352, 2:119.

3. **Rāṇī Kachvāhī Sobhāgdejī** (*pīhar* name Kisnāvatībāī)[5]

Daughter of Sekhāvat Kachvāho Durjaṇsāḷ Karamsīyot.

The Mughal Emperor Akbar took this girl as his daughter. He married her to Sūrajsiṅgh at Lahore on Sunday, June 23, 1588 while Sūrajsiṅgh was a *kuṃvar*. She died at Burhanpur in the Deccan in July or August of 1609.

S - Gajsiṅgh: born on Thursday, October 30, 1595[6] at Lahore. He succeeded Rājā Sūrajsiṅgh to the Jodhpur throne.

S - Jasvantsiṅgh: born in 1588-89 in Gujarat. He died at the age of five months.

D - Manbhāvatībāī: born in 1598-99. She was married to Prince Parvīz in 1623-24 in return for Parvīz's grant of Meṛto Pargano to her uterine brother, Rājā Gajsiṅgh. She remained a resident of Emperor Jahāngīr's household after Prince Parvīz's death in 1626.

D - Kalyāṇkuṃvar: died young.

4. **Rāṇī Āhāṛī Surtāṇdejī** (*pīhar* name Jasodābāī)[7]

Daughter of Āhāṛo Gahlot Rāvaḷ Sahasmal Āskaraṇot of Ḍūṅgarpur (ca. 1580-1606).

Surtāṇdejī was married on Friday, May 21, 1591 in Ḍūṅgarpur. She died on Monday, March 25, 1633 (*adhika vaiś*) or April 24, 1633 (*nija vaiś*) while at Baijnāthjī enroute home from a pilgrimage.

S - Sabaḷsiṅgh: born on Saturday, August 15, 1607. He held Phaḷodhī in *jāgīr* from Emperor Akbar, in addition to areas in Gujarat. He died at Phaḷodhī on Friday, January 24, 1647 from poison administered to him by a slave.

5. **Rāṇī Baṛī Jādam/Jādav Suhāgdejī** (*pīhar* name Pohpāṃbāī)

Daughter of Jādav Rāv Maṇḍlik.

Suhāgdejī was sent in *ḍoḷo* to Rājā Sūrajsiṅgh and married at Jodhpur on Friday, June 4, 1591.

6. **Rāṇī Paṃvār Caturaṅgdejī** [8]

Daughter of Paṃvār Sāṅgo Māldevot (of the Paṃvārs of Cāṭsū),

---

[5] ***Bāṅkīdās***, p. 26; ***Khyāt***, 1:325; ***Murārdān***, no. 2, p. 187; Ojhā, 4:1:386-387; Jahāngīr, 2:295; ***Vigat***, 1:108.

[6] ***Bāṅkīdās***, p. 27, ***Jodhpur Rājya kī Khyāt***, pp. 157, 161, and Ojhā, 4:1:388, all record this date. ***Vigat***, 1:105, gives the alternate date of October 15, 1595.

[7] ***Bāṅkīdās***, pp. 26-27, 107; G. H. Ojhā, ***Ḍūṅgarpur Rājya kā Itihās*** (Ajmer: Vedic Yantralaya, V. S. 1992 [A. D. 1935]), p. 103, n. 1; ***Khyāt***, 1:79; ***Murārdān***, no. 2, 652-653; Ojhā, 4:1:386, n. 4; ***Vigat***, 1:94-95, 104, 108.

[8] ***Bāṅkīdās***, pp. 27, 138; ***Khyāt***, 1:298-299; ***Paṃvār Vaṃś Darpaṇ***, p. 30.

Caturaṅgdejī was married in the village of Ārāī on Sunday, June 20, 1591. She died at Lahore in 1593-94.

D - Āskuṃvarbāī: given in adoption to Rāṇī Sūjāṇdejī (see *supra*, Rāṇī no. 2). Āskuṃvarbāī was married to Kachvāho Rājā Bhāvsiṅgh Mānsiṅghot of Āmber (1614-21). The marriage took place on either June 20 or July 3, 1616. She became a ***satī*** at Burhanpur in the Deccan at the time of Rājā Bhāvsiṅgh's death. She had only one daughter, Rūpkuṃvar, who died young.

7. **Rāṇī Soḷaṅkaṇī Manorathdejī** [9]

Daughter of Soḷaṅkī Khetsī Sāṃvatsīyot of Desurī in Goḍhvāṛ.[10] Khetsī was a military servant of Sīsodīyo Rāṇo Amarsiṅgh Pratāpsiṅghot of Mevāṛ (1597-1620).

Manorathdejī was married in the village of Sīrīyārī[11] in Mārvāṛ on Monday, February 18, 1594. She died in November or December of 1606.

8. **Rāṇī Jāṛecī Sahibdejī** (***pīhar*** name Lāḍbāī)

Daughter of Jāṛeco Jām Satrasāḷ of Nayanagar.

Sahibdejī was given in ***ḍoḷo*** to Rājā Sūrajsiṅgh. The marriage took place at Ahmadabad on Monday, January 24 or Tuesday, January 25, 1597. She died at the fort of Jodhpur on Friday, March 23, 1649.

9. **Rāṇī Boṛī Ratanādejī** (***pīhar*** name Phulāṃbāī)[12]

Daughter of Boṛo Cahuvāṇ Rāv Vāgho Vījāvat of Sayāṇo village.

Ratanādejī was sent in ***ḍoḷo*** to Rājā Sūrajsiṅgh and married to him at Ahmadabad on January 30 or February 14, 1597. She died in 1651-52.

S - Vijāysiṅgh: lived only fourteen (or twenty-four) months.

10. **Rāṇī Soḍhī Uchraṅgdejī** [13]

Daughter of Soḍho Paṃvār Rāv Candrasen Pātāvat (or Soḍho Bāṅkīdās) of Ūmarkoṭ.

Uchraṅgdejī was married at Ahmadabad on Saturday, April 22, 1598.

---

[9] ***Bāṅkīdās***, p. 135.

[10] Desūrī: located ten miles southeast of Nāḍūl in Goḍhvāṛ.

[11] Sīrīyārī village: located twenty miles southeast of Sojhat in eastern Mārvāṛ.

[12] ***Bāṅkīdās***, p. 161.

[13] ***Khyāt***, 1:359; ***Paṃvār Vaṃś Darpaṇ***, p. 33.

11. **Rāṇī Devṛī Hīrādejī** (*pīhar* name Kaṃvlāvatībāī)[14]

Daughter of Devṛo Cahuvāṇ Rāv Kalo Mehājalot.

Hīrādejī was sent in *ḍoḷo* to Rājā Sūrajsiṅgh. She came first to Agra, then to Mathurajī, where the marriage took place on Monday, June 25, 1604. She died at Jodhpur on Saturday, August 8, 1647.

S - Vīramde: born in 1607-08. He died at the age of six years.
S - (name unknown): died young.

12. **Rāṇī Vīrampurī Nāraṅgdejī** (*pīhar* name Cāmpābāī)

Daughter of Rāṇo Vaṇvīr.

Nāraṅgdejī was married at Ahmadabad on Sunday, August 17, 1606. She died at Jodhpur in either October/November of 1623, or November/December of 1633.

13. **Rāṇī Bhāṭiyāṇī Amolakhdejī** (*pīhar* name Parvatībāī)[15]

Daughter of Bhāṭī Sahasmal Māldevot, a son of Bhāṭī Rāvaḷ Mālde Lūṇkaraṇot of Jaisaḷmer (1551-61). Sahasmal had settled in Mārvāṛ.

Amolakhdejī was married at the village of Bīlāṛo[16] in 1607-08 while Rājā Sūrajsiṅgh was on his way to Agra. She died on Friday, September 7, 1677.

D - Mrigāvatībāī: married to Kachvāho Rājā Jaisiṅgh Mahāsiṅghot of Āmber (1621-67). Her marriage took place at Jodhpur on Monday, November 25, 1622, three years after Rājā Sūrajsiṅgh's death in 1619.

14. **Rāṇī Paṃvār Gāṅgādejī** (or Raṅgādejī)[17]

Daughter of Paṃvār Sādūḷ Māldevot (of the Paṃvārs of Cāṭsū).

Gāṅgādejī was married at Burhanpur in the Deccan in 1609-10 to settle the ***vair*** that had arisen between the Rāṭhoṛs of Jodhpur and the Paṃvārs of Cāṭsū over the death of Kuṃvar Bhopatsiṅgh Udaisiṅgh (see ***supra***, Moṭo Rājā Udaisiṅgh Māldevot, Rāṇī no. 2, S - Bhopatsiṅgh). Kuṃvar Bhopatsiṅgh was killed several years prior in either 1596-97 or 1606-07.

Gāṅgādejī became a ***satī*** at the time of Rājā Sūrajsiṅgh's death.

---

[14] ***Bāṅkīdās***, p. 155.

[15] ***Ibid.***, pp. 27, 125; ***Khyāt***, 1:297, 2:96.

[16] Bīlāṛo village: located forty-one miles east-southeast of Jodhpur.

[17] "Aitihāsik Bātāṃ," p. 96; ***Bāṅkīdās***, p. 138; ***Paṃvār Vaṃś Darpaṇ***, p. 30; ***Vigat***, 1:96-97.

15. **Rāṇī Lohṛī Jādam/Jādav Sūjandejī**[18]

Daughter of Jādav Pahāṛ Khān (or Pāḍkhān).

Sūjandejī was married at Burhanpur in the Deccan in 1609-10. She was at Jodhpur when Rājā Sūrajsiṅgh died in the Deccan in September of 1619. She proceeded to Maṇḍor on Wednesday, June 21, 1620 and became a ***satī*** there.

16. **Rāṇī Kachvāhī Noraṅgdejī** (***pīhar*** name Amrāṃ)[19]

Daughter of Sekhāvat Kachvāho Tirmaṇrāy Rāysalot and granddaughter of Kachvāho Rāysal "Darbārī" Sūjāvat.

Noraṅgdejī was married at the village of Khaṇḍeḷo on Sunday, June 7, 1612. She became a ***satī*** at the time of Rājā Sūrajsiṅgh's death.

D - Indrakuṃvar: born on Tuesday, July 28, 1618. She died at the age of four years in 1622-23.

17. **Rāṇī Kachvāhī Siṅgardejī** (or Raṅgādejī)[20]

Granddaughter of Dhīrāvat Kachvāho Rāmdās Darbārī Ūdāvat (no. 19).

Siṅgardejī was sent in ***ḍoḷo*** and married at the village of Maṇḍal on December 2, 1614 while Rājā Sūrajsiṅgh was proceeding from Udaipur in Mevāṛ to north India. She died on Sunday, November 23, 1628 at Puṣkarjī (near Ajmer). She was beginning a pilgrimage to the Ganges River.

Miscellaneous

D - Prabhāvatībāī: a daughter of Rājā Sūrajsiṅgh's by his concubine, Mohaṇī. Prabhāvatībāī was married following the Rājā's death to Bhāṭī Candrasen Pāñcāvat of Jaisaḷmer by her half-brother, Rājā Gajsiṅgh Sūrajsiṅghot (1619-38). Her marriage was conducted in Jodhpur at the home of Jeso Bhāṭī Goyanddās Mānāvat, who had been ***pradhān*** of Jodhpur under Rājā Sūrajsiṅgh. Rājā Gajsiṅgh gave Bhāṭī Candrasen a ***paṭo*** village in dowry, and retained him in his personal service.[21]

Marriage Lists

Lists of Rājā Sūrajsiṅgh's marriages and of his sons and daughters are contained in the following primary sources:

Jodhpur Rājya kī Khyāt, pp. 131, 156-161.

---

[18] ***Vigat***, 1:93.

[19] ***Khyāt***, 1:320, 323.

[20] ***Ibid.***, 1:331.

[21] ***Ibid.***, 2:81.

Murārdān, no. 2, pp. 207-213 (***Murārdān*** does not reference Rājā Sūrajsiṅgh's daughter, Prabhāvatībāī, born of his concubine, Mohaṇī).
Rāṭhoṛāṃ rī Vaṃśāvalī, MS no. 20130, ff. 99-100.

Other general sources include:

Bāṅkīdās, pp. 25-26; ***Khyāt***, 1:303; ***Murārdān***, no. 2, pp. 205-207; Ojhā, 4:1:362, 364; "Rāṭhauḍ Vaṃś rī Vigat," pp. 14-15; Reu, 1:198; ***Vigat***, 1:92; ***Vīr Vinod***, 2:816-818.

Rājā Gajsiṅgh Sūrajsiṅghot (12-1)

Born: Thursday, October 30, 1595
Died: Sunday, May 6, 1638
Ruled: October 6, 1619 - May 6, 1638
Mother: Rāṇī Kachvāhī Sobhāgdejī, daughter of Sekhāvat Kachvāho Durjaṇsāḷ Karamsīyot.

Rāṇīs, Sons and Daughters

1. **Baṛī Rāṇī Kachvāhī Kalyāṇdejī** (***pīhar*** name Rūpvatībāī or Rūpmatībāī)[1]

Daughter of Kachvāho Kuṃvar Jagrūp Jagnāthot, a son of Rājā Jagnāth Bhārmalot of Toḍo.

Kalyāṇdejī was born on Tuesday, September 9, 1595. Her marriage to Gajsiṅgh took place at Toḍo in 1605-06. She died in October or November of 1648.

D - Candrāvatībāī (or Candramatībāī): born on Wednesday, August 24, 1614. She was married to Vāghelo Soḷaṅkī Rājā Amarsiṅgh Vikramādityot of Bāndhavgaḍh, Rīvāṃ and Mukandpur on Saturday, February 22, 1634. She returned to Jodhpur in 1650-51 after Rājā Amarsiṅgh's death, and she died at Jodhpur in 1669-70.
D - Pūrbāī: died young.
D - Aṇdībāī: died young.
D - Pimaikuṃvar: died young.

2. **Rāṇī Cahuvāṇ Amratdejī** (or Imaratdejī; ***pīhar*** name Rāykuṃvarbāī)[2]

Daughter of Sācoro Cahuvāṇ Sikhro Mahkaraṇot, a son of Mahkaraṇ Rāṇāvat, who had married a daughter to Moṭo Rājā Udaisiṅgh Māldevot of Jodhpur (see ***supra***, Moṭo Rājā Udaisiṅgh Māldevot, Rāṇī no. 7). Sikhro Mahkaraṇot was a military servant of the Moṭo Rājā. He received the village of Khejaṛlo[3] and three others in ***paṭo*** from the Moṭo Rājā.

Amratdejī was married at the village of Khejaṛlo in January or February of 1608. She died at Jodhpur on Tuesday, January 20, 1663.

S - Acaḷsiṅgh: born in 1613-14; died young.

---

[1] ***Bāṅkīdās***, pp. 28-29, 102; ***Khyāt***, 1:133, 300-301; Ojhā, 4:1:408.

[2] ***Bāṅkīdās***, pp. 28, 162; ***Khyāt***, 1:233; Ojhā, 4:1:408, n. 1.

[3] Khejaṛlo village: located thirty-nine miles east of Jodhpur.

3. **Rānī Sīsodṇī Pratāpdejī** (*pīhar* name Rukhmāvatībāī)[4]

Daughter of Saktāvat Sīsodīyo Gahlot Bhāṇ Saktāvat of Mevāṛ.

Pratāpdejī was born on Monday, October 2, 1598. Her marriage took place at Mathurajī on Monday, September 19, 1607 and was arranged by her maternal grandfather, Varsiṅghot Meṛtīyo Rāṭhoṛ Kesodās "Mārū" Bhīṃvot. She received the rank of ***rāṇī*** at Jodhpur on Wednesday, November 27, 1622. She died in Lahore on Friday, May 30, 1634.

S - Jasvantsiṅgh: born on Tuesday, December 26, 1626 at Burhanpur in the Deccan. He succeeded Rājā Gajsiṅgh to the throne of Jodhpur.

4. **Rāṇī Candrāvat Kasmīrdejī**[5]

Daughter of Candrāvat Sīsodīyo Gahlot Rāv Cāndo Durgāvat of Rāmpuro.

Kasmīrdejī was married at Rāmpuro on Friday, April 24, 1612 while Gajsiṅgh was a ***kuṃvar***.

5. **Rāṇī Bhāṭiyāṇī Lachaḷdejī** (or Lāldejī) (***pīhar*** name Rāmkuṃvarbāī)[6]

Daughter of Bhāṭī Rāvaḷ Kalyāṇdās Harrājot of Jaisaḷmer (ca. 1613-27).

Lachaḷdejī was born on Sunday, November 25, 1593. Her marriage took place at Jaisaḷmer on Friday, January 1, 1613 and was arranged by her paternal uncle, Rāvaḷ Bhīṃv Harrājot (1577-1613). She died at Mathurajī in 1667-68.

6. **Rāṇī Sonagarī Mansukhdejī** (***pīhar*** name Bhagvatībāī)[7]

Daughter of Sonagaro Cahuvāṇ Jasvant Mānsiṅghot of Pālī village.[8]

Mansukhdejī was born on Tuesday, January 21, 1595. Her marriage took place at the village of Mīṇīyārī in Goḍhvāṛ on Saturday, April 9, 1614.[9] She left Jodhpur with her son, Amarsiṅgh, on Sunday, March 1, 1635 and settled with him at Nāgaur. She died at Nāgaur on Tuesday, June 15, 1641.

---

[4] ***Bāṅkīdās***, pp. 29, 93; ***Mahārāj Śrī Gajsiṅghjī kī Khyāt***, MS no. 15666, Rājasthān Prācyavidyā Pratiṣṭhān, Jodhpur, pp. 17-18; ***Khyāt***, 1:26; ***Murārdān***, no. 3, pp. 125-126; Ojhā, 4:1:408; ***Vigat***, 1:110, 123.

[5] ***Bāṅkīdās***, p. 33; ***Khyāt***, 3:248.

[6] ***Bāṅkīdās***, pp. 28, 34, 113; ***Khyāt***, 2:98.

[7] ***Bāṅkīdās***, p. 34; ***Khyāt***, 1:208; Ojhā, 4:1:407-408.

[8] Pālī village: located forty miles south-southeast of Jodhpur.

[9] This Rāṇī's marriage apparently took place almost five months after the birth of her son, Amarsiṅgh. The circumstances behind this late marriage are unknown.

S - Amarsiṅgh: born on Friday, December 11, 1613.[10] He received the title of ***rāv*** from the Mughal Emperor Shāh Jahān along with the ***jāgīr*** of Pargano Nāgaur.

7. **Rāṇī Vāghelī Kasūmbhadejī** [11]

Daughter of Vāghelo Soḷaṅkī Sāṅgo.

Kasūmbhadejī was born on Friday, December 5, 1595. She was married at Jodhpur in June of 1615 in the home of ***sikdār*** Sobho (tentatively identified as Jāṅgaḷvo Sāṅkhlo Paṃvār Sobho Harbhāmot). She had been sent in ***ḍoḷo*** from Īḍar to Rājā Gajsiṅgh.

8. **Rāṇī Jāṛecī Noraṅgdejī**

Daughter of Jāṛeco Jām Sāh, master of Nayanagar.

Noraṅgdejī was sent in ***ḍoḷo*** to Rājā Gajsiṅgh at Burhanpur in the Deccan. She was married at the village of Rāvar on Friday, April 12, 1622. She died during the night at Jodhpur on Wednesday, January 21, 1663.

9. **Rāṇī Kachvāhī Sūrajdejī** [12]

Daughter of Kachvāho Rājā Bhāvsiṅgh Mānsiṅghot of Āmber (1614-21).

Sūrajdejī was married at Āmber on Monday, November 4, 1622. The marriage was arranged by Rājā Jaisiṅgh Mahāsiṅghot (1621-67). She became a ***satī*** at the time of Rājā Gajsiṅgh's death at Agra in May of 1638.

D - (name unknown): born in 1636-37. She died young at Burhanpur in the Deccan.

10. **Rāṇī Narūkī Kachvāhī Kesardejī** [13]

Daughter of Narūko Kachvāho Candrabhāṇ Jaitsīyot, the master of Panvāṛ. Candrabhāṇ had settled in Mārvāṛ in 1611-12, and he held the village of Rāhaṇ[14] in ***paṭo*** from Rājā Sūrajsiṅgh Udaisiṅghot. He later took service under Mughal Emperor Jahāṅgīr.

Kesardejī was born on June 10, 1608. Her marriage took place on Tuesday, May 27, 1623 at the village of Panvāṛ during the time Rājā Gajsiṅgh

---

[10] ***Jodhpur Rājya kī Khyāt***, p. 199, converts this date to December 30, 1614, which is incorrect, but on p. 272, converts this same date correctly to December 11, 1613. Ojhā, 4:1:408, lists the date correctly.

[11] ***Bāṅkīdās***, p. 34.

[12] ***Ibid.***; ***Khyāt***, 1:298-299; ***Vigat***, 1:111.

[13] ***Bāṅkīdās***, p. 34; ***Khyāt***, 1:315.

[14] Rāhaṇ village: located ten miles north-northeast of Meṛto.

was traveling in the area of Rāmpuro on the Chambal River. She was in Jodhpur when the Rājā died, and she became a ***satī*** at Maṇḍor on Monday, May 14, 1638.

11. **Rāṇī Bhāṭiyāṇī** (***pīhar*** name Udaikuṃvarbāī) [15]
Daughter of Bhāṭī Rāvaḷ Manohardās Kalyāṇdāsot of Jaisaḷmer (ca. 1627-50).

Marriage Lists

Lists of Rājā Gajsiṅgh's marriages and of his sons and daughters are contained in the following primary sources. These sources reference all marriages except that of Rāṇī no. 11:

Jodhpur Rājya kī Khyāt, pp. 161, 197-201.
Murārdān, no. 2, pp. 225-228.
Rāṭhoṛāṃ rī Vaṃśāvalī, MS no. 20130, ff. 118-119.

Other general references include:

Khyāt, 1:325; ***Mūndiyāṛ rī Rāṭhoṛāṃ rī Khyāt***, no. 2, pp. 100-101; ***Murārdān***, no. 1, pp. 545-561; Ojhā, 4:1:388, 407-408, 413; "Rāṭhauḍ Vaṃś rī Vigat," p. 15; Reu, 1:209; ***Vigat***, 1:105; ***Vīr Vinod***, 2:819-821.

---

[15] ***Jaisalmer rī Khyāt***, p. 74; ***Tavārīkh Jaisalmer***, p. 56.

Rājā Jasvantsiṅgh Gajsiṅghot (13-1)

Born: Tuesday, December 26, 1626
Died: Thursday, November 28, 1678
Ruled: May 25, 1638 - November 28, 1678
Mother: Rāṇī Sīsodṇī Pratāpdejī, daughter of Saktāvat Sīsodīyo Gahlot Bhāṇ Saktāvat of Mevāṛ.

Rāṇīs, Sons, and Daughters

1. **Rāṇī Bhāṭiyāṇī Jasrūpdejī** (***pīhar*** name Pemkuṃvarbāī)[1]
Daughter of Bhāṭī Rāvaḷ Manohardās Kalyāṇdāsot of Jaisaḷmer (ca. 1627-50).
Jasrūpdejī was born on Saturday, September 15, 1627. She was married to Jasvantsiṅgh while he was a ***kuṃvar*** on Tuesday, April 25, 1637 at Jaisaḷmer. She died on Wednesday, April 10, 1650 and was cremated on the banks of the Jumna River in Delhi.

2. **Rāṇī Hāḍī Jasvantdejī**[2]
Daughter of Hāḍo Cahuvāṇ Rāv Catrasāḷ Gopīnāthot of Būndī (ca. 1631-58).
The texts list several different ***pīhar*** names for Jasvantdejī. These include Kalyāṇbāī, Kāṅkuṃvar, and Rāmkuṃvar. From sources available, it is not possible to determine which name is correct.
Jasvantdejī was born on either July 10 or August 9, 1627. She was married to Jasvantsiṅgh while he was a ***kuṃvar*** on Saturday, May 5, 1638 at Būndī. She received the rank of ***mahārāṇī*** on Friday, April 22, 1670 at Aurangabād. She died in Būndī.

3. **Rāṇī Cahuvāṇ Jagrūpdejī** (***pīhar*** name Rāykuṃvarbāī)[3]
Daughter of Sācoro Cahuvāṇ Dayāḷdās Sikhrāvat.
Jagrūpdejī was born on Monday, June 4, 1632.[4] She was sent in ***ḍoḷo*** to Rājā Jasvantsiṅgh and married at Bīlāṛo village[5] on either January 19 or February 2, 1641 while the Rājā was returning to Jodhpur from Lahore.

---

[1] ***Bāṅkīdās***, pp. 33, 113.

[2] ***Ibid***., pp. 34, 146; ***Vigat***, 2:462.

[3] ***Bāṅkīdās***, p. 34; ***Khyāt***, 1:233.

[4] ***Jodhpur Rājya kī Khyāt***, p. 262, records this date. ***Rāṭhoṛāṃ rī Vaṃśāvalī***, MS no. 20130, f. 155, gives the date of June 11, 1626, which is incorrect.

[5] Bīlāṛo village: located forty-one miles east-southeast of Jodhpur.

4. **Rāṇī Kachvāhī Jasmādejī** [6]

Daughter of Sekhāvat Kachvāho Rājā Dvārkādās Girdhardāsot of Khaṇḍeḷo.

Jasmādejī was born on Friday, August 20, 1624. She was married at Khaṇḍeḷo on Wednesday, February 24, 1641.

D - Pratāpkuṃvar: born on Tuesday, August 21, 1649. She died one day after birth.

5. **Rāṇī Jādav (Jādam) Jaivantdejī**

Daughter of Jādav Prithīrāj Rāysiṅghot.

Jaivantdejī came in ***ḍoḷo*** from the village of Corāū near Juṇāgaḍh. She was married at Jodhpur on Monday, May 13, 1644.

D - Mahākuṃvar: born on Saturday, May 31, 1645. She died on Wednesday, January 6, 1647.

6. **Rāṇī Gauṛ Jasraṅgdejī** (***pīhar*** name Cārmatībāī)[7]

Daughter of Gauṛ Manohardās Gopāḷdāsot.

Jasraṅgdejī was born on Saturday, June 27, 1635. She was married to Rājā Jasvantsiṅgh at the order of Emperor Shāh Jahān to end the ***vair*** between the Rāṭhoṛs of Jodhpur and the Gauṛs that emerged following the death of Rājā Jasvantsiṅgh's half-brother, Rāv Amarsiṅgh Gajsiṅghot.[8] The marriage took place at Riṇthambhor on Friday, February 8, 1650 under the supervision of Gauṛ Rājā Vīṭhaḷdās. Jasraṅgdejī died on Monday, September 1, 1662.

7. **Rāṇī Kachvāhī Atraṅgdejī** (***pīhar*** name Jānkuṃvarbāī)[9]

Daughter of Sekhāvat Kachvāho Rājā Varsiṅgh Dvārkādāsot of Khaṇḍeḷo, and daughter's daughter (***dohitrī***) of Hāḍo Cahuvāṇ Rāvrājā Ratansiṅgh Bhojrājot of Būndī (ca. 1607-58).

Atraṅgdejī was born on Tuesday, August 19, 1634. She was married at Khaṇḍeḷo on Tuesday, May 28, 1650 or May 17, 1651.

S - Prithīrāj: born at Jodhpur on Thursday, July 1, 1652. He died in Delhi on Wednesday, May 8, 1667.

---

[6] ***Khyāt***, 1:321-322.

[7] ***Bāṅkīdās***, p. 34; Ojhā, 4:1:409-410.

[8] See **Endnote** to this section for a discussion of the circumstances surrounding Rāv Amarsiṅgh Gajsiṅghot's death and Rājā Jasvantsiṅgh's resultant marriage of a daughter of the Gauṛs.

[9] ***Bāṅkīdās***, pp. 34-35; ***Khyāt***, 1:322.

D - Ratanāvatī: born in 1655-56.

8. **Rāṇī Sīsodṇī Jasrūpdejī** (*pīhar* name Rūpkuṃvarbāī)[10]

Daughter of Sīsodīyo Gahlot Vīramde Sūrajmalot, a grandson of Sīsodīyo Rāṇo Amarsiṅgh Pratāpsiṅghot of Mevāṛ (1597-1620).

Jasrūpdejī was born in 1643-44. She was married to Rājā Jasvantsiṅgh at Mathurajī on Wednesday, April 20, 1657. She died on Tuesday, October 21, 1662.

9. **Rāṇī Devṛī Atisukhdejī** (*pīhar* name Āṇandkuṃvarbāī)[11]

Daughter of Devṛo Cahuvāṇ Rāv Akhairāj Rājsiṅghot of Sīrohī (ca. 1618-65).

Atisukhdejī was born in 1643-44. She was married on Wednesday, March 30, 1659 in Sīrohī while Rājā Jasvantsiṅgh was enroute to Gujarat. Atisukhdejī died at the fort of Jodhpur on Sunday, December 29, 1658.[12]

Mūndiyāṛ rī Rāṭhoṛāṃ ri Khyāt, pp. 138-139, states that the Devṛos presented this Rāṇī in ***ḍoḷo*** to the Rājā in order to settle the ***vair*** which had arise between the Devṛos of Sīrohī and Jodho Rāṭhoṛs of Jodhpur. This ***vair*** arose when Jodho Rāṭhoṛ Rāv Rāysiṅgh Candrasenot was killed at the battle of Datāṇī in Sīrohī on October 17, 1583.[13] Rāv Rāysiṅgh was a son of Rāv Candrasen Māldevot of Jodhpur (see ***supra***, Rāv Candrasen Māldevot, Rāṇī no. 2, S - Rāysiṅgh).

10. **Rāṇī Candrāvat Jaisukhdejī** (*pīhar* name Nabhāvatībāī)[14]

Daughter of Candrāvat Sīsodīyo Gahlot Rāv Amarsiṅgh Harīsiṅghot of Rāmpuro.

Jaisukhdejī was born on Saturday, February 21, 1646. Her marriage took place at Rāmpuro on April 9, 1665 while Rājā Jasvantsiṅgh was enroute from Poona in the Deccan to north India. The Rājā received forty horses and one elephant in dowry. Jaisukhdejī became a ***satī*** at the time of Rājā Jasvantsiṅgh's death.

S - Jagatsiṅgh: born on Friday, January 4, 1667. He died during the night on Saturday, March 4, 1676.

---

[10] ***Khyāt***, 1:30.

[11] Ojhā, 4:1:448; ***Vigat***, 1:138.

[12] ***Jodhpur Rājya kī Khyāt***, p. 270, records this date. ***Rāṭhoṛāṃ rī Vaṃśāvalī***, MS no. 20130, f. 156, gives the date of December 16, 1708. It is not possible to know which date is correct, and the difference may be due to scribal error.

[13] See ***infra***, "Devṛo Cahuvāṇs," Rāv Surtāṇ Bhāṇot (no. 5), for more details about this battle and its aftermath.

[14] ***Vigat***, 1:150.

D - Udaikuṃvarbāī: born in January or February of 1676[15]; died young.

11. **Rāṇī Jādav Jaskuṃvarjī** [16]

Sources are in conflict regarding the identity of this Rāṇī's father. He is listed as both Jādav Rājā Chatramaṇ (or Chatrasāḷ) Mukandot of Karaulī, and Jādav Kuṃvar Bhupāḷ Chatramaṇot, a son of Rājā Chatramaṇ's. From sources available, it is not possible to determine his identity with certainty.

Jaskuṃvarjī was married on Saturday, April 15, 1665 in the village of Hibhavaṇ near Karaulī, while Rājā Jasvantsiṅgh was returning to Mārvāṛ from Poona in the Deccan.

S - Ajītsiṅgh: born in Lahore on Wednesday, February 19, 1679 following Rājā Jasvantsiṅgh's death. He succeeded Rājā Jasvantsiṅgh to the throne of Jodhpur.

12. **Rāṇī Kachvāhī Narūkījī** [17]

Daughter of Narūko Kachvāho Phatahsiṅgh Lāḍkhānot of Kaṇkoṛ village.

S - Dalthambhaṇ: born on Wednesday, February 19, 1679 following Rājā Jasvantsiṅgh's death at Lahore; died young.

Marriage Lists

Lists of Rājā Jasvantsiṅgh's marriages and of his sons and daughters are contained in the following primary sources:

Jodhpur Rājya kī Khyāt, pp. 203, 267-272.
Mūndiyāṛ rī Rāṭhoṛāṃ rī Khyāt, pp. 138-139 (this source does not reference Rāṇī no. 4).
Ojhā, 4:1:468-469.
Rāṭhoṛāṃ rī Vaṃśāvalī, MS no. 20130, ff. 155-156.

Other general sources include:

Ojhā, 4:1:413, 459; "Rāṭhauḍ Vaṃś rī Vigat," pp. 15-16; Reu, 1:238; ***Vīr Vinod***, 2:821-828.

---

[15] ***Rāṭhoṛāṃ rī Vaṃśāvalī***, MS no. 20130, f. 156, records this date. It is preferable to that given in ***Jodhpur Rājya kī Khyāt***, p. 271, which lists the date of January/February, 1665 for the child's birth. This latter date appears incorrect.

[16] ***Vigat***, 1:150; ***Vīr Vinod***, 2:1499-1500.

[17] ***Bāṅkīdās***, p. 35; ***Khyāt***, 1:318.

Endnote

Rāv Amarsiṅgh Gajsiṅghot's Death
and
Rājā Jasvantsiṅgh's Marriage of a Daughter of the Gauṛs

Rājā Jasvantsiṅgh's marriage of a daughter of the Gauṛs is of interest because the Gauṛs were not directly responsible for Rāv Amarsiṅgh's death. Rāv Amarsiṅgh was the eldest son of Rājā Gajsiṅgh Sūrajsiṅghot (1619-38). He was a Mughal ***mansabdār*** of rank, who at the time of his death, held Nāgaur in ***jāgīr*** from Emperor Shāh Jahān. He had received Nāgaur in 1638 on the death of Rājā Gajsiṅgh.

On July 25, 1644 Amarsiṅgh stabbed and killed Ṣalābat Khān Raushan Ḍamīr, the second Imperial Bakhshī, with his dagger in the private parlor of Sultān Dārā Shikoh's house at Agra, where the Emperor was living and holding court. Imperial mace-bearers in attendance upon the Emperor then took Amarsiṅgh's life. These killings occurred after the evening prayers, while the Emperor was writing a ***farmān*** with his own hand. Rāv Amarsiṅgh had been absent from the Imperial ***darbār*** for some time due to illness, and he had come to court this evening during his convalescence in order to pay his respects to Shāh Jahān and to present him with a customary gift. After performing obeisance before the Emperor, he took his assigned position standing to the right of the throne. But he suddenly drew his dagger and attacked Ṣalābat Khān who was on the Emperor's left. He caught the Khān unawares, stabbing him under the breast and killing him instantly.

Khalīl Ullah Khān and Gauṛ Arjaṇ Vīṭhaḷdāsot, a son of Gauṛ Rājā Vīṭhaḷdās's, who were among those present, both drew weapons and attacked Rāv Amarsiṅgh on the Emperor's order. The Rāv was able to ward off Khalīl Khān's blows, but Gauṛ Arjuṇ struck and wounded him while himself sustaining a cut to his ear from Amarsiṅgh's dagger. Imperial mace-bearers then fell on the Rāv and killed him. A series of pitched battles followed with Amarsiṅgh's Rajpūts. ***Maāthir-ul-Umarā***, 1:234, reports:

> After [Rāv Amarsiṅgh was killed], Mīr Khān Mīr Tūzak, and Mulak Chand the accountant of the daulātkhānakhāṣ, brought the body of Amar Singh, in accordance with orders, outside the vestibule (***dihlīz***) of the khilwatkhāna (private chamber) and sent for his [Rāv Amarsiṅgh's] men, in order that they might take it to his house. Fifteen of his servants heard of the affair and laid hands on their swords and daggers; Mulak Chand was killed, and Mīr Khān was wounded and died on the following night. Meanwhile the Aḥadīs and others came out and sent that rabble to hell. Six of the mace-bearers were killed and

six were wounded. Not content with this, a number of Amar Siṅgh's servants resolved what they would go to [Gauṛ] Arjan's house and kill him.

The Emperor learned what had occurred and attempted to have matters explained to Amarsiṅgh's men, and to quiet and disperse them to their homes. They would not be dissuaded, however, and the Emperor finally sent Saiyyid Khān Jahān Bārha along with a number of the Imperial bodyguard to oppose these Rajpūts, and many of them were killed.

Maāthir-ul-Umarā (***ibid.***) notes that "Though the king made inquiry into the origin of this uproar, nothing appeared except the long use of intoxicants aggravated by the illness of some days." Contrary to this assertion, there appear to have been a number of factors contributing to this outbreak of hostilities. Earlier that year a boundary dispute had arisen between Jākhaṇīyo village of Nāgaur and Sīlvo village of Bīkāner, and fighting had broken out between opposing forces. A number of men on both sides were killed, but the ***sāth*** from Bīkāner had gained the upper hand. Rāv Amarsiṅgh wrote to his men at Nāgaur afterwards, ordering them to assemble another ***sāth*** and prepare to attack Bīkāner. He then entreated the Emperor to allow him to attack Bīkāner in retaliation for his earlier defeat, but the Emperor forbade this action. Bīkāner Rājā Karaṇsiṅgh Sūrsiṅghot (1631-68), upon learning of Rāv Amarsiṅgh's plans, petitioned Ṣalābat Khān to appoint an ***amīn*** to settle the dispute. Ṣalābat Khān did appoint an ***amīn***, and appears openly to have sided with Bīkāner. This slight greatly offended Amarsiṅgh.

It is unclear why Ṣalābat Khān sided with Bīkāner, but he seems to have taken a personal dislike to Rāv Amarsiṅgh. ***Mūndiyāṛ rī Rāṭhoṛāṃ rī Khyāt***, pp. 125-126, reports that Rāv Amarsiṅgh had formed a relationship with Ṣalābat Khān's wife, whom he is said to have visited in Agra when the Khān was away on Imperial business. This liaison angered Ṣalābat Khān, who according to this ***khyāt***, tried unsuccessfully on a number of occasions to kill the Rāv.

On the evening of July 25 when Rāv Amarsiṅgh came to pay his respects to the Emperor, Ṣalābat Khān approached him and spoke disrespectfully to him. Their exchange led to angry words, and the Khān's provocation contributed directly to Rāv Amarsiṅgh's attack in the ***darbār***. According to "Mahārāv Śrī Amarsiṅghjī Rāṭhoṛ rī Vāt," pp. 113-114, a text composed in 1649 just five years after Rāv Amarsiṅgh's death, Ṣalābat Khān approached Amarsiṅgh as he entered the private chamber, questioning why he had been absent for so many days, and asking if he had brought a gift for the Emperor. Amarsiṅgh explained about his illness, but Ṣalābat Khān persisted, saying, "Rāvjī, have you remained absent because of the news of the fighting with Bīkāner?" implying directly that the Rāv could not show his face because he had been shamed by his loss. The Khān then openly stated, "Rāvjī, your ***sāth*** has run away before, and now again it will flee." Rāv Amarsiṅgh then cursed the Khān, retorting, "Spider (***makṛā***)! Shut up!" The exchange of insults continued until Amarsiṅgh drew away to pay his respects to the Emperor and present his gift. As he then went to his place in the chamber, the Khān taunted him, saying, "What, does the Rāvjī act like an [ignorant] villager (*gamārī karau*)?" These words enraged Amarsiṅgh and he drew his dagger and attacked Ṣalābat Khān.

Regardless of the reasons behind this enmity and the immediate cause of Amarsiṅgh's death, the Rāṭhoṛs held the Gauṛs responsible.

For information about Rāv Amarsiṅgh Gajsiṅghot, see: ***Jodhpur Rājya kī Khyāt***, pp. 199, 269-283; ***Maāt͟hir-ul-Umarā***, 1:232-236, 2:2:702-703; Ojhā, 4:1:409-410; "Mahārāv Śrī Amarsiṅghjī Rāṭhoṛ rī Vāt," in ***Rājasthānī Vāt-Saṅgrah***, Manohar Śarma, Śrīlāl Nāthmaljī Jośī, eds. (Naī Dillī: Sāhitya Akādemī, 1984), pp. 109-117; ***Mūndiyāṛ rī Rāṭhoṛāṃ rī Khyāt***, pp. 124-129.

BIOGRAPHICAL NOTES

RAJPŪTS

MUSLIMS

ADMINISTRATIVE *JĀTIS*

Jeso Bhāṭīs

(no. 1) **Pītho Āṇandot** (5-1)
(no. 2) **Sāṅkar Sūrāvat** (6-3)
(no. 3) **Tiloksī Parbatot** (6-1)

The Jeso Bhāṭīs are an important group of Rajpūts in Mārvāṛ. Their association with the Rāṭhoṛs and with Jodhpur dates from the mid-fifteenth century, when a sister of Bhāṭī Jeso Kalikaraṇot, the founder of this brotherhood (***bhāībandh***), was married to Jodho Rāṭhoṛ Kuṃvar Sūjo Jodhāvat (Rāv of Jodhpur, ca. 1492-1515). Within a short span of years, members of the Jeso Bhāṭīs emerged among the staunchest supporters of the Jodhpur throne, and a number of them became important ***ṭhākur***s in Mārvāṛ with influential positions at court.

Early History of the Jeso Bhāṭīs

The Jeso Bhāṭīs descend from Bhāṭī Jeso Kalikaraṇot (3-1). Jeso was the son of Kalikaraṇ Keharot (2-1) and grandson of Rāvaḷ Kehar Devrājot (1-1), ruler of Jaisaḷmer (1361-97).[1] No information is available about Jeso's father,

---

[1] Sources reviewed all state explicitly that Jeso Kalikaraṇot was a son of Kalikaraṇ Keharot and grandson of Rāvaḷ Kehar Devrājot. However, the ***Khyāt*** of Naiṇsī, 2:116, 144, also lists a Kalikaraṇ as son of Rāvaḷ Kelhaṇ Keharot of Pūṅgaḷ, who was himself a son of Rāvaḷ Kehar Devrājot of Jaisaḷmer (see ***infra***, Figure 2. **Bhāṭī Ruling Family of Jaisaḷmer**). ***Khyāt*** records that the descendants of the latter Kalikaraṇ were associated with a village called Tāṇāno. There appears to be no village by this name in the area of Pūṅgaḷ, and the name is suspiciously close to that of Tāṇo village of Mevāṛ, which Jeso Kalikaraṇot received from the Rāṇo of Cītoṛ. The confusion about the village and the recurrence of the name Kalikaraṇ for a son and grandson of Rāvaḷ Kehar's, which is most unusual, especially considering that Kalikaraṇ and Kelhaṇ were uterine brothers (***Khyāt***, 2:75-76), casts some doubt on the Jeso Bhāṭī genealogy.

The sources compound the confusion between the Kalikaraṇs in the following manner: Naiṇsī's ***Khyāt***, 3:7, refers to a Kalikaraṇ Bhāṭī (father unspecified, but presumably Kelhaṇ Kaharot), who rode with the Kelhaṇ Bhāṭīs against Rāṭhoṛ Bīko Jodhāvat (no. 42) and was killed in battle near Koṛamdesar (located eleven miles due west of present-day Bīkāner). This battle occurred while Bīko Jodhāvat was establishing a foothold in the area which later became known as Bīkāner. Ojhā, 5:1:94-95, mentions this same battle in his history of Bīkāner. But he identifies the Bhāṭī involved as Kalikaraṇ Keharot of Jaisaḷmer, noting that Rāvaḷ Kehar Devrājot's son, then aged eighty, went to help the Kelhaṇs against Bīko Jodhāvat and was killed there in 1478-79.

Jaisalmer rī Khyāt, p. 62, lists no son of Rāvaḷ Kelhaṇ Keharot's by the name of Kalikaraṇ. However, it does list a son by the name of Lūṇkaraṇ. It is possible that Lūṇkaraṇ is the correct name and that the name confusion is due to "scribal error" in the transmission and recording of names.

Kalikaraṇ Keharot, except the name of his mother. She was the Devṛī Cahuvāṇ Lāchāṃ. Regarding Jeso Kalikaraṇot himself, uncertainty extends both to questions about his family and to issues of chronology relating to events of his life.

There is detail in local sources only about the maternal side of Jeso's family. This information is difficult to interpret, however. The relationships in question concern those among Bhāṭī Jeso Kalikaraṇot, the Sāṅkhlo Paṃvār Harbhū Mahirājot of Baiṃhgaṭī village,[2] and Bhāṭiyāṇī Likhmībāī (***pīhar*** name) who was married to Jodho Rāṭhoṛ Sūjo Jodhāvat and lived at the Jodhpur court as Rāṇī Bhāṭiyāṇī Sāraṅgdejī.[3]

Sources record the following contradictory information about these individuals:

1. "Aitihāsik Bātāṃ," p. 37, states that Likhmībāī was Jeso's daughter (***beṭī***) and Harbhū's daughter's daughter (***dohitrī***).
2. ***Khyāt***, 3:7, states that Jeso was Harbhū's sister's son (***bhāṇej***).
3. ***Khyāt***, 3:103-104, records that Jeso was Harbhū's daughter's son (***dohitro***) and Likhmībāī was Jeso's sister, presumably born of the same mother (the text is unclear).

Given the broad range of possible degrees of kinship evident here, with Jeso either Harbhū's daughter's husband, daughter's son or sister's son, and Likhmībāī either Jeso's daughter or sister, these accounts are impossible to reconcile. The weight of both this and other evidence, however, points to the probability that Jeso was Harbhū's daughter's son, and that Likhmībāī was Jeso's uterine sister. These relationships appear most logical, given other details available about the lives of these individuals.

The ***Khyāt*** of Naiṇsī, 3:103-104, records, for example, that Jeso and Likhmībāī were brother and sister, that Bhāṭī Kalikaraṇ Keharot of Jaisaḷmer had married at Sāṅkhlo Harbhū's home, and that the Sāṅkhlo Harbhū was Jeso and

---

To add to the confusion, ***Bhaṭṭivaṃś Praśasti*** (see: Ojhā, 5:1:94-95, n. 3, for a complete reference to this text) also mentions a Lūṇkaraṇ with relation to the Bhāṭī attack on Koṛamdesar. The ***Praśasti*** identifies this Lūṇkaraṇ, however, as Rāv Lūṇkaraṇ Bīkāvat, who was Rāv Bīko Jodhāvat's son and ruler of Bīkāner, 1505-26. The ***Praśasti*** was composed by Vyās Govind Madhuvan during the rule of Bhāṭī Rāvaḷ Kalyāṇdās Harrājot of Jaisaḷmer (ca. 1612-26) It is apparent that the individuals involved have become confused over the passage of time. Ojhā, who references the ***Praśasti*** in his discussion of the history of Bīkāner, discounts the passage dealing with this Lūṇkaraṇ. It may be, however, that while certain parts of the ***Praśasti*** are in error, the name Lūṇkaraṇ and his association with the Kelhaṇ attack against Bīko Jodhāvat are correct.

[2] Baiṃhgaṭī: located eleven miles due west of Phaḷodhī village in northern Mārvāṛ.

[3] See ***supra***, **Marriage and Family Lists of the Rulers of Jodhpur**, Sūjo Jodhāvat, Rāṇī no. 1.

Likhmībāī's maternal grandfather (***nāno***). There is no evidence that another of Harbhū's daughters was married to Bhāṭī Kalikaraṇ. Jeso and Likhmībāī, therefore, appear to have been uterine brother and sister. This same entry in ***Khyāt*** also notes that Harbhū's daughter remained at her father's home (***pīhar***) following her marriage to Kalikaraṇ Bhāṭī, and that she gave birth to Likhmībāī at Baiṃhgaṭī village.

Khyāt, 2:152-153, records a slightly different version of Likhmībāī's birth. It states:

> [Jeso] went to the open fields [before] Kiraṛo[4] and stayed; there Rāṇī Likhmī was born . . ; then she was sent to Harbhū's [home], the maternal grandfather's home (***nānāṇo***).

Finally, ***Khyāt***, 3:7, places Jeso Kalikaraṇot at Harbhū's home during a time he would have been a child or early adolescent, and it appears that Jeso and Likhmībāī were both closely associated with their maternal grandfather's home throughout much of their early lives.

Information concerning events of Jeso Kalikaraṇot's life covers the period from the early 1440s to the late 1460s or early 1470s. Again there are difficulties with chronology and fact. The events recorded in the texts include the following:

1. Jeso was in Baiṃhgaṭī village in the early 1440s.
2. He left Jaisaḷmer and proceeded first to the village of Kiraṛo (near Phaḷodhī) and then to Bhāuṇḍo village of Nāgaur.[5]
3. He had a fort built at Bhāuṇḍo village.
4. He came to live in the ***vās*** ("residence, dwelling") of Rāṭhoṛ Sūjo Jodhāvat of Jodhpur.
5. He went to Cītoṛ and received the village of "Tāṇo, the one [formerly] belonging to Māḷo Soḷaṅkī (***Tāṇo Māḷo Soḷaṅkivāḷo***)"[6] and 140 others in ***paṭo*** from Sīsodīyo Rāṇo Kūmbho Mokaḷot (ca. 1433-68).
6. He left Cītoṛ for Delhi in order to organize an attack upon Jaisaḷmer.
7. He died "two months" after reaching Delhi.

Khyāt, 3:7, places Jeso in Baiṃhgaṭī village with his maternal grandfather, Sāṅkhlo Harbhū Mahirājot, in the early 1440s. It is unclear from the text whether Jeso was living in Baiṃhgaṭī at this time or merely visiting there with his mother. Regardless, the dating of the early 1440s rests upon Jeso's presence in this village at the time Rāṭhoṛ Jodho Riṇmalot came to Baiṃhgaṭī to visit Harbhū Sāṅkhlo, who was a well-known omen-reader and seer (***pīr***). Jodho

---

[4] Kiraṛo: located twelve miles north of Phaḷodhī.

[5] Bhāuṇḍo: located twenty-five miles southwest of Nāgaur.

[6] Tāṇo: located near Toḍgaṛh some sixty-four miles northwest of Cītoṛ.

Riṇmalot was living in Jāṅgaḷu[7] at the time. His father, Rāv Riṇmal Cūṇḍāvat, had been murdered at Cītoṛ ca. 1438, and in the wake of his death, Jodho had fled Mevāṛ for Mārvāṛ and Jāṅgaḷu while the Sīsodīyos under Rāṇo Kūmbho occupied Maṇḍor and much of eastern Mārvāṛ. Jodho himself then began the process of collecting Rajpūts and horses for the conquest of Maṇḍor which finally bore fruit ca. 1453, fifteen years after his father's murder. There is no indication that Jeso Kalikaraṇot was included in the discussions which took place at Baiṃhgaṭī or that he took part in any of the subsequent Rāṭhoṛ actions against the Sīsodīyos. Both omissions lend support to the probability that Jeso was a boy at this time.

Jeso's presence in Baiṃhgaṭī in the early 1440s appears to have coincided with Likhmībāī's birth. Her birth is also placed in the early 1440s for the following reasons: Entries regarding Likhmībāī's birth (***Khyāt***, 3:103-104) record that she was born under the ***vaḍo*** or ***mūl nakhatra***. This lunar asterism, considered by some the twenty-fourth, and by others the seventeenth or nineteenth, contains eleven stars which appear to be the same as those in the tail of Scorpio and are, therefore, considered unlucky.[8] Prospective bridegrooms whom Harbhū Sāṅkhlo approached with offers of marriage all considered Likhmībāī unacceptable. She was, therefore, married "late" to Rāṭhoṛ Sūjo Jodhāvat. Her first son by Sūjo was Vāgho Sūjāvat (no. 83), born in December of 1457. If Vāgho's birth took place shortly after Likhmībāī's marriage, this marriage would have occurred in the mid-1450s,[9] not long after Sūjo's father, Rāv Jodho Riṇmalot, conquered Maṇḍor from the Sīsodīyos ca. 1453. Furthermore, if Likhmībāī was in her late teens at the time of her marriage, she would have been born in the early 1440s. This dating coincides with Jeso's presence in Baiṃhgaṭī village at the time of Rāṭhoṛ Jodho Riṇmalot's visit.

Khyāt, 2:152, indicates that Jeso "left Jaisaḷmer." This departure must refer to his journey to Baiṃhgaṭī village as a boy. He and his mother may have quit Jaisaḷmer at his father's direction because of conflicts either within his own family or within the Bhāṭī brotherhood. ***Khyāt*** records only that Jeso went to Kiraṛo village (near Phaḷodhī) and that Likhmībāī was born there. However, Kiraṛo appears to have been a stopping place only and, as noted above, it is probable that Likhmībāī was born at Baiṃhgaṭī village itself.

Khyāt (***ibid.***) also notes that when Jeso left Jaisaḷmer, he "did not stay in any village of Phaḷodhī at any time." This passage is difficult to interpret given the fact that Jeso either lived in or visited Baiṃhgaṭī, a village of Phaḷodhī, and that his mother and sister were there. The statement in the ***Khyāt*** appears to refer not to Jeso himself, but rather to his sons and for the following reasons: Jeso's sister, Likhmībāī, gave birth to two sons by Sūjo Jodhāvat, Vāgho and Naro

---

[7] Jāṅgaḷu: located sixty-five miles northeast of Phaḷodhī and twenty-four miles south of present-day Bīkāner.

[8] See: Platts, ***Dictionary***, p. 1093.

[9] Sūjo Jodhāvat would have been between fourteen and eighteen years of age at this time. He was born on August 2, 1439.

Sūjāvat. Her second son, Naro, received Phaḷodhī and its surrounding area for his maintenance from Rāv Sūjo. An inscription at the fort of Phaḷodhī dated Monday, March 27, 1475 (*Caitrādi*) or Monday, April 15, 1476 (*Śrāvaṇādi*)[10] records the erection of the main gate of the fort during Naro's rule. ***Khyāt***, 3:103-114, records that Naro went to Phaḷodhī with his mother, and that he was involved there for a number of years in the consolidation of these lands under his authority. Because Naro was Jeso Kalikaraṇot's sister's son (***bhāṇej***), Naro was the "receiver" in the network of kinship. It would have been inappropriate for Jeso's sons to take from him or from Likhmībāī, their father's sister, or to occupy and live in villages under Naro's control. Jeso's sons themselves first settled in Khairvo and Sojhat, villages of Mārvāṛ located some distance to the south and southeast respectively of Phaḷodhī.

This prohibition appears not to have extended past the second generation. Another inscription at the fort of Phaḷodhī dated Wednesday, December 3, 1516 records the erection of pillars on the outer gateway of the fort during the time of Naro Sūjāvat's son, Hamīr Narāvat. The inscription includes mention of a Bhāṭī Nībā who was at the fort with Hamīr. This Bhāṭī may have been Jeso Kalikaraṇot's grandson, Nīmbo Āṇandot (5-3). Nīmbo was a military servant of Rāv Mālde Gāṅgāvat of Jodhpur (1532-62) and held the important village of Lavero[11] in ***paṭo*** from the Rāv. This village was to become a central place for the Jeso Bhāṭīs of Mārvāṛ for many generations to come.

It is difficult to say when Jeso reached Bhāuṇḍo village of Nāgaur. ***Khyāt***, 2:153, states only that Jeso went to Bhāuṇḍo and had a fort built there. His arrival may have coincided with the period of political unrest in Nāgaur that began in the mid-1450s. The ruler of Nāgaur, Khānzāda Khān Firūz Khān I, died in 1451-52. A succession struggle between his son, Shams Khān II, and his brother, Mujāhid Khān,[12] followed his death, which was not settled until 1454-55. This dispute, into which Sīsodīyo Rāṇo Kūmbho Mokaḷot of Cītoṛ (ca. 1533-68) also entered, may have allowed Jeso to occupy Bhāuṇḍo and to consolidate his position there. He may have been recruited by one of the sides in this struggle. Jeso eventually left Bhāuṇḍo for Cītoṛ, but he retained control over Bhāuṇḍo. ***Khyāt***, 2:153, states that Jeso's ***vasī*** stayed behind him there. This village remained in his family for one more generation.

Jeso was probably drawn to Cītoṛ by the growing power and influence of Sīsodīyo Rāṇo Kūmbho Mokaḷot, who was able to assert direct control in the area of Nāgaur for a brief period before being drawn into a series of conflicts

---

[10] See: L. P. Tessitori, "A Progress Report on the Preliminary Work done during the year 1915 in connection with the Proposed Bardic and Historical Survey of Rajputana," ***Journal of the Asiatic Society of Bengal***, N.S. 12 (1916), p. 94. Tessitori gives the date as ***V.S. 1532***, ***Vaisākh***, ***vadi 2 (?)***, ***Somvār***, noting that the number for the day of the month is unclear on the inscription. Dates given here are, therefore, calculated for ***Somvār*** ("Monday"), which is ***vadi 5*** and ***vadi 6***, respectively, for the ***Caitrādi*** and ***Śrāvaṇādi*** dates.

[11] Lavero: located thirty-four miles north-northeast of Jodhpur.

[12] See ***infra***, "Khānzāda Khāns."

with the rulers of Gujarat and Malwa. Jeso received a sizable ***paṭo*** grant from Rāṇo Kūmbho when he reached Cītoṛ. This grant included Tāṇo village and 140 others. Tāṇo is located along the eastern base of the Arāvallī hills near Toḍgaṛh, some sixty-four miles northwest of Cītoṛ. If it is assumed that the 140 other villages of this grant were contiguous with Tāṇo, Jeso would have controlled an important tract of lands along the northern edge of Mevāṛ fronting Ajmer. Unfortunately, no information is available about Jeso's years in Mevāṛ or the services which he may have performed for Rāṇo Kūmbho. It is known only that Jeso killed a man at Tāṇo village who was the father of Rāmdās, a Cahuvāṇ Rajpūt of the Mālhaṇ branch (***sākh***). The hostilities (***vair***) that arose from Rāmdās's father's murder continued into the next two generations of Jeso Bhāṭīs.

Much uncertainty surrounds the date of Jeso's arrival in Jodhpur, where he lived in the ***vās*** of Rāṭhoṛ Sūjo Jodhāvat. ***Khyāt***, 3:105, records only that "Likhmī's brother, Jeso, came [and] stayed [in] Sūjo's ***vās***." Jeso's coming may have occurred at the time of Likhmībāī's marriage to Sūjo, placed in the mid-1450s. But it is more likely that he came to live in Sūjo's ***vās*** either while enroute to Cītoṛ or after he had been in Mevāṛ for some time. ***Khyāt***, 2:153, states only that "Here [at Bhāuṇḍo, Jeso] had a fort built and kept [his] men, and he [himself] went to the Rāṇo at Cītoṛ."

It is also unclear how long Jeso remained in Mevāṛ before proceeding on to Delhi. ***Khyāt***, 2:153, records of his life in Mevāṛ only that:

> After coming [to Mevāṛ] during the time of Rāṇo Kūmbho, the ***paṭo*** [of Tāṇo and 140 other villages] was established. [Then Jeso] said to the Dīvāṇ [Rāṇo Kūmbho] - "[If you] say [that is, give me permission], then I would go to the ***dargāh*** [at Delhi] one time; I would attack Jaisaḷmer."

Regardless of the time, Jeso would have reached Delhi during the reign of the Afghan Bahlūl Lodī (1451-89). His intention appears to have been to enlist the aid of the Sultān in an attack against Jaisaḷmer. However, he died two months after reaching the city. It is difficult to connect Jeso's trip to Delhi with any event in Jaisaḷmer that might have occasioned it. Jeso's arrival in Delhi can be placed in the late 1460s, during the final years of Rāṇo Kūmbho's rule, or in the early 1470s some years after the Rāṇo's death in 1468.

* * *

Jeso had four sons of whom there is record: Āṇand (4-1), Bhairavdās (4-2), Jodho (4-3), and Vaṇvīr (4-4). About Jodho there is no information, and of Vaṇvīr it is known only that he received the village of Khairvo[13] in ***paṭo*** (probably from Rāv Jodho Riṇmalot, ca. 1453-1489).

Bhairavdās succeeded to Jeso's lands in Mevāṛ. ***Khyāt***, 2:153, records that the Rāṇo of Mevāṛ "gave Bhairavdās Jesāvat the title of ***rāv*** and Tāṇo

---

[13] Khairvo: located fifty miles south-southeast of Jodhpur.

village [along with] 140 [others] in *paṭo*." At the same time, Bhairavdās kept at least part of the *vasī* he inherited from his father at Bhāuṇḍo village of Nāgaur. Bhairavdās also received Dhauḷharo[14] from Sūjo Jodhāvat, and is said to have settled this village. The date of the grant is uncertain. ***Khyāt***, 2:178, records that "Rāv Sūjo" made the grant. But Sūjo did not succeed to the rulership of Jodhpur until ca. 1492. It is probable, therefore, that the grant was made during the rule of Sūjo's father, Rāv Jodho Riṇmalot.

The circumstances surrounding Bhairavdās's death are also unclear. One entry in ***Khyāt***, 2:153, states:

> [Bhairavdās's] ***vasī*** was at Bhāuṇḍo village of Nāgaur. The Baloc took the herd of Bhairavdās's ***vasī***. Bhairavdās caught up to [the Baloc] with 40 [of his own] men, and [he] died in battle.

Elsewhere, ***Khyāt***, 2:178, relates that at the time Bhairavdās settled Dhauḷharo village of Sojhat, a military servant of Sūjo Jodhāvat's named Sūrmālhaṇ held the nearby village of Copṛo.[15] A disagreement arose over the border between these two villages, and a battle broke out, during which Sūrmālhaṇ killed Bhairavdās.

These accounts are difficult to reconcile. The name "Sūrmālhaṇ" is of interest, however. Sūrmālhaṇ appears to be an incorrect rendering of Sūr Mālhaṇ, a Cahuvāṇ Rajpūt named Sūr of the Mālhaṇ ***sākh***. This Sūr Mālhaṇ may have been a relation of Rāmdās Mālhaṇ's, whose father Jeso Kalikaraṇot killed at Tāṇo village in Mevāṛ a number of years before. If so, Sūr Mālhaṇ's killing of Bhairavdās would be related to the settlement of the ***vair*** between the Jeso Bhāṭīs and the Mālhaṇ Cahuvāṇs.

Bhairavdās married a daughter named Karametībāī to Rāṭhoṛ Mahirāj Akhairājot. Her son by Mahirāj was Rāṭhoṛ Kūmpo Mahirājot (no. 95), the founder of the Kūmpāvat branch of Mārvāṛ Rāṭhoṛs and commander of the armies of Jodhpur under Rāv Mālde Gāṅgāvat (1532-62).

Little is known about Bhairavdās's brother, Āṇand Jesāvat, other than the fact that he avenged Bhairavdās's death. Again, the accounts from Naiṇsī's ***Khyāt*** are contradictory. ***Khyāt***, 2:153, records that Āṇand lived in Rāv Sūjo's ***vās*** at Jodhpur. Āṇand is said to have sought out Sūrmālhaṇ and killed him at Ahilāṇī village of Goḍhvāṛ.[16] ***Khyāt***, 2:178, relates that Sūrmālhaṇ fled Mārvāṛ after killing Bhairavdās and went to Mevāṛ. Āṇand is then said to have brought

---

[14] Dhauḷharo: located eighteen miles west-northwest of Sojhat in eastern Mārvāṛ.

[15] Copṛo: located eight miles to the north of Dhauḷharo village, and eighteen miles northwest of Sojhat.

[16] Ahilāṇī: located twelve miles south of Khairvo village on the south side of the Sumerī River.

a company of men (***sāth***) from Jaisaḷmer and to have killed Sūrmālhaṇ near the villages of Ahilāṇī and Indravaṛo.[17]

That Āṇand brought a ***sāth*** from Jaisaḷmer is difficult to accept if he were living in Rāv Sūjo's ***vās***. It would appear either that Āṇand originally went to live in Jaisaḷmer after his father Jeso's death, and only came to Jodhpur to avenge Bhairavdās's murder, or that the reference to Jaisaḷmer is simply wrong. No other information is available about Āṇand Jesāvat.

The Rāṇo of Cītoṛ (probably Rāṇo Rāymal Kūmbhāvat, ca. 1473-1509) gave Bhairavdās's son, Acaḷdās (5-4), the ***paṭo*** of Tāṇo village when Bhairavdās died. ***Khyāt***, 2:153, states that the ***vasī*** could not remain at Bhāuṇḍo village of Nāgaur, however, when Acaḷdās succeeded Bhairavdās. The reasons are unclear from the texts. This association with Bhāuṇḍo was not re-established until the early seventeenth century when one of Jeso Kalikaraṇot's descendants, Surtāṇ Mānāvat (7-1), held it for a short time. To compensate for this loss, Rāṇī Likhmī requested that Rāv Sūjo grant Acaḷdās the village of Copṛo, formerly held by the Mālhaṇ Cahuvāṇ, Sūr, for his ***vasī***. Acaḷdās then moved the ***vasī*** to Copṛo while he himself remained in Mevāṛ. He was eventually killed in Copṛo village by Rāmdās Mālhaṇ, whose father Bhāṭī Jeso Kalikaraṇot had killed at Tāṇo village of Mevāṛ some year earlier, thus bringing the ***vair*** full circle.

> "Aitihāsik Bātāṃ," p. 37; ***Bāṅkīdās***, pp. 118-119, 141; ***Jaisalmer rī Khyāt***, pp. 59, 61-62; ***Khyāt***, 2:2, 75-77, 152-157, 164, 178, 192, 3:7, 20, 34, 103-114, 116, 144, 216, 221; M. A. Chaghtā'ī, "Nagaur - A Forgotten Kingdom," ***Bulletin of the Deccan College Research Institute***, Vol. 2, nos. 1-2 (November, 1940), pp. 174-178; Māṅgīlāl Vyās, ***Mārvāṛ ke Abhilekh*** (Jodhpur: Hindī Sāhitya Mandir, 1973), pp. 72, 75; ***Murārdān***, no. 2, pp. 103-104; Ojhā, 2:582, 590, 613-618, 4:1:269, n. 4, 5:1:94-96, and 94-95, n. 3; Reu, 1:107, 109; Tessitori, "A Report on the Preliminary Work done during the year 1915 in connection with the Proposed Bardic and Historical Survey of Rajputana," ***Journal of the Asiatic Society of Bengal***, N.S. 12 (1916), pp. 94-95; ***Tavārīkh Jaisalmer***, pp. 40, 42, 45-49, 101, 104; ***Vigat***, 2:1-2, 421; ***Vīr Vinod***, 2:332.

(no. 1) **Pītho Āṇandot** (5-1)

Pītho Āṇandot was a son of Āṇand Jesāvat (4-1) and grandson of Jeso Kalikaraṇot (3-1), the founding ancestor of the Jeso Bhāṭīs of Mārvāṛ. He was a military servant of Rāv Mālde Gāṅgāvat of Jodhpur (1532-62). All that is known about him is that he was killed at Meṛto in 1562. He was fighting there under Rāṭhoṛ Devīdās Jaitāvat (no. 65) against Meṛtīyo Rāv Jaimal Vīramdevot

---

[17] Indravaṛo: located one mile to the north of Ahilāṇī on the north side of the Sumerī River.

(no. 107) and the Mughal forces of Akbar under the command of Mīrzā Sharafu'd-Dīn Ḥusayn.

"Aitihāsik Bātāṃ," p. 56; ***Bāṅkīdās***, pp. 16-17; ***Khyāt***, 2:163; ***Vigat***, 1:62, 2:66.

(no. 2) **Sāṅkar Sūrāvat** (6-3)

Sāṅkar Sūrāvat was a great-grandson of Bhāṭī Jeso Kalikaraṇot (3-1) through Jeso's son, Bhairavdās Jesāvat (4-2) and Bhairavdās's son, Sūro Bhairavdāsot (5-4). The texts refer to Sāṅkar as a ***vaḍo Rajpūt*** ("great warrior") of Rāv Mālde Gāṅgāvat of Jodhpur (1532-62). Sāṅkar came into prominence at the time of Rāv Mālde's occupation of Ajmer ca. 1535 when the Rāv made him ***kiledār*** of the fort at Ajmer and gave him the village of Bhiṇāī[18] in ***paṭo***. When Rāv Mālde's Rajpūts began to vacate the fort of Ajmer in 1543 in the face of Sher Shāh Sūr's advance from north India, ***Vigat***, 1:58, states that Sāṅkar wished to remain at the fort and die in its defense. His Rajpūts eventually took him away, however, and brought him to Jodhpur. Rāv Mālde then posted him at the Jodhpur fort.

Sāṅkar remained at the fort during the battle of Samel (near Ajmer)[19] in January of 1544. He was later killed at the fort when Sher Shāh attacked and occupied Jodhpur following his victory at Samel. One of Sāṅkar's descendants, Jeso Bhāṭī Goyanddās Mānāvat (7-2), the ***pradhān*** of Jodhpur under Rājā Sūrajsiṅgh Udaisiṅghot (1595-1619), had a cenotaph built in Sāṅkar's remembrance. This cenotaph is no longer present at the fort of Jodhpur and there is some confusion about its original location. "Aitihāsik Bātāṃ," p. 45, states that it was built at the fort near the small mosque that Sher Shāh had constructed there during his occupation. But ***Khyāt***, 2:180, records that the cenotaph was built on the embankment of a tank (***pāj***) of the fort. Without further evidence, it is not possible to establish which one of these locations is correct.[20]

Sāṅkar Sūrāvat had two sons, Hamīr and Vairsal. Both served under Rājā Udaisiṅgh Māldevot of Jodhpur (1583-95) and died in battle on his behalf.

"Aitihāsik Bātāṃ," p. 45; ***Bāṅkīdās***, p. 13; ***Khyāt***, 2:178, 180-181; ***Murārdān***, no. 2. pp. 124-126; ***Vigat***, 1:44, 58, 2:57.

---

[18] Bhiṇāī: located twenty-nine miles south-southeast of Ajmer.

[19] Samel village is located twenty-four miles southwest of Ajmer.

[20] Norman Ziegler questioned the Director of the Jodhpur Fort and Museum, Nāhar Siṅgh Mahevco, about the location of this cenotaph during a visit to Jodhpur in 1981. Nāhar Siṅgh indicated that although a great deal of investigation had been done, no one had been able to identify either the location of Sher Shāh's mosque, no longer in existence, or the location of Sāṅkar Sūrāvat's cenotaph. There are several tanks built at varying levels and distances from the main fort itself. None of these showed any indication that their embankments had once held the cenotaph.

(no. 3) **Tiloksī Parbatot** (6-1)

Tiloksī Parbatot was a great-grandson of Bhāṭī Jeso Kalikaraṇot (3-1). No information is available about Tiloksī's father, Parbat Āṇandot (5-2). Of Tiloksī himself it is known only that he was a military servant of Rāv Mālde Gāṅgāvat of Jodhpur (1532-62). Tiloksī was killed along with his paternal uncle, Pītho Āṇandot (5-1) (no. 1), and other Jeso Bhāṭīs at the battle of Meṛto in 1562. Here Rāv Mālde's Rajpūts under the command of Rāṭhoṛ Devīdās Jaitāvat (no. 65) fought against Meṛtīyo Rāv Jaimal Vīramdevot (no. 107) and the Mughal forces of Akbar under Mīrzā Sharafu'd-Dīn Ḥusayn.

"Aitihāsik Bātāṃ," p. 56; ***Bāṅkīdās***, pp. 16-17; ***Khyāt***, 2:162; ***Vigat***, 1:62, 2:66.

Figure 2. Bhāṭī Ruling Family of Jaisaḷmer

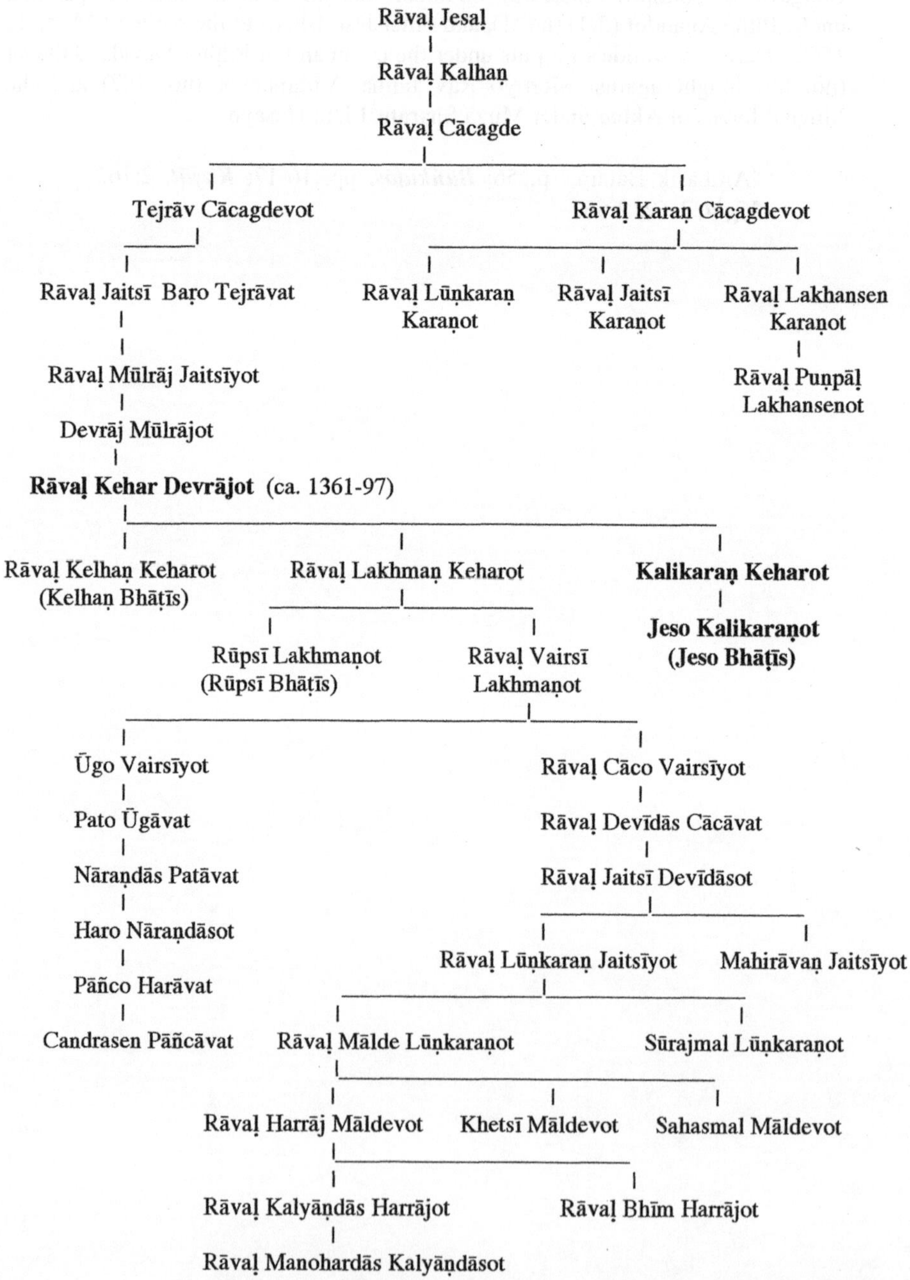

Figure 3. Jeso Bhāṭīs of Mārvāṛ

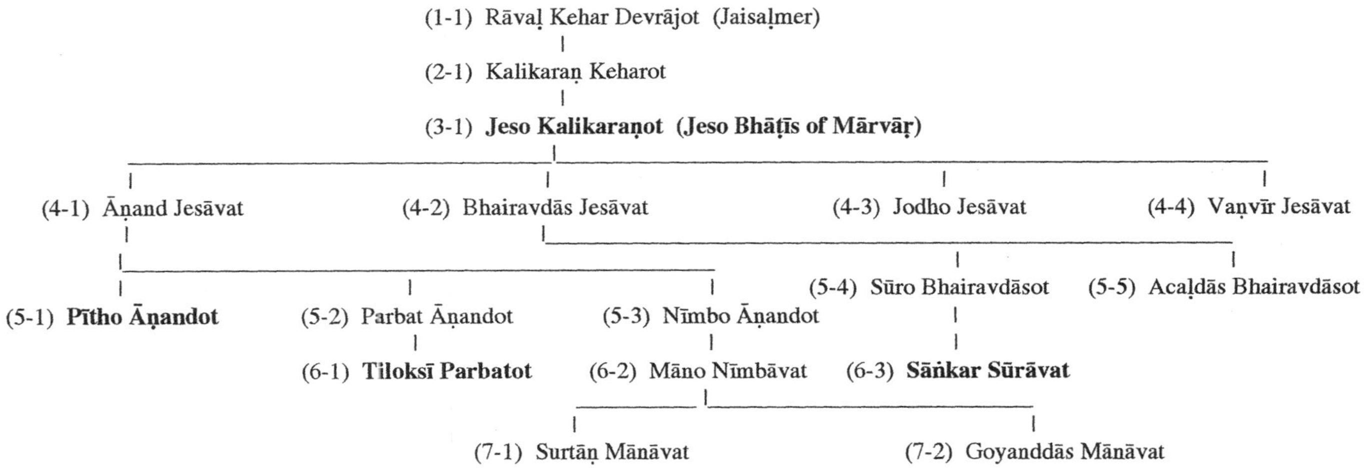
(1-1) Rāvaḷ Kehar Devrājot (Jaisaḷmer)
(2-1) Kalikaraṇ Keharot
(3-1) **Jeso Kalikaraṇot (Jeso Bhāṭīs of Mārvāṛ)**
(4-1) Āṇand Jesāvat
(4-2) Bhairavdās Jesāvat
(4-3) Jodho Jesāvat
(4-4) Vaṇvīr Jesāvat
(5-1) **Pītho Āṇandot**
(5-2) Parbat Āṇandot
(5-3) Nīmbo Āṇandot
(5-4) Sūro Bhairavdāsot
(5-5) Acaḷdās Bhairavdāsot
(6-1) **Tiloksī Parbatot**
(6-2) Māno Nīmbāvat
(6-3) **Sāṅkar Sūrāvat**
(7-1) Surtāṇ Mānāvat
(7-2) Goyanddās Mānāvat

Bālīso Cahuvāṇs

(no. 4) **Sūjo Sāṃvatot**

The Bālīso Cahuvāṇs

Little is known about the origins of the Bālīso branch (***sākh***) of the Cahuvāṇs. There is reason to associate this brotherhood with the village of Bālī[1] in southern Mārvāṛ and to link its name with that of the village. As with other Rajpūt branches whose names derive from places with which they were originally associated,[2] it seems probable that the name "Bālīso" comes from Bālī village. In this regard, Sākariyā, ***RHSK***, 2:891, defines the term ***Bālīs dharā*** as:

> 1. Bālī Pargano of Mārvāṛ. 2. The region in the vicinity of Bālī town in Goḍhvāṛ. 3. The land under the authority of the Vālīsā [*sic*] Cahuvāṇs.

This definition is supported by the association of the Bālīso Rajpūts as a group with the town and area of Nāḍūl[3] in the ***Khyāt*** of Naiṇsī, 3:48.

The Bālīsos held lands under the Rāṇos of Mevāṛ prior to 1540. The texts do not specify which lands or for what periods, other than to locate the Bālīso ***sākh*** in Goḍhvāṛ around Nāḍūl and Bālī. Their location in Goḍhvāṛ, the traditional Sīsodīyo influence in and control over much of Goḍhvāṛ prior to the rule of Rāṭhoṛ Rāv Mālde Gāṅgāvat of Jodhpur (1532-62), and the designation of the Bālīsos as ***poḷ rā cākar*** ("servants of the gate") of Mevāṛ (cf. ***Vigat***, 1:49) also indicate that the Bālīsos' relationship with Mevāṛ and the Rāṇos of Cītoṛ was a long standing one.

(no. 4) **Sūjo Sāṃvatot**

Sūjo Sāṃvatot appears in local texts first in relation to events that occurred in Mārvāṛ in 1540-41. He then disappears, only to re-emerge some fifteen years later as a participant in events in Mevāṛ in 1556-57. Sūjo came to Jodhpur in 1540-41 to seek service under Rāṭhoṛ Rāv Mālde Gāṅgāvat. Rāv Mālde welcomed him and granted him an important village in ***paṭo***. In 1556-57,

---

[1] Bālī village is located seventy-seven miles south-southwest of Jodhpur in Goḍhvāṛ, the area of southern Mārvāṛ fronting the western edge of the Arāvallī hills.

[2] Examples include the Mahevco Rāṭhoṛs, whose name comes from their association with the village and area of Mahevo in western Mārvāṛ, the Meṛtīyo Rāṭhoṛs of Meṛto in eastern Mārvāṛ, and the Īḍareco Rāṭhoṛs of Īḍar in southwestern Rājasthān.

[3] Nāḍūl lies just sixteen miles northeast of Bālī village in Goḍhvāṛ.

Sūjo was one of the ***pradhāns*** of Sīsodīyo Rāṇo Udaisiṅgh Sāṅgāvat of Mevāṛ (ca. 1537-72; no. 17). He played an important role in events leading up to Rāṇo Udaisiṅgh's battle at Harmāṛo[4] with Rāv Mālde of Jodhpur and Paṭhāṇ Hājī Khān. He was killed at Harmāṛo on January 24, 1557.

The texts do not specify Sūjo's reasons for coming to Jodhpur ca. 1540. They indicate only that he was angry with Rāṇo Udaisiṅgh and left Mevāṛ to settle in the ***vās*** ("residence, dwelling") of Rāv Mālde. ***Vigat***, 1:48, records that upon Sūjo's arrival in Jodhpur, Rāv Mālde showed him great respect and retained him, granting him the ***paṭo*** of Khairvo village.[5] The Rāv also "performed a great many kindnesses [for Sūjo] and questioned [him] in detail."

That a local ruler would welcome and retain a warrior who had left another kingdom to seek service in his own was not uncommon in this period. Rāv Mālde's more than favorable reception of Bālīso Sūjo bears explanation, however. It appears based upon the enmity that had emerged between Rāv Mālde and Rāṇo Udaisiṅgh shortly before Sūjo's arrival in Jodhpur.

Relations between these two rulers had grown suddenly hostile in 1540-41. Only shortly before ca. 1537, Rāv Mālde's warriors under the leadership of Sonagaro Cahuvāṇ Akhairāj Riṇdhīrot (no. 9), who had married a daughter to Rāṇo Udaisiṅgh, had ridden into Mevāṛ to unseat a pretender to the rulership of Cītoṛ, Sīsodīyo Vaṇvīr Prithīrājot, and bring Udaisiṅgh to the Sīsodīyo throne at Kumbhaḷmer. This supportive relationship altered ca. 1540 when Rāṇo Udaisiṅgh married a sister of Rāv Mālde's wife, Rāṇī Jhālī Sarūpdejī, who was a daughter of Jhālo Jaito Sajāvat.[6] ***Vigat***, 1:47-48, presents the circumstances surrounding this marriage as follows:

Jhālo Jaito Sajāvat was a military servant of Rāv Mālde's, holding the village of Khairvo in ***paṭo*** from the Rāv. The Rāv had come to Khairvo in 1540-41 as a guest of the Jhālos, bringing his wife, Jhālī Sarūpdejī, and other wives from the court at Jodhpur with him. While at Khairvo, the Rāv heard many taunts from the co-wives (***saukāṃ***) about Jhālī Sarūpde's sister, who was said to be exceptionally beautiful (***nipaṭ rūpvant***). The co-wives told the Rāv that "Sarūpde's sister is so pretty, there is no other as pretty as she." The Rāv himself saw the girl shortly after hearing these remarks, and he immediately desired to marry her. He had the Jhālos informed of his wish, but they were not agreeable, responding that they had already married one of their daughters to the Rāv. When the Rāv persisted and the Jhālos still refused, the Rāv threatened to marry their daughter by force.

At this point, Jhālī Sarūpdejī attempted to persuade her brothers and fathers (***bhāī bāpāṃ***) to comply with Rāv Mālde. The Jhālos hedged, but finally agreed with the Rāv's demands, at the same time secretly planning a deception.

---

[4] Harmāṛo village: located fifty-five miles south-southwest of Ajmer and six miles south of Vadhnor in northern Mevāṛ.

[5] Khairvo village: located fifty miles south-southeast of Jodhpur.

[6] See ***supra***, **Marriage and Family Lists of the Rulers of Jodhpur**, Mālde Gāṅgāvat, Rāṇī no. 5.

They set the marriage date for one and one-half months from that time and convinced the Rāv to return to Jodhpur until it was time for the wedding. As soon as the Rāv departed, they sent word to Sīsodīyo Rāṇo Udaisiṅgh of Mevāṛ, offering their daughter to him. This offer undoubtedly arose from the Jhālos' prior ties with Mevāṛ dating from the rule of Sīsodīyo Rāṇo Sāṅgo Rāymalot (1509-28). The Jhālos had first migrated into Mevāṛ during his reign. They left only after Rāṇo Sāṅgo's defeat in battle at Khanua in north India in 1527, fighting against the Mughal Bābur. Upon Rāṇo Udaisiṅgh's agreement to the marriage, the Jhālos left Khairvo and proceeded toward Mevāṛ. The Rāṇo met them enroute and married Jhālī Sarūpdejī's sister at their camp.

Rāv Mālde quickly learned of the Jhālos' deception and directed his anger for this slight at Rāṇo Udaisiṅgh. He placed outposts throughout Goḍhvāṛ and sent a contingent of Rajpūts (***sāth***) against the Rāṇo's fortress of Kumbhaḷmer. Rāv Mālde's attack against this fortress was unsuccessful, but both he and the Rāṇo directed raiding parties into each other's lands for some months thereafter.

It was during this period that Bālīso Sūjo Sāṃvatot arrived in Jodhpur. Rāv Mālde retained him and granted him the Jhālos' former ***paṭo*** of Khairvo village in return for his pledge of service. The Rāv also ordered Sūjo to join a force riding against Mevāṛ. Before setting out from Jodhpur for his village, however, Sūjo told the Rāv:

> five to seven times - "We are the servants of the gate (***poḷ rā cākar***) of Mevāṛ. Rāvjī! There are thousands of different tasks [I might do; you] may dispatch me to that place, but [you] should excuse me from this service" (***Vigat,*** 1:49).

Rāv Mālde did not listen to Sūjo and obstinately repeated his order. Bālīso Sūjo then asked permission to leave for Khairvo, stating that when the army arrived on its way to Mevāṛ, he and his men would be ready to join it.

Sūjo proceeded on to his ***paṭo*** village. But while settling there, conflict arose with some Cāmpāvat Rāṭhoṛs living in villages neighboring Khairvo. ***Vigat*** (***ibid.***) states that this conflict emerged because Sūjo and the Bālīsos were outsiders (***pardesī***) whom the Cāmpāvats wanted to drive away. In response, Sūjo decided to quit Mārvāṛ, and as he was leaving, his men attacked and looted two villages in the ***paṭo*** of the Cāmpāvats, killing "twenty Rajpūts of Mārvāṛ." [7]

Sūjo returned to Mevāṛ when he departed Khairvo, and he sent ***pradhān***s to Rāṇo Udaisiṅgh. The ***pradhān***s reported to the Rāṇo all that had happened, and the Rāṇo was very pleased. He sent his man (***ādmī***) to Sūjo, in turn, with a horse and a ***sirpāv*** in gift. The man presented these to Sūjo and then brought him into the presence of the Rāṇo. Rāṇo Udaisiṅgh took Sūjo into his service

---

[7] Other, later sources indicate that Sūjo "refused" to do as the Rāv ordered, that is, to ride against Mevāṛ, and that he left Mārvāṛ as a consequence of this refusal. Cf. Ojhā, 2:270, n. 2; ***Vīr Vinod***, 2:70-7.

once again and granted him the former ***paṭo*** of the Bālīsos (unspecified in the texts) along with the town of Nāḍūl [8] and twelve other villages.

Vigat, 1:49, states that Rāv Mālde was both very saddened (***ghaṇo dukh pāyo***) and greatly distressed with Sūjo (***ghaṇo darad Sūjā suṃ rākhīyo chai***) when he learned what had happened. But then, when Sūjo took occupation of Nāḍūl, the Rāv could not abide this affront and summoned Bālāvat Rāṭhoṛ Nago Bhārmalot (no. 38), ordering him to proceed against Nāḍūl and kill Sūjo by any means possible. Nago Bhārmalot and his two brothers, Vīñjo and Dhano (no. 39), were important Rajpūts in Mārvāṛ at this time. Together these Bālāvats set out against Nāḍūl with five hundred horse (***asvār***) and an unspecified number of foot (***pāḷā***). The battle they fought with Sūjo near Nāḍūl is of interest and is recounted here in some detail, based on information from ***Vigat***, 1:50-52.

The Bālāvats moved by stealth to within a ***kos*** of Nāḍūl, then sent twenty to twenty-five horsemen before the gates of the town as a ruse, ordering the horsemen to cause a disturbance by breaking the water pots of the women at the wells and stealing off with the herds. The Bālāvats reasoned that the Bālīsos would come in pursuit of these horsemen and that the Bālāvats' main force could then fall on and kill them. While the ruse worked at first, as the outcry was raised, Bālīso Sūjo suspected a trick, and he stopped his brothers and sons from following the raiders. He then ordered men summoned from the nearby villages and gathered a force of two thousand horse and foot. He set out in pursuit of the raiders with this small army. Ten ***kos*** from Nāḍūl the Bālīsos caught up with the Bālāvats, and in the battle which ensued, one-hundred and forty of the Bālāvats were slain. ***Vigat***, 1:50, records that Nago Bhārmalot was wounded and both of his brothers, Vīñjo and Dhano, were killed. Other sources indicate that Dhano did not die in this battle, but was killed later in another battle fought in the service of Rāv Mālde of Jodhpur (see "Bālāvat Rāṭhoṛs," ***infra***, for details).

The Bālāvat force fled from the field following their defeat, stopping at the village of Ḍahaṛo some twelve miles east-northeast of Nāḍūl. The Bālīsos pursued them there, and as they approached, Sūjo and his brothers, brothers' sons, and sisters' sons (***bhāī bhatījīṃ bhāṇejāṃ***) saw Nago Bhārmalot riding away. Two of Sūjo's brothers' sons, two of his sisters' sons and a Sahlot Rajpūt with them wanted to stop Nago and kill him. Sūjo attempted to stop them, saying:

> There is no deep-seated hostility (***vair***) between us and them; do not follow after Nago. [He] is not such a Rajpūt that he would run away, but [his] military servants [and his] brotherhood persuaded [and] forcefully took him away. He is an exceptional warrior (***baṛī balāy***); you should not speak his name (***Vigat***, 1:51).

Despite Sūjo's words, five or six horsemen rode after Nago. When Nago saw them coming, he stopped to confront them. He struck one man in the chest with

---

[8] Nāḍūl town: located some twenty miles south of Khairvo village in Goḍhvāṛ.

his lance, throwing it with such force that it passed out of the man's back, into the hindquarters of the horse and through the horse's testicles. Nago gave a great shout while removing the lance, and it is said that another two of the Bālīso men fell senseless and did not speak for six months afterwards out of fear.

Rāv Mālde sent no further armies against Nāḍūl, and the Bālāvats exacted no revenge for their humiliating defeat at Bālīso Sūjo's hands. The chronicles contain no further information about Sūjo until he is mentioned again with reference to the battle of Harmāṛo. He reappears here as a ***pradhān*** of Sīsodīyo Rāṇo Udaisiṅgh of Mevāṛ, and he played an important role in the events leading up to and during this battle against Hājī Khān and Rāv Mālde's forces from Jodhpur.

Hājī Khān was a noble of Sher Shāh Sūr. Following Sher Shāh's death in 1545, he assumed control over Alvar (Mevāt) and was there at the time of Akbar's succession to the Mughal throne in 1556. Akbar sent Nāṣiru'l-Mulk Pīr Muḥammad Sarvānī to drive Hājī Khān from Alvar. Hājī Khān fled with his army to Ajmer, where he usurped control. But he quickly came into conflict with Rāv Mālde of Jodhpur, who had heard of his coming with a large treasury in train. Rāv Mālde dispatched a force against Ajmer. This venture ended in stalemate, however, because Hājī Khān appealed to Sīsodīyo Rāṇo Udaisiṅgh for aid. The Rāṇo agreed to help and sent a force of Rajpūts to Ajmer. Their arrival halted the Rāṭhoṛ advance on the city, and both armies then turned back to their own lands and dispersed.

The Rāṇo sent two of his ***pradhān***s, Ūdāvat Rāṭhoṛ Tejsī Ḍūṅgarsīyot (no. 138) and Bālīso Sūjo Sāṃvatot, to Ajmer shortly thereafter to demand payment from Hājī Khān for his support against Rāv Mālde. The ***Khyāt*** of Naiṇsī. 1:60-61, states that the Rāṇo ordered his ***pradhān***s to tell Hājī Khān:

> I supported you against Rāv Mālde. [In payment] give me several elephants [and] some gold, [and] you have a band [of women]; in it is the dancing girl (***pātar***), Raṅgrāy, so give [her] to me.

Both Tejsī and Sūjo requested that the Rāṇo not demand this form of payment from Hājī Khān. But the Rāṇo persisted and sent them to Ajmer against their will.

Ūdāvat Tejsī and Bālīso Sūjo informed Hājī Khān of the Rāṇo's demands when they arrived in Ajmer. Hājī Khān refused the demands, saying that he had nothing to give and that the ***pātar***, Raṅgrāy, was his wife and therefore could not be given away. He then dismissed the Rāṇo's ***pradhān***s who returned to Mevāṛ, and he dispatched two of his men to Rāv Mālde at Jodhpur to ask for his support against the Rāṇo. "Aitihāsik Bātāṃ," p. 50, records that he offered Rāv Mālde the city of Ajmer in return for this support.

Both sides in this affair now prepared for battle. Rāv Mālde sent fifteen hundred chosen warriors under the command of Rāṭhoṛ Devīdās Jaitāvat (no. 65) to Ajmer to join with Hājī Khān's army, while the Rāṇo assembled an equally large force comprised of local rulers allied with Mevāṛ and their Rajpūts. They met at the village of Harmāṛo to the south of Ajmer on January 24, 1557 as Hājī

Khān was leaving Ajmer for Gujarat. The ***Khyāt*** of Naiṇsī, 1:61, records that Ūdāvat Tejsī Ḍūṅgarsīyot and Bālīso Sūjo mediated between the opposing armies before the battle and said to the Rāṇo: "[You] should not fight [this] battle. Five thounsand Paṭhāṇs and a thousand Rāṭhoṛs both will die." But the Rāṇo would not accept their counsel. The field was then cleaned (***khet buhārīyo***) for battle.

During the fighting that followed, the armies of Hājī Khān and Rāv Mālde defeated the Rāṇo's forces. Both Ūdāvat Tejsī and Bālīso Sūjo were killed along with many others. Bālīso Sūjo's death came at the hands of Rāṭhoṛ Devīdās Jaitāvat. ***Vigat***, 1:52, states that Devīdās challenged Sūjo to single-handed combat, saying: "Sūjo, [be] alert, [for] today I demand [revenge for the deaths of] Rāṭhoṛs Vīñjo and Dhano [Bhārmalot]." Devīdās then killed Bālīso Sūjo with his spear.

Vigat, 2:60, refers to Bālīso Sūjo as one of the renowned nobles (***nāṃvjādik umrāv***) of the Rāṇo's who died at Harmāṛo by Rāṭhoṛ Devīdās's hand. Devīdās's challenge to Sūjo stemmed from the defeat and humiliation of the Bālāvat Rāṭhoṛs at Nāḍūl some seventeen years earlier. By 1557 the leading Bālāvat ***ṭhākur***s were all dead and it was left to Devīdās Jaitāvat to end the ***vair***. Vīñjo Bhārmalot had been killed near Nāḍūl ca. 1540. Nago Bhārmalot died at Samel in January of 1544, and his remaining two brothers, Dhano and Vīdo, were both killed at Meṛto in 1554.

> "Aitihāsik Bātāṃ," pp. 50-51; ***Bāṅkīdās***, pp. 14-15, 141, 166; ***Khyāt***, 1:60-62, 89, 2:262-264, 3:48; Jānā, ***Kyāṃ Khāṃ Rāsā***, edited with extensive notes by Daśarath Śarma, Agarcand Nāhṭā, and Bhaṃvarlāl Nāhṭā (Jaypur: Rājasthān Puratattva Mandir, 1953), p. 5, v. 54; Lāḷas, ***RSK***, 3:2:3034-3035; Ojhā, 2:716-720, 4:1:290-291, 316-320; Sākariyā, ***RHSK***, 2:891; ***Vigat***, 1:47-52, 60, 65, 2:59-60; ***Vīr Vinod***, 2:70-71.

Devṛo Cahuvāṇs

(no. 5) **Surtāṇ Bhāṇot, Rāv** (8-3)
(Ruler of Sīrohī, ca. 1571-1610)

Surtāṇ Bhāṇot descends from a collateral line of the ruling house of Sīrohī. He was born in 1559-60 and succeeded to the rulership of this kingdom in 1571-72 at the age of twelve years. His succession inaugurated a period of internal disruption and local factionalism similar to that which had characterized the reign of his predecessor, Rāv Mānsiṅgh Dūdāvat (8-2). The Sīsodīyo Gahlots under Rāṇo Pratāpsiṅgh Udaisiṅghot of Mevāṛ (1572-97) and the Mughals under Akbar both entered into the affairs of this kingdom, adding to the turmoil. Rāv Surtāṇ ruled intermittently during the first twenty years following his accession. It was only in the 1590s that he was able to consolidate his authority. He maintained it thereafter as a nominal subordinate of the Mughals until his death in 1610 at the age of fifty-one years. His reign spanned some thirty-nine years during which he is said to have fought and emerged victorious from fifty-two battles. Local chronicles speak of him as a great warrior and a generous ruler who granted some eight-four villages in ***sāṃsaṇ*** to Brāhmaṇs and Cāraṇs.

The ***Khyāt*** of Naiṇsī, 1:141, provides detail about events leading to Surtāṇ's succession. These events speak to the internal rivalries and factionalism that plagued the Sīrohī ruling family of this period. The ***Khyāt*** records that on some occasion shortly before Surtāṇ's succession, Surtāṇ's predecessor, Rāv Mānsiṅgh Dūdāvat, poisoned Surtāṇ's ***pradhān***, Paṃvār Pañcāiṇ, in an attempt to force contributions from Surtāṇ's ***vasī***. Rāv Mānsiṅgh afterwards went to Ābū in the hilly region of southwestern Sīrohī, where he became involved in a disagreement with one of his personal attendants (***khavās***) and "shoved" him. This ***khavās*** was Paṃvār Kalo, a brother's son (***bhatījo***) of Paṃvār Pañcāiṇ's. In retaliation for being shoved, Paṃvār Kalo stabbed Rāv Mānsiṅgh one evening with a dagger, mortally wounding him.

Rāv Mānsiṅgh had no sons. The Devṛos in attendance upon the Rāv asked him to whom the ***ṭīko*** of succession should be given. Rāv Mānsiṅgh's last wish was that Surtāṇ Bhāṇot succeed him. The ***Khyāt*** provides no rationale for Rāv Mānsiṅgh's choice of Surtāṇ, who was a paternal relation several times removed from his family. Following the Rāv's wishes, however, the Devṛos, led by Ḍūṅgarot Devṛo Vījo Harrājot (10-1), brought the young boy, Surtāṇ Bhāṇot, forward and seated him on the throne at Sīrohī.

Rāv Surtāṇ thus came to power with the primary support of the Ḍūṅgarot Devṛos. The Ḍūṅgarots were the most powerful branch of Devṛos outside of the ruling family. The ***Khyāt*** of Naiṇsī, 1:162, refers to them as the "defenders/protectors of the land" (***des rā āgaḷ*** - lit. "wooden bar or bolt [for fastening a door] of the land," and ***bhaṛ kiṃvāṛ*** - lit. "warrior-door"), that is, those who remained steadfast in battle and barred the advance of the enemy into the land.

The leader of the Ḍūṅgarots, Vījo Harrājot, had been a primary influence around the throne prior to Surtāṇ's succession, and Vījo quickly asserted his power over the new ruler. He became Surtāṇ's ***dhaṇī-dhorī*** (lit. "master-leader"), assuming a primary role in managing the affairs of the kingdom at the same time that he plotted against Surtāṇ for control of the throne. Rāv Mānsiṅgh's wife, a Bāhaṛmerī Rāṭhoṛ, was pregnant at the time of his death. She gave birth to a son not long after Surtāṇ was placed on the throne. The birth of this son marked the outbreak of open hostilities at the Sīrohī court, for it was around this boy that Vījo Harrājot began laying plans to unseat Rāv Surtāṇ.

The Bāhaṛmerī quickly perceived the threat to her son, and she took him from Sīrohī to her paternal home (***pīhar***) to ensure his safety. With Mānsiṅgh's infant son gone from the capitol, Devṛo Vījo sought further to consolidate power around himself in order to exclude Rāv Surtāṇ and seat Mānsiṅgh's infant son on the throne in Surtāṇ's stead. To accomplish this end, Ḍūṅgarot Vījo had first to remove the influence of Surtāṇ's father's brother (***kāko***), Devṛo Sūjo Riṇdhīrot (7-5), who was Surtāṇ's primary support at the Sīrohī court. Devṛo Sūjo was a powerful and influential Rajpūt, "who had gathered many fine Rajpūts [and] many fine horses [in his service]" (***ibid***., 1:143). Vījo Harrājot talked with those Ḍūṅgarots around him about the need to kill Sūjo Riṇdhīrot. Many spoke against him, saying, "Do not do this thing. Surtāṇ has already become the master (***dhaṇī***) of Sīrohī" (***ibid***.). But Vījo would not heed their advice and proceeded on his own. Through a paternal cousin, Ḍūṅgarot Rāvat Sekhāvat (10-4), he sent Rajpūts to Devṛo Sūjo Riṇdhīrot's home when an opportunity arose, and had him murdered. Vījo then proceeded to take possession of all of Sūjo's lands and possessions. Sūjo's wife managed to escape with two of her sons, Prithīrāj Sūjāvat (8-5) and Syāmdās Sūjāvat (8-6), while a third son, Māno Sūjāvat (8-4), died fighting against Vījo Harrājot.

Vījo now summoned Rāv Mānsiṅgh's infant son from Bāhaṛmer in western Mārvāṛ, where his mother had taken him. The Bāhaṛmerī complied with this summons and returned to Sīrohī with her son. Upon receipt of news of their coming, Vījo Harrājot went out to receive them and escort them to the capitol. Rāv Surtāṇ, in the meantime, realizing that his primary support was now gone and that he had little chance of survival if he remained at Sīrohī, left the capitol one day on the pretext of going hunting, and went to Rāmseṇ village[1] where he took refuge. Devṛo Sūjo Riṇdhīrot's wife, who had fled to Ābū with her two sons, now came and joined him there.

With Surtāṇ gone from the capitol, Ḍūṅgarot Vījo welcomed Rāv Mānsiṅgh's son there. The mother brought the boy (***ḍāvṛo***) and placed him in Vījo's lap (gave him over for adoption). However, the infant died suddenly, thwarting Vījo's plans to place him on the throne and rule through him. Not to be deterred, Vījo attempted to assert his own right to the throne. He spoke with the Ḍūṅgarots, Samro Narsiṅghot (9-5) and Sūro Narsiṅghot (9-6), the sons of

---

[1] Rāmseṇ village: located eighteen miles northwest of Sīrohī town.

Narsiṅgh Tejsīyot (8-8), saying, "Give the *ṭīko* to me" (*ibid*., 1:144). But these Devṛos refused to recognize his claim, stating that there were many of the former ruler of Sīrohī, Rāv Lākho's (4-1), belly (***Rāv Lākho rai peṭ rā***), and that even if there were but a year old baby boy (of his line) living, that child would be recognized before Vījo as the legitimate ruler of Sīrohī.

Vījo remained undeterred. While alienating the support of these influential Ḍūṅgarots who left Sīrohī in anger, he placed himself on the throne and began to rule. His usurpation was very short-lived, lasting only some four months, for Sīsodīyo Rāṇo Pratāpsiṅgh Udaisiṅghot of Mevāṛ now entered into local affairs on behalf of Devṛo Kalo Mehājaḷot (7-3). Kalo Mehājaḷot was a grandson (***potro***) of Sīrohī Rāv Jagmāl Lākhāvat (5-1) and a sister's son (***bhāṇej***) of the Sīsodīyo ruling family. Rāṇo Pratāp sent a force in support of Kalo into Sīrohī and forced Ḍūṅgarot Vījo to flee south to Īḍar. He then seated Kalo on the throne and provided him with a firm base of operations from Kumbhaḷmer, his fortress on the western edge of the Arāvallīs some forty-five miles east-northeast of Sīrohī town. Once Rāv Kalo established himself at the capitol, Surtāṇ Bhāṇot came from Rāmseṇ village and made obeisance before him. Rāv Kalo then took Surtāṇ into his service as one of his military servants. Surtāṇ received several villages in ***paṭo*** from the new Rāv and "from time to time" performed service.

Rāv Kalo's rule at Sīrohī proved short-lived as well. Just as the Ḍūṅgarot Devṛos were the primary power behind the throne during Rāv Surtāṇ's brief rule and in prior years, the Cībo Devṛos led by Cībo Khīṃvo Bhārmalot[2] assumed this role under Rāv Kalo. And while those Ḍūṅgarots who left Vījo Harrājot took service under Rāv Kalo, they quickly became dissatisfied with him because the Cībos alienated their support and in turn undermined Rāv Kalo himself.

The ***Khyāt*** of Naiṇsī, 1:145-146, relates a story which characterizes this alienation. The ***Khyāt*** tells that Rāv Kalo arose from his ***darbār*** one day while several Ḍūṅgarots, including Samro and Sūro Narsiṅghot, remained seated in the chamber on a small carpet (***dulīco***). Seeing them there, a Cībo named Pāto ordered the ***pharās*** ("spreader of carpets"[3]) to "pick up and bring the ***dulīco***." The ***pharās*** went to the ***darbār*** only to find the Ḍūṅgarots seated on it. He then came back without it. When Cībo Pāto asked him why he had not brought the carpet, he replied that those men were sitting on it. Cībo Pāto rebuked him, exclaiming, "What! Are they [like] your father [that you treat them with such deference]? Take up the carpet and bring it!" The servant then returned to the ***darbār*** and requested the carpet from the Ḍūṅgarots. They arose in disgust, knowing the Cībo's designs, and stated, "Even if Parmeśvar wished it, we will

---

[2] See ***Khyāt***, 1:169, for an attenuated genealogy of the Cībo Devṛos listing Khīṃvo Bhārmalot.

[3] ***Pharās*** (Arabic ***farrāś***): a spreader (of carpets); tent-pitcher, bed-maker; servant. See: Sākariyā, ***RHSK***, p. 830; R. S. McGregor, ***The Oxford Hindi-English Dictionary*** (Oxford, Delhi: Oxford University Press, 1997), p. 678.

not now sit upon Rāv Kalo's floor cloth (*jājam*[4])," that is, they would not sit in Rāv Kalo's ***darbār*** again.

They proceeded to their homes, greatly offended. And they informed Surtāṇ of what had taken place, saying, "If you would come, we would join with you." They met with Surtāṇ at Rāmseṇ village where they again placed the ***ṭīko*** on his forehead and began to treat him as ruler. From this time forward, they endeavored once again to seat Surtāṇ on the throne at Sīrohī.

This faction of Devṛos urged Rāv Surtāṇ to summon Ḍūṅgarot Vījo Harrājot from Īḍar, where he had fled. Despite earlier problems, Rāv Surtāṇ agreed to their suggestion. Vījo was a very influential Devṛo. ***Khyāt***, 1:146, 148, speaks of him both as a fearsome warrior (***balāy***) and as a discerning, far-sighted Rajpūt who was skilled in battle (***rāh-vedhī Rajpūt***).[5] Given Surtāṇ's age and position of weakness, it is understandable that he might again turn to Vījo Harrājot. Vījo himself seized upon this opportunity to return. Rāv Kalo quickly learned of his coming, and he sent a force of some five hundred men under the command of Devṛo Rāvat Hāmāvat to bar his way. But Vījo defeated this army with a small force of one hundred and fifty of his own Rajpūts.

Ḍūṅgarot Vījo afterwards presented himself before Rāv Surtāṇ and begged forgiveness for his past offenses. Without other visible support, Rāv Surtāṇ joined forces with him. Vījo immediately urged the Rāv to enlist further aid from the ruler of Jāḷor, Mālik Khān-ī-Jahān. Rāv Surtāṇ then sent a man to Jāḷor with an offer of a ***lākh*** of rupees in return for the Mālik's aid. Khān-ī-Jahān replied that he would not ask the members of his brotherhood (***bhāībandh***) to die in battle for a ***lākh*** of rupees, but he would be ready to come if Surtāṇ would agree to give four ***pargano***s of Sīrohī. While there was disagreement within Rāv Surtāṇ's ranks, the Mālik's demands were finally met. Mālik Khān-ī-Jahān then joined the Rāv with fifteen hundred horse. Three thousand additional warriors had gathered by the Rāv in the meantime, and this combined force defeated Rāv Kalo's army of four thousand in a decisive battle near the village of Kāḷandharī.[6] The ***Khyāt*** of Naiṇsī, 1:147, records that the Khān's Vihāriyos (Bīhārī Paṭhāṇs) showed exceedingly great valor at this battle, and contributed much to the victory. Ḍūṅgarot Samro Narsiṅghot died fighting on behalf of Rāv Surtāṇ. Rāv Kalo was forced to flee with great loss. Among his Rajpūts killed was Cībo Pāto. Rāv Kalo's wives and family (***Kalā rā māṇas***) were at Sīrohī when Rāv

---

[4] ***Jājam***: a checkered or figured linen cloth spread on the floor or over a carpet for sitting; a floor cloth. See: Sākariyā, ***RHSK***, p. 437; McGregor, ***The Oxford Hindi-English Dictionary***, p. 366.

[5] The term ***rāh-vedhī*** has the additional meanings of "plunderer, looter, and ***bhomīyo***," all of which might be applied to Ḍūṅgarot Vījo. See: Sākariyā, ***RHSK***, p. 1159.

[6] Kāḷandharī village: located eleven miles west-northwest of Sīrohī town.

Surtāṇ occupied the city. The Rāv made certain the women were treated with respect, and he had them seated in ***sejhvāḷos***[7] and delivered to Kalo.

Surtāṇ then ascended the throne at Sīrohī a second time in 1574-75, three years after his initial succession. He was now fifteen years old.

Relying on Ḍūṅgarot Vījo quickly proved a mixed blessing for Rāv Surtāṇ. Within a short time, Vījo began again forcefully to assert his authority over the Rāv and to take on the airs of a ruler. While Surtān was master (***dhaṇī***), Vījo controlled the administration of the kingdom. Day by day Devṛo Vījo grew more powerful, and soon open enmity reasserted itself between Surtāṇ and Vījo. But Surtāṇ had little power in his own person and could do nothing to assert himself against Vījo. During this time, the Rāv married a Bāhaṛmerī Rāṭhoṛ. When the Bāhaṛmerī came to Sīrohī and saw the manner in which Vījo acted, she exclaimed, "What is the situation here in this kingdom (***ṭhākurāī***)? Are you master, or is Vījo?" (***ibid***., 1:148). Rāv Surtāṇ replied that there were no Rajpūts in the land who would oppose a fearsome warrior (***balāy***) like Vījo. But the Bāhaṛmerī counseled that if Surtāṇ would fill their stomachs, he would have many Rajpūts in the land. Rāv Surtāṇ then had his wife call twenty men from her paternal home (***pīhar***), and twenty exceedingly powerful (***nipaṭ prabaḷ***) men came. These men became Surtāṇ's personal bodyguards (***pāsvāṇ***).

Rāv Surtāṇ's circumstances now appeared brighter. Other Rajpūts began to gather by him. Even Devṛo Vījo's two brothers, Lūṇo Harrājot (10-2) and Māno Harrājot (10-3), separated themselves from Vījo and joined with Rāv Surtāṇ, whose authority continued to increase. One day thereafter, the Rāv had Vījo driven from the capitol. Ḍūṅgarot Vījo then proceeded to the village of his ***vasī***, where he waited.

The year 1576 ushered in a new set of circumstances for Rāv Surtāṇ, for Sīrohī came under direct pressure from the Mughals. Early in this year, Emperor Akbar had received word that Tāj Khān of Jāḷor and Devṛo Rāv Surtāṇ of Sīrohī had joined in support of Sīsodīyo Rāṇo Pratāpsiṅgh of Mevāṛ in his rebellion against the Mughals. Given Surtāṇ's age and circumstances in Sīrohī, it is uncertain what his actions were. But it would seem probably that the Devṛos offered support to the Sīsodīyos.

Akbar sent Bīkāvat Rāṭhoṛ Rājā Rāysiṅgh Kalyāṇmalot of Bīkāner (ca. 1574-1612), Tarson Khān, Saiyyid Hāshim Bārha and others against them, with instructions that "they were to begin by using soothing and admonitory language in order that they might guide the recalcitrants into the highway of obedience" (***Akbar Nāma***, 3:267). When the Imperial army reached Jāḷor, Tāj Khān quickly swore allegiance to the Emperor. The army then moved on toward Sīrohī. Rāv Surtāṇ, deeming it prudent, took this opportunity to meet with Rājā Rāysiṅgh, whom he welcomed to Sīrohī with great respect and hospitality. ***Akbar Nāma*** states that "The Rai of that place also awoke from his somnolent fortune, and came with an ashamed countenance to the servants of dominion." Ḍūṅgarot Vījo

---

[7] ***Sejhvāḷo***: a carriage used to convey women in purdah, with sides that are enclosed with curtains, and in which bedding has been spread for seating. See: Lāḷas, ***RSK***, 4:3:5797.

gathered a large ***sāth*** and also ventured forth to meet with the Rājā. Vījo sought to entice the Rājā's allegiance to his cause, but the Rājā would not agree to support him in his bid for rulership in Sīrohī. The Rājā held further talks with Rāv Surtāṇ, and he promised to drive Ḍūṅgarot Vījo from Sīrohī in return for the Rāv's pledge of one-half the lands of Sīrohī to the Mughal throne.

Rāv Surtāṇ accepted this offer. Rājā Rāysiṅgh then drove Devṛo Vījo from the land. The Rājā sent word to the Emperor, informing him of the cession of lands and his assistance to the Rāv in driving out the bandit (***grāsīyo***)[8] Vījo. He made the ceded lands ***khālso*** and placed an outpost (***thāṇo***) there with five hundred horse (***asvār***) under Rāṭhoṛ Madno Pātāvat. He asked the Emperor to send revenue officials (***karoṛīs***) to assume charge, and closed by stating, "Rāv Surtāṇ is [your Majesty's] obedient military servant (***hukmī cākar***)" (***Khyāt***, 1:150).

Rāv Surtāṇ, "together with Tāj Khān, set off to perform the worship of prostration at the holy threshold" (***Akbar Nāma***, 3:267), while the Rājā and Saiyyid Hāshim Bārha took up quarters at Nāḍūl[9] in order to close the routes to and from Mevāṛ during their on-going campaign against Sīsodīyo Rāṇo Pratāpsiṅgh. Rāv Surtāṇ left the Imperial court shortly afterward, however, without permission from the Emperor, and "from his ill-fate, and native savagery, came to his own country with an evil intention" (***ibid.***, 3:278). Akbar, in turn, dispatched Rājā Rāysiṅgh and Saiyyid Hāshim once again against this kingdom in early 1577. Word of their conquest of Sīrohī reached the Emperor on February 27, 1577. ***Akbar Nāma***, 3:278-279, includes a brief account of this conquest from records that Rājā Rāysiṅgh sent to court:

> At the signal from H. M. [Akbar], Rai Rai Singh, Saiyad Hāshim and other servants went to conquer that country [Sīrohī], and to punish that evil-disposed person [Rāv Surtāṇ]. They began by entering the country and besieging him. As the fort was strong, and he was without calculating reason, he thought that the lofty hills would protect him, and his arrogance increased. The warriors took up their abode there and proceeded to act leisurely instead of rapidly. Rai Rai Singh sent for his family from his home. He whose fortune was slumberous (the Rai of Sirohī) attacked the caravan on the road with a number of determined men. Many Rajputs who were with the convoy . . . fought bravely and there was a great fight. Many fell on both sides, but by the blessing of daily-increasing fortune that audacious highlander was defeated and became a vagabond in the desert of failure. He abandoned Sirohī and went off to Abūgarh. . . The victorious bands came to the fort [of Ābū] by the aid of daily-increasing fortune, and so strong a fortress, such

---

[8] See ***Glossary***, Volume I, for full meaning of this term.

[9] Nāḍūl: located fifty miles to the northeast of Sīrohī.

> as great princes would have found difficult to conquer, came into the hands of the party of loyalists with little effort. [Devṛo Rāv Surtāṇ] was bewildered by the majesty of the Sultanate of the Shāhinshāh and fell to supplications. He took refuge with the auspicious servants, and made the key of the fort the means of opening the knot of his fortune, by delivering it to them. Rai Rai Singh left the fort in charge of able men, and proceeded to court along with the Rai of Sirohī.

While administrative and revenue officials (*dīvāṇ-bagsī*) had, in the meantime, come to Sīrohī and begun taking control of the ceded lands in the Emperor's name, another outsider intruded into the affairs of the kingdom, this time in the person of Sīsodīyo Jagmāl Udaisiṅghot. Sīsodīyo Jagmāl was a son of Rāṇo Udaisiṅgh Sāṅgāvat (ca. 1537-72; no. 17) who had been passed over in succession to the throne of Cītoṛ in favor of Rāṇo Udaisiṅgh's eldest son, Pratāpsiṅgh, who now ruled in Mevāṛ. Jagmāl was a son of Rāṇo Udaisiṅgh's favored Bhāṭiyāṇī wife, and the Rāṇo had designated him as his chosen successor. But the leading Sīsodīyos at court passed him over in favor of Pratāpsiṅgh. Jagmāl in turn left Mevāṛ in anger and offered his service to the Mughal Emperor.

Jagmāl had married one of the daughters of the former ruler of Sīrohī, Devṛo Rāv Mānsiṅgh Dūdāvat, and was familiar with Sīrohī lands. Once at the Imperial court, he used his relationship with Rāv Mānsiṅgh's family to support his petition for the grant of Sīrohī lands in *jāgīr*. The ***Khyāt*** of Naiṇsī, 1:150, also indicates that the ***dīvāṇ*** and ***bagsī***s sent word to Akbar about Sīsodīyo Jagmāl. Akbar was well disposed to accept Jagmāl's petition and he granted him the lands. Ḍūṅgarot Vījo had also gone to court at this time to represent his own cause against Rāv Surtāṇ. But Akbar denied his petition, and when Sīsodīyo Jagmāl left for Sīrohī, Ḍūṅgarot Vījo joined with him.

Rāv Surtāṇ came forward to meet Sīsodīyo Jagmāl when he arrived bearing the Imperial certificate of appointment (***tālīko***), and he handed over to Jagmāl one-half of the lands of his kingdom. But hostilities quickly developed between Rāv Surtāṇ and Sīsodīyo Jagmāl. The Rāv continued to live in the ruler's quarters of the palace (***pāṭ rā gharāṃ***) at Sīrohī, while Sīsodīyo Jagmāl and his family were relegated to quarters elsewhere. Naiṇsī's ***Khyāt***, 1:150, indicates that Sīsodīyo Jagmāl's wife, Rāṇī Devṛī, complained to her husband, saying, "Why is another living in my father's home while we are here?" She encouraged the enmity between her husband and Rāv Surtāṇ. On one occasion shortly thereafter when Rāv Surtāṇ left the palace, Sīsodīyo Jagmāl and Ḍūṅgarot Vījo attempted to usurp control at the capitol. However, they met with stout resistance from military servants loyal to Rāv Surtāṇ, who included Soḷaṅkī Sāṅgo and the Āsiyo Cāraṇs Dūdo and Khaṅgār. Shamed by this defeat, Jagmāl took Ḍūṅgarot Vījo and returned to the Mughal court to seek redress before the Emperor.

Rāv Surtāṇ brought other difficulties upon himself during the late 1570s. He provided refuge for Rāṭhoṛ Rāv Candrasen Māldevot of Jodhpur (1562-81) after the Mughals drove him from Mārvāṛ. Rāv Candrasen remained for two years in Sīrohī before proceeding on to Vāṃsvāḷo and Ḍūṅgarpur in southern Rājasthān. When he left Sīrohī, he entrusted the safety of his mother and wives to Rāv Surtāṇ at the Devṛo court.

Then in 1581-82 the Rāv had Saiyyid Hāshim Bokhārī murdered. Akbar had appointed Saiyyid Hāshim to oversee affairs in Sīrohī along with Mīr Kalān and Kamālū'd-Dīn Ḥusayn Diwāna. Rāv Surtāṇ's Rajpūts fell on and killed the Saiyyid during a moment of negligence on the part of the Mughals. Rāv Surtāṇ remained in control of Sīrohī during this time, however, and he continued to maintain a nominal allegiance to the Mughal throne. ***Vigat***, 2:70, records, for example, that in 1582-83 the Rāv escorted a wet-nurse of Akbar's from Gujarat to Meṛto in Mārvāṛ.

Akbar finally revoked Rāv Surtāṇ's rights to rulership in Sīrohī in 1583. He granted Sīrohī, in turn, to Sīsodīyo Jagmāl Udaisiṅghot. Jagmāl returned to Sīrohī with the support of an Imperial army under I'timād Khān, Rāv Rāysiṅgh Candrasenot, a son of Rāv Candrasen Māldevot of Jodhpur who held Sojhat in eastern Mārvāṛ in ***jāgīr*** from Akbar, and Kolīsiṅgh, master of Dāntīvāṛo. Akbar ordered I'timād Khān to occupy Sīrohī and to make the lands over to Jagmāl. The Khān was able to accomplish this task, forcing Rāv Surtāṇ to flee once again into the hills. I'timād Khān afterwards retired from Sīrohī, leaving Sīsodīyo Jagmāl to assume final control with the assistance of Rāv Rāysiṅgh Candrasenot and Kolīsiṅgh. But with the departure of many of the Imperial troops for Gujarat, Rāv Surtāṇ emerged from hiding and met Jagmāl's and Rāv Rāysiṅgh's forces near the village of Datāṇī.[10] Both Sīsodīyo Jagmāl and Rāṭhoṛ Rāysiṅgh were killed there along with a large number of their Rajpūts, and the field fell to Rāv Surtāṇ.[11] Rāv Surtāṇ had reached twenty-four years of age at the time of this great victory.

The ***Khyāt*** of Naiṇsī, 1:151-152, records that prior to this battle, the Rāṭhoṛs in Jagmāl's army thought it would be best if they weakened Rāv Surtāṇ's forces by attacking the villages of the Rajpūts in his ***vasī*** (***Rāv Surtāṇrai vasīrā Rajpūtāṃrā gāṃv***), thereby drawing these Rajpūts away from the Rāv as they sought to protect their own lands. They decided to dispatch Ḍūṅgarot Vījo

---

[10] Datāṇī: located thirty-one miles southwest of Sīrohī town.

[11] ***Akbar Nāma***, 3:614, records incorrectly that the battle in which Rāṭhoṛ Rāv Rāysiṅgh and Sīsodīyo Jagmāl were killed was fought at Sīrohī, where the Rāv and Jagmāl had set up quarters. It notes:

> . . . Jagmāl entered Sirohī [town]. The presumptuous one (S. Deorah) retired to the ravines. Rai Singh [and others] were left to help Jagmāl. When the victorious troops marched to Gujarāt, that wayward one [Rāv Surtāṇ] renewed his turbulence, . . The wicked man came upon their quarters by secret paths. Those two men (Jagmāl and Rai Singh) awoke out of the sleep of neglect and preserved their honour by bravely sacrificing their lives.

See also: Ojhā, ***Sīrohī Rājya kā Itihās*** (Rev. 2nd. ed. Jodhpur: Rājasthān Granthāgār, 1999 [1936]), p. 239, for his comments on this passage.

Harrājot along with Rāṭhoṛ Khīṃvo Māṇḍaṇot, Rāṭhoṛ Rām Ratansīyot and a number of Turks (Muslims) against the ***pargano*** of Bhītroṭ to accomplish this end. Ḍūṅgarot Vījo spoke out against this plan to Rāṭhoṛ Rāv Rāysiṅgh and Sīsodīyo Jagmāl. He said, "[Beware]. If you separate me off from yourselves, then Rāv [Surtāṇ] will attack you." But the Rāṭhoṛ ***ṭhākurs*** made light of his words and replied sarcastically, "Even in a village with no rooster [to greet the dawn] night still ends" (***Khyāt***, 1:151), thereby saying, we don't need you; we can take care of ourselves without you.[12] Ḍūṅgarot Vījo then departed in the direction of Bhītroṭ, and Rāv Surtāṇ, true to Vījo's words, took full advantage of Vījo's absence. He had the kettledrums sounded, and with the help of Vījo's paternal cousin, Ḍūṅgarot Samro Narsiṅghot (9-5), quickly fell upon the Rāṭhoṛ camp at Datāṇī.[13]

This historic battle took place on October 17, 1583.[14]

---

[12] See ***Khyāt***, 1:151, n. 18, for the editor's explanation of this proverb.

[13] Ojhā, ***Sīrohī Rājyā kā Itihās***, pp. 232-233, notes that the well-known Cāraṇ Kavi Āḍho Durso was with Rāṭhoṛ Rāv Rāysiṅgh at Datāṇī and fell wounded in battle there. Rāv Surtāṇ found him on the field after the fighting. A Rajpūt with him was ready to kill the Cāraṇ, not knowing who he was, but Āḍho Durso declared that it was not proper for Rajpūts to kill men like himself, that he was a Cāraṇ. Rāv Surtāṇ replied that if he were a Cāraṇ, he should recite a ***dūho*** in honor of Dūṅgarot Samro Narsiṅghot, who had fallen in battle that day. Āḍho Durso recited a poem that pleased the Rāv very much, and the Rāv had the Cāraṇ seated in a palanquin and taken from the battlefield. He had his wounds tended, and when the Cāraṇ returned to health, the Rāv made him his ***pauḷpāt*** Cāraṇ and granted him several villages in ***sāṃsaṇ***.

Āḍho Durso was widely known throughout Rājasthān for his poetry, and rulers of Jodhpur and Udaipur alike gave him and his sons villages, showing them great respect and deference. In 1586 Moṭo Rājā Udaisiṅgh Māldevot of Jodhpur sequestered lands that Rāṭhoṛs Kalo and Karaṇ Rāmot had given in ***sāṃsaṇ*** to the Cāraṇs (and Brāhmaṇs) in Sojhat Pargano of eastern Mārvāṛ. To protest the Moṭo Rājā's actions, a large number of Cāraṇs gathered at Āūvo village and cut their throats with daggers in a mass suicide. Āḍho Durso was present at Āūvo. He also cut his throat, but ***Murārdān***, no. 2, p. 186, records that he did not die on that day.

[14] During the reign of Rājā Sūrajsiṅgh Udaisiṅghot of Jodhpur (1595-1619), efforts were made to settle the ***vair*** that arose between the Rāṭhoṛs of Jodhpur and the Devṛos of Sīrohī over Rāv Rāysiṅgh Candrasenot's death, and to arrange for the return to Jodhpur of all of the stolen property, which included Rāṭhoṛ Rāv Rāysiṅgh's kettledrums. Rāv Surtāṇ Bhāṇot's son, Rājsiṅgh, had succeeded him to the throne in 1610. Rāv Rājsiṅgh soon became involved in hostilities with his younger brother, Sūrsiṅgh, who sought a way to usurp control of the throne for himself and his family. Sūrsiṅgh met with Jodhpur Rājā Sūrajsiṅgh in 1611-12 to gain his support in his bid for power. He offered to marry one of his daughters to Kuṃvar Gajsiṅgh Sūrajsiṅghot (Rājā of Jodhpur, 1619-38), and the daughters of his Devṛo supporters to twenty-nine of Rājā Sūrajsiṅgh's Rajpūts whose family members had been killed at Datāṇī. He also promised to give Kuṃvar Gajsiṅgh the bejeweled dagger of Vījo Harrājot's, and ensure the return of all Rāv Rāysiṅgh's belongings, including his kettledrums, which Rāv Surtāṇ had stolen. The Rājā for his part was to support Sūrsiṅgh in his bid for power, seat him on the throne at Sīrohī, and then present him before the Mughal Emperor and see that he and his sons were recognized as the legitimate rulers of Sīrohī. An official agreement

Rāv Surtāṇ again assumed control at Sīrohī following this decisive victory. He ruled there in relative security until 1588. During this short period of five years, the peace was disturbed only when Sīsodīyo Sāgar Udaisiṅghot raided into Sīrohī to avenge the death of his brother, Jagmāl.[15] Ḍūṅgarot Vījo also left Sīrohī and returned to the Mughal court to petition the Emperor for the grant of Sīrohī to him in ***jāgīr***. This time Akbar agreed. Vījo's petition to the Emperor appears to have been aided by the support he received from Dhīrāvat Kachvāho Rājā Rāmdās Ūdāvat (no. 19), who was Emperor Akbar's petition-bearer (***arajvegī***). Ḍūṅgarot Vījo had approached Kachvāho Rāmdās in 1587 with offers of the marriage of one of his daughters. Kachvāho Rāmdās accepted this offer, and helped to arrange the marriage of this daughter to his sister's son. This alliance undoubtedly helped Vījo's bid for power in Sīrohī.

Vījo returned to Sīrohī in February of 1588 with an Imperial army under the command of Rāṭhoṛ Moṭo Rājā Udaisiṅgh Māldevot of Jodhpur (1583-95) and Jāmbeg. Rāv Surtāṇ again fled Sīrohī for Ābū on the approach of Imperial troops. The Mughals encamped at the village of Nītoro for one month, raiding and looting the surrounding lands. Moṭo Rājā Udaisiṅgh carried out a series of inconclusive operations, as much to avenge the death of his brother's son, Rāv Rāysiṅgh Candrasenot, as to punish Rāv Surtāṇ. The Imperial forces also planned a deception, and using the offices of Kūmpāvat Rāṭhoṛ Ṭhākur Vairsal Prithīrājot of Bagṛī village[16] in Mārvāṛ, had several of Rāv Surtāṇ's leading Rajpūts summoned to the Imperial camp on the pretext of holding settlement talks. These Rajpūts included the Ḍūṅgarots Pato Sāṃvatsīyot, Sūro Narsiṅghot (9-6), Sūro's son, Togo Sūrāvat (10-4), and Cībo Devṛo Jeto Khīṃvāvat. Once these men were in camp, they were murdered at the hands of Rāṭhoṛ Rām Ratansīyot. Rāṭhoṛ Vairsal Prithīrājot only learned of this deception afterwards, and he rode into the Moṭo Rājā's camp in anger and killed Rām Ratansīyot

---

stipulating all of the above was written down and signed on February 12, 1612. This agreement came to naught, however, for Sūrsiṅgh soon came to battle with Rāv Rājsiṅgh and was defeated and forced to flee Sīrohī. See: ***Jodhpur Rājya kī Khyāt***, pp. 145-149, for a detailed listing of this agreement and all of the marriages it entailed; Ojhā, 4:1:373-374; Ojhā, ***Sīrohī Rājya kā Itihās***, p. 232.

[15] Ojhā, ***Sīrohī Rājya kā Itihās***, pp. 243-244, writes that Sīsodīyo Rāṇo Pratāp refused to be party to these raids into Sīrohī on the part of his brother, but instead allied himself through marriage with Rāv Surtāṇ. When talk of the marriage of his son Amarsiṅgh's daughter, Kesarkuṃvar (Sukhkuṃvar), to Rāv Surtāṇ had first begun, Rāṇo Pratāp's brother, Sāgar, had remonstrated before the Rāṇo, saying that he should seek revenge for Jagmāl's death at Rāv Surtāṇ's hands. But Rāṇo Pratāp disregarded his words. He told Sāgar that he should go ahead and do as he wished, but he should understand that his family had not gained their honor by going to Delhi and filling their bellies serving the Muslims. Rāṇo Pratāp proceeded with the marriage of his granddaughter to Rāv Surtāṇ, whom, according to Ojhā, he considered one of his equals.

[16] Bagṛī village: located nine miles east-southeast of Sojhat in eastern Mārvāṛ.

before the Moṭo Rājā. He then committed suicide by stabbing himself in the stomach with his dagger.[17]

Ḍūṅgarot Vījo himself was killed during one of these operations in Sīrohī when he and Jāmbeg rode off with a separate raiding party apart from the Moṭo Rājā. With a void now in the rulership, the Moṭo Rājā seated Devṛo Kalo Mehājaḷot (7-3)[18] once again on the throne of Sīrohī. The Moṭo Rājā also demanded a large tribute from Rāv Surtāṇ including two ***lākh***s of rupees and a number of horses, and he held several of Rāv Surtāṇ's family members hostage to ensure the payment of this tribute.

Despite these events and the sanctions placed against him, Rāv Surtāṇ soon emerged from the hills and reasserted his own authority in Sīrohī. Rāv Kalo Mehājaḷot was forced to flee without fighting to Mārvāṛ, where he entered the service of Moṭo Rājā Udaisiṅgh. The Moṭo Rājā granted Kalo the village of Bhādrājuṇ[19] in ***paṭo***. Devṛo Kalo remained there until his death in 1604.

With Ḍūṅgarot Vījo now dead, Rāv Kalo in Mārvāṛ, and Mughal forces employed elsewhere, Rāv Surtāṇ spent the remaining years of his rule in relative peace. There is mention of only two episodes of outside interference. ***Akbar Nāma***, 3:985, records that in 1593 Moṭo Rājā Udaisiṅgh of Jodhpur "took leave to go to Sirohī in order that he might reduce the proprietor there to obedience, or else prepare punishment for refractoriness." These operations appear to have been inconclusive. However, in 1595 Rāv Surtāṇ was forced to pay a penalty (***daṇḍ***) to the Moṭo Rājā's son and successor, Rāṭhoṛ Rājā Sūrajsiṅgh Udaisiṅghot of Jodhpur (1595-1619). Rājā Sūrajsiṅgh exacted this penalty on behalf of Emperor Akbar while he was was enroute from Jodhpur to Gujarat on Imperial business.

Rāv Surtāṇ died on September 12, 1610. He had twelve wives and two sons. His eldest son by his Sīsodṇī Rāṇī was Rājsiṅgh Surtāṇot (9-1). Rājsiṅgh succeeded Rāv Surtāṇ to the throne of Sīrohī. A second son named Sūrsiṅgh Surtāṇot (9-2) was also born.

> ***Akbar Nāma***, 3:266-267, 278-279, 544-545, 614, 985; ***Bāṅkīdās***, pp. 155-156; ***Khyāt***, 1:135-169; ***Murārdān***, no. 2, pp. 171-173, 185-186; Ojhā, 2:736-738, 4:1:352-353, 359-360, 5:1:172-174, 176-177; Ojhā, ***Sīrohī Rājya kā Itihās***, pp. 217-244; ***Vigat***, 1:92, 2:70; ***Vīr Vinod***, 2:161-163, 221-222, 1097-1098.

---

[17] There is a memorial stone to Ṭhākur Vairsal Prithīrājot at the village of Nītoro. See: Ojhā, 4:1:359.

[18] The Moṭo Rājā received one of Devṛo Kalo's daughters in marriage in 1589-90. See **Marriage and Family Lists of the Rulers of Jodhpur**, Moṭo Rājā Udaisiṅgh Māldevot, Rāṇī no. 16.

[19] Bhādrājuṇ: located forty-eight miles south-southwest of Jodhpur.

Figure 4. Devṛo Cahuvāṇs of Sīrohī
(continued on the following page)

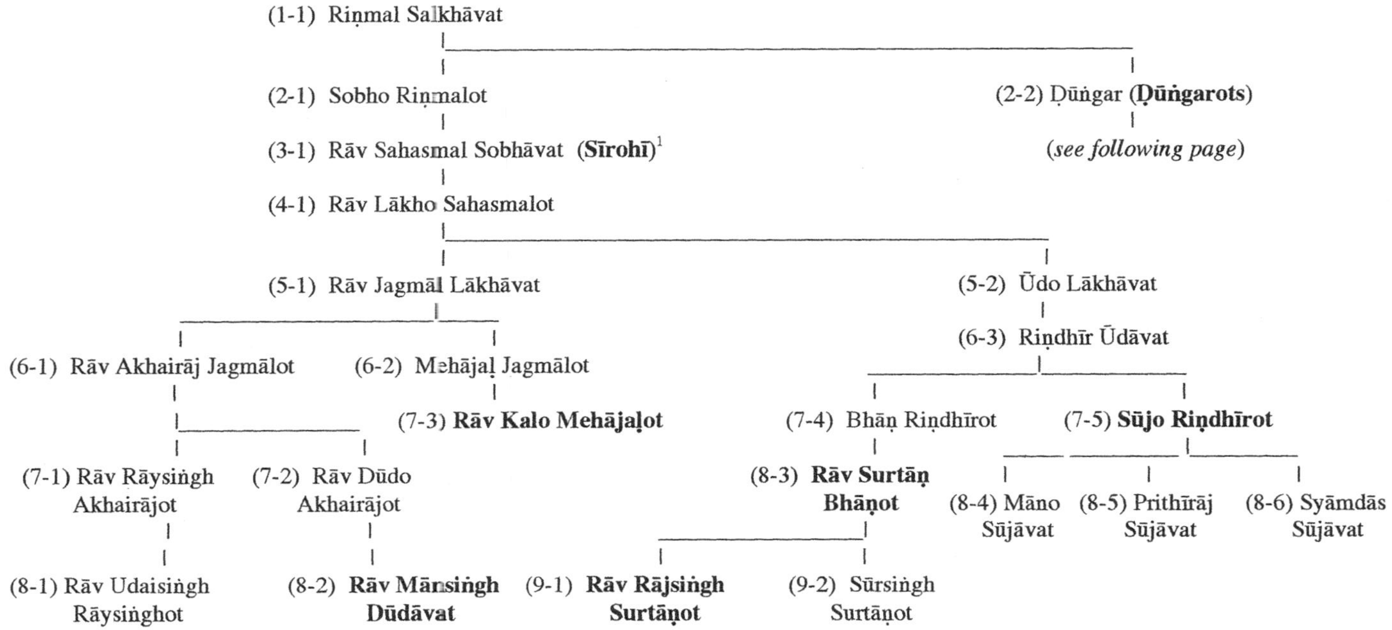

[1] The texts offer differing dates for Rāv Sahasmal Sobhāvat's founding of Sīrohī. ***Khyāt***, 1:135, records the date of March 27, 1396, while ***Vīr Vinod***, 2:1096, states that the original city of Saraṇvāhī (Sīrohī) was founded near the mountain named Saraṇvo on April 7, 1395.

Figure 4. Devṛo Cahuvāṇs of Sīrohī
(continued from the preceding page)

- (1-1) Riṇmal Salkhāvat
  - (2-1) Sobho Riṇmalot
    - (3-1) Rāv Sahasmal Sobhāvat (**Sīrohī**)
      - (*see previous page*)
  - (2-2) Ḍūṅgar (**Ḍūṅgarots**)[2]
    - (3-2) Jhāñjho
      - (4-2) Gajo
        - (5-2) Bhīndo
          - (6-4) Ālaṇ Bhīndāvat
            - (7-6) Tejsī Ālaṇot
              - (8-7) Rūdo Tejsīyot[3]
                - (9-3) Harrāj Rūdāvat
                  - (10-1) **Vījo Harrājot**
                  - (10-2) **Lūṇo Harrājot**
                  - (10-3) **Māno Harrājot**
                - (9-4) Sekho Rūdāvat
                  - (10-4) **Rāvat Sekhāvat**
              - (8-8) Narsiṅgh Tejsīyot
                - (9-5) **Samro Narsiṅghot**
                - (9-6) **Sūro Narsiṅghot**
                  - (10-4) **Togo Sūrāvat**

---

[2] Presented here is the genealogy of the Ḍūṅgarots as recorded in the ***Khyāt*** of Naiṇsī, 1:162-168. Ojhā, ***Sīrohī Rājya kā Itihās***, p. 217, and Ojhā, 2:727, n. 2, list a differing order for the first four generations, as follows: Gajo, Ḍūṅgar, Jhāñjho, Bhīndo.

[3] Ojhā, ***Sīrohī Rājya kā Itihās***, p. 217, gives the name "Dūdo Tejsīyot".

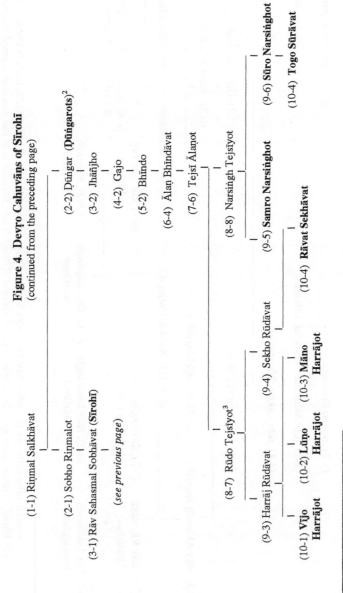

Hāḍo Cahuvāṇs

(no. 6) **Surjan Urjaṇot, Rāv** (12-2)

Hāḍo Rāv Surjan Urjaṇot, ruler of Būndī (ca. 1554-78), began his career as a military servant of Sīsodīyo Rāṇo Udaisiṅgh Sāṅgāvat of Mevāṛ (ca. 1537-72; no. 17).[1] He became a close companion of the Rāṇo and served under him until shortly after the fall of Cītoṛ to Akbar in 1568. Both his rise to power in Būndī and his position of local authority were intimately tied to the Rāṇo and to Cītoṛ. He then made obeisance to Akbar in 1569 and served under the Mughals in varying capacities until 1578-79, when he retired from Mughal service. He went to Benares to live with his family and died there in 1585-86. Rāv Surjan achieved the rank of 2,000 ***zāt*** as a ***mansabdār*** in Mughal service. Despite this prominence, he always carried with him the shame of being the Rajpūt commander of Riṇthambhor who submitted to Akbar without battle.

As a military servant of Sīsodīyo Rāṇo Udaisiṅgh's in the period prior to 1554-55, Surjan initially held twelve villages in ***paṭo***. The Rāṇo then gave him the ***pargano*** of Phūliyo as an increase after he was wounded while performing some service for the Sīsodīyo ruler. The Rāṇo later revoked this grant and gave Surjan Vadhnor[2] in northern Mevāṛ in exchange.

Rāṇo Udaisiṅgh supported Surjan's struggle for power in Būndī in 1554-55 against a paternal relation, Hāḍo Rāv Surtāṇ Sūrajmalot (12-1), who proved incompetent. Rāv Surjan continued in the Rāṇo's service during the early years of his rule, holding Būndī in grant from him. He was a major ally of the Rāṇo's at the battle of Harmāṛo[3] in January of 1557, during which the Rāṇo's forces were defeated by the combined armies of Rāṭhoṛ Rāv Mālde Gāṅgāvat of Jodhpur (1532-1562) and Paṭhāṇ Hājī Khān. Soon after Harmāṛo, Rāṇo Udaisiṅgh expressed his increased confidence in Rāv Surjan, giving him seven ***pargano***s in ***paṭo*** and entrusting him with the keys to the fortress of Riṇthambhor. The seven ***parganos*** included in addition to Būndī with its three-hundred and sixty villages, the following: Pāṭaṇ, Koṭo, Kaṭakhaṛo, Naiṇvāy, Āṃratdo, and Khairāvad.

Rāv Surjan remained in control of the fortress of Riṇthambhor from 1557 until early 1569. He was a constant companion of the Rāṇo during this period, and he accompanied the Rāṇo on his pilgrimage to Dvārkājī in Saurashtra, which the Rāṇo made in order to perform a penance for his murder of a close kinsman at Cītoṛ. While at Dvārkājī, Rāv Surjan asked the Rāṇo's

---

[1] Rāv Surjan's father, Urjaṇ Narbadot, was Rāṇo Udaisiṅgh's mother's father (***nāno***).

[2] Vadhnor: located forty-seven miles south-southwest of Ajmer.

[3] Harmāṛo: a village lying fifty-five miles south-southwest of Ajmer and six miles south of Vadhnor in northern Mevāṛ.

permission to have the temple of Riṇchoṛjī at Riṇthambhor rebuilt, which he did following his return.

The Mughal Emperor Akbar invested Cītoṛ in 1568. After his defeat of Rāṇo Udaisiṅgh's forces and his occupation of this fortress, Akbar sent an army under the command of Ashraf Khān against Riṇthambhor. Akbar himself soon followed, reaching Riṇthambhor in early February of 1569. He ordered batteries set in place and the siege of the fortress to commence. Desultory fighting occurred for more than a month between Rāv Surjan's Rajpūts and the Mughal army. Rāv Surjan then sent his two sons, Dūdo (13-1) and Bhoj (13-2), to meet with Akbar and arrange an end to the siege and a transfer of the fortress to the Mughals. ***Akbar Nāma***, 2:494, records that Rāv Surjan's sons

> succeeded, by the instrumentality of some high officers, in obtaining an interview [with Akbar] and placed the foreheads of supplication on the threshold of sincerity. They begged the pardon of their father's offenses and requested that they might perform the prostration (***sijda***).[4]

Maāt͟hir-ul-Umarā, 2:2:917-918, adds the following details:

> It is said that in the end of the month of Ramaḍān Emperor said that if the garrison did not surrender that day, the fort on the morrow-- which was the 'Īd day-- would be the ***qabaq-bāzī*** (archery or gunnery) target. Surjan became frightened and losing heart sent as emissaries to the Presence his sons Dūdā and Bhoj together with a number of his officers. After the interview orders were passed for presenting both of them with robes of honor. When they were taken out of the royal enclosure for putting on the K͟hil'ats, one of the companions, whose brain was deranged, thought that an order had been issued for the arrest of Surjan's sons. Consequently out of loyalty he lost control and drew his sword. One of the servants of Rāja Bhagwān Dās tried to restrain him, but that mad man used his sword on him. He ran to the royal enclosure, and wounded Pūran Mal son of Kān Shaik͟hāwat and two others, and with his sword cut into two Shaik͟h Bahā'-ud-Dīn Majd͟hūb Badāyūnī. Thereupon a servant of Muzaffar K͟hān killed him.
>
> The sons of Surjan were stricken with remorse at this occurrence, but as they were innocent, the Emperor excused them, and after granting them robes of honour allowed them to return to their father.

---

[4] ***Sijda***: bowing the forehead to the ground (as in prayer to Allah). See: R. S. McGregor, ed., ***The Hindi-English Dictionary*** (Oxford, Delhi: Oxford University Press, 1997), p. 1013.

Rāv Surjan himself later met with the Emperor. ***Akbar Nāma***, 2:245, notes:

> Sūrjan, in order that his honor might be preserved, begged that one of [Akbar's] . . . intimate courtiers might come and introduce him to the court . . .

Akbar agreed to this request and sent Ḥusayn Qulī Khān to escort the Rāv. Rāv Surjan then emerged from the fort, and on March 22, 1569 "prostrated himself at the threshold."

The ***Khyāt*** of Naiṇsī, 1:112, records that Rāv Surjan told Akbar during their meeting that while he was submitting to Mughal authority, he was under an oath of allegiance to the Rāṇo of Mevāṛ and would not be sent on any military campaigns against him. Akbar accepted this condition at the time of Rāv Surjan's submission. He then brought the Rāv into Mughal service and granted him four ***pargano***s in the area of Benares for his maintenance.

Akbar appears to have been pleased that Rāv Surjan submitted to his authority. But he held a low estimation of him as a warrior, for when he returned to Agra, he had the likenesses of two of the great Rajpūts who had been killed fighting at Cītoṛ, Meṛtīyo Rāṭhoṛ Jaimal Vīramdevot (no. 107) and Sīsodīyo Gahlot Pato Jagāvat, carved in stone seated upon elephants and placed as columns at the main doorway to the Red Fort, while he had Rāv Surjan's likeness carved in the form of a dog on one of these same columns. This slight from the Emperor greatly shamed Rāv Surjan.

For a number of years thereafter, Rāv Surjan held the Gadha-Katanga territory of Jabalpur in ***jāgīr*** from Akbar. The Emperor exchanged this land in 1575 for Fort Canadh (Cunar). Then in 1578 Akbar decided on the conquest of Būndī. This action arose in response to local disruptions in the area which Surjan's elder son, Dūdo, had caused. Rāv Surjan's younger son, Bhoj, had come to court to live at the Emperor's "foot" following Rāv Surjan's capitulation at Riṇthambhor in 1569. Rāv Surjan's elder son, Dūdo, left Riṇthanmbhor without the Emperor's permission, fleeing to Mevāṛ. There he took service under Rāṇo Udaisiṅgh, who "established some daily wage and gave [it to him]." Dūdo then proceeded to enter into the affairs of Būndī, and Akbar sent a force under Rāv Surjan, his son, Bhoj, and Zain Khān Kokaltāsh to chastise Dūdo and bring Būndī securely within the orbit of the Mughal throne. This operation proved successful, and afterwards Akbar promoted Rāv Surjan to the rank of 2,000 ***ẓāt***.

Rāv Surjan remained at court in attendance upon the Emperor for a short period after the conquest of Būndī. He then went to live at Benares with his family in 1578-79. He had a palace constructed there. Surjan apparently left active service under the Mughals at this time. While he was in Benares, his younger son, Bhoj, continued to live at court. His elder son, Dūdo, was pardoned in 1579, and he also came to live at court. Akbar then stationed him in the Punjab. But he again left his station without permission from the Emperor and returned to Mevāṛ and Būndī.

Rāv Surjan died in Benares in 1585-86. Emperor Akbar gave the ***ṭīko*** of succession to Surjan's younger son, Bhoj, and granted him Būndī in ***jāgīr***.

Bhoj's succession precipitated a ***grāsvedh*** (lit. "share-battle") between Bhoj and his elder brother, Dūdo, over the rulership of Būndī, a conflict into which the Mughals also entered.

Ā'īn-ī-Akbari, p. 510, records that Bhoj Surjanot, who carried the title of ***rāv***, received Būndī from Akbar in ***jāgīr*** in 1578, and that he served under Kachvāho Rājā Mānsiṅgh Bhagvantdāsot of Āmber (1589-1614) against the Afghans in Orissa, and under Shaikh Abū'l-Fazl in the Deccan. Rāv Bhoj then committed suicide in 1607-08. This action was the result of his refusal to consent to the marriage of his daughter's daughter to Emperor Jahāngīr. The ***Ā'īn*** notes:

> In the first year of his reign, Jahāngīr wished to marry Jagat Singh's daughter.[5] Rāy Bhoj, her grandfather, refused to give his consent, and Jahāngīr resolved to punish him on his return from Kabul. But Rāy Bhoj, in the end of 1016 [1607-08], committed suicide. The marriage, however, took place . . .
>
> It is said that Rāthoṛ and Kachhwāha princesses entered the imperial Harem; but no Hāḍā princess was ever married to a Timuride.

Rāv Surjan was a sister's son (***bhāṇej***) of the Gahlots. His son, Dūdo, was the daughter's son (***dohitro***) of Cāmpāvat Rāṭhoṛ Jeso Bhairavdāsot (no. 48) of Mārvāṛ, and his son, Bhoj, was the daughter's son of Āhāṛo Gahlot Rāv Jagmāl Udaisiṅghot of Vāṃsvāḷo (ca. 1518-44).

> ***Ā'īn-ī-Akbari***, pp. 449-450, 482, 510; "Aitihāsik Bātāṃ," p. 51; ***Akbar Nāma***, 2:484-496, 3:223, 258, 284-287, 851, 855; Athar Ali, ***Apparatus***, p. 15; ***Bāṅkīdās***, pp. 14, 143-145; Jahāngīr, 1:144; ***Khyāt***, 1:109-112, 291, 297; ***Maāthir-ul-Umarā***, 2:2:917-919; ***Vigat***, 2:60; ***Vīr Vinod***, 2:108-111.

[5] Rājāvat Kachvāho Jagatsiṅgh Mānsiṅghot, eldest son of Rājā Mānsiṅgh Bhagvantdāsot of Āmber (1589-1614).

Figure 5. Hāḍo Cahuvāṇs of Būndī

(1-1) Hāḍo Vijaipāḷot (Nāḍūl ***sākh*** of Cahuvāṇs)
|
(2-1) Bāṅgo Hāḍāvat
|
(3-1) Devo Bāṅgāvat (**Hāḍos of Būndī**)
|
(4-1) Jītmal Devot
|
(5-1) Nāpo Jītmalot
|
(6-1) Hāmo Nāpāvat
|
(7-1) Varsiṅgh Hāmāvat
|
(8-1) Vairo Varsiṅghot
|
(9-1) Bhāṇḍo Vairāvat

(10-1) Rāv Nāraṇdās Bhāṇḍāvat
|
(11-1) Rāv Sūrajmal Nāraṇdāsot
|
(12-1) **Rāv Surtāṇ Sūrajmalot**

(10-2) Narbad Bhāṇḍāvat
|
(11-2) Urjaṇ Narbadot
|
(12-2) **Rāv Surjan Urjaṇot**

(13-1) **Dūdo Surjanot**
|
(14-1) Rāv Ratansī Dūdāvat
|
(15-1) Gopīnāth Ratansīyot
|
(16-1) Rāv Catrasāl Gopīnāthot

(13-2) **Rāv Bhoj Surjanot**

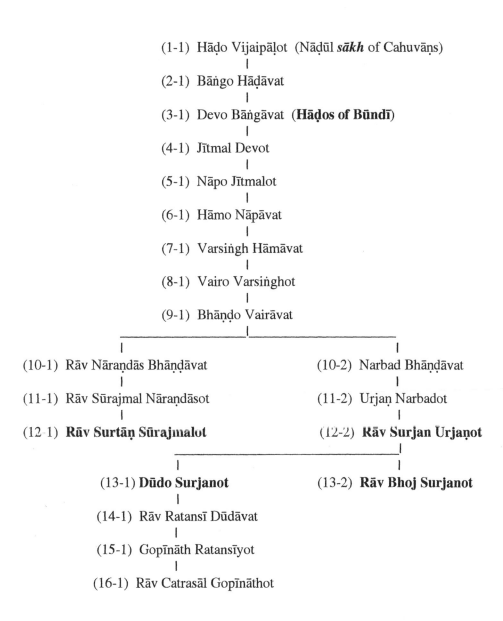

Sācoro Cahuvāṇs

(no. 7) **Jhāñjhaṇ Bhairavdāsot** (4-1)
(no. 8) **Megho Bhairavdāsot** (4-2)

The Sācoro Cahuvāṇs

The Sācoro Cahuvāṇs take their name from the town of Sācor in southern Rājasthān.[1] The ***Khyāt*** of Naiṇsī, 1:229, records that Sācor came under Cahuvāṇ rule on January 24, 1085 when Vijaisī Ālaṇot seized it from the Dahīyo Rajpūt Vijairāj. This information is incorrect. This area was under the control of the Solaṅkī Rajpūts of Gujarat between the tenth and the twelfth centuries. Cahuvāṇ control began in the late thirteenth century when the Cahuvāṇ ruler of Jāḷor[2] extended his authority over Sācor. It continued into the early fifteenth century, finally ending in 1421. In this year, Mīr Mālik defeated Sācoro Rāv Varjāṅg Pātāvat (1-1) in battle and captured the town. The ***Khyāt*** of Naiṇsī, 1:232, states that Varjāṅg's son, Jaisiṅghde Varjāṅgot (2-1), was also master (***dhaṇī***) of Sācor, but it is not known to what degree he exercised authority in this area.

Rāv Jaisiṅghde was a contemporary of Sīsodīyo Rāṇo Udaisiṅgh Sāṅgāvat of Mevāṛ (ca. 1537-72; no. 17), whose sister he married, and of Rāṭhoṛ Rāv Mālde Gāṅgāvat of Jodhpur (1532-62).

K. C. Jain, ***Ancient Cities and Towns of Rajasthan*** (Delhi: Motilal Banarsidass, 1972), pp. 198-201; ***Khyāt***, 1:229-232.

(no. 7) **Jhāñjhaṇ Bhairavdāsot** (4-1)

Jhāñjhaṇ Bhairavdāsot is listed in the texts under review simply as Jhāñjhaṇ Cahuvāṇ. He was a military servant of Rāv Mālde Gāṅgāvat of Jodhpur, and was attached to the Rāv's personal service. The genealogy of the Sācoro Cahuvāṇs in the ***Khyāt*** of Naiṇsī, 1:238, indicates that he resided in the ***vās*** ("residence, dwelling") of Rāv Mālde. Jhāñjhaṇ held the village of Mehagṛo[3] in ***paṭo*** from the Rāv. He is mentioned only once in the texts, his presence noted at the time Rāv Mālde granted one-half of the villages of Meṛto to Meṛtīyo Rāṭhoṛ Jagmāl Vīramdevot (no. 124). This grant took place in July of 1559 following the laying of foundations for the Mālgadh at Meṛto. Jhāñjhaṇ was a

---

[1] Sācor town is located one hundred thirty miles southwest of Jodhpur and seventy miles west of Sīrohī.

[2] Jāḷor is situated sixty-six miles northeast of Sācor.

[3] Mehagṛo: located twelve miles west of Sīvāṇo.

witness to the grant and to the swearing of Meṛtīyo Jagmāl at the temple of Mahāmāyā in Phaḷodhī village near Meṛto[4] along with Rāv Mālde's son, Kuṃvar Candrasen, and other Rajpūts in Rāv Mālde's service (see *Vigat*, 2:59 of the **translated text** for details of this swearing).

According to *Bāṅkīdās*, p. 162, Jhāñjhaṇ lived at Pokaraṇ in northern Mārvāṛ and was killed there during an outbreak of hostilities with the Devrājot Rāṭhoṛs.

Bāṅkīdās, p. 162; *Khyāt*, 1:238; *Vigat*, 2:62, 249.

(no. 8) **Megho Bhairavdāsot** (4-2)

Megho Bhairavdāsot was Jhāñjhaṇ Bhairavdāsot's (4-1) brother. He was killed at Meṛto in 1554 fighting with Rāṭhoṛ Prithīrāj Jaitāvat (no. 63) against Meṛtīyo Rāv Jaimal Vīramdevot (no. 107). Megho was apparently in Rāṭhoṛ Prithīrāj's personal service. He died along with a paternal nephew named Vīram Ūdāvat (5-2). Vīram Ūdāvat's son, Netsī Vīramot (6-1), was killed at Meṛto some eight years later in March of 1562 fighting with Rāṭhoṛ Prithīrāj's brother, Devīdās Jaitāvat (no. 65), against Meṛtīyo Rāv Jaimal and the Mughal forces of Akbar under Mīrzā Sharafu'd-Dīn Ḥusayn.

"Aitihāsik Bātāṃ," p. 49; *Khyāt*, 1:238, 240-241; *Vigat*, 1:59, 2:59.

[4] Phaḷodhī: located nine miles northwest of Meṛto town.

Figure 6. Sācoro Cahuvāṇs

(1-1) Rāv Varjāṅg Pātāvat (**Sācor**)

(2-1) Rāv Jaisiṅghde Varjāṅgot

(3-2) Bhairavdās Jaisiṅghdevot

(4-1) **Jhāñjhaṇ Bhairavdāsot**

(4-2) **Megho Bhairavdāsot**

(4-3) Gāṅgo Bhairavdāsot

- (5-1) Jīvo Gāṅgāvat

(4-4) Ūdo Bhairavdāsot

- (5-2) **Vīram Ūdāvat**
  - (6-1) **Netsī Vīramot**

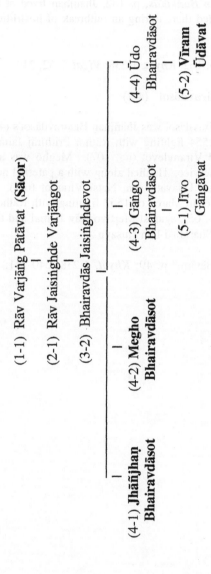

Sonagaro Cahuvāṇs

(no. 9) **Akhairāj Riṇdhīrot** (5-1)
(no. 10) **Mānsiṅgh Akhairājot** (6-1)

The Sonagaros Cahuvāṇs of Mārvāṛ

The Sonagaro Cahuvāṇs of Pālī village[1] in eastern Mārvāṛ descend from a branch of the Cahuvāṇs of Nāḍūl[2] in southern Mārvāṛ. Their association with the Rāṭhoṛs of Maṇḍor and Jodhpur dates from the time of Rāṭhoṛ Rāv Riṇmal Cūṇḍāvat (ca. 1428-38).

Rāv Riṇmal was a ***sago*** of the Sonagaros of Nāḍūl. He had married a daughter of theirs prior to his usurpation of power at Maṇḍor ca. 1428 from his uterine brother, Rāv Sato Cūṇḍāvat (no. 54). The chronicles of Mārvāṛ relate that the Sonagaros grew suspicious of Rāv Riṇmal and his growing power following his assumption of rulership, and they began to plot his murder. They used their ties through marriage to gain access to the court at Maṇḍor to further their ends. Word of the Sonagaro plot reached Rāv Riṇmal's Sonagarī wife, however, and she informed her husband of the danger and helped him to escape unharmed. In retaliation, Rāv Riṇmal organized a systematic campaign to rid Mārvāṛ of all Sonagaros. This campaign culminated in an attack on Nāḍūl, during which Rāv Riṇmal pillaged and burned the town and had all the Sonagaro men who had escaped his earlier retribution killed and their bodies thrown into the wells of the fort.

One Sonagaro who survived Rāv Riṇmal's revenge was Lolo Rāṇāvat (1-1). His mother was pregnant with him at the time of Rāv Riṇmal's attack. She was a Bhāṭiyāṇī from the ruling family of Jaisaḷmer and went to her paternal home (***pīhar***) to live following Rāv Riṇmal's attack on Nāḍūl. She remained at Jaisaḷmer thereafter, raising Lolo at his maternal grandfather's home (***nānāṇo***) at the Bhāṭī court. Rāv Riṇmal came to Jaisaḷmer sometime later to marry, and one afternoon while hunting with members of the Bhāṭī ruling family, noticed Sonagaro Lolo, then aged twelve years. The Rāv was impressed with the physical strength and prowess Lolo displayed during a fight with a lion. The Bhāṭīs told Rāv Riṇmal about this Sonagaro, saying that the Rāv had killed all the Sonagaros of Nāḍūl except this one who had been spared because he had been in his mother's belly. Rāv Riṇmal then requested Lolo from the Rāvaḷ, and brought him along when he left Jaisaḷmer. Upon his return to Maṇḍor, Rāv Riṇmal married Sundarbāī, the daughter of his son Jodho Riṇmalot, to Lolo.[3]

---

[1] Pālī: located forty miles south-southeast of Jodhpur.

[2] Nāḍūl: located sixty-seven miles south-southeast of Jodhpur.

[3] See ***supra***, **Marriage and Family Lists of the Rulers of Jodhpur**, Jodho Riṇmalot, D - Sundarbāī.

The Rāv also took the village of Pālī from the Nīmbāvat Sīndhaḷs then in control, and granted it to Lolo for his maintenance. Lolo Rāṇāvat later married a daughter to Rāv Riṇmal in exchange. Sonagaro attachments as military servants to the Rāṭhoṛ rulers of Maṇḍor and Jodhpur date from this time forward.

Little information is available about Lolo Rāṇāvat's immediate descendants. They maintained their position at Pālī as military servants of Jodhpur. Lolo Rāṇāvat's grandson, Khīṃvo Satāvat (3-1), married a daughter named Cāmpābāī to Rāv Riṇmal's son and successor, Rāv Jodho Riṇmalot (ca. 1453-1489),[4] in exchange for the daughter of Jodho that Rāv Riṇmal had given to Lolo. This Sonagarī's two sons, Varsiṅgh (no. 145) and Dūdo Jodhāvat (no. 104), established Rāṭhoṛ rule at Meṛto in eastern Mārvāṛ during the early 1460s.

"Aitihāsik Bātāṃ," p. 18; ***Bāṅkīdās***, p. 151; ***Khyāt***, 1:206-207; ***Vigat***, 1:39.

(no. 9) **Akhairāj Riṇdhīrot** (5-1)

Akhairāj Riṇdhīrot was fourth in line of descent from Lolo Rāṇāvat (1-1). He was a military servant of Rāv Mālde Gāṅgāvat of Jodhpur (1532-1562), under whom he rose to considerable prominence among the ***ṭhākur***s of Mārvāṛ. Following the death of his father, Riṇdhīr Khīṃvāvat (4-1), he succeeded to the rule of his ancestral village of Pālī, which Rāv Mālde granted him in ***paṭo***. While ***ṭhākur*** of Pālī, Akairāj became known as a warrior with few equals among the Rajpūts of Mārvāṛ. Local chronicles honor him as a great patron (***vaḍo dātār***), a great adept on the battlefield (***vaḍo ākhāṛsidh***), and a great warrior (***vaḍo jhūñjhār***).

Akhairāj Riṇdhīrot is mentioned in the texts in connection with several of Rāv Mālde's major campaigns between the years 1532 and 1544. He played a leading role in Rāv Mālde's occupation of Meṛto and Ajmer ca. 1535, when Meṛtīyo Rāv Vīramde Dūdāvat (no. 105) was driven from the land. Two years later ca. 1537, he led the contingent of Rajpūts who went to the aid of the fifteen-year-old heir to the throne of Cītoṛ, Sīsodīyo Udaisiṅgh Sāṅgāvat (Rāṇo of Mevāṛ, ca. 1537-72; no. 17). Udaisiṅgh's elder uterine brother, Rāṇo Vikramaditya, had been murdered at Cītoṛ ca. 1536. Udaisiṅgh himself escaped to Kumbhaḷmer and was under threat from a pretender to the throne, Sīsodīyo Vaṇvīr Prithīrājot. Udaisiṅgh's supporters called upon Sonagaro Akhairāj, offering to arrange the marriage of one of Akhairāj's daughters to Udaisiṅgh in return for Akhairāj's support. Akhairāj demurred, saying he would be honored to marry a daughter to Udaisiṅgh, but that there were rumors that this Udaisiṅgh was not the real heir to the throne. Sīsodīyo Vaṇvīr, the pretender, had been spreading rumors of Udaisiṅgh's death. Akhairāj said that if the Rajpūts around Udaisiṅgh would eat Udaisiṅgh's leavings (***jūṭhā***), he would accept this Udaisiṅgh as the legitimate heir. Udaisiṅgh's Rajpūts ate his leavings to prove

---

[4] See *supra*, **Marriage and Family Lists of the Rulers of Jodhpur**, Jodho Riṇmalot, Rāṇī no. 4.

his identity, and Akhairāj brought his daughter to Kumbhaḷmer and married her to Kuṃvar Udaisiṅgh. The ***Khyāt*** of Naiṇsī, 1:207, records that later, when Udaisiṅgh came under attack, he had a letter sent to Akhairāj, saying: "[You] should help me." Akhairāj then rode to Kumbhaḷmer in concert with other powerful Rāṭhoṛs and their Rajpūts including Kūmpo Mahirājot (no. 95), who was stationed at the ***thāṇo*** of Madārīyo village[5] in Goḍhvāṛ at the time, and Jeso Bhairavdāsot (no. 48), who had taken service under Udaisiṅgh a short time before and had been in close contact with Kūmpo Mahirājot. The ***Khyāt*** credits Akhairāj with defeating Vaṇvīr's forces, driving Vaṇvīr from Cītoṛ, and seating Udaisiṅgh on the Sīsodīyo throne at Kūmbhaḷmer.

In January of 1544 Akhairāj remained in the forefront of Rāv Mālde's army which faced Sher Shāh Sūr at Samel.[6] He was killed there along with one of his sons, Bhojrāj Akhairājot (6-2). Bhojrāj was a personal retainer of Rāṭhoṛ Kūmpo Mahirājot. Kūmpo and Kūmpo's paternal cousin, Jaito Pañcāiṇot (no. 61), were the commanders of Rāv Mālde's armies at Samel.

Akhairāj married daughters to several of the most powerful rulers of Rājasthān. He gave one daughter to Rāv Mālde Gāṅgāvat of Jodhpur.[7] He married another, as noted above, to Sīsodīyo Rāṇo Udaisiṅgh Sāṅgāvat of Mevāṛ (ca. 1537-72) while Udaisiṅgh was a ***kuṃvar***. This daughter's son (***dohitro***) was Pratāpsiṅgh Udaisiṅghot, who succeeded Rāṇo Udaisiṅgh to the throne of Cītoṛ and ruled 1572-97. A third daughter he married to Bīkāvat Rāṭhoṛ Kalyāṇmal Jaitsīyot (no. 46), a son of Bīkāner Rāv Jaitsī Lūṇkaraṇot (ca. 1526-42; no. 45). Kalyāṇmal succeeded Rāv Jaitsī to the throne of Bīkāner (ca. 1542-74), and his son, Rāysiṅgh by Akhairāj's daughter, also succeeded to the rulership of Bīkāner (ca. 1574-1612).

> "Aitihāsik Bātāṃ," pp. 45, 60; ***Bāṅkīdās***, pp. 151, 153; ***Khyāt***, 1:20, 28, 206-208, 212-213, 3:31, 95-96, 100; ***Murārdān***, no. 2, pp. 99, 121; Ojhā, 2:714-716, 4:1:306, n. 2; ***Vigat***, 1:56, 2:57; ***Vīr Vinod***, 2:63.

(no. 10) **Mānsiṅgh Akhairājot** (6-1)

Mānsiṅgh Akhairājot was a son of Sonagaro Akhairāj Riṇdhīrot (5-1) (no. 9) of Pālī village in central Mārvāṛ. Mānsiṅgh succeeded his father at Pālī following his father's death at the battle of Samel in 1544. He continued to hold this village in ***paṭo*** from Jodhpur for the next twenty years. He then left Mārvāṛ

---

[5] Madārīyo village: located thirteen miles south-southwest of Nāḍūl, and thirteen miles west-northwest of Kumbhaḷmer.

[6] Samel village: located twenty-four miles southwest of Ajmer.

[7] See ***supra***, **Marriage and Family Lists of the Rulers of Jodhpur**, Mālde Gāṅgāvat, Rāṇī no. 15.

for Mevāṛ in 1566-67, where he remained for the next ten years until his death in June of 1576.

Mānsiṅgh was one of Rāv Mālde Gāṅgāvat's most prominent ***ṭhākur***s following Samel. His name is mentioned with reference to several of the Rāv's important military campaigns. He took part in Rāv Mālde's abortive attempt to re-conquer Meṛto from Meṛtīyo Rāv Jaimal Vīramdevot (no. 107) in 1554, ten years after Samel. Some eight years later in 1562, Rāv Mālde sent Mānsiṅgh and a select number of Rajpūts with his son, Kuṃvar Candrasen Māldevot, to support Rāṭhoṛ Devīdās Jaitāvat (no. 65) in the defense of the Mālgaḍh at Meṛto against Meṛtīyo Rāv Jaimal and the Mughal forces of Akbar under Mīrzā Sharafu'd-Dīn Ḥusayn. Mānsiṅgh appears to have withdrawn from Meṛto with Kuṃvar Candrasen prior to the battle. His association with the Kuṃvar at this time may indicate that he was in the Kuṃvar's personal service.

Mānsiṅgh continued to serve under Rāv Mālde's son and successor, Rāv Candrasen Māldevot (1562-81), following Rāv Mālde's death in 1562. Mānsiṅgh supported Rāv Candrasen against his elder uterine brother, Udaisiṅgh, shortly after Rāv Candrasen's accession, when the brothers met in battle at the village of Lohiyāvaṭ in northern Mārvāṛ[8] ca. 1563. Udaisiṅgh attempted unsuccessfully at Lohiyāvaṭ to challenge Rāv Candrasen's authority in Mārvāṛ.

An elder half-brother of Rāv Candrasen, Rām Māldevot, took control of Sojhat in eastern Mārvāṛ with Mughal assistance in 1564. A year later in 1565, Mughal forces under Ḥusayn Qulī Khān attacked first Pālī and then Jodhpur. Mānsiṅgh took part in the engagement at Pālī, and then joined Rāv Candrasen at the fort of Jodhpur. Rāv Candrasen's forces were able to maintain control of the fort for several months, but on December 2, 1565 the Rāv finally handed over authority to Ḥusayn Qulī Khān and proceeded first to Bhādrājuṇ[9] and then to Sīvāṇo[10] in southern Mārvāṛ where he sought refuge during this time of distress (***vikhau***).

Mānsiṅgh remained with the Rāv for a short period after quitting Jodhpur. He then left Mārvāṛ for Mevāṛ in 1566-67, where he took service under his sister's husband (***bahanoī***), Sīsodīyo Rāṇo Udaisiṅgh Sāṅgāvat (ca. 1537-72; no. 17), and then his sister's son (***bhāṇej***), Rāṇo Pratāpsiṅgh Udaisiṅghot (1572-97). He was killed in June of 1576 at the battle of Haḷdīghāṭī in northern Mevāṛ,[11] when a Mughal force of Akbar's some five thousand strong met and defeated an army of three thousand Rajpūts under Sīsodīyo Rāṇo Pratāp.

---

[8] Lohiyāvaṭ: located eighteen miles southeast of Phaḷodhī in northern Mārvāṛ.

[9] Bhādrājuṇ: located forty-eight miles south-southwest of Jodhpur.

[10] Sīvāṇo: located fifty-eight miles southwest of Jodhpur.

[11] Haḷdīghāṭī is a narrow defile set amongst the Arāvallī hills eleven miles southwest of Nāthdvāra village and eighteen miles northeast of Gogūndo. The village of Khamṇor is nearby. Nāthdvāra lies twenty-six miles to the north of Udaipur in south-central Mevāṛ.

While *ṭhākur* of Pālī, Mānsiṅgh granted the village of Rāvaḷvās[12] to the Brāhmaṇ Purohit Māhāv Rāygur.

"Aitihāsik Bātāṃ," pp. 48, 53-54, 80; ***Bāṅkīdās***, pp. 21, 151; ***Khyāt***, 1:207-208; Ojhā, 4:1:335; ***Vigat***, 1:61, 68, 80, 83, 267-268, 2:63.

[12] Rāvaḷvās: located eight miles east of Pālī village in eastern Mārvāṛ.

Figure 7. Sonagaro Cahuvāṇs of Mārvāṛ

(1-1) **Lolo Rāṇāvat**

|

(2-1) Sato Lolāvat

|

(3-1) Khīṃvo Satāvat

|

(4-1) Riṇdhīr Khīṃvāvat

|

(5-1) **Akhairāj Riṇdhīrot**

(6-1) **Mānsiṅgh Akhairājot**	(6-2) **Bhojrāj Akhairājot**

Āhāṛo Gahlots

(no. 11) **Āskaraṇ Prithīrājot, Rāvaḷ of Ḍūṅgarpur**
(no. 12) **Pratāpsiṅgh Jaisiṅghot, Rāvaḷ of Vāṃsvāḷo**

(no. 11) Āskaraṇ Prithīrājot, Rāvaḷ

Āskaraṇ Prithīrājot succeeded to the rulership of Ḍūṅgarpur in 1549-50 and ruled for over thirty years until 1580. His accession followed a decade of division and hostility among the Āhāṛo Gahlots of southern Rājasthān, who held control of territory directly to the south of Mevāṛ. The Rāṇo of Cītoṛ, Sīsodīyo Ratansiṅgh Sāṅgāvat (ca. 1528-31), had entered into these hostilities as an arbiter, and during the rule of Rāvaḷ Āskaraṇ's father, Rāvaḷ Prithīrāj Udaisiṅghot (ca. 1527-49), this territory had been divided into the two kingdoms of Ḍūṅgarpur and Vāṃsvāḷo. Rāvaḷ Āskaraṇ came to the throne of Ḍūṅgarpur at a time when overt hostilities had momentarily settled between the two main branches of the Āhāṛos, and Rāvaḷ Āskaraṇ could look forward to an uncontested reign.

Few details are available about Rāvaḷ Āskaraṇ's period of rule. He figures in local chronicles largely because of the location of his kingdom in the hilly region of southern Mevāṛ and the Bāgaṛ, where he provided refuge on several occasions for rulers and prominent men from nearby kingdoms. One of the first of such men was Sujā'at Khān, whom Sher Shāh Sūr had made ***hākīm*** of Malwa in 1543. Sujā'at Khān fell out of favor with Sher Shāh's successor, Islām Shāh, following Sher Shāh's death in 1545, and declared himself the independent ruler of Malwa. Islām Shāh then sent an army against Sujā'at Khān, forcing him to flee Malwa and seek refuge in Ḍūṅgarpur with Rāvaḷ Āskaraṇ. Sujā'at Khān remained in Ḍūṅgarpur for some time, finally leaving to reassert his authority over Malwa.

Due to Ḍūṅgarpur's proximity to Mevāṛ, Sīsodīyo influence was strong throughout the kingdom. Rāvaḷ Āskaraṇ maintained a close but inconstant alliance with Mevāṛ. He was one of the allies of Sīsodīyo Rāṇo Udaisiṅgh Sāṅgāvat (ca. 1537-72; no. 17) at the ill-fated battle of Harmāṛo[1] in January of 1557. He rode to defeat here along with a number of other local rulers who had gathered in support of the Rāṇo against Paṭhāṇ Hājī Khān and the Rajpūts of Rāṭhoṛ Rāv Mālde Gāṅgāvat of Jodhpur (1532-62). Rāvaḷ Āskaraṇ's support of Rāṇo Udaisiṅgh appears short-lived, however, for an inscription at the Viṣṇu temple near Baneśvar Mahādev in Ḍūṅgarpur dated V.S. 1617 (1560-61) speaks of an attack from Mevāṛ and a victory for Ḍūṅgarpur against the Rāṇo. Specific details regarding these hostilities are unavailable.

---

[1] Harmāṛo village: located fifty-five miles south-southwest of Ajmer and six miles south of Vadhnor in northern Mevāṛ.

The Mughal Emperor Akbar sent an army under Aḥmad Khān Kokā against Malwa in 1561. This army forced Bāz Bahādur, son and successor of Sujā'at Khān, to flee the region. Bāz Bahādur sought refuge in Ḍūṅgarpur in 1562. Later in 1564, Akbar sent 'Abdu-llah Khān Uzbek against Ḍūṅgarpur in pursuit of Bāz Bahādur, who then fled to Mevāṛ. Bāz Bahādur soon returned to Ḍūṅgarpur and to Rāvaḷ Āskaraṇ's protection, however. The series of inconclusive Mughal operations against him finally ended in 1570 when he formally submitted to the Mughal throne.

Akbar sent another army under the command of Kachvāho Kuṃvar Mānsiṅgh Bhagvantdāsot (Rājā of Āmber, 1589-1614) in the direction of Ḍūṅgarpur and Mevāṛ in the period following his crushing of the rebellion in Gujarat in 1573. Kuṃvar Mānsiṅgh engaged Rāvaḷ Āskaraṇ in battle and forced him to flee and to seek refuge in the hills. The Kuṃvar then looted Ḍūṅgarpur town and proceeded on toward Udaipur. It was not until three years later in 1576 that Rāvaḷ Āskaraṇ finally submitted to the Mughals. ***Akbar Nāma***, 3:277, includes the following entry about the Rāvaḷ's submission:

> while the splendour of the august standards was casting glorious rays on the territory of Bānswāra, Rāūl Pertāp the head of that district - who was always stubborn - and Rāūl Askaran ruler of Dūngarpūr and other turbulent spirits of that country came and paid the prostration of repentance. Inasmuch as H. M. [Akbar's] nature is to accept excuses, and to cherish the humble, he accepted the shame of their having rendered little service, at the rate of good service, and took the life, the honour and the country of this faction under the protection of his justice and kindness. They were exalted by special favours.

Rāvaḷ Āskaraṇ offered one of his daughters to Akbar in marriage not long after his submission. Akbar sent a mission under Rājā Bīrbar to Ḍūṅgarpur to bring the Āhāṛī to his harem.

While earning a respite from Mughal depredations into his land through these actions, Rāvaḷ Āskaraṇ gained the ire of Sīsodīyo Rāṇo Pratāpsiṅgh Udaisiṅghot of Mevāṛ (1572-97). Rāṇo Pratāp sent an army against both Ḍūṅgarpur and Vāṃsvāḷo in 1578 to exact punishment. A battle took place along the Som Nadī, but it was inconclusive and ended only when the Rāṇo's commander was wounded and a number of Rajpūts on both sides had been killed.

Rāvaḷ Āskaraṇ extended help to Rāṭhoṛ Rāv Candrasen Māldevot of Jodhpur (1562-81) when the Rāv fled Mārvāṛ in 1576 for southern Rājasthān, and spent several years in exile. The Rāv stayed in Ḍūṅgarpur for a number of months, then moved on to Vāṃsvāḷo with the approach of Mughal forces. Rāvaḷ Āskaraṇ had married a daughter of Rāv Mālde Gāṅgāvat of Jodhpur named Pohpāṃvatībāī, and he was Rāv Candrasen's sister's husband (***bahaṇoi***).[2]

---

[2] See, ***supra*****, Marriage and Family Lists of the Rulers of Jodhpur**, Mālde Gāṅgāvat, Rāṇī no. 3, D - Pohpāṃvatībāī.

Rāvaḷ Āskaraṇ was succeeded to the rulership of Ḍūṅgarpur by his son, Sahasmal. Sahasmal married one of his daughters to Rāṭhoṛ Rājā Sūrajsiṅgh Udaisiṅghot of Jodhpur (1595-1619).[3]

"Aitihāsik Bātāṃ," p. 51; ***Akbar Nāma***, 3:277-278; ***Bāṅkīdās***, pp. 14, 106; G. H. Ojhā, ***Ḍūṅgarpur Rājya kā Itihās*** (Ajmer: Vedic Yantralaya, V. S. 1992 [A. D. 1935]), pp. 84-101; ***Khyāt***, 1:79; ***Murārdān***, no. 2, pp. 140, 208; ***Vigat***, 2:60; ***Vīr Vinod***, 2:1006-1007.

(no. 12) **Pratāpsiṅgh Jaisiṅghot, Rāvaḷ**

Few details are available about the life and rule of Rāvaḷ Pratāpsiṅgh Jaisiṅghot of Vāṃsvāḷo (ca. 1550-79). He was a close but inconstant ally of Mevāṛ like his Āhāṛo relation, Rāvaḷ Āskaraṇ Prithīrājot of Ḍūṅgarpur (no. 11). He did participate in the ill-fated battle of Harmāṛo in January of 1557 with Sīsodīyo Rāṇo Udaisiṅgh Sāṅgāvat (ca. 1537-72; no. 17). During Rāṭhoṛ Rāv Candrasen Māldevot's exile from Jodhpur and Mārvāṛ in the years 1576-79, he gave refuge to the Rāv and granted him several villages for his maintenance. Rāvaḷ Pratāpsiṅgh maintained his independence from Mughal rule until the mid-1570s. He finally submitted to Akbar in 1576 along with Rāvaḷ Āskaraṇ of Ḍūṅgarpur and other local rulers.

Rāvaḷ Pratāpsiṅgh was succeeded by his only son, Mānsiṅgh, born of a concubine.

"Aitihāsik Bātāṃ," p. 51; ***Akbar Nāma***, 3:277; ***Bāṅkīdās***, pp. 14, 107-108; ***Khyāt***, 1:70-88; Ojhā, 3:2:75-81; ***Vigat***, 2:60; ***Vīr Vinod***, 2:1031-1032.

---

[3] See, ***supra***, **Marriage and Family Lists of the Rulers of Jodhpur**, Sūrajsiṅgh Udaisiṅghot, Rāṇī no. 4.

Mānglīyo Gahlots

(no. 13) **Dedo**
(no. 14) **Vīram Devāvat**

Mānglīyo Vīram Devāvat is an obscure but important figure in the Rāṭhoṛ chronicles. He lived during the period of Rāv Mālde Gāngāvat's rule at Jodhpur (1532-62) and served under the Rāv in what appears to have been an administrative capacity.

Vīram's family had been associated with the house of Jodhpur for several generations. His grandfather, Mānglīyo Bhādo, had initiated this contact. Bhādo was from the village of Vāvṛī in northern Mārvāṛ.[1] He presented several hunting dogs to Rāv Mālde one day when the Rāv was hunting in the vicinity of his village. The Rāv, in turn, accepted Bhādo's son, Devo Bhādāvat, into his military service (*cākrī*). Devo must have taken part in the Rāv's conquest of Sīvāṇo from the Jaitmālot Rāṭhoṛs in June of 1538 and distinguished himself in some capacity during this campaign, for the Rāv honored Devo afterwards by placing him in charge of Sīvāṇo fort. Devo later died at the fort.

Mānglīyo Devo's son, Vīram Devāvat, followed his father into Rāv Mālde's service. ***Bānkīdās***, p. 60, refers to Vīram as a worthy and dutiful son (***vaḍo sapūt***). Vīram became a ***hujdār*** of Rāv Mālde's, responsible for the collection of revenues. His name is first mentioned in the chronicles with relation to Rāv Mālde's grant of one-half of the villages of Meṛto to Meṛtīyo Jagmāl Vīramdevot (no. 124) in July of 1559. Mānglīyo Vīram was present along with Rāv Mālde's son, Kuṃvar Candrasen, and other Rajpūts during Meṛtīyo Jagmāl's swearing at the temple of Mahāmāyā in Phaḷodhī village near Meṛto[2] prior to Meṛtīyo Jagmāl's receipt of this grant. Rāv Mālde afterwards stationed Vīram at Meṛto and entrusted him with the management of his affairs there.

Three years later on March 20, 1562 Mānglīyo Vīram was killed at Meṛto.[3] He was stationed at the Mālgaḍh along with other Rajpūts under the command of Rāv Mālde's commander, Rāṭhoṛ Devīdās Jaitāvat (no. 65). He died fighting there when Meṛtīyo Rāv Jaimal Vīramdevot (no. 107) and the Mughal forces of Akbar under Mīrzā Sharafu'd-Dīn Ḥusayn laid siege to Meṛto in early 1562 and succeeded in taking the fort and town. Among the Rajpūts in the Mālgaḍh was a relation of Vīram's, Mānglīyo Dedo (no. 13). Mānglīyo Dedo's reason for being at Meṛto and the role he played during the siege are uncertain. His specific relation to Mānglīyo Vīram is also unknown.

---

[1] Vāvṛī village: located twenty-one miles north of Phaḷodhī.

[2] Phaḷodhī village: located nine miles northwest of Meṛto.

[3] ***Vigat***, 1:63, incorrectly lists Mānglīyo Vīram as "Cahuvāṇ Vīram Ūdāvat."

"Aitihāsik Bātāṃ," p. 56; ***Bāṅkīdās***, pp. 16, 60; Ojhā, 4:1:288; ***Vigat***, 1:62-63, 2:62-63, 66.

Sīsodīyo Gahlots

(no. 15) **Bhīm Amrāvat, Rājā** (Mevāṛ) (8-1)
(no. 18) **Candrāvat Durgo Acḷāvat, Rāv** (Rāmpuro)
(no. 16) **Tejo Bīkāvat, Rāvat** (Devaḷīyo) (7-2)
(no. 17) **Udaisiṅgh Sāṅgāvat, Rāṇo** (Mevāṛ) (5-3)

(no. 15) **Bhīm Amrāvat, Rājā** (8-1)

Bhīm Amrāvat (Amarsiṅghot) was a son of Sīsodīyo Rāṇo Amarsiṅgh Pratāpsiṅghot (7-1) of Mevāṛ (1597-1620), and grandson of Rāṇo Pratāpsiṅgh Udaisiṅghot (6-1) (1572-97). He was a daughter's son (***dohitro***) of Akhairāj Kānhāvat of Bīrpur, tentatively identified as a Soḷaṅkī Rajpūt.

The ***Khyāt*** of Naiṇsī, 1:30, refers to Bhīm as a great warrior (***vaḍo Rajpūt***). During the rulership of his father, Rāṇo Amarsiṅgh, and until 1615 when Rāṇo Amarsiṅgh submitted to the Mughal Emperor Jahāngīr, Kuṃvar Bhīm participated in the Sīsodīyo struggles against the Mughals. Rāṇo Amarsiṅgh met with Prince Khurram (Shāh Jahān) in 1615 at the village of Gogūndo near Udaipur. This meeting marked the culmination of a concerted Mughal campaign against Mevāṛ led by Prince Khurram and begun over a year earlier in December of 1613. Rāṇo Amarsiṅgh sent his son, Karaṇsiṅgh (8-2), to the Mughal court with Prince Khurram following his submission. Bhīm was among the contingent of Sīsodīyos in accompaniment, and he remained at court and soon became a personal servant of Prince Khurram's. ***Maāṯhir-ul-Umarā***, 2:1:572, notes that Bhīm distinguished himself in the Prince's service. He also gained the respect and affection of Emperor Jahāngīr. Bhīm continued to serve under Prince Khurram for the remainder of his life.

Bhīm became involved with operations against ***zamīndārs*** in Gujarat and against the Deccanis soon after joining the Prince's service. He also took part in operations in Gondwana, where he proved valuable in collecting tribute, and he acquired a considerable reputation for bravery and courage. Prince Khurram granted Bhīm the revenues of the ***ghāsmārī*** tax of Jāḷor Pargano in 1619, which he held for approximately one year. Bhīm was in Kashmir with Emperor Jahāngīr in 1620 when his own father, Rāṇo Amarsiṅgh, died at Udaipur in Mevāṛ. Jahāngīr notes in his ***Memoirs***:

> On this day came the news of the death of Rānā Amar Singh, who had died a natural death at Udaipur (became a traveler on the road of non-existence). Jagat Singh, his grandson, and Bhīm, his son, who were in attendance on me, were presented with dresses of honor . . . (Jahāngīr, 2:123).

Emperor Jahāngīr also honored Bhīm with the title of ***rājā*** during this time. Rājā Bhīm served with Prince Khurram in the Deccan in 1621 during operations there against Mālik 'Ambar. He was placed in charge of one of the five armies used in these operations. Then in 1622 while Khurram was ***sūbedār*** of Ajmer (including Meṛto), Bhīm received 204 villages of Meṛto Pargano in Mārvāṛ along with the town of Meṛto in ***jāgīr***. ***Vigat***, 2:73, records that Rājā Bhīm himself came to Meṛto at this time.

Rājā Bhīm held Meṛto for only a short period, for in 1623 Prince Khurram rebelled against Emperor Jahāngīr. Rājā Bhīm followed the Prince into the Deccan, eastern India, and finally the Gangetic plains, and remained one of the Prince's foremost supporters during his rebellion. In May of 1624 Khurram's forces of some 10,000 men under Rājā Bhīm's command met an Imperial force of 40,000 led by Prince Parvīz and Mahābat Khān at the village of Damdama on the confluence of the Tons and the Ganges Rivers. Rājā Bhīm was killed during the battle that ensued.

> Athar Ali, ***Apparatus***, pp. 74, 86; ***Bāṅkīdās***, pp. 95-96; Jahāngīr, 2:123, 162; ***Khyāt***, 1:30-31; ***Maāthir-ul-Umarā***, 1:60, 417, 419, 455-456, 730, 2:1:572; Ojhā, 2:280, n. 4, 824-828; R. P. Tripathi, ***The Rise and Fall of the Mughal Empire*** (Reprint ed. Allahabad: Central Book Depot, 1966), pp. 400-401; ***Vigat***, 1:106, 112, 2:73.

(no. 16) **Tejo Bīkāvat, Rāvat** (7-2)

Tejo (Tejmāl) Bīkāvat, Rāvat of Devaḷīyo and Partābgaḍh (ca. 1564-93), came from a collateral line of the ruling house of Mevāṛ, stemming from Rāṇo Mokaḷ Lākhāvat (1-1), an early fifteenth century ruler of Cītoṛ. He was the eldest son of Rāvat Bīko (also referred to as Vikramsiṅgh) Rāysiṅghot (6-2). His mother was the daughter of Chapaṇīyo Rāṭhoṛ Jaimal Jaicandot. Tejo's father had ruled Partābgaḍh and founded his own capitol at Devaḷīyo. The dates for Rāvat Bīko's rule are obscure, and it appears from inscriptional evidence[1] that the ruling family was divided among a number of factions during this period, with unclear and disrupted periods of rulership. Ojhā, 3:3:101, 104, gives the date of 1563-64 for Rāvat Bīko's death, while ***Vīr Vinod***, 2:1056, offers the later date of 1578. Ojhā's earlier date is preferable, but still problematic, for Bīko's son, Tejo, is mentioned with the title of ***rāvat*** with relation to events that occurred as early as 1557.

Rāvat Tejo Bīkāvat is also an obscure figure in local history. Only a few references to him appear in the texts. He is mentioned as an ally of Sīsidīyo Rāṇo Udaisiṅgh Sāṅgāvat of Mevāṛ (ca. 1537-72; no. 17) and fought with him at the battle of Harmāṛo[2] on January 24, 1557 against the forces of Paṭhāṇ Hājī Khān, a former noble of Sher Shāh Sūr's, and Rāṭhoṛ Rāv Mālde Gāṅgāvat of Jodhpur (1532-62). ***Vigat***, 2:60, which lists him as a participant in the battle, gives him the designation "Rāvat Tejo, master of Devaḷīyo."

---

[1] See: Ojhā, 3:3:90-101.

[2] Harmāṛo village: located fifty-five miles south-southwest of Ajmer.

It is known that Rāvat Tejo was much involved with Sīsodīyo Rāṇo Pratāpsiṅgh Udaisiṅghot of Mevāṛ (1572-97) (6-1) during the latter's long struggle against Mughal domination of his lands. Akbar had conquered Cītoṛ in 1568. With the death of Rāṇo Udaisiṅgh in 1572, his son, Rāṇo Pratāpsiṅgh, maintained a running battle with the Mughals for several years thereafter. Rāvat Tejo assisted the Rāṇo with men and supplies, and he sent one of his sons to fight with Rāṇo Pratāp at the battle of Haḷdīghāṭī in northern Mevāṛ[3] in June of 1576. Tejo's son was killed in this battle. Rāvat Tejo submitted to the Mughals this same year, but he continued to assist the Rāṇo as opportunity allowed.

Rāvat Tejo died in 1593-94.

"Aitihāsik Bātāṃ," p. 51; ***Bāṅkīdās***, pp. 14, 105-106; ***Khyāt***, 1:90-96; Ojhā, 3:3:90-108; ***Vigat***, 2:60; ***Vīr Vinod***, 2:1056.

(no. 17) **Udaisiṅgh Sāṅgāvat, Rāṇo** (5-3)

Udaisiṅgh Sāṅgāvat was a son of Sīsodīyo Rāṇo Sāṅgo Rāymalot (4-1), ruler of Cītoṛ and Mevāṛ (1509-28). His rise to power and rulership in Mevāṛ ca. 1537 came at the end of a decade of turbulence in Mevāṛ following the death of his father, Rāṇo Sāṅgo, in 1528. Rāṇo Sāṅgo was poisoned by his Rajpūts following their defeat at the battle of Khanua in 1527 against the Mughal Bābur, to prevent him from organizing another force to oppose the Mughals. Ten years of political turmoil in Mevāṛ ensued. Udaisiṅgh Sāṅgāvat, a younger son of the Rāṇo's by his wife, Hāḍī Karametī, the daughter of Hāḍo Urjaṇ Narbadot of Būndī, succeeded to the seat of power ca. 1537.

Events leading to Udaisiṅgh's accession are as follows: Rāṇo Sāṅgo's elder son, Ratansiṅgh Sāṅgāvat (5-1), born of the daughter of Rāṭhoṛ Vāgho Sūjāvat of Jodhpur (no. 83), succeeded to the throne of Mevāṛ at Cītoṛ in February of 1528. Immediately after his accession, he became involved in a dispute with Hāḍo Rāv Sūrajmal Nāraṇdāsot of Būndī (ca. 1527-31). This dispute centered upon control of the fort of Riṇthambhor, then under nominal Sīsodīyo authority but entrusted to the Hāḍos of Būndī. The fort was in the ***paṭo*** of two of Rāṇo Ratansiṅgh's younger half-brothers, Vikramaditya (5-2) and Udaisiṅgh (5-3). Vikramaditya and Udaisiṅgh were uterine brothers, related to the ruling house of Būndī through their mother, Hāḍī Karametī, and therefore under the protection of the Hāḍos. Rāṇo Sāṅgo had given this ***paṭo*** to Vikramaditya and Udaisiṅgh during the latter years of his rule in order to protect as well as sustain them.

Rāṇo Ratansiṅgh attempted to assert his authority over Riṇthambhor, and issued a summons to his half-brothers and their mother to come to Cītoṛ. This summons brought immediate Hāḍo resistance which enraged Rāṇo Ratansiṅgh. Hāḍī Karametī then initiated negotiations with the Mughal Bābur to enlist his aid in seating one of her sons on the throne of Cītoṛ. These

[3] Haḷdīghāṭī is a narrow defile in the Arāvallī hills eleven miles southwest of Nāthdvāra village and eighteen miles northeast of Gogūndo. The village of Khamṇor is nearby. Nāthdvāra lies twenty-six miles to the north of Udaipur in south-central Mevāṛ.

negotiations came to naught, but they helped to inflame an already difficult situation among the different factions around the ruling house of Mevāṛ. In 1531 the personal hostility between Hāḍo Rāv Sūrajmal and Sīsodīyo Rāṇo Ratansiṅgh reached a peak. While hunting together near Cītoṛ, they fell to fighting and killed each other from wounds inflicted.

Both Vikramaditya and Udaisiṅgh were summoned from Riṇthambhor to Cītoṛ in the wake of Rāṇo Ratansiṅgh's death. Succession passed to Vikramaditya, the elder of the two brothers, then aged thirteen or fourteen years. His was a very short reign, lasting only five years ca. 1531-36. By all standards, Vikramaditya was incompetent to rule both because of age as well as personal idiosyncracies. He is said to have dismissed all of the regular palace servants and attendants and to have brought in a large number of wrestlers and strong men to court in order to make himself feel more secure. He also alienated many of the leading ***ṭhākur***s of Mevāṛ because of the frivolities of his rule. They left his attendance to remain sequestered in their own strongholds.

Cītoṛ came under attack from troops of the Sultān of Gujarat, Bahādur Shāh (1526-37) in 1533. Bahādur Shāh was expanding from Gujarat into Malwa and southern Rājasthān in this period. Cītoṛ fell to his troops on March 8, 1535 and was held until later that same year when the Mughal Emperor Humāyūn defeated Bahādur Shāh's army in north India. As news of this defeat reached Cītoṛ, Bahādur Shāh's men abandoned the fortress, allowing Vikramaditya and his followers to reoccupy it. Sīsodīyo Vaṇvīr Prithīrājot (5-4), a son of Rāṇo Vikramaditya's paternal uncle, Sīsodīyo Prithīrāj Rāymalot (4-2) by a concubine of the Khātī ***jāti***, had become a close companion and sycophant of the Rāṇo's during this time. In 1536 Vaṇvīr stabbed and killed Rāṇo Vikramaditya and made himself master of Cītoṛ.

Servants of Udaisiṅgh's smuggled him out of Cītoṛ on the night of Rāṇo Vikramaditya's murder, taking him first to Devaḷīyo, then Ḍūṅgarpur to the south of Mevāṛ, and finally to the fortress of Kumbhaḷmer, located among the Arāvallī hills in western Mevāṛ. Udaisiṅgh was then fifteen years old. Rajūts around him quickly organized support for his cause against Vaṇvīr, pretender to the throne. The chronicles relate that one of the prominent Rajpūts they called upon to assist Udaisiṅgh was Sonagaro Cahuvāṇ Akhairāj Riṇdhīrot (no. 9), who was a military servant of Rāṭhoṛ Rāv Mālde Gāṅgāvat of Jodhpur (1532-62). Udaisiṅgh's supporters arranged the marriage of one of Akhairāj's daughters to Udaisiṅgh in turn for Akhairāj's support. Akhairāj agreed to this marriage and brought his daughter to Kumbhaḷmer for the wedding. He later returned to Mevāṛ with a large force of Rajpūts from Mārvāṛ, including Kūmpo Mahirājot (no. 95), Rāṇo Akhairājot (no. 28), and Bhado Pañcāiṇot (no. 32). The assembled force defeated Vaṇvīr's army and marched on Cītoṛ. Vaṇvīr is reported to have either been killed or to have run away in the face of the attack.

Udaisiṅgh's succession took place ca. 1537 at Kumbhaḷmer. His reign as Rāṇo of Mevāṛ spanned thirty-five years until his death in 1572 at the age of fifty. The first part of his rulership involved several confrontations with Rāṭhoṛ Rāv Mālde of Jodhpur. Rāv Mālde sent a force under Bālāvat Rāṭhoṛ Nago Bhārmalot (no. 38) against Kumbhaḷmer in 1540-41 in an ill-fated attempt to take this fortress and the surrounding territory from the Rāṇo. The Rāṇo's marriage of a daughter of Jhālo Jaito Sajāvat, a military servant of Rāv Mālde's holding Khairvo in ***paṭo***, precipitated this attack. The Jhālos initially promised this daughter to Rāv Mālde, but later deceived the Rāv and gave their daughter to Sīsodīyo Rāṇo Udaisiṅgh.[4] Later in 1557 the Rāṇo and an allied force of Rajpūts fought at the ill-fated battle of Harmāṛo[5] against Paṭhāṇ Hājī Khān, a former noble of Sher Shāh Sūr's, and Rajpūts of Rāv Mālde Gāṅgāvat of Jodhpur led by Rāṭhoṛ Devīdās Jaitāvat (no. 65).

Rāṇo Udaisiṅgh had the foundations for the new fort and town of Udaipur laid in the heart of the Arāvallī hills in southern Mevāṛ in 1559-60. This construction had not been completed by the time of the Rāṇo's death in 1572.

In late 1567 Akbar marched into Mevāṛ and laid siege to Cītoṛ. Bitter fighting took place there in January and February of 1568, with Akbar's final establishment of authority over Cītoṛ on February 25, 1568. The battle for Cītoṛ was one of the most intense and bloody in India during this period, with more than 40,000 dead. Among those killed were Meṛtīyo Rāv Jaimal Vīramdevot (no. 107) and his brother, Īsardās Vīramdevot (no. 109), both of whom were military servants of the Rāṇo's.

For the remainder of his reign, Rāṇo Udaisiṅgh lived in the hills of Mevāṛ and at the fortress of Kumbhalmer, evading Mughal troops in an attempt to remain free of Muslim domination. He died on February 28, 1572, four years after the fall of Cītoṛ to Akbar.

Rāṇo Udaisiṅgh had a large family, including fifteen sons. His successor to the throne of Mevāṛ was Pratāpsiṅgh Udaisiṅghot (6-1), daughter's son of Sonagaro Cahuvāṇ Akhairāj Riṇdhīrot of Pālī, Mārvāṛ. Rāṇo Pratāp ruled Mevāṛ from 1572-97. There were five other sons by Udaisiṅgh's wife, Rāṇī Bhāṭiyāṇī, a daughter of Bhāṭī Rāvaḷ Lūṇkaraṇ Jaitsīyot of Jaisaḷmer (1527-49), and nine additional sons by other wives.

> "Aitihāsik Bātāṃ," pp. 50-51; ***Akbar Nāma***, 2:442-446, 465-477; ***Bāṅkīdās***, pp. 91-92; ***Khyāt***, 1:20-21, 102, 109; Ojhā, 2:695-735; ***Tavārīkh Jaisalmer***, p. 50; ***Vigat***, 2:59-60, 68-69; ***Vīr Vinod***, 2:1-8, 25-34, 61-87, 142.

(no. 18) Candrāvat Durgo Acḷāvat, Rāv of Rāmpuro

The origin of the Candrāvat branch (***sākh***) of the Sīsodīyo Gahlots is shrouded in obscurity. The ***Khyāt*** of Naiṇsī, 3:239, 247-248, whose authority if generally accepted,[6] records that the founder of this branch was Cāndro

---

[4] See ***supra***, Bālīso Cahuvāṇ Sūjo Sāṃvatot (no. 4), for details regarding this marriage and its aftermath.

[5] Harmāṛo village: located fifty-five miles south-southwest of Ajmer and six miles south of Vadhnor in northern Mevāṛ.

[6] Śyāmaldās, author of ***Vīr Vinod***, notes, 2:982, that the Baṛvā Bhāṭs with whom he spoke regarding the Candrāvat genealogy, stated that the founder of the Candrāvats was Cāndro Arīsiṅghot, second son of Arīsiṅgh Lakhmaṇot and grandson of Sīsodīyo Rāṇo

Bhavaṇsīyot, a son of Sīsodīyo Rāṇo Bhavaṇsī (Bhīṃvsī), a thirteenth century ruler of Mevāṛ. The following genealogy emerges from Naiṇsī:

Figure 8. Candrāvat Sīsodīyo Gahlots

Rāṇo Bhavaṇsī (Bhīṃvsī) of Mevāṛ
|
Cāndro Bhavaṇsīyot (**Candrāvat Sīsodīyos**)
|
Sajan Candrāvat
|

Chājū Sajanot	Jhāñjhaṇsī Sajanot
Rāv Sivo Chājūot	Bhākharsī Jhāñjhaṇsīyot
Rāv Rāymal Sivāvat	
Rāv Acḷo Rāymalot	
Rāv Durgo Acḷāvat	

During the time of Bhākharsī Jhāñjhaṇsīyot and his paternal uncle, Chājū Sajanot, the Candrāvats are said to have established themselves in the ***pargano*** of Āntrī in the land of Āmand in south-central Rājasthān. Following their establishment of control in Āntrī, Chājū fell out with his paternal uncle, Bhākharsī, and left this area, settling in the land of Māṇḍū to the south. His son, Sivo Chājūot, is credited with bringing this branch of the family into pre-eminence among the Candrāvats. According to tradition, Sivo rescued one of the wives of Hūshang Ghūrī, ruler of Māṇḍū (1405-34), from drowning. In reward for this feat of bravery and for the service to his family, the ruler of Māṇḍū granted Sivo the title of ***rāv*** and made him one of his military servants. The Māṇḍū ruler is also said to have granted Sivo title to his homeland (***utan***) of Āntrī. Rāv Sivo and his family then returned to the ***pargano*** of Āntrī.

Rāv Sivo's son, Rāv Rāymal Sivāvat, became a military servant of Sīsodīyo Rāṇo Kūmbho Mokaḷot of Cītoṛ (ca. 1433-68). The Candrāvats under Rāv Rāymal's son and grandson, Rāv Acḷo Rāymalot and Rāv Durgo Acḷāvat, remained based in Āntrī and continued as supporters and servants of the Sīsodīyos of Mevāṛ until the fall of Cītoṛ in 1568.

Lakhmaṇ of Mevāṛ (ca. 1382-1420). Śyāmaldās also makes note of another variation in the ***Tārīkh Mālvā***, a history written in the 18th century by Saiyyid Karīm Alī, which lists Cāndro as a son of Sīsodīyo Rāṇo Hamīr (ca. 1326-65) and a brother of Sīsodīyo Rāṇo Kheto (ca. 1366-81).

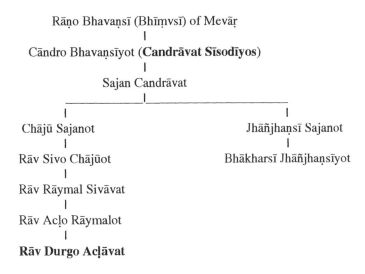

The ***Khyāt*** of Naiṇsī, 3:246, describes Rāv Durgo as a ***vaḍo desot*** ("great ruler of the land"), a ***vaḍo dātār*** ("great giver"), and as a ***kāraṇīk ṭhākur*** ("proven and tested master"). When he succeeded to the rulership of the Candrāvats, he founded his own capitol of Rāmpuro.[7] He named his capitol in honor of Ṭhākur Śrī Rāmcandrajī, the patron deity of the Candrāvats. Rāv Durgo emerged as a powerful and influential Rajpūt due to his more than forty years of active and devoted service to the Mughal throne.

In the early years of his rulership, Rāv Durgo maintained an alliance with the Sīsodīyo Rāṇos of Mevāṛ, for whom he performed military service. ***Khyāt***, 3:248, notes, however, that while the Candrāvats were servants of Mevāṛ, they always maintained a measure of their own independence. As servants, the Candrāvats under Rāv Durgo participated with Sīsodīyo Rāṇo Udaisiṅgh Sāṅgāvat (ca. 1537-72; no. 17) in the ill-fated battle of Harmāṛo[8] in 1557, when the Rāṇo met defeat at the hands of Paṭhāṇ Hājī Khān, a former noble of Sher Shāh Sūr's, and the Rajpūts of Rāṭhoṛ Rāv Mālde Gāṅgāvat of Jodhpur (1532-62).

Rāv Durgo continued in the service of the Rāṇo until after the battle of Cītoṛ in 1568. He then met with Akbar and swore allegiance to the Mughal throne. From this time torward until his death in 1608 at the age of eighty-two, Rāv Durgo remained a loyal servant of the Mughals. He was active in Mughal campaigns in the Deccan, Gujarat, Malwa, and elsewhere from the 1580s onwards. In 1582 he accompanied Prince Murād on an expedition against Mīrzā Muḥammad Ḥakīm of Kabul. Several years later, he was attached to Mīrzā Khān's troops and distinguished himself in Gujarat. He followed Mīrzā 'Azīz Kokā to the Deccan, and then again joined Prince Murād in operations in Malwa and the Deccan.

In 1586 Akbar appointed Rāv Durgo and Rājāvat Kachvāho Jagnāth Bhārmalot (no. 20) as governors of the ***sūbo*** of Ajmer. This joint appointment was part of Akbar's attempt to reorganize the administrative machinery of the empire, with two governors for each ***sūbo***, each governor having his own ***dīvāṇ***s and ***bakhshī***s. Rāv Durgo held this assignment for a short time only.

In 1593-1594 Rāv Durgo rose to the rank of 1,500 ***zāt***, which was confirmed in 1595-1596. He reached the rank of 2,000 ***zāt*** in 1605, then was raised to 4,000 ***zāt*** in 1606 not long before his death.

Rāv Durgo died at the end of the second year of Emperor Jahāṅgīr's reign. The Emperor mentioned him in his ***Memoirs***, remarking on the Rāv's many years of devoted service to his father, Akbar:

> He had been in attendance for forty years and more in the position of an Amīr of my revered father, until, by degrees, he had risen in rank to 4,000. Before he obtained the good fortune of waiting on my father, he was one of the trusted servants of

---

[7] Rāmpuro is located one hundred forty-five miles south-southeast of Ajmer and one hundred ten miles east of Udaipur.

[8] Harmāṛo village: located fifty-five miles south-southwest of Ajmer and six miles south of Vadhnor in northern Mevāṛ.

Rānā Ūday Singh . . . He was a good military man . . (Jahāngīr, 1:134).

Ā'īn-ī-Akbarī, pp. 459-460; "Aitihāsik Bātāṃ," p. 51; ***Akbar Nāma***, 3:599, 613, 632, 634-635, 1052, 1071, 1142, 1150, 1153, 1173, 1184, 1188; Athar Ali, ***Apparatus***, pp. 11, 17, 21, 33, 46; ***Bāṅkīdās***, p. 14; Jahāngīr, 1:134; ***Khyāt***, 1:61-62, 95, 3:239-248; ***Maāthir-ul-Umarā***, 1:505-509; ***Vigat***, 2:60; ***Vīr Vinod***, 2:982-984.

Figure 9. Sīsodīyo Gahlots

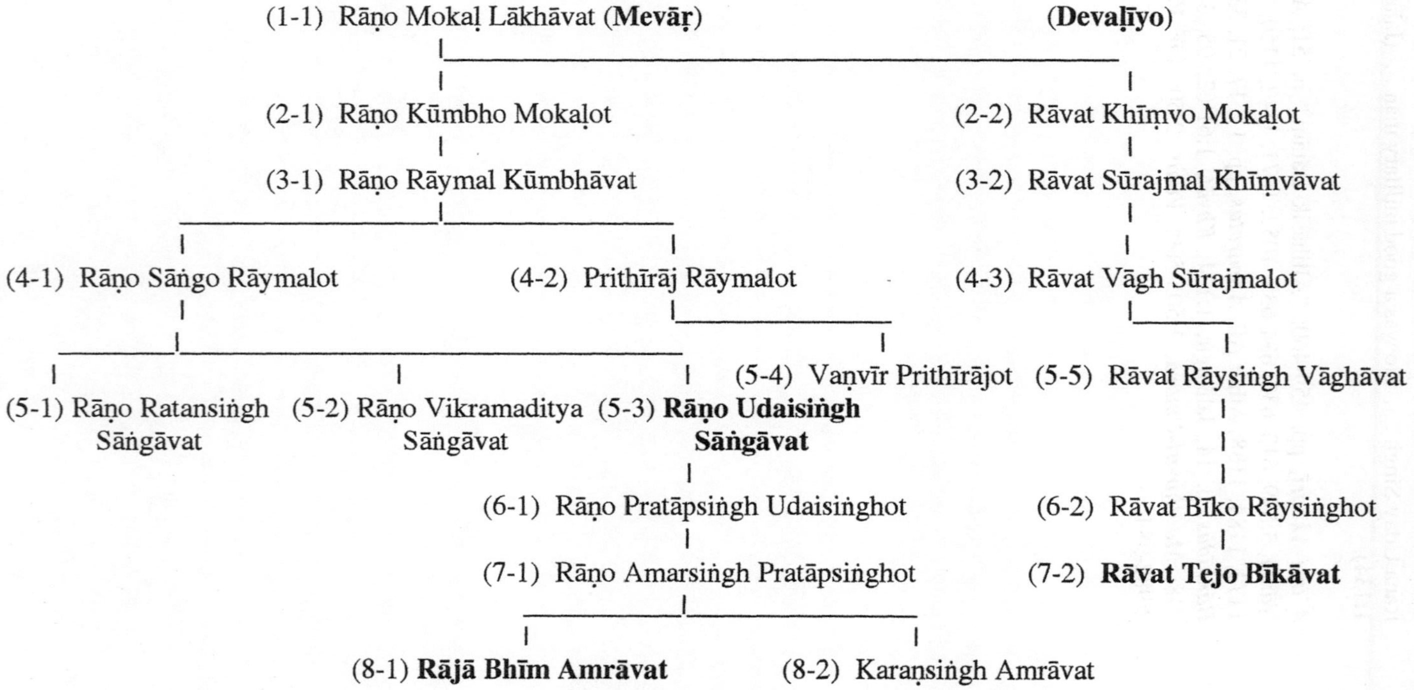

Dhīrāvat Kachvāhos

(no. 19) **Rāmdās Ūdāvat**

Rāmdās Ūdāvat was a Rajpūt who rose from very simple beginnings to a position of great prestige and influence at the Mughal court. He served under both Emperors Akbar and Jahāngīr, and, except for brief periods when he was sent on special assignments, spent most of his forty-three years of service under the Mughals in personal attendance upon the person of the Emperor. His rise to high position rested upon Akbar's personal friendship and esteem. Rāmdās became an ***amīr*** under Akbar, and he was able to maintain this position under Akbar's successor, Jahāngīr.

Discrepancies exist among the sources regarding Rāmdās's family and ancestry. ***Maāthir-ul-Umarā***, 2:2:587, and Blochman's note on Rāmdās in ***Ā'īn-ī-Akbarī***, 1:539, record only that Rāmdās's father was a man named "Urdat" or "Ordat." Both names appear to be corruptions of Ūdāvat (lit. "son of Ūdo"), a man by the name of Ūdo being listed in the ***Khyāt*** of Naiṇsī as Rāmdās's father (see ***infra***).

"Patal-Pota," a Rājasthānī document about Rāmdās Kachvāho,[1] provides more detailed (though also problematic) information about Rāmdās's family. This source traces Rāmdās's ancestry back to Pātaḷ, a son of Rājā Udaikaraṇ Juṇsīyot of Āmber, who ruled during the fourteenth century. It is from this Pātaḷ that the name *Patal-Potā* (lit. "Pātaḷ's descendants") derives (see ***infra***, **Figure 10. Rāmdās's Genealogy According to "Patal-Pota"**).

This genealogical list stands in considerable disagreement with that found in the ***Khyāt*** of Naiṇsī. Naiṇsī's material traces Rāmdās's ancestry to Rājā Kalyāṇde Rājādevot of Āmber, some three generations preceding Rājā Udaikaraṇ Juṇsīyot. ***Khyāt*** also records that Rāmdās's father was a man named Ūdo Cāndot, who was a descendant of Dhīro Māḷakot's, from whom Rāmdās's ***sākh*** took the name of Dhīrāvat (lit. "son of Dhīro") (see ***infra***, **Figure 11. Rāmdās's Genealogy According to Naiṇsī's *Khyāt***).

Given the degree of divergence between these two genealogical lists, no reconciliation is possible. The material in Naiṇsī appears preferable, however. Naiṇsī's ***Khyāt*** records that the Kachvāho genealogy was copied from material that the Bhāṭ Rājpāṇ of Udehī had collected and written down. Given the traditional role that families of Bhāṭs performed as genealogists for Rajpūts, Bhāṭ Rājpāṇ's information may be given credence and considered material handed down over generations within Rāmdās's family. No similar credence can be given the genealogy in "Patal-Pota." Of significance is the fact that Naiṇsī's

---

[1] B. P. Ambastha, "Patal-Pota: Biographical Account of Ram Das Kachhawaha," in his ***Non-Persian Sources on Indian Medieval History*** (Delhi: Idarah-i-Adabiyat-i Delli, 1984), pp. 75-128.

Khyāt, 1:286-332, does not include a man by the name of Pātaḷ in its list of sons of Rājā Udaikaraṇ, nor do any other of the later Middle Mārvāṛī sources, such as ***Bāṅkīdās rī Khyāt***. Lastly, no information is available about the dating of "Patal-Pota" or the material upon which it is based. While other information in this text agrees with and supplements material from other sources contemporary to Rāmdās, the genealogy tracing Rāmdās's descent from a Pātaḷ Udaikaraṇot appears suspect. Final judgment must rest, of course, upon further elucidation from local sources.

Discrepancies also exist among sources regarding Rāmdās's place of birth and the village in which he lived during the early part of his life. ***Maāthir-ul-Umarā***, 2:2:587, records that the village of Lūṇī was his home, and ***Ā'īn-ī-Akbarī***, 1:539, gives his home as Lūṇī (or Baulī) village. ***Akbar Nāma***, 3:91, states, however, that Akbar stopped at the village of Newata (Lucknow ed. "Hūna") in September of 1573 while enroute from Ajmer to Agra, and that Newata was Rāmdās Kachvāho's home. In this instance, "Patal-Pota," p. 77-78, provides clarifying information. It states that Rāmdās was born in the village of Baulī ,[2] but that he later left Baulī and settled in the village of Nevāta (location uncertain).

Sources generally agree that Rāmdās's father, Ūdo Cāndot, was a man of limited means who lived in difficult circumstances, and that Rāmdās could not provide for his family from his lands at the village of Nevāta. He, therefore, left his family to seek his livelihood elsewhere. The ***Khyāt*** of Naiṇsī, 1:331, records that Rāmdās was a supporter (***bālār*** - lit. "the main beam of a house; a son dutiful to his mother") of Rājāvat Kachvāho Salhaidī, who was a son of Rājā Bhārmal Prithīrājot of Āmber (d. ca. 1573), for a period of time. Then in 1568-69 he entered the service of Sekhāvat Kachvāho Rāysal Sūjāvat, better known as Rāysal Darbārī.

Rāysal Darbārī was a trusted servant and attendant of the Mughal Emperor Akbar's. It was Rāysal who brought Rāmdās to the Mughal court and provided him with his first opportunities there. "Patal-Pota," pp. 79-80, records:

> After being properly tutored in the arts of court-estiquettes [*sic.*], he (Ram Das) was given a horse (by Rai Sal) and was taken into the market of ahadis [personal servants and retainers of the Emperor's]. The emperor [Akbar] came to inspect the prospective ahadis. Being pleased with the manners of Ram Das, the emperor enquired [*sic.*] of the man who had brought Ram Das into the market. Ram Das made a *Kurnish* [salutation, with an inclination of the body and head; obeisance, made only before the Emperor] before the emperor, and, after making obesiance [*sic.*] with proper respects, he represented that it was Rai Sal who had brought him (Ram Das) into the market. . . [Rāysal] made a request that he (Ram Das) might be admitted

[2] Baulī village: located fifty-five miles southeast of Āmber.

to the cadre of the royal ahadis. The emperor appointed Ram Das as one of the ahadis.

"Patal-Pota," p. 80, notes that Akbar was pleased with the service that Rāmdās performed and soon appointed him as one of the ***khās bardār aḥādīs*** (special attendants who carried the Emperor's arms). Rāmdās continued to rise in the Emperor's esteem, and within a short period thereafter, was again promoted, this time to the position of ***jam'dār*** ("the one in charge") of 200 ***khās suwār*** (personal horsemen of the Emperor's). Over and above his performance of exceptional service, Rāmdās gained Akbar's affection for his songs. Rāmdās's liking for heroic songs had quickly come to the Emperor's attention, and Akbar would often call Rāmdās into his presence to hear him sing.

On July 4, 1572 Akbar left Fatehpur Sikri with his army for Gujarat. Rāmdās accompanied Akbar on this campaign as one of his personal attendants, and except for a brief visit to his home at Nevāta while enroute back to north India, he remained with Akbar until June of 1573 when the Emperor returned to the capitol. Rāmdās arranged the marriage of one of his daughters, Nāgīna Bāī, to Paṃvār Kisansiṅgh Daulatsiṅghot, a military servant of Kachvāho Rāysal Darbārī's, while he was at Nevāta. In August of 1573 Rāmdās again accompanied Akbar to Gujarat. The Emperor traveled this time by rapid march to suppress the rebellion against his rule and to reassert Mughal authority. While returning to the capitol in early October of 1573, Akbar displayed his affection for Rāmdās by stopping at Rāmdās's village for a short time at Rāmdās's special request. Rāmdās then followed the Emperor to Agra, accompanied by his daughter's husband (***jamāī***), Paṃvār Kisansiṅgh. In return for his devoted service during the Gujarat campaign, Akbar awarded Rāmdās the ***mansab*** rank of 500 ***zāt*** upon Rāmdās's arrival at the capitol.

Shortly thereafter, in August of 1574 Akbar appointed Rāmdās deputy of the revenue department under Rājā Todarmāl, whom he dispatched to Bihar to assist Khān Khānān in the reorganization of the Mughal army involved in operations there. "Patal-Pota," pp. 86-87, records that Rāmdās performed well in Bihar under Todarmāl, and that Todarmāl in turn made recommendations to the Emperor on his behalf. During this same period, Rāmdās held the position of ***koṭvāḷ*** of the town of Sāṅganer (near Āmber). Because of his capable service, the Emperor called him into his presence and awarded him with the favored position of petition-bearer (***arajvegī*** [Persian ***'arzbegī***]) in Mughal service. This position allowed Rāmdās direct access to the Emperor. ***Maāthir-ul-Umarā***, 2:2:588, notes that Rāmdās gained Akbar's affection as petition-bearer, and that because of this affection, the Emperor accepted most of Rāmdās's petitions and representations.

Akbar sent Rāmdās and Mujāhid Kambu to Bengal in late 1584. Their departure followed the earlier dispatch of Peshrau Khān and Khwājagī Fath Ullah to assist Shāhbāz Khān with operations against the Afghans, against whom the Mughals had suffered a series of defeats. By September/October of 1584, news of these defeats and of Shāhbāz Khān's difficulties in maintaining order among his own units and among the ***zāmīndār***s of Bengal and Bihar had reached the Mughal court. Rāmdās and Mujāhid Kambu were "by sharp words to produce a beneficial effect and make them [the *zāmīndārs* and the Mughal officers under Shāhbāz Khān] keen for service" (***Akbar Nāma***, 3:660). Rāmdās performed his duties well in Bengal, and in the period between December, 1584 and January, 1585 he and Khwājagī Fath Ullah were responsible for a Mughal victory against the Afghans. This victory entailed a dangerous crossing of the Jumna River in pursuit of the Afghans. "Patal-Pota," p. 90, notes that upon Rāmdās's return from Bengal, Akbar increased his ***mansab*** rank to 1,500 *zāt*.

Little information is available about Rāmdās's activities between 1585 and the time of Akbar's death in October of 1605. During most of this period, Rāmdās appears to have remained in personal attendance upon the Emperor. While he had a spacious mansion built in the fort at Agra near the Hatiapol with the wealth he had begun to amass, ***Maāṯhir-ul-Umarā***, 2:2:942, records that he always lived in the guard-room (***peshkhāna***) of the fort and attended upon the Emperor with two hundred of his own Rajpūts armed with lances.

Rāmdās's position of influence at the Mughal court attracted many to his person. "Patal-Pota," p. 91, records that numerous nobles claimed to enjoy his love and affection, and others sought alliance with him through marriage in order to consolidate their own positions of power. One such Rajpūt was Ḍūṅgarot Devṛo Vījo Harrājot of Sīrohī,[3] who came to the Mughal court between the years 1583 and 1588 seeking Akbar's support for his pretensions to rulership in Sīrohī. Devṛo Vījo approached Rāmdās in 1587-88 with a proposal for the marriage of his daughter to Rāmdās's sister's son (***bhāṇej***), Sambhusiṅgh. Devṛo Vījo's daughter was the granddaughter of Rāṭhoṛ Rāv Candrasen Māldevot of Jodhpur. Rāv Candrasen had married one of his daughters to Devṛo Vījo at Bhādrājuṇ in Mārvāṛ in 1569, during his period of exile from Jodhpur.[4] While Rāmdās had refused other offers, he accepted this one from Devṛo Vījo and helped to arrange the marriage to his sister's son. This alliance appears to have helped Devṛo Vījo in his bid for power in Sīrohī, and it is probable that Rāmdās made representations on Vījo's behalf before Akbar, for in 1588 Akbar granted Devṛo Vījo's petition for rulership in Sīrohī.

In May/June of 1589 Rāmdās accompanied Akbar to Kashmir during Mughal operations there. ***Akbar Nāma***, 3:942, states that Akbar named the gardens of a mansion situated north of the Ravi River on the route to Kashmir, Rāmbārī Bāgh ("Rāmdās's garden") in honor of Rāmdās.

Rāmdās also played an important role in Rajpūt affairs under Akbar. ***Vigat***, 2:73, records that in 1601-02 he was involved in the transfer of one-half of the villages of Meṛto Pargano in Mārvāṛ from Meṛtīyo Rāṭhoṛ Jagnāth Gopāḷdāsot (no. 116) to the ruler of Jodhpur, Rājā Sūrajsiṅgh Udaisiṅghot (1595-1619). According to ***Vigat***, this transfer was due, at least in part, to some discord that had arisen between Rāmdās and Meṛtīyo Jagnāth. The nature of this discord is unspecified.

---

[3] For further information about Devṛo Vījo Harrājot, see ***supra***, "Devṛo Cahuvāṇs."

[4] See ***supra***, **Marriage and Family Lists of the Rulers of Jodhpur**, Candrasen Māldevot, Rāṇī no. 1, D - Jamotībāī.

The only other official duties Rāmdās performed under Akbar involved the supervision of the Imperial roads. Akbar entrusted Rāmdās in 1602-03 with the supervision of the routes leading from north India to the Deccan and to Malwa. Rāmdās held specific responsibility for protecting travelers and merchants along these routes from the undue levying of transit duties by local ***zāmīndār***s.

Because of Akbar's personal friendship with and esteem for Rāmdās, he involved himself in Rāmdās's personal life. In 1601 Rāmdās married one of his daughters to a Rajpūt named Syāmsiṅgh (identity uncertain). Akbar attended the wedding ceremony on this occasion, and beforehand "went to the ante-chamber (***peshkhāna***) of the bride's father and bestowed favours, and presented five lakhs of ***dāms*** for the marriage celebration" (***Akbar Nāma***, 3:1197). A year later, Akbar again became involved with Rāmdās when Rāmdās's son, Dinmiṇdās (the ***Akbar Nāma*** has "Datman Das"), was killed. Dinmiṇdās had left the Imperial court for his home without permission from the Emperor, and once in his own territory, had begun to oppress local inhabitants. Rāmdās requested that Akbar have Dinmiṇdās brought back to court, and Akbar dispatched Shāh Qulī Khān for this purpose. Dinmiṇdās was apprehended, but he began a fight when he was returned to court and was killed in the exchange that ensued. ***Akbar-Nāma***, 3:1181, notes:

> That chosen servant (Rām Dās) was grieved on account of his child. H. M. [Akbar] went to his ante-chamber (***peshkhāna***) and administered consolation, and applied balm to the inward wound.

Rāmdās had risen to the rank of 2,000 ***zāt***, 200 ***suwār*** by the time of Akbar's death in 1605.

During the brief succession struggle that developed in Akbar's last days, Rāmdās remained steadfast in his loyalty to Akbar and to Akbar's choice of successor in Prince Salīm (Jahāngīr). In taking this position, he came into conflict with his paternal relation, Kachvāho Rājā Mānsiṅgh Bhagvantdāsot (1589-1614), who used his influence at the Mughal court to further the cause of Prince Salīm's son, Sultān Khusrau. Sultān Khusrau was Rājā Mānsiṅgh's sister's son. With Rājā Mānsiṅgh was Azam Khān, who was Sultān Khusrau's wife's father. While they tried to influence Akbar's choice of successor and the opinions of other nobles of the court, Akbar remained unmoved. Rāmdās himself withdrew from any involvement in the factionalism and maintained an unswerving guard with his Rajpūts over the Imperial treasury and the magazine at Agra. Jahāngīr later noted in his ***Memoirs*** that at the time of his accession, he promoted Rāmdās, "whom my father had favoured" to the rank of 3,000 ***zāt*** (Jahāngīr, 1:21). Under Jahāngīr, Rāmdās's position at the Mughal court increased in stature.

Jahāngīr appointed Rāmdās as the personal advisor (***atiliq***) to Kachvāho Mahāsiṅgh Jagatsiṅghot in June of 1607. Kachvāho Mahāsiṅgh was a grandson of Rājā Mānsiṅgh of Āmber. Jahāngīr sent both to help pacify the area of Bangash north of the Indus River. Following operations in Bangash, Jahāngīr ordered Rāmdās to accept ***jāgīr*** lands in the area of Swat (Sawad Bajaur) and to be enrolled among the auxiliaries of this ***sūbo*** under the command of Shāh Beg Khān Khān-daurān. Sources do not indicate how long Rāmdās remained in the area of Swat, but he appears to have returned within a short period to his duties as personal attendant upon the Emperor. Jahāngīr's ***Memoirs*** next mention Rāmdās as being among those who accompanied the Emperor on a hunting expedition in 1610.

During the next year, Jahāngīr appointed Rāmdās, "who was one of the sincere servants of my revered father," to accompany 'Abdu-llah Khān, the Governor of Gujarat, to the Deccan (Jahāngīr, 1:201). Jahāngīr recorded that he had sent Rāmdās with 'Abdu-llah Khān

> in order that he might in every place look after ['Abdu-llah Khān], and not allow him to be too rash and hasty. For this purpose I bestowed on him great favours, as well as the title of Raja, which he had not thought of for himself. I also gave him drums and the fort of Ranthanbūr, which is one of the noted castles in Hindustan, and honouring him with a superb robe of honour and an elephant and horse I dismissed him (Jahāngīr, 1:202).

While Rāmdās sought to urge due caution and deliberation upon 'Abdu-llah Khān during the operations in the Deccan, the Khān paid little heed. He sent no intelligence reports by runner to other sections of the Mughal army also proceeding toward Daulatabad, nor did he attempt to coordinate his movements with theirs. The result was a sharp defeat for the Mughals at Daulatabad at the hands of Mālik 'Ambar, and a forced retreat of Mughal contingents that had survived the fighting.

Two versions of the aftermath of this defeat and its effect upon Rāmdās appear in the sources. ***Maāthir-ul-Umarā***, 2:2:588, records that when Jahāngīr received news of the defeat, he had portraits made of all the officers who had taken part in the campaign and fled, and out of anger, made disparaging remarks about each as he viewed their portrait in the Imperial ***darbār***. About Rāmdās he is reported to have said:

> You were a servant of Rāīsāl at a *tankah* a day, my father cherished you and made you an *Amīr*. It is a disgrace for a Rājpūt to run away (from a field of battle). Alas! that you did not even have respect for the title of Rāja Karan [the name by which Rāmdās was known at the Mughal court].[5] I hope that you will lose faith and fortune (***dīn u duniyā***).

---

[5] "Patal-Pota," pp. 111-112, records that Emperor Jahāngīr himself gave Rāmdās the name of "Karaṇ." This occurred after Jahāngīr learned of a pious act that Rāmdās had performed. Following the death of one of his sons, Rāmdās is said to have withdrawn from the world for a time into a religious life, filling his house with both Muslim and Hindu holy men and poets. He performed many pious acts of feeding and caring for the poor, and he bathed twice daily in the Ganges River. One day during the cold season, a

Maāthir-ul-Umarā, 2:2:588-589, further states that Jahāngīr refused Rāmdās an audience upon his return to the capitol from the Deccan, and that he sent Rāmdās to Bangash as a punishment. When Rāmdās died in Bangash shortly thereafter, Jahāngīr is reported to have remarked: "My prayer worked, for, according to the Hindū religion, whoever dies after crossing the river Indus, goes to hell."

Jahāngīr provides a different and more preferred version of events in his own ***Memoirs***. He records that Rāmdās came to court "from the victorious army of the Deccan and paid his respects, and made an offering of 101 muhrs." He then states:

> For the purpose of advising the Amirs of Kabul, and on account of the disagreements that had sprung up between them and Qilīj Khān, I sent Rāja Rām Dās, and bestowed on him a horse and robe of honour and 30,000 rupees for expenses (Jahāngīr, 1:233).

"Patal-Pota," p. 125, provides additional details of events during this time which clarify the discrepancies between these two accounts. According to this source, Rāmdās had indeed been ineffective in his efforts to direct operations in the Deccan. Despite his good counsel, the Mughal forces met defeat. Rāmdās then fled the field with his Rajpūts. He considered suicide in the face of this defeat, but dismissed suicide as a cowardly act, deciding instead to go into hiding for a time until the truth of the affair became known to the Emperor. While he remained away from court, Rāmdās learned that Kachvāho Rājā Mānsiṅgh blamed him publicly for the defeat. Emperor Jahāngīr was much angered and had Rāmdās's palace and ***jāgīr*** confiscated. "Patal-Pota" corroborates the passage from ***Maāthir-ul-Umarā***, stating that the Emperor

> took each of the pictures in his hand and maligned the man there. When his turn (the turn of the picture of Ram Das) came up, after being properly reprimanded, his jagir was confiscated and his palace occupied.

This source goes on to say, however, that some days later, Jahāngīr came to know that the defeat was not due to Rāmdās's actions, that Rāmdās had given good counsel on the field. The Emperor then had a change of heart, and when word of this change reached Rāmdās, he returned to court (December 17, 1612). The Emperor was pleased and conferred a robe of honor upon him along with a reward of horses, elephants, and 30,000 rupees. Rāmdās was then allowed to proceed to his palace.

---

bad hail storm came, and during the storm Rāmdās met an old man by the road to whom he gave his costly shawl for warmth, exposing himself to the elements. This pious act came to the Emperor's attention and led him to give Rāmdās the name of Karaṇ.

The term "karaṇ" means "action, act, deed; making, doing; the instrumental cause." See: Platts, ***Dictionary***, p. 827.

Rāmdās died shortly thereafter on July 30, 1613[6] while on duty for the Emperor in Bangash. When news of his death arrived at the capitol, fifteen women and twenty men burned themselves in the company of his turban at the famous Hindu place of worship known as Rangta Hilalabad on the Jumna River near Agra.

Rāmdās had acquired the ***mansab*** rank of 5,000 ***zāt*** by the time of his death.

Both Persian and Middle Mārvāṛī sources comment on Rāmdās's generosity and on his liberal bestowal of favors on Cāraṇ bards and others. The ***Khyāt*** of Naiṇsī, 1:331, describes him as a ***vaḍo dātār*** ("great giver"), while ***Maāthir-ul-Umarā***, 2:2:589, states:

> He was unequal for his generosity and liberality. For one good story he would give a large sum of money. When he once gave a present to a *chāran*, a *bādfarōsh*[7] or a musician, they every year in the same month received the same amount from his treasurer, and there was no necessity of altering the receipt.

Rāmdās was also extremely fond of the game of ***caupar***.

The ***Khyāt*** of Naiṇsī, 1:331, lists Rāmdās's name as "Rāmdās Darbārī Ūdāvat."

One of Rāmdās's granddaughters named Siṅgarde (or Raṅgāde) was married to Rājā Sūrajsiṅgh Udaisiṅghot of Jodhpur (1595-1619) in 1614, shortly after Rāmdās's death.[8]

> ***Ā'īn-ī-Akbarī***, 1:539-540; ***Akbar Nāma***, 2:538, 3:48, 55, 69, 91, 660, 673, 819, 825, 942, 1181, 1197, 1200, 1253; Athar Ali, ***Apparatus***, pp. 18, 23, 32, 42, 52, 54; B. P. Ambastha, "Patal-Pota: Biographical Account of Ram Das Kachhawaha," in his ***Non-Persian Sources on Indian Medieval History*** (Delhi: Idarah-i-Adabiyat-i Delli, 1984), pp. 75-128; ***Bāṅkīdās***, pp. 123-130; F. Steingass, ***A Comprehensive Persian-English Dictionary*** (Reprinted ed. New Delhi: Oriental Books Reprint Corporation, 1973), p. 150; Jahāngīr, 1:21, 29, 111, 128, 201-202, 220, 233, 252, 285-286; ***Khyāt***, 1:287, 295-297, 302, 313, 318-320, 329, 331-332; Kunwar Refaqat Ali Khan, ***The Kachhwahas Under Akbar and Jahangir*** (New Delhi: Kitab Publishing House, 1976), pp. 172-175; ***Maāthir-ul-Umarā***,

---

[6] See: "Patal-Pota," p. 127, n. 151. This reference has an obvious misprint of 30th July, 1630 A. D. for Rāmdās's death. The next page (p. 128) notes that Jahāngīr received word of Rāmdās's death on September 10, 1613.

[7] A Bhāṭ, a musician or minstrel. See: Platts, ***Dictionary***, p. 119.

[8] See ***supra***, **Marriage and Family Lists of the Rulers of Jodhpur**, Sūrajsiṅgh Udaisiṅghot, Rāṇī no. 17.

2:2:587-589; ***Murārdān***, no. 2, p. 213; R. P. Tripathi, ***The Rise and Fall of the Mughal Empire*** (Reprint ed. Allahabad: Central Book Depot, 1966), pp. 208-212; V. S. Bhargava, ***The Rise of the Kachhawas in Dhundhār (Jaipur)*** (Ajmer, New Delhi: Shabd Sanchar, 1979), p. 15, n. 1; ***Vigat***, 2:73.

Figure 10. Rāmdās's Genealogy According to the "Patal-Pota"[1]

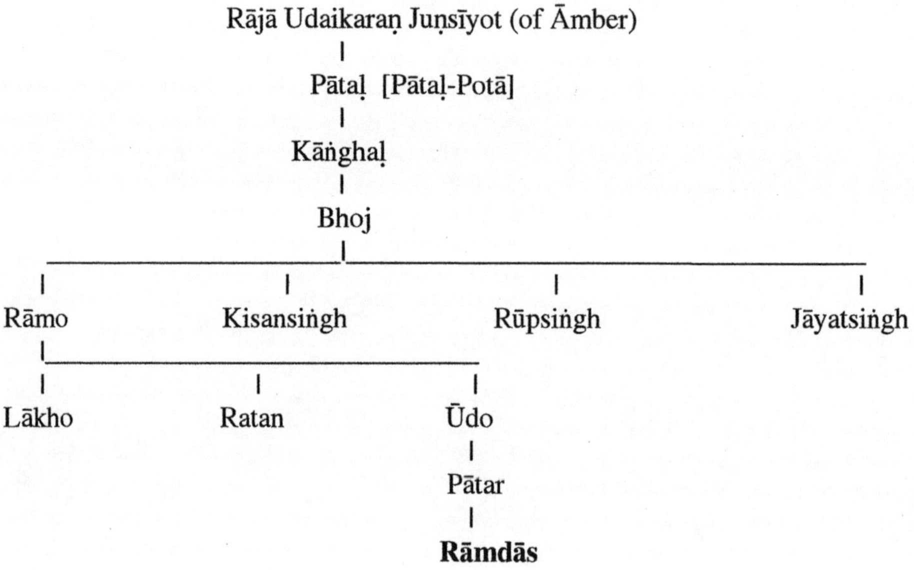

[1] Ambastha, "Patal-Pota (Biographical Account of Ram Das Kachhawaha)," p. 77.

Figure 11. Rāmdās's Genealogy According to Naiṇsī's *Khyāt*[2]

```
Rājā Kalyāṇde/Kilāṇde Rājādevot (of Āmber)
                    |
      ______________|______________
     |                             |
Rājā Kuntal                  Rājā Akhairāj
     |                             |
Rājā Juṇsī                       Mālak
     |                             |
Rājā Udaikaraṇ                   Dhīro  (Dhīrāvats)
                                   |
                                 Nāpo
                                   |
                                 Khān
                                   |
                                 Cānd
                                   |
                                 Ūdo
                                   |
                                 Rāmdās
```

[2] ***Khyāt***, 1:295-296, 331-332.

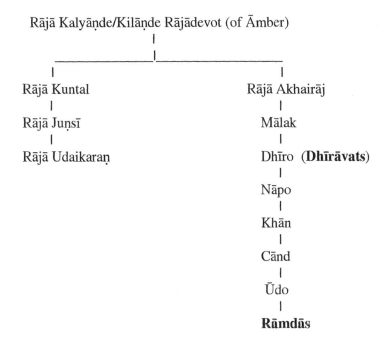

Rājāvat Kachvāhos

(no. 20) **Jagnāth Bhārmalot, Rājā** (4-2)
(no. 21) **Jagrūp Jagnāthot, Kuṃvar** (5-2)

(no. 20) **Jagnāth Bhārmalot, Rājā** (4-2)

Rājāvat Kachvāho Jagnāth Bhārmalot was a son of Rājā Bhārmal Prithīrājot of Āmber (1547-74) (3-1). He was born on December 10, 1552. Few details are available about his early life prior to 1562. In this year he and two of his paternal relations, Khaṅgār Jagmālot (4-6) and Rājsiṅgh Āskaraṇot (5-4), were taken hostage. Mīrzā Sharafu'd-Dīn Ḥusayn was governor of Ajmer at this time, having received the area of Mevāt along with Ajmer and Nāgaur in ***jāgīr*** from Akbar in 1561. The Mīrzā was eager to increase his holdings and had thoughts of acquiring Āmber, and he quickly became involved in the internal disputes of the Kachvāhos of Ḍhūṇḍhāṛ (Āmber). Kachvāho Bhārmal Prithīrājot was then Rājā of Ḍhūṇḍhāṛ. Mīrzā Sharafu'd-Dīn accepted the homage of Rājā Bhārmal's elder brother's son, Sūjo Pūraṇmalot (4-5), and then encouraged Sūjo's rivalry with Āmber. Following a series of skirmishes in which the Mīrzā took part, Rājā Bhārmal was forced into the hills. The Rājā finally came to terms, and the Mīrzā levied a fixed sum on the Rājā and took his son, Jagnāth, and two of his brothers' sons hostage as surety for the payment.

Akbar Nāma, 2:240-243, contains an interesting description of the events of this time, and records how Chaghatā'ī Khān represented Kachvāho Bhārmal to Akbar, speaking of his loyalty to the throne and of the bad treatment he and his family had received at the hands of Mīrzā Sharafu'd-Dīn:

> When the tale of the loyalty of this old family had been communicated to His Majesty he graciously gave permission for the introduction of the Rajah [Bhārmal]. When the cavalcade reached Deosa [near Āmber] most of the inhabitants fled from fear. His Majesty said, "We have no other intention than to do good to all mankind. What can be the reason of the flight of these people? Apparently these rustics of the valley of desolation have drawn an inference from the oppression they have undergone from Sharifu-d-dīn Ḥusain and so have run away" . . . Next day when the village of Sāngānīr [seven miles southwest of Āmber] was made the camping ground Caghatai Khān introduced Rajah Bihārī Mal together with many of his relations and leading men of his clan. Rajah Bhagwant Das, the Raja's eldest son, was excepted as he had been left in charge of the families. His Majesty with his discerning glance read devotion and sincerity in the behavior of the Rajah and his relatives. He captured his heart by kindness and exalted his rank. The Rajah from right-thinking and elevated fortune

> considered that he should . . . make himself one of the distinguished ones of the Court. In order to effect this purpose he thought of a special alliance, to wit that he should by means of those who had the right of entree introduce his eldest daughter, in whose forehead shone the light of chastity and intellect . . . his petition was accepted and His Majesty sent him off from this station along with Caghatai Khān in order that he might arrange for this alliance . . . and quickly bring his daughter.
>
> . . . When the standards were pitched at Sāmbar Sharifu-d-dīn Ḥusain Mīrzā had the bliss of doing homage, and brought suitable gifts. His Majesty the Shāhinshāh demanded Jagannath, Rāj Singh and Kangār, whom the Mīrzā had taken as hostages, in order that Rajah Bihārī Mal might be entirely free from apprehension. The Mīrzā agreed to surrender them, but put off the time of doing so by subterfuges . . . A stringent order was [later] issued for the production of the hostages and . . . the Mīrzā brought before His Majesty Jagannath, Rāj Singh, and Kangār. Rajah Bihārī Mal from the sincerity of his disposition made arrangements for the marriage in the most admirable manner and brought his fortunate daughter to the station and placed her among the ladies of the harem. . .

Jagnāth entered Mughal service at this time and remained a loyal supporter of the Mughal throne for the rest of his life. He was a much favored ***mansabdār*** of both Akbar and Jahāngīr. Under Akbar, he was often in attendance at the royal stirrup. When not in the Emperor's presence, he performed much of his service alongside his paternal nephew, Kuṃvar Mānsiṅgh Bhagvantdāsot (5-1) (Rājā of Āmber, 1589-1614).

Jagnāth's active military career began in 1573 when he was twenty-one years old. He accompanied Akbar on his rapid march to Gujarat to suppress the rebellion that had emerged here, and he took part in the successful campaign to reassert Mughal authority. Akbar afterwards sent Jagnath with Kuṃvar Mānsiṅgh, Shāh Qulī Khān and others to Ḍūṅgarpur by way of Īḍar to seek the homage of the various Rajpūt rulers of this area. Jagnāth's specific role in these activities is unknown, but he did take part in actions in Mevāṛ against Sīsodīyo Rāṇo Pratāpsiṅgh Udaisiṅghot (1572-97), who refused to come to terms with Akbar.

Later in 1575-76 Jagnāth again joined Kuṃvar Mānsiṅgh, who led a Mughal force seeking to bring Rāṇo Pratāp to battle. Jagnāth was placed with the van of the Mughal army and fought well against Rāṇo Pratāp's Rajpūts at Haḷdīghāṭī[1] in June of 1576. Local chronicles credit him with killing Meṛtīyo

---

[1] Haḷdīghāṭī is a narrow defile set amongst the Arāvallī hills eleven miles southwest of the village of Nāthdvāra and eighteen miles to the northeast of Gogūndo. The village of Khamṇor is nearby. Nāthdvāra lies twenty-six miles to the north of Udaipur in south-central Mevāṛ.

Rāṭhoṛ Rāmdās Jaimalot, a son of Rāv Jaimal Vīramdevot (no. 107), who was in the Rāṇo's service.[2]

Akbar sent Jagnāth and his brother, Rājā Bhagvantdās Bhārmalot of Āmber (ca. 1574-89) (4-1), to the Punjab in 1578, allotting ***jāgīr***s there to them and presenting them with horses, robes of honor, and advice regarding proper deportment with their commander, Saiyyid Khān. Jagnāth spent three years in the Punjab on military operations, some of which were directed against Mīrzā Hakīm in an attempt to prevent his re-entry into India from Kabul. Akbar allowed Jagnāth and other Kachvāhos to leave the Punjab in 1581, and Jagnāth then returned to Agra.

Akbar had sent Kachvāho Jaimal Rūpsīyot (4-3), a grandson of Rājā Prithīrāj Candrasenot of Āmber (1503-28) (2-1), on an expedition to Bengal in 1583. Jaimal became ill during the expedition, and died near Causa of heat prostration and exhaustion. His wife, Dāmetībāī, was a daughter of Rāṭhoṛ Moṭo Rājā Udaisiṅgh Māldevot of Jodhpur (1583-95).[3] She refused to become a ***satī*** when news of Jaimal's death reached Agra. Jaimal's son, Udaisiṅgh (5-3), and other Kachvāhos then took Dāmetībāī to the burning grounds and sought to force her to become a ***satī***. Word of this situation quickly reached the Emperor, who himself rode to save the woman from burning. Jagnāth Bhārmalot was in attendance upon the Emperor at this time, and he and Sekhāvat Rāysal Darbārī Sūjāvat seized Udaisiṅgh and prevented him from harming Dāmetībāī. ***Akbar Nāma***, 3:594-596, records the following description of these events:

> One of the occurrences was that the grand-daughter (***nabīra***) of Māldeo obtained a new life. In the wide country of India, on account of truth-choosing, and jealous honour, when the husband dies, his wife, though she have spent her days in distress, gives herself to the fire with an expanded heart and an open brow. And if from wickedness (***tardāmanī***) and love of life she refrain from doing this, her husband's relatives (***kheshāwandān***) assemble and light the flame, whether she be willing or unwilling. They regard this as preserving their honor and reputation. . .
>
> At this time H. M. had sent Jaimal by relays of horses to the Bengal officers. On account of immoderate expedition, and the excessive heat, the torch of his existence was extinguished in the neighborhood of Causā. His wife, the daughter of the Mota Rajah (The Fat Rajah), had not the courage to burn herself. Udai Singh her son and some bold and foolish persons set themselves to work this injustice (to make her burn). It was high dawn when the news came to H. M.'s female apartments. The just

[2] The Meṛtīyo genealogy in ***Murārdān***, no. 2, p. 487, gives the date ***V. S. 1632***, ***Śrāvaṇ***, ***vadi 7*** (June 30, 1575) for Rāmdās Jaimalot's death.

[3] See ***supra***, **Marriage and Family Lists of the Rulers of Jodhpur**, Udaisiṅgh Māldevot, Rāṇī no. 4, D - Dāmetībāī.

> sovereign fearing that if he sent others there would be delay, mounted a swift horse and went off to the spot. . . When the cavalier of fortune's arena had come near the spot, Jagannāth and Rai Sal went ahead and seized the ringleader . . .

Akbar initiated a series of innovations in the administration of the empire during this same year. He appointed Jagnāth along with Qulīj Khān and others to look after the care of armor and the security and condition of the roads as part of these changes.

In 1584 Akbar placed Jagnāth in command of the Mughal forces sent once again against Sīsodīyo Rāṇo Pratāpsiṅgh of Mevāṛ. This was the first time Akbar gave an independent command to Jagnāth. Jagnāth spent a number of months involved in inconclusive operations there. Two years later in 1586 Akbar assigned Jagnāth as governor of the ***sūbo*** of Ajmer along with Candrāvat Sīsodīyio Gahlot Rāv Durgo Acḷāvat (no. 18). This joint appointment reflected Akbar's attempt further to reorganize the administrative machinery of the empire, with two governors for each ***sūbo***, each having his own ***dīvāṇ***s and ***bakhshī***s. Jagnāth had acquired a great deal of military acumen by this time. He was also quite familiar with this area. Both of these qualities recommended his appointment to Akbar.

Jagnāth's governorship of Ajmer lasted only a short time. In 1587 he accompanied Mīrzā Yusuf Khān to Kashmir. Jagnāth was soon given leave to return to Agra, which he did in the accompaniment of the former governor of Kashmir, Qasīm Khān. But Akbar then sent him again north under the command of Zain Khān Kokā to take part in military operations against the Yusufzai tribesmen of Swat. Jagnāth remained in the north until 1589, when he joined Akbar in Kashmir as one of his personal attendants. Akbar presented Jagnāth with a personal gift of the spacious mansion of Qara Beg in Kashmir at this time. This gift caused great wonder among the other officers in Akbar's attendance.

Two years later in 1591, Jagnāth was sent with Prince Murād to Malwa and the Deccan. He remained involved with Mughal operations there until 1598, and is reported to have performed distinctive military service. He then received permission from Prince Murād to return home. Jagnāth proceeded first to the fortress of Riṇthambhor, which was in his ***jāgīr***, and afterwards into the presence of Akbar in the Punjab. Because he came into Akbar's presence on this occasion without permission, Akbar denied him an audience. However, Akbar eventually received Jagnāth and pardoned him. During Jagnāth's absence from the Deccan, one of his sons, Jagrūp Jagnāthot (5-2) (no. 21), was killed fighting at Ahmadnagar in 1599-1600.

Jagnāth was promoted to the rank of 3,000 ***zāt*** in 1593-1594. This rank was lowered to 2,500 ***zāt*** in 1595-1596, but then raised to 5,000 ***zāt*** in 1601, a great distinction for a Rajpūt ***amīr*** of the empire. Following this honor, Akbar visited Jagnāth at Riṇthambhor while enroute from the Deccan and "Jagannāth obtained auspiciousness by scattering money, and by presenting ***peshkash*** [to Akbar]" according to the custom of devoted servants (***Akbar Nāma***, 3:1189). Jagnāth then returned to the Deccan, where he remained until Akbar's death in 1605. Several years prior to this time, in 1602, Akbar had placed Jagnāth in charge of Mīrzā Kaiqubād, the son of Mīrzā Muḥammad Hakīm, entrusting Jagnāth to school Kaiqubād in the prison at Riṇthambhor. The Mīrzā was kept there as punishment for his drunkenness and unworthy deeds, and as a political safeguard.

Jahāngīr presented Jagnāth with a robe of honor and a jeweled waist-sword upon his succession to the Mughal throne in 1605, and sent him under the command of Prince Parvīz and Asaf Khān against Sīsodīyo Rāṇo Amarsiṅgh Pratāpsiṅghot of Mevāṛ (1597-1620). Prince Parvīz was soon recalled to Agra because of the rebellion of Prince Khusrau. He left Jagnāth in command of the Mughal army in Mevāṛ during his absence, taking Sīsodīyo Vāgho Amarsiṅghot, a son of Rāṇo Amarsiṅgh's whom the Rāṇo had offered in truce, with him to north India. Some months later, Jagnāth was himself sent to Nāgaur to put down the rebellion of Rāṭhoṛ Rājā Rāysiṅgh Kalyāṇmalot of Bīkāner (ca. 1574-1612) and his son, Daḷpat Rāysiṅghot (Rājā of Bīkāner, 1612-14).

Jahāngīr promoted Jagnāth again in 1609 to the rank of 5,000 ***zāt***, 3,000 ***suwār***. Jagnāth died shortly thereafter at the garrison of Māṇḍaḷ in eastern Rājasthān. During his life, he held not only the fort of Riṇthambhor in ***jāgīr***, but also the district of Toḍo in Rājasthān along with ***pargano***s in the Punjab and elsewhere. The ***Khyāt*** of Naiṇsī, 1:300-301, records that Toḍo, which lies to the east of Āmber, became his capitol (***rājthān***). A cenotaph (***chatrī***) was built in his honor along the banks of a tank at Māṇḍaḷ village.

> ***Ā'īn-ī-Akbarī***, pp. 421-422; ***Akbar Nāma***, 2:240-243, 3:48, 69, 237, 244-246, 380, 494, 546, 595-596, 599, 661, 705-706, 779, 798, 802, 810, 819, 825, 834, 923, 1052, 1071, 1110, 1136, 1178, 1189, 1236; Athar Ali, ***Apparatus***, pp. 11, 29, 41, 50; Jahāngīr, 1:16, 74, 76, 156; ***Khyāt***, 1:297, 300-301, 303-304, 312-313, 3:248; ***Maāthir-ul-Umarā***, 1:724-725, 2:1:580, 618; ***Murārdān***, no. 2, p. 487; Refaqat Ali Khan, ***The Kachhwahas Under Akbar and Jahangir*** (New Delhi: Kitab Publishing House, 1976), pp. 143-149; ***Vigat***, 2:72

(no. 21) **Jagrūp Jagnāthot, Kuṃvar** (5-2)

Jagrūp Jagnāthot was one of the eight sons of Rājā Jagnāth Bhārmalot (3-1) (no. 20). He took part with his father in Mughal operations in the Deccan under Prince Murād, and he remained there in 1598 when Rājā Jagnāth received permission to return home. While the Rājā was in north India, Jagrūp was killed outside Bīḍ city in 1599-1600, fighting in the Mughal van against the forces of Ahmadnagar. ***Vigat***, 2:72, notes that Jagrūp's cenotaph (***chatrī***) was built there.

Jagrūp had no sons. His one daughter named Rūpvatībāī was married to Rāṭhoṛ Rājā Gajsiṅgh Sūrajsiṅghot of Jodhpur (1619-38).[4] The marriage took place at Toḍo in central Rājasthān in 1605-06, some years after Jagrūp's death.

---

[4] See ***supra*****, Marriage and Family Lists of the Rulers of Jodhpur**, Gajsiṅgh Sūrajsiṅghot, Rāṇī no. 1.

Akbar Nāma, 3:1136; *Khyāt*, 1:1136; *Vigat*, 2:72.

Figure 12. Rājāvat Kachvāhos (Toḍo and Gwalior)

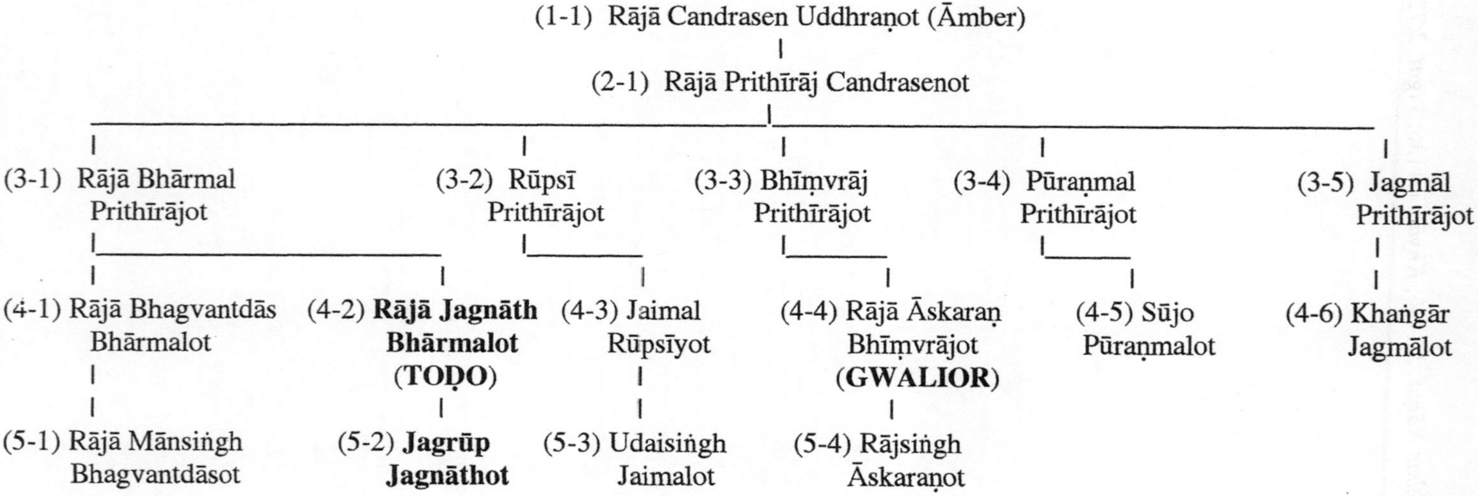

Sekhāvat Kachvāhos

(no. 22) **Rāymal Sekhāvat** (5-1)

The Sekhāvat Kachvāhos

The Sekhāvat Kachvāhos descend from Sekho Mokaḷot (4-1), a son of Mokaḷ Bālāvat (3-1) and great-grandson of Rājā Narsiṅgh Udaikaraṇot (1-1) of Āmber. Sekho's date of birth is placed in 1433-34. Both his birth and his name, Sekho, have important local significance. According to Sekhāvat traditions, Sekho's father, Mokaḷ, was without sons until he received the blessing of the Muslim saint, Sheikh Burhān Chishtī. One of Mokaḷ's wives, Nirvāṇ Cahuvāṇjī, gave birth to a son following the saint's blessing, and in honor of this saint, Mokaḷ named his son Sheikh (Middle Mārvāṛī "Sekho").

Sekho asserted his independence from Āmber as a young man, and with the help of his father, established his seat of rule in territory to the north and west of Āmber that became known as Sekhāvaṭī (lit. "Sekho's share/portion"). Sekho founded his capitol of Amarsar[1] between the years 1449-60, and then in 1477, laid foundations for the town of Sikargaḍh.[2] Some years later on April 4, 1489 Sekhojī was killed in battle defending his lands from attack by the Gauṛ Rajpūts of Maroṭh.[3]

(no. 22) **Rāymal Sekhāvat** (5-1)

Rāymal Sekhāvat was the youngest of the twelve sons of Sekhojī (4-1). He succeeded his father to the rule of Amarsar on April 15, 1489. Kachvāho Kuṃvar Prithīrāj Candrasenot (Rājā of Āmber, ca. 1503-27), a son of Rājā Candrasen Uddhraṇot of Āmber (d. ca. 1503), came to Amarsar to attend the succession ceremonies.

During the early years of his rule, Rāymal consolidated his position at Amarsar and carried out a series of raids against the Gauṛs of Maroṭh who were responsible for the death of his father, Sekhojī. The Gauṛs finally married a daughter to Rāymal and ceded a number of villages to him to end the ***vair***.

Much of Rāymal's life until his death in 1537-38 was spent in the defense of his territory against Muslim encroachments from north India. Navāb Hindāl, a noble of Sikandar Lodī of Delhi (1489-1517), attacked Sikargaḍh in 1498-99. Rāymal appealed to the Kachvāhos of Āmber for aid to counter this

---

[1] Amarsar: situated forty miles due north of Jaipur.

[2] Sikhargaḍh: located sixty miles northwest of Jaipur.

[3] Maroṭh: located fifty miles west-northwest of Jaipur and thirty miles south of Sikargaḍh.

raid, and the combined force of Rajpūts from Sekhāvaṭī and Āmber defeated the Navāb's army in battle.

Some years later in 1526, Rāymal and Rāymal's daughter's son (***dohitro***), Vīdāvat Rāṭhoṛ Kalyāṇmal Udaikaraṇot (no. 153) of Chāpar-Droṇpur (southeastern Bīkāner territory), joined Rāṭhoṛ Rāv Lūṇkaraṇ Bīkāvat of Bīkāner (1505-26; no. 44) in an expedition against Sheikh Abīmīrā and the Muslims of Narnol. While Kalyāṇmal and Rāymal were, at first, willing supporters of Rāv Lūṇkaraṇ's, their loyalty altered as they moved through Chāpar-Droṇpur enroute to Narnol. Kalyāṇmal overheard the Rāv speak of taking this land for himself, and suspecting deception, Kalyāṇmal and his maternal grandfather (***nāno***), Rāymal, withheld support during the fighting near Narnol. Rāv Lūṇkaraṇ and three of his sons were killed in battle there. Rāv Lūṇkaraṇ's son and successor, Rāv Jaitsī Lūṇkaraṇot (1526-42; no. 45), held Kalyāṇmal responsible for his father's death, and he mounted a series of expeditions against Chāpar-Droṇpur, finally forcing Kalyāṇmal to flee the area. Rāv Jaitsī placed a collateral relation of Kalyāṇmal's on the seat of rule and maintained close control over these lands from Bīkāner. Rāymal Sekhāvat's specific role in the latter conflict is unknown.

A contingent of Kachvāhos from Āmber joined the large force of Rajpūts under Sīsodīyo Rāṇo Sāṅgo Rāymalot of Cītoṛ (1509-28) that traveled to north India in 1527 to meet the Mughal Bābur in battle at Khanua. It is probable that Rāymal Sekhāvat took part in this expedition. However, local sources do not specify. Later in 1533 Mīrzā Hindāl, the younger brother of Mughal Emperor Humāyūn, attacked Amarsar. Humāyūn had made Mīrzā Hindāl the ***jāgīrdār*** of Mevāt,[4] and Hindāl attempted unsuccessfully to incorporate both Amarsar and Sikargaḍh within his territory. The Kachvāhos of Āmber once again came to Rāymal's aid during the fighting at Amarsar.

Two years later in 1535-36 Rāymal took Meṛtīyo Rāṭhoṛ Rāv Vīramde Dūdāvat (no. 105) under his protection at Amarsar. Rāv Vīramde was in exile from Meṛto and Ajmer, his lands having been occupied by Rāṭhoṛ Rāv Mālde Gāṅgāvat of Jodhpur (1532-62). Rāv Vīramde remained at Amarsar for approximately one year before proceeding on to Riṇthambhor and then Delhi, where he met with Sher Shāh Sūr (1540-1545). Rāv Mālde of Jodhpur sent armies in pursuit of Rāv Vīramde, following him north and east from Ajmer to Sāmbhar and Ḍīḍvāṇo, and then south as far as Cāṭsū (near Āmber).[5] This force did not encroach on Sekhāvaṭī. The Rāṭhoṛs of Jodhpur and the Sekhāvats were ***sagos***, and it is probable that their relationship through marriage deterred the Rāv from sending his armies into Rāymal's lands.

Marriage ties between the Jodho Rāṭhoṛs and the Sekhāvat Kachvāhos of Amarsar and Sikargaḍh include the following:

---

[4] Mevāt: the territory lying in the vicinity of modern Alvar, to the north and east of Jaipur.

[5] Cāṭsū lies thirty-five miles to the south of Jaipur.

1. Rāṭhoṛ Vāgho Sūjāvat (no. 83), a son of Rāv Sūjo Jodhāvat of Jodhpur (ca. 1492-1515), married his daughter, Ratankuṃvar, to Rāymal Sekhāvat's son, Sūjo Rāymalot (6-3).

2. Rāṭhoṛ Rāv Mālde Gāṅgāvat of Jodhpur married his daughter, Haṃsbāī, to Rāymal Sekhāvat's grandson, Lūṇkaraṇ Sūjāvat (7-5).[6]

3. Rāymal Sekhāvat's brother, Ratansī Sekhāvat (5-2), married his daughter, Lāchaḷde, to Rāṭhoṛ Rāv Mālde Gāṅgāvat of Jodhpur.[7]

The ***Khyāt*** of Naiṇsī, 3:98, records that the Sekhāvats were also ***sago***s of the Meṛtīyo Rāṭhoṛs of Meṛto in eastern Mārvāṛ, but provides few details.[8] ***Murārdān***, no. 2, pp. 473, 504, 506-507, lists several sons of Meṛtīyo Rāv Jaimal Vīramdevot (no. 107) who were born of Kachvāhī wives, but does not indicate the families from which these women came. Dunlod, p. 10, notes that a "Meṛtīyo Rāymal" of "Rāhaṇ" village married a daughter to Rāymal Sekhāvat's son, Sūjo Rāymalot. This Meṛtīyo Rāymal of Rāhīṇ is identified as Meṛtīyo Rāymal Dūdāvat, a brother of Rāv Vīramde Dūdāvat of Meṛto. Rāymal Dūdāvat held the village of Rāhaṇ[9] in ***paṭo*** from Rāv Vīramde and was killed fighting at Khanua against the Mughal Bābur in 1527.

Rāymal Sekhāvat is also known to have married daughters to Rāṭhoṛ Rāv Lūṇkaraṇ Bīkāvat's son, Kuṃvar Vairsī Lūṇkaraṇot, of Bīkāner, and to Vīdāvat Rāṭhoṛ Udaikaraṇ Vīdāvat of Chāpar-Droṇpur. Udaikaraṇ Vīdāvat was the father of Kalyāṇmal Udaikaraṇot (no. 153).

Akbar Nāma, 1:327, and ***Maāthir-ul-Umarā***, 2:1:564, both record that Mīyāṃ Ḥasan Khān Sūr, the father of Sher Shāh Sūr, was a military servant of Rāymal Sekhāvat's for a period of time.

Rāymal died in 1537-38 and was succeeded by his eldest son, Sūjo Rāymalot (6-3).

Akbar Nāma, 1:327; ***Bāṅkīdās***, p. 18; Harnath Singh Dunlod, ***The Sheikhawats and Their Lands*** (Jaipur: Raj Educational Printers, 1970), pp. 8-10; ***Khyāt***, 1:295-296, 318-327, 3:98, 151, 166; ***Maāthir-ul-Umarā***, 2:1:564; ***Murārdān***, no. 1, p. 241, no. 2, pp. 473, 504, 506-507, 555; Ojhā, 5:1:117-118; Refaqat Ali Khan, ***The Kachhwahas Under Akbar and Jahangir*** (New

---

[6] See ***supra***, **Marriage and Family Lists of the Rulers of Jodhpur**, Mālde Gāṅgāvat, Rāṇī no. 3, D - Haṃsbāī.

[7] See ***supra***, **Marriage and Family Lists of the Rulers of Jodhpur**, Mālde Gāṅgāvat, Rāṇī no. 16.

[8] ***Khyāt***, 1:320, lists only one specific marriage. A grandson of Rāymal Sekhāvat's, Rāysal Sūjāvat (7-4), married a daughter of Meṛtīyo Rāv Vīramde's grandson, Vīṭhaḷdās Jaimalot (no. 117). This marriage appears removed in time, however, from the events of 1535, when Meṛtīyo Rāv Vīramde took refuge with the Sekhāvats.

[9] Rāhaṇ (or Rāhīṇ) village: located ten miles north-northeast of Meṛto.

Delhi: Kitab Publishing House, 1976), p. 155; Ṭhākur Surjansiṃh Śekhāvat, ***Rāv Śekhā: Śekhāvāṭī-Saṅgh tathā Śekhāvat Vaṃś ke Pravarttak Rāv Śekhā kā Jīvan-Vṛtt*** (Sīkar: Mahārāv Śekhā Smārak Samiti, V. S. 2030 [A. D. 1973]), pp. 13-17, 107-114, 130-142; ***Vigat***, 1:55, 2:54; ***Vīr Vinod***, 2:1270-1271.

Figure 13. Sekhāvat Kachvāhos of Amarsar and Khaṇḍeḷo

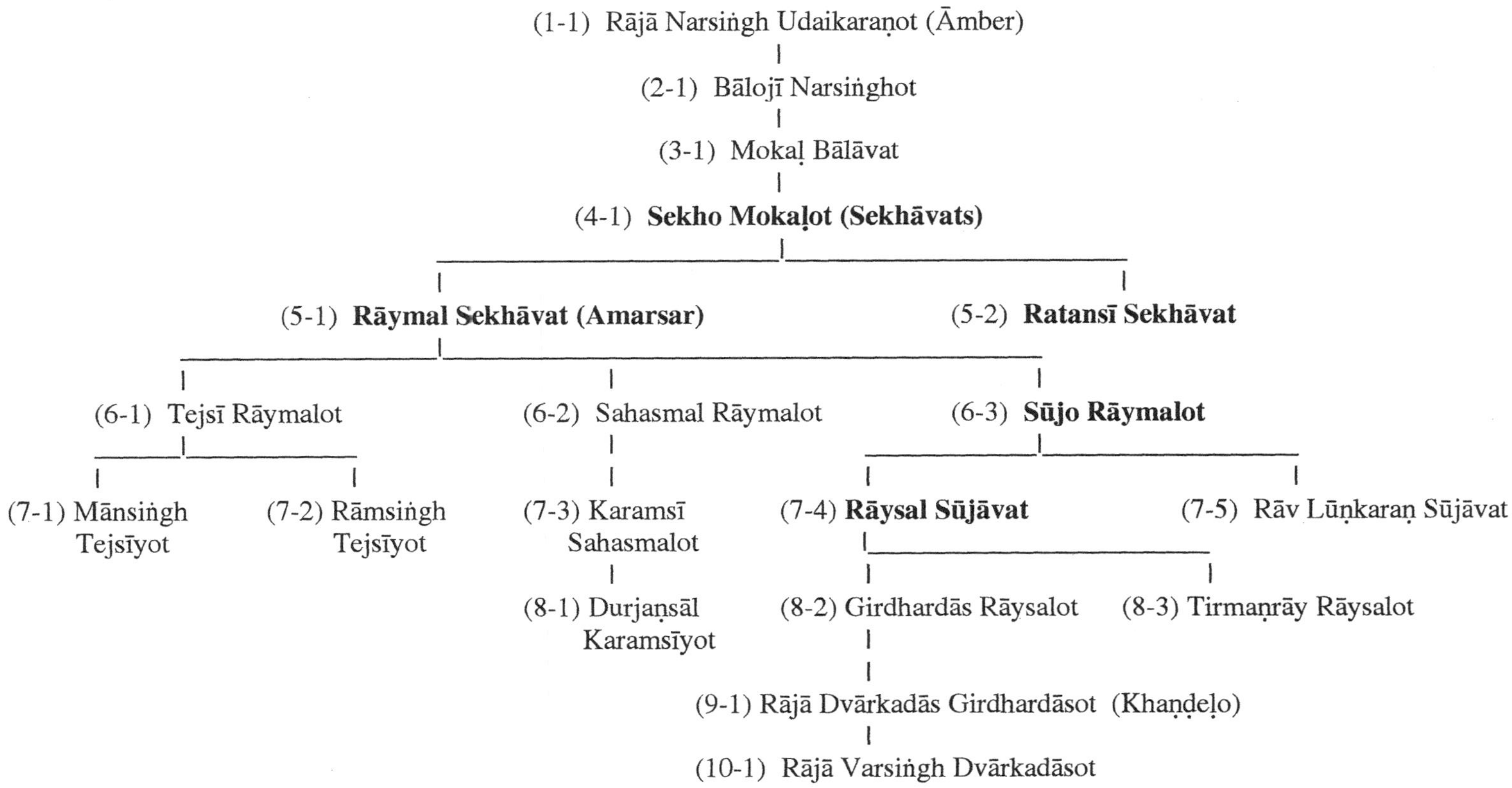

Paṃvārs of Cāṭsū

(no. 23) **Akho Soḍhāvat**
(no. 25) **Jagmāl Karamcandot, Rāvat** (5-2)
(no. 24) **Pañcāiṇ Karamcandot, Rāvat** (5-1)

The Paṃvārs of Cāṭsū[1] played an important but minor role in events discussed in the texts under consideration. Their involvement in several ***vairs*** with different ***sākhs*** of Mārvāṛ Rāṭhoṛs provided the context.

"Aitihāsik Bātāṃ," pp. 60-62, details a ***vair*** that developed between the Paṃvārs of Cāṭsū and the Ūdāvat Rāṭhoṛs of Jaitāraṇ[2] in eastern Mārvāṛ. This ***vair*** began during the time of Paṃvār Rāvat Karamcand Rāghavdāsot (4-1). According to the "Aitihāsik Bātāṃ," Rāvat Karamcand had gone on a trip to Mevāṛ to visit his ***sagos*** at the court of Cītoṛ. On return, he took a circuitous route across the Arāvallīs into Mārvāṛ and encamped at the village of Nīmbāj,[3] near Jaitāraṇ.

Karamcand noticed the prosperity of the residents of Nīmbāj, and seeing that they were unprotected, proceeded to loot the village. Complaints were immediately taken to Ūdāvat Rāṭhoṛ Rāv Ḍūṅgarsī Ūdāvat (no. 137) at Jaitāraṇ. Rāv Ḍūṅgarsī was an aged ***ṭhākur*** at the time and did nothing to recover the stolen goods nor to punish the Paṃvārs. The Paṃvārs then moved against Jaitāraṇ itself and upon arrival on the outskirts of the town, sent two ***pradhāns*** to Rāv Ḍūṅgarsī demanding that the Rāv give Rāvat Karamcand one of his daughters in marriage, or the Paṃvārs would attack the town. Rāv Ḍūṅgarsī acceded to the Paṃvārs' demands and gave them one of his daughters. Rāvat Karamcand then left Mārvāṛ and returned to Cāṭsū.

It was left for Rāv Ḍūṅgarsī's son, Tejsī Ḍūṅgarsīyot (no. 138), to take revenge for this insult. Tejsī was a young boy at the time Rāvat Karamcand looted Nīmbāj and extorted a daughter from his father. Even then, he vowed to avenge his family's honor. Tejsī organized a force of Rajpūts in the years after 1535 and raided Cāṭsū, looting much wealth and killing many Paṃvārs. One of Paṃvār Karamcand's son's, Jagmāl Karamcandot (5-2) (no. 25), who was then ***rāvat*** at Cāṭsū, is said to have left Cāṭsū prior to the raid and to have gone to live near Āmber (see ***infra***), leaving the town open to Tejsī's raid.

Tejsī Ḍūṅgarsīyot attacked Cāṭsū again sometime later. Following this raid, the Paṃvārs sent ***pradhāns*** to Jaitāraṇ to plead for an end to the ***vair***. They offered one of their daughters in marriage to a member of Rāv Ḍūṅgarsī's family. Tejsī agreed, but only if the daughter were married to the Rāv himself.

---

[1] Cāṭsū: located thirty-five miles south of Jaipur in central Rājasthān.

[2] Jaitāraṇ: located fifty-six miles east of Jodhpur.

[3] Nīmbāj : located six miles southeast of Jaitāraṇ.

Considering the advanced age of Rāv Ḍūṅgarsī, the Paṃvārs balked, but then conceded and the ***vair*** was finally settled.

The circumstances surrounding this ***vair***, including who specifically was murdered, are difficult to verify and are not corroborated in other sources. That a ***vair*** did exist seems entirely possible. However, Tejsī's attacks on Cāṭsū appear not to have been isolated ventures under his sole direction. ***Vigat***, 1:44, records that Rāv Mālde Gāṅgāvat of Jodhpur (1532-62) held Cāṭsū and had a fort built there in the years following his occupation of Ajmer ca. 1535. In this year he sent an army under his military commander, Rāṭhoṛ Kūmpo Mahirājot (no. 95), to drive Meṛtīyo Rāv Vīramde Dūdāvat (no. 105) from Ajmer and then Rājasthān. Kūmpo brought a wide area of central Rājasthān under Rāv Mālde's authority, including the areas of Ḍīḍvāṇo, Sāmbhar, Fatehpur, Jhūñjhaṇūṃ and Cāṭsū. It is probable that there were a series of raids on Cāṭsū itself. Ūdāvat Tejsī Ḍūṅgarsīyot may have taken part in these raids both as a military servant of Rāv Mālde's and as a private party interested in carrying out his own personal vendetta.

* * *

Paṃvār Karamcand and his family held traditional attachments to the area of Cāṭsū in central Rājasthān. They were also associated with Ajmer and lands in its vicinity, and it was while master of Śrīnagar (near Ajmer)[4] in the years prior to 1508, that Paṃvār Karamcand became closely involved with the Sīsodīyo ruling family of Cītoṛ, which greatly altered his political fortunes.

Vīr Vinod, 1:344, characterizes Karamcand as a ***luṭerā Rajpūt*** ("plunderer/robber Rajpūt") who ruled from Śrīnagar with three or four thousand warriors under his command. Several years prior to 1508, Sīsodīyo Kuṃvar Sāṅgo Rāymalot (Rāṇo of Cītoṛ, 1509-28) came to Karamcand in disguise and entered into his service as an ordinary military retainer. Kuṃvar Sāṅgo was then in exile from Mevāṛ, having fled and assumed anonymity during a period of conflict with elder brothers over precedence and rights to succesion at Cītoṛ. Sāṅgo remained with Karamcand at Śrīnagar, where he was able to conceal his whereabouts from members of the Sīsodīyo ruling family and protect himself.

Karamcand eventually learned of Sāṅgo's true identity, and he then pledged himself to the ***kuṃvar***'s service and married one of his daughters to the him.[5] Kuṃvar Sāṅgo's elder brother, Prithīrāj, was then killed in battle in Sīrohī ca. 1508, and his father, Rāṇo Rāymal Kūmbhāvat (1473-1509), learned shortly after that Sāṅgo was alive and with Paṃvār Karamcand at Śrīnagar. The Rāṇo summoned Sāṅgo back to Mevāṛ, and Karamcand accompanied him to Cītoṛ. The Rāṇo was pleased with Paṃvār Karamcand's service to his family, and he

---

[4] Śrīnagar village: located ten miles due east of Ajmer.

[5] Paṃvār Karamcand married several of his daughters to members of the Sīsodīyo ruling family. Sources indicate that these daughters were given both to Kuṃvar Sāṅgo Rāymalot, and also to two of Rāṇo Sāṅgo sons, Udaisiṅgh and Ratansī. See: ***Khyāt***, 1:21, 106; Ojhā, 2:655; ***Vīr Vinod***, 1:354.

rewarded Karamcand with a grant of lands in Mevāṛ. He also conferred on Karamcand a prominent rank among Rajpūts at his court.

Sāṅgo Rāymalot succeeded to the throne of Cītoṛ as ***rāṇo*** shortly thereafter in 1509. He in turn granted Karamcand a large ***paṭo*** in central Rājasthān including the ***parganos*** Ajmer, Parbatsar, Māṇḍal, Phūliyo, and Banero. Ojhā, 2:659, states that it was from Rāṇo Sāṅgo that Karamcand received the title of ***rāvat***. Rāvat Karamcand's son, Jagmāl Karamcandot (no. 25; see ***infra***), joined his father in the Rāṇo's service, and the Rāṇo is said to have given Jagmāl the title of ***rāv*** in return for his actions against Gauṛ Rajpūts in Mevāṛ who had "raised their heads" in rebellion.

Paṃvār rule over areas of central Rājasthān and Ajmer in particular continued through the reign of Rāṇo Sāṅgo, and following the Rāṇo's death by poison in 1528 after his defeat at the battle of Khanua against the Mughal Emperor Bābur, the Paṃvārs established a short-lived rule of their own at Ajmer. A ***praśasti*** dated V.S. 1589 (1532-33), which Somānī, p. 17, references, records that "Śrī Jagmal [Paṃvār]" was ruling at Ajmer in that year. Then in 1533, the troops of Sultān Bahādur Shāh of Gujarat (1526-37) occupied the city, ending the Paṃvārs' independent rule in this area.

Paṃvār association with Ajmer apparently extended back several generations. ***Paṃvār Vaṃś Darpaṇ***, p. 16, records that Karamcand and Jagmāl's ancestor, Rāvat Māhapo Sāṅgāvat (2-1), received Ajmer in ***paṭo***. The text gives no date for the grant, nor does it indicate from whom the ***paṭo*** was received. In all likelihood, it came from a Sīsodīyo ruler of Cītor. Sīsodīyo influence in central Rājasthān dates from the time of Rāṇo Kūmbho Mokaḷot (ca. 1433-68).

* * *

Vigat, 2:49-50, mentions a second ***vair*** in which the Paṃvārs were involved. It records that shortly after his succession to the throne of Jodhpur in 1532, Rāv Mālde Gāṅgāvat sent word to Paṃvār Karamcand's son, Rāvat Pañcāiṇ Karamcandot of Cāṭsū (5-1) (no. 24), to goad him into an attack against Merto. The ***Vigat*** alludes to the ***vair*** of Akho Soḍhāvat (no. 23), which the Paṃvārs had yet to settle. Akho Soḍhāvat was a Paṃvār Rajpūt of Pīsāṅgaṇ village[6] whom Meṛtīyo Rāṭhoṛ Ratansī Dūdāvat had murdered. Ratansī Dūdāvat was a brother of Rāv Vīramde Dūdāvat (no. 105). At the time he killed Paṃvār Akho, Ratansī was living in Kuṛkī village,[7] which Rāv Vīramde had granted him in ***paṭo***. The murder would have occurred before March 17, 1527 when Ratansī was killed in battle. He had accompanied Sīsodīyo Rāṇo Sāṅgo Rāymalot to north India in March of 1527 to fight against the Mughal Bābur, and he died at Khanua along with one of his brothers, Meṛtīyo Rāymal Dūdāvat. The fact that Rāvat Pañcāiṇ was responsible for avenging Akho's death suggests that Akho

---

[6] Pīsāṅgaṇ: located fifteen miles west-southwest of Ajmer.

[7] Kuṛkī: located eight miles west-northwest of Pīsāṅgaṇ village.

was under Pañcāiṇ's protection and probably a junior member of the Paṃvār brotherhood, perhaps holding Pīsāṅgaṇ in grant from the Rāvat himself.

Pañcāiṇ Karamcandot had succeeded his father, Rāvat Karamcand Rāghavdāsot (4-1), as ***rāvat*** of Cāṭsū sometime after 1522-23. The ***Khyāt*** of Naiṇsī, 1:122, records that Sāh Parbat, a ***kiroṛī*** of the Pātsāh of Māṇḍū, came and settled the town of Parbatsar (near Ajmer)[8] in 1522-23, "in the time of Paṃvār Karamcand."[9]

Rāvat Pañcāiṇ did become involved in an attempt to settle Akho's ***vair***. Rāv Mālde had formed an army to attack the Sīndhaḷs of Bhādrājuṇ[10] shortly after his accession in 1532, and he summoned members of the brotherhood including the Meṛtīyos, to participate in this campaign. Meṛtīyo Rāv Vīramde reluctantly agreed to comply with the summons and reported with his Rajpūts, leaving Meṛto virtually unprotected. As the expeditionary force gathered near Jodhpur, Rāv Mālde sent word to Rāvat Pañcāiṇ, encouraging him to come and settle the ***vair***. Rāv Mālde declared that with Rāv Vīramde involved elsewhere, the land of Meṛto was empty and the Paṃvārs could now exact their revenge.

Goaded by Rāv Mālde, Rāvat Pañcāiṇ proceeded to attack the village of Āḷṇīyāvās.[11] Pañcāiṇ's brother, Paṃvār Jagmāl, who succeeded him as ***rāvat*** of Cāṭsū, was with Pañcāiṇ on this raid. He likely joined him from Ajmer, where he appears to have held rule. Very little was accomplished, however, for the Paṃvārs fled without a fight when Meṛtīyo Rāysal Dūdāvat (no. 106), who had remained behind Rāv Vīramde at Meṛto, advanced against them with a force of Rajpūts.

Sources do not mention any other raids the Paṃvārs made against Meṛto. The ***vair*** of Akho Soḍhāvat appears to have remained unsettled.

* * *

Rāvat Pañcāiṇ was the maternal grandfather of Kachvāho Rājā Mānsiṅgh Bhagvantdāsot of Āmber (1589-1614). He was killed at Cītoṛ on May 25, 1533 fighting in the service of Rāṇo Vikramaditya Sāṅgāvat of Mevāṛ (ca. 1531-36) against the invading troops of Sultān Bahādur Shāh of Gujarat.

One of Rāvat Pañcāiṇ's sons, Rājā Mālde Pañcāiṇot (6-1), was for a time a ***mansabdār*** under Mughal Emperor Akbar. He left Imperial service, however, and went to Mevāṛ to serve under Sīsodīyo Rāṇo Udaisiṅgh Sāṅgāvat (ca. 1537-72; no. 17), under whom he held the ***paṭo*** of Jājpur.[12] One of Mālde's sons, Rājā

---

[8] Parbatsar: located thirty miles north of Ajmer, near Sāmbhar.

[9] It is possible that Rāvat Karamcand had accompanied Rāṇo Sāṅgo to north India in 1527 and was killed at the battle of Khanua, but sources available provide no information about the date or circumstances of his death.

[10] Bhādrājuṇ village: located forty-eight miles south-southwest of Jodhpur.

[11] Āḷṇīyāvās village: located twenty miles southeast of Meṛto.

[12] Jājpur: modern Jahāzpur, located seventy miles southeast of Ajmer.

Sādūḷ Māldevot (7-1), was also in Mughal service. ***Bāṅkīdās***, p. 138, records that Jahāngīr granted him the ***sūbo*** of Ajmer in ***jāgīr***. The extent of Rājā Sādūḷ's authority at Ajmer is unknown, and this grant is not confirmed in other sources. ***Bāṅkīdās*** states that at the behest of Sīsodīyo Rājā Bhīm Amarsiṅghot (no. 15), Paṃvār Sādūḷ acknowledged the authority of Prince Khurram (Shāh Jahān) over Ajmer. Sādūḷ was in all likelihood a military servant of the Prince's and received his authority at Ajmer from him.

It may have been at this time that Sādūḷ became involved in a ***vair*** with the Rāṭhoṛ ruling family of Jodhpur. Kuṃvar Bhopatsiṅgh Udaisiṅghot, a son of Moṭo Rājā Udaisiṅgh Māldevot, was killed at Masūdo village near Ajmer[13] by either Sādūḷ or one of his men. Paṃvār Sādūḷ married a daughter to Rājā Sūrajsiṅgh Udaisiṅghot of Jodhpur (1595-1619) to settle this ***vair***. The marriage took place in 1609-10 at Burhanpur in the Deccan. Sādūḷ's brother, Sāṅgo (7-2), had already married one of his daughters to Rājā Sūrajsiṅgh in 1590-91.[14]

* * *

After Rāvat Pañcāiṇ's death at Cītoṛ in May of 1533, his brother, Paṃvār Jagmāl Karamcandot, assumed authority at Cāṭsū. As noted above, Paṃvār Jagmāl had succeeded his father, Karamcand, to rule at Ajmer, but was forced to give up authority there in 1533 when the city was taken by troops of Sultān Bahādur Shāh's of Gujarat under Sham Sheru'l-Mulk.

Vigat, 2:54, records that Meṛtīyo Rāv Vīramde Dūdāvat stopped with the Paṃvārs at Cāṭsū during his flight from Meṛto and Ajmer in 1535.[15] The fact that he did stop at Cāṭsū may have been an additional pretext for Rāv Mālde's raid on this town. Sources do not clarify how Rāv Vīramde was able to stay at Cāṭsū when a ***vair*** between the Meṛtīyos and the Paṃvārs remained unsettled. However, Paṃvār Pañcāiṇ was killed in 1533 at Cītoṛ, and his brother, Paṃvār Jagmāl, may not have wished to continue the hostilities. Sources available provide no explanation.

Jagmāl Karamcandot was ***rāvat*** of Cāṭsū when Ūdāvat Rāṭhoṛ Tejsī Ḍūṅgarsīyot (no. 138) attacked the town (probably in 1540-41, but perhaps as early as 1536-37). For some reason, Jagmāl left Cāṭsū prior to this attack and

---

13 Masūdo village: located twenty-six miles south-southwest of Ajmer.

14 See *supra*, **Marriage and Family Lists of the Rulers of Jodhpur**, Sūrajsiṅgh Udaisiṅghot, Rāṇī no. 6 and Rāṇī no. 14.

15 The ***Khyāt*** of Naiṇsī, 3:95, states that the Paṃvār Rajpūts were in control of Ajmer at the time Meṛtīyo Rāv Vīramde asserted his authority over this city. This reference is incorrect. Ajmer came under the authority of the Sultān of Gujarat, Bahādur Shāh, in 1533. It was administered directly by his ***hākīm***, Sham Sheru'l-Mulk, who was in charge of the city just prior to Rāv Vīramde's occupation. The ***hākīm*** vacated Ajmer upon the fall of Māṇḍū to the Mughal Emperor Humāyūn, leaving the city open to Meṛtīyo Rāv Vīramde. See: ***Vigat***, 2:51, n. 212, of the **translated text** for details.

took up residence in Khoh village near Āmber. Cāṭsū was then left open to Tejsī's depredations.

A certain Paṃvār Jagmāl rose to the rank of 500 ***zāt*** in Mughal service and is mentioned several times in ***Akbar Nāma***. It is unclear from sources available whether this Paṃvār Jagmāl was the same person as Paṃvār Rāvat Jagmāl Karamcandot of Cāṭsū.

Ā'īn-ī-Akbarī, p. 532; "Aitihāsik Bātāṃ," pp. 60-62; ***Akbar Nāma***, 2:509, 3:69, 380, 519, 587, 599; Athar Ali, ***Apparatus***, p. 22; ***Bāṅkīdās***, pp. 24, 27, 124, 131, 137-138; ***Khyāt***, 1:21, 106, 122, 3:95, 176; ***Murārdān***, no. 2, pp. 194, 209, 212, 573-574; Ojhā, 2:654-655, 659, 706-709; ***Paṃvār Vaṃś Darpaṇ***, pp. 16, 23, 30; Rāmvallabh Somānī, "Mālde aur Bīramde Meṛtiyā kā Saṅgarṣ," ***Mārū-Bhāratī***, 15:4 (January, 1968), pp. 17-19; ***Vigat***, 1:43-44, 2:49-50, 54; ***Vīr Vinod***, 1:344, 351-352, 354.

Figure 14. Paṃvārs of Cāṭsū

(1-1) Rāvat Sāṅgo

(2-1) Rāvat Māhapo Sāṅgāvat

(3-1) Rāvat Rāghavdās Māhapāvat

(4-1) **Rāvat Karamcand Rāghavdāsot**

- (5-1) **Rāvat Pañcāiṇ Karamcandot**
  - (6-1) **Rājā Mālde Pañcāiṇot**
    - (7-1) **Rājā Sādūḷ Māldevot**
    - (7-2) **Sāṅgo Māldevot**
- (5-2) **Rāvat Jagmāl Karamcandot**

Sāṅkhlo Paṃvārs

(no. 26) **Jāṅgaḷvo Nāpo Māṇakrāvat, Rāṇo** (14-1)
(no. 27) **Jāṅgaḷvo Tejsī Bhojāvat** (15-1)

The Sāṅkhlo Paṃvārs

The ***Khyāt*** of Naiṇsī, 1:337-339, records that the Sāṅkhlo and Soḍho ***sākh***s of Paṃvār Rajpūts emerged from a common ancestor, a certain Bāhaṛ, the son of Dharṇīvarāh. Bāhaṛ had two sons said to have been born of a fairy (***apcharā***) who lived in his home. One son was called Soḍho and the other Sāṅkhlo Vāgh. The Sāṅkhlos trace direct descent from this Sāṅkhlo Vāgh (1-1), who lived in the areas of Bāhaṛmer and Chahoṭaṇ (Cohaṭaṇ) in western Mārvāṛ, while the Soḍhos established themselves at Ūmarkoṭ.[1] Sāṅkhlo Vāgh's son, Vairsī Vāghāvat (2-1), is said to have migrated from western Mārvāṛ to the vicinity of Meṛto, where he founded the village of Rūṇ.[2]

From Vairsī's descendants emerged two branches of Sāṅkhlos. Those who remained associated with the village of Rūṇ became known as Rūṇecos. A cadet line split off from this group and settled in the village of Jāṅgaḷu,[3] which they took from the Dahīyo Rajpūts then in control. This group became known as Jāṅgaḷvo Sāṅkhlos. A memorial stone (***devḷī***) found at Rāysīsar village near Jāṅgaḷu dated May 3, 1231 establishes Sāṅkhlo occupation in this area from the early thirteenth century onwards.

These two branches of Sāṅkhlo Paṃvārs can be traced genealogically from material recorded in the ***Khyāt*** of Naiṇsī, 1:338-354.[4] This information appears only partially acceptable, however. Rāṇo Nāpo Māṇakrāvat (14-1) and Tejsī Bhojāvat (15-1) are listed in the fourteenth and fifteenth generations, respectively, from Sāṅkhlo Vāgh (1-1). Yet these two individuals were separated in time by more than a century. Lists from Rājasthān which trace descent of ruling or prominent families for periods prior to the mid-fifteenth century share a common failing, that of turning lists of brothers or members of collateral lines into ascendant "king lists" tracing lineal descent. Questions about generation and relationship are thereby rendered difficult to ascertain. The genealogical lists of the Sāṅkhlos appear to partake of this failing.

---

[1] Ūmarkoṭ is located in modern-day southeastern Pakistan.

[2] Rūṇ village: located twenty miles northwest of Meṛto and fifty-nine miles northeast of Jodhpur.

[3] Jāṅgaḷu village: located sixty-five miles northeast of Phaḷodhī and forty-five miles north of Nāgaur.

[4] See *infra*, **Figure 15. Sāṅkhlo Paṃvārs of Rūṇ and Jāṅgaḷu.**

K. C. Jain, ***Ancient Cities and Towns of Rajasthan*** (Delhi: Motilal Banarsidass, 1972), pp. 310-311; ***Khyāt***, 1:337-354; Ojhā, 5:1:72.

(no. 26) **Jāṅgaḷvo Nāpo Māṇakrāvat, Rāṇo** (14-1)

Jāṅgaḷvo Sāṅkhlo Rāṇo Nāpo Māṇakrāvat played an important role as a military servant, advisor, and supporter of Rāṭhoṛ Rāv Jodho Riṇmalot of Maṇḍor and Jodhpur (ca. 1453-1489) and of his son, Bīko Jodhāvat (no. 42), who founded the new kingdom of Bīkāner in northern Rājasthān. Nāpo succeeded his father, Rāṇo Māṇakrāv Punpāḷot (13-1) as master (***dhaṇī***) of Jāṅgaḷu village in the 1420s or 1430s. Shortly thereafter, he came into close contact with Jodho Riṇmalot. Jodho Riṇmalot's father, Rāv Riṇmal Cūṇḍāvat (ca. 1428-38) had been murdered at Cītoṛ ca. 1438, and Jodho, who was present at Cītoṛ when his father was killed, had fled back across the Arāvallīs into Mārvāṛ, eventually seeking refuge at Jāṅgaḷu while the Sīsodīyos under Rāṇo Kūmbho Mokaḷot (ca. 1433-68) occupied Maṇḍor and overran much of eastern Mārvāṛ.

The ***Khyāt*** of Naiṇsī, 3:8-9, records that Nāpo Sāṅkhlo lived for some years at the court of Cītoṛ as Jodho Riṇmalot's representative. This would have been between the early 1440s, when Jodho first arrived in Jāṅgaḷu, and ca. 1453 when Jodho placed Rāṭhoṛ authority once again over Maṇḍor. Jodho Riṇmalot spent the fifteen years from 1438 to 1453 collecting horses and Rajpūts, and raiding Sīsodīyo outposts in Mārvāṛ as he sought to re-assert Rāṭhoṛ authority in Mārvāṛ. It is uncertain how long Nāpo remained at Cītoṛ, but he was an important advocate of Jodho's before Sīsodīyo Rāṇo Kūmbho, strongly urging the Rāṇo to work toward a reconciliation. ***Khyāt***, 3:9, records:

> [The Rāṇo] said to Nāpo Sāṅkhlo: "In what manner would there be a reconciliation?" Then Nāpo entreated: "Long live the Dīvāṇ. Resolution of the hostilities (***vair***) [with] the Rāṭhoṛs is a very difficult matter. Entwined in this matter is the hostility [caused by the murder] of Rāv Riṇmal." Thus the Dīvāṇ began to grow very fearful. And Nāpo entreated: "Dīvāṇ! The hostilities are intense. If by giving the land [back] in some manner, [the hostilities] could be averted, then Dīvāṇ! [You] should give the land [back]!" These words also appealed to the Dīvāṇ.

Nāpo kept Jodho informed about developments at the Sīsodīyo court during these years, and he counseled Jodho about the most opportune time to reassert Rāṭhoṛ hegemony in Mārvāṛ.

Nāpo returned to Jāṅgaḷu following Jodho Riṇmalot's conquest of Maṇḍor ca. 1453 and Jodho's assumption of his rightful position as ***rāv*** of Mārvāṛ. Sometime thereafter, Jāṅgaḷu and its neighboring areas came under heavy attack from the Baloc, who began raiding herds and looting villages, and forcing the Sāṅkhlos to flee. Unable to prevent these inroads, Nāpo Sāṅkhlo came to Rāv Jodho's court at Jodhpur to appeal for aid. Rāv Jodho responded by sending his two sons, Bīko Jodhāvat (no. 42) and Bīko's younger uterine brother, Vīdo,[5] to Jāṅgaḷu. ***Khyāt***, 1:346, records in its genealogy of the Jāṅgaḷvo Sāṅkhlos:

> Nāpo Māṇakrāvat. Master at Jāṅgaḷu. Then the Baloc pressed upon [the lands of Jāṅgaḷu]; for this reason, [Nāpo] came before Rāv Jodho at Jodhpur, brought Kuṃvar Bīko [Jodhāvat and his brother, Vīdo,] to Jāṅgaḷu, and made [Bīko] master. The Sāṅkhlos became [Bīko's] military servants (***cākar***s).

Bīko Jodhāvat and his brother's arrival in Jāṅgaḷu is placed in 1465-66. With the support of Nāpo Māṇakrāvat and the Sāṅkhlos, Bīko was able to secure the area against further attacks from the Baloc. Nāpo remained in attendance upon Bīko from this time forward. ***Khyāt***, 3:19-20, records that Nāpo participated with Bīko in the conquest of the territory that became Bīko's new kingdom of Bīkāner, and that he was responsible for advising Bīko about the most appropriate site for his new capitol and fort. The foundations for these were laid in 1485. ***Khyāt***, 1:353, also records that the Sāṅkhlos of Jāṅgaḷu became Bīko's most trusted servants. It was to Nāpo and his direct descendants that the keys to the fort of Bīkāner were entrusted.

During the period from 1464-74, Rāv Jodho and his sons, Bīko and Vīdo, were also active in the conquest of the area of Chāpar-Droṇpur.[6] Rāv Jodho eventually gave this territory to Vīdo Jodhāvat to rule. While operations were being undertaken here, Rāv Jodho's brother, Kāndhaḷ Riṇmalot, was killed by Sāraṅg Khān, the Muslim governor of Hisar. News of Kāndhaḷ's death came first to Bīko Jodhāvat, and he sent Nāpo Sāṅkhlo to Rāv Jodho at Jodhpur to ask for the Rāv's support in exacting revenge for this killing.

No further information is available about Nāpo Sāṅkhlo, and the date and circumstances of his death are unknown.

> ***Bāṅkīdās***, p. 74; ***Khyāt***, 1:346, 353-354, 3:5, 8-9, 11, 19-21, 31; Ojhā, 5:1:72-73, 90-91, 95-96, 102-103; ***Vigat***, 1:31, 39.

(no. 27) **Jāṅgaḷvo Tejsī Bhojāvat** (15-1)

Jāṅgaḷvo Sāṅkhlo Tejsī Bhojāvat was a military servant of Rāv Mālde Gāṅgāvat of Jodhpur (1532-62). He was killed in 1562, fighting at Meṛto under Rāṭhoṛ Devīdās Jaitāvat (no. 65) against Meṛtīyo Rāv Jaimal Vīramdevot (no. 107) and the Mughal forces of Akbar under the command of Mīrzā Sharafu'd-Dīn Ḥusayn.

No further information is known about Tejsī or his family from sources available.

---

[5] For more information about Vīdo Jodhāvat, see ***infra***, "Vīdāvat Rāṭhoṛs."

[6] Chāpar-Droṇpur constitutes the area of modern-day southeastern Bīkāner territory.

"Aitihāsik Bātāṃ," p. 56; ***Bānkīdās***, pp. 16-17; ***Khyāt***, 1:354; ***Vigat***, 2:66.

Figure 15. Sāṅkhlo Paṃvārs of Rūṇ and Jāṅgaḷu

(1-1) **Sāṅkhlo Vāgh**

(2-1) **Vairsī Vāghāvat (Rūṇ village)**

(3-1) Rājpāḷ Vairsīyot

- (4-1) Mahipāḷ Rājpāḷot (**Jāṅgaḷvos**)
  - (5-1) Rāṇo Rāysī Mahipāḷot (ca. 1231)
  - (6-1) Rāṇo Aṇakhsī Rāysīyot
  - (7-1) Rāṇo Khīṃvsī Aṇakhsīyot
  - (8-1) Rāṇo Kuṃvarsī Khīṃvāvat
  - (9-1) Rāṇo Rājsī Kuṃvarsīyot
  - (10-1) Mūñjo Rājsīyot
  - (11-1) Ūdo Mūñjāvat
  - (12-1) Rāṇo Punpāḷ Ūdāvat
    - (13-1) Rāṇo Māṇakrāv Punpāḷot
      - (14-1) **Rāṇo Nāpo Māṇakrāvat** (contemporary of Rāv Jodho Riṇmalot of Jodhpur, ca. 1453-89)
    - (13-2) Sāṇḍo Punpāḷot
      - (14-2) Bhojo Sāṇḍāvat
      - (15-1) **Tejsī Bhojāvat** (d. 1562 at Meṛto)
- (4-2) Chohil Rājpāḷot (**Rūṇecos**)
  - (5-2) Pālaṇsī Chohilot
  - (6-2) Mehado Pālaṇsīyot
  - (7-2) Haṃspāḷ Mehadot
  - (8-2) Soḍhal Haṃspāḷot
  - (9-2) Vīram Soḍhalot
  - (10-2) Cācag Vīramot
  - (11-2) Rāṇo Sīhar Cācagot
  - (12-2) Rāṇo Māṇḍaṇ Sīharot (contemporary of Rāv Jodho Riṇmalot of Jodhpur, ca. 1453-89)

Akhairājot Rāṭhoṛs

(no. 32) **Bhado Pañcāiṇot** (7-4)
(no. 29) **Goind Rāṇāvat** (7-1)
(no. 30) **Īsardās Rāṇāvat** (7-2)
(no. 33) **Lakhmaṇ Bhadāvat** (8-1)
(no. 36) **Netsī Sīhāvat** (7-7)
(no. 35) **Pato Kānhāvat** (8-4)
(no. 28) **Rāṇo Akhairājot** (6-1)
(no. 34) **Tejsī Urjaṇot** (8-3)
(no. 31) **Vairsī Rāṇāvat** (7-3)

The Akhairājot Rāṭhoṛs

The Akhairājot Rāṭhoṛs descend from Akhairāj Riṇmalot (5-1), a son of Rāv Riṇmal Cūṇḍāvat (4-1), ruler of Maṇḍor (ca. 1428-38). In the broadest sense, all descendants of Akhairāj Riṇmalot are included among the Akhairājots. However, several powerful and important branches (***sākh***s) of Rāṭhoṛs emerged in later periods from among Akhairāj's sons and grandsons. These are discussed separately under their individual ***sākh*** names and include, among others, the Jaitāvat Rāṭhoṛs and the Kūmpāvat Rāṭhoṛs who descend from two of Akhairāj Riṇmalot's grandsons. Rāṭhoṛs discussed here as Akhairājots are referred to in the texts by this designation, and are, for the most part, less important sons and descendants of Akhairāj Riṇmalot. In certain cases, these descendants and their families did found ***sākh***s in their own names. Where this occurred, mention is made in the discussion of the individuals involved.

Akahirāj Riṇmalot was Rāv Riṇmal Cūṇḍāvat's eldest son, and sister's son (***bhāṇej***) of the Sonagaros Cahuvāṇs of Nāḍūl. He spent his early life with his father, first at the village of Dhaṇlo[1] which was his father's initial seat of rule, and then at the court of Maṇḍor after ca. 1428 when Rāv Riṇmal usurped power from his younger uterine brother, Rāv Sato Cūṇḍāvat (no. 54). Akhairāj participated in Rāv Riṇmal's consolidation of authority at Maṇḍor, and in his extension of authority over eastern Mārvāṛ in 1429-30. Areas brought under control included Jaitāraṇ,[2] Bagṛī,[3] and Sojhat,[4] all of which were taken from the Sīndhaḷ Rāṭhoṛs. Reu, ***Mārvāṛ kā Itihās***, 1:73, states specifically that Rāv

[1] Dhaṇlo village: located twenty-seven miles due south of Sojhat in eastern Mārvāṛ.

[2] Jaitāraṇ town: located fifty-five miles east-southeast of Maṇḍor.

[3] Bagṛī village: located nine miles east-southeast of Sojhat and twenty-six miles north-northeast of Dhaṇlo village.

[4] Sojhat town: located forty-eight miles southeast of Maṇḍor.

Riṇmal entrusted Akhairāj with the rule of Sojhat following its conquest, but Bagṛī village became Akhairāj's seat of rule. Texts vary in their discussion of how Bagṛī was acquired, one stating that it was Rāv Riṇmal himself who killed Caṛro (Caṛdo) Sīndhaḷ at Bagṛī and established authority there, while others state that it was Akhairāj who defeated and killed Caṛro Sīndhaḷ in battle and conquered Bagṛī. In all likelihood, Akhairāj played a leading role in the eastward expansion of Rāṭhoṛ authority from Maṇḍor and established a strong presence at Bagṛī early in his father's reign. Kānotā, ***Cāmpāvatoṃ kā Itihās***, 1:8, notes that Akhairāj's younger brother, Cāmpo Riṇmalot,[5] assisted him in the conquest of Bagṛī, and that afterwards, Akhairāj left Maṇḍor and settled with his family there.

Rāv Riṇmal left Maṇḍor for Mevāṛ in 1433-34, and spent the latter years of his rule there. His sister, Haṃsbāī, had been married to Sīsodīyo Rāṇo Lākho Khetsot (ca. 1382-1420), and her son by Rāṇo Lākho, Sīsodīyo Rāṇo Mokaḷ Lākhāvat (ca. 1421-33), was murdered at Cītoṛ ca. 1433. Haṃsbāī then summoned her brother to Cītoṛ to protect her young grandson, Kūmbho Mokaḷot (Rāṇo of Cītoṛ, ca. 1433-68), then aged nine years, and ensure his succession to the throne. During his absence from Mārvāṛ, Rāv Riṇmal entrusted the rule of his kingdom to his two sons, Akhairāj and Cāmpo.

Their authority at Maṇḍor was short-lived, for ca. 1438 Rāṇo Kūmbho had Rāv Riṇmal murdered at Cītoṛ to rid Mevāṛ of Rāṭhoṛ influence and control. The Sīsodīyos then proceeded to overrun eastern Mārvāṛ and to occupy Maṇḍor. They maintained a hold over Mārvāṛ for the next fifteen years. Akhairāj spent these years fighting in support of his younger half-brother, Jodho Riṇmalot, who was Rāv Riṇmal's chosen successor. The Rāṭhoṛs finally succeeded in reasserting their authority at Maṇḍor ca. 1453. Akhairāj was present at Maṇḍor to place the ***ṭīko*** of succession on Jodho's forehead when Jodho assumed his rightful position as ***rāv***. This honor fell to Akhairāj as Rāv Riṇmal's eldest son.[6] During this period, Akhairāj also reestablished his own authority at Bagṛī.

Rāv Jodho founded his new capitol of Jodhpur five miles to the south of Maṇḍor in 1459. He then divided the lands of Mārvāṛ among his brothers and sons, and confirmed Akhairāj in his possession of Bagṛī village.[7] Āsopā, ***Āsop kā Itihās***, pp. 16-17, writes that after Akhairāj established himself at Bagṛī, he extended his authority over Sojhat as well, and granted rule of Sojhat to his son, Mahirāj Akhairājot.[8] This information appears incorrect. Akhairāj was

---

[5] See ***infra***, "Cāmpāvat Rāṭhoṛs," for more information about Cāmpo Riṇmalot.

[6] The honor of placing the ***ṭīko*** of succession on the new ruler of Jodhpur has been retained by a branch of Akhairāj Riṇmalot's family, the Jaitāvat ***ṭhākur***s of Bagṛī village in eastern Mārvāṛ.

[7] ***Vigat***, 1:38, and Bhāṭī, ***Sarvekṣaṇ***, 3:91, record that Rāv Jodho granted Bagṛī to Akhairāj in 1459, but it seems certain that Akhairāj's association with this village dates from an earlier period during the rule of his father, Rāv Riṇmal, at Maṇḍor.

[8] See ***infra***, "Kūmpāvat Rāṭhoṛs," for more information about Mahirāj Akhairājot.

associated with rule at Sojhat for a brief period during his father Rāv Riṇmal's rule at Maṇḍor, as noted above. His authority at Sojhat extended only during the initial establishment of Rāṭhoṛ authority in this area immediately after 1428. It is known that Jodho Riṇmalot lived at Sojhat as a ***kuṃvar*** sometime between the years 1428-38, and following his succession ca. 1453, Rāv Jodho placed his son and chosen successor, Kuṃvar Nīmbo Jodhāvat, at Sojhat. ***Vigat***, 1:390, records that Nīmbo had one of the arched gateways (***prauḷ***) to the fort of Sojhat constructed while he was there. Nīmbo Jodhāvat remained at Sojhat until his death in 1464 from wounds received in battle. Rāv Jodho then called his son, Sūjo Jodhāvat (Rāv of Jodhpur, ca. 1492-1515), from Phaḷodhī and placed him in charge at Sojhat.

No other information is available about Akhairāj's activities, and his date of death is uncertain.

> "Aitihāsik Bātāṃ," p. 36; ; ***Āsop kā Itihās***, pp. 16-17; ***Bāṅkīdās***, p. 52; Bhāṭī, ***Sarvekṣaṇ***, 3:91; ***Jodhpur Rājya kā Itihās***, p. 44; L. P. Tessitori, "A Progress Report on the Work done during the year 1917 in connection with the Bardic and Historical Survey of Rajputana," ***Journal of the Asiatic Society of Bengal***, N. S. 15 (1919), pp. 69-70; Mohansiṃh Kānotā, ***Cāmpāvatoṃ kā Itihās*** (Jāypur: Raṇbāṅkur Prakāśan, 1990-1991), 1:8, 10; Ojhā, 4:1:224-225; Reu, 1:73, 93, 97; ***Vigat***, 1:38, 389-390.

(no. 28) **Rāṇo Akhairājot** (6-1)
(no. 29) **Goind Rāṇ āvat** (7-1)
(no. 30) **Īsardās Rāṇāvat** (7-2)
(no. 31) **Vairsī Rāṇāvat** (7-3)

Rāṇo Akhairājot was a son of Akhairāj Riṇmalot (5-1) and grandson of Rāv Riṇmal Cūṇḍāvat (4-1), ruler of Maṇḍor (ca. 1428-38). Little information is available about Rāṇo and his three sons, Goind, Īsardās, and Vairsī. Rāṇo himself was a military servant of Rāv Mālde Gāṅgāvat of Jodhpur (1532-62). Sources mention him primarily in the company of several of his close paternal relations. These included Jeso Bhairavdāsot (no. 48), Jaito Pañcāiṇot (no. 61), and Kūmpo Mahirājot (no. 95). All of these Rāṭhoṛs were stationed at the garrison of Raṛod[9] ca. 1535 when word came of a battle developing with Meṛtīyo Rāv Vīramde Dūdāvat (no. 105). Rāṇo rode to Reyāṃ village[10] with the contingent from Raṛod to aid Rāv Mālde's Rajpūts there. During the fierce and bloody fighting against the Meṛtīyos that followed, Rāṇo was badly wounded.

Rāṇo took part in an expedition into Mevāṛ ca. 1537. He was included among the contingent of Rāṭhoṛs and other Rajpūts of Rāv Mālde's who went to

---

[9] Raṛod village: located forty-four miles northeast of Jodhpur and six miles west of Āsop.

[10] Reyāṃ village: located forty-nine miles east-southeast of Raṛod and fifteen miles southeast of Meṛto.

the aid of Sīsodīyo Udaisiṅgh Sāṅgāvat (Rāṇo of Mevāṛ, ca. 1437-72; no. 17), then under attack at Kumbhaḷmer by a pretender to the throne of Cītoṛ, Sīsodīyo Vaṇvīr Prithīrājot. Following the defeat of Vaṇvīr forces, Rāṇo participated in Sīsodīyo Udaisiṅgh's accession at the fortress of Kumbhaḷmer where Udaisiṅgh had established his court during his forced exile from Cītoṛ. The Sonagaro Cahuvāṇ ***ṭhākur*** of Pālī village[11] in Mārvāṛ, Akhairāj Riṇdhīrot (no. 9), who was Sīsodīyo Udaisiṅgh's wife's father, had led this campaign into Mevāṛ and presided over Udaisiṅgh's succession.

The texts do not mention Rāṇo Akhairājot with reference to events after this time. The date and circumstances of his death are also unknown. During his life, he held the village of Palṛī [12] in ***paṭo*** from Rāv Mālde. A ***sākh*** of Rāṭhoṛs known as Rāṇāvat later emerged bearing his name.

Rāṇo's three sons, Goind, Īsardās, and Vairsī, were also military servants of Rāv Mālde of Jodhpur. Vairsī Rāṇāvat took part alongside his father in the battle at Reyāṃ village ca. 1535. Then in January of 1544 he was killed at the battle of Samel[13] fighting against Meṛtīyo Rāv Vīramde Dūdāvat and Sher Shāh Sūr.

Vairsī's two brothers, Goind and Īsardās, were both killed during the battle of Meṛto in 1562. They fought there under the command of Rāṭhoṛ Devīdās Jaitāvat (no. 65) against Meṛtīyo Rāv Jaimal Vīramdevot (no. 107) and the Mughal forces of Akbar under Mīrzā Sharafu'd-Dīn Ḥusayn.

"Aitihāsik Bātāṃ," pp. 40, 45, 55; ***Bāṅkīdās***, pp. 16-17; Bhāṭī, ***Sarvekṣaṇ***, 3:91; Gehlot, ***Mārvāṛ***, p. 160; ***Khyāt***, 1:22-23; ***Murārdān***, no. 2, p. 120; ***Vigat***, 1:57, 61, 2:52-53, 65.

(no. 32) **Bhado Pañcāiṇot** (7-4)
(no. 33) **Lakhmaṇ Bhadāvat** (8-1)

Bhado Pañcāiṇot was a grandson of Akhairāj Riṇmalot's (5-2). He was a prominent ***ṭhākur*** of Mārvāṛ during the reign of Rāv Mālde Gāṅgāvat of Jodhpur (1532-62), under whom he served as a military retainer. References in the texts to Bhado associate him primarily with his paternal uncle, Rāṇo Akhairājot (6-1) (no. 28), and two other close paternal relations, Jaito Pañcāiṇot (no. 61) and Kūmpo Mahirājot (no. 95), who were the commanders of Rāv Mālde's armies of Mārvāṛ.

Bhado was stationed at the garrison of Raṛod ca. 1535 with Rāṇo Akhairājot, Jaito Pañcāiṇot and Kūmpo Mahirājot when word came of the battle developing with Meṛtīyo Rāv Vīramde (no. 105) at Reyāṃ village. Bhado rode to Reyāṃ with the contingent from Raṛod, and fought valiantly against Rāv Vīramde's Rajpūts. Rāv Vīramde came before him during the battle, and

[11] Pālī village: located forty miles south-southeast of Jodhpur.

[12] Palṛī village: located eighteen miles south-southeast of Sojhat.

[13] Samel village: located twenty-four miles southwest of Ajmer.

"Aitihāsik Bātāṃ," p. 40, records that Bhado voiced great contempt for him, calling him "black-faced" and a ***rāv*** worth only a ser of grain.

Despite these insulting remarks, Bhado did Rāv Vīramde the honor of striking his body during the fighting at Reyāṃ. *Vigat*, 2:53, also records that Bhado and Rāṭhoṛ Kūmpo Mahirājot were responsible for sparing Meṛtīyo Rāv Vīramde's life when he was badly wounded and the field had fallen to Rāv Mālde's Rajpūts. Rāv Vīramde was allowed to flee Mārvāṛ and seek refuge in parts of eastern Rājasthān.

Later, ca. 1537, Bhado was among the contingent from Mārvāṛ that Sonagaro Akhairāj Riṇdhīrot (no. 9) of Pālī village led to Kumbhaḷmer to help defend Sīsodīyo Udaisiṅgh Sāṅgāvat (no. 17) against a pretender to the throne of Cītoṛ, Sīsodīyo Vaṇvīr Prithīrājot.

Bhāṭī, ***Sarvekṣaṇ***, 3:96, associates Bhado with the village of Dāntīvāṛo.[14] He may have held this village in ***paṭo*** from Rāv Mālde, though the text does not specify. The date and circumstances of his death are also unclear. ***Murārdān***, no. 2, p. 120, records that he was killed at the battle of Samel in January of 1544, fighting against Meṛtīyo Rāv Vīramde and Sher Shāh Sūr. Bhāṭī, ***Sarvekṣaṇ***, 3:96, 113, indicates, however, that sometime after 1535, Ūhaṛ Rāṭhoṛ Bhāṇ Kājāvat (no. 145) organized a plot against Bhado Pañcāiṇot and his brother, Kānho Pañcāiṇot (7-6), and had them poisoned at a feast given by Rāv Mālde. According to this source, Rāv Mālde, who had undoubtedly instigated this intrigue, gave Bhado and Kānho ***bīṛo***s (betel leaves filled with spices, and folded to be eaten) that had been laced with poison at the feast of Dīvāḷī. Bhado set out afterwards for his village of Dāntīvāṛo, but died on the way. Kānho's fate is uncertain. The circumstances leading to the plot and murder are unknown.

In later generations, a Rāṭhoṛ ***sākh*** called Bhadāvat emerged bearing Bhado's name.

Bhado's son, Lakhmaṇ Bhadāvat, was also a military servant of Rāv Mālde of Jodhpur. No information is available about Lakhmaṇ prior to 1557, but in this year he was one of the select warriors whom Rāṭhoṛ Devīdās Jaitāvat (no. 65), the commander of Rāv Mālde's forces, chose to accompany him to Mevāṛ to fight alongside Paṭhāṇ Hājī Khān, a former noble of Sher Shāh Sūr's, at Harmāṛo.[15] This battle was fought against an allied force under Sīsodīyo Rāṇo Udaisiṅgh Sāṅgāvat of Mevāṛ (ca. 1537-72; no. 17).

Lachmaṇ's name does not appear with reference to other local events until the late 1560s, during the rule of Rāv Mālde's son and successor, Rāv Candrasen Māldevot (1562-81). "Aitihāsik Bātāṃ," p. 98, records that Lakhmaṇ held a place of defense (***gūḍho***) near the village of Jojāvar[16] in Goḍhvāṛ. A Mughal force attacked this stronghold on December 25, 1567, destroying the

---

[14] Dāntīvāṛo village: located eighteen miles due east of Jodhpur.

[15] Harmāṛo village: located fifty-five miles south-southwest of Ajmer and six miles south of Vadhnor in northern Mevāṛ.

[16] Jojāvar village: located in the Goḍhvāṛ some twenty-eight miles south-southeast of Sojhat.

small fort there and looting all its goods. Lakhmaṇ and his Rajpūts rode after these raiders and fought a pitched battle with them near the village of Kāṇḍū,[17] during which a number of Mughals were killed. Though Lakhmaṇ's ***gūḍho*** was destroyed, the text says that Lakhmaṇ was deserving of praise, for four elephants "came [to him, i.e., fell into his hands]." Another text records a slightly different version, stating that Lakhmaṇ "cut down" four elephants.[18]

No other information is available about Lakhmaṇ. The circumstances of his death are unknown.

"Aitihāsik Bātāṃ," pp. 40-41, 51, 92, 98; ***Bāṅkīdās***, p. 14; Bhāṭī, ***Sarvekṣaṇ***, 3:95-96, 113; "Jodhpur Hukūmat rī Bahī," pp. 208-210; ***Khyāt***, 1:21, 61, 207; ***Murārdān***, no. 2, p. 120; ***Vigat***, 1:60, 68, 2:52-53, "Pariśiṣṭ - 4: Ḍāvī ne Jīvṇī Mislāṃ rī Vigat," 2:475.

---

[17] Kāṇḍū village: located eight miles northwest of Jojāvar and twenty-three miles due south of Sojhat.

[18] The reference to the attack on Lackmaṇ's ***gūḍho*** appears as a fragment of text set toward the end of a larger section of the "Aitihāsik Bātāṃ" entitled "The Story of the Rule of Mahārājā Sūrajsiṅghjī." This section deals in some detail with events that occurred during the reign of Rājā Sūrajsiṅgh Udaisiṅghot of Jodhpur (1595-1619), but appears to be an amalgam of material, for there is mention of fiscal matters pertaining to the reigns of Rājā Sūrajsiṅgh and his two successors in addition to other fragments placed without seeming order and referencing events as early as 1553-54 during the latter part of Rāv Mālde Gāṅgāvat's reign (1532-62).

The fragment about Lakhmaṇ records that "Ismāyal Kulī" (Ismā'īl Qulī) attacked his stronghold. It has not been possible to identify this Muslim warrior with certainty, or to understand the context for the raid. The territory of eastern Mārvāṛ was being parceled up in this period. Rāv Candrasen's half-brother, Rām Māldevot, had acquired Sojhat in 1564 with Mughal assistance, and Rāv Candrasen's elder uterine brother held Phaḷodhī in northern Mārvāṛ. Rāv Candrasen himself had handed over the fort of Jodhpur to a Mughal force under Ḥusayn Qulī Khān in December of 1565, after a siege of several months. He was in exile from Jodhpur until November of 1570, when he met with and submitted to Akbar at Nāgaur. Lakhmaṇ's ***gūḍho*** was in the area of Sojhat, and the general unrest in this period may have provided opportunity and context for (random ?) Mughal attacks against local strongholds.

This fragment of text lists several Rajpūts by name who fought with Lakhmaṇ near the village of Kāṇḍū. These men included Rāṭhoṛs Sāṃvaḷdās Rāmot (9-1), Sūjo Rāymalot (9-2) and Sādūḷ Rāymalot (9-3), all of whom appear to have been members of Lakhmaṇ's brotherhood, Sāṃvaḷdās being a brother's son, and Sūjo and Sādūḷ related through a collateral line descending from Akhairāj Riṇmalot's son, Nagrāj (6-4) to Rāypāl (7-8) and then Rāymal (8-5). "Jodhpur Hukūmat rī Bahī," pp. 208-210, and Bhāṭī, ***Sarvakṣaṇ***, 3:91-96, provide genealogical information about the Akhairājot Rāṭhoṛs. But these sources unfortunately do not specifically mention the names of the three Rāṭhoṛs who were with Lakhmaṇ. They reference only the fathers' names, Rām Bhadāvat (8-2) and Rāymal Rāypāḷot (8-5).

(no. 34) **Tejsī Urjaṇot** (8-3)

Tejsī Urjaṇot was a great-grantson of Akhairāj Riṇmalot's (5-1). He served under Rāv Mālde Gāṅgāvat of Jodhpur (1532-1562) and was killed in 1562 at the battle of Meṛto. He fought there alongside Rāṭhoṛ Devīdās Jaitāvat (no. 65), Rāv Mālde's commander at the Mālgaḍh. No other information is available about Tejsī from sources at hand.

"Aitihāsik Bātāṃ," p. 55; Bhāṭī, ***Sarvekṣaṇ***, 3:91; "Jodhpur Hukūmat rī Bahī," p. 209; ***Vigat***, 1:61, 2:65.

(no. 35) **Pato Kānhāvat** (8-4)

Pato Kānhāvat was a great-grandson of Akhairāj Riṇmalot's (5-1). His father, Kānho Pañcāiṇot (7-6), had been part of the contingent of Rajpūts from Mārvāṛ under Sonagaro Cahuvāṇ Akhairāj Riṇdhīrot (no. 9), who went to the aid of Sīsodīyo Udaisiṅgh Sāṅgāvat (no. 17) ca. 1537 and helped to seat him on the throne of Mevāṛ at Kumbhaḷmer. It is possible that Pato was with his father at this time. However, texts available record only that Pato was a military servant of Rāv Mālde of Jodhpur, and that he was killed at the battle of Samel (near Ajmer) in January of 1544.

"Aitihāsik Bātāṃ," pp. 43-44; ***Khyāt***, 1:21, 207; ***Vigat***, 1:57.

(no. 36) **Netsī Sīhāvat** (7-7)

Netsī Sīhāvat was a grandson of Akhairāj Riṇmalot's (5-1). He served under Rāv Mālde Gāṅgāvat of Jodhpur (1532-1562), and was killed at the battle of Meṛto in 1562. He fought there alongside Rāv Mālde's commander at the Mālgaḍh, Rāṭhoṛ Devīdās Jaitāvat (no. 65), against Meṛtīyo Rāv Jaimal Vīramdevot (no. 107) and the Mughal forces of Akbar under Mīrzā Sharafu'd-Dīn Ḥusayn.

No other information is available about Netsī from sources at hand.

"Aitihāsik Bātāṃ," p. 56; Bhāṭī, ***Sarvekṣaṇ***, 3:91, 95; ***Vigat***, 1:52, 2:65.

Figure 16. Akhairājot Rāṭhoṛs
(continued on the following page)

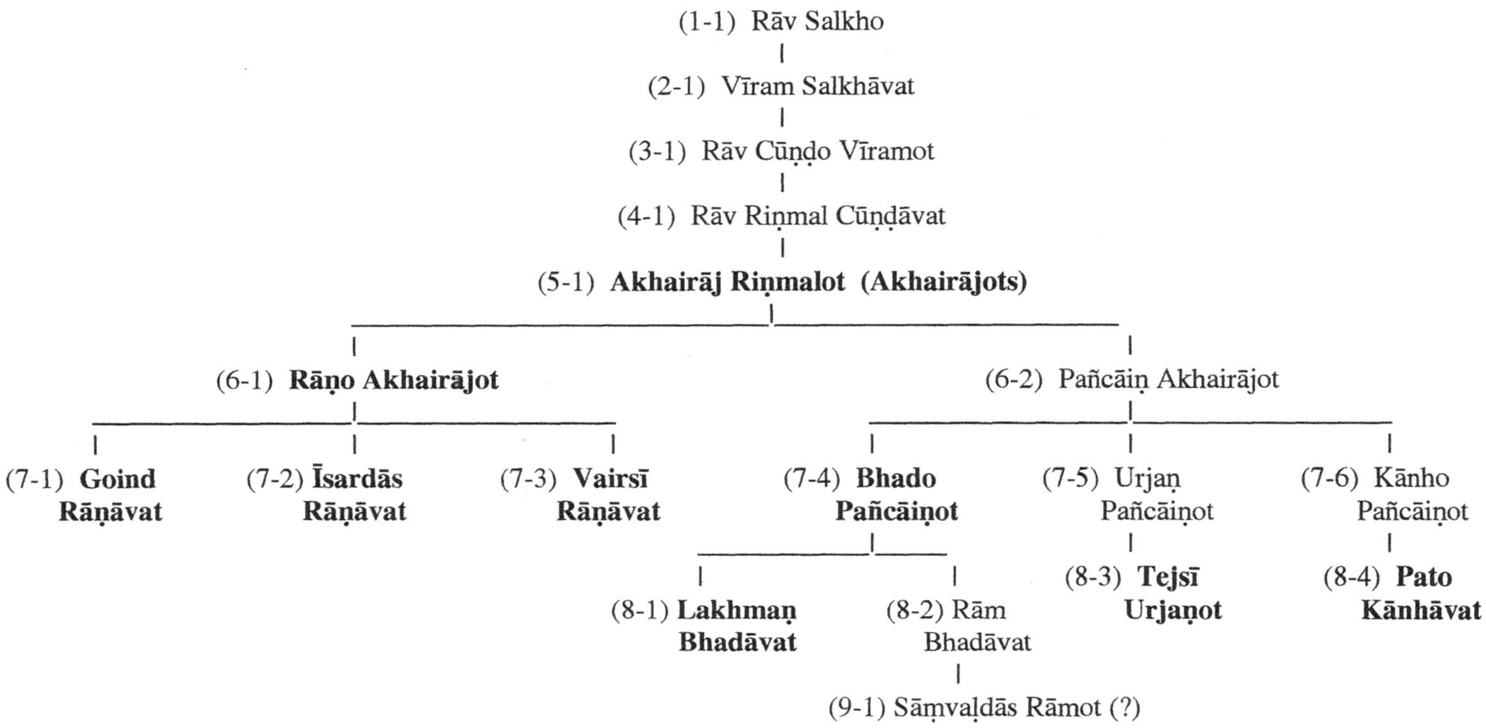

Figure 16. Akhairājot Rāṭhoṛs
(continued from previous page)

(1-1) Rāv Salkho

(2-1) Vīram Salkhāvat

(3-1) Rāv Cūṇḍo Vīramot

(4-1) Rāv Riṇmal Cūṇḍāvat

(5-1) **Akhairāj Riṇmalot (Akhairājots)**

- (6-3) Sīho Akhairājot
  - (7-7) **Netsī Sīhāvat**
- (6-4) Nagrāj Akhairājot
  - (7-8) Rāypāḷ Nagrājot
    - (8-5) Rāymal Rāypāḷot
      - (9-2) Sūjo Rāymalot (?)
      - (9-3) Sādūḷ Rāymalot (?)

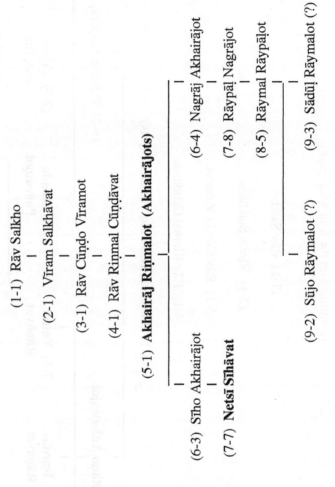

Bālāvat Rāṭhoṛs

(no. 39) **Dhano Bhārmalot** (8-3)
(no. 38) **Nago Bhārmalot** (8-2)
(no. 37) **Vīdo Bhārmalot** (8-1)

The Bālāvat Rāṭhoṛs

The Bālāvat branch (***sākh***) of Mārvāṛ Rāṭhoṛs descends from Bālo Bhākharot (6-1), a grandson of Rāv Riṇmal Cūṇḍāvat (4-1), the ruler of Maṇḍor (ca. 1428-38). Little is known from the chronicles about Bālo's father, Bhākhar Riṇmalot (5-2). He either died or was killed prior to 1459, for when Rāv Jodho Riṇmalot (ca. 1453-89) divided the lands of Mārvāṛ among his brothers and sons following his founding of Jodhpur in this year, Rāv Jodho gave his brother Bhākhar's son, Bālo, three villages as Bhākhar's share of lands. These villages were:

1. Khāṛṛī: located twenty-two miles due southeast of Jodhpur,
2. Kharlo: located twenty-five miles south-southeast of Khāṛṛī,
3. Sāhlī: located twenty miles south-southwest of Kharlo.

Vigat, 1:38, records the names of these villages, but does not include any explanation for Rāv Jodho's choice of them. It is possible that they afforded access to or control over an important route across central-eastern Mārvāṛ. The villages lie in a line extending to the south from Jodhpur.

No further information is available about the Bālāvat family until the time of Bālo's grandsons, Vīdo (8-1), Nago (8-2), and Dhano Bhārmalot (8-3). These three sons of Bhārmal Bālāvat's (7-1) were all military servants of Rāv Mālde Gāṅgāvat of Jodhpur (1532-62). They held positions of varying importance in Mārvāṛ and were all killed within a short time of each other in major military engagements involving the Meṛtīyo Rāṭhoṛs.

> ***Bāṅkīdās***, p. 57; Gehlot, ***Mārvāṛ***, p. 160; "Jodhpur Hukūmat rī Bahī," pp. 133-136; ***Vigat***, 1:38, "Pariśiṣṭ - 4: Ḍāvī ne Jīvṇī Mislāṃ rī Vigat," 2:476.

(no. 37) **Vīdo Bhārmalot** (8-1)

Vīdo Bhārmalot's name is associated with events that occurred earlier in the reign of Rāv Mālde of Jodhpur than his two brothers, Nago and Dhano. Vīdo was among a number of important Rāṭhoṛs and other Rajpūts whom Rāv Mālde posted at the garrison of Raṛod[1] ca. 1535 under the command of Rāṭhoṛs Jaito Pañcāiṇot (no. 61) and Kūmpo Mahirājot (no. 95). Vīdo rode with the Rajpūts from this garrison to participate in the battle that developed at Reyāṃ village[2] with Meṛtīyo Rāv Vīramde Dūdāvat (no. 105). Rāv Vīramde's forces suffered a severe defeat at this battle, and afterwards Rāv Vīramde was forced to quit Mārvāṛ and relinquish Ajmer, which he and his Meṛtīyos had only recently occupied.

A few years later in 1538-39 the Bīhārī Paṭhāṇ ruler of Jāḷor,[3] Sikandar Khān, sent an appeal to Rāv Mālde for aid against the Baloc who had driven him from his capitol. The Rāv responded by sending Vīdo Bhārmalot with an army against Jāḷor. ***Vigat***, 1:43-44, and "Aitihāsik Bātāṃ," p. 41, record that Vīdo and his Rajpūts captured Jāḷor fort from the Baloc, but details are lacking about the course of events and the length of time they remained in occupation.

Two years later in 1540-41 Vīdo participated in an unsuccessful attack on Kumbhaḷmer, the Sīsodīyo fortress that guarded the western passes through the Arāvallī hills into Mevāṛ. Rāv Mālde launched this expedition while he was placing garrisons throughout Goḍhvāṛ and sending raiding parties into Mevāṛ in an attempt to humiliate Sīsodīyo Rāṇo Udaisiṅgh Sāṅgāvat (ca. 1537-72; no. 17) for marrying a sister of his wife, Jhālī Sarūpdejī. The Jhālos had originally promised this daughter to Rāv Mālde, albeit under duress.[4]

In January of 1544 Vīdo was among Rāv Mālde's leading warriors who assembled before Samel village[5] to do battle against the combined forces of Meṛtīyo Rāv Vīramde and Sher Shāh Sūr. The ***Khyāt*** of Naiṇsī, 3:99-100, speaks of the great esteem in which Vīdo Bhārmalot was held as a warrior, equating his prowess and strength with that of three of Sher Shāh's Paṭhāṇ warriors. There had been discussion in Sher Shāh's ***darbār*** prior to the battle about the best means to settle the dispute. A noble of Sher Shāh's had suggested single-handed combat between one of Sher Shāh's Paṭhāṇs and one of Rāv Mālde's Rajpūts. Meṛtīyo Rāv Vīramde is said to have responded that Vīdo Bhārmalot would be sent from Rāv Mālde's side, and if he were to fight, he could easily defeat three of Sher Shāh's Paṭhāṇs in single-handed combat, take their weapons, and return to his side unharmed (see **translated texts** for details of this discussion).

Vīdo Bhārmalot was killed during the battle at Samel.

---

[1] Raṛod village: located forty-four miles northeast of Jodhpur and six miles west of Āsop.

[2] Reyāṃ village: located fifteen miles southeast of Meṛto and forty-nine miles east-southeast from Raṛod.

[3] Jāḷor: located sixty-eight miles south-southwest of Jodhpur in southern Mārvāṛ.

[4] For details about this marriage and the disruption is caused, see ***infra***, Nago Bhārmalot (no. 38), and ***supra***, Bālīso Cahuvāṇ Sūjo Sāṃvatot (no. 4).

[5] Samel village: located twenty-four miles southwest of Ajmer.

"Aitihāsik Bātāṃ," pp. 41-42, 45; ***Khyāt***, 3:95, 99-100; ***Murārdān***, no. 2, pp. 118, 120; Ojhā, 4:1:288, 291, 306-307, n. 2; ***Vigat***, 1:43-44, 48, 57, 2:57.

(no. 38) **Nago Bhārmalot** (8-2)

Vigat, 1:49, states that Nago and his brothers, Dhano (8-3) and Vīñjo (8-4), were great warriors of Rāv Mālde of Jodhpur. There is no information about specific lands that Nago and the Bālāvats held in ***paṭo*** from the Rāv. But these may have included the villages Rāv Jodho Riṇmalot (ca. 1453-89) originally gave to his brother's son, Bālo Bhākharot (6-1), following the founding of Jodhpur in 1459 (see ***supra***).

Nago Bhārmalot is first mentioned in the chronicles as part of an expedition Rāv Mālde of Jodhpur sent against Bālīso Cahuvāṇ Sūjo Sāṃvatot (no. 4) at Nāḍūl[6] in 1540-41. The Rāv launched this expedition to punish and humiliate Bālīso Sūjo. Sūjo had been a military servant of his holding the village of Khairvo[7] in ***paṭo***, but had quit Mārvāṛ in anger. While leaving, he had allowed his Rajpūts to loot several Cāmpāvat Rāṭhoṛ villages in the vicinity of Khairvo and kill a number of Cāmpāvats. Bālīso Sūjo had then gone to Mevāṛ and taken service under Sīsodīyo Rāṇo Udaisiṅgh Sāṅgāvat (ca. 1537-72; no. 17).

Bālīso Sūjo reappeared soon after in Mārvāṛ as a servant of the Rāṇo's, having been given the ***paṭo*** of Nāḍūl and surrounding villages for his maintenance. ***Vigat***, 1:49, records that Rāv Mālde became very distressed upon learning of Bālīso Sūjo's return. He immediately summoned Nago Bhārmalot to Jodhpur and ordered him to attack Nāḍūl and killed Bālīso Sūjo by any possible means. Nago send word to his Rajpūts, Rāṭhoṛ Dāso Pātaḷot, Ūhaṛ Rāṭhoṛ Jaimal and others, ordering them to assemble with all due haste. He gathered a force of some 500 horsemen and a number of footmen, and set out for Nāḍūl.

The Bālāvats and their men rode by stealth to within a short distance of Nāḍūl, then sent 20-25 riders before the gates of the town as a ruse. They instructed these riders to cause a disturbance by breaking the pots of the women drawing water at the wells, and by stealing the herds. They thought that the Bālīsos would pursue these men and allow the main force of the Bālāvats to fall upon and kill them by surprise. The ruse failed, however, for Bālīso Sūjo quickly suspected a trick. He prevented his brothers and sons from riding in pursuit of the party and instead, gathered a large force from the surrounding villages. With some 2,000 men consisting primarily of his close relations by blood and marriage, he rode out to confront the Bālāvats. He drew near to them some ten ***kos*** from Nāḍūl.

During the battle which followed, Bālīso Sūjo and his Rajpūts defeated the Bālāvat force with great loss. Some 140 of the Bālāvats were killed, among

---

[6] Nāḍūl: located sixty-seven miles south-southeast of Jodhpur.

[7] Khairvo village: located fifty miles south-southeast of Jodhpur.

them Vīñjo Bhārmalot.[8] Nago himself was badly wounded and his horse slain. The field fell to Bālīso Sūjo as Nago Bhārmalot, Dāso Pātaḷot, Uhaṛ Jaimal and the remaining force of Bālāvats fled. They finally halted before the village of Ḍehaṛo.[9] *Vigat*, 1:50-51, states that Nago sat on the ground there, apparently in wait for the Bālīsos. One of his Rajpūts approached him with concern, saying:

> You [must] go away! Why give the enemies any chance [to kill you]? One [thing is that] Vīñjo . . . [has] already died in battle, and if you also die, then the ***ṭhākurāī*** of the Bālāvats will diminish.

Nago was very obstinate, refusing to listen to the Rajpūt. He replied:

> Vīñjo having been killed, where would I go? And my horse died in battle. I cannot mount a horse [in my condition].

The Rajpūt then left to catch Vīñjo's horse, which had been wounded. He brought it and gave it to Nago, helping him to mount.

The Bālīsos arrived at the village just as Nago turned to ride off with the other Bālāvats. Several of Bālīso Sūjo's men saw Nago and wanted to ride after and kill him. Sūjo tried to stop them, saying:

> There is no deep-seated hostility (***vair***) between us and them; do not follow after Nago. [He] is not such a Rajpūt that he would run away, but [his] military servants [and his] brotherhood persuaded him [and] forcefully took him away. He is an exceptional warrior (***baṛī balāy***); you should not speak his name.

Despite Sūjo's words, five or six horsemen rode after Nago. When Nago saw them coming, he stopped to confront them. He threw his spear at one man, striking him with such force that the spear passed out of the man's back and into the hindquarters of the man's horse, striking its testicles. Nago then gave a great shout as he pulled his lance free from the horse and rider. It is said that when he shouted, two other of the Bālīsos became senseless and did not speak for six months thereafter out of fear. Having silenced his pursuers, Nago joined Dāso Pātaḷot and Ūhaṛ Jaimal to proceed home in defeat.

Rāv Mālde sent no further armies against Nāḍūl, and the Bālāvats exacted no revenge that is recorded for their humiliation at Bālīso Sūjo's hands.

Nago's activities over the next five years are uncertain. His name does not appear in the chronicles with relation to any events of this period, including the battle of Samel in January of 1544, at which Rāv Mālde's Rajpūts suffered a humiliating defeat at the hands of the combined forces of Meṛtīyo Rāv Vīramde

---

[8] ***Vigat***, 1:50, records that Dhano Bhārmalot also died in battle here, but other sources indicate that he died in battle later, which appears to be correct.

[9] Ḍehaṛo village: located tweleve miles east-northeast of Nāḍūl.

Dūdāvat and Sher Shāh Sūr. Nago was undoubtedly recovering from his wounds during this time, but how extensive these were and how debilitating is again not known. In all probability, Nago was with Rāv Mālde in the period before the battle of Samel, withdrawing with him just prior to the main engagement and returning to Jodhpur.

"Aitihāsik Bātāṃ," p. 40, includes Nago among the renowned (***nāṃvjādik***) warriors that Rāv Mālde sent against the Muslim outpost at Bhāṅgesar village[10] in 1545, shortly after Sher Shāh's death. This attacked marked the start of the Rāv's campaign to reassert his authority in Mārvāṛ following his defeat at Samel. Nago was again wounded during the fighting at Bhāṅgesar.

Nago then appears among the warriors Rāv Mālde led against Meṛtīyo Rāv Jaimal Vīramdevot (no. 107) at Meṛto in 1554. "Aitihāsik Bātāṃ," p. 48, states that Nago Bhārmalot and other of the Rāv's Rajpūts counseled against this attack. Their counsel was to no avail, however. The Rāv met in ***darbār*** with the Jaitmālot Rāṭhoṛ ***pradhān***s of Rāv Jaimal, Akhairāj Bhādāvat (no. 69) and Cāndrāj Jodhāvat (no. 74), prior to the main engagement on April 4, 1554. Nago Bhārmalot and Rāṭhoṛ Prithīrāj Jaitāvat (no. 63) sat alongside the Rāv during this meeting as his leading military servants and advisors. The ***pradhān***s had come seeking a means of accommodation with Rāv Mālde. They offered the promise of military service in return for the grant of Meṛto in ***paṭo*** to Rāv Jaimal. Rāv Mālde would not agree to this request, however. He offered another ***paṭo*** in Meṛto's place, unable to countenance Meṛtīyo rule over Meṛto. The ***pradhān***s then challenged the Rāv's authority to take possession of Meṛto at all, saying that the Meṛtīyos had equal rights, that he who had given the Rāv Jodhpur, had given Meṛto to the Meṛtīyos. Rāv Mālde's posture remained unbending, and the talks ended in mutual recrimination and insult, with the ***pradhān***s leaving Rāv Mālde's ***darbār*** in anger and returning to Meṛto without accommodation (see ***Khyāt***, 3:117-118, of the **translated text** for details of this meeting).

Rāv Mālde's forces were disorganized the following day and unprepared for the stout resistance they encountered from Rāv Jaimal and the Meṛtīyos. Nago Bhārmalot rode alongside Rāv Mālde, and for part of the fighting occupied a position near Meṛto's Jodhpur Gate. Both Nago and his brother, Dhano, were killed on this day, and by the end of the fighting, Rāv Mālde's force had been driven from the field in defeat.

> "Aitihāsik Bātāṃ," pp. 40, 48-49; ***Bāṅkīdās***, pp. 13, 57; ***Khyāt***, 3:117-121, 121; ***Murārdān***, no. 2, p. 129; ***Vigat***, 1:48-51, 65, 2:59.

(no. 39) **Dhano Bhārmalot** (8-3)

The chronicles mention Dhano Bhārmalot less frequently than his two brothers, Vīdo (8-1) and Nago (8-2). His name appears only twice. He was

---

[10] Bhāṅgesar village: located sixteen miles west of Sojhat in eastern Mārvāṛ.

among the Bālāvats who proceeded against Bālīso Cahuvāṇ Sūjo Sāṃvatot (no. 4) at Nāḍūl in 1540-41, where he was probably wounded, and he is listed among those killed at the battle of Meṛto on April 4, 1554. But there is disagreement among sources regarding the place and date of Dhano's death. ***Vigat***, 1:50, records that Dhano was killed during the fighting against the Bālīso Cahuvāṇs near Nāḍūl in 1540-41. Other sources including "Aitihāsik Bātāṃ," p. 49, ***Bāṅkīdās***, p. 13, and ***Vigat***, 1:59, 2:59, all list Dhano among those killed at Meṛto on March 20, 1554. He was probably only wounded at the fighting near Nāḍūl, as was his brother, Nago.

> "Aitihāsik Bātāṃ," p. 49; ***Bāṅkīdās***, p. 13; ***Murārdān***, no. 2, p. 130; ***Vigat***, 1:49-52, 59, 2:59.

Avenging the Bālāvat Defeat at Nāḍūl

Neither the Bālāvats nor Rāv Mālde of Jodhpur exacted any revenge for the humiliating defeat the Bālāvats suffered at the hands of Bālīso Cahuvāṇ Sūjo Sāṃvatot (no. 4) near Nāḍūl in 1540-41, or for Vīñjo Bhārmalot's (8-4) death during the fighting there. These were not avenged for seventeen years. Vīdo Bhārmalot (8-1) was killed four years later at Samel in 1544, and his two brothers, Nago (8-2) and Dhano (8-3), both died ten years later at Meṛto in 1554. There were apparently no opportunities in the interim to exact this revenge. It was left for Rāṭhoṛ Devīdās Jaitāvat (no. 65) to end the hostility (***vair***). Devīdās accomplished this feat at the battle of Harmāṛo[11] in January of 1557. During the fighting there between the combined armies of Rāv Mālde of Jodhpur and Paṭhāṇ Hājī Khān, and an allied force under Sīsodīyo Rāṇo Udaisiṅgh Sāṅgāvat of Cītoṛ, Devīdās challenged Bālīso Sūjo to single-handed combat. He killed him there with his spear.

> ***Vigat***, 1:52.

---

[11] Harmāṛo village: located fifty-five miles south-southwest of Ajmer and six miles south of Vadhnor in northern Mevāṛ.

Figure 17. Bālāvat Rāṭhoṛs

(1-1) Rāv Salkho
|
(2-1) Vīram Salkhāvat
|
(3-1) Rāv Cūṇḍo Vīramot
|
(4-1) Rāv Riṇmal Cūṇḍāvat
|
- (5-1) Rāv Jodho Riṇmalot
- (5-2) Bhākhar Riṇmalot
  - (6-1) Bālo Bhākharot (**Bālāvats**)
    - (7-1) Bhārmal Bālāvat
      - (8-1) **Vīdo Bhārmalot**
      - (8-2) **Nago Bhārmalot**
      - (8-3) **Dhano Bhārmalot**
      - (8-4) Vīñjo Bhārmalot

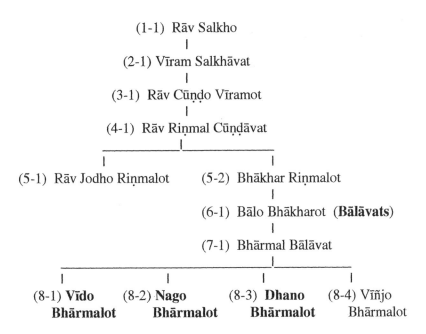

Bhārmalot Rāṭhoṛs

(no. 40) **Prithīrāj Baḷūvot** (11-1)

The Bhārmalot Rāṭhoṛs

The Bhārmalot Rāṭhoṛs descend from Bhārmal Jodhāvat (6-1), a son of Rāv Jodho Riṇmalot (5-1), ruler of Maṇḍor and Jodhpur (ca. 1453-89). Bhārmal was born of Rāṇī Hulṇī Jamnādejī (or Jāṇāndejī), a daughter of Hul Gahlot Vaṇvīr Bhojāvat.[1] During Rāv Jodho's division of the lands of Mārvāṛ among his brothers and sons following the founding of Jodhpur in 1459, the Rāv granted Bhārmal and his elder uterine brother, Jogo (6-2), the village of Koḍhṇo[2] and its surrounding lands in western Mārvāṛ.

The lands of Koḍhṇo were then under the control of the Ūhaṛ Rāṭhoṛs. Bhārmal and Jogo proceeded to take those lands from the Ūhaṛs and settle themselves at Koḍhṇo proper in the early 1460s. They remained there together for some years. Jogo Jodhāvat then left upon Rāv Jodho's death in 1489 and returned to Jodhpur, while Bhārmal remained at Koḍhṇo and established his line there. ***Murārdān***, no. 2, p. 97, records that Bhārmal had a fort constructed at Koḍhṇo. He also eventually left, however, moving his residence to the village of Bīlāṛo[3] in eastern Mārvāṛ, where he spent the remainder of his days. The texts give no date for this resettlement nor the context under which it occurred, but it would have taken place toward the end of the fifteenth or during the early sixteenth century.

Members of this group of Rāṭhoṛs display rather tenuous ties to the house of Jodhpur. The cause of this appears related to dealings over land that began during the first generation after Bhārmal Jodhāvat.

Jaisiṅghde Bhārmalot (7-1) succeeded his father, Bhārmal Jodhāvat, to rule at Koḍhṇo village. This succession probably took place when Bhārmal moved from Koḍhṇo to Bīlāṛo. ***Murārdān***, no. 2, p. 403, records that while Jaisiṅghde was master of Koḍhṇo, he was unable to protect his lands and maintain control in the face of Bhāṭī raids from Jaisaḷmer. These raids became serious enough to draw the attention of Rāv Gāṅgo Vāghāvat of Jodhpur (1515-32). To deal with the problem, the Rāv began summoning Ūhaṛ Rāṭhoṛs from Mahevo in southwestern Mārvāṛ, where they had gone after losing their lands to Bhārmal and Jogo Jodhāvat in the mid-fifteenth century, and parceling out the lands of Koḍhṇo among them. ***Murārdān*** (*ibid.*) notes, for example, that Rāv

---

[1] See ***supra***, **Marriage and Family Lists of the Rulers of Jodhpur**, Jodho Riṇmalot, Rāṇī no. 5.

[2] Koḍhṇo village: located twenty-eight miles west-southwest of Jodhpur.

[3] Bīlāṛo village: located forty-one miles east-southeast of Jodhpur.

Gāṅgo gave the village of Rājvo[4] and twelve others to the Ūhaṛ Mokaḷ Kharhathot. The Ūhaṛs were able to stop the Bhāṭī raids into this area, and thereby regained their former position of control. Koḍhṇo was lost to the Bhārmalots from this time forward.

The texts give no further information about Jaisiṅghde Bhārmalot or indicate what happened to him or his family when they lost Koḍhṇo. Little is known about his son, Jaitmāl Jaisiṅghdevot (8-1). ***Murārdān***, no. 2, pp. 410-411, records only that Jaitmāl and a brother named Rām Jaisiṅghdevot (8-2) were both killed on order from Rāv Mālde Gāṅgāvat of Jodhpur (1532-62). A number of years earlier in November of 1529 these same brothers had supported Rāṭhoṛ Sekho Sūjāvat (no. 86) at the battle of Sevakī village,[5] when Sekho Sūjāvat and his ally from Nāgaur, Khānzāda Khān Daulat Khān (no. 154), had challenged Rāv Mālde's father, Rāv Gāṅgo Vāghāvat (1515-32), over the rulership of Mārvāṛ. Sekho Sūjāvat's forces were badly defeated at Sevakī and Sekho himself killed. It appears that Jaitmāl Jaisiṅghdevot and his brother, Rām, had joined with Sekho Sūjāvat against the house of Jodhpur because of their enmity toward Rāv Gāṅgo, who had taken Bhārmalot lands and given them to the Ūhaṛ Rāṭhoṛs. They gained the ire of Rāv Gāṅgo's son, Kuṃvar Mālde, who had them murdered after he succeeded to the Jodhpur throne in 1532.

No further information is available about members of this family until the time of Baḷū Tejsīyot (10-1) some fifty years later. Baḷū first appears in the texts as a military servant of Moṭo Rājā Udaisiṅgh Māldevot of Jodhpur (1583-95), from whom he received the village of Bheṭnaṛo[6] in ***paṭo*** in 1584-85. ***Murārdān***, no. 2, p. 404, states the he revolted from the Moṭo Rājā in 1592-93 while at Lahore, and fled to Rājasthān, where he took service under Bīkāvat Rāṭhoṛ Rājā Rāysiṅgh Kalyāṇmalot of Bīkāner (1574-1612). Baḷū then returned to Mārvāṛ in 1595 upon the death of the Moṭo Rājā and offered his service to the Moṭo Rājā's successor, Rājā Sūrajsiṅgh Udaisiṅghot (1595-1619). The Rājā accepted Baḷū's offer and granted him the ***paṭo*** of Āū (Āūvo) village.[7] Baḷū again revolted in 1598-99, this time from Ahmadabad in Gujarat while on tour with the Rājā, and he fled to Mevāṛ, where he offered his services to Sīsodīyo Rāṇo Amarsiṅgh Pratāpsiṅghot (1597-1620). He was killed some years thereafter along the border of northern Mevāṛ during an outbreak of hostilities with the Soḷaṅkī Rajpūts.

Bāṅkīdās, p. 8; ***Khyāt***, 3:31; ***Murārdān***, no. 2, pp. 97-98, 403-404, 410-411, 422-423; ***Vigat***, 1:39.

---

[4] Rājvo village: located fifteen miles northeast of Koḍhṇo and fourteen miles west of Jodhpur.

[5] Sevakī village: located twenty-three miles northeast of Jodhpur.

[6] Bheṭnaṛo village: located twenty-three miles southeast of Jodhpur.

[7] Āū village: located twenty-one miles south of Sojhat in eastern Mārvāṛ.

(no. 40) **Prithīrāj Baḷūvot** (11-1)

Baḷū Tejsīyot's son, Prithīrāj Baḷūvot, had a career of military service similar to that of his father's in its erratic movements among different kingdoms and territories. Unlike his father, however, Prithīrāj eventually took service under the Mughals, and he became a loyal supporter of Prince Khurram (Shāh Jahān) with whom he remained for much of the remainder of his life.

Prithīrāj began performing military service in Mevāṛ while his father was still living. After his father's death, he left Mevāṛ and came to Mārvāṛ, where he took service under Jodhpur Rājā Sūrajsiṅgh Udaisiṅghot (1595-1619). Prithīrāj received his first village in ***paṭo*** from the Rājā in 1609-10. This was Khārlo village.[8] Shortly thereafter, he appears to have returned to Mevāṛ, for ***Murārdān***, no. 2, p. 405, records that in 1614-15 he revolted from Udaipur where he had killed a Dahīyo Rajpūt named Mohaṇdās, and returned to Mārvāṛ. Rājā Sūrajsiṅgh re-instated Prithīrāj with his former ***paṭo*** of Khārlo village in 1615-16.

Prithīrāj again left Mārvāṛ after only four months, however, this time for Ajmer where he took service under Prince Khurram. Emperor Jahāṅgīr (1605-1627) had appointed Prince Khurram ***sūbedār*** of Ajmer during the period of increased Mughal operations against the Sīsodīyos of Mevāṛ between 1613-1615. With the effective reduction of Sīsodīyo opposition by the end of 1615, Prince Khurram moved on to the Deccan, and Prithīrāj followed him there.

Prithīrāj appears to have remained in Khurram's service between the years 1616-1624. However, ***Vigat***, 2:74, records that Prithīrāj received the village of Reyāṃ[9] in ***jāgīr*** from Khurram's brother, Prince Parvīz, in 1623. Prince Parvīz was ***sūbedār*** of Ajmer at this time, having been appointed to this position by Emperor Jahāṅgīr upon the revolt of Khurram from the Deccan. Emperor Jahāṅgīr also transferred Meṛto Pargano from the house of Jodhpur when Rājā Sūrajsiṅgh Udaisiṅghot died in 1619, placing it first under Prince Khurram and then under Prince Parvīz. It was not until August of 1623 that the new Jodhpur ruler, Rājā Gajsiṅgh Sūrajsiṅghot (1619-38), regained authority over the area (see ***Vigat***, 2:73-75, of the **translated text** for details).

That Prithīrāj ever joined Prince Parvīz's service seems doubtful from what is known of later events of his life. It seems equally doubtful that he ever took possession of Reyāṃ village. Prince Parvīz may simply have awarded this ***jāgīr*** to Prithīrāj in an attempt to win his support away from his brother, Khurram.

Prithīrāj's continuing support for Khurram in this period is born out by a passage from ***Murārdān***, no. 2, p. 407, which states:

---

[8] Khārlo village: located thirty-two miles south-southeast of Jodhpur and nine miles southeast of Rohaṭh.

[9] Reyāṃ village: located fifteen miles southeast of Meṛto.

> In V.S. 1680 [1623-24], Prince [Khurram] stayed in the village of Kuḍaṇo[10] which Śrījī [Rājā Gajsiṅgh] had given to Prithīrāj for his ***vasī***.

A brother of Prithīrāj's named Mohaṇdās (11-2) was living in the village of Kuḍaṇo at this time. Prince Khurram's sojourn in the village probably occurred in early 1623 just prior to Khurram's flight from Rājasthān. Prithīrāj followed Khurram to eastern and northern India, and fought with him at the battle of Damdama on the confluence of the Tons and Ganges Rivers in October of 1624. He was wounded there when Imperial troops under Prince Parvīz and Mahābat Khān defeated Khurram in his bid for control of the empire.

Rājā Gajsiṅgh of Jodhpur, who was present at Damdama with the Imperial troops, took Prithīrāj from the field and cared for him following the battle. When Prithīrāj recovered from his wounds, the Rājā retained him and gave him Gūndoc[11] and several other villages in ***paṭo***. Then in early 1628, upon Khurram's succession to the Mughal throne as Shāh Jahān, Prithīrāj once again left Mārvāṛ and proceeded to north India along with a brother named Rāmsiṅgh (11-3). He remained in north India for the remainder of his life. ***Murārdān***, no. 2, p. 406, notes that "The Pātsāh gave him a ***mansab***." Few details are available from local chronicles about Prithīrāj's life while he served under Shāh Jahān. They record only that the people of his ***vasī*** remained behind in Mārvāṛ, living in the village of Jāvlī.[12]

Maāthir-ul-Umarā, 2:1:481-483, however, does present information about a "Prithīrāj Rāthor." This sources does not indicate who Prithīrāj's father was, but it does give the names of a brother, Rāmsiṅgh, and a son, Kesarīsiṅgh. In its genealogy of the Bhārmalot Rāṭhoṛs, ***Murārdān***, no. 2, pp. 404, 408, does not list any of Prithīrāj's sons, but it does record the name of Prithīrāj's brother, Rāmsiṅgh. We can, therefore, identify this "Prithīrāj" with some certainty as Prithīrāj Balūvot.

According to ***Maāthir-ul-Umarā***, Prithīrāj was one of Prince Khurram's household troopers or bodyguards, entrusted with the safety of the royal person. He was always in attendance during Khurram's rebellion, and "had thus assumed a position of reliance and trust." Khurram granted him the rank of 1,500 ***zāt***, 600 ***suwār*** following his succession to the Mughal throne as Shāh Jahān in February of 1628. Local sources confirm that Prithīrāj left Mārvāṛ when Khurram became Emperor in order to enter Mughal service. ***Maāthir-ul-Umarā*** records further that:

> In the 2nd year [A. D. 1629], [Prithīrāj] in company with Khwāja Abūl Ḥasan Turbatī was deputed to pursue Khān Jahān Lodī who had fled from Akbarābād (Āgra). Out of his zeal he

[10] Kuḍaṇo village: located seven miles west of Gūndoc village and some thirteen miles to the south of Pālī.

[11] Gūndoc village: located fifty miles south-southeast of Jodhpur.

[12] Jāvlī village: located ten miles north of Meṛto, near Rāhaṇ.

did not wait for others, but went off with a few officers, who all excelled in this noble quality, and overtook him near Dholpūr. During the fight, he, following the Rajpūt tradition, dismounted, and engaged in a single combat with Khān Jahān who was on horseback. He wounded him with a spear, and himself received wounds. The Emperor graciously summoned him to the Presence, and raised his rank to 2,000 with 800 horse, and presented him with a horse and an elephant.

Prithīrāj progressed steadily in rank as he continued to serve in varying military capacities under Shāh Jahān. When Mahābat Khān became Viceroy of the Deccan (1632-33), he was appointed one of his officers and was promoted to the rank of 2,000/1,500. During the siege of Daulatabad, he again fought in single-handed combat with a Deccani horseman who challenged him. He "left the ranks [of the other troopers], and finished [the Deccani] in a sword duel."

In 1644-45 Prithīrāj was made ***kiledār*** of the fort of Daulatabad. A year later, he was promoted to the rank of 2,000/2,000, and shortly thereafter, recalled to Agra and placed in charge of the fort there along with Bāqī Khān. In following years, he served under Prince Aurangzeb and then Prince Dārā Shikoh in northern India at Qandahar, and then under Prince Aurangzeb once again, this time in the Deccan.

Prithīrāj died in 1656. He ***mansab*** rank remained at 2,000 ***zāt***, 2,000 ***suwār***. He would have been over seventy years of age at this time. ***Maāthir-ul-Umarā*** records that his brother, Rāmsiṅgh, and his son, Kesarīsiṅgh, had also received small ***mansab***s.

"Aitihāsik Bātaṃ," p. 94; Athar Ali, ***Apparatus***, pp. 101, 107, 119, 126, 134, 140, 145, 192, 199, 205, 209, 214, 303; ***Bāṅkīdās***, p. 26; "Jodhpur Hukūmat rī Bahī," p. 207; ***Murārdān***, no. 2, pp. 220, 403-411; ***Maāthir-ul-Umarā***, 2:1:481-483; ***Vigat***, 1:111, 272, 2:74.

Figure 18. Bhāramlot Rāṭhoṛs

(1-1) Rāv Salkho
- (2-1) Vīram Salkhāvat
  - (3-1) Rāv Cūṇḍo Vīramot
    - (4-1) Rāv Riṇmal Cūṇḍāvat
      - (5-1) Rāv Jodho Riṇmalot
        - (6-1) Bhārmal Jodhāvat (**Bhārmalots**)
          - (7-1) Jaisiṅghde Bhārmalot
            - (8-1) Jaitmāl Jaisiṅghdevot
              - (9-1) Tejsī Jaitmālot
                - (10-1) Baḷū Tejsīyot
                  - (11-1) **Prithīrāj Baḷūvot**
                  - (11-2) Mohaṇdās Baḷūvot
                  - (11-3) Rāmsiṅgh Baḷūvot
            - (8-2) Rām Jaisiṅghdevot
        - (6-2) Jogo Jodhāvat

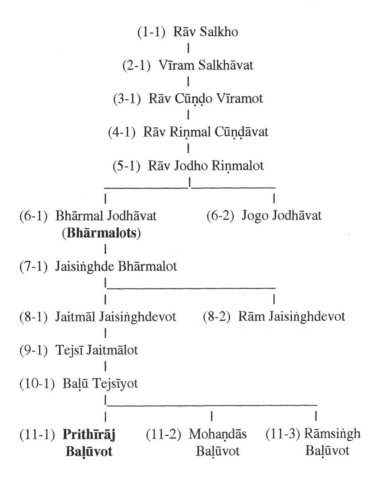

Bhīṃvot Rāṭhoṛs

(no. 41) **Varjāṅg Bhīṃvot, Rāv** (5-2)

Varjāṅg Bhīṃvot is an interesting though enigmatic figure in the Rāṭhoṛ chronicles. These chronicles refer to him by the title of ***rāv*** and speak of him as a powerful and influential ***ṭhākur*** and a great warrior who, along with his brothers, Vairsal (5-3) and Vījo (5-4), became "a pillar of Mārvāṛ." Stories about his life span the reigns of several Rāṭhoṛ rulers of Maṇḍor and Jodhpur from the time of Rāv Riṇmal Cūṇḍāvat (ca. 1428-38) (4-1) to the early years of Rāv Sūjo Jodhāvat (ca. 1492-1515) (6-2), when Varjāṅg would have been an elderly Rajpūt in his late seventies or early eighties. Some of the stories about him have gained with the telling but reflect the honor of one who was seen to have been "victorious in countless battles" and was praised as a protector who was the equal of 100,000 protectors. While a pillar of Mārvāṛ, Varjāṅg also had another side, for the chronicles portray him as a ***ṭhākur*** who looked to his own self-interest and who was not above extorting favors from the house of Jodhpur. He also stirred trouble among Rāv Jodho Riṇmalot's sons over issues of precedence and rights to rulership.

Varjāṅg first appears in the chronicles alongside his father, Bhīṃv Cūṇḍāvat (4-2). He would have been a young man in his late teens at this time. They were together at Cītoṛ with Bhīṃv Cūṇḍāvat's brother, Rāv Riṇmal. Bhīṃv was serving under his brother and had accompanied him to Mevāṛ. The Rāv spent much of the latter part of his reign in the company of his sister's grandson, Sīsodīyo Rāṇo Kūmbho Mokaḷot (ca. 1433-68), whose protector he had become.[1]

The Sīsodīyos under Rāṇo Kūmbho deceived and killed Rāv Riṇmal one night ca. 1438 in order to free Mevāṛ from Rāṭhoṛ influence and control. Immediately following the murder, the Sīsodīyos attacked the Rāṭhoṛ camp in the valley of Cītoṛ in an effort to find Rāv Riṇmal's son and chosen successor, Jodho Riṇmalot (5-1). Jodho managed to flee with a small band of warriors. Among them was Varjāṅg Bhīṃvot. But they had to leave Varjāṅg's father, Bhīṃv, behind. ***Murārdān***, no. 2, p. 69, records:

> When Jodho [Riṇmalot] escaped [from Cītoṛ, the Rāṭhoṛs] came to wake Bhīṃv and Varjāṅg, but Bhīṃv would not awaken. Then Jodho took Varjāṅg and left.

According to the chronicles, Bhīṃv Cūṇḍāvat was asleep in a drunken stupor at the time of the Sīsodīyo attack and could not be aroused. The Rāṭhoṛs

---

[1] Rāv Riṇmal's sister, Haṃsbāī, was married to Sīsodīyo Rāṇo Lākho Khetsot (ca. 1382-1420). Her son by Rāṇo Lākho was Rāṇo Mokaḷ Lākhāvat (ca. 1421-33). Rāṇo Mokaḷ was murdered at Cītoṛ ca. 1433 when his son, Kūmbho, was only nine years old.

fleeing the camp were forced to leave him, and he fell into the hands of the Sīsodīyos and was imprisoned. He managed his release, however, through the good offices of a Brāhmaṇ ***purohit*** named Damo.

Bhīṃv's name does not appear in the chronicles with relation to events after this time. ***Murārdān***, no. 2, p. 70, notes that while Bhīṃv was a great ***ṭhākur***, he did not become renowned. He did found a ***sākh*** of Mārvāṛ Rāṭhoṛs and his name is associated with several villages in Mārvāṛ which he held from Rāv Riṇmal. ***Murārdān***, no. 2, p. 6, lists seven villages. Six of these, situated in two groups of three, were located to the south and east of Maṇḍor. The location of the seventh village is uncertain. The villages were:

1. Sālāvās: a large village located sixteen miles south of Maṇḍor
2. Nandvāṇo: located one-half mile due west of Sālāvās
3. Mogṛo: located four miles due east of Sālāvās

4. Bhāvī: a large village located thirty-six miles east-southeast of Maṇḍor
5. Jhuṛlī: located two and one-half miles east-southeast of Bhāvī village
6. Lāmbo: located three and one-half miles west-southwest of Bhāvī village

7. Guṛo: (location uncertain).

Varjāṅg fled from Cītoṛ with Jodho Riṇmalot and the other Rāṭhoṛs toward the Arāvallīs. Near the pass of Delvāro, the Rāṭhoṛs fought one of a series of pitched battles with the pursuing Sīsodīyos. Varjāṅg was wounded during the battle at Delvāro and was left on the field as Jodho and the other Rāṭhoṛs made their escape. The Sīsodīyos later picked Varjāṅg up and carried him back to Cītoṛ. ***Murārdān***, no. 2, p. 70, records that the Sīsodīyos did not kill Varjāṅg because he was their "sister's son." The specific tie by marriage is unclear, but the Rāṇo did take Varjāṅg into custody at Cītoṛ and have his wounds cleaned and bound. A Cāraṇ and a Nāī ("barber") who were Varjāṅg's ***cākar***s, cared for Varjāṅg and wrapped his wounds. Unbeknownst to his captors, they used extra cloth to wrap the wounds, and when the wounds were healed, Varjāṅg was able to make a rope from the cloth, and escape over the walls of the fortress.

Once outside, Varjāṅg disguised himself and proceeded by bullock cart along a circuitous route back to Mārvāṛ. His journey took him past the village of Gāgrūṇ (Gāgūraṇ), where he stopped by the tank and encamped under the shade of a tree. The Khīcī Cahuvāṇ Acaḷdās Bhojāvat was the master of Gāgrūṇ. Khīcī Acaḷdās was a renowned warrior of Mevāṛ and had married one of his daughters to the Sīsodīyo ruling family of Cītoṛ.[2] Varjāṅg soon met Khīcī

---

[2] ***Bāṅkīdās***, p. 143, records that Acaḷdās Khīcī performed a ***sāko*** (lit. "event that begins an era"), or heroic defense of the fort of Gāgrūṇ ca. 1425, when it came under attack from the Muslim ruler of Malwa. There are several celebrated literary compositions about Khīcī Acaḷdās, including Sivdās, ***Acaldās Khīcī rī Vacnīkā: Śodhpūrṇ Bhūmikā***

Acaḷdās and was given one of his daughters in marriage. The story of this meeting is told as follows (***Murārdān***, no. 2, pp. 71-74):

While Varjāṅg was encamped near the tank at Gāgrūṇ, several slave girls came from the fort to fill their water pots in the wells. Varjāṅg overheard them talking about one of Khīcī Acaḷdās's daughters and learned that there was much concern within the family because no suitable husband could be found for her. Varjāṅg then stepped forward and presented himself, saying to the girls, "If you would give the sister (***bāī***) to us, we would marry her." The slave girls were amused by this remark, seeing only Varjāṅg's dirty clothing, his bearded face and dark complexion, and they responded with laughter, "Why don't you marry [someone of] lower [rank more suitable to yourself]?" They returned to the fort, and one reported what had happened, saying with amusement, "Today the sister has found a good husband."

Word quickly reached Khīcī Acaḷdās, who became suspicious, thinking no ordinary man would ask for the hand of his daughter in marriage. He then remembered that several days prior, news had arrived from the Rāṇo about Varjāṅg and his escape from Cītoṛ. Acaḷdās asked his ***ṭhākur***s and Rajpūts if they had seen Varjāṅg. Several replied that they had seen him by the tank. He then sent them to verify that the man they had seen was indeed Varjāṅg. These men returned saying they had found Varjāṅg himself. Even at this young age, Varjāṅg had already made a considerable reputation for himself as a warrior. Khīcī Acaḷdās sent a ***purohit*** to Varjāṅg with a betrothal coconut and an offer of marriage for his daughter. Varjāṅg complained to the ***purohit***, however, that he had nothing, neither clothing nor horses nor money for expenses, and questioned how he should be able to marry. The ***purohit*** replied, "What is this you are worried about? You are a ***ṭhākur*** of royal blood (***rājvī ṭhākur***). Everything will be provided for you." Varjāṅg then accepted the coconut with great humility.

Varjāṅg remained at Gāgrūṇ for several days during the wedding ceremony and the celebration afterwards. He then took his leave, saying he needed to go, that Jodho was alone and there was distress in the land of Mārvāṛ. Khīcī Acaḷdās gave Varjāṅg a large dowry including horses and men. Varjāṅg left his wife at Gāgrūṇ with her father and rode out for Mārvāṛ to find Jodho. Once in Mārvāṛ, he and his followers fell on and destroyed a Sīsodīyo outpost at the village of Cokṛī [3] (near Meṛto), killing a number of the Rāṇo's men. The Sīsodīyos had overrun much of eastern Mārvāṛ following Rāv Riṇmal's murder and had stationed men at various outposts in addition to occupying Maṇḍor. Varjāṅg soon joined Jodho Riṇmalot, and he spent the next fifteen years helping him gather Rajpūts and horses and raiding Sīsodīyo outposts in an attempt to dislodge Sīsodīyo control of Rāṭhoṛ lands. Jodho was finally able to capture Maṇḍor ca. 1453. He then assumed his rightful position as ***rāv*** of Mārvāṛ.

---

sahit. Edited by Śambhusiṃh Manohar (Jodhpur: Rājasthān Prācyavidyā Pratiṣṭhān, 1991).

[3] Cokṛī village: located twenty-four miles southwest of Meṛto in eastern Mārvāṛ.

Following his accession, the Rāv granted Varjāṅg the village of Rohaṭh[4] in return for his long years of devoted service.

Varjāṅg took his family and retainers and settled at Rohaṭh. Not long thereafter, a force of Sīsodīyos raided into Mārvāṛ and attacked Rohaṭh. Varjāṅg and his Rajpūts successfully defended the village, but Varjāṅg was again wounded. According to ***Murārdān***, no. 2, p. 75, he received a severe cut on the back of his neck from the blow of a sword. A bone from Varjāṅg's neck had to be removed because of this wound, and a peg of wood from the ***kair*** tree (*Acacia catechu*) substituted in its place. The Bhīṃvots of Rohaṭh have honored and performed ***pūja*** to the ***kair*** tree since this time.

Varjāṅg and his brother, Vairsal, kept many mares at Rohaṭh. The horses used to graze in the open fields near the village. As the story is told, they wandered off one day in the direction of Tilvāṛo,[5] which lies in Mahevo some sixty miles to the west of Rohaṭh. They were found and captured by the sons of Mahevco Rāvaḷ Vīdo of Kheṛ.[6] Varjāṅg and his brother soon discovered that the horses were missing and sent military servants in search of them. These servants followed the horses' tracks to Tilvāṛo, and when they discovered them in the possession of the Mahevcos, they requested their return. The Rāvaḷ's sons were not hospitable, however. They had been drinking and were rude and abusive. They refused to give the horses back and said mockingly, "Put one hand on your head, and one hand on your ass," and go away. The military servants responded, "You have abused us, but Varjāṅg is behind us."

They returned to Rohaṭh and told Varjāṅg what had happened. Varjāṅg became filled with anger. He summoned his brothers, Vairsal and Vījo, gathered his ***sāth***, and rode into Mahevo, looting and burning as he went. He fought a great battle against the Mahevcos at Tilvāṛo, killing many and capturing the town, which he also looted and burned. Varjāṅg lost his riding horse named "Gāṅgājaḷ" this day, but he and his ***sāth*** returned to Rohaṭh in triumph.

Varjāṅg and the Bhīṃvots were among the primary supporters of the Jodhpur throne following Rāv Jodho Riṇmalot's death in 1489. Varjāṅg himself became ***kiledār*** of the Jodhpur fort, while his brother, Vairsal, later rose to become ***pradhān*** under Rāv Sūjo Jodhāvat (ca. 1492-1515). "The weight of rulership (***ṭhākurāī***) was upon the Bhīṃvots" (***Murārdān***, no. 2, p. 78).

Varjāṅg used his position of influence to extort lands from the new ***rāv*** of Jodhpur, Sātal Jodhāvat (ca. 1489-92) (6-1). A confrontation had been developing between Rāv Sātal's half-brother, Rāv Varsiṅgh Jodhāvat of Meṛto, and the Muslim governor of Ajmer, Malū Khān, a subordinate of the Pātsāh of Māṇḍū. Varsiṅgh had sacked Sāmbhar and angered Malū Khān and then withheld tribute promised to him. Rāv Sātal was drawn into their dealings when Varsiṅgh turned to him for support against the Khān. Malū Khān gathered an

---

[4] Rohaṭh village: located twenty-five miles south-southeast of Jodhpur.

[5] Tilvāṛo village: located sixty miles west of Rohaṭh on the Lūṇī River.

[6] Kheṛ village: located five miles east of Tilvāṛo and sixty-two miles southwest of Jodhpur.

army and began ravaging the lands of Meṛto and Jodhpur, and Rāv Varsiṅgh and Rāv Sātal then joined forces to oppose him. Their armies gathered near each other in February of 1492, and Rāv Sātal called upon Rāv Varjāṅg to "decide about the battle."

Here responsibility for decision-making "was upon the head [of] Rāv Varjāṅg Bhīṃvot." But Varjāṅg displayed discontent and procrastinated in the face of the Rāv's requests for his service. He then demanded the village of Bhāvī, which his father Bhīṃv Cūṇḍāvat had held before him. Rāv Sātal readily agreed to the grant in order to appease Varjāṅg, after which Varjāṅg became much more "enthusiastic" about taking part in the action against Malū Khān. While Rāv Sātal and Rāv Varsiṅgh's forces waited, Varjāṅg went to spy on the Muslim army which was encamped at the village of Kusāṇo.[7] He disguised himself as a grass-bearer and stole into the enemy camp, returning to lead a daring night attack. The attack caused great panic among the ranks of the Muslims, and the Rāṭhoṛs were able to route Malū Khān's forces and take the field. Rāv Varjāṅg's efforts on that day (March 1, 1492) were "particularly outstanding" (see *Vigat*, 2:43-44, of the **translated text** for complete details of this attack and Varjāṅg's role in it).

Little information is available about Varjāṅg's activities following this battle. He was by now a man of advanced age, probably in his late seventies or early eighties. He remained an influential ***ṭhākur*** in Mārvāṛ during the early years of Rāv Sūjo Jodhāvat's rule (ca. 1492-1515) and continued in his position as ***kiledār*** of the Jodhpur fort.[8] He used this position to involve himself in political intrigues surrounding the rulership of Jodhpur. ***Murārdān***, no. 2, pp. 81-82, records that when Rāv Sūjo succeeded to the throne, Varjāṅg sent messages to Rāṭhoṛ Rāv Bīko Jodhāvat (no. 42), ruler of the newly founded kingdom of Bīkāner (ca. 1485-1504), saying, "If you come, then we will capture Jodhpur."

Rāv Bīko did bring a force against Jodhpur and lay siege to the fort. Rāv Varjāṅg had promised to open the gates of the fort to him, but this plot was discovered and foiled. Rāv Bīko then withdrew and returned to Bīkāner. ***Ṭhākur***s at Jodhpur confronted Varjāṅg afterwards, questioning his role in this affair. He is reported to have replied, "Jodho's puppies are growling." Varjāṅg's brother, Vairsal, was ***pradhān*** of Jodhpur under Rāv Sūjo. His role during this episode is unknown.

Mention of Rāv Bīko Jodhāvat's attack on Jodhpur is noticeably absent from the accounts of Rāṭhoṛ Rāv Sūjo's reign in the chronicles of Mārvāṛ. Ojhā, 4:1:266, writes that it is acknowledged only in the accounts of Varjāṅg Bhīṃvot. There were issues of precedence to rulership among Rāv Jodho's sons by his different wives. Rāv Jodho had apparently obtained an oath from Bīko that he would support his half-brother Sātal's succession to the throne as Rāv Jodho's chosen successor. At the same time, Rāv Jodho promised Bīko that a number of

---

[7] Kusāṇo village: located thirty-eight miles east-northeast of Jodhpur and seven miles northeast of Pīmpāṛ.

[8] Bhāṭī, *Sarvekṣaṇ*, 3:102, states that Varjāṅg was ***thanedār*** at the fort under Rāv Sūjo.

the prized family heirlooms would be his. When Rāv Sātal died after a reign of only three years and his uterine brother, Sūjo Jodhāvat, succeeded to the throne, Bīko was no longer constrained by oath to his father and sought to assert his rights as eldest living son to precedence in questions of rulership. Rāv Sūjo's mother, Rāṇī Hāḍī Jasmādeji, apparently interceded with Rāv Bīko when he laid siege to Jodhpur, and made arrangements for the heirlooms to be transferred to him in return for his withdrawal. These heirlooms included the image of Nāgṇecījī, the ***kuḷdevī*** of the Rāṭhoṛs, a pair of kettledrums, Rāv Jodho's sword, and the sandalwood throne, all of which Rāv Bīko carried back to Bīkāner.

There is record among sources available of only one of Varjāṅg's wives, a daughter of Khīcī Acaḷdās, and one son, Surjan Varjāṅgot (6-3). ***Murārdān***, no. 2, p. 91, records about this son that he fought for the Rāṇo of Mevāṛ and died in battle on his behalf. It is uncertain when he would have left Mārvāṛ and under what circumstances his death occurred.

Two of Surjan's sons are listed, Kalo Surjanot (7-1) and Vīdo Surjanot (7-2). Kalo held the villages of Sālāvās and Nandvāṇo from the ruler of Jodhpur, which his great-grandfather, Bhīṃv Cūṇḍāvat, had originally received from his brother, Rāv Riṇmal. Kalo's descendants also retained possession of these villages. Kalo's brother, Vīdo, was killed at the battle of Sevakī on November 2, 1529 when Rāv Gāṅgo Vāghāvat of Jodhpur (1492-1515) came to battle with his paternal uncle, Sekho Sūjāvat, over rulership in Mārvāṛ. ***Murārdān***, no. 2, p. 92, does not specify for which side Vīdo fought in this conflict.

"Aitihāsik Bātāṃ," p. 37; ***Bāṅkīdās***, p. 143; Bhāṭī, ***Sarvekṣaṇ***, 3:101-102; ***Jodhpur Rājya kī Khyāt***, pp. 60-64; L. P. Tessitori, "A Progress Report on the Work done during the year 1917 in connection with the Bardic and Historical Survey of Rajputana," ***Journal of the Asiatic Society of Bengal***, N.S. 15 (1919), pp. 73-75; ***Murārdān***, no. 2, pp. 5-6, 58, 69-82, 91-92; Ojhā, 4:1:261-266, 5:1:86-89; ***Vigat***, 1:31, 40, 2:43-44, "Ṭippaṇiyeṃ: Pratham Bhāg (Mahatvapūrṇ Vyaktiyoṃ tathā Sthānoṃ ādi para Ṭippaṇiyeṃ), Parganā Jodhpur," 3:66-69.

Figure 19. Bhīṃvot Rāṭhoṛs

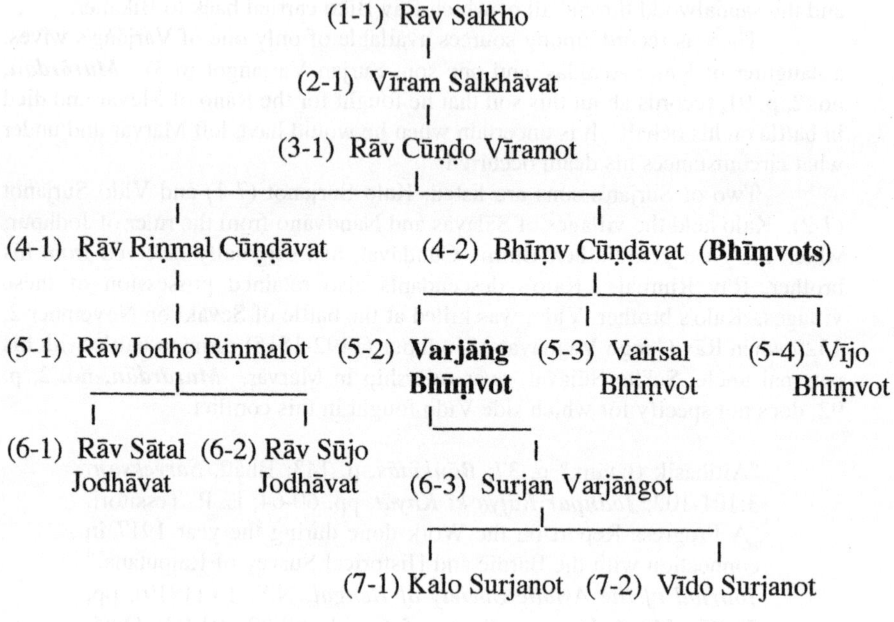
(1-1) Rāv Salkho
(2-1) Vīram Salkhāvat
(3-1) Rāv Cūṇḍo Vīramot
(4-1) Rāv Riṇmal Cūṇḍāvat
(4-2) Bhīṃv Cūṇḍāvat **(Bhīṃvots)**
(5-1) Rāv Jodho Riṇmalot
(5-2) **Varjāṅg Bhīṃvot**
(5-3) Vairsal Bhīṃvot
(5-4) Vījo Bhīṃvot
(6-1) Rāv Sātal Jodhāvat
(6-2) Rāv Sūjo Jodhāvat
(6-3) Surjan Varjāṅgot
(7-1) Kalo Surjanot
(7-2) Vīdo Surjanot

Bīkāvat Rāṭhoṛs

(no. 47) **Bhīmrāj Jaitsīyot** (9-2)
(no. 42) **Bīko Jodhāvat, Rāv** (6-1)
(no. 45) **Jaitsī Lūṇkaraṇot, Rāv** (8-1)
(no. 46) **Kalyāṇmal Jaitsīyot, Rāv** (9-1)
(no. 44) **Lūṇkaraṇ Bīkāvat, Rāv** (7-2)
(no. 43) **Naro Bīkāvat, Rāv** (7-1)

Set out below are brief discussions of the Rāṭhoṛ rulers of Bīkāner mentioned in the texts under review, beginning with Rāv Bīko Jodhāvat (ca. 1485-1504) (6-1) and ending with Rāv Kalyāṇmal Jaitsīyot (ca. 1542-74) (9-1). References are provided at the end of this section for more detailed information about these individuals and their reigns with mention of sources readily available in published form in English.

(no. 42) **Bīko Jodhāvat, Rāv** (ca. 1485-1504) (6-1)

The Bīkāvat Rāṭhoṛs descend from Bīko Jodhāvat, a son of Rāv Jodho Riṇmalot (5-1), ruler of Maṇḍor and Jodhpur (ca. 1453-89). His mother was the Sāṅkhlī Paṃvār Nāraṅgdejī, daughter of Rūṇeco Sāṅkhlo Paṃvār Māṇḍaṇ Jaitāvat.[1] Bīko was born August 5, 1438[2] and was thirty-one years old at the time his father founded Jodhpur in 1459. The Jodhpur chronicles state that Rāv Jodho divided the lands of Mārvāṛ among his brothers and sons following the founding of Jodhpur, and ***Vigat***, 1:39, records that he granted Bīko and his younger uterine brother, Vīdo Jodhāvat (6-2),[3] the area of Jāṅgaḷu,[4] located some one hundred miles to the north of Jodhpur, and the desert tract to the east and northeast of Jāṅgaḷu that became known as Bīkāner.

In fact, Bīko's and Vīdo's association with these areas did not begin until the mid-1460s. Bīkāner chronicles relate that this association emerged from a casual remark made one day in Rāv Jodho's ***darbār*** at Jodhpur. Bīko is said to have arrived late in the ***darbār*** on this day and to have taken a seat alongside his paternal uncle (***kāko***), Kāndhaḷ Riṇmalot (5-2), with whom he quickly became

---

[1] See ***supra***, **Marriage and Family Lists of the Rulers of Jodhpur**, Jodho Riṇmalot, Rāṇī no. 3, for a discussion of the uncertainties surrounding the identity of this Rāṇī's father.

[2] Reu, 1:103, n. 3, gives the date of July 14, 1440 (***adhika vaiś***) or August 14, 1440 (***nija vaiś***) for Bīko's birth.

[3] For information about Vīdo Jodhāvat, see ***infra***, "Vīdāvat Rāṭhoṛs."

[4] Jāṅgaḷu village: located twenty-four miles south of present-day Bīkāner.

involved in a whispered conversation. Rāv Jodho took note of Bīko's late arrival and his secretive discussion with Kāndhaḷ and remarked to the side that they must be scheming about the conquest of new lands. Kāndhaḷ Riṇmalot overheard the Rāv's aside and took it as a personal challenge. He pledged before Rāv Jodho that he would lead the conquest of new lands with Bīko at his side.

The Jāṅgaḷvo Sāṅkhlo Paṃvār, Nāpo Māṇakrāvat (no. 26), was in the ***darbār*** at the time. He had come to Jodhpur to seek aid in the recovery of the Sāṅkhlos' lands of Jāṅgaḷu, which the Sāṅkhlos had abandoned in the face of attacks from the Baloc. This land now lay vacant. Sāṅkhlo Nāpo urged Bīko and his uncle, Kāndhaḷ, to consider the conquest and occupation of Jāṅgaḷu, offering his support and that of the Sāṅkhlos in this enterprise.

Bīko set out from Jodhpur for Jāṅgaḷu with his brother, Vīdo, several of his paternal uncles, including Kāndhaḷ Riṇmalot, and a contingent of retainers and servants on September 30, 1465. While Vīdo eventually returned to assist his father, Rāv Jodho, in the conquest of Chāpar-Droṇpur, an area lying east-southeast of Jāṅgaḷu,[5] and then assumed authority there at the direction of his father, Bīko spent the next twenty years establishing his own foothold in Jāṅgaḷu and then in the lands further to the north. He established himself at Koṛamdesar[6] in 1472, and several years later in 1478, began construction of a fort near the tank at Koṛamdesar. He also formed an important alliance through marriage with Bhāṭī Rāv Sekho and the Bhāṭīs of Pūgaḷ, an area to the northwest of Koṛamdesar. Then in 1485 he had the foundations for a new fort laid some twelve miles to the east of Koṛamdesar and three years later in 1488, settled in his new capitol of Bīkāner.

Bīko's success in consolidating his authority at Bīkāner rested upon the support he received from two important sources. The first was from Cāraṇī Bhāgvatī Śrī Karṇījī, who resided at the village of Desnok, nineteen miles to the south of Bīkāner. It was to her that Bīko had proceeded for blessings and advice prior to each of his campaigns. Bīko's power also rested upon an important alliance with the Godāro Jāṭs. Different groups of Jāṭs controlled areas of land around Bīkāner, and Bīko's alliance with the Godāros led to the defeat of other Jāṭ opposition to his rule. From this time, a Godāro Jāṭ has placed the ***ṭīko*** of succession on the forehead of the new ruler of Bīkāner.

Rāv Bīko turned his attention to the south after consolidating his power at Bīkāner. He rode to aid his uterine brother, Vīdo Jodhāvat, who had been driven from Chāpar-Droṇpur by the Mohil Cahuvāṇs and a Muslim force under Sāraṅg Khān, the ***sūbedār*** of Hisar. Rāv Bīko succeeded in driving this force from the area, and then placed Vīdo once again upon the seat of rule.

A short time thereafter, ca. 1489, Rāv Bīko's paternal uncle, Kāndhaḷ Riṇmalot, whose support had been central to his establishment of authority at Bīkāner, was killed in battle against Sāraṅg Khān. Bīko vowed to avenge Kāndhaḷ's death to settle the ***vair***, and he called upon the aid of his father, Rāv Jodho Riṇmalot of Jodhpur, and his half-brothers from Meṛto, Varsiṅgh (no.

[5] Chāpar village: located seventy miles east-southeast of Jāṅgaḷu.

[6] Koṛamdesar village: located eleven miles west of present-day Bīkāner.

146) and Dūdo Jodhāvat (no. 104). Their combined force met and defeated Sāraṅg Khān, and Bīko's son, Naro Bīkāvat (7-1) (no. 43), is credited with killing Sāraṅg Khān.[7]

Bīko halted at Droṇpur with his father, Rāv Jodho, upon returning from this battle. It is here that Rāv Jodho is said to have taken an oath from Bīko, who was then his eldest living son. Bīko now had his own kingdom of Bīkāner, and Rāv Jodho asked that he lay no claim to Jodhpur, but leave this kingdom to those of his brothers who were Rāv Jodho's chosen successors. Bīko promised to abide by this request, but he asked in return that he be given several of the prized heirlooms of the Rāṭhoṛ ruling family. These included the sandalwood throne, the royal umbrella and fly whisk, Rāv Jodho's sword and shield, the kettledrums, Sāṅkhlo Paṃvār Harbhū Mehrājot's dagger, the Hiraṇyagarbha idol of Lakśmīnārāyaṇjī, and the large silver idol of Nāgṇecījī, the ***kuḷdevī*** of the Rāṭhoṛs. Rāv Jodho is said to have acceded to Bīko's request, promising to send these prized possessions to him upon his return to Jodhpur. Rāv Jodho died soon after his return, however, and the heirlooms remained at Jodhpur.

Rāv Bīko rode to Jodhpur several years later in 1492 to aid his half-brother, Rāv Sātal Jodhāvat (ca. 1489-92), and his two half-brothers from Meṛto, Varsiṅgh and Dūdo Jodhāvat, during a period of conflict with the Muslim ***sūbedār*** of Ajmer, Malū Khān. Soon thereafter, during the reign of Rāv Sātal's successor, Rāv Sūjo Jodhāvat (ca. 1492-1515), Rāv Bīko marched on Jodhpur itself, claiming the prized heirlooms which Rāv Jodho had promised him. Issues of precedence to rulership among Rāv Jodho's sons by different wives were involved here, and there is evidence of factions at the Jodhpur court around different sons. The chronicles relate that Rāṭhoṛ Varjāṅg Bhīṃvot (no. 42), ***kiledār*** of the Jodhpur fort under Rāv Sūjo Jodhāvat, secretly summoned Rāv Bīko to Jodhpur, saying that if he came, they could capture the town. He offered to open the gates of the fort to him. This plot was foiled, but Rāv Bīko did march on Jodhpur and lay siege to the town and fort. He finally agreed to lift his siege only after meeting with Rāv Sūjo's mother, Rāṇī Jasmādejī Hāḍī, who arranged to have the prized Rāṭhoṛ symbols of rulership and authority given to Rāv Bīko. He carried these back to Bīkāner with him.

Some years later, on June 17, 1504, Rāv Bīko died at the age of sixty five years.

(no. 43) **Naro Bīkāvat, Rāv** (ca. 1504-05) (7-1)

Naro Bīkāvat, Rāv Bīko's eldest son, succeeded him to the rulership of Bīkāner. Naro ruled only four months. He died on January 13, 1505. He had no sons and was succeeded by his younger brother, Lūṇkaraṇ Bīkāvat (7-2).

---

[7] The circumstances of Sāraṅg Khān's death are uncertain. The date of his death is given variously in the sources as 1489 and 1490. The latter date falls after the date given for Rāv Jodho Riṇmalot's death on April 6, 1489. This date is unconfirmed by inscriptional evidence, however, further complicating issues of chronology. See: Ojhā, 4:1:247-250.

(no. 44) **Lūṇkaraṇ Bīkāvat, Rāv** (1505-26) (7-2)

Lūṇkaraṇ Bīkāvat was born on January 12, 1470. His mother was Bhāṭiyāṇī Rāṇī Raṅgkuṃvar, the daughter of Bhāṭī Rāv Sekho of Pūgaḷ. He ascended the throne of Bīkāner on January 23, 1505 at the age of thirty-five years, and ruled until June of 1526, when he was killed along with three of his sons fighting Muslims near Narnol in central-eastern Rājasthān.

Rāv Lūṇkaraṇ spent the twenty-one years of his reign consolidating and expanding the territories that his father, Rāv Bīko Jodhāvat (6-1) (no. 42), had originally settled. He attacked the Cahuvāṇs of Dadrevo in eastern Bīkāner territory in 1509-10 and placed this land under his control, and then led a series of raids against the Kyāṃ Khānī Muslims of Fatehpur in 1512, bringing back much spoil to his capitol. In 1513, he defeated the Khānzāda Khān ruler of Nāgaur, Muḥammad Khān I (ca. 1495-1520), in battle and, a year later, proceeded to Cītoṛ to marry a daughter of Sīsodīyo Rāṇo Rāymal Kūmbhāvat (ca. 1473-1509).

Then in early 1526, he became involved in a dispute with Bhāṭī Rāvaḷ Jaitsī Devīdāsot of Jaisaḷmer (1491-1528). This dispute is said to have arisen over a slight. Cāraṇ Lāḷo of Bīkāner happened to be at the Jaisaḷmer court one day and overheard the Rāvaḷ mocking the Rāṭhoṛs. The Cāraṇ remarked to the Rāvaḷ that he should not speak ill of the Rāṭhoṛs, whereupon Rāvaḷ Jaitsī replied that he would give the Brāhmaṇs of his kingdom as much of his land as the Rāṭhoṛs could ride over. Cāraṇ Lāḷo quickly reported the Rāvaḷ's boast to Rāv Lūṇkaraṇ at Bīkāner, and the Rāv took up the challenge and rode with his warriors into the Bhāṭī lands. They penetrated as far as Jaisaḷmer itself, laying siege to the town and fortress and capturing Rāvaḷ Jaitsī. The Rāv lifted his siege and released the Rāvaḷ only after the Rāvaḷ agreed to marry one of his daughters to a son of Rāv Lūṇkaraṇ.

Rāv Lūṇkaraṇ rode with a force of Rajpūts from Bīkāner against the Muslims of Narnol in March of 1526. With him on this expedition were three of his sons, a contingent of Bhāṭīs from Pūgaḷ, Vīdāvat Rāṭhoṛ Kalyāṇmal Udaikaraṇot (no. 153) (8-5) and his Rajpūts from Chāpar-Droṇpur, and Sekhāvat Kachvāho Rāymal Sekhāvat (no. 22) of Amarsar. They halted in Chāpar-Droṇpur on their way to Narnol, and Vīdāvat Kalyāṇmal is said to have overheard the Rāv speak of coveting this land for his own family. These words raised grave suspicions in Kalyāṇmal's mind, and when Rāv Lūṇkaraṇ came to battle with Sheikh Abīmīrā at the village of Ḍhosī near Narnol, Kalyāṇmal told his close companion, Rāymal Sekhāvat, that he would not support Rāv Lūṇkaraṇ. Kalyāṇmal and the Vīdāvats then withdrew from the field and refused to participate in the fighting. Rāymal Sekhāvat is also said to have sided with Sheikh Abīmīrā.

Rāv Lūṇkaraṇ was killed at Ḍhosī on March 30, 1526 along with his sons, Netsī (8-2), Pratāpsī (8-3) and Vairsī (8-4).

(no.45) **Jaitsī Lūṇkaraṇot, Rāv** (ca. 1526-42) (8-1)

Rāv Lūṇkaraṇ's eldest son, Jaitsī Lūṇkaraṇot, succeeded him to the throne of Bīkāner. Jaitsī was born on October 31, 1489 and came to the throne at the age of thirty-six years. His first actions upon succession were to protect his capitol from Vīdāvat Kalyāṇmal Udaikaraṇot, who had proceeded to Bīkāner after the fighting at Narnol, asking to be allowed into the city to mourn the Rāv's death. Rāv Jaitsī wisely forbade him entry and soon after organized an expedition against the Vīdāvats of Chāpar-Droṇpur to avenge his father's and his brothers' deaths. The Rāv was able to drive Kalyāṇmal from the area, and he afterwards placed one of Kalyāṇmal's paternal nephews, Vīdāvat Sāṅgo Samsārcandot, on the seat of rule at Chāpar-Droṇpur.

Several years later, in 1529, Rāv Jaitsī rode to Jodhpur to aid Rāv Gāṅgo Vāghāvat (1515-32) in Rāv Gāṅgo's dispute with his paternal uncle (***kāko***), Sekho Sūjāvat (no. 86), over land and authority in Mārvāṛ. Rāv Gāṅgo was victorious at the battle of Sevakī [8] on November 2, 1529 with Rāv Jaitsī's help. Rāv Gāṅgo and Rāv Jaitsī found Sekho Sūjāvat lying on the field after the fighting, and, before dying, Sekho is reported to have reproached Rāv Jaitsī for interfering in a dispute between a father's brother (***kāko***) and a brother's son (***bhatījo***). He also stated that Rāv Jaitsī would meet the same fate that he, Sekho, had met.

Bīkāner came under attack from a Mughal army under Prince Kamran, brother to Emperor Humāyūn, some years later in 1534. The Mughals had first attacked and taken Bhaṭner (Hanumāngaṛh) from Rāv Jaitsī's son, Khetsī Jaitsīyot (9-4), who was killed. They then besieged Bīkāner and eventually took the fort. Rāv Jaitsī was forced to flee, but he returned in October of 1534 to retake the fort from the Mughals in a daring night attack.

Then in late 1541 Rāv Mālde Gāṅgāvat of Jodhpur (1532-62) sent an army under Rāṭhoṛ Kūmpo Mahirājot (no. 95) against Bīkāner. Rāv Jaitsī was killed fighting in the defense of his kingdom at Sobho village (near Bīkāner) on February 26, 1542. Rāv Mālde's forces occupied Bīkāner city and fort, and held it for the next two years. The Bīkāner Rāṭhoṛs under Rāv Jaitsī's successor were only able to occupy the city again in December of 1543.

(no. 46) **Kalyāṇmal Jaitsīyot, Rāv** (ca. 1542-1574) (9-1)
(no. 47) **Bhīmrāj Jaitsīyot** (9-2)

Rāv Jaitsī's son, Kalyāṇmal Jaitsīyot, succeeded him to the throne of Bīkāner in 1542. Kalyāṇmal was born on January 6, 1519. His accession in 1542 took place in the village of Sirso because of the occupation of Bīkāner by Rāv Mālde Gāṅgāvat's forces from Jodhpur. For the next several years, Kalyāṇmal moved about the countryside seeking to consolidate a foothold in the face of Rāv Mālde's superior force at the capitol. Rāv Kalyāṇmal sent his younger brother, Bhīmrāj Jaitsīyot, and a trusted court administrator, Muṃhato Nago, to Delhi to meet with Sher Shāh Sūr (1540-45) and plead the case of

[8] Sevakī village: located twenty-three miles northeast of Jodhpur.

Bīkāner against Rāv Mālde of Jodhpur. ***Daḷpat Vilās***, pp. 4-5, a local chronicle of Bīkāner dating from just after this period, notes that Sher Shāh had gone to Bīkāner during the time of hardship prior to his assumption of authority in north India, and that he had been cared for by Rāv Kalyāṇmal's family. Sher Shāh's earlier association with the Bīkāner ruling family undoubtedly played a role in his decision to move against Rāv Mālde of Jodhpur and assist in the recovery of their homeland.

Sher Shāh marched from north India against Mārvāṛ in early 1544. His forces met those of Rāv Mālde's at Samel[9] in February of that year, defeating them after a long and costly battle. Rāv Kalyāṇmal came with a contingent of warriors to aid Sher Shāh in this battle, and Muṃhato Nago had Sher Shāh place the ***ṭīko*** of succession on Kalyāṇmal's forehead afterwards to confirm him as ruler of Bīkāner. Rāv Kalyāṇmal then proceeded to his capitol. Rāv Mālde's defeat at Samel effectively removed all of his authority from this area and allowed Rāv Kalyāṇmal to consolidate his position for the first time.

Rāv Kalyāṇmal once again sent forces against Rāv Mālde in 1554, this time to aid Meṛtīyo Rāv Jaimal Vīramdevot (no. 107) at the battle of Meṛto. Rāv Jaimal emerged victorious here, and the Bīkāner chronicles record that Rāv Jaimal was much indebted to Rāv Kalyāṇmal and his warriors for their support. Three years later, in January of 1557, Rāv Kalyāṇmal again sent warriors south from Bīkāner, on this occasion to aid Sīsodīyo Rāṇo Udaisiṅgh Sāṅgāvat of Cītoṛ (ca. 1537-72; no. 17) and his allies against the forces of Hājī Khān Paṭhāṇ, a former noble of Sher Shāh Sūr, and Rāv Mālde of Jodhpur. They met in battle at Harmāṛo,[10] where the Rāṇo's army met defeat.

Rāv Kalyāṇmal went with his son, Kuṃvar Rāysiṅgh Kalyāṇmalot (10-1), to meet with the Mughal Emperor Akbar at Nāgaur on November 16, 1570. The Rāv offered his service to Akbar at this time, and he gave a daughter of his brother, Kānho Jaitsīyot (9-3), to the Emperor in marriage. His son, Rāysiṅgh, remained in attendance upon the Emperor after his return to Bīkāner. This meeting marked the beginning of the long and enduring bond of service between the Bīkāvat Rāṭhoṛs of Bīkāner and the Mughal throne.

Rāv Kalyāṇmal died on January 24, 1574 and was succeeded by his son, Rāysiṅgh Kalyāṇmalot.

Akbar Nāma, 2:159, 518; ***Bāṅkīdās***, pp. 74-75; Captain P. W. Powlett, ***Gazetteer of the Bikaner State*** (Calcutta: Office of the Superintendent of Government Printing, 1874), pp. i-v, 1-22; ***Daḷpat Vilās***, edited by Rāvat Sarasvat (Bīkāner: Sādūl Rājasthānī Resarc Insṭīṭyūt, 1960), pp. 4-5; ***Jodhpur Rājya kī Khyāt***, pp. 54-58; Karni Singh, ***The Relations of the House of Bikaner with the Central Powers, 1465-1949*** (New Delhi: Munshiram Manoharlal Publishers Pvt. Ltd., 1974), pp. 20-42;

---

[9] Samel village: located twenty-four miles southwest of Ajmer.

[10] Harmāṛo village: located fifty-five miles south-southwest of Ajmer and six miles south of Vadhnor in northern Mevāṛ.

L. P. Tessitori, "A Progress Report on the Work done during the year 1917 in connection with the Bardic and Historical Survey of Rajputana," ***Journal of the Asiatic Society of Bengal***, N. S. 15 (1919), pp. 43-50, 67-79; Major K. D. Erskine, ed., ***Rajputana Gazetteers***: Volume III-A, ***The Western Rajputana States Residency and the Bikaner Agency*** (Allahabad: The Pioneer Press, 1909), pp. 309-330; Ojhā, 4:1:247-250, 5:1:83, 90-162; Reu, 1:103, n. 3; ***Vigat***, 1:39, 2:45-46, 56, 58, 60; ***Vīr Vinod***, 2:478-485.

Figure 20. Bīkāvat Rāṭhoṛs

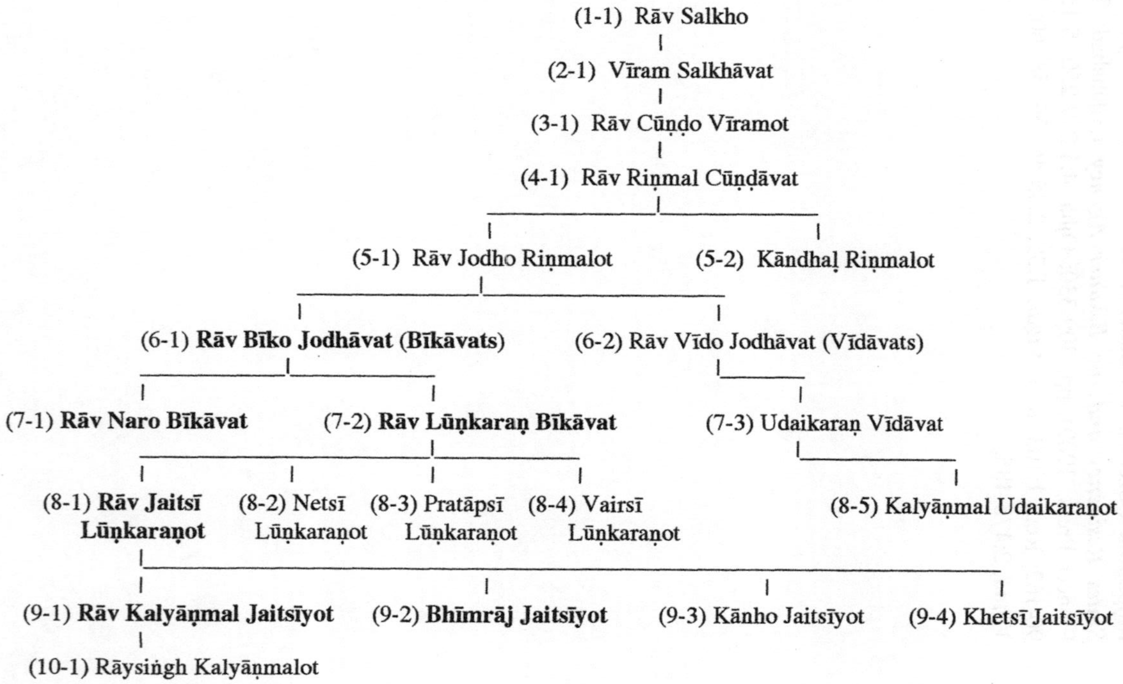
(1-1) Rāv Salkho
(2-1) Vīram Salkhāvat
(3-1) Rāv Cūṇḍo Vīramot
(4-1) Rāv Riṇmal Cūṇḍāvat
(5-1) Rāv Jodho Riṇmalot
(5-2) Kāndhaḷ Riṇmalot
(6-1) **Rāv Bīko Jodhāvat (Bīkāvats)**
(6-2) Rāv Vīdo Jodhāvat (Vīdāvats)
(7-1) **Rāv Naro Bīkāvat**
(7-2) **Rāv Lūṇkaraṇ Bīkāvat**
(7-3) Udaikaraṇ Vīdāvat
(8-1) **Rāv Jaitsī Lūṇkaraṇot**
(8-2) Netsī Lūṇkaraṇot
(8-3) Pratāpsī Lūṇkaraṇot
(8-4) Vairsī Lūṇkaraṇot
(8-5) Kalyāṇmal Udaikaraṇot
(9-1) **Rāv Kalyāṇmal Jaitsīyot**
(9-2) **Bhīmrāj Jaitsīyot**
(9-3) Kānho Jaitsīyot
(9-4) Khetsī Jaitsīyot
(10-1) Rāysiṅgh Kalyāṇmalot

Cāmpāvat Rāṭhoṛs

(no. 51)	**Amro Rāmāvat**	(8-2)
(no. 49)	**Jaitmāl Jesāvat**	(8-1)
(no. 48)	**Jeso Bhairavdāsot**	(7-1)
(no. 50)	**Rāmo Bhairavdāsot**	(7-2)
(no. 52)	**Sahaiso Rāmāvat**	(8-3)

The Cāmpāvat Rāṭhoṛs

The Cāmpāvat Rāṭhoṛs descend from Cāmpo Riṇmalot (5-1), one of the elder sons[1] of Rāv Riṇmal Cūṇḍāvat (4-1), ruler of Maṇḍor (ca. 1428-38). He was born of Rāṇī Sonagarī Rāmkuṃvar of Nāḍūl. Sources give widely differing dates for Cāmpo's birth. The most reasonable is January 5, 1413. He would have been fifteen years of age when his father came to power at Maṇḍor ca. 1428. Cāmpo took an active role in the affairs of the kingdom and spent much of his early life in his father's service at Maṇḍor.

Not long after his father's assumption of power, Cāmpo founded a village that became his seat of rule. The site he chose for the village, it is said, was where he had captured a caravan of camels that was passing near Maṇḍor on its way from Sindh to north India. The camels were loaded with "chunks" or "large pieces" of raw sugar (***guṛ ke kāpe***[2]), considered an auspicious sign. In recognition of this omen, Cāmpo established the village on this site and named it Kāparṛo.[3]

Cāmpo's father's sister, Haṃsbāī, had been married to Sīsodīyo Rāṇo Lākho Khetsot of Cītoṛ (ca. 1382-1420). Her son by Rāṇo Lākho, Mokaḷ Lākhāvat, had succeeded to the throne of Mevāṛ and ruled ca. 1421-33. When he was murdered at Cītoṛ ca. 1433, Haṃsbāī had summoned her brother, Rāv Riṇmal, to Mevāṛ to safeguard her grandson, Kūmbho Mokaḷot, then aged nine years, and ensure his succession to the throne. Cāmpo initially accompanied his father to Cītoṛ, where the Rāv was able to establish authority and seat Kūmbho Mokaḷot on the Sīsodīyo throne. The Rāv then spent much of the latter part of his reign in Mevāṛ as the Rāṇo's protector, while Cāmpo returned to Mārvāṛ, where he and his elder brother, Akhairāj, assumed management of the kingdom in their father's absence. The Sīsodīyos under Rāṇo Kūmbho (ca. 1433-68) later murdered Rāv Riṇmal ca. 1438 to rid Mevāṛ of Rāṭhoṛ influence and control and

---

[1] Mohansiṃh Kānotā, ***Cāmpāvatoṃ kā Itihās*** (Jāypur: Raṇbāṅkur Prakāśan, 1990-91), 1:5, states that Cāmpo was Rāv Riṇmal's third son after Akhairāj and Kāndhaḷ.

[2] For a definition of ***kāpo***, see: Lāḷas, ***RSK*** (2nd edition, 1988), 1:625.

[3] Kāparṛo village: located twenty-eight miles east of Maṇḍor and nine miles south-southwest of Pīmpāṛ.

afterwards proceeded to overrun much of eastern Mārvāṛ and occupy Maṇḍor. Cāmpo spent the next fifteen years fighting alongside Rāv Riṇmal's chosen successor, Jodho Riṇmalot, during Jodho's attempts to reassert Rāṭhoṛ authority in Mārvāṛ.

Jodho finally succeeded in the conquest of Maṇḍor ca. 1453. He then made Cāmpo his ***pradhān*** and delegated to him responsibility for managing the affairs of the kingdom. Cāmpo played a leading role in campaigns to drive the Sīsodīyos from their remaining outposts in Mārvāṛ. When Rāv Jodho organized a large force of Rāṭhoṛs to attack Pālī,[4] the last of the Sīsiodīyo garrisons, Cāmpo conducted negotiations with Sīsodīyo Rāṇo Kūmbho prior to the engagement. The ***Vigat*** of Naiṇsī, 1:35, records:

> One time later, Rāṇo Kūmbho assembled all the contingents (*sāth*) of Mevāṛ and came and halted at Pālī. News [of the arrival of the Sīsodīyos] reached Rāv Jodho. Rāv Jodho had very few horses at this time. Then 10,000 Rāṭhoṛs [seated in] 2,000 bullock carts resolved to die. And Rāv Jodho went and encamped above Pālī. The news reached the Rāṇo, "Jodho has come sitting in a [bullock] cart."

The Rāṇo determined to quit Mārvāṛ following negotiations rather than confront a Rāṭhoṛ army dedicated to death in battle. He agreed to marry his uterine sister to Rāv Jodho to seal the peace,[5] and he gave Rāv Jodho the lands of Sojhat in dowry.

Cāmpo participated in the general settlement of Mārvāṛ following the Sīsodīyo withdrawal, and sources note that he attacked and subdued the Sīndhaḷ Rāṭhoṛs under Narsiṅgh Sīndhaḷ at Jaitāraṇ[6] and made Narsiṅgh Rāv Jodho's subordinate.

Rāv Jodho founded his new capitol of Jodhpur five miles south of Maṇḍor in 1459. During the Rāv's subsequent division of lands in Mārvāṛ among his brothers and sons, he confirmed Cāmpo's possession of Kāparṛo village and in addition granted him the village of Baṇāṛ[7] as a reward for his devoted service to the throne.

Few details are available about the remainder of Cāmpo's life. He participated with Rāv Jodho in several campaigns against the Mohil Cahuvāṇs of Chāpar-Droṇpur[8] between the years 1464-1474. Then, on April 2, 1479

---

[4] Pālī village: located forty-five miles south-southeast of Maṇḍor.

[5] See *supra*, **Marriage and Family Lists of the Rulers of Jodhpur**, Jodho Riṇmalot, Rāṇī no. 9.

[6] Jaitāraṇ town: located fifty-six miles east of Jodhpur.

[7] Baṇāṛ village: located ten miles east-northeast of Jodhpur.

[8] Chāpar-Droṇpur: southeastern Bīkāner territory.

(*Caitrādi*) or March 22, 1480 (*Śrāvaṇādi*) Cāmpo was killed fighting against the Sīndhaḷ Rāṭhoṛs of Jaitāraṇ. Sources note that Cāmpo made an offering to the land of flesh and blood from his own hand prior to his death. He was approximately sixty-seven years of age.[9]

Cāmpo had between two and eight wives and five to eight sons, the most important of whom was Bhairavdās Cāmpāvat (6-1).

Bāṅkīdās, p. 54; Kānotā, *Cāmpāvatoṃ kā Itihās*, 1:5-38; *Murārdān*, no. 1, p. 655; Paṇḍit Badrī Śarmā, *Dāsapoṃ kā Itihās* (Jodhpur: Seṇāsadana, V. S. 2011[A. D. 1954]), pp. 11-17; *Cāmpāvat Rāṭhauṛ*, pp. 1-10; *Vigat*, 1:35, 38, "Pariśiṣṭ - 4: Ḍāvī ne Jīvṇī Mislāṃ rī Vigat," 2:475; *Vīr Vinod*, 2:805.

Bhairavdās Cāmpāvat (6-1)

Bhairavdās Cāmpāvat was born in 1434-35 during the last years of Rāv Riṇmal Cūṇḍāvat's (4-1) rule at Maṇḍor (ca. 1428-38). He was three or four years old when Rāv Riṇmal was murdered and grew up during the fifteen year Rāṭhoṛ struggle against the Sīsodīyos. No specific information is available about Bhairavdās's activities in this period, but when he came of age, he undoubtedly served with his father, Cāmpo Riṇmalot, in the Rāṭhoṛ campaigns that Jodho Riṇmalot led to reassert his family's authority in their homeland. Bhairavdās proved to be an ardent supporter of the Jodhpur throne and of Rāv Jodho's family. The Jodhpur chronicles speak of him as a great pillar of Mārvāṛ.

Following Rāv Jodho's assumption of rule at Maṇḍor, the Rāv sent Bhairavdās with an army of Rāṭhoṛs to attack Rāṭhoṛ Narbad Satāvat (no. 56) at his village of Kāylāno in Goḍhvāṛ.[10] Narbad Satāvat had participated with the Sīsodīyos in the occupation of Maṇḍor and eastern Mārvāṛ, and Rāv Jodho sought to take revenge for these actions. The Rāṭhoṛs under Bhairavdās were successful in driving Narbad Satāvat from Kāylāṇo and looting his village.

Bhairavdās was also vigilant in the protection of his family lands at the village of Kāparro. When these came under attack from Bāgho Sīndhaḷ of Kaṃvlāṃ[11] in 1459-60 and the cattle were driven off, Bhairavdās rode in pursuit. He brought Bāgho Sīndhaḷ to battle near Kaṃvlāṃ and killed him there.

Soon thereafter in 1461-62, Bhairavdās accompanied Rāv Jodho on his pilgrimage to Mathurajī and other holy sites at the behest of his father, Cāmpo. Some years later in 1472-73, Rāv Jodho called upon Bhairavdās to assist his son, Bīko Jodhāvat (Rāv of Bīkāner, ca. 1485-1504; no. 42), in the consolidation of

---

9 A brother's son, Bālo Bhakharsīyot, avenged Cāmpo's death a short time later, killing Narsiṅgh Sīndhaḷ in battle.

10 Kāylāṇo village: located thirty-eight miles south of Sojhat and nine miles east-northeast of Nāḍūl.

11 The identity of this village is obscure. It is perhaps Kāṃvlīyo, located seventeen miles south of Meṛto and twenty-eight miles west of Pīmpāṛ.

his authority at Jāṅgaḷu[12] and then at Koṛamdesar[13] against Bhāṭī inroads. Bhairavdās remained with Bīko Jodhāvat for over seven years and was with him when his father, Cāmpo, was killed in 1479. Bhairavdās returned to Kāparṛo following Cāmpo's death to assume his position of rule there. Rāv Jodho granted Bhairavdās the additional village of Coṭīlo[14] at this time.

Bhairavdās was apparently busy with family affairs over the following years for the texts next speak of him with relation to events of the mid-1480s. He once again became involved with Rāv Bīko Jodhāvat when Rāv Bīko went to aid his uterine brother, Vīdo Jodhāvat,[15] in the recovery of the lands of Chāpar-Droṇpur. These had been taken from Vīdo by the Mohil Cahuvāṇs and their ally, Sāraṅg Khān, the ***sūbedār*** of Hisar. Bhairavdās was badly wounded in the fighting in Chāpar-Droṇpur. He also rode with Rāv Jodho when the Rāv's son, Rāv Bīko Jodhāvat, called upon the Rāv to aid in avenging the death of Rāṭhoṛ Kāndhaḷ Riṇmalot ca. 1489. Kāndhaḷ had been killed near Hisar fighting against Sāraṅg Khān. Bhairavdās was again wounded in battle here.

Bhairavdās continued his service to the house of Jodhpur following Rāv Jodho's death in 1489, under Rāv Jodho's successors, Rāv Sātal Jodhāvat (ca. 1489-92) and Rāv Sūjo Jodhāvat (ca. 1492-1515). He fought at the battle of Kusāṇo[16] on March 1, 1492, when Rāv Sātal came to the aid of his half-brothers, Rāv Varsiṅgh Jodhāvat (no. 146) and Dūdo Jodhāvat (no. 104), whose lands of Meṛto were being attacked and pillaged by the ***sūbedār*** of Ajmer, Malū Khān. Rāv Varsiṅgh had precipitated Malū Khān's encroachments by an earlier attack on the rich trading city of Sāmbhar to the north. The Rāṭhoṛs were victorious at Kusāṇo, but Bhairavdās was again wounded, and one of his brothers, Ratansī Cāmpāvat (6-2), was killed. Rāv Sātal Jodhāvat was himself mortally wounded at Kusāṇo and died soon after. He was succeeded to the Jodhpur throne by his uterine brother, Sūjo Jodhāvat.

Under Rāv Sūjo, Bhairavdās participated in a campaign against the Mahevco Rāṭhoṛs of Pokaraṇ who had attacked Phaḷodhī[17] and besieged Rāv Sujo's son, Naro Sūjāvat. Later, in 1503-04, he and other Rāṭhoṛs took action against the Mers of Sojhat to avenge the death of Mahirāj Akhairājot.[18] Mahirāj was Bhairavdās's father's brother's son. Bhairavdās also joined Rāv Sūjo in the

---

[12] Jāṅgaḷu village: located twenty-four miles south of present-day Bīkāner.

[13] Koṛamdesar village: located eleven miles west of present-day Bīkāner.

[14] Coṭīlo village: located seven miles southeast of Rohaṭh in eastern Mārvāṛ.

[15] See ***infra***, "Vīdāvat Rāṭhoṛs," for more information about Vīdo Jodhāvat.

[16] Kusāṇo village: located thirty-eight miles east-northeast of Jodhpur.

[17] The towns of Pokaraṇ and Phaḷodhī lie eighty-three miles northwest and seventy-two miles north-northwest of Jodhpur, respectively.

[18] See ***infra***, "Kūmpāvat Rāṭhoṛs," for more information about Mahirāj Akhairājot.

conquest of Jaitāraṇ in eastern Mārvāṛ from the Sīndhaḷ Rāṭhoṛs and participated in the consolidation of this area under Rāv Sūjo's son, Ūdo Sūjāvat.[19]

Bhairavdās and other Rāṭhoṛ *ṭhākurs* close to the throne, including Bhairavdās's father's brother's son, Pañcāiṇ Akhairājot,[20] were instrumental in securing the succession to the Jodhpur throne of Rāv Sūjo's grandson, Gāṅgo Vāghāvat, over the claims of an elder half-brother, Vīramde Vāghāvat (no. 84), upon Rāv Sūjo's death in 1515. There is no information about Bhairavdās's activities after 1515, but he apparently remained closely involved with the affairs of Jodhpur. He was killed in battle some years later fighting in the service of the Jodhpur ruler. Sources differ regarding the date and circumstances of his death. One states that he was killed in November of 1529 at the battle of Sevakī,[21] while others record that he was killed in 1521-22 during a skirmish with Rāv Vīramde Vāghāvat's Rajpūts near Sojhat. He would have been ninety-five years old in 1529.

Bhairavdās had twelve wives and from eleven to seventeen sons, the most important of whom was Jeso Bhairavdāsot (no. 48) (7-1).

> ***Bāṅkīdās***, p. 54; ***Cāmpāvat Rāṭhauṛ***, pp. 11-17; Kānotā, ***Cāmpāvatoṃ kā Itihās***, 1:42-56; ***Murārdān***, no. 1, p. 655; Śarmā, ***Dāsapoṃ kā Itihās***, pp. 18-23; ***Vigat***, "Pariśiṣṭ - 4: Ḍāvī ne Jīvṇī Mislāṃ rī Vigat," 2:477.

(no. 48) **Jeso Bhairavdāsot** (7-1)

Jeso Bhairavdāsot was a son of Bhairavdās Cāmpāvat (6-1) and grandson of Cāmpo Riṇmalot (5-1), the founding ancestor of the Cāmpāvat Rāṭhoṛs. He was born on January 12, 1467, as Bhairavdās's fourth son. His mother was Bhāṭiyāṇī Bhagvānkuṃvar. Jeso's birth took place eight years after the founding of Jodhpur in 1459, and he grew up during the period of Rāṭhoṛ consolidation and expansion in Mārvāṛ, rising to a position of great influence and power under both Rāv Gāṅgo Vāghāvat (1515-32) and his successor, Rāv Mālde Gāṅgāvat (1532-62).

Little is known about Jeso's life prior to his father's death in 1521-22. The only recorded event is his founding of the village Riṇsīgāṃv[22] on November 3, 1502 when he was thirty-five years old. The texts offer varying reasons for Jeso's move from his father's village of Kāparṛo. The most cogent appears to be the curse of a holy man who lived in a garden at Kāparṛo. The holy man is said

---

[19] See ***infra***, "Ūdāvat Rāṭhoṛs," for more information about Ūdo Sūjāvat.

[20] See ***infra***, "Jaitāvat Rāṭhoṛs," for more information about Pañcāiṇ Akhairājot.

[21] Sevakī village: located twenty-three miles northeast of Jodhpur.

[22] Riṇsīgāṃv village: located seventeen miles east-northeast of Kāparṛo and forty-three miles east of Jodhpur.

to have foretold that if Bhairavdās's descendants remained at Kāparṛo, they would perish.

Jeso was fifty-four years old when his father died. He maintained his father's influential position in Mārvāṛ, and it is recorded that he lived another thirty-seven years and died in 1558-59 at the age of ninety-one at his village of Āū.[23]

Jeso's first major campaign following his father's death took place in 1527. He was part of the contingent of warriors from Mārvāṛ whom Rāv Gāṅgo Vāghāvat of Jodhpur sent to north India with Sīsodīyo Rāṇo Sāṅgo Rāymalot of Cītoṛ (1509-28) to meet the Mughal Bābur in battle at Khanua. Among this force was a contingent of Meṛtīyos under Rāv Vīramde Dūdāvat (no. 105) and his two brothers, Rāymal and Ratansī, both of whom were killed at Khanua. Jeso himself was wounded there, and a large number of Rajpūts who accompanied him killed.

Jeso fought alongside Rāv Gāṅgo of Jodhpur on November 2, 1529 at the battle of Sevakī[24] against the Rāv's paternal uncle, Sekho Sūjāvat (no. 86), and Sekho's ally from Nāgaur, Khānzāda Khān Daulat Khān (ca. 1526-36; no. 154). Sekho Sūjāvat, who sought broader authority and control in Mārvāṛ, had precipitated this conflict between father's brother (***kāko***) and brother's son (***bhatījo***).

Rāv Gāṅgo again turned his attention to Sojhat following his victory at Sevakī. He sequestered this land from his half-brother, Rāv Vīramde Vāghāvat (no. 84), with whom there had been on-going conflict since his accession in 1515. Rāv Vīramde was given the village of Khairvo[25] in compensation, but he was not content with this offer and continued his depredations against Jodhpur, forcing Rāv Gāṅgo to drive him from Mārvāṛ. Rāv Vīramde then went to Mevāṛ. He gained the support of Sīsodīyo Rāṇo Vikramaditya Sāṅgāvat (ca. 1531-36) and led a small force back into Mārvāṛ and attacked Jeso's village of Riṇsīgāṃv. Rāv Vīramde suffered defeat here, but he returned again for a decisive confrontation at the village of Sāraṇ[26] on the edge of the Arāvallīs southeast of Sojhat. Here Rāv Gāṅgo defeated Rāv Vīramde and removed all of his authority from Sojhat and Mārvāṛ. Jeso was an active participant in all of these actions and, during the latter conflict, was again wounded.

Rāv Gāṅgo's son, Mālde Gāṅgāvat, succeeded to the Jodhpur throne in 1532, and, with his succession, Jeso rose to become one of the principal ***ṭhākur***s of Mārvāṛ alongside Rāv Mālde's leading military commanders, Rāṭhoṛs Jaito Pañcāiṇot (no. 61) and Kūmpo Mahirājot (no. 95). Rāv Mālde's accession took place at Sojhat, and, following ceremonies there, the Rāv proceeded first to Jeso's village of Riṇsīgāṃv to pay his respects and to accept Jeso's oath of

---

[23] Āū village: located twenty-one miles south of Sojhat.

[24] Sevakī village: located twenty-three miles northeast of Jodhpur.

[25] Khairvo village: located twenty-two miles southwest of Sojhat.

[26] Sāraṇ village: located eighteen miles southeast of Sojhat.

loyalty and service. He made Jeso one of his ***pradhāns*** at this time. Shortly thereafter in 1534 Rāv Mālde sent Jeso with a force of Rajpūts to assist Sīsodīyo Rāṇo Vikramaditya in his unsuccessful defense of the fortress of Cītoṛ against Sultān Bahādur Shāh of Gujarat (1526-37).

A year later, ca. 1535, Jeso became more directly involved in the hostilities that had developed between Rāv Mālde and the Meṛtīyo Rāṭhoṛs. "Aitihāsik Bātāṃ," p. 57, records that early in Rāv Mālde's reign, Rāṭhoṛ Jaito Pañcāiṇot had confronted the Rāv when he spoke of his desire to conquer Meṛto, Bīkāner, and Sīvāṇo and had objected to these conquests because Rāṭhoṛs ruled all of these kingdoms. He stated forcefully, "The offense of killing one's family members/brothers (***gotrakadamb*** - lit. '***gotra***-destruction') will not be committed by me." ***Vigat***, 2:48, also notes that when Rāv Mālde plotted against Rāv Vīramde Dūdāvat (no. 105) and the Meṛtīyos, Kūmpo Mahirājot and Jeso Bhairavdāsot "would not get involved in this matter."

Neither Jeso nor the other leading Rajpūts in Rāv Mālde's service could blunt the Rāv's enmity toward Meṛto, however, nor were they willing to challenge his commands. They participated in open battle against Meṛtīyo Rāv Vīramde at Reyāṃ village[27] ca. 1535. This conflict was precipitated by Rāv Vīramde's occupation of Ajmer when the Muslim ***kiledār*** fled the city and left it open upon the fall of Māṇḍū to the Mughal Emperor Humāyūn. Rāv Mālde demanded Ajmer from Rāv Vīramde, and when Rāv Vīramde refused to hand over the city, Rāv Mālde sent his Rajpūts into the lands of Meṛto and began dividing them among his warriors. Rāv Vīramde then mounted a precipitous attack on Reyāṃ village in order to chastise Varsiṅghot Meṛtīyo Sahaiso Tejsīyot (no. 151), who had been one of his Rajpūts, but had sided with Rāv Mālde and received Reyāṃ from him in ***paṭo***. News of this coming attack reached the garrison at Raṛod,[28] where Jeso was stationed along with Jaito Pañcāiṇot, Kūmpo Mahirājot, and other important ***ṭhākurs*** of Mārvāṛ. They rode to Reyāṃ and took part in the bloody fighting at this village, during which Meṛtīyo Rāv Vīramde was badly defeated and many of his Rajpūts killed. Jeso was again wounded here (see ***Vigat***, 2:51-54, of the **translated text** for details about this engagement).

"Aitihāsik Bātāṃ," p. 59, records that ca. 1537 Jeso was a military servant of Sīsodīyo Ūdaisiṅgh Sāṅgāvat (Rāṇo of Cītoṛ, ca. 1537-72; no. 17) at Kumbhaḷmer. How Jeso came to take service under Sīsodīyo Udaisiṅgh is unclear. Kumbhaḷmer had come under siege in this period from the forces of a pretender to the throne, Sīsodīyo Vaṇvīr Prithīrājot, who had murdered Udaisiṅgh's uterine brother, Rāṇo Vikramaditya (ca. 1531-36) at Cītoṛ. Sīsodīyo Udaisiṅgh turned to Jeso and asked how he might liberate Kumbhaḷmer from Vaṇvīr's threat. Jeso counseled Udaisiṅgh to summon Rāṭhoṛ Kūmpo Mahirājot,

---

[27] Reyāṃ village: located fifteen miles southeast of Meṛto.

[28] Raṛod village: located forty-four miles northeast of Jodhpur and six miles west of Āsop.

whom Rāv Mālde had stationed at the garrison of Madārīyo in Goḍhvāṛ.[29] Jeso stated that when Kūmpo received word, he would come and provide the assistance and protection needed. Udaisiṅgh was unsure of how to respond, being fearful because of Rāv Mālde's forceful expansion out from Mārvāṛ following his accession in 1532, particularly after his occupation of Ajmer ca. 1535, when he sent his armies to occupy large areas of central Rājasthān. The Rāv had also placed garrisons along the northern borders of Mevāṛ and in Goḍhvāṛ. Sīsodīyo Udaisiṅgh remarked to Jeso:

> Rāv Mālde became [as it were] Rāhū[30] and attacked our land, and Kūmpo is a military servant of Rāv Mālde's. [If we were] to summon [him in] our distress, why would [he] come? (*ibid.*)

Jeso responded that Kūmpo was his brother's son[31] and that if Jeso's men came to Udaisiṅgh's assistance, Kūmpo and his men would also come without delay. Messages were then sent to Kūmpo at Madārīyo, and Kūmpo immediately rode to Kumbhaḷmer with five hundred warriors. The Sonagaro Cahuvāṇ, Akhairāj Riṇdhīrot (no. 9) of Pālī village,[32] who was Udaisiṅgh's wife's father,[33] had been much involved in supporting Udaisiṅgh as well. He played a leading role in coordinating this effort in Udaisiṅgh's behalf. He arrived with his own force of Rajpūts after Sīsodīyo Udaisiṅgh sent messages directly to him, requesting his aid. With their arrival, Vaṇvīr's men lifted their siege and retreated before this concerted force of Mārvāṛ Rajpūts. Sonagaro Akhairāj was then instrumental in seating Udaisiṅgh on the Sīsodīyo throne at Kumbhaḷmer.

Little information is available about Jeso's activities during the period between 1537 and 1544. Texts next record his presence at the battle of Samel[34] in January of 1544. Jeso was again a military servant of Rāv Mālde and he participated in the initial phases of this conflict. He is credited with killing one of Sher Shāh's leading warriors, Jalāl Khān Jalvāṇī, and with stealing Jalāl Khān's horses from under the eyes of Sher Shāh himself. Jeso was apparently

---

[29] Madārīyo village: located thirteen miles south-southwest of Nāḍūl and thirteen miles west-northwest of Kumbhaḷmer.

[30] Rāhū: the name of a Daitya or demon who is supposed to seize the sun and moon, thereby causing eclipses (Platts, ***Dictionary***, p. 585).

[31] Kūmpo Mahirājot's and Jeso Bhairavdāsot's grandfathers were brothers. These men were Akhairāj and Cāmpo Riṇmalot, both sons of Rāv Riṇmal Cūṇḍāvat of Maṇḍor.

[32] Pālī village: located forty miles south-southeast of Jodhpur.

[33] Kānotā, ***Cāmpāvatoṃ kā Itihās***, 1:69, notes that it was because of Jeso Bhairavdāsot's strong advice that Sonagaro Akhairāj married a daughter to Sīsodīyo Udaisiṅgh. The marriage took place some months prior to Udaisiṅgh's succession to the throne at Kumbhaḷmer ca. 1537.

[34] Samel village: located twenty-four miles southwest of Ajmer.

wounded at Samel prior to the main engagement, and he withdrew to join Rāv Mālde during his exile from Jodhpur in the hills near Sīvāṇo.

Rāv Mālde immediately sought to reassert his authority in Mārvāṛ following Sher Shāh's death in May of 1545. He moved first against the important and strongly manned garrison at Bhāṅgesar,[35] then under the charge of Hājī Alī Fateh Khān. Jeso was among the leading warriors sent against this garrison. According to "Aitihāsik Bātāṃ," p. 39, Jeso approached Rāv Mālde prior to this campaign and entreated him, saying, "I was not able to die fighting in the great battle [at Samel]." Jeso appears to have requested that he be sent against Bhāṅgesar to have another opportunity to die honorably in battle. He was seventy-eight years old. Rāv Mālde gave him a prominent role in this attack, and Jeso was wounded when the Rāv's Rajpūts overwhelmed the Muslims of the garrison and then proceeded on to Jodhpur, which they also took into their possession. Rāv Mālde paid Jeso great honor following this battle, giving him an elephant, a litter in which to ride, and costly jewels.

Jeso now emerged as Rāv Mālde's most important ***ṭhākur***. The Rāv's leading Rajpūts from the period before Samel, Jaito Pañcāiṇot and Kūmpo Mahirājot, were both dead. "Aitihāsik Bātāṃ," p. 46, states that "among the ***ṭhākur***s and important men, Rāṭhoṛ Jeso Bhairavdāsot became [the Rāv's] foremost counselor (***pūchaṇai pradhān***)." Jeso received the lands for the village of Āū (Āūvo) in ***paṭo*** at this time.[36] Jeso is said to have founded Āū following a trip to Goḍhvāṛ on a site where he had seen several lions. The sighting of lions was a most auspicious sign.

Jeso used his position of influence with Rāv Mālde during this period to have Bagṛī,[37] the ancestral village of Jaito Pañcāiṇot's family, returned to this family. The Rāv had taken Bagṛī from the Jaitāvats following the failure of one of Jaito's sons, Mānsiṅgh Jaitāvat, to perform military service after the battle of Samel. At Jeso's persistence, the Rāv relented and granted Bagṛī to another of Jaito's sons, Prithīrāj Jaitāvat (no. 63). Much of Jeso's persistence appears based upon his desire to ally Prithīrāj Jaitāvat firmly with the house of Jodhpur. Prithīrāj was himself a prominent ***ṭhākur*** of Mārvāṛ, and he soon thereafter gained the esteem of the Rāv and emerged as one of his leading military commanders.

Jeso was also concerned for Mārvāṛ. Following Rāv Mālde's return to Jodhpur after Samel, Sīsodīyo Rāṇo Udaisiṅgh Sāṅgāvat of Cītoṛ began preparations to send raiding parties against him. Jeso knew that:

---

[35] Bhāṅgesar village: located sixteen miles west of Sojhat.

[36] ***Murārdān***, no. 1, p. 655, states that Bhairavdās received Āū in 1545-46 after Rāv Mālde's reoccupation of Jodhpur, while Kānotā, ***Cāmpāvatoṃ kā Itihās***, 1:64, writes that Rāv Gāṅgo gave Jeso the lands of Āū some years earlier in 1529 following the battle of Sevakī.

[37] Bagṛī village: located nine miles east-southeast of Sojhat.

> Today Rāṇo Udaisiṅgh [is] powerful, [and] we have just now returned from a period of distress (***vikhau***). The Rajpūts [and] all the important men died fighting in the great battle [at Samel]. The Rāvjī's rulership (***ṭhākurāī***) will become weak [from] a confrontation today" ("Aitihāsik Bātāṃ," p. 46).

Rāv Mālde paid great deference to Jeso as his ***pradhān***, and, on Jeso's advice, agreed to marry one of his daughters to the Sīsodīyo Rāṇo and to give the Rāṇo horses, elephants, and fifty villages of Sojhat along with the whole of Goḍhvāṛ in dowry in order to placate him and ward off his attacks.

When Prithīrāj Jaitāvat learned that these arrangements were being considered, however, he remonstrated strongly with the Rāv, urging him not to display any weakness before the Rāṇo. Rāv Mālde then took heart and determined to withhold his offer of marriage and dowry. Prithīrāj Jaitāvat was later able to turn the Sīsodīyos back when they began raiding into Mārvāṛ and to prevent any humiliation of Rāv Mālde.

Rāv Mālde's confidence in Jeso remained undiminished, for he gave Jeso full responsibility for the army of Jodhpur sent to conquer Pokaraṇ[38] from the Bhāṭīs of Jaisaḷmer in 1550. Following Jeso's success there, Rāv Mālde sent him first against Bāhaṛmer in far western Mārvāṛ and then against Jaisaḷmer itself in 1552. Jeso besieged the fortress of Jaisaḷmer and pillaged the villages in the surrounding countryside. When he returned to Jodhpur, the Rāv awarded him full responsibility for administration of the kingdom. Jeso was an old warrior now of some eighty-five years.

Confusion surrounds the date and circumstances of Jeso's death. Both Bhagavatsiṃh, ***Cāmpāvat Rāṭhauṛ***, p. 31, and Śarmā, ***Dāsapoṃ kā Itihās***, p. 29, indicate that Jeso was killed in battle at Meṛto in 1562, fighting in the defense of the Mālgaḍh alongside Devīdās Jaitāvat (no. 65). However, Kānotā, ***Cāmpāvatoṃ kā Itihās***, 1:83, states that Jeso died at Āū village in 1558-59 at the age of ninety-one. He notes correctly that there is no mention in contemporary sources of Jeso's death at Merto in 1562.

Jeso had eight wives and from twelve to twenty-one sons. One of his daughters was married to Hāḍo Rāv Surjan Urjaṇot of Būndī (ca. 1554-68) (no. 6). Her son by Rāv Surjaṇ was Hāḍo Dūdo Surjanot.

> "Aitihāsik Bātāṃ," pp. 39-40, 44-47, 56-69; ***Baṅkīdās***, pp. 54; ***Cāmpāvat Rāṭhauṛ***, pp. 18-31; Gehlot, ***Mārvāṛ***, p. 160; Kānotā, ***Cāmpāvatoṃ kā Itihās***, 1:58-88; ***Khyāt***, 1:27, 111, 207, 2:164, 3:266; ***Murārdān***, no. 1, p. 655, no. 2, pp. 123, 128; Śarma, ***Dāsapoṃ kā Itihās***, pp. 23-29; ***Vigat***, 1:57, 63, 2:4-5, 48, 52-53, "Pariśiṣṭ - 4: Ḍāvī ne Jīvṇī Misḷāṃ rī Vigat," 2:475, 477.

---

[38] Pokaraṇ: located eighty-three miles northwest of Jodhpur.

(no. 49) **Jaitmāl Jesāvat** (8-1)

Jaitmāl Jesāvat was a son of Jeso Bhairavdāsot (7-1) (no. 48) and a great-grandson of Cāmpo Riṇmalot (5-1), the founding ancestor of the Cāmpāvat Rāṭhoṛs. He was born on January 10, 1489 of Hulṇī Prabhākuṃvar, daughter of Hul Mahesdās of Sojhat. Little is known about his life prior to the mid-1550s. He was a military servant of Rāv Mālde Gāṅgāvat of Jodhpur (1532-1562) and was among the select group of Rajpūts from Mārvāṛ whom Rāv Mālde sent under Rāṭhoṛ Devīdās Jaitāvat (no. 65) to fight at Harmāṛo[39] in January of 1557. Rāv Mālde's warriors joined with those of Paṭhāṇ Hājī Khān, a former noble of Sher Shāh Sūr. Together they defeated Sīsodīyo Rāṇo Udaisiṅgh Sāṅgāvat (ca. 1537-72; no. 17) and his allied force of Rajpūts.

In 1558, with the death of his father, Jaitmāl succeeded to the rule of Āū village. His family retained possession of this village for the next several generations. As ***ṭhākur*** of Āū, Jaitmāl assumed a position of great influence in Mārvāṛ, particularly under Rāv Mālde's successor, Rāv Candrasen Māldevot (1562-81). Local texts indicated that Jaitmāl developed a disagreement with Rāv Candrasen early in the Rāv's reign. This disagreement arose when Rāv Candrasen had one of his stablehands, with whom he had become angry, seized and killed in Jaitmāl's camp where the stablehand had fled for protection. Jaitmāl afterwards proceeded to the home of Rāṭhoṛs Prithīrāj Kūmpāvat (no. 97) and Mahes Kūmpāvat (no. 98) and wept before them. Prithīrāj then told Jaitmāl not to weep, saying:

> [If] Parameśvar bestows [his blessing on me], then I, [born] of Kūmpo's stomach, would cause Candrasen to weep [and to regret this act]. You should not be distressed for any reason.

Jaitmāl apparently departed for his village of Āū afterwards, where he stayed for some time. But he remained involved with affairs at court, and a faction of Rāṭhoṛs emerged in Mārvāṛ around both Jaitmāl Jesāvat and Prithīrāj Kūmpāvat that encouraged inroads into the kingdom on the part of several of Rāv Candrasen's brothers. These included the Rāv's elder uterine brother, Udaisiṅgh Māldevot, who was then at Phaḷodhī in northern Mārvāṛ, a half-brother, Rām Māldevot, who was in Mevāṛ, and another half-brother, Rāymal Māldevot, who came north from Sīvāṇo and began raiding in the area of Dunāṛo village.[40]

Udaisiṅgh Māldevot's advance from Phaḷodhī led to the battle of Lohīyāvaṭ[41] ca. 1563 when Rāv Candrasen defeated Udaisiṅgh's attempt to usurp control of Jodhpur. Kānotā, ***Cāmpāvatoṃ kā Itihās***, 3:771, notes that Jaitmāl was among those who counseled the Rāv not to pursue and drive his brother

---

[39] Harmāṛo village: located fifty-five miles south-southwest of Ajmer and six miles south of Vadhnor in northern Mevāṛ.

[40] Dunāṛo village: located thirty-two miles southwest of Jodhpur.

[41] Lohīyāvaṭ village: located eighteen miles southeast of Phaḷodhī in northern Mārvāṛ.

from Phaḷodhī following his victory, but to allow peace between them. Rāv Candrasen had summoned Jaitmāl from Āū, for Jaitmāl is listed among Rāv Candrasen's principal *ṭhākurs* at this battle. Given his enmity toward the Rāv, his specific role in the fighting is unknown.

The faction of Rāṭhoṛs opposing Rāv Candrasen next approached Rām Māldevot and urged him to seek Mughal support for his cause. Rām did seek aid from the Mughals, and the Rāṭhoṛs supporting his cause took part in mediations between him and Rāv Candrasen and were instrumental in Rām's acquisition of Sojhat in *jāgīr* in 1564.

Jaitmāl's specific role in Mārvāṛ after this time is unclear. He seems to have retired to his village of Āū, for when the Mughals forced Rāv Candrasen into exile in the Arāvallīs in the mid-1570s, Jaitmāl was not listed among those military servants who accompanied him.[42] Jaitmāl's name does not appear with relation to events after this time. No information is available about the circumstances surrounding his death.

"Aitihāsik Bātāṃ," pp. 51, 78; ***Bāṅkīdās***, p. 56; ***Cāmpāvat Rāṭhauṛ***, pp. 29-31; Kānotā, ***Cāmpāvatoṃ kā Itihās***, 3:769-774; ***Murārdān***, no. 1, p. 655, no. 2, p. 155; Śarmā, ***Dāsapoṃ kā Itihās***, p . 29; ***Vigat***, 1:60, 67, 80, 2:59.

(no. 50) **Rāmo Bhairavdāsot** (7-2)
(no. 51) **Amro Rāmāvat** (8-2)
(no. 52) **Sahaiso Rāmāvat** (8-3)

Little information is available about Rāmo (Rāmsiṅgh) Bhairavdāsot and his two sons, Amro and Sahaiso Rāmāvat.[43] Rāmo was a son of Bhairavdās Cāmpāvat's (6-1) and grandson of Cāmpo Riṇmalot's (5-1), the founding ancestor of the Cāmpāvat Rāṭhoṛs. He was Bhairavdās's ninth son, born in 1485-86 some eighteen years after the birth of his brother, Jeso Bhairavdāsot (no. 48) (7-1). He served under Rāv Mālde Gāṅgāvat of Jodhpur (1532-62) and held the village of Lodrāū (or Kāchrāū) of Jāḷor in *paṭo*. He and his sons, Amro and Sahaiso, were all killed in 1562 during the battle of Meṛto. They served under

[42] Kānotā, ***Cāmpāvatoṃ kā Itihās***, 3:772, writes that Jaitmāl did accompany Rāv Candrasen into exile and remained with him until his death in 1581. This statement appears to be in error.

[43] Amro Rāmāvat and Sahaiso Rāmāvat have been identified on a name basis only as sons of Rāmo Bhairavdāsot, appearing together as they do in lists of Rāv Mālde's warriors who were killed at Meṛto in 1562. This writer has been unable to identify them more precisely from genealogical materials available for the Cāmpāvat Rāṭhoṛs, and their names do not appear in genealogical materials for other groups which would provide an alternative identification. To complicate matters, Kānotā, ***Cāmpāvatoṃ kā Itihās***, 3:879, writes that Rāmo Bhairavdāsot had only one son named Chatrasiṅgh. Without other defining material, the placement of these Rajpūts genealogically remains moot.

Rāv Mālde's commander, Rāṭhoṛ Devīdās Jaitiāvat (no. 65), and were stationed at the Mālgaḍh with Devīdās when Meṛtīyo Rāv Jaimal Vīramdevot (no. 107) and Mīrzā Sharafu'd-Dīn Ḥusayn laid siege to the town. Following two months of desultory fighting, Rāv Mālde's Rajpūts agreed to give up the fort to Rāv Jaimal. As they left the Mālgaḍh and made their way toward Sātalvās.[44] the Mughals attacked, and Rāmo and his sons died alongside Rāṭhoṛ Devīdās as they fought on the open plain (see ***Vigat***, 2:65, of the **translated text** for details).

"Aitihāsik Bātāṃ," p. 56; ***Bāṅkīdās***, pp. 16-17; ***Cāmpāvat Rāṭhauṛ***, pp. 16-17; Kānotā, ***Cāmpāvatoṃ kā Itihās***, 3:877-879; Śarmā, ***Dāsapoṃ kā Itihās***, p. 23, n. 1; ***Vigat***, 1:62, 2:65.

---

[44] Sātalvās village: located just four miles southwest of Meṛto proper.

Figure 21. Cāmpāvat Rāṭhoṛs

(1-1) Rāv Salkho

(2-1) Vīram Salkhāvat

(3-1) Rāv Cūṇḍo Vīramot

(4-1) Rāv Riṇmal Cūṇḍāvat

(5-1) Cāmpo Riṇmalot (**Cāmpāvats**)

(6-1) Bhairavdās Cāmpāvat — (6-2) Ratansī Cāmpāvat

(7-1) **Jeso Bhairavdāsot** — (7-2) **Rāmo Bhairavdāsot**

(8-1) **Jaitmāl Jesāvat** — (8-2) **Amro Rāmāvat** — (8-3) **Sahaiso Rāmāvat**

Cūṇḍāvat Rāṭhoṛs

(no. 55) **Āskaraṇ Satāvat** (5-2)
(no. 57) **Īsar Ghaṛsīyot** (7-1)
(no. 53) **Kānho Cūṇḍāvat, Rāv** (4-1)
(no. 58) **Mahes Ghaṛsīyot** (7-2)
(no. 56) **Narbad Satāvat** (5-3)
(no. 59) **Rājsiṅgh Ghaṛsīyot** (7-3)
(no. 54) **Sato Cūṇḍāvat, Rāv** (4-2)

Rāv Cūṇḍo Vīramot and the Cūṇḍāvat Rāṭhoṛs

The Cūṇḍāvat Rāṭhoṛs comprise a loosely structured grouping of Mārvāṛ Rāṭhoṛs tracing descent from Rāv Cūṇḍo Vīramot (3-1), ruler of Maṇḍor in the late fourteenth and early fifteenth centuries. In the broadest sense, all descendants of Rāv Cūṇḍo's may be included within this grouping. However, by the sixteenth and seventeenth centuries, many branches (***sākh***s) of Rāṭhoṛs had emerged from among Rāv Cūṇḍo's sons and grandsons that became identified by the names of more recent "founders." The designation Cūṇḍāvat came to be applied only to members from less prominent lines of descent from Rāv Cūṇḍo, for whom Rāv Cūṇḍo was himself their most important ancestor.

By way of example, "Jodhpur Hukūmat rī Bahī," pp. 142-143, a manuscript whose compilation was begun during the reign of Jodhpur Rājā Jasvantsiṅgh Gajsiṅghot (1638-78), contains the names of nine Cūṇḍāvat Rāṭhoṛs to whom the rulers of Jodhpur granted ***paṭo***s between the years 1623-68. The Cūṇḍāvats listed are descendants of only two of Rāv Cūṇḍo's sons, Kānho (4-1) and Araṛkamal (4-4).

The Cūṇḍāvats discussed in this section include Rāv Kānho Cūṇḍāvat, Rāv Sato Cūṇḍāvat, two of Rāv Sato's sons, and three of Rāv Kānho's great-grandsons. While Kānho's line continued after him, Sato's appears to have died out after the deaths of his two sons. The ***Khyāt*** of Naiṇsī, 3:38, records that neither had sons of his own. The descendants of these individuals are traced with difficulty in the texts, however, and ***Vīr Vinod***, 2:804, notes that a branch of Rāṭhoṛs did emerge among Sato's descendants bearing the name Satāvat. In general, Cūṇḍāvats are mentioned rarely in the chronicles dealing with events of the sixteenth and seventeenth centuries, and they do not figure prominently in the later history of Jodhpur.

Much uncertainty surrounds the people and events of the early period of Rāṭhoṛ history in Mārvāṛ. It is not until the time of Rāv Jodho Riṇmalot (5-5), ruler of Maṇḍor and founder of Jodhpur (ca. 1453-89), that a strict chronology begins to emerge. Of Rāv Cūṇḍo himself it is possible to say with certainty only that:

1. He was raised in the household of a paternal relation, Rāṭhoṛ Rāvaḷ Mālojī (Mallināth) of Mahevo in western Mārvāṛ, in the mid-fourteenth century;

2. He became a Rajpūt of importance by the latter half of the fourteenth century, and he established his seat of rule at Maṇḍor in central Mārvāṛ;

3. He became involved in hostilities with Bhāṭī Rāv Rānagde of Pūṅgaḷ, whom he killed in battle;

4. He died in the early fifteenth century and was succeeded by three of his sons in rapid succession: Kānho (4-1), Sato (4-2), and then Riṇmal (4-5).

In these volumes, ca. 1423 has been employed to designate the date of Rāv Cūṇḍo's death in order to establish a rough chronology for this early period. This dating is conjectural, however. Among historians of Rājasthān and Mārvāṛ, there is wide disagreement. G. H. Ojhā states in his ***Rājpūtāne kā Itihās***, 4:1:231, for example, that there are only two certain dates for Rāṭhoṛ history during the thirteenth, fourteenth, and early fifteenth centuries:

1. The date of Rāv Sīho Setrāmot's death in 1273, noted on a memorial stone (***devḷī***) found at the village of Bīṭhū near Pālī in eastern Mārvāṛ[1] (Sīho Setrāmot is considered the founding ancestor of the Mārvāṛ Rāṭhoṛs);

2. The date of Rāv Riṇmal Cūṇḍāvat's death ca. 1438. This date is based upon the Ranpur Inscription of Sīsodīyo Rāṇo Kūmbo Mokaḷot (ca. 1433-68). This inscription is dated V.S. 1496 (1439-40) and records the Sīsodīyo conquest of Maṇḍor that followed immediately upon Rāv Riṇmal's murder at Cītoṛ.

Ojhā, 4:1:212-213, also makes reference to two copper plate inscriptions of Rāv Cūṇḍo's from Mārvāṛ dated 1396 and 1421. But he discredits these as not being authentic.

B. N. Reu is more direct in applying dating in his ***Mārvāṛ kā Itihās***. He states, 1:65, that Rāv Cūṇḍo died on March 15, 1423. He does not substantiate this date with any source reference, however. In addition, he notes, 1:60-61, that Rāv Cūṇḍo originally took possession of Maṇḍor in 1394, basing this dating upon an inscription found in the temple of Cāmuṇḍā Devījī, the ***kuḷdevī*** of the Rāṭhoṛs, in the village of Cāṃvḍo[2] which bears this date. The inscription does not refer directly to Rāv Cūṇḍo by name and it is fragmentary. But Reu argues that Cūṇḍo would have been responsible for building this temple after his conquest. Ojhā does not mention this temple inscription at all. Kavirājā Śyāmaldās, the author of ***Vīr Vinod***, 2:803, gives the date of 1394 for Rāv

---

[1] Bīṭhū village: located thirty miles south of Jodhpur and fourteen miles northwest of Pālī.

[2] Cāṃvḍo village: located fourteen miles west-northwest of Maṇḍor.

Cūṇḍo's conquest of Maṇḍor, and then offers the date of 1408 for his death. Both dates are presented without substantiation from primary source material.

These early historians of Mārvāṛ based their chronologies on the available inscriptional evidence and on secondary sources from periods much later than the events they referenced. The only local text of note to which they had access was Naiṇsī's ***Khyāt***. The ***Vigat*** of Naiṇsī was not available to them. One short passage in ***Vigat***, 1:38, provides some additional evidence about the date of Rāv Cūṇḍo's death to add to the controversy. It states that Rāv Jodho Riṇmalot's mother, a Bhāṭiyāṇī, was married to Rāv Riṇmal Cūṇḍāvat, "in [the settlement of] Cūṇḍo's ***vair***." Local chronicles all contain stories about Rāv Cūṇḍo having been killed in battle fighting against the Bhāṭīs from Jaisaḷmer. Jodho Riṇmalot was born April 1, 1416. This date of birth would mean that Rāv Cūṇḍo was killed some years prior, perhaps as early as 1408, a date given in several sources.

It is not our purpose here to define a more exact chronology for this early period of Rāṭhoṛ history, only to note that the period as a whole requires extensive reworking from both Mārvāṛī and other local sources.

> ***Bāṅkīdās***, p. 6; "Jodhpur Hukūmat rī Bahī," pp. 142-143; ***Khyāt***, 1:353, 2:306-316, 3:30-31; ***Murārdān***, no. 1, p. 64, no. 2, pp. 5, 56-65, 83-90; Ojhā, 4:1:200-213; Reu, 1:58-67; ***Vigat***, 1:21-26, 38; ***Vīr Vinod***, 2:803-804.

(no. 53) **Kānho Cūṇḍāvat, Rāv** (4-1)
(no. 54) **Sato Cūṇḍāvat, Rāv** (4-2)

Very little is known about Rāv Cūṇḍo Vīramot's two sons, Kānho and Sato Cūṇḍāvat, who succeeded him to the rulership of Maṇḍor. The length of their reigns is also uncertain. Figures given in the various texts range from eleven months to two or three years for Kānho, and up to four years for Sato. The chronicles consider both to have been weak and ineffective rulers, and both were unseated in turn by half brothers who turned against them. Rāv Riṇmal Cūṇḍāvat (4-5) eventually emerged as the ruler of Maṇḍor, and it is his descendants, beginning with Jodho Riṇmalot (5-5), who firmly established Rāṭhoṛ rule in central Mārvāṛ from the mid-fifteenth century onwards.

Kānho was Rāv Cūṇḍo's youngest son, born of Rāṇī Mohilāṇī Sonāṃ, the daughter of Mohil Cahuvāṇ Īsardās of Chāpar-Droṇpur.[3] Rāṇī Sonāṃ was Rāv Cūṇḍo's favorite wife in his old age, and the chronicles relate that he designated her son to succeed him to the throne of Maṇḍor over older, more capable sons by other wives. The only significant event ascribed to Rāv Kānho's reign is his successful raid against the Sāṅkhlo Paṃvārs of Jāṅgaḷu.[4] The chronicles present varying reasons for this attack including a desire on the Rāv's

---

[3] Chāpar-Droṇpur: an area that later became part of southeastern Bīkāner territory.

[4] Jāṅgaḷu: located one hundred miles to the north of Maṇḍor.

part of avenge his father, Rāv Cūṇḍo's, death, and hostilities between the Rāṭhoṛs and the Sāṅkhlos unrelated to Rāv Cūṇḍo.

Vigat, 1:385-386, includes mention of Bhāgvatī Karṇījī in its short record of Rāv Kānho's reign. Karṇījī was an important Cāraṇī of the late fourteenth and early fifteenth centuries, who became integrally involved in the affairs of Jodhpur and Bīkāner.[5] According to the *Vigat*, Karṇījī visited Rāv Kānho prior to his march on Jāṅgaḷu in order to bless him and empower his kingdom with an auspicious rite. The rite consisted of placing whole grains of rice on the ruler's forehead, seen as a propitious sign. When Karṇījī began the ceremony, the Rāv is said to have questioned her, asking why she was performing the rite. When the Cāraṇī replied that the kingdom would acquire merit from it, the Rāv only responded that he had no faith in such a ceremony. He relied only upon his own devotions. The Cāraṇī then became angry and cursed the Rāv, saying that the Rāv would lose his kingdom and the rice would forecast the number of days the kingdom would remain. It was not long thereafter that Rāv Kānho's half-brothers, Sato (4-2) and Riṇmal (4-5), attacked Maṇḍor and usurped rule of the kingdom.

Sato Cūṇḍāvat, an older son of Rāv Cūṇḍo's born of his wife, the Gahlot Tārāde, then assumed control of Maṇḍor as *rāv*. He also ruled only a short time. According to the chronicles, he gave one-half of the lands of Maṇḍor to his uterine brother, Rāvat Riṇdhīr Cūṇḍāvat (4-3), and delegated most of his authority for managing the affairs of the kingdom to him. Riṇdhīr soon gained

[5] Karṇījī was a Cāraṇī of the Kiṇīyo *sākh*. She is worshipped as a tutelary deity (*lokdevī*, *kuḷdevī*) among Rajpūts of Rājasthān in general, and of Mārvāṛ and Bīkāner in particular, and is considered an incarnation of Śaktī or the Divine Mother. According to local belief, such incarnations generally only occur within the Cāraṇ *jāti*. Karṇījī and before her, Avadjī, the *kuḷdevī* of the Bhāṭīs of Jaisaḷmer, are both seen as successive incarnations of Bhāgvatī Hiṅglāj, a former manifestation whose shrine is near Las Belas in Pakistan. Collectively, these manifestations are referred to as "Caurāsī Cāraṇ" and are worshipped widely in Rājasthān and other parts of western India by Rajpūts and Cāraṇs.

Karṇījī's traditional date of birth is September 21, 1387. She was born in the village of Adho on the border between Jaisaḷmer and Mārvāṛ. Her birth name was Ridhīkuṃvar, but during her life, she became known as Karṇī ("the Doer"), or more affectionately, Karnal Kiniyāṇī. Karṇījī lived much of her life in the village of Desnok, located nineteen miles south of Bīkāner, where a series of shrines grew up dedicated to her. They are still much attended today. She emerged during a formative period in the history of Rājasthān and was closely associated with the establishment of both the Rāṭhoṛ kingdoms of Jodhpur and Bīkāner. Rāv Bīko Jodhāvat (ca. 1485-1504; no. 42), the founder of Bīkāner, was a fervent devotee of hers. Karṇījī is considered responsible for initiating a series of marriage alliances between the Rāṭhoṛs of Mārvāṛ and Bīkāner, and the Bhāṭīs of Jaisaḷmer that helped to unify and stabilize political relationships in this area. Over and above these accomplishments, Karṇījī is widely known for her many miracles performed on behalf of members of all *jāti*s in western Rājasthān.

For more information about Karṇījī, see: Kr. Kailash Dan S. Ujwal, ***Bhagwati Shri Karniji Maharaj*: *A Biography*** (Ujlan [Marwar], n.d.).

the enmity of Rāv Sato's son, Narbad Satāvat (5-3) (no. 56), which led both to his and to Rāv Sato's downfall (see *infra*).

Murārdān, no. 2, p. 289, records that Rāv Sato married one of his sisters to the Muslim ruler of Nāgaur, Khānzāda Khān Shams Khān I Dāndāṇī (ca. 1405-18).[6]

"Aitihāsik Bātāṃ," pp. 18-19; ***Bāṅkīdās***, p. 6; ***Khyāt***, 2:309-314, 336-337, 3:30-31, 129-134; ***Murārdān***, no. 2, pp. 59-60, 66-68, 289, 299, 331-333; Ojhā, 4:1:213-219; Reu, 1:68-70; ***Vigat***, 1:25-27, 385-386; ***Vīr Vinod***, 2:804.

(no. 55) **Āskaraṇ Satāvat** (5-2)
(no. 56) **Narbad Satāvat** (5-3)

Narbad Satāvat was Rāv Sato Cūṇḍāvat's (4-2) eldest son. He assumes a much greater prominence in the chronicles of Mārvāṛ than his younger brother, Āskaraṇ, who finds mention by name only in passages dealing with his death in battle. Narbad was sister's son (***bhāṇej***) of the Sonagaro Cahuvāṇs of Pālī village in eastern Mārvāṛ.[7] ***Vigat***, 1:26, records that "Sato's son, Narbad, was a black-tailed scoundrel (***kāḷ-pūñchīyo bhaṃvrāḷo huvo***)." During Rāv Sato's rule, he played the role of spoiler at Maṇḍor. Narbad quickly came into conflict with both his father's uterine brother, Rāvat Riṇdhīr, and with Riṇdhīr's son, Nāpo Riṇdhīrot (5-4), over control of the lands and resources of the kingdom.

The ***Khyāt*** of Naiṇsī, 3:130, states that Narbad approached his mother's brother (***māmo***), a Sonagaro Cahuvāṇ of Pālī, and asked him whom he favored more, Narbad or Riṇdhīr's son, Nāpo, who was also a relation of the Sonagaros. Narbad's mother's brother replied that they were both equal, but that Narbad was special because he (the mother's brother) was living at Narbad's home. Narbad then asked him to give Nāpo poison and kill him. The Sonagaro refused, whereupon Narbad had one of his own servants kill Nāpo with poison. Narbad then gathered an army (***kaṭak bheḷo kīyo***) and drove Riṇdhīr from the kingdom.

Narbad now assumed control over the affairs of Maṇḍor, while Riṇdhīr joined his other uterine brother, Riṇmal Cūṇḍāvat (4-5) in Mevāṛ. He said to Riṇmal, "Let's go! I will have the ***ṭīko*** of Maṇḍovar [Maṇḍor] given to you" (***Khyāt***, 3:132). They met with their sister's son, Sīsodīyo Rāṇo Mokaḷ Lākhāvat of Cītoṛ (ca. 1421-33), and asked for his aid. The Rāṇo gave them an army to attack Maṇḍor. Riṇdhīr and Riṇmal defeated Rāv Sato and Narbad in battle ca. 1428. The Rāṇo of Cītoṛ then seated Riṇmal Cūṇḍāvat on the throne at Maṇḍor, and took Sato and Narbad back to Mevāṛ with him. Narbad had been badly wounded during the fighting at Maṇḍor, losing one of his eyes. The Rāṇo had his wounds cleaned and bound, and cared for him.

---

[6] For further information about Shams Khān, see ***infra***, "Khānzāda Khāns."

[7] Pālī village: located forty-five miles south-southeast of Maṇḍor.

Sato Cūṇḍāvat died shortly after arriving in Mevāṛ, but Narbad lived for some years after. "The Rāṇo showed [him] great affection (***bahot pyār***)" (***Khyāt***, 3:141). He became a favorite of both Rāṇo Mokaḷ and of his son and successor, Rāṇo Kūmbho Mokaḷot (ca. 1433-68). Rāṇo Mokaḷ granted Narbad the village and lands of Kāylāṇo[8] in Goḍhvāṛ in ***paṭo***. Narbad lived both there and at the court of Cītoṛ, and he became widely renowned in Mevāṛ for his bravery and prowess as a warrior, and for his devotion to the throne of Cītoṛ.

While "Narbad Satāvat was ruling (***rāj karai***) at Maṇḍor" (***ibid.***), the Sāṅkhlo Paṃvār, Sīhaṛ Cācagot, master of Rūṇ village,[9] had offered his daughter, Supiyārde, to Narbad in marriage. This offer was accepted and the betrothal completed prior to Rāv Sato's loss of Maṇḍor to his brothers, Riṇmal and Riṇdhīr. News of the Rāv's defeat quickly reached Rūṇ, and the Rūṇeco Sāṅkhlos then withdrew their offer of marriage to Narbad and married their daughter instead to the Sīndhaḷ Rāṭhoṛ, Narsiṅghdās Khīndāvat (no. 131), the master of Jaitāraṇ town in eastern Mārvāṛ.[10]

Narbad lived with this shame in Mevāṛ. When the Rāṇo learned of it, he sent a camel rider (***oṭhī***) to Sāṅkhlo Sīhaṛ with the message, "Give the betrothed to Narbadjī." The Rūṇeco Sāṅkhlos replied that Supiyārde was already married, but they would give a younger sister of Supiyārde's to Narbad. "Come and marry her," they said. Narbad would only accept the offer if Supiyārde herself performed ***ārtī***[11] at the wedding ceremony at Rūṇ village, and to this condition the Sāṅkhlos agreed. "Supiyārde will perform ***ārtī***," they assured the Rāṇo. But when Sīndhaḷ Narsiṅghdās learned of this news, he refused to let Supiyārde attend the wedding until she vowed that she would not perform ***ārtī***. He then allowed her to proceed to her father's home (***pīhar***), but he sent a barber (***Nāī***) to spy on her.

It was impossible for Supiyārde to live up to her vow in the face of threatened censure from the Sāṅkhlos and fear of Narbad's withdrawal from the marriage. So Supiyārde performed ***ārtī*** as Narbad entered her father's home, an act which Narbad had purposely initiated. It set in motion a chain of events that culminated in Supiyārde's flight from Jaitāraṇ with Narbad, and the death of Narbad's brother, Āskaraṇ, in battle against the Sīndhaḷs. When Supiyārde returned to Jaitāraṇ, she was confronted by her husband with the fact that she had broken her vow. Narisṅghdās Sīndhaḷ then beat Supiyārde, bound her hands and

---

[8] Kāylāṇo village: located thirty-eight miles south of Sojhat and nine miles east-northeast of Nāḍūl.

[9] Rūṇ village: located fifty-eight miles northeast of Maṇḍor.

[10] Jaitāraṇ town: located fifty-six miles east of Maṇḍor.

[11] ***Ārtī***: a ceremony of adoration performed for a god or goddess by moving a platter containing a five-wicked burning lamp, flour and incense around the head of the deity in a circular motion. At weddings, this ceremony of adoration is performed before the groom as he enters the bride's home, and is usually done by the eldest female member of the bride's family. Lāḷas, ***RSK***, 1:215; Platts, ***Dictionary***, p. 39.

threw her beneath her bed in her room. He summoned another of his wives to the room and told her to sleep in Supiyārde's bed. Supiyārde protested, but Narsiṅghdās refused to relent. Supiyārde then "took her husband's name," and said:

> Narsiṅghdās Sīndhaḷ! You have done what you must do, but now [if I] were to come to your bed, [it would be as if I] were coming to the bed of a brother (***Khyāt***, 3:144).

A slave girl (***chokrī***) quickly reported what had happened to Supiyārde's husband's mother (***sāsū***), and she took Supiyārde under her protection. Supiyārde arranged to send a message to Narbad at his village of Kāylāṇo. Narbad had said at the time of the wedding in Rūṇ that if there were any trouble, she should send word to him and he would come for her. Narbad traveled to Jaitāraṇ as soon as her received Supiyārde's message, and arranged through a servant for Supiyārde to slip away from the village. Narbad then fled with her toward Goḍhvāṛ in a cart. His brother, Āskaraṇ, met them on the return and remained behind to confront the pursuing Sīndhaḷs, who killed him in a pitched battle. The Sīndhaḷs proceeded on into Goḍhvāṛ where they looted Narbad's village of Kāylāṇo and took a number of Rāṭhoṛ women back to Jaitāraṇ as prisoners.

Narbad did not avenge his brother's death during his lifetime. Neither he nor Āskaraṇ had sons of their own, so the ***vair*** remained unsettled for some twenty years until the time of Rāv Jodho Riṇmalot of Maṇḍor and Jodhpur (ca. 1453-89). In the mid-1450s, Rāv Jodho sent his son, Dūdo Jodhāvat (no. 104), to Jaitāraṇ to kill Sīndhaḷ Narsiṅghdās Khīndāvat's son, Megho Narsiṅghdāsot (no. 132), and end the ***vair***. Dūdo accomplished this feat in single-handed combat with Megho on the field before Jaitāraṇ village (see "Aitihāsik Bātāṃ, pp. 38-40, of the **translated text** for details).

Narbad remained in the Rāṇo's service for the rest of his life. He took part in the Sīsodīyo occupation of Mārvāṛ under Rāṇo Kūmbho Mokaḷot (ca. 1433-68) in 1439-40. This occupation followed Rāṇo Kūmbho's murder of Rāv Riṇmal Cūṇḍāvat at Cītoṛ ca. 1438 and the subsequent Sīsodīyo conquest of Maṇḍor. Rāṇo Kūmbho stationed Narbad at Maṇḍor along with a number of his leading warriors. ***Vigat***, 1:32, records that the Rāṇo said to Narbad:

> Have Jodho [Riṇmalot] killed quickly. [When you] have killed Jodho, I will give you Maṇḍor.

Narbad participated in operations against Rāv Riṇmal's chosen successor, Jodho. But he was unable to capture or to kill him.

How long Narbad remained in Mārvāṛ is unclear from the chronicles. Although the Sīsodīyos held control of Maṇḍor until ca. 1453, Narbad appears to have returned to Mevāṛ after only a few years for his name does not appear in connection with any later events in Mārvāṛ. The chronicles record only one other occurrence during his life. This concerned his gift of his one remaining eye to the Rāṇo of Cītoṛ. This act of self-sacrifice occurred in the following manner (*Khyāt*, 3:149-150):

Narbad's people were heard praising Narbad one day at the court of Cītoṛ, saying, "Today there is no Rajpūt the equal of Narbadjī in [all the] land. Narbad is a great warrior." The Rāṇo asked why they were praising Narbad so, and they answered, "[When something is] asked of Narbad, [he] keeps nothing [to himself]." The Rāṇo then asked half in jest if Narbad would give whatever was demanded, and Narbad's people replied that he would. The Rāṇo thereupon sent his personal attendant (*khavās*) to Narbad's camp to request from Narbad his one remaining eye. Narbad immediately responded, "Very well, I will give [it]." He took up one of his daggers and cut out his eye, placing it in a cloth and handing it to the attendant who blanched white with shock. The attendant quickly returned to the Rāṇo with Narbad's eye. The Rāṇo saw the eye and was immediately filled with remorse. He went to Narbad and praised him for this selfless act. He later increased Narbad's *paṭo* by one and a half times.

> Bhāṭī, *Sarvekṣaṇ*, 3:106; *Khyāt*, 2:336, 3:38-40, 129-133, 141-150; *Murārdān*, no. 2. pp. 289-299; Ojhā, 2:504-507, 4:1:216-219; Reu, 1:69-70; *Vigat*, 1:26-27, 32-33, 387, 493-494; *Vīr Vinod*, 2:804.

(no. 57) **Īsar Gharṣīyot** (7-1)
(no. 58) **Mahes Gharṣīyot** (7-2)
(no. 59) **Rājsiṅgh Gharṣīyot** (7-3)

Only scant information is available about Rāv Kānho Cūṇḍāvat's (4-1) descendants, Īsar, Mahes and Rājsiṅgh Gharṣīyot. They all served in the armies of Rāv Mālde Gāṅgāvat of Jodhpur (1532-62) alongside their father, Gharṣī Bhārmalot (6-1). Both Mahes and his father rose to prominence following Rāv Mālde's occupation of Meṛto and Ajmer ca. 1535. *Vigat*, 1:43-44, records that Gharṣī Bhārmalot received the *paṭo* of Jājpur[12] from the Rāv, while his son, Mahes, was given Ajmer itself in *paṭo*.[13]

Mahes was forced to withdraw from Ajmer in late 1543, in the face of Sher Shāh Sūr's approach from north India. In January of 1544 Mahes participated in the initial fighting at the battle of Samel.[14] But he withdrew from

---

[12] Jājpur: modern Jahāzpur, located seventy miles southeast of Ajmer.

[13] Bhāṭī, *Sarvekṣaṇ*, 3:105, states that Gharṣī Bhārmalot was a great *ṭhākur*, and that he was stationed at the garrisons (*thāṇos*) of Kelvo, Kumbhalmer, and Kanhelo of Mevāṛ as a military servant under Rāv Mālde. This text also records that Gharṣī held the *paṭo* of Thāṃvlo village, located twelve miles northwest of Ajmer and twenty-eight miles east-southeast of Meṛto. Regarding Gharṣī's son, Mahes, this text notes that he held the village of Pīmpāṛ in *paṭo* from Rāv Mālde. Pīmpāṛ is located thirty-three miles east-northeast of Jodhpur.

[14] Samel village: located twenty-four miles southwest of Ajmer.

Samel along with Rāṭhoṛ Jeso Bhairavdāsot (no. 48) and others to join the Rāv during his exile in the hills of southern Mārvāṛ near Sīvāṇo. He remained with the Rāv during Sher Shāh's occupation of central Mārvāṛ and Jodhpur.

The chronicles do not mention Mahes or his brothers, Īsar and Rājsiṅgh, in connection with any events between the years 1544 and 1553. But Mahes did take part in an attack on Ajmer which would have occurred prior to 1554, when Rāv Mālde again attempted the conquest of Meṛto (see "Aitihāsik Bātāṃ," pp. 56-57, of the **translated text** for details).

"Aitihāsik Bātāṃ" notes that Rāv Mālde gave an army to Rāṭhoṛ Prithīrāj Jaitāvat (no. 63), one of his military commanders following Samel, and sent him against Ajmer. Mahes Ghaṛsīyot, who had previously held Ajmer in ***paṭo***, was with this army. Several of Mahes's military servants managed to climb the walls of the fort during the fighting, and proclaim a victory for Mahesjī. The chronicle states that this action deterred the Riṇmalots[15] who did not wish to advance further, saying:

> We would die [in battle], and the victory [would be the Cūṇḍāvat] Mahesji's, so for what reason [should we advance]?

This attack was withdrawn soon after because of the intervention of the Rāṇo of Cītoṛ on the side of the Muslims in the fort. Mahes's role following the withdrawal is unclear. But the chronicle records that Prithīrāj Jaitāvat was much ashamed, and went neither to the Rāv's court nor to his home village of Bagṛī.[16] When Rāv Mālde sent his armies against Meṛto in 1554, Prithīrāj argued that he should also be allowed to attack Ajmer once again. But the Rāv disagreed, and Prithīrāj then rode against Meṛto and was killed there in battle.

Mahes Ghaṛsīyot was one of the select ***ṭhākur***s of Mārvāṛ whom Rāv Mālde's commander, Rāṭhoṛ Devīdās Jaitāvat (no. 65), chose to accompany him in alliance with Paṭhāṇ Hājī Khān, a former noble of Sher Shāh Sūr's, against Sīsodīyo Rāṇo Ūdaisiṅgh Sāṅgāvat of Cītoṛ (ca. 1537-72; no. 17). These armies met at Harmāṛo village[17] in January of 1557, and were victorious against the Rāṇo and his allies. Then, in 1562, Mahes was among Rāv Mālde's military servants stationed at the Mālgaḍh in Meṛto under the command of Rāṭhoṛ Devīdās Jaitāvat. He was killed here along with his two brothers, Īsar and Rājsiṅgh, fighting against Meṛtīyo Rāv Jaimal Vīramdevot (no. 107) and the Mughal forces of Akbar under Mīrzā Sharafu'd-Dīn Ḥusayn.

Mahes Ghaṛsīyot granted the village of Bīñjā ro Vās[18] to the Vīṭhū Cāraṇ Dūdo Vīdāvat in ***sāṃsaṇ***. No date is recorded for this grant, but Mahes probably

---

[15] Riṇmalots: descendants of Rāv Riṇmal Cūṇḍāvat of Maṇḍor, ca. 1428-38.

[16] Bagṛī village: located nine miles east-southeast of Sojhat in eastern Mārvāṛ.

[17] Harmāṛo village: located fifty-five miles south-southwest of Ajmer and six miles south of Vadhnor in northern Mevāṛ.

[18] Bīñjā ro Vās: located twenty-one miles east of Jodhpur and twelve miles southwest of Pīmpāṛ.

made it during the time he held Ajmer in *paṭo* from Rāv Mālde between 1535 and 1543.

"Aitihāsik Bātāṃ," pp. 44-45, 51, 56-57, 74-75; ***Bāṅkīdās***, pp. 14-17; Bhāṭī, ***Sarvekṣaṇ***, 3:105; "Jodhpur Hukūmat rī Bahī," pp. 142-143; ***Vigat***, 1:43-44, 57, 62, 255, 2:66.

Figure 22. Cūṇḍāvat Rāṭhoṛs

- (1-1) Rāv Salkho
  - (2-1) Vīram Salkhāvat
    - (3-1) Rāv Cūṇḍo Vīramot (**Cūṇḍāvats**)
      - (4-1) **Rāv Kānho Cūṇḍāvat**
        - (5-1) Bhārmal Kānhāvat
          - (6-1) Gharṣī Bhārmalot
            - (7-1) **Īsar Gharṣīyot**
            - (7-2) **Mahes Gharṣīyot**
            - (7-3) **Rājsiṅgh Gharṣīyot**
      - (4-2) **Rāv Sato Cūṇḍāvat**
        - (5-2) **Āskaraṇ Satāvat**
        - (5-3) **Narbad Satāvat**
      - (4-3) Rāvat Riṇḍhīr Cūṇḍāvat
        - (5-4) Nāpo Riṇḍhīrot
      - (4-4) Araṛkamaḷ Cūṇḍāvat
      - (4-5) Rāv Riṇmal Cūṇḍāvat (**Riṇmalots**)
        - (5-5) Rāv Jodho Riṇmalot (**Jodhos**)

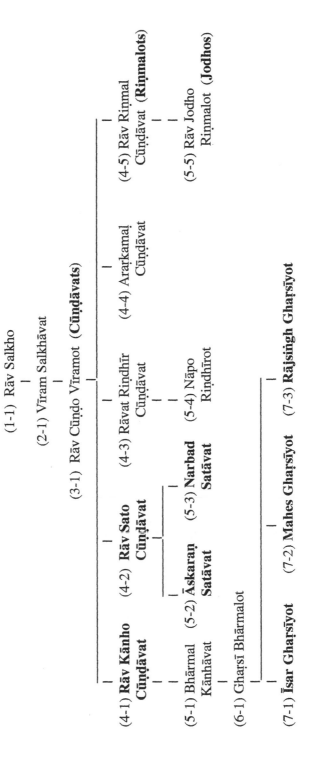

Īḍareco Rāṭhoṛs

(no. 60) **Narāyaṇdās Pūñjāvat, Rāv of Īḍar**

The Īḍareco Rāṭhoṛs

The Īḍareco (or Īḍarīyo) Rāṭhoṛs descend from Sonag Sīhāvat. Sonag was a son of Rāv Sīho Setramot's (d. 1273), who is considered the founding ancestor of the Mārvāṛ Rāṭhoṛs. Among Rāv Sīho's sons, Āsthān Sīhāvat established his rule at Kheṛ[1] and Mahevo in western Mārvāṛ, while Sonag established himself at Īḍar. A third brother, Ajo (Ajmāl), is said to have ruled at Dhaṭ in the Umarkot-Parkar area of what is now southwestern Pakistan.

According to Rāṭhoṛ traditions (*Vīr Vinod*, 2:994-995), Sonag left Mārvāṛ as a young man and went to Gujarat, where he took service under Solaṅkī Rājā Bhīmdev of Anhilvāṛo-Paṭṭan. He received lands there in return for his service, and soon established himself in a position of power. Īḍar was then under the rule of Kolī Sāṃvliyo Soṛ. His father, Kolī Hāthī Soṛ, had been a servant of Parihār Rājā Amarsiṅgh's. The Rājā entrusted Hāthī Soṛ with the administration of Īḍar when he joined Prithīrāj Cahuvāṇ in 1192 in battle against Shīhāb-al-dīn Moḥammad Ghorī (d. 1206). Rājā Amarsiṅgh was killed in this battle, and Hāthī Soṛ then assumed the rulership of Īḍar. This rule passed to his son, Sāṃvliyo, on his death.

Sāṃvliyo was not a benevolent ruler. He is said to have gained the distrust of his ***pradhān***, Nāgar Brāhmaṇ, because he sought to force Nāgar to marry a daughter to him. Nāgar complained to Rāṭhoṛ Rāv Sonag. Rāv Sonag saw an opportunity and agreed to help. He gathered three hundred of his Rajpūts and came in secret to hide at Nāgar's residence. Nāgar then called Sāṃvliyo Soṛ for the marriage. Sāṃvliyo arrived with his ***sāth*** in grand procession, and Nāgar received them with suitable hospitality, supplying them with much liquor to drink. As soon as they were intoxicated, the Rāṭhoṛs fell on them with their swords. Only Sāṃvliyo escaped, fleeing toward the fort of Īḍar. Sonag's Rajpūts found and killed him there before the gate of the fort, and they used his blood to place the ***ṭīko*** of succession on Sonag's forehead, confirming him as the new ruler of Īḍar.

Sonag's assumption of rulership at Īḍar is placed in 1256-57.

(no. 60) **Narāyaṇdās Pūñjāvat, Rāv**

Little information is available about Rāv Narāyaṇdās Pūñjāvat. He ruled Īḍar from the 1550s into the 1580s. He figures in the texts under consideration

---

[1] Kheṛ village: located sixty-two miles southwest of Jodhpur, near the great bend in the Lūṇī River.

because he took part in the battle of Harmāṛo[2] in January of 1557 as an ally of Sīsodīyo Rāṇo Udaisiṅgh Sāṅgāvat (ca. 1537-72; no. 17). Rāṇo Udaisiṅgh's forces suffered defeat at Harmāṛo against the combined armies of Paṭhāṇ Hājī Khān and Rāv Mālde Gāṅgāvat of Jodhpur (1532-62) under the command of Rāṭhoṛ Devīdās Jaitāvat (no. 65).

Rāv Narāyaṇdās maintained a presence in Īḍar during this period as an ally of the Rāṇos of Mevāṛ. He remained outside of Mughal control into the mid-1570s. ***Akbar Nāma***, 3:48-49, mentions that following Akbar's conquest of Gujarat in early 1573, Akbar sent a force to Ḍūṅgarpur by way of Īḍar, and notes:

> The Rānā [of Udaipur] and other zamindars of the neighborhood [including Rāv Narāyaṇdās of Īḍar] were to be treated with princely favours and to be brought to do homage, and the disobedient were to be punished.

There was no recognition of Mughal suzerainty until a number of years later, however, and Rāv Narāyaṇdās remained ambivalent toward Mughal control. ***Akbar Nāma***, 3:59, mentions that in July/August of 1573, "Rai Narain," the ***zamīndār*** of Īḍar, joined with Ikhtīyār-il-mulk in his revolt against Akbar, but then notes, 3:92, that in September of 1573, following Akbar's suppression of the revolt in Gujarat:

> The Zamindār [of Īḍar], Narain Dās Rāthor, recognized the arrival of the imperial officers as a great honour and went forward to welcome them. He presented suitable gifts . . .

A note to this passage[3] records that Abu'l Fazl noted of Rāv Narāyaṇdās that he was such an austere Hindu he only ate the grains of corn that had been voided by a cow.

Recognition of the Mughals was short-lived, for ***Akbar Nāma***, 3:268, mentions that in September/October of 1576, Rāv Narāyaṇdās "lifted his head in sedition" with the Rāṇo of Mevāṛ, Pratāpsiṅgh Udaisiṅghot (ca. 1572-97). Rāv Narāyaṇdās was Rāṇo Pratāpsiṅgh's wife's father (***susro***), and had joined with him in his running battle against the Mughals. ***Vīr Vinod***, 2:995, states that Akbar sequestered Īḍar at this time, but Akbar did not consolidate his control over this area until his conquest of Īḍar in 1577. This Mughal victory was a bloody, hard-fought affair, during which:

> The daring Rajpūts made ready their spears and encountered [the Mughal force under Sher Khān]. There were wondrous hand-to-

---

[2] Harmāṛo village: located fifty-five miles south-southwest of Ajmer and six miles south of Vadhnor in northern Mevāṛ.

[3] ***Akbar Nāma***, 3:92, n. 2.

hand combats. The jewel of courage was brought to the test and acquired fresh brilliancy (***Akbar Nāma***, 3:281).

Rāv Narāyaṇdās submitted to Akbar following the conquest and agreed to send his son, Kuṃvar Vīramde Narāyaṇdāsot, to the Mughal court. Akbar granted Īḍar to the Rāv in return. No details are available about events following the conquest, but Rāv Narāyaṇdās appears to have been inconstant in his loyalty. ***Akbar Nāma***, 3:389, notes that in early 1579:

> As the government of Gujarat had been entrusted to Shihābu'd-dīn Aḥmad K., he (Wazīr) had been ordered to Īḍar. In a short time the Rai of that country submitted and fell to supplication. The country was given to him (the Rai) and he came to do homage.

A last entry about Rāv Narāyaṇdās in ***Akbar Nāma***, 3:632, indicates that the Rāv remained in Mughal service after 1579. In December of 1583 he rode as part of the left wing of the Mughal army which marched to put down Sultān Muzaffar's rebellion at Ahmadabad in Gujarat. Rāṭhoṛ Moṭo Rājā Udaisiṅgh Māldevot (1583-95), who had only recently been confirmed as ruler of Jodhpur, was also part of the left wing.

No further information is available about Rāv Narāyaṇdās. The date and circumstances of his death are unknown. He was succeeded in Īḍar by his son, Vīramde Narāyaṇdāsot.

> ***Akbar Nāma***, 3:48-49, 59, 92, 280-282, 268, 389, 632; "Aitihāsik Bātāṃ," p. 51; ***Bāṅkīdās***, p. 14; L. P. Tessitori, "A Progress Report on the Work done during the year 1917 in connection with the Bardic and Historical Survey of Rajputana," ***Journal of the Asiatic Society of Bengal***, N.S. 15 (1919), p. 32; Ojhā, 4:1:158-165; Stanley Lane-Poole, ***The Mohammadan Dynasties: Chronological and Genealogical Tables with Historical Introductions*** (New York: Frederick Ungar Publishing Co., republished 1965), p. 292-294; ***Vigat***, 2:60; ***Vīr Vinod***, 2:994-995.

Jaitāvat Rāṭhoṛs

(no. 66) **Bhākharsī Jaitāvat** (8-3)
(no. 65) **Devīdās Jaitāvat** (8-2)
(no. 61) **Jaito Pañcāiṇot** (7-1)
(no. 63) **Prithīrāj Jaitāvat** (8-1)
(no. 64) **Pūraṇmal Prithīrājot** (9-1)
(no. 62) **Udaisiṅgh Jaitāvat** (8-4)

(no. 61) **Jaito Pañcāiṇot** (7-1)
(no. 62) **Udaisiṅgh Jaitāvat** (8-4)

The Jaitāvat Rāṭhoṛs descend from Jaito Pañcāiṇot, a son of Pañcāiṇ Akhairājot's (6-1) and grandson of Akhairāj Riṇmalot's (5-1),[1] whose father, Rāv Riṇmal Cūṇḍāvat, (4-1), ruled Maṇḍor (ca. 1428-38). Among the Rāṭhoṛs of the early sixteenth century, Jaito rose to a position of great power and influence alongside his paternal cousin, Kūmpo Mahirājot (no. 95). For more than twenty years, from the early 1520s until his death in January of 1544 at the battle of Samel,[2] Jaito served under the Jodhpur rulers, Rāv Gāṅgo Vāghāvat (1515-32), and his son, Rāv Mālde Gāṅgāvat (1532-62), as one of their foremost Rajpūts. Jaito assumed a preeminent position alongside Kūmpo Mahirājot during Rāv Mālde's rule as a commander of the Rāv's armies in battle, as an administrator of his kingdom, and as his close personal advisor.

Little information is available about Jaito's family. His father, Pañcāiṇ Akhairājot, appears to have succeeded to the rule of Bagṛī village[3] sometime in the latter half of the fifteenth century, following the death of his grandfather, Akhairāj Riṇmalot (5-1). Bagṛī had become Akhairāj's seat of rule in 1429-30 during his father, Rāv Riṇmal's, consolidation of authority at Maṇḍor and extension of his rule over areas of eastern Mārvāṛ. Texts vary in their discussion of how Bagṛī came under Rāṭhoṛ rule. Some attribute its conquest from the Sīndhaḷs to Rāv Riṇmal, while others state that is was Akhairāj himself who defeated and killed Caṛro Sīndhaḷ before Bagṛī. In all likelihood, Akhairāj played a leading role in this eastward expansion of Rāṭhoṛ authority from Maṇḍor, and established a strong presence at Bagṛī early in his father's reign. These lands were lost to Akhairāj and the Rāṭhoṛs ca. 1438, when Rāv Riṇmal was murdered at Cītoṛ and the Sīsodīyos overran eastern Mārvāṛ and occupied

---

[1] See ***supra***, "Akhairājot Rāṭhoṛs," for more information about Akhairāj Riṇmalot. ***Vigat***, 1:56, refers to Jaito Pañcāiṇot as an "Akhairājot," which was consistent with the time in which he lived.

[2] Samel village: located twenty-four miles southwest of Ajmer.

[3] Bagṛī village: located nine miles east-southeast of Sojhat in eastern Mārvāṛ.

Maṇḍor. But when Rāv Riṇmal's son and chosen successor, Jodho Riṇmalot, reasserted Rāṭhoṛ rule at Maṇḍor ca. 1453 and then founded Jodhpur in 1459, he confirmed Akhairāj in his possession of Bagṛī village.

Pañcāiṇ Akhairājot's activities in Mārvāṛ are unknown save for his involvement in the promotion of Rāv Sūjo Jodhāvat's (ca. 1492-1515) successor to the Jodhpur throne in 1515. Rāv Sūjo's chosen successor (***pāṭvī kuṃvar***) was his grandson, Vīramde Vāghāvat (no. 84). Vīramde did succeed to the throne, but he was quickly deposed in favor of another of Rāv Sūjo's grandsons, Gāṅgo Vāghāvat. According to the ***Khyāt*** of Naiṇsī, 3:80-81, the choice of successor lay with a faction of Rāṭhoṛs who favored Gāṅgo over Vīramde. The ***Khyāt*** tells the following story about Gāṅgo's selection:

Four Mārū ***ṭhākur***s came to Jodhpur on some occasion during the latter part of Rāv Sūjo's rule. The rains began while they were at Jodhpur, preventing them from returning to their camps. Being in need of provisions, the ***ṭhākur***s sent word to Vīramde Vāghāvat's mother, the Devṛī Cahuvāṇ Raṅgāde,[4] asking her to provide for them. The Rajpūtāṇī replied that the ***ṭhākur***s should cover themselves with their own woolen garments and proceed to their camps. She questioned, "Who will feed you here?" The ***ṭhākur***s then sent word to Gāṅgo Vāghāvat's mother, the Cahuvāṇ Udanbāī. This Rajpūtāṇī responded in a very different manner:

> ***Ṭhākur***s! Please be seated in the hall of audience (***darīkhāno***). We will perform many services [for you].

The ***ṭhākur***s came away very satisfied, and they sent a message to Gāṅgo's mother as they were leaving:

> "Your son, Gāṅgo, has the good fortune of [receiving] Jodhpur." . . . Then the Rāṇī had blessings conveyed [to the ***ṭhākur***s]. And [she] said: "***Jī***, we acquired Jodhpur only because of your influence. He alone receives to whom you give."

This favoritism for Gāṅgo Vāghāvat's family played a key role in securing Gāṅgo's later succession to the throne. Local texts indicate that following Rāv Sūjo's death in 1515, this faction of ***ṭhākur***s seated Gāṅgo on the throne in place of his elder half-brother, Vīramde. "Aitihāsik Bātāṃ," p. 37, records that these ***ṭhākur***s, who included Pañcāiṇ Akhairājot and Bhairavdās Cāmpāvat,[5] unseated Vīramde and placed Gāṅgo on the throne in his stead. The ***Khyāt*** of Naiṇsī, 3:81, notes that the ***ṭhākur***s:

---

[4] ***Khyāt***, 3:80, incorrectly identifies Vīramde's mother as a Sīsodṇī. One of Vīramde's father, Vāgho Sūjāvat's, wives was a Rāṇāvat Sīsodṇī. She was the mother of Vīramde's half-brother, Jaitsī Vāghāvat (no. 85).

[5] For further information about Bhairavdās Cāmpāvat, see ***supra***, "Cāmpāvat Rāṭhoṛs."

> grasped Vīramde [Vāghāvat] by the arm and took him down from the fort [of Jodhpur], and [then] gave the ***ṭīko*** to Gāṅgo.

In compensation, Vīramde Vāghāvat received the lands of Sojhat as his share of patrimony, a share with which he was never satisfied.

Pañcāiṇ's son, Jaito Pañcāiṇot, succeeded his father to the rule of Bagṛī village. Under Jaito, this village became the homeland (***utan***) of the Jaitāvat Rāṭhoṛs. Bagṛī was located very near Sojhat and came within Vīramde Vāghāvat's share of land, and Jaito quickly became involved in the conflict that emerged between Rāv Gāṅgo of Jodhpur and his elder, half-brother, Vīramde, who was ***rāv*** of Sojhat.

The feeling pervaded Rāv Gāṅgo's court that as long as Jaito held Bagṛī village and kept his ***vasī*** there, Rāv Gāṅgo's Rajpūts would be unable to gain an upper hand against Rāv Vīramde and his ***pradhān***, Muṃhato Rāymal Khetāvat (no. 159). Jaito was seen to straddle both sides of this conflict. The ***Khyāt*** of Naiṇsī, 3:81-82, states:

> So [Rāv] Vīramde does not [wish to] drive Jaito away. For what reason? [Those with Rāv Gāṅgo] said, "***Jī***, Jaito [is] a ***sirdār*** in the [Jodhpur] army, [but] he enjoys [the rule of] Bagṛī. [Therefore] he desires the well-being [lit. "the good"] of Sojhat." Then Rāv Gāṅgo said: "Jaitojī! Bring your carts to Bīlāṛo village.[6] Leave Bagṛī!"

Jaito kept his ***vasī*** at Bagṛī under the supervision of his ***dhāy-bhāī*** (lit. "milk-brother"), Reṛo, who refused to vacate the ancestral lands. In an attempt to prevent their having to leave, Reṛo went to Sojhat to seek out Muṃhato Rāymal and kill him. Muṃhato Rāymal's wife discerned Reṛo's designs, however, and Muṃhato Rāymal then killed Reṛo when Reṛo drew a weapon to attack him. News of Reṛo's death quickly reached Bagṛī and spread fear among the people of the ***vasī***. Only then did they make ready and depart the village for Jodhpur territory.

When Jaito's people left Bagṛī, Rāv Gāṅgo ordered Jaito to recruit Rāv Vīramde's leading warrior, Rāṭhoṛ Kūmpo Mahirājot (no. 95), and bring him to Jodhpur. Jaito accomplished this feat with the lure of a large grant of villages worth one ***lakh***, to be chosen from among Jodhpur's finest. He also had Rāv Gāṅgo send word to Kūmpo stating that the conflict between Sojhat and Jodhpur was of no real consequence, for Rāv Vīramde had no sons, and after his death, Sojhat would revert to Jodhpur. Kūmpo finally agreed to come to Jodhpur if Rāv Gāṅgo would not to attack Sojhat for one year. Rāv Gāṅgo readily accepted this condition, and shortly after Kūmpo's arrival at Jodhpur ca. 1529, Rāv Gāṅgo

---

[6] Bīlāṛo village: located twenty-one miles north-northwest of Bagṛī in Jodhpur territory.

was able to gain the upper hand against his half-brother. He eventually drove Rāv Vīramde from Sojhat and then from Mārvāṛ altogether.

While Jaito played an important role in Mārvāṛ under Rāv Gāṅgo, he rose to particular prominence under Rāv Gāṅgo's son and successor, Rāv Mālde Gāṅgāvat (1532-62). Jaito became a leader of Rāv Mālde's armies and one of the closest advisors to the throne.

Local texts present a picture of Jaito during Rāv Mālde's rule as a powerful figure torn between loyalty and duty to the Rāv and concern for the lands of Mārvāṛ and the values of brotherhood among the Rāṭhoṛs, which Rāv Mālde openly violated. "Aitihāsik Bātāṃ," p. 57, describes Jaito as:

> a great ***ṭhākur***, one who upheld a great vow. [He] did not allow Rāv Mālde to act improperly.

Jaito fell into disagreement with the Rāv over the Rāv's desire to conquer areas of Mārvāṛ and beyond that were under the control of Rāṭhoṛs. Rāv Mālde spoke of these conquests shortly after his accession, and Jaito remarked:

> "The offense of killing one's family members/brothers (***gotrakadamb*** - lit. '***gotra***-destruction') will not be committed by me" (***ibid***.).

Jaito's reply made the Rāv feel downhearted, so Jaito quickly responded:

> "Do not be downhearted. We will perform the tasks you tell [us to do]. . . ." Then Jaitojī summoned Kūmpo Mahirājot and had the Rāvjī grasp [his] arm. [And he] said to the Rāvjī, "***Rāj***, [you] should uphold Kūmpo's honor and prestige." And to Kūmpo, [he] said, "You should perform [whatever] tasks the Rāv tells [you to do]" (***ibid***., pp. 57-58).

The conflict between duty to one's master and the values of brotherhood came most sharply into focus with respect to Rāv Mālde's hostility toward the Meṛtīyo Rāṭhoṛs. Rāv Mālde had held enmity toward the Meṛtīyos since he was a ***kuṃvar***. When he became ***rāv*** of Jodhpur, he pursued this hostility at every opportunity. But ***Vigat***, 2:48, 51, notes that Jaito, Kūmpo Mahirājot, and other of the Rāv's Rajpūts would not involve themselves in his plots and deceptions. Following one unsuccessful intrigue planned in secret from Jaito and Kūmpo, Rāv Mālde "was disgraced in Jaito and Kūmpo's presence." This intrigue involved Rāv Mālde's drawing Meṛtīyo Rāv Vīramde Dūdāvat (no. 105) to Jodhpur to participate in an expedition against the Sīndhaḷs of Bhādrājuṇ.[7] At the same time, he incited Khānzāda Khān Daulat Khān of Nagaur (no. 154) to attack Meṛto, which had been left unprotected, and he drew Paṃvār Pañcāiṇ of Cāṭsū (no. 24) into the area to settle an old ***vair*** with the Meṛtīyos. He also

---

[7] Bhādrājuṇ village: located forty-eight miles south-southwest of Jodhpur.

urged Varsiṅghot Meṛtīyo Rāv Gāṅgo Sīhāvat (no. 149) to move against Meṛto and cause additional disruption. None of these ploys proved successful.

"Aitihāsik Bātāṃ," p. 58, records that when these intrigues against Meṛto began, Meṛtīyo Rāv Vīramde sent word to Jaito, asking him to entreat Rāv Mālde to allow the Meṛtīyos to perform the Rāv's service. Jaito did so, but to no avail, for the Rāv would not countenance any accommodation with the Meṛtīyos.

Rāv Mālde's Rajpūts finally met Rāv Vīramde in battle at the village of Reyāṃ[8] ca. 1535. This battle followed Rāv Vīramde's occupation of Ajmer and his refusal to hand over this city to Rāv Mālde when the Rāv demanded it. Rāv Mālde then moved into Meṛto lands and occupied them, distributing the villages among Rajpūts in his own service, one of whom was Varsiṅghot Meṛtīyo Sahaiso Tejsīyot (no. 151). Sahaiso was a former military servant of Rāv Vīramde's, but he had left Rāv Vīramde and taken service under Rāv Mālde. Sahaiso received the village of Reyāṃ in ***paṭo*** from Rāv Mālde in return for his offer of service. This action so enraged Rāv Vīramde that he launched a precipitous attack against Reyāṃ in opposition to the advice of his own Rajpūts. Jaito rode to Reyāṃ along with Kūmpo Mahirājot and other of Rāv Mālde's Rajpūts from the garrison of Raṛod[9] where he had been stationed, and he took part in the bloody fighting there. Rāv Vīramde was badly defeated and many of his Rajpūts killed. But Jaito was among those Rāṭhoṛs who prevented Rāv Vīramde's death and allowed him to leave Mārvāṛ. Several sources state that Jaito felt Rāv Vīramde should live because he was a great warrior. ***Bāṅkīdās***, p. 12, records that Jaito remarked to Kūmpo Mahirājot:

> Vīramde should not be killed: Vīramde is a great Rajpūt. If he remains alive, he will bring someone [to aid him against Rāv Mālde], and [thereby] shape his own death.

It was perhaps because of Jaito's outspokenness against ***gotrakadamb*** that Rāv Mālde placed Jaito in command of his armies only when they marched against Nāgaur, which they conquered in 1536. The Rāv's other campaigns against both Rāṭhoṛs and other Rajpūts prior to the battle of Samel in 1544 were led by Jaito's paternal cousin, Kūmpo Mahirājot. Jaito was stationed at the garrison of Raṛod prior to the conquest of Nāgaur. Raṛod is located midway between Jodhpur and Nāgaur, and one of Jaito's brothers, Acḷo Pañcāiṇot (7-2), was killed when the garrison came under attack from Nāgaur. The Rāṭhoṛs launched a series of raids into Nāgaur territory in retaliation, and ultimately undertook the conquest of Nāgaur itself. To end the ***vair*** that had arisen with Acḷo's death, a daughter of the Ṭāṅk Rajpūts was married to Jaito, while Rāv Mālde received Harsolāv village[10] and twenty-one others from Nāgaur.

---

[8] Reyāṃ village: located fifteen miles southeast of Meṛto.

[9] Raṛod village: located forty-nine miles west-northwest of Reyāṃ, and forty-four miles northeast of Jodhpur.

[10] Harsolāv village: located twenty-nine miles south of Nāgaur and six miles east of Āsop.

Jaito himself received a gift of *rs*.15,000 from the residents of Hīrāvaṛī village[11] of Nāgaur. He had made his camp in this village and the residents are said to have made this gift in gratitude to Jaito for preventing the looting of their homes. Jaito had a stepwell constructed with this gift in the nearby village of Rājlāṇī.[12]

Jaito's activities during the years between 1536 and the battle of Samel in 1544 are not recorded in the sources at hand. It is possible that he spent most of his time with Rāv Mālde, either at Jodhpur or on tour during military operations. The texts do not mention Jaito except in connection with the conquest of Bīkāner in 1542. Despite Jaito's concerns about the Rāṭhoṛ brotherhood, there are indications that he could be both haughty and cruel in his attitudes toward both Rāṭhoṛs and other Rajpūts whom he met in battle. Jaito's participation in the battle for Bīkāner provides an example. It was on this occasion that he accompanied Kūmpo Mahirājot and the armies of Jodhpur against Bīkāvat Rāṭhoṛ Rāv Jaitsī Lūṇkaraṇot (1526-42). They met at the village of Sohavo (near Bīkāner) in February of 1542. Rāv Jaitsī was killed there and his army routed with great loss.

Jaito and Kūmpo's actions at Sohavo are recorded in a manuscript from Bīkāner,[13] which states that prior to the main engagement, Jaito and Kūmpo sent ***pradhān***s to Rāv Jaitsī to order his submission to Rāv Mālde of Jodhpur. The ***pradhān***s were directed to say to Rāv Jaitsī, "You go before [Rāv] Mālde [and] bow your nose." This manuscript indicates that while the Bīkāner Rāṭhoṛs with Rāv Jaitsī wished to submit to Rāv Mālde, a Sāṅkhlo Paṃvār , Mahes, who was a military servant of Rāv Jaitsī's holding villages of Bīkāner in ***paṭo***, shamed them into fighting by proclaiming that "being killed on the field is honorable."

The ***pradhān***s reported back to Jaito and Kūmpo that they had been unable to reach a settlement with the Bīkāner Rāṭhoṛs because of the Sāṅkhlo's words. Jaito and Kūmpo then sent for Sāṅkhlo Mahes and asked him angrily why he was trying to "ruin" the Rāṭhoṛs. Sāṅkhlo Mahes replied that he had merely caused the Bīkāner Rāṭhoṛs to answer the Jodhpur proposal in an appropriate manner.

---

[11] Hīrāvaṛī village: located four miles west-northwest of Harsolāv village.

[12] Rājlāṇī village: located ten miles south of Hīrāvaṛī and eight miles south-southwest of Harsolāv. An inscription to one side of the stepwell contains details about its construction. It was begun on October 23, 1537 and completed on October 29, 1540. 171 men and 221 women laborers worked along with 151 artisans and craftsmen. The construction required 15 ***mans*** of cotton for cord and string, 520 ***mans*** of iron for clamps and balls placed on the heads of hammers, 321 wagons to bring the iron from the Arāvallī hills, and 121 ***mans*** of jute. In addition, 221 ***mans*** of poppy, 721 ***mans*** of salt, 1,121 ***mans*** of ***ghī***, 2,555 ***mans*** of wheat, 11,121 ***mans*** of other grains, and 5 ***mans*** of opium were brought to feed the laborers and craftsemen. See: Reu, 1:117, n. 1.

[13] See: L. P. Tessitori, "A Progress Report on the Work done during the year 1917 in connection with the Bardic and Historical Survey of Rajputana," ***Journal of the Asiatic Society of Bengal***, N. S. 15 (1919), pp. 44-46, for a complete reference to this work.

After their victory at Sohavo, Jaito and Kūmpo walked over the field counting the fallen. They searched especially for Sāṅkhlo Mahes's body, and when they could not find it, they chided the Sāṅkhlo in his absence, saying:

> It looks as if the Sāṅkhlo has fled. Nice indeed! After all the fine things he was saying! [Now be sure that] if the Sāṅkhlo is [lying] anywhere, he is lying on the field of battle in [his] women's apartments!

Soon thereafter, however, they found the Sāṅkhlo lying on the field, moaning. They asked him derisively if he moaned because he was in pain. He replied that he moaned because inferior men had killed Rāv Jaitsī. Jaito and Kūmpo then abused the Sāṅkhlo, exclaiming, "Throw dust in his mouth." An augur who witnessed these happenings remarked, "This land, the Sāṅkhlo [now] hold it in [his] jaws."

In January of 1544 Jaito again assumed a major role in the affairs of Mārvāṛ along with his paternal cousin, Kūmpo Mahirājot. They gathered to meet Meṛtīyo Rāv Viramde Dūdāvat and Sher Shāh Sūr in battle at Samel.

Jaito's position before Samel, like that of his cousin, Kūmpo's, was both as leader of the Rāv's forces and as protector of the lands of Mārvāṛ. The circumstances that brought the rupture among Rāv Mālde's warriors and caused the Rāv to retreat from his camp at Girrī[14] prior to battle are unclear. It seems certain, however, that Meṛtīyo Rāv Vīramde was able to instill suspicions within Rāv Mālde's mind about the loyalty of his Rajpūts. Jaito and Kūmpo both spent much time in negotiations with the Rāv through intermediaries. In the end, they refused to obey his command to retreat before the Muslim army and leave the land their ancestors had conquered open to the enemy. Rāv Mālde left his camp precipitously on the night before the main engagement without informing either Jaito or Kūmpo, taking a large number of Rajpūts with him in retreat.

With Rāv Mālde's departure, Jaito and Kūmpo both realized that they could not defeat the opposing forces in open battle. They decided, therefore, to organize a surprise night attack. This stratagem failed, however, for the Rāṭhoṛs were unable to locate Sher Shāh's camp in the dark. The next day as the battle closed, Jaito and Kūmpo dismounted from their horses in the safety of a river bank and ate opium with the water of the river, then rode off against the opposing forces. They managed to destroy an advance guard of Sher Shāh's army, and Jaito himself is credited with knocking Jalāl Jalūko, an Afghan chief in Sher Shāh's service, from his horse with his lance. He is said to have hurled his lance with such force that he broke both of the horse's front legs (see "Aitihāsik Bātāṃ," pp. 42-44 of the **translated text** for details of this battle).

Jaito was killed at Samel fighting alongside two of his sons, Devīdās Jaitāvat (8-2) (no. 65), who was wounded (see ***infra***), and Udaisiṅgh Jaitāvat (8-4), who was killed. Udaisiṅgh appears to have been one of Rāv Mālde's personal retainers. The texts mention his being posted outside the Rāv's tent as a bodyguard prior to the battle.

---

[14] Girrī village: located ten miles west-southwest of Samel.

"Aitihāsik Bātāṃ," p. 44, records that after the battle and the Rāṭhoṛ defeat, Sher Shāh found the bodies of both Jaito and Kūmpo lying on the field. He had his men hold up Jaito's body in order to look at him. He then said to Meṛtīyo Rāv Vīramde, who was with him, that Jaito had done so much, and that if Rāv Mālde had stayed to fight, he might have lost the Empire of Delhi.

Jaito was sixty years old when he was killed at Samel.

"Aitihāsik Bātāṃ," pp. 37, 39, 42-45, 57-58; ***Āsop kā Itihās***, pp. 16-17; ***Bāṅkīdās***, pp. 12, 52-53; Gehlot, ***Mārvāṛ***, p. 160; ***Khyāt***, 3:80-86, 95, 99-100; ***Murārdān***, no. 1, p. 639, no. 2, pp. 116-120, 449-450; Reu, 1:117-118; Tessitori, "A Progress Report on the Work done during the year 1917 in connection with the Bardic and Historical Survey of Rajputana," ***Journal of the Asiatic Society of Bengal***, N. S. 15 (1919), pp. 43-46; ***Vigat***, 1:46, 57, 63, 65, 2:48-49, 51, 57.

(no. 63) **Prithīrāj Jaitāvat** (8-1)

Jaito Pañcāiṇot's son, Prithīrāj Jaitāvat, was a powerful and influential Rāṭhoṛ ***ṭhākur*** in Mārvāṛ under Rāv Mālde Gāṅgāvat of Jodhpur (1532-62). He was born in 1524-25 during the rule of Rāv Gāṅgo Vāghāvat (1515-32). He rose to a position of authority equal to that of his father's at an early age. Mahevco Rāvat Bhīṃvo of Bāhaṛmer and Koṭṛo in western Mārvāṛ, against whom Prithīrāj came in battle, spoke of him as a Rajpūt with a "brown mustache, [whose] body [is] of great height and stature, a ***ṭhākur***," and "a brother, a most excellent [one]" ("Aitihāsik Bātāṃ," p. 47).

Following Prithīrāj's death at the battle of Meṛto in 1554, a local chronicle records that Rāv Mālde grew worried, for "there was no Rajpūt like [Prithīrāj]" (***ibid.***, p. 50). Prithīrāj was both ruthless and haughty as a warrior. But he was also a man who commanded great respect on the field of battle. It was said that he had received a boon from a Jogī that prevented any weapon from striking him from the front (***Khyāt***, 3:120).

As early as 1540-41, when Prithīrāj was approximately sixteen years of age, he accompanied his friend, Ūdāvat Rāṭhoṛ Tejsī Ḍūṅgarsīyot (no. 138), on a raid against the Paṃvārs of Cāṭsū in central Rājasthān.[15] Cāṭsū lies some thirty-five miles to the south of Āmber. It was one of the areas over which Rāv Mālde asserted his authority following his occupation of Ajmer ca. 1535. But the raid on Cāṭsū also appears to have been initiated by Tejsī Ḍūṅgarsīyot who desired to take revenge to settle an old ***vair*** against the Paṃvārs. He sent nine elephants to Rāv Mālde as spoils of his success there. Rāv Mālde had a small fort built at Cāṭsū as an outpost of his kingdom.

---

[15] See ***supra***, "Paṃvārs of Cāṭsū," and ***infra***, "Ūdāvat Rāṭhoṛs." It is possible that there were a series of raids against Cāṭsū in which Ūdāvat Tejsī Ḍūṅgarsīyot participated, with the first of these coming as early as ca. 1536.

Local chronicles do not record any of Prithīrāj's activities between 1541 and January of 1544, when his father, Jaito Pañcāiṇot (7-1) (no. 61), and his brother, Udaisiṅgh Jaitāvat (8-4) (no. 62), were killed in battle at Samel. Prithīrāj was at Samel, but he accompanied Rāv Mālde into exile in the hills near Sīvāṇo. It is possible that he, like his brother, Udaisiṅgh, had served as a personal attendant of the Rāv's, but unlike Udaisiṅgh, he withdrew with the Rāv instead of remaining behind to fight and die.

Mānsiṅgh Jaitāvat (8-5), another of Prithīrāj's brothers, refused to follow Rāv Mālde into exile, even when summoned to do so. He remained behind in Mārvāṛ and met with Sher Shāh's people to effect an accommodation. Mānsiṅgh was thereby able to remain in possession of the Jaitāvat village of Bagṛī.[16] However, the Muslims later killed Mānsiṅgh for unexplained reasons.

Rāv Mālde quickly reoccupied Jodhpur following Sher Shāh's death in 1545, and began returning villages to his Rajpūts in *paṭo*. But he withheld Bagṛī from Prithīrāj, because of his anger about Mānsiṅgh's actions. It was not until Rāv Mālde's ***pradhān***, Cāmpāvat Jeso Bhairavdāsot (no. 48), intervened on Prithīrāj's behalf that Rāv Mālde granted Bagṛī to Prithīrāj. "Aitihāsik Bātāṃ," p. 46, records:

> Jeso Bhairavdāsot persisted very stubbornly and had Bagṛī given [to Prithīrāj]. Prithīrāj was yet a young man.

A short time thereafter, Sīsodīyo Rāṇo Udaisiṅgh Sāṅgāvat of Mevāṛ (ca. 1537-72; no. 17) formed an army to march against Mārvāṛ in order to seize lands that Rāv Mālde had taken from him earlier. The threat of this attack worried Rāv Mālde greatly because most of his leading warriors had been killed at Samel. He was forced to rely heavily upon his ***pradhān***, Jeso Bhairavdāsot, to reach an accommodation with the Rāṇo. Jeso advised the Rāv to marry one of his daughters to the Rāṇo to placate him, and to give him a large dowry of horses and elephants along with fifty villages from Sojhat and Goḍhvāṛ. The Rāv agreed to do as Jeso advised, and letters of endorsement were made ready. But Prithīrāj then learned of this plan, and he strongly objected to any accommodation with the Rāṇo. He organized a concerted front of Mārvāṛ Rāṭhoṛs instead. There was the "sway of the Rāvjī. [And] the paramount influence of Rāṭhoṛ Prithīrāj" ("Aitihāsik Bātāṃ," p. 47).

In the face of this resolve, the Sīsodīyos withdrew from Mārvāṛ and hostilities were averted. Rāv Mālde's grant of Bagṛī to Prithīrāj at Jeso Bhairavdāsot's bidding had proven beneficial.

One of Rāv Mālde's sons, Kuṃvar Rām Māldevot by his wife, Rāṇī Kachvāhī Lachapdejī,[17] imprisoned his father at the fort of Jodhpur in 1547 in an attempt to seize power in Mārvāṛ. Kuṃvar Rām then approached Prithīrāj and asked him to join with him in the overthrow of the Rāv. Prithīrāj delayed his

---

[16] Bagṛī village: located nine miles east-southeast of Sojhat.

[17] See ***supra***, "**Marriage and Family Lists of the Rulers of Jodhpur**," Mālde Gāṅgāvat, Rāṇī no. 16, S - Rām.

reply and informed the ***pradhān***, Jeso Bhairavdāsot, who then formulated a plan with Prithīrāj to free the Rāv and to blockade the gates of the fort at Jodhpur while Kuṃvar Rām was at a feast at Maṇḍor. Prithīrāj and Jeso Bhairavdāsot put their plan successfully into action, thereby preventing Rāv Mālde's overthrow, and Kuṃvar Rām was forced to abandon Jodhpur for Gūndoc[18] along with his mother and his personal retainers.

Prithīrāj participated in several campaigns in western and northwestern Mārvāṛ between 1550 and 1552 in order to bring these areas under Rāv Mālde's control. In 1550 Prithīrāj rode against Phaḷodhī and Pokaraṇ.[19] Narāvat Rāṭhoṛ descendants of Naro Sūjāvat, a son of Rāv Sūjo Jodhāvat (ca. 1492-1515), held these forts. The Narāvats were closely allied with the Bhāṭīs of Jaisaḷmer, from whom they had received daughters in marriage. When Rāv Mālde's force under the command of his ***pradhān***, Jeso Bhairavdāsot, approached Phaḷodhī, Narāvat Jaitmāl Goindot sent word to Jaisaḷmer Rāvaḷ Mālde Lūṇkaraṇot (1549-60) for aid. Rāvaḷ Mālde dispatched his son, Kuṃvar Harrāj Māldevot, to Pokaraṇ. Fighting broke out at Phaḷodhī and then Pokaraṇ, but Rāv Mālde's Rajpūts were able to occupy both forts. The Rāv then sent his warriors against the Mahevco Rāṭhoṛs of Bāhaṛmer and Koṭro in western Mārvāṛ. They were also victorious there and they brought Mahevco Rāvat Bhīṃvo into Rāv Mālde's service.

It was during these expeditions that Prithīrāj's prowess as a warrior came to Rāv Mālde's notice. Local chronicles differ regarding detail. ***Vigat***, 2:4-5, records that it was during the battle for Pokaraṇ against Bhāṭī Kuṃvar Harrāj Māldevot that Prithīrāj's prowess was first evidenced. The ***Vigat*** relates that when the fighting ended, several Rajpūts came before the presence of the Rāv carrying lances that were red with the blood of battle, while Prithīrāj approached with a clean lance. The Rāv noticed this difference and questioned Jeso Bhairavdāsot, concerned that Prithīrāj had done no fighting that day. Jeso then showed the Rāv the underside of Prithīrāj's shirt, where Prithīrāj had cleaned his lance, and he told the Rāv in great detail about Prithīrāj's exploits during the battle. He said, "The battle was won because of his valor." Rāv Mālde was very pleased with Prithīrāj.

"Aitihāsik Bātāṃ," p. 47, tells that it was following the campaign against Bāhaṛmer and Koṭro that Prithīrāj came to Rāv Mālde's notice, and that it was then that Prithīrāj was promoted to be the commander of his army (***senāpati***). During the action against Rāvat Bhīṃvo and the Mahevcos, Prithīrāj is said to have struck Rāvat Bhīṃvo with his lance (***barchī***) and then wiped the lance clean of blood stains with his shirt. There were again questions about Prithīrāj's performance because his lance was clean, while those of other Rajpūts still bore the marks of fighting. When Rāvat Bhīṃvo was brought before the Rāv, however, he praised Prithīrāj, saying:

[18] Gūndoc village: located fifty miles south-southeast of Jodhpur.

[19] Phaḷodhī and Pokaraṇ are located seventy-two miles north-northwest and eighty-three miles northwest of Jodhpur, respectively.

> [this one with the] brown mustache, [whose] body [is] of great height and stature, a *ṭhākur* . . . [he] struck me [with his] lance.

Rāvat Bhīṃvo added that Prithīrāj was "a brother, a most excellent [one]." Rāv Mālde is said to have held Prithīrāj in very high esteem and to have made him the commander of his army.

Rāv Mālde sent his Rajpūts under Prithīrāj and his ***pradhān***, Jeso Bhairavdāsot, against Jaisaḷmer in September or October of 1552. Prithīrāj proceeded to Maṇḍor before his departure along with Rāv Mālde's son, Kuṃvar Rāymal Māldevot, and two ***purohit***s, Rāymal and Neto, in order to worship at the shrines there. He was then given leave to proceed against the Jaisaḷmer. Upon reaching the land of the Bhāṭīs, he looted and burned along the way to the city of Jaisaḷmer, where he encamped with his men in the city's gardens and orchards. The Rāvaḷ of Jaisaḷmer remained closed within the fort during this occupation. Scattered fighting took place in the city, but the Rāṭhoṛs left without capturing the fort. Prithīrāj did much damage while there, and had all of the trees in the gardens and orchards cut down with the exception of one pīpaḷ tree, alongside which he made his camp. This tree became known as "Prithīrāj's pīpaḷ."

The ***Khyāt*** of Naiṇsī, 1:60, and "Aitihāsik Bātāṃ," pp. 56-57, both record that Prithīrāj led Rāv Mālde's warriors in an attack against Ajmer. No date is given for this expedition, but the ***Khyāt*** states that Paṭhāṇ Hājī Khān was in occupation of Ajmer at the time. This statement would be incorrect if Prithīrāj were involved in this attack. Hājī Khān did not take possession of Ajmer until 1556, shortly before the battle of Harmāṛo[20] against Sīsodīyo Rāṇo Udaisiṅgh Sāṅgāvat (ca. 1537-72; no. 17), which took place in January of 1557. These events took place two years after Prithīrāj's death at the battle of Meṛto in 1554.

If Prithīrāj did lead this attack against Ajmer, it would have taken place in 1553-54. The sources relate that Prithīrāj rode on the campaign with Cūṇḍāvat Rāṭhoṛ Mahes Gharsīyot (no. 58), who had held Ajmer in ***paṭo*** from Rāv Mālde during the years 1535-43. The Rāṭhoṛ army is said to have raided the town and attacked the fort. Several of Mahes's retainers managed to climb the walls of the fort and proclaim a victory for Mahesjī. "Aitihāsik Bātāṃ," p. 57, notes that this action deterred the Riṇmalots[21] who were with Prithīrāj, dampening their enthusiasm to advance further. They said:

> We would die [in battle], and the proclamation [of victory would be the Cūṇḍāvat] Mahesji's, so for what reason [should we advance]?

The Muslims in the fort called upon the aid of Sīsodīyo Rāṇo Udaisiṅgh, and while Prithīrāj wished to do battle with the Rāṇo, his Rajpūts resisted, saying:

---

[20] Harmāṛo village: located fifty-five miles south-southwest of Ajmer and six miles south of Vadhnor in northern Mevāṛ.

[21] Riṇmalots: the descendants of Rāv Riṇmal Cūṇḍāvat, ruler of Maṇḍor, ca. 1428-38.

> We will all die [together here]. Once before Rāv Mālde had great *ṭhākurs*, so [they] were all killed in battle. And if we die, then the rulership (*ṭhākurāī*) [of Rāv Mālde] will become weak (*Khyāt*, 1:60).

The Rajpūts then brought Prithīrāj back to Mārvāṛ.

This action shamed Prithīrāj. He stayed away from Rāv Mālde's court and would not even enter his village of Bagṛī. He preferred to encamp outside it. In the following days, Prithīrāj argued with the Rāv in favor of another attack on Ajmer. But the Rāv would not hear of it. He sent Prithīrāj instead against Meṛtīyo Rāv Jaimal Vīramdevot (no. 107) at Meṛto in March of 1554.

Prithīrāj played a leading role in the events leading up to and during this attack on Meṛto. He was again in command of Rāv Mālde's forces that encamped at the village of Gāṅgarṛo[22] just to the northwest of Meṛto proper. Prithīrāj sent out raiding parties that pillaged the lands around the town. Both he and Bālāvat Rāṭhoṛ Nago Bhārmalot (no. 38) negotiated with Meṛtīyo Rāv Jaimal's *pradhāns*, the Jaitmālots Akhairāj Bhādāvat (no. 69) and Cāndrāj Jodhāvat (no. 74), when Rāv Jaimal sent them to Rāv Mālde's camp to seek an accommodation. Local sources present differing views of Prithīrāj's role in these negotiations. "Aitihāsik Bātāṃ," p. 48, records that Prithīrāj and a number of other Rajpūts entreated Rāv Mālde on behalf of the Meṛtīyos. But the ***Khyāt*** of Naiṇsī, 3:116-118, portrays Prithīrāj as a haughty and prideful ***ṭhākur*** who was himself fully committed to the subordination of Meṛto to Jodhpur.

During the main battle for Meṛto, which occurred on the day following the abortive negotiations at Rāv Mālde's camp, Prithīrāj was in personal command of a large ***aṇī*** ("division of the army") that came before the Jodhpur Gate at Meṛto proper. He divided this ***aṇī*** into two groups as the fighting began. Here also, Prithīrāj showed great prowess as a warrior. He is said to have killed fourteen of Meṛtīyo Rāv Jaimal's Rajpūts with his own hands. At some time during the battle, he met with Rāv Jaimal's young son, Surtāṇ Jaimalot (no. 113), whom he chided for coming before him, saying that Surtāṇ should have sent his father instead. Prithīrāj then took Surtāṇ's sword from him and awarded it to one of his military servants, Pīpāṛo Gahlot Hīṅgoḷo, to whom he had promised a sword.

Prithīrāj later confronted Jaitmālot Akhairāj Bhādāvat, who had sought him out. Prithīrāj used an exceptionally demeaning tone with Akhairāj, calling him a "dwarf" and asking him why had had delayed so long in coming. Akhairāj then attacked Prithīrāj and managed to strike him from behind, knowing that this was the only way he could defeat him. Prithīrāj fell from Akhairāj's blows. As he died, he is said to have left his curse upon Akhairāj.

Prithīrāj's sister's son (***bhāṇej***), Hul Gahlot Rāysal Rāmāvat, who was a military servant of Meṛtītyo Rāv Jaimal's, found Prithīrāj lying on the field after the battle, and he built a cover to shade Prithīrāj's body from the sun. Rāv

[22] Gāṅgarṛo village: located seven miles west-northwest of Meṛto.

Jaimal learned of this action, and he became angry with Rāysal. Rāysal then left Meṛto for the lands of Rāv Mālde of Jodhpur (see "Aitihāsik Bātāṃ," pp. 48-49, of the **translated text** for a complete description of this battle and the events that followed).

Prithīrāj was thirty years old when he was killed at Meṛto.

There was much talk about Prithīrāj at the court of Sīsodīyo Rāṇo Udaisiṅgh at Cītoṛ in the wake of Prithīrāj's death. Prithīrāj's friend, Ūdāvat Tejsī Ḍūṅgarsīyot, was at Cītoṛ at this time. The Rajpūts there all acclaimed Prithīrāj and his killing of fourteen men with his own hands. They asked if there were any among them who were his equal.

"Aitihāsik Bātāṃ," pp. 46-50, 56-57, 60-62, 66; ***Akbar Nāma***, 2:72; ***Bāṅkīdās***, p. 13; ***Khyāt***, 1:60, 3:116-121; Maṅgilāl Vyās, ***Jodhpur Rājya kā Itihās*** (Jaypur: Pañcśīl Prakāśan, 1975), pp. 157-163; ***Murārdān***, no. 2, pp. 128-129, 459; Ojhā, 4:1:310-312, 317-318; ***Vigat***, 1:59, 64-65, 2:4-5, 59.

(no. 64) **Pūraṇmal Prithīrājot** (9-1)

Pūraṇmal Prithīrājot was a son of Prithīrāj Jaitāvat's (8-1) (no. 63) and grandson of Jaito Pañcāiṇot's (7-1) (no. 61), the founding ancestor of the Jaitāvat Rāṭhoṛs. Pūraṇmal received his family's village of Bagṛī [23] in ***paṭo*** from Rāv Mālde following his father's death. But he held this village only three years, for in 1557 Rāv Mālde took it from Pūraṇmal and granted it to Pūraṇmal's paternal uncle, Devīdās Jaitāvat (8-2) (no. 65). The Rāv granted the village to Devīdās in reward for Devīdās's success in battle at Harmāṛo[24] against Sīsodīyo Rāṇo Udaisiṅgh Sāṅgāvat of Mevāṛ (ca. 1537-72; no. 17). Pūraṇmal received the village of Pacīāk [25] and twelve others in ***paṭo*** from Rāv Mālde in compensation.

No information is available about Pūraṇmal's activities while he was a military servant of Rāv Mālde's. He was killed within eight years of his father's death when he fought alongside his paternal uncle, Devidās Jaitāvat, at the battle of Meṛto in 1562. Rāv Mālde's Rajpūts stood here against Meṛtīyo Rāv Jaimal and the Mughal forces of Akbar under the command of Mīrzā Sharafu'd-Dīn Ḥusayn.

"Aitihāsik Bātāṃ," pp. 50, 52, 55; ***Bāṅkīdās***, pp. 16-17; "Jodhpur Hukūmat rī Bahī," p. 191; ***Vigat***, 1:61, 2:65.

---

[23] Bagṛī village: located nine miles east-southeast of Sojhat in eastern Mārvāṛ.

[24] Harmāṛo village: located fifty-five miles south-southwest of Ajmer and six miles south of Vadhnor in northern Mevāṛ.

[25] Pacīāk village: located three miles north of Bīlāṛo and twenty-three miles north-northwest of Bagṛī.

(no. 65) **Devīdās Jaitāvat** (8-2)
(no. 66) **Bhākharsī Jaitāvat** (8-3)

Devīdās Jaitāvat was a son of Jaito Pañcāiṇot's (7-1) (no. 61), the founding ancestor of the Jaitāvat Rāṭhoṛs. Devīdās appears in the chronicles of Mārvāṛ as a valorous if somewhat foolhardy warrior who possessed great personal strength and determination. He always carried the honor of the Jaitāvats and of the Rāṭhoṛs before himself. He was involved in all of the major campaigns of Rāv Mālde Gāṅgāvat of Jodhpur (1532-62) between the years 1553 and 1562, and he rose to a position of influence under Rāv Mālde that paralleled that of his elder brother, Prithīrāj Jaitāvat (8-1) (no. 63), and his father, Jaito Pancāiṇot.

Devīdās was approximately fifteen years old when he was wounded at Samel in January of 1544 fighting alongside his father. He was born in 1528-29 during the latter years of Rāv Gāṅgo Vāghāvat's rule at Jodhpur (1515-32), and he grew up during the years of Rāṭhoṛ conquest and expansion out from Jodhpur under Rāv Mālde Gāṅgāvat (1532-62).

Jodhpur Rājya kī Khyāt, pp. 90-91, relates that following the battle of Samel, it was initially thought that both Devīdās and his father had been killed. The women of the family heard this news at Bagṛī village,[26] and they shaved their heads and assumed the posture of widows in mourning as funerary rites were performed for both Devīdās and Jaito. However, Devīdās was in fact not killed. A wandering ascetic found him lying wounded on the battlefield and took and cared for him. When Devīdās's wounds were healed, he joined the ascetic's band and became one of them, and he remained with these ascetics (***atītāṃ***) for the next "five to seven years."

The band of ascetics left Mārvāṛ not long after and traveled to Sīrohī. Devīdās's sister had been married to the Rāv of Sīrohī (identity uncertain), and on one occasion, the Rāv invited the ascetics to come to the palace and take food. Devīdās went unrecognized at the court for he had assumed the garb and posture of a holy man. But he did keep his sword and shield with him, and the Rāv saw these weapons and determined to steal them. He called seven Maiṇos and said to them, "With such and such an ascetic are a sword and shield. So [if you] take and bring [these weapons], I would give a reward."

One night at midnight shortly thereafter, the seven Maiṇos stole into the quarters where Devīdās and the ascetics slept. Devīdās kept the weapons at his side, and when the Maiṇos tried to take them, they inadvertently awakened him. He immediately arose, took up his sword, and killed three of the Maiṇos. The remaining four fled with Devīdās in close pursuit. Nearby was a watercourse filled from the rains, across which the Maiṇos ran. But Devīdās could not follow because he had been wounded and lamed by a sword blow to the foot. Unable to continue his pursuit, Devīdās exclaimed, "Ṭhākurs! I shall not allow Jaitojī's honor/reputation to depart," thereby declaring his readiness to fight and defend his and his father's honor.

---

[26] Bagṛī village: located nine miles east-southeast of Sojhat in eastern Mārvāṛ.

The Maiṇos returned to the Rāv of Sīrohī and reported all that had happened to him. The Rāv then reasoned, "He brought up/mentioned Jaitojī's honor/reputation; perhaps he is Devīdās." The Rāv went to the women's quarters (***rāvḷo***) of the palace afterwards and said to his young wife (***bahu***), if this were her brother, she should recognize him. When the ascetics came to the ***rāvḷo*** to eat the next day, Devīdās's sister stood behind a curtain to view them. She immediately recognized her brother and had word conveyed to the Rāv, "He certainly is Devīdās."

The ascetics ate and then rose to leave after their meal, and as they did, the Rāvjī grasped Devīdās. Though Devīdās protested that he was only an ascetic, the Rāv said they had recognized him. The Rāv then took Devīdās into his company and treated him well, feeding him and making him comfortable, and he arranged a marriage for him.

Rāv Mālde at Jodhpur learned soon after that Devīdās was alive. He was overjoyed. He sent his son, Kuṃvar Candrasen Māldevot (Rāv of Jodhpur, 1562-81), to Sīrohī with a litter, horses, and camels for Devīdās, and with orders to bring him back to Jodhpur.

Devīdās returned to Mārvāṛ in 1550-51. It is uncertain how he began his military career, but he appears initially to have taken service under Ūdāvat Rāṭhoṛ Ratansī Khīṃvāvat (no. 141), from whom he held the village of Bāñjhāṅkuṛī [27] in ***paṭo***. It appears likely that he met Ūdāvat Ratansī through the ***kuṃvar***, for Ratansī himself served under Kuṃvar Candrasen. Devīdās took part in the Rāṭhoṛ occupation of Jāḷor in southern Mārvāṛ in 1553 as a military servant of Ratansī's, and ***Jodhpur Rājya kī Khyāt***, p. 91, records that Devīdās "[helped to] establish authority [there]." A year later in 1554 Devīdās participated in the battle for Meṛto as a member of Ratansī's ***sāth***. Though he played a much less distinguished role here than did his brother, Prithīrāj Jaitāvat, he did confront Meṛtīyo Rāv Jaimal Vīramdevot (no. 107) during the fighting. He would have attempted to kill Rāv Jaimal if Ratansī Khīṃvāvat had not stopped him and told him that Rāv Jaimal's life should be spared.

Devīdās left Ūdāvat Ratansī Khīṃvāvat's service following the battle for Meṛto and Rāv Mālde's defeat there, and he entered into Rāv Mālde's service. It is unclear why Devīdās chose this time to join Rāv Mālde. A number of things may have influenced his decision. His brother, Prithīrāj, had been killed at Meṛto and Devīdās then sought a means to avenge his death. Ratansī Khīṃvāvat had stopped him from striking and killing Meṛtīyo Rāv Jaimal during the fighting at Meṛto, and this undoubtedly angered him. He also desired to acquire his ancestral village of Bagṛī.

Rāv Mālde honored Devīdās when he entered his service. He knew the strength that Devīdās brought, and he reasoned that Devīdās might be able to achieve what Prithīrāj was no longer able to do, namely, to conquer and hold Meṛto.

Upon joining the Rāv's service, Devīdās immediately asked to be sent against Meṛto. He wanted to avenge his brother's death. Rāv Mālde praised

---

[27] Bāñjhāṇkuṛī village: located five miles north of Jaitāraṇ in eastern Mārvāṛ.

Devīdās and gave him 1,000 horses. Devīdās took this ***sāth*** and besieged the village of Reyāṃ[28] near Meṛto. No significant action took place, however. Rāv Jaimal wisely remained enclosed within the fort at Meṛto, not even venturing forth to disturb Devīdās's supply carts as they moved past Meṛto. Devīdās was forced to leave the area without having engaged the Meṛtīyos.

Devīdās's activities during the next several years are unclear. There is no record of Rāv Mālde's having granted him any villages in ***paṭo***, and it is possible that he remained in personal attendance on the Rāv at Jodhpur, living in his ***vās*** ("residence, dwelling"). Then in late 1556 and early 1557, when Paṭhāṇ Hājī Khān, a former noble of Sher Shāh Sūr's, occupied Ajmer and asked for Rāv Mālde's support against Sīsodīyo Rāṇo Udaisiṅgh Sāṅgāvat of Mevāṛ (ca. 1537-72; no. 17), Devīdās, who was now a seasoned warrior of some thirty years, volunteered to lead the Rāv's Rajpūts into battle. Rāv Mālde was again pleased. He allowed Devīdās to hand-pick 1,500 warriors for his ***sāth***, and he gave him a horse and a ***sirpāv***, exclaiming that "the shame of Mārvāṛ" rested upon his shoulders ("Aitihāsik Bātāṃ," p. 50).

Devīdās and his Rajpūts performed well at Harmāṛo[29] in January of 1557, when they and Hājī Khān's Muslim warriors defeated the allied force under Sīsodīyo Rāṇo Udaisiṅgh of Mevāṛ. "Aitihāsik Bātāṃ," p. 68, records that the victory at Harmāṛo was due to the "paramount influence of Rāṭhoṛ Devīdāsjī." Devīdās sought out and killed the Bālīso Cahuvāṇ Sūjo Sāṃvatot (no. 4) during the fighting there. Bālīso Sūjo was a military servant of the Rāṇo's, and Devīdās challenged him on the field, saying:

> Sūjo, [be] alert, [for] today I demand [revenge for the deaths of]
> Rāṭhoṛs Vīñjo and Dhano [Bhārmalot] (***Vigat***, 1:52).

Bālīso Sūjo's death settled a long-standing ***vair*** that had arisen twenty years earlier when Bālīso Sūjo and his brothers defeated the Bālāvat Rāṭhoṛs in battle near Nāḍūl [30] in southern Mārvāṛ, and killed the Bālāvat Vīñjo Bhārmalot.[31]

Rāv Mālde wished to make Devīdās a large grant of villages including Khairvo[32] and eighty-four others in reward for his victory at Harmāṛo. But the administrative officials concerned with revenue advised the Rāv to ask Devīdās what he wanted. Devīdās requested his home village of Bagṛī. Rāv Mālde then granted Bagṛī village and eighty-four others in ***paṭo*** to Devīdās, revoking the

---

[28] Reyāṃ village: located fifteen miles southeast of Meṛto.

[29] Harmāṛo village: located fifty-five miles south-southwest of Ajmer and six miles south of Vadhnor in northern Mevāṛ.

[30] Nāḍūl: located sixty-seven miles south-southeast of Jodhpur.

[31] See ***supra***, "Bālāvat Rāṭhoṛs" and "Bālīso Cahuvāṇs" for complete details about this battle and the ***vair*** that emerged from it.

[32] Khairvo village: located fifty miles south-southeast of Jodhpur.

grant he had earlier made to Devīdās's paternal nephew, Pūraṇmal Prithīrājot (9-1) (no. 64). He granted Pūraṇmal the village of Pacīāk[33] and twelve others in compensation.

Meṛtīyo Rāv Jaimal, who had been an ally of the Rāṇo's at the battle of Harmāṛo, was forced to vacate Meṛto and leave it open to Rāv Mālde's occupation after the Rāṇo's defeat. Rāv Mālde, in turn, sent Devīdās to Meṛto to place his authority over the town. Devīdās secured Meṛto and then assumed charge of the fort at Jodhpur, while Rāv Mālde had the old town and fort at Meṛto razed. Nearby he had a new town built along with a fort called the Mālgaḍh. Prior to beginning construction, Rāv Mālde asked Devīdās about the advisability of building the Mālgaḍh. Devīdās's response was not sanguine. He argued that such a fort would mean death for those who occupied it, for the fort would be built on the plain, open to continuing attack by the Meṛtīyos who would not easily relinquish their land. Rāv Mālde would not listen to Devīdās, however. He had the foundations for the new fort laid in March of 1558. The fort was completed two years later, in 1560.

Rāv Mālde appointed Meṛtīyo Jagmāl Vīramdevot (no. 124), to whom he had granted one-half of the villages of Meṛto, as ***kiledār*** of the Mālgaḍh, and he placed Devīdās at the fort with a large ***sāth*** of Rajpūts. Devīdās again protested to the Rāv about being stationed at Meṛto. He asked the Rāv to put someone else in his place, and stated that when the Meṛtīyos attacked the fort, he would not leave even if the Rāv ordered him to do so. Rāv Mālde would not listen to Devīdās's objections. He felt that this Rajpūt was perhaps the only one who would be able to withstand an attack and preserve his authority at Meṛto.

Meṛtīyo Rāv Jaimal and the Mughal forces of Akbar under Mīrzā Sharafu'd-Dīn Ḥusayn laid siege to the Mālgaḍh in February of 1562. This was an eventuality that Devīdās had long foreseen. Rāv Mālde sent reinforcements to Devīdās with his son, Kuṃvar Candrasen Māldevot. But Kuṃvar Candrasen found the situation at Meṛto untenable, and he withdrew with a large number of Rajpūts as his father had ordered him to do. He requested that Devīdās also leave. But neither the Kuṃvar's remonstrations nor those of Rāv Mālde would alter Devīdās's position. He would not appear ignoble by leaving Meṛto without a fight.

Devīdās proceeded to close himself within the fort with his Rajpūts, among whom were thirty-eight of Meṛtīyo Jagmāl Vīramdevot's, who had elected to remain with Devīdās and defend the fort. Jagmāl himself had withdrawn earlier after talking with the Mughals. In the days that followed, skirmishes occurred as Devīdās's Rajpūts emerged from the fort to harass their besiegers. But it was not until the Mughals exploded a mine beneath one of the towers of the fort that the situation changed. Devīdās then held talks with the Mughals, agreeing to withdraw with his own belongings and not to burn the stores inside.

The withdrawal from the fort began as an orderly process, but then Devīdās's Rajpūts fired the stores to prevent them from falling into the Mughals'

---

[33] Pacīāk village: located three miles north of Bīlāṛo and twenty-three miles north-northwest of Bagṛī.

hands. Devīdās was himself injured by a kick from a horse which broke one of his legs, and Devīdās killed a Muslim who tried to lay hands on one of Rāv Mālde's personal muskets, which a servant of Devīdās's was carrying. Once outside the fort, the Rajpūts began moving off toward Sātalvās, which lay four miles to the southwest of Meṛto in the direction of Jodhpur. Meṛtīyo Rāv Jaimal then urged an attack on Devīdās. He said to Mīrzā Sharafu'd-Dīn that Devīdās was not the sort of Rajpūt to abandon the fort, that he would quickly bring Rāv Mālde against them ("Aitihāsik Bātāṃ," p. 55).

The Mīrzā agreed, and the Mughals and Rāv Jaimal's Rajpūts attacked Devīdās and his men on the open plain near Meṛto. Here on March 20, 1562 Devīdās was killed along with one of his brothers, Bhākharsī Jaitāvat (8-3) (no. 66), and his paternal nephew, Pūraṇmal Prithīrājot (9-1) (no. 64).

Devīdās was approximately thirty-five years of age at the time of his death.

There are many stories in the chronicles of this period that say Devīdās did not die on this day near Meṛto, but was only wounded and lived to reappear some years later. ***Akbar Nāma***, 2:250, states, for example:

> Some said that Deo Dās [Devīdās] came out of this battle, wounded; and some ten or twelve years afterwards a person appeared in jogi's dress and assumed this name. Some acknowledged him, and many rejected him. He lived for a while and then was killed in some adventure.

Elsewhere, ***Akbar Nāma***, 3:224-225, relates a story about a "Debī Dās" who reappeared in Mārvāṛ in 1575. Similar accounts appear in the Mārvāṛī chronicles with slight variations.[34] They all record that Devīdās was not killed at Meṛto, but was taken from the field of battle by a holy man who cared for his wounds and brought him back to health. Devīdās became a ***sannyāsī*** and wandered about northern India with the holy man, visiting the shrines and holy places. After some years, the holy man gave him leave, and Devīdās then reappeared as Devīdās Rāṭhoṛ. He is said to have taken service under the Mughals in order to make his name known. It was with the Mughals that he returned to Mārvāṛ in the period of Rāv Candrasen Māldevot's exile from Jodhpur in the latter-1570s. He took up residence once again at Bagṛī and became involved with the Mughals in their operations against Rāv Candrasen. He also became involved with Rāv Kalo Rāmot, a paternal nephew of Rāv Candrasen's, who held Sojhat in ***jāgīr*** from the Mughals. This Devīdās eventually left service under the Mughals and sided with Rāv Kalo during hostilities that developed between him and the Mughals. According to ***Akbar Nāma***, 3:225, he was killed at Sojhat after he and a number of Rajpūts with him murdered Jalāl Khān Qurchī in his tent and then attacked Shimāl Khān Chela.

[34] See, for example: "Aitihāsik Bātāṃ," pp. 82-84; ***Aitihāsik Tavārīkhvār Vārtā***, MS no. 1234 (Caupāsnī: Rājasthānī Śodh Saṃsthān), ff. 71-74.

Other sources relate that Devīdās then fled into the hills to join Rāv Candrasen, with whom he continued to fight against the Mughal occupation of Mārvāṛ.

Ā'īn-ī-Akbarī, pp. 491, 531; "Aitihāsik Bātāṃ," pp. 49-55, 67-68, 82-84; ***Akbar Nāma***, 2:248-250, 3:224-225; ***Bāṅkīdās***, pp. 14-17; "Bāt Rāṭhoṛ Devīdās Jaitāvat rī," ***Aitihāsik Tavārīkhvār Vārtā***, MS no. 1234 (Caupāsnī: Rājasthānī Śodh Saṃsthān), ff. 71-74; ***Jodhpur Rājya kī Khyāt***, pp. 89-91; ***Khyāt***, 1:61-62, 240, 354, 2:162-163; ***Murārdān***, no. 2, pp. 418, 447, 571, 602; ***Vigat***, 1:47, 52, 60-61, 2:59-67.

Figure 23. Jaitāvat Rāṭhoṛs

(1-1) Rāv Salkho
|
(2-1) Vīram Salkhāvat
|
(3-1) Rāv Cūṇḍo Vīramot
|
(4-1) Rāv Riṇmal Cūṇḍāvat
|
(5-1) Akhairāj Riṇmalot
|
(6-1) Pañcāiṇ Akhairājot

- (7-1) **Jaito Pañcāiṇot (Jaitāvats)**
  - (8-1) **Prithīrāj Jaitāvat**
    - (9-1) **Pūraṇmal Prithīrājot**
  - (8-2) **Devīdās Jaitāvat**
  - (8-3) **Bhākharsī Jaitāvat**
  - (8-4) **Udaisiṅgh Jaitāvat**
  - (8-5) Mānsiṅgh Jaitāvat
- (7-2) Acḷo Pañcāiṇot

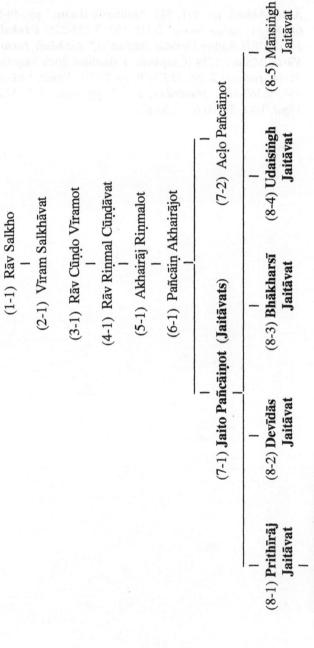

Jaitmālot Rāṭhoṛs

Of Meṛto:

(no. 69)	**Akhairāj Bhādāvat**	(M8-1)
(no. 68)	**Bhādo Mokaḷot**	(M7-1)
(no. 70)	**Bhairavdās Bhādāvat**	(M8-2)
(no. 76)	**Bhojo Gāṅgāvat, Rāvat**	(M7-5)
(no. 74)	**Cāndrāj Jodhāvat**	(M8-3)
(no. 73)	**Jodho Mokaḷot**	(M7-2)
(no. 75)	**Narāiṇdās Cāndrājot**	(M9-1)
(no. 78)	**Sagto Sāṅgāvat**	(M9-2)
(no. 71)	**Sāndho Mokaḷot**	(M7-4)
(no. 77)	**Sāṅgo Bhojāvat**	(M8-4)
(no. 72)	**Sīdho Mokaḷot**	(M7-3)
(no. 67)	**Ūdo Kānhaṛdevot**	(M5-1)

Of Sīvāṇo:

(no. 79)	**Moṭo Jogāvat**	(S9-2)

The Jaitmālot Rāṭhoṛs

The Jaitmālot Rāṭhoṛs descend from Jaitmāl Salkhāvat (2-1), a son of Rāṭhoṛ Rāv Salkho (1-1), the fourteenth century ruler of Mahevo[1] in western Mārvāṛ. Jaitmāl was a daughter's son (***dohitro***) of the Īndo Parihārs.

According to Rāṭhoṛ traditions, Jaitmāl received the area of Sīvāṇo[2] in southwestern Mārvāṛ from his paternal relation, Rāvaḷ Mālojī (Mallīnāth), who had succeeded Rāv Salkho to the rule of Mahevo. Jaitmāl's exact relation to Rāvaḷ Mālojī is unclear. Traditions concerning these early lines of Rāṭhoṛs vary considerably in the texts. In some, Jaitmāl is seen as Mālojī's uterine brother, while in others he is either a paternal nephew or a more distant paternal relation.

Jaitmāl established himself at Sīvāṇo during the latter half of the fourteenth century. Eight generations of Jaitmālots ruled there after him. Within three generations of Jaitmāl himself, however, the Jaitmālots became divided between Sīvāṇo and Meṛto branches (see ***infra***, **Figure 24** and **Figure 25**).

> ***Bāṅkīdās***, pp. 5-6; B. N. Reu, ***Glories of Marwar and the Glorious Rathors*** (Jodhpur: Archaeological Department, 1943), pp. xii-xiii; Bhāṭī, ***Sarvekṣaṇ***, 3:108; D. P. Henige, ***The Chronology of Oral Tradition: Quest for a Chimera*** (Oxford:

---

[1] Mahevo town: located sixty-six miles southwest of Jodhpur.

[2] Sīvāṇo town: located fifty-eight miles southwest of Jodhpur.

Clarendon Press, 1974), pp. 201-206; ***Khyāt***, 2:280-284; ***Murārdān***, no. 2, pp. 55, 308; ***Vigat***, 1:16, 2:215-216.

The Jaitmālots of Sīvāṇo

Little is known about the first five generations of Jaitmālot rulers of Sīvāṇo, descending from Jaitmāl Salkhāvat (2-1) to Rāvat Vījo Tīhaṇot (S6-1), Jaitmāl's great-great-grandson. Information becomes more plentiful for the rule of Rāvat Vījo's son, Rāṇo Devīdās Vījāvat (S7-1). Rāṇo Devīdās was a contemporary of Rāṭhoṛ Rāv Jodho Riṇmalot of Jodhpur (ca. 1453-89). His name figures in the Mārvāṛī chronicles because he came into direct conflict with Rāv Jodho over control of Sīvāṇo.

This conflict emerged following Rāv Jodho's grant of Sīvāṇo to his son, Sivrāj Jodhāvat, during his division of the lands of Mārvāṛ among his brothers and sons following the founding of Jodhpur in 1459. Rāv Jodho was aware that Sīvāṇo was under the control of the Jaitmālots, and he devised a stratagem to weaken their defenses and help his son wrest control of this area. He summoned Jaitmālot Kuṃvar Devīdās Vījāvat and one of his brothers, Karaṇ Vījāvat (S7-2), to Jodhpur on some official pretext, and while they were absent, dispatched a force of Rajpūts under Sīndhaḷ Āpmal of Bhādrājuṇ village[3] against Devīdās's father, Rāvat Vījo Tīhaṇot (S6-1). Sīndhaḷ Āpmal succeeded in taking Sīvāṇo, and during the fighting at the fort, killed Rāvat Vījo.

Sīndhaḷ Āpmal sent two camel messengers to Rāv Jodho following his victory, each carrying a bag of water from a well at Sīvāṇo as a visible sign of the conquest. Jaitmālot Devīdās saw these messengers approaching Jodhpur in great haste from the direction of Sīvāṇo one day following the battle, as he made his way to his camp on the outskirts of the city. He stopped them on the road to question them. He learned that they were servants of Sīndhaḷ Āpmal's of Bhādrājuṇ on their way to Rāv Jodho. Seeing the bags of water, Devīdās quickly discerned that Sīvāṇo had fallen. He fled Jodhpur for Jāḷor and Sācor[4] to the southwest, where he took refuge.

Rāv Jodho proceeded to establish an outpost at Sīvāṇo fort, and he dispatched his son, Sivrāj, to assume authority there. However, as Sivrāj traveled to Sīvāṇo with his family and retainers to take occupation in his own name, Jaitmālot Devīdās Vījāvat attacked the fort and occupied it. He assumed full authority there in his own name and adopted the title of ***rāṇo***. News of Rāṇo Devīdās's victory quickly reached Sivrāj and Rāv Jodho. The Rāv then declined further attempts to take control of the area and left the Jaitmālots in possession. Rāṇo Devīdās later attacked Bhādrājuṇ and killed Sīndhaḷ Āpmal along with a number of his Rajpūts in revenge for the death of his father.

Rāṇo Devīdās died several years later and was succeeded by his son, Jogo Devīdāsot (S8-1). Jaitmālot rule at Sīvāṇo continued for another half

[3] Bhādrājuṇ village: located forty-eight miles south-southwest of Jodhpur.

[4] Jāḷor is located sixty-eight miles south-southwest of Jodhpur, with Sācor sixty-six miles further southwest of Jāḷor.

century. Then in June of 1538, Rāv Mālde Gāṅgāvat of Jodhpur (1532-62) defeated Jaitmālot Rāṇo Ḍūṅgarsī Karamsīyot (S10-1) in battle before Sīvāṇo. From this time forward except for brief periods, Sīvāṇo remained under the authority of the house of Jodhpur.

Some Jaitmālots from the Sīvāṇo branch migrated to Meṛto and took service under the Meṛtīyo Rāṭhoṛs. Moṭo Jogāvat (no. 79) (S9-2), a grandson of Rāṇo Devīdās's, was one such Rajpūt (see ***infra***).

Murārdān, no. 2, p. 115; Ojhā, 4:1:288; ***Vigat***, 1:39, 2:216-219.

The Jaitmālots of Meṛto

(no. 67) **Ūdo Kānhaṛdevot** (M5-1)

The Jaitmālots of Meṛto descend from Ūdo Kānhaṛdevot, whose family appears to have established the initial Jaitmālot foothold in this area. Ūdo himself apparently left Sīvāṇo sometime during the mid-fifteenth century, traveling first to Nāgaur and then on to the area of Meṛto where he finally settled. He met Rāṭhoṛs Varsiṅgh Jodhāvat (no. 145) and Dūdo Jodhāvat (no. 104) in 1461-62. They had received Meṛto from their father, Rāv Jodho Riṇmalot (ca. 1453-89), during his division of the lands of Mārvāṛ among his brothers and sons following the founding of Jodhpur in 1459. Ūdo took service under the brothers. It was he who introduced them to the site near two ancient tanks that later became Meṛto town. Varsiṅgh and Dūdo Jodhāvat founded Meṛto in March of 1462, and Varsiṅgh then assumed authority there and adopted the title of ***rāv***. He made Ūdo Kānhaṛdevot his ***pradhān***, and he placed full responsibility upon Ūdo for managing the affairs of the new kingdom (see ***Vigat***, 2:37-39 of the **translated text** for details).

Little in known about the Jaitmālots who lived at Meṛto and served under the Meṛtīyo Rāṭhoṛs after Ūdo Kānhaṛdevot, except that they were important military servants of the Meṛtīyos, and at least through the period of Meṛtīyo Rāv Jaimal Vīramdevot (no. 107), served as ***pradhān***s of Meṛto. A number of Jaitmālots followed Rāv Jaimal to Cītoṛ in 1562, when the Rāv was forced to vacate Meṛto in the wake of Mīrzā Sharafu'd-Dīn Ḥusayn's rebellion from Akbar, in which he was implicated. Many of these Jaitmālots were killed in 1568 during Akbar's bloody conquest of Cītoṛ.

(no. 68) **Bhādo Mokaḷot** (M7-1)
(no. 69) **Akhairāj Bhādāvat** (M8-1)
(no. 70) **Bhairavdās Bhādāvat** (M8-2)
(no. 71) **Sāndho Mokaḷot** (M7-4)
(no. 72) **Sīdho Mokaḷot** (M7-3)

Bhādo Mokaḷot served as ***pradhān*** of Meṛto under Meṛtīyo Rāv Vīramde Dūdāvat (no. 105). ***Vigat***, 2:48, records that Bhādo took part in a battle at Kusāṇo village[5] ca. 1530, during the latter period of Rāv Gāṅgo Vāghāvat's rule at Jodhpur (1515-32). The battle developed when Rāv Gāṅgo's son, Kuṃvar Mālde Gāṅgāvat, incited the dispossessed sons of Varsiṅghot Meṛtīyo Rāv Sīho Varsiṅghot (no. 147), Rāv Bhojo Sīhāvat (no. 148) and Rāv Gāṅgo Sīhāvat (no. 149), to attack Meṛto in an attempt to reassert their rights to this land. They raided the market square at Meṛto and then moved away. Meṛtīyo Rāv Vīramde sent a contingent of Rajpūts under Jodho Rāṭhoṛ Khaṅgār Jogāvat (no. 82) in pursuit. This ***sāth*** caught up with the raiders at the village of Kusāṇo. Bhādo Mokaḷot and his brother, Sāndho Mokaḷot (M7-4), both took part in the fighting here. Rāv Vīramde's Rajpūts emerged victorious, but both Bhādo Mokaḷot and Khaṅgār Jogāvat were badly wounded.

Bhādo's son, Akhairāj Bhādāvat (M8-1), also served under Rāv Vīramde as one of his trusted warriors. He held the position of ***pradhān*** under both Rāv Vīramde and his successor, Rāv Jaimal Vīramdevot (no. 107). It is not known when Akhairāj assumed this position, but it is possible that his father, Bhādo, died from wounds received at Kusāṇo and that Akhairāj became ***pradhān*** shortly thereafter. Bhāṭī, ***Sarvekṣaṇ***, 3:109, records that Akhairāj held the six villages of Akhuvas, Dholerāv, Lāmbīyo, Mugaddo Vaḍo, Netṛī, and Pālṛī in ***paṭo***.[6]

Local texts portray Akhairāj as an astute and brave Rajpūt who had dedicated his life to the preservation of Meṛtīyo rule at Meṛto. Following Rāv Mālde Gāṅgāvat's succession to the Jodhpur throne in 1532, Akhairāj's capacities were sorely tested, beginning immediately after the Rāv's accession. Rāv Mālde initiated an expedition against the Sīndhaḷ Rāṭhoṛs of Bhādrājuṇ in 1532-33, and he summoned Rāv Vīramde from Meṛto to take part in this campaign. Rāv Vīramde complied with this summons for military service and rode with his warriors to Jodhpur, leaving Meṛto largely unprotected. Rāv Mālde then used this opportunity to instigate yet another attack on Meṛto, this time urging Daulat Khān (no. 154) to attack from Nāgaur, and Paṃvār Pañcāiṇ (no. 24) to come from Cāṭsū in central Rājasthān and settle an old ***vair*** with the Meṛtīyos.

Rāv Vīramde suspected subterfuge on Rāv Mālde's part, but he dutifully remained in the Rāv's camp. Jaitmālot Akhairāj Bhādāvat returned to Meṛto, however, without Rāv Vīramde's knowledge. Once at Meṛto, he prepared the fort for an attack. Scouts he sent to the countryside soon informed him of the approach of Daulat Khān's force from Nāgaur. Akhairāj closed himself within the fort while Daulat Khān's men pillaged the town. When they came before the

---

[5] Kusāṇo village: located twenty-eight miles southwest of Meṛto.

[6] These villages are located as follows:

Akhuvas (i.e. Ākhuvās): four miles south of Reyāṃ and eighteen miles southeast of Meṛto.

Dholerāv (i.e. Dholelāv): location uncertain, but in the vicinity of Reyāṃ which lies fifteen miles southeast of Meṛto.

Lāmbīyo: eighteen miles south of Meṛto.

Mugaddo Vaḍo (i.e. Mugadṛo): fourteen miles south-southwest of Meṛto.

Netṛī: location uncertain, but in the vicinity of Reyāṃ.

Pālṛī: nineteen miles east-northeast of Meṛto.

fort, Akhairāj led a small force of some fifteen to twenty warriors outside in a desperate attempt to retain control, and he succeeded in routing the Khān's forces. Akhairāj's brother, Bhairavdās Bhādāvat (M8-2), was killed during the fighting here.

Akhairāj and his paternal uncle, Sīdho Mokaḷot (M7-3), were with Rāv Vīramde later on, ca. 1535, when Rāv Vīramde took possession of Ajmer. They were also among the Rapūts who attempted to prevent Rāv Vīramde from proceeding against Varsiṅghot Meṛtīyo Sahaiso Tejsīyot (no. 151), a former military servant of Rāv Vīramde's who had received Reyāṃ village[7] in ***paṭo*** from Rāv Mālde of Jodhpur. It is not known whether Akhairāj participated in the fighting at Reyāṃ. But his paternal uncle, Sīdho Mokaḷot, was badly wounded there and many Meṛtīyos killed, leaving Rāv Vīramde with no choice but to flee Meṛto and Ajmer in the face of Rāv Mālde's superior force.

Akhairāj accompanied Rāv Vīramde to eastern Rājasthān during his exile form Meṛto. Both Akhairāj and Muṃhato Khīṃvo (no. 157) served as Rāv Vīramde's ***pradhān***s at Riṇthambhor in representations there before the ***sūbedār***. Their initial efforts failed, and Akhairāj was among those who counseled Rāv Vīramde that he should turn elsewhere to find support to regain his lands. It was Muṃhato Khīṃvo who was able finally to arrange a meeting with the offer of one of Rāv Vīramde's daughters in marriage to the ***sūbedār***'s young son.

Akhairāj's role in the affairs of Meṛto during the years 1536-54 is unknown. The texts next mention him and his paternal cousin, Cāndrāj Jodhāvat (M8-3), in connection with the battle of Meṛto in 1554. In March of this year, Rāv Mālde of Jodhpur prepared an expeditionary force to attack Meṛto and came and encamped at the village of Gāṅgāṛo.[8] His warriors moved out from there to raid the countryside around Meṛto proper. As news of these raids reached Meṛtīyo Rāv Jaimal, he dispatched his ***pradhān***s, Jaitmālots Akhairāj Bhādāvat and Cāndrāj Jodhāvat, to Rāv Mālde's camp in an attempt to reach an accommodation. Akhairāj showed great uncertainty about the wisdom of proceeding to Rāv Mālde's camp. He told Rāv Jaimal that even if he went, Rāv Jaimal should prepare for battle.

Akhairāj and Cāndrāj met in Rāv Mālde's ***darbār*** with the Rāv and his two leading advisors, Rāṭhoṛ Prithīrāj Jaitāvat (no. 63), the commander of his armies, and Rāṭhoṛ Nago Bhārmalot (no. 38). Neither the Rāv nor his advisors showed any desire for conciliation, and the discussions quickly dissolved into verbal abuse and intimidation. Akhairāj and Cāndrāj left filled with anger (see ***Khyāt***, 3:116-118, of the **translated text** for details of this meeting).

The battle joined the following day, and Akhairāj himself sought out Rāṭhoṛ Prithīrāj Jaitāvat. Prithīrāj heaped abuse on Akhairāj when they met, calling him a "dwarf" and asking him why he had delayed so long in coming. Akhairāj then deceived Prithīrāj. He knew that Prithīrāj had received a boon that prevented his being struck from the front. Akhairāj managed to strike Prithīrāj from behind, and killed him. The ***Khyāt*** of Naiṇsī, 3:121, records that before

---

[7] Reyāṃ village: located fifteen miles southeast of Meṛto.

[8] Gāṅgāṛo village: located seven miles west-northwest of Meṛto.

Prithīrāj died, he left his curse upon Akhairāj. Akhairāj was later killed in this battle along with his paternal cousin, Cāndrāj Jodhāvat.

(no. 73) **Jodho Mokaḷot** (M7-2)
(no. 74) **Cāndrāj Jodhāvat** (M8-3)
(no. 75) **Narāiṇdās Cāndrājot** (M9-1)

Little information is availabe in the texts about these Jaitmālots. Jodho Mokaḷot was a ***pradhān*** of Meṛto under Rāv Vīramde Dūdāvat (no. 105). He served in this capacity along with his brother, Bhādo Mokaḷot (M7-1) (no. 68). Jodho's son, Cāndrāj Jodhāvat (M8-3), also served as ***pradhān*** of Meṛto under Rāv Vīramde's successor, Rāv Jaimal Vīramdevot (no. 107). The texts mention Cāndrāj only with reference to events that occurred prior to and during the battle for Meṛto in 1554. Cāndrāj took part in the abortive negotiations at Rāv Mālde's camp at the village of Gāṅgāṛo along with his paternal cousin, Akhairāj Bhādāvat (M8-1) (no. 69). He was killed during the fighting at Meṛto the following day. His son, Narāiṇdās Cāndrājot (M9-1), was also killed there along with his paternal cousin, Akhairāj Bhādāvat.

(no. 76) **Bhojo Gāṅgāvat, Rāvat** (M7-5)
(no. 77) **Sāṅgo Bhojāvat** (M8-4)
(no. 78) **Sagto Sāṅgāvat** (M9-2)

No information is available about these Jaitmālots other than the dates of their deaths. All were military servants of the Meṛtīyos. Rāvat Bhojo Gāṅgāvat was killed in the battle at Reyāṃ village ca. 1535, when Meṛtīyo Rāv Vīramde (no. 105) unwisely led an attack on this village and was met by a superior force of Rāv Malde's Rajpūts from the garrison at Raṛod[9]. Rāvat Bhojo's son, Sāṅgo Bhojāvat, and his grandson, Sagto Sāṅgāvat, both died in battle at Meṛto twenty years later in 1554, also fighting against Rāv Mālde of Jodhpur.

(no. 79) **Moṭo Jogāvat** (S9-2)

Moṭo Jogāvat was a Jaitmālot of the Sīvāṇo branch who came to serve under the Meṛtīyo Rāṭhoṛs. All that is known about him is that he was killed during the battle for Meṛto in 1554, fighting under Meṛtīyo Rāv Jaimal (no. 107) against Rāv Mālde's Rajpūts from Jodhpur.

* * *

Bāṅkīdās, p. 167, records an additional footnote about the Jaitmālots. He writes that by the early nineteenth century, many Jaitmālots had become Muslims and had settled in areas of Nāgaur.

---

[9] Raṛod village: located forty-nine miles west-northwest of Reyāṃ and forty-four miles northeast of Jodhpur.

Bāṅkīdās, p. 167; Bhāṭī, ***Sarvekṣaṇ***, 3:108-109; "Jodhpur Hukūmat rī Bahī," pp. 130-133; ***Khyāt***, 3:115-122; ***Murārdān***, no. 2, pp. 130-131; ***Vigat***, 1:59-60, 65, 2:37-39, 41, 48-50, 52-55, 58-59.

Figure 24. Jaitmālot Rāṭhoṛs of Sīvāṇo

(1-1) Rāv Salkho
|
(2-1) Jaitmāl Salkhāvat (**Jaitmālots**)
|
(S3-1) Rāvat Hāpo Jaitmālot
|
(S4-1) Rāvat Karaṇ Hāpāvat
|
(S5-1) Rāvat Tīhaṇo Karaṇot
|
(S6-1) Rāvat Vījo Tīhaṇot
|
- (S7-1) Rāṇo Devīdās Vījāvat
  - (S8-1) Rāṇo Jogo Devīdāsot
    - (S9-1) Rāṇo Karamsī Jogāvat
      - (S10-1) Rāṇo Ḍūṅgarsī Karamsīyot
    - (S9-2) **Moṭo Jogāvat**
- (S7-2) Karaṇ Vījāvat

Figure 25. Jaitmālot Rāṭhoṛs of Meṛto

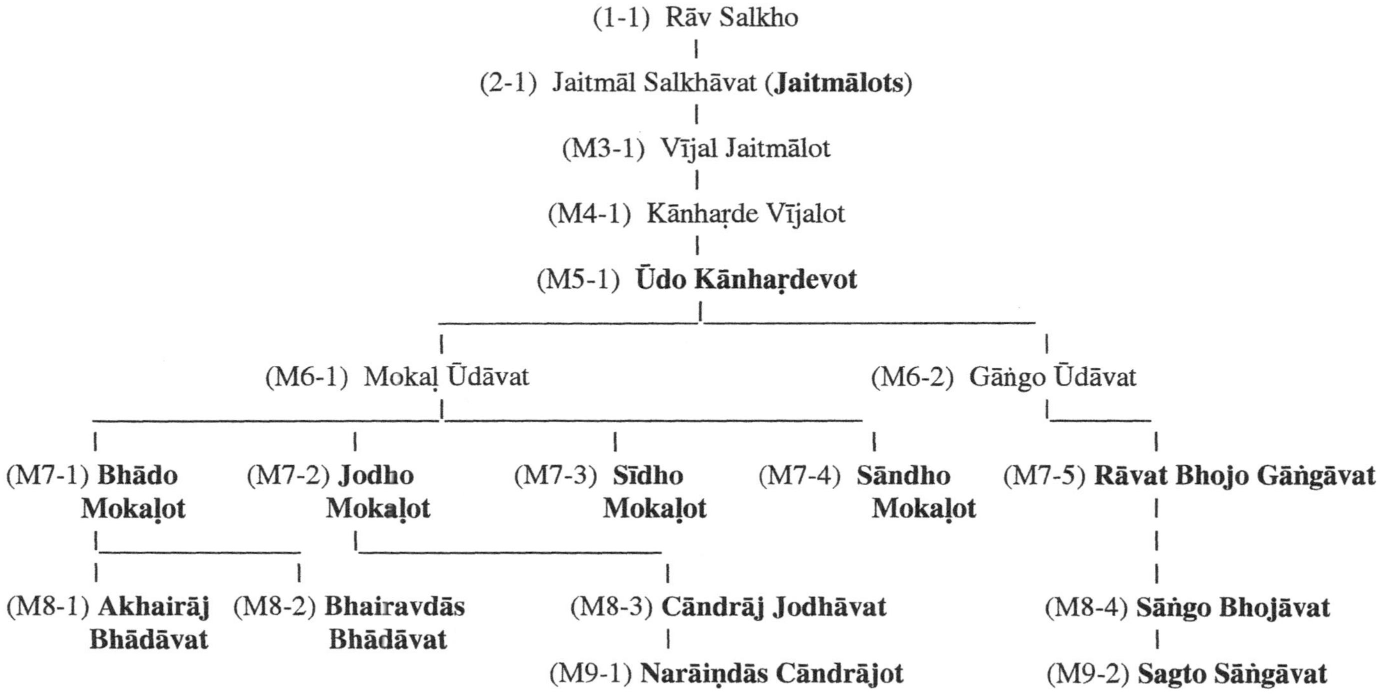

Jodho Rāṭhoṛs

(no. 80)	**Acḷo Sivrājot**	(7-6)
(no. 81)	**Bhākharsī Ḍūṅgarsīyot**	(9-3)
(no. 88)	**Īsardās Kalyāṇdāsot**	(12-7)
(no. 85)	**Jaitsī Vāghāvat**	(8-3)
(no. 82)	**Khaṅgār Jogāvat**	(7-4)
(no. 87)	**Kisandās Gāṅgāvat**	(9-2)
(no. 89)	**Mahesdās Daḷpatot, Rāv**	(12-2)
(no. 86)	**Sekho Sūjāvat**	(7-2)
(no. 83)	**Vāgho Sūjāvat, Kuṃvar**	(7-1)
(no. 84)	**Vīramde Vāghāvat, Rāv**	(8-2)

The Jodho Rāṭhoṛs

The Jodho Rāṭhoṛs descend from Rāv Jodho Riṇmalot (5-1), ruler of Maṇḍor and Jodhpur (ca. 1453-89). In the broadest sense, this branch (***sākh***) of Rāṭhoṛs includes all the descendants of Rāv Jodho. Many important cadet lines emerged from his descendants, however, and established separate identities of their own. "Jodhpur Hukūmat rī Bahī," a Middle Mārvāṛī text whose compilation was begun during the reign of Mahārājā Jasvantsiṅgh Gajsiṅghot of Jodhpur (1638-78) (13-1), lists ten major branches of Rāthoṛs, for example, that originated from Rāv Jodho's sons and grandsons.[1] These include:

From Rāv Jodho's sons:

Bhārmalots - from Bhārmal Jodhāvat
Bīkāvats - from Bīko Jodhāvat
Karamsots - from Karamsī Jodhāvat
Meṛtīyos - from Dūdo Jodhāvat
Rāypāḷots - from Rāypāḷ Jodhāvat
Sūjāvats - from Sūjo Jodhāvat
Vīdāvats - from Vīdo Jodhāvat

From Rāv Jodho's grandsons:

Khaṅgārots - from Khaṅgār Jogāvat, a son of Jogo Jodhāvat
Narāvats - from Naro Sūjāvat, a son of Sūjo Jodhāvat
Ūdāvats - from Ūdo Sūjāvat, a son of Sūjo Jodhāvat

---

[1] "Jodhpur Hukūmat rī Bahī," pp. 125, 161, 192, 198, 202, 204-205, 207.

With the exception of the Khaṅgārot, Narāvat, Rāypālot, and Sūjāvat ***sākh***s, all of the branches listed above are treated in individual sections of these Biographical Notes. These four above are not treated separately because their members do not figure in the texts under concern, and only the founders of the Khaṅgārot and Sūjāvat branches are named in the translated materials. For simplicity's sake, therefore, these founders are treated as Jodho Rāṭhoṛs, a designation which is consistent with the periods in which they lived, before groups emerged from among their descendants under separate identities.

Individuals included among the Jodhos are, then, members of the ruling house of Jodhpur and their immediate families to the third or fourth degree of removal. They do not include those individuals whose families, within one or two generations after Rāv Jodho, took on separate identities under designations other than Jodho, i.e., Meṛtīyo, Bhārmalot, Bīkāvat, etc.

(no. 80) **Acḷo Sivrājot** (7-6)

Acḷo Sivrājot was a son of Sivrāj Jodhāvat's (6-6) and grandson of Rāv Jodho Riṇmalot (5-1), ruler of Maṇḍor and Jodhpur (ca. 1453-89). Acḷo's father, Sivrāj, received the lands of Sīvāṇo[2] in southern Mārvāṛ from Rāv Jodho following the founding of Jodhpur in 1459. This area was then under the control of the Jaitmālot Rāṭhoṛs,[3] who considered Sīvāṇo their homeland (***utan***).

Rāv Jodho attempted to extend his control over Sīvāṇo on behalf of his son. He planned a deception against the Jaitmālots, summoning two sons of the ruler, Jaitmālot Rāvat Vījo Tīhaṇot, to Jodhpur on some pretext in order to weaken the Jaitmālot force at Sīvāṇo, and then dispatched a contingent of warriors under Sīndhaḷ Āpmal of Bhādrājuṇ village[4] against Sīvāṇo. Sīndhaḷ Āpmal attacked Sīvāṇo fort and was able to kill Rāvat Vījo and occupy the town and fort in Rāv Jodho's name. Rāv Jodho then established an outpost at the fort, and sent his son, Sivrāj, to occupy it in his own name.

While Sivrāj was enroute to Sīvāṇo with his family and retainers, however, Jaitmālot Devīdās Vījāvat, a son of the former ruler, was able to retake Sīvāṇo fort. He established his own authority there and declared himself ***rāṇo***. News of this turn of events quickly reached Jodhpur, and Rāv Jodho then relinquished all plans of conquest. He gave the village of Dunāṛo[5] to Sivrāj in place of Sīvāṇo, and Sivrāj established his line there. Within several generations, a minor branch of the Mārvāṛ Rāṭhoṛs emerged bearing the name "Sivrājot Jodhos."

---

[2] Sīvāṇo town: located fifty-eight miles southwest of Jodhpur.

[3] See ***supra***, "Jaitmālot Rāṭhoṛs."

[4] Bhādrājuṇ village: located forty-eight miles south-southwest of Jodhpur and twenty-seven miles east of Sīvāṇo.

[5] Dunāṛo village: located thirty-two miles southwest of Jodhpur along the Lūṇī River.

Sivrāj Jodhāvat's son, Arjaṇ (7-5), succeeded him as master (*dhaṇī*) of Dunāṛo village. Arjaṇ's brother, Acḷo Sivrājot (7-6), took service under the house of Jodhpur and is mentioned in the texts as a military servant of Rāv Mālde Gāṅgāvat's (1532-62) (9-1). He appears to have lived in Rāv Mālde's *vās* ("residence, dwelling"), for during much of his career, he was stationed at the fort of Jodhpur.

Acḷo was killed at the Jodhpur fort in January of 1544 while defending it against attack from the Muslim forces of Sher Shāh Sūr's. Sher Shāh's army overran central and eastern Mārvāṛ following Rāv Mālde's defeat at the battle of Samel[6] on January 5 of that year. Acḷo is credited with killing Mamārak Khān, a noble of Sher Shāh's, during the fighting at the fort. This feat is commemorated in a *sākh*:

Khādho Acaḷ Mamārakh Khān

(Acaḷ [Acḷo] ate up Mamārak Khān)

Acḷo's wife, the Bālīsī Cahuvāṇ, became a *satī* following his death. Acḷo's thumb was severed from his hand for her, and she held it in her own while she burned. This event was commemorated in a *dūho*:

Acaḷ jikā akhiyāt, aṅgūṭho āpe abaḷ,
Sāyar jāṃ lag sākh, sāñjotāṃ Sivrāj ut.

(The oceans shall long bear testimony to Sivrāj's son,
Of the fame Acḷo easily won by sending his wife his thumb.)

A cenotaph (*chatrī*) was built at the fort of Jodhpur in Acḷo's memory. Alongside it stood two other cenotaphs for Jeso Bhāṭī Sāṅkar Sūrāvat (no. 2) and Ūdāvat (Baiṭhvāsīyo) Rāṭhoṛ Tiloksī Varjāṅgot (no. 143), who died with Acḷo in the defense of the fort.

"Aitihāsik Bātāṃ," p. 45; Gehlot, *Mārvāṛ*, p. 201; *Khyāt*, 2:180; *Murārdān*, no. 2, pp. 417, 420; *Vigat*, 1:39, 58, 65, 2:57, 217-218.

(no. 81) **Bhākharsī Ḍūṅgarsīyot** (9-3)

Bhākharsī Ḍūṅgarsīyot was a grandson of Acḷo Sivrājot's (7-6) (no. 80). The only information available about him is that he was a military servant of Rāv Mālde Gāṅgāvat of Jodhpur (1532-62) (9-1). He was killed at Meṛto in 1562 fighting under Rāṭhoṛ Devīdās Jaitāvat (no. 65), Rāv Mālde's commander at the Mālgaḍh, against Meṛtīyo Rāv Jaimal Vīramdevot (no. 107) and the Mughal forces of Akbar under Mīrzā Sharafu'd-Dīn Ḥusayn.

---

[6] Samel village: located twenty-four miles southwest of Ajmer.

"Aitihāsik Bātāṃ," p. 56; ***Bāṅkīdās***, pp. 16-17; ***Murārdān***, no. 2, p. 418; ***Vigat***, 1:52, 2:65.

(no. 82) **Khaṅgār Jogāvat** (7-4)

Khaṅgār Jogāvat was a son of Jogo Jodhāvat's (6-4) and a grandson of Rāv Jodho Riṇmalot (5-1), ruler of Maṇḍor and Jodhpur (ca. 1453-89). He spent much of his life in the service of Meṛtīyo Rāv Vīramde Dūdāvat (no. 105) of Meṛto. He was one of Rāv Vīramde's leading warriors entrusted with the command of the Rāv's forces in battle. ***Murārdān***, no. 2, p. 430, records that he was a devout Rajpūt who held eleven vows regarding personal bravery and prowess in battle. He twice ventured forth to avenge the deaths of close relations.

Khaṅgār's association with Meṛto and the Meṛtīyos originated with his father Jogo Jodhāvat's settlement in the village of Khārīyo[7] in the early 1490s. This settlement occurred late in Jogo's life, for he was originally associated with the village of Koḍhṇo[8] in western Mārvāṛ. Jogo was born of Rāṇī Hulṇī Jamnādejī, a daughter of Hul Gahlot Vaṇvīr Bhojāvat.[9] With the founding of Jodhpur in 1459, Rāv Jodho divided the lands of Mārvāṛ among his brothers and sons, and he gave Jogo and his uterine brother, Bhārmal,[10] the village of Koḍhṇo.

Jogo and Bhārmal settled at Koḍhṇo in the early 1460s. Jogo remained much involved in the affairs of Jodhpur, however, and in 1474-75 Rāv Jodho placed him in control of the territory of Chāpar-Droṇpur to the north of Jodhpur, which he had just conquered from the Mohil Cahuvāns. This test of Jogo's ability to rule proved his undoing. The ***Khyāt*** of Naiṇsī, 3:164-165, records that after the conquest of Chāpar-Droṇpur:

> There was a great gathering [in] the realm of the Rāṭhoṛs. Rāv Jodhojī looked over this place [Chāpar-Droṇpur], [and he] gave [it] to Kuṃvar Jogo. Afterwards he proceeded to Maṇḍor.
>
> This Kuṃvar Jogo was a simple ***ṭhākur*** (***bhoḷo so ṭhakur***). The land did not prosper with Jogo, and the Mohils began to despoil [it].

---

7 Khārīyo village: located forty-four miles northeast of Jodhpur and twenty-five miles west of Meṛto.

8 Koḍhṇo village: located twenty-eight miles west-southwest of Jodhpur.

9 See ***supra***, **Marriage and Family Lists of the Rulers of Jodhpur**, Jodho Riṇmalot, Rāṇī no. 5, S - Jogo.

10 See ***supra***, "Bhārmalot Rāṭhoṛs."

When it became clear that Jogo was not able to assert his authority and protect the land, his wife, the Jhālī, sent word to her husband's father (***susro***), saying:

> There is no auspiciousness (***lakhaṇ***) in your son. And the land you/we have conquered is being lost [to the Mohils]. It would appear [that] you should devise a remedy (***ilāj kījyo***) (***ibid.***, 3:165).

Upon receipt of this news, Rāv Jodho recalled Jogo to Jodhpur, and he gave authority over Chāpar-Droṇpur to Jogo's half-brother, Vīdo Jodhāvat.[11]

Jogo's specific activities in the years following his failure in Chāpar-Droṇpur are unknown. He did emerge briefly as one of the candidates for the Jodhpur throne ca. 1489. But he was quickly passed over in favor of another of his half-brothers, Sātal Jodhāvat (6-2) (Rāv of Jodhpur, ca. 1489-92). ***Murārdān***, no. 2, pp. 422-423, records that all at court were initially prepared to grant succession to Jogo. They made ready to place the ***ṭīko*** on his forehead. But then Jogo stopped them and said, "I washed just now; allow my forehead to dry a little." The gathering then considered Jogo "unworthy of the ***rāj***," and they gave the kingdom to Jogo's half-brother, Sātal, in his stead.

Jogo left Jodhpur afterwards and settled in the village of Khārīyo. He also appears to have quit Koḍhṇo at this time, leaving it entirely to his uterine brother, Bhārmal, who established his line there. Jogo spent the remainder of his life at Khārīyo apart from the affairs of Jodhpur.

Jogo's son, Khaṅgār Jogāvat, grew up within the realm of the Meṛtīyo Rāṭhoṛs. He succeeded to the rule of Khārīyo upon Jogo's death. Meṛtīyo Rāv Vīramde Dūdāvat granted the village to him in ***paṭo*** along with twelve others. Although Khaṅgār rose to be a leading Rajpūt of Rāv Vīramde's at Meṛto, little in fact is known about his life. The chronicles record only his involvement in a few military operations in the area of Meṛto, and his venturing forth on two occasions to avenge the deaths of close relations.

Khaṅgār's activities are first mentioned when he took part in operations ca. 1530 to protect Meṛto from the depredations of members of a rival branch of the family. Kuṃvar Mālde Gāṅgāvat of Jodhpur had formed a conspiracy with the Varsiṅghot Meṛtīyos, Rāv Bhojo Sīhāvat (no. 147) and Rāv Gāṅgo Sīhāvat (no. 148), whose family had originally controlled Meṛto. Kuṃvar Mālde urged them to re-claim their rightful shares of these lands which the family of Meṛtīyo Rāv Vīramde had taken from them. Kuṃvar Mālde nursed his own ill-will against the Meṛtīyos for their failure to comply with his command to have an elephant of the Nāgaurī Khān's given to him following the battle of Sevakī[12] in November of 1529. This elephant had run amok during the battle and fled wounded toward Meṛto, and the Meṛtīyos had taken and cared for it.

---

[11] See ***infra***, "Vīdāvat Rāṭhoṛs."

[12] Sevakī village: located twenty-three miles northeast of Jodhpur.

Kuṃvar Mālde's conspiracy led to a Varsiṅghot Meṛtīyo raid on the market square at Meṛto. It was here that Rāṭhoṛ Khaṅgār Jogāvat became involved. He was one of the members of the pursuit party that went after the raiders. They came to battle near the village of Kusāṇo.[13] ***Vigat***, 2:48, records that Rāv Vīramde placed full responsibility for the command of his forces upon Rāṭhoṛ Khaṅgār Jogāvat, and the Meṛtīyo force under Khaṅgār emerged victorious. Both Varsiṅghots Rāv Bhojo and Rāv Gāṅgo were wounded during the fighting at Kusāṇo, as were Khaṅgār and a ***pradhān*** of Rāv Vīramde's, Jaitmālot Rāṭhoṛ Bhādo Mokaḷot (no. 68).

These Varsiṅghot Meṛtīyos remained disruptive figures in the area for several years thereafter. Khaṅgār met Rāv Bhojo Sīhāvat again in battle near the village of Kekīdṛo.[14] Here Khaṅgār and his Rajpūts killed Rāv Bhojo and a number of his men.

It is probable that Khaṅgār died shortly after this time, for the chronicles do not mention his name with relation to later events. The only other information about him concerns his taking revenge for the deaths of two close relations. The first occasion was ca. 1531 when he avenged the death of his paternal uncle, Karamsī Jodhāvat,[15] against the Muslims of Narnol. Karamsī was killed at Narnol in 1526, fighting in support of Bīkāner Rāṭhoṛ Rāv Lūṇkaraṇ Bīkāvat (1505-26; no. 44), who himself died there along with three of his sons. ***Murārdān***, no. 2, pp. 429-430, records that Khaṅgār took service under a Paṭhāṇ in order to gain entry to the closely guarded fort at Narnol. In an opportune moment, he then killed several of the Muslims at the fort and fled back to his village of Khārīyo unharmed.

Some time later, Khaṅgār is said to have avenged the death of a sister's son (***bhāṇej***) named Khīṃvo against the Muslims of Multan. He was again wounded during the venture and had to be carried back to Khārīyo.

A ***sākh*** of Rāṭhoṛs emerged from among Khaṅgār's descendants known as Khaṅgārot Jodhos. ***Vigat***, 2:145, lists his village by the name ***Khārīyo Khaṅgār ro*** ("Khaṅgār's Khārīyo").

Gehlot, ***Mārvāṛ***, p. 201; "Jodhpur Hukūmat rī Bahī," p. 205; ***Khyāt***, 3:31, 164-165; L. P. Tessitori, "A Progress Report on the Work done during the year 1917 in connection with the Bardic and Historical Survey of Rajputana," ***Journal of the Asiatic Society of Bengal***, N.S. 15 (1919), pp. 72-73; ***Murārdān***, no. 2, pp. 403, 422-423, 429-430, 586-587, 600-602; Ojhā, 5:1:117-118; ***Vigat***, 1:39, 2:48, 145.

---

[13] Kusāṇo village: located twenty-eight miles southwest of Meṛto.

[14] Kekīdṛo village: located fifteen miles south-southeast of Meṛto.

[15] See ***infra***, "Karamsot Rāṭhoṛs."

(no. 83) **Vāgho Sūjāvat, Kuṃvar** (7-1)

Vāgho Sūjāvat was one of the younger of Rāv Sūjo Jodhāvat's (6-3) eleven sons. He was born of Rāṇī Bhāṭiyāṇī Sāraṅgdejī (***pīhar*** name Likhmībāī),[16] daughter of Jaisaḷmer Bhāṭī Kalikaraṇ Keharot and sister of Bhāṭī Jeso Kalikaraṇot, whose descendants became the important military servants of Jodhpur known as the Jeso Bhāṭīs.

Vāgho was born in 1457 or 1458. The chronicles agree neither upon the year nor the day, giving dates ranging from December 4, December 7, and December 16, 1457 to April 2, April 5, and April 6, 1458.[17] Vāgho was Rāv Sūjo's chosen successor (***pāṭvī kuṃvar***) to the Jodhpur throne. He died during the Rāv's lifetime, however, and one of his sons, Gāṅgo Vāghāvat (8-1), succeeded to the throne following Rāv Sūjo's death in 1515.

The chronicles contain few details about Vāgho's life. He was born approximately two years before the founding of Jodhpur in 1459, and he grew up under the rule of his grandfather, Rāv Jodho Riṇmalot (ca. 1453-89) (5-1). When his own father, Sūjo Jodhāvat, ascended the throne ca. 1492 following the brief rule of his paternal uncle, Rāv Sātal Jodhāvat (ca. 1489-92) (6-2), he was already thirty-five years old.

The ***Khyāt*** of Naiṇsī, 3:105, associates Vāgho with the village of Bagṛī[18] and records that after Rāv Sūjo's accession, "Rāv Sūjo make incursions into and encompassed all of Mārvāṛ. [And he] stationed [his] son, Vāgho, at Bagṛī." No details are available about Vāgho's activities at Bagṛī, nor is Vāgho's relationship with the family of Rāṭhoṛ Akhairāj Riṇmalot known, for this family was closely associated with Bagṛī and considered it their homeland (***utan***).[19]

Vigat, 1:392, includes mention of one tank called Vāghelāv, which Vāgho had constructed just to the south of Sojhat. At the time of the compilation of the ***Vigat*** in the mid-seventeenth century, this tank held water for a short period following the rains, and two stepwells Vāgho built inside the tank gave sweet water for drinking. ***Vigat***, 1:41, also records that Vāgho gave one elephant in charity as an honorable and pious gesture. The text does not indicate to whom the elephant was given.

Vāgho died at Jodhpur on September 3, 1514 from an illness. He was fifty-seven years of age. His death occurred just one year prior to the death of his own father, Rāv Sūjo Jodhāvat, on October 2, 1515. ***Murārdān***, no. 1, pp. 225-226, no. 2, p. 104, records that before his death, Vāgho told his father that if

---

[16] See ***supra***, **Marriage and Family Lists of the Rulers of Jodhpur**, Sūjo Jodhāvat, Rāṇī no. 1, and "Jeso Bhāṭīs" for a discussion of Rāṇī Sāraṅgdejī's family and the uncertainties surrounding the identity of her father.

[17] See: "Aitihāsik Bātāṃ," p. 36; ***Bāṅkīdās***, p. 9; ***Murārdān***, no. 1, p. 226, no. 2, p. 104; Ojhā, 4:1:269, n. 5; ***Vigat***, 1:41. ***Jodhpur Rājya kī Khyāt***, p. 68, gives the widely varying date of Friday, April 15, 1468.

[18] Bagṛī village: located nine miles east-southeast of Sojhat in eastern Mārvāṛ.

[19] See ***supra***, "Akhairājot Rāṭhoṛs" and "Jaitāvat Rāṭhoṛs."

one of his own sons were chosen to succeed to the Jodhpur throne, he would rest in peace. Rāv Sūjo spoke with Vāgho's elder half-brother, Sekho Sūjāvat (7-2) (no. 86), seeking his support for such a choice. Sekho agreed to comply with his father's wishes, and Rāv Sūjo then promised Vāgho that he would designate Vāgho's son, Vīramde Vāghāvat (8-2) (no. 84), as his successor. This choice ushered in seventeen years of conflict within the ruling family of Jodhpur, for the Rāṭhoṛ ***ṭhākur*s** close to the throne rejected Vīramde as successor in favor of his half-brother, Gāṅgo Vāghāvat (8-1) (Rāv of Jodhpur, 1515-32). Vīramde was relegated to Sojhat, where he ruled as ***rāv*** until driven from Mārvāṛ in 1532.

Vāgho had five wives, seven sons, and eight daughters of whom there is record:

His sons listed under their mothers' names were:

1. Cahuvāṇ Udanbāī (***pīhar*** name)

    S - Gāṅgo (8-1) - born May 6, 1484; succeeded Rāv Sūjo to the Jodhpur throne in 1515 at the age of thirty-one years.

    S - Sīṅghaṇ - became an ancestral spirit (***pitar***).

2. Bhāṭiyāṇī

    S - Bhīṃv - had the fort of Dasorkoṭ constructed; sometime later, his half-brother, Gāṅgo Vāghāvat, poisoned and killed him.

    S - Khetsī

3. Devṛī Cahuvāṇ Raṅgāde of Sīrohī
    She received the title of ***rāṇī***.

    S - Vīramde (8-2) (no. 84).

4. Rāṇāvat Sīsodṇī

    S - Jaitsī (8-3) (no. 85).

5. Cahuvāṇ Pohpāṃbāī (***pīhar*** name)

    S - Pratāpsī

Vāgho's daughters are not listed by mother in the texts. They were married into the following families:

D - Dhanbāī - married to Sīsodīyo Rāṇo Sāṅgo Rāymalot of Cītoṛ (1509-28). Her son by Rāṇo Sāṅgo was Ratansī Sāṅgāvat (Rāṇo of Mevāṛ, ca. 1528-31).

D - (name unknown) - married to Sīsodīyo Rāṇo Sāṅgo Rāymalot of Cītoṛ.

D - (name unknown) - married to Sīsodīyo Rāṇo Sāṅgo Rāymalot of Cītoṛ.

Murārdān, no. 2, p. 105, notes that Rāṇo Sāṅgo was satisfied after he had married a third daughter of the Rāṭhoṛs of Jodhpur.

D - Khetūbāī - married to Hāḍo Cahuvāṇ Rāv Narāyaṇdās Bhāṇḍāvat of Būndī (d. ca. 1527). Her son by Rāv Narāyaṇdās was Sūrajmal Narāyaṇdāsot (Rāv of Būndī, ca. 1527-31). Sūrajmal and Sīsodīyo Rāṇo Ratansī Sāṅgāvat, his mother's sister's son (see ***supra***), killed each other during an outbreak of hostilities in Mevāṛ.[20]

D - Ratankuṃvar - married to Sekhāvat Kachvāho Sūjo Rāymalot of Amarsar in central Rājasthān. Her married name was Amadsarī. Her son by Sūjo Rāymalot was Rāysal Sūjāvat, who rose to a position of great influence under Emperor Akbar, and was known at the Mughal court as "Rāysal Darbārī."

D - Lāṛbāī - married to Soḷaṅkī Surtāṇ Harrājot of Toḍo.

D - Bāī - married to Kelhaṇ Bhāṭī Pañcāiṇ Jaitsīyot of Vairsaḷpur.

D - Gāṅgābāī - died at the age of three years.

"Aitihāsik Bātāṃ," p. 36; ***Bāṅkīdās***, p. 9; Gehlot, ***Mārvāṛ***, pp. 202-203; ***Jodhpur Rājya kī Khyāt***, pp. 67-70; ***Khyāt***, 1:19, 102-109, 319-320, 2:119, 3:86, 103-105, 215; ***Murārdān***, no. 1, pp. 225-226, 238-241, no. 2, pp. 103-106, 670; Ojhā, 4:1:269; ***Vigat***, 1:41, 162, 392.

(no. 84) **Vīramde Vāghāvat, Rāv** (8-2)

Vīramde Vāghāvat was a son of Vāgho Sūjāvat's (7-1) (no. 83) by the Devṛī Cahuvāṇ Raṅgāde of Sīrohī, and grandson of Rāv Sūjo Jodhāvat (6-3), ruler of Jodhpur (ca. 1492-1515). Vīramde became designated successor (***pāṭvī kuṃvar***) to the Jodhpur throne upon the death of his father, Vāgho, in 1514. According to ***Murārdān***, no. 1, pp. 225-226, no. 2, p. 104, Vāgho told his father when he was dying that if one of his sons were chosen successor, he would rest in peace. Rāv Sūjo conferred with an elder son and half-brother of Vāgho's, Sekho Sūjāvat (7-2) (no. 86), to gain his support for this choice, and then promised Vāgho that he would designate his son, Vīramde, as successor.

Vīramde did succeed briefly to the Jodhpur throne. But he and his mother had alienated the ***ṭhākur***s of Mārvāṛ who were close to the throne, and these ***ṭhākur***s unseated Vīramde and placed his half-brother, Gāṅgo Vāghāvat (8-1) (Rāv of Jodhpur, 1515-32), on the throne in his stead. Vīramde was then

---

[20] See ***supra***, "Sīsodīyo Gahlots," Rāṇo Udaisiṅgh Sāṅgāvat (no. 17), for further details.

relegated to the lands of Sojhat. These were his ***bhāīvaṇṭ*** ("brother's share") of Mārvāṛ, which he received along with the title of ***rāv***. Once at Sojhat, Vīramde became "deranged" and spent the next seventeen years fighting his half-brother, Rāv Gāṅgo, over land and authority in Mārvāṛ. He was finally driven from Sojhat and then Mārvāṛ itself. He died some years after his banishment in Mevāṛ, where he had sought protection from the Sīsodīyo Rāṇo of Cītoṛ.

Local chronicles are unanimous in their portrayal of Vīramde Vāghavat as a ***kuṃvar*** of the royal family of Jodhpur who was unfit to rule. ***Murārdān***, no. 2, p. 106, states, for example:

> Vīramde used to make senseless statements, because of which the Rajpūts summoned Vāgho's son, Gāṅgo, and gave him the throne.

The ***Khyāt*** of Naiṇsī, 3:80-86, relates in some detail the sequence of events that occurred prior to and following Vīramde's succession, which led to his dethronement and relegation to Sojhat.

According to the ***Khyāt***, four Mārū ***ṭhākur***s came to Jodhpur on some occasion during Rāv Sūjo's later years of rule. While they were in the city, the rains began, preventing them from returning to their camps. The ***ṭhākur***s were in need of provisions and sent word to Vīramde Vāghāvat's mother, the Devṛī Raṅgāde, asking her to provide for them. They received only a curt reply from the Devṛī that they should cover themselves with their own woolen garments and proceed to their camps. The Devṛī stated, "Who will feed you here?" The ***ṭhākur***s then sent word to Gāṅgo Vāghāvat's mother, the Cahuvāṇ Udanbāī, who responded deferentially, saying:

> ***Ṭhākur***s! Please be seated in the hall of assembly (***darīkhāno***). We will perform many services [for you] (***ibid.***, 3:80).

The ***ṭhākur***s came away very satisfied with their treatment, and when they left Jodhpur, they sent a message to the Cahuvāṇ Udanbāī with the words:

> "Your son, Gāṅgo, has the good fortune of [receiving] Jodhpur." . . . Then the Rāṇī had blessings conveyed [to the ***ṭhākur***s]. And [she] said, "***Jī***, we acquired Jodhpur only because of your influence. He alone receives to whom you give" (***ibid.***).

Later, when Vīramde succeeded to the throne, these ***ṭhākur***s, who included Rāṭhoṛ Pañcāiṇ Akhairājot [21] and Rāṭhoṛ Bhairavdās Cāmpāvat,[22] led a faction at court that deposed Vīramde. They then had Gāṅgo Vāghāvat summoned from Īḍar, where he had gone to live, and they placed Gāṅgo on the throne. Gāṅgo's accession took place on November 8, 1515. The ***Khyāt*** of

---

[21] See ***supra***, "Jaitāvat Rāṭhoṛs."

[22] See ***supra***, "Cāmpāvat Rāṭhoṛs."

Naiṇsī, 3:81, records that when these ***ṭhākur***s took Vīramde from the fort of Jodhpur, they met Muṃhato Rāymal Khetāvat (no. 159), a strong supporter of Vīramde's and his family. The Muṃhato is reported to have said:

> "Hey! Why are [you] taking this chosen successor (***pāṭvī kuṃvar***) from the fort?" Rāymal then brought Vīramde back [to the fort]. Then all [the Rajpūts with Rāymal] gathered right there and said [to Rāv Gāṅgo], "***Jī***, [you] should give Sojhat to Vīramde." [And Rāv Gāṅgo] made Vīramde ***rāv*** of Sojhat.

Vīramde did acquire Sojhat as his share of the lands of Mārvāṛ due to Muṃhato Rāymal's efforts. The ***Khyāt*** of Naiṇsī, 3:81, notes, however, that once at Sojhat:

> Vīramde became deranged (***gehlo***). [He] babbled [to himself], "Hey! Is this Jodhpur?" Then Muṃhato Rāymal [became the] protector [of] Sojhat. Vīramde remained sitting [in his] bed.

This situation, defined by Rāv Vīramde's apparent bed-ridden madness following his dethronement and his unwillingness to assume a position subordinate to Rāv Gāṅgo of Jodhpur, led to the subsequent hostilities between Sojhat and Jodhpur.

Muṃhato Rāymal served as Rāv Vīramde's ***pradhān*** and the commander of his warriors in battle during these years. He proved himself to be a capable leader and enabled Sojhat to stand its ground before Jodhpur. Much of the history of this struggle from the Jodhpur perspective relates to Rāv Gāṅgo's attempts to control alliances among the Rajpūts involved in the fighting. Among these Rajpūts were Jaito Pañcāiṇot (no. 61) and Kūmpo Mahirājot (no. 95). Jaito Pañcāiṇot, son of Pañcāiṇ Akhairājot, was a member of the original faction of ***ṭhākur***s who had seated Rāv Gāṅgo on the throne. Jaito quickly emerged as Rāv Gāṅgo's leading warrior, but Jaito maintained ties with his ancestral village of Bagṛī[23] which had come within Rāv Vīramde's share of lands. The ***Khyāt*** of Naiṇsī, 3:81-82, records the following observation:

> So [Rāv] Vīramde does not [wish to] drive Jaito away. For what reason? [Those with Rāv Gāṅgo] said, "***Jī***, Jaito [is] a ***sirdār*** in the [Jodhpur] army, [but] he enjoys [the rule of] Bagṛī. [Therefore], he desires the well-being [lit. "the good"] of Sojhat." Then Rāv Gāṅgo said, "Jaitojī! Bring your carts to Bīlāṛo village[24]. Leave Bagṛī."

The people of Jaito's ***vasī*** eventually left Bagṛī in compliance with Rāv Gāṅgo's orders. But their departure did not occur until Muṃhato Rāymal had killed

---

[23] Bagṛī village: located nine miles east-southeast of Sojhat.

[24] Bīlāṛo village: located twenty-one miles north-northwest of Bagṛī in Jodhpur territory.

Jaito's ***dhāy-bhāī*** ("milk-brother"), Reṛo, at Sojhat. When the news of his death reached Bagṛī, the people of the ***vasī*** became afraid and fled to the lands of Jodhpur.

Rāv Gāṅgo's next move was to bring one of Rāv Vīramde's leading warriors, Kūmpo Mahirājot, to Jodhpur. He managed this change of allegiance through the offices of Jaito Pañcāiṇot. Jaito offered Kūmpo a ***paṭo*** worth a ***lakh***, to be selected from among the finest villages of Jodhpur, and he had Rāv Gāṅgo send a writing to Kūmpo arguing that he should leave Sojhat because the fighting between Sojhat and Jodhpur was of no import. Rāv Vīramde had no sons and after his death, the lands of Sojhat would inevitably pass to Jodhpur.

Kūmpo saw the wisdom of this reasoning and agreed to leave if Rāv Gāṅgo would not attack the villages of Sojhat for one year.[25] Rāv Gāṅgo readily accepted this condition and brought Kūmpo to Jodhpur ca. 1529. With Kūmpo came all the Riṇmalots[26] who were at Sojhat, and their departure further weakened Rāv Vīramde's position.

The ***Khyāt*** of Naiṇsī, 3:84, records that Kūmpo became Rāv Gāṅgo's army commander and established a stable of horses on the borders of Sojhat:

> Then [Kūmpo Mahirājot] brought [horses] to Dhauḷharo [village[27] near Sojhat] and established a stable. [He] stationed four thousand of Rāv Gāṅgo's household warriors (***cīndhaṛ***)[28] at [this] outpost . . . [and he] stationed [four of the Rāv's] nobles (***umrāv***) with [these men] and the horses.[29]

Kūmpo used this large mobile force of Rajpūts to raid into Sojhat and harass Muṃhato Rāymal's forces. Even then, Muṃhato Rāymal was able to inflict a severe defeat upon Rāv Gāṅgo's warriors at Dhauḷharo, and when he returned to Sohat after the battle, he went before Rāv Vīramde and said:

---

[25] This timeframe seems a formality only, for in fact Kūmpo himself appears to have led raids into Sojhat within a short time after his coming to Jodhpur.

[26] Riṇmalots: descendants of Rāv Riṇmal Cūṇḍāvat, ruler of Maṇḍor, ca. 1428-38.

[27] Dhauḷharo village: located eighteen miles west-northwest of Sojhat.

[28] ***Cīndhaṛ***: this term also refers to men who were hired soldiers working for short periods of time and who sometimes held small land grants. See: Lāḷas, ***RSK***, 2:1:920-921.

[29] The establishment of this stable was an important military innovation in Mārvāṛ at this time. For a discussion of this development and its significance, see: N. P. Ziegler, "Evolution of the Rathor State of Marvar: Horses, Structural Change and Warfare," in ***The Idea of Rajasthan: Explorations in Regional Identity***, edited by Karine Schomer et al. (Columbia, MO.: South Asia Publications by arrangement with Manohar Publishers & Distributors; New Delhi: American Institute of Indian Studies, 1994), Vol 2, pp. 193-201.

"I have brought your father's and grandfather's horses (*bāp-dādairā ghoṛā*)." The *baniyo* [Muṃhato Rāymal] had caused so much destruction that for two years, Rāv Gāṅgo could not recover (*ibid*, 3:85).[30]

Rāv Vīramde did not help his own cause during this time, however. He alienated a powerful Rāṭhoṛ who sought to ally himself with Sojhat, and he became involved with his paternal uncle, Sekho Sūjāvat (7-2) (no. 86), through the ministrations of his wife, the Sīsodṇī. This latter involvement estranged Muṃhato Rāymal and ultimately brought Rāv Vīramde's downfall.

The Rāṭhoṛ who sought to ally himself with Sojhat was Ūhaṛ Hardās Mokaḷot (no. 144). Hardās had held the lands of Koḍhṇo village[31] in *paṭo* from Rāv Gāṅgo, but he acquired the enmity of the Rāv's son, Kuṃvar Mālde Gāṅgāvat (Rāv of Jodhpur, 1532-62) (9-1), because of his failure to perform expected service. Kuṃvar Mālde had Hardās's *paṭo* revoked, and Hardās then came to Sojhat. He offered his service to Rāv Vīramde on the sole condition that the Rāv fight against Rāv Gāṅgo and the house of Jodhpur. Rāv Vīramde readily accepted this condition and settled Hardās at Sojhat.

The *Khyāt* of Naiṇsī, 3:88, notes, however, that Rāv Vīramde soon alienated Ūhaṛ Hardās because of insensitive remarks he (Vīramde) made about him. Hardās rode into battle one day on a horse from Rāv Vīramde's stable. Both Hardās and the horse were wounded during the fighting, but when Hardās returned to Sojhat, Rāv Vīramde could only find fault with him for allowing his horse to be injured. Hardās rebuked Rāv Vīramde, calling him an unworthy Rajpūt (*kurajpūt*), and he left Sojhat in anger for Nāgaur, where he entered into the household (*vās*) of Sarkhel Khān (no. 155) for a short period before moving on to Pīmpāṛ.[32] At Pīmpāṛ he allied himself with Rāv Vīramde's paternal uncle, Sekho Sūjāvat.

Sekho Sūjāvat, whom the *Khyāt* of Naiṇsī, 3:86, describes as Rāv Vīramde's *got-bhāī* (lit. "*gotra*-brother"), came to Sojhat in this same period to meet with Rāv Vīramde's wife, the Sīsodṇī. He told her that if she would have him included on Rāv Vīramde's side in the struggle with Jodhpur, Rāv Vīramde would gain the upper hand. Sekho was well aware that Rāv Vīramde had no sons, and that any victory over Jodhpur would ultimately be to his favor. The Sīsodṇī turned to Muṃhato Rāymal Khetāvat for advice. Muṃhato Rāymal told her not to form an alliance with Sekho. But the Sīsodṇī did not listen and proceeded to include Sekho in the affairs of Sojhat. This alliance opened the

---

[30] ***Jodhpur Rājya kī Khyāt***, p. 74, records that Muṃhato Rāymal attacked Dhauḷharo in February of 1532, considerably later than the time set forth in Naiṇsī's ***Khyāt***, and that he did not capture any horses. This text speaks of Muṃhato Rāymal's disappointing performance at Dhauḷharo as a prelude to his defeat before Sojhat shortly thereafter.

[31] Koḍhṇo village: located twenty-eight miles west-southwest of Jodhpur.

[32] Pīmpāṛ village: located thirty-three miles east-northeast of Jodhpur.

possibility that the lands of Sojhat would pass from Vāgho Sūjāvat's family to another of Rāv Sūjo Jodhāvat's sons. Muṃhato Rāymal reasoned:

> "Now [it is] not my ***dharma*** [to remain here as Rāv Vīramde's ***pradhān***]."
>
> Then Rāymal had word sent to Rāv Gāṅgo, . . "I will die in battle. [And I] will give the land [of Sojhat] to you" (***ibid.***).

The battle for Sojhat between Rāv Gāṅgo and Muṃhato Rāymal was delayed for some time. The Rāv's attention was drawn first to the rebuilding of his own forces, and then to a confrontation with his father's brother (***kāko***), Sekho Sūjāvat, which culminated in the battle of Sevakī[33] on November 2, 1529. Both Sekho Sūjāvat and Hardās Mokaḷot were killed at Sevakī.

This conflict ended Sekho Sūjāvat's involvement in the affairs of Sojhat, but it did not change Muṃhato Rāymal's position nor mitigate the hostilities that lay between Sojhat and Jodhpur. In the early months of 1532, Rāv Gāṅgo and his son, Kuṃvar Mālde, brought the army of Jodhpur before Sojhat to challenge Muṃhato Rāymal.[34] ***Khyāt*** (***ibid.***) records that before riding out to fight against the forces of Jodhpur, Muṃhato Rāymal came before Rāv Vīramde and circumambulated his bed with his right side facing the Rāv in reverential salutation. He grasped the Rāv's feet in the manner of a son. He then left to gather his ***sāth*** to meet Rāv Gāṅgo and Kuṃvar Mālde. Rāymal was killed on this day by Kūmpo Mahirājot's hand.[35]

---

[33] Sevakī village: located twenty-three miles northeast of Jodhpur.

[34] Local chronicles give the following dates for the conquest of Sojhat: "Aitihāsik Bātāṃ," p. 38, states that Sojhat was taken on March 16, 1532, while ***Murārdān***, no. 2, pp. 110-111, gives the date of March 2, 1532 for the battle at Sojhat, and April 9, 1532 for the occupation of the fort. ***Bāṅkīdās***, p. 9, provides the alternate date of March 17, 1532 for the battle. ***Jodhpur Rājya kī Khyāt***, p. 74, also gives the date of Sunday, March 17, 1532 for the battle with Muṃhato Rāymal.

For an alternative opinion about the dating of this event, see Ojhā, 4:1:277, n. 1. Ojhā acknowledges the dates given in the ***khyāts***, but takes issue with them, stating that they "cannot be considered trustworthy." He feels that the conquest of Sojhat should be placed before the battle of Sevakī, which took place in November of 1529. He sites as evidence the fact that Sīsodīyo Rāṇo Sāṅgo Rāymalot (1509-28) is mentioned in several ***khyāts*** as having come to Rāv Vīramde's aid, but then returned to Mevāṛ when he saw the strength of Rāv Gāṅgo's army before Sojhat. ***Murārdān***, no. 2, p. 111, has such a reference to Rāṇo Sāṅgo. But it records that Rāṇo Sāṅgo attacked Rāv Gāṅgo after he had captured Sojhat. Adding to the confusion, mention of this event occurs following discussion of the conquest of Sojhat itself on March 2, 1532, as noted above. Rāṇo Sāṅgo was killed in 1528.

[35] ***Bāṅkīdās***, p. 10, records that during the battle for Sojhat, Muṃhato Rāymal became a ***kabandh***, a body that keeps fighting after its head has been severed in battle. It is said that when the ***kabandh***'s head falls off, a new eye opens in the area of its breast, by which it "sees" (see Lāḷas, ***RSK***, 1:413). ***Bāṅkīdās*** notes that during the battle at

Rāv Gāṅgo now forced Vīramde from Sojhat, relegating him to the village of Khairvo[36]. But ***Murārdān***, no. 1. p. 641, notes that Vīramde became even more deranged at Khairvo and continued his depredations into the lands of Jodhpur. Rāv Gāṅgo then drove him from Mārvāṛ altogether. Vīramde went to Mevāṛ, where Sīsodīyo Rāṇo Vikramaditya Sāṅgāvat (ca. 1531-36) granted him the village of Indravaṛo in Goḍhvāṛ[37] for his maintenance. Even here Rāv Vīramde continued to organize expeditions against Rāv Gāṅgo's lands. On one occasion his Rajpūts attacked Cāmpāvat Rāṭhoṛ Jeso Bhairavdāsot's (no. 48) village of Riṇsīgāṃv.[38] His forces suffered a severe defeat here. Shortly thereafter, Rāv Vīramde met Rāv Gāṅgo's warriors at Sāraṇ village,[39] and he was again defeated with great loss. Vīramde then returned to Goḍhvāṛ, where he remained for the rest of his life. He died at Indravaṛo some years later. A cenotaph was built in his memory above a tank at the village.

While at Sojhat, Rāv Vīramde granted the village of Pāñcvo[40] to the Sīvaṛ Brāhmaṇ Purohit Narsiṅgh Cothot in ***sāmsaṇ***.

> "Aitihāsik Bātāṃ," pp. 37, 58; ***Bāṅkīdās***, pp. 9-10; ***Jodhpur Rājya kī Khyāt***, p. 74; ***Khyāt***, 3:80-86; ***Murārdān***, no. 1, pp. 226, 238-239, 639-641, no. 2, pp. 104, 106, 109-110, 302; Ojhā, 4:1:271, 274-277; ***Vigat***, 1:41-42, 389, 480.

Sojhat, a ***lākhā lovṛī*** ("costly woolen") was thrown over the ***kabandh*** when it fell down from its horse and lay on the ground.

An informant from Jodhpur, Śrī Kailāś Dānjī Ujjval, describes the ***lovṛī*** as a woolen mantle or shawl (***oḍhṇī***) of light chocolate or maroon color (white and black colors are permissable among certain groups) that is worn by a widow and remarks that covering the ***kabandh*** with a fine, costly mantle was a respectable way for friends to silence it. Śrī Ujjval also notes that during a battle, opponents traditionally sprinkled an "impious liquid," usually indigo water (***nīl ro pāṇī***), on the ***kabandh***'s body in order to still it and make it fall down.

See ***infra***, Muṃhato Rāymal Khetāvat (no. 159), for further discussion about Muṃhato Rāymal's career and death in battle before Sojhat and about ***kabandh***.

[36] Khairvo village: located fifty miles south-southeast of Jodhpur and twenty-two miles southwest of Sojhat.

[37] Indravaṛo village: located in Goḍhvāṛ one mile north of Ahilāṇī village and twelve miles south of Khairvo, on the north side of the Sumerī River.

[38] Riṇsīgāṃv village: located forty-three miles east of Jodhpur.

[39] Sāraṇ village: located eighteen miles southeast of Sojhat.

[40] Pāñcvo village: located sixteen miles northwest of Sojhat.

(no. 85) **Jaitsī Vāghāvat** (8-3)

Jaitsī Vāghāvat was a grandson of Rāv Sūjo Jodhāvat (6-3), ruler of Jodhpur (ca. 1492-1515), and a son of Vāgho Sūjāvat (7-1) (no. 83) by his wife, the Rāṇāvat Sīsodṇī. Little information is available about Jaitsī's life. He was a military servant of Rāv Mālde Gāṅgāvat (9-1) of Jodhpur (1532-62). ***Murārdān***, no. 1, p. 641, records that his "seat" was at the village of Bramhamī[41]. ***Vigat***, 1:455, observes that the village of Sīdhā Vāsṇī, located just three miles to the southeast of Braṃhamī, was settled during Jaitsī's time. It is likely that this land was incorporated within his ***paṭo***. ***Vigat***, 1:44, also lists Kosīthaḷ and Bīsalpur in Goḍhvāṛ[42] as areas Jaitsī held following Rāv Mālde's seizure of this land from Mevāṛ in the years immediately following his accession to the throne in 1532.

Jaitsī is credited with the murder of Varsiṅghot Meṛtīyo Rāv Gāṅgo Sīhāvat (no. 149) at Gāṅgo's village of Āsop[43] in 1543-44. Local sources do not specify the reason for this murder. They state only that Jaitsī surprised Rāv Gāṅgo one day while the Rāv was sitting on the porch of his home, and killed him.

One year later in 1544, Jaitsī was among the ***ṭhākur***s of Mārvāṛ who rode with Rāv Mālde to confront Meṛtīyo Rāv Vīramde Dūdāvat (no. 107) and Sher Shāh Sūr at the battle of Samel.[44] Jaitsī took part in the initial fighting at Samel on January 5. But "Aitihāsik Bātāṃ," p. 44, lists him as one of the great ***ṭhākur***s who withdrew from Samel and joined Rāv Mālde in exile in the hills of Sīvāṇo during the Muslim occupation of eastern Mārvāṛ and Jodhpur.

No further information is available about Jaitsī. It is possible that he was wounded at Samel and later died from these injuries. He had no sons. ***Murārdān***, no. 1, p. 641, records that after his death, Rāv Mālde presented all the ***hujdār***s, Brāhmaṇs, and Rajpūts of Jaitsī's ***vasī*** to his own son, Kuṃvar Udaisiṅgh Māldevot (Rājā of Jodhpur, 1583-95) (10-2), who kept them stationed at Braṃhamī village.

> "Aitihāsik Bātāṃ," pp. 44-45; ***Bāṅkīdās***, p. 9; ***Murārdān***, no. 1, pp. 239, 641-642, no. 2, pp. 104, 586-597; ***Vigat***, 1:44, 57, 220, 455.

(no. 86) **Sekho Sūjāvat** (7-2)

Sekho Sūjāvat was an elder son of Rāv Sūjo Jodhāvat (6-3), ruler of Jodhpur (ca. 1492-1515). His mother was a daughter of Sācoro Cahuvāṇ

---

[41] Braṃhamī village: located fifteen miles southeast of Jodhpur on the Lūṇī River.

[42] Bīsalpur village: located twenty-five miles southwest of Nāḍūl. The location of Kosīthaḷ is uncertain.

[43] Āsop village: located fifty miles northeast of Jodhpur.

[44] Samel village: located twenty-four miles southwest of Ajmer.

Pithamrāv Tejsīyot,[45] whose father, Tejsī Varjāṅgot, was Rāv of Sācor in southern Mārvāṛ.

Rāv Sūjo did not choose Sekho to succeed him to the Jodhpur throne. The Rāv conferred this honor first upon a younger son, Vāgho Sūjāvat (7-1) (no. 83) by his wife, Rāṇī Bhāṭiyāṇī Sāraṅgdejī.[46] Vāgho fell ill and died in 1514, however, at which time Rāv Sūjo promised Vāgho that his son, Vīramde Vāghāvat (8-2) (no. 84), would succeed to the throne. ***Murārdān***, no. 1, p. 226, records that before making this promise, Rāv Sūjo sought out his son, Sekho, to obtain his support for this choice. Sekho assented to Vīramde's selection.

Sekho appears to have lived apart from Jodhpur during the latter part of Rāv Sūjo reign. ***Murārdān***, no. 2, p. 302, notes that he had received the lands of Pīmpāṛ[47] from his father, and that he established himself there.

Rāv Sūjo died at Jodhpur on October 2, 1515 and was succeeded first by his grandson, Vīramde Vāghāvat, and then by Vīramde's half-brother, Gāṅgo Vāghāvat (8-1), whom a powerful faction of Rāṭhoṛ ***ṭhākurs*** seated on the throne. Local chronicles relate that Sekho did not hold loyalties or obligations toward Gāṅgo Vāghāvat, and that enmity quickly emerged between father's brother (***kāko***) and brother's son (***bhatījo***) as Sekho sought wider control of lands in central Mārvāṛ and finally, the throne of Jodhpur itself.

Murārdān, no. 2, p. 106, and ***Bāṅkīdās***, p. 11, both include a story which speaks of the emergence of enmity between Sekho and Rāv Gāṅgo. Sekho and Rāv Gāṅgojī are said to have been bathing together one day at a spring with their Rajpūts. The Rajpūts began splashing water on each other in fun, but their play soon turned serious as the sides opposed one another in mock battle, each vowing not to retreat. Sekho is said to have set his mind against Rāv Gāṅgo at this time, while Rāv Gāṅgo sought some means of conciliation. Rāv Gāṅgo later proposed a division of lands in Mārvāṛ, offering Sekho all the land with ***karaṛ*** grass, while he took the land with ***bhuraṭ*** grass.[48] Sekho is said to have considered this proposal, but his ***pradhān***, Ūhaṛ Hardās Mokaḷot (no. 144), would not hear of any accommodation with the house of Jodhpur and turned Sekho against the offer. Ūhaṛ Hardās had settled in Sekho's ***vās*** (residence, dwelling") and taken service under him solely on the condition that he fight against Jodhpur. He spent all of his time with Sekho plotting battle strategy against Rāv Gāṅgo.

Sekho also involved himself in the affairs of Sojhat during this time, where he sought an alliance with his brother's son, Rāv Vīramde Vāghāvaṭ (8-2)

---

[45] See ***supra***, **Marriage and Family Lists of the Rulers of Jodhpur**, Sūjo Jodhāvat, Rāṇī no. 2, S - Sekho.

[46] See ***supra***, **Marriage and Family Lists of the Rulers of Jodhpur**, Sūjo Jodhāvat, Rāṇī no. 1, S - Vāgho.

[47] Pīmpāṛ village: located thirty-three miles east-northeast of Jodhpur.

[48] ***Karaṛ*** is a tall, thin-leafed grass much used for fodder. It is more common in eastern Mārvāṛ. ***Bhuraṭ*** is a burr-grass more common in the sandier tracts of central Mārvāṛ.

(no. 84). Rāv Vīramde was himself engaged in on-going hostilities with Rāv Gāṅgo over contol of land in Mārvāṛ, and he accepted Sekho as an ally at the behest of his wife, the Sīsodṇī.

Murārdān, no. 2, pp. 302-303, records that following Sekho's alliance with Sojhat, Rāv Gāṅgo's son, Kuṃvar Mālde Gāṅgāvat (9-1), and Kuṃvar Mālde's mother's brother (***māmo***), Devṛo Cahuvāṇ Rāv Akhairāj Jagmālot of Sīrohī, stopped to visit Sekho one day at Pīmpāṛ while hunting together on the plains of central Mārvāṛ. Sekho showed them great hospitality, but Akhairāj quickly noted the many horses, men, and provisions at Sekho's, and he grew suspicious. He said to his sister's son (***bhāṇej***):

> "Sekho is not under your control." Mālde replied, "He is not? How so?" Then Akhairāj said, "If he is, then seize one of his villages and see. If he is under your command, he will not raise his head."

Kuṃvar Mālde afterwards had one of Sekho's villages sequestered. This action enraged Sekho and led him to begin overt preparations for battle against Jodhpur.

Sekho and Hardās then met with Khānzāda Khān Muḥammad Khān II (Daulat Khān or Daulatīyo) (ca. 1526-36; no. 154) at Nāgaur to enlist his aid against Jodhpur. The ***Khyāt*** of Naiṇsī, 3:90, records that Ūhaṛ Hardās promised to marry daughters to the Muslims in return for their support. When Sekho questioned whose daughters Hardās meant, Hardās replied that if they were victorious against Jodhpur, there would be many girls from whom to choose, while if they lost, what would it matter (see ***Khyāt***, 3:89-90, of the **translated text** for details). With this promise and assurances of victory over Rāv Gāṅgo, Daulat Khān agreed to join them. He brought eighty armored elephants and a large number of Muslim warriors from Nāgaur with him.

Rāv Gāṅgo summoned the aid of his paternal relation, Bīkāvat Rāṭhoṛ Rāv Jaitsī Lūṇkaraṇot of Bīkāner (ca. 1526-42; no. 45), for this confrontation. The opposing armies met at the village of Sevakī[49] on November 2, 1529. Rāv Gāṅgo again attempted to conciliate Sekho before battle with another proposal for the division of lands in Mārvāṛ. But neither Sekho nor his ***pradhān*** would consider the offer. Sekho sent word back to Rāv Gāṅgo that he had prepared the field for battle.

When the opposing forces closed, Rāv Gāṅgo's warriors were able to scatter the Nāgaurī Khān's elephants with a shower of arrows, and Rāv Gāṅgo himself is credited with wounding the Khān's lead elephant, Dariyājoīs, and its mahout. The Muslims then fled the field, leaving Sekho and Hardās alone with their Rajpūts to confront Rāv Gāṅgo and Rāv Jaitsī. The ***Khyāt*** of Naiṇsī, 3:92, records that "Sekho dismounted along with seven hundred men" to join with Rāv Gāṅgo in battle and that both Sekho and Hardās Ūhaṛ died fighting along with their sons. The field fell to Rāv Gāṅgo of Jodhpur who took with him many of the Khān's elephants as the spoils of victory. "Aitihāsik Bātāṃ," p. 37, notes

[49] Sevakī village: located twenty-three miles northeast of Jodhpur.

that at Sevakī, the efforts of the Akhairājot Rāṭhoṛs, who had come with Rāv Gāṅgo, were much praised for their role in achieving this victory.

Rāv Gāṅgo and Rāv Jaitsī of Bīkāner found Sekho Sūjāvat after the battle. He was lying on the field where he had fallen, still alive. Rāv Jaitsī provided shade for Sekho and gave him opium to eat along with some water. ***Khyāt***, 3:92, states that Sekho questioned who Jaitsī was and why he had entered hostilities between a father's brother and a brother's son, who quarreled over land. He then warned Rāv Jaitsī that Jaitsī's fate would be the same as his own had been.

Rāv Jaitsī Lūṇkaraṇot was killed on February 26, 1542 fighting against Rāv Mālde Gāṅgāvat's army of Jodhpur that conquered Bīkāner.

"Aitihāsik Bātāṃ," p. 60, records another statement Sekho made before he died. According to this text, Sekho said, "You should say to Rāṭhoṛ Jaitsī Ūdāvat, [and you] should say to Tejsī Ḍūṅgarsīyot, [that] they should settle the ***vair***." Sekho referred to hostilities that existed between the Rāṭhoṛs of Jodhpur and the Cahuvāṇs of Sūrācand.[50] The ***vair*** had begun when the Cahuvāṇ ruler of Sūrācand murdered a servant of Sekho Sūjāvat's. Sekho was unable to avenge the death of this servant during his lifetime, and he asked these Ūdāvat Rāṭhoṛs to settle the hostilities for him. Sekho was Jaitsī Ūdāvat's (no. 139) paternal uncle and Tejsī Ḍūṅgarsīyot's (no. 138) great uncle. Jaitsi Ūdāvat later mounted an attack on Sūrācand in 1534-35 to end the ***vair***.[51]

Sekho's uterine brother, Devīdās Sūjāvat, was with him at Sevakī, but he survived the fighting. ***Murārdān***, no. 2, pp. 431-432, notes that his Rajpūts took him from the field and would not allow him to die, telling him that Sekho himself had already retreated in order to convince him to leave. Devīdās then withdrew along with his mother's brother, Sācoro Cahuvāṇ Ajo Pithamrāvat (Prithīrāvat). Both soon quit Mārvāṛ and took service under the Sīsodīyo Rāṇo of Cītoṛ, Vikramaditya Sāṅgāvat (ca. 1531-36). They were killed at Cītoṛ in 1533 when it came under attack from the forces of Sultān Bahādur Shāh of Gujarat (1526-37).

Most of Sekho's family left Mārvāṛ following his death. ***Murārdān***, no. 2, pp. 306-307, reports that Sekho's son, Sahasmal Sekhāvat (8-4), was driven from the land and went to Bāgaṛ in the hills of western Mevāṛ. One of Sahasmal's sons did hold a ***paṭo*** village in Sojhat Pargano many years later, but then revolted and left Mārvāṛ. A grandson is also said to have come back to Mārvāṛ from Būndī in 1661, during the rule of Rājā Jasvantsiṅgh Gajsiṅghot (1638-78) (13-1).

Some years after Sevakī, a ***sākh*** of Rāṭhoṛs emerged known as Sekhāvat. Both ***Bāṅkīdās***, p. 11, and ***Murārdān***, no. 3, p. 76, note that many of Sekho's descendants became Muslims and that in Hāḍautī, the Rāṭhoṛ master of Nāhargaḍh was called ***navāb***.

---

[50] Sūrācand: a town located 125 miles southwest of Jodhpur.

[51] See ***infra***, "Ūdāvat Rāṭhoṛs," for further details about this ***vair*** and its settlement.

"Aitihāsik Bātāṃ," pp. 37, 60; ***Bāṅkīdās***, pp. 9, 11; ***Khyāt***, 1:135-136, 241-244, 3:88-92; ***Murārdān***, no. 1, p. 226, no. 2, pp. 102-108, 302-307, 410-411, 431-432, no. 3, p. 76; Ojhā, 4:1:270, n. 1, 276-280, 5:1:135-136; ***Vigat***, 1:41, ***Vīr Vinod***, 2:808.

(no. 87) **Kisandās Gāṅgāvat** (9-2)

Kisandās Gāṅgāvat was a son of Rāv Gāṅgo Vāghāvat (8-1), ruler of Jodhpur (1515-32). He was born of Rāṇī Bhāṭiyāṇī Lāḍbāī (***pīhar*** name), whose father is unidentified in local chronicles.[52]

Only a few details are available about Kisandās's life. He appears first in the texts as a military servant of Meṛtīyo Rāv Jaimal Vīramdevot of Meṛto (no. 107). He fought at the battle of Meṛto in 1554, when the Meṛtīyos defeated Rāv Mālde Gāṅgāvat of Jodhpur (1532-62) and his Rajpūts under Rāṭhoṛ Devīdās Jaitāvat (no. 63). "Aitihāsik Bātāṃ," p. 50, mentions that when Rāv Mālde began to leave his camp at the village of Gāṅgārṛo[53] after his defeat, a military servant of Rāv Jaimal's named Sīsodīyo Megho drew near him and attempted to strike him with his lance. Kisandās Gāṅgāvat and another Rāṭhoṛ, Ḍūṅgarsī Ūdāvat (no. 137), saw Megho and killed him before he could harm Rāv Mālde. Meṛtīyo Rāv Jaimal and others with him were infuriated when they learned what had happened. Kisandās then fled Meṛto for Rāv Mālde's ***vās*** ("residence, dwelling"), where he sought safety.

Kisandās remained in the service of Jodhpur for a time thereafter. ***Murārdān***, no. 1, p. 632, notes that he held the ***paṭo*** of Nandvāṇ village,[54] but provides no details about his activities. He was inconstant in his loyalty to Jodhpur, however, for when Rāv Mālde's son and successor, Rāv Candrasen Māldevot (1562-81) (10-1), fled Jodhpur to live in exile in the Arāvallīs and in southern Rājasthān in the mid-1570s, Kisandās remained behind in Mārvāṛ. He was unable to retain possession of his lands at Nandvāṇ, however, in the face of the Mughal occupation.

When and where Kisandās died is uncertain. ***Murārdān*** (***ibid.***) notes only that he was killed by the Thorīs.

"Aitihāsik Bātāṃ," p. 50; ***Murārdān***, no. 1, p. 632, no. 2, pp. 112-113.

---

[52] See ***supra***, **Marriage and Family Lists of the Rulers of Jodhpur**, Gāṅgo Vāghāvat, Rāṇī no. 5, S - Kisandās.

[53] Gāṅgārṛo village: located seven miles west-northwest of Meṛto.

[54] Nandvāṇ village: located twelve miles south-southwest of Jodhpur.

(no. 88) **Īsardās Kalyāṇdāsot** (12-7)

Īsardās Kalyāṇdāsot was a son of Rāṇo Kalyāṇdās Rāymalot (11-9) of Sīvāṇo[55] and a great-grandson of Rāv Mālde Gāṅgāvat (1532-62) (9-1). Īsardās and his family played only minor roles in the affairs of Mārvāṛ during the period under review. For the most part, they were military servants of the Mughals following the departure of Īsardās's grandfather, Rāymal Māldevot (10-3), from Mārvāṛ in the early 1560s, and they maintained only sporadic and inconstant alliances with Jodhpur.

Rāymal Māldevot (10-3)

Īsardās's grandfather, Rāymal Māldevot, was born of Rāṇī Jhālī Hīrādejī, a daughter of Jhālo Māno (Mansiṅgh) Jaitsīyot of Haḷvad.[56] He served under his father, Rāv Mālde Gāṅgāvat, during the early part of his life. Rāv Mālde stationed Rāymal at the fort of Sīvāṇo in southwestern Mārvāṛ after his conquest of this area in 1538. Rāymal was in possession of Sīvāṇo at the time of his half-brother Candrasen Māldevot's succession to the Jodhpur throne in 1562. Shortly thereafter, Rāymal joined two of his other half-brothers, Udaisiṅgh Māldevot (10-2) and Rām Māldevot (10-4), in attempts to seize lands in Mārvāṛ from Rāv Candrasen and to challenge his authority to rule.

Rāv Candrasen was successful in countering these moves against him. He was able to force Rāymal from the area of Dunāṛo[57] where he had begun raiding. He halted Rām Māldevot's depredations in the area of Sojhat and drove him back across the Arāvallīs into Mevāṛ. And he defeated his uterine brother, Udaisiṅgh Māldevot, in battle at Lohīyāvaṭ village[58] ca. 1563.

Rāv Candrasen later took Sīvāṇo from Rāymal, forcing him to leave Mārvāṛ for Mevāṛ. Local chronicles do not indicate how long Rāymal remained in Mevāṛ nor do they say anything about his activities there. He eventually moved on to north India, where he took service under Mughal Emperor Akbar. It is probable that Rāymal was among the contingent of troops that Akbar sent under the command of Shāh Qulī Maḥramī against Rāv Candrasen at Sīvāṇo in 1574-75, but the chronicles do not mention Rāymal's name. ***Murārdān***, no. 1, p. 605, notes that following Sīvāṇo's conquest, however, Rāymal received Sīvāṇo in ***jāgīr***. It is unclear from the sources how long he remained in possession.

Rāymal Māldevot died in 1581-82.

Local sources record two of Rāymal's marriages, one to a daughter of Hāḍo Rāv Surjan Urjaṇot of Būndī (ca. 1568-1607) named Ratankuṃvar, and a

---

[55] Sīvāṇo town: located fifty-eight miles southwest of Jodhpur.

[56] See *supra*, **Marriage and Family Lists of the Rulers of Jodhpur**, Mālde Gāṅgāvat, Rāṇī no. 4, S - Rāymal.

[57] Dunāṛo village: located thirty-two miles southwest of Jodhpur.

[58] Lohīyāvaṭ village: located eighteen miles southeast of Phaḷodhī in northern Mārvāṛ.

second to a daughter of a Kachvāho Rajpūt also named Rāymal. The identity of this Kachvāho and the name of his daughter are unknown.

One of Rāymal's daughters was married to Akbar's son, Prince Dānyāl, on October 2, 1595. ***Akbar Nāma***, 3:1040, mentions this marriage in passing, and it is unclear from the text which of Rāymal's sons or grandsons took part in the marriage arrangements. It is possible that Rāymal's grandson, Īsardās Kalyāṇdāsot, arranged the marriage in an attempt to create a firmer alliance with the Mughals following his father Kalyāṇdās Rāymalot's revolt from Akbar and death in battle at Sīvāṇo in January of 1589.

> ***Akbar Nāma***, 3:1040; ***Bāṅkīdās***, p. 19; ***Jodhpur Rājya kī Khyāt***, pp. 98, 105, 122; ***Khyāt***, 3:152; Maṅgilāl Vyās, ***Jodhpur Rājya kā Itihās*** (Jaypur: Pañcśīl Prakāśan, 1975), pp. 187-188, 198-203; ***Murārdān***, no. 1, p. 605, no. 2, p. 142, no. 3, p. 53; Ojhā, 4:1:326, n. 4, 333-334, 342-346, 360; ***Vigat***, 1:55, 2:219-220.

Kalyāṇdās Rāymalot (11-9)

Īsardās's father, Kalyāṇdās Rāymalot, and Kalyāṇdās's brother, Pratāpsī Rāymalot (11-11), were also Imperial servants of Mughal Emperor Akbar's. ***Vigat***, 2:219-220, notes that, following Rāymal Māldevot's death in 1581-82, both Kalyāṇdās and Pratāpsī approached the Emperor regarding Sīvāṇo, and that Akbar granted it to them in ***jāgīr***, giving the title of ***rāṇo*** to Kalyāṇdās. ***Murārdān***, no. 1, pp. 610-611, records in its genealogy of this family that Pratāpsī received only a number of villages of Sīvāṇo from Akbar, not Sīvāṇo itself.

Little is known about Rāṇo Kalyāṇdās's activities during the years between 1581 and 1588. ***Murārdān***, no. 1, p. 605, mentions that Kalyāṇdās performed military service at Lahore. He also spent time in Mārvāṛ, for ***Murārdān***, no. 2, pp. 629-631, records his involvement in a local dispute that included two of his brothers, Pratāpsī and Kānho Rāymalot (11-10), and a number of their military servants. According to ***Murārdān***, Kalyāṇdās's brothers quarreled over the division of villages in Sīvāṇo following Kalyāṇdās's receipt of Sīvāṇo in ***jāgīr***. A military servant of Kānho Rāymalot's named Jasvant Dāsāvat blamed this quarrel on Muṃhato Narāyaṇdās, who served under Pratāpsī Rāymalot. Jasvant is said to have told Kānho that "the cause of this enmity is that shopkeeper (***banīyo***), Narāyaṇ." Muṃhato Narāyaṇdās became angry when he learned of Jasvant's remarks. He confronted him, and they fell into an open quarrel during which weapons were drawn. But others around them intervened and stopped the fight before anyone was hurt. ***Murārdān*** notes that there was much affection between Kalyāṇdās and his brother, Kānho, and that Kalyāṇdās then gathered his ***sāth*** and attacked Muṃhato Narāyaṇdās at his brother, Pratāpsī's, home. During the fighting there, a servant of Kalyāṇdās's named Rāso Nagrājot was killed, and Muṃhato Narāyaṇdās was badly wounded. ***Murārdān*** gives no further details about this skirmish, except to say that some time later, a Rāṭhoṛ friend of Muṃhato Narāyaṇdās stole a number of Kalyāṇdās's horses, putting Kalyāṇdās in a difficult position.

Rāṇo Kalyāṇdās revolted from Akbar in 1588. The circumstances surrounding his revolt and his death in battle at Sīvāṇo in January of 1589 are of interest and are recounted here in some detail:

Murārdān records two different accounts of the revolt. In its section on the reign of Moṭo Rājā Udaisiṅgh Māldevot of Jodhpur (1583-95) (10-2), ***Murārdān***, no. 2, p. 188, states that, while at Lahore, Kalyāṇdās killed a Saiyyid who was an Imperial servant of Akbar during a quarrel. When Akbar learned of this murder, he ordered the Moṭo Rājā to kill Kalyāṇdās. Kalyāṇdās then fled from the Imperial camp for Mārvāṛ, and he took refuge in the fort of Sīvāṇo.

Elsewhere in its genealogy of Rāymal Māldevot's family, ***Murārdān***, no. 1, p. 605, states that Rāṇo Kalyāṇdās took offense when the Moṭo Rājā married his daughter, Manāvatībāī (popularly known as Jodhbāī), to Akbar's son, Prince Salīm (Jahāṅgīr) ca. 1586.[59] Kalyāṇdās is said to have been angered by the Moṭo Rājā's actions and to have remarked:

> Why has a daughter been married to the Turks? I will kill Prince [Salīm] and the Moṭo Rājā!

When the Moṭo Rājā learned of this remark, he informed Akbar. Akbar then ordered the Moṭo Rājā to kill Kalyāṇdās, whereupon Kalyāṇdās fled the Imperial camp.

Vigat, 2:220, supports ***Murārdān***'s latter entry, noting:

> The Moṭo Rājā married a daughter to Prince [Salīm]. Then there was a fight with Rāṭhoṛ Kalyāṇdās.

In compliance with the Emperor's orders, the Moṭo Rājā sent an expedition against Sīvāṇo under Bhaṇḍārī Māṇo and two of his sons, Kuṃvar Bhopat Udaisiṅghot (11-4) and Kuṃvar Jaitsiṅgh Udaisiṅghot (11-6). But Kalyāṇdās entrenched himself in the fort and proved too strong an opponent. He also led a daring night attack against the army from Jodhpur with fifty or sixty of his men, creating havoc among its ranks and forcing its flight from the area. In the face of this defeat, the Moṭo Rājā received permission from the Emperor to leave the Imperial camp. He returned to Mārvāṛ to lead a second, stronger expedition against Sīvāṇo himself. This force allowed Kalyāṇdās no quarter. Realizing that his defeat was imminent, Kalyāṇdās had his wives perform ***jauhar***,[60] and he then led his Rajpūts outside to fight to the death.

---

[59] See ***supra***, **Marriage and Family Lists of the Rulers of Jodhpur**, Udaisiṅgh Māldevot, Rāṇī no. 10, D - Manāvatībāī.

[60] ***Jauhar***: a mass ritual suicide, performed by burning on pyres or leaping to death from the walls of a fort in the face of defeat. The ***jauhar*** is generally performed by women before their men sally forth to fight to the death in battle.

The texts provide different dates for the events that occurred at Sīvāṇo. ***Murārdān***, no. 2, pp. 190-191, records that the ***jauhar*** at the fort took place on Thursday, January 2, 1589, and that Kalyāṇdās then emerged with his Rajpūts and was killed in battle immediately thereafter. ***Vigat***, 2:220, and "Aitihāsik Bātāṃ," p. 92, give the date of November 19, 1589 for the Moṭo Rājā's conquest of Sīvāṇo and Kalyāṇdās's death. The latter date appears incorrect and is unsupported in modern histories of Mārvāṛ. Ojhā, 4:1:360, for example, following ***Jodhpur Rājya kī Khyāt***, p. 123, gives the earlier date of Thursday, January 2, 1589 for the Moṭo Rājā's entry into Sīvāṇo.

The Moṭo Rājā received Sīvāṇo in ***jāgīr*** from Akbar following this victory.

> "Aitihāsik Bātāṃ," pp. 91-92; ***Bāṅkīdās***, p. 19; ***Jodhpur Rājya kī Khyāt***, pp. 122-123; ***Khyāt***, 1:239, 2:164-165, 173; ***Murārdān***, no. 1, pp. 605-606, 610-611, no. 2, pp. 187-191, 629-631; Ojhā, 4:1:360-361; V. S. Bhargava, ***Marwar and the Mughal Emperors*** (Delhi: Munshiram Manoharlal, 1966), pp. 58-59; ***Vigat***, 1:75-77, 2:219-220; ***Vīr Vinod***, 2:815.

(no. 88) **Īsardās Kalyāṇdāsot** (12-7)

No information is available about the activities of Rāṇo Kalyāṇdās Rāymalot's son Īsardās Kalyāṇdāsot prior to 1599-1600. He was then a military servant of Rāṭhoṛ Sakatsiṅgh Udaisiṅghot (11-3). Rāṭhoṛ Sakatsiṅgh was a son of Moṭo Rājā Udaisiṅgh Māldevot of Jodhpur (1583-95), who had received the ***pargano*** of Sojhat in ***jāgīr*** from Akbar in 1599-1600. He held this ***jāgīr*** for one year. Īsardās was with him at the time.

Īsardās appears to have left service under Sakatsiṅgh in 1601-02, following Sakatsiṅgh's loss of Sojhat. He then went to live with his brother, Narsiṅghdās Kalyāṇdāsot (12-8), at the village of Bhāuṇḍo[61] of Nāgaur. Narsiṅghdās held Bhāuṇḍo in ***paṭo*** from Sīsodīyo Rāṇo Sagar Udaisiṅghot, who had received Nāgaur in ***jāgīr*** from Emperor Jahāngīr upon his succession to the Mughal throne. Īsardās became involved in a ***vair*** at Bhāuṇḍo with the Jeso Bhāṭīs of Mārvāṛ which lasted for several years and which determined the subsequent course of his life. This ***vair*** emerged in the following manner:

It is uncertain when Īsardās arrived at Bhāuṇḍo, but it was sometime between the years 1601 and 1612-13, for in the latter year Rāṇo Sagar sequestered Bhāuṇḍo village from Īsardās's brother, Rāṭhoṛ Narsiṅghdās. The Rāṇo[62] then granted this village to another of his military servants, Jeso Bhāṭī

---

[61] Bhāuṇḍo village: located fifty-three miles north-northeast of Jodhpur and twenty-five miles southwest of Nāgaur.

[62] Local texts including ***Khyāt***, 1: 23-24, 2:156-158, ***Murārdān***, no. 2, 505-506, and ***Bāṅkīdās***, p. 119, all record that Sīsodīyo Rāṇo Sagar held Nāgaur at this time, and that both Rāṭhoṛ Narsiṅghdās and Bhāṭī Surtāṇ received Bhāuṇḍo village from him. A late 19th century source, "Pariśiṣṭ 1 (gh), Pargane Nāgor rau Hāl," ***Vigat***, 2:422, states that Sīsodīyo Rāṇo Sagar held Nāgaur for only one year from 1605-06, and that Emperor

Surtāṇ Mānāvat, who was a brother Jeso Bhāṭī Goyanddās Mānāvat, the ***pradhān*** of Jodhpur under Rājā Sūrajsiṅgh Udaisiṅghot (1595-1619). Bhāṭī Surtāṇ had taken service under Rāṇo Sagar in 1612-13, and he occupied Bhāuṇḍo by the end of this year.

While Rāṭhoṛ Narsiṅghdās vacated Bhāuṇḍo for Bhāṭī Surtāṇ, he harbored resentments over the loss of this village. He then returned to Bhāuṇḍo in May of 1613 with his two brothers, Īsardās and Mādhodās (12-9), and other Jodhos in his ***sāth*** to challenge Bhāṭī Surtāṇ's rights to the village. Bhāṭī Surtāṇ had constructed a small fort at Bhāuṇḍo, but he emerged from this fort with his Rajpūts to meet Rāṭhoṛ Narsiṅghdās before the village. In the pitched battle that followed on May 16, 1613,[63] both Rāṭhoṛ Narsiṅghdās and Jeso Bhāṭī Surtāṇ were killed.

Jodhpur ***pradhān*** Jeso Bhāṭī Goyanddās mounted a punitive expedition against Bhāuṇḍo to avenge his brother's death when news of his brother's killing reached him. Both Īsardās and Mādhodās Kalyāṇdāsot fled Mārvāṛ in the face of his actions. But Bhāṭī Goyanddās killed one of their paternal cousins, Jodho Rāṭhoṛ Gopāḷdās Bhagvāndāsot, at Kāṅkaṛkhī village[64] near Meṛto, where he had pursued him, to end the ***vair***. This murder raised the ire of other Jodhos and eventually led to Bhāṭī Goyanddās's own death two years later in 1615.[65]

Īsardās and Mādhodās next appeared at Burhanpur in the Deccan in 1616-17. Here they sought out Rājā Sūrajsiṅgh of Jodhpur and entreated him to end the hostilities with the Jeso Bhāṭīs. ***Murārdān***, no. 1, p. 606, records that they told the Rājā:

> whatever happened, we were not at fault. We are the sons of the ***Rāj***, and you should not take it badly and refuse to retain us. You should end the ***vair***.

The Rājā took these Rajpūts under his protection, and he prevailed upon Mahābat Khān to bring them into his service.

Jahāngīr then granted Nāgaur in ***jāgīr*** to Kachvāho Mādhosiṅgh Bhagvantdāsot, a brother of Rājā Mānsiṅgh Bhagvantdāsot of Āmber (1589-1614). Kachvāho Mādhosiṅgh is said to have held Nāgaur from 1606-16. It has not been possible to verify Kachvāho Mādhosiṅgh's involvement with Nāgaur from other sources. In its genealogy of the Kachvāhos of Āmber, Naiṇsī's ***Khyāt***, 1:299, for example, states only that Mādhosiṅgh "was [a servant] of Emperor Akbar's [and held] the [***jāgīr***] of Ajmer and Mālpuro."

63 This is the date given by Ojhā, 4:1:374 and ***Jodhpur Rājya kī Khyāt***, p. 150. ***Murārdān***, no. 1, p. 608, gives the date of May 18, 1613, while ***Bāṅkīdās***, p. 119, records the date of May 27, 1612.

64 Kāṅkaṛkhī village: located nine miles south-southwest of Meṛto.

65 See ***infra***, "Kūmpāvat Rāṭhoṛs," Kānhāsiṅgh Khīṃvāvat (no. 100), for further discussion of this matter.

Īsardās remained in Mahābat Khān's service for several years thereafter. But *Vigat*, 2:74, notes that Īsardās was one of four Rāṭhoṛs who received villages of Meṛto Pargano in *jāgīr* from Prince Parvīz. Emperor Jahāngīr had made Parvīz *sūbedār* of Ajmer (including Meṛto) in 1623 following Prince Khurram's revolt. Prince Parvīz divided the villages of Meṛto among his retainers, and he granted four villages to Rāṭhoṛs who held service attachments either to Prince Khurram or Mahābat Khān in an apparent attempt to influence their loyalties. Īsardās received the *jāgīr* of Rohīso village.[66] He apparently left Mahābat Khān's service at this time, for *Murārdān*, no. 2, p. 506, notes that Īsardās killed a Meṛtīyo Rāṭhoṛ named Govardhan Dvārkādāsot "on the border." No village is named, but Meṛtīyo Govardhan's brothers held villages of Meṛto, and this incident may refer to an outbreak of hostilities that occurred when Īsardās took possession of Rohīso.

Murārdān, no. 1, pp. 606-607, also records that Īsardās left Mahābat Khān's service to become an Imperial servant of Emperor Jahāngīr's. It is possible that this change occurred in 1623 when he received the *jāgīr* of Rohīso village, or shortly thereafter. Īsardās was killed a few years later in 1628-29 during an outbreak of hostilities in the Deccan. *Murārdān* (*ibid.*) does not specify the circumstances surrounding these hostilities, but they may have been connected with Khān-ī-Jahān's revolt from Shāh Jahān shortly after Shāh Jahān's succession to the Mughal throne in 1628.

Īsardās's brother, Mādhodās, accompanied him to the Deccan. He became a favorite of Mahābat Khān's. But he later offended the Khān when they were in Kabul over a family matter involving Emperor Shāh Jahān and his wife, Nur Mahal. A fight broke out at the Imperial camp with some of the Imperial gunners, during which Mādhodās and a paternal cousin, Akhairāj Kānhāvat (12-10), were both shot and killed. The specific date of this incident is uncertain.

> ***Bāṅkīdās***, p. 119; ***Khyāt***, 1:23-24, 291, 299, 2:156-158; ***Murārdān***, no. 1, pp. 606-610, 612, no. 2, pp. 505-506; ***Vigat***, 1:390, 2:74, "Pariśiṣṭ 1 (gh), Pargane Nāgor rau Hāl," 2:422.

(no. 89) **Mahesdās Daḷpatot, Rāv** (12-2)

Mahesdās Daḷpatot was a son of Daḷpat Udaisiṅghot (11-2) and a grandson of Moṭo Rājā Udaisiṅgh Māldevot of Jodhpur (1583-95) (10-2). His father, Daḷpat, was the fourth of sixteen sons of the Moṭo Rājā, born July 18, 1568 of Rāṇī Cahuvāṇ Ajāyabdejī (*pīhar* name Kaṅkābāī), a daughter of Sācoro Cahuvāṇ Mahkaraṇ Rāṇāvat.[67]

Only a few details are available from the chronicles about Daḷpat Udaisiṅghot's life. He was born during the period in which his father, Udaisiṅgh Māldevot, held the lands of Phaḷodhī as his share of Mārvāṛ, while Udaisiṅgh's

---

[66] Rohīso village: located fifteen miles southeast of Meṛto.

[67] See *supra*, **Marriage and Family Lists of the Rulers of Jodhpur**, Udaisiṅgh Māldevot, Rāṇī no. 7, S - Daḷpat.

uterine brother, Rāv Candrasen Māldevot (1562-81) (10-1), ruled at Jodhpur. Daḷpat spent his life in his father's service. The chronicles first mention his taking part in an expedition against the Sīndhaḷs in 1586-87 along with three of his brothers, Kuṃvars Bhopat (11-4), Bhagvāṇdās (11-5) and Jaitsiṅgh (11-6), but the particulars of this expedition are unknown. Daḷpat also spent time at Lahore, both with his father and then, after his father's death in 1595, in service to the Mughals.

Naiṇsī's ***Khyāt***, 1:233-235, records the names of several Sācoro Cahuvāṇs who were ***cākar***s of Daḷpat. They included Daḷpat's mother's brother (***māmo***), Sāṃvatsī Mahkaraṇot, a brother's son of Sāṃvatsī named Bhāṇ Rāymalot, and a paternal cousin of his, Sūjo Rāmāvat.

The chronicles do not record whether Daḷpat was with the Moṭo Rājā when he died at Lahore. ***Bāṅkīdās***, p. 28, notes only that Daḷpat was at Lahore in 1597 and that he took part in an expedition against Bundelo Ran Dhavaḷ along with Jeso Bhāṭī Goyanddās Mānāvat, ***pradhān*** of Jodhpur under Rājā Sūrajsiṅgh Udaisiṅghot (1595-1619) (11-1).

Mughal Emperor Akbar granted Moṭo Rājā Udaisiṅgh sixty-five village of Jaitāraṇ Pargano in eastern Mārvāṛ and one-half of the town of Jaitāraṇ[68] in ***jāgīr*** in 1583 upon his succession to the Jodhpur throne. The other portions of Jaitāraṇ remained under the Ūdāvat Rāṭhoṛs.[69] When the Moṭo Rājā died, Akbar divided these sixty-five villages of Jaitāraṇ among five of the Moṭo Rājā's sons. Daḷpat received the ***jāgīr*** of eighteen and one-half villages; the others were shared among his brothers, Sakatsiṅgh (11-3), Bhopat (11-4), Mādhosiṅgh (11-7), and Mohaṇdās (11-8). ***Vigat***, 1:73-75, includes a list of these villages and notes of Daḷpat's that fourteen were suitable for ***khālso*** (***khālsā lāyak***), while four and one-half were villages given either in ***paṭo*** to military servants or in gift (***sāṃsaṇ***) to Brāhmaṇs and Cāraṇs. These villages are listed below with their locations noted in relation to Jaitāraṇ town:

14 - suitable for ***khālso***

1 - Āgevo - four miles south-southwest of Jaitāraṇ
1 - Boghāṇī/Beghāṇī - ten miles southwest
1 - Balāhaṛo - ten miles northeast
1 - Cāvṛīyo - six miles south
1 - Gaḷṇīyo - four miles west
1 - Koṭṛo - twenty-two miles east
1 - Mahelvo - (location uncertain)
1 - Murṛāho - seven miles northeast
1 - Nīmbol - nine miles northwest
1 - Nīboṛo - (location uncertain)
1 - Rahelṛo - sixteen miles east-southeast
1 - Rāmāvās Baḍo - five miles northwest

[68] Jaitāraṇ town: located fifty-six miles east of Jodhpur.

[69] See ***infra***, "Ūdāvat Rāṭhoṛs."

1 - Rāmpuro - eleven miles south-southwest
1 - Rātṛīyo - twenty miles east-southeast
14

4 1/2 - written and given in *paṭo* or in ***sāṃsaṇ***
1 - Bhākhar Vāsṇī - three miles southeast of Jaitāraṇ
1/2 - Bīkarlāī - eight miles northwest
1 - Bohoguṇ rī Vāsṇī - ten miles northwest
1 - Khetāvās - four miles west
1 - Tejā rī Vāsṇī - ten miles south
4 1/2

Daḷpat gave the village Tejā rī Vāsṇī in ***sāṃsaṇ*** to Āsīyo Cāraṇ Tejo Karamsīyot in 1596. ***Vigat***, 1:551-552, records in its description of this village that this gift consisted of some fields (***khet***) lying along the border between the villages of Rāmpuro[70] and Nīmbāheṛo.[71] A new settlement (***kheṛo***) was established there. ***Vigat*** states further:

> Rāṭhoṛ Daḷpat formerly held 10 villages; [they] were ***paṭo*** [villages], then [he] gave [Tejā rī Vāsṇī to Cāraṇ Tejo Karamsīyot].

The reference to ***paṭo*** villages in this passage is confusing, but it may refer to villages Daḷpat originally held in ***paṭo*** from his father.

Daḷpat died in 1600 at the age of thirty-one years. He had from five to nine wives, five sons, and three to four daughters. His wives and sons born of them (where known) included:

1. Kachvāhī Rāykuṃvar, a daughter of Rājāvat Kachvāho Rājā Bhagvantdās Bhārmalot of Āmber (ca. 1574-89). Rājā Mānsiṅgh Bhagvantdāsot (1589-1614) was her brother.

2. Bhāṭiyāṇī Kusumkuṃvar, a daughter of Kelhaṇ Bhāṭī Goyanddās Pañcāiṇot of Pūṅgaḷ and Vairsaḷpur. Her sister was married to Rājā Sūrajsiṅgh Udaisiṅghot of Jodhpur (1595-1619).[72]

S - Mahesdās (12-2) (no. 89)

3. Vāghelī (of Pīthāpur)

---

[70] Rāmpuro village: located eleven miles south-southwest of Jaitāraṇ.

[71] Nīmbāheṛo village: located nine miles south of Jaitāraṇ.

[72] See ***supra***, **Marriage and Family Lists of the Rulers of Jodhpur**, Sūrajsiṅgh Udaisiṅghot, Rāṇī no. 2.

S - Jhūñjhārsiṅgh (12-4)
S - Rājsiṅgh (12-3)

4. Tuṃvar Sāhibkuṃvar, a daughter of Tuṃvar Kesrīsiṅgh of Lākhāsar.

S - Jasvantsiṅgh (12-5)
S - Kanhīrām (12-6)

The places of marriage of three of Daḷpat's daughters are known:

D - married to Sīsodīyo Rāṇo Karaṇsiṅgh Amarsiṅghot of Mevāṛ (1620-28).

D - married to Jaisaḷmer Bhāṭī Khetsi Māldevot, a son of Rāvaḷ Mālde Lūṇkaraṇot (1551-61).

D - married to Hāḍo Harisiṅgh Ratansiṅghot, a son of Rāv Ratansiṅgh Bhojāvat (ca. 1607-31).

Mahesdās Daḷpatot was born on December 27, 1596 during the period his father held the ***jāgīr*** of eighteen and one-half villages of Jaitāraṇ Pargano from Emperor Akbar.

Little is known about Mahesdās's early life. In his ***Ratlām kā Pratham Rājya***,[73] pp. 7, 15, Raghubīrsiṃh associates Mahesdās's father, Daḷpat, with the village and area of Pīsāṅgan[74] near Ajmer and states that Mahesdās, being three years old when his father died, received Pīsāṅgan and surrounding villages in ***jāgīr*** and that he grew up at Pīsāṅgan.

Murārdān, no. 2, p. 663, and ***Jodhpur Rājya kī Khyāt***, p. 229, both record that Mahesdās began his career as a military servant of Prince Khurram's (Shāh Jahān's). He may have taken service under Prince Khurram when the Prince received Meṛto Pargano from the Emperor on the death of Rājā Sūrajsiṅgh Udaisiṅghot in 1619. But he appears to have remained in the Prince's service only a short time, for ***Vigat***, 2:74, lists Mahesdās as the recipient of Baḍlī village[75] of Meṛto Pargano from Prince Parvīz in 1623. Emperor Jahāṅgīr had appointed Prince Parvīz ***sūbedār*** of Ajmer (including Meṛto) in 1623 following the revolt of Prince Khurram from the Deccan. Upon assuming his position, Prince Parvīz divided villages among his retainers, and he gave four villages of Meṛto to Rāṭhoṛs who held service attachments either to Prince Khurram or to Mahābat Khān. Mahesdās received one of these villages.

Jodhpur Rājā Gajsiṅgh Sūrajsiṅghot (1619-38) (11-1) soon after received Meṛto Pargano from Prince Parvīz in ***jāgīr*** and placed his authority over this area

---

[73] Raghubīrsiṃh, ***Ratlām kā Pratham Rājya: Uskī Sthāpnā evaṃ Ant [Īsā kī 17vīṃ Śatābdī]*** (Nāī Dillī: Rājkamal Prakāśan, 1950).

[74] Pīsāṅgan village: located fifteen miles west-southwest of Ajmer.

[75] Baḍlī village: located twelve miles south-southeast of Meṛto and eight miles northwest of Kuṛkī.

in August of 1623. It was apparently during this period that Mahesdās took service under the Rājā, for he also received the village of Kuṛkī[76] in ***paṭo*** from Rājā Gajsiṅgh. Because of the proximity of Kuṛkī to Baḍlī, Mahesdās may have held these villages jointly in this period. However, it is unclear exactly how Mahesdās directed his loyalties and service attachments at this time.

Raghubīrsiṃh, ***Ratlām kā Pratham Rājya***, pp. 16-18, notes that Mahesdās accompanied his father's mother (***dādī***), Sācorī Cahuvāṇ Ajāyabdejī, on a pilgrimage to the holy places along the banks of the Narmada River in 1627-28. Fatigued by the long journey, Ajāyabdejī fell ill and died at Sītāmaū[77] on the return. Mahesdās had his paternal grandmother cremated along the banks of a tank at Sītāmaū and built a cenotaph (***chatrī***) in her memory on this spot.

In January or February of 1628, Mahesdās and his brothers, Jhūñjhāṛsiṅgh (12-4), Rājsiṅgh (12-3), and Jasvantsiṅgh (12-5), left the service of Jodhpur and became military servants of Mahābat Khān. Emperor Jahāngīr had died on October 27, 1627, and Prince Khurram (Shāh Jahān) then succeeded to the Mughal throne on February 4, 1628. While enroute from the Deccan to Agra, the Prince stopped at Ajmer and on January 14, 1628 appointed Mahābat Khān ***sūbedār*** of Ajmer. It is then that Mahesdās and his brothers entered the Khān's service.

Mahesdās and his brothers remained with Mahābat Khān over the next six years. During this period, Mahesdās acquired a considerable reputation for courage and valor in battle, and he was badly wounded in the Deccan during Mughal operations against Ahmadnagar and Bijapur. With him in this period were Kelhaṇ Bhāṭīs Rūghnāth Jogīdāsot and Jagnāth Jogīdāsot, who were sons of his mother's brother, Bhāṭī Jogīdās Goyanddāsot. Jagnāth Jogīdāsot's son, Harnāth Jagnāthot, was also with him. His Sācoro Cahuvāṇ relations including his father's mother's brother, Sāṃvatsī Mahkaraṇot, and Sāṃvatsī's four sons, Sādūḷ, Balū, Gopāḷdās, and Acaḷdās, were also with Mahābat Khān's army. During the siege of Daulatabad, Mahesdās's Kelhaṇ Bhāṭī relations were all killed along with his own brothers, Jhūñjhāṛsiṅgh and Rājsiṅgh.

When Mahābat Khān died of fistula in the Deccan on October 26, 1634 Mahesdās proceeded north to present himself before the Emperor at the Imperial ***darbār*** and to offer his services once again to the Mughal throne. His reputation preceded him, for the Emperor welcomed him into his service on January 5, 1635, and ***Murārdān***, no. 2, p. 663, notes that Mahesdās received Jājpur[78] for his ***vasī*** at this time. He was also awarded a ***mansab*** rank of 500 ***zāt***, 400 ***suwār***. The Emperor honored him at this time with a sword which he presented to Mahesdās with his own hands.

Raghubīrsiṃh, ***Ratlām kā Pratham Rājya***, pp. 33-34, notes that up until this time, Mahesdās had held Pīsāṅgan and surrounding villages, which were his

---

[76] Kuṛkī village: located twenty miles southeast of Meṛto.

[77] Sītāmaū: located in Madhya Pradesh forty-eight miles north-northeast of Ratlām and one hundred ten miles east-southeast of Udaipur.

[78] Jājpur: modern Jahāzpur, located seventy miles southeast of Ajmer.

family *jāgīr*, along with several villages of Titrod Pargano (modern Sītāmaū). After receiving Jājpur in *jāgīr*, Mahesdās had his family moved from Pīsāṅgan, and his family remained at Jājpur for the next seven years.

In September of 1635, Mahesdās accompanied Prince Aurangzeb to the East. The Prince had been placed in charge of the Imperial army sent against Jhūñjhāṛsiṅgh Bundelo, who was in revolt against the Empire. Mahesdās was with Kachvāho Rājā Jaisiṅgh Mahāsiṅghot (1621-67) and Khān Daurān during operations against Bijapur and Golkunda in 1636-37. He returned to Agra with Khān Daurān in March of 1637, and his *mansab* rank was increased at this time to 800/600. Mahesdās remained in close attendance upon the Emperor from this time forward. He was included among those *mansabdārs* who were responsible for the Imperial guard and who were in attendance at the stirrup (*hāzir rakāb*).

Mahesdās's *mansab* rank was again increased to 1000/600 on March 11, 1638, and in August of that year, he accompanied Shāh Jahān to Lahore. He remained with the Emperor during his travels to Kabul and back to Lahore between November of 1638 and February of 1640. While at Lahore, Mahesdās granted a village of Jājpur Pargano to his *rājguru* in *sāṃsaṇ*. He had previously granted the village of Ḍābṛī of Pargano Titrod to his *rājguru*, and he now changed the name of this village of Mahesdāspur. In addition, Mahesdās granted the village of Caurāṇo of Ratlām Pargano to his *rājpurohit* in *sāṃsaṇ*.

Mahesdās took leave of the Emperor while the latter was in Kashmir in August of 1640 in order to travel to Prayag to bathe in the Ganges. His eldest son, Ratansiṅgh Mahesdāsot (13-2), accompanied him on this pilgrimage. Mahesdās again joined the Emperor in November of 1640 upon the Emperor's return from Kashmir.

Raghubīrsiṃh, ***Ratlām kā Pratham Rājya***, pp. 50-51, records an incident involving Mahesdās's son, Ratansiṅgh, which brought the Emperor's close attention to the family and contributed to Mahesdās and his son, Ratansiṅgh's, favor at court. There was great celebration at the Imperial camp on the occasion of the Emperor's fifty-first birthday in January of 1641, and the Emperor gave the order for an elephant fight to take place as part of the festivities. One of the Emperor's favorite elephants, Kaharkop, was brought forward for the fight. Kaharkop was difficult to control, however, being in a perpetual state of rut, and, while entering the arena, broke free from his attendants and ran loose in the bazaar. He finally wandered into the vicinity of the Imperial *darbār* where a large crowd had gathered to watch the fight. Mahesdās and his son, Ratansiṅgh, were present there. Seeing the elephant loose and drawing near to the Imperial presence, Ratansiṅgh drew his dagger and ran forward to distract the elephant and turn it away. The elephant charged Ratansiṅgh when it saw him approach, and grabbed him with its trunk, lifting him off the ground. But Ratansiṅgh showed great presence of mind, stabbing the elephant several times. In an opportune moment, he was able to free himself from the elephant's trunk, climb on the elephant's head and seat himself behind its ears, where he continued to use his dagger to try and turn the elephant away. The elephant finally fled from the crowd, and Ratansiṅgh leaped down and escaped unharmed.

The Emperor was very pleased with Ratansiṅgh's display of courage. He praised him and considered that he deserved to be Mahesdās's designated successor. The Emperor is said to have spoken to Mahesdās about this matter, and to have greatly influenced Mahesdās's choice of Ratansiṅgh as his successor over another more favored son named Kalyāṇdās (13-4). The Emperor afterwards presented the elephant Kaharkop to Mahesdās, and he gave Ratansiṅgh a cavalry sword inlaid with gold.

Mahesdās's good fortune now began to increase. In April of 1641 his ***mansab*** was increased to 1000/800. He took leave for Jājpur shortly after, and in October of this year, on the occasion of the eclipse of the sun, was at the holy town of Puśkar, near Ajmer. He took this opportunity to grant lands in Jājpur Pargano in ***sāṃsaṇ*** to the Brāhmaṇ Devo. Mahesdās then returned to Lahore to be with the Emperor, who increased his ***mansab*** yet again on January 11, 1642 to 1000/1000.

In April of 1642 Mahesdās was at Lahore with the Imperial army during operations against the Shāh of Iran. When the army set out from Lahore, he received a robe of honor and a horse as was customary and, in addition, was given the gift of a banner. The banner was green and red in color, with gold wire embroidery and border, a gift given to a ***mansabdār*** upon attaining the rank of 1000 ***suwār***. Mahesdās accompanied Dārā Shikoh to Qandahar at this time and then returned with him to Lahore.

Mahesdās's ***mansab*** was again increased on August 31, 1642 to 2000/2000. He received Jāḷor Pargano[79] in ***jāgīr*** along with the title of ***rāv*** from Emperor Shāh Jahān at this time. Jāḷor now became Mahesdās's place of residence. He took leave of Shāh Jahān and proceeded to Jāḷor in order to place his authority over the area. His son, Ratansiṅgh, was with him, and he had his family come from Jājpur to join him.

Among those in Mahesdās's ***sāth*** when he went to Jāḷor were his sons, Ratansiṅgh, Rāysal (13-3), Kalyāṇdās (13-4), Phatehsiṅgh (13-5) and Rāmcandro (13-6), and several of his brothers' sons. A number of Sācoro Cahuvāṇs were in Ratansiṅgh's ***sāth***. These Cahuvāṇs were relations of Mahesdās through his father's mother's brother.

At the time Mahesdās took control of Jāḷor, an incident occurred at the village of Kāksī of Sīvāṇo, of which ***Vigat***, 2:265, speaks in its description of Kāksī village. Kāksī was a deserted hamlet (***kheṛo***) located twenty-five miles west of Sīvāṇo town at the time of the compilation of the ***Vigat*** in the mid-seventeenth century. Farmers and herdsmen from nearby villages cut grass there, and the farmers also cultivated some of its lands. A Rāṭhoṛ Rajpūt named Kisandās Jasvantot settled this village around the time Mahesdās received Jāḷor in ***jāgīr***. But Kāksī was included within Mahesdās's lands, and when Mahesdās took control at Jāḷor, he killed Rāṭhoṛ Kisandās during a border dispute that

---

[79] Jāḷor town and fort: located sixty-eight miles south-southwest of Jodhpur in southern Mārvāṛ. Jāḷor had been part of Jodhpur Rājā Gajsiṅgh Sūrajsiṅghot's ***jāgīr***. Upon his death in 1638 it reverted to Imperial ***khālso***, remaining as such until the Emperor granted it to Mahesdās in 1642.

broke out near this village. *Vigat* notes that the boundaries were later re-drawn, and Kāksī was then taken from Jāḷor and officially included within the ***pargano*** of Sīvāṇo.

Mahesdās soon returned to Agra to attend upon the Emperor, and in March of 1645 he accompanied Shāh Jahān once again to Lahore. The Emperor appointed him ***kiledār*** of Lahore at this time, a position he held for one year. On the occasion of the Emperor's birthday in January of 1646, Mahesdās's ***mansab*** was again increased to 2500/2000. In February of this year, he rode in the vanguard of the Imperial army under Prince Murād Bakhsh and Rājā Vīṭhaḷdās Gauṛ that was sent against Balkh and Badakhashan.

On March 26, 1646 Mahesdās's rank was again increased to 3000/2000, and he was presented with a kettledrum. Mahesdās was now among the leading ***amīr***s of the Empire. His rank increased further to 3000/2500 as reward for the Mughal victory when Shāh Jahān received news of it at Kabul in July of 1646.

Following this campaign, Mahesdās remained in close attendance upon the Emperor. The Emperor returned to Lahore on November 9, 1646, and Mahesdās's rank was again increased to 4000/3000 in early 1647. He died shortly thereafter on March 7, 1647 at the age of fifty-one years. He was cremated at Lahore, and a cenotaph was built for him there. His turban was sent to Jāḷor with news of his death, and his seventh wife, Candrāvat Sīsodṇī Saraskuṃvar, became a ***satī*** at Jāḷor.

Maāthir-ul-Umarā, 2:1:35, notes of Mahesdās that he was an experienced soldier upon whom Shāh Jahān placed great reliance. It states:

> In the audience hall he used to stand behind the throne by the side of a bench (***sandalī***), which was placed at a distance of two yards from the royal sword and quiver. During riding he followed at a fair distance.

Mahesdās had seven wives, six sons and five daughters. His wives and sons born of them (where known) were:

1. Rājāvat Kachvāhī Kusumkuṃvarde, a daughter of Rājāvat Kachvāho Lūṇkaraṇ of Āmber.

S - Ratansiṅgh (13-2) - born on Saturday, March 6, 1619 at Balāhaṛo village[80] of Jaitāraṇ Pargano in Mārvāṛ.

2. Sonagarī Amlokdekuṃvar, a daughter of Sonagaro Sakatsiṅgh of Jāḷor.

S - Rāysal (13-3)
S - Kalyāṇdās (13-4)

---

[80] Balāhaṛo village: located ten miles northeast of Jaitāraṇ town.

3. Hāḍī Sūrajkuṃvar, a daughter of Hāḍo Rajsiṅgh of Būndī.

S - Phatehsiṅgh (13-5)
S - Rāmcandro (13-6)

4. Gauṛ Pepkuṃvar, a daughter of Gauṛ Bhopatsiṅgh of Sarvāṛ Manoharpur.

S - Sūrajmal (13-7)

5. Candrāvat Sīsodṇī Saraskuṃvar, daughter of Candrāvat Sīsodīyo Harisiṅgh of Rāmpuro.

The places of marriage of three of Mahesdās's daughters are known:

D - married to Jaisaḷmer Bhāṭī Rāvaḷ Sabaḷsiṅgh Dayāḷdāsot (ca. 1651-60).
D - married to Candrāvat Sīsodīyo Mohakamsiṅgh Amarsiṅghot, a son of Rāv Amarsiṅgh Harisiṅghot of Rāmpuro. Mohakamsiṅgh succeeded to the Rāmpuro throne.
D - married to Būndī Hāḍo Rāv Catrasāḷ Gopīnāthot (ca. 1631-58).

Mahesdās was succeeded at Jāḷor by his eldest son, Ratansiṅgh Mahesdāsot. Ratansiṅgh held the rank of 400 *zāt*, 200 ***suwār*** prior to his father's death. When Shāh Jahān confirmed his ***jāgīr*** of Jāḷor, he raised Ratansiṅgh's rank to 1500/1500. This rank was later increased to 2000/2000. Ratansiṅgh held Jāḷor until 1658, in which year he accompanied Rāṭhoṛ Rājā Jasvantsiṅgh Gajsiṅghot of Jodhpur (1638-78) to north India and was killed at the battle of Ujjain fighting against the forces of Prince Aurangzeb, who was then in rebellion against the Empire.

Athar Ali, ***Appuratus***, pp. 127, 149, 157, 180, 182, 185, 198, 200-202, 204-205, 210, 216, 238, 306, 319, 327; ***Bāṅkīdās***, pp. 23-24; ***Jodhpur Rājya kī Khyāt***, pp. 129-130; ***Khyāt***, 1:233-236, 246, 2:119, 177; ***Maāthir-ul-Umarā***, 2:1:34-35; ***Murārdān***, no. 1, p. 636, no. 2, pp. 187, 193, 197, 663-665; R. P. Tripathi, ***The Rise and Fall of the Mughal Empire*** (Reprint ed. Allahabad: Central Book Depot, 1966), p. 442; Raghubīrsiṃh, ***Ratlām kā Pratham Rājya***, pp. 5-67; Reu, 1:178, n. 5; ***Vigat***, 1:73-74, 496, 551-552, 2:74, 265, 415.

Figure 26. Jodho Rāṭhoṛs
(continued on the following pages)

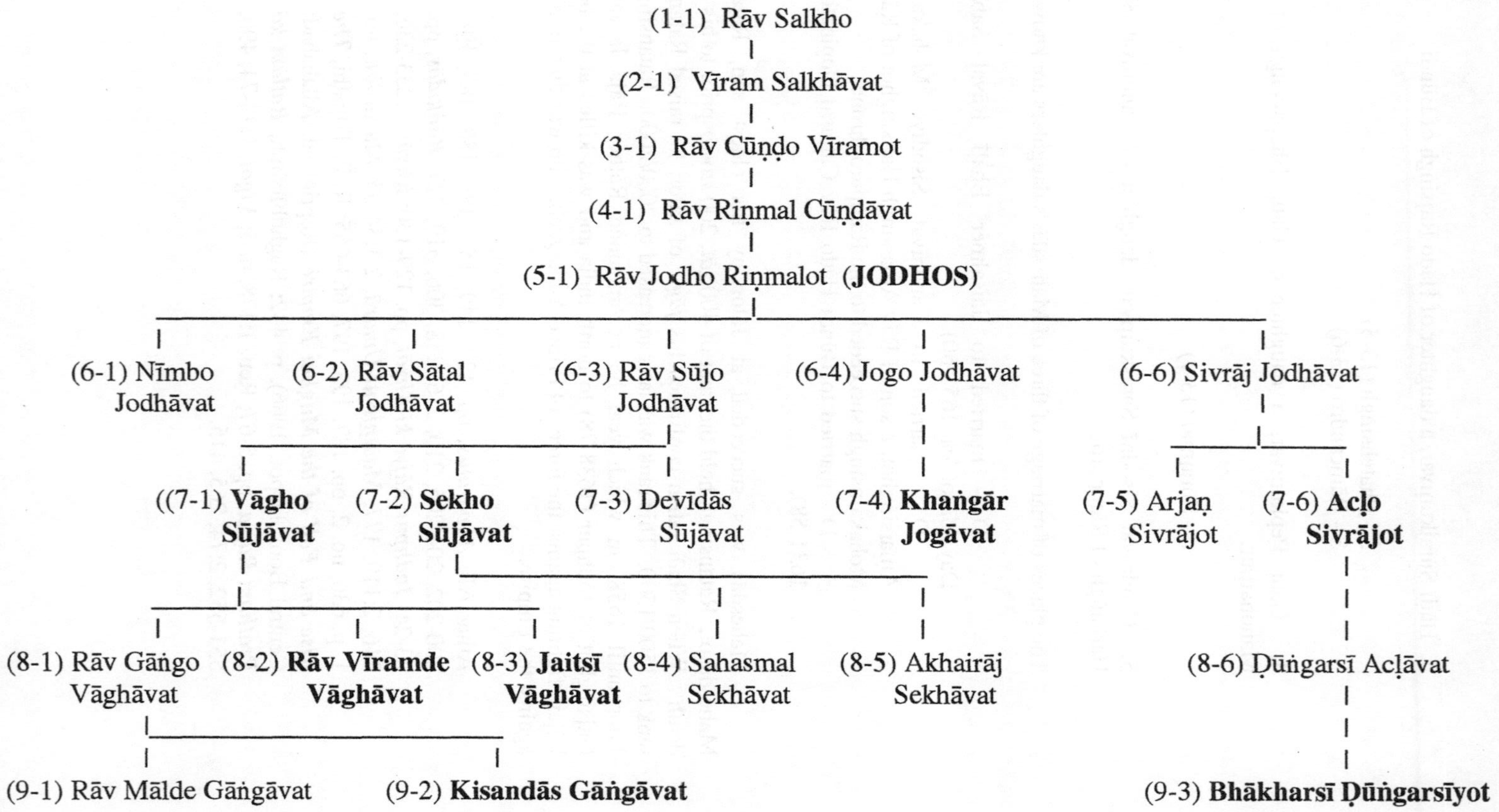

Figure 26. Jodho Rāṭhoṛs

(continued from the previous page and onto the following pages)

(4-1) Rāv Riṇmal Cūṇḍāvat

(5-1) Rāv Jodho Riṇmalot (**JODHOS**)

(6-3) Rāv Sūjo Jodhāvat

(7-1) Vāgho Sūjāvat

(8-1) Rāv Gāṅgo Vāghāvat

(9-1) Rāv Mālde Gāṅgāvat

(10-1) Rāv Candrasen Māldevot | (10-2) Rājā Udaisiṅgh Māldevot | (10-3) Rāymal Māldevot | (10-4) Rām Māldevot

Children of (10-2) Rājā Udaisiṅgh Māldevot:

(11-1) Rājā Sūrajsiṅgh Udaisiṅghot | (11-2) Dalpat Udaisiṅghot | (11-3) Sakatsiṅgh Udaisiṅghot | (11-4) Bhopat Udaisiṅghot | (11-5) Bhagvāṇdās Udaisiṅghot | (11-6) Jaitsiṅgh Udaisiṅghot | (11-7) Mādhosiṅgh Udaisiṅghot | (11-8) Mohaṇdās Udaisiṅghot

(12-1) Rājā Gajsiṅgh Sūrajsiṅghot

(13-1) Rājā Jasvantsiṅgh Gajsiṅghot

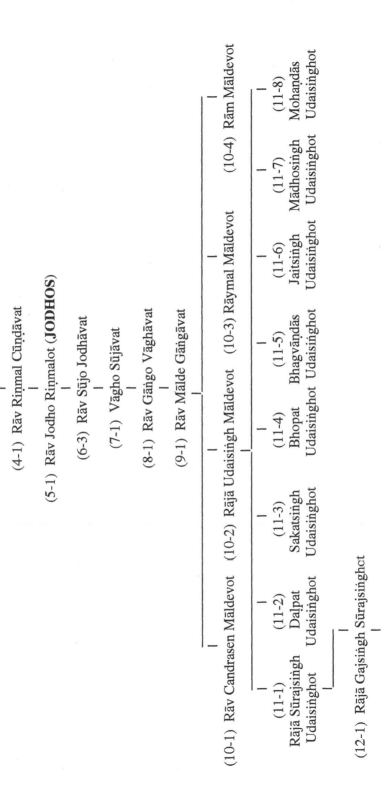

Figure 26. Jodho Rāṭhoṛs

(continued from previous pages and onto following page)

(5-1) Rāv Jodho Riṇmalot (**JODHOS**)

(6-3) Rāv Sūjo Jodhāvat

(7-1) Vāgho Sūjāvat

(8-1) Rāv Gāṅgo Vāghāvat

(9-1) Rāv Mālde Gāṅgāvat

(10-2) Rājā Udaisiṅgh Māldevot

(11-2) Daḷpat Udaisiṅghot

(12-2) **Rāv Mahesdās Daḷpatot**
(12-3) Rājsiṅgh Daḷpatot
(12-4) Jhūñjhāṛsiṅgh Daḷpatot
(12-5) Jasvantsiṅgh Daḷpatot
(12-6) Kanhīrām Daḷpatot

(13-2) Ratansiṅgh Mahedāsot
(13-3) Rāysal Mahesdāsot
(13-4) Kalyāṇdās Mahesdāsot
(13-5) Phatehsiṅgh Mahesdāsot
(13-6) Rāmcandro Mahesdāsot
(13-7) Sūrajmal Mahesdāsot

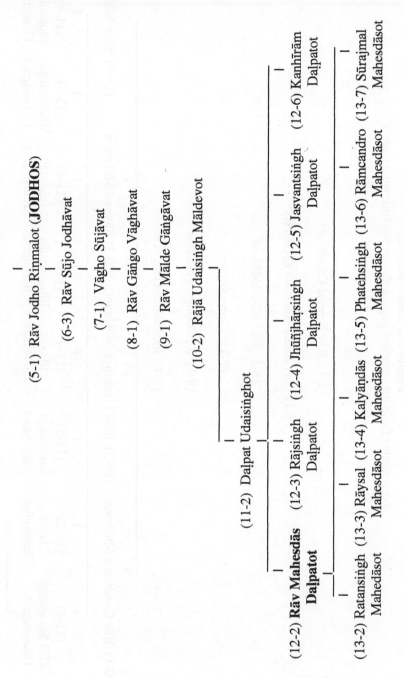

Figure 26. Jodho Rāṭhoṛs
(continued from the previous pages)

(4-1) Rāv Riṇmal Cūṇḍāvat

(5-1) Rāv Jodho Riṇmalot (**JODHOS**)

(6-3) Rāv Sūjo Jodhāvat

(7-1) Vāgho Sūjāvat

(8-1) Rāv Gāṅgo Vāghāvat

(9-1) Rāv Mālde Gāṅgāvat

(10-3) Rāymal Māldevot

(11-9) Rāṇo Kalyāṇdās Rāymalot

(12-7) **Īsardās Kalyāṇdāsot**

(12-8) Narsiṅghdās Kalyāṇdāsot

(12-9) Mādhodās Kalyāṇdāsot

(11-10) Kānho Rāymalot

(12-10) Akhairāj Kānhāvat

(11-11) Pratāpsī Rāymalot

Karamsot Rāṭhoṛs

(no. 94) **Dhanrāj Karamsīyot** (7-2)
(no. 91) **Jagmāl Udaikaraṇot** (8-2)
(no. 93) **Mahes Pañcāiṇot** (8-1)
(no. 92) **Pañcāiṇ Karamsīyot** (7-1)
(no. 90) **Udaikaraṇ Karamsīyot** (7-5)

The Karamsot Rāṭhoṛs

The Karamsot Rāṭhoṛs descend from Karamsī Jodhāvat (6-1), a son of Rāv Jodho Riṇmalot (5-1), ruler of Maṇḍor and Jodhpur (ca. 1453-89). His mother was Rāṇī Bhāṭiyāṇī Pūrāṃ, a daughter of Kelhaṇ Bhāṭī Rāv Vairsal Cācāvat, the ruler of Pūṅgaḷ and founder of Vairsalpur in northeastern Jaisaḷmer territory.[1]

During his division of the lands of Mārvāṛ among his brothers and sons following the founding of Jodhpur in 1459, Rāv Jodho granted Karamsī and his uterine brother, Rāypāḷ Jodhāvat (6-2), the village of Nāhaḍhsaro.[2] Both brothers initially settled there. Shortly after, their uterine sister, Bhāgāṃ, was married to Khānzāda Khān Salho Khān (Ṣalāh Khān, ca. 1467-69) of Nāgaur, and they received the two important villages of Khīṃvsar and Āsop in ***sāḷā kaṭārī***[3] in return for the gift of their sister. Karamsī then settled at Khīṃvsar, while Rāypāḷ occupied Āsop.

The villages of Khīṃvsar and Āsop lie sixteen miles apart along the border separating Jodhpur from Nāgaur, with Khīṃvsar situated fifty-four miles north-northeast and Āsop fifty miles northeast of Jodhpur, respectively. These villages had been separate from lands the Rāṭhoṛs held since the time of Rāv Cūṇḍo Vīramot of Maṇḍor (d. ca. 1423) (3-1). Rāv Cūṇḍo had been killed defending these lands against an army of Bhāṭīs and Muslims from the north.

---

[1] See ***supra***, **Marriage and Family Lists of the Rulers of Jodhpur**, Jodho Riṇmalot, Rāṇī no. 2, S - Karamsī.

[2] Nāhaḍhsaro village: located forty-five miles northeast of Jodhpur and eight miles south of Āsop.

[3] ***Sāḷā kaṭārī*** (lit. "wife's brother-dagger"): the customary gifts of clothing, money and/or land a sister's husband (***bahanoi***) gives to his wife's brother (***sāḷo***) in return for the gift of his sister. The giving of ***sāḷā kaṭārī*** forms a special part of the wedding ceremony, taking place after the bride and groom circumambulate the sacred fire. At the appropriate time, the wife's brothers grasp either a sword or dagger, and then grab the ear of the groom, demanding his gifts. See: Lāḷas, ***RSK***, 4:3:5538; ***Census Report, 1891***, pp. 33-34.

They now returned to the Rāṭhoṛs and remained important border villages demarcating the lands of Mārvāṛ from those of Nāgaur.

Little is known about Karamsī's life from this time forward until his death in eastern Rājasthān in 1526. Sometime after his settlement at Khīṃvsar, he joined his paternal nephew, Rāṭhoṛ Rāv Lūṇkaraṇ Bīkāvat of Bīkāner (1505-26; no. 44), in an expedition against the Muslims of Narnol, then under the rule of Sheikh Abīmīrā.[4] The Rāṭhoṛs fought at the village of Ḍhosī near Narnol on March 30, 1526, and Karamsī was killed there along with Rāv Lūṇkaraṇ and three of the Rāv's sons. Jodho Rāṭhoṛ Khaṅgār Jogāvat (no. 82), a paternal nephew of Karamsī, avenged his death against these Muslims some years later.

The texts record one marriage of Karamsī to Māṅgliyāṇī Dulde, a daughter of Māṅglīyo Gahlot Bhoj Hamīrot. Karamsī had four sons by Māṅgliyāṇī Dulde: Pañcāiṇ (7-1), Dhanrāj (7-2), Narāiṇ (7-3), and Pithurāv (7-4). Karamsī had a fifth son, Udaikaraṇ (7-5), by a second wife whose name is not recorded.

(no. 90) **Udaikaraṇ Karamsīyot** (7-5)
(no. 91) **Jagmāl Udaikaraṇot** (8-2)
(no. 94) **Dhanrāj Karamsīyot** (7-2)

Karamsī's son, Udaikaraṇ Karamsīyot, succeeded him to the rule of Khīṃvsar in 1526. Udaikaraṇ held this village for several years while a military servant of Rāv Gāṅgo Vāghāvat of Jodhpur (1515-32). Khīṃvsar was taken from him in 1530, however, for his failure to report for military service at the time of the battle of Sevakī[5] in November of 1529. Rāv Gāṅgo fought at Sevakī against his father's brother, Jodho Rāṭhoṛ Sekho Sūjāvat (no. 86), over the division of land and authority in Mārvāṛ.

No other information is available about Udaikaraṇ Karamsīyot.

Udaikaraṇ's son, Jagmāl Udaikaraṇot, was a military servant of Rāv Mālde Gāṅgāvat of Jodhpur (1532-62). Jagmāl received Khīṃvsar in ***paṭo*** from Rāv Mālde, but sources are unclear when this grant was made. They do not specify Jagmāl's relationship with his paternal cousin, Mahes Pañcāiṇot (8-1) (no. 93), who also held Khīṃvsar in ***paṭo*** from the Rāv in this same period. Jagmāl was killed in 1554 at Meṛto along with his paternal uncle, Dhanrāj Karamsīyot, fighting under Rāv Mālde's commander, Rāṭhoṛ Prithīrāj Jaitāvat (no. 63), against Meṛtīyo Rāv Jaimal Vīramdevot (no. 107).

Udaikaraṇ and Dhanrāj's brother, Narāiṇ Karamsīyot (7-3), also served under Rāv Mālde of Jodhpur. He held the ***paṭo*** of Nāhaḍhsaro village.

---

[4] ***Bāṅkīdās***, p. 67, records that Karamsī was in the service of Rāv Lūṇkaraṇ at this time.

[5] Sevakī village: located twenty-three miles northeast of Jodhpur.

(no. 92) **Pañcāiṇ Karamsīyot** (7-1)
(no. 93) **Mahes Pañcāiṇot** (8-1)

Pañcāiṇ Karamsīyot was an important military servant of Rāv Mālde Gāṅgāvat of Jodhpur (1532-62). Rāv Mālde stationed Pañcāiṇ at the garrison of Nāḍūl[6] after the conquest of southern Mārvāṛ during the early years of his reign, and he apportioned a substantial income from this area to him. Pañcāiṇ was also among Rāv Mālde's Rajpūts who rode from the garrison at Raṛod village[7] to Reyāṃ[8] ca. 1535 to do battle with Meṛtīyio Rāv Vīramde Dūdāvat (no. 105). Following Rāv Mālde's victory there and the occupation of Meṛto, Pañcāiṇ participated in the occupation of Ajmer that same year. He was finally killed at the battle of Samel[9] in 1544, fighting against Meṛtīyo Rāv Vīramde and Sher Shāh Sūr.

Pañcāiṇ's son, Mahes Pañcāiṇot, held the ***paṭo*** of Khīṃvsar village from Rāv Mālde after his father's death and served as one of his military retainers. Sources do not indicate the year he received Khīṃvsar in ***paṭo***, nor do they indicate Mahes's relationship with his paternal cousin, Jagmāl Udaikaraṇot (8-2) (no. 91), who also held Khīṃvsar in ***paṭo*** in this period. Mahes was killed at the battle of Meṛto in 1562, fighting under Rāv Mālde's commander at the Mālgaḍh, Rāṭhoṛ Devīdās Jaitāvat (no. 65), against Meṛtīyo Rāv Jaimal Vīramdevot (no. 107) and the Mughal forces of Akbar under Mīrzā Sharafu'd-Dīn Ḥusayn.

Mahes granted the village of Ḍāṃvrai rī Vāsṇī[10] in ***sāṃsaṇ*** to the Cāraṇ Gāḍaṇ Devo.

"Aitihāsik Bātāṃ," pp. 49, 56, 75; ***Bāṅkīdās***, p. 67; ***Khyāt***, 3:96-97; ***Murārdān***, no. 2, pp. 96-97, 118, 120, 600-602, 621, 636, 641; Ojhā, 4:1:252, 5:1:117-118; ***Vigat***, 1:40, 62, 336, 2:59, 65.

---

[6] Nāḍūl town: located sixty-seven miles south-southeast of Jodhpur in southern Mārvāṛ.

[7] Raṛod village: located forty-four miles northeast of Jodhpur and six miles west of Āsop.

[8] Reyāṃ village: located fifteen miles southeast of Meṛto.

[9] Samel village: located twenty-four miles southwest of Ajmer.

[10] Ḍāṃvrai rī Vāsṇī: located thirty miles northeast of Jodhpur.

Figure 27. Karamsot Rāṭhoṛs

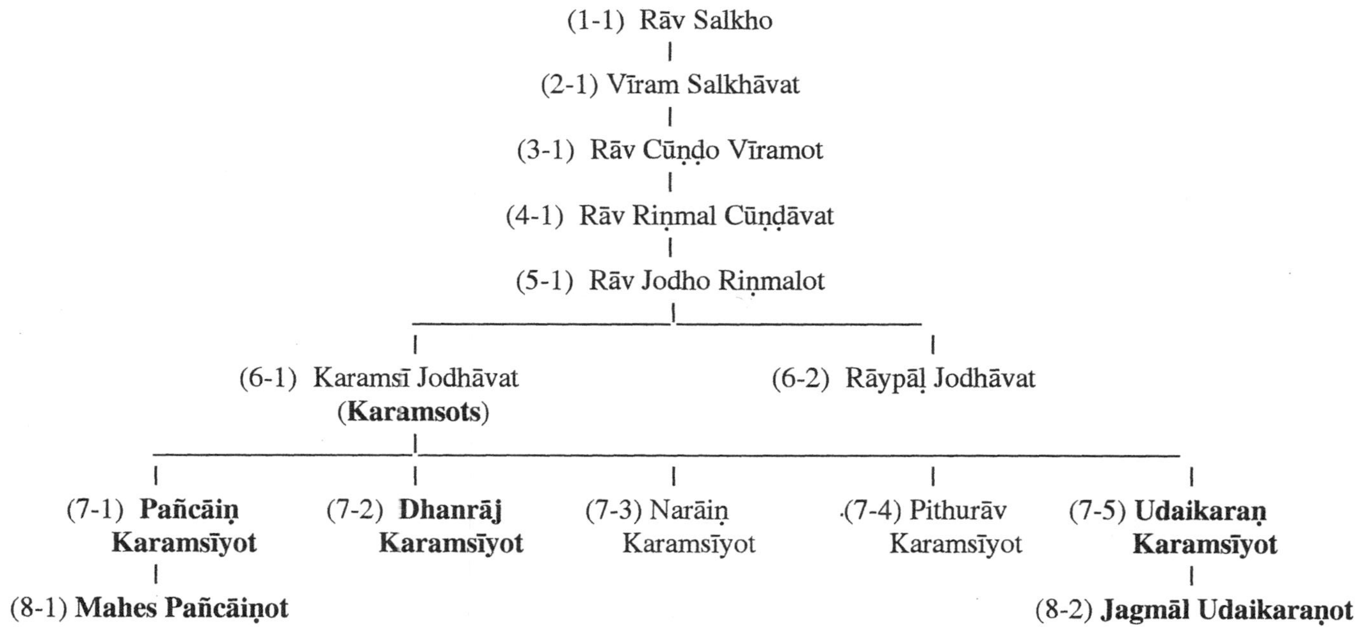
(1-1) Rāv Salkho
(2-1) Vīram Salkhāvat
(3-1) Rāv Cūṇḍo Vīramot
(4-1) Rāv Riṇmal Cūṇḍāvat
(5-1) Rāv Jodho Riṇmalot
(6-1) Karamsī Jodhāvat (**Karamsots**)
(6-2) Rāypāḷ Jodhāvat
(7-1) **Pañcāiṇ Karamsīyot**
(7-2) **Dhanrāj Karamsīyot**
(7-3) Narāiṇ Karamsīyot
(7-4) Pithurāv Karamsīyot
(7-5) **Udaikaraṇ Karamsīyot**
(8-1) **Mahes Pañcāiṇot**
(8-2) **Jagmāl Udaikaraṇot**

Kūmpāvat Rāṭhoṛs

(no. 100) **Kānhāsiṅgh Khīṃvāvat** (10-1)
(no. 95) **Kūmpo Mahirājot** (7-1)
(no. 98) **Mahes Kūmpāvat** (8-3)
(no. 99) **Māṇḍaṇ Kūmpāvat** (8-4)
(no. 96) **Pato Kūmpāvat** (8-1)
(no. 97) **Prithīrāj Kūmpāvat** (8-2)
(no. 101) **Rājsiṅgh Khīṃvāvat** (10-2)

(no. 95) **Kūmpo Mahirājot** (7-1)

The Kūmpāvat Rāṭhoṛs descend from Kūmpo Mahirājot, a son of Mahirāj Akhairājot (6-1) and a grandson of Akhairāj Riṇmalot (5-1). Akhairāj's father, Rāv Riṇmal Cūṇḍāvat (4-1), was ruler of Maṇḍor (ca. 1428-38).

Kūmpo's family was originally associated with the village of Bagṛī[1] in eastern Mārvāṛ. ***Vigat***, 1:38, and Bhāṭī, ***Sarvekṣaṇ***, 3:91, record that Rāv Jodho Riṇmalot (ca. 1453-89) granted Bagṛī to Akhairāj Riṇmalot following the founding of Jodhpur in 1459, but it seems clear from other sources that Akhairāj's association with Bagṛī dates from as early as 1429-30. Akhairāj participated with his father in the consolidation of Rāṭhoṛ authority at Maṇḍor ca. 1428 and in Rāv Riṇmal's extension of rule over areas of eastern Mārvāṛ in 1429-30. Following Rāv Jodho's reassertion of authority at Maṇḍor ca. 1453 and then the founding of Jodhpur in 1459, he confirmed Akhairāj in his possession of Bagṛī village.[2]

Kūmpo's father, Mahirāj Akhairājot, was born in 1458-59, the year before the founding of Jodhpur. His eldest brother, Pañcāiṇ Akhairājot (6-2), had succeeded to Bagṛī village on Akhairāj's death. Mahirāj received the village of Dhaneṛī[3] and twelve others of Sojhat in ***paṭo*** on April 23, 1490 (***Caitrādi***) or April 12, 1491 (***Śrāvaṇādi***). He had a small fort built on a hill near the village and established his residence there. Mahirāj lived another twenty-three years and

---

[1] Bagṛī village: located nine miles east-southeast of Sojhat.

[2] See ***supra***, "Akhairājot Rāṭhoṛs," for more specific information about Akhairāj Riṇmalot.

[3] Dhaneṛī (variously spelled Dhanahṛī/Dhanehṛī) village: located four miles northeast of Sojhat town. Śivnāthsiṃh, ***Kūmpāvat Rāṭhauṛoṃ kā Itihās*** (Gārāsaṇī, Mārbāṛ: Rāṭhoṛ Bhīmsiṃh Kūmpāvat, 1946), p. 115, lists the village as "Ghaneṛī," which is incorrect.

died on January 20, 1514[4] according to an inscription found at Dhaneṛī village commemorating the ***satī*** of one of his wives, Hulṇī Padmā Devī.

Mahirāj died as a result of wounds received while fighting against Mers who had stolen cattle from his village. The circumstances surrounding Mahirāj's death are closely connected with the birth of his son, Kūmpo (see ***infra***). According to ledgers of the Rāṇī Maṅgās and Bholāvat Bhāṭs of Khagriyo village of Bīlāṛo Pargano,[5] Mahirāj had four wives and one son:

1. Jeso Bhāṭiyāṇī Karametībāī (***pīhar*** name), daughter of Jeso Bhāṭī Bhairavdās Jesāvat.[6]

   S - Kūmpo

2. Solaṅkaṇī Dammā Devī, daughter of Solaṅkī Pithal Gokuldāsot.

3. Hulṇī Padmā Devī, daughter of Hul Hemrāj.

4. Bhāṭiyāṇī Harakhā Devī, daughter of Bhāṭī Kanīrām Rājāvat.

A memorial was built for Mahirāj at Dhaneṛī village before the temple of Vaijnāth Mahādev.[7]

Mahirāj's only son, Kūmpo Mahirājot, rose to a position of preeminent power in Mārvāṛ. His rise began during the reign of Rāv Gāṅgo Vāghāvat of Jodhpur (1515-32), whose army commander (***senādhipat***) he became. It reached its zenith under Rāv Gāṅgo's son and successor, Rāv Mālde Gāṅgāvat (1532-62), in the years between 1532 and 1544. Kūmpo was killed at the battle of Samel[8] in January of 1544.[9]

"Aitihāsik Bātāṃ," p. 58, describes Kūmpo Mahirājot as a great patron (***vaḍo dātār***), a great warrior (***vaḍo jhūñjhāṛ***), and a warrior who was adept in battle (***akhāṛsidh rajpūt***). This text also acclaims him as the ***avtār*** of Śrī Vaijnāth Mahādev because of his fine abilities as a leader of men and as a warrior in battle. Under Rāv Mālde of Jodhpur, Kūmpo became the most

---

[4] Bhāṭī, ***Sarvekṣaṇ***, 3:96, incorrectly gives the date of October/November, 1503, and ***Āsop kā Itihās***, p. 17, records the date of October 20, 1503.

[5] Śivnāthsiṃh, ***Kūmpāvat Rāṭhauroṃ kā Itihās***, p. 120.

[6] See ***supra***, "Jeso Bhāṭīs."

[7] Śrī Vaijnāth Mahādev is a manifestation of the Hindu God, Śiva.

[8] Samel village: located twenty-four miles southwest of Ajmer.

[9] ***Vigat***, 1:56, gives Kūmpo's name as "Kūmpo Mahirājot Akhairājot" in its listing of Rajpūts killed at the battle of Samel. The designation of Kūmpo as an "Akhairājot Rāṭhoṛ" is appropriate for the period. A separate ***sākh*** bearing the name "Kūmpāvat" did not emerge until several generations after Kūmpo's death.

powerful and influential of the Rāv's ***ṭhākur***s alongside his paternal cousin, Jaito Pañcāiṇot (no. 61).[10] He was Rāv Mālde's most excellent protector (***sirāī caukī***), and in deference to him, a cotton-stuffed gown (***labāyco***) of Jaito Pañcāiṇot's was provided for him to wear during the cold season. Unlike his paternal cousin, Jaito, who appears from local texts to have been a man often torn between his duty to Rāv Mālde and his concern for the values of brotherhood among the Rāṭhoṛs, Kūmpo emerges as a single-minded military commander and warrior who set the example for bravery and cunning in battle, and for lavish display, with which other prominent ***ṭhākur***s of Rāv Mālde's often vied.

The sources give different dates for Kūmpo's birth. These include November 9, November 11, and December 26, 1502.[11] According to Kūmpāvat traditions, his birth occurred under the following circumstances. His father, Mahirāj, was without sons and is said to have received a boon from Vaijnāth Mahādev in return for his devotions and offerings before Mahādev's temple at his village of Dhaneṛī. The God was pleased and manifested himself, impregnating water from a nearby well which was then given to Mahirāj's wife, Jeso Bhāṭiyāṇī Karametībāī, to drink. She bore a son named Kūmpo, who was said to be the ***avtār*** of Mahādev. Kūmpāvat traditions related in Śivnāthsiṃh, ***Kūmpāvat Rāṭhauṛoṃ kā Itihās***, pp. 115-118, state that a condition of this birth was that Mahirāj not look at his son. It he did, he would bring his own death. Karametībāī and Kūmpo were therefore sent to a nearby village to live, and is it there that Kūmpo was raised.

A number of years following Kūmpo's birth, Mers rustled cattle from Mahirāj's village. Mahirāj set out in pursuit and drew near them at the village of Sāraṇ.[12] Kūmpo, who was a now a growing boy of some twelve years, is said to have learned of this raid and to have ridden after the Mers with a ***sāth*** from his village. Both he and his father met and defeated the Mers before Sāraṇ. Afterwards Mahirāj happened to come before his son. He did not recognize him, but someone then told him who the boy was and reminded him of the circumstances surrounding his birth. Knowing that his death was imminent, Mahirāj called Kūmpo to him and introduced himself, commending Kūmpo for his actions that day. Mahirāj then rode off with his men. Mers who had not been killed in the battle had regrouped, and they now surrounded Mahirāj, attacking and killing him.

Śivnāthsiṃh, ***Kūmpāvat Rāṭhauṛoṃ kā Itihās***, p. 120, states that following Mahirāj's death, Kūmpo's mother, Karametībāī, took Kūmpo to her

---

[10] Jaito Pañcāiṇot and Kūmpo Mahirājot were brothers' sons. Their fathers, Pañcāiṇ Akhairājot and Mahirāj Akhairājot, were both sons of Akhairāj Riṇmalot. See ***supra***, "Jaitāvat Rāṭhoṛs," for more information about Jaito Pañcāiṇot.

[11] See: ***Bāṅkīdās***, p. 53; Śivnāthsiṃh, ***Kūmpāvat Rāṭhauṛoṃ kā Ītihās***, p. 117; ***Āsop kā Itihās***, p. 19.

[12] Bhāṭī, ***Sarvekṣaṇ***, 3:96; Sāraṇ village is located eighteen miles southeast of Sojhat. Śivnāthsiṃh, ***Kūmpāvat Rāṭhauṛoṃ kā Ītihās***, p. 119, lists the village as Sīriyārī, located 10 miles north of Sojhat.

pīhar at the village of Tāraṇ, where he was raised by his mother's brother (***māmo***), Acaḷdās. This information appears to be incorrect. ***Vigat*** lists no village by the name of Tāraṇ for any of the ***pargano***s of Mārvāṛ. Jeso Bhāṭiyāṇī Karametībāī's ***pīhar*** village was Dhauḷharo village[13] of Sojhat, but Karametībāī's brother, Jeso Bhāṭī Acḷo Bhairavdāsot, was a prominent ***cākar*** of the Rāṇo of Cītoṛ (probably Rāṇo Rāymal Kūmbhāvat, ca. 1473-1509, or his son, Rāṇo Sāṅgo Rāymalot, 1509-28), from whom he held the village of Tāṇo[14] and 140 other in ***paṭo***. Acḷo also held the village of Copṛo[15] of Sojhat, where he kept his ***vasī***. It is perhaps this Tāṇo village which is meant, in which case, Karametībāī took Kūmpo not to her ***pīhar***, but to her brother, asking him to assume responsibility for raising Kūmpo.

When Kūmpo came of age, he proceeded to Meṛto, where he entered the household of Meṛtīyo Rāv Vīramde Dūdāvat (no. 105). Rāv Vīramde granted him the village of Mugadṛo[16] for his maintenance. Little information is available about Kūmpo's activities while he was a military servant at Meṛto. There is record only of his participation in an attack against the Sonagaro Cahuvāṇs of Pālī village,[17] who were military servants of Jodhpur. The texts give no reasons for this attack. They are also unclear about subsequent events which led to Kūmpo's departure from Meṛto.

Āsop kā Itihās, p. 20, states simply that Kūmpo fell out with Rāv Vīramde and left Meṛto for Sojhat, while "Aitihāsik Bātāṃ," p. 58, records that following the raid against the Sonagaros, Kūmpo said to Rāv Vīramde that he wished to avenge the death of his father, Mahirāj, "bare-headed" (***ughāṛai māthai***), that is, with the single-minded devotion with which one comes before a god or goddess. It then notes, cryptically, that a particular garrison (***thāṇo vises***), location undefined, became Kūmpo's, and that afterwards he left Rāv Vīramde of Meṛto for Sojhat, where he took service under Jodho Rāṭhoṛ Rāv Vīramde Vāghāvat (no. 84) in 1515-16. Śivnāthsiṃh, ***Kūmpāvat Rāṭhauṛoṃ kā Itihās***, p. 122, adds that when Kūmpo arrived at Sojhat, he entered into the Rāv's household. The Rāv granted him the village of Dhaneṛī which his father had held before him in return. Rāv Vīramde is also said to have made him the commander of his army (***senādhyakś***).

---

[13] ***Khyāt***, 2:178. Dhauḷharo village is located eighteen miles west-northwest of Sojhat town.

[14] Tāṇo village: located in northern Mevāṛ near Toḍgaṛh some sixty-four miles to the northwest of Cītoṛ. Jeso Bhāṭī Acḷo's father, Bhairavdās Jesāvat, and grandfather, Jeso Kalikaraṇot, had held this ***paṭo*** from the Rāṇo before Acḷo. See ***supra***, "Jeso Bhāṭīs," for details.

[15] Copṛo village: located eighteen miles northwest of Sojhat.

[16] Mugadṛo village: located fourteen miles south-southwest of Meṛto.

[17] Pālī village: located seventy-two miles southwest of Meṛto.

Rāv Vīramde Vāghāvat was an elder half-brother of Rāv Gāṅgo Vāghāvat of Jodhpur (1515-32). Kūmpo quickly became involved in the struggles between Rāv Vīramde of Sojhat and Rāv Gāṅgo of Jodhpur over the division of land and authority in Mārvāṛ. This conflict emerged following Rāv Sūjo Jodhāvat's death in 1515. His grandson, Vīramde Vāghāvat, had succeeded him to the Jodhpur throne, only to be deposed by a faction of Mārvāṛ Rāṭhoṛs who favored Vīramde's younger half-brother, Gāṅgo Vāghāvat. Once in power, Rāv Gāṅgo granted Vīramde the title of ***rāv*** and the lands of Sojhat as his share of Mārvāṛ.[18] Rāv Vīramde never accepted this division, and during much of Rāv Gāṅgo's rule, he sought to recover his lost prestige and power. Rāv Vīramde relied much on the support and leadership of his ***pradhān***, Muṃhato Rāymal Khetāvat (no. 159), during these years. Alongside Muṃhato Rāymal, Kūmpo was Rāv Vīramde's foremost warrior, and he led many successful attacks against the villages and garrisons of Jodhpur.

Unable to gain an upper hand against Sojhat, Rāv Gāṅgo ordered his leading warrior, Jaito Pañcāiṇot, to bring Kūmpo to Jodhpur. Jaito was Kūmpo's paternal cousin, and he lured Kūmpo with an offer of a ***paṭo*** worth a ***lakh***, to be selected from among Jodhpur's finest villages. He also had the Rāv send a writing to Kūmpo, stating that Rāv Vīramde had no sons and that after his death, the lands of Sojhat would pass to Jodhpur. The import of these words was that the conflict between Sojhat and Jodhpur was of no consequence and that Kūmpo should side with Rāv Gāṅgo. Kūmpo saw the correctness of this argument. He sent word that he would come to Jodhpur if Rāv Gāṅgo would agree not to attack Sojhat for one year. The Rāv readily accepted this condition, and ca. 1529 Kūmpo took his leave of Rāv Vīramde Vāghāvat and Muṃhato Rāymal.

All of the Riṇmalots[19] in Rāv Vīramde's service left Sojhat with Kūmpo, greatly reducing Muṃhato Rāymal's forces. Kūmpo became the commander of Rāv Gāṅgo's army (***senādhipat***) at Jodhpur. The ***Khyāt*** of Naiṇsī, 3:84, records that he organized a council of war and proceeded to lead many attacks against Sojhat, taking many of its villages for Jodhpur. He also:

> brought [horses] to Dhauḷharo [village near Sojhat][20] and established a stable. [He] stationed four thousand of Rāv Gāṅgo's household warriors (***cīndhaṛ***)[21] at [this] outpost . . .

---

[18] Śivnāthsiṃh, ***Kūmpāvat Rāṭhauṛoṃ kā Itihās***, p. 122, states that it was upon Kūmpo Mahirājot's counsel that Vīramde was given Sojhat as his share. This information is not corroborated in contemporary sources and is, perhaps, a later addition to the lore about Kūmpo.

[19] Riṇmalots: descendants of Rāv Riṇmal Cūṇḍāvat, ruler of Maṇḍor (ca. 1428-1438).

[20] Dhauḷharo (or Dhavaḷairo) village: located eighteen miles west-northwest of Sojhat.

[21] ***Cīndhaṛ***: this term also refers to men who were hired soldiers working for short periods of time and who sometimes held small land grants. See: Lāḷas, ***RSK***, 2:1:920-921.

> [and he] stationed [four of the Rāv's] nobles (***umrāv***) with [these men] and the horses.[22]

Rāv Gāṅgo and his warriors were eventually able to defeat Muṃhato Rāymal in battle before Sojhat in early 1532. ***Murārdān***, no. 2, p, 110, credits Kūmpo himself with killing Muṃhato Rāymal. Rāv Gāṅgo then assumed full authority over these lands, and he banished his elder half-brother, Vīramde, first to Khairvo village[23] and then from Mārvāṛ altogether. Kūmpo made a number of attacks against the Mers of Sojhat during this same period, looting and burning their villages and killing many of their men in revenge for the death of his father.

With the succession of Rāv Mālde Gāṅgāvat to the throne of Jodhpur in 1532, Kūmpo quickly rose to a preeminent position of power alongside his paternal cousin, Jaito Pañcāiṇot. It was to Kūmpo and to Jaito that Rāv Mālde entrusted the leadership of his armies and the administration of his kingdom. Both of these Rajpūts were also his closest advisors.

Kūmpo became involved in Rāv Mālde's desire to conquer lands under the control of other Rāṭhoṛ brotherhoods and surrounding territories under the rule of other Rajpūts very early in the Rāv's reign. "Aitihāsik Bātāṃ" records that Kūmpo's paternal cousin, Jaito, spoke out strongly against the killing of brothers (***gotrakadamb*** - lit. "***gotra***-destruction") to Rāv Mālde on one occasion in his ***darbār***, saying:

> The offense of killing one's family members/brothers will not be committed by me (***ibid***., p. 57).

Seeing the Rāv become downhearted because of his objections, Jaito quickly attempted to soothe his feeling, however. And he said:

> "Do not be downhearted. We will perform the tasks you tell [us to do]" . . . Then Jaitojī summoned Kūmpo Mahirājot and had the Rāvjī grasp [his] arm. [And he] said to the Rāvjī, "***Rāj***, [you] should uphold Kūmpo's honor and prestige." And to Kūmpo, [he] said, "You should perform [whatever] tasks the Rāv tells [you to do]" (***ibid***., pp. 57-58).

---

[22] The establishment of this stable manned with household warriors was an important military innovation at this time in Mārvāṛ. For further discussion of its significance, see: Norman P. Ziegler, "Evolution of the Rathor State of Marvar: Horses, Structural Change and Warfare," in ***The Idea of Rajasthan: Explorations in Regional Identity***, edited by Karine Schomer et al (Columbia, Mo.: South Asia Publications by arrangement with Manohar Publishers & Distributors; New Delhi: American Institute of Indian Studies, 1994), pp. 193-201.

[23] Khairvo village: located fifty miles south-southeast of Jodhpur and twenty-one miles southwest of Sojhat.

Rāv Mālde proceeded to plot against other Rāṭhoṛ brotherhoods despite Jaito's objections, especially against the Meṛtīyos, for whom he had held great enmity since he was a ***kuṃvar***. ***Vigat***, 2:48, 51, notes that Kūmpo, Jaito and other of the Rāv's Rajpūts would not involve themselves in these plots. Following one unsuccessful intrigue against Meṛtīyo Rāv Vīramde, planned when Rāv Vīramde was summoned to Jodhpur to participate in an expedition against the Sīndhaḷs of Bhādrājuṇ,[24] Rāv Mālde "was disgraced in Jaito and Kūmpo's presence."

Kūmpo took part in his first major battle against the Meṛtīyos ca. 1535. Meṛtīyo Rāv Vīramde had occupied Ajmer this year, and when he refused to hand this city over to Rāv Mālde upon demand, the Rāv sent his Rajpūts to occupy Meṛto. He then began dividing Meṛto's villages among his military servants. Rāv Mālde gave Reyāṃ village[25] to Varsiṅghot Meṛtīyo Sahaiso Tejsīyot (no. 151), a former military servant of Meṛtīyo Rāv Vīramde. Sahaiso's actions in taking service under Rāv Mālde and accepting one of Meṛto's villages from him so enraged Rāv Vīramde that he unwisely mounted an attack on Sahaiso at Reyāṃ against the better judgement of his own Rajpūts.

Word of Rāv Vīramde's advance on Reyāṃ reached the garrison at Raṛod village,[26] where Kūmpo was stationed along with Jaito Pañcāiṇot, Rāṇo Akhairājot (no. 28), and other of Rāv Mālde's ***ṭhākur***s. These Rajpūts rode to Reyāṃ and took part in the bloody fighting there, during which Rāv Vīramde and his warriors were badly defeated. ***Vigat***, 2:53, states that Kūmpo and Bhado Pañcāiṇot (no. 32) had ***saidāno***s played in celebration of the auspicious occasion, but that Kūmpo was among those Rajpūts who prevented Rāv Vīramde from being killed and allowed him to leave Mārvāṛ. Texts indicate, however, that Kūmpo took this position only at Jaito Pañcāiṇot's urging.

Bāṅkīdās, p. 12, records that on another occasion, Jaito specifically stopped Kūmpo from harming Rāv Vīramde, remarking:

> Vīramde should not be killed; Vīramde is a great Rajpūt. If he remains alive, he will bring someone [to aid him against Rāv Mālde] and [thereby] shape his own death.

Rāv Mālde sent his warriors under the command of Kūmpo and Jaito against Nāgaur in January of 1536. They conquered this land from the Khānzāda Khāns,[27] and in return for the victory, Rāv Mālde awarded Nāgaur to Kūmpo in ***paṭo***. Shortly thereafter, ca. 1537, Kūmpo was stationed at the garrison village

---

[24] Bhādrājuṇ village: located forty-eight miles south-southwest of Jodhpur.

[25] Reyāṃ village: located fifteen miles southeast of Meṛto.

[26] Raṛod village: located forty-nine miles west-northwest of Reyāṃ.

[27] See ***infra***, "Khānzāda Khāns."

of Madārīyo[28] in Goḍhvāṛ, which he also held in ***paṭo*** from the Rāv. While there, Kūmpo received a summons for aid from Sīsodīyo Udaisiṅgh Sāṅgāvat (Rāṇo of Mevāṛ, ca. 1537-72). Sīsodīyo Udaisiṅgh's elder uterine brother, Rāṇo Vikramaditya Sāṅgāvat (ca. 1531-36), had been murdered at Cītoṛ earlier that year by a pretender to the throne, Sīsodīyo Vaṇvīr Prithīrājot. Udaisiṅgh had fled Cītoṛ for Kumbhaḷmer in western Mevāṛ in the wake of this murder, but Vaṇvīr's forces had pursued him and besieged him there. Kūmpo was in communication with Cāmpāvat Jeso Bhairavdāsot (no. 48), who had taken service under Udaisiṅgh in this period, and with Sonagaro Cahuvāṇ Akhairāj Riṇdhīrot (no. 9) regarding the situation in Mevāṛ, and he rode to Kumbhaḷmer along with these ***ṭhākur***s in response to Udaisiṅgh's appeal. They succeeded in defeating Vaṇvīr's forces and either killing or driving Vaṇvīr from Mevāṛ. They then participated in Udaisiṅgh's succession to the throne of Mevāṛ at Kumbhaḷmer fortress, in which Udaisiṅgh's wife's father, Sonagaro Akhairāj, played a leading role.[29]

Rāv Mālde ordered Kūmpo to ride in pursuit of Meṛtīyo Rāv Vīramde during this same period. Rāv Vīramde had fled Meṛto and Ajmer for Ḍīḍvāṇo and then for the home of his ***sago***s, the Sekhāvat Kachvāhos of Sikargaḍh and Amarsar in central Rājasthān. Kūmpo proceeded first against Ḍīḍvāṇo, which he brought under the Rāv's authority, then moved on to Fatehpur, Jhūñjhaṇūṃ, Revās, Cāṭsū, Lālsoṭ and Malārṇo in central Rājasthān, all of which he incorporated within Rāv Mālde's expanding domain.[30]

Then in late 1541 Rāv Mālde placed Kūmpo in command of the army he sent against the Bīkāvat Rāṭhoṛs of Bīkāner. Once again, Kūmpo emerged victorious, defeating and killing Rāv Jaitsi Lūṇkaraṇot (1526-42) in battle before the village of Sohavo (near Bīkāner) on February 26, 1542. Rāv Mālde awarded Kūmpo with the additional grants of Fatehpur and Jhūñjhaṇūṃ when he learned of Kūmpo's victory. These were given as an increase (***vadhāro***) on the news of conquest. Later, when Rāv Mālde entered the occupied city of Bīkāner, he granted Bīkāner itself to Kūmpo in ***paṭo***, and soon after the additional ***paṭo***s of

---

[28] Madārīyo village: located thirteen miles south-southwest of Nāḍūl and thirteen miles west northwest of Kumbhaḷmer.

[29] Śivnāthsiṃh, ***Kūmpāvat Rāṭhauroṃ kā Itihās***, pp. 131-132, 150, states that Kūmpo had also married a daughter to Sīsodīyo Udaisiṅgh and that Kūmpo's position as Udaisiṅgh's wife's father was a strong incentive for his providing support to Udaisiṅgh at this time. This marriage is not confirmed in seventeenth century sources such as Naiṇsī's ***Khyāt***, which mentions only Sonagaro Akhairāj Riṇdhīrot's marriage of a daughter to Udaisiṅgh prior to Udaisiṅgh's succession. Kūmpo's marriage of a daughter to Udaisiṅgh appears to be another later addition to the lore about this prominent Rajpūt.

[30] Rāv Mālde did not send Kūmpo against the Sekhāvat Kachvāhos. The reasons behind his sparing of the Sekhāvats are unclear. It is possible the Rāv avoided such a confrontation because the Sekhāvats were ***sago***s. See ***supra***, Sekhāvat Kachvāho Rāymal Sekhāvat (no. 22), for details about the Sekhāvat marriages with the house of Jodhpur and with the Meṛtīyos in this period.

Sāmbhar and Ḍīḍvāṇo. By the end of 1542, Kūmpo controlled a vast territory in central and northern Rājasthān in his capacity as commander of Rāv Mālde's armies of Jodhpur.

Kūmpo's dramatic rise to power and authority in Mārvāṛ came to an abrupt end at the battle of Samel in January of 1544. Here again, Kūmpo was the leader of Rāv Mālde's forces along with his cousin, Jaito Pañcāiṇot. Kūmpo had been at Bīkāner at the time Sher Shāh began his march toward Mārvāṛ, but he had quickly vacated the fort there and returned to Mārvāṛ. Together he and Jaito assumed roles as both army commanders and protectors of the lands of Mārvāṛ. Sources are in conflict about the circumstances that brought the rupture between Rāv Mālde and his Rajpūts and caused the Rāv to retreat precipitously from his camp at Girrī[31] on the day before the main engagement. It seems certain, however, that Meṛtīyo Rāv Vīramde was able to instill suspicions within Rāv Mālde about the loyalty of his warriors. Kūmpo and Jaito spent much time in negotiations with the Rāv through intermediaries. They could come to no agreement, however, and in the end, they refused to obey his command to retreat in the face of Sher Shāh's army. They refused to leave the lands of their ancestors open to an invader.

Kūmpo and Jaito both realized after Rāv Mālde's departure with a large force of Rajpūts, that they could not defeat the Muslim army in open battle on the plain. They then decided on a surprise night attack. But this action failed because they could not located the Muslim camp in the dark. When the battle closed the following morning, "Aitihāsik Bātāṃ," p. 42, speaks of Kūmpo and Jaito dismounting from their horses in the safety of a river bank and eating opium with the water of the river, then riding off to fight against the Muslims. They were able to defeat an advance guard of Sher Shāh's, but soon after were both killed (see "Aitihāsik Bātāṃ," pp. 42-44, ***Khyāt***, 3:98-101, and ***Vigat***, 2:56-57, of the **translated text** for full details of this battle).

The ***Khyāt*** of Naiṇsī, 2:192, records that prior to this battle, Kūmpo sent one of his personal military servants, Jeso Bhāṭī Gāṅgo Varjāṅgot, as his ***pradhān*** to negotiate with Sher Shāh. Sher Shāh imprisoned Jeso Bhāṭī Gāṅgo for some days. Gāṅgo then either managed to escape or was released, for he joined the Rāṭhoṛs in the fighting at Samel and was also killed there. Gāṅgo was Kūmpo's ***māvḷiyāī bhāī***, his mother's family brother.[32]

Kūmpo was forty-two years old at the time of his death at Samel.[33] He is said to have had twelve wives, elevens sons and three daughters.[34] The most

---

[31] Girrī village: located ten miles west-southwest of Samel.

[32] See ***infra***, **Rājasthānī Kinship Terminology**, for a more complete definition of this term. Gāṅgo was a son of Jeso Bhāṭī Varjāṅg Bhairavdāsot, whose father, Bhairavdās Jesāvat, was the father of Kūmpo's mother, Bhāṭiyāṇī Karametībāī. Gāṅgo was then Kūmpo's mother's brother's son.

[33] "Aitihāsik Bātāṃ," p. 58, incorrectly states that Kūmpo was 35 years old when he was killed at Samel.

important of his sons were Prithīrāj (8-2) (no. 97), Mahes (8-3) (no. 98), and Māṇḍaṇ (8-4) (no. 99), all born of his Bhāṭiyāṇī wife, the daughter of Bhāṭī Rāypāḷ Jaitsīyot.

"Aitihāsik Bātāṃ," pp. 40-44, 54, 57-59, 74-75; ***Āsop kā Itihās***, pp. 16-44; ***Bāṅkīdās***, pp. 12-13, 53; Bhāṭī, ***Sarvekṣaṇ***, 3:96; ***Khyāt***, 1:20-21, 207, 212, 2:152-153, 178, 181, 192, 3:81, 83-84, 95, 99-100; Śivnāthsiṃh, ***Kūmpāvat Rāṭhauṛoṃ kā Itihās***, pp. 115-150; ***Murārdān***, no. 2, pp. 110, 115-121, 429, 449-450, 453; ***Vigat***, 1:43-44, 56, 65, 2:48-49, 51-54, 57.

(no. 96) **Pato (Pratāpsiṅgh) Kūmpāvat** (8-1)

Little is known from the texts about Kūmpo Mahirājot's (7-1) son, Pato Kūmpāvat. Sources under review mention him only twice: at Rāv Mālde's camp at Girrī prior to the battle of Samel in January of 1544, and at the battle of Meṛto in 1562, when he was killed.[35]

Pato appears to have been a personal retainer of Rāv Mālde's during the period before Samel, holding the village of Siṇlo[36] in ***paṭo***. "Aitihāsik Bātāṃ," p. 42, records his being present at Rāv Mālde's camp at Girrī, sleeping on the ground near the Rāv's bed. He was in the company of Rāṭhoṛ Udaisiṅgh Jaitāvat (no. 62), Jaito Pañcāiṇot's (no. 61) son. Both Pato and Udaisiṅgh served as personal bodyguards for the Rāv.

Pato apparently withdrew from Girrī with Rāv Mālde before the main battle at Samel. Local texts do not mention that he took part in the fighting there. Texts next mention him as one of the Rajpūts stationed with Rāṭhoṛ Devīdās Jaitāvat (no. 65) at the Mālgaḍh at Meṛto in 1562. He died there alongside Devīdās Jaitāvat, fighting against Meṛtīyo Rāv Jaimal Vīramdevot (no. 107) and the Mughal forces of Akbar under Mīrzā Sharafu'd-Dīn Ḥusayn.

"Aitihāsik Bātāṃ," pp. 42, 55; ***Āsop kā Itihās***, p. 44; ***Bāṅkīdās***, pp. 15-16; Śivnāthsiṃh, ***Kūmpāvat Rāṭhauṛoṃ kā Itihās***, p. 151; ***Vigat***, 1:62, 2:65.

---

[34] See: Śivnāthsiṃh, ***Kūmpāvat Rāṭhauṛoṃ kā Itihās***, pp. 148-150, for a complete listing.

[35] ***Āsop kā Itihās***, p. 44, incorrectly lists Pato as having been killed at the battle of Samel.

[36] Śivnāthsiṃh, ***Kūmpāvat Rāṭhauṛoṃ kā Itihās***, p. 151, lists the name of this village as "Saṇlā." ***Vigat*** has no listing for a village by this name. Siṇlo is probably meant. The exact location of Siṇlo is obscure. It is not evident on modern maps, but it was an important village in 17th century Mārvāṛ. ***Vigat***, 1:463, states that is was located just near the village of Jogrāvās, which lay fourteen miles west of Sojhat town.

(no. 97) **Prithīrāj Kūmpāvat** (8-2)
(no. 98) **Mahes Kūmpāvat** (8-3)

These two sons of Kūmpo Mahirājot (7-1) (no. 95) rose to be important ***ṭhākur***s in Mārvāṛ. They had careers as military servants that followed different paths but were also much intertwined.

Prithīrāj was Kūmpo's eldest son, born in 1522-23. He succeeded to the village of Dhaneṛī[37] following Kūmpo's death. He was a prominent ***ṭhākur*** during the latter part of Rāv Mālde Gāṅgāvat's rule at Jodhpur (1532-62) and in the early years of Rāv Candrasen Māldevot's reign (1562-81). He then left Mārvāṛ in 1565-66 and took service under the Mughals. He remained in Mughal service thereafter until his death in 1574-75.

Prithīrāj's name first appears in the texts in a list of ***ṭhākur***s whom Rāv Mālde sent against Meṛtīyo Rāv Jaimal Vīramdevot (no. 107) at Meṛto in 1554. Prithīrāj fought there under the command of Rāṭhoṛ Prithīrāj Jaitāvat (no. 63) during Rāv Mālde's abortive attempt to usurp control of this land from the Meṛtīyos.

Later in January of 1557, Prithīrāj was among the select warriors of Rāv Mālde's whom Rāṭhoṛ Devīdās Jaitāvat (no. 65) took under his command to join with Paṭhāṇ Hājī Khān at the battle of Harmāṛo.[38] They defeated an allied force of Rajpūts there under Sīsodīyo Rāṇo Udaisiṅgh Sāṅgāvat of Mevāṛ (ca. 1537-72; no. 17).

Prithīrāj's brother, Mahes Kūmpāvat, appears in the texts for the first time at the battle of Harmāṛo. He fought on the opposing side in this engagement. "Aitihāsik Bātāṃ," p. 51, records that Mahes was a military servant of Sīsodīyo Rāṇo Udaisiṅgh and states:

> Mahes had little wealth. [He] had one village of Mevāṛ, Nīpraṛ,[39] [in] *paṭo*. [At] that battle [of Harmāṛo], Mahesjī seized an elephant of the Rāṇo's [and] protected it. [He] brought [it to the Rāṇo], because of which Mahes gained esteem. Afterwards, the Rāṇojī gave Mahesjī [the village of] Bālī[40] [along] with seventeen [other] villages.

Mahes remained in Mevāṛ for several years thereafter while Prithīrāj continued to serve under Rāv Mālde of Jodhpur. Prithīrāj was included among the Rajpūts whom Rāv Mālde sent with his son, Kuṃvar Candrasen Māldevot, to reinforce Rāṭhoṛ Devīdās Jaitāvat at the Mālgaḍh at Meṛto in 1562. Meṛto had

---

[37] Dhaneṛī village: located four miles northeast of Sojhat town.

[38] Harmāṛo village: located fifty-five miles south-southwest of Ajmer and six miles south of Vadhnor in northern Mevāṛ.

[39] Nīpraṛ village: the location of this village is uncertain.

[40] Bālī village: located sixteen miles south-southwest of Nāḍūl in Goḍhvāṛ.

come under siege from the forces of Meṛtīyo Rāv Jaimal Vīramdevot and Mīrzā Sharafu'd-Dīn Ḥusayn. Kuṃvar Candrasen found the situation at Meṛto untenable and withdrew along with a large number of Rāv Mālde's Rajpūts stationed at the Mālgaḍh. Prithīrāj left with the Kuṃvar, but one of his brothers, Pato Kūmpāvat (8-1) (no. 96), elected to remain behind with Devīdās Jaitāvat. Both Pato and Devīdās were later killed in battle on the plain near Meṛto.

Prithīrāj emerged as one of the leading ***ṭhākur*s** of Mārvāṛ following Rāv Mālde's death in November of 1562 and Kuṃvar Candrasen Māldevot's succession in December of this year. He quickly joined a faction of Riṇmalots who initiated a series of intrigues to unseat Rāv Candrasen and place one of his brothers on the throne at Jodhpur. Prithīrāj's brother, Mahes, appears to have returned to Mārvāṛ at this time, for he was also involved in the conspiracies that surrounded the throne.

"Aitihāsik Bātāṃ," p. 78, reports that these intrigues arose shortly after Rāv Candrasen's accession and were due to the Rāv's alienation of a number of his ***ṭhākur*s**. The text relates that one day Rāv Candrasen became angry with one of his stablehands. This servant fled and sought refuge in the camp of Cāmpāvat Rāṭhoṛ Jaitmāl Jesāvat (no. 49). The Rāv sent several of his Rajpūts to Jaitmāl Jesāvat's camp upon learning that the stablehand was there, and these Rajpūts seized and killed the servant. Jaitmāl Jesāvat later came before Prithīrāj and Mahes Kūmpāvat wept about this incident. Prithīrāj tried to calm Jaitmāl and told him not to weep, saying:

> [If] Parameśvar bestows [his blessing upon me], then I, [born] of Kūmpo's stomach, would cause [Rāv] Candrasen to weep [and to regret this act]. You should not be distressed for any reason.

The Riṇmalots then encouraged Rāv Mālde's banished son, Rām Māldevot, to make inroads into Mārvāṛ from his base in Mevāṛ, and they were in communication with Rāv Candrasen's elder uterine brother, Udaisiṅgh Māldevot (Rāv of Jodhpur, 1583-95), at Phaḷodhī in northern Mārvāṛ, which Udaisiṅgh had received as his share of lands of Mārvāṛ upon Rāv Mālde's death. They also encouraged another of Rāv Candrasen's half-brothers, Rāymal Māldevot, to come north from Sīvāṇo and begin raiding Jodhpur lands.

Rāv Candrasen was able to drive both Rām Māldevot and Rāymal Māldevot from Mārvāṛ, and he defeated his brother, Udaisiṅgh, in battle at Lohīyāvaṭ[41] ca. 1563. Prithīrāj Kūmpāvat and another of his brothers, Tiloksī Kūmpāvat (8-5), were among Rāv Candrasen's ***ṭhākur*s** at Lohīyāvaṭ, but given their enmity toward the Rāv, it is not known what role they played in the actual fighting.

Following Udaisiṅgh's defeat at Lohīyāvaṭ, the Riṇmalots realized that they had accomplished nothing through these intrigues. Prithīrāj Kūmpāvat and Jaitāvat Rāṭhoṛ Āskaraṇ Devīdāsot, a son of Devīdās Jaitāvat with whom Mahes Kūmpāvat was later closely involved, then sent a large sum of money to Rām Māldevot for expenses and urged him to seek Mughal support for his cause.

---

[41] Lohīyāvaṭ village: located eighteen miles southeast of Phaḷodhī.

Rām Māldevot soon appeared in Mārvāṛ with an army of Mughals. Prithīrāj and Āskaraṇ served as mediators in the negotiations between Rāv Candrasen and his half-brother, Rām Māldevot. They were influential in having Rāv Candrasen agree to grant Sojhat to Rām as his share of Mārvāṛ. Rām in turn received Sojhat in ***jāgīr*** from Emperor Akbar along with the title of ***rāv***.

Mahes Kūmpāvat apparently took service under Rāv Rām Māldevot at Sojhat following this award, while his brother, Prithīrāj, left Mārvāṛ to offer his service to Akbar. By 1572 Prithīrāj had assumed a position of some influence at Akbar's court as a son of Rāṭhoṛ Kūmpo Mahirājot, whose name and renown were well-known to the Emperor.

Prithīrāj and Mahes again came into contact in 1572 during events that followed Rāṭhoṛ Rāv Rām Māldevot's death this year. A dispute arose between Rāv Rām's two sons, Karaṇ and Kalo, over succession to rule at Sojhat. Mahes Kūmpāvat and Āskaraṇ Devīdāsot became involved in this disputed succession as arbiters. According to ***Murārdān***, no. 2, p. 591, Rāv Rām's eldest son, Karaṇ, initially succeeded his father. Karaṇ then showed favor for a Rajpūt named Sūrajmal Prithīrājot,[42] which angered both Mahes Kūmpāvat and Āskaraṇ Devīdāsot. They then withheld their support from Karaṇ and met with Karaṇ's younger brother, Kalo, offering their support to him. Within a short time, they proceeded with Kalo to Emperor Akbar's court to petition the Emperor on Kalo's behalf.

Mahes sought out his brother, Prithīrāj, once at court. Prithīrāj agreed to present Kalo's petition to Akbar on the condition that Mahes speak with Kalo and arrange to have the village of Khairvo[43] given to him for his ***vasī***. "Aitihāsik Bātāṃ," p. 82, records that when Prithīrāj presented Kalo's petition, Akbar asked him for a full accounting of the situation in Mārvāṛ, but that

> [Prithīrāj] invented a story, saying that the Rajpūts [who are] the pillars of Mārvāṛ are [on] Kalo's side. Afterwards, the Emperor [who] had recognized the names of [Mahes's and Āskaraṇ's] fathers and grandfathers (***māitrāṃ*** - lit. "mothers and fathers"), also summoned [Mahes and Āskaraṇ] and questioned [them about the succession at Sojhat].

According to ***Murārdān***, no. 1, p. 592, Akbar asked Mahes:

> "Who is the eldest?" The ***ṭhākur*** [Mahes] said, "The eldest is Karaṇ. But we are Kalo's military servants."

The Emperor spoke with other Rāṭhoṛs including Sūrajmal Prithīrājot, who presented Karaṇ's petition. But he judged in favor of Rāv Rām's younger son,

---

[42] The identity of this Rajpūt remains obscure.

[43] Khairvo village: located twenty-one miles southwest of Sojhat and included administratively within Sojhat Pargano at this time.

Kalo, and awarded Sojhat to him in ***jāgīr*** along with the title of ***rāv***. Akbar afterwards retained Karaṇ Rāmot and Sūrajmal Prithīrājot in his own service.

Akbar gave Rāv Kalo and his party leave to return to Mārvāṛ. Mahes avoided meeting his brother, Prithīrāj, as they departed, and upon arrival in Sojhat, had Rāv Kalo grant the village of Khairvo to him for his own ***vasī***. Prithīrāj learned of this duplicity and complained before Akbar, saying that Khairvo belonged with Jodhpur, not Sojhat. The Emperor then had Khairvo and its surrounding villages included administratively with Jodhpur Pargano. Khairvo remained attached to Jodhpur from this time forward.

Mahes remained in the area of Sojhat for several years thereafter, serving under Rāv Kalo Rāmot. He held several villages in ***paṭo*** including Māṇḍho and Kaṇṭālīyo.[44] Śivnāthsiṃh, ***Kūmpāvat Rāṭhauṛoṃ kā Itihās***, p. 674, states that Mahes drove the Jhālo Rajpūts from Khairvo village and made it his seat of rule in 1573-74. Little else is known about his activities during this time.

Prithīrāj apparently remained in Mughal service in north India following this incident with his brother, except for one other occasion. Local texts mention his return to Mārvāṛ for a brief period prior to his death in 1574-75 to help his brothers, Mahes and Māṇḍaṇ (8-4) (no. 99), avenge the death of another brother against the Sīndhaḷ Rāṭhoṛs of Sojhat.[45]

Within a short time after the settlement of these hostilities, Mahes himself was killed in battle near Sojhat fighting against a contingent of Mughals under Jalāl Khān Qurchī. The Mughals had entered Sojhat in order to find Rāv Kalo Rāmot, who had gained Emperor Akbar's disfavor. ***Murārdān***, no. 1, p. 593, records that while Rāv Kalo was at the Imperial court on some occasion, one of the women from the Imperial harem had visited his camp at Fatehpur Sikri. Rāv Kalo then fled before the Emperor's displeasure and took refuge in a stronghold in the hills near Sojhat. When the Mughals arrived in Mārvāṛ, they occupied Sojhat and many of its villages, and severe fighting broke out in several areas.

Mahes was with Rāv Kalo during this time, but he appears to have withheld his full support. "Aitihāsik Bātāṃ," p. 83, states that the people of his ***vasī*** including several ***mahājan***s, cobblers, milkmen and others, came and spoke disrespectfully to him. They said if Mahes would exert himself instead of leaving everything to Rāv Kalo and his people, the Mughals could be driven from Sojhat.

The Mughal army drew near the hills where the Rāṭhoṛ camps were located some days later. Fighting broke out, but the Mughals withdrew to wait for the Rajpūts to come out onto the plain to fight. Mahes's ***sāth*** then began moving out from the hills. Mahes objected strongly, but his Rajpūts disobeyed him, leaving Mahes with no choice but to follow. Once the Rajpūts were on the plain, the Mughals advanced against them with their elephants, stampeding their

---

[44] Māṇḍho and Kaṇṭālīyo are located six miles apart from each other, some fifteen miles to the south-southeast of Sojhat proper.

[45] See ***infra***, Māṇḍaṇ Kūmpāvat (no. 99), for details regarding this ***vair*** and its settlement.

horses and causing many to flee. One elephant came after Mahes's horse and caused the horse to bolt and throw Mahes. The elephant then pressed forward to trample Mahes, but Mahes raised himself to a squatting position and threw his lance, lodging it deeply in the elephant's face and forcing the elephant aside. Mahes was later killed as the Mughals took the field.

Mahes Kūmpāvat died on January 9, 1576.[46] The Mughals captured Rāv Kalo in 1577. They carried him in a bullock cart to Nāḍūl in southern Mārvāṛ, where they killed him.

* * *

Prithīrāj Kūmpāvat granted two villages of Sojhat in ***sāṃsaṇ*** to Cāraṇs. The dates of these grants are uncertain, but the villages and the Cāraṇs to whom they were given were:

1. Repṛāvās Tījo[47] - granted to Cāraṇ Bārhaṭh Devīdās Bhairavdāsot.
2. Rāmā rī Vāsṇī[48] - granted to Cāraṇ Sāndu Rāmo Dharamsīyot.

"Aitihāsik Bātāṃ," pp. 48, 51, 53-54, 78-79, 82-84; ***Āsop kā Itihās***, p. 44; ***Bāṅkīdās***, p. 53; "Bāt Rāṭhoṛ Tejsī Kūmpāvat rī," ff. 65-66, and "Bāt Māṇḍaṇ Kūmpāvat rī," ff. 66-70, in ***Aitihāsik Tavarīkhvār Vārtā***, MS no. 1234, Rājasthānī Śodh Saṃsthān, Caupāsnī; Bhāṭī, ***Sarvekṣaṇ***, 3:99; ***Khyāt***, 3:123-128; Śivnāthsiṃh, ***Kūmpāvat Rāṭhauṛoṃ kā Itihās***, pp. 155-157, 674; ***Murārdān***, no. 1, pp. 591-593; ***Vigat***, 1:61, 71, 80, 82-83, 418, 485, 487, 489, 492, 2:63.

(no. 99) **Māṇḍaṇ Kūmpāvat** (8-4)

Among Kūmpo Mahirājot's (7-1) (no. 95) sons, Māṇḍaṇ Kūmpāvat achieved perhaps the greatest renown as a warrior. The texts portray him as a Rajpūt who tolerated no ridicule of his family nor slight to his name. He was much feared for his prowess in battle. Māṇḍaṇ led a migratory existence among the kingdoms of Mārvāṛ, Mevāṛ, and Vāṃsvāḷo following the death of his father, Kūmpo's, and the defeat of Rāv Mālde Gāṅgāvat's Rajpūts at the battle of Samel in January of 1544. He then took service under the Mughals like his brother, Prithīrāj Kūmpāvat (8-2) (no. 97), and finally returned to Mārvāṛ with Moṭo Rājā

[46] Śivnāthsiṃh, ***Kūmpāvat Rāṭhauṛoṃ kā Itihās***, p. 674, and ***Murārdān***, no. 1, p. 593, both give the date ***V. S. 1632, Māgh, sudi 8*** for Mahes's death. ***Kūmpāvat Rāṭhauṛoṃ kā Itihās*** converts the date to January 3, 1576, which is incorrect. The correct conversion is as given above.

[47] Repṛāvās Tījo village: located eleven miles northwest of Sojhat.

[48] Rāmā rī Vāsṇī village: located fourteen miles north of Sojhat.

Udaisiṅgh Māldevot (1583-95). He became a prominent *ṭhākur* of Mārvāṛ who served under the Jodhpur ruler while holding the village of Āsop[49] and surrounding lands in *jāgīr* directly from the Mughal Emperor. He died in 1594 from wounds received in battle.

Māṇḍaṇ was born in 1526-27 in the village of Phulīyo[50] of Sojhat. He was approximately eighteen years old when his father was killed at Samel. Local chronicles contain little information about Māṇḍaṇ's life or activities in Mārvāṛ during the years leading up to and immediately following the battle of Samel. He appears to have served with his father in Rāv Mālde's armies along with one of his brothers, Prithīrāj Kūmpāvat.[51] Like his other brother, Mahes Kūmpāvat (8-3) (no. 98), he left Mārvāṛ in the late 1540s or early 1550s and proceeded to Mevāṛ, where he sought service under the Rāṇo of Cītoṛ, Sīsodīyo Udaisiṅgh Sāṅgāvat (ca. 1537-72; no. 17). Sources vary in their presentation of events leading to his departure from Mārvāṛ. Bhāṭī, ***Sarvekṣaṇ***, 3:97, records that Rāv Mālde had given Māṇḍaṇ a village in ***paṭo***, but that he became ill/diseased and was unable to walk. He therefore could not report for military service. Rāv Mālde then revoked his ***paṭo***, and Māṇḍaṇ left Mārvāṛ soon after. Śivnāthsiṃh, ***Kūmpāvat Rāṭhauroṃ kā Itihās***, p. 161, states that Māṇḍaṇ was driven from the land by the Muslims following Samel, while ***Āsop kā Itihās***, p. 49, suggests that Māṇḍaṇ quit Mārvāṛ because of Rāv Mālde's much reduced area of control after Samel, and his inability to provide lands for his Rajpūts.

Māṇḍaṇ arrived at Cītoṛ with a large contingent of warriors (***sāth***). For some reason, he was not well received there. People at the Rāṇo's court insulted him and cast aspersions upon his band of retainers, saying they were only members of his brotherhood, not his personal military servants. The Rāṇo suggested that his ***sāth*** was not his at all but rather that of Sāṅkhlo Paṃvār Abho Bhojāvat, a former military servant of Rāv Mālde of Jodhpur who was associated with the Kūmpāvats. Māṇḍaṇ was a young man at this time and apparently did not yet command sufficient respect among other Rajpūts despite his father Kūmpo's stature. Angered by these insults, Māṇḍaṇ left Mevāṛ and proceeded to Vāṃsvāḷo, where the Rāvaḷ welcomed him and granted him lands in ***paṭo*** for his maintenance. Māṇḍaṇ remained in Vāṃsvāḷo for approximately one year. He then returned to Cītoṛ.

While enroute from Vāṃsvāḷo, Māṇḍaṇ received word from one of his men who had remained behind at the Rāvaḷ's court about a Varsiṅghot Meṛtīyo Rāṭhoṛ named Sāṃvaḷdās Udaisiṅghot (no. 152). This Rajpūt had come to Vāṃsvāḷo and been given lands Māṇḍaṇ had previously held from the Rāvaḷ.

---

[49] Āsop village: located fifty miles northeast of Jodhpur.

[50] Phulīyo village: located twelve miles south-southeast of Sojhat town.

[51] Śivnāthsiṃh, ***Kūmpāvat Rāṭhauroṃ kā Itihās***, p. 161, states that Māṇḍaṇ was at the village of "Raḍḍāvās" of Sojhat at the time of the battle of Samel, and that he succeeded to the rule of this village following his father's death. ***Vigat*** has no listing of a village by this name for any of the ***pargano***s of Mārvāṛ. Perhaps Harḍhāvas village is meant. Harḍhāvas was a sizeable village eighteen miles east-southeast of Sojhat town.

Māṇḍaṇ's servant reported that when the Rāvaḷ presented the lands to Sāṃvaḷdās and told Sāṃvaḷdās that he had great honor to uphold for he had received the ***paṭo*** of Māṇḍaṇ Kūmpāvat, a great Rajpūt of Mārvāṛ, along with a ***paṭo*** belonging to another great Rajpūt of Vāṃsvāḷo, that Varsiṅghot Sāṃvaḷdās, who appears in the texts as a rather obtuse, thoughtless Rajpūt, replied that he had received many such ***paṭo***s and did not know any Māṇḍaṇ, son of Kūmpo.

This slur greatly angered Māṇḍaṇ, who vowed to avenge his honor before Sāṃvaḷdās. Several of Māṇḍaṇ's Rajpūts cautioned him against involving two Rāṭhoṛ brotherhoods in hostilities, but he would not be dissuaded despite the sanctions against such actions. Māṇḍaṇ then returned to Vāṃsvāḷo and sought out Sāṃvaḷdās at his village. Māṇḍaṇ's ***sāth*** broke into Sāṃvaḷdās's male apartment (***koṭṛī***) and killed thirty of his Rajpūts there. Māṇḍaṇ himself then climbed up to the second floor bedroom (***māḷīyo***) where Sāṃvaḷdās was hiding with his wife, a Vaḍgūjar woman. There he confronted Sāṃvaḷdās's wife, who remained behind alone while her husband fled into the neighboring house of a Brāhmaṇ. The Vaḍgūjar faced Māṇḍaṇ wearing her husband's garments and said, "Your brother has indeed fled; I stand [before you]" ("Bāt Māṇḍaṇ Kūmpāvat rī," f. 68). Māṇḍaṇ then went away, but he killed Sāṃvaḷdās's mother and wounded one of Sāṃvaḷdās's elephants before he quit the village.[52]

News of this deed preceded Māṇḍaṇ's arrival in Mevāṛ, and when he returned to the Rāṇo's court, he was summoned before the Rāṇo and received with great respect. The Rāṇo praised his actions against Sāṃvaḷdās and retained him, presenting him with a sizeable grant of villages.

Māṇḍaṇ's activities during the ten year period from the mid-1550s to the mid-1560s are uncertain. Rāmkaraṇ Āsopā writes that Māṇḍaṇ went to Delhi at the time of Akbar's succession to the Mughal throne in 1556, and that he received the village of Āsop and thirteen others in ***jāgīr*** from the Emperor in 1557 (***Āsop kā Itihās***, p. 49). Contemporary sources do not corroborate this assertion. The Mughals had no authority in Mārvāṛ at this time. Āsopā's statement, therefore, must be disregarded. Māṇḍaṇ did take service under the Mughals, however, for the ***Khyāt*** of Naiṇsī, 3:274, records:

> [for] so many days, Emperor Akbar had granted Jhūñjhaṇūṃ [in north-central Rājasthān] in ***jāgīr*** to Māṇḍaṇ Kūmpāvat.

The ***Khyāt*** offers no date for the grant. But based on other facts known about Māṇḍaṇ's life, the ten year period from 1555-65 appears the most probable time he would have held this ***jāgīr***.

Māṇḍaṇ left service under the Mughals in the mid-1560s to return to Mārvāṛ and join Rāv Candrasen Māldevot (1562-81). His reasons for leaving at this time are unclear, but Bhāṭī, ***Sarvekṣaṇ***, 3:97, records that "Emperor Akbar requested a daughter [from Māṇḍaṇ], but [Māṇḍaṇ] would not give [him one]." This text offers no further information, but Māṇḍaṇ's refusal may have provided

---

[52] See n. 111 to "Aitihāsik Bātāṃ," p. 53, of the **translated text** for further discussion of this incident.

the impetus for his return to Mārvāṛ. Rāv Candrasen had been forced to abandon Jodhpur in December of 1565 in the face of pressure from the Mughals, and had proceeded to the stronghold at Bhādrājuṇ[53] where he established his court. Few facts are available from sources, but Māṇḍaṇ appears to have remained with Rāv Candrasen into the early 1570s, when he again left Mārvāṛ, this time for Mevāṛ where he took service under Sīsodīyo Rāṇo Pratāpsiṅgh Udaisiṅghot (1572-97). Māṇḍaṇ's departure from Mārvāṛ may have coincided with Rāv Candrasen's forced exile in the hills of Sīvāṇo beginning in 1574 and his subsequent retreat across the Arāvallīs into Mevāṛ and Vāṃsvāḷo.

Māṇḍaṇ received villages in ***paṭo*** from the Rāṇo for his maintenance, and Śivnāthsiṃh, ***Kūmpāvat Rāṭhauṛoṃ kā Itihās***, pp. 168-169, indicates that Māṇḍaṇ took part with Rāṇo Pratāpsiṅgh in his running battle with the Mughals as they sought to impose their control in Mevāṛ. Māṇḍaṇ was posted at the ***thāṇo*** of Gogūndo, and he fought in an important battle there against the Mughals in 1578-79.

While serving under Rāṇo Pratāp, Māṇḍaṇ returned to Mārvāṛ and joined his brothers, Prithīrāj Kūmpāvat (8-2) (no. 97) and Mahes Kūmpāvat (8-3) (no. 98), in the settlement of an old ***vair*** with the Sīndhaḷ Rāṭhoṛs of Sojhat. This ***vair*** had begun some years earlier when Sīndhaḷ Sīho Bhāṇḍāvat and his Rajpūts had killed one of the Kūmpāvat brothers near the village of Khairvo.[54] Local sources are in conflict about which brother was killed, naming both Goind (8-6) and Tejsī (8-7). There is also confusion about the reason for the murder. Its occurrence is related both to a dispute over horses and to a Sīndhaḷ raid on a Kūmpāvat village.

The ***Khyāt*** of Naiṇsī, 3:123-128, contains an interesting account of this ***vair*** and its settlement. Sīho Sīndhaḷ, the master of Kamḷāṃ-Pāvā village,[55] was in difficult circumstances, it is told. All of his horses had died. He remarked one day while sitting with his Rajpūts:

> "***Ṭhākur***s! [We have] no horses." Then Sīho asked, "[Does anyone knows] who has any horses?" [His] Rajpūts said, "***Rāj***! [There] are horses at Dhūḷharo village.[56] But Goind Kūmpāvat lives there." [Someone] said, "If [you] kill Goind, the horses would come to hand." Then Sīho said, "[We] must bring the horses" (***Khyāt***, 3:123).

Sīho and his men then set out for Dhauḷharo village. They killed Goind Kūmpāvat there (according to this version) and took away two hundred of the Kūmpāvats' horses.

---

[53] Bhādrājuṇ village: located forty-eight miles south-southwest of Jodhpur.

[54] Khairvo village: located fifty miles south-southeast of Jodhpur.

[55] The identification and location of this village are obscure.

[56] Dhauḷharo or Dhavaḷairo village: located eighteen miles west-northwest of Sojhat.

"Tejsī Kūmpāvat rī Bāt," f. 65, states that Sīho Sīndhaḷ was filled with remorse after Goind Kūmpāvat was killed. Goind's death brought back memories of a costly ***vair*** with the Cāmpāvat Rāṭhoṛs, in the settlement of which Sīho's father, Bhāṇḍo, had been involved. Some days after the Sīndhaḷ attack on Dhauḷharo village, Sīho rode to Mahes Kūmpāvat's village near Sojhat. He put his weapons aside when he arrived and seated himself before Mahes's doorway, saying:

> Feed me ***khīc***.[57] This deed was committed by me (***ibid***.).

A Cāraṇ named Sāndu Rāmo Dharamsīyot, to whom Mahes's brother, Prithīrāj Kūmpāvat, had given the village of Rāmā rī Vāsṇī in ***sāṃsaṇ***, was present at this time. Cāraṇ Rāmo greeted Sīho Sīndhaḷ and went to inform Mahes of his arrival.

Mahes was at a loss about what to do. He asked Rāmo for his advice. Rāmo said he should have ***khīc*** prepared and given to Sīho with the formalities appropriate for such an occasion. He also suggested that Mahes could end the ***vair*** in the same manner the Cāmpāvats had settled hostilities earlier with the Sīndhaḷs. At that time, Sīho's father, Bhāṇḍo, had cut off one of his fingers as an offering to equalize the loss between the two brotherhoods. Mahes did not have Sīho fed ***khīc***, but he agreed with the other part of Cāraṇ Rāmo's proposal. When Rāmo approached Sīho, however, Sīho took offense and left Mahes's village in anger.

Māṇḍaṇ later learned of these events and reproached his brother, Mahes, saying:

> Mahes did a stupid thing (***bhūṇḍo kām kīyo***). If Sīho had come, then [Mahes] should have fed [him] ***khīc***. Mahes did [something] unprincipled [and destructive] (***buro kīyo***) (***ibid***.).

Sīho Sīndhaḷ was a powerful local Rajpūt. Hostilities with him could only prove costly for the Kūmpāvats.

Both Māṇḍaṇ and Sīho were military servants of the Rāṇo of Cītoṛ during this period. They came together by chance during a feast at the Rāṇo's court. While Sīho sat picking at his food (he could not eat for fear of Māṇḍaṇ), Māṇḍaṇ came and stood in a mock confrontation before Sīho's shoes, which Sīho had placed in the entryway to the hall. The Sīndhaḷs saw Māṇḍaṇ's actions and exclaimed:

---

[57] ***Khīc***, a simple preparation of boiled wheat or millet and pulses (see **Glossary** to Volume I), is a very ordinary subsistence food. Sākariyā, editor of the ***Khyāt***, glosses this passage (n. 7) as meaning, "Please punish [me]." Siho was seeking a means by which the Kūmpāvats could take something from him to equalize their loss. He offered his honor/reputation. He would be lowering himself to eat ***khīc*** which they served.

"Bravo! Oh, Sīho! Your fate [stands there]; has Māṇḍaṇ himself begun preparations for battle?" Then Sīho spoke, "Māṇḍaṇ will kill me. This act was a warning" (*ibid.*, 1:124).

Sīho left the ***vās*** ("residence, dwelling") of the Rāṇo shortly thereafter and proceeded to Jāḷor, where he entered the service of the Muslim ruler. Māṇḍaṇ perceived, "Now Sīho is gone." And he also left the Rāṇo's ***vās*** and returned to Mārvāṛ. There he began collecting a ***sāth***. He went to the home of Rāṭhoṛ Kalo Vīdāvat. He released his dagger, saying:

"Kalo! You [are] Vīdo's son. If you would have [me] tie [this] dagger on [you], then I would tie [it on]." Then [with] as many of his ***sāth*** as were [present], with that many Kalo mounted and joined [Māṇḍaṇ] (*ibid.*).

Māṇḍaṇ proceeded to the village of Devṛo Cahuvāṇ Udaisī. Udaisī was a ***sirdār*** with many ***sāth***, all good Rajpūts (***bhalā bhalā rajpūt***). But Udaisī had married at the homes of both Māṇḍaṇ and Sīho Sīndhaḷ. He was in a difficult position, having alliances with both brotherhoods. The ***Khyāt*** of Naiṇsī, 3:124, states that Māṇḍaṇ's daughter was first wife and, therefore, favored in her marriage (***suhāgaṇ***), while Sīho's daughter was second wife and less favored (***duhāgaṇ***). Māṇḍaṇ sent a Cāraṇ to Udaisī's home with a message for his daughter. "Entreat Udaisī [on our behalf]." Māṇḍaṇ intended that Udaisī look the other way. It was not his ***vair*** to settle with the Sīndhaḷs.

Māṇḍaṇ afterwards went off with his ***sāth*** to lie in wait, and he ambushed Sīho, killing him along with a number of his Rajpūts. He then left with his men, fearful of what Devṛo Udaisī would do when he learned of Sīho's death. Udaisī soon received word of the battle and grew angry. He cried out against Māṇḍaṇ:

"Fuck Māṇḍaṇ's mother! (***Mā jāṛūṃ Māṇḍaṇrī***!) [Māṇḍaṇ] killed Sīho [in] our valley?" Then Māṇḍaṇ's daughter grasped hold of the edge of Udaisī's shirt and said, "What must you do [now]? Do you go to take revenge? [Do not forget that you married at my father's home and that my father] has placed curds (***dahī***) [on] your forehead" (*ibid.*, 3:127).

Udaisī would not be mollified. He cried out angrily that Māṇḍaṇ had made him an unworthy Rajpūt (***kurajpūt***).

Udaisī's Rajpūts now gathered in the male apartment of his home (***koṭṛī***) and waited, armed and ready, for him to come and lead them. Sīho Sīndhaḷ's daughter then appeared before them. She exclaimed:

Hey, unworthy Rajpūts! . . . Māṇḍaṇ's daughter has prevented [Udaisī from coming to lead you]. Is there no one born of a Rajpūtāṇī among you, [who is] protector of the shame of this fort (***iṇ koṭ rī lājro rakhvāḷo***) (*ibid.*)?

This Rajpūtāṇī's words inflamed the Devṛos. One hundred and sixty armored men (***jaṇā bagatriyā***) then moved out from the village, riding double on horseback. When they reached Māṇḍaṇ's camp, they dismounted in a group and attacked Māṇḍaṇ and his men on foot, knocking down their shields and killing all the ***sāth***. Kalo Vīdāvat died fighting along with fifty of his Rajpūts. ***Khyāt***, 3:128, records that he was only fifteen years old. Māṇḍaṇ himself was badly wounded.

According to ***Khyāt*** (***ibid.***), Rāv Candrasen Māldevot of Jodhpur emerged from his exile in the hills of Gūghroṭ at this time and came to the Kūmpāvats' aid. He led his Rajpūts in an attack against the Devṛos, killing all of the ***sāth***. "There was such a battle (***isṛo māmlo huvo***)." The Rāv's men also fought with the Sīndhaḷs and inflicted a severe defeat on them. And Māṇḍaṇ was carried from the field and his wounds were bound.[58]

Māṇḍaṇ joined Rāv Candrasen during the final years of his exile from Jodhpur following the settlement of this ***vair***, and he remained with the Rāv until the Rāv's death in 1581. Māṇḍaṇ then returned to Mevāṛ where he served under Sīsodīyo Rāṇo Pratāpsiṅgh Udaisiṅghot for a short period. Then in 1582-83 he left Mevāṛ for north India to join Rāv Candrasen's elder uterine brother, Udaisiṅgh Māldevot (Moṭo Rājā of Jodhpur, 1583-95), at Samavali (near Gwalior). Udaisiṅgh was a Mughal ***mansabdār*** holding Samavali in ***jāgīr*** from Emperor Akbar.

When Udaisiṅgh Māldevot succeeded to the throne of Jodhpur in 1583, Māṇḍaṇ acompanied him back to Mārvāṛ. He continued to serve under the Moṭo Rājā until his death in 1594. Bhāṭī, ***Sarvekṣaṇ***, 3:97, states that he died in Lahore, while ***Āsop kā Itihās***, p. 54, notes that he was killed during operations against the Mahevco Rāṭhoṛs of western Mārvāṛ who refused to submit to the authority of the Jodhpur ruler.[59]

---

[58] The dating of the settlement of this ***vair*** in the mid-1570s is conjectural. The different sources indicate that Māṇḍaṇ and his two brothers, Prithīrāj and Mahes, were all present in Mārvāṛ in this period and that they all took part in the fighting against the Sīndhaḷs. One of the sources places the start of the ***vair*** in Khairvo village ("Bāt Māṇḍaṇ Kūmpāvat rī," f. 69). This village was granted to Mahes in 1572, when Rāv Kalo Rāmot received Sojhat in ***jāgīr*** from Akbar. Mahes was then killed in battle in the area of Sojhat in 1576, but his brother, Prithīrāj, died in 1574-75. The events must have taken place between 1572-74.

The ***Khyāt*** of Naiṇsī, 2:188-189, also records that Jeso Bhāṭī Gopāḷdās Merāvat was with Māṇḍaṇ Kūmpāvat when he attacked and killed Sīho Sīndhaḷ and that Bhāṭī Gopāḷdās died in this battle. Bhāṭī Gopāḷdās received a village in ***paṭo*** from Moṭo Rājā Udaisiṅgh Māldevot (1583-95) in 1583. This date adds confusion to attempts at chronology. In addition, ***Bāṅkīdās***, p. 53, writes that Sīho Sīndhaḷ was killed in 1570. This date appears incorrect given other information available about Māṇḍaṇ's and his brothers' whereabouts in this period but adds to the uncertainty about chronology.

[59] Alternatively, Śivnāthsiṃh, ***Kūmpāvat Rāṭhauroṃ kā Itihās***, p. 172, states that Moṭo Rājā Udaisiṅgh sent Māṇḍaṇ against Rāvaḷ Vīram of Jasoḷ. Following his victory there, he proceeded toward Sojhat, where he met Mughal troops of Prince Salīm (Jahāṅgīr).

Māṇḍaṇ held the village of Āsop and surrounding lands in ***jāgīr*** directly from the Mughal Emperor Akbar during this period. This award may relate to services Māṇḍaṇ rendered while he held Jhūñjhaṇūṃ in ***jāgīr*** some years earlier. Local texts are also unclear how long Māṇḍaṇ held Āsop separately from Jodhpur while he served under the Moṭo Rājā. Rāmkaraṇ Āsopā writes:

> In one old ***khyāt***, a description of the giving of the kingdom of Jodhpur is written in this manner: "The Emperor, Śrī Akbar, gave the ***ṭīko*** [of succession] and Jodhpur to Rājā Udaisiṅghjī; [he] gave [Jodhpur] in the month ***jait*** (April/May) of 1583. He sequestered [these lands] from the Saiyyids Hāsam and Kāsam. Jodhpur came [with] a ***sirpāv***, horses, [and a] ***mansab*** of 1,500 ***zāt***, 700 ***suwār***. [It came] in 12 subdivisions (***tapho***s) . . . Among these [the Emperor] gave Bīlāṛo [***tapho***] to [Jaitāvat Rāṭhoṛ] Rāv Vāgh Prithīrājot. [And] Āsop was given to Māṇḍaṇjī" (***Āsop kā Itihās***, p. 53).

Vigat, 1:77, confirms this record. It states:

> [The Emperor] gave Jodhpur [to Rājā Udaisiṅgh] in April/May of 1583. At this time, 2 ***tapho***s were [administratively] outside [of Jodhpur Pargano]. Āsop ***tapho*** was [given] directly to Rāṭhoṛ [Māṇḍaṇ][60] Kūmpāvat. Bīlāṛo to Rāṭhoṛ Vāgh Prithīrājot; 2 ***tapho***s separate . . .

Elsewhere, "Aitihāsik Bātāṃ," p. 91, records that:

> The 1 ***tapho*** of Āsop had been [given] to Rāṭhoṛ Māṇḍaṇ Kūmpāvat, so [in] 1585 the ***tapho*** of Āsop became [the Moṭo Rājā's].

This entry seems to indicate that while Māṇḍaṇ held Āsop in ***jāgīr*** from Akbar during the first years after Rājā Udaisiṅgh's accession, this order changed in 1585 when Āsop was included within the ***pargano*** of Jodhpur and made part of the Moṭo Rājā's ***jāgīr***. Māṇḍaṇ may then have received Āsop from the Moṭo Rājā in ***paṭo*** while he continued to serve under him. It is also possible that he continued to hold Āsop directly from Akbar.[61]

Fighting broke out with these troops, during which he is said to have been mortally wounded. This text gives the date of January 27, 1594 for Māṇḍaṇ's death.

[60] ***Vigat*** lists the name incorrectly as "Bhāṇ Kūmpāvat," not Māṇḍaṇ Kūmpāvat, probably a scribal error.

[61] Śivnāthsiṃh, ***Kūmpāvat Rāṭhauṛoṃ kā Itihās***, p. 171, gives the date of March 11, 1586 (***Caitrādi***) = February 28, 1587 (***Śrāvaṇādi***) for Māṇḍaṇ's receipt of Āsop (and 11 other villages) in ***jāgīr*** directly from the Emperor. This date cannot be verified from other more contemporary sources and appears to be late. These villages are said to

An inscription on a cenotaph built near the temple of Mahādev in Dhaneṛī village records the date of Māṇḍaṇ's death along with the names of the three wives who became *satīs*:

> Memorial (*devḷī*[62]) [dated] January 27, 1594 - Rāj Śrī Māṇḍaṇjī Kūmpāvat Rāṭhauṛ, Mahāsatī Dammā Bhāṭiyāṇī, Mahāsatī Kinkā Cahuvāṇ, Mahāsatī Jasodā Sīsodṇī.

Māṇḍaṇ had eleven wives, nine sons, and two daughters. His son, Khīṃvo Māṇḍaṇot (9-1), succeeded him to the rule of Āsop.

> "Aitihāsik Bātāṃ," pp. 53-54, 91; ***Āsop kā Itihās***, pp. 48-56; ***Bāṅkīdās***, p. 53; "Bāt Rāṭhoṛ Tejsī Kūmpāvat rī," ff, 65-66; "Bāt Māṇḍaṇ Kūmpāvat rī," ff. 66-70; Bhāṭī, ***Sarvekṣaṇ***, 3:97; ***Khyāt***, 2:172, 181, 184, 187-189, 3:123-128, 274; Śivnāthsiṃh, ***Kūmpāvat Rāṭhauṛoṃ kā Itihās***, pp. 161-175; ***Vigat***, 1:77.

(no. 100) **Kānhāsiṅgh Khīṃvāvat** (10-1)
(no. 101) **Rājsiṅgh Khīṃvāvat** (10-2)

Kānhāsiṅgh Khīṃvāvat and his younger brother, Rājsiṅgh Khīṃvāvat, were sons of Khīṃvo Māṇḍaṇot (9-1), born of his first wife, Devṛī Koṛamdevī, daughter of Devṛo Jaimal Harrājot, and grandsons of Māṇḍaṇ Kūmpāvat (8-4) (no. 99). Both achieved prominence in Mārvāṛ as important ***ṭhākurs***, and under Rājsiṅgh, Āsop village returned to this family. It now became the homeland (***utan***) of the Kūmpāvat Rāṭhoṛs following Māṇḍaṇ Kūmpāvat's establishment of his rule there. These Kūmpāvats continued the strong tradition of Kūmpāvat service to the Jodhpur throne which had begun with their ancestor, Kūmpo Mahirājot (7-1) (no. 95).

Khīṃvo Māṇḍaṇot (9-1)

Kānhāsiṅgh and Rājsiṅgh's father, Khīṃvo Māṇḍaṇot, was born in 1549-50. He remained behind in Mārvāṛ while his father, Māṇḍaṇ Kūmpāvat, traveled first to Mevāṛ and then to north India to join Udaisiṅgh Māldevot at Samavali (near Gwalior) in 1581-82. Khīṃvo took service under Rāv Candrasen Māldevot's son, Rāv Rāysiṅgh Candrasenot, who had received Sojhat in ***jāgīr*** from Emperor Akbar in 1581. Bhāṭī, ***Sarvekṣaṇ***, 3:97, states that he received Īḍvo village[63] of Meṛto from Rāv Rāysiṅgh for his ***vasī***. Khīṃvo was at Sojhat

---

have been given in reward for Māṇḍaṇ's valorous performance against rebels in the East against whom he was sent 1586-1587. The other villages included in this grant were: Bāṛṇī Baṛī, Bāṛṇī Khurad, Chāplo, Dāṛmī, Hiṅgolī, Kubhāro, Kūkaṛdo, Lohārī, Narāsṇī, Pelṛī, Rājlāṇī, Raṛod, Rāḍsar, Rāmpuro, and Surpuro.

[62] ***Devḷī***: a memorial (image/effigy) to a ***satī***.

[63] Īḍvo village: located eighteen miles northeast of Meṛto.

when Rāv Rāysiṅgh was killed in battle in Sīrohī in October of 1583,[64] and he and Rāṭhoṛ Āskaraṇ Devīdāsot, a son of Devīdās Jaitāvat (no. 65), were among the Rajpūts of Rāv Rāysiṅgh's ***vasī*** who were sent from Sojhat to Jodhpur after Rāv Rāysiṅgh's death. Moṭo Rājā Udaisiṅgh retained these Rajpūts in his own service, and he posted Khīṃvo to the garrison at Sojhat.

Khīṃvo held the village of Dhaṇlo[65] in ***paṭo*** from the Moṭo Rājā while he was stationed at Sojhat. ***Murārdān***, no. 2, p. 183, records that the Moṭo Rājā drove Khīṃvo from this village, however, and gave it to Khīṃvo's brother, Prayāgdās Māṇḍaṇot (9-2). The date of this occurrence is not recorded, but the sequence in which the text lists this event indicates that the village was sequestered ca. 1584. ***Āsop kā Itihās***, p. 56, states that Khīṃvo then succeeded his father, Māṇḍaṇ, to Āsop village in 1593-94. Seventeenth century sources available do not confirm that Āsop village was granted to Khīṃvo in ***paṭo***, and the dating is also problematic. The Moṭo Rājā's actions against Khīṃvo at Dhaṇlo village also indicate some uncertainty about Khīṃvo's position.

It is known, however, that Khīṃvo continued in the service of Jodhpur under the Moṭo Rājā's successor, Rājā Sūrajsiṅgh Udaisiṅghot (1595-1619). He spent much of his time between the years 1595-1608 on military tour with the Rājā in the Deccan. Khīṃvo and several other of Rājā Sūrajsiṅgh's Rajpūts distinguished themselves at the battle of Bīḍ city (near Ahmadnagar) in 1599-1600 by capturing the red and white flag of Ahmadnagar. Rājā Sūrajsiṅgh adopted these colors as his own, and in reward for Khīṃvo's valor in this battle, he granted Khīṃvo the ***paṭo*** of Īḍvo village which he had held before while serving under Rāṭhoṛ Rāv Rāysiṅgh Candrasenot.

Sources differ regarding details of Khīṃvo's death. ***Āsop kā Itihās***, p. 57, states that Khīṃvo was killed in 1608-09 during an outbreak of hostilities with Hāḍo Rajpūts in Būndī, southern Rājasthān. Śivnāthsiṃh, ***Kūmpāvat Rāṭhauṛoṃ kā Itihās***, p. 184, asserts that he was killed in November or December of 1611 during a battle near Bhādrājuṇ village.[66] The fighting near Bhādrājuṇ is said to have taken place against Rajpūts of Sīsodīyo Rāṇo Amarsiṅgh Pratāpsiṅghot (1597-1620) who had raided into Mārvāṛ after an Imperial caravan. Alternatively, Bhāṭī, ***Sarvekṣaṇ*** 3:97, records that Khīṃvo died at Burhanpur in the Deccan in 1617-18.

Khīṃvo had four wives and from six to nine sons.

> ***Āsop kā Ītihās***, pp. 56-58; Bhāṭī, ***Sarvekṣaṇ***, 3:97; Śivnāthsiṃh, ***Kūmpāvat Rāṭhauṛoṃ kā Itihās***, pp. 177-185; ***Murārdān***, no. 2, pp. 182-183; ***Vigat***, 1:89, 105.

---

[64] Śivnāthsiṃh, ***Kūmpīvat Rāṭhauṛoṃ kā Itihās***, p. 177, states that Khīṃvo Māṇḍaṇot was present in Sīrohī with Rāv Rāysiṅgh. This assertion appears to be incorrect.

[65] Dhaṇlo village: located twenty-seven miles due south of Sojhat.

[66] Bhādrājuṇ village: located forty-eight miles south-southwest of Jodhpur.

(no. 100) **Kānhāsiṅgh Khīṃvāvat** (10-1)

Kānhāsiṅgh Khīṃvāvat (also known as Kisansiṅgh Khīṃvāvat) was a sister's son (***bhāṇej***) of the Devṛos. He was born on November 7, 1583. Little is known about his early life. He appears to have entered the service of Jodhpur as a young man and become a military servant of Jodho Rāṭhoṛ Gajsiṅgh Sūrajsiṅghot, under whom he served while Gajsiṅgh was a ***kuṃvar*** and later when Gajsiṅgh succeeded to the Jodhpur throne as ***rājā*** in 1619.

Kānhāsiṅgh was with Kuṃvar Gajsiṅgh in 1614-15 during Mughal operations in Mevāṛ against Sīsodīyo Rāṇo Amarsiṅgh Pratāpsiṅghot (1597-1620). Emperor Jahāngīr had placed Prince Khurram in charge of these operations, and the Prince established outposts at a number of different locations throughout Mevāṛ. He appointed Jodhpur Rājā Sūrajsiṅgh Udaisiṅghot (1595-1619) to the ***thāṇo*** of Sādṛī in Goḍhvāṛ.[67] It was here that Kānhāsiṅgh was stationed, and he is said quickly to have earned a reputation for courage and resourcefulness. Kānhāsiṅgh went on to attain considerable prominence in Mārvāṛ as a warrior and as an administrator.

Both ***Āsop kā Itihās***, p. 58, and Śivnāthsiṃh, ***Kūmpāvat Rāṭhauṛoṃ kā Itihās***, p. 185, assert that Kānhāsiṅgh succeeded to Āsop village when his father, Khīṃvo, died. Seventeenth century sources available do not confirm this assertion, and it is unclear if Kānhāsiṅgh ever received this village in ***paṭo***. Śivnāthsiṃh, ***Kūmpāvat Rāṭhauṛoṃ kā Itihās***, p. 193, also states that Jodhpur Rājā Sūrajsiṅgh sequestered Āsop from Kānhāsiṅgh because Kānhāsiṅgh took part with Jodho Rāthoṛ Rāv Kisansiṅgh Udaisiṅghot of Kisangaḍh in the actions that resulted in the death of Rājā Sūrajsiṅgh's ***pradhān***, Jeso Bhāṭī Goyanddās Mānāvat, at Ajmer in 1615. Rāṭhoṛ Kisansiṅgh was a son of Moṭo Rājā Udaisiṅgh Māldevot (1583-95) and half-brother to Rājā Sūrajsiṅgh. He appears to have nursed several grievances against Bhāṭī Goyanddās. Goyanddās had driven him from Mārvāṛ in 1600-01 following a series of disputes over land holdings. He nevertheless remained involved in affairs in Mārvāṛ, and when Bhāṭī Goyanddās killed a paternal cousin of his in 1613 he sought to avenge his death against the ***pradhān***. He and his Rajpūts attacked Bhāṭī Goyanddās's camp at Ajmer on May 26, 1615 and murdered him to settle the ***vair***. The above source states that when Rājā Sūrajsiṅgh took Āsop from Kānhāsiṅgh, Kānhāsiṅgh left Mārvāṛ for Rāṭhoṛ Kisansiṅgh's kingdom of Kisangaḍh and returned to Mārvāṛ only in 1619 when Gajsiṅgh succeeded to the Jodhpur throne.

There are a number of problems with the account in Śivnāthsiṃh, ***Kūmpāvat Rāṭhauṛoṃ kā Itihās***. As noted above, it seems doubtful that Kānhāsiṅgh ever held Āsop in ***paṭo***. ***Khyāt***, 2:155, records that Jeso Bhāṭī Goyanddās received Āsop in 1606-07 and held it along with Lavero[68] and other villages while he served as ***pradhān*** of Jodhpur under Rājā Sūrajsiṅgh. Āsop

---

[67] Sādṛī village: located fifteen miles south of Nāḍūl.

[68] Lavero village: located thirty-four miles north-northeast of Jodhpur.

remained in Bhāṭī Goyanddās's ***paṭo*** until his death in 1615, and on his death, it passed to his two sons, Rāmsiṅgh and Prithīrāj. It appears that one reason Kānhāsiṅgh may have joined Rāv Kisansiṅgh in the hostilities at Ajmer was because Goyanddās held possession of Āsop. This village did not return to Kānhāsiṅgh's family until 1619, when Rājā Gajsiṅgh took it from Jeso Bhāṭīs Rāmsiṅgh and Prithīrāj Goyanddāsot and awarded it to Kānhāsiṅgh's younger brother, Rājsiṅgh Khīṃvāvat (see ***infra***).

Kānhāsiṅgh may also have joined with Rāv Kisansiṅgh to help settle the ***vair*** between the Jodho Rāṭhoṛs and the Jeso Bhāṭīs which emerged when Jeso Bhāṭī Goyanddās killed Jodho Rāṭhoṛ Gopāḷdās Bhagvāndāsot. Rāṭhoṛ Gopāḷdās was a son of Rāv Kisansiṅgh's brother, Bhagvāndās Udaisiṅghot.[69] He had been in the ***sāth*** of his paternal relation, Jodho Rāṭhoṛ Narsiṅghdās Kalyāṇdāsot,[70] who had held Bhāuṇḍo village[71] of Nāgaur as a ***cākar*** of Sīsodīyo Rāṇo Sagar Udaisiṅghot. Rāṇo Sagar had taken this village from Narsiṅghdās in 1612-13 and given it to another of his ***cākar***s, Jeso Bhāṭī Surtāṇ Mānāvat, who took service under him that year. Bhāṭī Surtāṇ was a brother of Bhāṭī Goyanddās Mānāvat. Bhāṭī Surtāṇ took possession of Bhāuṇḍo in December of 1612, but hostilities broke out some months later in May of 1613, when Rāṭhoṛ Narsiṅghdās and his ***sāth*** returned to Bhāuṇḍo and challenged Bhāṭī Surtāṇ's rights to possession of the village. Bhāṭī Surtāṇ emerged from the small fort at Bhāuṇḍo to meet them, and during the pitched battle before the village which followed, Rāṭhoṛ Narsiṅghdās and Bhāṭī Surtāṇ were both killed. Rāṭhoṛ Gopāḷdās Bhagvāndāsot was wounded but managed to flee along with others of Narsiṅgdās's ***sāth***, including Narsiṅghdās's brothers, Īsardās and Mādhodās Kalyāṇdāsot. When Bhāṭī Goyanddās learned what had happened, he rode from Jodhpur to avenge Surtāṇ's death. Īsardās and Mādhodās Kalyāṇdāsot managed

---

[69] The relationships among the Jodho Rāṭhoṛs listed here is as follows:

Rāv Mālde Gāṅgāvat
- Moṭo Rājā Udaisiṅgh Māldevot
  - **Rāv Kisansiṅgh Udaisiṅghot**
  - Bhagvāndās Udaisiṅghot
    - **Gopāḷdās Bhagvāndāsot**
- Rāymal Māldevot
  - Kalyāṇdās Rāymalot
    - **Narsiṅghdās Kalyāṇdāsot**

[70] See ***supra***, "Jodho Rāṭhoṛs," Īsardās Kalyāṇdāsot (no. 88), for more information about Narsiṅghdās Kalyāṇdāsot.

[71] Bhāuṇḍo village: located fifty-three miles north-northeast of Jodhpur and twenty-five miles southwest of Nāgaur.

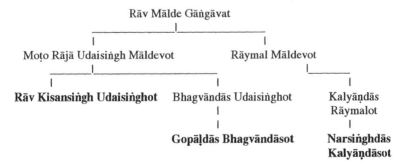

to escape. But Bhāṭī Goyanddās caught up with Gopāḷdās at the village of Kāṅkaṛkhī[72] near Meṛto and killed him there to settle the ***vair***.

Gopāḷdās Bhagvāndāsot's paternal uncle, Rāv Kisansiṅgh Udaisiṅghot, sought to avenge his death in turn. Angered that his brother, Rājā Sūrajsiṅgh of Jodhpur, would take no action against his ***pradhān***, Rāv Kisansiṅgh made a precipitous attack on Bhāṭī Goyanddās's camp at Ajmer and killed him on the night of May 26, 1615 while he was with Rājā Sūrajsiṅgh in attendance upon Emperor Jahāṅgīr.

Local sources including ***Khyāt***, 2:155, ***Murārdān***, no. 2, pp. 255-258, and ***Jodhpur Rājya kī Khyāt***, pp. 130, 145, 150-152, assert that the Emperor himself was involved in Bhāṭī Goyanddās's murder. The latter two sources openly state that Rāv Kisansiṅgh complained before the Emperor about Rāṭhoṛ Gopāḷdās's death and that the Emperor then ordered him to kill Bhāṭī Goyanddās. That Emperor Jahāṅgīr ordered Kisansiṅgh to kill Bhāṭī Goyanddās is questionable, the best contemporary source for what happened being the Emperor's own writing:

> On the night of Friday, the 15th, a strange affair occurred. By chance on that night I was at Pushkar. To be brief, Kishan, own brother to Rāja Sūraj Singh, was in great perturbation through Gobind Dās, the Vakil of the said Raja having some time ago killed his nephew, a youth of the name of Gopāl Dās. . . Kishan Singh expected that, as Gopāl Dās was also the nephew of the Raja (Sūraj Singh), the latter would kill Gobind Dās. But the Raja, on account of the experience and ability of Gobind Dās, relinquished the idea of seeking revenge for his nephew's death. When Kishan saw this neglect on the part of the Raja, he resolved to take revenge for his nephew, and not allow his blood to pass away unnoticed. For a long time he kept this matter in his mind, until on that night he assembled his brothers, friends, and servants, and told them that he would go that night to take Gobind Dās's life, whatever might happen, and that he did not care what injury might happen to the Raja. The Raja was ignorant of what was happening, and when it was near dawn Kishan came with Karan [Ugrasenot], his brother's son, and other companions. When he arrived at the gate of the Raja's dwelling he sent some of the experienced men on foot to the house of Gobind Dās, which was near the Raja's. He himself (Kishan) was on horseback, and stationed himself near the gate. The men on foot entered Gobind Dās's house, and killed some of those who were there on guard. Whilst this fight was going on Gobind Dās awoke, and seizing his sword in a state of bewilderment was comng out from one side of the house to join the outside watchmen. When the men on foot had finished killing some of the people, they came out of the tent to

[72] Kāṅkaṛkhī village: located nine miles south-southwest of Meṛto.

endeavour to find out Gobind Dās, and, meeting him, they finished his affair (killed him). Before the news of the killing of Gobind Dās reached Kishan, he, unable to bear it any more, dismounted and came inside the dwelling. Although his men protested in a disturbed state that it was not right to be on foot, he would in no way listen to them. If he had remained a little longer and the news of his enemy having been killed had reached him, it is possible that he would have escaped safe and sound, mounted as he was. As the pen of destiny had gone forth after another fashion, as soon as he alighted and went in, the Raja, who was in his *maḥall* (female apartment) awoke at the uproar among the people, and stood at the gate of his house with his sword drawn. People from all sides were aroused and came in against the men who were on foot. They saw what the number of men on foot was, and came out in great numbers and faced Kishan Singh's men, who were about ten in number. In short, Kishan Singh and his nephew Karan, when they reached the Raja's house, were attacked by these men and both of them killed. Kishan Singh had seven and Karan nine wounds. Altogether in this fight 66 men on the two sides were killed, on the Raja's side 30 and on Kishan Singh's 36. When the sun rose and illumined the world with its light, this business was revealed, and the Raja saw that his brother, his nephew, and some of his servants, whom he considered dearer than himself, were killed, and the whole of the rest had dispersed to their own places. The news reached me in Pushkar, and I ordered them to burn those who were killed, according to their rites, and inform me of the true circumstances of the affair. In the end it became clear that the affair had happened in the manner in which it has been written here, and that no further enquiry was necessary (Jahāngīr, 1:291-293).

Bhāṭī, ***Sarvekṣaṇ***, 3:98, states that Kānhāsiṅgh became an Imperial servant in 1620-21 and that he did service in the Deccan and at Burhanpur. He is said to have received the village of Pīpāvaṛ,[73] where he stationed his ***rāvḷo***. This information is difficult to reconcile with other information known about Kānhāsiṅgh, unless it is assumed that he served under Rājā Gajsiṅgh at this time. Kānhāsiṅgh did become an important military servant under Rājā Gajsiṅgh. ***Āsop kā Itihās***, p. 58, mentions that Rājā Gajsiṅgh granted several villages to Kānhāsiṅgh in ***paṭo*** in reward for his military services in the Deccan. These villages included Baṛlū, Rātkūṛīyo and Khārīyo of Jodhpur Pargano, Pīmpāṛ subdivision (***tapho***), and the village of Nāhaḍhsaro of Āsop ***tapho***.[74]

[73] ***Vigat*** does not list a village by this name for any of the ***parganos*** of Mārvāṛ. Perhaps Pīmpāṛ is meant. Pīmpāṛ is located thirty-three miles east-northeast of Jodhpur.

[74] These villages are located as follows:
Baṛlū : twenty miles north of Pīmpāṛ town.

Kānhāsiṅgh was placed in charge of the internal affairs of Mārvāṛ during the early 1620s and worked with the assistance of Pañcolī Rāghodās, a ***kāmdār*** of Rājā Gajsiṅgh. He also took part in the transfer of Meṛto Pargano from Prince Parvīz to Rājā Gajsiṅgh when the Prince granted Meṛto to him in ***jāgīr***. This transfer took place on August 8, 1623, and both Kānhāsiṅgh and Bhaṇḍārī Lūṇo (no. 156), the ***pradhān*** of Jodhpur, proceeded to Meṛto to present the orders from Prince Parvīz to Abu Kābo (Abu Muḥammad Kambu), the ***amīn***, and to see that the transfer was made in an orderly fashion.

Āsop kā Itihās, p. 59, notes that Rājā Gajsiṅgh sent a force under Kānhāsiṅgh to confront Rajpūts of Sīsodīyo Rāṇo Karaṇsiṅgh Amarsiṅghot of Mevāṛ (1620-28) who were raiding and looting villages in Mārvāṛ in the area of Nāḍūl[75] in Goḍhvāṛ. Kānhāsiṅgh achieved a significant victory here, but this text states that as a result of this victory, Kānhāsiṅgh "became very arrogant and stopped reporting for service." The Rājā then sequestered his ***paṭo*** of Āsop village and granted it to his younger brother, Rājsiṅgh (see ***infra***). The validity of this information regarding Āsop is in doubt, as noted above.

Some uncertainty also surrounds the date and circumstances of Kānhāsiṅgh's death. ***Murārdān***, no. 2, p. 221, records that he was killed in battle in 1624 during the conflict at Damdama on the confluence of the Tons and the Ganges Rivers (near Allahabad). It was here that Imperial troops under Mahābat Khān fought with Prince Khurram (Shāh Jahān), then in rebellion from his father, Emperor Jahāngīr. Rājā Gajsiṅgh was present with the Imperial troops at this battle.

Vigat, 1:114, and ***Jodhpur Rājya kī Khyāt***, p. 186, indicate that Kānhāsiṅgh was killed near Balūndo village[76] of Jaitāraṇ during an outbreak of hostilities with Abu Kābo and his men. Dates given for this occurrence range from 1621-22 in the ***Vigat***, which seems clearly wrong, to 1622-23 in ***Jodhpur Rājya kī Khyāt***. ***Āsop kā Itihās***, p. 59, notes alternatively that a history of Āsop Ṭhikāṇo asserts Kānhāsiṅgh was killed during a battle with an army from Udaipur (no date given), while Bhāṭī, ***Sarvekṣaṇ***, 3:98, records that he died at Burhanpur in the Deccan and offers yet another date of 1630-31 for his death.

Kānhāsiṅgh had five wives and seven sons.

Āsop kā Itihās, pp. 58-60; Bhāṭī, ***Sarvekṣaṇ***, 3:98; ***Mahārāj Śrī Gajsiṅghjī kī Khyāt***, MS no. 15666, Rājasthān Prācyavidyā Pratiṣṭhān, Jodhpur, pp. 23-24; Jahāngīr, 1:291-293; ***Jodhpur Rājya kī Khyāt***, pp. 130, 145, 150-152, 186; ***Khyāt***, 2:155-156; Śivnāthsiṃh, ***Kūmpāvat Rāṭhauṛoṃ kā Itihās***, pp. 185, 192-

---

Rātkūṛīyo: twelve miles north-northeast of Pīmpāṛ.
Khārīyo: six miles east-southeast of Pīmpāṛ.
Nāhaḍhsaro: eight miles due south of Āsop.

[75] Nāḍūl vilage: located sixty-seven miles south-southeast of Jodhpur.

[76] Balūndo village: located fifty-five miles east of Jodhpur and eight miles north of Jaitāraṇ.

196; ***Murārdān***, no. 2, p. 221, 255-258; Ojhā, 4:1:379-382; ***Vigat***, 1:108, 113-114, 2:75.

(no. 101) **Rājsiṅgh Khīṃvāvat** (10-2)

Following Kūmpo Mahirājot (7-1) (no. 95) and Māṇḍaṇ Kūmpāvat (8-4) (no. 99), Rājsiṅgh Khīṃvāvat was perhaps the most illustrious of the Kūmpāvat Rāṭhoṛs of the sixteenth and seventeenth centuries. He held varying positions of influence in Mārvāṛ from personal retainer to Kuṃvar Gajsiṅgh Sūrajsiṅghot (Rājā of Jodhpur, 1619-38) to ***pradhān*** of Jodhpur. He served as ***pradhān*** under both Rājā Gajsiṅgh Sūrajsiṅghot and his son and successor, Rājā Jasvantsiṅgh Gajsiṅghot (1638-78) from 1624-25 until his death in 1640. While a servant of Jodhpur, he was also a Mughal ***mansabdār*** holding the village of Āsop in ***paṭo*** from the Jodhpur ruler and in ***jāgīr*** from the Mughal Emperor. His life was as much involved with the affairs of Mārvāṛ as with the Mughal court, and he performed the role of diplomat on numerous occasions.

Rājsiṅgh was born on either April 11, 1586 (***Caitrādi***) or March 31, 1587 (***Śrāvaṇādi***). He initially served in the Deccan with his father, Khīmvo Māṇḍaṇot, then returned to Mārvāṛ in 1606-07 and, at the order of Rājā Sūrajsiṅgh, was taken into Kuṃvar Gajsiṅgh's service as one of his personal retainers. He received the village of Bāhlo[77] from the ***kuṃvar*** this same year. ***Vigat***, 1:101, also notes that he accompanied Kuṃvar Gajsiṅgh from Pīsāṅgaṇ village[78] to Mārvāṛ in 1614-15, when Rājā Sūrajsiṅgh was posted to the Deccan under orders from Emperor Jahāṅgīr.

Śivnāthsiṃh, ***Kūmpāvat Rāṭhauṛoṃ kā Itihās***, p. 214, indicates that Rājsiṅgh was with Rājā Sūrajsiṅgh when the Rājā traveled to the Deccan in 1615. The Rājā received leave on June 5 of that year to return to Jodhpur and, pleased with Rājsiṅgh's attendance upon him, awarded him the village of Īḍvo of Meṛto[79] which his father, Khīṃvo, had held before him. Emperor Jahāṅgīr granted Jāḷor Pargano to Kuṃvar Gajsiṅgh in ***jāgīr*** in 1616-17, and ordered him to take authority there from the Bīhārī Paṭhāṇs. Rājsiṅgh accompanied the ***kuṃvar*** on this campaign. They successfully took control of Jāḷor fort, but they had to repeat this feat three years later in 1619 following the Paṭhāṇs reassertion of their rule.

Rājā Sūrajsiṅgh of Jodhpur died in September of 1619 at the ***thāṇo*** of Mehkar in the Deccan. Upon Gajsiṅgh Sūrajsiṅghot's succession to the throne as ***rājā*** at Burhanpur on October 5, 1619, he placed Rājsiṅgh in charge of the fort at Jodhpur and awarded him with the ***paṭo*** of Āsop village. Śivnāthsiṃh, ***Kūmpāvat Rāṭhauṛoṃ kā Itihās***, p. 217, states that Rājsiṅgh received Āsop in

[77] Bāhlo village: located thirty-two miles east-southeast of Jodhpur.

[78] Pīsāṅgaṇ village: located fifteen miles west-southwest of Ajmer.

[79] Īḍvo village: located eighteen miles northeast of Meṛto.

reward for his earlier services during the Jāḷor campaign.[80] Āsop was taken from Jeso Bhāṭīs Rāmsiṅgh and Prithīrāj Goyanddāsot at this time. Rājsiṅgh was later with Rājā Gajsiṅgh and Prince Khurram in the Deccan in 1621-22. He again displayed great courage and resourcefulness and was rewarded with the additional ***paṭo*** of Rāṛod village.[81] Rāṛod was taken from Jeso Bhāṭī Veṇīdās Goyanddāsot, a brother of Rāmsiṅgh and Prithīrāj.

In 1619-20, not long after Rājā Gajsiṅgh's succession to the Jodhpur throne, military retainers of his seized the ***māl*** and ***ghāsmārī*** revenues of Meṛto from Prince Khurram's officers there under Abu Kābo (Abu Muḥammad Kambu), the ***amīn***. Rājsiṅgh spent several weeks in negotiations with Abu Kābo over this seizure. He finally agreed to a cash settlement of rs. 50,000 and he stationed Muṃhato Velo (no. 160) at Meṛto to look after the Rājā's interests. Hostilities broke out soon after between Muṃhato Velo's and Abu Kābo's servants. Muṃhato Velo then asked Abu Kābo for a written release from all obligations, and the ***amīn*** had a deed of discharge made and brought it to Velo at Meṛto.

A final settlement about Meṛto was delayed for several years. Following Prince Khurram's rebellion in 1623, Prince Parvīz was appointed ***sūbedār*** of Ajmer (including Meṛto), and negotiations began with him over the transfer of Meṛto Pargano to Rājā Gajsiṅgh. Rājsiṅgh played an important role in petitioning Prince Parvīz through Navāb Mahābat Khān for this transfer. The Prince eventually agreed to the transfer, and he had the certificate of appointment (***tālīko***) written and given to Rājā Gajsiṅgh. Rājsiṅgh's brother, Kānhāsiṅgh Khīṃvāvat, and Bhaṇḍārī Lūṇo (no. 156) brought the ***tālīko*** to Meṛto. Hostilities broke out with Prince Parvīz's men there, but Rājā Gajsiṅgh was able to assume full authority on August 8, 1623.

Rājsiṅgh continued to play a diplomatic role in the affairs of Mārvāṛ throughout his life. Meṛto had not been written into the ***dargāhī mansab*** of Rājā Gajsiṅgh at the time of the original transfer to him in 1623. It had only been granted to the Rājā in ***jāgīr***. After Rājsiṅgh became the new ***pradhān*** of Jodhpur upon the death of Bhaṇḍārī Lūṇo in 1624, he proceeded to Lahore with Fidāī Khān to petition the Emperor himself to have Meṛto written officially into Rājā Gajsiṅgh's Imperial ***mansab***. Rājsiṅgh accomplished this task and returned to Mārvāṛ in 1625-26.

---

[80] ***Āsop kā Itihās***, p. 59, states that Rājsiṅgh received Āsop village in ***paṭo*** after it was sequestered from his brother, Kānhāsiṅgh, shortly before Kānhāsiṅgh's death. This information appears to be incorrect (see ***supra***, Kānhāsiṅgh Khīṃvāvat). ***Khyāt***, 2:157, states very clearly that Rājsiṅgh received Āsop village in 1619-20, when it was taken from Jeso Bhāṭī Rāmsiṅgh and his brother, Prithīrāj. Their father, Jeso Bhāṭī Goyanddās Mānāvat, had received Āsop in 1606-07 in ***paṭo*** from Jodhpur Rājā Sūrajsiṅgh (1595-1619) while he was ***pradhān*** of Jodhpur. He held Āsop under his death in 1615, at which time this village was granted to his two sons, Rāmsiṅgh and Prithīrāj.

[81] Rāṛod village: located forty-four miles northeast of Jodhpur and six miles west of Āsop.

Rājsiṅgh performed other military service for Rājā Gajsiṅgh. He accompanied Kuṃvar Amarsiṅgh Gajsiṅghot and an Imperial force sent against Mahābat Khān, who had rebelled against Emperor Jahāngīr and fled the Imperial camp while enroute from Lahore to north India in 1626-27. Mahābat Khān took refuge in the hills of Mevāṛ, and then made contact with Prince Khurram in the Deccan. Rājsiṅgh was again in Jodhpur with Rājā Gajsiṅgh at the time of Jahāngīr's death in October of 1627.

Emperor Shāh Jahān appointed Rājsiṅgh ***pradhān*** of Jodhpur following Rājā Gajsiṅgh's death in early May of 1638. The Emperor made this appointment while Rājsiṅgh was at Agra in attendance upon the Emperor and Rājā Gajsiṅgh's eleven year old son, Jasvantsiṅgh Gajsiṅghot. The Emperor himself placed the ***ṭīko*** on Jasvantsiṅgh's forehead, confirming his succession to the Jodhpur throne on May 29, 1638. Shāh Jahān paid specific recognition to Rājsiṅgh at this time for his services to the throne. On August 16, 1638[82] the Emperor gave him a ***sirpāv*** of one ***lakh*** rupees and granted Āsop village to him in ***jāgīr*** along with the ***mansab*** rank of 1,000 ***zāt***, 400 ***suwār***.[83] Rājsiṅgh also received a ***paṭo*** from the Rājā worth a ***lākh***.

Rājsiṅgh was much involved with the affairs of Mārvāṛ at the Mughal court during the next several years. Much of his effort there related to settling Rājā Gajsiṅgh's accounts with the Imperial treasury and ensuring that the different ***pargano***s of Mārvāṛ were written correctly into Rājā Jasvantsiṅgh's ***dargāhī mansab***. Rājsiṅgh's ***mansab*** rank was increased in 1639-40 to 1,000 ***zāt***, 600 ***suwār***, which he held until his death very shortly after.

Rājsiṅgh died suddenly at Jodhpur on Monday, November 23, 1640. The manner in which he died, as related in ***Āsop kā Itihās***, pp. 62-64, is of interest and is recorded here in some detail:

It is said that young Rājā Jasvantsiṅgh slipped out of the fort of Jodhpur in disguise on the night of November 22 and went into the city with one of the ***koṭvāḷ***s stationed at the fort. It was a hot night, and the Rājā entered into one of the tanks of the city to swim while the ***koṭvāḷ*** patrolled the area. The tank in which the Rājā swam was considered to be the dwelling place of evil spirits (***bhūt***), and one is said to have entered the Rājā's body. When the people of the city came to the tank at first light to bathe, they found the Rājā lying unconscious and feverish along its edge. They quickly raised the alarm and had him carried back to the fort.

The Rājā's body was placed on a bed at the fort, and those present, who included all of the high officials of the kingdom, proceeded to bargain with the spirit possessing Jasvantsiṅgh's body. The spirit refused to depart. The officials finally obtained a promise from the spirit that it would leave the Rājā's body if someone of equal stature offered himself in the Rājā's stead. Rājsiṅgh

---

[82] ***Jodhpur Rājya kī Khyāt***, p. 263, n. 5 gives this date. Śivnāthsiṃh, ***Kūmpāvat Rāṭhauroṃ kā Itihās***, p. 222, records the date July 12, 1638 (***Adhika Śrāvaṇa***), August 11, 1638 (***Nija Śrāvaṇa***).

[83] Śivnāthsiṃh, ***Kūmpāvar Rāṭhauroṃ kā Itihās***, p. 222, has written incorrectly that he received a ***mansab*** of 1000/4000.

immediately stepped forward. He drank water consecrated with a spell while circumambulating Rājā Jasvantsiṅgh's body, and the spirit then left the Rājā's body and took possession of Rājsiṅgh's, whereupon Rājsiṅgh immediately died.

A cenotaph was built in Rājsiṅgh's memory at the Kāgā Bāgh in Jodhpur. Shāh Jahān himself offered two pairs of golden urns in Rājsiṅgh's memory, one of which was placed in the fort of Jodhpur and the other in Rājsiṅgh's home at Āsop. Rājsiṅgh's wife, Bhāṭiyāṇī Rājkuṃvar, daughter of Jaisaḷmer Bhāṭī Vardesjī, and three *khavās* became *satīs* at Jodhpur when his body was cremated.

According to Śivnāthsiṃh, *Kūmpāvat Rāṭhauroṃ kā Itihās*, pp. 226-227, Rājsiṅgh had eight wives, nine sons and three daughters. His son, Mukaṇdās (Nāhar Khān) Rājsiṅghot by his wife, Sekhāvat Kachvāhī Śirekuṃvar, daughter of Sekhāvat Kachvāho Īsardās Jālamsiṅghot, succeeded him to the rule of Āsop.

> *Āsop kā Itihās*, pp. 60-70; Athar Ali, *Apparatus*, pp. 164, 167, 183; *Bāṅkīdās*, pp. 29-30; Bhāṭī, *Sarvekṣaṇ*, 3:97; *Mahārāj Śrī Gajsiṅghjī kī Khyāt*, pp. 22-23, 36-37; *Śrī Mahārāj Śrī Jasvantsiṅghjī kī Khyāt*, MS no. 15661, Rājasthān Prācyavidyā Pratiṣṭhān, Jodhpur, pp. 183-184; *Jodhpur Rājya kī Khyāt*, pp. 149-150, 263; *Khyāt*, 2:154-157; *Mūndiyāṛ rī Rāṭhoṛāṃ rī Khyāt*, pp. 133, 136; Ojhā, 4:1:382-384, 413-16; Śivnāthsiṃh, *Kūmpāvat Rāṭhauroṃ kā Itihās*, pp. 185, 213-227; *Vigat*, 1:101, 108-111, 124-125, 496, 2:74-75.

Figure 28. Kūmpāvat Rāṭhoṛs

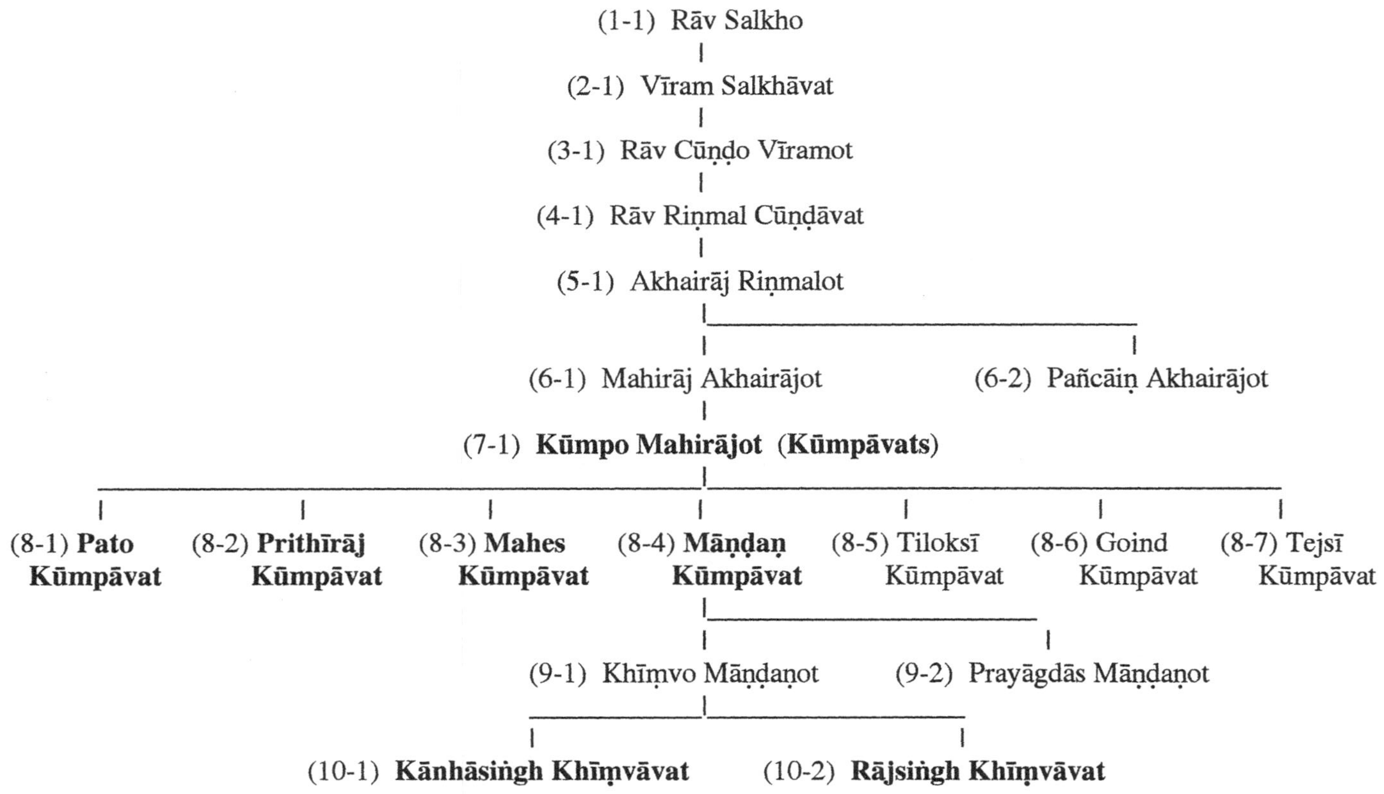
(1-1) Rāv Salkho
(2-1) Vīram Salkhāvat
(3-1) Rāv Cūṇḍo Vīramot
(4-1) Rāv Riṇmal Cūṇḍāvat
(5-1) Akhairāj Riṇmalot
(6-1) Mahirāj Akhairājot
(6-2) Pañcāiṇ Akhairājot
(7-1) **Kūmpo Mahirājot (Kūmpāvats)**
(8-1) **Pato Kūmpāvat**
(8-2) **Prithīrāj Kūmpāvat**
(8-3) **Mahes Kūmpāvat**
(8-4) **Māṇḍaṇ Kūmpāvat**
(8-5) Tiloksī Kūmpāvat
(8-6) Goind Kūmpāvat
(8-7) Tejsī Kūmpāvat
(9-1) Khīṃvo Māṇḍaṇot
(9-2) Prayāgdās Māṇḍaṇot
(10-1) **Kānhāsiṅgh Khīṃvāvat**
(10-2) **Rājsiṅgh Khīṃvāvat**

Mahevco Rāṭhoṛs

(no. 102) **Hāpo Varsiṅghot, Rāvaḷ** (9-1)
(no. 103) **Meghrāj Hāpāvat, Rāvaḷ** (10-1)

The Mahevco Rāṭhoṛs

The Mahevco Rāṭhoṛs descend from Mālojī Salkhāvat (Rāvaḷ Mallīnāth) (2-1), a fourteenth century Rāṭhoṛ warrior. Rāvaḷ Mallīnāth is said to have established Rāṭhoṛ rule at the village of Kheṛ[1] in Mahevo,[2] western Mārvāṛ. He is a prominent figure in local traditions, much celebrated for his legendary prowess as a warrior. There is a fair held each year in March at the village of Tilvāṛo (near Kheṛ) in his remembrance.

Rāvaḷ Mallīnāth's son, Jagmāl Mālāvat (3-1), succeeded him to the rule of Mahevo and Kheṛ. The area of Mahevo then became divided into four portions among Jagmāl's sons. Maṇḍlīk Jagmālot (4-1) succeeded to Mahevo, the most prominent of these sections. It is from Maṇḍlīk that the Mahevco rulers known by the title of ***rāvaḷ*** descend.

(no. 102) Hāpo Varsiṅghot, Rāvaḷ of Mahevo (9-1)

Rāvaḷ Hāpo Varsiṅghot of Mahevo and his brother, Ūgo Varsiṅghot (9-2), became involved in the fortunes of the Jodhpur throne during the period of Rāv Mālde Gāṅgāvat's rule (1532-62). The Mahevcos had maintained a separate and independent existence from Jodhpur prior to this time. Then in 1545 Rāvaḷ Hāpo and his brother, Ūgo, joined Rāv Mālde's warriors in an attack on the Muslim garrison at the village of Bhāṅgesar.[3] Sher Shāh Sūr had placed an outpost at this village following his victory at the battle of Samel[4] in January of 1544, in the aftermath of which he had occupied Jodhpur and much of eastern Mārvāṛ.

The Mahevco involvement in the fortunes of Jodhpur appears linked to a series of marriage alliances between the Mahevcos and the Jeso Bhāṭīs of Mārvāṛ, who served under Rāv Mālde and were some of the most steadfast

---

[1] Kheṛ village: located on the northern side of the Lūṇī River some sixty-two miles southwest of Jodhpur and five miles due east of Tilvāṛo, which is situated on the southern side of the Lūṇī River. Both villages are near the Pacpadro salt pits.

[2] Mahevo (modern Mallāṇī): the name of an area of western Mārvāṛ and also a village located sixty-six miles southwest of Jodhpur and five miles south of Kheṛ.

[3] Bhāṅgesar village: located sixteen miles west of Sojhat.

[4] Samel village: located twenty-four miles southwest of Ajmer.

supporters of the throne.[5] Rāvaḷ Hāpo's mother was a Jeso Bhāṭiyāṇī, daughter of Jeso Bhāṭī Rāṇo Jodhāvat, who held the village of Vālarvo[6] and fifteen others in ***paṭo*** from Rāv Mālde. Jeso Bhāṭī Rāṇo's son, Kisno Rāṇāvat, had taken a wife from the Mahevcos in return. During the period of Rāv Mālde's exile from Jodhpur following his defeat at Samel, Jeso Bhāṭī Kisno went to Mahevo to live with his sister's son (***bhāṇej***), Rāvaḷ Hāpo. Then upon Sher Shāh's death in 1545, Kisno received summons from Rāv Mālde to report for military service. The Rāv was organizing an expedition against the Muslim garrison at Bhāṅgesar. Jeso Bhāṭī Kisno brought Rāvaḷ Hāpo, Hāpo's brother, Ūgo, and several hundred other Mahevcos with him. They assembled with Kisno's father, Jeso Bhāṭī Rāṇo Jodhāvat, and the rest of Rāv Mālde's warriors under the command of Cāmpāvat Rāṭhoṛ Jeso Bhairavdāsot (no. 48).

Both Mahevco Ūgo Varsiṅghot and Jeso Bhāṭī Rāṇo Jodhāvat were killed during the fighting at Bhāṅgesar. Rāvaḷ Hāpo and his mother's brother (***māmo***), Jeso Bhāṭī Kisno Rāṇāvat, were wounded. Rāvaḷ Hāpo then returned to Mahevo and apparently died shortly thereafter, perhaps from wounds received at Bhāṅgesar. The texts do not mention his name with reference to events after this battle.

(no. 103) **Meghrāj Hāpāvat, Rāvaḷ of Mahevo** (10-1)

Rāvaḷ Hāpo's son, Meghāj Hāpāvat, succeeded him to rule at Mahevo. The Mahevco involvement with Jodhpur continued under Rāvaḷ Meghrāj. His name appears first in a listing of Rāv Mālde's warriors chosen to fight under Rāṭhoṛ Devīdās Jaitāvat (no. 65) at the battle of Harmāṛo[7] in January of 1557. Here Rāv Mālde's army joined with Paṭhāṇ Hājī Khān, a former noble of Sher Shāh Sūr's, in battle against an allied force under Sīsodīyo Rāṇo Udaisiṅgh Sāṅgāvat of Mevāṛ (ca. 1537-72; no. 17). Rāvaḷ Meghrāj returned to Mahevo following this engagement, and continued his rule there, offering nominal allegiance to Jodhpur until the time of Rāv Mālde's son and successor, Moṭo Rājā Udaisiṅgh Māldevot (1583-95), when Mahevo came officially under the Jodhpur throne.

Rāvaḷ Meghrāj participated in several military expeditions under Rāv Mālde's immediate successor, Rāv Candrasen Māldevot (1562-81). Shortly after Rāv Candrasen's accession to the Jodhpur throne, Candrasen became involved in conflict with his elder uterine brother, Udaisiṅgh Māldevot, over the division of land and authority in Mārvāṛ. Rāval Meghrāj was with Rāv Candrasen when the Rāv met Udaisiṅgh in battle at the village of Lohīyāvaṭ[8] in northern Mārvāṛ ca.

---

[5] See ***supra***, "Jeso Bhāṭīs."

[6] Vālarvo village: located eighteen miles north-northwest of Jodhpur.

[7] Harmāṛo village: located fifty-five miles south-southwest of Ajmer and six miles south of Vadhnor in northern Mevāṛ.

[8] Lohīyāvaṭ village: located eighteen miles southeast of Phaḷodhī in northern Mārvāṛ.

1563. Ten years later in 1573, Rāvaḷ Meghrāj again fought alongside Rāv Candrasen, this time unsuccessfully against Mughal forces at Sīvāṇo in southwestern Mārvāṛ.

Udaisiṅgh Māldevot succeeded to the throne of Jodhpur in 1583 following the death of his brother, Rāv Candrasen, in 1581 and a short interim period in rulership during continuing Mughal operations in Mārvāṛ. At the time of the Moṭo Rājā's succession, Emperor Akbar granted the Rājā the ***jāgīr*** of Mahevo along with Jodhpur and other areas of Mārvāṛ. The Moṭo Rājā met with Rāvaḷ Meghrāj afterwards and granted Mahevo to him in ***paṭo*** in return for his pledge of support and service. That same year, Rāvaḷ Meghrāj accompanied the Moṭo Rājā to Sīvāṇo, which they occupied. The Rāvaḷ again accompanied the Moṭo Rājā in 1585 when Akbar sent him to Gujarat on an expedition against Sultān Muzaffar III (1561-73; 1583; in revolt until 1593). The Moṭo Rājā granted the Rāvaḷ four additional villages near Mahevo in ***paṭo*** in return for his services in Gujarat.

Rāval Meghrāj's son, Kalo Meghrājot (11-1), died while a young man. The Rāvaḷ designated his grandson, Vīramde Kalāvat (12-1), in 1586-87 as his successor to Mahevo. He then went on pilgrimage to Mathurajī, where he is reported to have sacrificed himself in the Ganges River. He died in 1590-91.

"Aitihasik Bātāṃ," pp. 39-40; ***Bāṅkīdās***, pp. 14, 49; Hardayal Singh, ***Brief Account of Mallani*** (Jodhpur: n.p., 1892), pp. 19-21, 28-29; "Jodhpur Hukūmat rī Bahī," p. 117; ***Khyāt***, 2:164; ***Murārdān***, no. 2, pp. 127, 155-157, 308-315; ***Vigat***, 1:54, 60, 63, 73, 2:59, 220.

Figure 29. Mahevco Rāṭhoṛs

(1-1) Rāv Salkho
|
(2-1) Rāvaḷ Mallīnāth Salkhāvat (**Mahevcos**)
|
(3-1) Rāvaḷ Jagmāl Mālāvat
|
(4-1) Rāvaḷ Maṇḍḷīk Jagmālot
|
(5-1) Rāvaḷ Bhojrāj Maṇḍḷīkot
|
(6-1) Rāvaḷ Vīdo Bhojrājot
|
(7-1) Rāvaḷ Nisaḷ Vīdāvat
|
(8-1) Rāvaḷ Varsiṅgh Nisaḷot

(9-1) **Rāvaḷ Hāpo Varsiṅghot** — (9-2) Ūgo Varsiṅghot

Descendants of (9-1):

(10-1) **Rāvaḷ Meghrāj Hāpāvat**
|
(11-1) Kalo Meghrājot
|
(12-1) Rāvaḷ Vīramde Kalāvat

Meṛtīyo Rāṭhoṛs

(no. 110)	**Acḷo Rāymalot**	(8-7)
(no. 111)	**Arjaṇ Rāymalot**	(8-8)
(no. 114)	**Balbhadar Surtāṇot**	(10-1)
(no. 123)	**Cāndo Vīramdevot**	(8-3)
(no. 104)	**Dūdo Jodhāvat, Rāv**	(6-1)
(no. 118)	**Dvārkādās Jaimalot**	(9-8)
(no. 128)	**Gopāḷdās Sūndardāsot**	(11-3)
(no. 115)	**Gopāḷdās Surtāṇot**	(10-2)
(no. 122)	**Indrabhāṇ Kānhīdāsot**	(11-2)
(no. 109)	**Īsardās Vīramdevot**	(8-5)
(no. 124)	**Jagmāl Vīramdevot**	(8-6)
(no. 116)	**Jagnāth Gopāḷdāsot**	(11-1)
(no. 107)	**Jaimal Vīramdevot, Rāv**	(8-1)
(no. 127)	**Jaitmāl Pañcāiṇot**	(8-9)
(no. 126)	**Kalo Jagmālot**	(9-17)
(no. 121)	**Kānhīdās Kesodāsot**	(10-3)
(no. 119)	**Kesodās Jaimalot**	(9-3)
(no. 120)	**Narhardās Īsardāsot**	(9-15)
(no. 112)	**Prayāgdās Arjaṇot**	(9-18)
(no. 106)	**Rāysal Dūdāvat**	(7-2)
(no. 108)	**Sādūḷ Jaimalot**	(9-14)
(no. 113)	**Surtāṇ Jaimalot**	(9-1)
(no. 125)	**Vāgh Jagmālot**	(9-16)
(no. 105)	**Vīramde Dūdāvat, Rāv**	(7-1)
(no. 117)	**Vīṭhaḷdās Jaimalot**	(9-11)

Meṛtīyo and Varsiṅghot Meṛtīyo Rāṭhoṛs

The Meṛtīyo and Varsiṅghot Meṛtīyo Rāṭhoṛs descend from Dūdo Jodhāvat (no. 104) and his elder uterine brother, Varsiṅgh Jodhāvat (no. 146), respectively. These two brothers, sons of Rāv Jodho Riṇmalot (ca. 1453-89) (5-1), received the area of Meṛto from their father following the founding of Jodhpur in 1459.

Dūdo and Varsiṅgh participated together in the founding of Meṛto and in the establishment of a strong Rāṭhoṛ presence in eastern Mārvāṛ. But they soon became divided among themselves, and both they and their descendants proceeded along different lines of development.

Those Rāṭhoṛs treated in this section descend from Dūdo Jodhāvat. They assumed authority at Meṛto and became known as **Meṛtīyos**. Those who descend from Dūdo's brother, Varsiṅgh Dūdāvat, became known as **Varsiṅghots** or **Varsiṅghot Meṛtīyos**. They are treated in a separate section entitled **Varsiṅghot Meṛtīyo Rāṭhoṛs** (see ***infra***).

(no. 104) **Dūdo Jodhāvat, Rāv of Meṛto** (6-1)

Dūdo Jodhāvat was born on September 28, 1440 of Sonagarī Cāmpā,[1] a daughter of Sonagaro Cahuvāṇ Khīṃvo Satāvat[2] of Pālī village[3] in eastern Mārvāṛ. He grew up during a period of Sīsodīyo rule in Mārvāṛ. Rāv Jodho's father, Rāv Riṇmal Cūṇḍāvat (ca. 1428-38) (4-1), was murdered at Cītoṛ ca. 1438. Jodho Riṇmalot fled Cītoṛ in the wake of his death for Mārvāṛ and then Jāṅgaḷu, an area some one hundred miles to the north of Maṇḍor, while the Sīsodīyos under Rāṇo Kūmbho Mokaḷot (ca. 1433-68) overran eastern Mārvāṛ and occupied Maṇḍor. Jodho Riṇmalot and his Rajpūts spent the next fifteen years re-establishing Rāṭhoṛ authority. Jodho finally succeeded in the conquest of Maṇḍor ca. 1453, and he then assumed his rightful position as ***rāv*** of Mārvāṛ.

Dūdo was approximately thirteen years old when his father became ***rāv***, and he grew to maturity at his father's court. The ***Khyāt*** of Naiṇsī, 3:38-40, tells of his becoming involved in the settlement of an old ***vair*** with the Sīndhaḷ Rāṭhoṛs of Jaitāraṇ[4] while a ***kuṃvar***. This ***vair*** had arisen some twenty years earlier when the Sīndhaḷs killed Dūdo's grandfather's brother's son, Cūṇḍāvat Rāṭhoṛ Āskaraṇ Satāvat (no. 55).[5] The ***Khyāt*** records that Rāv Jodho sent Dūdo to Jaitāraṇ to end the hostilities. Dūdo killed Sīndhaḷ Narsiṅghdās's son, Megho (no. 132), in single-handed combat before the village. Rāv Jodho gave Dūdo a horse and a ***sirpāv*** in recognition of this feat.

Rāv Jodho divided the lands of Mārvāṛ among his brothers and sons following the founding of his new capitol of Jodhpur in 1459. He granted the lands of Meṛto to Dūdo and Dūdo's elder uterine brother, Varsiṅgh Jodhāvat (no. 146). Dūdo and Varsiṅgh brought their carts to this area in 1461-62, and with guidance from Jaitmālot Rāṭhoṛ Ūdo Kānhaṛdevot (no. 67), located the site of two ancient tanks known by the names of Kuṇḍaḷ and Bejpo. The chronicles record that they founded Meṛto near these tanks on March 7, 1462.

Dūdo and Varsiṅgh then proceeded to settle the land. They made Jaitmālot Ūdo Kānhaṛdevot their ***pradhān***, and together they secured the area from the Sāṅkhlo Paṃvārs who inhabited many of the villages. They brought

---

[1] See ***supra***, **Marriage and Family Lists of the Rulers of Jodhpur**, Jodho Riṇmalot, Rāṇī no. 4, S - Dūdo.

[2] See ***supra***, "Sonagaro Cahuvāṇs."

[3] Pālī village: located forty miles south-southeast of Jodhpur.

[4] Jaitāraṇ village: located fifty-six miles east of Jodhpur and thirty-six miles south-southwest of Meṛto.

[5] For details about the beginning of this ***vair***, see ***supra***, Āskaraṇ Satāvat (no. 55) and Narbad Satāvat (no. 56) under "Cūṇḍāvat Rāṭhoṛs."

Ḍāṅgo Jāṭs from the Savāḷakh area of Nāgaur to settle and farm the land, and they recruited Rajpūts from many different branches (***sākh*s**) to serve under them.

Varsiṅgh, the elder brother, assumed control as ***rāv*** of Meṛto during this early period, while Dūdo lived at the village of Rāhaṇ.[6] Although Dūdo and Varsiṅgh worked as one, ***Vigat***, 2:38-39, relates that an omen appeared on the site of Meṛto before its founding, foretelling the eventual emergence of Dūdo and his descendants to dominance at Meṛto. The omen assumed the form of two lions, one larger (representing Varsiṅgh) and one smaller (signifying Dūdo). The larger lion roared, but was then driven away, while the smaller one went into a nearby cave and sat down. An augur who witnessed this event forecast that Varsiṅgh's sons and grandsons would not live at Meṛto after his death, but that Dūdo's descendants would.

Discord eventually arose between the two brothers. Dūdo then left Meṛto and traveled north to join his half-brother, Bīko Jodhāvat (no. 42). Bīko was in the process of establishing his own kingdom to the north of Nāgaur in an area that became known as Bīkāner.

A famine fell across Meṛto not long after Dūdo's departure, and for want of provisions the people attached to Varsiṅgh began to leave. Rāv Varsiṅgh attacked the rich trading city of Sāmbhar to the northeast of Meṛto and looted much wealth in an effort to provide for his people and retain them at Meṛto. The Cahuvāṇ ruler of Sāmbhar appealed to the ***sūbedār*** of Ajmer, Malū Khān, who was a subordinate of the Pātsāh of Māṇḍū, to punish Varsiṅgh for this aggression. Rāv Varsiṅgh also became involved in a dispute with Rāv Sātal Jodhāvat of Jodhpur (ca. 1489-92) at this time over the division of land and authority in Mārvāṛ. Malū Khān entered into this dispute as well, as an arbiter. Demanding a heavy tribute for the looting of Sāmbhar and for a favorable settlement in Mārvāṛ, Malū Khān drew Rāv Varsiṅgh to Ajmer and then imprisoned him. News of Varsiṅgh's capture quickly reached Dūdo, who brought Rāv Bīko Jodhāvat from Bīkāner to join forces with Rāv Sātal of Jodhpur and confront Malū Khān at Ajmer. Malū Khān released Varsiṅgh in the face of this threat, but he soon after brought an army against Meṛto, looting and burning villages and taking prisoners. He was finally met and defeated in battle at the village of Kusāṇo[7] on March 1, 1492 by the combined force of Rajpūts under Rāv Sātal, Dūdo and Rāv Varsiṅgh. Dūdo himself is credited with killing two of Malū Khān's leading warriors, Siriyā Khān and Mīr Gaṛulā, and with the capture of Siriyā Khān's elephants.

Rāv Varsiṅgh died within a short time thereafter. ***Vigat***, 2:46, relates that his death resulted from a slow poison that Malū Khān had given him while he was imprisoned at Ajmer. Varsiṅgh was succeeded by his son, Sīho Varsiṅghot (no. 147), as ***rāv*** of Meṛto. Sīho quickly proved incompetent, and from all sides, people began to press upon the lands of Meṛto. ***Murārdān***, no. 2, p. 445, records that those around Rāv Sīho struck a bargain with Rāv Sūjo

---

[6] Rāhaṇ village: located ten miles north-northeast of Meṛto.

[7] Kusāṇo village: located twenty-eight miles southwest of Meṛto.

Jodhāvat of Jodhpur (ca. 1492-1515), giving him one-third of the villages of Meṛto in return for his protection. But the Rāv moved quickly to occupy not only those villages granted to him, but Meṛto itself. Rāv Sīho's mother, the Sāṅkhlī Paṃvār, then called an assembly of the *pañco*:

> Then Sīho's mother said, "If you were to give the land to Rāv [Sūjo[8]], all the land would be lost. Because of this [eventuality], if you summon Dūdo and give [him] the land, then what harm [would come]? If you were to give the land to Dūdo [and] make Dūdo master of Meṛto, then the land will pass from [those of] my womb, but it will not leave the issue of the mother of my husband (*sāsū*). The land will remain within this house. But if you were to give the land to [Rāv Sūjo], then the land would pass from [this] house. There is no doubt about this [eventuality]. For this reason, I say, have Dūdo summoned, place the *ṭīko* [of succession on his forehead], and having made him master, protect yourselves (***Murārdān***, no. 2, pp. 445-446).

The *pañco* heeded the Sāṅkhlī's words and summoned Dūdo ca. 1492 secretly from Sarvāṛ village[9] where he had established himself after returning from Bīkāner, taking "the best villages in all directions," and where members of his *bhāībandh* also settled. The *pañco* granted Dūdo one-half the revenues of Meṛto in return for his protection, the other half remaining with Rāv Sīho Varsiṅghot. Dūdo quickly drove Rāv Sūjo's men from the area and established his own authority. A short time later in 1495-96, he moved Rāv Sīho himself from Meṛto one night while Sīho was intoxicated, and placed him in the village of Rāhaṇ to the north of Meṛto proper. From this time forward, Dūdo asserted preeminent control over Meṛto for himself and his sons, and he assumed the title of *rāv*.

Rāv Dūdo died two years later in 1497-98 at the age of fifty-seven years.

Rāv Dūdo established a strong tradition within his family of granting villages in *sāṃsaṇ* to Brāhmaṇs and Cāraṇs in the style of a local ruler. Four of Rāv Dūdo's village grants are recorded in the texts:

> 1. Bāmbhaṇ Vās[10] - granted to the Gūjargauṛ Brāhmaṇ Rām Tīlāvat.
> 2. Bījolī[11] - granted to the Rohaṛīyo Cāraṇ *bārhaṭh*s, Pato and Devo Īcot.

---

[8] The text has incorrectly entered the name "Gāṅgo." Rāv Gāṅgo Vāghāvat was Rāv Sūjo's successor and ruler of Jodhpur (1515-32).

[9] Sarvāṛ village: located forty-nine miles due north of Meṛto and twenty-five miles east-northeast of Nāgaur.

[10] Bāmbhaṇ Vās: located nine miles north-northwest of Meṛto proper.

[11] Bījolī: located twenty-eight miles northeast of Meṛto.

3. Khānpur[12] - granted to the Jaghaṭh Cāraṇ Poṭalo, son of Kalo Samrāvat.

4. Parbat kā Khet[13] - granted to the Ratnuṃ Cāraṇ Palo Ūdāvat.

Dūdo had two wives of whom there is record, one daughter and five sons. His wives were the Sīsodṇī Candrakuṃvar, daughter of Sīsodīyo Varsiṅgh of Devaḷīyo, and the Cahuvāṇ Mrigkuṃvar, daughter of Cahuvāṇ Mānsiṅgh of Bambāvdo. His daughter's name was Gulābkuṃvar. Her place of marriage is unknown. Dūdo's sons were:

Vīramde (7-1) (no. 105)
Rāysal (7-2) (no. 106)
Ratansī (7-3)[14]
Rāymal (7-4)
Pañcāiṇ (7-5)

Bāṅkīdās, pp. 8, 59; ***Khyāt***, 1:21, 3:39-40; Gopāḷsiṃh Rāṭhoṛ Meṛtiyā, ***Jaymalvaṃśprakāś, arthāt, Rājasthān Badnor kā Itihās = Jayamal Vansa Prakasha, or, The History of Badnore*** (Ajmer: Vaidik Yantrālay, 1932), pp. 59, 71-72; ***Murārdān***, no. 2, pp. 96-99, 101, 444-446; Ojhā, 4:1:251, 253-254, 261, n. 1, 262, 263, n. 1; Reu, 1:99, 103, n. 5, 105, 106, n. 1, 107; ***Vigat***, 1:39-40, 2:37-39, 41-42, 45-47, 108, 152, 165-166, 175-176, 184-185.

(no. 105) **Vīramde Dūdāvat, Rāv of Meṛto** (7-1)

Vīramde Dūdāvat was a son of Rāv Dūdo Jodhāvat (6-1) (no. 104) and grandson of Rāv Jodho Riṇmalot, ruler of Maṇḍor and Jodhpur (ca. 1453-89). He was born on November 19, 1477, during the period that his father, Dūdo, lived in northern Rājasthān with his half-brother, Bīko Jodhāvat (no. 42). Little is known about Vīramde's early life. He was fifteen years old when his father was summoned back to Meṛto and eighteen years old when his father assumed rulership as ***rāv*** at Meṛto in 1495-96. Two years later in 1497-98, Vīramde himself succeeded his father as ***rāv*** of Meṛto.

It was perhaps in this period from 1492 to 1497 that Vīramde came into conflict with Rāṭhoṛ Ūdo Sūjāvat of Jaitāraṇ village.[15] Ūdo Sūjāvat was a son of

---

[12] Khānpur: located seventeen miles east-northeast of Meṛto.

[13] Parbat rā Khet: a ***khero*** of Rāhaṇ village, located ten miles north-northeast of Meṛto.

[14] Ratansī Dūdāvat had no sons and only one daughter of record. Her name was Mīrāṃbāī. She was married to Sīsodīyo Gahlot Bhojrāj Sāṅgāvat, a son of Rāṇo Sāṅgo Rāymalot of Cītoṛ (1509-28). Her marriage took place in 1516-17. Mīrāṃbāī achieved considerable prominence in Rājasthān as a ***bhaktī*** poetess (***Khyāt***, 1:21).

Rāv Sūjo Jodhāvat of Jodhpur (ca. 1492-1515) who had established his seat of rule at Jaitāraṇ in the early 1480s.

According to Ūdāvat traditions, Vīramde came to Jaitāraṇ on some occasion when Ūdo had fallen ill and was unable to defend the town, and he rode off with a number of Ūdo's mares. Ūdo set out in pursuit as soon as he was able and came upon Vīramde and his party at a village to the south of Meṛto proper. Ūdo demanded the return of his horses. When Vīramde refused, a battle ensued during which Ūdo is said to have emerged victorious. Ūdo then retrieved his mares and, according to Ūdāvat traditions, made Vīramde lay down his dagger and promise that from that day forward, Meṛtīyo ***sirdār***s would not strap on daggers.

This story is not mentioned elsewhere in the Rāṭhoṛ chronicles, and the date given in the Ūdāvat material for Vīramde's stealing the horses is problematic. The event is said to have taken place in 1484-85. Vīramde was only seven years old at this time, and he was in all likelihood in northern Rājasthān with his father, not in the vicinity of Jaitāraṇ. While the date is incorrect, it is possible that if there was conflict between Vīramde and Ūdo, it emerged at the time Dūdo Jodhāvat was establishing himself at Meṛto following his return ca. 1492. It may have been part of a wider series of conflicts that took place with Rāv Sūjo Jodhāvat and the house of Jodhpur over control of territory, with Ūdo Sūjāvat drawn in because he was Rāv Sūjo's son.[16] The Meṛtīyo promise not to strap on daggers appears dubious, however.

Rāv Vīramde's succession to rule at Meṛto in 1497-98 ushered in a period of turmoil, for his reign is a chronicle of conflict between the Meṛtīyos and the rulers of Jodhpur. The beginnings of this conflict were seen during the early struggles of Rāv Varsiṅgh and Dūdo Jodhāvat with their half-brothers, Rāv Sātal (ca. 1489-92) and Rāv Sūjo Jodhāvat (ca. 1492-1515) of Jodhpur. Rāv Vīramde Dūdāvat maintained a truce with Rāv Sūjo's successor, Rāv Gāṅgo Vāghāvat (1515-32), based on occasional military service to Jodhpur. He accompanied Rāv Gāṅgo to Īḍar to assist the Rāṭhoṛ ruler there in the defense of his territory against encroachments from Sultān Muzaffar II (1511-1526) of Gujarat. Rāv Vīramde and his two brothers, Ratansī Dūdāvat (7-3) and Rāymal Dūdāvat (7-4), also came with a contingent of Meṛtīyos to join the force Rāv Gāṅgo sent with Sīsodīyo Rāṇo Sāṅgo Rāymalot of Cītoṛ (1509-28) to fight against the Mughal Bābur at Khanua.[17] Both Ratansī and Rāymal were killed at Khanua on March 17, 1527 during Rāṇo Sāṅgo's abortive attempt to stem the Mughal advance into north India.

---

[15] Jaitāraṇ village: located fifty-six miles east of Jodhpur and thirty-six miles south-southwest of Meṛto.

[16] See ***infra***, "Ūdāvat Rāṭhoṛs," for more information about Ūdo Sūjāvat and the traditions surrounding the conflict between Ūdo and the Meṛtīyos.

[17] ***Akbar Nāma***, 1:261, lists a "Dharam Deo, ruler of Mirtha," with 4,000 Rajpūts at Khanua. This Dharam Deo was Rāv Vīramde Dūdāvat of Meṛto.

The lines of conflict became more firmly drawn toward the end of Rāv Gāṅgo's reign with the growing influence of Rāv Gāṅgo's son, Kuṃvar Mālde Gāṅgāvat, at the court of Jodhpur. According to the chronicles, Kuṃvar Mālde's enmity toward the Meṛtīyos emerged following the battle of Sevakī[18] on November 2, 1529. Rāv Gāṅgo of Jodhpur and his ally from Bīkāner, Rāṭhoṛ Rāv Jaitsī Lūṇkaraṇot (1526-42) (no. 45), met and defeated Rāv Gāṅgo's paternal uncle (***kāko***), Jodho Rāṭhoṛ Sekho Sūjāvat (no. 86), and his ally from Nāgaur, Khānzāda Khān Daulat Khān (no. 154), at Sevakī. A prize elephant of Daulat Khān's named Dariyājoīs ran amok during the battle and fled toward Meṛto, where it was captured and its wounds bound. Kuṃvar Mālde later demanded the elephant from the Meṛtīyos. But they demurred, requesting that Kuṃvar Mālde first come to Meṛto and take food with them. Kuṃvar Mālde came, but he refused to eat until the elephant was delivered. The Meṛtīyos in their turn also refused, leaving Kuṃvar Mālde with no choice but to return to Jodhpur empty-handed. Mālde carried this insult with him for the rest of his life. Despite Rāv Vīramde's later attempts at reconciliation, Mālde would only countenance a Meṛto strictly subordinate to the rule of Jodhpur.[19]

Kuṃvar Mālde plotted against Meṛto soon after Sevakī with the sons of Rāv Sīho Varsiṅghot, Rāv Bhojo (no. 148) and Rāv Gāṅgo Sīhāvat (no. 149). He used as a goad their desire to reassert their father's authority. This intrigue led to their raid on the market square at Meṛto ca. 1530. They fled to the southwest in the direction of Jodhpur following the raid, only to be caught by a pursuit party from Meṛto under the command of one of Rāv Vīramde's leading warriors, Jodho Rāṭhoṛ Khaṅgār Jogāvat (no. 82). They fought a pitched battle near Kusāṇo village,[20] where Rāv Bhojo and Rāv Gāṅgo suffered a severe defeat and were both badly wounded.

Rāv Vīramde again attempted a reconciliation after Mālde's succession to the Jodhpur throne in 1532. He answered Rāv Mālde's summons for service for an expedition against the Sīndhaḷ Rāṭhoṛs of Bhādrājuṇ.[21] But Rāv Mālde used the opportunity provided by Rāv Vīramde's absence from Meṛto to plot further against him. Rāv Mālde sent word secretly to Daulat Khān at Nāgaur, urging him to attack and pillage Meṛto, now left unprotected, to settle the old score with the Meṛtīyos for their taking his prize elephant after the battle of Sevakī in 1529. He prodded Paṃvār Pañcāiṇ Karamcandot (no. 24) of Cāṭsū in central Rājasthān to come against the Meṛtīyos to settle a long-standing ***vair*** that had arisen some time before with the murder of Paṃvār Akho Soḍhāvat (no. 23).

---

[18] Sevakī village: located twenty-three miles northeast of Jodhpur.

[19] Meṛtīyo Rāv Vīramde was not the only victim of Mālde's overweening pride. Mālde had two Bhārmalot Rāṭhoṛs who had fought with Sekho Sūjāvat at Sevakī, killed upon his succession to the Jodhpur throne in 1532. For further details, see ***supra***, "Bhārmalot Rāṭhoṛs."

[20] Kusāṇo village: located twenty-eight miles southwest of Meṛto.

[21] Bhādrājuṇ village: located forty-eight miles south-southwest of Jodhpur.

And he had Varsiṅghot Rāv Gāṅgo Sīhāvat ride into the area of Meṛto with a contingent of warriors.

While Rāv Vīramde suspected subterfuge, he remained in Rāv Mālde's camp as expected. But his ***pradhān***, Jaitmālot Akhairāj Bhādāvat (no. 69), slipped away without leave and reached Meṛto in time to prevent Daulat Khān's force from taking the fort. He was able to drive the Muslims from Meṛto with a small but determined band of warriors. Rāv Vīramde's brother, Rāysal Dūdāvat (7-2) (no. 106), also drove Paṃvār Pañcāiṇ from Āḷṇīyāvās village.[22] preventing his attempt to exact revenge. Varsiṅghot Rāv Gāṅgo's depredations also came to naught.

Then all opportunities for reconciliation ended, for ca. 1535 Rāv Vīramde occupied Ajmer when the Muslims evacuated the city upon the fall of Māṇḍū to the Mughal Emperor Humāyūn. Rāv Mālde of Jodhpur in turn demanded that Rāv Vīramde hand over Ajmer to the house of Jodhpur, under whose authority Mālde felt it properly belonged. When Rāv Vīramde refused, Rāv Mālde occupied Meṛto town and began parceling out the villages of Meṛto among his military servants. Rāv Mālde gave the village of Reyāṃ[23] to Varsiṅghot Meṛtīyo Sahaiso Tejsīyot (no. 151), who had left Rāv Vīramde's service to become his military servant. This action on Sahaiso's part so enraged Rāv Vīramde that he mounted a precipitous attack on Reyāṃ against the better judgment of his Rajpūts. Rāv Vīramde was handed a severe defeat by Sahaiso Tejsīyot and his men who, prior to the battle, donned saffron robes and emerged to seat themselves on blankets before the village, signifying their readiness to die in battle, and Rāv Mālde's Rajpūts, who rode to Reyāṃ from their garrison at the village of Raṛod.[24] Rāv Vīramde himself narrowly escaped death that day. Only the efforts of several of Rāv Mālde's leading warriors including Jaito Pañcāiṇot (no. 61), Kūmpo Mahirājot (no. 95), Jeso Bhairavdāsot (no. 48), and Bhado Pañ cāiṇot (no. 32), prevented his being killed. These Rāṭhoṛs carried reservations about Rāv Mālde's open hostility toward other Rāṭhoṛ brotherhoods. Jaito Pañ cāiṇot in particular considered his actions against them ***gotrakadamb*** (lit. "***gotra***-destruction"), against which there were severe sanctions.

Rāv Vīramde was driven from Meṛto and Ajmer following his defeat at Reyāṃ, and all of his lands were usurped by the house of Jodhpur. He fled north to Ḍīḍvāṇo and then east to Sīkar territory (near Āmber), where he remained for some time with his ***sago***, Kachvāho Rāymal Sekhāvat (no. 22). He eventually moved on to Riṇthambhor and then Delhi, where he met with Sher Shāh Sūr (1540-45).

Sher Shāh showed much sympathy for Vīramde's cause. He had heard similar complaints from the Rāṭhoṛs of Bīkāner, whose lands Rāv Mālde's armies occupied in 1542. Sher Shāh proceeded with a substantial force against Jodhpur

---

[22] Āḷṇīyāvās village: located twenty miles southeast of Meṛto.

[23] Reyāṃ village: located fifteen miles southeast of Meṛto.

[24] Raṛod village: located forty-four miles northeast of Jodhpur and forty-nine miles west-northwest of Reyāṃ.

in late 1543. The opposing armies met at Samel[25] on January 5, 1544. Some five thousand or more of Rāv Māldeʼs warriors died here in battle. Rāv Vīramde was with Sher Shāhʼs force before Samel, and the chronicles relate that he was able to divide the ranks of Jodhpur and raise enough suspicion in Rāv Māldeʼs mind that the Rāv retreated from the field precipitously on the night before the main engagement. Rāv Vīramde received Meṛto in *jāgīr* from Sher Shāh following the victory, and he returned there to rule until his death a short time thereafter in February or March of 1544. He was approximately sixty-seven years of age.

There are discrepancies in the sources regarding the number of wives Rāv Vīramde had, as well as the number of his children. ***Murārdān***, no. 2, pp. 459, 549, mentions two wives, a Ṭāṅkaṇī who was the mother of his son, Jaimal Vīramdevot (8-1) (no. 107), and a Soḷaṅkaṇī who was the mother of his son, Sāraṅgde (8-2). A modern source, Meṛtiyā, ***Jaymalvaṃśprakāś***, p. 106, which draws upon the "***khyāt***s of the Kuḷgurūs, Bhāṭs and Rāṇīmaṅgs," lists four wives. This text unfortunately does not indicate which wives bore which sons. The wives were:

1. Soḷaṅkaṇī Kalyāṇkuṃvar, daughter of Rāṇo Kesavdās of Nīvarvāṛo.
2. Soḷaṅkaṇī Gaṅgakuṃvar, daughter of Rāv Phatehsiṅgh of Nīvarvāṛo and Vīsalpur.
3. Sīsodṇī Gorjyākuṃvar, daughter of Rāṇo Rāymal Kūmbhāvat of Cītoṛ (ca. 1473-1509).
4. Kachvāhī Mānkuṃvar, daughter of Rājā Kisandās of Kālvāṛo (near Āmber).

This source also lists three daughters and their places of marriage:

D - Syāmkuṃvar - married to Sīsodīyo Rāvat Sāṅgo of Madārīyo in Goḍhvāṛ.

D - Phūlkuṃvar - married to Sīsodīyo Rāvat Pato Jagāvat of Kelvo.

D - Abhaykuṃvar - married to Cahuvāṇ Rāv Rāghavdās of Gaṅgor.

These references are of interest because they show that Rāv Vīramde married a daughter from the ruling family of Cītoṛ and gave one of his daughters in marriage to the important Sīsodīyo Rajpūt, Pato Jagāvat,[26] whom the Mughal Emperor Akbar was later to acclaim a great warrior alongside Rāv Vīramdeʼs son, Jaimal, at the battle of Cītoṛ in 1568.

---

[25] Samel village: located twenty-four miles southwest of Ajmer.

[26] Cūṇḍāvat Sīsodīyo Gahlot Pato Jagāvat, son of Jago Siṅghot. See ***Khyāt***, 1:66-70, for a genealogy of the Cūṇḍāvat ***sākh*** of the Sīsodīyo Gahlots, which includes mention of Pato Jagāvat.

Rāv Vīramde had between nine and thirteen sons.[27] Some of these sons figure in the texts under discussion. They have been given biographical note numbers and are included on the genealogical charts. These sons were:

S - Jaimal (8-1) (no. 107)
S - Sāraṅgde (8-2)
S - Cāndo (8-3) (no. 123)
S - Māṇḍaṇ (8-4)
S - Īsardās (8-5) (no. 109)
S - Jagmāl (8-6) (no. 124)

The names of other sons listed in the various sources are mentioned here for reference only. They include:

S - Pratāpsiṅgh
S - Prithīrāj
S - Karaṇ (Khemkaraṇ)
S - Acḷo
S - Bīko
S - Sekho
S - Kān

Rāv Vīramde granted several villages in ***sāṃsaṇ*** to Brāhmaṇs and Cāraṇs. These were:

1. Bhāṃvalī Cāraṇāṃ rī[28] - granted to the Khiṛīyo Cāraṇ Māṇḍaṇ Khīṃvsurāvat.

2. Gohṛo Khurad[29] - granted to the Ratnūṃ Cāraṇ Karaṇ Sukhāvat.

3. Kheṛī Campo[30] - granted to the Jāgarvāḷī Brāhmaṇ Rāmo Ḍuṅgāvat.

4. Sāṃvaḷīyāvās Khurad[31] - granted to the Śrīmāḷī Brāhmaṇ Vyās Jagde Rāmdevot.

"Aitihāsik Bātāṃ," pp. 42-44; ***Akbar Nāma***, 1:261; ***Bāṅkīdās***, pp. 12, 59-60, 62; ***Khyāt***, 3:93-102, 115; Meṛtiyā,

---

[27] For the variant lists, see: ***Bāṅkīdās***, p. 60; Meṛtiyā, ***Jaymalvaṃśprakāś***, pp. 107-111; ***Murārdān***, no. 2, pp. 459, 507, 520-521, 526, 549, 550, 555.

[28] Bhāṃvalī Cāraṇāṃ rī: located twenty-two miles northeast of Meṛto, near Deghāṇo.

[29] Gohṛo Khurad: located just near Altāvo, to the northeast of Meṛto.

[30] Kheṛī Campo: located ten miles northeast of Meṛto, near Moḍro.

[31] Sāṃvaḷīyāvās Khurad: located fifteen miles due north of Meṛto, near Rāhaṇ.

Jaymalvaṃśprakāś, pp. 63, 106-111; *Murārdān*, no. 2, pp. 116-120, 124-125, 128, 447-459, 507, 520-521, 523-524, 526, 549-550, 554-555, 574; Ojhā, 4:1:274, 279-280, 285-287, 296-309, 314; *Vigat*, 1:42, 2:47-58, 163-164, 175, 185-186, 198.

(no. 106) **Rāysal Dūdāvat** (7-2)

Rāysal Dūdāvat was a son of Rāv Dūdo Jodhāvat (6-1) (no. 104) and a grandson of Rāv Jodho Riṇmalot (5-1), ruler of Maṇḍor and Jodhpur (ca. 1453-89). The chronicles describe Rāysal as a great warrior who was skilled in battle. He was one of the influential *ṭhākurs* of Meṛto during Rāv Vīramde's reign, and he was a strong internal force against the house of Jodhpur. Rāysal played a prominent role in the early conflicts between Meṛto and Jodhpur, and he appears primarily responsible for the Meṛtīyo refusal to accede to Kuṃvar Mālde Gāṅgāvat's demand that they hand over the Nāgaurī Khān's elephant following the battle of Sevakī[32] on November 2, 1529.

Rāysal was with Rāv Vīramde during the occupation of Ajmer ca. 1535, and he fought with the Meṛtīyos against Rāv Mālde's Rajpūts at Reyāṃ village[33] that same year. He was badly wounded there and had to be carried back to Ajmer where he died shortly after. He was a Rajpūt whom Rāv Mālde greatly feared, and the Rāv sought specific news of Rāysal after his victory at Reyāṃ before proceeding against Ajmer.

Bāṅkīdās, p. 59; *Khyāt*, 3:94-95, 97-98; *Murārdān*, no. 2, p. 571; *Vigat*, 2:50-52.

(no. 107) **Jaimal Vīramdevot, Rāv of Meṛto** (8-1)

Jaimal Vīramdevot was a son of Rāv Vīramde Dūdāvat (7-1) (no. 105) by his Ṭāṅkaṇī wife and a grandson of Rāv Dūdo Jodhāvat (6-1) (no. 104), the founding ancestor of the Meṛtīyo Rāṭhoṛs. Jaimal was born on July 8, 1508 and succeeded his father to the rulership of Meṛto in 1544 at the age of thirty-six years. He ruled Meṛto intermittently for a quarter of a century until his death in early 1568 at the battle of Cītoṛ.

Rāv Jaimal reigned in relative peace at Meṛto for the first ten years of his rule after the battle of Samel in 1544. Rāv Mālde of Jodhpur (1532-62) was engaged in rebuilding his armies and in the conquest of other territories in both Mārvāṛ and surrounding areas during these years. In 1554, however, Rāv Mālde again turned his attention toward Meṛto, and Jaimal, like his father, then spent the remainder of his life engaged in conflict with the house of Jodhpur. Rāv Jaimal emerged victorious from the first of these encounters, a skirmish on the outskirts of Meṛto town near the ancient tank of Kuṇḍaḷ. The chronicles state that Śrī Caturbhujjī, the patron deity of the Meṛtīyos, of whom Jaimal was a

[32] Sevakī village: located twenty-three miles northeast of Jodhpur.

[33] Reyāṃ village: located fifteen miles southeast of Meṛto.

fervent devotee, became manifest during this battle and was responsible for the Meṛtīyo victory.

In this engagement, Rāv Mālde lost one of his most able commanders, Rāṭhoṛ Prithīrāj Jaitāvat (no. 63). The Hul Rajpūt Rāysal Rāmāvat, a military servant of Rāv Jaimal's holding Phālko village[34] and twelve other in ***paṭo***, was a sister's son (***bhāṇej***) of Prithīrāj. Rāysal found Prithīrāj lying on the ground after the battle, and he built a cover to shade his body from the sun. This action greatly angered Rāv Jaimal, and Hul Rāysal then abandoned Meṛto and took service under Rāv Mālde.

Some desultory fighting continued after the battle for Meṛto in 1554. Rāṭhoṛ Devīdās Jaitāvat (no. 65), Prithīrāj Jaitāvat's brother, led a strong force of several thousand Rajpūts against Reyāṃ village[35] in an attempt to avenge his brother's death. Rāv Jaimal remained enclosed within the fort at Meṛto, however, and no significant engagements with Devīdās occurred. Devīdās was eventually forced to withdraw from the area.

Rāv Jaimal left Meṛto with an army in late 1556 to join Sīsodīyo Rāṇo Udaisiṅgh Sāṅgāvat of Mevāṛ (ca. 1537-72; no. 17) during his conflict with Paṭhāṇ Hājī Khān, a former noble of Sher Shāh Sūr's. Hājī Khān had occupied Ajmer in this year. By January of 1557, both sides had assembled large forces, with Rāv Mālde of Jodhpur sending warriors under Rāṭhoṛ Devīdās Jaitāvat to support Hājī Khān. The opposing armies finally met at Harmāṛo[36] on January 24, 1557.

Hājī Khān's and Rāv Mālde's forces emerged victorious at Harmāṛo, and when Rāv Jaimal returned to Meṛto, he found Rāv Mālde already in the process of consolidating his authority over the area. Sīsodīyo Rāṇo Udaisiṅgh himself came to Meṛto and took Rāv Jaimal back to Mevāṛ, refusing to allow him to die in battle there. Jaimal then took up residence at the court of Cītoṛ and began a period of service under the Rāṇo.

Sometime earlier, two of Rāv Jaimal's brothers, Sāraṅgde (8-2) and Māṇḍaṇ (8-4), had been killed during an outbreak of hostilities with some Soḷaṅkī Rajpūts near Toḍo in central Rājasthān. Sāraṅgde was a sister's son (***bhāṇej***) of the Soḷaṅkīs, and Rāv Jaimal himself had married a Soḷaṅkaṇī and was their daughter's husband (***jamāī***). These relationships may in some way have been related to the killings, but sources do not specify. Rāv Jaimal's brother, Cāndo Vīramdevot (8-3) (no. 123), killed a Soḷaṅkī named Narāiṇdās at Cītoṛ to settle this ***vair***, but it finally ended only when the Soḷaṅkīs gave Rāv Jaimal another of their daughters in marriage.

Rāv Jaimal met with the Mughal Emperor Akbar at Sāmbhar in early 1562 while Akbar was enroute from Ajmer to north India. Akbar agreed to assist Jaimal in the recovery of his lands from Rāv Mālde. He sent Mīrzā Sharafu'd-

---

[34] Phālko village: located fourteen miles south-southwest of Meṛto.

[35] Reyāṃ village: located fifteen miles southeast of Meṛto.

[36] Harmāṛo village: located fifty-five miles south-southwest of Ajmer and six miles south of Vadhnor in northern Mevāṛ.

Dīn Ḥusayn and a force of some 7,000 Mughals with Rāv Jaimal against Meṛto. This force laid siege to the Mālgaḍh in February of 1562 and, following several weeks of desultory fighting, were finally able to explode a mine under one of the towers of the fort. Only then did Rāv Mālde's commander, Rāṭhoṛ Devīdās Jaitāvat, hold talks with Rāv Jaimal and the Mughals and agree to vacate the fort. Rāv Jaimal could not allow Devīdās simply to leave the fort, however, for he feared later retribution. He urged the Mīrzā to attack and kill Devīdās and his Rajpūts as they moved off in the direction of Sātaḷvās, a village four miles to the southwest of Meṛto, on March 20, 1562. He argued that Devīdās was not the sort of Rajpūt who would abandon the fort, but was only leaving in order to bring Rāv Mālde against them. The Mīrzā and Rāv Jaimal rode after Devīdās and his men, killing many of them including Devīdās on the plain before Meṛto.

Rāv Jaimal afterwards assumed full authority at Meṛto in his own name and received these lands in ***jāgīr*** from Akbar. After a period of consolidation during which Rāv Jaimal developed a close relationship with Mīrzā Sharafu'd-Dīn, Akbar's governor of Ajmer and Nāgaur, he sent his son, Vīṭhaḷdās (9-11) (no. 117), with the Mīrzā to Agra to wait upon the Emperor at court. The Mīrzā then rebelled against Akbar in October of 1562, and Rāv Jaimal and his sons immediately became involved. Jaimal's son, Vīṭhaḷdās, fled Agra with the Mīrzā and came to Meṛto to report the turn of events to his father. Another son, Sādūḷ Jaimalot (9-14) (no. 108), was killed bringing the Mīrzā's family and retainers from Nāgaur. Rāv Jaimal himself escorted Sharafu'd-Dīn to the borders of southern Mārvāṛ to ensure his safety and, afterwards, knowing that his association with the Mīrzā meant certain censure from Akbar and the revocation of his ***jāgīr***, returned to the Sīsodīyo court at Cītoṛ by way of the Arāvallīs. He had already sent his family to Vadhnor.[37] The Rāṇo again accepted Jaimal into his military service and granted him a large ***paṭo*** of villages for his maintenance.[38]

Rāv Jaimal remained at Cītoṛ in the Rāṇo's service for the remainder of his life. One of his brothers, Īsardās Vīramdevot (8-5) (no. 109), was with him, as were a large number of Rajpūts who had accompanied them from Meṛto. In February of 1568 both Jaimal and Īsardās were killed at the battle of Cītoṛ against Emperor Akbar, along with some two hundred other Meṛtīyos and a large number of Jaitmālot Rāṭhoṛs, who were military servants of the Meṛtīyos. Akbar himself shot Rāv Jaimal as Jaimal directed operations to fill a breech in the wall of the fort, and Jaimal died shortly afterwards.[39] His death is said to have greatly dampened resistance at the fort against the Mughal attack.

Akbar took possession of Cītoṛ on February 24 or 25, 1568. In tribute to Rāv Jaimal's bravery, Akbar had a stone column placed before a door to the Red

---

[37] Vadhnor village: located forty-seven miles south-southwest of Ajmer in northern Mevāṛ.

[38] See: ***Vigat***, 2:69, of the **translated text** for details.

[39] For a discussion of the controversy surrounding Rāv Jaimal's death at Cītoṛ, see n. 484 to ***Vigat***, 2:68, of the **translated text**.

Fort at Agra with Rāv Jaimal's likeness carved seated upon an elephant. Alongside him on a second column Akbar placed the likeness of Cūṇḍāvat Sīsodīyo Pato Jagāvat,[40] another brave Rajpūt killed in this battle. Sīsodīyo Pato Jagāvat had married a daughter of Rāv Jaimal's father, Rāv Vīramde Dūdāvat, and Jaimal was Pato's wife's brother (*sāḷo*).

Rāv Jaimal had seven wives, fourteen sons and two daughters of whom there is record. His wives and their sons were:[41]

1. Soḷaṅkaṇī (elder)

    S - Surtāṇ (9-1) (no. 113)

2. Soḷaṅkaṇī (junior)

    S - Kesodās (9-3) (no. 119)
    S - Mādhodās (9-2)
    S - Goyanddās (9-4)

3. Kachvāhī

    S - Kalyāṇdās (9-5)

4. Kachvāhī - daughter of Rājāvat Kachvāho Rājā Āskaraṇ Bhīṃvrājot of Gwalior.

    S - Narāiṇdās (9-6)
    S - Narsiṅghdās (9-7)
    S - Dvārkādās (9-8) (no. 118)

5. Kachvāhī

    S - Harīdās (9-9)

6. Vāghelī

---

[40] See ***Khyāt***, 1:32, 66-70, for references to this Rajpūt and a genealogy of the Cūṇḍāvat Sīsodīyos.

[41] This listing is taken from ***Murārdān***, no. 2, pp. 462-463, 470-471, 473, 480, 487, 489, 491-493, 499, 502, 504-507. The recent history, Meṛtiyā, ***Jaymalvaṃśprakāś***, p. 159, lists only three wives. According to this source, they were Soḷaṅkaṇī Kevalkuṃvar, daughter of Rāṇo Riṇdhīrsiṅgh of Lūṇavāṛo, Nīrvāṇ Cahuvāṇ Vinaykuṃvar, daughter of Rājā Kesavdās of Khaṇḍelo, and Soḷaṅkaṇī Padmākuṃvar, daughter of Rāy Kesrīsiṅgh of Desūrī. This source does not list sons by mother, and includes the names of two more sons than ***Murārdān***: Anopsiṅgh and Acaḷdās (see pp. 160-164).

S - Rāmdās (9-10)
S - Vīṭhaldās (9-11) (no. 117)
S - Mukanddās (9-12)
S - Syāmdās (9-13)

7. (unknown)

S - Sādūḷ (9-14) (no. 108)

Rāv Jaimal's two daughters and their places of marriage were:[42]

D - Gumānkuṃvar - married to Cahuvān Rāv Bakhtāvarsiṅgh of Gaṅgor.
D - Gulābkuṃvar - married to Sīsodīyo Gahlot Rāvat Pañcāiṇ.

Rāv Jaimal granted the following villages in ***sāṃsaṇ*** to Brāhmaṇs and Cāraṇs:

1. Dābṛīyāṇī Khurad[43] - granted to the Pokaraṇo Brāhmaṇ Purohit Kelaṇ Cutrāvat.
2. Harbhu rī Vāsṇī[44] - granted to the Srīmāḷī Brāhmaṇ Vyās Gotam Gensar.
3. Jodhṛāvās Khurad[45] - granted to the Vīṭhū Cāraṇ Mālo Tejāvat.
4. Moḍṛīyo[46] - granted first by Varsiṅghot Meṛtīyo Rāv Sīho Varsiṅghot (no. 147) to Khiṛīyo Cāraṇ Sīho Candrāvat and later by Rāv Jaimal to Khiṛīyo Cāraṇ Cāhaṛ Māṇḍaṇot.
5. Raḷīyāvṭo Khurad[47] - granted to the Khiṛīyo Cāraṇ Moṭoḷ Māṇḍaṇot.
6. Rāmā Cāraṇāṃ rī Vāsṇī[48] - granted to the Jaghaṭh Cāraṇ Rāmo Dharamāvat.

"Aitihāsik Bātāṃ," pp. 48-55; ***Akbar Nāma***, 2:248-249; A. L. Srivastava, ***Akbar the Great***, Vol. 1, ***Political History: 1542-***

---

[42] This list comes from Meṛtiyā, ***Jaymalvaṃśprakāś***, p. 159.

[43] Dābṛīyāṇī Khurad: located eight miles north of Meṛto, near Rāhaṇ.

[44] Harbhu rī Vāsṇī: located three miles southwest of Meṛto, near Mokālo.

[45] Jodhṛāvās Khurad: located sixteen miles north-northeast of Meṛto, near Rāhaṇ.

[46] Moḍṛīyo village: located sixteen miles northeast of Meṛto, near Moḍro.

[47] Raḷīyāvṭo Khurad: located twenty-six miles east-northeast of Meṛto, near Deghāṇo.

[48] Rāmā Cāraṇāṃ rī Vāsṇī: located just four miles from Meṛto.

1605 A.D. (2nd ed. Agra: Shiva Lala Agarwala & Co., 1972), p. 109; ***Bāṅkīdās***, pp. 13-16, 60-62; ***Khyāt***, 1:32, 112, 3:115-19, 121-22 ; Meṛtiyā, ***Jaymalvaṃśprakāś***, pp. 159-164; ***Murārdān***, no. 2, pp. 128-129, 459-463, 470-471, 473, 480, 487, 489, 491-493, 499, 502-508, 549, no. 3, p. 172; ***Vigat***, 2:58-60, 63-69, 110-111, 119, 139, 163-164, 176, 197; ***Vīr Vinod***, 2:75, 80, 82.

(no. 108) **Sādūḷ Jaimalot** (9-14)

Sādūḷ Jaimalot was a son of Rāv Jaimal Vīramdevot (8-1) (no. 107) and a great-grandson of Rāv Dūdo Jodhāvat (6-1) (no. 104). He held the village of Kuṛkī[49] in ***paṭo*** from Rāv Jaimal.

Sādūḷ appears to have spent most of his short life in his father's service at the court of Meṛto. He became caught up in the aftermath of Mīrzā Sharafu'd-Dīn Ḥusayn's rebellion from Akbar in October of 1562 and his flight from Agra to Rājasthān. Sāḍūl was sent to Nāgaur with a small ***sāth*** to bring the Mīrzā's family and military retainers to Meṛto. They managed their escape from Nāgaur, but the Mughal officers in pursuit caught up with them on the outskirts of Meṛto. In the pitched battle that ensued, Sādūḷ was killed along with forty of his men.

Bāṅkīdās, p. 61; ***Murārdān***, no. 2, p, 470; ***Vigat***, 2:67-68.

(no. 109) **Īsardās Vīramdevot** (8-5)

Īsardās Vīramdevot was a son of Rāv Vīramde Dūdāvat (7-1) (no. 105) and grandson of Rāv Dūdo Jodhāvat (6-1) (no. 104), the founding ancestor of the Meṛtīyo Rāṭhoṛs. Only a few details are available about Īsardās's life. He lived at Meṛto, holding the villages of Kekīnd[50] and Āḷṇīyāvās[51] in ***paṭo*** from Rāv Jaimal. The chronicles record that during the battle of Meṛto in 1554 against Rāv Mālde Gāṅgāvat of Jodhpur (1532-62), Īsardās stole some of Rāv Mālde's horses while they were watering at a local tank. He appears to have been only a young man at this time. Īsardās later followed Rāv Jaimal to Mevāṛ in 1562, when Jaimal was forced to forfeit Meṛto in the wake of Mīrzā Sharafu'd-Dīn's rebellion against Akbar. He was killed at Cītoṛ in early 1568 during the great battle against Emperor Akbar.

Bāṅkīdās, p. 60; ***Khyāt***, 1:32, 3:118; ***Murārdān***, no. 2, pp. 507-508.

(no. 110) **Acḷo Rāymalot** (8-7)

[49] Kuṛkī village: located twenty miles southeast of Meṛto.

[50] Kekīnd village: located fourteen miles south-southeast of Meṛto.

[51] Āḷṇīyāvās village: located twenty miles southeast of Meṛto.

Acḷo Rāymalot was a son of Rāymal Dūdāvat (7-4) and a grandson of Rāv Dūdo Jodhāvat (6-1) (no. 104). Little information is available about Acḷo or his family. Acḷo's father, Rāymal, held the village of Rāhaṇ[52] in ***paṭo*** from his brother, Rāv Vīramde Dūdāvat (7-1) (no. 105). Rāymal accompanied Rāv Vīramde and a contingent of Meṛtīyos to north India with Sīsodīyo Rāṇo Sāṅgo Rāymalot of Cītoṛ (1509-28) to meet the Mughal Bābur at Khanua. He was killed there in battle on March 17, 1527. Rāymal had married a daughter to Sekhāvat Kachvāho Sūjo Rāymalot, a son of Kachvāho Rāymal Sekhāvat's (no. 22).

Acḷo Rāymalot succeeded his father to Rāhaṇ village and appears to have spent much of his life there while nominally in the service of Meṛtīyo Rāv Jaimal Vīramdevot (8-1) (no. 107). The chronicles present Acḷo as a Meṛtīyo who sought his own advantage and who preferred not to become involved in the series of conflicts between Meṛto and Jodhpur. He chose to sit at home instead of responding to Rāv Jaimal's summons for military service and did not report, for example, during the battle for Meṛto in 1554 against Rāv Mālde Gāṅgāvat of Jodhpur (1532-62). He died a natural death some years later.

Acḷo granted the village of Acḷā rā Khet[53] in ***sāṃsaṇ*** to the Vīṭhū Cāraṇ Ābo Tejāvat.

Harnath Singh Dunlod, ***The Sheikhawats & their Lands*** (Jaipur: Raj Educational Printers, 1970), p. 10; ***Khyāt***, 3:116; ***Murārdān***, no. 2, pp. 555, 560; ***Vigat***, 2:165.

(no. 111) **Arjaṇ Rāymalot** (8-8)

Arjaṇ Rāymalot was a son of Rāymal Dūdāvat (7-4) and grandson of Rāv Dūdo Jodhāvat (6-1) (no. 104). He served under Rāv Jaimal Vīramdevot (7-1) (no. 107) of Meṛto, holding the village of Īḍvo[54] in ***paṭo*** from the Rāv. The chronicles portray Arjaṇ, like his brother, Acḷo Rāymalot (8-7) (no. 110), as an uncertain supporter of Rāv Jaimal in his conflicts with the house of Jodhpur. Arjaṇ also hesitated to answer Rāv Jaimal's summons for service during the battle for Meṛto in 1554. But unlike Acḷo, he eventually came, and he fought well during the main engagement. Then in 1562 he followed Rāv Jaimal to Mevāṛ in the wake of Mīrzā Sharafu'd-Dīn's rebellion against Akbar. He was killed at Cītoṛ in early 1568 in the great battle against Emperor Akbar.

Bāṅkīdās, p. 104; ***Khyāt***, 3:115-116, 119; ***Murārdān***, no. 2, p. 556.

---

[52] Rāhaṇ village: located ten miles north-northeast of Meṛto.

[53] Acḷā rā Khet: specific location uncertain, but probably in the vicinity of Rāhaṇ.

[54] Īḍvo village: located eighteen miles northeast of Meṛto.

(no. 112) **Prayāgdās Arjaṇot** (9-18)

Prayāgdās Arjaṇot was a son of Arjaṇ Rāymalot (8-7) (no. 111) and a great-grandson of Rāv Dūdo Jodhāvat (6-1) (no. 104). Little is known about Prayāgdās's life from sources at hand. He appears only once in the chronicles of Naiṇsī (***Khyāt***, 3:119-120) as a military servant of Rāv Jaimal Vīramdevot (8-1) (no. 107), who participated in the battle for Meṛto in 1554 against Rāv Mālde Gāṅgāvat of Jodhpur (1532-62). Prayāgdās was a young man at this time. The ***Khyāt*** portrays him as both a loyal and enthusiastic supporter of Rāv Jaimal, and as an untried, injudicious warrior in battle. Rāv Jaimal welcomed him to the battle and exclaimed that he always forgave Prayāgdās for his indiscretions because he appeared for service.

The ***Khyāt*** records that Prayāgdās was killed in this battle while trying to force his bow over Rāv Mālde's head. Other information from ***Murārdān***, no. 2, p. 557, indicates that this was not the case. This text states that Prayāgdās followed his father, Arjaṇ Rāymalot, to Cītoṛ in 1562. He remained there with his father and other Meṛtīyos in Rāv Jaimal's service until after the battle of Cītoṛ in 1568, in which his father was killed. He then became a military servant of Rāv Jaimal's son, Surtāṇ Jaimalot (9-1) (no. 113). He received the ***paṭo*** of Sīrāsṇo village[55] from Surtāṇ in 1572. Prayāgdās continued his service under Surtāṇ's son, Gopāḷdās Surtāṇot (10-2) (no. 115), following Surtāṇ Jaimalot's death in Bihar in 1589-90. ***Murārdān*** records that he was killed at Bīḍ city in the Deccan with Gopāḷdās in 1599-1600 during Mughal operations there against Ahmadnagar.

Khyāt, 3:119-120; ***Murārdān***, no. 2, p. 557.

(no. 113) **Surtāṇ Jaimalot** (9-1)

Surtāṇ Jaimalot was the son and chosen successor of Rāv Jaimal Vīramdevot (8-1) (no. 107) of Meṛto. He was born of Rāv Jaimal's elder Soḷaṅkaṇī wife. Surtāṇ's name first appears in the texts with reference to the battle of Meṛto in 1554, at which time he was only a youth. He came before Rāv Mālde's commander, Rāṭhoṛ Prithīrāj Jaitāvat (no. 63), near Meṛto's Jodhpur Gate, and he thrust his lance at Prithīrāj. Prithīrāj easily warded off this blow, and he then took Surtāṇ's sword away from him and presented it to one of his own military servants, Pīpāṛo Gahlot Hīṅgoḷo, to whom he had promised such a weapon. Prithīrāj afterwards chided Surtāṇ that his father, Rāv Jaimal, should have come in his stead.

Surtāṇ accompanied his father to Cītoṛ in late-1562 in the wake of Mīrzā Sharafu'd-Dīn's rebellion from Akbar. Then in 1568, following Rāv Jaimal's death in battle at Cītoṛ, Surtāṇ took up residence at the fort of Bor[56] near the village of Rūpjī in the hilly area of western Mevāṛ. The Rāṇo of Mevāṛ,

---

[55] Sīrāsṇo village: located twelve miles northeast of Meṛto.

[56] Bor village: located twelve miles northeast of Kumbhaḷmer in western Mevāṛ.

Sīsodīyo Udaisiṅgh Sāṅgāvat (ca. 1537-72; no. 17), had granted this fort to Surtāṇ and his younger half-brother, Kesodās (9-3) (no. 119), in ***paṭo***. Surtāṇ's ***vasī*** remained in this village for a number of years. The Meṛtīyos constructed a temple to their patron deity, Śrī Caturbhujjī, at Bor.

Murārdān, no. 2, p. 462, records that after Rāv Jaimal's death at Cītoṛ, the Mughal Emperor Akbar sought the offices of Rājāvat Kachvāho Bhagvantdās Bhārmalot (Rājā of Āmber, ca. 1574-89) to call Surtāṇ from Mevāṛ. The Emperor wished to offer Meṛto in ***jāgīr*** to Surtāṇ in return for Surtāṇ's obeisance. Surtāṇ is said to have replied that his ***dharma*** demanded he remain in the service of the Rāṇo for one year, after which he would be free to leave.

The texts disagree about events during this period of Surtāṇ's life. The following basic chronology emerges:

Surtāṇ remained in Mevāṛ at Bor fort for one or two years after the battle of Cītoṛ along with his half-brother, Kesodās, and other Meṛtīyos. He then proceeded to the Mughal court in 1570-71 and made obeisance to Akbar. The Emperor awarded him with the ***jāgīr*** of Malārṇo in eastern Rājasthān (near Riṇthambhor). Then in 1572-73 Akbar granted Surtāṇ the ***jāgīr*** of one-half the villages of Meṛto. Akbar had already granted the other half of Meṛto's villages in ***jāgīr*** to Surtāṇ's half-brother, Kesodās. The chronicles note that there was friction between Surtāṇ and Kesodās when Surtāṇ returned to Meṛto and began dividing his villages among his retainers. This disagreement caused Kesodās to leave Meṛto to seek redress from the Emperor.

Akbar sequestered all the villages of Meṛto from Surtāṇ and Kesodās in 1577-78. ***Vigat***, 2:70, records that Akbar's action resulted from the Meṛtīyos' mistreatment of a wet-nurse of the Imperial court who passed through Meṛto enroute from Gujarat to north India. Akbar gave Surtān the ***jāgīr*** of Sojhat Pargano in eastern Mārvāṛ in exchange. Surtāṇ held this ***jāgīr*** until 1582-83. Surtāṇ's assumption of authority at Sojhat fell on the death of Rāv Kalo Rāmot, a grandson of Rāv Mālde Gāṅgāvat of Jodhpur (1532-62), who was killed by the Mughals in 1577. Akbar also granted Surtāṇ the village of Sarvāṛ[57] where Surtāṇ's ***vasī*** remained for several years. Surtāṇ's great-grandfather, Rāv Dūdo Jodhāvat (6-1) (no. 104), had occupied this village in the late fifteenth century.

Several years later, Rāv Candrasen Māldevot of Jodhpur (1562-81) emerged from his exile and overran the area of Sojhat. Sources are unclear whether Surtāṇ retained Sojhat during this time. There was a great deal of disruption locally until Rāv Candrasen's death in 1581. Akbar then granted Sojhat in ***jāgīr*** to Rāv Candrasen's son, Rāv Rāysiṅgh Candrasenot, in 1582-83, at which time Surtāṇ's involvement with this area ended.

Surtān did not hold lands in Meṛto again until 1586. He was much involved in Imperial military service in the interim between 1582 and 1586, particularly in Gujarat with the ***sūbedār***, Khān Khānān Mīrzā 'Abdu'r-Rahīm. ***Akbar Nāma***, 3:632, 656, records that Surtāṇ was in Gujarat both in December of 1583 and in September of 1586. In 1583 he had campaigned against Muzaffar

---

[57] Sarvāṛ village: located forty-nine miles north of Meṛto and twenty-five miles east-northeast of Nāgaur.

Khān III (1561-73; 1583; in revolt until 1593), riding as part of the Mughal army center. Moṭo Rājā Udaisiṅgh Māldevot of Jodhpur (1583-95) was also present riding in the Mughal right wing. In 1586 several of Surtāṇ's retainers were responsible for killing two Jāṛeco Rajpūt bandits who had plagued the city of Ahmadabad. As a reward for this service, the ***sūbedār*** used his offices to obtain the return of Surtāṇ's (and Kesodās's) ***jāgīrs*** of Meṛto. ***Vigat***, 2:70, records that Surtāṇ's ***vasī*** came back to Meṛto on February 12, 1586 after an absence of nine years.

During the next few years, Surtāṇ spent most of his time on military tour for the Mughals in eastern India. He was killed in 1589-90 in Gokul (Bihar) during Mughal operations under Kachvāho Rājā Mānsiṅgh Bhagvantdāsot of Āmber (1589-1614) against the Afghans.

Surtāṇ granted the following villages of Meṛto in ***sāṃsaṇ*** to Cāraṇs:

1. Lūṅgīyo[58] - granted to the Āḍho Cāraṇ Durso Mehāvat.
2. Netā rī Vāsṇī[59] - granted to the Ratnūṃ Cāraṇ Sāṅkar Hīṅgoḷāvat.
3. Ratanāvās[60] - Ratansī Dūdāvat (7-3) had originally granted this village to the Mīsaṇ Cāraṇ Ratno Ḍāhāvat. Surtāṇ Jaimalot later took it from Ratno and granted it to the Cāraṇ Bārhaṭh Cutro Jaimalot.

The chronicles record the following ***dūho*** about Surtāṇ Jaimalot:

Surtāṇ said to the Pātsāh,
"I shall enjoy my land so long as two things are not done,
Giving [you] a daughter [in marriage],
And allowing you to see [my] wife."

"Aitihāsik Bātāṃ," p. 48; ***Akbar Nāma***, 3:632, 656; ***Bāṅkīdās***, pp. 62, 104; ***Khyāt***, 1:291, 297, 302, 3:120; ***Murārdān***, no. 2, pp. 462-464, 471; R. P. Tripathi, ***The Rise and Fall of the Mughal Empire*** (Reprint ed. Allahabad: Central Book Depot, 1966), pp. 308-311; ***Vigat***, 1:389-390, 2:69-72, 111, 165, 185, 212.

(no. 114) **Balbhadar Surtāṇot** (10-1)

---

[58] Lūṅgīyo village: located fifteen miles southeast of Meṛto, near Reyāṃ.

[59] Netā rī Vāsṇī: located seventeen miles north-northeast of Meṛto, near Rāhaṇ.

[60] Ratanāvās village: located thirty miles northeast of Meṛto, near Altavo.

Balbhadar Surtāṇot was a son of Surtāṇ Jaimalot (9-1) (no. 113) and grandson of Rāv Jaimal Vīramdevot (8-1) (no. 107) of Meṛto. He was a sister's son (***bhāṇej***) of the Bhāṭī Rajpūts. Following the death of his father, Surtāṇ, in Bihar in 1589-90, Balbhadar received the ***jāgīr*** of one-half of Meṛto from Akbar. His paternal uncle, Kesodās Jaimalot (9-3) (no. 119), continued to hold the other half of Meṛto from Akbar during this same period.

Little is recorded about other aspects of Balbhadar's life. He was killed in the Deccan while in Mughal service in 1596-97. ***Murārdān***, no. 2, pp. 464-465, records that Balbhadar became involved in a fight with a Turk one day at his camp, and died from wounds received. The text provides no explanation for the hostilities.

Balbhadar granted the village of Ḍāgsūrīyo[61] in ***sāṃsaṇ*** to the Dhadhvāṛīyo Cāraṇ Moko Māṇḍaṇot.

Balbhadar achieved the the rank of 300 ***zāt*** as a ***mansabdār*** in Mughal service. He died without sons and was succeeded at Meṛto by his brother, Gopāḷdās Surtāṇot (10-2) (no. 115).

Ā'īn-i-Akbarī, p. 563; Athar Ali, ***Apparatus***, pp. 24, 28; ***Murārdān***, no. 2, pp. 464-465; ***Vigat***, 2:72, 140, 491; ***Vīr Vinod***, 2:208.

(no. 115) **Gopāḷdās Surtāṇot** (10-2)

Gopāḷdās Surtāṇot was a son of Surtāṇ Jaimalot (9-1) (no. 113) and a grandson of Rāv Jaimal Vīramdevot (8-1) (no. 107) of Meṛto. The chronicles describe Gopāḷdās as a stout, powerfully build Rajpūt who was very generous. Upon the death of his brother, Balbhadar Surtāṇot (10-1) (no. 114), in 1596-97 in the Deccan, Gopāḷdās received Balbhadar's share of one-half the village of Meṛto in ***jāgīr*** from Akbar. He had been in Mughal service prior to this time and he continued to serve until his death in 1599-1600 at Bīḍ city in the Deccan during Mughal operations against Ahmadnagar under the command of Sher Khwāja. He died there along with two of his paternal uncles, Kesodās Jaimalot (9-3) (no. 119), who also held one-half of Meṛto in ***jāgīr*** from Akbar, and Dvārkādās Jaimalot (9-8) (no. 118).

The ***Khyāt*** of Naiṇsī, 2:97-98, notes that Bhāṭī Surtāṇ Harrājot, a son of Bhāṭī Rāvaḷ Harrāj Māldevot of Jaisaḷmer (1561-77), was also killed at Bīḍ city with Gopāḷdās. Gopāḷdās's brother, Balbhadar, was a sister's son (***bhāṇej***) of the Bhāṭīs. Bhāṭī Surtāṇ Harrājot may have been a ***sago*** of Gopāḷdās's family.

Gopāḷdās had two wives of whom there is record, a Cahuvāṇ and a Sīsodṇī. The Sīsodṇī was a daughter of Rāṇo Pratāpsiṅgh Udaisiṅghot of Mevāṛ (1572-97) and mother of Gopāḷdās's son, Jagnāth Gopāḷdāsot (11-1) (no. 116).

Akbar Nāma, 2:1136; ***Bāṅkīdās***, p. 62; ***Khyāt***, 2:97-98; ***Murārdān***, no. 2, pp. 465-466; ***Vigat***, 2:72.

---

[61] Ḍāgsūrīyo village: located twenty-four miles west-southwest of Meṛto.

(no. 116) **Jagnāth Gopāḷdāsot** (11-1)

Jagnāth Gopāḷdāsot was a son of Gopāḷdās Surtāṇot (10-2) (no. 115) and great-grandson of Rāv Jaimal Vīramdevot (8-1) (no. 107) of Meṛto. He was born of Gopāḷdās's Sīsodṇī wife and was daughter's son (***dohitro***) of Sīsodīyo Rāṇo Pratāpsiṅgh Udaisiṅghot (1572-97). Jagnāth served under the Mughals as had his father, and, following his father's death at Bīḍ city in the Deccan in 1599-1600, he succeeded to Gopāḷdās's share of one-half the villages of Meṛto. He held this ***jāgīr*** for only a short time, however. Beginning with the spring crop (***unāḷī***) of 1602, Akbar granted Jagnāth's ***jāgīrī*** rights to Rājā Sūrajsiṅgh Udaisiṅghot of Jodhpur (1595-1619). In compensation, Jagnāth received the village of Rūṇ[62] in ***jāgīr***.

Vigat, 2:72-73, suggests that part of the reason for Jagnāth's loss of his share of Meṛto was discord between himself and Dhīrāvat Kachvāho Rājā Rāmdās Ūdāvat (no. 19). Rāja Rāmdās was a personal favorite of Emperor Akbar's with the position of petition-bearer at the Mughal court. No details are available about the source of conflict. But it is suggested that Rājā Rāmdās petitioned the Emperor in favor of Rājā Sūrajsiṅgh. A granddaughter of Rājā Rāmdās was married to Rājā Sūrajsiṅgh following Rāmdās's death.[63]

Jagnāth died in 1609-10 at Ahmadabad in Gujarat. He had a large number of sons and a segment of Meṛtīyo Rāṭhoṛs called Jagnāthot later emerged bearing his name.

Bāṅkīdās, p. 62; ***Murārdān***, no. 2, pp. 465-466; ***Vigat***, 2:72-73.

(no. 117) **Vīṭhaḷdās Jaimalot** (9-11)

Vīṭhaḷdās Jaimalot was a son of Rāv Jaimal Vīramdevot (8-1) (no. 107) and sister's son (***bhāṇej***) of the Vāghelo Rajpūts. He spent his early years at the court of his father, Rāv Jaimal, at Meṛto. During Rāv Jaimal's forced exile from Meṛto in the period between 1557-1562, he accompanied him to Mevāṛ. Then with the reoccupation of Meṛto in 1562 following the Mughal siege of the Mālgaḍh and the defeat of Rāv Mālde's commander, Rāṭhoṛ Devīdās Jaitāvat (no. 65), Rāv Jaimal sent Vīṭhaḷdās to the Mughal court in the accompaniment of Mīrzā Sharafu'd-Dīn Ḥusayn. Vīṭhaḷdās was at court only a short time, for he was forced to flee Agra with Mīrzā Sharafu'd-Dīn when the Mīrzā rebelled against Akbar in October of 1562. He returned to Meṛto with the Mīrzā, bringing news of the events to his father.

The chronicles supply no details, but Vīṭhaḷdās undoubtedly went with Rāv Jaimal to Cītoṛ this same year and lived there until his father's death during the battle of Cītoṛ in 1568. Vīṭhaḷdās then apparently remained with his half-

---

[62] Rūṇ village: located twenty miles northwest of Meṛto.

[63] See ***supra***, **Marriage and Family Lists of the Rulers of Jodhpur**, Sūrajsiṅgh Udaisiṅghot, Rāṇī no. 17.

brother, Surtāṇ Jaimalot (9-1) (no. 113), in Mevāṛ at the Bor fort.[64] When Surtāṇ received one-half of Meṛto in ***jāgīr*** from Akbar in 1572-73, Surtāṇ gave Vīṭhaḷdās the two villages of Kekīnd[65] and Āḷṇīyāvās,[66] which his paternal uncle (***kāko***), Īsardās Vīramdevot (8-5) (no. 109), had held before his death at the battle of Cītoṛ.

Vīṭhaḷdās occupied these villages for several years. He then left Meṛto to become a military servant of Sīsodīyo Rāṇo Pratāpsiṅgh Udaisiṅghot of Cītoṛ (1572-97). He was killed in Mevāṛ at the battle of Haḷdīghāṭī[67] in June of 1576 fighting against the Mughals. Vīṭhaḷdās's uterine brother, Rāmdās Jaimalot (9-10), was also killed at Haḷdīghāṭī.

Vigat, 2:71-72, states that in 1583 Vīṭhaḷdās was in Gujarat with his brother, Surtāṇ Jaimalot, on military tour with Khān Khānān. While Vīṭhaḷdās may have accompanied Surtāṇ to Gujarat on some occasion, the date of 1583 seems at variance with other facts known about Vīṭhaḷdās's life.

Vīṭhaḷdās married one of his daughters to the Sekhāvat Kachvāhos of Khaṇḍelo. Kachvāho Girdhardās Rāysalot, the ruler of Khaṇḍelo, was his daughter's son (***dohitro***). Girdhardās's father, Rāysal Sūjāvat, was the daughter's son of Jodho Rāṭhoṛ Vāgho Sūjāvat (no. 83).

Bāṅkīdās, p. 61; ***Khyāt***, 1:320-321; ***Murārdān***, no. 2, p. 489; ***Vigat***, 2:67-72.

(no. 118) **Dvārkādās Jaimalot** (9-8)

Dvārkādās Jaimalot was a son of Rāv Jaimal Vīramdevot (8-1) (no. 107) and a sister's son (***bhāṇej***) of the Kachvāhos, born of a daughter of Rājāvat Kachvāho Rājā Āskaraṇ Bhīṃvrājot of Gwalior.

Little is known about Dvārkādās's life prior to 1572-73. In this year his elder half-brother, Surtāṇ Jaimalot (9-1) (no. 113), received one-half of Meṛto in ***jāgīr*** from Akbar. Following receipt of this grant, Surtāṇ gave Dvārkādās the village of Lāmbīyo[68] in ***paṭo***. At some point, perhaps on Surtāṇ's death in 1589-90 in Bihar, Dvārkādās took service under the Mughals, and he then received Lāmbīyo in ***jāgīr***.

Dvārkādās was killed in 1599-1600 in the Deccan during the battle at Bīḍ city near Ahmadnagar. He was part of the Meṛtīyo contingent under Sher

---

[64] Bor village: located twelve miles northeast of Kumbhaḷmer in western Mevāṛ.

[65] Kekīnd village: located fourteen miles south-southeast of Meṛto.

[66] Āḷṇīyāvās village: located twenty miles southeast of Meṛto.

[67] Haḷdīghāṭī: a narrow defile in the Arāvallīs located some eighteen miles northeast of the fort of Gogūndo and eleven miles southwest of Nāthdvāra.

[68] Lāmbīyo village: located eighteen miles due south of Meṛto.

Khwāja. He died there along with his half-brother, Kesodās Jaimalot (9-3) (no. 119), and a son of Surtāṇ Jaimalot, Gopāḷdās Surtāṇot (10-2) (no. 115).

> ***Bāṅkīdās***, p. 62; ***Khyāt***, 1:290, 303, 2:177; ***Murārdān***, no. 2, pp. 504-505; ***Vigat***, 2:72.

(no. 119) **Kesodās Jaimalot** (9-3)

Kesodās Jaimalot was a son of Rāv Jaimal Vīramdevot (8-1) (no. 107) and a sister's son ***(bhāṇej)*** of the Soḷaṅkī Rajpūts, born of Rāv Jaimal's junior Soḷaṅkaṇī wife.

Some unclarity exists in the texts regarding events of Kesodās's life, particularly in the immediate aftermath of Rāv Jaimal's death at Cītoṛ in 1568. The following basic chronology emerges:

Kesodās joined his half-brother, Surtāṇ Jaimalot (9-1) (no. 113), at the fort of Bor[69] near Rūpjī village in the hills of western Mevāṛ after the battle of Cītoṛ. Sīsodīyo Rāṇo Udaisiṅgh Sāṅgāvat (ca. 1537-72; no. 17) had granted this fort jointly to Kesodās and Surtāṇ in ***paṭo***. Kesodās appears to have left Mevāṛ in 1570-71 and proceeded without Surtāṇ to the Mughal court, where he made obeisance to Akbar. Akbar then granted Kesodās the ***jāgīr*** of one-half the villages of Meṛto.

Kesodās's primary ally at the Mughal court was his paternal uncle, Narhardās Īsardāsot (8-5) (no. 120), a son of Rāv Jaimal's brother, Īsardās Vīramdevot (8-5) (no. 109). ***Murārdān***, no. 2, pp. 512-513, records that after Narhardās's father, Īsardās, and Rāv Jaimal were killed at Cītoṛ, Narhardās broke allegiance with Surtāṇ Jaimalot, who was Rāv Jaimal's chosen successor, in favor of Kesodās. While Kesodās and Surtāṇ both remained in Mevāṛ, Narhardās proceeded to the Mughal court and advocated Kesodās's rights to Meṛto before Akbar. ***Murārdān*** further states that Narhardās gave his sister, Pūrāṃbāī, in marriage to Akbar at this time and then joined the Imperial service. Narhardās was successful at court, for he later had an official writ from the Emperor granting ***jāgīrī*** rights to one-half of Meṛto sent to Kesodās in Mevāṛ. Kesodās then proceeded to the Mughal court and made obeisance to the Emperor in return for the confirmation of his ***jāgīr***. ***Murārdān***, no. 2, p. 471, specifically records that Kesodās received one-half of Meṛto prior to Surtāṇ Jaimalot.

This chronicle is at variance with information recorded in ***Vigat***, 2:69-70. The ***Vigat*** states that neither Kesodās nor Surtāṇ went to the Mughal court until 1571-72 and even then did not receive Meṛto in ***jāgīr*** for some years thereafter. Surtāṇ Jaimalot held the ***jāgīr*** of Malārṇo (near Riṇthambhor) from Akbar during this interim period, and it was only later that both brothers received shares of Meṛto. The ***Vigat*** gives precedence to Surtāṇ's story as Rāv Jaimal's chosen successor to rule at Meṛto, but this information appears incorrect. As noted above, ***Murārdān***, no. 2, p. 471, states specifically that Kesodās received

---

[69] Bor village: located twelve miles northeast of Kumbhaḷmer in western Mevāṛ.

his share of Meṛto prior to Surtāṇ. In addition, Kesodās did have representation at the Mughal court in the person of Meṛtīyo Narhardās Īsardāsot.

There are other precedents from this period to indicate that Emperor Akbar made decisions about whom to award lands and position based upon the support those individuals received at his court. An example comes from the family of Rāṭhoṛ Rāv Rām Māldevot. Rāv Rām was one of the sons of Rāv Mālde Gāṅgāvat of Jodhpur (1532-62). He received Sojhat in ***jāgīr*** from Akbar. On his death in 1572, Akbar presented Sojhat in ***jāgīr*** to Rām's younger son, Kalo, along with the title of ***rāv***, bypassing Rāv Rām's elder son, Karaṇ. Akbar appears to have made this decision based upon the strong support Kalo received at court from two influential Rāṭhoṛs from Mārvāṛ, Prithīrāj Kūmpāvat (no. 97) and Mahes Kūmpāvat (no. 98).[70]

Kesodās assumed control of his villages in Meṛto in 1570-71. His half-brother, Surtāṇ, was not granted ***jāgīrī*** rights in Meṛto until 1572-73, at which time conflict broke out between the two brothers over the division of villages. Kesodās left Meṛto with his paternal uncle, Narhardās Īsardāsot, and proceeded once again to the Mughal court to seek redress. ***Vigat***, 2:70, states that Kesodās married his daughter to the Emperor at this time in return for the ***jāgīr*** of one-half of Meṛto. ***Murārdān*** does not mention this marriage at all. From the ***Ā'īn-i-Akbarī***, pp. 323, 594, it is apparent that Kesodās married a daughter to Prince Salīm (Jahāngīr), not to Emperor Akbar.[71] Kesodās then returned to Meṛto where he remained in possession of his village until 1577-78.

---

[70] For more about these Rajpūts and their involvements in Sojhat, see ***supra***, "Kūmpāvat Rāṭhoṛs."

[71] There is some question about which "Kesodās Rāṭhoṛ" married a daughter to Prince Salīm. The question is complicated by conflicting evidence in the texts, and by the fact that three different Kesodās Rāṭhoṛs are mentioned in the Mughal sources of the period: Meṛtīyo Rāṭhoṛ Kesodās Jaimalot, Varsiṅghot Meṛtīyo Rāṭhoṛ Kesodās "Mārū" Bhīṃvot, and Bīkāvat Rāṭhoṛ Kesodās Amarsiṅghot.

Blochmann mentions in his notes to the ***Ā'īn-i-Akbarī***, p. 232, n. 4, that a daughter of a "Rājā Keshū Dās Rāṭhor" was one of Jahāngīr's wives and the mother of his daughter, Bahār Bānū Begam, born A. H. 988 (A. D. 1591).

Elsewhere in this same text, p. 563, n. 302, Blochmann lists a "Kesū Dās, son of Jai Mal," as a ***mansabdār*** of Akbar's with the rank of 300 ***zāt***. He confuses this Kesodās Jaimalot with "Kesū Dās Mārū," who is mentioned several times in Jahāngīr's ***Memoirs*** (Jahāngīr, 1:21, 79, 170, 296-297, 390, 410). This Kesodās Mārū was Kesodās Bhīṃvot, a Meṛtīyo Rāṭhoṛ of the Varsiṅghot ***sākh***, descended from Rāv Varsiṅgh Jodhāvat (no. 146), one of the original founders of Meṛto. Kesodās Mārū rose to a position of considerable influence under Akbar, from whom he held the ***jāgīr*** of Vadhnor in northern Mevāṛ. Under Jahāngīr, Kesodās Mārū remained active in the affairs of the empire, and he reached the ***mansab*** rank of 2000/1200. Toward the end of Jahāngīr's reign, he apparently went mad and frittered away his lands and wealth. He is said to have begun beating his wives and causing disturbances locally, and he was eventually shot and killed by his son, Karaṇ Kesodāsot, who was in turn poisoned by one of Kesodās's wives (see: ***Murārdān***, no. 2, pp. 584-585).

Lastly, Blochmann, p. 594, n. 408, refers to a "Keshū Dās, the Rāṭhor" who was a ***mansabdār*** of 200 ***zāt***, and notes that he served in Gujarat in early 1585.

Kesodās accompanied Rājā Rāysiṅgh Kalyāṇmalot of Bīkāner (1574-1612), Shāh Qulī Maḥram-i Bahārlū, Shimāl Khān Chela, and others during operations in Mārvāṛ in 1574 against Rāv Candrasen Māldevot of Jodhpur (1562-81). Then in 1577-78 Akbar sequestered both Kesodās's and Surtāṇ's ***jāgīr***s of Meṛto because of the Meṛtīyos' mistreatment of a wet-nurse from the Imperial court who passed through Meṛto while enroute from Gujarat to north India. Akbar granted Kesodās the village of Nāgelāv[72] in compensation. Kesodās then moved his ***vasī*** to Nāgelāv, where they were to remain for the next nine years.

Meṛto was finally returned to both Kesodās and his half-brother, Surtāṇ, in 1586 and Kesodās then resumed residence at Meṛto.[73] Nothing is recorded about his activities during the period from 1577-86, nor during the period following the return of Meṛto in ***jāgīr*** from 1586-99. In all probability, Kesodās spent much of his time on military tour for the Mughals. He was killed in 1599-1600 in the Deccan during Mughal operations against Ahmadnagar. He undoubtedly took part in the battle at Bīḍ city where the Mughals were hard-pressed by the troops of Sultāna Cānd Bībī until reinforcements arrived under the command of Abū'l-Fazl.

Kesodās was a ***mansabdār*** in the Imperial service with the rank of 300 ***zāt***.

Blochmann identifies this Kesodās as a son of "Rāy Rāy Singh's brother" of Bīkāner and states that he was killed in a private quarrel in Akbar's 36th Regnal year (1592). Blochmann states that it was this Kesodās Rāṭhoṛ who married a daughter to Prince Salīm (Jahāngīr). This Kesodās was Bīkāvat Rāṭhoṛ Kesodās Amarsiṅghot, a son of Amarsiṅgh Kalyāṇmalot, the brother to Rājā Rāysiṅgh Kalyāṇmalot, ruler of Bīkāner (1574-1612). Kesodās Amarsiṅghot was killed in 1590 as a result of hostilities which arose following his father's rebellion against Akbar in the same year (see: Ojhā, 5:1:180).

Without further evidence, it is difficult to know for certain which of these Kesodās Rāṭhoṛs married a daughter into Akbar's family. It appears that Blochmann is incorrect in his judgement that it was Kesodās Amarsiṅghot's daughter who was married to Prince Salīm. The fact that the Rāṭhoṛ who married a daughter to Salīm is referred to in Mughal sources as "Rājā" points rather toward Kesodās Jaimalot or to Kesodās Bhīṃvot, both of whom had greater stature than Kesodās Amarsiṅghot.

Vigat, 2:70, appears in error in its statement that Kesodās Jaimalot married a daughter to Akbar, but the reference to a marriage into Akbar's family would seem to point to Rāṭhoṛ Kesodās Jaimalot as the Kesodās Rāṭhoṛ who gave his daughter to the Mughals.

The date of the marriage is uncertain. According to Mughal sources, Prince Salīm's first marriage took place in February of 1585 to the daughter of Kachvāho Rājā Bhagvantdās of Āmber (ca. 1574-89). Kesodās Jaimalot's marriage of his daughter to Prince Salīm would then have occurred sometime thereafter, ca. 1586.

(A note of thanks to Frances Taft for details regarding the Āmber marriage).

[72] Nāgelāv village: located eighteen miles southwest of Ajmer.

[73] See ***supra***, Surtāṇ Jaimalot (no. 113) for details about Meṛto's return to Surtāṇ and Kesodās.

Ā'īn-i-Akbarī, pp. 323, 563, 594; Abd al-Qādir ibn Mulūk Shāh Badā'ūnī, ***Muntakhabut-Tawārikh***. Translated from the Original Persian and Edited by George S. A. Ranking (Reprint ed. Karachi: Karimsons, 1976 [1898-1925]), 2:352; ***Akbar Nāma***, 3:113, 678; Athar Ali, ***Apparatus***, p. 25; ***Bāṅkīdās***, p. 62; Jahāngīr, 1:21, 55-56, 79, 170, 296-297, 390, 410; ***Murārdān***, no. 2, pp. 462-464, 471, 512-513, 584; Ojhā, 5:1:170, 180; Tripathi, ***The Rise and Fall of the Mughal Empire***, pp. 329-335; ***Vigat***, 2:69-70, 72, 491; ***Vīr Vinod***, 2:209.

(no. 120) **Narhardās Īsardāsot** (9-15)

Narhardās Īsardāsot was a son of Īsardās Vīramdevot (8-5) (no. 109) and a grandson of Rāv Vīramde Dūdāvat (7-1) (no. 105). He is described in the texts as a very powerfully built, brave Rajpūt warrior. No information is available about Narhardās's life prior to the death of his father at the battle of Cītoṛ in 1568. Īsardās Vīramdevot had fought and died there along with his brother, Rāv Jaimal Vīramdevot (8-1) (no. 107), in the great battle against the Mughal Emperor Akbar. Narhardās was apparently at Cītoṛ with his father and the other Rajpūts in Rāv Jaimal's service. But his specific activities during the battle are unknown. Narhardās broke relations with Rāv Jaimal's son and chosen successor to rule at Meṛto, Surtāṇ Jaimalot (9-1) (no. 113), following this battle, and sided with Surtāṇ's younger half-brother, Kesodās Jaimalot (9-3) (no. 119). While Surtāṇ and Kesodās remained in Mevāṛ for some time living at the fort of Bor in the hills of western Mevāṛ which Sīsodīyo Rāṇo Udaisiṅgh Sāṅgāvat (ca. 1537-72; no. 17) had granted them in ***paṭo***, Narhardās proceeded alone to the Mughal court to petition Emperor Akbar on Kesodās's behalf for the lands of Meṛto. According to ***Murārdān***, no. 2, p 471, Narhardās's petition was successful. Narhardās obtained an Imperial writ assigning one-half of the villages of Meṛto in ***jāgīr*** to Kesodās and had this sent to Kesodās in Mevāṛ, summoning him to court to perform obeisance before the Emperor.

Narhardās then joined the Imperial service and received the ***jāgīr*** of Vadhnor[74] in northern Mevāṛ from Akbar. He married his sister, Pūrāṃbāī, to Akbar at this time. Kesodās also granted Narhardās villages in Meṛto in ***paṭo*** when he took possession of his lands there. These villages included Reyāṃ[75] and Padūkhāṃ rī Vāsṇī.[76]

Narhardās had no sons. He spent his later years at Meṛto serving under Kesodās Jaimalot. No information is available about the date or circumstances of his death.

---

[74] Vadhnor village: located forty-seven miles south-southwest of Ajmer.

[75] Reyāṃ village: located fifteen miles southeast of Meṛto.

[76] Padūkhāṃ rī Vāsṇī: located four miles north-northwest of Meṛto.

Narhardās granted the village of Santhāṇo Sāraṅgvās[77] in *sāṃsaṇ* to the Pārīkh Golvāḷ Brāhmaṇ Bāṇopāḷ (or Gopāḷ) Lakhāvat.

Murārdān, no. 2, pp. 471, 512-513; *Vigat*, 2:69-70, 112, 211.

(no. 121) **Kānhīdās Kesodāsot** (10-3)

Kānhīdās Kesodāsot was a son of Kesodās Jaimalot (9-3) (no. 119) and grandson of Rāv Jaimal Vīramdevot (8-1) (no. 107). Little is known about Kānhīdās from records available. He received Kesodās's share of one-half the villages of Meṛto in *jāgīr* from Akbar in 1599-1600, following Kesodas's death in the Deccan. He held this *jāgīr* until his death a short time thereafter in 1601-02.

There is some disagreement in the chronicles about the date of Kānhīdās's death. *Vigat*, 2:77, places his death in 1604-05, while *Murārdān*, no. 2, p. 471, records that he died in the Deccan in 1601-02. He apparently served under the Mughals all of his life, and he was active in Akbar's Deccan campaign against Ahmadnagar. The date of 1601-02 for Kānhīdās's death appears appropriate, given what is known about his son, Indrabāṇ Kānhīdāsot (11-2) (no. 122) (see *infra*).

While holding the *jāgīr* for one-half of Meṛto, Kānhīdās granted the village of Ghāṇām[78] in *sāṃsaṇ* to the Jaghaṭh Cāraṇ Khīmvo Veṇīdāsot.

Murārdān, no. 2, p. 471; *Vigat*, 2:72-73, 112, 185.

(no. 122) **Indrabhāṇ Kānhīdāsot** (11-2)

Indrabhāṇ Kānhīdāsot was a son of Kānhīdās Kesodāsot (10-3) (no. 121) and great-grandson of Rāv Jaimal Vīramdevot (8-1) (no. 107) of Meṛto. Indrabhāṇ succeeded to his father Kānhīdās's position at Meṛto in 1601-02 but with much attenuated *jāgīrī* rights to villages there. According to *Murārdān*, no. 2, p. 472, Indrabhāṇ received only the village of Kekīnd[79] and twenty-two others from Akbar in *jāgīr*. The remainder of his father's share was given to the Rājā of Jodhpur, Sūrajsiṅgh Udaisiṅghot (1595-1619). Indrabhāṇ's attentuated share of villages was then taken from him in 1604-05 and granted to the Jodhpur Rājā. Ojhā, 4:1:370, gives the date of May 30, 1605 for the Rājā's receipt of all of Meṛto.

No information is available about whether Rājā Sūrajsiṅgh in turn granted Indrabhāṇ his villages of Meṛto in *paṭo*. *Vigat*, 2:73, records only that in 1604-05 the important *ṭhākur*s of Meṛto went to the Mughal court with a contingent of some 2,000 horse to petition Akbar in favor of Indrabhāṇ's rights

---

[77] Santhāṇo Sāraṅgvās village: located eighteen miles east-southeast of Meṛto.

[78] Ghāṇām village: located twenty-five miles northeast of Meṛto, near Altāvo.

[79] Kekīnd village: located fourteen miles south-southeast of Meṛto.

to Meṛto. Their petition was denied. Akbar gave full support to the rights of the ruler of Jodhpur to authority over Meṛto, rights which the Mughals continued to recognize for the next three-quarters of a century.

No information is available about the date and circumstances of Indrabhāṇ's death.

Murārdān, no. 2, p. 472; ***Vigat***, 2:73.

(no. 123) **Cāndo Vīramdevot** (8-3)

Cāndo Vīramdevot was a son of Rāv Vīramde Dūdāvat (7-1) (no. 105) and a grandson of Rāv Dūdo Jodhāvat (6-1) (no. 104). The chronicles describe Cāndo as a large, powerfully built Rajpūt. His life stands in contrast to those of most of his brothers, for Cāndo stood apart from Meṛto and served much of his life in the armies of Rāv Mālde Gāṅgāvat of Jodhpur (1532-62). For reasons unexplained in the texts, Cāndo gained the enmity of his father, Rāv Vīramde, and he was driven from Meṛto during his youth. It is possible that he posed a threat to his brother, Jaimal Vīramdevot (8-1) (no. 107), who was Rāv Vīramde's chosen successor. No specific information is available about their mothers or the circumstances leading to Cāndo's banishment.

The chronicles do not specify when Cāndo left Meṛto and took service under Rāv Mālde. But in 1546-47 Cāndo received the ***paṭo*** of Āsop village[80] from Rāv Mālde. Āsop is an important village in Mārvāṛ, and Cāndo's receipt of this grant indicates that he held a position of some influence at Rāv Mālde's court. Cāndo retained Āsop until 1552-53 when he received Balūndo village[81] in ***paṭo***.

Cāndo was present with Rāv Mālde during the Rāv's abortive attack on Meṛto in 1554, and following Rāv Mālde's defeat there, Cāndo appears to have become disaffected, for he retired to his village of Balūndo. He did not participate in Rāv Mālde's occupation of Meṛto after the battle of Harmāṛo[82] in January of 1557, nor was he included in the division of Meṛto's villages among Rāv Mālde's military servants that followed.

Cāndo's failure to report for service gained Rāv Mālde's ire, and in 1559 the Rāv sent his ***hujdār***, Māṅglīyo Gahlot Vīram Devāvat (no. 14), the ***hākīm*** of Meṛto, to Balūndo with a contingent of Rajpūts to drive Cāndo from the village. This action occurred just prior to Rāv Mālde's grant of one-half the villages of Meṛto on July 28, 1559 to Cāndo's brother, Meṛtīyo Jagmāl Vīramdevot (8-6) (no. 124). On the day Meṛtīyo Jagmāl received his ***paṭo*** of villages, the Rāv had Jagmāl swear an oath (***devaco***) that he would not retain Cāndo in his service.

80 Āsop village: located fifty miles northeast of Jodhpur.

81 Balūndo village: located fifty-five miles east of Jodhpur and eight miles due north of Jaitāraṇ.

82 Harmāṛo village: located fifty-five miles south-southwest of Ajmer and six miles south of Vadhnor in northern Mevāṛ.

Cāndo then quit Mārvāṛ and joined his brother, Rāv Jaimal Vīramdevot (8-1) (no. 107) in Mevāṛ. Rāv Jaimal was at Cītoṛ in the service of Sīsodīyo Rāṇo Udaisiṅgh Sāṅgāvat (ca. 1537-72; no. 17) from 1557-62. While at Cītoṛ, Cāndo became involved in the settlement of the Meṛtīyo *vair* with the Soḷaṅkī Rajpūts. The Soḷaṅkīs had killed two of his brothers, Sāraṅgde (8-2) and Māṇḍaṇ (8-4), some years earlier near Toḍo in central Rājasthān. In revenge, Cāndo killed a Soḷaṅkī named Narāiṇdās at Cītoṛ. He left Mevāṛ afterwards, apparently because of difficulties that arose from this killing, and returned to Mārvāṛ. The *vair* with the Soḷaṅkīs was finally ended only after Rāv Jaimal was given another daughter of the Soḷaṅkīs' in marriage. Rāv Jaimal was himself a *sago* of the Soḷaṅkīs, having married a Soḷaṅkaṇī. His brother, Sāraṅgde, was also sister's son (*bhāṇej*) of the Soḷaṅkīs. These relationships may in some way have been responsible for the outbreak of hostilities which started the *vair*.

Cāndo joined Rāv Mālde's service once again following his return to Mārvāṛ, and in 1560-61 Rāv Mālde returned the *paṭo* of Āsop village to him. Cāndo held this grant until 1562-63. He was stationed at the fort of Jodhpur as *kiledār* during these two years. He assumed this position following Rāṭhoṛ Devīdās Jaitāvat's (no. 65) posting at the Mālgaḍh at Meṛto.

With the fall of Meṛto to Rāv Jaimal Vīramdevot and the Mughals under Mīrzā Sharafu'd-Dīn Ḥusayn in early 1562, Cāndo again left Rāv Mālde's active service to sit in his village of Āsop. When Mīrzā Sharafu'd-Dīn rebelled from Akbar in October of 1562, Ḥusayn Qulī Khān became Akbar's new governor at Nāgaur. He summoned Cāndo to Nāgaur on some pretext in 1563-64 and had him killed there. *Murārdān*, no. 2, p. 527, records that the Khān had his men fall upon Cāndo as Cāndo ascended the ladder leading up to the platform upon which the Khān was seated. No reason is given for this murder. The Mughals may have felt that Cāndo posed a threat, and was by association, implicated in the Mīrzā's rebellion.

"Aitihāsik Bātāṃ," pp. 48-49, 99; *Khyāt*, 2:121; *Murārdān*, no. 2, pp. 526-527, 549, no. 3, pp. 171-172; *Vigat*, 1:47, 2:63.

(no. 124) **Jagmāl Vīramdevot** (8-6)

Jagmāl Vīramdevot was a son of Rāv Vīramde Dūdāvat (7-1) (no. 105) and grandson of Rāv Dūdo Jodhāvat (6-1) (no. 104), the founding ancestor of the Meṛtīyo Rāṭhoṛs. Like his brother, Cāndo Vīramdevot (8-3) (no. 123), Jagmāl left Meṛto early in his life and became a military servant of Rāv Mālde Gāṅgāvat of Jodhpur (1532-62). He received the village of Khairvo[83] in *paṭo* from the Rāv.

Jagmāl's name is not mentioned in the chronicles with regard to any of Rāv Mālde's important military undertakings prior to the battle of Harmāṛo,[84]

---

[83] Khairvo village: located fifty miles south-southeast of Jodhpur.

[84] Harmāṛo village: located fifty-five miles south-southwest of Ajmer and six miles south of Vadhnor in northern Mevāṛ.

which took place on January 24, 1557. Jagmāl's name appears in a list of prominent ***ṭhākur***s of Mārvāṛ who fought at Harmāṛo under the command of Rāṭhoṛ Devīdās Jaitāvat (no. 65). Rāv Mālde's troops had joined with Paṭhāṇ Hājī Khān against an allied force under Sīsodīyo Rāṇo Udaisiṅgh Sāṅgāvat of Cītoṛ (ca. 1537-72; no. 17).

Jagmāl continued in Rāv Mālde's service after Harmāṛo and was rewarded with the ***paṭo*** of one-half of the villages of Meṛto in July of 1559. This grant followed Rāv Mālde's occupation of Meṛto. Meṛtīyo Rāv Jaimal Vīramdevot (8-1) (no. 107) had been an ally of the Rāṇo's at Harmāṛo, and the Rāṇo's defeat left Meṛto forfeit to Rāv Mālde.

Rāv Mālde had Jagmāl swear an oath (***devaco***) on July 28 in the temple of Mahāmāyā at Phaḷodhī village[85] near Meṛto before his son, Kuṃvar Candrasen, and several members of his administrative staff including Māṅglīyo Vīram Devāvat (no. 14), Pañcolī Neto Abhāvat (no. 162) and Cahuvān Jhāñjhaṇ Bhairavdāsot (no. 7). Jagmāl brought Meṛtīyo Jaitmāl Pañcāiṇot (8-9) (no. 127) and Purohit Bhāṇīdās to Phaḷodhī to witness this swearing. Jagmāl affirmed enduring loyalty to Rāv Mālde and his son, Kuṃvar Candrasen, and swore that he would neither retain his half-brother, Cāndo Vīramdevot (8-3) (no. 123), nor one of his own sons, Vāgh Jagmālot (9-16) (no. 125), in his service. The texts give no reasons for the inclusion of Jagmāl's son, Vāgh, in this prohibition.[86]

Jagmāl divided his villages among his own personal retainers, and took up residence at Meṛto proper as ***kiledār*** of the Mālgaḍh. Construction on this fort was completed in 1560-61. Then in early 1562 the Mughals under Mīrzā Sharafu'd-Dīn Ḥusayn laid siege to the Mālgaḍh in league with Jagmāl's half-brother, Rāv Jaimal Vīramdevot. Jagmāl was present at the Mālgaḍh during the initial stages of the siege. But he held negotiations with the Mughals and Rāv Jaimal, and then withdrew with a small contingent of his military servants, leaving all of his personal property behind in the fort. Rāṭhoṛ Devīdās Jaitāvat (no. 65), who was posted with Jagmāl at the Mālgaḍh, remained inside with a large force of Rajpūts including thirty-eight of Jagmāl's own men who had refused to leave. Most of these men were later killed when the Mughals and Rāv Jaimal attacked Rāṭhoṛ Devīdās and his men as they withdrew from the fort in the direction of Sātaḷvās, a village four miles to the southwest of Meṛto.

With the loss of Meṛto and Rāv Mālde's death in November of 1562, Jagmāl left Mārvāṛ and proceeded to the Mughal court. He offered his service to Emperor Akbar. Within a year, Jagmāl's half-brother, Rāv Jaimal, to whom Akbar had given Meṛto in ***jāgīr*** following its conquest in 1562, had fled Meṛto for Mevāṛ in the wake of Mīrzā Sharafu'd-Dīn's rebellion in October of that year. Akbar thereupon granted one-half of Meṛto to Jagmāl in ***jāgīr***, reserving the other half as Imperial ***khālso***. Jagmāl married one of his daughters to Akbar at this time. He lived for several more years at Meṛto and died a natural death in 1570-71.

---

[85] Phaḷodhī village: located nine miles northwest of Meṛto.

[86] See ***Vigat***, 2:62, of the **translated text** for specific details of this swearing.

Jagmāl granted several villages in ***sāṃsaṇ*** to Brāhmaṇs. These included:

1. Cāṃvaḍīyo Ādho[87] - half of this village was granted to the Sīvaṛ Brāhmaṇ Purohit Bhavānīdās Tejsīyot.
2. Jagnāthpuro[88] - granted to the Śrīmāḷī Brāhmaṇs Davo and Jagnāth Sadāphaḷot. This grant was made in 1559-60.

Ā'īn-i-Akbarī, pp. 339-340; "Aitihāsik Bātāṃ," pp. 48, 51; ***Akbar Nāma***, 2:248-249, 305; ***Bāṅkīdās***, pp. 14, 16, 60; ***Murārdān***, no. 2, pp. 520-524; Ojhā, 4:1:322-324; Reu, 1:138-139; ***Vigat***, 1:60, 2:59, 61-63, 110, 138, 212; ***Vīr Vinod***, 2:812-813.

(no. 125) **Vāgh Jagmālot** (9-16)
(no. 126) **Kalo Jagmālot** (9-17)

Vāgh and Kalo Jagmālot were sons of Jagmāl Vīramdevot (8-6) (no. 124) and grandsons of Rāv Vīramde Dūdāvat (7-1) (no. 105). About Vāgh we know only that Rāv Mālde Gāṅgāvat of Jodhpur (1532-62) forbade his father, Jagmāl, from retaining him in his personal service while Jagmāl held the ***paṭo*** of one-half of the villages of Meṛto between July of 1559 and March of 1562. The circumstances behind this censure are not known.

Of Kalo Jagmālot there is more information. It was his uterine sister whom his father married to Akbar in 1562. Kalo followed his father into Mughal service at this time, and he received the ***jāgīr*** of Thāṃvḷo village,[89] near Ajmer. His activities after this time are unknown. ***Murārdān***, no. 2, p. 524, states only that he died at Thāṃvlo village.

A paternal uncle of Kalo's, Meṛtīyo Jaitmāl Pañcāiṇot (8-9) (no. 127), had no sons, and adopted Kalo into his family. The date of this adoption is unrecorded.

Murārdān, no. 2, pp. 447, 524; ***Vigat***, 2:63.

(no. 127) **Jaitmāl Pañcāiṇot** (8-9)

Jaitmāl Pañcāiṇot was a son of Pañcāiṇ Dūdāvat (7-5) and a grandson of Rāv Dūdo Jodhāvat (6-1) (no. 104). No information is available about Jaitmāl's father. Jaitmāl himself was a military servant of Rāv Mālde Gāṅgāvat of Jodhpur (1532-62). He appears in the chronicles first in association with

---

[87] Cāṃvaḍīyo Ādho village: located seven miles southeast of Meṛto.

[88] Jagnāthpuro village: located sixteen miles southest of Meṛto, near Reyāṃ.

[89] Thāṃvḷo village: located twenty-eight miles east-southeast of Meṛto and twelve miles northwest of Ajmer.

Meṛtīyo Jagmāl Vīramdevot (8-6) (no. 124). Jaitmāl was present as a witness on behalf of Jagmāl on July 28, 1559 when Jagmāl swore an oath of loyalty to Rāv Mālde in the temple of Mahāmāyā at Phaḷodhī village near Meṛto, prior to his receipt of one-half of the villages of Meṛto in *paṭo* from the Rāv.

Jaitmāl is mentioned later as part of the contingent of Rajpūts under Rāṭhor Devīdās Jaitāvat (no. 65) who fought in defense of the Mālgaḍh at Meṛto in 1562 against Meṛtīyo Rāv Jaimal Vīramdevot (8-1) (no. 107) and the Mughal forces of Akbar under the command of Mīrzā Sharafu'd-Dīn Ḥusayn. Jaitmāl was killed at Meṛto during this conflict.

Jaitmāl had no sons. He adopted Meṛtīyo Jagmāl Vīramdevot's son, Kalo Jagmālot (9-17) (no. 126), into his family. The date of this adoption is unrecorded.

"Aitihāsik Bātāṃ," p. 56; ***Bāṅkīdās***, pp. 16, 51; ***Murārdān***, no. 2, pp. 447, 524; ***Vigat***, 1:62, 2:63, 66.

(no. 128) **Gopāḷdās Sūndardāsot** (11-3)

Gopāḷdās Sūndardāsot was a son of Sūndardās Mādhodāsot (10-4) and great-grandson of Rāv Jaimal Vīramdevot (8-1) (no. 107). Among the Meṛtīyos of the mid-seventeenth century, Gopāḷdās alone rose to a position of great power and influence as ***pradhān*** of Jodhpur under Rājā Jasvantsiṅgh Gajsiṅghot (1638-78).

Little information is available about Gopāḷdās's family. His grandfather, Mādhodās Jaimalot (9-2), was the uterine brother of Kesodās Jaimalot (9-3) (no. 119), born of Rāv Jaimal's junior Soḷaṅkaṇī wife. Mādhodās apparently served under Kesodās, from whom he held the village of Reyāṃ[90] in ***paṭo***. Local chronicles do not specify when the grant was received. Kesodās Jaimalot himself received his ***jāgīr*** of one-half the villages of Meṛto in 1570-71, retained it until 1577-78, then held this grant again between the years 1586-1599/1600. About Mādhodās it is known only that he held Reyāṃ in ***paṭo*** for a number of years and that he died prior to Kesodās's death in 1599-1600.

Gopāḷdās's father, Sūndardās Mādhodāsot, also held Reyāṃ in ***paṭo***. But he did not immediately succeed to this village on his father's death. ***Murārdān***, no. 2, pp. 493, 498, records that Sūndardās's brother's son, Jasvant Mohandāsot (11-4), received Reyāṃ in ***paṭo*** from Kesodās Jaimalot on Mādhodās Jaimalot's death. Jasvant Mohandāsot served with Kesodās in the Deccan, and he took part along with Kesodās in Mughal operations against Ahmadnagar. Both Jasvant and Kesodās were killed in 1599-1600 during the battle of Bīḍ city. Upon Jasvant's death, Sūndardās Mādhodāsot then received Reyāṃ in ***paṭo*** in 1600-01 from Kesodās's son and successor, Kānhīdās Kesodāsot (10-3) (no. 121).

How long Sūndardās continued to hold Reyāṃ is unclear. It appears that it was only for a short time, for in 1601-02 Kānhīdās was also killed in the Deccan, and his son, Indrabhāṇ Kānhīdāsot (11-2) (no. 122), succeeded to an

---

[90] Reyāṃ village: located fifteen miles southeast of Meṛto.

attenuated ***jāgīr*** in Meṛto including Kekīnd[91] and twenty-two other villages. Akbar then took these villages from Indrabhāṇ in 1604-05 and granted them to the ruler of Jodhpur, Rājā Sūrajsiṅgh Udaisiṅghot (1595-1619). No further information is available about Sūndardās Mādhodāsot.

Sūndardās's son, Gopāḷdās Sūndardāsot, was a military servant of Kānhīdās Kesodāsot and of his son, Indrabhāṇ Kānhīdāsot. Gopāḷdās left Indrabhāṇ Kānhīdāsot in 1615-16, however, and settled in the lands of Rājā Sūrajsiṅgh of Jodhpur, under whom he took service. He received the ***paṭo*** of Reyāṃ village from the Rājā soon thereafter.

Meṛto was sequestered from Jodhpur in 1619 upon the death of Rājā Sūrajsiṅgh. The new ruler, Rājā Gajsiṅgh Sūrajsiṅghot (1619-38), then granted Gopāḷdās the village of Gūndoc[92] in compensation for his loss of Reyāṃ. Gopāḷdās again received Reyāṃ in ***paṭo*** in 1623-24 upon the return of Meṛto in ***jāgīr*** to the house of Jodhpur. Reyāṃ remained in Gopāḷdās's ***paṭo*** until his death in 1668. ***Vigat***, 2:199, notes in its description of Reyāṃ that while Gopāḷdās held the village, the people of his ***vasī*** lived on the east side of the village, the remainder of the village being inhabited by Jāṭ cultivators.

Only limited information is available about Gopāḷdās's life. He became involved in the transfer of authority over Meṛto to the Rājā of Jodhpur during the early years of Rājā Gajsiṅgh's rule. Prince Khurram (Shāh Jahān) had received Meṛto in ***jāgīr*** following Rājā Sūrajsiṅgh's death in September of 1619. He then sent the ***amīn***, Abu Kābo, to Meṛto, and Abu in turn entrusted the two halves of Meṛto to ***kiroṛīs***. Abu's ***hākmī*** lasted two years, after which Prince Khurram divided Merto among his military servants and retainers. Sīsodiyo Gahlot Rājā Bhīm Amrāvat (no. 15) was one of Prince Khurram's servants who held villages in Meṛto at this time. Abu's presence continued in the area, however, in the continued assessment of revenue and the collections of taxes through the ***kiroṛīs*** and their men. Meṛtīyo Gopāḷdās was wounded at Meṛto on May 9, 1622 during a disagrement over taxes with Abu Kābo's men that turned into a running battle during which a number were killed and wounded on both sides.[93]

Gopāḷdās's specific activities during the next twenty years are not recorded in local texts at hand. But he remained in the service of the Jodhpur rulers, for in 1642-43, he was appointed ***pradhān*** of Jodhpur under Rājā Jasvantsiṅgh Gajsiṅghot (1638-78). Gopāḷdās's appointment came upon the Rājā's dismissal of Cāmpāvat Rāṭhoṛ Mahesdās Sūrajmalot from this post. Gopāḷdās held the position of ***pradhān*** for the next six years until 1648-49.

During his tenure as ***pradhān***, Gopāḷdās took part in Mughal operations under Prince Augangzeb against the Uzbeks in Balkh and Kabul in 1646-47. Although very costly to the Mughals, this campaign was nominally successful in settling affairs in this area. Rājā Jasvantsiṅgh gave Gopāḷdās a village as a

---

[91] Kekīnd village: located fourteen miles south-southeast of Meṛto.

[92] Gūndoc village: located fifty miles south-southeast of Jodhpur.

[93] See ***Vigat***, 1:113-114, for details of this confrontation and lists of dead and wounded and also ***Vigat***, 2:73, of the **translated text** for background information.

bonus (*vadhāro*) upon news of the success. This grant was later converted to a cash payment of *rs*. 4,000.

Gopāḷdās stepped down as ***pradhān*** of Jodhpur in 1648. Two years later, in 1650-51, he took part in one of the most important military undertakings in Mārvāṛ during this period, the conquest of the fort of Pokaraṇ from the Bhāṭīs of Jaisaḷmer. The ***pargano*** of Pokaraṇ had been written into the ***jāgīr*** of the Jodhpur rulers since the time of Rājā Sūrajsiṅgh Udaisiṅghot (1595-1619), but they had possessed no authority over the area from the time Rāv Candrasen Māldevot (1562-81) mortgaged Pokaraṇ to the Bhāṭīs in the latter-1570s to raise money during his exile in the Arāvallīs. The Jodhpur rulers had not attempted to take possession after their award of ***jāgīr*** because the ruling family of Jaisaḷmer were ***sago***s of Jodhpur. The ruling line of Jaisaḷmer changed in 1650, however, and Rājā Jasvantsiṅgh then chose to reassert Rāṭhoṛ authority over Pokaraṇ. He placed Gopāḷdās in command of one of the three wings of his army of 2,000 horse and 4,000 foot. The Rāṭhoṛ campaign against Pokaraṇ was Rājā Jasvantsiṅgh's first major military undertaking and his first victory following his succession to the Jodhpur throne at the age of twelve years in 1638. Rājā Jasvantsiṅgh awarded Gopāḷdās a cash bonus of ***rs***. 4,000 following the victory at Pokaraṇ.

Gopāḷdās died on July 24, 1668. He had held a ***paṭo*** with a valuation of ***rs***. 35,700, including Reyāṃ and twenty-one other villages. He had also received a monthly salary of ***rs***. 275 while he was ***pradhān*** of Jodhpur between the years 1642-1648.

"Aitihāsik Bātāṃ," p. 55; ***Bāṅkīdās***, pp. 30, 64; "Jodhpur Hukūmat rī Bahī," p. 161; ***Śrī Mahārāj Śrī Jasvantsiṅghjī kī Khyāt***, MS no. 15661, Rājasthān Prācyavidyā Pratiṣṭhān, Jodhpur, p. 186; ***Khyāt***, 2:201; ***Mūndiyāṛ rī Rāṭhoṛāṃ rī Khyāt***, p. 136; ***Murārdān***, no. 2, pp. 493-494, 498; Ojhā, 4:1:422-423; Tripathi, ***The Rise and Fall of the Mughal Empire***, pp. 454-458; ***Vigat***, 1:113-115, 2:199, 291, 299, 302-303, 305.

RULERSHIP AT MEṚTO

ca. 1462-92	Varsiṅghot Meṛtīyo Rāv Varsiṅgh Jodhāvat (no. 146)
ca. 1492	Varsiṅghot Meṛtīyo Rāv Sīho Varsiṅghot (no. 147)
ca. 1492-95	Meṛto divided between Varsiṅghot Meṛtīyo Rāv Sīho Varsiṅghot and Meṛtīyo Dūdo Jodhāvat (no. 104)
ca. 1495-97	Meṛtīyo Rāv Dūdo Jodhāvat (Rāv Sīho Varsiṅghot relegated to the village of Rāhaṇ)
ca. 1497-1535	Meṛtīyo Rāv Vīramde Dūdāvat (no. 105)
ca. 1535-January, 1544	Rāv Mālde Gāṅgāvat of Jodhpur
ca. 1544	Meṛtīyo Rāv Vīramde Dūdāvat
ca. 1544-January, 1557	Meṛtīyo Rāv Jaimal Vīramdevot (no. 107)
January, 1557-July, 1559	Rāv Mālde Gāṅgāvat
July, 1559-March, 1562	Rāv Mālde Gāṅgāvat (1/2 Meṛto)
	Meṛtīyo Jagmāl Vīramdevot (no. 124) (***paṭo*** grant from Rāv Mālde for the other 1/2 of Meṛto)
ca. 1562	Meṛtīyo Rāv Jaimal Vīramdevot (Meṛto in ***jāgīr*** from Emperor Akbar)
ca. 1563-70	Meṛtīyo Jagmāl Vīramdevot (1/2 Meṛto in ***jāgīr*** from Emperor Akbar; the remainder held as Imperial ***khālso***)

ca. 1570-77	Meṛtīyo Kesodās Jaimalot (no. 119) (1/2 Meṛto in ***jāgīr*** from Emperor Akbar)
ca. 1572-77	Meṛtīyo Surtāṇ Jaimalot (no. 113) (1/2 Meṛto in ***jāgīr*** from Emperor Akbar)
ca. 1577-86	Meṛto became Imperial ***khālso*** (*jāgīrs* of both Kesodās and Surtāṇ revoked in 1577-78)

Jāgīr of 1/2 Meṛto from Emperor Akbar

ca. 1586-89	Meṛtīyo Surtān Jaimalot (no. 113)
ca. 1589-96	Meṛtīyo Balbhadar Surtāṇot (no. 114)
ca. 1596-99	Meṛtīyo Gopāḷdās Surtāṇot (no. 115)
ca. 1599-Spring crop, 1602	Meṛtīyo Jagnāth Gopāḷdāsot (no. 116)
Spring crop, 1602-1605	Rājā Sūrajsiṅgh Udaisiṅghot of Jodhpur

Jāgīr of 1/2 Meṛto from Emperor Akbar

ca. 1586-99	Meṛtīyo Kesodās Jaimalot (no. 119)
ca. 1599-1601	Meṛtīyo Kānhīdās Kesodāsot (no. 121)
ca. 1601-05	Meṛtīyo Indrabhāṇ Kānhīdāsot (no. 122) (held only an attenuated share of villages)
ca. 1601-05	Rājā Sūrajsiṅgh Udaisiṅghot of Jodhpur (held 1/2 share of Meṛto's villages minus Indrabhāṇ's share)

May, 1605-September, 1619	Rājā Sūrajsiṅgh Udaisiṅghot of Jodhpur (received all of Meṛto in ***jāgīr*** from Akbar; confirmed by Emperor Jahāngīr)
September, 1619-May/June, 1623	Prince Khurram made ***sūbedār*** of Ajmer and given Meṛto in ***jāgīr***
May/June, 1623- August, 1623	Prince Parvīz made ***sūbedār*** of Ajmer and given Meṛto in ***jāgīr*** on rebellion of Prince Khurram from the Deccan
August, 1623-1625	Rājā Gajsiṅgh Sūrajsiṅghot of Jodhpur (***jāgīr*** of Meṛto from Mahābat Khān)
1625-May 1638	Rājā Gajsiṅgh Sūrajsiṅghot of Jodhpur (Emperor Jahāngīr confirmed ***jāgīr*** of Meṛto in 1625)
May, 1638- November, 1678	Rājā Jasvantsiṅgh Gajsiṅghot of Jodhpur (Meṛto in ***jāgīr*** from the Mughal Emperor)

Figure 30. Meṛtīyo Rāṭhoṛs
(continued on the following pages)

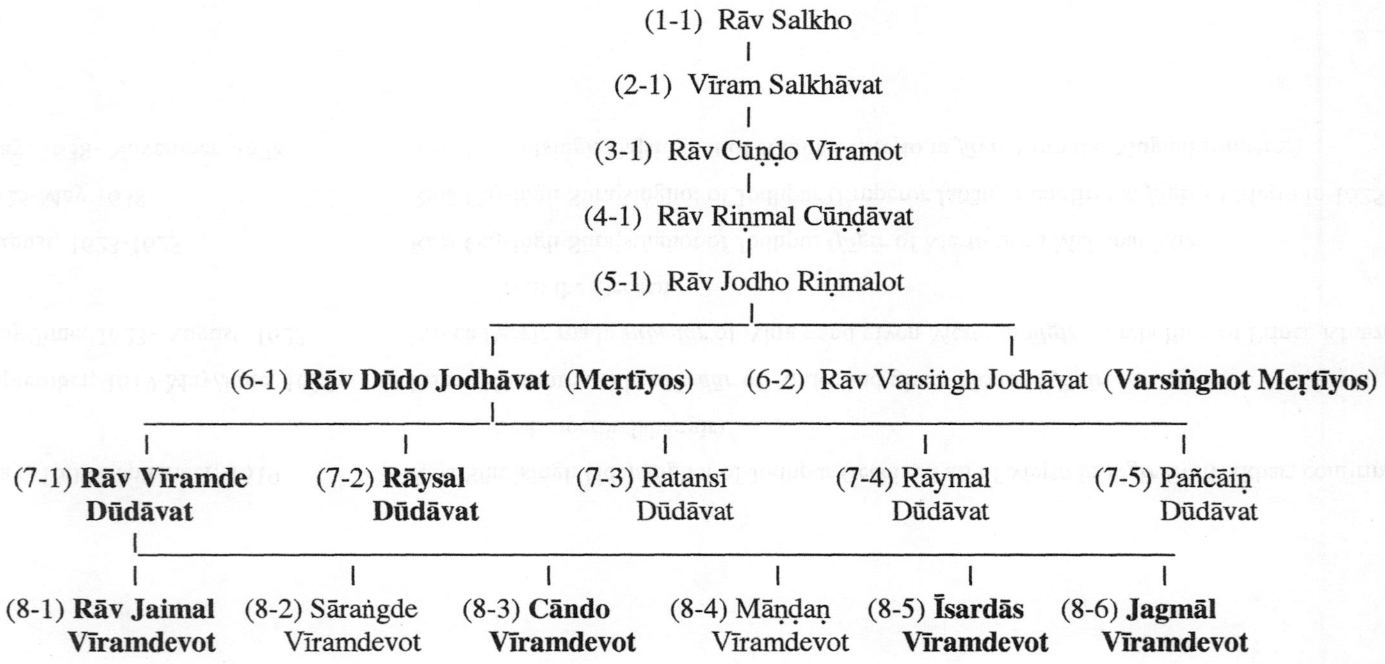

Figure 30. Meṛtīyo Rāṭhoṛs

(continued from the previous page and onto the following pages)

- (5-1) Rāv Jodho Riṇmalot
  - (6-1) **Rāv Dūdo Jodhāvat (Meṛtīyos)**
    - (7-1) **Rāv Vīramde Dūdāvat**
      - (8-1) **Rāv Jaimal Vīramdevot**
        - (9-1) **Surtāṇ Jaimalot**
          - (10-1) **Balbhadar Surtāṇot**
          - (10-2) **Gopāḷdās Surtāṇot**
            - (11-1) **Jagnāth Gopāḷdāsot**
        - (9-4) Goyanddās Jaimalot
        - (9-2) Mādhodās Jaimalot
        - (9-3) **Kesodās Jaimalot**
          - (10-3) **Kānhīdās Kesodāsot**
            - (11-2) **Indrabhāṇ Kānhīdāsot**
        - (9-8) **Dvārkādās Jaimalot**
        - (9-5) Kalyāṇdās Jaimalot
        - (9-6) Narāiṇdās Jaimalot
        - (9-7) Narsiṅghdās Jaimalot
        - (9-12) Mukanddās Jaimalot
        - (9-9) Harīdās Jaimalot
        - (9-10) Rāmdās Jaimalot
        - (9-11) **Vīṭhaḷdās Jaimalot**
        - (9-13) Syāmdās Jaimalot
        - (9-14) **Sādūḷ Jaimalot**

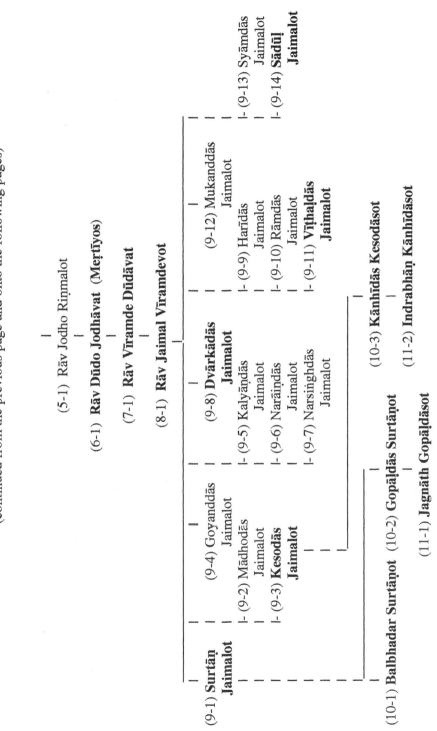

Figure 30. Meṛtīyo Rāṭhoṛs
(continued from the previous pages and onto following page)

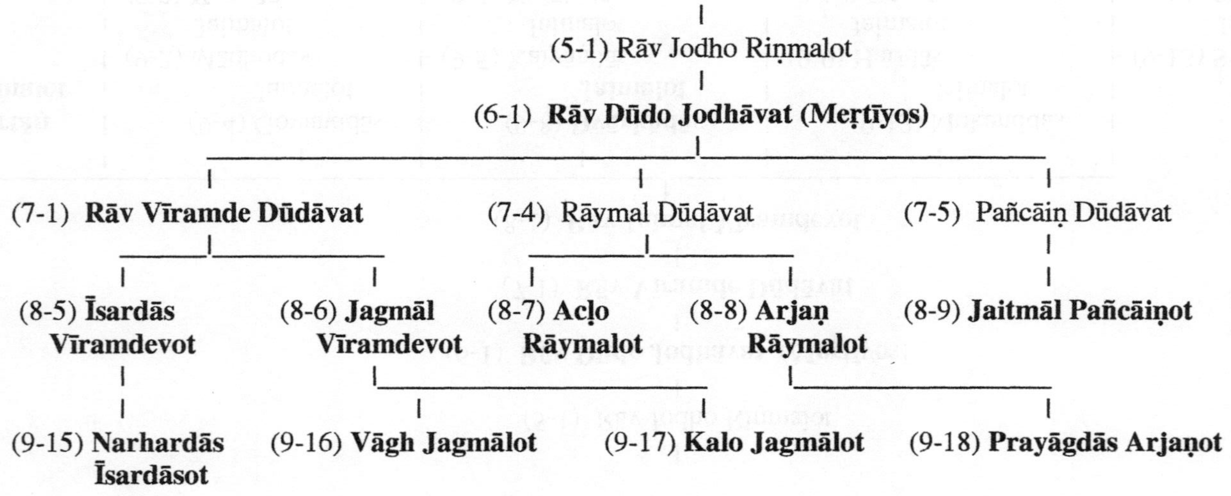

Figure 30. Meṛtīyo Rāṭhoṛs
(continued from previous pages)

(5-1) Rāv Jodho Riṇmalot

(6-1) **Rāv Dūdo Jodhāvat (Meṛtīyos)**

(7-1) **Rāv Vīramde Dūdāvat**

(8-1) **Rāv Jaimal Vīramdevot**

(9-2) Mādhodās Jaimalot

(10-4) Sūndardās Mādhodāsot

(11-3) **Gopāḷdās Sūndardāsot**

(10-5) Mohaṇdās Mādhodāsot

(11-4) Jasvant Mohandāsot

Riṇmalot Rāṭhoṛs

(no. 130) **Bhān Bhojrājot, Rāv** (8-1)
(no. 129) **Sīṅghaṇ Khetsīyot** (7-1)

The Riṇmalot Rāṭhoṛs

The Riṇmal or Riṇmalot Rāṭhoṛs descend from Rāv Riṇmal Cūṇḍāvat (4-1), ruler of Maṇḍor (ca. 1428-38). In the broadest sense, this group includes all of Rāv Riṇmal's sons and descendants. The texts from the period under review use the term "Riṇmal/Riṇmalot" to refer to those Rāṭhoṛs who were Rāv Riṇmal's heirs to the lands of Mārvāṛ. The term is applied in this broad sense to distinguish these Rāṭhoṛs from other Rāṭhoṛs, such as the Sīndhaḷs and the Ūhaṛs, and from Rajpūts of clans different from the Rāṭhoṛs.[1]

Many powerful branches (***sākh***s) of Rāṭhoṛs emerged from Rāv Riṇmal's sons and their descendants. These ***sākh***s include, to name but a few, the Jodho Rāṭhoṛs from Riṇmal's son, Jodho (ruler of Maṇḍor and Jodhpur, ca. 1453-89), the Akhairājot Rāṭhoṛs from Riṇmal's son, Akhairāj, and the Kūmpāvat Rāṭhoṛs from Riṇmal's great-grandson, Kūmpo Mahirājot (no. 95). By the mid-seventeenth century, lists of Rāṭhoṛ ***sākh***s such as those found in "Jodhpur Hukūmat rī Bahī," do not refer to a Riṇmal or Riṇmalot ***sākh***. They refer, rather, to the more particularistic groupings of Mārvāṛ Rāṭhoṛs that emerged from prominent descendants of Rāv Riṇmal's dating from more recent periods.

The heading "Riṇmalot" is used in this section to designate two of the less prominent descendants of Rāv Riṇmal about whom there is limited information. Where appropriate, mention is made of Rāṭhoṛ ***sākh***s that later emerged among their descendants.

(no. 129) **Sīṅghaṇ Khetsīyot** (7-1)

Sīṅghaṇ Khetsīyot was a great-grandson of Rāv Riṇmal Cūṇḍāvat, descending from Rāv Riṇmal's son, Jagmāl Riṇmalot (5-1), and Jagmāl's son, Khetsī Jagmālot (6-1). Jagmāl Riṇmalot died as a young man during his father Rāv Riṇmal's lifetime. During Rāv Jodho Riṇmalot's division of the lands of Mārvāṛ among his brothers and sons following the founding of Jodhpur, Rāv Jodho gave Jagmāl's son, Khetsī Jagmālot, the village of Netṛāṃ[2] as his share. Khetsī settled at Netṛāṃ and a ***sākh*** of Mārvāṛ Rāṭhoṛs known as Khetsīyot later

---

[1] See: "Aitihāsik Bātāṃ," pp. 48, 50, 54, and ***Vigat***, 2:66, of the **translated text** for examples of this usage.

[2] Netṛāṃ village: located twenty-one miles north-northeast of Jodhpur.

emerged bearing his name. No further information is available from texts at hand about this Riṇmalot.

Khetsī's son, Sīṅghaṇ Khetsīyot, appears in the chronicles as a military servant of Rāv Mālde Gāṅgāvat of Jodhpur (1532-62). Sīṅghaṇ was posted at the fort of Jodhpur, and he died in the defense of the fort when it came under attack from the forces of Sher Shāh Sūr following the battle of Samel[3] in January of 1544.

No other information is available about this Rajpūt.

Gehlot, ***Mārvāṛ***, p. 161; "Jodhpur Hukūmat rī Bahī," pp. 141-142; ***Khyāt***, 2:12, 141; ***Vigat***, 1:39, 58, 2:57, "Pariśiṣṭ 4 - Ḍāvī ne Jīvṇī Mislāṃ rī Vigat," 2:476.

(no. 130) **Bhāṇ Bhojrājot, Rāv of Cāḍī** (8-1)

Bhāṇ Bhojrājot was fourth in line of descent from Rāv Riṇmal Cūṇḍāvat (4-1) through Riṇmal's son, Rūpo Riṇmalot (5-2), and his grandson, Sādo Rūpāvat (6-2). It was Rūpo Riṇmalot who received the village of Cāḍī[4] from his brother, Rāv Jodho Riṇmalot, following the founding of Jodhpur in 1459. This village was the homeland (***utan***) of the Lahuvo Bhāṭīs. Rūpo was able to take this area from the Bhāṭīs and then establish himself and his family at Cāḍī. A ***sākh*** of Rāṭhoṛs later emerged from among his descendants bearing the name of Rūpāvat. Cāḍī village became the homeland of these Rūpāvat Rāṭhoṛs.

Bhāṇ Bhojrājot was a contemporary of Rāv Mālde Gāṅgāvat of Jodhpur (1532-62). The ***Khyāt*** of Naiṇsī, 2:137-138, describes him as the master (***dhaṇī***) of Cāḍī and refers to him by the title of ***rāv***. He appears to have led a relatively independent existence at Cāḍī, a village which lay near the northern borders of Mārvāṛ territory. He became involved with Jodhpur in 1552 during Rāv Mālde's operations against the Kelhaṇ Bhāṭīs of Pūṅgaḷ and the Bhāṭī ruling family of Jaisaḷmer.

References in Naiṇsī's ***Khyāt*** to relations between the Bhāṭīs of Pūṅgaḷ and the Rāṭhoṛs of Jodhpur in this period are difficult to interpret. It appears that prior to 1552 when Rāv Mālde moved against Pūṅgaḷ and Jaisaḷmer, the Kelhaṇ Bhāṭīs attacked and overran Cāḍī and other villages of this area. The ***Khyāt*** mentions three battles that Rāv Mālde's Rajpūts fought in and around Cāḍī and Karṇū.[5] They were severely tested during these battles by the Kelhaṇ Bhāṭīs under Rāv Jeso Varsiṅghot of Pūṅgaḷ. Bhāṇ Bhorājot's brother, Prithīrāj Bhojrājot (8-2), was killed at the battle for Cāḍī, and another of Bhāṇ's brothers, Rāṇagde Bhojrājot (8-3), died along with seventeen of his men at a battle near the village of Lākhāsar in the territory of Bīkāner.

---

[3] Samel village: located twenty-four miles southwest of Ajmer.

[4] Cāḍī village: located fifty-eight miles north of Jodhpur.

[5] Karṇū village: located six miles east-northeast of Cāḍī.

Rāv Bhāṇ remained in Rāv Mālde's service following operations in the early 1550s. In 1562, he was stationed at the Mālgaḍh at Meṛto with Rāṭhoṛ Devīdās Jaitāvat (no. 65). The Mālgaḍh came under siege this year, and Rāv Bhāṇ was killed during the fighting against Meṛtīyo Rāv Jaimal Vīramdevot (no. 107) and the Mughal forces of Akbar under Mīrzā Sharafu'd-Dīn Ḥusayn.

"Aitihāsik Bātāṃ," p. 55; ***Bāṅkīdās***, pp. 16-17; Gehlot, ***Mārvāṛ***, p. 161; "Jodhpur Hukūmat rī Bahī," p. 129; ***Khyāt***, 2:137-138; ***Vigat***, 1:38, 61, 2:65, "Pariśiṣṭ 4 - Ḍāvī ne Jīvṇī Mislāṃ rī Vigat," 2:476.

Figure 31. Riṇmalot Rāṭhoṛs

(1-1) Rāv Salkho
|
(2-1) Vīram Salkhāvat
|
(3-1) Rāv Cūṇḍo Vīramot
|
(4-1) Rāv Riṇmal Cūṇḍāvat

- (5-1) Jagmāl Riṇmalot
  - (6-1) Khetsī Jagmālot
    - (7-1) **Sīṅghaṇ Khetsīyot**
- (5-2) Rūpo Riṇmalot
  - (6-2) Sādo Rūpāvat
    - (7-2) Bhojrāj Sādāvat
      - (8-1) **Rāv Bhāṇ Bhojrājot**
      - (8-2) Prithīrāj Bhojrājot
      - (8-3) Rāṇagde Bhojrājot

Sīndhaḷ Rāṭhoṛs

(no. 136) **Cāmpo Karamsīyot**
(no. 134) **Dedo Kojhāvat**
(no. 133) **Ḍūṅgarsī**
(no. 132) **Megho Narsiṅghdāsot**
(no. 131) **Narsiṅghdās Khīndāvat**
(no. 135) **Riṇdhīr Kojhāvat**

The Sīndhaḷ Rāṭhoṛs

The Sīndhaḷs are a very old Rajpūt group in Mārvāṛ. According to local chronicles, they descend from Sīndhaḷ Jopsāhot, a great-grandson of Rāv Sīho Setrāmot, who is considered the founding ancestor of the Mārvāṛ Rāṭhoṛs. Little is known in fact about Rāv Sīho other than the date of his death: October 9, 1273. This date is recorded on a memorial stone (***devḷī***) dedicated to a Raṭhaḍā (Rāṭhoṛ) Sīho, son of Setrām, found at the village of Bīṭhū[1] in central Mārvāṛ. Sīho's son, Āsthān, is associated in the chronicles with the villages of Pālī[2] in eastern Mārvāṛ and with Kheṛ[3] in western Mārvāṛ. Āsthān is said to have founded his capitol at Kheṛ. No specific information is available regarding Āsthān's son, Jopsāh Āsthānot, or Jopsāh's son, Sīndhaḷ Jopsāhot.

The precise genealogical relationship of the Sīndhaḷs to other branches of Mārvāṛ Rāṭhoṛs is very conjectural given the extremely doubtful nature of this type of information prior to the time of Rāv Riṇmal Cūṇḍāvat of Maṇḍor (ca. 1428-38) and his son, Rāv Jodho Riṇmalot (ca. 1453-89). Richard Saran has suggested that the Sīndhaḷs may be an old Rajpūt group from Mārvāṛ that became incorporated within the Rāṭhoṛ clan (***kuḷ***) at some time during the early history of this area. Saran notes that, by the end of the sixteenth century, the Sīndhaḷs were probably firmly established as Rāṭhoṛ Rajpūts.

Bhāṭī, ***Sarvekṣaṇ***, 3:114, records that Sīndhaḷ was the uterine brother of Ūhaṛ, the founding ancestor of the Ūhaṛ Rāṭhoṛs (see ***infra***). Sīndhaḷ is said to have settled in central-western Mārvāṛ and to have founded the village of Bhādrājuṇ,[4] while Ūhaṛ settled at Koḍhṇo[5]. This same text, 3:114-115, presents

---

[1] Bīṭhū village: located thirty miles south of Jodhpur and fourteen miles northwest of Pālī in central Mārvāṛ.

[2] Pālī village: located forty miles south-southeast of Jodhpur.

[3] Kheṛ village: located sixty-two miles southwest of Jodhpur, just near the great bend in the Lūṇī River.

[4] Bhādrājuṇ village: located forty-eight miles south-southwest of Jodhpur.

[5] Koḍhṇo village: located twenty-eight miles west-southwest of Jodhpur.

an abbreviated genealogy for the Sīndhaḷs, listing thirteen generations of names in direct line of descent from Sīndhaḷ Jopsāhot, beginning with his son, Āsal Sīndhaḷot, and ending with Sādul Acḷāvat. No information is given about these Sīndhaḷs, nor is there specific genealogical information about the Sīndhaḷs mentioned in the texts under review. These Rajpūts figure in the history of this period primarily because of their presence in areas of eastern Mārvāṛ that came under increasingly heavy attack from the Rāṭhoṛs of Jodhpur from the time of Rāv Sūjo Jodhāvat (ca. 1492-1515). These lands were eventually incorporated within the sphere of Jodhpur.

> B. N. Reu, ***Glories of Marwar and the Glorious Rathors*** (Jodhpur: Archaeological Department, 1943), p. x; Bhāṭī, ***Sarvekṣaṇ***, 3:114-115; Gehlot, ***Mārvāṛ***, p. 72; "Jodhpur Hukūmat rī Bahī," 146; Ojhā, 4:1:152-160.

(no. 131) **Narsiṅghdās Khīndāvat**
(no. 132) **Megho Narsiṅghdāsot**

Sīndhaḷ Narsiṅghdās Khīndāvat was the master (***dhaṇī***) of Jaitāraṇ village[6] in eastern Mārvāṛ during the time of Rāṭhoṛ Rāv Sato Cūṇḍāvat's rule at Maṇḍor (ca. 1424-28). He appears in the chronicles because of a ***vair*** that emerged between the Sīndhaḷs of Jaitāraṇ and the Rāṭhoṛs of Maṇḍor and Jodhpur over the death of Rāv Sato's son, Āskaraṇ Satāvat (no. 55).

The emergence of this ***vair*** involved a complex set of circumstances surrounding Rāv Sato's son, Narbad Satāvat (no. 56), the betrothal of a daughter of the Sāṅkhlo Paṃvārs of Rūṇ village[7] named Supiyārde to Narbad, the withdrawal of this betrothal, the marriage of Supiyārde to Sīndhaḷ Narsiṅghdās Khīndāvat of Jaitāraṇ, and finally the flight of Supiyārde from Jaitāraṇ with Narbad Satāvat. It was during Narbad's flight from Jaitāraṇ with Supiyārde that Āskaraṇ Satāvat became involved. The Sīndhaḷs had come in pursuit, and Āskaraṇ was killed in a pitched battle near Narbad's village of Kāylāṇo[8] in Goḍhvāṛ as he sought to prevent their advance. The Rāṇo of Mevāṛ became involved with both sides in this affair as arbiter. The ***vair*** was settled finally during the reign of Rāṭhoṛ Rāv Jodho Riṇmalot of Jodhpur (ca. 1453-89). Rāv Jodho sent his son, Dūdo Jodhāvat (no. 104), to kill Sīndhaḷ Narsiṅghdās's son, Megho Narsiṅghdāsot, and end the hostilities. Dūdo accomplished this feat in single-handed combat before Jaitāraṇ.[9]

---

[6] Jaitāraṇ town: located fifty-six miles east-southeast of Maṇḍor.

[7] Rūṇ village: located fifty-eight miles northeast of Maṇḍor.

[8] Kāylāṇo village: located thirty-eight miles south of Sojhat and nine miles east-northeast of Nāḍūl.

[9] See ***supra***, "Cūṇḍāvat Rāṭhoṛs," Āskaraṇ Satāvat (no. 55) and Narbad Satāvat (no. 56), for full details of events surrounding Āskaraṇ's death and "Aitihāsik Bātāṃ," pp. 38-40,

The Sīndhaḷs maintained their hold over Jaitāraṇ into the early fifteenth century. The Rāṇo of Cītoṛ, Sīsodīyo Kūmbho Mokaḷot (ca. 1433-68), asserted his authority over the area following his murder of Rāṭhoṛ Rāv Riṇmal Cūṇḍāvat at Cītoṛ ca. 1438, but the Sīndhaḷs remained in possession of these lands as nominal servants of the Rāṇo. Rāv Sūjo Jodhāvat of Jodhpur (ca. 1492-1515) and/or his son, Ūdo Sūjāvat, later attacked Jaitāraṇ and drove the Sīndhaḷs away. Jaitāraṇ then came under the authority of Jodhpur. Rāv Sūjo granted this land to his son, Ūdo Sūjāvat, from whom descend the Ūdāvat Rāṭhoṛs of Jaitāraṇ.[10]

Bāṅkīdās, p. 48, records that the descendants of Narsiṅghdās Khīndāvat took up residence in Mevāṛ after they were driven from Jaitāraṇ, occupying villages the Rāṇo granted to them.

Bāṅkīdās, p. 48; ***Khyāt***, 3:38-40, 141-148; ***Vigat***, 1:493-495.

(no. 133) **Ḍūṅgarsī**

Ḍūṅgarsī Sīndhaḷ was a military servant of Rāv Mālde Gāṅgāvat of Jodhpur (1532-62). He was killed at the battle of Meṛto in March of 1554, fighting under Rāv Mālde's commander, Rāṭhoṛ Prithīrāj Jaitāvat (no. 63), against Meṛtīyo Rāv Jaimal Vīramdevot (no. 107).

"Aitihāsik Bātāṃ," p. 49; ***Murārdān***, no. 2, p. 129; ***Vigat***, 1:59, 2:59.

(no. 134) **Dedo Kojhāvat**
(no. 135) **Riṇdhīr Kojhāvat**

These two Sīndhaḷs are mentioned in a list of Rajpūts who were killed at the battle of Harmāṛo[11] on January 24, 1557. They were military servants of Rāv Mālde Gāṅgāvat of Jodhpur and fought at Harmāṛo under Rāṭhoṛ Devīdās Jaitāvat (no. 65). They were among the 1,500 Rajpūts from Mārvāṛ that Devīdās selected to ride under his command and join with Paṭhāṇ Hājī Khān against an allied force of Rajpūts under Sīsodīyo Rāṇo Udaisiṅgh Sāṅgāvat of Mevāṛ (ca. 1537-72; no. 17).

No other information is available about these two Rajpūts.

"Aitihāsik Bātāṃ," pp. 51-52; ***Bāṅkīdās***, p. 15.

---

of the **translated text** for the story of how Dūdo Jodhāvat killed Sīndhaḷ Megho Narsiṅghdāsot.

[10] See ***infra***, "Ūdāvat Rāṭhoṛs," for information about Ūdo Sūjāvat and a more complete discussion of the issues surrounding the conquest of Jaitāraṇ.

[11] Harmāṛo village: located fifty-five miles south-southwest of Ajmer and six miles south of Vadhnor in northern Mevāṛ.

(no. 136) **Cāmpo Karamsīyot**

Sīndhaḷ Cāmpo Karamsīyot was a military servant of Meṛtīyo Surtāṇ Jaimalot's (no. 113). His name appears in the Mārvāṛī chronicles because of an important service he performed for Surtāṇ in Gujarat. Meṛtīyo Surtāṇ was on tour for the Mughals in Gujarat in the early 1580s. Cāmpo Sīndhaḷ and other of Surtāṇ's military servants killed two Jāṛeco Rajpūt bandits who had been terrorizing the city of Ahmadabad. This action came to the attention of the ***sūbedār*** of Gujarat. In reward, the ***sūbedār*** used his office to help Surtāṇ regain his ***jāgīr*** of one-half the villages of Meṛto from Emperor Akbar.[12]

Vigat, 2:70-72.

[12] See ***supra***, "Meṛtīyo Rāṭhoṛs," Surtāṇ Jaimalot (no. 113), for details. Surtāṇ's brother, Kesodās Jaimalot (no. 119), also regained his ***jāgīr*** of one-half the villages of Meṛto as a result of Surtāṇ's actions.

Ūdāvat Rāṭhoṛs

(no. 142)	**Bhīṃv Kilāṇdāsot**	(11-1)
(no. 137)	**Ḍūṅgarsī Ūdāvat**	(8-1)
(no. 139)	**Jaitsī Ūdāvat**	(8-3)
(no. 140)	**Khīṃvo Ūdāvat**	(8-2)
(no. 141)	**Ratansī Khīṃvāvat**	(9-3)
(no. 138)	**Tejsī Ḍūṅgarsīyot**	(9-1)

The Ūdāvat Rāṭhoṛs

The Ūdāvat Rāṭhoṛs descend from Ūdo Sūjāvat (7-1), son of Rāv Sūjo Jodhāvat (Jodhpur ruler, ca. 1492-1515) and grandson of Rāv Jodho Riṇmalot (ruler of Mandor, ca. 1453-89; founder of Jodhpur, 1459). Ūdo was born on November 16, 1462, from the womb of Rāṇi Māṅgliyāṇī.[1] His descendants, the Ūdāvats, are also called Jaitāraṇīyo Rāṭhoṛs, a name derived from Jaitāraṇ town,[2] which he (or possibly his father) had taken from the Sīndhaḷ Rāṭhoṛs. Jaitāraṇ and its surrounding villages became the homeland (***utan***) of the Ūdāvat ***sākh***.

According to one tradition, the first settlement (***ād sahar***) in the Jaitāraṇ region was the village of Āgevo.[3] Jaitāraṇ town itself is said by Naiṇsī to have been settled in 1468-69 during the reign of Rāv Jodho. This tradition is at variance with the information given in the story of Dūdo Jodhāvat (no. 104) and Sīndhaḷ Megho (no. 132) (***Khyāt,*** 3:38-40), which indicates that Dūdo had not yet obtained Meṛto when he fought Megho at Jaitāraṇ. Since Dūdo and Varsiṅgh Jodhāvat (no. 145) settled Meṛto on March 7, 1462, Jaitāraṇ town must have been founded before this date, unless the date for the foundation of Meṛto is incorrect. It appears, however, that the date given for the settling of Jaitāraṇ is simply wrong. Traditions concerning the lives of Cūṇḍāvat Rāṭhoṛs Āskaraṇ (no. 55) and Narbad Satāvat (no. 56) indicate that Jaitāraṇ was under the rule of the Sīndhaḷs during the reign of Rāv Rinmal of Maṇḍor (ca. 1428-38). The ***Vigat*** states that Rāv Jodho took Jaitāraṇ and Sojhat from Rāṇo Kūmbho of Mevāṛ (ca. 1433-68) shortly after his conquest of Maṇḍor (1453). Thus the date given by Naiṇsī for the founding of Jaitāraṇ cannot be accepted.

Even though Rāv Jodho had taken Jaitāraṇ from the Rāṇo, the Sīndhaḷs, who had been serving the Sīsodīyo ruler, could not be driven from the area. They continued to hold Jaitāraṇ until at least 1482. The ***Vigat*** notes that before

---

[1] See ***supra***, **Marriage and Family Lists of the Rulers of Jodhpur**, Sūjo Jodhāvat, Rāṇī no. 3, S - Ūdo.

[2] Jaitāraṇ town: located fifty-six miles east of Jodhpur.

[3] Āgevo village: located four miles south-southwest of Jaitāraṇ.

Sūjo became ruler of Jodhpur (ca. 1492), he settled his son Ūdo in Jaitāraṇ and drove away the Sīndhaḷs, but another tradition relates that Ūdo, angry with his father, had entered the service of the ruler of Jaitāraṇ, Sīndhaḷ Khīṃvo, who had given him the village Loṭaudhrī[4] in grant. While living there, Ūdo plotted to take Jaitāraṇ. One day all the Sīndhaḷs except Khīṃvo left in a marriage procession. Ūdo went to Khīṃvo's residence and killed him. Rāmkaraṇ Āsopā and Kiśansiṃh Ūdāvat, two twentieth-century historians of the Ūdāvat family, have argued that this event took place in V.S. 1539 (A.D. 1482-83).

Alternatively, Māṅgilāl Vyās recently suggested that Ūdo, aided by his father, established control over Jaitāraṇ much later. He quotes as evidence a couplet giving the date of March 8, 1509, for Ūdo's grant of the village Tālūkīyo[5] to his purohit, Bhojrāj. Bhojrāj had consecrated Ūdo as ruler of Jaitāraṇ; in exchange, Ūdo gave him this village. Vyās believes that the consecration and the grant of the village must have occurred at roughly the same time; by this reasoning, Ūdo's taking of Jaitāraṇ with Rāv Sūjo's aid occurred around 1508 or 1509.

An anonymous local ***khyāt*** from Ṭhikāṇo Rāypur indicates that Ūdo conquered Jaitāraṇ in 1482 and sat on the throne there on April 10, 1483.[6] Then, between February of 1485 and December of 1486, he had a fort built in the town, at a cost of 81,000 rupees. The earlier date for the conquest of Jaitāraṇ seems more likely. Ūdo would have been about twenty years old if he took Jaitāraṇ in 1482, but nearly fifty if he accomplished this in 1508 or 1509. One of his father Sūjo's other sons, Naro Sūjāvat, had already established a separate domain for himself by 1476. 1482 would not have been too soon for Ūdo to have done the same.

Some years later the Sīndhaḷs, driven from Jaitāraṇ, went to Mevāṛ and appealed to Rāṇo Rāymal (ca. 1473-May 24, 1509) for aid. The Rāṇo gave them twelve villages and military assistance for an attack on Jaitāraṇ. Ūdo was able to repell the attack, but in it the Cāraṇ Nībsī Khetsīyot was killed. Āsopā (p. 22) states that in gratitude for this sacrifice Ūdo gave Nībsī's son the village Giyāsṇī (i.e., Gehāvāsṇī).[7] The defeated Sīndhaḷs returned to Mevāṛ.

Very little else is known about Ūdo's reign at Jaitāraṇ. According to one story, he became involved in a dispute with Rāv Vīramde Dūdāvat (no. 105), the ruler of Meṛto from 1497-1544. The circumstances of the dispute are as follows:

When Khīmvo Sīndhaḷ was killed in 1482, his Māṅgliyāṇī wife (Ūdo's mother's sister), before becoming a ***satī***, cursed Ūdo, saying that his body would become leprous and his descendants would be unable to retain his kingdom.

---

[4] Loṭaudhrī village: located eight miles northwest of Jaitāraṇ.

[5] Tālūkīyo village: located five miles northeast of Jaitāraṇ.

[6] The Rāypur ***khyāt*** is described in Bhāṭī, ***Sarvekṣaṇ***, 1:48-52.

[7] Naiṇsī (***Vigat***, 1:551) indicates that Khīmvo Ūdāvat (no. 140; 8-2) gave this village to the Kavīyo Cāraṇ Nīmbo Khetāvat. Gehāvāsṇī village is located eight miles south-southwest of Jaitāraṇ.

And indeed, soon afterward Ūdo developed leprosy. In 1484-85, while he was very ill, Rāv Vīramde of Meṛto stole some of his mares. Too sick to take immediate action, he appealed to a holy man, Gūdaṛ Bābā, for whom he had performed many devotions. With the blessing of Gūdaṛ Bābā, his body was miraculously restored, and he set out after Vīramde.

Vīramde had encamped at Līlīyāṃ village[8] about ten ***kos*** from Jaitāraṇ. He and his companions were about to eat a meal when Ūdo arrived with his retainers in pursuit of the horses. After Vīramde refused to return all of the horses, a battle occurred. Vīramde was defeated. Then Ūdo told Vīramde to put down his dagger and promise that in the future the Meṛtīyos would never tie on a dagger. And in fact from that day forward the Meṛtīyo ***sirdārs*** never tied one on again. Thus the story ends.

The date given, 1484-85, cannot be correct, as Vīramde would have been only seven years old at that time. Nor was he Rāv of Meṛto until 1497. If there was a conflict between Vīramde and Ūdo, it must have occurred after 1497, or the representation of Vīramde as Rāv of Meṛto in this story is inaccurate. An old song (***gīt***) quoted by Āsopā (p. 22) mentions the quarrel but does not refer to Vīramde by name. One cannot say if the "son of Dūdo" (Dūdāvat) in the ***gīt*** was Vīramde at all. Possibly there was enmity between Ūdo and one of Dūdo Jodhāvat's other sons. Without further evidence, a final judgment is not possible. Either the story about Vīramde and Ūdo is a complete fabrication, or the date is wrong, or someone other than Vīramde was involved.[9]

According to the anonymous Rāypur ***khyāt*** (Bhāṭī, ***Sarvekṣaṇ***, 1:49), Ūdo died on May 5, 1503. Both Āsopā and Kiśansiṃh Ūdāvat have given a later date, May 12, 1511, for his death. The later date seems much more likely. Sources also differ about the number of his wives and sons. Āsopā (pp. 23-26) provides the following lists:

Four wives, all of whom became ***satīs*** when Ūdo died:

1. Senior wife Sīsodṇī Anopkuṃvar of Cītoṛ.
2. A Gauṛ wife, Phūlkuṃvar of Rājgaḍh.
3. Jādvaṇjī Mānkuṃvar of Karolī.
4. Sonagarī Nandkuṃvar of Mallārgaḍh.

Seven sons:

1. Mālamsiṃh (i.e, Mālde).
2. Ḍūṅgarsī.
3. Jaitsī.

---

[8] Līlīyāṃ (i.e., Nīlīyāṃ) village: located eighteen miles north-northeast of Jaitāraṇ and thirteen miles south-southwest of Meṛto.

[9] See ***supra***, "Meṛtīyo Rāṭhoṛs," for additional discussion concerning the conflict between Ūdo Sūjāvat and the Meṛtīyos

4. Netsī.
5. Khetsī.
6. Vaṇvīr.
7. Khīṃvkaraṇ (i.e., Khīṃvo).

Kiśansiṃh Ūdāvat has examined (p. 16, n. 3) the ***Udaibhāṇ Cāmpāvat rī Khyāt***, a seventeenth-century text containing a genealogy of the Ūdāvats, which records that he had eleven sons:

1. Khīṃvkaraṇ (i.e., Khīṃvo).
2. Ḍūṅgarsī.
3. Mālde.
4. Bhāṇ.
5. Jaitsī.
6. Khetsī.
7. Netsī.
8. Mānsiṃh.
9. Lūṇkaraṇ.
10. Bhojrāj.
11. Bhīm.

A ***guṭakā***, or anthology of documents, also noticed by Kiśansiṃh Ūdāvat (p. 18, n. 1), provides a list of five wives, eight sons, and one daughter, as follows:

1. Sekhāvatjī Rāṇī Javār Kuṃvar, daughter of Durjansāl Maheśdāsot of Cokḍī. She had one son, Lūṇkaraṇ.
2. Rāṇī Hul[ṇī] Naval Kuṃvar, daughter of Samarathsiṃh Sālamsiṃhot of Pīsaṇ. She had two sons, Ḍūṅgarsī and Khīṃvo.
3. Rāṇī Sāṅkhlī Aṇand Kuṃvar, daughter of Mānsiṃh Riḍmalot of Koṭā. She had two sons, Netsī and Khetsī.
4. Rāṇī Cahuvāṇ Chel Kuṃvar, daughter of Pa[h]āṛsiṃh Padamsiṃhot of Cītalvāṇo. Her two sons were Vaṇvīr and Mālde.
5. Rāṇī Rāṇāvat Sire Kuṃvar, daughter of Mādhosiṃh Dalpatsiṃhot of Rāmpur. She had one son, Jaitsī, and one daughter, Jaḍāv Kuṃvar.

During his reign at Jaitāraṇ, Ūdo gave two villages to Brāhmaṇs: Tālūkīyo, to Purohit Bhojrāj Kūmpāvat, a Sīvaṛ Brāhmaṇ, and Bhākharvāsṇī,[10] to the Śrīmāḷī Brāhmaṇ Bhākhar Narharot.

Rāmkaraṇ Āsopā, ***Itihās Nībāj, arthāt, Marūdeśāntargat Svasthān Nībājādhipati Ūdāvat Rāṭhauṛ Rājvaṃś kā Itihās*** (Mārvāṛ: Ṭhikānā Śrī Nībāj, [1931]), pp. 11-26; ***Khyāt***, 3:38-40; Kiśansiṃh Ūdāvat, ***Ūdāvat Rāṭhauṛ Itihās*** (Jaitāraṇ: Vīr Rāv

[10] Bhākarvāsṇī village: located six miles west of Jaitāraṇ.

Śrī Ratansiṃh Rāṭhauṛ Smṛti Bhavan Niyās, 1982-83), pp. 8-18; Bhāṭī, ***Sarvekṣaṇ***, 1:48-52; ***Vigat***, 1:35, 493-495, 513, 543, 547; Māṅgilāl Vyās, ***Jodhpur Rājya kā Itihās*** (Jaypur: Pañcśīl Prakāśan, 1975), pp. 66-69, 307.

(no. 137) **Ḍūṅgarsī Ūdāvat** (8-1)

After Ūdo Sūjāvat died in 1511, his eldest son, Mālde (8-4), sat on the throne in Jaitāraṇ, while Ḍūṅgarsī held Nīmbāj,[11] Netsī Rāypur,[12] Jaitsī (no. 139; 8-3) Chīmpīyo Khusyālpur,[13] Khīṃvo (no. 140; 8-2) Girrī,[14] and Khetsī Jūṇṭho.[15] Vaṇvīr was living in Chīmpīyo Khusyālpur, apparently under the supervision of Jaitsī. Probably several of these sons had received their lands prior to Ūdo's death, just as he had obtained Jaitāraṇ during his father's lifetime.[16]

Exactly how long Mālde remained in control of Jaitāraṇ is uncertain. Naiṇsī does not include Mālde among the Ūdāvat rulers of Jaitāraṇ in the list he provides in his ***Vigat*** (1:495). Perhaps this omission signifies that Mālde's reign was short and unremarkable. But Āsopā, in his history of Nīmbāj (p. 25), suggests that Mālamsiṃh (i.e, Mālde) adopted Ratansī Khīṃvāvat (no. 141; 9-3), one of the sons of Khīṃvo Ūdāvat. Since Ratansī was born August 18, 1520, possibly Mālde was still ruling Jaitāraṇ at this time. The anonymous ***khyāt*** from Rāypur, however, contains the following story:

> ... Māldejī went to the Bhāṭīs' [residence], Bīkamkor, to marry a second time. At that time, his brother Rāv Khīṃvkaraṇjī [i.e., Khīṃvo] was ruling in Girrī. Jaitsī, who was in Chīmpīyo, said to him: "Brother, the throne of Jaitāraṇ is ours; [if] you command, we shall go [there] and establish [our] authority." Khīṃvkaraṇjī spoke: "These words are correct; the throne is ours ...." Then Khīṃvkaraṇjī rode from Girrī with 1,000 horses. He went to Jaitāraṇ and established [his] authority .... The people

---

[11] Nīmbāj village: located six miles southeast of Jaitāraṇ.

[12] Rāypur village: located ten miles south-southeast of Jaitāraṇ.

[13] Chīmpīyo Khusyāpur village: located seven miles south of Jaitāraṇ.

[14] Girrī village: located thirteen miles east-southeast of Jaitāraṇ.

[15] Jūṇṭho village: located eleven miles south of Jaitāraṇ.

[16] Ūdo's uterine brother, Prāg, had obtained Devḷī village of Jaitāraṇ (which the ***Vigat***, 1:513, calls Devḷī Pirāg ro) during Rāv Sūjo's reign. He had come with Ūdo from Jodhpur and was very close to his brother. His descendants are known as Prāgdāsot Ūdāvats although they do not descend from Ūdo himself. ***Jodhpur Rājya kī Khyāt***, p. 67; Kiśansiṃh Ūdāvat, ***Ūdāvata Rāṭhauṛa Itihās***, p. 16.

> [and] Rajpūts all came and paid respects [to him] (*Sarvekṣaṇ*, 1:49).

The ***khyāt*** notes that Ḍūṅgarsī Ūdāvat was also involved in the taking of Jaitāraṇ. Apparently not long after deposing Mālde, Khīṃvo left Jaitāraṇ under Ḍūṅgarsī's control and concerned himself more with the affairs of Girrī and of Vadhnor, which he had received from Rāṇo Sāṅgo of Mevāṛ (ca. 1509-28; see B.N. for Khīṃvo Ūdāvat, ***infra***).[17]

The exact date of Ḍūṅgarsī's acquisition of Jaitāraṇ is unknown, but it is evident that he was ruling at least as early as 1529, when Rāṭhoṛ Sekho Sūjāvat (no. 86) was killed at the battle of Sevakī. The chronicles relate that at the time of this battle the Rāṭhoṛs had a ***vair*** involving the Cahuvāṇs of Sūrācand, a town about 125 miles southwest of Jodhpur near the mouth of the Lūṇī River. Sekho, dying on the battlefield, sent a message to Jaitsī Ūdāvat (no. 139; 8-3), Ḍūṅgarsī's brother, and Tejsī (9-1; no. 138), Ḍūṅgarsī's son, telling them to retaliate against the Cahuvāṇs. Several years later, in 1534, Jaitsī attacked Sūrācand. Tejsī also had prepared to attack, but Jaitsī moved first.

The tradition indicates that, at the time of Sekho Sūjāvat's death in 1529, Tejsī was an Ūdāvat of some prominence, old enough to be considered capable of settling a ***vair***. This fact is important for dating Ḍūṅgarsī's period of rule in conjunction with details given in another tradition. It is recorded that when Ḍūṅgarsī was ***ṭhākur*** of Jaitāraṇ, Paṃvār Karamcand, Rāvat of Cāṭsū (no. 24;), a town about thirty-five miles south of Jaipur, had come to the village of Nīmbāj (six miles southeast of Jaitāraṇ) and looted it. When Ḍūṅgarsī did nothing, Karamcand sent his ***pradhān***s to Ḍūṅgarsī and forced him to marry a daughter to the Paṃvārs. At this time Tejsī was a young boy, incapable of avenging the insult. Thus one can conclude that the sack of Nīmbāj took place before Tejsī matured and began taking an active part in the affairs of the Ūdāvat ***sākh***, beginning around 1529, and so Ḍūṅgarsī's rule must have begun in Jaitāraṇ before this date.

Ḍūṅgarsī is described as an indolent (***susto***) ***ṭhākur***, a strongly pejorative term for a Rajpūt in a warrior society that commended heroic actions. Paṃvār Karamcand, after looting Nīmbāj and observing that Ḍūṅgarsī had done nothing at all, remarked to his companions that there was an "empty field" in Jaitāraṇ, a slur demeaning Ḍūṅgarsī's ability to protect his people. It was left to Tejsī to settle with the Paṃvārs, which he did probably around 1540-41, but possibly before 1536 (see B.N. no. 138 for Tejsī, ***infra***). Tejsī sacked and looted Cāṭsū, took the ***koṭṛī*** in the city, and captured nine elephants, which he sent back to Rāv Mālde (Jodhpur ruler, 1532-62). The Paṃvārs subsequently sent their ***pradhān***s to Jaitāraṇ to arrange a peace. They offered a daughter in marriage to the Ūdāvats. At this time Ḍūṅgarsī spoke up, suggesting that he be the one to marry the Paṃvār woman. Tejsī agreed, but the Paṃvārs objected, saying that Ḍūṅgarsī was an eighty-year old man who required servants to tie the cord of his

---

[17] Ḍūṅgarsī was Khīṃvo's uterine brother, a bond which may explain why Khīṃvo would have entrusted him with Jaitāraṇ.

pajama bottoms. Finally they relented, but observed that they would know "a daughter died," a statement suggesting that they felt Ḍūṅgarsī himself would soon die and the Paṃvār woman would have to become a ***satī***. They sent the betrothal coconut to Ḍūṅgarsī. Tejsī accepted it on his behalf.

It seems that soon after the raid on Cāṭsū (1540-41) Ḍūṅgarsī relinquished his rather feeble control of the ***ṭhākurāī*** of Jaitāraṇ to his more ambitious son, Tejsī. Naiṇsī lists Tejsī as Ḍūṅgarsī's successor, and it is known that Tejsī himself left Mālde's service around 1545, when Mālde punished him for certain transgressions. Thus at some time between 1540-41 and 1545 he must have succeeded Ḍūṅgarsī at Jaitāraṇ. Probably he did so after his heroic feats against the Paṃvārs.

Possibly, however, Ḍūṅgarsī remained on as the nominal ruler of Jaitāraṇ while Tejsī managed the affairs of the ***ṭhākurāī***. According to one story, Rāvaḷ Pratāpsiṅgh of Vāṃsvāḷo (ca. 1550-70; no. 12) told Jasvant Ḍūṅgarsīyot (9-2), who had entered the Rāvaḷ's service, that Rāv Mālde had done wrong in taking Jaitāraṇ from Ḍūṅgarsī while sons like Jasvant were living. In reply, Jasvant referred to Tejsī as the master (***dhaṇī***) of Jaitāraṇ and suggested that Tejsī's actions in 1545 were to blame for Mālde's seizure of Jaitāraṇ. The story might mean that Ḍūṅgarsī had held Jaitāraṇ up to 1545 though Tejsī was the effective ruler (***dhaṇī***).

Ḍūṅgarsī, despite being very old (although undoubtedly not as old as the Paṃvārs had said in what must have been a moment of exaggeration sparked by anger), lived on for many years after the loss of Jaitāraṇ. He is mentioned as having been at the battle of Meṛto in 1554, where he and Rāṭhoṛ Kisandās Gāṅgāvat (no. 87) killed Sīsodīyo Megho before Megho could assassinate Mālde. He was Rāv Jaimal Vīramdevot's supporter at this time. At some point thereafter, he went to Mevār, where he stayed until his son, Jasvant Ḍūṅgarsīyot (9-2), received Jaitāraṇ from Rāv Mālde after the death of Ratansī Khīṃvāvat in 1558. He accompanied Jasvant to Jaitāraṇ and remained there with him until Mughal pressure on the area forced them both to withdraw to Boraṛ[18] in 1560. Ḍūṅgarsī is recorded still to have been living as late as 1566, when Jasvant was killed fighting the Mughals. A Josī had told Ḍūṅgarsī that his son would not come back alive from the battle with the Mughals; he had tried to stop Jasvant from leaving but to no avail.

Ḍūṅgarsī had six sons:

1. Tejsī (9-1), the eldest.
2. Jasvant (9-2).
3. Vīramde.
4. Sagto.
5. Pato.
6. Vairsal.

---

[18] Boraṛ village: located fifteen miles southeast of Jaitāraṇ.

During his rule of Jaitāraṇ, Ḍūṅgarsī granted the village Jainā Vāsṇī[19] to the Śrīmāḷī Vyās Brāhmaṇ Jaino Rāmāvat and the village Jodhāvās[20] to the Mehudu Cāraṇ Jodho Sāraṅgot.

"Aitihāsik Bātāṃ," pp. 50, 60-62, 72-73; Āsopā, ***Itihās Nībāj***, pp. 23-26; Kiśansiṃh Ūdāvat, ***Ūdāvat Rāṭhauṛ Itihās***, pp. 16-17, 27, 92-96; Bhāṭī, ***Sarvekṣaṇ***, 1:49, 234; ***Vigat***, 1:495, 497-498, 547, 550.

(no. 138) **Tejsī Dūṅgarsīyot** (9-1)

The account of Tejsī's life given in "Aitihāsik Bātāṃ" suggests that he was an extraordinarily rapacious and truculent Rajpūt. In the words of the author of his biography, "Tejsī was particularly outstanding in his individual actions (***kām***) and in the pursuit of personal gain (***arath***)." He is called "a great Rajpūt, victorious in innumerable battles." His career indeed was filled with heroic moments, but also with periods of poverty and years of wandering while in exile from his homeland in Mārvāṛ.

By the time of Sekho Sūjāvat's (no. 86) death at Sevakī in 1529, Tejsī had already become a ***ṭhākur*** of some prominence (see B.N. no. 137 for Ḍūṅgarsī Ūdāvat, ***supra***). Subsequently he acquired notice by avenging an old feud with the Paṃvārs of Cāṭsū. This event probably took place in 1540-41, when Rāv Mālde of Jodhpur (1532-62) is said to have asserted his authority over Cāṭsū.[21] It is likely that Tejsī's attack on Cāṭsū was sanctioned by Mālde, who then extended his suzerainty over the looted town. Tejsī sent nine elephants captured from the Paṃvārs back to Mālde.

Possibly the raid on Cāṭsū took place earlier, perhaps before 1536. The biography of Tejsī states that when he had matured, he decided to take revenge for the insult the Paṃvārs had done his father years before. He summoned his friend, Rāṭhoṛ Prithīrāj Jaitāvat (no. 63), and formed a ***sāth*** to attack Cāṭsū. On the way, they encountered a Paṭhāṇ, Burhān, an old friend of Prithīrāj's, who, it is said, had formerly been in the services of Rāv Mālde but later had left and settled in the household of the ruler of Nāgaur. At first Tejsī and Prithīrāj attempted to deceive Burhān, saying that the ***sāth*** was a wedding party and that Tejsī was going to marry a Kachvāho woman. Burhān noticed the armor and the lances, told them he knew the truth, then mounted up and joined them for the raid on Cāṭsū.

---

[19] Jainā Vāsṇī: located four miles southeast of Jaitāraṇ.

[20] Jodhāvās: located three miles southwest of Jaitāraṇ.

[21] Vyās, ***Jodhpur Rājya kā Itihās***, p. 95, notes that Rāv Mālde had control of Cāṭsū and other lands to the east of Mārvāṛ by 1540-41, but Somāṇi has suggested that the conquest of Cāṭsū occurred in 1538-39. See Rāmvallabh Somāṇī, "Māldev aur Bīramdev Meṛtiyā kā Saṅghaṛṣ," ***Maru-Bhāratī***, 15:4 (January, 1968), p. 19.

If it is true that Burhān was in the service of the ruler of Nāgaur at this time, then the raid may have taken place before Rāv Mālde took Nāgaur in 1536. However, the story is ambiguous: the chronicler may simply have been delineating events in the life of Burhān preceding his encounter with Tejsī and Prithīrāj and not asserting that he was still in the service of the Nāgaur ruler.

Shortly after the Cāṭsū raid, Tejsī seems to have taken control of Jaitāraṇ from his father, who perhaps remained the nominal *ṭhākur* (see B.N. no. 137 for Ḍūṅgarsī, *supra*).

In 1545, Tejsī's actions caused the loss of Jaitāraṇ. His biography says that hard times (***dukāḷ***) had come to the land. His ***hujdār***s wandered around trying to get loans, but nothing was obtained. Then the ***hujdār***s wrote a letter to Tejsī recommending that he seize half the funds in the possession of certain rich Vāṇīyos in his ***vasī***, but he refused, saying that God (***Paramesvar***) did not wish him to torment the people of this ***vasī***. At this time, Sher Shāh's soldiers, stationed in Mārvāṛ after the battle of Samel in 1544, attacked the fort at Sīvāṇo (southwestern Mārvāṛ). Rāv Mālde, who held Sīvāṇo but at the time of the siege was elsewhere, expressed a desire that someone go there and aid the besieged soldiers. Tejsī accepted the assignment on the condition that Mālde pay him 100,000 ***phadīyos***.[22] An agreement was worked out: his ***hujdār***s would remain with Mālde, who would pay them when news came of his successful entrance into the fort. He was able to get inside the besieged fort at Sīvāṇo, where he remained for several days. Then came news that the Pātsāh, Sher Shāh, had died (1545), and the Muslim soldiers immediately departed. When day broke, Tejsī and the other Rajpūts inside were astonished to see that the Muslims had given up the siege. Then Mālde sent a message explaining what had happened and summoning Tejsī into his presence. Tejsī went first to his ***vasī***, then proceeded to Mālde. His ***hujdār***s told him on the way that Mālde had paid them off, but he noticed that Mālde had given the ***hujdār***s ***phadīyo***s in only fair condition (***suhālā-sā***). A ***phadīyo*** in excellent condition (***suhālā gāḍhā***) was worth five ***dugāṇī***s (a ***dugāṇī*** was equal to one-fortieth rupee); one in fair condition fetched only four. He decided he had to take another 100,000 ***dugāṇī***s from Mālde's ***hujdār***s.

Tejsī came to the Rāv's ***darbār*** several days later. He was sitting outside Mālde's chamber; Abho Pañcolī (no. 161) attempted to pass by him and enter. He rudely told Abho to give him the 100,000 ***dugāṇī***s and be off. Abho stalled; meanwhile someone told Mālde what happened. Irritated, Mālde called Tejsī into his chamber. He told him not to hold up his ***hujdār***s and said that if there was anything to give, he (Mālde) would give it. Tejsī, using informal, blunt language, told Mālde to give him 100,000 ***dugāṇī***s. The Rāv, who had been eating before Tejsī came in, became so infuriated that he threw his gold plate on the ground, whereupon Tejsī picked it up and made off with it. This serious breach of conduct cost Tejsī and his father Jaitāraṇ.

---

[22] ***Phadīyo***: a small silver coin of varying value. See Daśarath Śarmā, "Phadiyā, Dukṛā aur Dugānī," ***Maru-Bhāratī***, 8:2 (July, 1960), pp. 49-51.

Prior to the episode with the plate, Tejsī had been staying in Bhādrājuṇ (a town forty-eight miles south-southwest of Jodhpur) along with many other ***ṭhākurs*** who had left their lands during the period of distress following Sher Shāh's great victory at Samel in 1544. While in Bhādrājuṇ, Tejsī acquired fame by killing the Sīndhaḷs Vīdo and Vīsaḷ. He had established a ***guṛo*** near the town. The Sīndhaḷs Vīdo and Vīsaḷ came to the ***guṛo*** and stole the livestock. He received word, formed a pursuit party of seven or eight horsemen, and set out after them. The Sīndhaḷs were quickly apprehended and a skirmish began. Tejsī had loaned his ***vāgo*** to one of his Rajpūts a few days previously; the Rajpūt was struck down in the fighting. The Sīndhaḷs thought they had killed Tejsī. They began shouting. Tejsī himself had fallen and was lying underneath his horse. He identified himself, and then, as both Sīndhaḷs came after him, rose up and struck the one in front, Vīdo, a blow in the chest with his lance. The lance penetrated to the backbone. In the process of jerking out the lance, Tejsī struck Vīsaḷ, who had come up from behind to strike him, a blow in the head, fracturing Vīsaḷ's forehead and driving pieces of bone into his brain. The two bodies, one lying in front of Tejsī, the other behind, were dragged away by the Sīndhaḷs' military servants.

Shortly afterward Tejsī was driven from Bhādrājaṇ by Mālde because of his misconduct involving the golden plate. Apparently around this time he went to Jāḷor, where in his youth he had been friends with the son of Mālik Buḍhaṇ Bīhārī, ʻAlī Sher (d. 1525), his ***pagṛībadal bhāī*** ("brother through the exchange of turbans"). He received in grant the village Seṇo,[23] formerly a possession of the Boṛo Cahuvāṇs, along with twelve others. He came to Seṇo and camped. During the night, thieves came and stole a small box of gold bars lying under his bed. He continued to sleep, but when the thieves were gone his wife, who had been awakened during the theft, woke him and told him what had happened. Tejsī picked up his sword and his stick and went after the thieves. He managed to get ahead of them, then concealed himself at a narrow gap through which passed the road on which they were coming. He struck down three of the thieves with his sword, then killed the fourth, who was running away with the box, with the stick. He hit him so hard the stick wrapped completely around the thief's body. Tejsī threw the dead thieves in the bushes and went back to camp. In the morning, the bodies were discovered along with his stick. In the words of the chronicle, "then all knew [that] Tejsī killed these men."

It is said that Rāv Mālde drove Tejsī from Seṇo village of Jāḷor as well. Tejsī continued his wanderings, settling finally in Lās Muṇād village[24] and entering the service of the Rāv of Sīrohī. While he was staying in Lās Muṇād, the Sultān of Gujarat, Maḥmūd III (1537-54), attacked Sīrohī. The Rāv fled. Tejsī, however, came to Sīrohī from his village, and when the Gujaratis learned he was there, they abandoned the attack. He acquired considerable renown for

---

[23] Seṇo village: located thirteen miles south-southeast of Jāḷor and twenty miles northwest of Sīrohī.

[24] Lās Muṇād village: identified as Lās village, located sixteen miles north of Sīrohī.

his part in the town's defense. The attack on Sīrohī probably took place in 1551, when Mahmūd began a series of assaults on Rajpūt principalities bordering Gujarat.

At some time thereafter, Tejsī entered the service of the Sultān of Gujarat. He was serving there at the time the slave Burhān assassinated Mahmūd III (February 5, 1554). Tejsī's biography mentions that he subsequently killed Burhān; another source is more specific, stating that he killed Burhān on February 16, 1554. Persian sources, however, make no mention of his involvement in Burhān's execution, which took place shortly after the Sultān's murder.

It is said that after the Sultān died, three of his ***umrāvs*** were dividing up his wealth. Tejsī went to where they were and was able to persuade them to give him a quarter-portion of the Sultān's personal valuables. After receiving his quarter-share, he had the gall to take in addition a golden vessel and a silver leg of the Sultān's ***ḍholīyo***. Despite this affront, the ***umrāvs*** allowed him to leave.

A few days afterward Tejsī left Gujarat, went to Mevāṛ, and settled in the service of Sīsodīyo Rāṇo Udaisiṅgh Sāṅgāvat (ca. 1537-72; no. 17). He was given a ***paṭo*** for the village Dhulop,[25] where he kept his ***vasī***, but he himself resided at the Rāṇo's court. In the ***darbār***, the talk was all about Rāṭhoṛ Prithīrāj Jaitāvat (no. 63), Tejsī's old friend, who had recently died fighting at Meṛto (1554), but who, before dying, had cut down fourteen men in combat. Tejsī heard the talk, but he disparaged Prithīrāj, saying "he did not kill one ***sirdār***." The Mevāṛ ***ṭhākurs*** began whispering among themselves: "Tejsī will kill a ***sirdār***."

A few years later, in 1557, Hājī Khān, a former noble in the service of Sher Shāh Sūr, and Rāṇo Udaisiṅgh joined in battle at Harmāṛo near Ajmer. Many great ***ṭhākurs*** fought on the side of the Rāṇo (see ***Vigat***, 2:60), and Hājī Khān was aided by Rāv Mālde, who sent Devīdās Jaitāvat (no. 65) with a hand-picked ***sāth*** of 1,500 Rāṭhoṛs to Harmāṛo. Before the battle, Tejsī recalled what he had said about Prithīrāj never killing a ***sirdār*** and announced that he personally would kill Hājī Khān and that "the palaces of the sons of Ḍūṅgarsī would be on the field of Harmāṛo." At this point Bālīso Sūjo (no. 4) retorted that he would "have a little hut built nearby." Tejsī's statement quickly became the talk of both camps. Hājī Khān heard about it. He asked Devīdās what sort of Rajpūt Tejsī was. Devīdās made rather a tongue-in-cheek remark, saying first that "dying and killing was in the hands of Fate," but then adding that Tejsī was a great Rajpūt of Mārvāṛ. Hājī Khān understood his meaning. At the time of the battle, he took many defensive precautions. He himself put on armor, then sat inside an armored compartment on an elephant. He had 500 foot soldiers take up clubs and surround the elephant. He also kept some horsemen nearby. Besides all this, he made the Rāṭhoṛs take up the ***harol*** ("vanguard") position ahead of the main body of his army.

[25] Dhulop village: perhaps the modern village of Dhanop, located fifty miles south-southeast of Ajmer.

Tejsī himself was heavily armored. Even his horse was covered with armor, so much so that "there was no uncovered spot." When the battle began, he was confronted by his brother Rāṭhoṛs in the ***harol***. They lifted their lances to kill him, but he put forth an appeal, saying that he was their brother and that if they killed him, his vow would be unfulfilled and the Sīsodīyos would laugh at the Rāṭhoṛs. They spared him. Urging on his horse, Tejsī forged ahead into the Muslim army. He was struck and wounded several times, but he fought his way to where Hājī Khān was. With his customary impudence, he shouted out: "Where is the little Sindhī?" (***Sindhuṛo***, a diminutive of ***Sindhu***, "man of Sindh," referring to Hājī Khān). Hājī Khān forbade his ***sāth*** to kill Tejsī. He descended from the elephant, mounted a horse, and joined weapons with him. He struck him in the head; Tejsī knocked out two of his teeth. After this brief skirmish, the Khān's nearby military servants cut down Tejsī. His death occurred on January 27, 1557.

> "Aitihāsik Bātāṃ," pp. 51, 60-69, 99; M. S. Commissariat, ***A History of Gujarat*** (vol. 1, Bombay: Longmans, Green & Co., Ltd., 1938; vol. 2, Bombay: Orient Longmans, 1957), 1:430-433; ***Gazetteer of the Bombay Presidency***: Volume V, ***Cutch, Pālanpur, and Mahi Kāntha*** (Bombay: Government Central Press, 1908), pp. 318-319; Kiśansiṃh Ūdāvat, ***Ūdāvat Rāṭhauṛ Itihās***, pp. 55-56; ***Vigat***, 1:60, 495, 2:60; Vyās, ***Jodhpur Rājya kā Itihās***, pp. 95-98.

(no. 139) **Jaitsī Ūdāvat** (8-3)

After Ūdo Sūjāvat's (7-1) death in 1511, Jaitsī became the ***ṭhākur*** of the village Chīmpīyo-Khusyālpur. This village was Jaitsī's share of his father's landholdings around the town of Jaitāraṇ. Soon Jaitsī, along with his two brothers, Ḍūṅgarsī (no. 8-1) and Khīṃvo (8-2), connived to dethrone another brother, Mālde (8-4), Ūdo's successor at Jaitāraṇ (see B.N. no. 137 and 140, respectively, for details).

Jaitsī was one of Rāv Mālde's (Jodhpur ruler, 1532-62) most important Rajpūts. He along with his brother, Khīṃvo Ūdāvat, are mentioned as being among the great ***ṭhākurs*** of Mārvāṛ who refused to enter into Mālde's plots against Mertiyo Rāṭhoṛ Rāv Vīramde Dūdāvat (no. 105) in 1532. In 1534, he led an attack against Sūrācand, a town 125 miles southwest of Jodhpur, to settle an old ***vair*** with the Cahuvāṇ Rajpūts there. According to one tradition, the Cahuvāṇ ruler of Sūrācand had murdered a servant of Sekho Sūjāvat (no. 86). Sekho, dying on the battlefield of Sevakī in 1529, had sent word to Jaitsī and Tejsī Ḍūṅgarsīyot (no. 138; 9-1) telling them to avenge the feud with the Cahuvāṇs. On September 17, 1534, Jaitsī took revenge for the murder of Sekho's servant by killing the ruler of Sūrācand during the attack on the town (see B.N. for Ḍūṅgarsī Ūdāvat, ***supra***).

A second account of this ***vair***, contained in the ***Jaitsī Ūdāvat rī Vāt*** ("Story of Jaitsī Ūdāvat"), provides more details and may be considered an example of how a story might grow in the telling over a period of centuries. In this account, Rāv Gāṅgo sends Ḍūṅgarsī, Tejsī, Jaitsī, and a certain Jagnāth (identity unknown), to comfort a dying Sekhojī after the battle of Sevakī. As they tend to him, he reveals the origin of the *vair* with the Rājā of Sūrācand. It seems his servant, Rājo Sūṇḍo, had been offered by the Rājā as a sacrifice to a mother goddess in a temple there. Before the sacrifice took place, the servant had said:

> Rājājī! I am a Sūṇḍo Rajpūt; I dwell in the *vās* of Sekho Sūjāvat, and I became angry with my master and brought [my] food [and] water here [to camp]. And you are killing me [now] without bloodshed [or other] offence on my part. But *ṭhākur*! I have a master who will not live without taking up the *vair* [incurred by my death] ("Jaitsī Ūdāvat," p. 159).

Sekho had never found an opportunity to avenge Rājo Sūṇḍo, but as he lay dying, he entrusted the task to Jaitsī:

> Jaitsī, brother's son! You excel in being a Rajpūt. You are one who pursues old *vairs*. Take up that *vair* [of Rājo Sūṇḍo] ("Jaitsī Ūdāvat," *ibid*.).

Jaitsī agreed to avenge Sekho. For many days he pondered the difficulties of the task:

> He constantly thought about ending that *vair*. Sleep did not come to him at night. He put [his] shield on [his] knees and remained seated above [his] *ḍholīyo* like the Lord of the Yogīs. He sighed all day long. In just this way lived Jaitsī ("Jaitsī Ūdāvat," p. 160).

Finally he made preparations to depart for Sūrācand. He took with him twenty-five of his Rajpūts. At every step along the way the omens were auspicious:

> ... The omen-readers interpreted the omens and said: "These omens [indicate that] the Rājā of Sūrācand shall come into [your] hands, and [that] we shall incur good fortune. There shall be the business of battle, [which] is the *dharma* of the Kṣatriya. Moreover, you will kill the Rājā of Sūrācand" ("Jaitsī Ūdāvat," p. 162).

On the seventh day, Jaitsī and his men arrived at Rājāvās, a village four or five *kos* from Sūrācand. Here they encountered a women drawing water from a well, whom they asked to serve them. After she had done so, she astonished them by remarking: "Who among you is Jaitsī Ūdāvat?" They had no idea how she knew he was with them. They thought she might be a goddess. As it happened, she was Harkuṃvarī, the daughter of a Cāraṇ from Balāhaṛo village[26] near Jaitāraṇ. Her father, Karamāṇand, had married her to the son of Cāraṇ Āīdān Khiṛīyo of Rājāvās. She knew all about Jaitsī and his obligation to avenge Sekho Sūjāvat. She warned him that the Rājā of Sūrācand had taken many precautions. Hundreds of Rajpūts were posted on watch around Sūrācand. She advised him as follows:

> Come to my father-in-law's [in Rājāvās]. There you should ask for me by name. Next, my father-in-law's people (***sāsriyā***) will ask you: "Where is [your] ***vās***? .... [Of] what ***sākh*** [are you]?" Then you should say: "I am [of] the Gauṛ ***sākh***;[27] [my] ***vās*** is Tīvījī [village]; my name is Sarvaṇ. I am going on to Sūrācand for military service" ("Jaitsī Ūdāvat," p. 165).

Then the people would ask Jaitsī what his connection with Harkuṃvarī was. He was to tell them that she was the sister's daughter (***bhāṇejī***) of Sāmdān Āsiyo, his Cāraṇ, who had asked him to meet with Harkuṃvarī when he passed through Rājāvās on his way to Sūrācand. He was to give her some presents.

When Jaitsī went to Rājāvās, everything happened as Harkuṃvarī had said. She was asked by her in-laws to identify him, and she confirmed the false identity she had given him previously. Thus no one suspected who he actually was, and the Rājā of Sūrācand knew nothing of his presence nearby. Soon Jaitsī was able to penetrate Sūrācand, where again the Rājā was about to offer a man as a sacrifice in the temple of the mother goddess. Jaitsī confronted him and said:

> Rājā [of] Sūrācand! I demand from you [revenge for] the ***vair*** [incurred by the death] of Rājo Sūṇḍo. [If] there is the essence of a Rajpūt (***Rajpūtī***) in you, display it ("Jaitsī Ūdāvat," p. 173).

But there was nothing from the Rājā. His retainers attempted to defend him and a struggle broke out. Many men were killed, but Jaitsī prevailed. He cut off the heads of the slain and constructed a tower of skulls (***Bābar-koṭ***)[28] before the mother goddess. He told her:

> "Mother! Are you satisfied, or are you not satisfied? If you are not satisfied, then once again I shall offer up [human sacrifices for you]." Then the mother goddess, pleased, said: "For so many days I would demand men [be sacrificed to me]. Now, as of today, I am satisfied" ("Jaitsī Ūdāvat," p. 174).

---

[26] Balāhaṛo village: located ten miles northeast of Jaitāraṇ.

[27] i.e., a Rajpūt of the Gauṛ family (one of the thirty-six Rajpūt ruling families).

[28] ***Bābar-koṭ***: literally, a "Bābar-tower," named after the Mughal Emperor Bābur (1526-30), who was believed to have constructed towers of skulls after his victories in north India.

She announced her support for Jaitsī. He left Sūrācand safely and returned to Chīmpīyo-Khusyālpur. Thus ends the story.[29]

Jaitsī subsequently received important positions under Rāv Mālde. He is recorded to have been made commander of two garrisons in the Goḍhvāṛ region of southeastern Mārvāṛ, Kosīthaḷ and Bīsalpur. Here he distinguished himself by driving off the Sīsodīyo Rāṇo of Mevāṛ, Udaisiṅgh Sāṅgāvat (ca. 1537-72; no. 17), who had attacked Kosīthaḷ. Jaitsī also held at least part of the region around Vadhnor (located forty-seven miles south-southwest of Ajmer) in ***paṭo*** from Rāv Mālde. One source states that he alone held Vadhnor; another indicates that he and his brother Khīṃvo Ūdāvat (no. 140; 8-2) shared the grant of Vadhnor and 700 surrounding villages. It is more probable that the grant was shared between the two, for Khīṃvo had taken the town from the Vāgaṛīyo Cahuvāṇs (see B.N. 140 for Khīṃvo Ūdāvat, ***infra***) and thus would have had a claim to the area.

Jaitsī is called a great Rajpūt, one who caused Death (Mṛtyu) to rise up among his foes and make them cry out for protection. It is said that he settled many ***vairs*** for the Rāṭhoṛs as well. He died along with sixteen of his men fighting against Sher Shāh Sūr at Samel in 1544. During his lifetime, he made three village grants to Brāhmaṇs: (1) Morvī Vaḍī,[30] to Purohit Rājā Cohothot Sīvaut; (2) Morvī Khurad,[31] to the Rājguru Brāhmaṇ Varsiṅgh Pīthāvat; (3) Brampurī,[32] to Ḍūṅgar Padmāvat, another Rājguru Brāhmaṇ.

> "Aitihāsik Bātāṃ," pp. 60, 75; "Jaitsī Ūdāvat," in ***Rājasthānī Vātāṃ: Rājasthānī Bhāṣā meṃ likhit Prācīn Kahāniyoṃ kā Saṅgrah***, ed. Sūryakaraṇ Pārīk (Dillī: Navayug-Sāhitya-Mandir, 1934), pp. 155-175; Kiśansiṃh Ūdāvat, ***Ūdāvat Rāṭhauṛ Itihās***, pp. 23-24, 38, n. 4; ***Khyāt***, 3:100; Reu, 1:113, n. 2; Bhāṭī, ***Sarvekṣaṇ***, 1:234; ***Vigat***, 1:44, 497-498, 543-544, 2:57; Vyās, ***Jodhpur Rājya kā Itihās***, p. 98.

(no. 140) **Khīṃvo Ūdāvat (8-2)**

Khīṃvo Ūdāvat was born on August 16, 1480. Before 1511, the year his father died, and while he was still a ***kuṃvar***, he obtained the village of Girrī. Girrī became the center of Khīṃvo's domain. Here he kept his ***vasī*** and had a

---

[29] Reu, 1:113, n. 2, states that after the battle of Sevakī, Sekho Sūjāvat, dying on the battlefield, asked Rāv Gāṅgo to avenge his servant, offered as a sacrifice by the Cahuvāṇs of Sūrācand. Subsequently Gāṅgo sent some men, who killed fourteen of the Cahuvāṇs' men and thus avenged Sekho. Reu does not mention Jaitsī as one of those sent to Sūrācand.

[30] Morvī Vaḍī village: located six miles east-southeast of Jaitāraṇ.

[31] Morvī Khurad village: located one-half mile east-northeast of Morvī Vaḍī village.

[32] Brampurī village: located five miles east-southeast of Jaitāraṇ.

fort built. A commemorative poem concerning his residence at Girrī has survived:

> Dwelling in the fort above Girrī [was Khiṃvo], a thorn to [his] enemies.
> The Kamdhaj [i.e., Rāṭhoṛ] drove the foe [from the land];
> he satisfied the demonness (*ḍakaṇ*) with offerings [of human flesh].

The sources say that Khīṃvo was a great ***ṭhākur***, one who upheld a vow to destroy the enemy on the battlefield. During the reign of his grand-father, Rāv Sūjo Jodhāvat (ca. 1492-1515), it is likely that Khīṃvo and Sūjo's other grandsons and sons were at least nominally loyal to Jodhpur, but after Rāv Gāṅgo's circuitous accession to the Jodhpur throne in 1515, Rāv Vīramde Vāghāvat (no. 84) of Sojhat, Sekho Sūjāvat (no. 86) of Pīṃpāṛ, and Khīṃvo aligned themselves with the growing power of Rāṇo Sāṅgo of Mevāṛ (ca. 1509-28). On January 16, 1518, Khīṃvo received Vadhnor from the Rāṇo. Probably shortly afterward he and his brothers Ḍūṅgarsī (8-1) and Jaitsī (8-3) joined together and wrested Jaitāraṇ from the rule of his half-brother Mālde (8-4). Perhaps, if it is true that Mālde adopted Ratansī, Khīṃvo's son (no. 141; 9-3), the seizure of Jaitāraṇ occurred after August 18, 1520, the date of Ratansī's birth. Khīṃvo evidently left Jaitāraṇ under the rule of his uterine brother, Ḍūṅgarsī, while he himself returned to manage the affairs of Girrī, his homeland, and Vadhnor (see B.N. no. 137, ***supra***).

For reasons unknown, Khīmvo abandoned Vadhnor in 1525. Perhaps the Rāṇo had transferred Vadhnor from Khīṃvo's control in that year. Khīṃvo apparently did not offer his allegiance to Rāv Gāṅgo at this time, nor did he involve himself in the dispute between his uncle Sekho and Gāṅgo. In 1529, following the battle of Sevakī, Khīṃvo was not one of the Ūdāvat ***ṭhākur***s addressed by Sekho with regard to the ***vair*** incurred by the murder of Sekho's retainer in Sūrācand. He seems to have had nothing to do with the politics of Mārvāṛ during this troubled period. Possibly he remained in the service of Rāṇo Sāṅgo even after leaving Vadhnor, but the sources are silent on his activities.[33]

The rapid rise of Rāv Mālde of Jodhpur following his accession in 1532 and a period of tumultuous political developments in Mevāṛ very likely persuaded Khīṃvo to enter the service of the young Jodhpur Rāv. Early in Mālde's reign he achieved a position of prominence among the Rāv's military servants. He is mentioned as one of the notable ***ṭhākur***s who refused to condone Mālde's early plotting against Meṛtīyo Rāṭhoṛ Rāv Vīramde Dūdāvat (no. 105) in 1532. Subsequently he took Vadhnor from the Vāgaṛīyo Cahuvāṇs, who had been granted the town during the reign of Rāṇo Sāṅgo. Khīṃvo had taken the village of Vāgad, in the domain of Rāṇo Udaisiṅgh Sāṅgāvat (ca. 1537-72; no.

---

[33] With one exception: the Rāypur ***khyāt*** states that he ruled Jaitāraṇ after leaving Vadhnor, but this is not correct. Bhāṭī, ***Sarvekṣaṇ***, 1:49.

17), from the Vāgaṛīyos; then, after he followed this triumph by taking Vyāvar (thirty miles southwest of Ajmer), the Vāgaṛīyos fled to Vadhnor, which Khīṃvo also captured. Rāv Mālde formalized his possession of the town by granting it and 700 neighboring villages to him and his brother Jaitsī in ***paṭo***.

Little else is known of Khīṃvo's life. He along with three hundred and nine of his men died fighting against Sher Shāh's troops in the great battle of Samel in 1544. He and his brother Jaitsī are said to have negotiated with Jaito Pañcāiṇot (no. 61) and Kūmpo Mahirājot (no. 95) and arranged Rāv Mālde's flight before the battle took place. Khīṃvo then set off with Mālde, the Rāv's hand on his. But Jaitsī told him that it was very far to Jodhpur (i.e., he wouldn't make it back to Samel in time for the battle), a subtle way of reminding him that his duty lay in fighting to the death against the armies of Sher Shāh and not in escorting Mālde in flight from the battlefield.

Khīṃvo had seven sons[34] and at least one daughter by two wives:

1. Rāṇī Sekhāvatjī of Navalgaṛh (Mehtāp Kuṃvar), who had five sons:

   1. Bhānīdās.
   2. Kānh.
   3. Bhopatsiṃh.
   4. Karaṇsiṃh.
   5. Mādhosiṃh.

2. Rāṇī Gauṛjī of Rājgaṛh (Indrakuṃvar), who had two sons and one known daughter:

   Sons:
   1. Ratansī.
   2. Suratsiṃh.

   Daughter:
   1. Sāyar Kuṃvar.

Both wives became ***satīs*** after Khīṃvo's death in 1544.

Khīṃvo gave one village in grant to a Cāraṇ: Gehāvāsṇī,[35] to Kavīyo Nīmbo Khetāvat.

"Aitihāsik Bātāṃ," pp. 59-60; Āsopā, ***Itihās Nībāj***, pp. 26-43; Bhāṭī, ***Sarvekṣaṇ***, 1:49; Kiśansiṃh Ūdāvat, ***Ūdāvat Rāṭhauṛ Itihās***, pp. 19-49; ***Khyāt***, 3:100-101; ***Vigat***, 1:56, 497-498, 518, 2:48, 57.

---

[34] Āsopā, ***Itihās Nībāj***, p. 43, only mentions three sons: Ratansī, Bhānīdās, and Kānh.

[35] Gehāvāsṇī village: located eight miles south-southwest of Jaitāraṇ.

(no. 141) **Ratansī Khīṃvāvat** (9-3)

The two twentieth-century historians of the Ūdāvats, Rāmkaraṇ Āsopā and Kiśansiṃh Ūdāvat, both suggest that Khīṃvo was the ruler of Jaitāraṇ during much of his life. Āsopā states that Khīṃvo succeeded his father in 1511 and continued to rule without interruption until his death in 1544. Kiśansiṃh Ūdāvat believes that Khīṃvo entrusted his brother Ḍūṅgarsī with Jaitāraṇ after Rāv Mālde gave him and Jaitsī Vadhnor in ***paṭo***. But this cannot be correct, as Ḍūṅgarsī was ruling Jaitāraṇ before 1529. If Ḍūṅgarsī received Jaitāraṇ from Khīṃvo, he most likely would have done so during Khīṃvo's period of service in Mevāṛ (see B.N. no. 137 and 140, ***supra***). Kiśansiṃh Ūdāvat also believes Khīṃvo was ruling Jaitāraṇ when he died in 1544, without saying how or why Ḍūṅgarsī might have abandoned the town. And both Āsopā and Kiśansiṃh Ūdāvat make Ratansī Khīṃvāvat Khīṃvo's immediate successor at Jaitāraṇ. They both ignore the evidence in seventeenth-century sources which suggests that Ḍūṅgarsī and then his son Tejsī ruled Jaitāraṇ until 1545 (see B.N. no. 138, ***supra***).

Ratansī Khīṃvāvat was born on August 18, 1520. Nothing is known of his activities from his birth until his father's death in 1544. At some time between 1545, when Jaitāraṇ was lost to Tejsī Ḍūṅgarsīyot, and 1558, the year of Ratansī's death, he acquired authority over Jaitāraṇ, for he is listed in the ***Vigat*** (1:495) as one of the Ūdāvats who held the town, which Rāv Mālde Gāṅgāvat (Jodhpur ruler, 1532-62) had given him. Possibly Surtāṇ Jaitsīyot, one of Jaitsī Ūdāvat's (no. 139; 8-3) sons, also controlled Jaitāraṇ for a brief period after 1545, for the ***Vigat*** (1:548) states that "when Rāṭhoṛ Surtāṇ [Jaitsīyot] held Jaitāraṇ, half of Khināvṛī [village] was in the ***khālso***." It is equally possible, however, that Surtāṇ held Jaitāraṇ at some point after Ratansī's death. The sources simply are too vague to allow a more concrete opinion.

Ratansī, unlike his famous father, Khīṃvo, had a mostly undistinguished career. In September-October of 1550, Rāv Mālde, beginning to reassert his dominance in Mārvāṛ, had taken Pokaraṇ town (about eighty-three miles northwest of Jodhpur) and then proceeded southwestward to seize Koṭro[36] and Bāhaṛmer.[37] A garrison (***thāṇo***) was left at Bāhaṛmer under Ratansī's authority. Rāvat Bhīm, the dispossessed ruler, went to Jaisaḷmer and obtained Bhāṭī assistance for an attack on the garrison. The ***Vigat*** (1:63-64) records that Ratansī fled ignominiously, with the result that all the camp equipment was looted. According to this source, Bāhaṛmer was lost in 1551-52; another source gives April-May, 1553.

Ratansī is also mentioned as one of the great ***ṭhākur***s who took part in Rāv Mālde's unsuccessful attack on Meṛto in 1554. Prior to the attack, Rāv Mālde divided his troops into two ***aṇī***s, one near the Jodhpur Gate of Meṛto under the command of Prithīrāj Jaitāvat (no. 63), the other under Ratansī near the

---

[36] Koṭro: located seventy miles southwest of Pokaraṇ.

[37] Bāhaṛmer: located eighty-four miles southwest of Pokaraṇ.

Bejpo Tank. Meṛtīyo Rāv Jaimal Vīramdevot (no. 107) successfully defeated Prithīrāj and his men near the Jodhpur Gate, then turned around to attack the other ***aṇī,*** which was at that moment coming to the entrance of the Bejpo after looting Meṛto town and taking the nearby villages under control. A fierce struggle broke out; Devīdās Jaitāvat (no. 65), a military servant of Ratansī's, was about to kill Jaimal when Ratansī asked that Jaimal be spared. Subsequently Devīdās left Ratansī's service and became an important retainer of Rāv Mālde's.

In 1557, Rāṇo Udaisiṅgh Sāṅgāvat, Sīsodīyo ruler of Mevāṛ (ca. 1537-72; no. 17), and Hājī Khān, a former noble of Sher Shāh's who had acquired independent control of Alvar in northeastern Rājasthān, engaged in battle at Harmāṛo near Ajmer. Rāv Mālde had sent a large contingent of troops under the command of Devīdās Jaitāvat to aid Hājī Khān. The Khān's victory in this battle attracted the attention of the Mughals, who sent troops to put him down. Subsequently, he fled into Mārvāṛ, where Rāv Mālde allowed him to stay in the villages of Loṭaudhrī and Nīmbol[38] in Jaitāraṇ Pargano. Shortly afterward he went to Gujarat. The Mughal Emperor, Akbar, ordered that whoever had protected Hājī Khān was to be killed, and, as a result, a Mughal contingent under the command of Muḥammad Qāsim Khān attacked Jaitāraṇ in 1558. On March 14[39] of that year Ratansī Khīṃvāvat died along with thirty-three other ***sirdār***s defending the town. At least four other Ūdāvats, Goyanddās, Kisandās, and Kāno (Kāndās), sons of Jaitsī (8-3), and Bhānīdās, a son of Khīṃvo's (8-2), died along with Ratansī.[40] The ***Akbar Nāma*** (2:102-103) has a brief but vivid description of the capture of Jaitāraṇ:

> (The victorious heroes by the strength of their swords and the might of their courage conducted many of the stiff-necked Rajpūts to the Abyss of annihilation and took possession of the fort.) The surface of that country was cleared from the rubbish of stubborn rebels.

---

[38] Nīmbol village is seven miles northwest of Jaitāraṇ; Loṭaudhrī village is one mile southwest of Nīmbol.

[39] ***Jodhpur Rājya kī Khyāt***, p. 91, gives March 13, 1558 (V.S. 1614, ***Caitra***, ***Vadi*** 9) as the date of the battle, but a contemporary inscription has March 14, 1558 (V.S. 1614, ***Caitra***, ***Vadi*** 10). Kiśansiṃh Ūdāvat (***Ūdāvat Rāṭhauṛ Itihās***, p. 68), has read the inscription as V.S. 1615, ***Caitra***, ***Vadi*** 10, which is correct for March 14, 1558 if the year is ***Caitrādi*** but converts to March 3, 1559 if the year is ***Śrāvaṇādi***. This later date would place the taking of Jaitāraṇ in Akbar's fourth regnal year, whereas the ***Akbar Nāma*** indicates that the event took place in his third. The text of the inscription is given by Āsopā, ***Itihās Nībāj***, p. 51, n. 1.

[40] Āsopā, ***Itihās Nībāj***, pp. 49-50, indicates that three other Ūdāvats, Nārāyaṇdās Sāṅgāvat, Nagrāj Gāṅgāvat, and Khetsī Parbatot, died along with Ratansī. We have not been able to trace their exact ancestry.

Vyās has suggested that Rāv Mālde, angered by Ratansī's allowing Jaimal Vīramdevot to escape death at Meṛto in 1554, may have refused to send aid to Ratansī in 1558. Inexplicably, Jaimal himself is said to have accompanied the Mughal contingent to Jaitāraṇ in 1558.

Ratansī had at least three wives, ten sons, and one known daughter, as follows:

1. Rāṇī Sekhāvatjī Kesarkuṃvar. She had three sons and one daughter:

Sons:

1. Kilāṇdās.
2. Rāghodās.
3. Kesavdās.

Daughter:

1. Mohankuṃvar (Kanakāvatī Bāī), who was married to Rājā Mānsiṅgh of Āmber.

2. Rāṇī Bhaṭīyāṇījī Jorāvarkuṃvar. She had three sons:

1. Rām.
2. Narhardās.
3. Manīrām.

3. Rāṇī Devṛījī. She had two sons:

1. Gopāldās.
2. Gokuldās.

Two other sons of Ratansī's are known:

1. Udaisiṅgh.
2. Bhavāṇīdās.

Two of Ratansī's wives, Rāṇī Sekhāvatjī and Rāṇī Bhaṭīyāṇījī, became *satī*s after he was killed in battle.

During his lifetime, Ratansī made three grants to Cāraṇs and Brāhmaṇs: (1) Dehūrīyo,[41] to Purohit Kāndhal Bhojāvat Sīvaṛ; (2) Gehāvās,[42] to the Cāraṇ Geī Ratnāvat Khaṛīyo; (3) Lākhāvāsṇī,[43] to the Cāraṇ Lākho Dāsāvat Kachelā.

Āsopā, ***Itihās Nībāj***, pp. 43-53; ***Ā'īn-ī-Akbarī***, p. 379; "Aitihāsik Bātāṃ," pp. 48-50, 99; ***Akbar Nāma***, 2:102-103; ***Jodhpur Rājya kī Khyāt***, p. 91; ***Khyāt***, 1:62, 297; Kiśansiṃh Ūdāvat, ***Ūdāvat Rāṭhauṛ Itihās***, pp. 50-91; ***Vigat***, 1:59, 63-64,

[41] Dehūrīyo village: located four miles northeast of Jaitāraṇ.

[42] Gehāvās village: located ten miles northeast of Jaitāraṇ.

[43] Lākhāvāsṇī village: located seven miles west-southwest of Jaitāraṇ.

70, 495, 498-499, 523, 542-543, 551-552; Vyās, *Jodhpur Rājya kā Itihās*, pp. 171-173.

(no. 142) **Bhīṃv Kilāṇdāsot** (11-1)

Following Ratansī Khīṃvāvat's death defending Jaitāraṇ in 1558, the Mughals apparently abandoned the area. Rāv Mālde (Jodhpur ruler, 1532-62) was able to assert his authority over Jaitāraṇ shortly afterward. The sources indicate he gave the town to Ḍūṅgarsī Ūdāvat's (no. 137; 8-1) son, Jasvant (9-2), who had been until then a military servant in Gujarat employed by Rāv Pūñjo of Īḍar.[44] Jasvant came to Jaitāraṇ along with his father, whom he brought from Mevāṛ. He was unable to hold the town for long because of increased Mughal pressure against Mārvāṛ. During 1560 he went to Borāṛ, a village in the Mer territory east of Jaitāraṇ, where he suppressed the local Mer people and built a large fort.[45] After Rāv Mālde died in 1562, Jasvant continued in the service of Jodhpur as a supporter of Rāv Candrasen (Jodhpur ruler, 1562-81), Mālde's successor. He died fighting against the encroaching Mughals at the battle of Rāmgaḍh (a small hamlet located just east of Borāṛ) on October 28, 1566, along with many others, including at least three Ūdāvats: Ratansī, son of Jaitsī (no. 139; 8-3), and Udaisiṅgh and Bhavāṇīdās, sons of Ratansī (9-3).

In 1571-72, four of Ratansī's surviving sons, Gopāldās, Narhardās, Rām, and Kilāṇdās (10-1) met with the Mughal ***mansabdar***s holding Jaitāraṇ and were allowed to bring their ***vasī*** to the village of Āsarlāī just east of the town. For the next few decades they held Jaitāraṇ town as military servants of the Mughal Empire. In 1583, Akbar gave Moṭo Rājā Udaisiṅgh Māldevot of Jodhpur (1583-95) sixty-five villages of Jaitāraṇ Pargano, but the sons of Ratansī continued to hold the town and the rest of the ***pargano***'s villages. When Moṭo Rājā died in 1595, his sons received sixty-five villages while Kilāṇdās and Gopāldās Ratansīyot each were given half of Jaitāraṇ town and a share of the remaining villages. This situation lasted until December, 1604, when Akbar gave Rājā Sūrajsiṅgh Udaisiṅghot (Jodhpur ruler, 1595-1619) all of the ***pargano***. In this same year Kilāṇdās Ratansīyot received Rāypur, a large village near Jaitāraṇ, from Sūrajsiṅgh. Kilāṇdas died fighting along with fifty retainers in a skirmish with some Cahuvāṇ Rajpūts in 1617-18.

Bhīṃv Kilāṇdāsot was one of the seven[46] sons of Kilāṇdās Ratansīyot. He first distinguished himself in 1599-1600, when Rājā Sūrajsiṅgh's troops

---

[44] Āsopā, ***Itihās Nībāj***, p. 53, states that Kilāṇdās Ratansīyot (10-1), one of Ratansī's sons, succeeded him at Jaitāraṇ in 1558, but Āsopā's opinion is not corroborated by any primary source; Kilāṇdas, who was born in 1543, would only have been fifteen in 1558, very likely too young to assume such an important post in such difficult times.

[45] ***Jodhpur Rājya kī Khyāt***, p. 92, notes that on June 13, 1560, one of Akbar's officers came to Meṛto Pargano, took prisoners from fifteen villages, and returned to Ajmer. Around that time, "from fear of the Mughals, Jaitāraṇ became deserted."

[46] Āsopā, ***Itihās Nībāj***, p. 56, mentions only five sons.

besieged Sojhat. Bhīṃv is listed among the ***sirdārs*** of the Rājā's who were wounded at this time. Only scattered references to Bhīṃv's activities in subsequent years appear in the sources available. He was one of a number of Rāṭhoṛs who together killed a certain Dalo Sāh at Burhanpur on December 1, 1610. On May 26, 1615, he was wounded when Jodho Rāṭhoṛ Kisansiṅgh Udaisiṅghot attacked Rājā Surajsiṅgh's camp at Ajmer and killed Jeso Bhāṭī Goyanddās Mānāvat.[47]

Bhīṃv is listed as a recipient of the village of Āṇandpur, headquarters of Tapho Āṇandpur, a subdivision of Meṛto Pargano. It would appear Shāhzāda Parvīz granted him the village in 1623-24 while Parvīz was ***sūbedār*** of Ajmer during the rebellion of Shāhzāda Khurram. Apparently Bhīṃv was Parvīz's servant during this period.[48] In May of 1624 an Imperial army under the command of Parvīz and Mahābat Khān met Khurram's forces at the village of Damdama on the confluence of the Tons and Ganges Rivers. Bhīṃv was wounded in this battle. ***Bāṅkīdās*** states that Bhīṃv survived only through the exertions of Rāja Gajsiṅgh Sūrajsiṅghot (Jodhpur ruler, 1619-38), who had him picked up and removed from the battlefield. Gajsiṅgh retained Bhīṃv in his service and gave him the villge Nīmbāj of Jaitāraṇ Pargano along with several others for his maintenance.

When Shāh Jahān became Mughal Emperor in 1628, Bhīṃv entered Imperial service once again. The Emperor gave him two large land grants in Ajmer Pargano on the Mārvāṛ border, Baṃvāl[49] village with thirty-two others, and Thāṃvḷo,[50] which he made his residence, with twelve. He received a ***mansab*** of 1,500 ***ẕāt***, 600 ***sawār*** at this time.[51] Bhīṃv continued to be an important Imperial military servant based in Thāṃvḷo for the next several years. In 1638, when Rājā Gajsiṅgh died, Bhīṃv made an attempt to secure Jaitāraṇ Pargano in ***jāgīr*** from Shāh Jahān. According to one source, the ***pargano*** had actually been transferred briefly to Bhīṃv, who had accepted the area at an assessment of 200,000 rupees (another source says 250,000 rupees), a sixty percent increase over the evaluation of the ***pargano*** under Gajsiṅgh. Such an arrangement effectively gave the Mughals a promise of more troops for their money, since Bhīṃv presumably would have to maintain forces in accordance

---

[47] Jeso Bhāṭī Goyanddās Mānāvat was Rājā Sūrajsiṅgh Udaisiṅghot's ***pradhān*** at this time.

[48] The ***Vigat*** (2:74) is not clear on this point. Bhīṃv is listed as having received (or having held) Āṇandpur, but one does not know for certain from whom. He may have been Prince Khurram's retainer.

[49] Baṃvāl village: located ten miles north of Ajmer and thirty miles east of Meṛto.

[50] Thāṃvḷo village: located twenty-eight miles east-southeast of Meṛto and twelve miles northwest of Ajmer.

[51] Bhīṃv is to be identified as the "Bhīm Rāṭhoṛ" or "Bhīm Sen (i.e., Bhīṃvsī or Bhīṃvsiṃh) Rāṭhoṛ" of the Mughal Persian chronicles. See Athar Ali, ***Apparatus***,, pp. 101, 133, 135, 147, 191.

with the new, higher evaluation. His motives in this case appear to have been a desire to regain the town of Jaitāraṇ, lost to the Ūdāvat ***sākh*** since 1604, and perhaps a wish to assert himself as the dominant Ūdāvat Rāṭhoṛ in Mārvāṛ. Whatever his aims, his plans were frustrated by Kūmpāvat Rāṭhoṛ Rajsiṅgh Khīṃvāvat (no. 101), Rājā Jasvantsiṅgh's (Jodhpur ruler, 1638-78) ***pradhān***. Rajsiṅgh petitioned the Mughals, saying that Jaitāraṇ was the source of expense money for Jasvantsiṅgh's army and that the new Rājā's power would be seriously reduced if the ***pargano*** were given to someone else. After a cash sum of 200,000 rupees was given to the Mughals, Jaitāraṇ was given to Jasvantsiṅgh, who agreed to hold the ***pargano*** at an evaluation of 200,000 rupees thereafter. The story is an excellent example of how evaluations of individual ***pargano***s were inflated by the actions of local officers attempting to improve their positions by making deals with the Mughals.

According to the ***Udaibhāṇ Cāmpāvat rī Khyāt***, an important seventeenth-century document examined by Kiśansiṃh Ūdāvat, Bhīṃv abandoned military service and went to Vṛndāvan after his unsuccessful attempt to obtain Jaitāraṇ Pargano. He may have died there in 1638-39. Alternatively, Lāhorī, a Mughal historian, indicates that he remained in Imperial service and died in 1644-45. At the time of his death, his Imperial rank was 1,500 ***ẓāt***, 1,000 ***sawār***.

"Aitihāsik Bātāṃ," pp. 68-73, 80, 86, 95, 97; Āsopā, ***Itihās Nībāj***, pp. 53-56; Athar Ali, ***Apparatus***, pp. 101, 133, 135, 147, 191; ***Bāṅkīdās***, p. 27; ***Jodhpur Rājya kī Khyāt***, p. 92; Kiśansiṃh Ūdāvat, ***Ūdāvat Rāṭhauṛ Itihās***, pp. 93-94, 1-8, 10-12 (second group); ***Vigat***, 1:69-70, 99-100, 124, 495-496, 2:74.

Figure 32. Ūdāvat Rāṭhoṛs

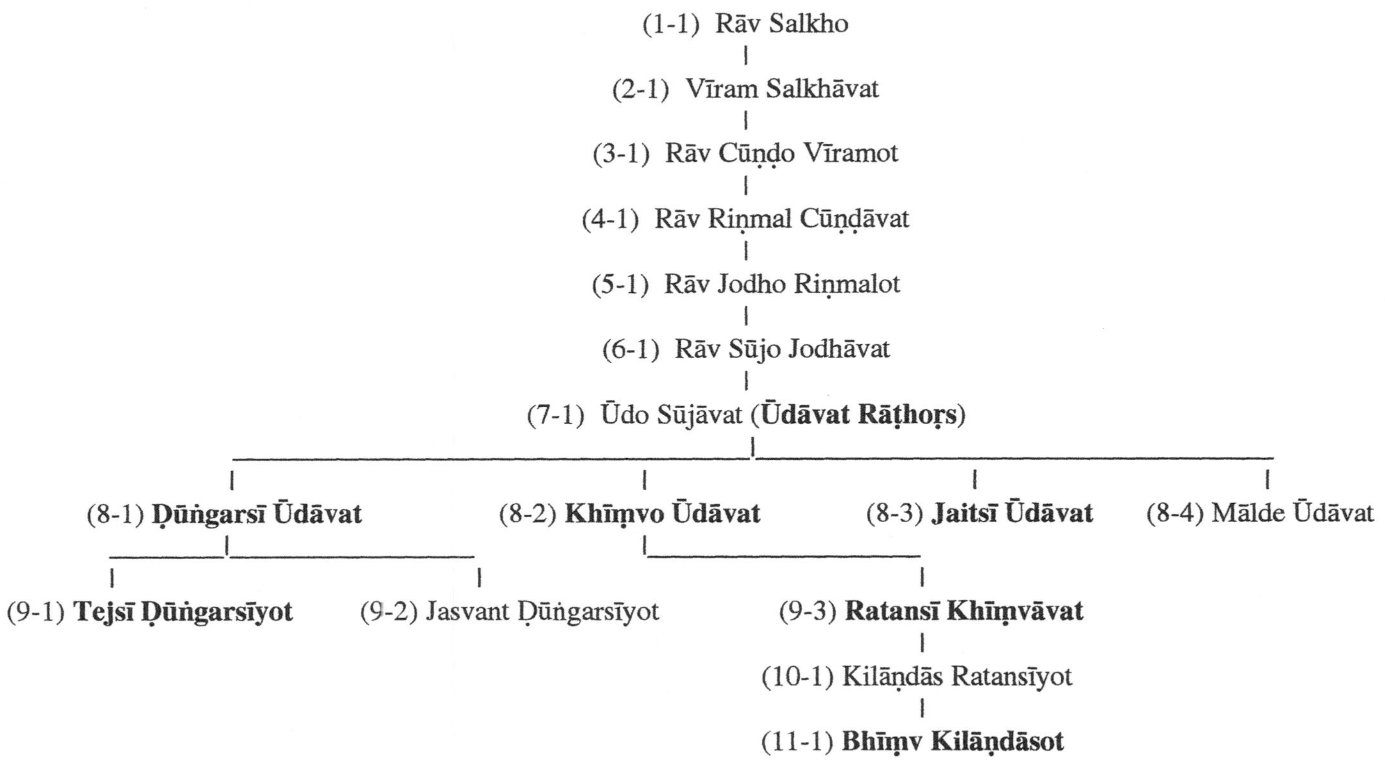
(1-1) Rāv Salkho
(2-1) Vīram Salkhāvat
(3-1) Rāv Cūṇḍo Vīramot
(4-1) Rāv Riṇmal Cūṇḍāvat
(5-1) Rāv Jodho Riṇmalot
(6-1) Rāv Sūjo Jodhāvat
(7-1) Ūdo Sūjāvat (**Ūdāvat Rāṭhoṛs**)
(8-1) **Ḍūṅgarsī Ūdāvat**
(8-2) **Khīṃvo Ūdāvat**
(8-3) **Jaitsī Ūdāvat**
(8-4) Mālde Ūdāvat
(9-1) **Tejsī Ḍūṅgarsīyot**
(9-2) Jasvant Ḍūṅgarsīyot
(9-3) **Ratansī Khīṃvāvat**
(10-1) Kilāṇdās Ratansīyot
(11-1) **Bhīṃv Kilāṇdāsot**

Ūdāvat (Baiṭhvāsīyo) Rāṭhoṛs

(no. 143) **Tiloksī Varjāṅgot** (5-2)

The Ūdāvat (Baiṭhvāsīyo) Rāṭhoṛs

One of the complexities of Rāṭhoṛ family history is that for some time two distinct Rāṭhoṛ branches in Mārvāṛ were referred to as "Ūdāvat Rāṭhoṛs": the Ūdāvats of Jaitāraṇ, discussed in the preceding section, and the Ūdāvats of Baiṭhvās village.[1] By the mid-seventeenth century, the term "Ūdāvat" was mainly used for the Ūdāvats of Jaitāraṇ, although they were also known as "Jaitāraṇīyo Rāṭhoṛs," and the Ūdāvats of Baiṭhvās were generally called "Baiṭhvāsīyo Rāṭhoṛs."

The Baiṭhvāsīyo Rāṭhoṛs are the descendants of Ūdo Tribhuvaṇsīyot. Tribhuvaṇsī (or Tribhāvaṇsī, as he is listed in one source) was the son[2] of Rāv Kānhaṛde Tīḍāvat, ruler of Mahevo in western Mārvāṛ during the early fourteenth century. After Rāv Tīḍo was killed at the siege of Sīvāṇo ca. 1308, Kānhaṛde succeeded him as Rāv of Mahevo. He had two sons, Kānhaṛde and Salkho, by different wives. Kānhaṛde was the heir-apparent, his mother was Tīḍo's favorite wife, and so Salkho was forced to wander about in his youth trying to find a livelihood. He was captured by the Muslims and imprisoned in Gujarat when Tīḍo was killed. Kānhaṛde, however, was able to succeed Tīḍo as the leader of the Mahevo household when the Muslims withdrew. Two yogis rescued Salkho from prison and brought him back to Mahevo, where he received a one-village land grant from Kānhaṛde as his share of Tīḍo's lands. He also inherited a small number of Tīḍo's retainers and servants, whom he took with him to populate his village, newly renamed Salkhāvāsī (***Khyāt***, 2:280, 3:23-24; ***Vigat***, 1:15, 2:216).

One day Salkho went to Mahevo for food. He impressed a laborer into service and had him carry the provisions back to his settlement. On the way, they came upon four lions seated in the road gnawing bones. As the lion is the symbol of the Rajpūt, Salkho immediately recognized them as an omen. He sat motionless in the road while the laborer summoned an augur. The augur perceived that the lions indicated that Salkho would have four sons, who would conquer much land, be powerful men, and possess much energy. Moreover they, not the sons of Kānhaṛde, would rule Mahevo. And indeed, soon four sons were born: two, Mālo (the eldest) and Jaitmāl, of one ***rāṇī***; two others, Vīramde and

---

[1] We have been unable to locate Baiṭhvās village, which is not listed in the ***Vigat*** of Naiṇsī.

[2] The ***Jodhpur Rājya kī Khyāt***, p. 31, indicates that Tribhuvaṇsī was Kānhaṛde's brother.

Sobhat, of another (***Khyāt***, 2:280-281; ***Rāṭhauṛāṃ rī Vaṃsāvaḷī nai Pīḍhiyāṃ nai Phuṭkar Vātāṃ***, partially edited and translated by L. P. Tessitori in ***idem***, "A Progress Report on the Work done during the year 1917 in connection with the Bardic and Historical Survey of Rajputana," ***Journal of the Asiatic Society of Bengal***, N.S. 15 (1919), pp. 31-43; ***Vigat***, 1:15).

Mālo is described as "a very far-sighted man, a portion of a god" (***Vigat***, 1:16). He was a boy when Salkho died, so he took up residence with his uncle, Kānhaṛde. He became one of Kānhaṛde's armed retainers. An extremely precocious and aggressive youth, Mālo shocked Kānhaṛde's Rajpūts one day during a hunt by grabbing his uncle's garment and refusing to let go until given some land:

> He said: "Kānhaṛdejī! I demand a portion of the land. I shall not let go!" He said much, but he did not let go. [Kānhaṛde's] Rajpūts remained standing apart. No one came close (***Khyāt***, 2:281).

Kānhaṛde admired his brash act. Impressed with his nephew, he gave him one-third of the Rāṭhoṛ lands and made him his ***pradhān***. The other Rajpūts observing all this remarked to themselves that "whoever appoints a kinsman ***pradhān*** is about to lose his domain" (***Khyāt***, 2:282).

Soon Mālo was presented with his first problem. The Sultān of Delhi had sent revenue collectors to each of the major fortresses held by the Muslims in Rājasthān with instructions to put the surrounding countryside under taxation. Kānhaṛde summoned all of his Rajpūts. He asked them what should be done about the collectors coming to Mahevo. Mālo suggested taking them into the various villages around Mahevo ostensibly to realize the land revenue and then killing them one by one. His plan pleased everyone. But, on the appointed day of the executions, while the other Rajpūts were killing the Sultān's agents in the villages, Mālo took the chief collector home as his guest. He told him, "Kānhaṛde has killed all of your men. But I will not kill you" (***Khyāt***, 2:282-283).

The collector, grateful, soon went back to Delhi. He petitioned the Sultān:

> Kānhaṛde has killed all of your men. And my enemy, Mālo, kept me alive. Mālo is an excellent servant of the Sultān. He is worthy. He is a man loyal to his master (***Khyāt***, 2:283).

The Sultān summoned Mālo to Delhi and granted him jurisdiction over Mahevo with the title of ***rāvaḷ***. He dismissed him when they learned that Kānhaṛde had died in Mahevo and had been succeeded by his son Tribhuvaṇsī.

Mālo returned to Mahevo with the backing of the Sultān. He fought and defeated Tribhuvaṇsī, who fled wounded into the Rājasthān Desert. Tribhuvaṇsī was saved by the Īndo Rajpūts, his relatives through marriage, who sheltered him and bandaged his wounds. But Mālo perceived that his supremacy in Mahevo would be insecure while Tribhuvaṇsī lived, and so he arranged for his assassination:

> Tribhuvaṇsī had a brother, Padamsī, whom [Mālo] deceived. He told him: "If you kill Tribhuvaṇsī, I shall give you the throne [of Mahevo]." Then Padamsī, being greedy, went and mixed arsenic in the ***nīm*** leaf bandages meant for Tribhuvaṇsī. The bandages were poisoned. Tribhuvaṇsī died (***Khyāt***, 2:283-284).[3]

Padamsī came to Mahevo to collect:

> He said: "Give me the throne." Mālo said: "One does not obtain a throne like this!" He said: "***Jī***, take two villages. Eat sitting [there]!"[4] Then he gave Padamsī two villages of Mahevo and dismissed [him] (***Khyāt***, 2:284).

Nothing is known of Tribhuvaṇsī's son Ūdo except that he took up residence in Baiṭhvās village and that he had at least two sons, Vijo and Varjāṅg Ūdāvat.

(no. 143) **Tiloksī Varjāṅgot** (5-2)

Tiloksī Varjāṅgot was one of Ūdo Tribhuvaṇsīyot's grandsons.[5] Although little information is available concerning Tiloksī's career, it is evident that he was a Rajpūt of some importance among Rāv Mālde's (Jodhpur ruler, 1532-62) military servants. He held the garrison of Bījāpur,[6] a former possession of the Bālīso Cahuvāṇs situated in the Godhvāṛ region of south-eastern Mārvāṛ. While stationed there, he had the fort and gates of Bījāpur constructed. Subsequently Rāv Mālde appointed him ***kiledār*** of Jodhpur fort, a position he held at the time of Sher Shāh's invasion of Mārvāṛ. He was one of several Rajpūts who died in heroic fashion defending the fort in 1544, holding out as long as possible and then sallying forth to fight to the death against the besieging army. Rāv Mālde had ***chatrīs*** built for Tiloksī and the other important Rajpūts who were killed during the siege.

---

[3] The date of Tribhuvaṇsī's death is not known. His daughter Kumarde was married to Rāvaḷ Kehar Devrājot of Jaisaḷmer (ca. 1361-97). After Rāvaḷ Kehar died in 1397, Kumarde became a ***satī***. An inscription commemorates this act. Cf. ***Khyāt***, 2:280, n. 1.

[4] This sentence implies that Padamsī may enjoy the rule of two villages (literally, "eat" them) and not make further attempts to acquire the throne of Mahevo (i.e, remain "sitting").

[5] The genealogical link between Ūdo Tribhuvaṇsīyot and Tiloksī Varjāṇgot is not certain; it is possible that Tiloksī was Ūdo's great-grandson and that Varjāṅg was in fact Ūdo's grandson, not his son.

[6] Bījāpur is twenty-five miles southwest of Nāḍūl in Goḍhvāṛ.

"Aitihāsik Bātāṃ," pp. 45, 75; Bhāṭī, ***Sarvekṣaṇ***, 3:110-111; ***Khyat***, 3:101; ***Vigat***, 1:58, 65, 2:57, 3:77

Figure 33. Ūdāvat (Baiṭhvāsīyo) Rāṭhoṛs

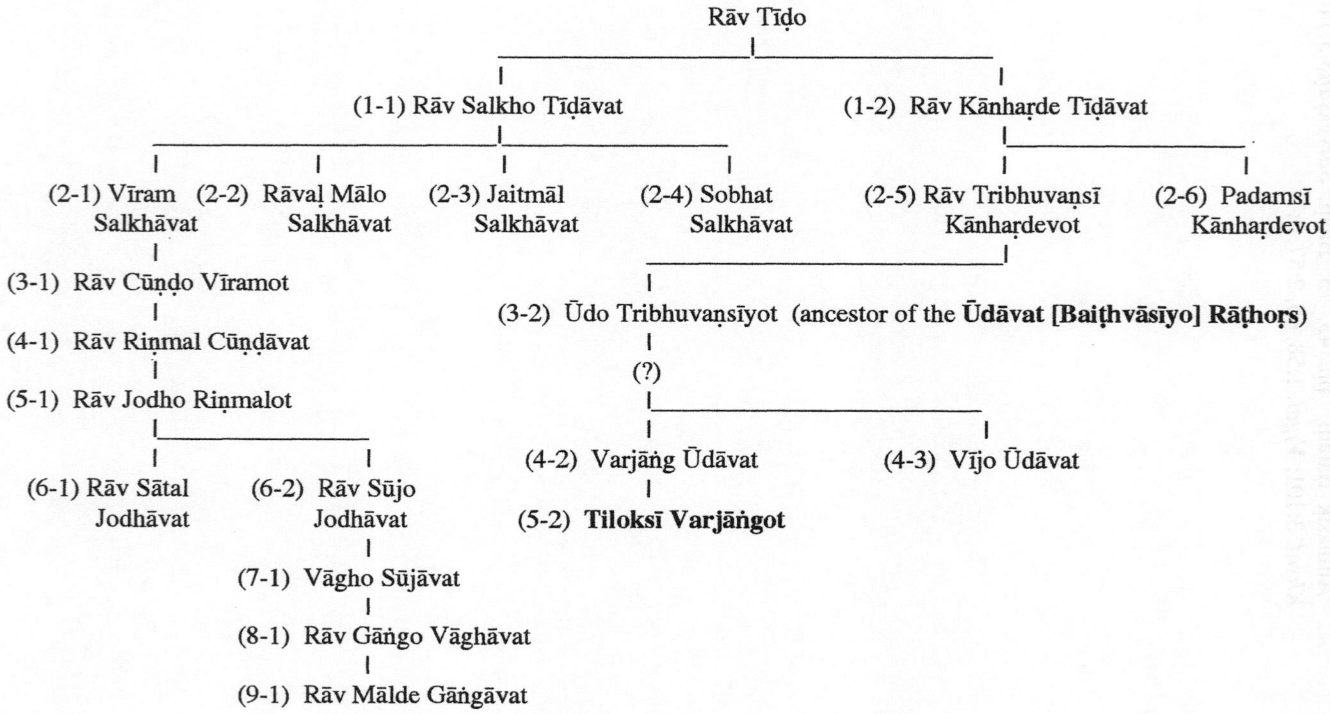

Ūhaṛ Rāṭhoṛs

(no. 144) **Hardās Mokaḷot**
(no. 145) **Bhāṇ Kājāvat**

The Ūhaṛ Rāṭhoṛs

The Ūhaṛ Rāṭhoṛs are a very old Rajpūt group in Mārvāṛ. According to Mārvāṛī traditions, they descend from Ūhaṛ Jopsāhot, a great-grandson of Rāv Sīho Setrāmot, who is considered the founding ancestor of the Mārvāṛ Rāṭhoṛs. Little is known in fact about Rāv Sīho other than the date of his death: October 9, 1273. This date is recorded on a memorial stone (***devḷī***) for a Raṭhaḍā (Rāṭhoṛ) Sīho, son of Setrām, found at the village of Bīṭhū[1] in central Mārvāṛ. The chronicles associate Sīho's son, Āsthān Sīhāvat, with the villages of Pālī[2] in eastern Mārvāṛ and with Kheṛ[3] in western Mārvāṛ. Āsthān is said to have established his capitol at Kheṛ village. No specific information is available about Āsthān's son, Jopsāh Āsthānot, or Jopsāh's son, Ūhaṛ Jopsāhot.

The genealogical relationship of the Ūhaṛs to other branches of the Mārvāṛ Rāṭhoṛs is very conjectural given the extremely doubtful nature of this type of information prior to the time of Rāv Riṇmal Cūṇḍāvat of Maṇḍor (ca. 1428-38) and his son, Rāv Jodho Riṇmalot (ca. 1453-89). Richard Saran has suggested of the Sīndhaḷ Rāṭhoṛs (see ***supra***) that they are a Rajpūt group that became incorporated within the Rāṭhoṛ clan (***kuḷ***) at some time during the early history of the Rāṭhoṛs of Mārvāṛ. The same may also be true of the Ūhaṛs.

Bhāṭī, ***Sarvakṣaṇ***, 3:114, records that Ūhaṛ was the uterine brother of Sīndhaḷ, the founding ancestor of the Sīndhaḷ Rāṭhoṛs. Ūhaṛ is said to have settled in the area of Koḍhṇo[4] in western Mārvāṛ while Sīndhaḷ settled in central-western Mārvāṛ and founded the village of Bhādrājuṇ.[5]

> B. N. Reu, ***Glories of Marwar and the Glorious Rathors*** (Jodhpur: Archaeological Department, 1943), p. x; Bhāṭī, ***Sarvekṣaṇ***, 3:112-114; Gehlot, ***Mārvāṛ***, p. 72; "Jodhpur

---

[1] Bīṭhū village: located thirty miles south of Jodhpur and fourteen miles northwest of Pālī in central Mārvāṛ.

[2] Pālī village: located forty miles south-southeast of Jodhpur.

[3] Kheṛ village: located sixty-two miles southwest of Jodhpur, just near the great bend in the Lūṇī River.

[4] Koḍhṇo village: located twenty-eight miles west-southwest of Jodhpur.

[5] Bhādrājuṇ village: located forty-eight miles south-southwest of Jodhpur.

Hukūmat rī Bahī," p. 138; ***Murārdān***, no. 2, pp. 46-47; Ojhā, 4:1:152-160.

(no. 144) **Hardās Mokaḷot**

Ūhaṛ Hardās Mokaḷot appears in the Mārvāṛī chronicles in association with two prominent Rāṭhoṛ figures of the early sixteenth century, Rāv Vīramde Vāghāvat (no. 84), a grandson of Rāv Sūjo Jodhāvat of Jodhpur (ca. 1492-1515), and Sekho Sūjāvat (no. 86), a son of Rāv Sūjo. Both Rāv Vīramde and Sekho Sūjāvat became involved in conflicts with Rāv Sūjo's successor to the Jodhpur throne, Rāv Gāṅgo Vāghāvat (1515-32), over land and authority in Mārvāṛ. Hardās Mokaḷot entered into these conflicts to avenge himself against the house of Jodhpur for perceived past wrongs that he and his brotherhood had suffered at their hands.

Details are unclear, but Hardas's enmity toward Rāv Gāṅgo and the house of Jodhpur appears to be related to the fortunes of the Ūhaṛ Rāṭhoṛs of Koḍhṇo in western Mārvāṛ. The Ūhaṛ Rāṭhoṛs had been in possession of Koḍhṇo and surrounding villages prior to and during the rule of Rāv Riṇmal Cūṇḍāvat of Maṇḍor (ca. 1428-38) and his son, Rāv Jodho Riṇmalot (ca. 1453-89). The Ūhaṛs considered these villages their homeland (***utan***). Rāv Jodho then divided the lands of Mārvāṛ among his brothers and sons following the founding of Jodhpur in 1459, and he granted Koḍhṇo to his two sons, Jogo and Bhārmal Jodhāvat.[6] Jogo and Bhārmal proceeded to take possession of Koḍhṇo in the early 1460s, and they forced the migration of the Ūhaṛs south to Mahevo.

By the time of Rāv Gāṅgo Vāghāvat of Jodhpur some sixty years later, the descendants of Bhārmal Jodhāvat, who had remained at Koḍhṇo, had begun to lose control of Koḍhṇo to the Bhāṭīs from Jaisaḷmer. Rāv Gāṅgo began recalling families of Ūhaṛs from Mahevo to reoccupy the villages in order to maintain Rāṭhoṛ authority there. Koḍhṇo itself eventually came under Ūhaṛ control, and in the 1520s Ūhaṛ Hardās Mokaḷot, who was a military servant of Rāv Gāṅgo, held Koḍhṇo in ***paṭo*** along with one hundred and forty other villages.

Khyāt, 3:87, records that Ūhaṛ Hardās was a powerful Rajpūt, much feared by other men, but that he would not perform even "the simplest service." He came to Jodhpur to pay his respects to the Jodhpur ruler and to reaffirm his vows of loyalty and service only at the time of the Dasrāho festival in the fall of the year. Hardās gained the ire of Rāv Gāṅgo's son, Kuṃvar Mālde Gāṅgāvat, for his lack of service, and the Kuṃvar had Hardās's ***paṭo*** revoked and given to another Ūhaṛ named Bhāṇ Kājāvat (no. 145). ***Khyāt*** relates in rather amusing fashion that because Hardās was such a fearsome warrior, no one dared come near him to inform him that his ***paṭo*** had been revoked. Ūhaṛ Bhāṇ allowed him to stay at Koḍhṇo while he went to perform military service for the house of Jodhpur. Several years passed in this manner. Then Bhāṇ's and Hardās's

[6] See ***supra***, "Jodho Rāṭhoṛs" and "Bhārmalot Rāṭhoṛs," respectively.

hujdār*s** fell to fighting at Koḍhṇo, and Hardās finally learned the truth of his situation (see ***Khyāt, 3:87-88, of the **translated text** for details).

Hardās now left Koḍhṇo and proceeded to Sojhat. Sojhat was under the control of Rāv Gāṅgo's half-brother, Rāv Vīramde Vāghāvat (no. 84), who was himself engaged in on-going hostilities with Jodhpur. Hardās offered his services to Rāv Vīramde solely on the condition that the Rāv continue his fight against Jodhpur. Rāv Vīramde readily accepted Hardās's offer of service, and Hardās quickly became involved in skirmishes with Rāv Gāṅgo's forces.

Khyāt, 3:88, records that Rāv Vīramde soon alienated Ūhaṛ Hardās, however, because of his lack of concern for Hardās's welfare as one of his military servants. Rāv Vīramde displayed this lack of concern one day after Hardās had ridden into battle on one of the horses from the Rāv's stable. Both Hardās and the horse were wounded during the fighting. Ūhaṛ Bhāṇ Kājāvat was present at this conflict as one of Rāv Gāṅgo's warriors. His relationship with Hardās had apparently remained amicable, for ***Khyāt*** notes that Bhāṇ "picked up Hardās" after the battle and had him sent him back to Sojhat.

When Hardās returned to Sojhat, Rāv Vīramde could only find fault with him because he had allowed his horse to be injured. The Rāv showed little concern for Hardās's own wounds. Hardās then rebuked the Rāv, calling him an "unworthy Rajpūt" (***kurajpūt***), and left Sojhat in anger for Nāgaur.

Hardās entered into the household (***vās***) of Sarkhel Khān (no. 155) at Nāgaur for a short period before proceeding on to Pīmpāṛ[7] and the home of Sekho Sūjāvat. Sekho was the paternal uncle of Rāv Gāṅgo Vāghāvat of Jodhpur. He had received Pīmpāṛ and surrounding villages as his share of Mārvāṛ on the death of his father, Rāv Sūjo Jodhāvat, in 1515. He sought wider control and authority in Mārvāṛ, however, and when Hardās offered his services under the same conditions he had specified to Rāv Vīramde of Sojhat, Sekho gladly welcomed him and retained him as his ***pradhān***. Sekho and Hardās then began to plot in earnest against the house of Jodhpur, and they drew in Khānzāda Khān Daulat Khān (no. 154) from Nāgaur as an ally. Their conspiracy culminated in the battle of Sevakī village[8] on November 2, 1529. Rāv Gāṅgo's superior stance at Sevakī forced Daulat Khān to flee with great loss, and both Sekho Sūjāvat and Hardās Mokaḷot were killed along with many of their Rajpūts (see ***Khyāt***, 3:87-92, of the **translated text** for details of this battle and the events which surrounded it).

Khyāt, 1:361, 3:87-92; ***Murārdān***, no. 2, pp. 97-98, 403-404, 422-423; ***Vigat***, 1:39, 293.

---

[7] Pīmpāṛ village: located thirty-three miles east-northeast of Jodhpur.

[8] Sevakī village: located twenty-three miles northeast of Jodhpur.

(no. 145) **Bhāṇ Kājāvat**

Bhāṇ Kājāvat was the son of Ūhaṛ Kājo Kharhathot, of whom nothing is known. The exact relationship between the families of Bhāṇ and Hardās Mokaḷot (no. 144), the two leading Ūhaṛs of the early sixteenth century, is also unknown.

Bhāṇ rose to a position of some prominence during the reign of Rāv Gāṅgo Vāghāvat of Jodhpur (1515-32). Rāv Gāṅgo had given him a ***paṭo*** for the village Bāvaḷlī[9], and then after Hardās failed to perform military service, Kuṃvar Mālde Gāṅgāvat gave Bhāṇ all of Koḍhṇo. Shortly thereafter Bhāṇ's and Hardās's ***hujdār***s fought in Koḍhṇo. Hardās left for Sojhat and military service under Rāv Vīramde Vāghāvat (no. 84) upon finding out that Bhāṇ, and not he, held the ***paṭo*** from Kuṃvar Mālde. Bhāṇ and Hardās continued to have an amicable relationship, however, for Bhāṇ had Hardās picked up and sent back to Sojhat after Hardās and the horse he was riding were badly wounded during a skirmish with Rāv Gāṅgo's Rajpūts from Jodhpur.

In 1529 at Sevakī, Hardās was killed fighting against the forces of Rāv Gāṅgo and Kuṃvar Mālde. Bhāṇ, still in possession of Koḍhṇo, was now the leading Ūhaṛ in Mārvāṛ. He was included among Rāv Mālde's ***pradhān***s. At some point after 1535 he constructed a plot against the Akhairājot Rāṭhoṛs Kānho and Bhado Pañcāiṇot (no. 32). He had them poisoned and killed at a feast given by Rāv Mālde.[10] Undoubtedly the initiative for this assassination came from Mālde himself. According to one source,

> Rāv Mālde gave [them] poison in the ***bīṛo***s.[11] It was the feast of Dīvāḷī. He stood up, gave them the ***bīṛo***s, and said: "You go home." During the night [Bhado Pañcāiṇot] went to [his home], Dāntīvāṛo.[12] While going, he died. Bhāṇ Ūhaṛ organized the plot against Bhado and Kānho both.

In 1544, the Sūr Emperor, Sher Shāh, came to Mārvāṛ to fight the battle of Samel against Rāv Mālde. Prior to the battle, Mālde had gone to Sojhat and begun to assemble his army. Bhāṇ did not show up. Mālde was not the sort of ruler who would fail to notice this breach of service. His ***pradhān***, Jaito Pañcāiṇot (no. 61), constructed a plan, and Mālde selected Jagmāl Ūhaṛ to carry it out. Afterward Bhāṇ did come to Sojhat; Jagmāl attacked him and killed him

---

[9] Bāvaḷlī village: located eleven miles southwest of Koḍhṇo proper.

[10] ***Murārdān***, no. 2, p. 120, lists Bhado as having been killed at the battle of Samel in January of 1544. See ***supra***, "Akhairājot Rāṭhoṛs."

[11] ***Bīṛo***: betel leaf with lime, spices, etc., folded to be eaten and distributed at ceremonial occasions.

[12] Dāntīvāṛo village: located eighteen miles due east of Jodhpur.

as he was climbing the embankment around the town. This event occurred either late in 1543 or early 1544, just before Samel.

Bhāṭī, ***Sarvekṣaṇ***, 3:96, 113; ***Khyāt***, 3:87-88.

Varsiṅghot Meṛtīyo Rāṭhoṛs

(no. 148) **Bhojo Sīhāvat, Rāv** (8-1)
(no. 149) **Gāṅgo Sīhāvat, Rāv** (8-2)
(no. 150) **Jeso Sīhāvat, Rāv** (8-3)
(no. 151) **Sahaiso Tejsīyot** (8-4)
(no. 152) **Sāṃvaḷdās Udaisiṅghot** (10-1)
(no. 147) **Sīho Varsiṅghot, Rāv** (7-1)
(no. 146) **Varsiṅgh Jodhāvat, Rāv** (6-2)

(no. 146) Varsiṅgh Jodhāvat, Rāv of Meṛto (6-2)

Varsiṅgh Jodhāvat was a son of Rāv Jodho Riṇmalot, ruler of Maṇḍor and Jodhpur (ca. 1453-89). He was born of Sonagarī Cāmpā,[1] daughter of Sonagaro Cahuvāṇ Khīṃvo Satāvat of Pālī village[2] in eastern Mārvāṛ. No information is available about Varsiṅgh's date of birth. But Varsiṅgh was the elder of Sonagarī Cāmpā's two sons, and was born prior to 1440, the year of the birth of Varsiṅgh's younger brother, Dūdo Jodhāvat's (6-1) (no. 104).

Varsiṅgh grew up during the period of Sīsodīyo rule in Mārvāṛ following the murder of his grandfather, Rāv Riṇmal Cūṇḍāvat (4-1), at Cītoṛ ca. 1438. For fifteen years thereafter, Varsiṅgh's father, Jodho Riṇmalot, fought to reassert Rāṭhoṛ authority at Maṇḍor. Jodho finally succeeded in the conquest of Maṇḍor ca. 1453. Six years later in 1459, he founded his new capitol of Jodhpur high on a sandstone ridge overlooking the central plain of Mārvāṛ, five miles to the south of Maṇḍor. Rāv Jodho then divided the lands of Mārvāṛ among his brothers and sons. He gave the lands of Meṛto to his two sons, Varsiṅgh and Dūdo.

The two brothers settled in the area of Meṛto in 1461-62. They became acquainted with the Jaitmālot Rāṭhoṛ Ūdo Kānhaṛdevot (no. 67), who lived in the area and offered his services. Ūdo showed them the site of two ancient tanks called Kuṇḍaḷ and Bejpo. They were pleased, and they founded Meṛto town near this site on March 7, 1462.

Varsiṅgh and Dūdo proceeded to establish their authority and to settle the land. They made Jaitmālot Ūdo their ***pradhān*** and gave him full responsibility for governing the land. The chronicles relate that they drove Sāṅkhlo Paṃvārs from several villages to secure the area and then brought Ḍāṅgo Jāṭs from the Savāḷakh area of Nāgaur to populate and farm the villages. During this initial settlement process, Varsiṅgh, the elder brother, assumed

---

[1] See ***supra*****, Marriage and Family Lists of the Rulers of Jodhpur**, Jodho Riṇmalot, Rāṇī no. 4, S - Varsiṅgh.

[2] Pālī village: located forty miles south-southeast of Jodhpur.

control at Meṛto proper and took the title of ***rāv***, while Dūdo, the younger, lived at the village of Rāhaṇ.[3]

Both brothers cooperated with each other in the founding of Meṛto and in the settlement of the land. They eventually quarreled, however, and Dūdo then left Meṛto to join his half-brother, Bīko Jodhāvat (no. 42) (Rāv of Bīkāner, ca. 1485-1504), who was in the process of founding his own kingdom in the area of northern Rājasthān that became known as Bīkāner. The time of Dūdo's departure is uncertain, but it probably occurred in the later 1480s, toward the end of the rule of his father, Rāv Jodho, at Jodhpur. Rāv Varsiṅgh appears to have ruled Meṛto in relative peace during the last ten years of Rāv Jodho's life. But with Rāv Jodho's death in 1489, Varsiṅgh became involved in a series of conflicts over land and authority in Mārvāṛ that soon brought his own death. These conflicts involved Rāv Jodho's successor to the throne of Jodhpur, Rāv Sātal Jodhāvat (ca. 1489-92), and the ***sūbedār*** of Ajmer, Malū Khān, a subordinate of the Pātsāh of Māṇḍū.

The chronicles tell of a famine that fell across Meṛto and other parts of Mārvāṛ at this time. They relate that poor harvests and lack of food caused many of Rāv Varsiṅgh's men, who had come with his family from Jodhpur, to leave Meṛto. Out of desperation, Rāv Varsiṅgh mounted an attack on Sāmbhar, the rich trading city to the northeast of Meṛto, which he looted of much wealth. This aggression brought him into direct conflict with Malū Khān of Ajmer, to whom the Cahuvāṇ ruler of Sāmbhar appealed for redress.

Rāv Varsiṅgh also fell out with his half-brother, Rāv Sātal Jodhāvat of Jodhpur. Varsiṅgh demanded additional lands and villages from Jodhpur, which he claimed were his by right of patrimony. Rāv Sātal eventually acceded to Rāv Varsiṅgh demands, but Malū Khān became involved in this dispute as an outside arbiter. Rāv Varsiṅgh struck a bargain with Malū Khān, agreeing to pay a tribute of ***rs***. 50,000 to settle his account regarding Sāmbhar, and to enlist Malū Khān's support in acquiring Jodhpur itself.

Exact chronology of events is unclear, but it appears Malū Khān brought an army from Māṇḍū and began to ravage the lands of Meṛto and Jodhpur when Rāv Varsiṅgh failed to live up to his part of the bargain. The three brothers, Rāv Varsiṅgh Jodhāvat of Meṛto, Rāv Sātal Jodhāvat of Jodhpur, and Sūjo Jodhāvat (Rāv of Jodhpur, ca. 1492-1515), then met and defeated Malū Khān in battle at Kusāṇo[4] on March 1, 1492. Malū Khān fled from the field, but he soon brought another army from Māṇḍū and demanded concessions from Varsiṅgh. Rāv Varsiṅgh finally met with Malū Khān at Ajmer, where the Khān allayed his suspicions with presents and much flattery, then imprisoned him in an unsuspecting moment. Word of Rāv Varsiṅgh's capture spread quickly both to Rāv Sūjo at Jodhpur and to Dūdo Jodhāvat in Bīkāner. Shortly thereafter, the combined forces of Rāv Sūjo of Jodhpur, Dūdo Jodhāvat, and Rāv Bīko Jodhāvat of Bīkāner marched on Ajmer to force Rāv Varsiṅgh's release. Malū Khān reluctantly agreed to release Varsiṅgh rather than confront the Rāṭhoṛs in

---

[3] Rāhaṇ village: located ten miles north-northeast of Meṛto.

[4] Kusāṇo village: located twenty-eight miles southwest of Meṛto.

battle, and Rāv Varsiṅgh then returned to Meṛto to assume his former position of authority.

Rāv Varsiṅgh died suddenly at Meṛto several months after this confrontation. *Vigat*, 2:46, records that Malū Khān had given Varsiṅgh a slow poison when he imprisoned him at Ajmer, which killed him in six months. Rule at Meṛto then passed to Varsiṅgh's son, Sīho Varsiṅghot (7-1) (no. 147).

Rāv Varsiṅgh granted the following villages in *sāṃsaṇ* to Brāhmaṇs and Cāraṇs:

1. Kāṃvḷīyo[5] - to the Khiṛīyo Cāraṇ Dharmo Cāndaṇot.
2. Kharṛī (Kharhāṛī)[6] - to the Khiṛīyo Cāraṇ Lumbo Cāndaṇot.
3. Pāñcḍoḷī rā Vās[7] - to the Sīvaṛ Brāhmaṇ Purohit Kānho Dūdāit.
4. Sīhā rī Vāsṇī[8] - to the Jaghaṭh Cāraṇ Bākhal Cāndaṇot.
5. Ṭukṛī[9] - to the Sīvaṛ Brāhmaṇ Purohit Khīdo Kānhāvat in exchange for Kāṃvḷīyo village (see *supra*).

Bāṅkīdās, p. 57; ***Khyāt***, 3:28; ***Murārdān***, no. 2, pp. 96-97, 99, 101, 444-446, 583-584; ***Vigat***, 1:39-40, 2:37-39, 41-46, 106-107, 128-129, 139, 151-152.

(no. 147) **Sīho Varsiṅghot, Rāv of Meṛto** (7-1)

Sīho Varsiṅghot was the son of Rāv Varsiṅgh Jodhāvat (6-2) (no. 146) and the grandson of Rāv Jodho Riṇmalot (ca. 1453-89). He succeeded Rāv Varsiṅgh to the rulership of Meṛto in 1492. The chronicles all relate that Sīho's accession to rule was not auspicious. It soon led to the decline of Varsiṅgh's line and to the ascendancy of Varsiṅgh's younger uterine brother, Dūdo Jodhāvat (no. 104), and his descendants. The fall of Varsiṅgh's line from Meṛto had been foretold in an omen that appeared on the site where the new city of Meṛto was to be founded. The omen took the form of two lions, one larger (representing Varsiṅgh, the elder) and one smaller (signifying Dūdo). The larger lion had roared and had then been driven away, while the smaller had gone into a nearby cave and sat down. An augur who witnessed this event forecast that Varsiṅgh's sons and grandsons would not live at Meṛto after his death, but that Dūdo's would.

---

[5] Kāṃvḷīyo village: located seventeen miles south of Meṛto, near Aṇandpur.

[6] Kharṛī village: located fifteen miles south of Meṛto, near Aṇandpur.

[7] Pāñcḍoḷī rā Vās: located five miles southeast of Meṛto.

[8] Sīhā rī Vāsṇī: located twelve miles west of Meṛto.

[9] Ṭukṛī village: located seventeen miles west of Meṛto.

By all the chronicles, Rāv Sīho was incompetent to rule. Most cast him as a drunkard who remained intoxicated much of the time. Others describe him as weak and stupid. Upon his succession, Meṛto became subject to inroads. To protect the lands, those around Rāv Sīho struck a bargain with Rāv Sūjo Jodhāvat of Jodhpur (ca. 1492-1515), offering him one-third of the villages of Meṛto in return for his protection. The Rāv accepted this offer and sent his men to occupy villages in Meṛto, but he quickly moved to sequester Meṛto itself. Alarmed at these developments, Sīho's mother, the Sāṅkhlī Paṃvār, called together the ***pañco***. ***Murārdān***, no. 2, pp. 445-446, records the following statement of the Sāṅkhlī's to the assembly:

> Then Sīho's mother said, "If you were to give the land to Rāv [Sūjo[10]], all the land would be lost. Because of this [eventuality], if you summon Dūdo and give [him] the land, then what harm [would come]? If you were to give the land to Dūdo [and] make Dūdo master of Meṛto, then the land will pass from [those of] my womb, but it will not leave the issue of the mother of my husband (***sāsū***). The land will remain within this house. But if you were to give the land to [Rāv Sūjo], then the land would pass from [this] house. There is no doubt about this [eventuality]. For this reason, I say, have Dūdo summoned, place the ***ṭīko*** [of succession on his forehead], and having made him master, protect yourselves" (***Murārdān***, no. 2, pp. 445-446).

The ***pañco*** considered the Sāṅkhlī's words prudent, and they called Dūdo Jodhāvat back to Meṛto and agreed to give him one-half of the revenues from the land in return for his protection. Dūdo returned in 1492-93. Within a short time, he was able to drive Rāv Sūjo's Rajpūts from the land and secure his family's territory. He then moved Rāv Sīho out of Meṛto as well in 1495-96, having him carried in a wagon to Rāhaṇ[11] village north of Meṛto one night while he was drunk. Dūdo then asserted preeminent rights over Meṛto for himself and his family, and he assumed the title of ***rāv***. The family of Varsiṅgh Jodhāvat remained subordinate to Dūdo's from this time forward.

Rāv Sīho granted the village of Moḍrīyo[12] in ***sāṃsaṇ*** to the Khiṛīyo Cāraṇ Sīho Candrāvat.

> ***Bāṅkīdās***, p. 59; ***Murārdān***, no. 2, pp. 444-446, 583-584; ***Vigat***, 2:46-48, 108, 176.

---

[10] The text had the name "Gāṅgo" in place of Sūjo here, which is incorrect. Rāv Gāṅgo Vāghāvat was Rāv Sūjo's successor to the rulership of Jodhpur (1515-32).

[11] Rāhaṇ village: located ten miles north-northeast of Meṛto.

[12] Moḍrīyo village: located sixteen miles northeast of Meṛto, near Moḍro.

(no. 148) **Bhojo Sīhāvat, Rāv** (8-1)
(no. 149) **Gāṅgo Sīhāvat, Rāv** (8-2)
(no. 150) **Jeso Sīhāvat, Rāv** (8-3)

Bhojo, Gāṅgo, and Jeso Sīhāvat were sons of Rāv Sīho Varsiṅghot (7-1) (no. 147) and grandsons of Rāv Varsiṅgh Jodhāvat ((6-2) (no. 146), one of the original founders of Meṛto. ***Vigat***, 2:47, refers to them by the title of ***rāv*** and describes them as "great, fearsome warriors." They appear to have succeeded jointly to Rāv Sīho's land and position at Rāhaṇ village as nominal heads of one-half of the territory and revenues of Meṛto. With the death of Rāv Dūdo Jodhāvat (6-1) (no. 104) in 1497-98 and the succession of Rāv Dūdo's son, Rāv Vīramde Dūdāvat (no. 105), to Meṛto, any possibility of their acquiring wider influence in Meṛto, however, quickly receded.

The three brothers had different careers with varying involvements in Meṛto itself. Of Rāv Jeso Sīhāvat we know only that he was a military servant of Sīsodīyo Rāṇo Sāṅgo Rāymalot of Mevāṛ (1509-28). He accompanied Rāṇo Sāṅgo to north India in 1527 and took part in preparations for the battle at Khanua, where an allied force of Rajpūts under Rāṇo Sāṅgo's leadership attempted to stem the Mughal Bābur's advance into India. ***Bāṅkīdās***, p. 58, records that Rāv Jeso died of dysentery on March 16, 1527, the day prior to the battle.

Rāv Jeso granted the village of Rābhlāvās[13] in ***sāṃsaṇ*** to the Ratnūṃ Cāraṇ Bharam Rūpāvat.

Jeso's brother, Rāv Bhojo Sīhāvat, moved away from Rāhaṇ to his own village of Kuṛkī,[14] which ***Murārdān***, no. 2, p. 586, says that he first settled. Rāv Bhojo emerged from this village to cause a great deal of local disturbance during attempts to reassert rights to a greater share of the land and authority in Meṛto. Sometime during the early to mid-1520s, Rāv Vīramde Dūdāvat drove Bhojo out of Kuṛkī and gave this village to his own brother, Ratansī Dūdāvat.

Rāv Bhojo then settled in the village of Jaitāvās (or Jaitgaḍh),[15] which he found deserted. He and his brother, Rāv Gāṅgo, soon became involved in an intrigue with Kuṃvar Mālde Gāṅgāvat (Rāv of Jodhpur, 1532-62).[16] Kuṃvar Mālde played upon the two brothers' enmity toward Rāv Vīramde Dūdāvat and goaded them into an attack on the market square at Meṛto ca. 1530. This attack proved a complete failure, and Rāv Vīramde's Rajpūts under the command of Jodho Rāṭhoṛ Khaṅgār Jogāvat (no. 82) pursued Bhojo and Gāṅgo and their men

---

[13] Rābhlāvās village: located thirteen miles southwest of Meṛto, near Mokālo.

[14] Kuṛkī village: located twenty miles southeast of Meṛto.

[15] Jaitāvās village: located fifteen miles southeast of Meṛto, just to the north of Reyāṃ.

[16] ***Vigat***, 2:48, incorrectly states that all three brothers were involved here. These events took place several years after Rāv Jeso's death at Khanua in 1527.

from Meṛto, finally bringing them to battle near the village of Kusāṇo,[17] where they killed many of their Rajpūts and wounded both of the brothers.

Rāv Mālde continued to plot with Rāv Bhojo and Rāv Gāṅgo following his accession to the Jodhpur throne in 1532. He organized a series of raids against Meṛto with the connivance of Rāv Gāṅgo Sīhāvat, Daulat Khān of Nāgaur (no. 154), and Paṃvār Pañcāiṇ Karamcandot of Cāṭsū (no. 24). Rāv Mālde instigated these actions at the time he called Rāv Vīramde Dūdāvat to Jodhpur to take part in an expedition against the Sīndhaḷ Rāṭhoṛs of Bhādrājuṇ.[18] With each of these parties, Rāv Mālde played on a different theme: With Rāv Gāṅgo, the possibility of reasserting Varsiṅghot rule at Meṛto; with Daulat Khān, the opportunity of settling an old score left unfinished from the battle of Sevakī on November 2, 1529, when the Meṛtīyos captured a prize elephant of the Khān's; and with Paṃvār Pañcāiṇ, the chance to end a ***vair*** with the Meṛtīyos. These intrigues failed, however, due in large measure to the valiant efforts of Rāv Vīramde's ***pradhān***, Jaitmālot Akhairāj Bhādāvat (no. 69), in protecting Meṛto.

Rāv Bhojo came into conflict with Rāv Vīramde sometime later at the village of Kekīdṛo.[19] And there, Rāv Vīramde's commander, Khaṅgār Jogāvat (no. 82), and his Rajpūts killed Rāv Bhojo along with a number of his men.

Rāv Bhojo's brother, Rāv Gāṅgo Sīhāvat, lived for a number of years outside Meṛto. He took service under Rāv Mālde Gāṅgāvat of Jodhpur in 1532-33 and remained with the Rāv for ten years. He held the village of Āsop[20] in ***paṭo***. Then for unexplained reasons, Rāv Mālde had one of his military servants, Jaitsī Vāghāvat (no. 85), kill Rāv Gāṅgo in 1543-44. ***Murārdān***, no. 2, p. 586, records only that Jaitsī Vāghāvat took Rāv Gāṅgo by surprise one morning and killed him while he was sitting on the porch in front of his house. This text records the following ***sākh*** regarding Rāv Gāṅgo's death:

> Gallery seated, Gāṅgo murdered.

> ***Bāṅkīdās***, p. 58; ***Murārdān***, no. 2, pp. 584, 586-587; ***Vigat***, 2:47-50, 112, 141.

(no. 151) **Sahaiso Tejsīyot** (8-4)

Sahaiso Tejsiyot was a son of Tejsī Varsiṅghot (7-2) and a grandson of Rāv Varsiṅgh Jodhāvat (6-2) (no. 146), one of the original founders of Meṛto. Little information is available about his family. His father, Tejsī, lived for some

---

[17] Kusāṇo village: located twenty-eight miles southwest of Meṛto.

[18] Bhādrājuṇ village: located forty-eight miles south-southwest of Jodhpur.

[19] Kekīdṛo village: located fifteen miles south-southeast of Meṛto.

[20] Āsop village: located fifty miles northeast of Jodhpur.

years at the village of Reyāṃ.[21] which his grandfather, Rāv Varsiṅgh, granted to Tejsī for his maintenance. Tejsī was killed there during an outbreak of hostilities with some Kachvāhos.

Sahaiso himself was initially a military servant of Meṛtīyo Rāv Vīramde Dūdāvat (no. 105), but it is unclear from sources at hand if he held any lands. It is possible that he did not succeed his father to Reyāṃ village, for he left Rāv Vīramde and took service under Rāv Mālde Gāṅgāvat of Jodhpur when Rāv Mālde occupied Meṛto ca. 1535 and began distributing the villages of Meṛto among his military servants. The Rāv gave Sahaiso the ***paṭo*** of Reyāṃ and five other villages in return for his service. The chronicles relate that Sahaiso's acceptance of this ***paṭo*** so enraged Rāv Vīramde that he mounted a precipitous attack against Reyāṃ from his base at Ajmer against the better judgment of his Rajpūts.

Word reached Sahaiso of Rāv Vīramde's impending attack, and appeals for aid were dispatched to Rāv Mālde at Jodhpur and to his garrison at Raṛod,[22] where the Rāv had stationed a large ***sāth*** with some of his best warriors including Kūmpo Mahirājot (no. 95), Rāṇo Akhairājot (no. 28), and Jeso Bhairavdāsot (no. 48). Sahaiso donned a saffron robe (***kesarīyo***) on the morning of battle and proceeded outside the village gates along with five hundred Rajpūts, where cloths were spread upon the ground. They all took seats to wait, ready to fight and die in the defense of their village. Rāv Mālde's ***sāth*** from Raṛod soon arrived to join in the bloody fighting that took place that day at Reyāṃ.

Sahaiso survived this battle and remained in Rāv Mālde's service for a number of years after. He then fled from Mārvāṛ. ***Murārdān***, no. 2, p. 587, records that Sahaiso feared for his life after Rāv Mālde had Sahaiso's paternal uncle, Rāv Gāṅgo Sīhāvat (8-2) (no. 149), killed at his ***paṭo*** village of Āsop[23] in 1543-44. Sources available do not provide reasons behind Rāv Gāṅgo's murder, nor do they give details about Sahaiso's flight from Reyāṃ.

Sahaiso's son, Veno Sahaisāvat (9-2), was killed during the battle at Reyāṃ ca. 1535.

Sahaiso granted the village of Lūṇkaraṇ rī Vāsṇī[24] in ***sāṃsaṇ*** to the Sīvaṛ Brāhmaṇ Purohit Girdhar Jīyāvat.

Bāṅkīdās, p. 58, 60; ***Khyāt***, 3:95; ***Murārdān***, no. 2, p. 586; ***Vigat***, 2:52-53, 112, 212.

---

[21] Reyāṃ village: located fifteen miles southeast of Meṛto.

[22] Raṛod village: located forty-nine miles west-northwest of Reyāṃ village.

[23] Āsop village: located thirty miles west-northwest of Meṛto.

[24] Lūṇkaraṇ rī Vāsṇī: located just to the south of Reyāṃ village.

(no. 152) **Sāṃvaḷdās Udaisiṅghot** (10-1)

Sāṃvaḷdās Udaisiṅghot was a grandson of Rāv Jeso Sīhāvat's (8-3) (no. 150) and fourth in line of descent from Rāv Varsiṅgh Jodhāvat (6-2) (no. 146), one of the original founders of Meṛto. No information is available about Sāṃvaḷdās's family or his early life. He appears first in the texts as a military servant of Rāv Mālde Gāṅgāvat of Jodhpur (1532-62) at the battle of Samel[25] in January of 1544. Sāṃvaḷdās survived the fighting at Samel, but he left Rāv Mālde's service soon afterwards in the wake of the Muslim occupation of eastern Mārvāṛ and Jodhpur, and traveled to Mevāṛ where he sought service under Sīsodīyo Rāṇo Udaisiṅgh Sāṅgāvat (ca. 1537-72; no. 17). Sāṃvaḷdās was refused patronage in Mevāṛ for rather curious reasons that display some interesting characteristics of this Rajpūt.

"Bāt Māṇḍaṇ Kūmpāvat rī,"[26] ff. 66-70, relates that Rāṇo Udaisiṅgh honored Sāṃvaḷdās when he first arrived at Cītoṛ, and sent several of his personal servants to assist Sāṃvaḷdās at his camp. Instead of receiving the Rāṇo's servants with appropriate regard, however, Sāṃvaḷdās proceeded to insult them by asking an older man among them to perform the menial task of warming water for his bath, and "putting his hands on" others when they did not respond quickly enough to his demands. This touching of the servants infuriated the Rāṇo who then refused to retain Sāṃvaḷdās as his military servant.

Other sources confirm that Sāṃvaḷdās was both crude and boastful, and that he often created problems for himself because of his loose tongue and his obtuse, insensitive manner. Incidents that occurred after his leaving Mevāṛ bear out these propensities.

Sāṃvaḷdās proceeded to Vāṃsvāḷo after his offer of service was refused in Mevāṛ. The Rāvaḷ of Vāṃsvāḷo welcomed him, and granted him two ***paṭo***s. One of these had been held by Rāṭhoṛ Māṇḍaṇ Kūmpāvat (no. 95), who was in Vāṃsvāḷo just prior to Sāṃvaḷdās's arrival. The other had been the ***paṭo*** of an important Rajpūt of Vāṃsvāḷo. When presenting these ***paṭo***s to Sāṃvaḷdās, the Rāvaḷ suggested that Sāṃvaḷdās should be honored to received lands held by Māṇḍaṇ Kūmpāvat, a great Rajpūt of Mārvāṛ, and lands held by a great Rajpūt of Vāṃsvāḷo. Sāṃvaḷdās could only reply in his oblique fashion that he had received many such grants, and that he did not know any Māṇḍaṇ, son of Kūmpo.

A servant of Māṇḍaṇ Kūmpāvat's happened to be at the Rāvaḷ's court at this time. He overheard Sāṃvaḷdās's slight and informed Māṇḍaṇ about what had happened. Māṇḍaṇ was greatly offended, and vowed to avenge his honor before Sāṃvaḷdās. Several of his Rajpūts cautioned him against involving two Rāṭhoṛ brotherhoods in hostilities, but he was not dissuaded.

---

[25] Samel village: located twenty-four miles southwest of Ajmer.

[26] "Bāt Māṇḍaṇ Kūmpāvat rī," in ***Aitihāsik Tavārīkhvār Vārtā***, MS no. 1234, Rājasthānī Śodh Saṃsthān, Caupāsnī, ff. 66-70.

Māṇḍaṇ then returned to Vāṃsvāḷo and sought out Sāṃvaḷdās at his village. Sāṃvaḷdās had learned of Māṇḍaṇ's vow, and he immediately became alarmed when he heard riders approaching. His wife, a Vaḍgūjar, tried to reassure him. But Sāṃvaḷdās explained to her that Māṇḍaṇ Kūmpāvat had come to challenge him because of his insult of Māṇḍaṇ at the Rāṇo's court.

Māṇḍaṇ and his Rajpūts broke into the male apartment (***koṭṛī***) of the house while Sāṃvaḷdās and his wife were talking, and killed thirty of Sāṃvaḷdās's Rajpūts. Māṇḍaṇ himself then climbed to the second floor bedroom (***māḷīyo***) where Sāṃvaḷdās was hiding. Sāṃvaḷdās leaped down into the house of a neighboring Brāhmaṇ and took refuge at the last minute. In his absence, Sāṃvaḷdās's Vaḍgūjar wife confronted Māṇḍaṇ wearing her husband's garments, and saying, "You brother has indeed fled; I stand [before you]." Māṇḍaṇ then went away. But while going, he killed Sāṃvaḷdās's mother and wounded one on Sāṃvaḷdās's elephants. Sāṃvaḷdās's actions of fleeing and leaving his wife to face Māṇḍaṇ in his stead, and then allowing Māṇḍaṇ to kill his mother and wound one of his elephants greatly dishonored him.

Sāṃvaḷdās's name disappears from the chronicles following this series of events until his re-emergence in Mārvāṛ in the early 1560s as a military servant of Rāv Mālde Gāṅgāvat of Jodhpur. He was at the Rāv's court prior to the battle of Meṛto in 1562. The Rāv sent him to Meṛto with his son, Kuṃvar Candrasen Māldevot, and other Rajpūts to reinforce Rāṭhoṛ Devīdās Jaitāvat (no. 65) and the Rajpūts stationed with him at the Mālgaḍh. While Kuṃvar Candrasen left Meṛto soon after when he realized that the situation there was untenable, Sāṃvaḷdās remained behind with his men to support Rāṭhoṛ Devīdās.

The chronicles relate that one night after Sāṃvaḷdās's arrival at the Mālgaḍh, he once again created problems for himself because of injudicious remarks he made. On this occasion, he offended Rāṭhoṛ Prithīrāj Kūmpāvat (no. 97), a brother of Māṇḍaṇ Kūmpāvat, and Sonagaro Mānsiṅgh Akhairājot (no. 10), both of whom were present at Rāv Mālde's camp. He called Prithīrāj a ***vāṇīyo*** ("moneylender, Baniya"), and referred to Mānsiṅgh as a little one-eyed man, casting aspersions upon the prowess of both these warriors. Prithīrāj Kūmpāvat and Mānsiṅgh Akhairājot reciprocated in kind, making disparaging remarks about Sāṃvaḷdās and his dishonorable actions before Māṇḍaṇ Kūmpāvat in Vāṃsvāḷo (see "Aitihāsik Bātāṃ," pp. 53-54, of the **translated text** for details of this interesting exchange).

Sāṃvaḷdās remained at the camp despite the ill-will he had generated, and soon after proved himself to be a brave if somewhat foolhardy warrior. He carried out a night attack against the Mughal camp, killing a number of Mughal soldiers and causing great commotion among their ranks. Several of his men were killed here, however, and Sāṃvaḷdās's foot was badly wounded. His Rajpūts finally remonstrated with him and brought him from the field in order to prevent further bloodshed.

Rāv Jaimal Vīramdevot (no. 107) and Mīrzā Sharafu'd-Dīn Ḥusayn brought a force from the Mughal camp the following morning and caught

Sāṃvaḷdās and his Rajpūts near the village of Reyāṃ,[27] where they had withdrawn. There the Mughals killed Sāṃvaḷdās.

"Aitihāsik Bātāṃ," pp. 53-54; ***Bāṅkīdās***, pp. 16, 58; "Bāt Māṇḍaṇ Kūmpāvat rī," in ***Aitihāsik Tavarīkhvār Vārtā***, MS 1234, Rājasthānī Śodh Saṃsthān, Caupāsnī, ff. 66-70; ***Vigat***, 2:63-64.

[27] Reyāṃ village: located fifteen miles southwest of Meṛto.

Figure 34. Varsiṅghot Meṛtīyo Rāṭhoṛs

(1-1) Rāv Salkho

(2-1) Vīram Salkhāvat

(3-1) Rāv Cūṇḍo Vīramot

(4-1) Rāv Riṇmal Cūṇḍāvat

(5-1) Rāv Jodho Riṇmalot

(6-1) Rāv Dūdo Jodhāvat   (6-2) **Rāv Varsiṅgh Jodhāvat**
(**Varsiṅghot
Meṛtīyos**)

(7-1) **Rāv Sīho Varsiṅghot**   (7-2) Tejsī Varsiṅghot

(8-1) **Rāv Bhojo Sīhāvat**   (8-2) **Rāv Gāṅgo Sīhāvat**   (8-3) **Rāv Jeso Sīhāvat**   (8-4) **Sahaiso Tejsīyot**

(9-1) Udaisiṅgh Jesāvat   (9-2) Veno Sahaisāvat

(10-1) **Sāṃvaḷdās Udaisiṅghot**

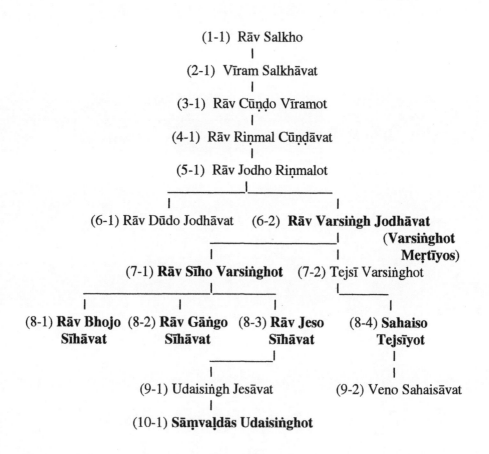

Vīdāvat Rāṭhoṛs

(no. 153) **Kalyāṇmal Udaikaraṇot** (8-1)

The Vīdāvat Rāṭhoṛs

The Vīdāvat Rāṭhoṛs descend from Vīdo Jodhāvat (6-1), a son of Rāv Jodho Riṇmalot (5-1), ruler of Maṇḍor and Jodhpur (ca. 1453-89). Vīdo was born of Rāṇī Sāṅkhlī Nāraṅgdejī, a daughter of Rūṇeco Sāṅkhlo Paṃvār Māṇḍaṇ Jaitāvat.[1] ***Vigat***, 1:39, records that Rāv Jodho gave Vīdo and his elder uterine brother, Bīko Jodhāvat (no. 42), the areas of Jāṅgaḷu[2] and an open desert tract to the north of Jāṅgaḷu. This tract was to become the new kingdom of Bīkāner during his division of the lands of Mārvāṛ among his brothers and sons following the founding of Jodhpur in 1459. ***Vigat*** then states with much foreshortening of time, that "Rāv Bīko sat on the throne [at Bīkāner]. And [Rāv Jodho] gave Vīdo Lāḍṇūṃ [and] Droṇpur, the lands of the Mohils, with one hundred and forty villages."

Vīdo's and his brother Bīko's association with Jāṅgaḷu dates more precisely from the mid-1460s, when they first went to this area at the request of Jāṅgaḷvo Sāṅkhlo Nāpo Māṇakrāvat (no. 26). Nāpo Sāṅkhlo had come to Rāv Jodho's court at Jodhpur to seek aid against the Baloc, who were raiding the Sāṅkhlos' lands and driving the Sāṅkhlos away. Nāpo Sāṅkhlo offered Bīko Jodhāvat his support and that of all the Sāṅkhlos in regaining these lands. Bīko and Vīdo Jodhāvat then rode forth with their contingents of retainers. While Bīko Jodhāvat made himself master ***(dhaṇī)*** at Jāṅgaḷu, securing this land for the Sāṅkhlos, and proceeded upon the conquest of his own kingdom (of Bīkāner) to the north,[3] Vīdo and his descendants settled in the areas of Lāḍṇūṃ and Chāpar-Droṇpur to the south and southeast of Bīkāner, respectively.

Vīdo's association with Lāḍṇū and Chāpar-Droṇpur followed the conquest of these areas by his father, Rāv Jodho, between the years 1466-74. The ***Khyāt*** of Naiṇsī, 3:158-166, relates the story of this conquest. It tells that Rāv Jodho had married one of his daughters, Rājāṃbāī,[4] to Ajīt Sāṃvatsīyot, the

---

[1] See ***supra***, **Marriage and Family Lists of the Rulers of Jodhpur**, Jodho Riṇmalot, Rāṇī no. 3, S - Vīdo. Uncertainties regarding the identity of this Rāṇī's father are discussed in this section.

[2] Jāṅgaḷu village: located some one hundred miles to the north of Jodhpur, and twenty-four miles due south of Bīkāner .

[3] For more information about Bīko Jodhāvat, see ***supra***, "Bīkāvat Rāṭhoṛs."

[4] See ***supra***, **Marriage and Family Lists of the Rulers of Jodhpur**, Jodho Riṇmalot, Rāṇī no. 2, D - Rājāṃbāī.

powerful leader of the Mohil Cahuvāṇs of Chāpar-Droṇpur. As Rāv Jodho himself grew in stature, he began to contemplate ways to bring the land of the Mohils under his own authority.

One time when Mohil Ajīt came to Maṇḍor, Rāv Jodho perceived, "If Ajīt were killed, then the land would come [into my hands]" (***Khyāt***, 3:158). The Rāv then began to plot Ajīt's murder. But Ajīt's wife's mother (***sāsū***), Rāṇī Bhāṭiyāṇī Pūrāṃ, learned of this plan and sent word to Ajīt's ***pradhān***s and personal attendants (***khavās***):

> The Rāvjī has conspired against you; if you stay, then [you] will [only] have trouble (***ibid.***, 3:159).

Ajīt's ***pradhān***s and nobles (***umrāv***s) quickly devised a means to take Ajīt from Maṇḍor without his knowledge of Rāv Jodho's plot. They knew that if they told him of the plot, he would not leave, for he had vowed never to flee from battle. They told him instead that the Yādavs had come against Ajīt's father's brother's son, Rāṇo Bachrāj Sāṅgāvat, and that Rāṇo Bachrāj was under siege in Chāpar-Droṇpur and had sent word asking Ajīt to come quickly to his aid.

Ajīt and his men had the drums sounded, announcing their departure, and they set out from Maṇḍor. When Rāv Jodho heard the drums, he immediately realized that his plot had been exposed, and he gave pursuit. The parties drew near each other in the vicinity of the towns of Chāpar and Droṇpur. It was here that Ajīt's ***pradhān***s confessed to Ajīt that they had brought him away from Jodhpur when they received a warning from his wife's mother. Their words greatly offended Ajīt, who said, "You have caused my firm vow (***sabḷo paṇ***) to be diminished" (***ibid.***, 3:160).

A battle followed, during which Ajīt was killed along with forty-five of his men. Rājāṃbāī became a ***satī*** after Rāv Jodho's return to Maṇḍor with news of her husband's death. A great enmity (***sabḷo vair***) then broke out between the Rāṭhoṛs and the Mohils.

> The Rāṭhoṛs [were] strong, [and] the ***ṭhākurāī*** of the Mohils was strong, but [there was] little unity between the brotherhoods (***bhāībandhe meḷ ghaṇo koī nahīṃ***) (***ibid.***)

A year slipped by as Rāv Jodho waited patiently for an opportunity to attack. When one arose, he gathered together the whole brotherhood and came upon the Mohils. He met Ajīt's father's brother's son, Rāṇo Bachrāj Sāṅgāvat, in battle and killed him along with two hundred and sixty-five of his men (***māṇas***). Rāv Jodho then assumed control over Chāpar-Droṇpur in his own name. ***Khyāt***, 3:166, gives the date of 1466-67 for Rāv Jodho's victory.

Rāṇo Bachrāj's son, Kuṃvar Megho Bachrājot, was not killed in this battle, and Rāv Jodho was unable to settle the land in the face of his attacks. The Rāv quickly perceived that while Megho lived, he would not be able to bring the land under his control. He returned to Maṇḍor after only two months, leaving the land once again to the Mohils.

Rāṇo Megho died some years later. Dissension then broke out among the Mohils. The land became divided among the brothers (*bhāyāṃ vaṇṭ huī*). ***Khyāt***, 3:161, states, "The kingdom (*ṭhākurāī*) grew weak. There became sixteen shares." The Mohils bickered among themselves over these shares, and seeing their weakness, Rāv Jodho again mounted an expedition against Chāpar-Droṇpur. The Mohils offered no resistance this time, and Rāv Jodho was able to establish his authority over the land in 1474-75.

Khyāt states that during this period, two Mohils from the former ruling family, Rāṇo Vairsal Meghāvat, the son and successor to Rāṇo Megho Bachrājot, and Vairsal's younger half-brother, Narbad Meghāvat, who was the daughter's son (*dohitro*) of Rāv Jodho's elder half-brother, Rāṭhoṛ Rāvat Kāndhaḷ Riṇmalot (5-2), left Mārvāṛ in search of support for the recovery of their lands. Narbad Meghāvat eventually proceeded to Delhi to petition Bahlūl Lodī, Afghan ruler of the Sultānate (1451-89), for his support. Rāṭhoṛ Vāgho Kāndhaḷot (6-4), who was Narbad Meghāvat's mother's brother (*māmo*), was with him. Sultān Bahlūl Lodī agreed to help, and he ordered Sāraṅg Khān Paṭhāṇ, ***sūbedār*** of Hisar, to march against Rāv Jodho with five thousand of his warriors.

Khyāt, 3:162-164, records that Rāv Jodho came with six thousand of his Rajpūts to confront Sāraṅg Khān and the Mohils. The armies encamped on the borders of Chāpar and Fatehpur and made preparations for battle. According to ***Khyāt***, 3:163, Rāv Jodho, knowing of Rāṭhoṛ Vāgho Kāndhaḷot's presence with the opposing army, summoned Vāgho in secret before the battle and reproached him, saying:

> Fine! You [there], brother's son (***bhatījo***)! [You] strap on a sword on behalf of the Mohils [and march] against us. Will you have [your] elder brothers' wives (***bhojāyāṃ***) and women (***bairāṃ***) imprisoned?

Vāgho Kāndhaḷot then realized that what he had done was not proper. He became Rāv Jodho's ally, promising to do what the Rāv thought best. Vāgho said to the Rāv that the Mohils' horses were weak and slow of foot, and that he would, therefore, have them fight on foot, while he would inform the Paṭhāṇs that they should fight on horseback.

> The Mohils will fight on foot; their force will be [on the] left, and the force of the Paṭhāṇs will be on the right. Thus, when [the armies] gather, the Mohils' ***sāth*** will be on foot; you should thrust [your] horses upon them. The ***sāth*** [will be] on foot, so [it] will run away. The Turks will be riding; [you] should attack them with your swords. Those who are to die will die; the other Turks will flee (***ibid***., 2:163-164).

On the day of the battle, the Rāṭhoṛ ***sāth*** rode upon the Mohils with their horses. The Mohils could not withstand this attack on foot and fled from the field. Rāv Jodho's warriors then fought a great battle with Sāraṅg Khān. ***Khyāt***, 3:164, records that Sāraṅg Khān was killed and remained on the field with five hundred and fifty-five of his men (***māṇas***), while the rest, being wounded, fled. The field came into Rāv Jodho's hands. He returned to Droṇpur and proceeded to consolidate his control over the land.

Rāv Jodho afterwards placed his son, Jogo Jodhāvat (6-3), in charge of the land. Jogo was a simple ***ṭhākur*** (***bhoḷo so ṭhākur***) and soon proved himself incompetent to rule. The Mohils made continuing inroads from the countryside. Kuṃvar Jogo's wife (***vahū***), the Jhālī, sent word to her husband's father (***susro***), saying:

> There is no auspiciousness (***lakhaṇ***) in your son. And the land you/we have conquered is being lost [to the Mohils]. It would appear [that] you should devise a remedy (***ilāj kījyo***) (***ibid***., 3:165).

Rāv Jodho gave Chāpar-Droṇpur to his son, Vīdo Jodhāvat, and he recalled Jogo to Jodhpur. Vīdo quickly reversed the misrule that had developed under Jogo and established a firm authority in his own name. To settle the conflict with the Mohils, he allowed them to return to their lands and granted these lands to them in ***paṭo*** in return for their military service (***cākrī***). Vīdo also married among the Mohils, taking a daughter of Mohil Jabo Sīṅgaṭot as his wife. Jabo Sīṅgaṭot was a rich and influential ***ṭhākur*** and he presented Vīdo with a large dowry of one hundred horses, two hundred camels, and wealth the equal of a ***lākh*** of rupees. In return, Vīdo helped Jabo drive a faction of Mohils from the area with whom Jabo was in conflict. Vīdo thereby:

> established firm authority. [He] again settled Droṇpur. [And he] made Droṇpur a large habitation (***vaḍī vastī***) (***ibid***., 3:166).

Vīdo now assumed the title of ***rāv***.

There are inconsistencies in the material in Naiṇsī's ***Khyāt*** regarding Rāv Jodho's conquest of Chāpar-Droṇpur and his battle with Sāraṅg Khān. Elsewhere, ***Khyāt***, 3:21-22, states that Rāv Jodho came to battle with Sāraṅg Khān when his son, Bīko Jodhāvat (6-2) (ruler of Bīkāner, ca. 1485-1504), called him to help settle the ***vair*** caused by the death of Rāṭhoṛ Kāndhaḷ Riṇmalot (5-2). This ***vair*** is said to have arisen a number of years after Rāv Jodho's conquest of Chāpar-Droṇpur. Kāndhaḷ Riṇmalot was instrumental in helping Bīko Jodhāvat consolidate his rule at Bīkāner, and after the foundation for the new fort at Bīkāner was laid in 1485, Kāndhaḷ went to live in the area of Hisar. There he began raiding and looting villages, and he soon came into conflict with the ***sūbedār***, Sāraṅg Khān. They met in battle ca. 1489. During the fighting, Kāndhaḷ was killed.

Rāv Jodho is then said to have ridden to join his son, Rāv Bīko, in avenging Kāndhaḷ's death. It is told that they met Sāraṅg Khān in battle near Chāpar and Droṇpur, and during this battle, Rāv Bīko's own son, Naro Bīkāvat, is credited with killing Sāraṅg Khān.[5] It appears from this material that Rāv Jodho's conflict with Sāraṅg Khān and Sāraṅg Khān's death came later, not at the time of Rāv Jodho's conquest of Chāpar-Droṇpur itself.

Ojhā, 4:1:246-248, notes that ***Dayāldās rī Khyāt***, which gives a detailed history of Bīkāner, also presents a different version of the conquest of Chāpar-Droṇpur. ***Dayāldās rī Khyāt*** records that it was after Vīdo Jodhāvat had assumed his position of rule in Chāpar-Droṇpur that the Mohils, Rāṇo Vairsal and Narbad Meghāvat, came against him with Sāraṅg Khān. Rāṭhoṛ Kāndhaḷ Riṇmalot's son, Vāgho Kāndhaḷot, was with the Mohils. Vīdo Jodhāvat was unable to maintain his position in the area in the face of pressure from the Mohils, and he retreated to Bīkāner where he took refuge with his uterine brother, Rāv Bīko Jodhāvat.

Rāv Bīko is said to have sent an appeal to his father, Rāv Jodho, at Jodhpur at this time, asking for help in recovering the lands of Chāpar-Droṇpur. But Rāv Jodho demurred and refused this request. The Rāv's wife, Rāṇī Hāḍī Jasmādejī,[6] was angry with Vīdo because he had refused her the lands of Lāḍṇūṃ, which she had requested. Vīdo thereby gained Rāv Jodho's displeasure.

Bīko Jodhāvat then gathered his own army and rode with his paternal uncle (***kāko***), Rāvat Kāndhaḷ Riṇmalot, and others against the Mohils. The Johīyo Rajpūts are said to have joined with Rāv Bīko on this campaign. Sometime before the battle, Rāv Bīko summoned Kāndhaḷ's, son, Vāgho Kāndhaḷot, in secret from the enemy camp, and reproached him, saying:

> My paternal uncle, Kāndhaḷ, became such [a great warrior] that he destroyed the kingdom of the Jāṭs and established authority over a new region [which became my kingdom of Bīkāner], while you [Kāndhaḷ's son] have come against me . . . Doing as you have done is not proper.

Bīko's words shamed Vāgho, and he then became Bīko's ally against the Mohils. As in the story from Naiṇsī's ***Khyāt***, he gave his word that he would advise the Mohils to fight on foot, and that Sāraṅg Khān's army would be on the right. Bīko's force emerged victorious. Rāv Bīko then entrusted his uterine brother, Vīdo, with the rule of Chāpar-Droṇpur and returned to Bīkāner.

---

[5] The dating of Kāndhaḷ's death and the following battle against Sāraṅg Khān are conjectural. Major K. D. Erskine, ed. ***Rajputana Gazetteers:*** Volume III-A, ***The Western Rajputana States Residency and the Bikaner Agency*** (Allahabad: The Pioneer Press, 1909), p. 315, places Kāndhaḷ's death in 1490. This date falls after Rāv Jodho's death, which according to most sources took place on April 6, 1489. This date is unconfirmed by inscriptional evidence, however, and is, therefore, also conjectural. See: Ojhā, 4:1:250, n. 2.

[6] Rāṇī Hāḍī Jasmādejī was Rāv Jodho's favored wife. It was her sons who succeeded Rāv Jodho to the throne of Jodhpur. See ***supra***, **Marriage and Family Lists of the Rulers of Jodhpur**, Jodho Riṇmalot, Rāṇī no. 1.

There is no mention in this account of Sāraṅg Khān's death, which appears to have occurred only later, when the combined Rāṭhoṛ armies met him in battle while avenging the death of Kāndhaḷ Riṇmalot. Ojhā prefers Dayāldās's account of the final conquest of Chāpar-Droṇpur. He notes that the Vīdāvats had always been closely allied with Bīkāner, not with Jodhpur. Vīdo and Bīko were uterine brothers who had come to this area together, and very early developed strong ties of support. Ojhā states that is appears more credible that Vīdo would have turned to his brother, Bīko, for support, than to his father, Rāv Jodho.

> ***Bāṅkīdās***, pp. 8, 80; Erskine, ed. ***Rajputana Gazetteers:*** Volume III-A, ***The Western Rajputana States Residency and the Bikaner Agency***, p. 315; Karni Singh, ***The Relations of the House of Bikaner with the Central Powers, 1465-1949*** (New Delhi: Munshiram Manoharlal, 1974), pp. 24-25; ***Khyāt***, 3:21-22, 31, 158-166, 230-231; ***Murārdān***, no. 2, p. 98; Ojhā, 4:1:244-250, 5:1:101-105; ***Vigat***, 1:39.

(no. 153) **Kalyāṇmal Udaikaraṇot** (8-1)

Kalyāṇmal Udaikaraṇot was a son of Udaikaraṇ Vīdāvat (7-1) and grandson of Rāv Vīdo Jodhāvat (6-1), ruler of Chāpar-Droṇpur in the late fifteenth century. No information is available about his family, except the date of the death of his father, Udaikaraṇ, in 1518-19. Local sources provide no details about the circumstances behind his death.

Kalyāṇmal succeeded to the rulership of Chāpar-Droṇpur. He was a military servant of his paternal grandfather's brother's son, Rāṭhoṛ Rāv Lūṇkaraṇ Bīkāvat (7-3), ruler of Bīkāner (1505-26; no. 44). Kalyāṇmal was also closely associated with the Sekhāvat Kachvāhos of Amarsar and Sīkargaḍh (near Āmber) in central Rājasthān. Kachvāho Rāymal Sekhāvat (no. 22) was Kalyāṇmal's maternal grandfather and close companion. He also served along with Kalyāṇmal under Rāv Lūṇkaraṇ of Bīkāner.

Accounts about Kalyāṇmal center upon his involvement in the Bīkāvat Rāṭhoṛ campaign against the Muslims of Narnol in eastern Rājasthān in 1526. Rāv Lūṇkaraṇ set out on an expedition against Narnol in this year with a contingent of Vīdāvats in accompaniment. They passed through Chāpar-Droṇpur on their way to Narnol. ***Khyāt***, 3:151, records that Rāv Lūṇkaraṇ remarked as he viewed Kalyāṇmal's lands, "This place is such that some ***kuṃvar*** [of mine] should be kept [here]."

Kalyāṇmal overheard this remark and immediately became suspicious of the Rāv's intentions. He and his men continued on with Rāv Lūṇkaraṇ to Narnol. But Kalyāṇmal withheld Vīdāvat support from Rāv Lūṇkaraṇ during the battle with the Muslims at the village of Ḍhosī (near Narnol). Rāv Lūṇkaraṇ was killed there on March 30, 1526 along with three of his sons.

Rāv Lūṇkaraṇ's son, Rāv Jaitsī Lūṇkaraṇot (8-3), succeeded him to the throne of Bīkāner (1526-42; no. 45). He brought Chāpar-Droṇpur under direct attack, holding Kalyāṇmal directly responsible for his father's and brothers' deaths. Kalyāṇmal was forced to flee his homeland in October of 1527, and take refuge at Nāgaur. Rāv Jaitsī then placed Kalyāṇmal's father's brother's son, Sāṅgo Saṃsārcandot (8-2), on the seat of rule at Chāpar-Droṇpur.

Kalyāṇmal's activities after this time are uncertain. The date and circumstances of his death are also unknown.[7]

> ***Khyāt***, 3:101-102, 151-152; L. P. Tessitori, "A Progress Report on the Work done during the year 1917 in connection with the Bardic and Historical Survey of Rajputana," ***Journal of the Asiatic Society of Bengal***, N.S. 15 (1919), p. 12; Ojhā, 5:1:117, n. 3, 118, 123-124.

---

[7] See: ***Khyāt***, 3:101-102, of the **translated text** for material that mentions Kalyāṇmal in association with Meṛtīyo Rāv Vīramde Dūdāvat in the period immediately following the battle of Samel in January of 1544. This material appears of dubious historical validity, and has, therefore, not been included in this Biographical Note (see n. 113 to ***Khyāt***, 3:101, for an explanation).

Figure 35. Vīdāvat Rāṭhoṛs

(1-1) Rāv Salkho

(2-1) Vīram Salkhāvat

(3-1) Rāv Cūṇḍo Vīramot

(4-1) Rāv Riṇmal Cūṇḍāvat

(5-1) Rāv Jodho Riṇmalot

(5-2) Rāvat Kāndhaḷ Riṇmalot

(6-1) Vīdo Jodhāvat (**Vīdāvats**)

(6-2) Rāv Bīko Jodhāvat (Bīkāvats)

(6-3) Jogo Jodhāvat

(6-4) Vāgho Kāndhaḷot

(7-1) Udaikaraṇ Vīdāvat

(7-2) Saṃsārcand Vīdāvat

(7-3) Rāv Lūṇkaraṇ Bīkāvat

(8-1) **Kalyāṇmal Udaikaraṇot**

(8-2) Sāṅgo Saṃsārcandot

(8-3) Rāv Jaitsī Lūṇkaraṇot

Khānzāda Khāns

(no. 154) **Muḥammad Daulat Khān (Daulatīyo)** (8-1)
(no. 155) **Sarkhel Khān**

The Khānzāda Khāns of Nāgaur

Nāgaur and its surrounding areas of the Savāḷakh[1] were under the control of a Muslim family known as "Khānzāda" or "Nāgaurī" from the beginning of the fifteenth century and into the mid-sixteenth century. This family adopted the title of ***khān*** and was related by blood to the sultāns of Gujarat.

The first ruler of this line was Shams Khān I (ca. 1405-18) (2-2). He was called "Dandānī" ("of the teeth") because of his large protruding front teeth. Shams Khān I Dandānī was a younger brother of Zafar Khān (2-1), who in 1405-06 became Sultān Muzaffar Shāh, the first independent Muslim ruler of Gujarat. Their common ancestor was a Ṭāṅk Rajpūt named Sadhāran from Thanesar in the Punjab, who had converted to Islam and taken service at the court of Sultān Muḥammad b. Tughluq (1325-51) at Delhi. Sadhāran found favor with the Sultān who awarded him the title of Wajīhu'l-Mulk and promoted him to the office of cupbearer (***sharābdār***). Sadhāran's two sons, the elder, Zafar Khān (b. June 30, 1342), and his younger brother, Shams Khān, became cupbearers at the court of Firūz Shāh Tughluq (1351-88), and were eventually promoted to the rank of ***amīr***.

In 1391 during the reign of Muḥammad Shāh III Tughluq (1389-92), Zafar Khān was sent to Gujarat to quell the rebellion of the local governor. Zafar Khān's brother, Shams Khān, either went with him or followed soon after. Zafar Khān placed his authority over Nāgaur and surrounding areas on his way to Gujarat, and placed Jalāl Khān Khokhar at Nāgaur as governor, while he proceeded on to Gujarat. He was able to assert his authority in Gujarat, and over the next decade as Sultānate rule under the Tughluqs at Delhi collapsed, he proclaimed independent rule and assumed the title of Sultān Muzaffar Shāh in 1405-06 at his capitol of Patan.

Following his assumption of rule, Sultān Muzaffar sent his brother, Shams Khān Dandānī, to replace Jalāl Khān Khokhar at Nāgaur. Shams Khān I Dandānī ruled there ca. 1405-18. He and his successors up until the time of

---

[1] The Savāḷakh constitutes an area of central and northwestern Rājasthān that includes Nāgaur, Ḍīḍvāṇo, Sāmbhar, Khāṭū, and Lāḍṇūṃ.

Nāgaur: located seventy-five miles north-northeast of Jodhpur.
Ḍīḍvāṇo: located fifty-four miles east-northeast of Nāgaur.
Sāmbhar: located ninety-five miles east-southeast of Nāgaur.
Khāṭū: located thirty-six miles east-southeast of Nāgaur.
Lāḍṇūṃ: located fifty-two miles northeast of Nāgaur.

Muḥammad Khān I (ca. 1495-1520) adopted the title of "Masnad-i 'ālī," which signified their independence at Nāgaur.

Shams Khān I was succeeded by his son, Firūz Khān I (3-1), who ruled for over thirty years, ca. 1418-51. He spent the first part of his reign protecting his territory against inroads from Sīsodīyo Rāṇo Mokaḷ Lākhāvat of Cītoṛ (ca. 1421-33). Rāṇo Mokaḷ was able to wrest control over the eastern regions of Nāgaur territory. An inscription of Firūz Khān's brother, Mujāhid Khān (3-2), dated May 31, 1437, records that the Rāṇo held authority over Ḍīḍvāṇo and Sāmbhar, areas over which Mujāhid Khān later reasserted his own authority. The Rāṭhoṛs of Maṇḍor also made inroads into Nāgaur in this period under Rāv Cūṇḍo Vīramot. Rāv Cūṇḍo is said to have captured Nāgaur and then to have been killed fighting a combined army of Bhāṭīs from Jaisaḷmer and Muslims ca. 1423.[2]

Mujāhid Khān exercised independent rule over these eastern areas from 1435-36 through the end of Firūz Khān's rule. Aḥmad Shāh, Sultān of Gujarat, was active in the area, making an expedition against Cītoṛ in 1432-33 and coming to Nāgaur. Firūz Khān offered the Sultān a large sum as booty, but the Sultān declined, an indication of the good relations that held between these two regions at this time.

With Firūz Khān's death in 1451-52 and the succession of Firūz Khān's son, Shams Khān II (4-1), to rulership at Nāgaur, Mujāhid Khān quickly entered into the affairs of Nāgaur and usurped rule from Shams Khān. Shams Khān fled to Mevāṛ where he sought the aid of Sīsodīyo Rāṇo Kūmbho Mokaḷot (ca. 1433-68) in the recovery of lands. Rāṇo Kūmbho agreed to help Shams Khān on the condition that part of the fortification walls at Nāgaur fort be destroyed when the town was recovered. Shams Khān accepted this condition and, with the Rāṇo's help, succeeded in the recovery of Nāgaur. Mujāhid Khān was forced to flee to Malwa where he sought the protection and aid of Sultān Maḥmūd (1436-69).

Shams Khān II soon fell out with Rāṇo Kūmbho and fled to Gujarat where he sought the aid of Sultān Quṭb-al-dīn Aḥmad Shāh (1451-58). Over the next several years, Shams Khān and Mujāhid Khān vied for control at Nāgaur. The Rāṇo, who maintained his authority in this area, had to deal not only with pressures from Gujarat and Malwa, but also with the Rāṭhoṛ resurgence in Mārvāṛ under Jodho Riṇmalot (ruler of Maṇḍor and Jodhpur, ca. 1453-89). The Rāṇo fought a decisive battle at Nāgaur in the period before 1454-55 against an army of the Sultān of Gujarat, during which the Sultān's army was badly defeated. The Kīrtistumbha inscription from Cītoṛ commemorates the Rāṇo's victory and proclaims that the Rāṇo stole Nāgaur from the Sultān, demolished the fort there, captured many elephants and took many Muslim women prisoners, and then turned Nāgaur into a pasture for grazing.

The Rāṇo was finally forced to withdraw from Nāgaur following his defeat at Ajmer in 1454-55, when Sultān Maḥmūd Khaljī regained control of this

---

[2] See ***supra***, "Cūṇḍāvat Rāṭhoṛs," for more information about Rāv Cūṇḍo. Some historians place Rāv Cūṇḍo's attack against Nāgaur and his death in battle as early as 1408, during the rule of Shams Khān I Dandānī.

town after a fierce battle lasting five days. Shortly thereafter, Sultān Quṭb-al-dīn Aḥmad brought an army from Gujarat onto Mevāṛ. He forced the Rāṇo to agree to abandon Nāgaur and never again to enter this territory. Mujāhid Khān was then able to assert his authority at Nāgaur in 1454-55, and he remained in power there for the next thirteen years until 1467-68.

Mujāhid Khān's descendants continued to rule at Nāgaur until January of 1536, but from 1495 onwards, the Khānzāda rulers ceased using the title "Majlis-i 'ālī." Omission of this title in inscriptions may indicate some diminished independence, but local inscriptions make no reference to Delhi or Gujarat, so their status is unclear. It is known that during the reign of Muḥammad Khān I (ca. 1495-1520) (6-1), there was acknowledgment of the Lodī Sultān in Delhi. Two of Muḥammad Khān's sons sought to overthrow and kill him (Muḥammad Khān). They fled to the court of Sikandar Lodī (1488-1517) at Delhi upon their plot being discovered, and Muḥammad Khān then sent gifts to the Lodī court and acknowledged the Sultān. He ordered the Sultān's name to be read in ***khuṭba*** at Nāgaur, and to be printed on coins minted at Nāgaur. This acknowledgment appeased the Sultān but appears to have been nominal, for the Khānzāda family continued to rule independently at Nāgaur. This independence was fostered by the fact that the Rāṇo of Mevāṛ was no longer a force in the region, and relations between the Khānzāda family and the Rāṭhoṛs of Mārvāṛ also remained peaceful. Rāṭhoṛ Rāv Jodho Riṇmalot's marriage of a daughter to Salho Khān (Ṣalāh Khān,[3] ca. 1467-69) may have contributed to these good relations. It appears that in this period the Khāns maintained control over a sizable region around Nāgaur including the towns of Ḍīḍvāṇo, Lāḍṇūṃ, Khāṭū and Jayel[4].

Muḥammad Khān II (ca. 1526-36) (8-1) was the last of the Khānzāda rulers at Nāgaur. He is mentioned in Middle Mārvāṛī sources by the name of Daulat Khān or Daulatīyo. Information about him is limited and details about Rāv Mālde's conquest of his kingdom in January of 1536 when he sent the army of Jodhpur under his commander, Rāṭhoṛ Kūmpo Mahirājot (no. 95), are few. One document about Nāgaur notes:

> The rule of the khans of Nagaur came to an end when Maldev, the Raja of Jodhpur, took possession of Nagaur, apparently not without fierce resistance. It still echoes in the memory of people of Nagaur that the collapse of Islamic rule was followed by the demolition of the palaces of the khans in the fort, and most of the mosques and tombs in and around the town. The upper parts of the fort and the parts of the town wall which were also destroyed were later reconstructed by Maldev, reusing the stones of the demolished buildings, including their inscriptions. It is in

---

[3] See *supra*, **Marriage and Family Lists of the Rulers of Jodhpur**, Jodho Riṇmalot, Rāṇī n. 2, D - Bhāgāṃ.

[4] Jāyel: located twenty-seven miles east of Nāgaur.

> these walls that the epigraphs of the buildings of the Ghurids, the Khaljīs, and the khans themselves are to be found.[5]

This same source also notes that:

> The descendants of the khans continued to live as a distinguished family in Nagaur, but apparently without [any] official position. They retained the title of ***khānzāda***, but their names do not appear among the nobles of the Mughal court.[6]

> Dasharatha Sharma, ***Lectures on Rajput History and Culture*** (Delhi: Motilal Banarsidass, 1970), pp. 63-69; ***Khyāt***, 2:310-315; M. A. Chaghtā'ī, "Nāgaur--A Forgotten Kingdom," ***Bulletin of the Deccan College Research Institute***, Vol. III, Nos. 1-2 (November, 1940), pp. 166-185; Mehrdad Shokoohy and Natalie H. Shokoohy, ***Nagaur: Sultanate and Early Mughal History and Architecture of the District Nagaur, India*** (London: Royal Asiatic Society, 1993), pp. 1-20, 173; Ojhā, 2:607-620; ***Vigat***, 1:25, "Pariśiṣṭ 1 (gh) - Pargane Nāgor rau Hāl," 2:421.

(no. 154) **Muḥammad Daulat Khān (Daulatīyo)** (8-1)
(no. 155) **Sarkhel Khān**

Members of the Khānzāda Khān family figure in the texts under review in connection with the following events:

The Battle of Sevakī[7] - November 2, 1529

Rāv Gāṅgo Vāghāvat of Jodhpur (1515-32) spent much of his reign immersed in conflict over territory and authority in Mārvāṛ with his half-brother, Rāv Vīramde Vāghāvat (no. 84) of Sojhat,[8] and with his paternal uncle, Sekho Sūjāvat (no. 86), ***ṭhākur*** of Pīmpāṛ village in central Mārvāṛ.[9] One of Rāv Gāṅgo's important military servants, Ūhaṛ Rāṭhoṛ Hardās Mokaḷot (no. 144), added to the Rāv's difficulties by shifting his allegiance first to Rāv Vīramde at Sojhat and then to Sekho Sūjāvat. Hardās also entered into the household (***vās***)

---

[5] Shokoohy and Shokoohy, ***Nagaur: Sultanate and Early Mughal History and Architecture of the District Nagaur, India***, p. 20.

[6] ***Ibid.***

[7] Sevakī village: located twenty-three miles northeast of Jodhpur.

[8] Sojhat: located forty-six miles southeast of Jodhpur

[9] Pīmpāṛ village: located thirty-three miles east-northeast of Jodhpur.

of Sarkhel Khān at Nāgaur for a short time before joining Sekho Sūjāvat. Hardās and Sekho's plotting led directly toward preparations for battle, with Rāv Gāṅgo summoning the aid of his paternal relation from Bīkāner, Rāv Jaitsī Lūṇkaraṇot (ca. 1526-42), while Sekho and Hardās approached the Khānzāda Khāns at Nāgaur. ***Khyāt***, 3:90, records that Hardās offered to marry daughters to Sarkhel Khān and Daulat Khān in exchange for their support. The Muslims accepted this offer, and Sekho Sūjāvat then brought them to the village of Berāī,[10] where they encamped in wait for the approaching army of Jodhpur.

The identity of Sarkhel Khān is uncertain. He appears to have been a member of the Khānzāda family with a position of importance, for he commanded the force of eighty elephants brought from Nāgaur to take part in the battle. The name Sarkhel is perhaps the Middle Mārvāṛī term for the Persian ***sar-khail***, commander of a troop of horse or company of men (***khail***).[11] The Rāṭhoṛ chronicles may mistakenly have used this term as the man's personal name, when in fact it was his title as Daulat Khān's military commander.

The battle at Sevakī was a decisive victory for Rāv Gāṅgo. Daulat Khān and Sarkhel Khān fled ignominiously from the field after suffering loss of men and elephants, and both Sekho Sūjāvat and Hardās Mokaḷot were killed.

The attack against Meṛto, ca. 1532

Soon after becoming ruler of Jodhpur in May of 1532, Rāv Mālde Gāṅgāvat began plotting against Meṛtīyo Rāv Vīramde Dūdāvat (no. 105). Rāv Mālde had held enmity toward the Meṛtīyos since the battle of Sevakī, when the Meṛtīyos captured one of Daulat Khān's prized elephants that had ran amok from this battle, and later refused to give this elephant to Kuṃvar Mālde when he demanded it. Rāv Mālde used the Meṛtīyos' capture of the elephant to goad Daulat Khān into attacking Meṛto while Rāv Vīramde and other Meṛtīyos were drawn from Meṛto to take part in an expedition against the Sīndhaḷs of Bhādrājuṇ.[12]

Rāv Vīramde grew suspicious of Rāv Mālde's intentions while in the Rāv's camp, and he sent a Rebārī messenger to Meṛto with a warning. Jaitmālot Rāṭhoṛ Akhairāj Bhādāvat (no. 69), a ***pradhān*** of Meṛto, also suspected subterfuge. He left Rāv Vīramde's camp without requesting leave from Rāv Vīramde and reached Meṛto just as the Rāv's messenger arrived with his warning. Akhairāj took refuge in the fort at Meṛto with a small band of Rajpūts. Soon after, Daulat Khān entered Meṛto and began to loot the town. He then invested the fort as Akhairāj watched from a tower. Akhairāj later sallied forth from the fort with a band of dedicated Rajpūts and drove the Khān and his retainers from Meṛto after a bloody clash.

---

[10] Berāī village: located five miles north of Sevakī.

[11] Platts, ***Dictionary***, pp. 498, 648.

[12] Bhādrājuṇ village: located forty-eight miles south-southwest of Jodhpur.

Daulat Khān retired to Nāgaur after this defeat. He is not mentioned again by name in the Mārvāṛī sources. The only other information about Daulat Khān is that he was given a daughter of Rāv Mālde's in marriage.[13] This marriage probably took place shortly after Rāv Mālde's accession in 1532, when he sought aid from the Khānzādas against the Meṛtīyos.

"Aitihāsik Bātāṃ," pp. 37, 74; Chaghtā'ī, "Nāgaur: A Forgotten Kingdom," p. 176; ***Khyāt***, 3:85, 90-93; ***Murārdān***, no. 2, pp. 106-108, 114, 145; Ojhā, 4:1:210-212, 276-279, 287; ***Vigat***, 1:43, 2:49-50.

---

[13] **See *supra*, Marriage and Family Lists of the Rulers of Jodhpur**, Mālde Gāṅgāvat, Rāṇī n. 16, D - Jasodābāī.

Figure 36. Khānzāda Khāns of Nāgaur

(1-1) Wajīhu'l-Mulk Sadhāran

(2-1) Zafar Khān
(Muzaffar Shāh)
(d. 1410-11)

(Sultāns of
Gujarat)

(2-2) Shams Khān I (Dandānī)
(ca. 1405-18)

(3-1) Firūz Khān I
(ca. 1418-51)

(4-1) Shams Khān II
(ca. 1451-52)

(3-2) Mujāhid Khān
(ca. 1454-67)

(4-2) Ṣalāh Khān
(ca. 1467-69)

(5-1) Firūz Khān II
(ca. 1469-95)

(6-1) Muḥammad Khān I
(ca. 1495-1520)

(7-1) Firūz Khān III
(ca. 1520-26)

(8-1) Muḥammad Khān II
(ca. 1526-January, 1536)

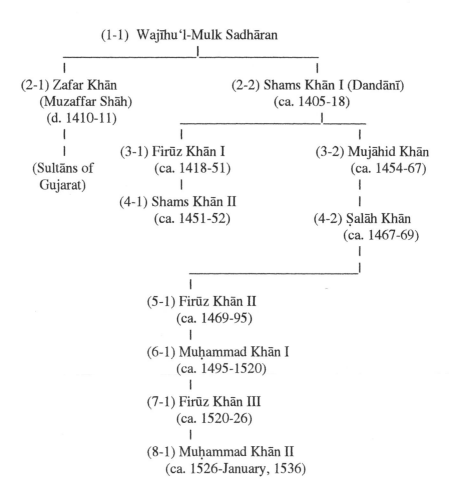

Bhaṇḍārīs

(no. 156) **Lūṇo Gorāvat**

The Bhaṇḍārīs

Bhaṇḍārī is the name of a branch of the Osvāḷ *jāti*. The members of this branch claim descent from the family of Cahuvāṇ Rāv Lākhaṇ (eleventh century) of Nāḍūl[1] in southern Mārvāṛ. Rāv Lākhaṇ's three sons are said to have been converted to Jainism by the Jain sage Jasbhadrasūri. Some of their descendants later took service under local Rajpūt rulers, and it is they who became known as "Bhaṇḍārī." The term itself means "one in charge of a treasury; a small treasury; one associated with the kitchen; also, a branch of the Cahuvāṇs."[2] Originally, Bhaṇḍārīs may have performed administrative functions in the local treasuries of Rajpūt rulers.

The Bhaṇḍārīs of Mārvāṛ trace descent from a Bhaṇḍārī Samro, who was a military servant of Sīsodīyo Rāṇo Kūmbho Mokaḷot of Cītoṛ (ca. 1433-68). holding the village of Nāḍūl in ***paṭo*** from the Rāṇo. When Rāṭhoṛ Rāv Riṇmal Cūṇḍāvat of Maṇḍor (ca. 1428-38) was murdered at Cītoṛ ca. 1438, Bhaṇḍārī Samro was among the Rāṇo's servants stationed at the garrison at Jīlvāṛo village, which guarded the entrance to a pass in the Arāvallī hills leading from Mevāṛ into Mārvāṛ. During the fighting between the Rāṭhoṛs and the pursuing Sīsodīyos that occurred as Rāv Riṇmal's son, Jodho Riṇmalot, and his Rajpūts fled Mevāṛ, Bhaṇḍārī Samro was killed. Before his death, Samro is said to have entrusted his son to Jodho Riṇmalot, who brought this son with him into Mārvāṛ. From that time onward, Bhaṇḍārīs were in the service of Jodhpur. One text refers to them as "servants from the beginning" (***theṭū cākar***).

> ***Census Report***, 1891, pp. 412, 417; "Jodhpur rā Cākrāṃ rī Vigat," in Muṃhato Naiṇsī, ***Mārvāṛ rā Parganāṃ rī Vigat***, vol. 2, edited by Nārāyaṇsiṃh Bhāṭī (Jodhpur: Rājasthān Prācyavidyā Pratiṣṭhān, 1969), pp. 478-479; Munshi Hardyal Singh, ***The Castes of Marwar: Being Census Report of 1891***, 2nd edition, with an introduction by Komal Kothari (Jodhpur: Books Treasure, 1990), p. 131-132.

(no. 156) **Lūṇo Gorāvat**

Bhaṇḍārī Lūṇo (Lūṇkaraṇ) Gorāvat was in the line of descent from Bhaṇḍārī Samro of Nāḍūl. Lūṇo was an important member of the Jodhpur administrative service under both Rājā Sūrajsingh Udaisiṅghot (1595-1619) and

---

[1] Nāḍūl is sixty-seven miles south-southeast of Jodhpur.

[2] Lāḷas, ***RSK***, 3:3:3255.

his son, Rājā Gajsiṅgh Sūrajsiṅghot (1619-38). Lūṇo first came into prominence in the year 1608, when he, Jeso Bhāṭī Goyanddās Mānāvat, and Munsī Kesav began the installation of the Sūrsāgar Tank in Jodhpur. In 1610-11 these same three men had the Padmanābhjī Temple in Gāṅgāṇī village[3] renovated. Then, during 1612-13, Sūrajsiṅgh's *paṭrāṇī*, Sobhāgde, had the Sobhāgdesar Tank built in Chījar village (in Kutch). After the tank was built, the village was resettled and Bhaṇḍārī Lūṇo had a garden begun there. Toward the end of Sūrajsiṅgh's reign, Luṇo became more involved in the activities of Kuṃvar Gajsiṅgh. In 1616-17 the Mughal Emperor Jahāngīr had written the ***pargano*** of Jāḷor[4] into Gajsiṅgh's ***jāgīr*** and ordered the Kuṃvar to take Jāḷor from Pahāṛ Khān and the Bīhārī Muslims then in control.[5] Kuṃvar Gajsiṅgh then organized an expedition against Jāḷor and seized the fort from the Bīhārīs on August 30, 1617. Bhaṇḍārī Lūṇo was included in this expedition. Then, in the year 1618-19, Rājā Sūrajsiṅgh departed for the Deccan and ordered Lūṇo, Gajsiṅgh, Vyās Nātho, and Kūmpāvat Rāṭhoṛ Rājsiṅgh Khīṃvāvat (no. 101) to assume supervision of the Jodhpur domains.

After Rājā Sūrajsiṅgh died in 1619, Bhaṇḍārī Lūṇo soon attained positions of high importance in the regime of the new Rājā, Gajsiṅgh. The ***Jodhpur Rājya kī Khyāt*** (p. 187) notes that in the year 1624 Bhaṇḍārī Lūṇo became Rājā Gajsiṅgh's ***pradhān***,[6] and that previously he had held the ***dīvāṇgī***, or position of ***dīvāṇ***, of Jodhpur. Probably while he was ***dīvāṇ***, Lūṇo participated in the transfer of authority over Meṛto Pargano from Prince Parvīz to Gajsiṅgh in 1623. In this year, Kūmpāvat Rāṭhoṛ Kānho (Kānhāsiṅgh) Khīṃvāvat (no. 100) brought the deed of transfer from Prince Parvīz's court to Meṛto. Bhaṇḍārī Lūṇo then became involved in negotiations with Prince Parvīz's men at Meṛto over the transfer, and both he and Kānho were entrusted with establishing Rājā Gajsiṅgh's authority there.

Very soon after Bhaṇḍārī Lūṇo was made ***pradhān*** in 1624, he died. He was succeeded in this office by Kūmpāvat Rāṭhoṛ Rājsiṅgh Khīṃvāvat. A line of Lūṇo's descendants became known as Rāvḍairā Bhaṇḍārīs.

Bāṅkīdās, p. 176; "Jodhpur rā Cākrāṃ rī Vigat," p. 479; ***Jodhpur Rājya kī Khyat***, pp. 152, 154, 168, 187; ***Mahārāj Śrī Gajsiṅghjī kī Khyāt*** (MS no. 15666, Rājasthān Prācyavidyā Pratiṣṭhān, Jodhpur), pp. 24, 112; ***Mūndiyāṛ rī Rāṭhoṛāṃ rī Khyāt*** (MS no. 15635, no. 2, Rājasthān Prācyavidyā Pratiṣṭhān,

---

[3] Gāṅgāṇī (or Ghāṅgāṇī) village is seventeen miles northeast of Jodhpur.

[4] Jāḷor town and fort are sixty-eight miles south-southwest of Jodhpur.

[5] According to a ms. entitled ***Jālor Parganā rī Vigat***, Prince Khurram held Jālor from Jahāngīr, and Khurram gave the ***pargano*** to Rājā Sūrajsiṅgh. But it was Kuṃvar Gajsiṅgh who took control of the town. ***Jodhpur Rājya kī Khyāt***, p. 152, n. 1.

[6] "Jodhpur rā Cākrāṃ rī Vigat," p. 479, indicates that Bhaṇḍārī Lūṇo was made ***pradhān*** in 1617 following Rājā Gajsiṅgh's conquest of Jāḷor. This statement appears incorrect and is not supported by other sources.

Jodhpur), p. 133; "Nīvāṇāṃ rī Vigat," in Muṃhato Naiṇsī, ***Mārvāṛ rā Parganāṃ rī Vigat***, vol. 1, edited by Nārāyaṇsiṃh Bhāṭī (Jodhpur: Rājasthān Prācyavidyā Pratiṣṭhān, 1968), pp. 583, 588, 594; ***Vigat***, 1:102, 108, 2:75.

Muṃhatos

(no. 157) **Khīṃvo Lālāvat**
(no. 158) **Nago**
(no. 159) **Rāymal Khetāvat**
(no. 160) **Velo**

The Muṃhatos

During the last few centuries, the term Muṃhato[1] has had several different meanings in Mārvāṛ. Derived from the Sanskrit *mahānt* ("great"),[2] it has been used to refer to the agents or officials of ruling men. Over time, since only members of certain subdivisions of the Osvāḷ *jāti* served in this capacity, members of these subdivisions became known as Muṃhatos. A list of these "*mutsaddī*[3] Osvāḷs," as they were called, was compiled during the reign of Rājā Ajītsiṅgh Jasvantsiṅghot (1707-24) of Jodhpur based on information contained in an old register (*bahī*) dated V.S. 1640 (A.D. 1583-84), from the reign of Moṭo Rājā Udaisiṅgh Māldevot (1583-95):

> **Bhaṇḍsālī Muṃhatos.** During the reign of Rāv Cūṇḍo Vīramot (d. ca. 1423), Bhaṇḍsālī Sukno became his servant. A few decades later, when Rāv Jodho Riṇmalot (ca. 1453-89) had fled Mevāṛ, and Mārvāṛ was occupied by Rāṇo Kūmbho Mokaḷot's (ca. 1433-68) troops, one of Sukno's descendants, Surto, attacked the Sīsodīyo military outpost in Maṇḍor. He killed Āhāro Hīṅgolo and Muṃhato Raiṇāyar, the commanders of the garrison, and took the town. From Surto's time onward the Bhaṇḍsālī Muṃhatos were in the service of the Jodhpur rulers.

---

[1] We have preferred the spelling Muṃhato, which occurs in the texts translated, to Muṃhatā, given by Sākariyā in his glossary of Middle Mārvāṛī terms, and Muhto, the form which appears in his *RHSK* (2:1075). Cf. Badrīprasād Sākariyā, "Khyāt meṃ Prayukt Pad, Upadhi aur Virudādi Viśiṣṭ Saṅgyāoṃ ya Śabdoṃ kī Arth sahit Nāmāvalī," in Muṃhato Naiṇsī, *Muṃhatā Naiṇsī viracit Muṃhatā Naiṇsīrī Khyāt*, edited by Badrīprasād Sākariyā, vol. 4 (Jodhpur: Rājasthān Prācyavidyā Pratiṣṭhān, 1967), p. 204. Lāḷas, in his *RSK*, 3:3:3779, gives the spelling Muṃhatā but defines the word under the spelling Mahtā (3:3:3612).

[2] R. S. McGregor, *The Oxford Hindi-English Dictionary* (Oxford: Oxford University Press, 1993), s.v. "mahto," p. 798.

[3] *Mutsaddī* (A. mutaṣaddī): a writer, clerk.

> **Samdaṛiyā Muṃhatos.** When Rāv Sūjo Jodhāvat (ca. 1492-1515) married Rāṇī Likhmī of Jaisaḷmer, they came with her to Jodhpur as part of her dowry (*dāyjo*). Rāv Sūjo gave one of them, Muṃhato Gumno, a ***sirpāv***, and from that time onward they were servants of the Jodhpur rulers.
>
> **Kocar Muṃhatos.** Their service also dates from the time of Rāv Sūjo Jodhāvat. Rāv Sūjo's wife, Rāṇī Likhmī (Bhaṭiyāṇī Sārangdejī) lived part of her life in Phaḷodhī in northern Mārvāṛ with her son, Naro Sūjāvat. While she was there, the Kocars became her servants. Later, during the reign of Moṭo Rājā Udaisingh Māldevot (1583-95), several Kocars, Belo, Phato, and Dhīro, entered his service and received ***sirpāv***s. They remained in the service of Jodhpur thereafter.
>
> **Bachāvat Muṃhatos.** Their service dates from the reign of Rāv Mālde Gāngāvat (1532-62).
>
> **Bāgrecā Muṃhatos.** Service attachments of this branch date from the reign of Moṭo Rājā Udaisingh Māldevot (1583-95).
>
> **Daphtarī Muṃhatos.** During the reign of Rājā Gajsingh Sūrajsinghot (1619-38), the son of Muṃhato Malū, Kesodās, took up residence at the Jodhpur ***daphtar***. The service of the Daphtarī Muṃhatos dates from this time.
>
> **Vaid Muṃhatos.** Originally they were Paṃvār Rajpūts who became Osvāḷs. They migrated from Bīkāner to Mārvāṛ at an unspecified time. Their name, Vaid ("physician"), comes from one of their ancestors, who successfully treated one of the Sultāns of Delhi for an eye ailment.

To this list one may add the Muhaṇots, the family in which Muhaṇot Naiṇsī was born. Naiṇsī himself is sometimes referred to as "Muṃhato Naiṇsī."[4]

By the late nineteenth century, an entire separate branch of the Osvāḷ ***jāti***, the Muṃhato or Mūto Osvāḷs, had emerged. The author of the Hindī ***Census Report***, 1891 (p. 418) notes that

> The officials of ***jāgīrdār***s, and also those Mahājans who for protection have become part of the ***bassī*** (i.e., ***vasī***) of ***jāgīrdār***s, are called Mūtos.

When a Mūto became wealthy enough, he could buy his freedom from the ***vasī***. But the claims of the ***jāgīrdār*** might still imperil him, as an old saying, "a Mūto does not become a ruined Baniyā," suggests. The implication is that the ***jāgīrdār***

---

4 Muṃhato is not to be considered a variant of Muhaṇot ("descendant of Mohaṇ") as suggested by Sākariyā, "Khyāt meṃ Prayukt Pad, Upadhi aur Virudādi Viśiṣṭ Sangyāoṃ ya Śabdoṃ kī Arth sahit Nāmāvalī," p. 204.

would not seize the funds of someone in his *vasī*, who would be under his protection, as easily as he would the funds of an independent Baniyā.

The Hindī ***Census Report*** of 1891 does not include the Bhaṇḍsālīs, Samdaṛiyās, or tothers mentioned above among the Mūtos; they are categorized as Osvāḷs only. But the English version of this report considers Bhaṇḍsālīs, Bāgrecās, Vaid Muṃhatos, and Kocars to be Mūtos. The Muhaṇots are not included among the Mūtos by either version of the report, although Muhaṇot Naiṇsi is referred to as "Mohta" or "Mūtā (Muṃhato) Naiṇsī."

> ***Census Report***, 1891, 3:411-412, 417-418; "Jodhpur rā Cākrāṃ rī Vigat," in Muṃhato Naiṇsī, ***Mārvāṛ rā Parganāṃ rī Vigat***, vol. 2, edited by Nārāyaṇsiṃh Bhāṭī (Jodhpur: Rājasthān Prācyavidyā Pratiṣṭhān, 1969), pp. 479-480; Munshi Hardyal Singh, ***The Castes of Marwar: Being Census Report of 1891***, 2nd edition, with an introduction by Komal Kothari (Jodhpur: Books Treasure, 1990), p. 131, 133-135.

(no. 157) **Muṃhato Khīṃvo Lālāvat**

Muṃhato Khīṃvo Lālāvat was a ***kāmdār*** in the service of Meṛtīyo Rāṭhoṛ Rāv Vīramde Dūdāvat of Meṛto (ca. 1497-1544; no. 105). The texts mention Khīṃvo as a member of Rāv Vīramde's forces ca. 1535, when Rāv Vīramde occupied Ajmer. Later in this same year, when Rāv Mālde Gāṅgāvat of Jodhpur (1532-62) drove Rāv Vīramde from Mārvāṛ and Ajmer, Muṃhato Khīṃvo accompanied him into the areas of central and eastern Rājasthān where Rāv Vīramde lived in exile. Upon reaching Riṇthambhor,[5] Rāv Vīramde sent Muṃhato Khīmvo and his ***pradhān***, Jaitmāl Rāṭhoṛ Akhairāj Bhādāvat (no. 69), to meet with the ***navāb*** of the fort. Muṃhato Khīṃvo is credited with devising the strategy that finally obtained an audience with the ***navāb*** and led to Rāv Vīramde's eventual meeting with Sher Shāh Sūr in Delhi ca. 1543. This strategy involved the offer of a daughter of Rāv Vīramde in marriage to the young son of the ***navāb***.

The sources at hand provide no further information about Muṃhato Khīṃvo and his life.

> ***Khyāt***, 3:95, 98-99; ***Vigat***, 2:54-55.

(no. 158) **Muṃhato Nago**

Muṃhato Nago was a ***kāmdār*** in the service of Bīkāvat Rāṭhoṛ Rāv Jaitsī Lūṇkaraṇot of Bīkāner (ca. 1526-42; no. 45). The texts under review mention Nago only once, as a companion of Kuṃvar Bhīmrāj Jaitsīyot, who accompanied the ***kuṃvar*** to Delhi to meet with Sher Shāh Sūr. Kuṃvar Bhīmrāj had been sent to Delhi following his father Rāv Jaitsī's death in battle in 1542,

[5] Riṇthambhor is sixty-five miles southeast of Jaipur.

fighting against the forces of Rāv Mālde Gāṅgāvat of Jodhpur (1532-62), which had occupied Bīkāner.

Ojhā, 5:1:136-138; Reu, 1:123; ***Vigat***, 2:56.

(no. 159) **Muṃhato Rāymal Khetāvat**

Muṃhato Rāymal Khetāvat belonged to the Vaid subdivision of Muṃhatos, who claim descent from Paṃvār Rajpūts. He played a prominent role in the affairs of Sojhat and Jodhpur between the years 1515 and 1532 when he was in the service of Rāv Vīramde Vāghāvat (no. 84), grandson of Rāv Sūjo Jodhāvat of Jodhpur (ca. 1492-1515). Rāymal became associated with Vīramde Vāghāvat and his family while Vīramde was a ***kuṃvar*** living in his grandfather's court at Jodhpur. According to the ***Khyāt*** of Naiṇsī, four Mārū ***ṭhākur***s came to Jodhpur on some occasion during Rāv Sūjo's last year of rule. One of these ***ṭhākur***s was Rāymal,[6] who went to his home in Jodhpur. The other three went to the hall of assembly (***darīkhāno***). Then the rains began. And then

> ... these ***ṭhākur***s sent word to Vīramde's mother, a Sīsodṇī:[7] "***Jī***, the rains have prevented us [from leaving the hall of assembly]. You should look after us." Then the Rāṇī sent word: "Wrap [yourselves with] woolens and depart for [your] camps, ***ṭhākurs***. Who will feed you here?" (***Khyāt***, 3:80).

The ***thākur***s were highly dissatisfied with her response, and so sent word to Gāṅgo Vāghāvat's mother, Udanbāī Cahuvāṇ, who had them stay in the hall of assembly, supplied them with what they required, and in general treated them with great deference. In gratitude, they promised the throne of Jodhpur to her son, Gāṅgo.

Very soon thereafter, Rāv Sūjo died. These ***ṭhākur***s, who included Rāṭhoṛ Bhairavdās Cāmpāvat[8] and Rāṭhoṛ Pañcāiṇ Akhairājot,[9] led a faction at court that deposed Vīramde. They then had Gāṅgo Vāghāvat summoned from Īḍar, where he had gone to live, and they placed him on the throne. His accession took place on November 8, 1515. The ***Khyāt*** of Naiṇsī (3:81) records that when these ***ṭhākur***s were leading the deposed Vīramde down from the fort

---

[6] To our knowledge, this is the only incidence in Middle Mārvāṛī chronicles of a non-Rajpūt being referred to as a ***ṭhākur***.

[7] According to other sources, Vīramde's mother was not a Sīsodṇī, she was Devṛī Raṅgāde. See "Jaitāvat Rāṭhoṛs," n. 4, ***supra***.

[8] See ***supra***, "Cāmpāvat Rāṭhoṛs."

[9] See ***supra***, "Jaitāvat Rāṭhoṛs."

of Jodhpur, they met Muṃhato Rāymal Khetāvat, a strong supporter of Vīramde and his family. Rāymal is reported to have said:

> "Hey! Why are you taking that chosen successor (***pāṭvī kuṃvar***) down from the fort?" Then Rāymal brought Vīramde back [to the fort]. Then they all gathered and they said: "***Jī***, give Vīramde Sojhat." They made Vīramde Rāv of Sojhat.

And so, through Muṃhato Rāymal's efforts, Vīramde acquired Sojhat as his share of the lands of Mārvāṛ. When Rāv Vīramde went to Sojhat, Muṃhato Rāymal accompanied him there.

The ***Khyāt*** of Naiṇsī (3:81) records that after Rāv Vīramde settled at Sojhat, he became deranged from his desire to take Jodhpur from Rāv Gāṅgo. And in the absence of Rāv Vīramde's leadership, it was Muṃhato Rāymal who led Rāv Vīramde's warriors in battle and organized his campaigns against Rāv Gāṅgo. As hostilities grew,

> If [Rāv] Gāṅgo would plunder one village of Sojhat, then [Muṃhato] Rāymal would plunder two villages of Jodhpur. They lived like this, as their battle continued.

For a period of years, Muṃhato Rāymal was very successful in his campaign against Jodhpur, and his warriors won a series of victories against those of Rāv Gāṅgo. The ***Khyāt*** of Naiṇsī explains this situation by noting that one of Rāv Gāṅgo's leading commanders, Rāṭhoṛ Jaito Pañcāiṇot (no. 61), kept his ***vasī*** in his ancestral village of Bagṛī (located nine miles east-southeast of Sojhat), which lay within Rāv Vīramde's share of lands. Jaito's position, therefore, straddled both sides of this conflict.

Rāv Gāṅgo eventually ordered Jaito to leave Bagṛī and bring the people of his ***vasī*** to lands that were under Jodhpur rule. Jaito sent messages to his ***dhāy-bhāī*** (lit. "milk-brother"), Reṛo, at Bagṛī, asking him to abandon the village and bring the people to Bīlāṛo. But Reṛo refused to leave, because the original order had come from Rāv Gāṅgo and not from Rāv Vīramde. When Muṃhato Rāymal then continued to defeat Rāv Gāṅgo's warriors in battle, Rāv Gāṅgo summoned Jaito and rebuked him for not vacating Bagṛī. Jaito, in turn, ordered Reṛo to leave the ancestral village immediately. This command brought Reṛo into potential direct conflict with Muṃhato Rāymal. Reṛo reasoned that if he were to kill Muṃhato Rāymal, he and the people of Jaito Pañcāiṇot's ***vasī*** would not have to leave Bagṛī. So he proceeded to Sojhat to seek out Muṃhato Rāymal, who welcomed him and took him to pay respects to Rāv Vīramde's Sīsodṇī Rāṇī:

> He took Reṛo and went [to pay] respects to the Rāṇī. Rāymal went and paid [his] repects. Then she said: "***Jī***, Sir! Who is he?" Then he said: "***Jī***, he is the ***dhāy-bhāī*** of Jaitojī." Then he had [him] touch [her] feet. While they were returning, she took him aside and said: "Sir! Do not trust him! I perceive he has an

inauspicious look." Then Rāymal said: "*Jī*, he is one of ours."
But the Sīsodṇī said: "Sir! Do not trust him."

Then Muṃhato Rāymal and Reṛo proceeded to the hall of assembly. Reṛo realized that if they entered the hall, there would be too many men present for him to murder Muṃhato Rāymal. He decided to kill him right there. He struck at the Muṃhato with his sword, but just then Rāymal bent down to pick up a stone to throw at a bird. The sword grazed his back. Rāymal turned around and with one blow of his own sword cut off Reṛo's head. After this fiasco, Jaito Pañcāiṇot's people fled Bagṛī in fear of the Muṃhato.

Although Muṃhato Rāymal was able to maintain his position in this period, he did lose one of his most capable warriors, Rāṭhoṛ Kūmpo Mahirājot (no. 95), to Jodhpur ca. 1529. Kūmpo had been lured to Jodhpur with the offer of a large grant of villages. He agreed to this offer upon the stipulation that Rāv Gāṅgo not attack Sojhat for one year. Rāv Gāṅgo accepted this condition, and Kūmpo then proceeded to Muṃhato Rāymal to request his leave. He told the Muṃhato that he was leaving because Rāv Vīramde had no sons and when he died, the lands of Sojhat would return to Jodhpur. He implied that there was no benefit to a continued struggle, a line of reasoning made plain to him during his prior negotiations with Jodhpur. Muṃhato Rāymal was displeased and said:

> Kūmpojī! [Rāv Gāṅgo] would put [his] foot on [Muṃhato Rāymal] Khetāvat's chest and remove Vīramde's ***ḍholīyo*** from Sojhat [and] you are leaving?

In other words, Kūmpo had chosen the wrong moment to abandon his allegiance to Sojhat. And worse, all of the Riṇmalots[10] in Sojhat followed him to Jodhpur. Rāymal was left with only seven hundred mounted retainers.

For a period of time thereafter, Rāv Gāṅgo appeared to have the upper hand. Kūmpo advised him to seize a few villages of Sojhat each year. He had the Rāv establish an outpost in Dhoḷharo village[11] on the border of Sojhat, where a large number of ***cīndhaṛ***s[12] were stationed along with a stable of horses. Four ***umrāv***s were placed in command of the men and horses. But Rāv Gāṅgo grew careless; he left the outpost to celebrate Hoḷi in the village where his ***vasī*** resided, on the assumption that Rāymal would also be observing Hoḷī and would not attack Ḍhoḷharo. Given an opportunity, Rāymal swept down on the outpost and put four thousand men to the sword. He brought the horses captured in the

---

[10] Riṇmalots: descendants of Rāv Riṇmal Cūṇḍāvat, ruler of Maṇḍor, ca. 1428-38.

[11] Dhoḷharo village is eighteen miles west-northwest of Sojhat.

[12] See ***supra***, "Jodho Rāṭhoṛs," n. 28.

battle back to Sojhat.[13] The ***Khyāt*** of Naiṇsī (3:85) states that Rāv Gāṅgo could not recover for two years.

It was during this time that Sekho Sūjavat (no. 86), the ruler of Pīmpāṛ, suggested to Rāv Vīramde's Sīsodṇī wife that she join forces with him. Naiṇsī has written:

> Then Sekho Sūjāvat, who was Vīramdejī's ***got-bhāī***,[14] came [to Sojhat]. He came and met with the Sīsodṇī [Rāṇī]. He said: "You should join me, in order that the weighing pan of your [scale] be heavy. Rāv Gāṅgo would not be a match [for us]." (***Khyāt***, 3:86)

The Sīsodṇī agreed to join Sekho against the advice of Muṃhato Rāymal. She joined forces with Sekho and Rāv Vīramde's retainers fought alongside him at the battle of Sevakī in 1529.

Rāymal, discouraged that his advice was no longer being followed, sent word to Rāv Gāṅgo. He enjoined the Rāv to come to Sojhat:

> Now you come, I will fight ... I will die fighting. [And] I will give the land [of Sojhat] to you.

Rāv Gāṅgo and his son, Kuṃvar Mālde Gāṅgāvat, then rode to Sojhat to meet Muṃhato Rāymal in battle early in 1532. Before he went out to confront them, Rāymal circumambulated Rāv Vīramde's bed in a clockwise direction (as a worshipper would an idol) and respectfully grasped the Rāv's feet in the manner of a loyal retainer or a son. Then he gathered his ***sāth*** and went to face Rāv Gāṅgo. He died fighting that day. Rāv Gāṅgo took Sojhat.

The ***Khyāt*** of Bāṅkīdās (p. 10) has an interesting description of what happened in this battle:

> The Vaid Muṃhato, Rāymal, [was] in Sojhat. Rāvjī Gāṅgojī [and] Kuṃvar Māldejī went upon Sojhat. [During the battle], when Rāymal became a ***kabandh***, [his] sword moved with [what had been] the intent of [his] eye [and] made pieces of a boy (***beṭārā baṭakā kiyā***). They wrapped the [headless] corpse with an expensive woolen when it fell from the horse to the ground.

A ***kabandh*** is a body that keeps fighting even after its head has been severed in battle.[15] The word comes from Kabandha, the name of a headless

---

[13] ***Jodhpur Rājya kī Khyāt***, p. 74, records that Muṃhato Rāymal attacked Ḍhoḷharo in February of 1532, considerably later than the time set forth in Naiṇsī's ***Khyāt***, and that he did not capture any horses.

[14] ***Got-bhāī***: close male relation. Vīramde was Sekho Sūjāvat's half-brother's son.

[15] Cf. B.N. no. 84 for Jodho Rāṭhoṛ Vīramde Vāghāvat, n. 35, ***supra***.

demon in the Araṇyakāṇḍa or Forest Book of the Rāmāyaṇa who confronts Rāma and his younger brother, Lakṣmaṇa:

> ... there, facing them, stood the giant Kabandha, a creature without head or neck, his face set in his belly. The hair on his body was bushy and wiry, he towered over them like a mountain, a savage creature like a black storm cloud and with a voice like thunder. And in his chest, darting glances, thick-lashed, tawny, prodigious, wide, and terrible, was a single eye.[16]

Bāṅkīdās, by saying that Rāymal had become a ***kabandh***, is indicating that he lost his head, but he also is implying that Rāymal had the evil, ugly, yet powerful demeanor of Kabandha in the Rāmāyaṇa. And just as Kabandha was struck down by Rāma and Lakṣmaṇa, so too was Muṃhato Rāymal struck down by their descendants, the Rāṭhors of Jodhpur, who, unlike Rāymal, were Rajpūts. To compare Rāymal to a ***rākṣasa***, or demonic creature, may be ***Bāṅkīdās***'s way of explaining what was to him an anomaly: an extraordinarily powerful man in middle period Mārvāṛ who was not a Rajpūt.

> ***Bāṅkīdās***, pp. 9-10; ***Khyāt***, 3:80-86; ***Murārdān***, no. 1, pp. 639-641; no. 2, pp. 109-111; ***Vigat***, 1:42.

(no. 160) **Muṃhato Velo**

Muṃhato Velo was a ***kāmdār*** in the service of Rājā Gajsiṅgh Sūrajsiṅghot of Jodhpur (1619-38). ***Vigat***, 2:74, mentions Velo in connection with Rājā Gajsiṅgh's occupation of Meṛto in 1619-20. Following his succession to the Jodhpur throne in 1619, Rājā Gajsiṅgh had sent Kūmpāvat Rāṭhoṛ Rājsiṅgh Khīṃvāvat (no. 101) and Muṃhato Velo along with a contingent of retainers to Meṛto with the order to seize the ***māl*** and ***ghāsmārī*** revenues of this ***pargano*** from the Mughal officers of Prince Khurram under the supervision of the ***amīn***, Abu Muḥammad Kambu (Abu Kābo). Rājsiṅgh Khīṃvāvat and Bhaṇḍārī Lūṇo (no. 156) spent several days in negotiations with Abu. And Muṃhato Velo was then stationed in Meṛto with the ***amīn***, during which time a fight broke out between their servants. When a settlement was finally reached, Muṃhato Velo accepted the deed of discharge which Abu Kābo had drawn up

---

[16] ***The Rāmāyaṇa of Vālmīki: An Epic of Ancient India***, vol. 3, ***Araṇyakāṇḍa***, introduction, translation, and annotation by Sheldon I. Pollack; edited by Robert P. Goldman (Princeton: Princeton University Press, 1991), p. 72. See also Siddheśvarśāstrī Citrāv, ***Bhāratavarṣīya Prācīn Caritrakoś*** (Pūnā: Bhāratīya Caritrakoś Maṇḍal, 1964), p. 115; Vettam Mani, ***Purāṇic Encyclopaedia: A Comprehensive Dictionary with Special Reference to the Epic and Purāṇic Literature*** (4th ed., reprinted. Delhi: Motilal Banaridass, 1979 [1974]), p. 362; Margaret and James Stutley, ***Harper's Dictionary of Hinduism*** (New York: Harper & Row, 1977), p. 136.

and sent to him at Meṛto. A final settlement of affairs at Meṛto and full transfer of this ***pargano*** to Rājā Gajsiṅgh was delayed until 1623.

Vigat, 2:74.

Pañcolīs

(no. 161) **Abho Jhājhāvat**
(no. 162) **Neto Abhāvat**
(no. 163) **Ratno Abhāvat**

The Pañcolīs

The Pañcolīs are a branch of the Kayasth *jāti*, which is widespread in north India. In Mārvāṛ, the Kayasths are divided into two main groups: the ***pardeśīs***, or outsiders, and the ***deśīs***, or natives. The ***deśī*** Kayasths are all Māthurs, one of the twelve major subdivisions of this *jāti*, and locally are known as Pañcolīs. Some say they received their name because they originally came to Mārvāṛ from Pañcolpurā, a village near Delhi. Others say they are called Pañcolīs because of their knowledge of the five (***pañc***) elements. Still others say that in the beginning there were four castes, the Brāhmaṇ, Kṣatriya, Vaiśya, and Śūdra; the Kayasths, who were not included in this scheme, formed a fifth, hence the name Pañcolī (from ***pañc***, "five," and ***olī***, "line," "occupation"). And finally, there is the tradition that five Māthur Kayasths came with Rāv Āsthān Sīhāvat from Kanauj to Mārvāṛ in the thirteenth century; they fought in a battle with an unnamed Muslim ruler's army at Pālī[1] and died along with the Rāv. Their descendants, who remained in Mārvāṛ, are called Pañcolīs.

It is believed that there are eighty-four ***khāmps*** of Pañcolīs, but in Mārvāṛ only seventeen are to be found, and of these only three are important: the Mānakbhaṇḍārīs, Jhāmariyās, and Bhivānīs, each of which may be discussed in turn:

(1) The Mānakbhaṇḍārīs. They are the Pañcolīs of most ancient origin in Mārvāṛ; their ancestor, Kulpatrāy, came to Sāmbhar[2] in the seventh century and was the first man to produce salt there, an endeavor which pleased the local ruler, Rājā Mānakdev Cahuvāṇ, who granted Kulpatrāy an annuity from the salt revenues. His ancestors enjoyed the rights to this annuity as late as the beginning of the twentieth century.

(2) The Jhāmariyās. Their ancestor, Khīmsī, received an appointment from Ghiyāsuddīn Tughluq to the position of ***sūbedār***, or local governor, at Khāṭū,[3] at around the time in the fourteenth century when Rāṭhoṛ Rāv Cūṇḍo Vīramot (d. ca. 1423) had taken the fort of Maṇḍor from its Muslim commander. Ghiyāsuddīn, angered by Cūṇḍo's action, was about to send an army to Mārvāṛ,

---

[1] Pālī town is forty miles south-southeast of Jodhpur.

[2] Sāmbhar town located fifty miles northeast of Ajmer and eighty miles east-northeast of Meṛto.

[3] Khāṭū town is thirty-five miles east of Nāgaur.

but Khīmsī negotiated a compromise by which Cūṇḍo was allowed to retain possession of Maṇḍor. In gratitude, Cūṇḍo made Dhanrāj, Khīmsī's son, his ***pradhān***. From then on, the Jhāmariyā Pañcolīs held important posts in Mārvāṛ and received rich rewards, as is apparent from the magnificence of the residences they built in Jodhpur after it was founded in 1459.

(3) The Bhivānīs. Sodā, the father of their ancestor Bhiān, was in the service of the ruler of Delhi, but incurred his displeasure and was ordered to be put to death. Bhiān went to Mārvāṛ and took refuge in Khāṭū, where he married Jhāmariyā Khīmsī's daughter.

Over the centuries the Pañcolīs of Mārvāṛ were active in court administration and military service, as suppliers and treasurers, and as agents or pleaders (***vakīl***). They have held important positions under the Jodhpur rulers, including ***dīvāṇ***, ***pradhān***, ***bagsī***, etc.

> ***Census Report***, 1891, pp. 397-400; Munshi Hardyal Singh, ***The Castes of Marwar: Being Census Report of 1891***, 2nd edition, with an introduction by Komal Kothari (Jodhpur: Books Treasure, 1990), pp. 124-126.

(no. 161) **Abho Jhājhāvat**
(no. 162) **Neto Abhāvat**
(no. 163) **Ratno Abhāvat**

Pañcolī Abho Jhājhāvat was an important ***kāmdār*** in the administrative service of Rāv Mālde Gāṅgāvat of Jodhpur (1532-62). He held responsibility for overseeing the fiscal affairs of the kingdom. The "Jodhpur Hukūmat rī Bahī" (pp. 116-117) records that Abho received the two villages of Nandvāṇ and Nahnaḍo (or Naheṛvo)[4] in ***paṭo*** from Rāv Mālde for his maintenance, while various important ***umrāv***s gave him eighteen others.[5]

Pañcolī Abho served under Rāv Mālde until his death at the battle of Meṛto in 1554. He was included in the contingent of warriors under the command of Rāṭhoṛ Prithīrāj Jaitāvat (no. 63) that Rāv Mālde sent against Meṛtīyo Rāṭhoṛ Rāv Jaimal Vīramdevot (no. 107) in this year. Pañcolī Abho was killed here along with one of his sons, Ratno Abhāvat. Another of his sons, Neto Abhāvat, is listed as also having been killed at Meṛto in 1554. However, Neto's name appears in the ***Vigat*** (2:62) under a listing of Rāv Mālde's servants who witnessed the swearing of Meṛtīyo Rāṭhoṛ Jagmāl Vīramdevot (no. 124) at the temple of Mahāmayā in Phaḷodhī village[6] of Meṛto ca. 1559. Meṛtīyo Jagmāl had proceeded to the Mahāmayā temple for his swearing of oaths to Rāv Mālde prior to his receipt of the ***paṭo*** for one-half the villages of Meṛto from the Rāv.

---

[4] Nandvāṇ is twelve miles south-soutwest of Jodhpur, and Naheṛvo is forty-seven miles south of Jodhpur.

[5] ***Vigat***, 1:54, says nineteen other villages.

[6] Phalodhī village is nine miles northwest of Meṛto.

No other information is available about these Pañcolī servants of Rāv Mālde.

"Aitihāsik Bātāṃ," p. 64; "Jodhpur Hukūmat rī Bahī," pp. 116-117; ***Murārdān***, no. 2, p. 130; ***Vigat***, 1:45, 54, 2:59, 62.

RĀJASTHĀNĪ KINSHIP TERMINOLOGY
(from Middle Mārvāṛī sources)

A

Antevar[1] — wife; woman; harem, zenana; the female apartment of a royal household.

Aulād[2] (var. ***Olād***) — family; issue, progeny, offspring; lineage, clan, dynasty.

B

Bābo[3] — father; father's elder brother; father's father or grandfather; term of respect for an elder.

Bahan[4] — sister; woman born of the same clan (*vaṃś*) or brotherhood (***bhāībandh***).

Bahanoī[5] — sister's husband.

Bahū[6] (var. ***Vahū***) — wife; newly married woman, bride; son's wife; woman, female.

Bāī[7] — sister, daughter; girl; mother; general term of reference for a woman or female.

Bair[8] (var. ***Vair***) — woman, female; wife; faithful and devoted wife; enmity, animosity, hostility.

Bāḷak[9] — infant, baby, child; one who is inexperienced, immature; one who is playful, frolicsome.

Bāp[10] — father; progenitor, procreator.

Beṭo[11] (f. ***Beṭī***) — son; boy, young male relation; term of affection for one who is like a son; offspring, progeny.

Bhābhī[12] — elder brother's wife.

Bhāī[13] — uterine brother, born of the same mother; brother; male of the same ***gotra***, clan (*vaṃś*) or brotherhood (***bhāībandh***).

Bhāībandh[14] — (lit. "brother-bound") brotherhood; those related by ties of male blood to a comman ancestor.

Bhāṇej[15] (var. ***Bhāṇejo***) — sister's son.

Bhāṇjī[16] (var. ***Bhāṇejī***) — sister's daughter.

Bhatījo[17] (f. ***Bhatījī***) — brother's son.

Bhāyap[18] (var. ***Bhāīpo***) — brotherhood; those who share ties of male blood to a common ancestor; alliance, friendship.

Bhojāī[19] — elder brother's wife.

C

Chokro[20] (f. ***Chokrī***) — boy, male child; son; issue, progeny; slave boy.

Chorū[21] — son; boy, male child; progeny, offspring; young servant, slave boy.

D

Dādo[22] (f. ***Dādī***) — father's father; term of respect for an elder brother or an elder male.

Ḍāvṛo[23] (f. ***Ḍāvṛī***) — son; young boy; male child.

Devar[24] — husband's younger brother.

Dhaṇī[25] — husband; master, lord.

Dhāy-bhāī[26] — milk-brother; male to whom one is related through sharing the nipple or milk of a wet-nurse (***dhāy***); son of the woman who suckles a boy.

Among Rajpūts, a wet-nurse was generally a Rajpūtāṇī who raised her own son with the son of the ruler or ***ṭhākur*** whom she nursed, as his ***dhāy-bhāī***.

Ḍīkro (var. ***Dikro***)[27] (f. ***Ḍīkrī***; var. ***Dīkrī***) — son; young boy.

Dohitro[28] (f. ***Dohitrī***) — daughter's son; grandson.

Ḍoḷo[29] marriage custom whereby a father sends his daughter, seated in a litter or sedan, to the groom's house for the wedding; generally indicative of a ranked relationship, where an inferior gives a daughter to a superior.

Duhāgaṇ[30] married woman who has lost the favor of her (living) husband; wife who is disregarded and out of favor; widow.

Dumāt-bhāī[31] brother born of the father's co-wife or step-mother; half-brother.

G

Ghardhaṇī[32] husband; master of the house.

Gharāṇo[33] family; clan, lineage, brotherhood; offspring, progeny; those related by ties of male blood to a common ancestor.

Got-bhāī man or brother born of the same ***gotra***.
Gotī/Gotiyo person born of the same ***gotra***.
Gotra[34] clan, lineage, family (***vaṃś***, ***kuḷ***); those sharing ties of male blood to a common ancestor and the same ***gotra*** designation (usually the name of a god or sage [***ṛṣī***]).

Goṭhiyo[35] friend, companion, boyhood friend; one with whom one shares food communally, as at a feast (***goṭh***).

J

Jamāī[36] daughter's husband.

Jeṭh[37] husband's elder brother.

K

Kabīlo[38] family, clan, lineage; offspring; progeny; harem, the women who reside with the wife of a ruler (***rāṇī***) in the women's quarters.

Kaḍūmbo[39] family, clan, lineage.

Kāko[40] father's brother; paternal uncle.

Kapūt[41] bad boy; unworthy, underserving son.

Khāmp[42] clan, lineage (***vaṃś***, ***kuḷ***), brotherhood (***bhāībandh***);

	those sharing ties of male blood to a common ancestor; segment, part, piece.
Kuḷ[43]	clan, lineage (***vaṃś***, ***gotra***), brotherhood; those sharing ties of male blood to a common ancestor.

L

Laṛko[44] (f. ***Laṛkī***)	boy; son; young male child.
Lohaṛo-beṭo	younger son.
Lohaṛo-bhāī[45]	younger brother.

M

Mā[46]	mother; paternal grandmother.
Mahaḷ[47]	woman, female; pretty, young woman; wife; beloved favorite.
Māīt[48]	parents, mothers and fathers; elders; elders honored as mothers and fathers; ancestors, forefathers.
Māmāṇo[49] (var. ***Mūmāṇo***)	mother's brother's home; maternal grandfather's home.
Māmī	mother's brother's wife.
Māmo[50]	mother's brother.
Māṇṭī[51]	husband, master, lord; man; relation; ally, friend; warrior, strong and powerful man.
Māsī[52]	mother's sister; maternal aunt.
Māvḷiyāī-bhāī[53]	blood or uterine brother; brother born of the same mother; half- or step-brother; mother's family brother, that is, first cousin on the mother's side; mother's brother's son (or) mother's sister's son.

N

Nānāṇo[54]	mother's father's home.
Nāno[55] (f. ***Nānī***)	mother's father; maternal grandfather.

P

Parvār[56]	family; dependents, relations; those who share ties of male blood to a common ancestor; those dependent on a particular person for their maintenance and nourishment.
Peṭ[57]	abdomen, belly, stomach; foetus; son; offspring, progeny; those sharing ties of male blood to a common ancestor.
Pīḍhī[58]	(lit. "generation") a genealogy.
Pīhar[59]	married woman's father's home; maternal parent's home.
Poto (var. ***Potro***)[60] (f. ***Potī***; var. ***Potrī***)	son's son; grandson.
Pūrvaj[61]	elder brother; ancestor, forefather.
Putra[62] (f. ***Putrī***)	son; young boy.

S

Sāḍu[63] (var. ***Sāḍhu***)	wife's sister's husband.
Sagāī[64]	betrothal; alliance; relationship, connection.
Sago[65]	relation through marriage; one to whom one gives and/or from whom one receives a daughter in marriage (also referred to as ***sagpaṇ***); ally; uterine, born of one mother.
Sago-bhāī	uterine brother.
Sago-bahan[66]	uterine sister.
Sākh[67]	(lit. "branch, as of a tree") clan, lineage (***vaṃṣ***, ***kuḷ***, ***gotra***), brotherhood; those related by ties of male blood to a common ancestor.
Sāḷo[68] (f. ***Sāḷī***)	wife's brother; term of abuse.

Sāmī[69]	husband; god, ruler, master.
Sapūt[70]	good, dutiful son; worthy son; warrior, fighter.
Sāsro[71]	home of one's husband or wife's father.
Sāsriyo[72]	those of the home of one's husband or wife's father.
Sāsū[73] (var. ***Sāsu/Sās***)	mother of one's husband or wife.
Sok[74] (var. ***Sauk***)	co-wife.
Suhīgaṇ[75]	woman whose husband is living; woman who is not a widow; woman who is favored/loved by her husband.
Susro[76] (var. ***Sasuro/Sasro***)	father of one's husband or wife.

T

Ṭābar[77]	boy (or girl) child.

V

Vaṃś[78]	family, clan, lineage (***gotra***, ***kuḷ***), brotherhood; offspring, descendants; those related by ties of male blood to a common ancestor.

---

[1] ***Khyāt***, 3:30-31; Lāḷas, ***RSK***, 1:11; Sākariyā, ***RHSK***, p. 85.

[2] ***Khyāt***, 1:2, 14, 51, 101, 336-337, 2:16, 31; Lāḷas, ***RSK***, 1:370, 379; Sākariyā, ***RHSK***, pp. 184, 188.

[3] ***Khyāt***, 2:20, 3:116; Lāḷas, ***RSK***, 3:2:3014; Sākariyā, ***RHSK***, p. 886; ***Vigat***, 1:58.

[4] ***Khyāt***, 1:76, 124, 265, 2:210, 3:69, 143, 244, 285; Lāḷas, ***RSK***, 3:2:2934; Sākariyā, ***RHSK***, p. 872; ***Vigat***, 1:8, 40, 52, 493, 2:219.

[5] ***Khyāt***, 1:265, 2:244-245, 3:43, 65; Lāḷas, ***RSK***, 3:2:2935; Sākariyā, ***RHSK***, p. 872.

[6] ***Khyāt***, 1:75, 2:115, 203, 3:66, 80, 146, 148; Lāḷas, ***RSK***, 3:2:2949; Sākariyā, ***RHSK***, p. 874; ***Vigat***, 1:14.

[7] *Khyāt*, 2:292, 306, 316, 3:62, 64, 271; Lāḷas, *RSK*, 3:2:2973-2974; Sākariyā, *RHSK*, p. 878; *Vigat*, 1:52, 111.

[8] *Khyāt*, 1:7, 15, 36, 2:40, 114, 228, 299, 341, 3:139, 144, 148, 258; Lāḷas, *RSK*, 3:2:3206-3207; Sākariyā, *RHSK*, p. 924; *Vigat*, 1:9, 20, 55, 72, 492, 2:46.

[9] *Khyāt*, 1:49, 75, 2:34, 296, 3:273; Lāḷas, *RSK*, 3:2:3027; Sākariyā, *RHSK*, p. 889; *Vigat*, 2:290, 293.

[10] *Khyāt*, 1:87, 2:11, 213, 3:60, 63, 79, 85; Lāḷas, *RSK*, 3:2:3007; Sākariyā, *RHSK*, p. 885; *Vigat*, 1:21, 48, 53, 493; 2:48.

[11] *Khyāt*, 1:19, 2:11, 41, 67-68, 109, 290, 3:38, 41, 57-58, 103, 293; Lāḷas, *RSK*, 3:2:1674; Sākariyā, *RHSK*, p. 918; *Vigat*, 1:2-3, 12, 29, 52, 69, 78, 111, 2:1, 11, 38.

[12] *Khyāt*, 3:64, 66-67; Lāḷas, *RSK*, 3:2:3346.

[13] *Khyāt*, 1:14, 2:50, 86, 290, 304, 3:63-64, 144, 244; Lāḷas, *RSK*, 3:2:3334; Sākariyā, *RHSK*, p. 953; *Vigat*, 1:8, 48, 51, 2:6, 43, 66.

[14] *Bātāṃ ro Jhūmakho*, edited by M. Śarma (Bisau: Rājasthān Sāhitya Samiti, V. S. 2021 [1964]), 3:40; *Khyāt*, 1:76, 82, 98, 2:213; Lāḷas, *RSK*, 3:3:3335; Sākariyā, *RHSK*, p. 954; *Vigat*, 1:33, 2:21, 43, 46, 51, 155, 160-162.

[15] *Khyāt*, 1:28, 103, 260, 264, 2:12, 66, 134, 269, 3:3, 7, 130; Lāḷas, *RSK*, 3:3:3328-3329; Sākariyā, *RHSK*, p. 957; *Vigat*, 1:8, 26, 38, 43, 51, 385.

[16] *Khyāt*, 3:104; Lāḷas, *RSK*, 3:3:3328-3329; Sākariyā, *RHSK*, p. 957.

[17] *Khyāt*, 1:50, 119, 260, 2:67, 82, 240, 250, 3:92, 163; Lāḷas, *RSK*, 3:3:3288-3289; Sākariyā, *RHSK*, p. 942; *Vigat*, 1:24, 171.

[18] *Khyāt*, 2:301; Lāḷas, *RSK*, 3:3:3334, 3347; Sākariyā, *RHSK*, p. 959.

[19] *Khyāt*, 3:64-65, 67, 163, 270; Lāḷas, *RSK*, 3:3:3450; Sākariyā, *RHSK*, p. 984.

[20] *Khyāt*, 2:41, 286, 341, 3:60-61, 64, 145-146; Lāḷas, *RSK*, 2:1:1019-1020, 1022; Sākariyā, *RHSK*, p. 414; *Vigat*, 1:21.

[21] "Aitihāsik Bātāṃ," p. 46; *Khyāt*, 2:66, 68, 210, 287, 333, 3:38, 83; Lāḷas, *RSK*, 2:1:1022; Sākariyā, *RHSK*, p. 415; *Vigat*, 1:84, 111, 2:52.

[22] *Khyāt*, 1:87, 93, 186, 3:85; Lāḷas, *RSK*, 2:2:1704-1705; Sākariyā, *RHSK*, pp. 604-605; *Vigat*, 2:3, 48.

[23] *Khyāt*, 1:2, 103, 2:19, 60, 210, 287, 3:94, 103; Lāḷas, *RSK*, 2:1:1377-1378; Sākariyā, *RHSK*, p. 513; *Vigat*, 1:21, 47.

[24] *Khyāt*, 3:64, 271; Lāḷas, *RSK*, 2:2:1807; Sākariyā, *RHSK*, p. 625.

[25] *Bātāṃ ro Jhūmakho*, 1:47; *Khyāt*, 1:1, 80, 2:12, 26, 3:3, 13, 148, 266; Lāḷas, *RSK*, 2:2:1865; Sākariyā, *RHSK*, p. 634; *Vigat*, 1:1-3, 27, 29, 72, 175, 2:1, 3, 57, 215.

[26] *Khyāt*, 1:71, 2:180, 3:82-83; Lāḷas, *RSK*, 2:2:1906; *Vigat*, 1:72, 76, 87, 449.

[27] *Khyāt*, 2:61, 254, 281, 3:41, 43, 127, 250; Lāḷas, *RSK*, 2:1:1382, 2:2:1741; Sākariyā, *RHSK*, p. 611.

[28] "Aitihāsik Bātāṃ," p. 37; *Khyāt*, 1:20, 2:85, 110, 139, 325, 336, 3:31, 49, 105, 161, 266; Lāḷas, *RSK*, 2:2:1829; Sākariyā, *RHSK*, p. 629; *Vigat*, 1:39-40, 65, 76, 92.

[29] Lāḷas, *RSK*, 2:1:1400; Sākariyā, *RHSK*, p. 521; *Vigat*, 1:3, 23, 103.

[30] *Khyāt*, 2:210, 297; Lāḷas, *RSK*, 2:2:1788; Sākariyā, *RHSK*, pp. 619-620.

[31] *Khyāt*, 1:263-264; Lāḷas, *RSK*, 2:2:1770; Sākariyā, *RHSK*, p. 616.

[32] *Khyāt*, 2:268; Lāḷas, *RSK*, 1:805; Sākariyā, *RHSK*, p. 344.

[33] Lāḷas, *RSK*, 1:806; Sākariyā, *RHSK*, p. 345; *Vigat*, 2:55.

[34] *Khyāt*, 1:9, 23, 111, 128, 3:86, 175; Lāḷas, *RSK*, 1:769; Sākariyā, *RHSK*, p. 335; *Vigat*, 1:115.

[35] *Khyāt*, 1:216; Lāḷas, *RSK*, 1:767; Sākariyā, *RHSK*, p. 334.

[36] *Khyāt*, 1:23, 133, 2:20, 34, 240, 3:107, 127, 202; Lāḷas, *RSK*, 2:1:1064; Sākariyā, *RHSK*, p. 426; *Vigat*, 1:71.

[37] *Khyāt*, 3:148; Lāḷas, *RSK*, 2:1:1157; Sākariyā, *RHSK*, p. 454.

[38] *Khyāt*, 2:29, 206; Lāḷas, *RSK*, 1:414; Sākariyā, *RHSK*, p. 201; *Vigat*, 1:12-13, 102.

[39] *Khyāt*, 2:65, 267, 3:104; Lāḷas, *RSK*, 1:392; Sākariyā, *RHSK*, p. 194.

[40] *Khyāt*, 1:143, 2:218, 282, 319, 3:63, 79, 116, 141; Lāḷas, *RSK*, 1:466-467; Sākariyā, *RHSK*, p. 222; *Vigat*, 1:58, 119, 171, 2:293.

[41] Lāḷas, *RSK*, 1:412; Sākariyā, *RHSK*, p. 200; *Vigat*, 2:293.

[42] *Bātāṃ ro Jhūmakho*, 1:47; Lāḷas, *RSK*, 1:605; Sākariyā, *RHSK*, p. 283.

[43] *Khyāt*, 1:2, 3:73, 104; Lāḷas, *RSK*, 1:605; Sākariyā, *RHSK*, p. 283.

[44] *Khyāt*, 3:273; Lāḷas, *RSK*, 4:1:4296; Sākariyā, *RHSK*, p. 1191.

[45] *Khyāt*, 1:13, 79, 2:100, 202, 206; Lāḷas, *RSK*, 4:1:4446.

[46] *Khyāt*, 1:101, 2:41, 211, 276, 3:57, 80, 270, 283; Lāḷas, *RSK*, 3:3:3677-3678; Sākariyā, *RHSK*, p. 1031; *Vigat*, 1:21, 2:46.

[47] *Khyāt*, 3:7, 31; Lāḷas, *RSK*, 3:3:3617, 3639; Sākariyā, *RHSK*, p. 1018.

[48] "Aitihāsik Bātāṃ," p. 82; *Khyāt*, 1:62, 2:21; Lāḷas, *RSK*, 3:3:3678; Sākariyā, *RHSK*, p. 1031; *Vigat*, 2:57.

[49] *Khyāt*, 1:206; Lāḷas, *RSK*, 3:3:3671, 3847; Sākariyā, *RHSK*, p. 1042.

[50] *Khyāt*, 1:25, 255, 2:21, 65, 217, 269, 302, 3:3, 41, 276; Lāḷas, *RSK*, 3:3:3672-3673; Sākariyā, *RHSK*, p. 1042.

[51] *Khyāt*, 1:54, 216, 2:25, 3:144, 257, 282; Lāḷas, *RSK*, 3:3:3654; Sākariyā, *RHSK*, p. 1053.

[52] *Khyāt*, 1:361, 3:104, 106; Lāḷas, *RSK*, 3:3:3730; Sākariyā, *RHSK*, p. 1050.

[53] *Khyāt*, 2:192; Lāḷas, *RSK*, 3:3:3728; Sākariyā, *RHSK*, p. 1050.

[54] *Khyāt*, 1:206, 2:153, 288, 291, 305, 3:7; Lāḷas, *RSK*, 2:2:2030; Sākariyā, *RHSK*, p. 674.

[55] *Khyāt*, 1:27, 109, 241-242, 2:203, 217, 254, 264, 3:112, 151; Lāḷas, *RSK*, 2:2:2030-2031; Sākariyā, *RHSK*, p. 674.

[56] *Khyāt*, 1:9, 26, 172, 2:16, 66, 84, 154, 196; Lāḷas, *RSK*, 3:1:2379, 2393; Sākariyā, *RHSK*, p. 730.

[57] *Khyāt*, 2:301, 303, 319; Lāḷas, *RSK*, 3:1:2580-2581; Sākariyā, *RHSK*, p. 791.

[58] *Khyāt*, 1:12, 77, 134, 2:9, 16, 92, 3:20, 153, 182, 220, 247; Lāḷas, *RSK*, 3:1:2520; Sākariyā, *RHSK*, p. 774; *Vigat*, 1:2, 15, 389, 2:216.

[59] *Khyāt*, 2:97, 276, 3:3, 32, 103-104, 282-283; Lāḷas, *RSK*, 3:1:2526; Sākariyā, *RHSK*, p. 776; *Vigat*, 1:9.

[60] *Bātāṃ ro Jhūmakho*, 3:40; *Khyāt*, 1:26, 2:2, 11, 33, 43, 290, 3:7, 239, 247; Lāḷas, *RSK*, 3:1:2605; Sākariyā, *RHSK*, p. 799; *Vigat*, 1:25-26, 37, 56, 173.

[61] *Khyāt*, 1:1, 10; Lāḷas, *RSK*, 3:1:2574.

[62] *Khyāt*, 1:1, 2:275-276, 3:7, 26; Lāḷas, *RSK*, 3:1:2540-2541; Sākariyā, *RHSK*, p. 779; *Vigat*, 2:5.

[63] "Aitihāsik Bātāṃ," p. 36; Lāḷas, *RSK*, 4:3:5501-5502.

[64] *Khyāt*, 1:134, 2:75, 112, 132, 292, 3:72, 104; Lāḷas, *RSK*, 4:3:5225; *Vigat*, 1:2, 14, 2:55.

[65] *Khyāt*, 1:26, 82, 2:253, 319, 332-333, 3:98, 134; Lāḷas, *RSK*, 4:3:5227; *Vigat*, 1:14, 2:60, 246, 298.

[66] *Khyāt*, 1:23, 49, 2:76, 92, 96, 110, 116; Lāḷas, *RSK*, 4:3:5227; *Vigat*, 1:39-40, 76, 89, 2:37.

[67] *Bātāṃ ro Jhūmakho*. 1:46, 3:40; *Khyāt*, 1:26, 88-90, 2:11, 78-79, 144, 3:7, 155, 157, 175, 239; Lāḷas, *RSK*, 4:3:5484; *Vigat*, 2:41, 68.

[68] *Bātāṃ ro Jhūmakho*, 1:46; *Khyāt*, 1:18, 265, 2:95, 245, 3:25, 107, 135, 281-282; Lāḷas, *RSK*, 4:3:5542, 5544; *Vigat*, 1:83.

[69] *Khyāt*, 2:24; Lāḷas, *RSK*, 4:3:5467.

[70] *Khyāt*, 1:183, 2:86, 309, 313, 325; Lāḷas, *RSK*, 4:3:5297-5298; *Vigat*, 2:57.

[71] *Khyāt*, 1:76, 253, 2:250, 3:31, 104, 158, 285; Lāḷas, *RSK*, 4:3:5552.

[72] *Khyāt*, 2:251; Lāḷas, *RSK*, 4:3:5552.

[73] *Khyāt*, 2:20, 23, 34, 328, 3:88-89, 133-134, 145-146, 258; Lāḷas, *RSK*, 4:3:5552.

[74] *Khyāt*, 3:63, 144; Lāḷas, *RSK*, 4:3:5857; *Vigat*, 1:47.

[75] *Khyāt*, 1:13, 253, 2:41, 210; Lāḷas, *RSK*, 4:3:5755.

[76] *Khyāt*, 1:242, 2:20, 90, 119, 202, 328, 3:74, 107, 165; Lāḷas, *RSK*, 4:3:5420, 5751.

[77] *Khyāt*, 2:287, 321, 3:58-60, 103; Lāḷas, *RSK*, 2:1:1294; Sākariyā, *RHSK*, p. 484.

[78] *Khyāt*, 1:15, 109, 291, 2:1, 3, 15-16, 209; Lāḷas, *RSK*, 4:2:4460-4461; *Vigat*, 2:289.

INDEX OF PERSONAL NAMES

A

B

C

D

F

G

H

K

L

N

Q

R

S

V

W

Y

Z

INDEX OF PLACE NAMES

A

B

F

G

H

I

J

M

N

O

P

S

Sācor 21, 104, 106, 248, 272
Sādṛī 322
Sāhlī 13, 171
Sālāvās 185
Salkhāvāsī 410
Samāvalī 42, 46, 48, 318, 320
Sāmbhar 146, 151, 153 n. 8, 202, 306, 338, 348, 421, 439 n. 1, 440, 458
Samel 4, 32-33, 48, 76, 109-110, 165-166, 168, 172, 174-176, 196, 206-208, 220-221, 231-233, 235, 240, 258, 271, 296, 299, 306-307, 312-313, 332-333, 344, 346, 379, 394-395, 400, 402, 418-419, 427, 437 n. 7
Sāṃvaḷīyāvās Khurad 345
Sāṃvatkuvo 34
Sānduro 13
Sāṅganer 129, 138
Sāngānīr -see Sāṅganer
Saṇlā 307 n. 36
Santhāṇo Sāraṅgvās 363
Sāraṇ 204, 270, 300
Saraṇvāhī 97 n. 1
Saraṇvo 97 n. 1
Sarvāṛ 339, 354 n. 57
Sarvāṛ Manoharpur 289
Sātalvās 211, 348, 366
Sathlāṇo 47
Saurashtra 99
Savāḷakh 338, 420, 439
Sayāṇo 52
Sekhāvaṭī 145-146
Seṇo 395
Sevakī 179, 195, 203-204, 207 n. 36, 260-261, 273-274, 295, 342, 346, 391, 393, 397-398, 400 n. 29, 401, 417, 425, 442-443, 455
Sīdhā Vāsṇī 271
Sīhā rī Vāsṇī 422
Sīkar 343
Sikargaḍh 145-146, 305, 436
Sīlvo 65
Sindh 199, 397
Siṇlo 307
Sīrāsṇo 353
Sīrīyārī 52, 300 n. 12
Sīrohī 5, 24-25, 27, 30 n. 15, 41, 62, 86-93, 94 n. 14, 95-98, 104 n. 1, 130, 240-241, 263-264, 273, 321, 395-396
Sirso 195
Sītāmaū 285-286

END

Printed and bound by CPI Group (UK) Ltd, Croydon, CR0 4YY
13/04/2025
14656855-0001